THE AGE OF GLOBAL WARMING

THE AGE OF GLOBAL WARMING
A HISTORY

RUPERT DARWALL

QUARTET

First published in 2013 by
Quartet Books Limited
A member of the Namara Group
27 Goodge Street, London W1T 2LD
Copyright © Rupert Darwall 2013
The right of Rupert Darwall to be identified
as the author of this work has been asserted
by him in accordance with the
Copyright, Designs and Patents Act, 1988
A catalogue record for this book
is available from the British Library
ISBN 978 0 7043 7299 3
Typeset by Josh Bryson
Printed and bound in Great Britain by
T J International Ltd, Padstow, Cornwall

Contents

1
THE IDEA

It is ideas that make history … Human society is an issue of the mind.

Ludwig von Mises[1]

The orthodoxy produced by intellectual fashions, specialisation, and the appeal to authorities is the death of knowledge, and that the growth of knowledge depends entirely upon disagreement.

Karl Popper[2]

Polar bears or swallows?

The two symbolise the dilemma posed by global warming.

A male polar bear's desperate struggle for food was captured in the 2006 BBC television series *Planet Earth*. Eventually the exhausted animal finds a pod of walruses. Three times he attacks. Each time he fails, retreating to lie down and die. The burgeoning number of polar bears has replaced the giant panda as the icon of a species on the verge of extinction and of fragile nature endangered by man.

Swallows crossing the Sahara can lose up to half their bodyweight as they fly from Northern Europe to Southern Africa burning hydrocarbons, one of the highest density sources of energy found in nature. For the same reason, mankind has come to depend on hydrocarbons.

Global warming's entrance into politics can be dated with precision – 1988; the year of the Toronto conference on climate change, Margaret Thatcher's address to the Royal Society, NASA scientist James Hansen's appearance at a congressional committee and the establishment of the Intergovernmental Panel on Climate Change (IPCC).

By then, the world was ready.

Rounds of international climate change conferences and treaties followed – the Rio Earth summit and the United Nations Framework Convention on Climate Change in 1992, the 1997 Kyoto Protocol – culminating in the 2009 Copenhagen climate conference, interspersed with periodic pronouncements from the IPCC with four assessment reports (1990, 1995, 2001 and 2007) sounding a crescendo of alarm.

The global warming idea is composed of three propositions which proceed from two facts. The first fact is that carbon dioxide is one of a number of so-called greenhouse gases (the most abundant being water vapour). The second is that the proportion of carbon dioxide in the atmosphere has risen by around thirty-five per cent from pre-industrial times.[3]

The first proposition is about the past. Increased carbon dioxide, together with other greenhouse gases emitted by human activities, has caused global temperatures to rise.* In the words of the IPCC's Fourth Assessment Report, 'It is likely that there has been significant anthropogenic warming over the past fifty years over each continent (except Antarctica).'[4]

The second is about the future. Left unchecked, rising global temperatures will cause immense damage to the environment and humanity.

The third proposition is political. Developed countries should lead the world in making deep cuts in carbon dioxide emissions, preferably by substituting fossil fuels with renewable energy sources such as wind and solar power.

Why was the world ready for this new idea?

Global warming did not make itself evident like a solar eclipse. People had to be told it was happening. An event of such historical magnitude does not come out of nothing. It can be understood in terms of ideas, which in turn reflect particular values and visions.

The British mathematician and philosopher A.N. Whitehead said that the spiritual precedes the material; philosophy works slowly before mankind suddenly finds it embodied in the world. It builds cathedrals before the workmen have moved a stone.[5]

So it is with global warming.

During the course of the twentieth century, mankind's relationship with nature underwent a revolution. At the beginning of the last century, human intervention in nature was regarded as beneficent and a sign of the progress of civilisation. By its end, such interventions were presumed harmful unless it could be demonstrated they were not.

The entry of nature into politics was of very different character on either side of the Atlantic. In the US, it was healthy. Unlike the European versions, it was not defined by opposition to democracy or capitalism.

In Germany and Britain, to the degree that the British variant was influenced by German thinking, it emerged from the same swamp in which Nazi doctrines festered. Accordingly, only the American variant was viable after the Second World War.

---

*   According to the IPCC's Fourth Assessment Report, increased carbon dioxide emissions accounted for just over one hundred per cent of the net man-made global warming effect. IPCC, *Climate Change 2007: Synthesis Report Summary for Policymakers* (2007), p. 39.

The pivotal year was 1962 with the publication of Rachel Carson's *Silent Spring*. Within a decade, the notion that mankind's pillaging of the planet was leading to an environmental catastrophe – risking man's extinction – had taken hold.

> If all man can offer to the decades ahead is the same combination of scientific drive, economic cupidity and national arrogance, then we cannot rate very highly the chances of reaching the year 2000 with our planet still functioning and our humanity securely preserved

– words written by Barbara Ward, the other seminal environmentalist of the era, in *Only One Earth*.[6] It had been commissioned for the first major UN conference on the environment at Stockholm in 1972.

Malthusian ideas had enjoyed previous bouts of popularity. The first was at the end of the eighteenth century, when Thomas Malthus predicted disaster as population growth would outstrip food production. In 1865, the foremost economist of the day, William Stanley Jevons, shifted the focus from food to resource depletion. Britain's economic demise was inevitable with the exhaustion of cheap coal. Similar scares afflicted the US before and after the First World War.

What was new in the late 1960s and early 1970s was the pervasiveness of doomsday predictions. 1972 also saw publication of the Club of Rome's *The Limits to Growth* and *A Blueprint for Survival*, signed by leading British scientists of the day, predicting the end of civilisation.

At Stockholm, the West's environmental awakening had to contend with another force of the post-war era – the ambition of newly independent Third World nations to industrialise. A Third World boycott was averted by Maurice Strong, the UN conference organiser, and Ward formulating a political compact between First World environmentalism and Third World development aspirations. Under it, economic growth was deemed double-edged. When rich countries got richer, it harmed the environment; when poor countries grew, the environment benefited.

Sustainable development – the link forged by Strong and Ward between environmentalism and the Third World development agenda – was pushed onto the international agenda by the 1980 Brandt Report and the 1987 Brundtland Report. Whatever its accuracy as a description of reality, sustainable development was the political fiction environmentalism needed to buy developing nations' neutrality, a fiction that broke down when the increase in developing countries' greenhouse gas emissions overtook those of the developed world.

Then, as Sherlock Holmes explained to the Scotland Yard detective, there is the curious incident of the dog in the night-time. But the dog did nothing. 'That,' Holmes replied, 'was the curious incident.'

Marx and Engels condemned Malthus and his population theory. In turn, their labour theory of value put no value on pristine nature. The timing of the demise of Marxism as a living ideology meant that global warming never had to contend with opposition from the Left of the political spectrum. It is hard to conceive of the pre-Gorbachev Soviet Union being a party to global environmental treaties on ideological grounds, let alone during a strategic race to bury the West.

Viewed as an ideology, environmentalism took the Marxist concept of the alienation of the working class from the means of production and applied it to the rich man's alienation from nature. In doing so, environmentalism triumphed in developed societies, dominating the mainstream politics of the West where Marxism had entirely failed. 'By losing sight of our relationship with Nature, and its interdependent and holistic characteristics, we have engendered a profoundly dangerous alienation,' the Prince of Wales stated in 2009. Poorer societies were, in many ways, 'infinitely richer in the ways in which they live and organise themselves as communities.'[7]

That's not how those societies viewed their level of economic development. The corollary of environmentalism's success in the West is its limited appeal in poorer countries. Communism, based on a doctrine of scientific materialism, had much greater success for most of the second half of the twentieth century.

Thus the West and the East (or North and South) took different approaches to the climate change negotiations. The West, particularly the Europeans, viewed global warming diplomacy as about persuading other countries to be virtuous, like themselves. The stance of countries such as China and India was driven by their economic interests.

The comparison with Marxism also illuminates an important dimension of environmentalism – its relationship with science. Environmentalism exists in a similar relationship to its scientific base as communism did to the economics of *Das Kapital*. Science and ideology become so deeply entwined that in practice it is difficult to separate the two, the scientist and the environmentalist becoming one and the same person.

In his 2002 presidential address to the American Association for the Advancement of Science, Professor Peter Raven (a botanist) argued that human society had outstripped the limits of global sustainability (a key tenet of environmentalism). 'Simply appropriating as much as possible of the world's goods and processing them as efficiently as possible can never be a recipe for long-term success,' Raven asserted. 'Success' was about finding 'new ways of thinking about our place in the world and the ways in which we relate to natural systems' – a clearly ideological construct.[8]

Similarly the response to adverse evidence is often an ideologue's denial rather than a scientist's questioning of their hypothesis. In 1968, the American zoologist Paul Ehrlich's *The Population Bomb* declared that the battle to feed humanity was over. It was inevitable that hundreds of millions of people would starve to death. Ehrlich specifically predicted that India was doomed.

Yet the falsification of Ehrlich's prediction led him to make only trivial changes to his thesis. Forty years later, Ehrlich was comparing humanity's ability to feed itself to fruit flies living off rotting bananas. 'Our problem is we only have one pile of bananas.'[9] The remarkable technological accomplishments of modern human beings had merely delayed the timetable of doom.[10]

When a Danish statistician (and an environmentalist to boot) decided to debunk the arguments of American economist Julian Simon that received views on the worsening state of the environment were mistaken, he found that, by and large, the evidence supported Simon's view. Would the evidence change minds? As Bjorn Lomborg recounts in *The Skeptical Environmentalist*,

> to begin with, I was surprised that the only reaction from many environmental groups was the gut reaction of complete denial ... but I would have thought as the debate progressed that refusal would give place to reflection on the massive amounts of data I had presented.[11]

Lomborg's optimism was misplaced. The hostility he encountered wasn't because he had changed his mind. It was because he was an apostate.*

Unlike the discovery of the link between tobacco smoking and lung cancer, with carbon dioxide and global warming there was a pre-existing structure of ideas about the incompatibility of industrial society and nature to co-exist in harmony. Environmentalists were predisposed to anticipate harmful consequences from industrial societies' reliance on hydrocarbons. Because global warming is the most powerful argument in the environmentalist

---

* Raven described Lomborg as the latest in a line of 'false prophets and charlatans', concluding his American Association for the Advancement of Science presidential homily with the plea that scientists should learn to respect one another.

armoury and because science provides its source code, global warming occasioned a profound and subtle shift in the nature of science.

According to Karl Popper, the twentieth century's leading thinker on the theory of science, the essence of the scientific method is critical argument and genuine attempts to refute theories with empirical tests yielding reproducible data. We cannot be sure of what is truthful. We can know what is false. Truth is therefore approached by discarding what has been proved false.

What hardened into the scientific orthodoxy of global warming does not meet the threshold of being a scientific theory because its predictions are not capable of being tested against nature and therefore refuted by evidence. Thus it would be more accurate to describe global warming as a speculation or conjecture. Instead, global warming must depend on the preponderance of scientific opinion in order to maintain its potency.

Popper's view of scientific theories as being provisional, only valid until they've been refuted, conflicts with the political need to characterise the science of global warming as settled. Science advances through challenge but maintaining the consensus subverts the needs of genuine scientific enquiry. Politicisation of climate science and the de-legitimisation of debate – risks inherent in the idea of global warming – led to a retreat from the standards that emerged during the Scientific Revolution of the seventeenth century to pre-scientific norms; principally, reliance on consensus, peer review and appeals to authority.

In contrast to the overstatement with respect to the science is the downplaying of the likely costs and the adverse consequences of adopting policies designed to delay the rise in global temperatures. This is the opposite of what can be reliably said about the science of global warming on the one hand and the economics on the other. The state of the climate in one hundred years' time and its impact on the environment are not just uncertain. They are unknowable. The impact on food prices of policies that divert corn into car fuel is not. We can be fairly certain that if more wind farms are built, more birdlife will be destroyed.

Yet the political imperative of global warming means that it is more important for governments to be seen to be doing something than assessing the likely consequences of their policies.

This licence leads to the logical outcome of the global warming idea: policies ostensibly designed to deal with global warming bring about the very outcomes as if global warming was left unchecked – rising food prices, instability caused by food shortages, reduced biodiversity, and, with their threat to the international trading system, a poorer and more dangerous world. These are all examples of the Global Warming Policy Paradox – the therapy causing the malady it was designed to avert. The logic of collective action leads to collectively harmful outcomes but, for individuals and interest groups advocating such action, potentially advantageous ones.

Global warming now affects almost every aspect of our lives. Where and how we travel; the amount we pay for power; the way houses are built; the lights we read by; the food we eat (no lamb please, they burp methane), and how much it costs; the destruction of local habitats to make way for wind farms, palm oil plantations and tidal barrages; what children are taught in schools.

It has re-defined what constitutes ethical behaviour. Virtue is being seen to tread with a small carbon footprint – offsets being offered for sale to obtain one – and changes how people behave towards each other. Being kind to the planet appears to involve being less kind to other people. A Canadian study found that people act less altruistically and are more likely to cheat and steal after purchasing green products.[12]

To explore global warming is to journey through the mind of contemporary Western man. Cultivating the habit of thinking what we are doing was much over-rated, Whitehead observed. 'Civilisation advances by extending the number of important operations which we can perform without thinking about them,' Whitehead argued.[13] Could it be that in an age when so much mental activity is automated and so much information is available instantaneously that it is harder to reason from first principles, making it more susceptible to global warming?

'Operations of thought,' Whitehead went on, 'are like cavalry charges in a battle – they are strictly limited in number, they require fresh horses, and must only be made at decisive moments.'

It is time to mount the cavalry.

2
PROMETHEAN REVOLUTION

Knowing the power and the action of fire, water, air, stars, heavens and all the other bodies which environ us as distinctly as we know the various trades and crafts of our artisans, we might in the same way be able to put them to all the uses to which they are proper, and thus make ourselves, as it were, masters and possessors of nature.

René Descartes

Accounts of global warming usually start with the observation that carbon dioxide is one of a number of greenhouse gases and that human activities have increased the amount of carbon dioxide in the atmosphere. This isn't the real beginning for it leaves out why modern civilisations evolved to exhale carbon dioxide. In the words of the Nobel economist Ronald Coase, we need to know the value of what is obtained, as well as what is sacrificed to attain it – the benefits as well as the costs.[1]

A better place to start is at the beginning, or rather before the beginning, with the man who foresaw a new beginning when he turned his back on the Middle Ages.

In 1577 or thereabouts, the record isn't precise, the sixteen-year-old Francis Bacon was studying at Trinity College, Cambridge. He had been a favourite of Elizabeth I, answering her questions with a gravity beyond his years. Bacon grew up in an age of vitality and exuberance. According to his Italian biographer Paolo Rossi, Bacon was a medieval philosopher haunted by a modern dream.[2] It was at Cambridge that the young Bacon had the decisive thought of his life, one that pointed to a new era in the history of mankind. In the words of his future private secretary, Bacon fell into the dislike of the philosophy of Aristotle, a pursuit strong only 'for disputations and contentions, but barren of the production of works, for the benefit of the life of man'.[3] That the pursuit of knowledge should be directed at deriving practical benefits for mankind and not the abstract hair-splitting of the medieval monastery became the guiding idea of Bacon's life.

Bacon spat at Aristotle, the pope of medieval philosophers, and Greek philosophy in general. Aristotle was a wretched sophist, his logic a manual of madness. Bacon denounced the 'degenerate learning' of the followers of Aristotle, who idled their lives in pointless disputes over logic and abstract speculation to prove points of no practical benefit. He also accused Plato of doing mankind a mortal injury by turning men's minds away from the observation of nature to 'grovel before our own blind and confused idols under the name of contemplative philosophy'.[4]

Examining the long history of human thought from the ancient Greeks, Bacon asked: Why had mankind's condition improved so little? Men's minds should turn to the observation of nature and to experimentation. By discovering what was written in nature's book, it could be harnessed to bettering man's lot and transforming his existence. 'We cannot command nature except by obeying her,' he wrote.[5]

Bacon saw himself as an experimenter, scientist and inventor. But his scientific contributions were minimal. Even his famous discourses on scientific method had little influence on the development of science. His mind had fastened on to something larger.

> If a man could succeed, not in striking out some particular invention but in kindling a light in nature – a light which should in its very rising touch and illuminate all the border-regions that continue to circle our present knowledge; and so spreading further and further should presently disclose and bring into sight all that is most hidden and secret in the world – that man (I thought) would be benefactor indeed of the human race – the propagator of man's empire over the universe, the champion of liberty, the conqueror and subduer of necessities.[6]

In *The New Atlantis*, Bacon advocated a scientific foundation, Salomon's House, to engage in discovering 'the knowledge of causes, and the secret motions of things; and the enlarging of the bounds of the Human Empire'.[7] In 1660, thirty-four years after Bacon died, the Royal Society was founded; its motto – *Nullius in verba*, take no one's word – an exhortation to healthy scepticism. For Bacon, knowledge about nature was not to be acquired for its own sake, but for the purpose of enabling man to use nature to better his material conditions of life – the invention of invention, as Whitehead put it. *Nam et ipsa scientia potestas est*, Bacon wrote. Knowledge is power.

Karl Marx called Bacon the prophet of the Industrial Revolution, his ideas looking forward to 'an alteration in the form of production and to effective control of nature by man' – as Marx wrote in *Das Kapital*.[8] Karl Popper called Bacon the spiritual father of modern science and the creator of the Industrial and Scientific Revolutions with his idea of 'a *material* self-liberation through knowledge'.[9] It made Western civilisation different from all others, past and present. 'European civilisation is an industrial civilisation … It uses engines, sources of energy which are non-muscular. In this, European and American civilisations differ fundamentally from all other great civilisations, which are or were mainly agrarian and whose industry depended on manual labour.'[10]

Power has a political as well as physical or scientific dimension; power over people as well as power over nature. Plato's republic was ruled by the wise. Scientists were to govern the New Atlantis. In a pre-democratic society where monarchs ruled by divine right, Bacon's political idea was revolutionary, especially from the pen of someone who had been Lord Chancellor of England, the highest political office under the crown.

Popper described Bacon and scientists generally as epistemological optimists. They believed humans can know with certainty the truth about the natural world. 'Once the truth stands revealed before us, it is impossible for us not to recognise it as truth,' is the way Popper characterised epistemological optimism. As Descartes put it, God does not deceive us, making explicit science's debt to religion. According to Whitehead, the scientific endeavour was driven by what he called 'the unexpugnable belief that every detailed occurrence can be correlated in a perfectly definite manner, exemplifying general principles.'[11] This belief, Whitehead thought, came from the prior epoch and 'the medieval insistence on the rationality of God'.[12]

The mental framework science inherited from religion also explains why some people rejected the manifest truth. Such people were, in Popper's words, 'epistemological sinners' who erred because they stubbornly clung to their prejudices, in contrast to those who saw truth when it was set before them. 'It is the unbiased mind, the pure mind, the mind cleansed of prejudice, that cannot fail to recognise the truth.'[13]

These pre-scientific traits – that the truth of a rational, predictable nature could be apprehended by the human mind and that non-believers were not just ignorant but, in some way, morally corrupted – would become leitmotifs in debates on the science of global warming. In November 2009, the Australian prime minister Kevin Rudd denounced climate change deniers. 'They are a minority. They are powerful. And invariably they are driven by vested interests,' Rudd warned. Small in number, they were 'literally holding the world to ransom'.[14]

Popper's own theory of scientific knowledge was provoked by his experience in Vienna after the First World War. The truth of Marxism, of Freudian psychoanalysis and Alfred Adler's psychology explained everything in their respective fields, including why people didn't believe them, because of their class interest or because of unanalysed repressions crying out for treatment.[15]

A confrontation with a young, uniformed member of the Nazi party armed with a pistol might, Popper thought, have planted the seed for his classic book, *Open Society*: 'What, you want to argue? I don't argue: I shoot.'[16] An open society is one that not merely tolerates dissenting opinions, but respects them: 'Democracy (that is, a form of government devoted to the protection of the open society) cannot flourish if science becomes the exclusive possession of a closed set of specialists.'[17]

By contrast, what Popper termed the 'critical optimists' based their views on the Socratic insight that to err is human. Less numerous, Popper numbered Locke among them. In this respect, the framers of the American constitution followed Locke. Checks and balances and the separation of powers are an implicit repudiation of the assumption that 'the people', or, at any rate, a majority of them, cannot err, a view made explicit in the *Federalist Papers*.

Bacon died in 1626, a decade and a half before the outbreak of the English Civil War, a conflict that was to lead to the development in England of the classical liberal political philosophy and find its most perfect expression in the constitution of the American republic. Thomas Hobbes' *Leviathan* was published in the last year of that war when John Locke, whose development of Hobbes' ideas inspired both Montesquieu and America's Founding Fathers, was not yet twenty years old.

The debate Bacon and Locke could not have, whether society should be governed by scientists or whether it should be based on popular sovereignty mediated by a liberal constitutional order, is one that, some three hundred years after Locke's death, sparked into life in debates on global warming. Writing in September 2009, *New York Times* columnist Thomas Friedman asked whether China's one-party system was better at tackling an issue like global warming because, Friedman argued, it could impose 'the politically difficult but critically important policies needed to move a society forward in the twenty-first century'.[18]

In his 2004 book on globalisation, Martin Wolf argues that after a millennium or more of flat-lining the decisive technological shift from human and animal power to inanimate energy, most importantly hydrocarbons, was the key factor in the sudden and extraordinary take-off in economic performance and living standards within the last two and half centuries. 'What is called the industrial revolution is better named the energy revolution.'[19] Its first stirrings were apparent in Bacon's lifetime. Production of pit coal in England rose from an average of two hundred and ten tonnes a year in the decade 1551-60 to nearly two million tonnes in the decade 1681–90, a growth rate of over seven per cent a year.[20]

Why coal? Why fossil fuels? Why did this energy revolution depend on the combustion of hydrocarbons and, as an unavoidable by-product, the emission of carbon dioxide into the atmosphere?

Hydrocarbon molecules are rich in energy. When fully oxidised as carbon dioxide (CO_2) there is no more energy to be extracted from a carbon atom. Carbon dioxide can be re-energised by exposure to sunlight and water in the presence of an enzyme catalyst, a process known as photosynthesis. Plant leaves are able to do this in abundance, producing energy-rich molecules like sugar and cellulose. Cellulose, as wood, is still the principal fuel for many in the developing world. The remains of plants of the carboniferous era (around three hundred million years ago) are the source of fossil carbon which is the result of the geological processes of time, heat, and pressure, increasing their energy density with the loss of their oxygen atoms.

At the start of the Industrial Revolution, it was more convenient to mine coal which, as a solid, could be easily transported and stored. Oil was obtained from plants (olive oil, linseed oil) or from animals like whales. Plants and animals, including humans, convert carbohydrate to hydrocarbons (fatty acids) to store energy efficiently. In using fossil fuels, mankind unlocked a store of energy used by plants and animal and, from the time of the Industrial Revolution, started to apply it on an industrial scale.

By the end of the eighteenth century, Britain was becoming the world's first industrialised economy. The Promethean Revolution was underway.

If Bacon was the prophet of man's material liberation through the advance of science and technology, Malthus was its Jeremiah – prophesying that mankind's future was to be trapped in an agrarian past which the Promethean Revolution was already making history.

If ever there was an inflection point in the economic history of mankind, this was it. It was a spectacularly inapposite moment to be writing a treatise on economic development and population based on the assumption of the static technological endowment of pre-industrial societies when industrialisation was taking mankind out of the Malthusian trap.

In his 1798 *Essay on the Principles of Population*, Malthus warned his readers that his view of human life had a melancholy hue. The great question of his age was, Malthus said, whether mankind was accelerating down a path of illimitable and hitherto unforeseen improvement (which it was) or instead whether humanity's destiny was to be condemned to perpetual oscillation between happiness and misery.

Malthus's argument proceeded from two propositions: the first, that food is necessary for the existence of man; the second, that, as this celibate Anglican cleric put it, 'the passion between the sexes is necessary and will remain nearly in its present state'.[21] From these two propositions – as trite as they are true – Malthus launched the core of his case: 'The power of population is indefinitely greater than the power in the earth to produce subsistence for man.'[22] Summarising the dilemma mathematically – any proposition that can be put into a mathematical form automatically improves its propagation – human population tended to expand at a geometric rate, whereas the means of subsistence expanded arithmetically. The two lines could not diverge for any length of time. The gap could only be closed by the population line moving back to the subsistence line through war, pestilence or famine.

Human progress would, Malthus surmised, be neither rapid nor unlimited. Instead, humanity would be subjected to repeated checks, forcing a reversion of human population growth back to the trend of the subsistence line. To Malthus, this appeared to be decisive proof against the possibility of a society 'all the members of which should live in ease, happiness, and comparative leisure; and feel no anxiety about providing the means of subsistence for themselves and their families'.[23]

As an ordained clergyman, Malthus had to square checks on population growth with the existence of a benevolent God. Misery and vice – the twin mechanisms by which human population growth would be corrected – were natural and therefore sanctioned by God. As Malthus explained, 'the ordeal of virtue is to resist temptation'.[24] The religious dimension of Malthus's theory of population growth was summarised by the nineteenth-century French economist Frédéric Bastiat. 'If you multiply inconsiderately, you cannot avoid the chastisement which awaits you in some form or other, and always in a hideous form – famine, war, pestilence etc.'[25]

Economic history demonstrates conclusively that Malthus was wrong to believe that, without population controls, no human society could completely escape a downward pull towards subsistence. If Malthus's *Essay* demonstrated anything, it is that the accuracy of forecasts of doom is inversely related to their political impact.

The *Essay*'s impact was immense, running to six editions in Malthus's lifetime. It speaks volumes for the potency of the scare Malthus created that in the middle of the Napoleonic wars, fighting France, a country whose population of nearly thirty million was nearly double Britain's (over one third of which was Irish and of doubtful loyalty), a growing population was seized on in Britain as a cause of alarm. Such was its effect in creating 'alarmist' views about the future (the word used by Britain's Office of National Statistics in describing the episode) that in 1800, Parliament passed the Census Act.[26]

The first official census took place in 1801, subsequent ones every ten years afterwards except during the Second World War.

The 1801 census found that England and Wales had a population of 8.9 million. At the 1851 census, it had doubled to 17.9 million, rising to 32.5 million in 1901.[27]

Had this nearly four-fold population increase led to greater disease and pestilence and put pressure on living standards?

While infant mortally rates remained almost unchanged during the nineteenth century, recent research suggests that the trend of increased life expectancy from around forty years in Malthus's day to between seventy and eighty years at the end of the twentieth century began around 1850.[28]

Living standards rose as well.

Farming cash wages rose by twenty-eight per cent. Cash wages in industry rose by over fifty per cent.[29] These rises understate the rise in living standards because prices fell and the purchasing power of money more than doubled.[30] Living standards benefited even more from falling prices than rising wages.

None of these trends is consistent with Malthus's prediction of population growth triggering reversions to subsistence. Instead, high population growth was associated with a sustained move from subsistence to becoming a society which Malthus claimed could not possibly exist.

How could the economy support a larger population that nearly quadrupled in one hundred years? Industrial production increased twelve-fold and the output from Britain's coalmines rose tenfold between 1815 and 1901.[31]

In the preface to the *Essay*, Malthus wrote that, even if in theory he could be shown to have been wrong, he would 'gladly retract his present opinions and rejoice in the conviction of his error'.[32]

Although he was to live thirty-four years into the new century, the economic evidence did not lead him to retract and rejoice. Neither did it lead to his views being quietly forgotten. The power of the Malthusian substructure of sin, punishment and redemption overwhelmed the contrary evidence to become a recurring feature of the consequences of man's relationship with the Earth and with nature. Modern man's escape from the Malthusian trap is either illusory or temporary.

Take for example Maurice Strong, the Canadian environmentalist who was secretary of first United Nations (UN) conference on the environment in Stockholm in 1972 and the Rio Earth Summit twenty years later. The first chapter of Strong's 1999 autobiography *Where on Earth are We Going?* is set in

2031. It foretells humanity's fate unless, that is, we are 'very, very lucky' or 'very, very wise'.[33] Nation-states have imploded; the international order completely broken down; there are food shortages, energy shortages, more people perishing from severe weather than in the two world wars of the previous century; a Great Earthquake strikes in 2026; Americans are dying like flies from excessive heat (there was not enough electricity for air conditioners).

A mystic figure by the name of Tadi emerges to synthesise all the main world religions into one. 'In this Time of Troubles God must call all to a new and transcendent unity,' Tadi concluded.[34] There was, however, a presentiment of a New Dawn. The human population was falling to what it had been at the beginning of the twentieth century, 'a consequence, yes, of death and destruction – but in the end a glimmer of hope for the future of our species and its potential for regeneration'.[35]

Sin, punishment, redemption.

Malthus's population theory's most lasting impact was not in economics but in biology. In his autobiography, Charles Darwin wrote about how it helped catalyse his theory of evolution:

> In October 1838, that is, fifteen months after I had begun my systematic inquiry, I happened to read for amusement Malthus on *Population*, and being well prepared to appreciate the struggle for existence which everywhere goes on from long-continued observation of the habits of animals and plants, it at once struck me that under these circumstances favourable variations would tend to be preserved, and unfavourable ones to be destroyed. The results of this would be the formation of a new species. Here, then, I had at last got a theory by which to work.[36]

In contrast to the struggle-for-existence models of Malthus and evolution-ary biologists, modern economics has incorporated the greatest finding of his friend and rival, David Ricardo.* 'Though an awareness of the benefits of specialisation must go back to the dim mists of antiquity in all civilisa-tions,' according to the *New Palgrave Dictionary of Economics*, 'it was not until Ricardo that this deepest and most beautiful result in all economics was obtained.'[37] Specialisation and the increasing division of labour dis-

---

*   Not all economists elevated Ricardo above Malthus. Keynes wrote in the 1930s, 'if only Malthus, instead of Ricardo, had been the parent stem from which nineteenth-century economics proceeded, what a much wiser and richer place the world would be today' – not that Keynes subscribed to fears about running out of resources.

tinguish advanced societies from primitive ones. It was trade that enabled Britain to specialise in manufacturing and coal mining, importing food from the Americas and other parts of the world which had a comparative advantage in agriculture.

In debates on the environment and global warming from the late 1960s to our own day, biologists and other natural scientists tend to see economic processes through Malthusian spectacles. Most economists follow Ricardo. Because the Malthusian narrative is about man's relationship with nature, the voices of natural scientists are generally given more weight in these debates.

Nature misleads when transposed to human society. It offers food chains, at the top of which are carnivores where the winner takes all and the loser forfeits their life. Nature also provides examples of symbiotic relationships (the closest to us physically being the flora lining our gut). But these latter relationships hardly compare to the conscious intent inherent in economic bargaining and to the specialisation of activities within a single species which exchange both enables and rewards.

There is nothing comparable in nature to Ricardo's elucidation of comparative advantage. Trade depends on arguably man's greatest invention – money. Trade is voluntary; the parties to an exchange only undertake it if each of them believes it will make them better off. Thus trade generates positive sum outcomes.

Natural scientists' thinking about economic issues is also conditioned by the first law of thermodynamics. This states that energy cannot be created or destroyed, only transformed. How can mankind's numbers grow and consumption increase, like an economic perpetual motion machine, without incurring some equivalent loss somewhere else? Economic activity must therefore have a limit because it consumes what it depends upon, so the argument goes. This leads scientists and environmentalists (often they're the same people) to worry about resource depletion and the planet's carrying capacity.

The analogy with physics does not hold because the driver pushing outwards the boundary of economic potential is the expansion of human knowledge. In this respect, the market economy has always been the 'knowledge economy'. Knowledge is not like one of Paul Ehrlich's rotting bananas. As Bacon put it, knowledge is power.

3
ANTECEDENTS

Most of the population-theory teachers are Protestant pastors.

Karl Marx[1]

So far then as our wealth and progress depend upon the superior command of coal we must not only stop – we must go back.

William Stanley Jevons[2]

By the beginning of the second half of the nineteenth century, Malthus's prediction – that it was impossible for any human society to escape subsistence without some form of population control – was no longer tenable. His theory had to be reformulated or discarded.

The critical responses of leading economists of the day prefigure those that accompanied the emergence of environmentalism at the end of the 1960s and the debates on global warming two decades later.

The first response is an ancestor of the global warming party. William Stanley Jevons was born in 1835, the year after Malthus died. The economist Joseph Schumpeter, a tough assessor of reputation – he thought Adam Smith much overrated – lauded Jevons for his 'brilliant conceptions and profound insights'. Jevons was 'without any doubt one of the most genuinely original economists who ever lived', Schumpeter wrote.[3] Praise in economics does not come higher.

'His definitive breakthrough came with the publication of *The Coal Question* in 1865, which predicted a decline in Britain's prosperity due to the future exhaustion of cheaply extractable coal,' Jevons' biographer Harro Maas wrote.[4]

The Coal Question begins by rehearsing Malthus's key argument: although human numbers tended to increase in a uniform ratio, the supply of food cannot be expected to keep up. 'We cannot double the produce of the soil, time after time, *ad infinitum*.'[5] Conceding that innovation would 'from time to time' allow a considerable increase, this would only buy time. 'Exterior nature presents a certain absolute and inexorable limit,' Jevons maintained.[6] Although Malthus's fundamental insight still held, Jevons argued that the growth of manufacturing and free trade 'take us out of the scope of Malthus's doctrine'.[7] But this would not free mankind from resource constraints. The inability to grow enough food was no longer the check on human progress. Now it was coal – 'the Mainspring of Modern Material Civilization', as he called the carbonaceous rock.[8] 'With coal almost any feat is possible or easy; without it we are thrown back into the laborious poverty of early times,' Jevons claimed.[9] How Britain should respond to this challenge was not merely an economic issue; it was a question of 'almost religious importance'.[10]

The transfer of the check on civilisation's progress from farm to coal mine had actually worsened humanity's material predicament. 'A farm,' Jevons argued, 'however far pushed, will under proper cultivation continue to yield for ever a constant crop. But in a mine there is no reproduction, and the produce once pushed to the utmost will soon begin to fail and sink to zero.'[11] Jevons thus anticipated both the idea of 'sustainability' that was to emerge in the 1970s and the rationale for renewable energy.

Whereas exporting farm products – 'the surplus yearly interest of the soil,' as Jevons put it – could be unalloyed gain, Jevons argued that to export coal was to be 'spendthrifts of our mineral wealth.'[12] 'Are we wise in allowing the commerce of this country to rise beyond the point at which we can long maintain it?' Jevons asked.[13]

His answer was unequivocal. Britain should understand that any increase in its prosperity and its power in the world was temporary.

> If we lavishly and boldly push forward in the creation and distribution of our riches, it is hard to over-estimate the pitch of beneficial influence to which we may attain in the present. *But the maintenance of such a position is physically impossible. We have to make the momentous choice between brief greatness and longer continued mediocrity.*[14]

The second response provided the most vigorous counter-attack to Malthus. If Malthus was right, Marx and Engels had to be wrong. So they deployed some of their most cutting invective against him. In 1865, the same year as *The Coal Question*, Marx called Malthus's essay a 'libel against the human race'.[15] Twenty years earlier, Engels described Malthus's law of population as 'the most open declaration of war of the bourgeoisie upon the proletariat'.[16] His *Essay* was 'nothing more than a schoolboyish, superficial plagiary', Marx said, ridiculing Malthus's vow of celibacy.[17]

'Where has it been proved that the productivity of the land increases in arithmetical progression?' Engels asked in his 1844 essay *The Myth of Overpopulation*. True, the area of land was limited. Even if it was assumed that additional labour did not always yield a proportionate increase in output, there was,

Engels argued a third element, which 'the economists, however, never consider as important' – science. 'What is impossible for science?' Engels asked.[18]

Jevons was emphatic. Science could not free mankind from resource constraints. 'A notion is very prevalent,' Jevons wrote, 'that, in the continuous progress of science some substitute for coal will be found, some source of motive power, as much surpassing steam as steam surpasses animal labour.'[19] He attacked a popular scientific writer of the time for spreading such notions as 'inexcusable.'[20] The potential of electricity was based on 'fallacious notions', comparable to belief in perpetual motion machines.[21]

What about petroleum? While superior in some respects to coal, it was nothing but the essence of coal. Besides, there wasn't very much of it. 'Its natural supply is far more limited and uncertain than that of coal,' its high price already reflected its scarcity.[22] According to Jevons, 'an artificial supply can only be had by the distillation of some kind of coal at considerable cost.'[23] The future, Jevons asserted, lay in the development of the steam engine and the possibility of multiplying by at least threefold its fuel efficiency. 'If there is anything certain in the progress of the arts and sciences it is that this gain will be achieved, and that all competition with the power of coal will then be out of the question,' Jevons wrote.[24]

Perhaps it needed someone with the imagination of H.G. Wells to envisage a world transformed by the internal combustion engine (which was being developed in the 1860s) and the gas turbine (1930s). However, by the 1860s, the dynamo, discovered by Michael Faraday in 1831, was being commercialised. During the 1870s, dynamos were generating electricity cheaply enough to power factories and begin to replace steam on railways and tramways.[25]

Marx and Engels displayed a much deeper grasp of the dynamic power of capitalism than Jevons. In the same year Jevons was making his assertions about the future's dependence on coal and steam, Engels received a letter commenting on the similarity between Darwin's account of plant and animal life and Malthusian theory.

'Nothing discredits modern bourgeois development so much as the fact that it has not yet succeeded in getting beyond the economic forms of the animal world,' Engels replied:

> We start from the premise that the same forces which have created modern bourgeois society – the steam engine, modern machinery, mass colonisation, railways, steamships, world trade – these same means of production and exchange will also suffice … to raise the productive

powers of each individual so much that he can produce enough for the consumption of two, three, four, five or six individuals.[26]

The third antecedent is Frédéric Bastiat. In Schumpeter's unkind estimation, Bastiat was like the swimmer who enjoys himself in the shallows but drowns when he swims out of his depth. 'I do not hold that Bastiat was a bad theorist,' Schumpeter commented, 'I hold that he was no theorist.'[27]

Theorist or not, when it came to enquiring why Malthus was mistaken, Bastiat asked the right question: Why did Europe no longer suffer from periodic famine? The answer, Bastiat thought, had been provided by another French economist, Jean Baptiste Say. As civilisation advances, the means of existence – the living standards people at any given time think are the minimum needed to maintain themselves and their families – diverge from the means of subsistence, the bare minimum needed to keep body and soul together.

> The means of existence, by reason of social progress, have risen far above the means of subsistence. When years of scarcity come, we are thus enabled to give up many enjoyments before encroaching on the first necessities of life. Not so in such countries as China or Ireland, where men have nothing in the world but a little rice or a few potatoes. When the rice or potato crops fail, they have absolutely no means of purchasing other food.[28]

Malthus's population principle should therefore be amended so that population growth is no longer linked with the means of subsistence, Bastiat argued, but with the means of existence; 'the point where the [population] laws of *multiplication* and *limitation* meet, is removed, and elevated.'[29] People will have as many children as they can afford and maintain a certain standard of living, one that tends to rise over time.

Bastiat's insight is relevant to the debate on global warming a century and a half later. The greater the gap between the means of existence and the means of subsistence, the greater a society's resilience to climatic disaster, however caused. Australia is the world's driest inhabited continent. In the early 1980s, it suffered an intense drought, causing an estimated A\$3 billion in losses.[30] If a similar drought hit sub-Saharan Africa, the issue wouldn't have been the scale of economic losses but the extent of the humanitarian disaster. The difference is a function of economic development. In rich countries, people don't die from drought and crop failure.

Bastiat's ameliorist position reflects a different cast of mind from the pessimistic outlook of Malthus and Jevons. Malthus, he thought, had 'fixed his regards too exclusively on the sombre side. In my own economical studies and inquiries, I have been so frequently led to the conclusion that *whatever is the work of Providence is good*, that when logic has seemed to force me to a different conclusion, I have been inclined to distrust my logic'.[31]

Bastiat's view of the harmony of class interests was in complete contradiction to Marxism's class warfare analysis of history. Marx and Engels viewed Bastiat, a liberal, bourgeois economist, with even greater disdain than Schumpeter did. But in responding to Malthusian views on environmental limits to population growth and economic activity, they were on the same side of the argument. Writing in 1895, towards the end of his life and of a century that had witnessed the greatest increase in production up to that point in history, Engels remarked:

> I do not understand how anyone can speak today of a completion of the Malthusian theory that *the population presses against the means of subsistence* at a time when corn in London cost twenty shillings a quarter, or half the average price of 1848–70, and when it is generally recognised that *the means of subsistence are pressing against the population* which is not large enough to consume them![32]

Capitalism would collapse because it produced too much too cheaply, Marxists used to argue.

That couldn't be said of the collapse of communism in 1989. For sure, the environmental degradation of the communist regimes of Eastern Europe revealed that communism had been faithful to its founders' Promethean ideology of man's subjugation of nature, just as it required the subjugation of mankind. However, communism did not fail because it had poisoned the Earth, polluted the skies or drained inland seas. Neither did it fail because it had run out of natural resources. As an economic system, it failed because it could not produce.

The functional extinction of Marxism as a living ideology was to have a profound impact on the success of the idea of global warming and its ascendancy in the early 1990s. The decline of Marxism removed one of the two economic antecedents from the nineteenth century that would have opposed environmentalism and alarmism about global warming. From the 1960s onwards, the growth of the environmental movement would expand to occupy the space on the political spectrum vacated by classical Marxism. It left the ameliorists, Bastiat's successors, to fight the battle alone against the depletionists, the descendants of Malthus and Jevons.

Jevons' forecasts, or prophecies as Keynes called them, also tell a story relevant to our day. We cannot definitively verify economic forecasts to justify calls to tackle global warming. Unlike Jevons' contemporaries, we can see whether the fame *The Coal Question* earned him was justified by events.

Jevons simply took a three and a half per cent annual growth rate and extended it for a century.[33] For the first decade, the forecast wasn't too bad with a 3.1 per cent average rate of growth a year.[34] But by 1881, the divergence was unmistakable, with actual output of coal nearly twelve per cent less than Jevons had reckoned. The divergence kept growing and coal output peaked and started to decline in the second decade of the twentieth century.

Out-turn vs. Jevons forecast – coal

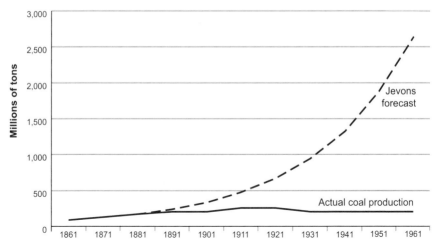

Sources: *Jevons, The Coal Question, p. 213; B.R. Mitchell, International Historical Statistics: Europe 1750–2000, Tables D2, D12, H1, J1*
Note: *1921 average of 1920 and 1922*

Overall, Jevons calculated that Britain would need to produce one hundred and two billion tonnes of coal in the period 1861–1970 with annual production in 1961 projected to be 2.2 billion tonnes. It was this colossal number, which Jevons argued was beyond Britain's physical resources, that led him to conclude that Britain's 'present happy progressive condition' was of limited duration.[35] In reality, total coal production in the hundred years to 1965 was a shade under two billion tonnes, less than the *annual* amount Jevons had forecast for 1965. The forecast by one of the most brilliant economists of his or any age was out by a factor greater than fifty. By 2007, British coal consumption had fallen to around sixty-three million tonnes, of which some twenty million was produced domestically – less than one per cent of what Jevons had projected for the last year of his series.

Even more spectacular than Jevons' over-estimation of the importance of coal was his dismissal of petroleum. Here is the Jevons coal curve again, this time with the rising curve of petroleum imports.

Out-turn vs. Jevons forecast – oil

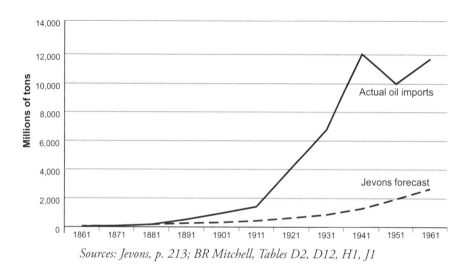

Sources: Jevons, p. 213; BR Mitchell, Tables D2, D12, H1, J1

Keynes said that Jevons wrote *The Coal Question* to shock and establish his public reputation. The book was a bestseller. It led to Jevons meeting Gladstone who told Jevons that his book was masterly. John Stuart Mill argued that because Britain's prosperity was limited, the National Debt should be paid down – a proposition that Keynes argued should have been dismissed with only 'a little reflection'. If demand for coal was to increase indefinitely at a geometric rate, future national income would be so much greater than present national income that the dead-weight represented by the National Debt would become of little account.[36]

How did Jevons get it so wrong?

One of his economist contemporaries said that not only was Jevons simply a genius, he was also a brilliant logician. Jevons believed that forecasting the future was a matter of logic. He once wrote in his journal of waking one sunny morning with the sure sensation that logic had disclosed the future to him, only for it to slip his grasp – epistemological optimism taken to a delusory extreme. Then there's the role of character, as explained by Keynes: 'There is not much in Jevons' scare which can survive cool criticism. His conclusions were influenced, I suspect, by a psychological trait, unusually strong in him, which many other people share, a certain hoarding instinct, a readiness to be alarmed by the idea of the exhaustion of resources.'[37]

Keynes went on to relate that he'd been told by Jevons' son, an economist of some note, about how his father

> held similar ideas as to the approaching scarcity of paper as a result of the vastness of demand in relation to the supplies of suitable material … He acted on his fears and laid in such large stores not only of writing paper, but also thin brown packing paper, that even today, more than fifty years after his death, his children have not used up the stock he left behind of the latter; though his purchases seem to have been more in the nature of speculation than for his personal use, since his own notes were mostly written on the backs of old envelopes and odd scraps of paper, of which the proper place was the waste-paper basket.[38]

The rationality of Jevons' response to his fear of resource depletion provides a contrast with the manner of his end. Ignoring the advice of his doctor that he avoid swimming, on holiday one August, Jevons drowned at sea.

In December 2007, NASA climate scientist James Hansen wrote to the British Prime Minister Gordon Brown, sending a copy of his letter to the Queen. Britain, along with the United States and Germany, had contributed more carbon dioxide emissions per capita than any other country, Hansen claimed. Accompanying the letter was a short analysis of 'basic fossil fuel facts'. There was a graphic totalling carbon dioxide emissions in the period 1751–2006. Coal was the single largest culprit. 'Fully half of the excess CO_2 in the air today (from fossil fuels), relative to pre-industrial times, is from coal,' the analysis said.[39]

Is this a bad thing? As the economist Ronald Coase reminded us, to answer the question, we need to know the value of what is obtained as well as what is sacrificed in obtaining it.

Suppose that at the beginning of the nineteenth century, as the Industrial Revolution was gaining momentum, a climate scientist had found a link between carbon dioxide emissions and global temperatures. And suppose the politicians of the time, invoking the precautionary principle that society should not do things that might involve unknown and un-quantifiable risk, had followed the advice of today's leading proponents of the global warming consensus. As a result, fossil fuel extraction would have been capped when Britain, the world's leading coal producer, was mining less than twenty million tonnes of coal a year.

Posing the counter-factual provides a reality check. If today we implemented deep emission cuts, we cannot be sure how different the future would be in terms of economic development or how the climate of the future might be. But we can be fully confident that if the combustion of coal and other hydrocarbons had been severely restricted from the start of the nineteenth century, the economic take-off of the Industrial Revolution would not have happened: we would all be a lot poorer, our lives would be shorter and most of us would be earning our living working in the fields.

We can also see that the benefits of the Industrial Revolution were not outweighed by the costs of any resultant change in the climate, insofar as such changes can be attributed to industrialisation. The Maldives, or any other inhabited islands, did not sink beneath the oceans – if Darwin was right about the formation of coral atolls, they would not have anyway.* Neither is Bengal inundated. There hasn't been a mass extinction of species due to climate change. It is quite possible that such changes in the climate as a result of industrialisation might, in fact, have been benign. Would a colder world have made us better off – with no coal, no electricity, no gas-fired central heating?

Around the time that Marx, Engels, Bastiat and Jevons were debating Malthus, a scientific breakthrough was occurring with the first experimental demonstration of the warming effect of carbon dioxide. Before it could happen, scientists needed to have identified and isolated carbon dioxide. And to do that, they had to discard one of chemistry's most cherished theories.

---

* In 1836, during the last year of his voyage on HMS Beagle, Darwin hypothesised that coral atolls had been formed by subsidence of the ocean bed of 'extreme slowness.' Witnessing the unrelenting power of the Indian Ocean, Darwin reflected that an island built of the hardest rock would ultimately be demolished by such irresistible forces. 'Yet these low, insignificant coral islets stand and are victorious: for here another power, as antagonist to the former, takes part in the contest. The organic forces separate the atoms of carbonate of lime one by one from the foaming breakers, and unite them into a symmetrical structure. Let the hurricane tear up its thousand huge fragments; yet what will this tell against the accumulated labour of myriads of architects at work night and day, month after month.' Charles Darwin, *Voyage of the Beagle* (first published 1839; Penguin 1989), p. 346 & 338.

It was in the 1750s, during the early stirrings of the Industrial Revolution, that Scottish chemist Joseph Black demonstrated what he called 'fixed air' had fundamentally different properties from ordinary atmospheric air. In the last three decades of the century, Joseph Priestley prepared and differentiated some twenty new 'airs.'[40] At this point, scientific understanding encountered a block in the form of the phlogiston theory of combustion. This explained chemical changes caused by combustion in terms of a substance, phlogiston, being lost into the atmosphere.

The invention of phlogiston wouldn't be the last time that scientists invented something to explain something else. In the nineteenth century, scientists invented ether because their materialistic assumptions required something through which light could undulate and electromagnetic occurrences happen. 'If you do not happen to hold the metaphysical theory which makes you postulate such an ether,' Whitehead wrote, 'you can discard it. For it has no independent vitality.'[41]

The overthrow of the phlogiston theory is a *locus classicus* in Thomas Kuhn's *The Structure of Scientific Revolutions* which describes how a scientific paradigm defines scientists' field of study, then experiences a crisis to be supplanted by a new paradigm in a process similar to a political revolution. Kuhn challenged the idea that scientific knowledge proceeded through cumulative breakthroughs. The depreciation of historical fact and context was deeply ingrained in the ideology of the scientific profession, Kuhn wrote. Science still needed heroes, so it revised or forgot their works that did not fit the present. The outcome was 'a persistent tendency to make the history of science look linear and cumulative'.[42] History, Kuhn argued, did not bear out this linear view of scientific progress: 'Cumulative acquisition of unanticipated novelties proves to be an almost non-existent exception to the rule of scientific development.'[43]

The phlogiston theory broke down because it demanded greater and greater contortions to explain how the escape of a substance was consistent with the increased weight of what was left behind: phlogiston was incorporeal; it was the lightest known substance; it had negative weight.[44] This enabled the Frenchman Antoine-Laurent Lavoisier, who had established his oxygen theory of combustion seven years earlier, to administer the *coup de grâce*. In an extraordinary passage anticipating Popper's theory of science, Lavoisier wrote in 1785:

> Chemists have made phlogiston a vague principle, which is not
> strictly defined and which consequently fits all the explanations

demanded of it. Sometimes it has weight, sometimes it has not; sometimes it is free fire, sometimes it is fire combined with an earth; sometimes it passes through the pores of vessels, sometimes they are impenetrable to it. It explains at once causticity and non-causticity, transparency and opacity, colour and the absence of colours. It is a veritable Proteus that changes its form every instant![45]

In 1800 Frederick William Herschel, a German astronomer settled in England, found that sunlight passing through a prism produced heat just beyond the red end of the visible spectrum. Herschel had stumbled upon infrared radiation. In the 1820s, Jean-Baptiste Fourier took Herschel's discovery as the basis of his speculation that the Earth's temperature could be 'augmented by the interposition of the atmosphere', because, as Fourier hypothesised, 'heat in the state of light find less resistance in penetrating the air, than in re-passing into the air when converted into non-luminous heat'.[46] Had Fourier 'discovered' the greenhouse effect? The self-styled Newton of heat wasn't sure. It was difficult to know how far the atmosphere influenced the average temperature of the globe. Fourier, a formidable mathematician, despaired of solving this problem: 'We are no longer guided by a regular mathematical theory.'[47]

Whether or not Fourier could be said to have discovered the greenhouse effect, it had not been demonstrated experimentally. In 1859, a few months before Charles Darwin published *The Origin of the Species*, the Irish scientist John Tyndall discovered that different gases absorb radiant heat of different qualities in different degrees. Provoked by an interest in glaciers and Alpinism, Tyndall set up a series of experiments to, as he said, put these questions to nature. After seven weeks of intense experimentation in his basement laboratory at the Royal Institution, Tyndall declared 'the subject is completely in my hands'.[48]

Three weeks later at a lecture attended by Prince Albert, Tyndall demonstrated his findings and concluded:

> The bearing of this experiment upon the action of planetary atmospheres is obvious … the atmosphere admits of the entrance of the solar heat, but checks its exit; and the result is a tendency to accumulate heat at the surface of the planet.[49]

Changes in the composition of the atmosphere, Tyndall wrote two years later, might have produced 'all the mutations of climate which the researches of geologists reveal'.[50]

Towards the end of the century, the Swedish scientist Svante Arrhenius was also attracted to the idea that changes in the composition of the atmosphere could explain what caused successive glacial cycles. After a colleague pointed out to him that industrial processes were releasing carbon dioxide into the atmosphere and would gradually alter its composition, Arrhenius did some calculations to quantify the effect. In 1896 Arrhenius produced a paper estimating that a doubling of carbon dioxide in the atmosphere would increase temperatures by 5-6°C.[51]

As an explanation of glacial cycles, Arrhenius' paper did not attract much scientific support. In the 1920s, the Serb mathematician Milutin Milanković proposed a competing theory relating glacial cycles to changes in the Earth's orbit, which scientists found more plausible. By the end of the twentieth century, the Milanković cycles had fallen out of favour. Scientists now favoured theories that explained climate change in terms of changes in the atmosphere.

A new paradigm held scientists in its grip.

4
FIRST STIRRINGS

Was it for this
That one, the fairest of all rivers, loved
To blend his murmurs with my nurse's song,
And, from his alder shades and rocky falls,
And from his fords and shallows, sent a voice
That flowed along my dreams? For this, didst thou,
O Derwent! winding among grassy holms
Where I was looking on, a babe in arms,
Make ceaseless music that composed my thoughts
To more than infant softness, giving me
Amid the fretful dwellings of mankind
A foretaste, a dim earnest, of the calm
That Nature breathes among the hills and groves.

William Wordsworth

At the beginning of the twentieth century, the rudiments of a mechanism of man-made global warming had been documented. And as if to confirm it, temperatures rose through the first decades of the new century. According to a 1922 newspaper report, the Arctic seemed to be warming up. Fishermen, seal hunters and explorers sailing the seas around Spitsbergen and the eastern Arctic pointed to 'a radical change in climatic conditions, and hitherto unheard-of high temperatures … Ice conditions were exceptional. In fact, so little ice has never before been noted'.[1]

The 1930s was a hot decade in North America. 1934 would vie with 1998 as the warmest year of the twentieth century (NASA's Goddard Institute, one of the custodians of the global temperature records, would have difficulty deciding which was the hotter). Six of the fifteen hottest Julys since 1895 were in that decade – each year from 1930 to 1936 except 1932.[2] The 1936 heat wave, which killed five thousand people, set temperature records, some of which have not been exceeded.[3] Dust bowl storms swept the American prairie, caused by severe drought and soil erosion, described by a NASA climate scientist as 'the major climatic event in the nation's history'.[4]

The Central England temperature series, the longest reliable temperature series in the world, shows temperatures rising from the middle of the 1890s, a partial decline in the first decade of the twentieth century, followed by a rising plateau over the next three decades.[5] Data from Nordic countries also conforms to a broad pattern of rising temperatures to peak around 1940.[6]

Might this have been caused by industrialisation?

One man thought so. Guy Stewart Callendar was born in 1898, two years after Arrhenius's 1896 paper. The son of a distinguished Cambridge physicist, Callendar was a talented scientist specialising in the thermodynamics of steam and kept copious notes on temperature and climate records. In 1938, Callendar published a paper on *The Artificial Production of Carbon Dioxide and Its Influence on Temperature*.

Temperatures, as measured by two hundred weather stations worldwide, had risen and the five years 1934–38 were easily the warmest such period at several stations whose records started up to one hundred and eighty years earlier. Humans had added one hundred and fifty billion tonnes of carbon dioxide to the atmosphere since the end of the nineteenth century, around three quarters of which was still in the atmosphere. Callendar estimated that the higher level of carbon dioxide was a major factor explaining the temperature rise, accounting for two thirds of the warming trend of 0.005 degrees centigrade a year experienced in the first half of the twentieth century.

Global warming was first known in scientific circles as the Callendar Effect.[7] If the 1930s' Dust Bowl had happened fifty or sixty years later, it doesn't require much imagination to guess what it would have been blamed on.* Why did it take half a century for the Callendar Effect to be transformed from a scientific curiosity into a planet-threatening crisis?

In the 1930s, there were more pressing issues – the Depression, recovery from the First World War and the threat of a Second, the rise of fascism and communism and the retreat of the nineteenth-century liberal order.

Something else had to change.

Attitudes towards man's interference in nature underwent a profound transformation over the course of the twentieth century. Nowadays, it is (pre-)judged as bad, manifested in opposition to genetically modified food crops; foregoing the opportunity to wipe-out malarial mosquitoes in Africa with the use of DDT and the banning of polychlorinated biphenyl (PCB), a non-toxic chemical used in a wide variety of applications believed by some to be a cancer-causing toxin. At the beginning of the twentieth century, science was allied with industrial progress in benefiting mankind.

---

*   The 1930s drought is now attributed to a cooler Pacific and warmer Atlantic diverting and weakening the jet stream blowing from the Atlantic away from the Midwest (http://www.nasa.gov/centers/goddard/news/topstory/2004/0319dustbowl.html).

This transformation is reflected in changed attitudes towards global warming. Arrhenius thought that burning fossil fuels would accelerate a virtuous cycle in preventing a rapid return to the conditions of the ice age, removing the need for a forced migration from temperate countries to Africa. It might even inaugurate a new carboniferous era of enormous plant growth.[8] Callendar shared this belief. Carbon dioxide emissions would extend agriculture northwards, stimulate plant growth and, quite possibly, indefinitely delay return of the 'deadly glaciers.'[9] Callendar was to have direct experience of the benefits of intervening in nature. During the Second World War, Callendar designed the FIDO fog dispersal system for the Royal Air Force. 'There is no need,' Churchill said, 'to fight the enemy and the weather at the same time.'[10]

America was first to experience the impact of concern about nature on politics. There, it reflected the cultural values of its leaders, especially Theodore Roosevelt.

After the First World War, Britain imported environmental ideas from Germany, where they were grafted on to an indigenous strain of urban nostalgia for the countryside. Far from America being an inspiration, British environmentalists saw America's commercial culture as embodying the features they most detested in their own. For many of them, Germany showed the path back to nature.

> It was still the Wild West in those days, the Far West, the West of Owen Wister's stories and Frederic Remington's drawings, the West of the Indian and the buffalo-hunter, the soldier and the cow-puncher. That land of the West has gone now, "gone, gone with lost Atlantis", gone to the isle of ghosts and of strange dead memories. It was a land of vast silent spaces, of lonely rivers, and of plains where the wild game stared at the passing horseman.[11]

Theodore Roosevelt's need for nature never left him. As president, Roosevelt would often take his companions on lengthy point-to-point walks, walking in a dead straight line.

> On several occasions we thus swam Rock Creek in the early spring when the ice was floating thick upon it. If we swam the Potomac, we usually took off our clothes. I remember one such occasion when the French ambassador, Jusserand … was along, and just as we were about to get in to swim, somebody said, 'Mr Ambassador, Mr Ambassador, you haven't taken off your gloves,' to which he promptly responded, 'I think I will leave them on; we might meet ladies.'[12]

It is hard to imagine the Marquis of Salisbury, the inhabitant of Downing Street when Roosevelt took office, leading such an expedition. Salisbury took no exercise other than riding a tricycle around his estate at Hatfield House and grew immensely fat.

The vigour espoused by Roosevelt contrasts with the solitary contemplation of Henry David Thoreau, who spent two years living on the edge of Walden Pond in the 1840s. Thoreau's was a radical rejection of civilisation. He pitied the young men who inherited farms and houses and cattle. Better to have been born in open pasture and suckled by wolves, so they might see their fields made them 'serfs of the soil.'[13] To Roosevelt, it was 'right and necessary' that the way of life of the Wild West should pass – 'the safety of our country lies in its being made the country of the small homemaker.'[14] Both men shared what Ralph Waldo Emerson called an original relation to the Universe. 'I am no worshipper of Hygeia,' the Greek goddess of health, Thoreau wrote, 'but rather of Hebe ... who had the power of restoring gods and men to the vigour of youth,'[15] a sentiment that accords with Roosevelt's philosophy of the strenuous life.

As a child, Roosevelt seemed destined to become a naturalist. He assembled a collection of rare birds and mammals that he later donated to the Smithsonian. He had an astonishing ear for birdsong. On a walk in England's Itchen Valley with Lord Grey, the British foreign secretary, having heard a bird sing, all he needed to know was its name, and it was unnecessary to tell him more. 'He knew the kind of bird it was, its habit and appearance. He just wanted to complete his knowledge by hearing the song,' Lord Grey recalled.[16]

'More was accomplished for the protection of wild life in the United States than during all the previous years, excepting only the creation of the Yellowstone National Park,' Roosevelt wrote of his time in the White House.[17] He acted, he said, 'to preserve from destruction beautiful and wonderful wild creatures whose existence was threatened by greed and wantonness', overseeing the creation of five national parks, four big game refuges, fifty-one bird reservations and the enactment of laws to protect the wildlife of Alaska.[18]

Roosevelt also subscribed to the depletionist scare first popularised by Jevons the previous century. 'The idea still obtained,' Roosevelt later wrote, 'that our natural resources were inexhaustible.'[19] He invited state governors and the presidents of societies concerned with natural resources – the environmental NGOs of the day – to a three day conference held in May 1908 at the White House. 'It is doubtful whether, except in time of war, any new idea of like importance has ever been presented to a Nation and accepted by it with such effectiveness and rapidity,' Roosevelt wrote.[20]

The conference established the National Conservation Commission, led by Gifford Pinchot, one of the leading conservationists of the era. Published six months later, the commission's report estimated that America's natural gas fields would run out within twenty-five years and its oilfields by the middle of the century. Coal was less of a worry. Reserves appeared adequate to the middle of the twenty-first century.[21] When it was sent to Congress in January 1909, the report was described as 'one of the most fundamentally important documents ever laid before the American people'.[22]

With less than three months of his presidential term left, Roosevelt decided to convene a North American Conservation Conference. It met in February (some things happened faster at the beginning of the twentieth century than at its end). The conference decided that the issue needed to be elevated from a continental to a global level – 'all nations should be invited to join together in conference on the subject of world resources, and their inventory, conservation and wise utilisation'.[23] Before February was out, the US government had sent invitations to forty-five governments. On 4th March, Roosevelt's term was over and the project lapsed. It would take another sixty-three years before the first global conference on the environment in Stockholm in 1972 and not, as Roosevelt had planned, in 1909 at The Hague.

Theodore Roosevelt's leadership had brought nature into American politics, uniting the nascent environmental movement already prone to division. Conservationists, led by Gifford Pinchot, were depletionists following in Jevons' footsteps and believed in taking a utilitarian approach to the use of natural resources. Preservationists such as John Muir, the first president of the Sierra Club, founded in 1892, rejected the Conservationists' utilitarianism. For Muir, as for Emerson and Thoreau, nature was a transcendental reality. Nature was needed for men's souls, not for meeting their material needs. Roosevelt vaulted over Muir's breach with Pinchot. Pinchot had advocated allowing sheep – hoofed locusts, Muir called them – to graze in forest reserves. Roosevelt spent three days with Muir in Yosemite and, acting at Muir's prompting, expanded the Yosemite National Park.

The First World War heightened American concerns about energy supplies, a 'case of national jitters' after the narrow escape from acute energy scarcity in 1917–18.[24] The 1917 Lever Act put the coal industry under government control, setting prices, allocating supply and requisitioning firms not acting in the public interest, all of which helped trigger America's first energy crisis – lightless nights, heatless Mondays, shutdowns of factories producing non-essential items, and fuel riots.[25]

Those jitters led to the creation of the United States Coal Commission in 1922. Its three-thousand-page report, assembled by a five-hundred-strong team, sounded the alarm of impending scarcity – the output of natural gas had begun to wane and the production of oil could not long maintain its present rate. As for coal, rather than analyse the impact of government regulation in restricting supply (the geology of the United States hadn't changed in the fourteen years since the findings of Roosevelt's National Conservation Commission), it argued that output of coal would struggle to meet demand.[26]

Appointed by President Harding, the commission's report was received by his successor, Calvin Coolidge. The new president responded to the commission's report in his first annual message to Congress in December 1923. Acknowledging that the price of coal was 'unbearably high', Coolidge gave the barest of nods to its depletionist case and made plain he was not going to intervene in the coal industry. 'The Federal Government probably has no peacetime authority to regulate wages, prices, or profits in coal at the mines or among dealers, but by ascertaining and publishing facts it can exercise great influence,' Coolidge declared. The real threat to coal supplies was not from imminent resource depletion. It was the coal industry's poor labour relations. On this front, Coolidge promised 'uncompromising action', urging passage of legislation to settle labour dispute as 'exceedingly urgent'.[27]

Coolidge's stand stemmed the depletionist tide for much of the Roaring Twenties. Although Pinchot contemplated running against Coolidge for the Republican nomination in the 1924 election, he decided not to. The Depression in the 1930s reversed the tide. The assumptions underpinning much of Franklin Roosevelt's Depression-era economic policies ran in the opposite direction. High prices and the dangers of scarcity gave way to low prices and glut, which were blamed for worsening the Depression.

In Europe, calls for a return to nature between the two world wars were a reaction to modernity rather than an articulation of modern man's need for it – with one major exception. Often they embodied a call to return to the ways of the past; sometimes they were linked to questions of national identity and, on occasion, more than tinged with blood-and-soil nationalism.

The few voices from the political Left tended to be outside the mainstream. The Marxist belief in scientific socialism and the coming dictatorship of the proletariat made communists such as Lenin ideologically hostile to attempts to battle the laws of history. The British Labour party, in the words of Ernest Bevin, emerging out of the bowels of the trade union movement, was hardly in the business of turning the working class into peasants. Elsewhere in Europe, peasant-orientated movements and parties were not about recovering man's relationship with nature, but pressing claims for land redistribution from landlord to tenant.[28]

In its attitude to nature, National Socialism, together with its British offshoot, was profoundly different from Italian fascism and similar movements elsewhere in Europe, which placed culture and nature as conflicting entities, elevating culture above nature. This led to tension between Italy and Germany when Mussolini embarked on a programme of cutting down trees in the South Tyrol.[29] According to Anna Bramwell in her courageous book, *Ecology in the 20th Century*,

> European fascism, where it had a programme, emphasised forward-looking technological planning and urban development … Germany was the exception, with a tradition, in practice as well as in theory, of looking to nature for philosophical guidance.[30]

That tradition pre-dated Hitler's rise and was appropriated rather than created by Nazi ideologists. Indeed, the word ecology, *Oekologie*, was invented in 1866 by Ernst Haeckel as the science of relations between organisms and their environment.[31]

In the 1920s and 1930s, German ideas permeated Britain. They added to an array of ideas championed by prominent literary figures of the age: D.H. Lawrence and the distinctive German brand of serious nature and sun worship and healthy exercise;[32] the Catholic socialism of Hilaire Belloc and G.K. Chesterton (advocates of giving every worker three acres and a cow); T.S. Eliot's revival of the Christian society and medieval parishes. These disparate voices shared a common loathing of (sub)urban bourgeois culture and hostility to liberal industrial capitalism.

In their criticisms of capitalism and its exploitation of nature, there was little to distinguish Left from Right. Just six months before the outbreak of the Second World War, T.S. Eliot wrote about 'the evil in particular institutions at particular times'. These included 'problems such as the hypertrophy of the motive of Profit into a social ideal, the distinction between the use of natural resources and their exploitation, the use of labour and its exploitation, the advantages unfairly accruing to the trader in contrast to the primary producer, the misdirection of the financial machine, the iniquity of usury, and other features of a commercialised society'.[33]

These ideas were seeded in the fertile political soil of nostalgic patriotism that located the essence of England in the English countryside, a country where the desire of people to have their own garden is visible to anyone flying over London into Heathrow airport. 'The sounds of England, the tinkle of hammer on anvil in the country smithy, the corncrake on a dewy morning, the sound of the scythe against the whetstone, and the sight of a plough team coming over the brow of a hill, the sight that has been in England since England was a land,' words spoken by Stanley Baldwin in a nostalgia-laden St George's Day address in 1924.[34]

British politicians began to respond to the consequences of the rapid expansion of England's cities. Electric trains had extended the reach of the suburbs and, in the inter-war years, the motorcar was further extending it. In 1935, Baldwin's government passed the Restriction of Ribbon Development Act, designed to limit unplanned suburban spread. Protecting the countryside from expanding cities was an outgrowth of nineteenth-century agitation for social reform of curing urban problems through town planning. Ebenezer Howard proposed the garden city as a peaceful path to reforming industrial society. 'The key to the problem,' Howard wrote in 1898, 'is how to restore the people to the land, that beautiful land of ours, with its canopy of sky, the air that blows upon it, the sun that warms it, the rain and dew that moisten it, the very embodiment of Divine love for man.'[35]

In 1926, Sir Patrick Abercrombie, one of the leading town planners of the age, founded the Council for the Protection of Rural England. Was this an English version of Muir's communion with nature in Yosemite and the foundation of the Sierra Club in California? Peter Hall, the leading authority on the English planning system, detects a different motive. Rural England was a place of segregation and social stratification.

> The more prosperous members of the old county society, joined by selected newcomers from the cities, have sought to defend a way of life which they regarded traditionally as their right. The weapon they have used, and it has been a powerful one, is conservationist planning. The result has been to segregate the less affluent newcomers as firmly as ever the medieval cottagers were.[36]

By contrast, George Orwell's England embraced the urban England where Labour drew its support, 'the clatter of clogs in the Lancashire mill towns, the to-and-fro of the lorries on the Great North Road, the rattle of pintables in the Soho pubs'.[37] There was a lively debate within the Left's intelligentsia between urban socialists and rural distributists, the former pushing for the nationalisation of the means of production, the latter for the expropriation of landowners and the redistribution of land to the rest of society.

In 1928, Hilaire Belloc chaired a debate between George Bernard Shaw, speaking for socialism, and G.K. Chesterton championing distributism. Belloc, himself a distributist, summed up. Industrial civilisation, he prophesied, 'will break down and therefore end from its monstrous wickedness, folly, ineptitude' or it will lead 'the mass of men to become contented slaves'.[38] Before the First World War, Chesterton had written of the need for a Peasant Proprietorship in *What's Wrong with the World*. 'If we are to save property, we must distribute property, almost as sternly and sweepingly as did the French Revolution,' a sentiment closer in spirit to Robespierre than Edmund Burke.

Orwell was dismissive of the distributists, writing that a return to small-scale peasant ownership was impossible.[39] In *The Road to Wigan Pier*, Orwell wrote of what he called the Chesterton-type of writer, who wanted 'to see a free peasant or other small-owner living in his privately-owned and probably insanitary cottage; not a wage-slave living in an excellently appointed Corporation flat and tied down by restrictions as to sanitation'.[40]

After the First World War, the younger generation espousing return-to-the-soil ideas broke off in an entirely new direction. In 1920, a leading member of Baden-Powell's Boy Scout movement, the twenty-six-year-old John Hargrave founded the Kindred of the Kibbo Kift, the name purportedly an ancient Kentish dialect meaning proof of great strength. Hargrave's movement had a programme of open-air education, camping and naturecraft and the Brotherhood of Man. A Quaker and a pacifist, Hargrave – White Fox to his followers – believed society could only be regenerated by training a cohort of the strongest few. Inspired by North American Red Indians (the movement adopted totem poles), the Kibbo Kift combined Nordic sagas and Saxon dress.

How could anyone have taken Hargrave and his movement seriously?

An idea seizing the imagination of the leading minds of one age can appear bizarre or absurd to a later one. Within three years of its founding, Hargrave had signed up some of the luminaries of the 1920s to his Kibbo Kift advisory council: Norman Angell, author of the celebrated pre-war book, *The Grand Illusion*, a future Labour Member of Parliament and winner of the 1933 Nobel Peace prize; the evolutionary biologist Julian Huxley; the Belgian playwright Maurice Maeterlinck and winner of the 1911 Nobel Prize in literature; the Indian poet Rabindrath Tagore and H.G.

Wells. D.H. Lawrence was put off by Hargrave's impractical ambition, but, for all that: 'He's right and I respect him for it … If it weren't for his ambition and lack of warmth, I'd go and Kibbo Kift with him.'[41]

In 1923, Hargrave first met Major C.H. Douglas, the theoretician of the Social Credit movement. Social credit, a now forgotten monetary explanation of the economic difficulties of the inter-war years, was based on Major Douglas's cranky A+B theorem. It earned Douglas a mention in Keynes' 1936 *General Theory of Employment, Interest and Money* – 'a private, perhaps but not a major in the brave army of heretics'.[42] Eight years later, the Kibbo Kift became the Green Shirt Movement for Social Credit. Now the Green Shirts had a comprehensive solution to society's problems, an economic prong and an environmentalist prong together providing a critique of capitalism and urban industrial society. Accompanied by a corps of drummers, Green Shirts marched through English towns and cities, singing the Anthem of the Green Shirt movement:

> *Dead Men arise*
> *From the catacombs of Death!*

went the refrain, the anthem ending with the stirring cry,

> *Wake, now, the Dead!*
> *By numbers held in thrall;*
> *On this fruitful Earth*
> *There is Earth-wealth for all!*

While Hargrave and the Green Shirts looked to the past and to Red Indians and Saxons, for inspiration, others looked across the English Channel. 'England is dying, capitulating to the forces which she herself has set in motion,' reads the preface to a book published in 1928.

> Germany is the sole country where there is a positive challenge to the mechanism and commercialism which we associate with America, but which we in England take lying down, without real protest or power to discover an alternative. If contact with Germany cannot stir the faint-heart hopes to a new quickness which will attune us with the forgotten genius of our own Britain, some of us might realise that Germany is fertile soil in which we may plant the seeds of our experience with the surety of their having increase.[43]

Britain and Germany: A Frank Discussion Instigated by Members of the Younger Generation, was co-edited by Rolf Gardiner, who had briefly been a member of the Kibbo Kift and had originally introduced Hargrave to Major Douglas and social credit.

In a chapter, 'Have the Northern Peoples a Common Destiny?', Gardiner repudiated sterile internationalism and rejected Hargrave's pacifism. 'Should some polity arise which calls forth a genuine star-like quality in the blood of men we should be prepared to fight and die for that quality,' Gardiner wrote.[44] Europe's artificial states should be dissolved to reveal the real frontiers of 'race and culture, and they are made manifest in the form and effluence of landscapes, of regions inhabited by past generations.'

Gardiner disdained the British Union of Fascists for being too lower middle class and urban for his taste. Instead, national regeneration would come about through an alliance of aristocracy and yeomanry.[45] Together with the Earl of Portsmouth, Gardiner was the leading advocate of organic farming, the pair paying a visit to Walther Darré, the Nazi agriculture minister. Their journal, *The New Pioneer*, was edited by an ex-member of the National Socialist League, an organisation that criticised Moseley's fascists for being insufficiently anti-Semitic, and devoted much of its space to Gardiner's back-to-the-land programme and organic farming.[46]

The complexity of the various cross currents of the non-traditional Right can be seen with Henry Williamson, author of *Tarka the Otter*, published in 1927, and one of the greatest nature writers of the twentieth century. Having fought in the First World War, Williamson ended it strongly sympathetic to Germany and a Bolshevik. On returning from the 1935 Nuremburg Rally, Williamson expressed his revulsion of the rootless civilisation he saw in London, 'hoardings, brittle houses, flashiness posing as beauty, mongrel living and cosmopolitan modernism.'[47] Two years later, he joined Moseley's British Union of Fascists. Agricultural reform was central to Moseley's plan to recreate British society. Under the Fascists, land use throughout Britain was to be centrally planned and organised, with programmes of re-afforestation, sewage disposal and building motorways to create jobs and re-cycle materials.[48]

Brown Shirts and Green Shirts clashed on the streets of Britain's cities. According to Bramwell, 'the Green Shirts had an element of Quaker niceness, of world unity pacifism' completely at variance with the violence and anti-semitism of Oswald Moseley's fascists.[49] In 1937, the Public Order Act swept the Brown Shirts and Green Shirts off the streets. The Second World War rendered environmentalism irrelevant, putting some of its more vocal pro-German supporters behind bars. In 1944, the Green Shirts were being written off by Labour MP Tom Driberg as a 'small, fantastic cult of nature worshippers'.[50] Hargrave dissolved the organisation in 1951.

Gardiner and his circle found a more successful route into the post-war era. In June 1945, he co-founded the Soil Association and for many years sat on its council.[51] Until the early 1960s, its journal, *Mother Earth*, was edited by the former British Union of Fascists' agricultural secretary, who had spent part of the war in prison. Sixty years after it was founded, eighty per cent of the organic food sold in Britain's supermarkets was being certified by the Soil Association.[52]

Thus British environmentalism emerged from an alien gene pool from the Progressive policies of Theodore Roosevelt a decade or two earlier, with a strong anti-democratic virus and narrative of national decay. To British environmentalists, American culture exemplified all that was wrong with the modern world. 'The English have now reached a point in their history where they must seek a new focus,' Gardiner wrote in 1928; 'the saga of our nationhood and Empire is finished.'[53] Britain had to reject materialism and accept where its true destiny lay: 'Germany is once again a young and puissant nation, pulsating with life and hope, and, like Faust, striving for possession of her own soul.'[54]

In German culture, nature – especially trees and forests – is part of national identity as in no other European country. The Nazi seizure of power in 1933 means that this aspect of German culture became entwined with National Socialist ideology. And here one comes to an awkward truth for the post-1945 environmental movement. Were it not for its crimes, the Nazi record on the environment would have been praised for being far in advance of its time. Nazi Germany introduced anti-vivisection laws. It was the first country in Europe to create nature reserves. In 1934, the Nazis required that new tree plantations should include deciduous trees as well as conifers. In 1940, the Nazis passed hedgerow and copse protection ordinances to protect wildlife as its armies were laying waste to Europe. Following the annexation of part of Poland, one sixth of the new territory's arable land was reserved for new forests and woodland. At the height of the war, Hitler vetoed Ministry of Agriculture schemes to drain and reclaim moorland.[55]

How far could these environmental policies be described as specifically Nazi rather than reflecting more generalised German values and priorities? Put another way, how central was protecting the environment to Nazi ideology?

The story of organic farming in the Third Reich illustrates the Nazis' real priorities. Walther Darré, in charge of the agriculture ministry until

1942, was a convinced Nazi; the titles of two of his books give a flavour: *The Peasantry as Life Source of the Nordic Race* (1928) and *A New Nobility of Blood and Soil* (1934). He was also a supporter of bio-dynamic (organic) farming that had been advocated by Rudolf Steiner in the 1920s, even though Steiner had been an early opponent of the Nazis before his death in 1925.

Rudolf Hess, Hitler's deputy, was a follower of Rudolf Steiner's teachings on the threat to human health posed by artificial fertilisers and Himmler, the head of the SS, encouraged organic farming. Others in the Nazi leadership, such as Goering, were strongly opposed. Following Hess's flight to Britain in 1941, Darré was marginalised, the Gestapo led a crack down on organic farmers and the technocrats in the regime focused on maximising what farms could produce. The Nazi project was not about saving the planet, but about world conquest, the extermination of the Jews and the enslavement of peoples deemed racially inferior.

To become an international movement and make a global impact in the post-war world, environmentalism needed what its European versions in the pre-war period would have abhorred; mass international travel and communications, multinationals and global consumer brands, a transnational entertainment culture – all the things that go to create a global village. Hitler's defeat in 1945 and the depth of Nazi barbarism meant that post-war environmentalism wouldn't speak German as its first language. In Britain, environmentalism's high Conservative lineage and the stain of its association with National Socialism also meant that the next burst of environmentalism would be led from a different social class and from a different part of the political spectrum.

Environmentalism needed to be Americanised. In the post-war world, environmentalism spoke with an American accent – descended from Thoreau and Emerson, Pinchot and Muir and the environmental politics of Theodore Roosevelt.

5
TURNING POINT

Human beings are now carrying out a large scale geophysical experiment of a kind that could not have happened in the past nor be reproduced in the future … This experiment, if adequately documented, may yield a far-reaching insight into the processes determining weather and climate.

Hans Suess and Roger Revelle, 1957[1]

In 1962, when Silent Spring *was first published, 'environment' was not even an entry in the vocabulary of public policy.*

Al Gore[2]

After the Second World War, Callendar exchanged ideas with the younger generation of climate scientists such as Gilbert Plass and Charles Keeling. In 1956, Keeling obtained funding for an observatory at Mauna Loa in Hawaii to record atmospheric concentrations of carbon dioxide. Over time, results from Mauna Loa would show rising levels of carbon dioxide, the Keeling Curve as it became known.

Five years later, Callendar finished the last of his essays. In his 1938 paper, he wrote that 'the course of world temperatures during the next twenty years should afford valuable evidence as to the accuracy of the calculated effect of atmospheric carbon dioxide'.[3] His 1961 paper concluded that the trend toward higher temperatures was significant. Yet Callendar's confidence was undermined by the downturn in global temperatures in the 1950s and 1960s. England's three skating Christmases of 1961, 1962 and 1963 – the coldest since 1740 – shook Callendar's belief in the Callendar Effect.[4]

The post-war era began by subscribing to Francis Bacon's belief that the progress of science and technology aid mankind's mastery of nature and improve his material wellbeing. That belief was to be challenged and then recede over the course the second half of the twentieth century. During it, the prime source of ideological hostility to the Baconian view of man's relationship with nature shifted from the Right to the Left of the political spectrum; the conservationism of the century's first half would be supplanted by environmentalism and the public role of scientists would change from illuminating and enabling mankind's progress along the path of greater material wellbeing to issuing warnings about economic growth and telling governments how they should mitigate the effects of such progress. For a development of such enormity, it all happened with surprising speed.

The end of the Second World War and the start of the Cold War saw the return of fears that the US might run out of raw materials, exacerbated by the Korean War. In January 1951, President Truman appointed William Paley, president of the CBS network, to head a Materials Policy Commission. 'We cannot allow shortages of materials to jeopardize our national security nor to become a bottleneck to our economic expansion,' Truman wrote to Paley.[5]

When its eight-hundred-and-nineteen-page report, *Resources for Freedom*, appeared the following year, it was unmistakably a product of its time.

> The United States, once criticised as the creator of a crassly materialistic order of things, is today throwing its might into the task of keeping alive the spirit of Man and helping beat back from the frontiers of the free world everywhere the threats of force and of a new Dark Age which rise from the Communist nations. In defeating this barbarian violence moral values will count most, but they must be supported by an ample materials base. Indeed, the interdependence of moral and material values has never been so completely demonstrated as today, when all the world has seen the narrowness of its escape from the now dead Nazi tyranny and has yet to know the breadth by which it will escape the live Communist one.[6]

Soaring demand, shrinking resources, upward pressure on costs, the risk of wartime shortages all threatened to stop or reverse Americans' rising standard of living. It sounded as if *Resources for Freedom* would be the latest product of the Jevons cookie cutter. Instead, *Resources for Freedom* turned out to be the most comprehensive official statement of the ameliorist position made by any government or intergovernmental body before or since. It was a popular fallacy, the report concluded, 'to regard our resource base as a fixed inventory which, when used up, will leave society with no means of survival'. American history showed why. 'In developing America,' the commission asserted, 'our forebears consumed resources extravagantly, but we are certainly better off in materials than they were. It would be unreasonable for us, their posterity, to suggest that they should have consumed less so that we might consume more.'[7]

> Using resources today is an essential part of making our economy grow
> ... Hoarding resources in the expectation of more important uses later

involves a sacrifice that may never be recouped; technological changes
and new resource discoveries may alter a situation completely.[8]

To act in this way, the report suggested, would be rather like the early settlers
of New England conserving bayberries to provide light for a generation
that lives by kilowatts.

At times, the report reads like a point-by-point refutation of Jevons.
On recycling, it sided with Keynes, who, as we saw in Chapter Three, had
criticised Jevons for hoarding scraps of paper. It was another popular fallacy, the commission said, to equate physical waste with economic waste,
an attitude which can lead to 'devoting a dollar's worth of work to "saving"
a few cents' worth of waste paper and old string.'[9] The waste paper bin does
have an economic function after all.

The commission had three fundamental convictions. Growth is good
('it seems preferable to any opposite, which to us implies stagnation and
decay,' was the common sense justification); belief in private enterprise,
the profit motive and the price system; and internationalism.[10] Trade was
good for America and America was stronger when its allies were stronger.
If the US did not work to raise living standards in the rest of the free
world, it would 'hamper and impede further rise of our own, and equally
lessen the changes of democracy to prosper and peace to reign the world
over.'[11]

Resources for Freedom made two fundamental recommendations – a do
and a don't to maximise economic efficiency. 'There is no magic formula
which will yield the right answers … Yet there is one basic economic principle which, if applied to the limit of available facts and injected consciously into each judgment, can provide a basic thread of consistency. THE
LEAST COST PRINCIPLE.'[12] The commission recognised the risk of interest groups exploiting political concern about the availability of resource
supplies to cut legal privileges and special deals for themselves.

The second recommendation was a plea to avoid protectionism and au-
tarky. 'The United States must reject self-sufficiency as a policy and instead
adopt the policy of the lowest cost acquisition of materials wherever secure
supplies may be found.' The idea of self-sufficiency, the commission observed, 'amounts to a self-imposed blockade and nothing more.'[13] It urged
that tariff and other barriers to trade be removed, as these were adding to the
free world's material problems. 'By interfering with market pressures of supply and demand, they prevent normal development of the tendency to move
toward the lowest cost sources of materials – a movement which, as the com-

mission has pointed out, is essential in promoting the most rapid economic growth of both the United States and the less developed countries.'[14]

The US should unilaterally eliminate import duties on any commodity if the US was likely to become dependent on it. In the case of petroleum – 'the great enigma of future energy supplies' – the commission envisaged with equanimity that by 1975 the US would have increasingly turned to foreign supplies, although it suggested stockpiling in case of war.[15] It went on to urge repeal of the Buy American Act 1933 and similar protectionist legislation, 'a relic of depression years and depression psychology'.

In the history of concern about industrialised societies running out of resources, which started in 1865 and continues to the present, *Resources for Freedom* stands apart. Based on its examination of history, the commission rejected the depletionists' assumption that there was a fixed lump of resource which, when used up, was gone forever. Compared to the drumbeat of depletionist reports that punctuated the 1970s prophesying resource-induced and environmental catastrophes before the end of the twentieth century, the view of the world set out in *Resources for Freedom* turned out to be right. The world reached 1975 (the time horizon adopted in the report) and the beginning of the twenty-first century closer to the state envisaged in *Resources for Freedom* than the predictions made by the depletionists. For that reason alone, *Resources for Freedom* demands attention and a respectful hearing.

It would have been easy for the Paley Commission to have lapsed in to paranoia. The international situation in 1952 was much riskier than fifty years later. The Soviet Union had acquired the Bomb, the Iron Curtain divided Europe, and the US and its allies were fighting a war in Korea in which the American commander had requested the use of atomic weapons against China.

The policy optimism of *Resources for Freedom* reflected the outlook of a governing elite that a few years earlier had led America to victory in the Second World War and had just put in place the architecture that would win the Cold War. It was confident about America's future and the capacity of its economy to keep growing. It had the self-confidence to be internationalist. Far from falling for the illusion of 'energy independence', *Resources for Freedom* recognised that American prosperity and security were enhanced by an open trading system.

The same year as the Paley Commission produced its report, Congress passed the Domestic Minerals Program Extension Act. It requires the federal government to reduce American dependency on foreign sources of critical or strategic materials and remains in force to this day. In 2003 congressional testimony, the director of the US Geological Survey admitted that shortly after passage of the Act, 'minerals were in surplus rather than shortage … by 1956, even uranium was in over-supply'.[16] Thus within months of the Paley Commission's report, the market had solved the problem it had been established to examine, insofar as there had been one in the first place. It would be another twenty years before politicians and policymakers thought that they, rather than markets, were needed to solve the problem of resource scarcity.

Long-term, the commission foresaw little risk of resource depletion. As land-based resources became more costly, and as technology improved, man would increasingly turn to the sea. 'Covering seventy-one per cent of the earth's surface, the sea is a great reservoir of minerals. In its three hundred million cubic miles of water, the sea probably contains, in solution, all the elements found in the earth's crust.'[17]

Such a view would have confirmed the worst fears of Rachel Carson, an aquatic biologist working for the US Fish and Wildlife Service, whose book, *The Sea Around Us*, had been published the previous year. 'We will become even more dependent upon the ocean as we destroy the land' – a view which reflected what one of her admirers has called her aesthetic of ocean-centrism.[18]

Although trained as a scientist, Carson had always assumed she was going to be a writer. She majored in English, switching to zoology. 'I thought I had to be one or the other; it never occurred to me, or apparently anyone else, that I could combine the two.'[19] Her favourite writers were Henry Thoreau and Henry Williamson. She kept Thoreau's journal beside her bed and her first book, *Under the Sea Wind*, was inspired by Williamson's *Salar the Salmon*.[20]

'I never predicted the book would have a smashing success,' Carson said of *Silent Spring*, which was published in 1962.[21] It spent much of that autumn at the top of the *New York Times* bestseller list and sold over one hundred thousand copies in the week before Christmas. In August, *Silent Spring* sparked a question at President Kennedy's press conference on the dangers of DDT, leading to a report by the President's Science Advisory Committee. It concluded that Carson had been right to warn about the dangers of pesticides. In his address to the UN General Assembly in September, President Kennedy tried to move international relations beyond Cold War divisions to the common challenge of improving the conditions of mankind. Plunder and pollution were the foes of every nation and Kennedy proposed a worldwide programme of conservation.[22]

At one level, Carson's crusade against pesticides failed.[23] According to an official Environmental Protection Agency appreciation of *Silent Spring* sixteen years on, 'Americans now apply more than twice the amount of pesticides they did before *Silent Spring* was published.'[24] What *Silent Spring* changed was vastly more consequential. In a review for the Book-of-the-Month Club, Supreme Court Justice William O. Douglas compared *Silent Spring* to *Uncle Tom's Cabin* for its revolutionary implications.

'You are a poet not only because you use words so well,' wrote one of her fans in a letter that evidently meant much to Carson as she copied it to a friend, 'but because by describing non-human life, you make us readers understand our place on earth so much better. As I drive home along the Hudson tonight I'll feel more human for having read your lovely, loving words today.'[25]

Silent Spring's title was a masterstroke, suggested to Carson by her editor. Discarded titles included 'Man against the Earth' and 'The War against Nature', which better describe the larger dimension of the book's purpose at the cost of the book's capacity to provoke the kinds of reaction (those lovely, loving words) if its purpose had been made plain in its title. Spring has an almost religious quality about it. 'In a pleasant spring morning all men's sins are forgiven,' Thoreau wrote in *Walden*. 'Through our own recovered innocence we discern the innocence of our neighbours ... There is not only an atmosphere of good will about him, but even a savour of holiness groping for expression.'[26] For modern man to destroy spring is tantamount to extinguishing the possibility of redemption.

The book opens with what Carson described as a fable for tomorrow, the silent spring. A rural town in the heart of America hit by a 'strange blight' casting an 'evil spell'; sudden deaths which doctors couldn't explain – children dead within a few hours; apple trees that yielded no fruit; birds that trembled violently and couldn't fly: 'No witchcraft, no enemy action had silenced the rebirth of new life in this stricken world. The people had done it to themselves.'[27] Although the town did not exist, Carson wrote that every one of the disasters had actually happened somewhere, allegedly silencing the voices of spring in countless towns across America.[28]

The book proceeds to catalogue a string of disasters. A dog and baby exposed to an insecticide. Within an hour the dog is dead and the baby little more than a vegetable.[29] Two children in Florida dead after touching a bag that contained a Parathion – a favourite means of committing suicide in Finland, we're told.[30] An unfortunate chemist who swallowed 0.0424 ounces of Parathion to assess its effects – paralysed before he could reach the antidotes.[31] The housewife scared of spiders who sprayed her house three times with an aerosol containing DDT and petroleum distillate. She felt unwell, saw a doctor and was found to be suffering from acute leukaemia – dead the next month.[32]

The threat of cancer lurked everywhere. People were living in a sea of carcinogens.[33] Worse still was the prevalence of cancer among children. Twenty-five years previously, cancer in children had been rare. 'Today more American school children die of cancer than from any other disease.'[34] Attempts to cure cancer were doomed, Carson wrote, 'because it leaves untouched the great reservoirs of carcinogenic agents which continue to claim new victims faster than the as yet elusive "cure" could allay the disease'.[35]

After her death in 1964 (the same year as Callendar), Carson acquired an iconic status as a lonely female scientist speaking up for nature against an entrenched male scientific establishment financed by vested interests. While working on *Silent Spring*, Carson was being treated for breast cancer, sanctifying *Silent Spring* as the product of a green martyrdom. Questioning its scientific basis is considered bad form or worse, especially from the wilder shores of eco-feminism.*

Although framed as an indictment of pesticides, Carson's general theory was that flora and fauna were threatened by any substance which they had not previously encountered.

> With the dawn of the industrial era the world became a place of continuous, even accelerating change. Instead of the natural environment there was rapidly substituted an artificial one composed of new chemical and physical agents, many of them possessing powerful capabilities for inducing biologic change.[36]

Each year, five hundred new chemicals were being introduced to which 'the bodies of men and animals are required somehow to adapt'.[37] Man's speed was nature's enemy. 'The rapidity of change and the speed with which new situations are created follow the impetuous pace of man rather than the deliberate pace of nature.'[38]

---

*   In *The Recurring Silent Spring*, Patricia Hynes, a former official of the EPA, wrote of her anger 'at living in a world in which nature and women are presumed to exist for the use and convenience of men, so that the destruction of nature and violence against women are interconnected, increasingly technologised, and infect all corners of the earth.' H. Patricia Hynes, *The Recurring Silent Spring*, Elmsford, (1989), p. 2.

This scientific hypothesis at the core of *Silent Spring* is not one that was subsequently developed with any success. Even her admirers do not ascribe pre-eminence to the science of *Silent Spring*. For them, its significance lies elsewhere. Linda Lear's 1997 biography describes *Silent Spring* as a 'fundamental social critique of a gospel of technological progress.'[39] A leading textbook of environmental issues in American history argues that *Silent Spring* was more important for what it said about modern society and its relationship to nature than about chemistry and biology.

> For all the debate about the specific merits of pesticide regulation that Carson's work ultimately produced, at bottom her profoundly radical and most enduring argument was that corporate and governmental institutions of power – whether out of arrogance or ignorance, or for base profit motives – had disrupted the balance of the natural world and now threatened human health.[40]

As social theory, the arguments in *Silent Spring* are decidedly patchy. Who was to blame? 'The authoritarian temporarily entrusted with power.'[41] But elsewhere, Carson castigated 'the mores of suburbia' which led to the use of herbicides to remove unwanted crabgrass. Power mowers, Carson complained, had been fitted with devices to disseminate pesticides, 'so to the potentially dangerous fumes from petrol added the finely divided particles of whatever insecticide the probably unsuspected suburbanite has chosen'.[42] Then there were farmers exceeding the prescribed dosages and using chemicals too close to harvest time or more insecticides than were necessary and in other ways displaying 'the common human failure to read the fine print.'[43] If Carson's reputation had rested on the power and originality of her analysis of social causation, she would have been a marginal figure.

During her life, Carson was accused by some of her critics of being unmarried, which was true but irrelevant – although not everyone thought so ('I thought she was a spinster. What's she so worried about genetics for?' exclaimed a member of the Federal Pest Control Review Board) – and a communist.[44] Classical Marxism was about reorganising industrial societies along socialist lines. Carson was against industrial societies altogether. Carson was not a communist; she was an ecologist. 'What is important is the relation of man to all life, when through our technology we are waging war against the natural world,' she said in 1963.[45] Writing to a friend, she put it more baldly: 'In truth, man is against the earth.'[46]

Carson summarised her credo in a 1964 CBS interview:

> I truly believe that we in this generation must come to terms with
> nature, and I think we're challenged as mankind has never been
> challenged before to prove our maturity and our mastery, not of
> nature, but of ourselves.[47]

In a statement written not long after *The Sea Around Us* was published,
Carson gave voice to an aesthetic, her belief system. 'I believe that whenever we destroy beauty, or whenever we substitute something man-made
and artificial for a natural feature of the earth, we have retarded some part
of man's spiritual growth.'[48]

The ecologism espoused by Carson conforms to what Nietzsche had
anticipated at the end of the nineteenth century. Since the time of Copernicus, science had been pushing man from the centre of the universe
and would push him to its periphery. 'It destroys my importance,' Kant
observed. According to Nietzsche, science was destroying the self-respect
humans once had. The faith in their dignity, their uniqueness, their irre-
placeable position in the chain of being, their position as children of God,
had gone. The human being was becoming a mere animal.[49]

Biologists in the second half of the twentieth century point out that
homo sapiens is one species among the countless that have existed since life
began, and, in their eyes, not an especially significant one. Palaeontologist
Stephen Jay Gould liked to counter the received picture of evolution working from simple forms of life toward complexity, with man at the summit.
'The most outstanding feature of life's history is that through 3.5 billion
years this has remained, really, a bacterial planet. Most creatures are what
they've always been: They're bacteria and they rule the world,' Gould told
an interviewer. 'We need to be nice to them.'[50]

Carson told the viewers of CBS that man still talked in terms of conquest. 'We still haven't become mature enough to think of ourselves as only
a tiny part of a vast and incredible universe.'[51] Carson's ocean-centrism
overwhelmed mankind's significance. 'He cannot control or change the
ocean as, in his brief tenancy of earth, he has subdued and plundered the
continent,' she wrote in *The Sea Around Us*.[52]

Ecologism differs from the transcendentalism of Emerson and Thoreau.
With the latter, the individual's openness to nature elevates him and shows
him his uniqueness. By contrast, ecologism preaches man's intrinsic insig-
nificance. Not that its followers find their own lives devoid of importance.

Towards the end of her life, Carson was drawn toward belief in the immortality of her soul. When consideration moves from a particular individual to the relationship of human society to the natural world, ecologism brings a radically altered perspective, one of a disruptive, out-of-control species, putting its survival and that of other species at risk by upsetting natural balances.

Ecologism was a child of the 1960s given the breath of life by Rachel Carson. It would be the philosophy used to evaluate man's impact on nature. The lasting effect was the presumption that human interventions in the natural world were potentially harmful. New ones should be avoided unless it could be demonstrated that they were harmless, giving rise to the precautionary principle. The logic of the precautionary principle runs counter to the development of human society, especially its acceleration with the Industrial Revolution. As environmentalism reached a peak in 1972, the Canadian economist Harry Johnson countered that 'man's whole history has been one of transforming his environment rather than accepting its limitations'.[53]

In focusing exclusively on mankind's impact on nature, ecologism – the ideological core of the environmental movement – opposed the claims of the poor to seek better lives for themselves. There were too many of them and meeting their demands would put further pressure on fragile ecological balances and accelerate resource depletion.

To succeed in its mission to save the planet, environmentalism depended on global participation. Its ability to persuade developing countries that doing so would be in their interests would be environmentalism's greatest challenge. Its success would determine the fate of its most ambitious project – saving the world from the perils of global warming.

6
SPACESHIP EARTH

We came all this way to explore the moon, and the most important thing is that we discovered the Earth.

Bill Anders on Apollo 8, 24th December 1968

On 23rd March 1964, the first session of the United Nations Conference on Trade and Development (UNCTAD) was held in Geneva. Four thousand delegates from one hundred and nineteen countries attended, making it the largest international event held up to that date. The United Nations had designated the 1960s the Decade of Development and the creation of UNCTAD reflected the growing weight of Third World countries in the UN General Assembly. In the 1950s, Latin America had twenty out of the fifty-one seats in the General Assembly. Decolonisation meant that in the 1960s, the Third World constituted the majority. The Geneva conference saw the formalisation of the G77 group as the largest voting bloc in the UN.

Only two speakers were given a standing ovation, the improbably pin-striped Che Guevara and the secretary-general of the conference, Raúl Prebisch. Like Guevara, Prebisch was an Argentine exile. Although the CIA had kept him under surveillance in the 1950s, Prebisch was no revolutionary. Born in 1901, he had a meteoric rise. Appointed under-secretary of finance at the age of twenty-nine, he quickly rose to become general manager of Argentina's central bank.

On the outbreak of the Second World War, realising it would lead to American economic leadership, Prebisch went to Washington to negotiate a trade deal. A three-minute courtesy call with Franklin Roosevelt turned into an hour-long meeting. Roosevelt urged Prebisch to nationalise Argentina's British-owned railways, at the same time warning him that railways were a poor investment.[1]

Following a coup in 1943, Prebisch was sacked. There was no place for him in the new regime, so he decided to develop the economic policies Argentina should adopt after the war. Prebisch believed that Argentina's reliance on agriculture condemned it to boom-bust cycles and decline relative to the industrialised world. At the centre of his economic thinking was a structural rift between the core and the periphery of the international trading system. Trends in commodity prices relative to prices of manufactured goods between 1873 and 1938 provided evidence, Prebisch argued, that the commodity-producing periphery was at a structural disadvantage to the industrialised core.

A UN conference at Havana in 1949 set the stage for Prebisch's new ideas. Tensions between the US and Latin America had been rising, fuelled by resentment of the US. Prebisch's speech electrified the conference. 'I gave consistency to ideas that were in the air. I did not create *ex novo*: I reflected an intellectual reality,' he explained towards the end of his life.[2] Prebisch's Havana Manifesto demonstrated why Third World countries were condemned to relative decline and provided their governments with policies that overturned the traditional ones prescribed by classical economics, just as Keynes had for economies during the Depression of the 1930s. 'One of the conspicuous deficiencies of general economic theory from the point of view of the periphery,' Prebisch told the conference, 'is its false sense of universality.'[3]

Exhilarated by the instant acclaim and attention, Prebisch suddenly disappeared. According to his biographer, 'His sensational public success had unleashed an unbridled sexuality heretofore contained by a life of disciplined work and family.'[4] Three weeks later, he re-emerged to be acknowledged as the intellectual leader of a new path for the economic development of the Third World, one which emphasised the need for governments to actively stimulate industrialisation.

The path of economic development advocated by Prebisch ran in diametrically the opposite direction to the demands of the environmental movement in the West unleashed by *Silent Spring*. Thus two new forces were emerging to re-shape the post-war world. Their inner logic was antithetical to each other. Unless they could identify a common foe or develop a new synthesis, only one of them could prevail.

One aspect of Prebisch's economic analysis meshed with the growing environmentalist movement in the West in the 1960s. Both were based on an assumption that markets failed. For Western environmentalists, markets led to environmental degradation and resource depletion. For Prebisch and his followers in the Third World, the benefits from trade between the core and the periphery – North and South as it would become in the UN development debates of the 1970s and 1980s – were distributed unequally.

But in other ways, the two clashed. Environmentalists blamed the ills of society and threats to the environment on industrialisation. Prebisch argued that Third World governments should intervene to accelerate industrialisation. Western environmentalists believed resources were running out, implying higher commodity prices. Prebisch argued that prices of commodities would fall relative to prices of manufactured goods. Who was right? A 1992 study of twenty-six individual commodity prices over the period 1900–1983 suggests neither of them were. Of the twenty-six, sixteen were trendless, five had statistically significant negative trends and the remaining had positive trends.[5]

Whatever its objective merits as an economic blueprint for developing countries, the Havana Manifesto was a political fact, one institutionalised with the creation of UNCTAD and the formation of the G77. In forming the most numerous voting bloc in the UN General Assembly, the Third World had succeeded in carving out a bargaining position in international negotiations wherever their agreement was required. Whenever it could, the G77 would insist that international issues be addressed through the General Assembly.

Environmentalists in the West were slow to recognise the dilemma this posed for environmentalism. During the 1960s, environmentalism went global – its mission became planetary. In July 1965, five days before a fatal heart attack, Adlai Stevenson, America's ambassador to the UN, spoke of humanity as passengers on a little spaceship dependent on its vulnerable reserves of air and soil.

> We cannot maintain it half fortunate, half miserable, half confident, half despairing, half slave – to the ancient enemies of man – half free in a liberation of resources undreamed of until this day. No craft, no crew can travel safely with such vast contradictions. On their resolution depends the survival of us all.[6]

The following year, economist Kenneth Boulding picked up Stevenson's theme. Entitled 'The Economics of the Coming Spaceship Earth', Boulding argued that past civilisations had imagined themselves to be living on an illimitable plane. 'There was almost always somewhere beyond the known limits of human habitation, and over a very large part of the time man has been on earth, there has been something like a frontier.'[7] This was the 'cowboy economy', symbolising 'the reckless, exploitative, romantic, and violent behaviour, which is characteristic of open societies'.[8] In the cowboy economy, consumption was regarded as a good thing, as was production. Now mankind was transitioning to the spaceman economy. Man's material wellbeing would be constrained by the economics of the closed sphere. Everyone in the world shared the same spaceship. On spaceships, supplies are rationed; 'The less consumption we can maintain a given state with, the better off we are.'[9]

The metaphor of the spaceship economy carried a strong presumption in favour of global governance. What anyone did anywhere was the concern of everyone, everywhere.

Stevenson's speech had been drafted by Barbara Ward, a British intellectual who, alongside Rachel Carson, has a strong claim to be the most consequential environmentalist of the twentieth century. In 1966, Ward gave a lecture, *Space Ship Earth*, in which she argued that mankind's survival depended on developing a government of the world.

The longevity of China's government, Mao being the latest dynasty, demonstrated that world government was possible. If two thousand years of rule can work for twenty-five per cent of the world's population, 'we can hardly argue that the task of government becomes *a priori* impossible simply because the remaining three-quarters are added', Ward argued.[10] Would a world government have to be authoritarian, she asked? No, look at the continental federation of the United States. 'If a free continent is possible, why not an association of free continents?'[11]

The expansion of environmentalism to embrace the future of the planet had huge implications for global politics and environmentalism. Whereas socialism within one country was a viable political doctrine, one-country environmentalism would be nothing more than symbolism. Saving the planet demanded global policies.

On Christmas Eve 1968, nearly a quarter of a million miles from Earth, the three crew members of Apollo 8 orbited the moon. Each took turns to read the first ten verses of the book of Genesis, ending their reading with 'God bless all of you, all of you on the good Earth'. The photographs were even more arresting; the first of the whole Earth, a blue disc suspended in a black void, and of the Earth rising above the curve of the moon's horizon, an unforgettable contrast between the only known planet that supported life and the grey, pitted emptiness of the lunar landscape. Environmentalism had acquired as its icon one of the most powerful images ever produced.

Back on Spaceship Earth, a growing number of the crew were gaining their independence from declining imperial powers. The newly independent states had little interest in replacing an antiquated form of imperialism with a newer version and were adopting economic policies that ran counter to the anti-industrialisation tenets of Western environmentalism. How could the irreconcilable be reconciled?

One man above all developed and popularised the notion that the solution to the environmental and spiritual crisis in the First World could be found in the Third World. Hailed by Jonathon Porritt, a leading British environmentalist and adviser to Prince Charles, as 'the first of the "holistic thinkers" of the modern Green Movement', Fritz Schumacher was born in Bremen three years before the First World War.[12] Revulsion at the Nazis led

Schumacher to flee Germany and settle in Britain. He quickly developed a reputation as an able economist, engaging Keynes in discussions about post-war currency reform and working on the 1944 Beveridge Report on full employment.

His input into the Beveridge Report impressed Hugh Gaitskell. When he became minister of fuel and power in the 1945 Labour government, Gaitskell suggested that the newly nationalised National Coal Board appoint Schumacher as its chief economist. Like Jevons before him, Schumacher became alarmed at the prospect of resource depletion, ironically just as post-war demand for coal started to fall. In a 1954 lecture, Schumacher articulated his concern by placing the depletion of finite energy resources in the context of man's relationship with nature.

> We are living off capital in the most fundamental meaning of the word. Mankind has existed for many thousands of years and has always lived off income. Only in the last hundred years has man forcibly broken into nature's larder and is now emptying it out at a breathtaking speed which increases from year to year ... The whole problem of nature's larder, that is the exhaustion of non-renewable resources, can probably be reduced to this one point – Energy.[13]

Schumacher's work at the Coal Board went hand in hand with a growing preoccupation with organic farming. He bought a house in Surrey with a four-acre garden, promptly joined the Soil Association and became an avid reader of its journal *Mother Earth*, edited by the former fascist Jorian Jenks. He invited an expert from the Soil Association to give a lecture to the Coal Board's gardening club. 'To listen to a lecture on food production in the Headquarters of fuel production,' was, Schumacher told his colleagues, 'the most significant concentration on the essential that I could imagine.'[14] He also developed an interest in Eastern mysticism and astrology, working out his children's horoscopes. If used 'correctly and wisely', astrology could be a useful instrument in understanding one's fellow men, Schumacher claimed.[15]

The event that pulled these diffuse strands together was an invitation to be an economic adviser to the government of Burma. The trip was the final stage in Schumacher's transformation. He left for Burma as an economist and returned as a soothsayer and guru. The Economic and Social Council of Burma, which had invited him, was not thrilled with its economic adviser seeking answers to economic questions from orange-robed monks.

Stopping off in New York, 'this American madhouse', the contrast with Burma led him to declare that he had found the cure for Western civilisation – Buddhist economics.[16] A Buddhist approach would distinguish between misery, sufficiency and surfeit. 'Economic "progress" is good only to the point of sufficiency, beyond that, it is evil, destructive, uneconomic,' Schumacher said.[17] Economics was based on materialism and the religions of the East offered an alternative, the new guru thought. Mahatma Gandhi had laid down the foundation for a system of economics that, Schumacher believed, would be compatible with Hinduism and Buddhism too.

'Buddhist economics' enabled Schumacher to recast the narrower depletionist arguments developed by Jevons ninety years before into a new language mixing ecologism and Eastern mysticism:

> A Buddhist economy would make the distinction between 'renewable' and 'non-renewable resources'. A civilisation built on renewable resources, such as products of forestry and agriculture, is by this fact alone superior to one built on non-renewable resources ... The former co-operates with nature, while the latter robs nature. The former bears the sign of life, while the latter bears the sign of death.'[18]

All this was poured into Schumacher's classic, *Small is Beautiful*. It gave him a huge cult following. The one thing it wasn't was what Schumacher claimed it to be: 'A study of economics as if people mattered.' Answering critics who asked what economics had to do with Buddhism, Schumacher replied. 'Economics without spirituality can give you temporary and physical gratification, but it cannot provide an internal fulfilment.'[19] Economics without Buddhism is like sex without love. The remark illustrates Schumacher's flawed premise. Economics is not a science of happiness. Economic welfare is only a part of human welfare; it has no claims to explain what falls outside its domain or resolve the problems of the spirit, ethical problems or indeed instruct people on how to find happiness.

Instead *Small is Beautiful* is a collection of *pensées* and injunctions, predominantly of a religious and philosophical character – many of them trite, trivial or bizarre. Why is small beautiful? 'Man is small, and, therefore, small is beautiful,' said the Sage of Surrey.[20] Technology must therefore be redirected to the actual size of man. Buddhist economics means simplicity and non-violence.[21] What might this mean in practice? 'It would be highly uneconomic, for instance, to go in for complicated tailoring, like the modern west, when a much more beautiful effect can be achieved by the skilful draping of uncut material,' Schumacher opined.[22]

What has this to do with economics? As Humpty Dumpty explained to Alice, 'When I use a word, it means what I choose it to mean' – an attitude that is the mark of a guru, not a philosopher or economist.

Schumacher liked trees. If people followed the Buddhist injunction to plant a tree every few years, the result would be a high rate of genuine economic development. 'Much of the economic decay of south-east Asia (as of many other parts of the world) is undoubtedly due to a heedless and shameful neglect of trees,' Schumacher wrote.[23] Anticipating a deeply held belief of the Green Movement, he argued that Buddhist economics was hostile to international trade, 'production from local resources for local needs is the most rational way of economic life, while dependence on imports from afar and the consequent need to produce for export to unknown and distant peoples is highly uneconomic and justifiable only in exceptional cases and on a small scale'.[24]

Similarly, Schumacher favoured renewable resources. 'Non-renewable goods must be used only if they are indispensable.'[25] As with his opposition to international trade, Schumacher did not provide anything that might be described as a chain of economic reasoning supported by evidence. Even the Buddhist tag was a misnomer. The Sermon on the Mount's blessing of the meek was reinterpreted to mean 'we need a gentle approach, a non-violent spirit, and small is beautiful'.[26] A militant atheist as a young man, Schumacher was received into the Catholic Church in 1971. Responding to a questioner on his final trip to the US, Schumacher said: 'It was what I call Buddhist economics. I might have called it Christian economics, but then no one would have read it.'[27] Schumacher was really the successor to Hilaire Belloc and G.K. Chesterton for the 1960s flower-power generation, reaching an audience of millions.

For all Schumacher's popularity among the impressionable and the credulous in the First World – in 1977, he visited the White House, where he gave a delighted Jimmy Carter a copy of *Small is Beautiful* – the reaction to ideas in the Third World was distinctly cool, perhaps reciprocating his own. 'India is a sewer,' he remarked in 1973.[28] His doctrine of 'intermediate technology' would have locked the Third World into permanent inferiority to the West and was patronising to boot:

> All development, like all learning, is a process of stretching. If you attempt to stretch too much, you get a rupture instead of a stretch, or you will lose contact and nothing happens at all.[29]

He was an ardent supporter of the Soil Association, bequeathing them the royalties from *Small is Beautiful*. 'Their methods bear the mark of non-violence and humility towards the infinitely subtle system of natural harmony,' absolving it of the Nazi sympathies of its founders, and was strongly opposed to the use of pesticides and chemical fertilisers to increase crop yields.[30]

Application of Schumacher's ideas to the Third World would have been disastrous. It was Norman Borlaug's Green Revolution, not Schumacher's intermediate technology or the Soil Association's organic farming, which fed the Third World and avoided the mass starvation and the deaths of millions of Indians confidently predicted by Paul Ehrlich in his 1968 bestseller *The Population Bomb*. As Borlaug, winner of the 1970 Nobel Peace Prize, pointed out in a 1972 newspaper article, wheat yields in India and Pakistan doubled in the six years from 1965, with similar progress in rice yields.[31] When Borlaug died in 2009, the Indian agriculture minister paid tribute. India and many other nations owed a debt of gratitude to 'this outstanding personality' for helping to forge world peace and saving the lives of two hundred and forty-five million people worldwide.[32]

Gratitude in the Third World, but what about in the West? For American radicals, the implications of the Green Revolution were quite different. Borlaug's achievement wasn't about feeding the hungry and saving lives; the Green Revolution had damaged the prospects of a Red Revolution and had extended capitalist agriculture to the tropics.[33]

From his perch at Berkeley in California, the leading ideologist of the New Left Herbert Marcuse re-formulated classical Marxism – a belief system entirely indifferent to nature – to capitalise on the surge in environmentalism. 'Violation of the Earth is a vital aspect of the counter-revolution,' Marcuse told a 1972 conference on ecology and revolution.[34] Monopoly capitalism is waging war against nature, 'the more capitalist productivity increases, the more destructive it becomes. This is one sign of the internal contradictions of capitalism.'[35] Marcuse yoked together the two issues bringing young people out onto the streets: 'The genocidal war against people is also "ecoside".'[36]

The passengers and crew of Spaceship Earth were nothing if not disputatious.

7
LIMITS TO GROWTH

The crux of the matter is not only whether the human species will survive, but even more whether it can survive without falling into a state of worthless existence.

Executive Committee of the Club of Rome, 1972[1]

22nd April 1970 – Americans celebrated the first Earth Day. A quarter of a million people gathered in Washington, DC. Altogether twenty million people took part in peaceful demonstrations across America.[2] President Nixon's 'Silent Majority', who sided with him over the Vietnam War against the anti-war protestors, was marching with them on the environment.

In preparing his first State of the Union Message in January 1970, Nixon noted that public concern on environmental issues had risen from twenty-five per cent in 1965 to seventy-five per cent at the end of 1969.[3] Nixon decided to pre-empt the Democrats on the environment and prevent them using it against him in the 1972 presidential election. His decision made, Nixon went the full distance: 'The time has come for a new quest – a quest not for a greater quantity of what we have, but for a new quality of life in America.' The question America would answer in the 1970s was whether it would make peace with nature. Using the language of environmentalism, Nixon spoke of making reparations to nature. 'Through our years of past carelessness we incurred a debt to nature, and now that debt is being called.' He would propose the 'most comprehensive and costly' environmental programme in America's history.[4]

In private, Nixon told one of his aides, 'In a flat choice between smoke and jobs, we're for jobs ... But just keep me out of trouble on environmental issues.'[6]

Cynical? The *New York Times* gave him the headline he wanted:

NIXON, STRESSING QUALITY OF LIFE, ASKS IN THE STATE OF THE UNION MESSAGE FOR BATTLE TO SAVE ENVIRONMENT; OFFERS 'NEW ROAD'[5]

Congress passed laws to regulate air and water pollution and in July, Nixon created the Environmental Protection Agency by carving out functions from existing federal departments. One of the Cabinet secretaries losing staff in the reorganisation asked Nixon whether it was all right for a Cabinet member to say, 'No comment.' Nixon shot back, 'Yes. And it's about time.'[7] He appointed William Ruckelshaus, a lawyer, to be the EPA's first administrator. Ruckelshaus then led a seven-month hearing into DDT. Despite the thinness of scientific evidence of DDT's threat to human health, in 1972 the EPA banned its use – ten years after publication of *Silent Spring* – in a highly political reaction to the over-use of the pesticide by American farmers.

America's second most important elected Republican approached environmental politics differently. In his campaign for governor in 1966, Ronald Reagan had caused consternation with his remark about California's redwoods: 'A tree is a tree – how many more do you need to look at?'[8] Environmental sensitivities in California had been raised by the blowout of an oil platform six miles off the coast of Santa Barbara in January 1969, leading to a drilling ban in federally controlled waters off the central Californian coast.

Once elected, Reagan's environmental policies turned out to be a lineal descendant of Teddy Roosevelt. He created a fifty-eight-thousand-acre Redwood National Park. He reached agreement with Nevada to restrict development of Lake Tahoe. Reagan also supported legislation to ban the registration and sale of automobiles that did not meet Californian auto emission standards. In what his long time biographer Lou Cannon called his finest environmental achievement, Reagan stopped the Dos Rios Dam construction project. 'Ike, I hate to see a beautiful valley destroyed,' he told Ike Livermore, the state's secretary for resources.[9] In 1973, Reagan saddled up and, followed by one hundred packhorses, rode to a meadow underneath Minaret Summit in the eastern Sierra. Waving a white hat, Reagan dismounted and made a speech opposing the Trans-Sierra highway project. It would have been the only road cutting the two-hundred-and-eleven-mile John Muir Trail between Yosemite and Mount Witney. The highway was never built.

Unlike the localised surges in environmental politics earlier in the twentieth century, environmentalism in the late 1960s and early 1970s was synchronised across the Western world. It was powered by a common concern that man's activities – the pollution of air and water – were poisoning the biosphere (Carson had called *Silent Spring* her poison book).[10] Governments across the Western world responded in similar ways. A 1976 UN survey found that seventy countries had created agencies or departments at national level with environmental protection as a core function.[11]

The wave would crest in 1972. Then, even more swiftly than it rose, it broke. Fifteen years would pass before the second wave began to roll, propelled by global warming.

Both drew their energy from fear that industrialised societies were destroying the balance of nature on which humans depended. The first wave was more extreme in its claims, the second more consequential in its effects. Both started during a long period of prosperity. The first began towards the end of what economic historian Angus Maddison called the Golden Age and the second during the growth phase of what Maddison dubbed the Neoliberal Order.

They had similar cheerleaders – NGOs and a cast of experts comprising scientists, mostly physicists and biologists, acting as Jeremiahs warning that time was running out to avert catastrophe. These experts, possessing the gift of seeing the future, were blind to the past – ignorant of the recurring pattern of alarmist forecasts from Malthus and Jevons onwards and incurious as to why similar prophecies in the past had all been wrong. Compared to those earlier efforts, in the sixties and early seventies, forecasts of collapse and doom were high decibel, Technicolor productions for worldwide release.

Might they share the misconceptions that pre-determined the predictive failure of earlier ones? A persistent feature of the environmentalist position is to ignore economic history and fail to ask how or why industrial societies had escaped the Malthusian trap in the past.*

More often, the boot was on the other foot, as if questioning forecasts of imminent collapse was irresponsible. Responding to the charge of being Micawbers for believing that society would continue to find solutions to problems of pollution, would increase food supplies and find sufficient raw materials for future growth, the economist Wilfred Beckerman wrote in 1974:

> Our predictions are firmly based on a study of the way these problems have been overcome in the past. And it is only the past that gives us any insight into the laws of motion of human society and hence enables us to predict the future.[12]

---

* Insofar as human rather than climatic history was used as a source for argument, it was of pre-industrial societies that had suffered the effects of resource depletion and natural climate variation. Thus Al Gore in *Earth in the Balance* (1993) writes of the impact of volcanoes on the climate and the disappearance of the Minoan civilisation (p.58), on the lead up to the French Revolution (pp. 59–60); on the ending of warm periods and the fall of the Roman Empire (p. 64) and in triggering the Black Death and wiping out the Viking settlers on Greenland towards the end of the Middle Ages (p. 67); other climatic changes, such as changes in rainfall, leading to the disappearance of the Mycenaean civilisation in 1200 BC (p. 65) and the abandonment of Fatepur Sikri in India in the sixteenth century (p. 64); the onset of warmer periods, possibly causing the collapse of the Mayan civilisation around AD 950 and the Irish potato famine in the middle of the nineteenth century (p. 69).

At the same time, environmentalists called for alternatives to modern industrial society – the only economic structure known to have kept widening the gap between subsistence and people's living standards. 'We can
free our imagination from bondage to the existing system and realise that
twentieth-century civilisation is only one, and not necessarily the best, of
the many possibilities among which mankind is free to choose.' Not the
words of a dope-smoking drop-out, but the view an official report to the
British government in 1972.[13]

The first environmental wave is close enough to enable ageing baby
boomers to look in the mirror and see a 1960s' student. It is sufficiently
distant for its predictions of eco-doom – a term coined at the time – to be
verified. These forecasts assumed economic growth would be ultimately
destructive and cause man's collision with nature. It should therefore be
deliberately halted though government action.

In addition to its alleged harm on the environment, it was argued that
growth didn't make people happy; that the way GDP numbers were put
together meant that the costs of growth were not fully accounted for; that
growth led to private affluence and public squalor. The president of the
European Commission, Dr Sicco Mansholt, called on European governments to change their economic policies. 'We should no longer orientate
our economic system towards the pursuit of maximum economic growth,'
he wrote in a 1972 newspaper article.[14]

The most famous anti-growth tract was produced by the Club of Rome.
Founded in 1968, the Club described itself as an 'invisible college' of some
seventy experts. They were united in the belief that 'the major problems
facing mankind are of such complexity and are so interrelated that traditional institutions and policies are no longer able to cope with them'.[15] The
Club commissioned a study based on a computer model developed by Jay
Forrester, a computer scientist and management professor, that purportedly demonstrated how the world economy would develop over the two
hundred years to 2170.

The results were summarised in *The Limits to Growth*, which appeared in
1972. Its headline finding generated global publicity, helping the book sell
four million copies. On an unchanged trend, the limits to growth would
be reached in one hundred years. 'The most probable result will be a rather
sudden and uncontrollable decline in both population and industrial capacity,' the authors claimed.[16] Similarly to Jevons' call in 1865 that Britain
should shrink its economy before it was forced to, the Club of Rome authors argued that precipitate decline could be avoided if immediate steps

were taken to stop further growth and thereby establish a condition of 'ecological and economic stability' which they asserted would be sustainable far into the future.[17]

Their doom-laden advice rested on a simple misconception which in turn led the authors to mis-specify the problem they were analysing as 'growth in a finite system'.[18] Resources are used up, not by growth, but by production and consumption. Given its premise of finite resources, the desired state of 'ecological and economic stability' would also run out of resources and collapse.* The only difference was timing; it would just happen a bit later. The two-hundred-year model runs illustrated in the book conveniently ended before they would have showed this happening. Catastrophe avoided, not postponed, by limiting growth.

Like Jevons, the Club of Rome authors expressed a particular animus towards those who reasonably thought technological progress could overcome the limits to growth. It was, they wrote 'the most dangerous reaction to our findings.'[19] Technology, they argued, had adverse side-effects. For sure, the Green Revolution had increased food production and the number of agricultural jobs. It had also widened inequality because larger farms adopted the better methods first.[20] Therefore an extreme version of the precautionary principle was required to deal with the threat posed by technology. Any mass-produced new technology should be forbidden unless all physical and social side effects could be demonstrated beforehand. If a new technology lifted one limit to growth, then it would have to be shown that the next check was more desirable than the one being lifted.[21]

It was Malthusianism for a technocratic age; its vision of a post-industrial society, where change would proceed at a pace the Pharaohs of ancient Egypt would have been comfortable with. Reduced to its essentials, the logic of *The Limits to Growth* implied that human beings were the fundamental problem because humans consume resources.

The conclusions of *The Limits to Growth* were by no means extreme for the time, but fairly representative of intellectual opinion. The Organisation for Economic Co-operation and Development (OECD) set up a study group

---

*   The authors evidently realised their error, because the argument was shifted to a different issue from resource depletion to the system's responsiveness to feedback loops. 'Delays in the feedback loops of the world system would be no problem if the system were [sic] growing very slowly or not at all.' Dennis L. Meadows et al, *The Limits to Growth: A Report for the Club of Rome's Project on the Predicament of Humanity* (1972), p. 144. No evidence was offered for this to conflict with the common sense observation that dynamic societies are more adaptable than static ones.

chaired by Harvey Brooks, a Harvard engineering professor. In a 1971 report, the group argued that developed societies were fast approaching a condition of near saturation. Even in higher education, people were suffering from information overload which risked stifling the production of new knowledge.[22]

The January 1972 edition of the *Ecologist* was devoted to 'A Blueprint for Survival'. It was endorsed by thirty-seven eminent experts, including five Fellows of the Royal Society and sixteen holders of science chairs at British universities, two Nobel laureates and Sir Julian Huxley, who was a subscriber to virtually every environmental cause, from the Kibbo Kift in the 1920s, eugenics and population control in the 1930s, the first director-general of UNESCO in 1946, co-founder of the World Wildlife Fund (WWF) in 1961, and writer of the preface to the British edition of *A Silent Spring*.

Environmental problems were not accidental malfunctions of modern society, the 'Blueprint' stated. They were 'warning signs of a profound incompatibility between deeply rooted beliefs in continuous growth and the dawning recognition of earth as a space ship.'[23] Industrial society, with its ethos of expansion, was unsustainable. Then came an unambiguous, cast iron prediction: 'Its termination within the lifetime of someone today is inevitable.'[24] A choice therefore had to be made between famine, epidemic and war (those three again) or initiating 'a succession of thoughtful, humane and measured changes' to spare our children the hardship and cruelty of the first option.[25] Even the most fervent proponents of global warming might be nervous of tying themselves to such a tight timetable for civilisation's rendezvous with catastrophe.

As with global warming, scientists weren't speaking from the fringes of the policy debate but given the role of defining what the problem was. In Britain, the Conservative government asked Sir Eric Ashby, a distinguished botanist and Fellow of the Royal Society, to chair a study ahead of the UN conference on the human environment in Stockholm. Its report, *Pollution: Nuisance or Nemesis?*, contains some of the most alarmist language presented to a British government in peacetime. Acknowledging that some members of the group considered that having less pollution and a better environment was a matter of political choice, like providing more hospitals, 'others among us felt such an attitude is dangerously complacent, and are convinced that a fundamental and painful restructuring of our industrial society is necessary if mankind is to survive'.[26] Growth had to be halted in 'a deliberate and controlled manner'. The sooner this happened, the better – 'the longer the change is delayed, the more the productivity of the biosphere will be damaged, and the lower will be the eventual sustainable level for our descendants'.[27] There was no analysis or evidence to support this dire conclusion.

Most alarming to the alarmist was the lack of alarm in the general population. 'The danger of entrusting the environment to the mandate of public opinion is that most people ascribe a higher priority to the present than the future,' the report said. 'Only in time of war do people willingly make such sacrifices.'[28] While some members of the working party believed that 'the normal pace of politics' was adequate to solve environmental problems, 'others of us feel that there is no hope of action capable of grappling with the complex environmental crisis unless the issues are presented to the public in the same stark terms of national and even racial survival as maintained in war'.[29]

Wilfred Beckerman's experience of serving on Ashby's working group sharpened his criticisms of natural scientists' approach to economic and social matters. Two years later, he wrote that scientists who might be world authorities on phenomena pertaining in the physical world 'do not have a minimal understanding of the way that the world of human beings operates in general, or, in particular, the way that society reacts to problems such as pollution and demands for raw materials'.[30] Understanding those problems required knowledge of human beings in a social context. Some scientists might have decided to become scientists, Beckerman suggested, 'precisely to shield themselves from these phenomena and to escape into a world where problems are not on a human scale, but microscopic or astronomic'.[31]

Beckerman argued against governments intervening to ensure the long-run supply of raw materials, as it would rest on the assumption that governments were better at forecasting future trends and developing new technology than private industry. 'There is no reason to make such an assumption,' Beckerman said. 'This does not mean private industry always gets it right; it doesn't, but it usually pays for its mistakes.'[32]

At that time, counter-arguments to environmentalism tended to come from the Left rather than the Right of political spectrum. Beckerman was an economic adviser to Tony Crosland, a senior Cabinet minister in the 1964–1970 Labour government and the Labour party's foremost intellectual. Environmental policies had a distributional impact because they were inevitably skewed towards meeting the wants of the better off in society at the expense of the poor, Beckerman argued. There was a natural hierarchy of human wants. As societies became richer, improved quality of life became more important. Collective policies favouring improved quality of life therefore favoured the better off.[33] Crosland himself had a famous difference of opinion with the American economist J.K. Galbraith. In a brilliant put-down, he mocked Galbraith and then set out a point-by-point defence of economic growth.

In a 1971 pamphlet, Crosland warned that parts of the environmental lobby were hostile to growth in principle and indifferent to the needs of ordinary people, reflecting manifest class bias and a set of middle and upper class value judgements:

> Its champions are often kindly and dedicated people. But they are affluent and fundamentally, though of course not consciously, they want to kick the ladder down behind them … We must make our own value judgment based on socialist objectives: and that objective must … be that growth is vital, and its benefits far outweigh its costs.[34]

The triumph of environmentalism during the West's years of plenty was assured by the structural weakness of its opponents. Right-of-centre political parties represented class interests favouring environmental initiatives, but left-of-centre parties were divided between representing blue-collar workers (Crosland's position) and members of the middle-class intelligentsia, such as Galbraith. There was one obstacle to environmentalism that could not be so easily overcome: obtaining Third World support needed for any global agreement on the environment.

In 1972, a representative of a leading member of the G77 challenged the fundamental basis of ecologism. Brazil's Miguel Alvaro Osório de Almeida, who served as ambassador to the US and the UN and led Brazil's preparations for the Stockholm conference, delivered an insight of great subtlety:

> the problem to be solved in fact is not achieving an 'ecological balance', but, on the contrary, obtaining the most efficient forms of 'long-term ecological imbalance'. The problem is not to exterminate mankind now, in the name of ecological equilibrium, but to prolong our ability to use natural resources for as long as possible.[35]

A year earlier, de Almeida had shocked western delegates at a preparatory meeting for the Stockholm conference. 'To be many and to be poor is offensive to the sights and feelings of developed countries,' he told them. 'Most of their suggestions do not concern cooperation for increasing income, but cooperation to reduce numbers.'[36]

Without a formula to reconcile rich countries' environmentalism and the developing world's hunger for economic growth, the Stockholm conference, due to convene on 5th June 1972, was heading for disaster. In fact, the germ of that formula was to be found in Adlai Stevenson's final speech, the passengers on the little spaceship, 'half fortunate, half miserable'.

The person who planted it there would do more than anyone else to fashion it into a political doctrine to form the basis of a treaty of convenience between environmentalism and the Third World. Her contribution was to be decisive in ensuring that the Stockholm conference would be a starting point rather than a showdown – something that could not be avoided, only postponed.

8
STOCKHOLM

Its real leader, the source of its inspiration and the directions it set for the future of our planet, was Lady Jackson, whom the world knows best as Barbara Ward.

Maurice Strong[1]

Swedish scientists were finding an increase in the acidity of rain falling across Scandinavia. The Swedish government raised their concern at the UN. In 1968, the General Assembly passed a resolution to convene the world's first intergovernmental conference on the environment.

For all its enthusiasm, hardly any preparations had been made for the conference, to be hosted by Sweden in 1972. Through a mutual friend, Sweden's ambassador to the UN approached Maurice Strong to head the conference secretariat. Undersecretary of state Christian Herter for the Nixon administration lobbied Strong to take the assignment. A formal offer from U. Thant, the UN secretary-general, followed. Strong did not need much persuading. It was the opportunity he had been preparing for all his adult life.

Born in Canada in 1929, as a boy growing up in Depression-era Manitoba, Strong remembers asking his mother: 'If nature could be so right, how could human society be so wrong?'[2] Inspired by Churchill and Roosevelt's vision of a global organisation to ensure world peace, 'I knew at once that I wanted to be part of that endeavour.'[3] Strong lived side by side with Inuit people in the Canadian Arctic working for the Hudson's Bay Company. At seventeen, he got his first job at the UN as a junior clerk in the passes office.

Reading *Silent Spring* deepened his concern about the environment, Carson's 'cry of alarm' confirming what he already believed.[4] It also reinforced his belief in global governance. The environment is supranational and transcends the nation state – 'one of the great underlying truths of environmental politics', according to Strong.[5] The establishment of effective global governance and management was the single most important challenge of the next generation, Strong said in a lecture marking the fifteenth anniversary of the Stockholm conference. 'I find it hard to conceive that civilisation could continue through the coming century if we fail to do this.'[6]

In a career straddling politics and business, Strong worked in the oil and mining industries before becoming head of the Canada's international aid agency in 1966. Where some saw a contradiction between his environmentalism and digging minerals out of the ground, Strong saw 'positive synergy' between mankind's economic and environmental needs.

> It's through our economic life that we affect our environment, and it's only through changes in economic behaviour, particularly on the part of corporations, which are the primary actors in the economy, that we can protect and improve the environment.[7]

Strong's sole foray into elective politics was not, he admitted, his finest hour. In 1977, Pierre Trudeau persuaded him to become a parliamentary candidate. Within weeks, Strong asked Trudeau if he could withdraw. It was the making of him. As an unelected politician, Strong could make a far greater impact on global affairs.

Strong's lack of educational qualifications, he believed, barred him from a traditional ascent in international politics, so he pursued a business career to get noticed and get on. Power is augmented by influence derived from extensive and diverse networks, he found.[8] Through them, Strong became powerful.

The list of his positions takes up four and a half pages of his autobiography. They include membership of the advisory boards of Toyota and Harvard's Centre for International Development, UN undersecretary and adviser to the UN secretary-general, senior adviser to the president of the World Bank (he talent-spotted the bank's president, Jim Wolfensohn, in the 1950s), Chairman of the Earth Council, trustee of the Rockefeller Foundation, a board member of the Davos World Economic Forum and of the regents of New York's Episcopalian cathedral St John the Divine, as well as being a member of the Vatican's Society for Development, Justice and Peace, Fellow of the Royal Society and member of the Club of Rome (*The Limits to Growth* was on the right lines but ahead of its time, he thought). He knew how to obtain political access and hedge his bets. In the 1988 American presidential election, Strong donated $100,000 to Mike Dukakis's campaign, became a trustee of the Democratic National Committee and fundraised for the Republican National Committee at the same time.[9]

He believed the best form of conflict resolution was conflict avoidance. 'I had learned never to confront but to co-opt, never to bully but to equivocate, and never to yield ... The oblique approach can often be the most direct one.'[10] Strong was the right man for the job, as the Stockholm environment conference was threatened by two sets of global divisions, between East and West and between North and South. Strong could not overcome the former. If East Germany was invited, the US and West Germany wouldn't attend. If East Germany wasn't invited, the Soviet Union and its main Warsaw Pact allies wouldn't show up, which is what happened. Nonetheless, Strong insisted on having a Soviet on his staff (he ended up with two) and at the conference itself he met the Soviet ambassador to Sweden almost daily to brief him on the conference.

The division between North and South was a bigger threat. In March 1971, Strong received a signal from Yugoslavia of a potential boycott by developing countries. It galvanised him. He decided he had to win over India and Brazil as the most important members of the G77. In June he went to New Delhi hoping to arrange a meeting with Indian Prime Minister Indira Gandhi. It was a long shot as rising tension with Pakistan would lead to war six months later. He got his meeting and persuaded Mrs Gandhi to deliver the keynote address to the conference.

Brazil felt its sovereignty threatened by environmentalists claiming the Amazon as a global preserve. Although Strong started a dialogue with the Brazilian government, it continued to lobby the rest of the G77 to back its hard line text at the UN emphasising national sovereignty, more additional aid and the curtailment of Strong's authority. A Swedish text supportive of Strong was adopted by a large majority while Brazil's position received the support of a smaller majority (the US and the UK voting against).

A split was averted due to Strong's recognition that bridging the divide required more than diplomatic skill. It needed something he did not possess: the intellectual creativity to devise a formula that would turn the conflict between the North's environmentalism and the South's ambitions for economic development into a new synthesis. Barbara Ward was the person he needed.

Although she did not have the instant fame Carson experienced with *Silent Spring*, it could be said that of the two, Ward's contribution was the more important. Few today take seriously the science in *Silent Spring* but Ward's concept of sustainable development has grown to be one of the dominant policy doctrines of our age.

The *New York Times* described Ward as a 'synthesiser and propagandist'.[11] She was much more than that. Perhaps the closest comparison is Harry Hopkins' relationship with Churchill and FDR. Whereas Hopkins lived and worked in the White House, Ward's arena was global, projecting her ideas through the numerous political leaders who trusted her. At a White House meeting between the British Prime Minister Harold Wilson and Lyndon

Johnson in February 1968, Johnson gave Wilson a note on the economic situation. Two and half pages of quarto, single spacing. 'It was drafted in terms which would appeal to him – the pure Roosevelt approach to the dangers of another 1931,' Wilson recalled. 'For the rest, I did not agree with the analysis. But, I said, I could trace a feminine hand in its drafting, English at that. He roared with laughter. No one knowing Washington would underrate the importance nor fail to recognise the handiwork of Barbara Ward.'[12]

Ward took her father's Quaker earnestness to improve the world and her Roman Catholicism from her mother. After graduating from Oxford, she lectured extensively and wrote her first book at the age of twenty-four. The next year she became assistant editor of the *Economist*, becoming its foreign editor four years later. She used to write the *Economist* leaders from her bed without effort or correction, what she called her 'fatal facility'.

Such was her remarkable talent as a speaker and broadcaster that in 1943 the British government sent her to the United States to win support for Britain's war effort. She stayed five months, lunching with Eleanor Roosevelt, dining with Vice President Wallace and amassing a circle of American admirers. In the 1945 election, she campaigned for Labour, escorting a young American naval officer, John F. Kennedy, whom Ward had come to know through his sister Kathleen. A speech she gave on full employment reduced the hard-bitten Ernest Bevin, Britain's most powerful trade union leader, to tears.

The next year she struck up a life-long friendship with J.K. Galbraith (a woman of rare and slender beauty, Galbraith recalled), who got her a post at Harvard's department of economics. Later she was appointed Albert Schweitzer Professor at Columbia (Nelson Rockefeller, Governor of New York, was also one of her circle) and her work received substantial backing from the Carnegie Foundation. Friendship with Adlai Stevenson opened doors to the leading figures in the Kennedy administration. She became a confidante of Robert McNamara, with whom she retained a strong influence during his time as president of the World Bank. Although she found Kennedy a cool personality who always kept his distance, the same was not true of his successor.[13] Ward fascinated Johnson. Her books were the only ones he ever read, Johnson once said.[14] She contributed to his speeches, including the 1964 Great Society speech. Two days before leaving the White House, Johnson wrote to her: 'Whatever mark we have made in these last five years clearly bears your stamp too.'[15]

In the 1950s, she lived in Africa and was friends with the first generation of African leaders – Kwame Nkrumah of Ghana, Tanzania's Julius Nyerere,

Jomo Kenyatta of Kenya and Zambia's Kenneth Kaunda – whose economic policies helped ruin their countries. Visiting India in 1952, she met Prime Minister Jawaharlal Nehru, who had better things to talk about than five-year plans, and met his daughter, Indira Gandhi, who became a life-long admirer, a relationship crucial in persuading Gandhi to come to Stockholm.[16]

She lobbied the Second Vatican Council on Third World development. In 1967, Pope Paul VI established the Pontifical Commission for Justice and Peace, with Ward as one of its members. The encyclical, *Populorum Progressio*, 'The Development of the Peoples', with its criticism of 'unbridled liberalism', its call for 'concerted planning' and the creation of a 'World Fund' are evidence of Ward's imprint.*[17] It's no wonder that, for Strong, the prospect of working with Ward was 'a dream come true'.[18]

Like Strong, Ward believed world government was necessary and achievable. 'We live physically and socially in a post-national order. But we still worship the "idols of the tribe,"' she wrote in a 1973 paper for the Vatican.[19] The urgent economic problems of the day required policies which could only be achieved at a 'planetary level'.[20] Underlying the debate on Third World development was the ethical issue of world distribution of income and resources, a debate sharpened because of the unsustainability of 'the reckless economic expansion of the last three hundred years'.[21]

The belief that without massive aid transfers, developing countries could not improve their living standards was central to Ward's worldview.

> The market alone cannot begin to accomplish the scale of readjustment that will be needed once the concept of unlimitedly growing wealth, mediated to all by a 'trickle down' process, ceases to be a rational possibility for tomorrow's world economy.[22]

In an *Economist* article on the eve of the Stockholm conference, Ward argued that the pursuit of 'destabilising growth' was not the answer because it didn't reduce the gap between the rich and poor nations. 'It has no built-in tendency to redistribute the surpluses and tends on the contrary to skew still further the patterns of income it creates' – a view that has not withstood the test of time in a new era grappling with the implications of China's huge trade surpluses.[23]

---

* The encyclical also gave the Catholic Church's sanction to the expropriation landed estates in the name of the 'common good' – a position espoused by Catholic distributists such as G.K. Chesterton earlier in the twentieth century. Ward, like Schumacher, was a successor to the distributists.

The Marshall Plan should be the model for the whole world, a case she made in 1957 from the same podium on the tenth anniversary of General Marshall's speech, when she became the first woman to give the Harvard commencement address. Five years later in *The Rich Nations and the Poor Nations*, Ward argued that high income countries should allocate one per cent of their national income to aid programmes. Selected by the Book of the Month club, the *New York Times* called it 'wise and inspiring'.

It was imperative, Ward argued, to manage the future. Collectively, human beings must know where they're going and what the world will look like in twenty years' time, she said in her 1966 paper *Space Ship Earth*. 'It is surely inconceivable that we should turn the whole human experiment over to forces of change which we can neither master nor even fully understand.'[24]

Marx and Engels have been heavily criticised for claiming to have discovered the scientific laws that govern history. Forecasts of environmental doom also depend on a deterministic view of history, in particular that the values and state of human knowledge of future societies are knowable by the present. In doing so, they presume the social organisation of the anthill or the beehive and the curtailment of individual freedom and initiative – forces we can never fully understand or predict.

Strong commissioned Ward and the microbiologist René Dubos to write a book summing up the 'knowledge and opinions' of leading experts Strong had selected on 'the relationships between man and his natural habitat at a time when human activity is having profound effects upon the environment'.[25]

Only One Earth couldn't hide the divide between experts from First World and Third World. One from the former argued that societies should retreat from industrialisation to agriculture. Representatives from the Third World argued the opposite. Industrial development should have priority over worries about future environmental damage and 'dreams of landscapes innocent of smokestacks', as one of them put it.[26]

Global warming made a somewhat tentative debut in 1972. Small changes in the planet's balance of energy could change average temperatures by two degrees centigrade, 'downwards, this is another ice age, upwards to an ice-free age. In either case, the effects are global and catastrophic'.[27] The greenhouse effect could mean that temperatures rise 0.5^0C by the end of the century. But if developing countries consumed energy at levels in the developed world, might that risk temperatures rising uncomfortably close to the catastrophic two degree centigrade threshold?[28]

At that stage, global warming was not considered the main threat to mankind's survival. What was? 'Pockets of urban degradation in affluent countries provide us with a foretaste of what could become man's greatest environmental risk,' the authors of *Only One Earth* wrote. 'Spreading urban misery, city quarters of unrelieved ugliness and squalor in which imaginative life of young children may be as systematically starved as their bodies are undernourished.'[29] Catastrophe was just around the corner.

Although living things had survived ice ages, volcanic eruptions, earthquakes and typhoons of 'our unstable planet', they served as a warning. 'Like the giant reptiles of the Jurassic ages, some species have gone the "way to dusty death."'[30] What was the lesson of the extinction of the dinosaurs, given that it wasn't caused by the human activities that were risking the planet's viability? 'A need for extreme caution, a sense of the appalling vastness and complexity of the forces that can be unleashed and of the egg-shell delicacy of the arrangements that can be upset,' was the answer.[31]

The more immediate eggshell was Third World hostility to the promotion of environmental concerns at the expense of their development agenda. Strong convened a group from the development movement in New York. He would assess progress with Ward at one-to-one dinner meetings, always over a bottle of Dom Perignon, her favourite champagne.[32] The message was simple and devastating. As expressed by Pakistan's Mahub ul Haq, industrialisation had given developed countries disproportionate benefits and huge reservoirs of wealth, at the same time causing the very environmental problems that they were now asking developing countries to help resolve. Those who had created the mess in the first place should pay the costs of cleaning it up.[33] Strong realised more needed to be done to save the conference.

In June 1971, Strong held a week-long seminar at Founex, fifteen minutes' drive from Geneva airport. 'One of the best intellectual exchanges I have ever participated in,' Strong recalled. 'It had a profound influence both on the Stockholm conference and on the evolution of the concept of the environment-development relationship.'[34] Founex produced a three-part deal which gave developing countries what they sought. In turn, it gave Strong what he wanted – the presence of Third World countries at the conference.

The first part was the assumption that the Third World would not emulate the developed world's path to industrialisation, expressed as a non-binding aspiration on the part of the Third World. Developing countries would 'wish' to avoid the patterns of development of industrialised countries.[35]

The second related to national sovereignty. Suppose this turned out to be wrong? Where environmental objectives conflict with development objectives, each country had the right to decide the trade-off for itself.[36]

The third part was about money: 'If the concern for human environment reinforces the commitment to development, it must also reinforce the commitment to international aid. It should provide a stimulus for augmenting the flow of resources from the advanced to the developing countries.'[37]

The Founex deal was packaged in a formula that bound together a contradiction – the environmental problems of developed countries are caused by too much development but the Third World's environmental problems are caused by too little. A political compromise lacking internal consistency or empirical validation, its second half contains an important truth. As societies get wealthier, they can afford to spend more and place a higher value on a clean environment and unspoiled nature. When Bjorn Lomborg produced evidence suggesting that far from getting worse, environmental indicators had been improving as wealth had increased, he was attacked for demonstrating the validity of one part of the Founex formula – only it was the wrong half. As a political formula, Founex did the trick.

On 5th June 1972, the first session of the world's first environmental conference took place in Stockholm's Royal Opera House. Traffic delayed the opening ceremony. None of the communist states turned up apart from China, Romania and Yugoslavia. But the Third World nations did come. Kurt Waldheim, the new UN secretary-general, warned against man's unplanned, selfish and ever-growing activities. 'While the environment is an emerging, new and very serious problem, we must not forget that development is still the highest priority,' Waldheim said, acknowledging the position of the largest bloc in the UN.[38]

At times, the conference was chaotic. 'There is a strange sensation here of large groups of people wandering aimlessly about looking for someone else,' a reporter wrote.[39] In addition to a fleet of Saabs and Volvos, the Swedish government provided two hundred bicycles painted in the UN's blue and white. Not enough, delegates complained. By the conference's second day, half had disappeared, most ending up in hotel rooms.

The sense of disorganisation was partly a result of one of Strong's masterstrokes. His most important allies in prosecuting the environmental agenda were the NGOs that had helped generate the political momentum for the conference in the first place. Despite resistance from the UN bureaucracy, Strong enlisted volunteers, led by the secretary-general of League of Red Cross Societies and Baron Axel von dem Bussche (a former member of Germany's anti-Hitler resistance) to encourage NGOs to come. More than four hundred NGOs did, attending a parallel Environment Forum at Hog Farm just outside the city.

Ward shuttled between Hog Farm and the main conference, arranging briefing sessions and tickets. According to one government insider, the NGOs had little discernible effect on 'the real action'. That wasn't why Strong wanted them there. It was to hold governments' feet to the fire after the agreements had been signed and everyone had gone home.[40]

The NGOs and prominent experts also helped generate press interest. Biologist Paul Ehrlich showered praise on Strong. It was an 'absolute miracle' that Strong had said that poor countries could not close the gap with rich countries.[41] It was just ten years before the start of China's growth spurt.* For Ehrlich's fellow biologist Barry Commoner, the culprits were capitalism, colonialism and especially the US. The environmental crisis 'wrenched open' the brutality of racial competition for survival. Producing for the common good, not for private profit, would solve it.[42] Colonialism had caused the population explosion, Commoner claimed. Rich countries should now pay reparations for it.[43]

Inside the conference, host Prime Minister Olof Palme also attacked the US, demanding the conference examine the environmental impact of the Vietnam War 'ecoside'. Even so, the Nixon administration managed the conference with considerable skill. On the conference eve, the EPA announced its DDT ban, leaving other countries to play catch up. Shortly before it ended, President Nixon announced a $100 million fund to finance new environmental activities, while France and China came under attack for jointly opposing a resolution calling for a halt to nuclear testing.

In her keynote address, Indira Gandhi blamed the profit motive for wrecking the environment and keeping people poor. The West's affluence had been achieved at the price of the domination of other countries, the wealth of the few coming about 'through sheer ruthlessness'. Modern man, she said, must re-establish an unbroken link with nature.[44] There were limits to how much should be done to protect the environment. India did not wish to impoverish the environment further, but could not forget its own people. 'When men feel deprived, how can we speak about preserving animals?'[45]

---

* Ehrlich has a record of making predictions that turn out spectacularly wrong. In 1970 he said that if he was a gambler, he would take even money that England would not exist in the year 2000. Quoted in Julian L. Simon, *The Ultimate Resource* (1981), p. 101.

Barbara Ward, the conference's other star, addressed delegates in her sunglasses; it was unsustainable if two thirds of humanity stayed poor so that one third could stay rich. Robert McNamara, president of the World Bank, claimed that the evidence was 'overwhelming' that a century of very rapid growth had contributed to a 'monstrous assault on the quality of life in the developed [sic] countries'.[46]

China, making its first appearance at a major international conference since taking its seat at the UN, used the conference to attack imperialism and colonialism. It tried to turn the proposed Preamble to the Declaration on the Human Environment into a Maoist diatribe. The environment had been endangered by 'plunder, aggression and war by colonialists, imperialists and neo-colonialists'. Theories of over-population were attacked along classic Marxist lines ('the notorious Malthusian theory is absurd in theory and groundless in fact').[47]

As the conference drew to a close, it was touch-and-go whether it would end in failure. Exhausted delegates haggled about the final wording of a draft declaration and argued what had been achieved during the eleven days of the conference. Strong had to deal with the prospect of a walk-out by the Chinese, as Beijing hadn't instructed them how to vote on the final declaration. He astutely suggested that instead of leaving the room, they should just stand behind their seats. That way, they'd neither vote, nor abstain, but be reported as present. It enabled the conference chairman to declare the resolution passed by consensus.

'What came out of Stockholm is about what we expected – not much,' said Brazil's Carlos Calero Rodrigues.[48] In his speech to the conference, Strong admitted that the draft declaration was less than the inspirational and comprehensive code of international environmental conduct that was needed. It was, he claimed, an indispensable beginning.[49]

The Stockholm declaration enshrined the Founex contradiction, that the economic development of advanced nations caused environmental problems; in developing countries, the same process reduced them. It then went on to set out twenty-six principles. These included a condemnation of apartheid and all foreign and colonial domination (principle one); that natural resources should be subject to 'careful planning or management' (2); the benefits from finite resources should be shared by all mankind (5); the need for the transfer of 'substantial' financial and technological aid to developing nations (9); that schools and the mass media should disseminate information on the environment (19); and that international policy should be decided cooperatively by all countries 'on an equal footing' (24), i.e., making it more difficult for the West to impose its environmental priorities on the rest of the world.[50]

The conference also agreed nearly a hundred recommendations ranging from the need for genetic cataloguing to measuring and limiting noise emissions. These included half a page of recommendations concerning the atmosphere. Governments should be 'mindful' of activities in which there is appreciable risk of effects on climate. Ten baseline stations should be established in remote areas to monitor changes in the atmosphere that might cause climatic changes. The World Meteorological Organisation should continue to carry out its Global Atmospheric Research Programme to understand whether the causes of climatic changes were natural or the result of man's activities.[51]

Compared to the half page given to global warming, the oceans and marine pollution took four and a half pages. Lured by the prospect of near limitless supplies of minerals on and beneath the seabed, in the first decade after Stockholm, the environmental and developing world agenda focused on the oceans. Attention only switched to the atmosphere and global warming from the mid-1980s.

The G77 backed Kenya's bid to host the new UN Environment Program based in Nairobi and Strong became its first head. Stockholm's most important legacy was the twinning of global environmentalism with the Third World's aid and development agenda as a way of managing their inherent contradictions.

The first environmental wave had risen with great suddenness and force. A decade separates *Silent Spring* and the Stockholm conference. Even more sudden was the speed of its apparent collapse.

When Barbara Ward died in 1981, obituarists ran out of superlatives, the *Guardian* calling her one of the most brilliant contributors to economic and political thought since the 1930s.[52] Her contribution to the forging of global environmentalism and her role at the world's first conference on the environment barely rated a mention.

9
BREAKING WAVE

It is almost impossible for historians to understand how in advance of some of history's great revolutions, it was often not even realised that a change was about to take place.

Henry Kissinger[1]

We have learned that more is not necessarily better, that even our great Nation has its recognized limits, and that we can neither answer all questions nor solve all problems.

Jimmy Carter, 20th January 1977[2]

At 2pm on 6th October 1973, over two hundred Egyptian aircraft flew over the Suez Canal and two thousand artillery guns started a series of barrages. Twenty minutes later, the first Egyptian troops crossed the canal. Using high-pressure water pumps, they blasted passages through the Bar Lev line, a fortification running the length of the canal made of sand and concrete. Sixteen hours later, ninety thousand troops, eight hundred and fifty tanks and eleven thousand additional vehicles were on the east side of the canal.[3] At the same time, the Syrians attacked Israel from the north.

A survey of polls in the US, Great Britain, and Germany suggest that 1972 marked the high point of concern about the environment.[4] The circulation of the *Ecologist* more than halved between 1973 and 1976.[5] Although membership of the largest environmental pressure groups continued to rise, only half a dozen of the environmental magazines started on or after Earth Day 1970 survived. Though in retreat, environmentalism broadened its reach. During this period, America's national security establishment became a functional ally of environmentalism as concerns about energy security coincided with environmentalists' campaign against fossil fuels.

The cause was the same event that led to the sudden disappearance of environmentalism from the world stage. Of all the wars of the twentieth century in which the major powers were not combatants, none had such an effect as the Yom Kippur war. To Henry Kissinger, it brought the curtain down on the post-war period.

> The seemingly inexorable rise in prosperity was abruptly reversed. Simultaneously, inflation ran like a forest fire through the industrialised countries and recession left millions unemployed. … Transcending even the economic revolution was the emergence of oil as a weapon of political blackmail. The industrial democracies saw imposed on them not only an economic upheaval but fundamental changes in their social cohesion and political life.[6]

Environmentalists seized on this as vindication of their arguments. The party is over, Barbara Ward declared. Fritz Schumacher poured scorn on those who expected 'to get back onto the happy road of economic growth'.[7]

> The present situation, I am certain, has nothing in common with any previous 'depression' or 'recession' … It is not part of a cycle, is not a 'correction' or 'shake-out' or anything of this sort: It is the end of an era.[8]

Those who couldn't see this, Schumacher said, were indulging in the psychological exercise of 'the refusal of consciousness'.[9]

One political leader decided to overcome the refusal of consciousness.

Barely mentioned in the 1976 presidential election, Jimmy Carter made the energy crisis the centrepiece of his presidency. In a June 1979 interview, it was put to Carter that a poll showed that sixty-five per cent of Americans did not believe there was a gasoline shortage. 'Is there a shortage?' the president was asked. 'Yes,' Carter replied.[10]

The facts suggested otherwise. In 1973 world oil production was 58.3 million barrels of oil a day. Output rose steadily to 65.7 million barrels a day in 1979. The energy crisis was created by governments, not geology. Shortages in the US were the result of government regulation rather than world supply. America's European allies were also enveloped in a refusal of consciousness. On the first day of the 1979 Tokyo G7 summit, Carter endured a bitter and unpleasant lunch when he was personally abused by German leader Helmut Schmidt. 'One of the worst days of my diplomatic life,' as Carter later called it.[11]

The world was not running out of oil. The major oil producers had formed a cartel and were exploiting their pricing power. But the circumstances of its sudden emergence enormously amplified its impact. The success of the initial Arab attacks was the single most traumatic event in Israel's history. Four days into the war, Israel decided to push deep into Syrian territory towards Damascus. To relieve the Syrians, the Egyptians launched further attacks, enabling the Israel Defence Forces to counter-attack. The Israelis crossed the canal and began to advance towards Cairo and cut off the Egyptian Third Army. Within a matter of days, Israel, Egypt and Syria had felt their existence at risk.

From mid October 1973, the US began a twenty-three-day airlift. It was meant to have been under the cover of darkness. When one of the first aircraft arrived in broad daylight, James Schlesinger, US defense secretary, said 'much of the population of Tel Aviv went out to the perimeter of the airport to cheer'.[12] The airlift ricocheted around the Arab world. Two days later, Arab oil producers announced they were increasing the oil price from $3.01 to $5.01 a barrel, described by Kissinger as stunning and unprecedented.[13] On 20th October, Saudi Arabia announced it was halting oil exports to the US. The next day Kuwait, Bahrain, Qatar and Dubai followed suit. The oil weapon had been unsheathed, triggering a wave of panic buying.

Throughout 1973, the Saudis had threatened to use oil as an economic weapon. In a TV interview in the late summer, King Faisal warned

> America's complete support of Zionism against the Arabs makes it extremely difficult for us to continue to supply the United States' petroleum needs and to even maintain our friendly relations.[14]

The threat had been discounted in Washington because of the failure of an attempted embargo in 1967.[15] Such had been the Nixon administration's complacency that when, in 1969, the Shah of Iran offered to sell Washington one million barrels of oil a day for ten years for a strategic reserve, it was rejected out of hand.[16]

By November 1973, President Nixon was telling Americans they faced the most severe energy shortage since the Second World War. They would have to use less heat, less electricity, less gasoline. 'The fuel crisis need not mean genuine suffering for any American, but it will require some sacrifice by all Americans.'[17] There would be a ten per cent reduction in flights and a fifteen per cent cut in supplies of domestic heating oil ('we must ask everyone to lower the thermostat in your home by at least six degrees') and requested highway speed limits be cut to fifty mph.

Invoking the Manhattan project and the Apollo space programme, Nixon announced Project Independence: by 1980, America would meet all its energy needs without any imports. It marked a one-hundred-and-eighty-degree turn from the lowest cost, free trade principles of the 1952

Paley Commission and set a course which Jimmy Carter, George W. Bush and Barack Obama followed. It was also a complete flop. In 1973, the US imported 6.3 million barrels of oil a day. By 1980, this had risen to 6.9 million and, in 2007, the last year before the onset of recession, America imported 13.5 million barrels of oil a day, more than double the 1973 level.[18]

A December meeting of Persian Gulf producers in Tehran decided to increase the oil price from $5.12 to $11.65 a barrel. 'One of the pivotal events in the history of this century,' according to Kissinger.[19] The oil price increase from the beginning of the Yom Kippur War was unprecedented. Expressed in March 2009 dollars, it rose by $41.14 in four months and peaked $2.40 higher in June 1975, before trending down to a low of $46.33 in November 1978. Unprecedented but not unsurpassed. The oil price increase from January 2007 of $72.24 (in March 2009 dollars) to $123.73 in July 2008 was two thirds bigger than the 1973 oil price shock.[20] By then, the world had learned to live with high and volatile oil prices without turning it into a crisis.

In February 1974 Western foreign ministers met in Washington to take forward Kissinger's proposal for an oil buyers' group. France was strongly opposed. 'I won't be able to accept, no matter what conditions are established, a situation which requires us to forego Arab oil, for even a year,' President Pompidou told Kissinger.[21] Major oil importing countries such as West Germany and Japan decided to let their economies adjust to higher oil prices. German motorists were not going to wait in long lines to fill up their cars. 'We're going to recognise that if we want oil, we're going to pay the world price,' West Germany's economics minister said.[22] The US went down the route of much greater regulation. The 1973 Emergency Petroleum Allocation Act authorised a raft of petroleum price, production, allocation and marketing controls, turning the oil price shock into an energy supply crisis.

The rift between Europeans and American policy became a defining feature of the Carter presidency. Carter was a true believer; he'd read *The Limits to Growth*. It had, he said, melded together scientific data 'to show a dismal prospect, even for the survival of mankind, if we fail to change some of those trends quickly'. Its language became a major theme of his inaugural address and his presidency.[23]

Politically Carter's problem was that he saw limits where his fellow countrymen did not. Convincing Americans about the energy crisis was like pulling teeth, Carter complained.[24] By 1979, according to a briefing by his pollster Pat Caddell, Americans did not believe his warnings about future energy shortages. They were convinced that both the government and oil companies were either incompetent, dishonest or both.[25]

'Tonight I want to have an unpleasant talk with you,' Carter told Americans three months into his presidency.[26] The energy crisis was the 'moral equivalent of war.' The alternative might be 'national catastrophe', Carter claimed. The lines at gas pumps had gone, but the energy problem was now worse; 'more waste has occurred, and more time has passed by without our planning for the future'. The immorality of waste was Carter's overarching theme. 'Our energy problems have the same cause as our environmental problems – wasteful use of resources.'[27]

The next day, Carter presented his energy plan to Congress. He wasn't expecting any applause and didn't get any. It was 'torn to pieces in Congress in much the same way puppies might rip the stuffing out of a rag doll', critics noted.[28] A month after declaring war on oil and natural gas usage, Carter sent Congress a message on the environment: 'The transition to renewable energy sources, particularly solar energy, must be made.'[29] He had solar panels installed on the roof of the White House (they got taken down for maintenance in 1986 and were never put back), backed gasohol (a mixture of ten per cent ethanol and ninety per cent petroleum), called for the creation of an energy security corporation financed by $5 billion of energy bonds, and a solar bank. Twenty per cent of America's energy should come from solar power by 2000, a target Carter said was crucial.[30] The target might as well never have existed. By 2007, renewable energy contributed less than seven per cent of America's needs while the contribution from solar energy was little more than a drop in the ocean – less than one tenth of one percent.[31]

The Nixon-era price controls inherited by Carter had a two-tier system so that the price of oil from developed reserves was capped at a lower price than oil from new fields. Selling gasoline at two different prices created local shortages and long lines at filling stations. During the 1976 primary campaign, Carter had pledged to remove price controls on natural gas prices, helping him win the crucial Texas primary. But he reversed himself once he got to the White House in what his domestic policy adviser Stu Eizenstat thought possibly the most fateful domestic decision of his presidency.[32]

Deregulating energy prices wouldn't work, Carter claimed, because OPEC dominated the global energy market. Instead Carter got former defense secretary James Schlesinger, who had been a Rand Corporation systems analyst in the 1960s, to design a national energy plan. Its aim was to put the market to work to conserve oil and gas. 'Why not then, use the real market?' asked the plan's conservative critics. 'Even a systems analyst, however brilliant, would find it impossible to simulate the complexities of a fairly simple market system, let alone one as huge as the energy market,' they argued.[33]

Carter's energy policy was based on the (false) premise that energy supplies were soon going to be exhausted. 1973 world oil production was 58.5 million barrels of oil a day and rose to sixty-six million barrels a day in 1979.[34] Neither was it the case that America's reserves of energy were running low. In April 1977, shortly before Carter launched his energy plan, the Energy Research and Development Agency concluded that America's natural gas reserves could be expected to exceed its total energy needs well into the twenty-first century. The director of the US Geological Survey, Dr Vincent McKelvey, said that following a slew of recent discoveries America's natural gas reserves were about ten times the energy value of all previously discovered oil and gas reserves in the US combined. He left his post shortly after.[35]

The more Carter talked about energy, the lower his poll rating sank. In 1977, he made three television addresses on the subject as well as one to Congress and countless appearances at public forums talking about the energy crisis. It left everyone confused, including Carter himself. In June 1979, Carter told an interviewer: 'I don't claim that the government has done a good job with the energy problem; it hasn't.'[36] When asked by Dan Rather in August 1980 to grade his performance, Carter gave himself a straight 'A' on energy. 'Very good, I think we've done better than we had anticipated, and that's one of the great achievements of our administration.'[37]

1979 was a particularly tough year for Carter's energy policy. In April he announced another energy package, including a windfall tax (preventing energy suppliers 'profiteering' from changes in energy prices was a constant theme). The public was cool and the attitude of Congress 'disgusting', Carter wrote in his diary.[38] At the end of June came his mauling by Helmut Schmidt in Tokyo. To save face, the Europeans agreed to a formula that would meet Carter's objective of cutting oil imports by counting oil from the British North Sea as pooled with the other European members of the G7.

On his return home, Carter planned another televised address on energy for Independence Day. After reading the draft, he cancelled it and went to Camp David to reflect. 'Some of the most thought-provoking and satisfying [days] of my presidency,' Carter wrote in his memoirs.[39] He emerged to give what he thought was one of his best speeches, one that history knows as Carter's malaise speech.

By this stage of his presidency, the energy crisis had mutated into a moral and spiritual crisis. Inflation, unemployment and all the economic ills that ailed America were blamed on imported oil. 'This intolerable dependence on foreign oil threatens our economic independence and the very security of our nation,' Carter told America. 'It is a clear and present danger.'[40] He asked Congress to give him authority to impose standby gasoline rationing and announced that he was setting import quotas on foreign oil. 'Beginning this moment, this nation will never use more foreign oil than we did in 1977 – never,' Carter emphasised.[41]

For a time, it looked like the tide had turned. Oil imports had peaked in 1977 and continued to decline until 1985. Since the trough that year, apart from during the early 1990s recession, oil imports grew each year. Every year since 1994, oil imports exceeded 1977 and in 2009 were over one third higher.[42]

Carter's energy policies provide a test run for similar policies Western governments adopted in response to global warming. Energy policies based on the assumption of energy shortages end up creating shortages. As one historian of the Carter years has written, the energy crisis was a politically constructed artefact.[43] German car drivers did not queue for petrol because the German government decided to let the market work.

Invoking national security is a useful indicator of poor quality policy. Compelling countries to use higher cost, less efficient sources of energy than those available from the world market inflicts a continuing penalty on economic performance. The Paley Commission's lowest cost principle is better economics: obtain the lowest cost energy in whatever form, from whatever source, and let the economy adapt to changes in energy prices is likely to be more efficient than pre-emptively imposing high-cost energy on energy consumers. The Shah of Iran's suggestion to the Nixon administration of building a strategic energy reserve is a better answer to the threat of temporary supply disruptions than permanently hobbling the economy with mandates for high cost domestic energy.

Carter left another bequest to posterity. In his May 1977 environmental message, Carter announced a study on the implications of world population growth for natural resources and the environment. Work on *The Global 2000 Report to the President* took almost the rest of his term. In his farewell address, Carter said that population growth and resource depletion were one of the top three issues confronting America. 'The report is credible,' Madeleine Albright told colleagues on the National Security Council when it appeared in 1980.[44] Measured by the one and a half million copies sold, it was also a success.[45]

'The world must expect a troubled entry into the twenty-first century,' the report predicted.[46] For sure, the report wasn't anticipating the possible effect of the millennium bug on computer programs. Neither did it anticipate what actually happened. Writing shortly after the century's end, Maddison found that

> the world economy performed better in the last half century than at any time in the past. World GDP increased six-fold from 1950 to 1998 with an average growth rate of 3.9 per cent a year compared to 1.6 per cent from 1820 to 1950, and 0.3 per cent from 1500 to 1820.[47]

As was the custom with such efforts, the study, led by Gerald Barney, a physicist, did not analyse why previous studies predicting a reversal of the benevolent economic trends since the Industrial Revolution had failed. Instead, the report's authors believed their methodology imparted an optimistic bias to their gloomy conclusions.[48] In 2000 people would be poorer than in 1980 and life for most would be more precarious.[49] Erosion of the Earth's 'carrying capacity' and the degradation of natural resources would give rise to global problems of 'alarming proportions'.[50]

The most serious environmental impact would be on food production, caused by 'an accelerating deterioration and loss of resources essential for agriculture'.[51] The report predicted that by 2000, more people, especially babies and children, would be dying from hunger and disease. Many of those (un)lucky enough to survive would be 'mentally and physically handicapped' by childhood malnutrition.[52] In fact, life expectancy continued to lengthen. According to the UN, over the last two decades of the century global life expectancy at birth rose by four years to sixty-five and, for the least developed, countries it rose by three years, from forty-eight to fifty-one.[53]

Food production of developing countries, the report conceded, would increase, but not by enough to keep ahead of population growth.[54] Wrong again. Compared to 1970, the supply of calories per head in developing countries rose by twenty-five per cent and the supply of nutrient per head grew by twenty percent.[55] Inevitably the report predicted that oil would be running out. During the 1990s, oil production would approach its geological estimate of maximum production capacity.[56] In 1980, world oil output, temporarily depressed by the Iranian Revolution, was 62.9 million barrels of oil a day. Ten years later, this had risen by four percent to 65.4 million barrels a day and increased by fourteen per cent during the 1990s to reach 74.8 million barrels a day in 2000.[57]

In one respect, *Global 2000* was prophetic of a new era. 'Rising carbon dioxide concentrations are of concern because of their potential for causing a warming of the earth,' it said.[58] A doubling of atmospheric carbon dioxide by the middle of the twenty-first century would lead to a 2-3°C rise in temperatures in the Earth's middle latitudes and greater warming of polar temperatures which could lead to the melting of the Greenland and Antarctic ice caps, a gradual rise in sea levels and the abandonment of many coastal cities.[59]

Had Carter been re-elected in 1980, might it have brought forward the age of global warming to the beginning of the 1980s? More likely, it would have meant a much more problematic launch than the one global warming was to have in 1988, when the stars were in perfect alignment. Environmentalism needs prosperity to thrive. Poor economic performance during the second half of the 1970s, especially in Britain and the US, meant that the economy came first.

Global warming also needs a benign global order. As *Global 2000* recognised: 'An era of unprecedented global cooperation and commitment is essential.'[60] On Christmas Eve 1979, the Soviet Union invaded Afghanistan. In response, Carter stopped further grain exports to the Soviet Union and banned the US from competing in the Moscow Olympics. The Cold War needed to be won first.

There was another factor. The planet wasn't warming, or at least not many people thought it was. The opposite seemed to be happening. According to James Rodger Fleming, one of the leading historians of the science of global warming,

> by the mid 1970s global cooling was an observable trend. The US National Science Board pointed out that during the last twenty to thirty years, world temperatures had fallen, 'irregularly at first but more sharply over the last decade'.[61]

Global warming needed a warming world – economically, geostrategically and climatically. The world was not ready.

'How much do you miss dinosaurs? Would your life be richer if those giant pre-historic flying lizards occasionally settled on your front lawn?' Ronald Reagan asked a radio audience in 1977.[62] Reagan often discussed the energy crisis and environmental issues in radio talks during the Carter years. The question about dinosaurs was his way of suggesting that species had become extinct before man's appearance, but that feeling guilty about species loss had led to legislative over-reaction.

Reagan described himself as an environmentalist at heart who, like the majority of people, was somewhere in the middle between those who'd pave over everything in the name of progress and those who wouldn't let us build a house 'unless it looked like a bird nest'.[63] He didn't buy a CIA report cited by Carter that claimed the oil would be gone in thirty years. Past government reports had consistently under-estimated oil reserves. If they'd been right, the oil would have run out by now. Even if true, what was the point of Carter's conservation measures to reduce consumption by ten per cent if all it meant was that the oil ran out three years later?[64] Gas-guzzling Californians were not to blame for the state's gasoline shortage, Reagan argued. The fault lay with government regulations that capped the price of oil and prevented Californian refineries from importing the low sulphur crude they were designed for.[65] Having reduced oil production, the government was now proposing to reduce consumption. 'Why don't we try the free market again?' Reagan asked.[66]

As president, that's what he did. One of Reagan's first acts was to lift all remaining domestic petroleum price and allocation controls. The price of oil peaked at $39 a barrel the month after Reagan took office. It fell to $18 a barrel five years later and ended the decade nearly fifty per cent lower than the peak after taking account of inflation.[67] The 1980s turned out to be a decade of oil glut. The 1970s energy crisis had been solved.

After 1973, it had been an article of faith among environmentalists such as Schumacher that economic growth had gone for good, as a result of its collision with environmental limits. The pursuit of high standards of consumption in an advertising-crazed society would condemn societies to perpetual inflation, Barbara Ward argued in 1973. If pursued across the world, it would precipitate such an exhaustion of resources and such a toll of pollution that the technological system would simply crack under the strain.[68]

And so, paradoxically, the renewed prosperity of the 1980s that environmentalism said could not happen became the prerequisite for environmentalism's own revival.

10
PUPATION

Does the flap of a butterfly's wings in Brazil set off a tornado in Texas?

Edward Lorenz, 1979

Before reaching their adult form, holometabolous insects such as butterflies undergo a complete metamorphosis. When they hatch, they are very different from the adult. Inside are the rudiments of the adult together with small blobs of tissue called imaginal disks. When the larva has grown enough, it stops moving to form a protective cocoon. The larva pupates and the imaginal disks grow into adult structures. What was a caterpillar becomes a butterfly.

In the decade and a half after the Stockholm conference, environmentalism underwent a form of pupation. It lost some features and gained others. Over time, the crusade against economic growth was replaced by talk of sustainable development and green growth. Environmentalists thought the sudden disappearance of growth was desirable. It took time for environmentalists to adapt to the new environment.

In 1974, the Club of Rome produced a sequel to *The Limits of Growth*. In some ways *Mankind at the Turning Point* was even more extreme. It too claimed to be a scientifically conducted assessment based on computer models. Mankind's 'crisis' was defined as two widening gaps, between man and nature and between North and South. 'Both gaps must be narrowed if world-shattering catastrophes are to be avoided,' although the book did not explain how a computer could measure the gap between man and nature.[1] Nonetheless, the authors argued that scientists had every right to make recommendations based on their subjective judgements, otherwise scientists would be barred from discussion of mankind's future, leaving the arena to those more ignorant about the world's future course.[2]

Nearly four decades later, the hypothesis that scientists can see the future better than non-scientists can be tested. Comparing economic growth to cancer, the authors, Mihaljo Mesarovic, a professor of systems engineering, and Eduard Pestel, a professor of mechanics, predicted a series of regional catastrophes.* In the

---

*   The impression of mankind as a form of malignant tumour was reinforced by a passage quoted at the beginning of the book's first chapter: 'The world has cancer and the cancer is man.' To add a Doctor Strangelove twist, in the second half of the 1970s Mesarovic and Pestel's 'World Integrated Model' was used by the Pentagon for planning purposes. Julian L. Simon & Herman Kahn (ed.), *The Resourceful Earth: A Response to Global 2000* (1984), pp. 37–8.

early 1980s, South Asia would be hit by a catastrophe which would peak around 2010. 'There is no historical precedent for this kind of slow destruction – the massive, agonising reduction of the population of an entire world region once inhabited by several billion people.'[3] Indeed.

Climate change was an additional threat. The continuous increase in carbon dioxide would lead to a rise in global temperatures, but the increase in particulate matter would cause falling temperatures. Either one would be disastrous, but cooling was more of a threat. 'Since 1945 the second trend has appeared to be prevailing. If it continues it will have grave consequences for [the] food production capacity of the globe.'[4]

The *Guardian* thought *Mankind at the Turning Point* might be the most important document of the year.[5] Otherwise it caused hardly a ripple. The world had moved on. At a conference in Philadelphia in 1976 to celebrate the bicentenary of America's independence the Club of Rome's founder, Aurelio Peccei, distanced the Club from its anti-growth crusade. *The Limits to Growth* had 'punctured the myth of exponential growth,' but further growth was needed to solve world poverty and threats to world peace.[6] Even so, the book had served its purpose of 'getting the world's attention'. Finding solutions to the problems it had identified required puncturing a second myth – 'the myth of national competence'.[7] Peccei's view that individual nations were powerless to shape their economic future would take some hard knocks in the 1980s.

As little noticed was a conference Barbara Ward chaired between representatives of UNCTAD and Maurice Strong's UN Environment Programme in the Mexican town of Cocoyoc in October 1974. The Cocoyoc Declaration codified the basis of an alliance of convenience between the G77 and environmentalism in terms of their mutual enemy rather than what divided them. Thus it was a synthesis of Raúl Prebsich's Havana Manifesto and Barbara Ward's environmentalism.

> Large parts of the world today consist of a centre exploiting a vast periphery and also our common heritage, the biosphere. The ideal we need is a harmonised cooperative world in which each part is a centre, living at the expense of nobody else in partnership with nature and solidarity with future generations.[8]

A North American or a European child, on average, consumes outrageously more than his Indian or African counterpart, the Declaration said.[9] The problem was not one of absolute physical shortage, but of the economic and social structures within and between countries, reflecting the legacy of colonialism.[10] The market enabled powerful nations to exploit poor countries' natural resources at low prices and then sell manufactures back to them 'often at monopoly prices'.[11] It demanded taxation of the 'global commons' as a first step towards a system of international taxation to generate automatic transfers from rich to poor countries.[12]

The global commons that mattered most was the ocean. In 1973, Ward had written that the Conference on the Law of the Sea was *the* critical conference of the world's 'commons' of the twentieth century. There should be a special maritime authority to administer the ocean's mineral reserves.[13] The Cocoyoc Declaration also said that a globally administered oceans regime had to be established 'with jurisdiction over a maximum area of the oceans'.[14]

The Law of the Sea Treaty, negotiated through the 1970s, embodied the redistributionist principles of the New International Economic Order. It was one of the reasons that led President Reagan in 1982 to reject it. When Al Haig, Reagan's secretary of state asked him why, Reagan replied: 'Al, that's what the last election was all about … It was about not doing things just because that's the way they've been done before.'[15]

After Cocoyoc, the New International Economic Order gained momentum. Responding to a suggestion made by Robert McNamara in September 1977 the former German Chancellor Willy Brandt announced his readiness to launch an independent commission. The Brandt Commission on International Development marked a decisive move away from the militant anti-growth rhetoric of First Wave environmentalism. 'Many people in the North have questioned whether it is feasible, and even desirable, to maintain high rates of growth,' the commission acknowledged. Growth, the Brandt Report argued, helped fund environmental protection. It wasn't growth as such that was environmentally damaging, but particular technologies, lifestyles and industries which should be controlled by selective intervention.[16]

The thrust of the report was that the gap between rich and poor was wide and getting wider, that it threatened the global economy and world peace, and could only be narrowed by a new architecture of global governance. 'Current trends point to a sombre future for the world economy and international relations,' the commission feared. Mankind was using up non-renewable resources. Pollution and exploitation of the atmosphere, sea and soil were all-embracing. 'Are we to leave our successors a scorched planet of advancing deserts, impoverished landscapes and ailing environ-

ments?' the commission asked.[17] 'The 1980s could witness even greater catastrophes than the 1930s,' it said.[18] For an anti-Nazi who had adopted the
pseudonym Willy Brandt to hide from the Gestapo, this was as bad a prognosis as it could possibly be, one that turned out to be totally ill-judged.

Among the twenty-five 'eminent persons' the commission invited to
testify were Barbara Ward and Maurice Strong – and Raúl Prebisch. It was
a close knit circle. One of the commissioners, former British Prime Minister Edward Heath, was a fervent admirer of Ward. Another commissioner,
Washington Post owner Katharine Graham, was one of only three people
McNamara would take a telephone call from before ten in the morning,
the other two being his wife and Barbara Ward.

North-South: A Programme for Survival concluded that the world community must shape a new international economic order to transfer more
resources from the North to the South. The welfare state had delivered
social harmony within nations by protecting the weak and promoting the
principles of justice. It had to be elevated to the global level. 'The world
too can become stronger by becoming a just and humane society. If it fails
in this, it will move towards its own destruction.'[19] Rich countries should
transfer 0.7 per cent of national income in aid to poorer countries, rising
to one percent by 2000. There should be global system of taxation, based
on a sliding scale of national income, and taxes on exploiting the seabed.[20]

The Brandt Report was one of the items of the 1980 G7 in Venice.
President Carter also briefed fellow leaders on the *Global 2000* report. The
summit communiqué agreed that the G7 needed a better understanding of
the long-term effects of global population growth and economic development generally. Formally welcoming the Brandt Report, the summit point-
edly said that providing aid must be equitably shared by the oil-exporting
countries and the Soviet bloc, which was tantamount to saying it wasn't
going to happen.[21] As Prebisch had privately remarked about OPEC, 'the
worst type of rich are the poor that have been enriched'.[22]

At the 1981 G7 in Ottawa, host Pierre Trudeau prevailed on Ronald
Reagan to attend the first North-South summit in Cancún later that year.
Margaret Thatcher wanted Reagan there for the opposite reason – to argue
against the New International Economic Order. At Cancún, Thatcher dismissed the Brandt Report as fashionable talk and attacked its underlying
idea of tackling poverty through redistribution rather than wealth creation
as wrongheaded. She and Reagan saw off proposals to change the voting
weights of the IMF and the World Bank. She wasn't going to have British
money in a bank run by those on overdrafts.[23]

Cancún and Reagan's rejection of the Law of the Sea Treaty the following year marked the end of North-South dialogue in response to the South's attempts to create the New International Economic Order. When world leaders met in Rio de Janeiro in 1992, it was at the West's behest in the context of its fears about global warming. The South's demands hadn't gone away.

The ideas championed by Carter and Brandt also began to attract the criticism of academics. In the US, economist Julian Simon led a critique of *Global 2000* by a group of academics which included one of Al Gore's favourite scientists, Roger Revelle. Simon's studies of population growth and economic history had led him to conclude that population growth, far from being a threat to prosperity, was associated with rising prosperity. People were the ultimate resource, he argued. Simon turned upside down *Global 2000*'s pessimistic end-of-century forecast: 'If present trends continue, the world in 2000 will be less crowded (though more populated), *less polluted, more stable ecologically*, and *less vulnerable to resource-supply disruption* than the world we live in now.'[24]

On the other side of the Atlantic, David Henderson, a former World Bank economist, wrote a searching analysis of the Brandt Report. Henderson argued that the commission's view that inequalities between nations caused war had no historical basis. War had been an endemic state of affairs throughout history, whereas the condition of extreme inequality between nations had arisen only in the recent past. The commission's understanding of why economies grew was naively political. Evidence of progress made by many poor countries had, in George Orwell's term, become an 'unfact'. Henderson's criticism centred on the commission's handling of uncertainty.

> It is a profound mistake to suppose that the issues of social and economic life are such that it makes sense to think in terms of 'solutions' to them, as though they were like the entries in a crossword puzzle, for which there can be found a recognised, uniquely correct and permanently valid set of responses.[25]

The belief that economic problems had determinate solutions, Henderson argued, embodied a definite magical element, 'so that the complexities and uncertainties of the world are wished away, and events are treated as though they could be made predictable and manipulable by formulae or spells'.[26]

In December 1983, the UN General Assembly adopted resolution 38/161 – without a vote – to establish a special commission to propose 'long term environmental strategies for achieving sustainable development by the year 2000 and beyond'.[27] To those who might have opposed it, the resolution appeared pretty innocuous. Member governments weren't bound by the commission's conclusions. Its costs were to be met by voluntary contributions from its sponsors, Canada, Japan, the Netherlands, Switzerland and the four Nordic nations.[28]

The issues hardly appeared momentous. The previous year, the governing council of the UN Environment Programme (UNEP) had selected three topics of concern – hazardous waste, acid rain and the possible adverse environmental impact of large-scale renewable energy farms.[29] The chairmanship was offered to the leader of the Norwegian Labour party and former prime minister, Gro Harlem Brundtland.

Like its forebears, the Brundtland Commission's report, *Our Common Future*, was predicated on impending doom. There was a trinity of crises: an environmental crisis, a development crisis and an energy crisis. 'They are one,' the report proclaimed.[30] According to Brundtland herself, a painful list of disasters had alerted 'all thinking people to the grave crisis facing our planet'.[31]

Hope was at hand. 'What we need is new concepts, new values and to mobilise will. We need a new global ethic.'[32] The planet could be redeemed and the poor saved from sliding down a spiral of economic and ecological decline by embracing the doctrine of sustainable development.

What was the magic formula possessing such power? 'Sustainable development is development that meets the needs of the present without compromising the ability of future generations to meet their own needs.'[33]

It had the merit of superficial plausibility. But as the Paley Commission put it, the needs of future generations are unknowable – the syndrome of conserving bayberries for the electric age. In his review of the Brandt Report, Henderson argued that the distinction between essential and non-essential needs was alien to the conception of economic choice which underlies the case for using market modes of allocation in which 'there are no needs to be met regardless of cost, and to think in terms of a sharp distinction from essential to non-essential is meaningless'.[34]

At times, the search for the meaning of sustainable development gets caught in a loop of tautology. Living standards higher than 'the basic minimum' are only sustainable if consumption standards everywhere have regard for long-term sustainability.[35] Should the use of non-renewable resources be forbidden? No. 'The rate of depletion and the emphasis on recycling and the economy of use should be calibrated to ensure that the resource does not run out before acceptable substitutes are available'[36] – a formulation that is meaningless because the world has never run out of a particular mineral. Species become extinct, not minerals.

In principle, the Brundtland formulation of sustainable development is consistent with having no policy at all other than to promote the efficient functioning of markets. This would, of course, clash with the report's presumption that markets were propelling the world towards some kind of planetary catastrophe.

So what does 'sustainable development' actually mean?

> In essence, sustainable development is a process of change in which the exploitation of resources, the direction of investments, the orientation of technological development, and institutional change are all in harmony and enhance both current and future potential to meet human needs and aspirations.[37]

In relation to the concept of needs, the Brundtland Report stated that the needs of the world's poor should have over-riding priority.[38] Poverty was a major cause and effect of global environmental problems, the report asserted.[39] Brundtland herself went further, telling the UNEP governing council that international economic inequalities were the root cause of poverty and environmental degradation.[40]

The need for more resources for developing countries could not be evaded. 'The idea that developing countries would do better to live within their limited means is a cruel illusion.'[41] Thus sustainable development provided green packaging for egalitarianism and global income redistribution policies. 'Perceived needs are socially and culturally determined, and sustainable development requires the promotion of values that encourage consumption standards that are within the bounds of the ecologically possible and to which all can reasonably aspire.'[42]

Sustainable development is not an economic concept, but a political doctrine with far-reaching economic implications. In her speech to the UNEP at Nairobi in 1987, Brundtland herself described sustainable development as the report's 'overriding political concept.' It would help provide 'the key to open new doors of perception and entail inspiration for humankind in its quest for progress and survival ... It requires fair access to knowledge and resources and a more equitable distribution within and among nations'.[43] Sustainable development, she claimed, turned on its head what she called the zero growth dogma of the early seventies. If done right, growth could be good and developing countries had no option but to seek to grow.

Yet the shedding of the limits-to-growth hair shirt was more in the nature of a re-branding statement than a substantive shift. There might not be absolute limits, but there were 'ultimate limits', the report said. The affluent would have to adopt lifestyles and live within 'the planet's ecological means'. 'Painful choices have to be made,' the report warned. 'In the final analysis, sustainable development must rest on political will.'[44]

A commission chaired by a Norwegian social democrat, financed by wealthy, high latitude, northern hemisphere countries was always going to advocate a form of globalised Scandinavian social democracy. Nearly nine hundred organisations and individuals gave their views to the commission or assisted it in some way. Seventy-seven came from Scandinavia and Finland, compared to thirty-five from the US and fifty-one from the Soviet Union, the last signifying an important step in the greening of international relations.

The Chernobyl nuclear accident in April 1986 and Mikhail Gorbachev's policy of *glasnost* had made discussion about Soviet attitudes to the environment permissible. 'No one even imagined the extent of our ecological disaster, how far we were behind the developed nations as a result of our barbaric attitude towards nature,' according to Gorbachev.[45] At one of the commission's public hearings in Moscow seven months after the Chernobyl accident, a member of the Soviet Academy of Sciences asked whether the development of civil nuclear power had not been premature, a position that before Gorbachev would have aroused the interest of the KGB (Gorbachev concluded that the Soviet Union could not dispense with nuclear power).[46]

While the commission achieved balance between the industrial and developing nations, there was a marked imbalance within the latter, with Indonesia (ninety-six) and Brazil (eighty-eight) to the fore. Despite the 1984 Bhopal industrial disaster, there were only six from India and two from China.

One nation stood above all the rest: seemingly every organ of the Canadian government, its provinces and territories and a multitude of societies, students and individuals – two hundred and seven in all – were mobilised and made it their business to be involved. Maurice Strong was a commissioner and fellow Canadian Jim MacNeill, a 1971 Founex participant, was in charge of drafting its report. It is reasonable to say that the Brundtland Report and its aftermath represent Canada's most singular impression on world affairs.*

---

* There were no participants from Australia and New Zealand.

Political success required sustainable development to have something it lacked. The Brundtland Report and its antecedents made big claims about adverse trends harming the poor and the planet, which some day, would end in catastrophe, in some form. Yet these assertions were remarkably free of hard data. While sustainable development implied limits, it couldn't say where they were or what exactly would happen if those thresholds were crossed. It was a doctrine in search of scientific authentication. As a political ideology, Marxism always claimed to be derived from scientific analysis. By contrast, sustainable development was an ideology, developed from a political formula, in search of science.

What transformed the impact of the Brundtland Commission was a joint conference of UNEP, the World Meteorological Organisation and the International Council of Scientific Unions in the Austrian town of Villach in October 1985. Called to assess the impact of increasing concentrations of carbon dioxide and other greenhouse gases on the climate, the conference concluded

> it is now believed that in the first half of the next century a rise of global mean temperature could occur which is greater than any in man's history.[47]

The estimated increase of between 0.3 and 0.7°C in global mean temperature during the previous one hundred years was, the conference said, consistent with the projected temperature increase attributable to the observed increase in CO_2 and other greenhouse gases, although the rise could not be ascribed in a scientifically rigorous manner to these factors alone.

An advisory group on greenhouse gases was formed, which liaised with MacNeill. Bert Bolin, a leading climate scientist and future chair of the Intergovernmental Panel on Climate Change, deemed the MacNeill channel to the Brundtland Commission essential in enabling the scientific community to get global warming onto the political agenda.[48]

Global warming was one of four environmental threats identified by the Brundtland Commission (the others being urban pollution, acid rain and the risk of nuclear reactor accidents). If the meeting at Villach had not taken place, the thrust of the Brundtland Report and the need for the world to adopt sustainable development would have been the same. Brundtland herself did not mention global warming in her June 1987 prepared remarks to UNEP on the report.

Without global warming, sustainable development would not have shifted the world's political axis. With global warming, environmentalism had found its killer app. In turn, global warming became embedded in a pre-existing ideology, built on the belief of imminent planetary catastrophe – which many scientists subscribed to – with a UN infrastructure to support it and a cadre of influential political personages to propagate it.

A butterfly was ready to spread its wings.

11
ANNUS MIRABILIS

Global Warming Has Begun, Expert Tells Senate.

New York Times, 24th June 1988

It was hot. The date had been chosen after consulting the Weather Bureau. The air conditioning wasn't working and the windows had been left open overnight. The television lights made it worse.

23rd June turned out to be a record-breaking day in a year when drought swept much of the United States.[1] NASA scientist James Hansen wiped away the sweat as he told the Senate Energy and Natural Resources Committee: 'The greenhouse effect has been detected, and it is changing our climate now.'[2]

If Philip Larkin could date 1963 as the year when sexual intercourse became a cultural phenomenon,

> Between the end of the Chatterley ban
> And the Beatles' first LP

then 1988 was the start of global warming as a political one. Parallels with the mid sixties were apposite. The rise of the Second Environmental Wave began towards the end of a decade of renewed prosperity after the lost decade of the 1970s.

> We got department stores and toilet paper
> Got Styrofoam boxes for the ozone layer

Neil Young sang in his 1989 'Rockin' in the Free World': 'Got fuel to burn, got roads to drive.' Britain experienced its Second Summer of Love, a return to the psychedelic 1960s with acid-fuelled rave parties and protests against road-building. Environmentalism needed ringing tills and gridlocked roads.

Global warming's arrival in the world was announced with a blaze of fanfares heralding potential catastrophe. Alarmism went hand-in-hand with predictions of temperature increases that turned out to be excessive. Although warnings that civilisation was doomed because economic activity was destroying the biosphere had become something of a routine, two things were different this time. First, mainstream political leaders from across the political spectrum quickly joined and amplified the chorus. Second, an institutional apparatus was constructed to keep attention on the issue. Unlike the 1972 Stockholm conference and the creation of the UNEP far away from the centres of power, the Intergovernmental Panel on Climate Change was an inter-governmental body with close and pervasive relations with its sponsoring governments. The rhythm of the publication of IPCC assessment reports would help feed media interest and keep governments engaged.

And there was something else. It wasn't just one event. It was many. It was in the air.

Four days before Hansen's Senate appearance, the G7 summit in Toronto declared that 'global climate change, air, sea and fresh water pollution, acid rain, hazardous substances, deforestation, and endangered species require priority attention'.[3] Climate change had first been mentioned in the 1985 Bonn summit, but the Toronto G7 went further. Canada had been the first western nation to support the Brundtland Report and host Brian Mulroney wanted to make sure environmental protection and the Brundtland Report were on the summit agenda.[4]

The summit noted that the Brundtland Report's call that environmental considerations should be integrated into all areas of economic policymaking for the globe to continue to support humankind and formally endorsed 'the concept of sustainable development'.[5] It had taken seventeen years from Founex to sustainable development being adopted by the G7. It was environmentalism's greatest international triumph up to that point.

Why did Ronald Reagan at his last G7 summit and Margaret Thatcher, then the longest-serving G7 leader, give their approval to a political doctrine that holds as its axiom that markets keep people in the developing world poor and devastate the environment? The answer is clearer with Thatcher. But there is little to suggest Reagan had changed his views. Most likely, sustainable development had been an issue the top levels of the administration had not considered that important. The first item on the summit communiqué had been the Soviet Union's withdrawal from Afghanistan and managing the de-escalation of the Cold War to a peaceful close.*

In his final year as president, Reagan continued to resist environmental regulations he thought might harm American economic interests. Earlier

---

* When asked in 2010, former secretary of state George Shultz had no specific recollection of discussions on the Brundtland Report or sustainable development (email to author from Susan Schendel, 14th October 2010).

in 1988, Mulroney had visited Washington to push the Reagan administration into signing a treaty on acid rain. Reagan and secretary of state George Shultz ignored Mulroney's pleas, although Mulroney's meeting with Vice President Bush produced a promise that he would, a pledge that he kept after he became president. As Mulroney put it in his memoirs, 'unlike his decisive actions in East-West relations and other important international issues, Ronald Reagan, as I was to find out in April in Washington, was unable to fully seize the moment'.[6]

Eight days after the G7, Mulroney hosted a second Toronto conference. Organised by Gro Harlem Brundtland and Jim MacNeill, it was on global warming and its implications for global security. The language at the conference was alarmist, as were the temperature forecasts. The dangers from the growth of greenhouse gases were second only to nuclear war. Harmful consequences were already evident over many parts of the globe, although it wasn't specified where these were or what they might be. Severe economic and social dislocation for present and future generations was predicted.

Average global temperatures were forecast to rise by between 1.5°C and 4.5°C before the middle of the twenty-first century.[7] By 2009, one third of the way into 1988–2050 forecast period, average global temperatures, according to Britain's Hadley/Met Office temperature series, had risen by just over one quarter of a degree centigrade (0.257°C) compared to the half-degree rise implied by the lower band assumed by the Toronto conference. The top of the forecast band is way off the scale – out by a factor of nearly six.[8]

The Toronto climate conference did make one correct forecast, anticipating the pattern of recommendations that should be adopted to combat global warming. Calling for a rapid reduction in North-South inequalities, the conference said that total emissions of carbon dioxide should be cut twenty per cent below their 1988 level by 2005, with all the cuts falling on the rich nations. Additional energy consumption by developing nations should be met by even steeper reductions on the part of the developed world. At some stage, rapid economic growth by developing nations implied that developed countries would have to cut their carbon emissions to less than zero.

In September came a powerful voice from an unexpected quarter. Echoing Revelle and Suess in their 1957 paper, Margaret Thatcher warned humans might have 'unwittingly begun a massive experiment with the system of the planet itself'.[9] Global warming now had a political champion of undoubted world stature. 'We are told,' although she didn't say by whom, 'that a warming of one degree centigrade per decade would greatly exceed the capacity of our natural habitat to cope,' she said in her speech to the Royal Society. Such a rapid rise might indeed have been a cause for alarm. The degree-per-decade rise alluded to by Mrs Thatcher implied that by 2010, the planet would have warmed a full two degrees centigrade compared to the 1.8°C to 4.0°C range predicted by the IPCC in its 2007 Fourth Assessment Report to the end of the twenty-first century.[10]

Two months later in Geneva, the Intergovernmental Panel on Climate Change met for the first time. Mustafa Tolba, executive director of the United Nations Environment Programme, asked Bert Bolin to be the IPCC's first chairman. An independent-minded meteorologist and some-time scientific adviser to Sweden's prime minister, Bolin was clear what the IPCC needed to do. It should provide a stringent assessment of the available scientific knowledge he thought had been lacking thus far. Bolin spared neither supporters nor opponents of anthropogenic global warming from criticism, whether it was Hansen's congressional testimony ('the data showing the global increase of temperature had not been scrutinised well enough'); the forecasts adopted by the Toronto climate conference ('not yet been generally accepted by the scientific community') or Mrs Thatcher ('seriously misinformed' on the scale of the warming effect).[11]

Bolin's opinions were not limited to scientific matters. He thought Mrs Thatcher's interest in global warming was motivated by a desire to close Britain's coal mines.[12] More importantly, his opinions on the economics and politics of global warming, which would become a large part of the IPCC's work, were coloured by his belief in sustainable development. For Bolin the scientist, there was no boundary demarcating the positivist world of science and the clash of normative values that characterises political debate. Writing of the IPCC's work in developing policies to combat global warming, Bolin said, 'striving for sustainable development and an equitable world must be central features of any study of this kind'.[13]

In his role as IPCC chairman Bolin adjudicated technical disputes far outside his field of expertise. For example, he opposed the use of Purchasing Power Parity indices (used to compare GDP across frontiers) in the IPCC's economic scenarios because he (wrongly) thought they made assumptions incompatible with 'the basic goal of a future equitable world.'[14] From the outset, the IPCC and its first chairman were not going to limit themselves to diagnosis; they were going to set the parameters for the cure as well. Politicisation of the IPCC's work was not an incidental risk that needed to be managed; it was inherent in the mandate the IPCC had devised for itself and Bert Bolin's expansive view of it.

The Geneva meeting also established IPCC's tripartite working group structure which has persisted to the present day; Working Group I to assess the available evidence, led initially by Sir John Houghton of Britain's Meteorological Office; Working Group II to assess the environmental and socioeconomic impacts, led by Dr Yuri Izrael of the USSR's Hydro-Meteorological Service; and Working Group III to formulate response strategies, led by Dr Frederick Bernthal of the US State Department – and thought the most important of the three.

Twenty years to the day after his 1988 testimony, Hansen gave a reprise. 'Now, as then, I can assert that these conclusions have a certainty exceeding ninety-nine per cent,' Hansen testified.[15] There were already present, Hansen stated, the elements of a 'perfect storm' and a 'global cataclysm'. Even without further greenhouse gas emissions, the Arctic would soon be ice-free during summer. If emissions followed a business-as-usual scenario, Hansen claimed there would be two metre sea level rises by the end of the century and hundreds of millions of refugees. His call for the chief executives of oil and coal companies to be tried for 'high crimes against humanity and nature' caught the media's attention, as such inflammatory language was designed to do.[16]

It also had the effect of diverting media scrutiny from other problematic aspects of Hansen's testimony. While complaining of a 'wide gap' between what the scientific community knew and the public believed, there was a widening gap Hansen was less keen to talk about – that between his 1988 temperature forecasts and what actually happened.

In his 1988 testimony, Hansen had presented long-term temperature projections based on three scenarios for future emissions of carbon dioxide and other greenhouse gases. These ranged from scenario A, which Hansen described as 'business as usual' through an intermediate scenario B to scenario C, which he described as illustrating the impact of 'draconian emission cuts' resulting in no net addition to concentration of greenhouse gases from 2000, i.e., by then, man-made emissions would be completely absorbed by natural sinks.[17]

Because Hansen's team over-forecast the growth of other greenhouse gases apart from carbon dioxide, Hansen's intermediate scenario B provided the best fit with actual emissions, but not, interestingly, with the trend in global temperatures. By 2008, the trend in observed temperatures was well below scenario B and, in some cases, below even that for scenario C. Of Hansen's three scenarios, his temperature increase projections for scenario C provide the best fit with observed temperatures.[18]

The message that the world didn't hear from Hansen's presentation was that it was getting the temperatures assumed by Hansen's no net emissions scenario without incurring any of its costs. Such a conclusion would have been consistent with the data, but would have undermined Hansen's characterisation of the 'global warming time bomb' and demolished his claim of a better than ninety-nine per cent certainty.

Unlike the blanket TV coverage Hansen generated at his 1988 appearance, there were no cameras when Mrs Thatcher addressed the Royal Society on 27th September 1988. Told that the prime minister's speech was going to be on climate change, the BBC decided it wouldn't make the TV news.[19]

The speech had been a long time in the making. Flying back from visiting President Mitterrand in Paris in May 1984, Mrs Thatcher asked her officials if any of them had any new policy ideas for the forthcoming G7 summit in London. Sir Crispin Tickell, then a deputy undersecretary at the Foreign Office, suggested climate change and how it might figure in the G7 agenda. The next day, Tickell was summoned to Number 10 to brief the Prime Minister. The eventual result was to make environmental problems a specific item, and a statement in the London G7 communiqué duly referred to the international dimension of environmental problems and the role of environmental factors, including climate change. Environment ministers were instructed to report back to the G7 meeting at Bonn the following year, and duly did so.[20]

Tickell's interest in climate change dated from the mid 1970s. Influenced by reading Hubert Lamb's book *Climate History and the Modern World*, Tickell took the opportunity of a one-year fellowship at Harvard to study the relationship between climate change and world affairs and wrote a book on the subject in 1977. Tickell recalls that people at the time thought his interest in the topic a bit eccentric, but he was the only non-American to have participated in the Carter administration's *Global 2000* project.

By 1987, Tickell had been appointed Britain's ambassador to the UN and informally was acting as Thatcher's envoy on global warming, his position at the UN making him privy to gossip from other nations.[21] On two occasions, Thatcher recalled him from New York to brief her. Tickell was always struck by her determined approach; in the world of politics, Thatcher was a woman in a man's world and someone with scientific training in a non-scientific world.[22] To meet the test, you had to know what you were talking about; if she challenged you, you needed to be sure of your ground; she could be remarkably vigorous, Tickell found. The prime minister wanted the government to grasp the importance of global warming.

Ministers were called to Number 10 for briefings by climate scientists. 'You are to listen, not to speak,' the prime minister told them.[23]

Returning to England for his summer holiday in 1988, Tickell called on Thatcher and suggested she make a major speech on global warming. She thought the Royal Society would be the perfect forum for it. She spent two weekends working on the draft with George Guise, one of her policy advisers.

In the speech, Thatcher addressed the Society as a scientist and a Fellow who happened to be prime minister. Environment policy was her main subject. Action to cut power station emissions and reduce acid rain was being undertaken 'at great and necessary expense', she said, building up to her main theme. 'The health of the economy and the health of the environment are totally dependent on each other,' implicitly rejecting the view of conventional economics of there being a trade-off between resources used for environmental protection which couldn't be used to raise output or increase consumption.[24] It was also clear that the G7's endorsement of sustainable development had not been an oversight or meant to be taken lightly, as far as she was concerned. 'The government espouses the concept of sustainable economic development,' she stated, although the new policy had not been discussed collectively by ministers beforehand or with Nigel Lawson, the Chancellor of the Exchequer.[25]

Thatcher concluded her speech by referring to one of the most famous events in the Royal Society's history, when in 1919 Arthur Eddington displayed the photographic plates taken during the total eclipse of the sun earlier that year. The eclipse enabled Eddington to record whether light from distant stars was bent by the sun's gravity and verify a prediction of Einstein's theory of relativity.

Whitehead witnessed Eddington's demonstration. The scene, tense as a Greek drama, he wrote, was played out beneath the portrait of Isaac Newton, the Society's twelfth president, 'to remind us that the greatest of scientific generalisations was now, after more than two centuries, to receive its first modification'.[26] In Vienna, reports of it thrilled the seventeen-year-old Karl Popper. What particularly impressed Popper was the risk implied by Einstein's theory, that light from distant stars would be deflected by the Sun's mass, because it could be subjected to a definitive test: 'If observation shows that the predicted effect is definitely absent, then the theory is simply refuted. The theory is *incompatible with certain possible results of observation* – in fact with results which everybody before Einstein would have expected.'[27]

These considerations led Popper to argue that the criterion for assessing the scientific status of a theory should be its capacity to generate predictions that could, in principle, be refuted by empirical evidence, what Popper called its falsifiability, or refutability, or testability.[28] Every 'good' scientific theory is a prohibition. The more a theory forbids, the better it is. Scientists should therefore devise tests designed to yield evidence that the theory prohibits, rather than search for what the theory confirms. If we look for them, Popper argued, it is easy to find confirmations for nearly every theory. 'Only a theory which asserts or implies that certain conceivable events will not, in fact, happen is testable,' Popper explained in a lecture in 1963. 'The test consists in trying to bring about, with all the means we can muster, precisely these events which the theory tells us cannot occur.'[29]

In 1988, proponents of global warming did not provide a similar black and white predictive test of the key proposition of global warming: the degree of warming with increasing levels of carbon dioxide in the atmosphere. It is therefore incapable of being falsified. The issue is not the capacity of carbon dioxide to absorb radiation in a test tube, which had first been demonstrated by John Tyndall in 1859, but the effect of increased levels of atmospheric carbon dioxide and other greenhouse gases on the temperature of the atmosphere. An answer can only be derived from empirical observation.

Revelle and Suess's characterisation of mankind carrying out a large-scale geophysical experiment, further illustrates global warming's weakness as a scientific statement and its strength as a political idea. While prejudging the results of an experiment constitutes bad science, the proposition simultaneously generates powerful calls to halt the experiment before it is concluded. Yet questioning the science would inevitably be seen as weakening the political will to act. It created a symbiotic dependence between science and politics that marks 1988 as a turning point in the history of science and the start of a new chapter in the affairs of mankind.

12
TWO SCIENTISTS

There's no doubt that any man with complete conviction, particularly who's an expert, is bound to shake anybody who's got an open mind. That's the advantage of having a closed mind.

John F. Kennedy[1]

Science is one of the very few human activities – perhaps the only one – in which errors are systematically criticised and fairly often, in time, corrected.

Karl Popper[2]

We cannot know how the future will judge the era of global warming that dawned in 1988. We can listen to the voices from the past. The past can provide perspective. History is fluid, events are contingent, seemingly immutable categories that condition thought and action, evolve over time. Many scientists were environmentalists, subscribing to the tenets of environmentalism. Until the advent of global warming, environmentalism could not claim the support of science.

Before science became set in the concrete of the present, it is timely to introduce two scientists from the past and preview the terrain across which the science unfolded. The first died well before the global warming era and the main body of professional work of the second also took place before then. Neither, therefore, had any affiliation in the disputes about global warming.

Percy W. Bridgman was a Harvard physicist, winner of the 1946 Nobel Prize for his discoveries in the field of high pressure physics and one of nine signatories of Albert Einstein and Bertrand Russell's 1955 manifesto on nuclear disarmament. Bridgman's is a voice that speaks of the critical importance of verification in science and of the inherent problem in talking about the future, which for him assumed an entirely different character from studying the past. Writing of the 'inscrutable character of the future', Bridgman thought that statements about the future belonged to the category of pseudo-statements.

> I personally do not think that one should speak of making statements about the future. For me, a statement implies the possibility of verifying its truth, and the truth of a statement about the future cannot be verified.[3]

Why is verification important? 'Where there is no possibility of verification there can be no error, and "truth" becomes meaningless.'[4] Bridgman accorded greater confidence to the astronomer than to the man in the street to a verification of whether the sun had risen that day. If it had not, it would have involved suspension of the laws of mechanics which the astronomer had observed were manifest in every moving thing.[5]

Global warming, of course, involves projecting increased levels of atmospheric carbon dioxide and other greenhouse gases into the inscrutability of the future. However it is not possible to determine global temperature in advance, solely by reference to the laws of physics and chemistry. The value of the climate sensitivity of carbon dioxide, the impact on average global temperatures from a doubling of the concentration of carbon dioxide, is unknown.

Though an upper limit can be inferred from global temperatures not increasing dramatically since the Industrial Revolution, there is no lower limit above zero.* Making an assumption more precise than this amounts to educated guesswork about what the forecaster believes *should* happen. If someone says, 'It will rain tomorrow,' what they mean is, 'I expect it will rain tomorrow.' Our predictions embody our expectations. As Bridgman put it, 'to "correctly-predict" is a verb which has only a past tense.'[6] Thus predictions of future temperature increases tell us less about whether the planet was heading for a climatic fever than the beliefs of the people making them.

Our second scientist was Britain's first leading climate scientist. Hubert Lamb was a friend of Guy Stewart Callendar. He had a long career in the Meteorological Office before being appointed founding director of the Climatic Research Unit in 1972 at what later became the University of East Anglia. Delving into weather records and other historical evidence such as diaries, pictures and population records, Lamb used his knowledge of weather patterns to argue that climate variability was an important but neglected factor in explaining the development and decline of various human societies.

In his last book, published in 1982, Lamb repeatedly used terms that no climate scientist would risk today. Warmer climates are genial, writing of the Medieval Warm Period, 'the genial climate of the high Middle Ages which coincided with the twelfth- and thirteenth-century climax of

---

* In a 1991 paper, Canadian mathematician Christopher Essex demonstrated that the effect on global surface temperature of increased levels of carbon dioxide could be less than zero. Christopher Essex, 'What Do Climate Models Tell Us About Global Warming?' in *Pure and Applied Geophysics PAGEOPH*, Vol. 135, Issue 1 (1991), pp. 125–33.

cultural development.'[7] The cooling trend of the fourteenth century is a 'climatic deterioration'.[8] His research into that cooling (a factor he thought behind recurrence of the Black Death in Europe) led Lamb to be worried by the post-Second World War cooling trend.[9] 1965 had been the year which halted the long recession of many Alpine glaciers and saw the return of Arctic sea ice around Iceland.[10] The cooling trend in the northern hemisphere reversed an earlier upward trend, which had led Callendar to doubt the Callendar Effect, as global warming was known in those days. Lamb acknowledged that some mild winters in the 1970s had 'caused judgement to hesitate and produced the impression that the spate of writings in the 1960s about climatic change had overstressed the subject', adding: 'That was before the winters of record severity in parts of North America and Europe in the later 1970s.'[11]

Lamb therefore assessed the growing belief in anthropogenic global warming against his deep immersion in meteorological history and of post-war cooling. Claims of a warming of between two and eleven [!] degrees centigrade by 2100 were, he wrote carefully, 'an opinion, seemingly founded on firm scientific knowledge, which has to be taken seriously, even though we may notice some grounds for doubt and scepticism'.[12] One cause of Lamb's scepticism was his observation that the World Meteorological Organisation and other modellers assumed a range for natural fluctuation of plus or minus one degree, later reduced by the IPCC to as little as plus or minus half a degree. Lamb understood probably better than anyone that natural variations could greatly exceed the limited ranges assumed by later climate modellers.

It is only by assuming a small range of natural variation that modellers could project that warming caused by greenhouse gas emissions will 'swamp' all other elements of natural variation so the global warming 'signal' can emerge from the background 'noise'. Lamb responded

> There is a fallacy in this part of the case since it is impossible to define a figure for the range of natural variation of climate which is meaningful in this connection. The record of prevailing temperatures, whether over the past few centuries or over the much longer-term record of ice ages and interglacial periods, shows that the range of variation is itself subject to variation.[13]

To establish the amplitude of natural climate variability requires analysis of the climate record of past centuries and millennia. The instrumental record does not stretch sufficiently far – the oldest, the Central England Temperature record, goes back to 1659 on a monthly basis and to 1772 on a daily one. Creating a temperature record going back to the beginning of the current inter-glacial period over ten thousand years ago depends on the use of controversial proxy data. These include evidence from lake sediment, ice cores, pollen records and tree ring and coral ring studies.

What the bounds of natural variability might be – whether it is plus or minus one or half a degree – alters the significance of the estimated 0.6 degree (plus or minus 0.2) rise over the course of the twentieth century. If the rise falls within the bounds of natural variability, there is no need for man-made global warming to explain it. Having a version of the climatic past that showed a narrow amplitude of natural fluctuation was therefore essential in prosecuting the case for global warming.

There was a second reason. Part of the idea of global warming is that elevated temperatures are harmful. This invites comparison with previous climatic episodes. Are current temperatures unprecedented in human history? If not, how badly did human societies and ecosystems fare during previous warm periods? On the other hand, might such episodes, far from being harmful, have been benign and, to borrow Lamb's term, genial?

After 1988, climate scientists and the IPCC expended great effort on reconstructing a global temperature record. In doing so, climate scientists descended from the impregnable heights of unverifiable assertion about the future to the arena of evidence of the past and the requirements of reproducibility and verifiability. 'Your statement that you have verified something is indifferent to me unless I believe that I could make the verification also,' was the way Bridgman described it.[14] It was on this field that the science of global warming suffered its first defeat, a strategic reversal from which it has not yet recovered.

A dramatic new version of the temperature record over the last thousand years was presented in 2001 in the IPCC's Third Assessment Report. The message appeared compelling: 1998 was the warmest year in the warmest decade in the last one thousand years. The Hockey Stick graph, which told a story of a declining temperature trend in the northern hemisphere for nine hundred years, then an abrupt uptick at the beginning of the twentieth century, could not meet a verification standard such as that required by Bridgman. Despite considerable obstruction, it was shown by independent researchers, notably Canadian mining analyst Steve McIntyre and his economist colleague Ross McKitrick, to be a statistical contrivance.

The counter-attack defending the Hockey Stick demonstrated even more clearly how rapidly scientific standards have changed. It was now argued that the universal principle of verification should be restricted to a select group of experts. Only papers in peer-reviewed literature that supported their views were to be considered legitimate in settling the dispute.

Popper issued a stark warning against such thinking with implications that go to the fundamental basis of Western civilisation.

> An open society (that is, a society based on the idea of not merely tolerating dissenting opinions but respecting them) and a democracy (that is, a form of government devoted to the protection of an open society) cannot flourish if science becomes the exclusive possession of a closed group of specialists.[15]

A further danger with having a closed group is in reinforcing the natural tendency of the human mind to fit facts into preconceived theory. To explain why planets and stars were in positions they shouldn't according to the Ptolemaic system of the Earth being at the centre of the universe, medieval astronomers added geometrically complex and implausible epicycles. Adding 'epicycles' has come to be synonymous with adopting stratagems to avoid questioning the basic premise of a scientific proposition.

The hypothesis of dangerous global warming is sufficiently accommodating to be consistent with a wide spectrum of outcomes, even if these were not specifically predicted beforehand. The observed pause in the warming trend in the first decade of the twenty-first century was not predicted by climate scientists. After the event, they explained it away by invoking the Pacific Decadal Oscillation and not questioning the premise of their models.

1988 came at the end of a first decade of warming, reversing the previous twenty-year trend of declining temperatures. This decline, which Lamb had thought indicated a long-term cooling trend, has since been interpreted as masking the rise that would have happened were it not for aerosols – microscopic particles formed in the atmosphere from coal-fired power station emissions – that reflect back the sun's incoming radiation.* As with

---

*   Coal-fired power stations occupy a unique place in the demonology of global warming, being held responsible as the main culprits of global warming and the cause of the cooling in the third quarter of the last century. In 2008, Hansen compared trains carrying coal to power stations to those that carried Jews to the concentration camps. Thus a speculative view of the future has been accorded the same evidential status as historical fact, moreover the fact of the greatest crime of all time, and doubters about the former are subliminally bracketed with deniers of the latter (James Hansen, 'Global Warming Twenty Years Later: Tipping Points Near' www.columbia.edu/~jeh1/2008/TwentyYearsLater_20080623.pdf).

the post-1998 cessation of warming, this rationalisation is of the same type as that applied by medieval astronomers in invoking their epicycles. 'The physicist has, and the rest of us should have a temperamental aversion to *ad hoc* constructions in his theorising,' Bridgman cautioned. For the use of ad hoc argument means there is no second method of arriving at a theory's terminus, and therefore, Bridgman argued, 'no method of verifying that the construction corresponds to anything "real"'.[16]

Instead of seeking to meet Popper's criterion of falsifiability, the activities of climate scientists conform to an earlier injunction pre-dating the Scientific Revolution: 'Seek, and ye shall find.' Climate scientists have followed this teaching from the Sermon on the Mount in their search for confirmatory evidence of global warming in shrinking ice caps, retreating glaciers and inferring past temperatures from tree rings.

The lack of a falsifiability test led scientists and governments into putting their faith in the existence of a scientific consensus as the guide to scientific truth. This too, according to Bridgman, is problematic. Consensus is one of the methods used to weed out individual error, but its role was strictly limited. He specifically rejected the notion of defining science as the consensus of all competent observers. Relying on verification by 'competent persons' during any epoch meant having a selection of people who had been subject to definite preconditioning.[17] It might, Bridgman thought, signify little more than the discovery that under similar conditions, different human animals react the same way

> merely because there are so many common features in the construction of all human animals. Verification by consensus is always to be accepted with extreme reservation.[18]

In contrast to Bridgman's caution, consensus-building is at the heart of what the IPCC does. It rests on a highly questionable claim: the subjective opinions of individual scientists can be transmuted into scientific knowledge through the process of being formed into an agreed judgement. In his 2009 book *Why We Disagree About Climate Change*, climate scientist and IPCC author Mike Hulme cited the IPCC's expressions of increasing confidence in attributing rising temperatures to human activities as how consensus works to establish scientific knowledge; from the caution of its First Assessment Report in 1990 to what Hulme called the bullishness of its Fourth Assessment Report in 2007. According to Hulme, at each stage of the process, substantial judgment on the part of the scientist(s) is required; a judgement formed through dialogue, dispute and compromise rather than through detached and disinterested truth-seeking.[19]

There was little alternative to relying on such procedures, Hulme argued. 'In complex and uncertain areas of knowledge "objective methods" alone are rarely adequate to establish what is known.'[20]

The purpose of consensus is to gain agreement with a view to taking collective action. Here, an altogether larger claim is being made: consensus can transform belief into knowledge. This requires us to accept that there is no fundamental difference between belief and knowledge, so long as there is collective agreement on it by those whose opinions count – the experts who don the mantle of scientific authority. In this way today's scientists have become modern day alchemists transforming the lead of subjective belief into the gold of objective knowledge.

Such a claim has profound implications for the nature of science itself. It permits scientists to slip the bounds of what had traditionally been understood as science into pseudo-science, to adopt Popper's term, and into the realm of futurology. For sure, eminent scientists can make more of an impact on the popular imagination with their essays in futurology than with their scientific research. In 2006 the physicist Stephen Hawking made headlines with his prediction that humans would have to leave Earth to avoid the risk of the species being wiped out by an asteroid or a nuclear disaster.[21] In 2003, Britain's Astronomer Royal and future president of the Royal Society Martin Rees wrote a book, *Our Final Century* (*Our Final Hour* in the American market), which estimated that mankind had only a fifty per cent chance of surviving the century thanks to threats even more dangerous than global warming.

The historian must accept a definition of science as being what scientists do. However, the historian can make two claims. The first is that the predictive record of scientists on the future of mankind is rather worse than a random selection of people off the street. The scientists who put their names to the *Blueprint for Survival* in 1972 – predicting civilisation would come to an end in the lifetimes of people then living – proved spectacularly poor guides to the future. The actions of ordinary people who maintained their commitment to the future, the most important one being the decision to have children, have been vindicated.

Second, the nature and purpose of science has undergone profound change in recent decades. Until around the middle of the last century, science was about making discoveries and solving problems by refining and modifying theories so that they better conformed to what had been found in laboratory experiments and seen through telescopes. The purpose of these activities was the advancement of scientific knowledge.

Bridgman for one rejected the idea of a purpose beyond the pursuit of knowledge. 'To attempt to broaden the concept of science to include social responsibility, as appears to the popular temper at present can result only in confusion,' he wrote in 1959.[22] Three years later, the scientist and philosopher Michael Polanyi said much the same thing in an article extolling the republic of science: 'I appreciate the generous sentiments which actuate the aspiration of [society] guiding the progress of science into socially beneficent channels, but I hold [this aspiration] to be impossible and indeed nonsensical.'[23]

The role of science became like medicine. The point of acquiring knowledge is to diagnose and cure malady. Thus climate science, particularly after 1988, developed as the most important branch of what might be called global therapeutics. The principal justification for climate science is not the pursuit of knowledge for its own sake, but diagnosing the world's ills and defining the parameters of the therapy required by the patient.

With the irruption of global warming into world affairs, scientists mounted a radical extension of Polanyi's republic, in the process turning it upside down. Scientists were now directing science into what they decided were socially and environmentally beneficent channels in a project that required governments to implement the prescription scientists and likeminded experts had devised. The justification for governments to do so was not subject to objective verification, because global warming precluded this. Henceforth, the word of scientists was to be taken on trust.

The rigorous methodology developed by Popper and the verification standards required by a physicist such as Bridgman were now replaced. This did not happen because of the emergence of a superior epistemological standard; that is to say from the development of a new and sharper theory of knowledge. The explanation is quite different. Far from becoming obsolete, they had become inconvenient. Dependence on consensus made it all the more important to ensure that the consensus continued to prevail, especially as the future of the planet was at stake.

This provided strong incentives to sustain the consensus and maintain the world's interest; otherwise, the action which the consensus required would not be taken. For exactly the same reasons, those who expressed their doubts represented a threat. Dissenters needed to be crushed and dissent de-legitimised. They were stooges of oil companies and fossil fuel interests, free market ideologues, or climate change deniers. In the years after 1988, much reputational capital of prestigious scientific bodies and of governments was sunk into global warming, further reducing the incentives for being open to debate and criticism.

For Popper, intolerance and lack of respect for dissenting opinions were antithetical to the precepts of an open society. Dissent is also linked to the success of science in expanding scientific knowledge because criticism is the engine of the growth of knowledge. 'What is called objectivity consists solely in the critical approach,' Popper wrote in 1963.[24] The growth of scientific knowledge came not from the accumulation of observations, Popper argued, but from the repeated overthrow of scientific theories and their replacement by better or more satisfactory ones. This marked science out from virtually all other fields of human endeavour. Since the beginning of the Scientific Revolution in the seventeenth century, the West left far behind all past civilisations – surpassing even the brilliance and originality of the ancient Greeks. Scientific advance represents the supreme intellectual accomplishment of Western civilisation.

A precondition for the Scientific Revolution was the freedom to question orthodoxy and the rejection of authoritarianism. Scientists based their claim to progress by pointing to the standards later distilled by Popper. Global warming's inability to meet the verifiability and falsifiability standards set by the Scientific Revolution constitutes a reversion to pre-modern modes of defining what should be accepted as knowledge based on appeals to authority.

The significance of global warming in the history of science is not that it represented a change of paradigm within a branch of science. It was a change in the paradigm of science itself.

13
GREEN WARRIOR

The core of Tory philosophy and for the case for protecting the environment are the same. No generation has a freehold on this earth. All we have is a life tenancy – with a full repairing lease.

Margaret Thatcher, 14th October 1988[1]

In 1988, climate scientists put global warming onto the international political agenda. In the three and a half years to the Rio Earth summit in June 1992, politicians joined scientists. In signing the UN Framework Convention on Climate Change, they committed themselves to the convention's objective of stabilising greenhouse gases at a level that would avoid 'dangerous anthropogenic interference in the climate system'. After Rio, debating the science of global warming became superfluous. Politics had settled the science.

The speed with which the rhetoric of alarm was ratcheted up is astonishing. A March 1989 article in the *Financial Times* on the Green Revolution in international relations spoke of heightened concern about the environment, 'rising panic is scarcely too strong a phrase'.[2] A conference the previous month in New Delhi warned of apocalyptic scenarios. 'Global warming is the greatest crisis ever faced collectively by humankind,' its final report claimed.[3] The next month saw an international conference at The Hague organised by the French, Dutch and Norwegian prime ministers. Twenty-four governments signed a declaration suggesting that human life was under imminent threat. 'The right to live [sic] is the right from which all other rights stem,' the Hague Declaration began. 'Today, the very conditions of life on our planet are threatened by the severe attacks to which the earth's atmosphere is subjected.'[4]

In addition to the three sponsoring governments, signatories included Canada, West Germany, Australia, New Zealand, Brazil, India and Zimbabwe, whose oppressed citizens had more reason to fear their ruler than the composition of the atmosphere. News of global warming reached Buckingham Palace. In her 1989 Commonwealth Day message, the Queen spoke of threats to the environment so far-reaching it was difficult to grasp them. 'We hear, for example, of the possibility of radical changes in our climate leading, among other things, to a rise in the sea level, with all that would mean for small islands and low-lying regions.'[5]

For some, the second environmental wave came just too late. A rival accused Al Gore of running for national scientist in his 1988 presidential campaign. 'I started to wonder whether the issues I knew to be important were peripheral after all,' Gore wrote in *Earth in the Balance*, 'I began to doubt my own political judgement.'[6] Global warming barely registered in the presidential election that year. True, the Democratic party platform called for regular world environmental summits to address global threats such as the 'greenhouse effect', but its presidential candidate Michael Dukakis framed the environment as a law enforcement issue. 'We're going to have an Environmental Protection Agency that is more interested in stopping pollution than in protecting the polluters,' he told the Democratic National Convention in Atlanta.[7]

Not to be outdone, Vice President Bush told the Republican Convention a month later that he was going to have the FBI trace medical wastes and infected needles dumped into America's lakes and rivers.[8] At a campaign stop in Michigan, Bush said he would use the 'White House effect' to tackle the greenhouse effect and pledged to convene a global conference on the environment at the White House during his first year as president.

James Baker, the new secretary of state, was quicker off the mark. His first speech was to the IPCC's Working Group III on developing response strategies, ten days after taking office. 'We face the prospect of being trapped on a boat that we have irreparably damaged, not by the cataclysm of war, but by the slow neglect of a vessel we believed impervious to our abuse,' Baker told representatives from forty countries.[9]

The World Resources Institute, one of Washington's leading environmental pressure groups, praised Baker's speech. It was 'a positive shift in commitment' compared to the Reagan administration. Bolin thought otherwise. Baker had not realised the scope of oncoming climate change or the scale of the response required.[10]

Things weren't so positive in a closed door session at which the US officials proposed a plan to collect more data before acting. Some observers blamed the call for delay on mid-level staff held over from the Reagan administration.[11] They couldn't have been more wrong. Opposition came not from remnants from the previous administration, but from the most senior White House staff.

Responding to international pressure, in May the Bush administration conceded that it would support the negotiation of a framework convention. At the G7 summit in Paris, host President Mitterrand observed that environmental issues had never before been the subject of as many conversations and so many decisions.[12] The G7 leaders agreed that 'decisive action' was urgently needed to understand and protect the Earth's ecological balance. This included 'common efforts to limit emissions of carbon dioxide and other greenhouse gases, which threaten to induce climate change, endangering the environment and ultimately the economy', adding that they strongly supported the work of the IPCC.[13] Protecting the environment required 'early adoption, worldwide, of policies based on sustainable development'.[14]

Risking international isolation, the Bush administration maintained a clear line: it would not agree to anything that legally bound the United States to targets or to reduce its emissions of carbon dioxide by a specific time. This led to fierce criticism. William Nitze, a deputy assistant secretary of state in the Reagan and Bush administrations until he resigned in 1990, charged that the eventual outcome had been a success for American diplomacy, but a failure of presidential leadership. (He went on to serve in the Clinton administration at the Environmental Protection Agency.) Al Gore compared Bush's policy to the Senate's refusal to ratify the Versailles Treaty that prepared the way for the Second World War. By not providing the world with leadership in the face of what Gore called the 'assault by civilisation on the global environment', Bush was 'inviting a descent toward chaos'.[15]

That the Bush administration's position was not a function of some hard-line ideology can be seen with the Reagan administration's response to fears about depletion of the ozone layer. In 1974 two American chemists alerted the world that stratospheric ozone could be destroyed by chlorofluorocarbons (CFCs) being broken down to release chlorine, increasing the amount of ultra-violet radiation reaching the surface of the planet. In the 1970s, countries began unilaterally to cut their consumption of CFCs. In 1985, two months after the Vienna Convention for the Protection of the Ozone Layer had been agreed, the British Antarctic Survey found a hole in the ozone layer (which had thinned by forty percent in eight years). The Reagan administration played a key role in negotiating the 1987 Montreal Protocol binding signatories to steep cuts in CFCs, which came into force at the beginning of 1989. President Reagan and George Shultz hailed it as a magnificent achievement. Former UN secretary-general Kofi Annan described it as perhaps the single most successful international agreement to date.[16]

US support was a product of hard-headed calculation. According to Richard Benedick, the US lead negotiator, a major breakthrough came with a cost-benefit analysis by the President's Council of Economic Advisers. Despite the scientific and economic uncertainties, the monetary benefits of preventing future deaths from skin cancer far outweighed the costs of CFC control as estimated either by the industry or by the Environmental Protection Agency.[17] However, if the US acted alone, there would be little long-term benefit. It was better for the US to get as many countries to join in as possible. At Reagan's insistence, US negotiators lowered the participation threshold at which the agreement would come into force.

The discovery of the ozone hole provided the world dramatic narrative of industrial pollutants exposing people to increased risk of skin cancers, premature skin ageing and eye cataracts. Finding substitutes for CFCs as aerosol propellants and refrigerants was straightforward and relatively inexpensive. As a result, politicians could and did act quickly and decisively. In the words of the political scientist Scott Barrett, from whose book this account is largely drawn, 'the achievements of the Montreal controls are truly outstanding'.[18] By providing governments with a template as to how they could tackle global warming, the Montreal Protocol misled most of them – the US being the most important exception – into believing that global warming might be amenable to similarly straightforward treatment. Prime among them was the world leader who first raised the alarm.

'Mrs Thatcher, looking back over your life,' the BBC's Michael Buerk asked, 'are you really a friend of the earth?' *The Greening of Mrs Thatcher*, broadcast on 2nd March 1989, drew from Thatcher some of the most surprising things she ever said.

There was more than a hint of green in her final years at Number 10. Unlike Nixon's green phase, hers was a product of conviction, not political calculation. She was changing the political weather, Nixon was reacting to it. On the environment, Thatcher had profound differences with her ideological soul mate Ronald Reagan. She supported action against acid rain, Reagan blocked it; she believed in the dangers of resource depletion, he thought they were baloney. Even when they agreed on the ozone layer, it was for different reasons, hers being environmental, his the health and economic wellbeing of Americans.

Environmental policies used to be mostly about cleaner rivers and smog-free cities, Thatcher answered Buerk. The problems had been localised, there hadn't been the realisation of a global dimension, 'there was no greenhouse effect up there somewhere. There was no ozone layer'. She said how she'd overruled scientific advice and saved the British Antarctic Survey. 'I have always been interested in Antarctica. There is some marvellous wildlife there, there is probably a good deal of mineral deposits.' It was a fantastic, icy place that wasn't a wasteland, and recounted a meeting with members of the survey. 'They came into the next room and gave me a marvellous account of everything they are doing just a few weeks ago.'

She was worried about the greenhouse effect: 'We still do not fully understand the greenhouse gases or how they are going to operate, but we do know that we have to do something.' At that stage, emissions cuts were not on that 'to do' list. Her priority was trees. 'We are giving very considerable help on research into forestry and into the planting of tropical forests and into the preservation of tropical forests.'

According to her policy aide, George Guise, Thatcher's thinking had been particularly influenced by her conversations with the billionaire financier, Sir James Goldsmith, who owned an eighteen-thousand-acre estate on the Pacific coast of Mexico and whose brother, Edward, had helped put together the 1972 *Blueprint for Survival*.[19] Thatcher told Buerk that planting trees would help solve Bangladesh's perennial flooding.

> When President Ershad was here recently, I said: 'Look this is quite absurd. You are getting floods year after year. Really, we want the silt out of your rivers, put back on to the hills into the country behind you, into Nepal and India, and planted with trees again.'

The real difficulty with the developing world, she said, was that they wanted higher standards of living and to get out of poverty. 'That is why we have the concept under Mrs Brundtland of sustainable development with which we firmly agree.' She also favoured nuclear energy. 'I would prefer more nuclear power because it is not fundamentally interfering with the world's eco-systems.'

'Finally Mrs Thatcher,' Buerk asked, 'if and when you finish being Prime Minister, would you want to be remembered as somebody who had helped to save the world in this environmental sense?' 'Enormously so, enormously so,' she replied. 'My whole sort of political philosophy is that what you have inherited from your forefathers, it is your duty to add to it … The problems science has created, science can in fact solve and we are setting about it.'

At the end of 1988, the Maltese government sponsored a resolution of the General Assembly of the United Nations on the conservation of the climate as mankind's common heritage. The resolution said rising greenhouse gases could produce global warming which 'could be disastrous for mankind' and encouraged the convening of global, regional and national conferences to raise awareness of global warming.[20] From 1989 there was a marked intensification in the rhythm of international conferences on global warming.

The most important were the ministerial meeting that produced the Hague Declaration in March, the Noordwijk ministerial conference in November, the Bergen Conference on sustainable development in May 1990, and the Second World Climate Conference in Geneva in November. Shortly before the Geneva conference, European Community (EC) environment ministers meeting in Luxembourg agreed an EC-wide goal of stabilising carbon dioxide emissions at current levels by 2000 (a target that would only be met because German emissions fell with the incorporation of East Germany and Britain's dash-for-gas).[21] The resolution also requested the IPCC to produce its report 'as soon as possible' and in time for the Geneva conference less than two years away.

At the UN, Crispin Tickell regularly held informal gatherings of the ambassadors of the five permanent Security Council members in his New York apartment and briefed the secretary-general afterwards. At one of his meetings, Tickell floated the idea of an environmental conference to mark the twentieth anniversary of the Stockholm conference. The idea was taken up.[22] Initially it was to be at Stockholm again. The Brazilian government wanted the conference in Rio de Janeiro. The Swedish government quickly agreed, so Rio it was.

The conference momentum soon put Thatcher onto the defensive. Asked in the House of Commons why she wasn't going to the twenty-four-nation conference at The Hague, Thatcher gave no quarter: 'The conference is to set up yet another organisation, which is not necessary, and it proposes that compensation should be paid – without saying how – and that sanctions should be applied if rules are not complied with – again without saying how.'[23] To the horror of civil servants, Britain did not even send an observer. According to a senior Dutch official, the new world ecological institutions could grow in the same way as the European Commission, Parliament and Court had grown out of an embryonic European coal and steel community.[24] No wonder Mrs Thatcher stayed away.

Seven months later at the Noordwijk conference in November, with more than three times the number of countries, the negotiations went in a different direction – emissions cuts. Britain brokered an agreement between the ambitions of the Europeans for firm commitments to stabilise emissions and the refusal of the US, joined by the Soviet Union and Japan, to do so. The declaration fudged the issue by recognising the need to stabilise greenhouse gas emissions 'as soon as possible,' while recording the view of many industrialised nations that this should be achieved at the latest by

2000.[25] No one could have foreseen that the disintegration of the Soviet Union and the implosion of its economy would enable the Russian Federation to record a forty-one per cent fall in carbon dioxide emissions between 1990 and 2000, a reminder of the inscrutability of even the near future.[26]

The Dutch government said it would implement previously announced plans for unilateral cuts in greenhouse emissions of eight per cent by 1994, a proposal which had led to the fall of the Dutch government the previous May. In fact, Dutch carbon dioxide emissions rose by 4.6 per cent over the period.[27] While the Dutch set a pattern other countries would follow, there was a one-off event. The delegation from Saudi Arabia told the conference that the world's largest oil producer considered global warming 'a life or death issue for considerable areas of the earth'. There was 'no argument' that carbon dioxide was the main culprit or question about the need to move to non-greenhouse gas energy generation.[28]

The same month, Thatcher addressed the UN General Assembly. The threat to the global environment was an insidious danger threatening irretrievable damage to the atmosphere, to the oceans and to the earth itself, Thatcher declared, comparing it to the risk of global annihilation from warfare.

The speech is significant in two respects. Although the subject of global warming occupies much of the text, its core message of undiluted Malthusianism could have been the same without it.

> More than anything, our environment is threatened by the sheer numbers of people and the plants and the animals which go with them … Put in its bluntest form: the main threat to our environment is more and more people.[29]

The tragedy of Easter Island was a warning of what might befall the rest of the world. Cutting down a primeval forest had led to warfare over the scarce remaining resources, the population fell and there wasn't enough wood to make boats to sail to another island. 'We must have continued economic growth in order to generate the wealth required to pay for the protection of the environment,' she told the General Assembly. 'But it must be growth which does not plunder the planet today and leave our children to deal with the consequences tomorrow.'[30] In the past, growth happened. Now it had to be the right sort.

The other notable feature of the Mrs Thatcher's speech was its impact on American politics. It generated far more media coverage in the US than the Noordwijk meeting and more in the US than in the UK. The National Governors Association Task Force on Global Warming was holding its first meeting at the United Nations. Its chair, Republican Jim Thompson of Illinois, called her address 'elegant, straightforward and full of common sense and leadership'. New York's Mario Cuomo used Thatcher's speech to criticise President Bush's refusal to set a timetable for emissions cuts at the Noordwijk conference earlier in the week (a position shared by the British government at that point), 'I would have preferred the President to manifest the leadership of the nation on that occasion.'[31] A copy of the speech was circulated to senior staff in the White House by Robert Grady, an associate director at the Office of Management and Budget (OMB). 'The President could easily have given this speech and taken credit for an aggressive posture with very little change in current policy required,' Grady commented.[32] The three names at the top of the circulation list, John Sununu, the president's chief of staff, Dick Darman, head of the OMB and chief science adviser Allan Bromley were doing all they could to ensure the president did not make such a speech and that US policy did not change.

In May 1990, Gro Harlem Brundtland hosted the Bergen conference on sustainable development. 'I am nervous that time is running out,' Brundtland warned.[33] But she was more rattled by journalists' questions on whether she supported a resumption of commercial whaling, Norway being accused of hypocrisy for hosting an environmental conference while hunting whales.[34] The Canadian government's attempt to line up with the US in opposing emissions targets was stymied by a leak to the Friends of the Earth of a State Department cable which said that Canada would be joining Britain and the US in opposing any move on emissions cuts that went beyond the position agreed at Noordwijk.[35] The outcry led environment minister Lucien Bouchard to pledge that Canada's emissions would be no higher in 2000 than in 1990.[36] Like the Dutch pledge six months earlier, it was an empty promise. Canada's carbon dioxide emissions increased by twenty-three per cent between 1990 and 2000, faster than the seventeen per cent for the US.[37]

British opposition to emissions caps also began to crack. A junior environment minister (Chris Patten, the environment secretary, decided to stay at home) signalled that Britain would have a target for stabilising or even reducing emissions. It marked a watershed in Britain's approach to global warming, according to the *Financial Times*.[38]

Abandonment by two of its most reliable allies did not change America's position. Timothy Atkeson, assistant administrator of the EPA, said the expected costs were 'as big as you can get.' 'We're talking about costs in excess of the gross national product of the United States,' he told reporters.[39] Although participants declared their willingness to 'assume a major responsibility to limit or reduce greenhouse gases', the outcome of the Bergen conference marked no movement from the position agreed at Noordwijk.[40] Political progress seemed stalled as the prospect of a transatlantic rift opened up.

14
RUSH TO JUDGEMENT

There are three roads to ruin; women, gambling and technicians. The most pleasant is with women, the quickest is with gambling, but the surest is with technicians.

President Georges Pompidou

Any remaining doubts must not be allowed to dissuade us from action.

Michel Rocard, 6ᵗʰ November 1990

While governments were engaged in an accelerating round of conferences, scientists were working to meet the deadline for the IPCC's First Assessment Report ahead of the World Climate Conference in November 1990. As chair, Bolin had to overcome a major disagreement between Working Group I, tasked with summarising scientific knowledge under Sir John Houghton, and Working Group II, led by Soviet academician Yuri Izrael to examine potential impacts of global warming.

One of the Soviet scientists in Working Group II argued that warming might be beneficial at northerly latitudes (an opinion that had been held by Svante Arrhenius and Guy Stewart Callendar in the first half of the twentieth century). Preventative action was therefore not justified. A meeting was held in Leningrad but, according to Bolin, there was still tension.[1] Even within Working Group I, agreement was not always easy.[2]

Bolin had wanted to document and explain reasons for disagreement. 'I had repeatedly pointed out to the working groups that the goal was not necessarily always to reach an agreement, but rather to point out different views when necessary and to clarify reasons for disagreements when possible, but this was still seldom tried,' he recalled.[3] Despite Bolin's encouragement, public airing of disagreements was counter-cultural.

Nonetheless, the First Assessment Report went further in meeting this objective than subsequent ones. It was also more open in highlighting not only uncertainties in the science (one can be uncertain about the particular outcome of tossing a coin, but the parameters of the outcome can be defined with certainty), but also ignorance, especially in the section dealing with past climate variations and change (Section Seven of the Working Group I report). As the IPCC developed, admissions of ignorance gave way to more qualified expressions of uncertainty, often couched in spurious degrees of confidence.

According to the Working Group I Summary for Policy Makers, the observed global mean surface air temperature had increased by between 0.3°C and 0.6°C over the previous hundred years.

> The size of this warming is broadly consistent with predictions of climate models, but it is also of the same magnitude as natural climate variability. Thus the observed increase could be largely due to this natural variability; alternatively this variability and other human factors could have offset a still larger human-induced greenhouse warming.[4]

The recent warming was neither unique nor could natural variability be ruled out. Section Seven of Working Group I on past climate variations noted that although the evidence pointed to a real but irregular warming over the last century, 'a global warming of larger size has almost certainly occurred at least once since the end of the last glaciations without any appreciable increase in greenhouse gases. Because we do not understand the reasons for these past warming events it is not yet possible to attribute a specific proportion of the recent, smaller warming to an increase of greenhouse gases'.[5]

Putting the twentieth-century warming in the context of past climatic changes, the report pointed out that the Little Ice Age involved global climate changes of comparable magnitude to the warming observed over the previous one hundred years to 1990, part of which could reflect cessation of Little Ice Age conditions. 'The rather rapid changes in global temperature around 1920–1940 are very likely to have had a natural origin,' the report went on. 'Thus a better understanding of past variations is essential if we are to estimate reliably the extent to which warming over the last century, and future warming, is the result of greenhouse gases,' a need that would give rise to the Hockey Stick and its prominence in the 2001 Third Assessment Report.[6]

The crucial section of the entire report was on the detection of the enhanced greenhouse effect (Section Eight of the Working Group I report). Its authors acknowledged that the 0.3°C to 0.6°C observed rise in average global temperatures permitted a number of explanations. If it had been caused by a 'man-induced' greenhouse effect, then the implied climate sensitivity of carbon dioxide (the warming resulting from a doubling of carbon dioxide in the atmosphere) would be at the bottom of the range. If a significant fraction of the warming had been due to natural variability, the implied value for the climate sensitivity would be even lower than model predictions. If a larger greenhouse warming had been offset by natural variability or other factors, then the climate sensitivity of carbon dioxide could be at the 'high end' of model predictions.[7] Scientists' inability to reliably detect predicted signals should not be taken to mean that 'the greenhouse theory is wrong, or that it will not be a serious problem for mankind in the decades ahead'.[8]

Section Eight also carried an implicit rebuke to James Hansen and his claim two years earlier to have detected the greenhouse effect.

> Because of the many significant uncertainties and inadequacies in the observational climate record, in our knowledge of the causes of natural climatic variability and in current computer models, scientists working in this field cannot at this point in time make the definitive statement: 'Yes, we have now seen an enhanced greenhouse effect.'[9]

With the possible exception of an increase in the number of intense showers, there was, the Summary for Policy Makers said, no clear evidence that weather variability would change in the future.[10] Neither was there evidence that tropical storms had increased or any consistent indication that they would be likely to increase in a warmer world.[11]

Nonetheless, belief in anthropogenic global warming shines through the pages of the Working Group I report, especially the twenty-eight-page Summary for Policy Makers. 'We calculate with confidence,' the summary claimed, 'that carbon dioxide has been responsible for over half the enhanced greenhouse effect in the past'.[12] At first glance, it might appear that here the IPCC had nailed its culprit. In actual fact, the claim teeters on the brink of meaninglessness. As the report admitted, scientists were unable to attribute the contribution of the enhanced greenhouse effect to the observed rise in global temperatures over the previous one hundred years. To have said that extra carbon dioxide was responsible for over half of an effect that couldn't be measured or even detected was the modern equivalent of medieval monks counting angels on pinheads.

Distilled to its essence, the message of the First Assessment Report was that global warming is happening, even though the evidence remained equivocal. In one of the most significant passages in the report, the IPCC stated: 'The unequivocal detection of the enhanced greenhouse effect from observations is not likely for a decade or more, when the commitment to future climate change will then be considerably larger than it is today.'[13] Thus for the IPCC, detection of the greenhouse effect was a question of 'when' not 'if', as Sir John Houghton wrote in the *Financial Times*. 'We are sure that human activities are leading to climate change – although we do not claim yet to have detected it.'[14]

The most loaded claim was the report's call for action. 'If there are concentration levels that should not be exceeded,' the Summary for Policy Makers warned, 'then the earlier emission reductions are made the more effective they are,' hinting at the possibility of undefined tipping points and climate catastrophism.[15] Yet buried in the body of the report, the IPCC noted growing evidence that worldwide temperatures had been higher than at present, at least in summer, around five to six thousand years ago, although carbon dioxide levels were thought to have been quite similar to the pre-industrial era.[16]

Alarm about global warming depended on a critical but unverifiable assumption: increased levels of carbon dioxide trigger positive feedbacks amplifying the direct warming effect from carbon dioxide. Water vapour plays the central role in assumptions about positive feedbacks. It is a more abundant and powerful greenhouse gas than carbon dioxide (the IPCC estimated that if water vapour were the only greenhouse gas present in the atmosphere, the greenhouse effect would be sixty to seventy per cent of the value of all gases included, but if carbon dioxide alone were present, the corresponding value would be about twenty-five per cent).[17] Without positive feedback from water vapour and other sources, the IPCC estimated a value of +1.2°C for the climate sensitivity of carbon dioxide.

However, the IPCC assumed that the impact of this initial warming is amplified by increasing the concentration of water vapour, raising the initial 1.2°C to 1.9°C.[18] There are many other feedbacks; overall, they might be positive and amplify the direct warming effect of added carbon dioxide, or they might be negative and dampen it. More water vapour might lead to more clouds being formed. 'Feedback mechanisms related to clouds are extremely complex,' Working Group I stated. 'There is no *a priori* means of determining the sign of cloud feedback.'[19]

Results from computer climate models cited in the 1990 report gave a range of 1.9°C to 5.2°C for the climate sensitivity of carbon dioxide. Taking into account these results together with observational evidence, the IPCC chose a value of 2.5°C as its best estimate, implying that over half the warming effect of carbon dioxide assumed by the IPCC came from positive feedbacks.[20]

The IPCC's handling of the role of clouds was criticised by Richard Lindzen, professor of meteorology at the Massachusetts Institute of Technology. Without the assumption of an overall positive feedback effect, the IPCC would have assumed a rise closer to 1°C from a doubling of carbon dioxide. If the IPCC and scientific orthodoxy had followed Lindzen, it is safe to say that the post-1988 era would not be an age defined by belief in global warming.

In addition to uncertainty and ignorance over the size and direction of feedbacks, the IPCC made an even more fundamental assumption based – literally – on hope, that, in the words of the IPCC, 'The climate system is in equilibrium with its forcing.'[21] Making any forecasts of long-term temperature depends on the extent to which this assumption holds. While the assumption is necessary and desirable from the perspective of climate modellers, it does not follow that nature will accommodate it. Although some elements of the climate system were chaotic on a century to millennium timescale, others were stable. 'That stability,' the report went on, 'gives us hope that the response of the atmospheric climate (including the statistics of the chaotic weather systems) to greenhouse forcing will itself be stable and that the interactions between the atmosphere and the other elements of the climate system will also be stable.'[22]

Large-scale features of the world ocean circulation system were deemed to be non-chaotic by the IPCC. 'The question,' according to the Working Group I report, 'is whether the existence of predictability in the ocean component of the Earth's climate system makes the system predictable as a whole. However this seems to be a reasonable working hypothesis,' the authors thought.[23] Absence of computing capacity meant that scientists were unable to model the response of the oceans, even though, as the 1990 report said, 'this is crucial for climate prediction'.[24] It is easy to see why. The entire heat capacity of the atmosphere is equivalent to less than three-metres-depth of water.[25] In the North Atlantic, the heat input carried by the ocean circulation is of similar magnitude to that reaching the ocean surface from the sun.[26]

The sheer length of time for the oceans to respond to a warming atmosphere opened up a huge disconnect between the timescales over which scientists were anticipating global warming and the 'children and grandchildren' timescale deployed by politicians to justify action against global warming. According to Working Group I, the global oceans need millennia to reach a new equilibrium, making a couple of generations a rounding error.[27] Even if it were possible to stop all man-made emissions of carbon dioxide, atmospheric concentrations would decline very slowly and would not approach their pre-industrial levels for 'many hundreds of years. Thus any reductions in emissions will only become fully effective after a time of the order of a century or more'.[28]

With positive feedbacks assumed in the climate models, the IPCC's business-as-usual scenario of emissions growth predicted a temperature rise of 0.3°C per decade (i.e., in the subsequent one to two decades, the world would get the whole of the 0.7°C temperature rise observed in the twentieth century), resulting in a 'likely' rise of 1°C by 2025.[29] By 2009, well past the halfway mark of this thirty-five-year forecast, the temperature had risen by 0.18°C since 1990, or an average of just under 0.1°C per decade.[30] To hit the predicted one-degree rise by 2025, the average global temperature would have to rise at an average rate of 0.5°C per decade for the rest of the period.

Throughout the time when the IPCC report was being prepared, one political leader took a particularly keen interest in the scientists' progress. Mrs Thatcher asked Houghton for regular updates. The week of 21st May 1990 was particularly intense. On the Monday afternoon, Houghton presented the conclusions of Working Group I report to the prime minister and other ministers in the Cabinet room at Number 10. The next three days, Houghton chaired the plenary of the working group at a hotel in Windsor, on Tuesday and Wednesday returning to Downing Street to help Thatcher with her speech for the opening on Friday of the Hadley Centre to coincide with publication of the IPCC's assessment report. Houghton was amazed at the prime minister, pencil and erasure in hand, determined to get the science right. She put a lot of her own time into it, Charles Powell, her chief aide, told him.[31]

Your task, she told the Hadley Centre's director and staff, was no less than 'to help us safeguard the future of the planet'.[32] Describing the IPCC's report as of historic significance, she said governments and organisations around the world were 'going to have to sit up and take notice'. She announced that Britain would set itself the target of cutting projected levels of carbon dioxide emissions by thirty per cent by 2005. Because the projected increases were so high, this meant returning to 1990 levels by that date. Unlike the Dutch and Canadians, the UK beat this target by more than five percentage points, largely thanks to privatising and liberalising the energy market, enabling the market to respond with a dash-to-gas for generating electricity.*

---

*   With coal, the ratio of hydrogen to carbon is 0.5 to one; with natural gas, it is four to one, i.e., the proportion of carbon in natural gas is one-eighth that of coal.

In October 1990, the second World Climate Conference met in Geneva. Unlike the all but forgotten first conference in 1979, it was addressed by six government leaders. Scientists and academics also came to spread the alarm that was not to be found in the IPCC's equivocation. German meteorologist Harmuth Grassl, a contributor to the Working Group I report, said that while scientists were 'basically here as ruminants, it is very important to get out the main message: that change on earth is now so fast there is no analogy during the last 10,000 years'.[33] It was a claim without any basis in the IPCC report.

Martin Parry, a British geographer and future chair of Working Group II, produced a report claiming that the world could suffer mass starvation and soaring food prices in just forty years.[34] True, there were sharp rises in food prices in the first decade of the twenty-first century. They weren't caused by rising temperatures but by climate change policies diverting agricultural resources to the production of biofuels, contributing to a wave of food riots in 2008.

The political response was divided between the minority of governments that took seriously the IPCC's equivocal verdict and those arguing that the need for action overrode it. Despite pressure from the European Community – 'I hope that Europe's example will help the task of securing world-wide agreement,' Thatcher told the conference – the US and the Soviet Union, the world's two largest carbon dioxide emitters, weren't budging.[35] Yuri Izrael for the Soviet delegation emphasised the doubt and uncertainty of climate change. More scientific research was needed, Izrael concluded.[36] John Knauss, director of the National Oceanic and Atmospheric Administration, who led the US delegation, said that Washington had refused to set targets because 'it does not believe in them', adding, 'it's as simple as that. We are not prepared to guarantee our projections'. American officials thought European targets lacked credibility, which they characterised as political goals not easily put into effect.[37]

Maurice Strong, recently appointed secretary-general of the Rio Earth Summit, described the evidence of global warming as 'compelling, if not yet definitive'. It posed 'the greatest threat ever to global security'. Action had to be taken before the scientific evidence was definitive, Strong told delegates. 'It is not feasible to wait for the post mortem on planet earth to confirm our diagnosis. If there is ever an instance in which we must act in accordance with the precautionary principle, this surely is it.'[38]

Michel Rocard, the French prime minister, declared that the time for words was over. 'What we need now is action,' Rocard told the conference. 'The race against time is on. The very survival of our planet is at stake.'[39] Despite the appeal for action made at The Hague and the summits at Noordwijk and Bergen, 'nothing decisive has yet been accomplished'. Beyond the problem of global warming, the world community faced a fundamental question on the enforcement of international environmental law. 'What point is there in holding meetings and conducting research if there is no certainty that the standards we adopt and the commitments we enter into will actually be respected?' Rocard asked.[40]

Acknowledging the need for more research, Mrs Thatcher argued it should not be used as an excuse to delay 'much needed' action. 'There is already a clear case for precautionary action at an international level,' she said. 'We must not waste time and energy disputing the IPCC's report.'[41]

Her argument did not impress *The Times* science correspondent Nigel Hawkes. 'Computer models predicting temperature rises very much smaller than their proven margins of error are being used by a prime minister who claims to be a scientist as grounds for imposing economic sacrifices on the entire world,' Hawkes wrote. 'A couple of cold winters will take the froth off the debate, and allow us the time we need to discover whether or not the earth is really warming up.'[42]

By this stage of her premiership, it says much for Thatcher's commitment to global warming that she was dedicating so much time to it. The week before, Sir Geoffrey Howe, her nominal deputy, had resigned. Before the month was out, she was no longer prime minister. In retirement, her views on global warming appear to have evolved. Her last book *Statecraft*, published in 2002, speaks of her concern about anti-capitalist arguments deployed by campaigners against global warming and the lack of scientific advice available to leaders from experts who were doubtful of the global warming thesis.[43]

These were not the sentiments of her Geneva speech, her last pronouncement on the subject as prime minister. Instead she used language straight out of the green lexicon, talking of the growing imbalance between 'our species and other species, between population and resources, between humankind and the natural order.'[44] She called for as many countries as possible to negotiate a framework convention on climate change for agreement in 1992 with binding emissions cuts, following the lead taken by European governments. In this endeavour,

> the International [sic] Panel's work should be taken as our sign post: and the United Nations Environment Programme and the World Meteorological Organisation as the principal vehicles for reaching our destination.[45]

The IPCC did play the role Thatcher envisaged, but the WMO and UNEP – neither of which can be remotely described as purveyors of doubt about global warming that Thatcher said in her 2002 book was needed – were sidelined as negotiating vehicles. The G77 group of developing countries have more leverage within UN fora than inter-governmental arrangements, in which it is easier for OECD countries to hold sway.*

The previous year, Brazil and Mexico had led an initiative to get increased representation with the formation of a special committee on the participation of developing countries. Both countries had objected to Bolin's draft of the synthesis report. Frankly admitting that IPCC was a political bargaining process, the report was changed: 'Recognising the poverty that prevails among the populations of developing countries, it is natural that they give priority to achieving economic growth,' it now reads. 'These sentences are of course politically inspired, but they are basically factual,' Bolin explained.[46] Bolin was right. Since the 1972 Stockholm conference, this has been the consistent position of the G77 on environmental issues, right the way through the negotiations to hammer out UN Framework Convention on Climate Change, the Kyoto Protocol in 1997 to the Copenhagen climate conference in 2009.

In December 1990, UN General Assembly adopted a resolution establishing the Intergovernmental Negotiating Committee for a Framework Convention on Climate Change (INC). Four intensive rounds of negotiations in the course of 1991 were marked by procedural wrangles and failure to produce a draft negotiating text. A fifth round in February 1991 was marked by deadlock. According to Daniel Bodansky's account of the INC negotiations, 'States still seemed engaged in a battle of nerves, hoping that, with the Rio Summit fast approaching, the other side would blink first.'[47]

In April – less than two months to go before the summit – INC chairman Jean Ripert held extended meetings with key participants in Paris. No one blinked.

'Don't go wobbly on me, George,' Thatcher is reported to have told President Bush on facing down Saddam Hussein in 1990. On climate

---

*   Mostafa Tolba, UNEP executive director at the time, complained that governments took the preparation of the framework convention away from UNEP. 'It has been speculated that the developed countries were not yet ready for the positive action and concrete action advocated by the UNEP executive director.' Other than his testimony, there is little evidence to support this view. Mostafa K Tolba with Iwona Rummel-Bulska, *Global Environmental Diplomacy: Negotiating Environmental Agreements for the World, 1973–1992* (1998), p. 95.

change, the Europeans wanted Bush to wobble. The prospect of the Rio Earth Summit without a convention on climate change was being taken right down to the wire.

15
A House Divided

I say this on climate change: we're not going to enter into commitments we don't keep.

President Bush, 7th June 1992[1]

Negotiations on the climate change framework convention were marked by what the head of India's delegation described as a 'fundamental and irresolvable difference' between the US and European Community.[2] Apart from the INC's first session, US negotiators maintained the line that they would not accept any text which bound them to timetables and targets for carbon dioxide emissions. Diluted formulations calling for countries to commit to measures 'aimed at' stabilising emissions were rejected.

The negotiations stalled.

Less than two months before the summit, British and American negotiators hammered out a compromise. Britain's environment secretary, Michael Howard, was sent to Washington to persuade key members of the administration that the President could sign the convention.

If history judges George H.W. Bush's supreme achievement to bring the Cold War to a peaceful conclusion, then global warming could have been designed to wrong foot him. In the post-Cold War New World Order, America found itself isolated. Fundamentally an internationalist, it would have been hard for Bush to stay away from the most numerous gathering of world leaders ever assembled. But there was no upside for him in going to Rio. Election year made the politics harder still and Bush did not have the political skills to pull it around. Bush lacked Nixon's cynicism in his handling of the Stockholm conference twenty years earlier or Bill Clinton's deftness in negotiating the Kyoto Protocol but not putting it to a vote in the Senate.

In the 1988 election, the Bush campaign had decided that the environment was critical to winning key battleground states. To win suburban voters in these states, the strategy was to go to the right on tax, defence and crime and to the centre on childcare and the environment. On election night, exit polls gave Bush and Dukakis a dead heat on the environment and Bush wound up winning New Jersey, Illinois and California, the last Republican candidate to do so.[3]

This was more than 'read my lips' campaign rhetoric. William Reilly, president of the Conservation Foundation, provided briefings to both presidential campaigns. Mostly ignored by the Dukakis camp, they were devoured by the Republicans. Bush hosted a dinner with leading environmental campaigners, the candidate sitting between Russell Train, who led the US delegation at the Stockholm conference, and Reilly. After the election, William Ruckelshaus, the Environmental Protection Agency's first administrator, suggested to Bush he appoint Reilly to lead the EPA.

Reilly became the first environmentalist to head the EPA. He would not have many allies in the administration, except the most important one. On one occasion, budget director Richard Darman commented, 'The problem is we have an environmentalist running the EPA and,' pointing to the Oval Office, 'the bigger problem is we've got an environmentalist sitting in there.'[4] According to Bush campaign manager Lee Atwater, Bush regarded people like Atwater as necessary tools, but had come into politics to work with people like Reilly.[5] Bush's interest in environmental policy was genuine, a conservationist in the mould of Teddy Roosevelt averse to command-and-control solutions to environmental problems.[6]

The priority of the senior White House staff was different: improving America's economic performance. With Bush mostly focused on foreign policy, Reilly's was an isolated voice. Nonetheless, the Bush administration notched up a number of achievements, notably the 1990 Clean Air Act Amendments, which pioneered the use of tradable emissions permits.

The prospect of the administration's differences being played out under the floodlights of the Rio Earth Summit meant that, one way or another, the divergence between the environment candidate and the priority accorded the economy needed to be resolved. That posed a particular challenge for an administration held together by loyalty to the president and, when John Sununu was chief of staff, the discipline he exerted, rather than a shared sense of mission. Reilly recalls remarking to Barbara Bush at a social event on how well everyone got on with each other. 'They're all old friends, except for you Bill,' the First Lady replied. 'You're the only one we didn't know.'[7] When loyalty gave way to other agendas, as happened during the Rio conference, the result was spectacularly damaging.

This vulnerability was accentuated by another. As a communicator, Bush did not use speeches to build a case, but to convey sentiments ('a kinder, gentler nation', most famously) or state policy positions ('the day of the open cheque book is over', with respect to the Earth Summit).[8] This mattered when the global warming policy adopted by the Bush administration ran counter to where the rest of the world was heading. It needed advocacy, but the administration had no advocate.

Technically, the Bush White House was unusually well equipped to appraise the science and economics of global warming. Sununu held a Ph.D. in mechanical engineering from MIT and had worked on thermal transfer problems. Darman held a Harvard Ph.D. Robert Watson, who later worked in the Clinton White House and succeeded Bolin as chairman of the IPCC, described Sununu and Darman as 'incredibly bright'.[9] Michael Boskin, chairman of the Council of Economic Advisers, had devoted much of his career as a Stanford professor to studying the interface between technology and the economy. Allan Bromley, the White House science adviser, was a nuclear physicist. (During his confirmation hearings, Al Gore tried to convince Bromley that Bromley did not understand the greenhouse effect.)[10] Bromley wrote a memoir of his time in the White House. There was no question that Sununu and Darman considered many of the claims of environmental activists to be seriously overblown, 'but they were prepared to listen to any reasonable argument. What they refused utterly to do was to stipulate that we were *already* in a crisis, as many of the activists demanded as a basis for discussion'.[11]

Of them, Darman was the most sceptical. He first brought Hansen's claims to Sununu's attention.[12] Darman's approach to micro-economic policy was much more conservative than on fiscal and size of government issues. He deployed a cost-benefit approach that a particular environmental measure would cost X thousand dollars per fish saved, a mode of analysis he'd learnt from David Stockman, Reagan's first budget director.[13]

Early in the Bush presidency, some of the leading global warming advocates had a meeting with Sununu, Darman and Bromley. Sununu probed the computer models. Did they couple the atmosphere and the ocean? No, came the reply. Sununu pointed out that the thermal capacity of the oceans could not be ignored. Computer models that only took account of the atmosphere were meaningless. Although his interlocutors were not happy that the White House chief of staff was unsupportive, Sununu authorised a large increase in funding for climate modelling.[14] In two years, spending more than doubled to $1.03bn.[15]

Reilly and Sununu often clashed. Shortly after James Baker's speech on global warming, Reilly made a similar speech on the subject. The next day, Sununu rang to tell him it wasn't administration policy. Reilly replied that he has taken the same line as Baker. 'He has?' asked Sununu, 'I'll talk to Jim.' Baker subsequently announced he was rescuing himself from involvement in the area to avoid potential conflicts of interest over his personal investments. 'You'll never win against the White House,' Baker's deputy, Bob Zoellick, told Reilly.[16]

In October 1989, Bush asked Bromley to chair the White House climate change working group. The next month he and Reilly led the US delegation to the Noordwijk ministerial conference. 'Neither we nor anyone known to us had any detailed economic or technical understanding of what would be involved in achieving this level of emissions [reductions],' Bromley recorded.

> The lack of economic analysis was astonishing … I asked the head of one of the major European delegations how exactly his country intended to achieve the projected emissions goals and was told, 'Who knows – after all it's only a piece of paper and they don't put you in jail if you don't actually do it.'[17]

At the Malta summit with President Gorbachev in December 1989, when the two announced the end of the Cold War, Bush said he would host a White House conference on the environment and global warming the following spring. The Council of Economic Advisers studied the economics of global warming, its conclusions forming part of the Council's 1990 annual report published in February that year. Its chairman, Michael Boskin, was concerned at reliance on primitive attempts to model the climate and the failure of other governments to analyse the economics. Global warming champions were environment ministries. Their lexicographical preference, to use Boskin's term, was to treat the impact on economic performance as ancillary. Boskin alerted the economic ministries of other governments, but was frustrated that they continued to take a back seat to environment ministries.[18]

The Council of Economic Advisers did some preliminary cost/benefit and risk analysis. Boskin brought in outside expertise, notably Yale economist William Nordhaus, a former Carter administration official and the leading economist in the field. The Council noted that there was 'an extremely high level of uncertainty' regarding possible future climate change. Unlike policies to combat depletion of the ozone layer, there were no low-cost substitutes for fossil fuels.[19] The cost of gradually reducing US carbon dioxide emissions by twenty per cent over the course of the next one hundred and ten years was estimated at between $800bn under optimistic scenarios to $3.6 trillion under pessimistic ones, between thirty-five to one hundred and fifty times greater than the EPA's estimates of the costs of completely phasing out CFCs by the end of the twentieth century.[20]

The study estimated the impact on the economy of carbon dioxide reduction policies by reference to the 1973 and 1979 oil price shocks and their impact in reducing the energy intensity of economic activity. With no growth in energy consumption between 1973 and 1985, carbon dioxide emissions were flat. But these were also years of economic weakness. Although caused by many factors, 'higher energy prices clearly played an important role', the report said. Policies designed to stabilise emissions could halve the growth rate of the global economy.[21]

Reducing emissions was even harder for the US because of its dependence on coal-fired power stations, which contributed fifty-six per cent of America's electricity in 1986. Canada, France and Sweden generated more than eighty per cent of their electricity from nuclear, hydroelectric or geothermal sources.[22] Germany had a similar reliance on coal, but had an ace up its sleeve.

With the costs of substantially slowing carbon dioxide emissions likely to reach trillions of dollars, what, the report asked, might be the benefits? Most sectors of industrialised economies were not climate sensitive. Estimates of the impact on world agriculture of a doubling of carbon dioxide ranged from $35–70 billion a year on pessimistic scenarios, with the US losing $1 billion annually, to small net gains.[23] By comparison, trade-distorting agricultural policies were reckoned to cost $35 billion a year for the world and $10 billion a year for the US.[24]

The report concluded that without improved understanding of the impacts and likelihood of global warming, there was no justification for imposing large costs on the American economy. The adoption of many small programmes, each of which failed a standard cost-benefit analysis, could significantly slow economic growth and eliminate jobs, the Council warned. Any strategy to limit aggregate emissions without worldwide participation was likely to fail, the report stated.

The Bush administration was the only Western government to seriously analyse the economics of global warming, widening the rift between it and the rest of the West. This became particularly evident in April at the White House conference on the environment. Held in a Marriot hotel, the president gave the opening and closing addresses. 'Two scientists, two diametrically opposed points of view – now where does that leave us?' Bush asked in his first address, pointing to a couple of scientists who had been arguing about the science on a TV talk show.[25] Unimpressed, was the verdict of many participants. After a round of polite applause, European delegates quickly headed for the lobby with critical comments for reporters. Germany's environmental minister, Klaus Töpfer, criticised the US. 'Gaps in information should not be used as an excuse for worldwide inaction,' Töpfer told the *Washington Post*.[26] Lucien Bouchard, Canada's environment minister, chimed in: 'The price of inaction is too high.'[27] Bert Bolin, who managed to get an invitation although he had not been on the original guest list, criticised those hiding behind 'the concept of uncertainty'. Because of the inertia of the climate system and the energy stored in the oceans, Bolin told the conference, 'We are [therefore] committed to a further change [of the climate] of perhaps [an additional] fifty per cent.'[28] Fifty per cent of what? Bolin didn't say.

Administration officials tried to push back. 'Up until now, the conferences I've been to haven't focused at all on economics,' Reilly told a journalist. 'I don't trust a commitment that is made without some knowledge of the cost.' But Allen Meyer of the Union of Concerned Scientists was dismissive. 'This conference is yet another example of the yawning chasm between George Bush's campaign rhetoric on global warming and the reality of his administration's policy of inaction.'[29]

Not everyone was hostile. 'President Bush is absolutely correct,' said Soviet Deputy Prime Minister Nikolay Laverov on Bush's comments linking environmental wellbeing and economic welfare. 'The two are interwoven, and that is what differentiates this conference from other conferences of this kind.'[30]

Negative reactions to the president's speech prompted a change of heart. Reilly suggested to Bush and Darman's deputy, Robert Grady, that it was possible to cool it down and join the ranks of the concerned without abandoning the administration's opposition to targets and timetables.[31] Grady produced a draft. 'Above all,' the president said in his closing address, 'the climate change debate is not about research versus action, for we've never considered research a substitute for action.'[32]

Travelling in the president's car, Bush asked Reilly if the speech had gone all right. Reilly began to answer but Bush cut him off: 'I know; I showed I give a shit.'[33]

'Bush does about-face at warming conference,' the headline said in *USA Today*.[34] Bolin was pleased. 'I take the president's speech to be a clear signal to proceed very vigorously with what we are trying to do with the IPCC,' he told journalists.[35] The president was inching closer to Rio.

Canada proposed that Maurice Strong be the conference secretary-general. Bush had known Strong from his days as American ambassador at the UN. Despite being seen as a Democrat, Bush, in 'typically gentlemanly fashion indicated that I was OK'.[36] The view was not reciprocated. 'A phoney' and a 'horse's rump' was how administration insiders came to view him.[37]

Rio was to be the culmination of a two-decade long effort to bring environmental issues from the side-lines to the centre of international politics. As Strong told the 1990 Geneva climate conference:

> It will focus on the need for fundamental changes in our economic behaviour and in international economic relations, particularly between North and South, to bring about a new, sustainable and equitable balance between the economic and environmental needs and aspirations of the world community.[38]

For the developing world, the Earth Summit promised to be a bonanza. 'This is about sharing power,' said Rizali Ismail, Malaysia's UN ambassador.

> When it was East vs. West, our development needs were ignored unless you were a marionette of the Soviet Union or the US. Now with the environment seriously frightening many people in comfortable paradise areas, for the first time people are taking us seriously.[39]

Pakistan's Mahbubul Haq estimated that the industrial countries would have a 'peace dividend' of $1,200 billion to distribute over the next ten years.[40] India's lead climate negotiator, Chandrashekhar Dasgupta, contrasted the split between the US and the rest, and the cohesiveness of the developing world, with China speaking on behalf of the G77 plus China, enhancing the effectiveness of the South in the negotiations.[41]

The potential for a feeding frenzy set alarm bells ringing in Brazil. José Goldemberg, the Brazilian minister in charge of preparing for the summit, became convinced that the summit was heading for disaster.[42] Brazil wanted to be seen making amends for its previous negative attitudes towards.[43] In the 1970s, Brazil had been wary of environmentalism as international concern about preservation of the Amazon rainforest was regarded by Brazil's military rulers as interference in the country's national sovereignty.

That changed when President Sarney came to power in 1985, ending military rule. Sarney pressed for Brazil to host the 1992 summit in response to an international outcry about forest fires in the Amazon. Brazilian scientists had concluded that deforestation was not as extensive as the international press had claimed, but that it could also significantly harm the regional climate of parts of the country.[44]

Fernando Collor de Mello, who succeeded Sarney in 1990, had an added incentive. Under a cloud of corruption charges, Collor hoped that hosting the world's largest summit might win him a reprieve (he was forced to resign at the end of 1992). To prepare for the summit Goldemberg, a physics professor, met Sununu, the engineering Ph.D. Although Sununu had, Goldemberg thought, a reasonable grasp of the science, he felt Sununu was typically American in thinking if temperatures did rise then technology and air conditioning were the answer.[45]

In April 1991, reinforcements landed in Brazil. Sailing up the Amazon, the Royal Yacht Britannia berthed at Belém. It was Prince Charles's idea to bring together politicians, businessmen and NGO representatives. The most important invitee to the seminar was Collor. When he got wind that Collor might not come, he sent a hand-written letter. 'The Royal Yacht is sailing all the way out to Brazil especially for this seminar so as to provide what I hoped to be a reasonably neutral and relaxed setting for such a gathering,' the prince wrote. If Collor didn't come, the prince continued, 'I think it would give the wrong signals to many people who are looking forward towards the importance of the 1992 United Nations Conference.'[46]

It was just as well Collor came, as the prince had also invited Reilly. Brazilian protocol meant that the venue for the meeting between Collor, Goldemberg and two other ministers in Collor's Cabinet was held on a vessel of the Brazilian navy. Sitting around a table on the boat's deck, there was a lively discussion on prospects for the conference. The planning looked chaotic, Reilly pitched in. The summit was heading for disaster. As things stood, he would recommend that the president should not go. Collor said that the presence of sixty-five heads of state was worth less than the president. If Bush comes, we will not allow him to be embarrassed, Collor promised. On his return, Reilly switched his recommendation. The Brazilians kept their side of the deal, Reilly believes. 'They put on a first rate show.'[47]

Sununu's departure from the White House at the end of 1991 raised hopes that the administration would soften its opposition to targets and timetables. They were quickly disappointed. On coming to the White House to head the Policy Coordinating Group, Clayton Yeutter was aghast. 'Why in the world is this summit meeting being held and, for heaven's sake, why in our presidential election year?' he asked.[48] Rio was putting the administration in an impossible position as the US was bound to be criticised whatever it did. Yeutter tried to find out who in the administration had agreed to the summit in the first place, but got no satisfactory answer. At the same time, the White House became increasingly aware that the other developed nations were playing by different rules and approaching Rio in a different spirit. Yeutter spoke to a senior European diplomat. Would his country be prepared to accept the pledges and commitments expected of them? Of course, came the reply. Would his country be able to carry out those pledges and commitments? Of course not.[49]

Hypocrisy has always played a role in international relations. Why couldn't the US play by the same rules as everyone else? When other governments sign a treaty, the hard work is over. For an American president, it is just the beginning. There is more risk in treaty ratification than in negotiating it in the first place. Treaties, especially ones with potentially enormous implications for domestic policy, present institutional challenges almost entirely absent in countries with parliamentary systems. In those, the government controls the legislature and writes the legislation that turns the provisions of a treaty into domestic law. If the courts start to interpret in ways not envisaged by the executive, the government can always amend the original legislation.

In the US, obtaining a two-thirds majority in the Senate requires the president to commit his time and prestige. Deals might have to be cut with reluctant senators. The Senate can attach 'reservations' or 'understandings', changing what the president proposes. Further uncertainty comes from how the courts might interpret the treaty. A global warming treaty with emissions cuts hardwired in the text risked being a blank cheque for Congress, with the courts determining the terms of payment.

Domestic and foreign policy advisers in the Bush White House disagreed whether it mattered if the US failed to meet its targets. Yeutter stated that the administration should not agree to binding targets. Brent Scowcroft, national security adviser, argued that in international conventions, every day, the US made commitments it wasn't sure it could keep.[50]

A meeting at the White House in April 1992 brought home to Goldemberg and the Brazilians just how precarious the prospects for American participation in the summit had become. Despite Goldemberg's lowly status, Scowcroft invited him to meet the president where he explained what the summit meant to Brazil.

The White House insisted that all language about guilt and crimes of the developed world be removed from the Earth Charter. Collor despatched Goldemberg to visit China and India to reconcile the G77 stance with the American position and tone down the language. It didn't prevent the April meeting of the G77 in Kuala Lumpur from reaffirming the developed world's crimes and guilt.[51]

If Bush was going to Rio, there had to be an agreement that he could sign. All the indications were that the US would not sign the biodiversity convention (President Clinton did in June 1993, but the Senate did not ratify it). That meant the administration had to agree the climate change convention or the president staying away. At crunch meetings in Paris, the American negotiating team tested the waters to see if there might be a way to bridge the gap with the Europeans. They knew there was no way that the US or, for that matter, most of the other developed nations could scale their carbon dioxide emissions back to 1990 levels. Staring into the abyss of failure, the British side approached the Americans to see if there might be language to finesse the issue. The Americans returned to Washington and worked up a text.[52]

At the end of April, Michael Howard went to Washington with a version of the text in his pocket. On 29th April he visited five different federal departments and agencies. At his 9am meeting at the EPA, Reilly told Howard that it was essential for the US to sign. The outcome depended on Howard's meeting later that day at the State Department. At the Energy Department, its secretary, Admiral Watkins, also told Howard that his meeting at the State Department was crucial, but that the US should have nothing to do with the convention. Howard had lunch at the British embassy with two senior White House aides who expressed diametrically opposite views. The only thing they could agree on was that the outcome depended entirely on Howard's meeting at the State Department.[53]

At his meeting with Zoellick, Howard went through the draft text of the convention line by line. At the end of it, Zoellick declared that it was a document that the US could sign. Then on to the White House and a meeting with Scowcroft. Howard reported the outcome of the meeting with Zoellick. 'If it's good enough for Bob, it's good enough for the president,' Scowcroft said.[54] The next day, he phoned Howard to say that the president wanted a minor change. Howard replied that the Europeans wouldn't wear it. Zoellick replied that he knew Howard was going to say that and that they would go ahead and sign anyway. The outcome was a coup for British diplomacy. It is doubtful any other country could have pulled it off. Zoellick's secretary told Howard that they had more calls to and from the British embassy than all the rest put together.

Bush called John Major to confirm the deal, and followed up with calls to President Mitterrand of France (who kept his side of the deal) and Chancellor Kohl of Germany (who didn't). The text agreed by Howard and Zoellick formed Article 4 2 (a) and (b) of the convention. It requires developed countries to adopt policies and measures to limit greenhouse gas emissions, thereby demonstrating that they are taking the lead in modifying the long-term trend in emissions. The Europeans got their favoured emissions path into the text. Returning to the 1990 emissions level by 2000, the convention states, would contribute to such a modification. The US got a non-binding formulation and recognition of the need to maintain strong and stable economic growth. The way Darman put it, the US was making a moral, but not legal, commitment to cut carbon dioxide emissions.[55]

'There is nothing in any of the language which constitutes a commitment to a specific level of emissions at any time,' Yeutter wrote to conservative Republicans, describing the outcome as masterfully vague.[56]

16
PRESIDENT BUSH GOES TO RIO

The time of the finite world has come.

UN secretary-general Boutros Boutros Ghali, 3rd June 1992

I did not come here to apologise.

President Bush addressing the Earth Summit, Rio de Janeiro
on 12th June 1992

Having agreed that the president could sign the convention, the next
question was whether he should go to Rio. If anything this debate provoked
even more discussion than the convention itself. The White House was
split down the middle. Darman was the most vocal opponent, but the
president wanted to go, even if it had a political cost back home. After
finding out that virtually all the leaders of important countries were going,
Bush felt he should be there.[1]

There was a logistical consequence of the lateness of President Bush's decision to attend. The White House staff and press corps were booked into
the VIP's Motel, one of Rio's famed guesthouses, offering comfort, privacy
and an impressive array of mirrors.[2]

Because of his relationships with fellow environment ministers, the
White House decided that Reilly should lead the American delegation
to Rio. The caveat was that he would not make any binding agreements
without first clearing them with Yeutter. According to Yeutter, Reilly did
a splendid job.[3] Reilly continued to press his agenda, but as a team player.
Even after agreement of the compromise text on the climate change convention, Reilly kept up the pressure for targets and timetables.

In early June, he arranged for Gro Harlem Brundtland to be seated next
to the president at a dinner to press the case. The next day, Bush called Reilly
from his running machine. Could he provide the president with a memo on
whaling? At the dinner, the chairman of the Brundtland Commission had
spent two hours lobbying the president on the need for 'scientific' whaling.[4]

Publicly, Brundtland had a different message. Speaking on the White
House driveway, she expressed her disappointment at American unwillingness to sign the biodiversity convention. 'I believe you can combine
environmental concern with an increase in jobs,' although she didn't specifically mention those of Norwegian whalers.[5]

Splits within the Bush administration and its differences with the rest of world served to shift the spotlight from splits between other nations. Europe's environment commissioner Carlo Ripa di Meana threatened to boycott the summit after failing to secure support for a European carbon tax and to express his disgust at the compromise with the US. It meant that Europe was being forced to accept a treaty with lower standards than it was adopting for its own members.[6]

There were also splits among the nations of the South. Saudi Arabia wanted forests to be seen as carbon sinks that remove carbon dioxide. Malaysia argued that the industrial countries had caused the climate problem, so should reduce their emissions rather than trying to solve the problem by locking up forests in the developing world.[7]

Once he got to Rio, Reilly met Goldemberg to explore possible changes to the biodiversity convention that would enable Bush to sign it. Reilly cabled Yeutter his suggestions. Shortly after, while being interviewed on live television, Reilly was handed a copy of the cable that had been leaked to the *New York Times*. He abruptly ended the interview. 'I was personally embarrassed just to be handed the goddamn thing,' he said later.[8]

The leak had a devastating impact on the administration's ability to contain what anyway was going to be a difficult situation. Two days later, an exasperated Bush told a joint press conference with the British prime minister, 'I'd like to find the leaker, and I'd liked to see the leaker filed – fired.' Once found, the culprit would be 'gainfully unemployed'.[9] All this was greeted with glee by Democrats in Rio. Al Gore, leading the Senate delegation to the conference, said it had set off a firestorm of criticism. 'Once again, the president has overruled his EPA chief. This time, the whole world is watching.' Reilly countered that his resignation was not on the cards, 'I do not want to give that satisfaction to my enemies.'[10]

Up till then, Gore had been more measured than some of his colleagues. Senator Wirth called America's position a disgrace. 'Instead of a commie under every bed, it's now an eco-terrorist behind every tree.'[11] Jerry Brown, the once and future governor of California, accused the president of being in the pocket of special interests. Greed and corruption would always win the day.[12] To applause from an audience of mostly American environmentalists, Brown added, 'Bush and the administration's position on the environment are completely crackpot.'[13] This kind of attack on foreign soil was too much even for Wirth. 'Our side is getting hammered,' he complained. 'It's the complete inability of the White House to explain what the US has been doing the last twenty years.'[14]

The *Washington Post* described the US as virtually under siege at the conference.[15] The Bush team's headaches didn't come from the Third World. Collor had been as good as his word. True, Fidel Castro received the loudest ovation with his claim that consumer societies were fundamentally responsible for environmental destruction, but at least kept to the allotted five minutes speaking time.[16] Austria, Switzerland and the Netherlands launched an initiative to get like-minded countries to sign up to the targets that had been taken out of the climate change convention. The administration made a clumsy counter-attack. 'They treated us like we are some kind of colony,' an Austrian diplomat complained, while a Swiss diplomat said the US was 'shooting sparrows with a cannon'.[17]

Soon the sparrows were joined by a German eagle. No American ally had benefited more from the Bush administration than Germany. Now it was payback time. Going back on the agreement between Bush and Kohl, Klaus Töpfer said Germany would seek to have all members of the EC sign a separate declaration at Rio reinstating specific emissions targets. Zoellick, who had joined Reilly in Rio, counter-briefed that Germany and Japan were engaged in a guilt-induced attempt to be politically correct. 'All this chaos … the circus and the rhetoric' at the summit were laid at the door of 'the guilty developed-world logic' in which the wealthiest feel they 'owe the rest of the world.'[18]

American difficulties didn't restrain the German government from playing its ace. It announced that it would cut its carbon dioxide emissions by between twenty-five to thirty per cent by 2005.[19] On 1st July 1990, the economies of the two Germanys were unified. Soon after, the economy of the former East Germany went into a deep slump. Industrial production fell by more than half and heavily polluting power stations were closed. Reunification enabled Germany to proclaim its virtuousness at Rio and Germany's emissions fell by nearly eighteen per cent between 1990 and 2005, the steepest achieved by any advanced economy.[20] At a conservatively estimated cost of DM750 billion ($523 billion) for the first five years, viewed as a policy to cut carbon emissions, reunification is the world's most costly global warming policy to date – equivalent to more than twenty per cent of Germany's 1995 Gross Domestic Product.

President Bush spent as little time at Rio as he decently could. He gave a speech, signed the climate change convention, and had his photo taken with the one hundred and seven other world leaders at the summit. Bush also had a private meeting with the ecologist and film maker Jacques Cousteau, who had given a lecture claiming that population growth would lead to a world where people could only survive like rats. 'Even if we found a way to feed this human tidal wave, it would be impossible to provide this multitude with decent living conditions,' Cousteau told an audience that included Collor and the King and Queen of Sweden.[21]

In reality, the summit was part ceremonial and part soap box, its substantive business having been concluded beforehand. The docking of a replica Viking ship, the Gaia, marked the opening of the Global Forum, an alternative summit for NGOs. Not everybody welcomed the Vikings. 'Go home Gaia. $5 million rich men show off,' said one banner.[22] Compared to the four hundred or so NGOs at Stockholm's Hog Farm, the number of NGOs accredited at Rio was some one thousand four hundred and fifty.[23] James Bond actor Roger Moore, who had been chased around the Sugarloaf by Richard Kiel's Jaws in *Moonraker*, proclaimed 3rd June to be 'the first day of the rest of the world' and Gro Harlem Brundtland argued that whales could be hunted if it was done on a sustainable basis.[24]

Four days later, the Beach Boys were doing a gig and pledging their support for the Global Forum. Its sound system had been turned off after failing to pay its electricity bills and run up a $2 million deficit amid allegations of corruption. In another part of Rio, tenor Plácido Domingo was singing for the great and the good and those who could pay $100.[25] The Rio Refuse Collection Authority complained that people were ignoring recycling signs on the one hundred and sixty special bins placed throughout the conference centre. 'I wouldn't trust him to save the planet,' grumbled one refuse collector as an Australian ecologist threw a large piece of pizza into a bin for recyclable material.[26]

Writing in the *New York Times* on the conference's first day, Czechoslovakia's president Vaclav Havel argued that two years after the collapse of Communism, a new polarization was developing, this time between the rich countries of the North and the poor ones of the South. 'The states of the South find it difficult to overcome their mistrust of the North,' Havel wrote.

> They believe that the northern countries should finally understand that today's patterns of production and consumption, besides not being sustainable, are the principal cause of the threat facing the global eco-system, and that the northern states therefore have to accept substantial blame for environmental degradation in the poorer countries.[27]

On the conference's fourth day, Greenpeace and three other NGOs organised a press conference at Rocinha, home to a quarter of a million of Rio's poorest people. The assistant editor of the British Medical Journal, Fiona Godlee, went with them. At a school, the NGOs outlined their plans to save the summit and the planet, with demands for legally binding cuts in greenhouse gas emissions and a reduction in the standard of living of the North.

Sabarina Uega, who ran the Rocinha residents' association, guided the visitors around over heaps of rubbish and open drains and answered journalists' questions. What did the people of Rocinha want? Lack of clean water and decent sanitation was the biggest problem. Many children died; perhaps as many as one in five before the age of one. What did Sabarina think of all the money that had been spent on prettifying Rio for the conference? She smiled. 'Just because we are poor it doesn't mean we don't want the city to be beautiful.'[28]

Opposition from Third World countries meant the proposed convention on forests became a statement of principles. Similarly the legal status of the Earth Charter, envisaged by Strong as the keystone of the summit's architecture, was downgraded to a non-binding 'Rio Declaration'. Everyone had thought that the charter would be a namby-pamby, platitudinous statement, said Barbara Bramble of the National Wildlife Federation, the largest US environmental group. Instead it turned into a knockdown, drag-out fight between North and South. 'They took a draft about ecologic philosophy and turned it into economic power politics.'[29]

The Declaration pronounced a 'new and equitable global partnership', in which developed countries acknowledged their responsibility for the pressure their societies placed on the global environment (principle seven). Sustainable development required states to eliminate unsustainable patterns of production and consumption and 'promote appropriate demographic policies', in a coy reference to belief in the benefits of population control (principle eight). In the absence of scientific certainty, the precautionary principle should be applied to protect the environment (principle fifteen). Signatories declared themselves in favour of eradicating poverty – 'an indispensable requirement for sustainable development' (principle five) – and against war – 'inherently destructive of sustainable development' (principle twenty-four). The roles of women, youth, and indigenous people in sustainable development were all highlighted and the rights of oppressed peoples (the Palestinians) to have their environment recognised (principles twenty to twenty-three) asserted.

Without a concrete plan of action, Strong believed the high sounding rhetoric in UN declarations would be just that. The purpose of Agenda

Twenty-One was to avoid the Rio Declaration following the same fate.[30] 'Humanity stands at a defining moment in history,' the preamble to Agenda Twenty-One claimed. The world was confronted with a perpetuation of disparities within and between nations; a worsening of poverty, hunger, ill health and the continuing deterioration of ecosystems.[31] In reality, the world had already crossed a threshold into an era that saw the largest numbers of people lifted out of poverty in human history, an accomplishment that the doctrine of sustainable development denied was or could ever happen within an internationally liberal economic order. Described by Goldemberg as a naïve attempt by NGOs to reorganise the basis of the world economy, Agenda Twenty-One's estimated cost of $600 billion a year, $125 billion of which was meant to come from developed countries, ensured its irrelevance.

At the time, climate change was not the all-consuming issue at Rio. Twenty years later, Rio's importance is defined by it. Without the summit, the convention would not have been brought into being so quickly – just four years after the alarm had been raised in 1988 – and possibly not at all. For European governments, the Convention's teeth had been pulled with the removal of legally binding targets. Strong expressed extreme disappointment over this, but wrote that the convention marked an historic milestone in the development of international law. 'It was clear from inception that it would involve some very fundamental changes in industrial civilisation.'[32]

The convention did not change the basis of industrial civilisation. Its significance lay elsewhere. In Article Two, the international community accepted the central proposition of global warming by committing themselves to stabilising greenhouse gas concentrations to prevent dangerous anthropogenic interference in the climate system.

Rio therefore was a decisive event in the history of global warming. Even though the IPCC in its First Assessment Report two years earlier had returned an open verdict, the science had been settled by environment ministries and diplomats. Thus President Bush's signing of the convention was more important than the convention's omission of legally binding targets for emissions reductions. One hundred and ninety-three nations of the world, including the most powerful one, remain formally bound by international treaty to accept the view that man-made global warming is dangerous.

Should President Bush have gone to Rio?

As Clayton Yeutter describes it, the White House was in a no-win position. It was a matter of choosing the least damaging option.[33] On the other hand, John Sununu believes the decision was the single biggest mistake of Bush's presidency. Until Sununu's departure from the White House, Bush was all set to have given it a miss.[34]

Suppose the conference had been held four years earlier, what might Bush's predecessor have done? Ed Meese, who served Ronald Reagan in the White House and as chief of staff when he was governor of California, thinks that Reagan would have gone to Rio to explain why he wouldn't sign the climate change convention. His record as governor showed he was keen on protecting the environment, but as president, he was wary of international conventions. He would have been very suspicious of the science on which the climate change convention was based, Meese told the author, and was opposed to 'environmental extremism' being used as a way of advancing the grasp of government.[35] If Reagan had been watching ABC's *This Week* on the eve of Rio, he would have had confirmation of that fear. 'The task of saving the Earth's environment is going to become the central organising principle in the post-Cold War world,' Al Gore told David Brinkley.[36]

In negotiating and signing a climate change convention without legally binding commitments to cut carbon dioxide emissions, the Bush administration ended up where the American political system and public wanted to be. The convention was swiftly and overwhelmingly ratified by the Senate that autumn. If Bush had not signed it, his successor would have. If the Bush administration had not negotiated in good faith, the convention would have ended up with similar provisions to the Kyoto Protocol that Clinton signed but couldn't get through the Senate. In retrospect, Bill Reilly, the most vocal supporter of targets and timetables within the administration, believes their removal had been the right call. The strong economy of the 1990s would have blown the emissions caps and any practical chance to stabilise carbon dioxide emissions.[37]

Not that Bush got any credit from voters. A CBS News poll, released towards the end of the conference, found that only nine per cent of those surveyed expected the summit to produce substantial results to help solve the world's environmental problems. Seventy per cent said the president had been insincere in his expression of support for environmental issues. Asked if protecting the environment was so important that requirements and standards should be set regardless of cost, sixty-seven per cent replied in the affirmative, an indicator of public sentiment at the time, but a meaningless guide to what voters would actually accept in the absence of a context or consequences to the question.[38]

There was a further irony, perhaps the biggest of all. In Rio, Bush administration officials were deeply frustrated that they were playing defence, as if America was the dirty man of the world. Since the presidency of Teddy Roosevelt, when America became the first nation to pass laws to preserve its natural heritage, no country had done more to preserve its wildernesses, canyons and coastline. Post-war environmentalism was born in America. In the 1970s, its government imposed the most comprehensive environmental standards of any major economy. Yet America was put in the dock at Rio, as was President Bush, accused by Bill Clinton of being Rio's lone holdout against environmental progress.[39] Demonstrating the political dexterity that Bush lacked, Clinton flipped the position that he wouldn't sign an agreement that took risks with jobs and the economy, and turned it against him. 'When you're weak at home, it weakens you abroad,' Clinton told a newspaper.[40]

Clinton would bring those skills to the politics of global warming, matchlessly outclassing his predecessor in his political handling of the issue, but ending up precisely where Bush had left off in 1992.

17
TWO PROTOCOLS

If there is one person in the world who has the history, understanding and reputation to bring this all together, it is Al Gore.

Michael Oppenheimer, Environmental Defence Fund, Kyoto, December 1997[1]

Rio begat Kyoto.

The Kyoto Protocol has not begotten a son, only a string of COPs – Conferences of the Parties – and MOPs – Meetings of the Parties. 'Since 1991, legions of well-meaning diplomats, scientists, and environmentalists have undertaken excruciatingly complicated negotiations in what is essentially a political exercise that creates the illusion of mitigating climate change while actually accomplishing little more than raising public consciousness,' Richard Benedick, who led the US team that negotiated the Montreal Protocol, has written.[2]

What accounts for the success of the Montreal Protocol in eliminating CFC emissions and the failure of the Kyoto Protocol ten years later? Writing in 2003, Scott Barrett argued that the Kyoto Protocol was likely to fail because it did not solve the enforcement problem. Appeals to a state's sense of its responsibilities, offers of assistance or threats of naming and shaming were, Barrett thought, inadequate substitutes for having a credible enforcement mechanism. Barrett would press negotiators on their hesitation to address the issue. 'Always I received the same unsatisfying response: enforcement was something that was best addressed later.'[3] Although the Kyoto Protocol specified that the parties should agree a compliance regime at the first COP after Kyoto, it only came up for discussion at The Hague COP6 in November 2000. By then, it was too late.

Unlike Kyoto, the Montreal Protocol has strong incentives for countries to join the Montreal regime and not to leave it. It provides the threat of trade sanctions on any goods produced using CFCs and other controlled substances by countries that had not ratified the protocol. Countries can be suspended if they have not complied with their obligations, freezing their rights and privileges.

Why, then, didn't the international community incorporate similar mechanisms being used to reverse stratospheric ozone depletion to the global warming treaties? Put another way, how was it that President Reagan, allegedly a unilateralist who once said trees cause more pollution than automobiles, led the international community to agree an environmental treaty with teeth, whereas President Clinton and a vice president who had compared global warming to an ecological *Kristallnacht* signed a toothless protocol which he did not ask the Senate to ratify?[4]

Robert Reinstein was alternate head alongside Benedick leading the US team that negotiated the Montreal Protocol and subsequently led the negotiations for the US on the climate change convention. In a 1992 paper, Reinstein highlighted differences in the nature and uses of the gases themselves and in the status of the science between ozone depletion and global warming. The initial international response to ozone depletion focused on eight synthetic gases that were manufactured for a limited range of specific applications, such as refrigerants and foam-blowing. Greenhouse gases such as carbon dioxide, methane and nitrous oxide occur naturally and are emitted mostly as by-products in processes that are basic to human survival. Whereas there were a limited number of chemical plants producing CFCs, every person who burns fossil fuels is a 'producer' of carbon dioxide and every farmer raising cattle or sheep is a 'producer' of methane.

Then there is the respective status of the scientific knowledge of ozone-layer depletion and global warming. Although the causes of stratospheric ozone depletion had not been proven, certain chemicals had been demonstrated to destroy ozone in laboratory tests under conditions comparable to those in the stratosphere. By comparison, Reinstein observes, the science concerning global climate is extremely complex. Many different layers of the atmosphere must be analysed, many different physical and chemical reactions; the role of clouds, oceans, land masses, vegetation must all be taken into account, as well as complex interactions with radiation from the sun and other parts of space.[5]

The 1992 Climate Change Convention was adopted on the basis of the precautionary principle, Article 3.3 speaking of the need for the parties to take 'precautionary measures'. Subsequently the official scientific consensus on global warming hardened with the IPCC's 1995 Second Assessment Report. 'The balance of evidence suggests that there is a discernible human influence on global climate,' although the IPCC acknowledged scientists' limited ability to quantify the effect because the expected 'signal' was still emerging from the noise of natural variability (another way of saying the signal hadn't unambiguously emerged).[6]

Even if the scientific uncertainties could be resolved, there was a gulf separating the respective economic cases for the Montreal Protocol and the Kyoto Protocol. In 2007 Cass Sunstein, a law professor at the University of Chicago who subsequently became President Obama's head of the White House office of information and regulatory affairs, compared the two. Sunstein's analysis focused on the differences between the ratios of perceived benefits to costs flowing from policies to reverse the depletion of the ozone layer and to slow down global warming, especially for the United States as the world's largest emitter of CFCs and carbon dioxide. These differences helped explain and drove the differing assessments of national interest, the response of consumers and the role of powerful private actors, Sunstein argued.[7]

The conclusion was stark. Of all the countries in the world, the US was expected to gain the most from the Montreal Protocol and lose the most from the Kyoto Protocol. The perceived costs of complying with Kyoto were $313 billion higher than the costs of Montreal while the perceived benefits of Kyoto were some $3,562 billion lower than the perceived benefits of Montreal.[8] Put another way, each $1 billion spent complying with Kyoto Protocol was estimated to yield $37 million in benefits.[9] By contrast, each $1 billion spent on complying with the Montreal Protocol was anticipated to yield $170 billion in benefits.[10] For the world as a whole, Montreal was estimated to produce net benefits greater than $900 billion.[11] Kyoto, on the other hand, was expected to generate *negative* net benefits of $119 billion to $242 billion (the band reflects different treatments of the money spent by the US buying other countries' excess emissions allowances).[12]

According to Sunstein, the difference in the cost benefit assessments of the two was corroborated by differences in consumer behaviour. These in turn drove political and business incentives. Vivid warnings about the consequences for human health of CFCs and the trivial costs to consumers of mitigating the risk led Americans to cut purchases of aerosol sprays by more than half. Politicians responded quickly. Who would want to run for election in the Sunbelt on a platform in effect favouring skin cancer for light-skinned people? In 1978, Congress banned the use of CFCs as an aerosol propellant. After DuPont developed HCFCs as viable (and profitable) substitutes for CFCs, businesses followed, pledging to phase out CFCs and lobbying for international controls.*

---

*   Reinstein argues that the success of the Montreal Protocol was achieved at an acceptable cost because negotiators used a 'bottom-up' approach, working closely with businesses on what was technically and economically feasible, in contrast to the 'top-down' negotiation of emissions caps under Kyoto which depend on 'technological forcing' of low cost substitutes for fossil fuels that do not exist at present (Robert Reinstein, 'Ozone Protection and Global Climate Change: Is the Montreal Protocol a Good Model for Responding to Climate Change?', 1996).

Given their comparative advantage over foreign competitors, American businesses could expect to benefit from global moves that generated higher demand for replacements for CFCs. 'If environmentally unfriendly products are unpopular in the market, industry is likely to respond with safer substitutes.'[13] Again, the contrast with global warming is telling. Despite the enormous media coverage of global warming, if judged by their actions as consumers, Americans do not rate climate change as a serious risk compared to the benefits they derive from the burning of fossil fuels. 'Contrary to their behaviour in the context of ozone layer depletion, American consumers and voters are now putting little pressure on either markets or officials,' Sunstein observed.[14]

To Sunstein, US leadership in obtaining international agreement to cut CFC emissions conforms to the model of a global hegemon providing public goods because it benefited from doing so.[15]

How does Kyoto fit this model?

Not very well. Insofar as there were any benefits accruing to the US from complying with Kyoto, they were a fraction of the costs. Although the Clinton administration pledged to reduce emissions by seven per cent compared to eight per cent for the European Union, it was vastly more challenging for the US. The 1990 base year chosen for the Kyoto Protocol was the trough of recession in America, which occurred in 1992 for Europe. In that period, US carbon dioxide emissions rose by 1.3 per cent. In Europe, thanks to recession and the implosion of the former communist economies, emissions fell by nearly five per cent.[16]

Special factors affected Europe's two largest emitters which had nothing to do with policies to reduce their carbon dioxide emissions. Helmut Kohl's Germany was one of the most strenuous in demanding deep emissions cuts, but its approach was based on extraordinarily shallow analysis. After the 1988 Toronto conference had called for developed countries to cut emissions by twenty per cent by 2005, a German study team concluded that the goal was under-ambitious.[17] In early 1990, Kohl asked the BMU, the federal ministry with responsibility for the environment, to prepare a carbon dioxide reduction target.

After only four weeks looking at the issue, the ministry concluded that a 30.5 per cent reduction was feasible. In June, the government adopted a twenty-five per cent target compared to 1987 levels for West Germany. The target for the former West Germany was reaffirmed in November, the government stating that it expected larger reductions from the former East Germany.[18] It proved wildly optimistic. Although German carbon dioxide emissions fell in twelve of the fifteen years from 1990 to 2005, at the end of the period they were 17.7 per cent below 1990 levels, half the fall coming in the first two years after reunification.[19]

For Britain, the speed of its fall in carbon dioxide emissions was in response to a major policy error in privatising the electricity industry. The original idea had been to create a power generating duopoly so the larger company could own the country's nuclear power stations. Preparations for privatisation revealed what many economists and environmental groups had long argued – after taking into account decommissioning costs, nuclear power was fundamentally uneconomic. The nuclear power stations were dropped from the initial privatisation package, but the generating duopoly was preserved. To provide some competitive pressure, the electricity regulator encouraged local electricity distributors to build their own gas-fired power stations by letting them earn temporary super-profits from vertical integration. According to Dieter Helm, the leading authority on the British energy industry, 'The consequence was that gas came on faster than would have been dictated by competitive markets, and the coal industry contracted more quickly.'[20] Together with the effect of a sharp recession at the beginning of the 1990s, the switch from coal to natural gas helped Britain's emissions to fall by nearly seven per cent from 1990 to 1997.[21]

As the negotiations progressed, the EU proposed their members share the British and German reductions under an EU 'bubble', even though they were simultaneously arguing that other countries should be held to flat rate reductions. Yet the high cost of meeting Kyoto's seven per cent cut for America was not the decisive factor behind America's non-ratification of Kyoto. The fundamental reason lay in the architecture of the Protocol, which followed the ground plan of the convention. This divided the world into two, with developed nations listed in Annex I of the convention. Non-Annex I nations therefore comprised the rest of the world – the least developed, oil-rich exporters, successfully industrialised and the world's fastest growing economies.

At the convention's first COP in Berlin in the spring of 1995, the parties agreed that the commitments of the Annex I parties needed to be strengthened. As a condition for allowing the process to proceed, the G77 plus China stipulated that no new commitments should be introduced for non-Annex I parties. This agreement was incorporated into the Berlin Mandate, which defined the objectives and parameters for the negotiations that resulted in the Kyoto Protocol.

At COP2 in Geneva the following July, Tim Wirth, now serving as undersecretary of state for global affairs, announced that the Clinton administration would be urging Annex I countries to negotiate 'realistic, verifiable and binding targets' to reverse the trend of rising greenhouse gas emissions. 'This is a big deal,' Wirth told the *New York Times*.[22]

It certainly was. A year later, the US Senate adopted the Byrd-Hagel resolution by ninety-five to zero; America should not sign any protocol which imposed limits on Annex I parties unless it also imposed specific, timetabled commitments on non-Annex I countries within the same compliance period. In some respects, the resolution represented the Senate taking a second look at the convention it had ratified less than five years earlier by a similar margin as it had adopted Byrd-Hagel. The principle of 'common but differentiated responsibilities' – the first of the convention's five principles – and the bifurcation between Annex I parties and the rest of the world were central to the convention's ground plan.

There was always a high risk of the Annex I bifurcation becoming unbridgeable, as the convention did not provide an automatic mechanism by which non-Annex I countries could or should graduate to Annex I. However it contained two provisions that might have served as a basis for bridging the divide. Article 4.2(f) stipulated that by the end of 1998, a future COP should have reviewed available information 'with a view to taking decisions' on the matter, so long as any move into Annex I was with the approval of the party concerned.[23] The provision was essentially stillborn, only being used to remove Turkey, considered a developed country for the purposes of global warming, from the Annex II donor countries, which mirrors Annex I, so Turkey remained in Annex I but does not have Annex II donor obligations. The second provision, Article 4.2(d), required the periodic review of adequacy of the commitments of Annex I and non-Annex I parties. As we shall see, the fate of this provision provides one of the most telling pieces of evidence as to the attitude of the developing world to the global warming negotiations.

The effect of the Berlin Mandate was not to change the structure of the convention, but to build a wall around the existing Annex I parties and thereby institutionalise the division between North and South. To date, only Malta has crossed this new Berlin Wall, and that was because it had joined the EU (Cyprus, the only other non-Annex I country to become a member of the EU, so far has not done so). If there was any issue that risked triggering the collapse of negotiations at Kyoto, it was in response to any attempt to fragment or erode the solidarity of the G77 plus China on this issue.

By contrast, the Montreal Protocol avoided this by having a unified ground plan based on objective criteria. While bearing in mind the developmental needs of developing countries, to use the words of the Montreal

Protocol's preamble, there is no list of countries subject to quantitative limits; the annexes simply list the various categories of controlled gases. Developing countries are subject to the full control regime while capping their per capita consumption of ozone depleting gases. In the case of CFCs, developing countries which consume less than 0.3 kg per capita of CFCs a year are granted a grace period of ten years 'in order to meet its basic domestic needs' before having to comply with the full rigour of the Protocol's controls, as long as they keep their per capita consumption below 0.3 kg a year.[24]

Thus the Montreal Protocol provides a tough, universal regime with powerful sanctions for compliance. The bifurcated regime adopted in the 1992 climate change convention and developed further by the Kyoto Protocol can only be judged superior to the Montreal Protocol if the principal objective is assumed not to be the reduction of greenhouse gas emissions.

History helps explain why such divergent approaches were taken. The Montreal Protocol was negotiated between 1985 and 1987, in the brief period after the rise of Mikhail Gorbachev and before the formal adoption of the doctrine of sustainable development in 1988. Agreement on the final text was secured five months after publication of the Brundtland Report in April 1987. By contrast, the climate change regime is an offspring of the doctrine of sustainable development, a term that does not appear anywhere in the Montreal Protocol, and its fusion of First World environmentalism and the Third World's demand for the New International Economic Order.

Of the world's top ten per capita carbon dioxide emitters in 2000, six are outside Annex I, including the top three, Qatar (with per capita emissions three times those of the US and nearly six times the average of the developed world), the United Arab Emirates and Kuwait.[25] Neither is per capita GDP a criterion for inclusion. By 2009 for example, non-Annex I South Korea had per capita GDP of $23,407, just $278 less than the EU's at $23,685.[26]

Instead of being based on objective criteria, the Annex I dividing line closely follows the 1980 Brandt Line, purportedly delineating the unbridgeable chasm dividing the rich North from the poor South. Thus Annex I countries comprise the old OECD (i.e., excluding Mexico, Chile, Israel and South Korea, which were not OECD members at the time) plus the countries of the former Soviet bloc, but excluding the Soviet Union's Asian republics, such as Turkmenistan and Kazakhstan. The resulting North-South demarcation, as carved in stone in global warming agreements, is a product of history. It has a political explanation, but no objective economic justification.

With the Montreal Protocol, developing countries had not engaged early in the process or *en bloc*. After it came into force in 1989, developing countries asserted their need for new and additional transfers, agreement being reached at the London ozone conference in July 1990, when the Chinese and Indian delegations announced that they were recommending that their countries ratify the protocol. Coming late to the party had a cost, because the developed nations, led by the US, had already settled the Protocol's main terms. They weren't going to make the same mistake twice. In 1989, Brazil and Mexico pressed for increased developing country representation in negotiations to tackle global warming, creating a Special Committee on the Participation of Developing Countries. The following year, the UN resolution establishing the INC specified that it should be open to all member states.

Putting developing countries on an equal footing had profound implications for the conduct of the negotiations as well as their outcome. The Montreal Protocol was negotiated by around thirty countries. Typically the climate change COPs have been attended by one hundred and fifty or more countries and more than one thousand, three hundred delegates.[27] Progress is achieved through UN-style consensus rather than majority voting, meaning that there must be no stated or formal objections to a decision.[28]

Given all these constraints, to have produced a treaty signed by over one hundred and ninety nations was the result of a diplomatic *tour de force*. Michael Oppenheimer, an astrophysicist subsequently specialising in atmospheric physics and chemistry, was in Kyoto as science adviser to the Environmental Defence Fund. Al Gore, Oppenheimer said, was the only person with the history, understanding and reputation to bring it together. 'If this fails, a large part of the blame falls on the administration.'[29] He was wrong on both counts.

There was one person who could and did bring the negotiations to a successful conclusion and that was Raúl Estrada-Oyuela, the Argentine diplomat who chaired the negotiations over a period of thirty-two months. The resulting agreement was, Estrada wrote two years later, the 'best compromise the international community was able to reach at that time'.[30] It was a diplomatic accomplishment of the highest order. 'I thought Raúl did a strong, credible job in a most challenging negotiation,' Tim Wirth told the author.[31]

To have blamed Gore if the conference had broken up without an agreement or for its failure to produce a treaty which met the requirements of the Byrd-Hagel resolution would also have been unfair. But it wasn't in the interests of NGOs like the Environmental Defence Fund to point their finger in the direction of the South, but at America and its most prominent environmentalist.

At a symbolic level, though, Gore invited the charge because he had made it himself: Western civilisation was the root cause of the environmental crisis. Nature was in crisis because Western man was sick. 'Ecology and the human spirit' is the somewhat Germanic sounding subtitle of *Earth in the Balance*, in which Gore set out these and other thoughts. At other times, Gore conceded that Western man might not be wholly to blame. Thinking about human beings and the environment led him to pose the biggest environmental question of all. Had God made a mistake when giving mankind dominion over the earth?[32]

Gore's ecological philosophy brought together an American tradition of environmentalism, extending from Thoreau and Muir, with crankier elements imported from Europe, notably Schumacher. What made Gore unique was that no ecologist before him had attained high political office, let alone being a heartbeat away from the presidency of the United States. The harsh criticism Gore directed at the preceding and succeeding administrations contrasts with the Clinton administration's performance with respect to the Kyoto Protocol, the subject of the next two chapters.

18
CHINA SYNDROME

It's the economy, stupid.

Clinton-Gore campaign war room, 1992

*Ours are survival emissions. Theirs are luxury emissions. They have
two people to a car and yet they don't want us to ride buses.*

Shukong Zhong, China's chief negotiator, Kyoto,
December 1997[1]

As a teenager, the future vice president and his sister read and talked about
Silent Spring. A happy and vivid memory, Al Gore recalled. Rachel Carson's
picture hangs in his office and her example inspired Gore to write *Earth in
the Balance*.[2] It is one of the most extraordinary books by any democratic
politician seeking high elective office, for it constitutes an attack on
Western civilisation and a fundamental rejection of two of its greatest
accomplishments – the Industrial and Scientific Revolutions.

Searching for a better understanding of his own life and how he was
going to rescue the global environment, Gore concluded that modern civilisation was suffering from a spiritual crisis.[3] Although one of a number
of environmental crises, global warming symbolised the collision between
civilisation and the Earth's ecological system.[4] Global warming turned the
internal combustion engine into a more deadly threat than any military foe
America was ever likely to face.[5] The current generation might even experience a year without a winter, Gore warned. [6]

Western man had only escaped the Malthusian trap by making a Faus-
tian pact.[7] Men were to blame, for Western civilisation had emphasised a
'distinctly male' way of relating to the world. A solution might be found by
'leavening the dominant male perspective with a healthier respect for female ways of experiencing the world'.[8] Western civilisation was a dysfunc-
tional family, impelled by addiction to inauthentic substitutes for direct
experience of real life, leading to the frenzied destruction of the natural
world. It was well known, Gore observed, 'that the vast majority of child
abusers were themselves abused as children'.[9]

The chain of abuse went back to the two philosophers who anticipated
the Scientific Revolution. 'The unwritten rules that govern our relationship
to the environment have been passed down from one generation to the

next since the time of Descartes, Bacon, and the other pioneers of the Scientific Revolution.'[10] Gore reinterpreted medieval metaphysics as an ecological philosophy connecting man to nature in a web of life, matter and meaning, now lost to the modern world. By breaking with Aristotleanism, Bacon and Descartes had separated man from nature and science from religion. For them, facts derived from science had no moral significance. 'As a consequence,' Gore wrote, 'the scientific method changed our relationship to nature and is now, perhaps irrevocably, changing nature itself.'[11] If science had kept its link with religion, Gore thought humans might not be threatening the earth's climate balance.[12]

Bacon was morally confused, because he had argued that science was about the advancement of knowledge and making scientific discoveries without reference to any moral purpose. The divorce of facts from values and morality had terrible consequences in the twentieth century, Gore argued, Bacon and the scientific method thereby contributing to the extreme evils perpetrated by Hitler and Stalin.[13] Gore's accusation against science shows an extraordinary misreading of history. The Nazis did not commit their crimes because they lacked values, but because their values were evil. Moreover the Nazis enacted the most environmentally friendly laws in Europe. They passed anti-vivisection laws (Gore criticised Bacon for dissecting animals for the sake of knowledge) but used humans instead. Nazi ideologists rejected the proposition that science is morally neutral, most horribly in their racial theories. Similarly, Stalin supported Trofim Lysenko's genetic theories, not because of their superior explanatory power, but because they conformed to Marxist-Leninist ideology.

Yet Gore's assault on the Scientific Revolution met with silence from leading academies and societies. Collectively scientists tolerated an extraordinary attack on the integrity and morality of their discipline because they were united by a common enemy – global warming and fossil fuel interests.

The book was well timed. Bill Clinton's Arkansas had one of the worst environmental records in America. Environmental policy was not, as Clinton admitted, his strong suit. Gore gave Clinton a signed copy. 'I read it, learned a lot, and agreed with his argument.'[14]

With Gore as vice president, there was no debate within the new administration on the science of global warming. Gore regularly hosted breakfast seminars with leading scientists, exposing agency heads to what scientists were thinking. Bob Watson, who worked in the White House during President Clinton's first term, recalls Gore being an avid reader of *Nature*. He would often telephone, 'Bob, what do you think of this paper?'

In preparing scientists for the seminars, Watson would tell them to speak for a maximum of seven minutes, as Gore will interrupt and ask questions. Gore's biggest strength was in synthesising and connecting issues and Watson had no hesitation in putting him in front of a pure science audience.[15]

The economics presented a greater challenge. In his book, Gore strongly criticised the Bush administration for threatening to torpedo the Rio summit because of its refusal to sign up to targets and timetables. Ratcheting back emissions to their 1990 level was a target the US could 'easily' meet.[16] Here debates within the Clinton administration in the run-up to Kyoto were similar to those in the Bush administration before Rio. 'Al has discovered it's a lot easier to write a book about the subject than to grapple with the economic costs,' one of Clinton's top aides said, 'but he's getting the hang of it.'[17]

From his position in the State Department, Tim Wirth advocated an aggressive plan for significant cutbacks in greenhouse gas emissions. The plan was scaled back as Clinton listened to warnings of senior economic advisers, notably Larry Summers and Janet Yellen of the Council of Economic Advisers. 'The spin is that we won,' an economic adviser told the *New York Times*. 'We agreed there needed to be goals, even aggressive goals. But there also needed to be escape hatches, in case the economic effects turned out to be a lot more damaging than we thought.'[18]

Rescuing the environment was not the central organising principle of the Clinton administration. Within four weeks of being sworn in, Clinton announced what was – deficit reduction to induce a bond market rally, encourage private investment to spur productivity, job creation and growth. He proposed cutting spending and raising taxes. Gore argued for a broad-based tax on energy. Clinton called the BTU energy tax his toughest tax call, particularly after he had dropped his election pledge of a middle-class tax cut. Lloyd Bentsen, the treasury secretary, joined Gore in pressing him. 'Finally, I gave in.'[19] A few days later, Clinton announced the BTU tax in his State of the Union speech in February.

Environmentalists were thrilled. A retrospective paper by one called it 'brilliantly conceived in every way. It was simple, clean, easy to administer and raised significant revenue'.[20] The BTU tax quickly became the most controversial part of Clinton's deficit reduction package. Manufacturers claimed it would cost more than half a million jobs. When the Senate deleted the BTU tax two months later and substituted a 4.3 cents a gallon gas tax, Clinton's relief was palpable. 'The bad news was that the gas tax would promote less energy conservation than the BTU tax; the good news was that it would cost middle-class Americans less.'[21]

The loss of the BTU tax was enormously consequential. Even when Democrats controlled Congress, taxation as a policy response to global warming was not politically feasible. So the Clinton administration turned away from energy taxes to champion the major environmental policy innovation of the Bush administration – tradable pollution permits. Emissions trading had solved a politically intractable problem that had stalled progress on tackling acid rain and led to a market-based way that enabled the Bush administration to propose the most ambitious target of a fifty per cent emissions cut with the most creative means.[22] Although Gore had been a bystander in the Clean Air Act debates, emissions trading and flexible market mechanisms became the central plank of the Clinton administration's negotiating strategy.

Transposing a mechanism designed to cut emissions from the chimneys of a few dozen power stations in one country to creating a market for the right to emit a gas used in processes too numerous to count, a gas, moreover, that is part of a naturally occurring cycle and therefore influenced by land use changes, then extending the market to cover developed countries and, through the Clean Development Mechanism, to embrace virtually every country in the world, posed technical, legal, verification and compliance challenges several orders of magnitude more complex.

Carbon taxes would have been simpler, easier and cleaner. Focusing negotiators on setting quantities, in the form of emissions caps, rather than setting prices, in the form of taxes, also created irresistible incentives for gaming. It incentivised countries to target emissions reductions that would have happened anyway (essentially the position of the European Union) or to negotiate trading mechanisms to take advantage of other nations' emission reductions that were happening anyway, principally those caused by the collapse of the Soviet bloc (the American goal).

The outcome was very different from the Montreal Protocol. All the reductions of CFCs and other substances controlled by the Montreal Protocol occurred as a direct result of regulatory actions designed to reverse the depletion of the ozone layer. On the other hand, the interest of the Annex I parties in negotiating the Kyoto Protocol was to free ride to the greatest extent possible reductions that would have happened anyway or existed only on paper.

The Clinton administration's journey along this road began in October 1993 with its climate change action plan. The forty-nine-page document listed forty-four actions designed to meet the president's personal commitment to reduce emissions to 1990 levels by the end of the decade (they actually increased by 16.1 per cent compared to the 3.4 per cent fall needed to return to 1990 levels).[23] It was thin stuff. All the actions were voluntary and the plan involved only $1.9 billion in new and redirected spending between 1994 and 2000.

Some environmental NGOs disguised their disappointment. Others couldn't. The Sierra Club said the administration had looked global warming in the eye and blinked. The National Wildlife Federation compared it to date rape. And there was an endorsement the administration could have done without. Fred Singer, a leading scientist opposed to the scientific consensus, wrote that the voluntary measures made 'a certain amount of sense'.[24]

Losing both houses of Congress in the November 1994 mid-term elections put the Clinton administration's climate policies on the defensive at home when its presence was required on the international stage. In March 1995, Helmut Kohl addressed the first COP in Berlin. There was a certain irony as Kohl urged delegates to remember the lesson of Berlin. Never again should walls of enmity be erected between peoples and nations, Kohl declared, for the Berlin Mandate institutionalised a new division across the world between North and South.[25]

The demarcation line had been agreed at a late stage in the negotiations on the Climate Change Convention three years earlier at an INC session in Paris during Holy Week. There were various attempts to define developed and developing countries. GDP per capita was felt not to be a good measure, as there were lots of countries in between. Because there were more developing countries, it was easier to define the developed countries, which was done on the basis of membership of the OECD (a definition that put Turkey in an anomalous position as a developing country which was also an OECD member) plus Eastern Europe.[26]

Angela Merkel, the German environment minister, had to fashion a compromise to reconcile the contradictory demands of North and South. Growing up in East Germany, Merkel was versed in the uselessness of inflexibility. She was helped by Britain's environment secretary, John Gummer, one of the most pro-European members of John Major's government who had replaced the Atlanticist Michael Howard two years earlier. Gummer's views were closely aligned with mainstream European attitudes and was an early admirer of Merkel. 'Very, very able,' Gummer found her.[27] China had to be kept onside, recognising Chinese sensitivities to anything that appeared to them to infringe their sovereignty (at times, Gummer recalls negotiators spent longer debating the rights and wrongs of the Boxer Rebellion than climate change). In Gummer's view, the difficulties America had over China were not fundamentally about climate change, but sprang from fears about China's rivalry with the US.

Apart from the EU and the G77 plus China, the other main negotiating bloc was the US-led Umbrella Group, loosely comprising Australia, Canada, Iceland, Japan, New Zealand, Norway, the Russian Federation, and the Ukraine as a counter-weight to the EU. Merkel's strategy was to target Canada's environment minister, Sheila Copps, the leading left-winger in Jean Chrétien's Liberal government. Copps was peeled away from the Umbrella Group, which helped convince the Chinese delegation that they should have confidence that Annex I parties genuinely accepted overwhelming responsibility for taking action to tackle global warming.[28] Shuttling between two rooms, one with developed countries, the other with developing countries, she produced a compromise text at six in the morning and declared the Mandate adopted despite protests from OPEC members.[29]

Throughout the rest of the negotiations, OPEC was carefully managed. At COP2, OPEC members were bought off with a fund to compensate oil producers for the loss of income resulting from policies to cut carbon dioxide emissions. There is evidence that Japan offered Saudi Arabia a side deal in return for its cooperation at Kyoto.[30]

No threats or inducements could subsequently shift the G77 plus China from what they had wrung from COP1. The text of the Berlin Mandate states that the process will not introduce any new commitments for Parties not included in Annex I.[31] Its implications went further than a literal reading might suggest, which neither added nor subtracted anything to what was already in the text of the convention, as it precluded even specifying what the obligations of non-Annex I parties in the original convention might be.

Other than the State Department, the Berlin Mandate did not receive high level attention in the Clinton administration. Although American negotiators in Berlin recognised that it might go down badly on the Hill, agreeing it was seen as a 'tactical step to keep the process moving'.[32] It proved a grave miscalculation.

A decade and a half on, the man who discharged the Berlin Mandate believes it was the only basis on which the process could have been taken forward.[33] As host, Japan would by custom hold the presidency of the conference. Internal splits meant it was unable to field a candidate of sufficient standing. Before taking up his new post as Argentina's ambassador to Beijing, Raúl Estrada-Oyuela was elected chair of the Ad Hoc Group of the Berlin Mandate.

As an Argentine, Estrada brought to the job the economic perspective of his fellow countryman, Raúl Prebisch, the intellectual grandfather of the development half of sustainable development. The two got to know each other when they were living in Washington in the early 1970s where their sons went to the same kindergarten. A decade later, Estrada attended Prebisch's funeral in Santiago; a complicated affair, with Prebisch's two concurrent wives each taking a share of his ashes.[34] Some of Estrada's most penetrating economic analyses of the climate change issues owe much to Prebisch's economics.

Estrada had been involved in climate change negotiations since attending the Geneva World Climate Conference in 1990. He consciously applied the approaches used by his predecessors to forge consensus: Ripert in consulting privately with delegations on every issue to understand their thinking; Tommy Koh of Singapore, who chaired the preparatory committee for the Rio summit and addressed delegations by their first names, making emotional appeals at plenary sessions; and Merkel's devotion to constructive compromise.[35] The chair needed to possess an instinct for the sense of the room; to know when to press forward and when to wait.[36] And he needed determination. 'You have to be optimistic. Particularly in Kyoto, I was paid to be optimistic … the Chairman has to be perseverant, persistent, otherwise you are lost.'[37]

Estrada was supported by the convention secretariat, headed by the Maltese Michael Zammit Cutajar for its first eleven years. Zammit Cutajar began his career in UNCTAD, providing a further link with Prebisch, who was his first boss. When questioned about the position of the climate change secretariat in the negotiations, Zammit Cutajar would recall what Prebisch used to say:

> 'As a secretariat we are objective, but we cannot be indifferent to development. We cannot be neutral. We are fighting for development.' So when people try to block the [climate change] process, we can admire their negotiating skill, but we cannot be indifferent … We have a commitment.[38]

Although the commitment to tackle global warming was seen through the prism of Prebisch's economics and the development needs of the South, the chair and secretariat did not permit their commitment to be about promoting the interests of the South. At one point, in Kyoto, Estrada accused Brazil of coming to the conference 'with an open hand', triggering a walk out by the Brazilian ambassador.[39] He opposed the Clean Development Mechanism, which was designed to pump money from North to South. When Saudi Arabia and Kuwait challenged one of his decisions, he rounded on them. 'From the very beginning … a group of countries was trying to stop the process … I will do everything to overcome those countries … I am not going to be [held] hostage.'[40] OPEC wouldn't risk a walk out and Estrada knew he had the votes.

This was not the case for the G77 plus China on the issue that bound them together: individually and collectively its members would be held totally immune from the costs of policies designed to tackle global warming. President Clinton tried; Estrada had more success – but nothing could break the solidarity of the South.

After the 1994 mid-term elections, the Clinton administration requested that the negotiations be slowed down. At COP2 in July 1996, with Clinton cruising to re-election, the Clinton administration called for an international agreement on binding targets to be met with the maximum flexibility. It also put its name to a ministerial declaration led by Canada, which stated the continued rise of greenhouse gas concentrations 'will lead to dangerous interference with the climate system'.[41] It was an important moment. The convention had been adopted on the precautionary principle. The ministerial declaration replaced the modal auxiliary 'might' with the future tense 'will'. The convention's objective is to avoid dangerous anthropogenic interference in the climate system, but it did not define what should be considered dangerous. Now the politicians had. Because delegations from Australia, New Zealand, Saudi Arabia and Venezuela disagreed (and Russia's Yuri Izrael continued to dispute that global warming would be harmful), the COP noted, but did not adopt, the declaration.[42]

The Kyoto conference had to resolve three sets of issues. The first was the level of emissions cuts for Annex I countries. This pitted the US and the EU against each other, a nervous Japan on the sidelines, worried about the burden on its economy, but as host not wanting to cause the conference to fail. The second set revolved around the flexibility of those targets and timetables and the means by which they should be achieved. This was another battle between the US and the EU, joined by a deeply suspicious South, that saw flexibility as a means by which Annex I countries could evade their responsibilities by cutting emissions of poorer countries rather than their own. The third was the extent to which non-Annex I parties should indicate willingness to assume some form of obligation to limit carbon dioxide emissions at some point in the future.

The stage for the confrontation on the first of these was set in June 1997 at the Denver G8 summit, the only one hosted by Bill Clinton. On his return to Washington, Clinton told Taylor Branch, his oral historian, how the Europeans, including Tony Blair and Helmut Kohl, had ganged up on him. 'They upbraided him, said the president, even though they had no idea how they would meet their standards,' Branch recorded.[43] Blair had been elected less than two months earlier on a manifesto which included the pledge to cut carbon dioxide emissions by twenty per cent by 2010 (a target the Labour government missed by fifty per cent).[44]

More painful was Kohl – 'almost like a blood brother', according to Branch. It had been eighteen years since a German chancellor had attacked an American president, but their respective positions had changed one hundred and eighty degrees since Helmut Schmidt had taken on Jimmy Carter in Tokyo in 1979. Then it was a realist German expressing his scorn for an American president's crusade against imported oil. In the intervening years, German politics had been transformed by the rise of the Greens.

Schmidt was a hard-headed pragmatist. His definition of a successful leader was to prevent his country being overrun by war or by need and hunger. Schmidt's call for a NATO response to the Soviet Union stationing of SS-20 nuclear missiles helped fuel the rise of anti-nuclear sentiment in Germany. In 1978 and 1979, massive, sometimes violent, demonstrations against nuclear power and nuclear weapons made the extra-parliamentary Left the voice of radical environmentalism that until then had mainly been the province of old and neo-Nazis. In October 1980, the Green Party was formed to bring the radicals into the parliamentary system for the first time in post-war Germany. The rise of the Greens was a gift to Kohl and the CDU, who used the Greens against the SPD to split the centre-left. At the same time, the CDU had to develop pro-environmental positions to prevent losing conservative voters to the Greens.

In July, the US Senate fired its warning shot across Clinton's bows on the third strategic issue by passing the Byrd-Hagel resolution. According to co-sponsor Chuck Hagel, there was not a single senator who had not been concerned about what might come out of Kyoto and worried that the president was going too far.[45]

Three months later, Clinton announced the instructions he was giving American negotiators in a speech at the National Geographic Society. The US would commit to stabilising emissions at 1990 levels between 2008 and 2012.* Although he talked of achieving meaningful reductions 'here

---

*   The original draft of the speech called for a five per cent cut, but a member of Clinton's economic team changed the text. Amy Royden, *U.S. Climate Change Policy Under President Clinton: A Look Back* (2002), fn. 119.

in America', that goal was contradicted by Clinton's second goal – flexible mechanisms including emissions trading and 'joint implementation', whereby firms could invest in projects in other countries and receive credits for those reductions at home. On bringing non-Annex I countries in to the net, Clinton could hardly have been clearer: 'The United States will not assume binding obligations unless key developing nations meaningfully participate in this effort.'[46]

Less than a month before the Kyoto conference was due to begin, Tim Wirth announced he was quitting. His place was taken by Stuart Eizenstat, who, at short notice, flew in from Switzerland where he had been negotiating the restitution of Nazi gold. Where Wirth's time in Congress had made him a somewhat divisive figure, Eizenstat was highly regarded by Democrats and Republicans. Clinton could hardly have made a better received appointment.

If the Kyoto conference had only been about flexibility mechanisms, the outcome would have been an unqualified success for the Clinton administration. US negotiators gained every one of their main objectives. America wouldn't have to cut its own emissions if it could buy other countries' excess emissions – the Russian Federation having enough 'hot air' to satisfy American needs, or so the thinking went. (It was never likely that the US Congress would approve a law which resulted in American businesses and consumers sending billions of dollars to Russia for its hot air.) It was on the third of Clinton's three objectives that no ground was given nor taken at Kyoto.

Rio had been a signing ceremony. The Kyoto COP3, which started on 1st December 1997, was a real time negotiating conference with cameras present at the final climatic session. NGOs came, but their purpose was to influence the negotiators and raise the stakes for failure. Scientists also played their customary Cassandra role. 1997 was expected to be the Earth's warmest year on record, they said. 'We are beginning to see the fingerprint of man's impact on the climate,' a scientist from Britain's Hadley Centre told the media.[47]

Not everyone was impressed. *Washington Post* columnist Charles Krauthammer reminded his readers of a leading climate scientist, Stephen Schneider, who was now arguing that it was 'journalistically irresponsible' to present both sides of the debate. Twenty-five years previously, Schneider had been arguing that the real threat was global cooling. Then, he had dismissed fears about global warming by claiming that a doubling of carbon dioxide would produce a temperature change of less than one degree centigrade.[48]

A congressional delegation was in Kyoto to provide oversight. 'This is not a conference about environment,' Hagel told a local newspaper. 'This is a conference about economics,' one with an underlying agenda of wealth transfer. 'I've never seen so many silly people,' the senator added.[49] Senator Liebermann was challenged by a Chinese delegate: 'Do you expect us to keep our people poor? Is that what you want?' To which the senator, a future sponsor of cap-and-trade legislation, replied, 'We can't ask our people in the US to accept the burdens associated with reducing greenhouse gas emissions, if at the same time, the developing nations accept no responsibility.'[50]

Senator Kerry took a more emollient approach. America must tell the Third World: 'The mistakes we made should not be repeated and we're willing to help you grow in thoughtful ways. So please, when you get cars, think about unleaded gasoline and emissions controls, about the virtues of mass transit and trains.'[51]

There had been an end of June deadline for countries to submit proposals for consideration. Out of more than two hundred pages, Estrada distilled a twenty-five-page draft protocol, closing minor issues but leaving open the large contentious ones. He then challenged the Annex I countries to put their cards on the table.

The EU's opening position had been a flat fifteen per cent cut. In March the EU re-allocated this among themselves under the 'EU bubble', in the process weakening their credibility in pressing for a flat rate for everyone else, although John Gummer believes it was perfectly reasonable for the world to view the EU as a single economy. Indeed he describes his support of the EU bubble as his proudest moment as a minister of the British crown. It meant Britain would have to do more so Ireland could do less, as some recompense for eight hundred years of oppression.[52]

On the third day of the COP, the US indicated that it might introduce a small symbolic cut to take its target below 1990 levels. Three days later, Estrada proposed a ten per cent cut for the EU, five per cent for the US and two and a half per cent for Japan. The EU objected, saying the three should have the same target.[53]

On 8th December, Gore arrived. 'A one day cosmetic trip that would not make up for years of neglect by the Clinton administration,' Philip Clapp, a former aide to Tim Wirth and president of the National Environmental Trust, called it.[54] Environmental groups chanted 'read your book' outside rooms where Gore was meeting.[55]

Gore's decision to go had been made only two weeks before. Although he had spent months wavering, he insisted that political calculation had not entered into his reasons for making the trip. Representative John Dingell, a Michigan Democrat and long-time opponent of tough emissions curbs, thought otherwise. Dingell warned that Gore's performance at Kyoto 'could affect many things, including his nomination and election'.[56] Harlan Watson, a senior congressional aide, had first known Gore in the early 1980s, when he had been a congressman. He had always been struck by how bright, quick and extraordinarily articulate Gore was. A different man was on stage in Kyoto, hesitant and looking around for prompts. Perhaps it was jet lag.[57]

Then Gore dropped his bombshell. In remarks added thirty minutes beforehand, the vice president said that after meeting the US negotiating team and speaking with President Clinton by phone, 'I am instructing our delegation right now to show increased negotiating flexibility if a comprehensive plan can be put in place.'[58]

The message was clear. The Clinton administration would do whatever it took to avoid being isolated. 'We were taken aback,' recalled Watson.[59] The congressional delegation had been completely frozen out; it hadn't been helpful not to know what its own government was doing, Hagel later recounted.[60] Perhaps the American negotiating team didn't know what was happening either. Watson remembers Eizenstat looking as surprised as everyone else.[61]

Estrada made a new proposal of eight, five, and four and a half per cent reductions for the EU, the US and Japan respectively.[62] Two days later on 10th December, at around midnight in Washington, Eizenstat called the White House to say they were close to agreement. Eight, seven, six would clinch the deal. At 2am Washington time, Gore telephoned Japanese Prime Minister Ryutaro Hashimoto. After reminding him how far the EU, the US and Japan had come, he laid it on the line. The last thing anyone wanted was for people to say that the thing that prevented a deal was the host country not moving a final percentage point.[63] And that's where the three main Annex I parties ended up, although during the conference's closing moments Australia got its cap raised from plus five to plus ten per cent.*

On flexibility, the US scored a string of wins; a five-year commitment period from 2008 to 2012, joint implementation and generous accounting for forest sinks. Emissions trading was strongly opposed by the G77 plus China. From their perspective (and to some in the EU), it was wrong to

---

* In post-conference briefings, Clinton administration officials claimed that -7 per cent was equivalent 'at most' to -3 per cent on their original proposal of stabilisation because of differences in accounting for forests and land management (sinks) and inclusion of extra greenhouse gases with a 1995 base year. See for example Stuart Eizenstat's testimony to the Senate Foreign Relations Committee, 11th February 1998 http://www.iitap.iastate.edu/gcp/kyoto/protocol.html

have a mechanism to enable America to cut other countries' emissions to avoid cutting its own. It provoked a confrontation between China and the US, drawing a rebuke from Estrada. 'It might be better if we have no agreement,' he said. 'I invite you to reflect.'

During the pause, Chinese and American negotiators stood nose-to-nose, snarling at each other in a pre-dawn showdown.[64]

The conference had been due to end on 10th December, but at four in the morning the following day Estrada announced he was deleting an OECD text on emissions trading, putting in its place a new article permitting trading but stating it must be supplemented by domestic action. Estrada banged his gavel. Emissions trading was in the Protocol.

The US also got a bonus that wasn't in its original list. Three days before the June deadline for proposals for Kyoto, Brazil tabled a complex plan to allocate greenhouse gas emission commitments based on countries' historic contributions to the increase in global temperatures. Although none of it was adopted, the G77 plus China used the hook of a Clean Development Fund to be financed by fines levied on Annex I countries for non-compliance. In November, Brazilian and American negotiators realised that paying a fine for non-compliance was functionally identical to buying a licence to remain compliant without the stigma. The US had found another flexibility mechanism. Even better, it could in principle extend emissions trading to the whole world.

The Clean Development Mechanism (CDM) turned out to be one of the most controversial parts of the Kyoto Protocol. After the conference, the Clinton administration argued that the CDM represented a 'down payment' on developing countries' future efforts to reduce greenhouse gas emissions.[65] In reality, it was nothing of the sort. 'Though I facilitated approval of this proposal, I did not like it,' Estrada wrote in 1998. 'I do not understand how commitments can be implemented jointly if only one of the parties involved is committed to limit or reduce emissions and the other party is free from the quantitative [restrictions].'[66] The hypothesis that mitigation costs are lower in developing countries is true only if market distortions are adjusted, Estrada argued, otherwise everything is cheaper in developing countries – a disparity that has been the root cause of every colonisation since the time of the Greeks.[67]

The US only won emissions trading because it had comprehensively lost on the third of Clinton's three objectives. The response to Gore's instruction of flexibility on the part of the US was met by total inflexibility on the part of the G77 plus China. Early in the conference, a US negotiator indicated that all they were looking was for some movement on the issue of developing country participation, while Hagel said not all one hundred and forty developing nations need sign on. Those that did need only agree to a general commitment to limit emissions. The G77's response was swift. 'We have said categorically *no*.'[68]

Estrada tabled a draft article to enable non-Annex I countries to make voluntary commitments. A number of non-Annex I countries gave it qualified support, including the Association of Small Island States, Argentina, South Korea and the Philippines. The majority didn't. OPEC members, perhaps recognising that the article might increase the chance of Senate ratification, argued that the article be deleted. They were joined by the host of the Earth summit, along with India and China. Recognising there was no consensus, Estrada said the article should be deleted.

Then New Zealand launched an initiative for future commitments from non-Annex I countries based on Annex I countries delivering theirs, with talks beginning in 1998. The G77 plus China said that it would not participate in them as a matter of principle. In his speech to the conference, the spokesman for the G77 plus China concluded with one word: 'No.' The proposal was not discussed again.[69]

Some delegations had already left. Contracts for the conference translators had expired, leaving the Russian and Chinese delegations without interpreters. Having worked through the night, at around 1pm on 11th December, Estrada said he was happy to submit a Kyoto Protocol and declared that it had been unanimously recommended.

At a wrap-up briefing for the congressional delegation, Watson was sitting next to Dingell and a member of his staff. Eizenstat came over to them. 'Well, Mr Chairman, I did the best I could,' Eizenstat said. 'Don't worry Stu,' Dingell replied. 'You can't make chicken salad when you're handed chicken shit.'[70]

Nine hundred and seventy-nine days after COP1, Estrada had discharged the Berlin Mandate. After it was formally adopted, Estrada took a nap. Then he went to see the city with his wife.

19
THE MORNING AFTER

Our most fateful new challenge is the threat of global warming; 1998 was the warmest year ever recorded. Last year's heat waves, floods, and storms are but a hint of what future generations may endure if we do not act now.

President Clinton, 19th January 1999[1]

During his twenty-four hours in Kyoto, Al Gore told reporters he welcomed the prospect of a 'knock-down, drag-out' fight to ratify the Kyoto Protocol. 'It would be high stakes and a lot of fun.'[2]

His bravado scarcely lasted the return flight. The Protocol faced 'bleak prospects', Trent Lott, the Senate majority leader, warned. 'I have made clear to the President personally that the Senate will not ratify a flawed climate change treaty,' Lott reassured Chuck Hagel.[3]

A tug of war ensued between the Senate and the White House. The day after the Protocol's adoption, the *Washington Times* reported that the Clinton administration had decided to delay submitting it to Congress. 'As we said from the very beginning, we will not submit this agreement for ratification until key developing nations participate in this effort,' an administration spokesman said. Lott argued that Clinton should not withhold the treaty from the Senate for 'cynical, political reasons.'[4]

Clinton nominated Frank Loy to succeed Tim Wirth as undersecretary of state for global affairs. On taking up his post, Loy immediately recognised that even with a friendly Senate, the Protocol was not in a state to be ratified. The text was an outline, being totally silent or sparse in setting out how the Protocol's emissions goals should be met. While Loy and his colleagues recognised they were never going to get absolute quantified emissions targets from even the richest of the G77, getting something from some of them was high on the administration's agenda both in terms of meeting the convention's objective of avoiding dangerous interference and for its political importance.[5]

In doing what they could to improve the prospects for ratification, the Clinton administration got little help from the Europeans, in particular Germany, France and the Scandinavians, which had Green environment ministers. Far and away the most thoughtful and realistic was the UK and John Prescott, environment secretary and deputy PM. Prescott was 'extremely helpful', according to Loy.[6]

In October 1997, Clinton had visited Argentina. Speaking in the magnificence of the Nahuel Huapi National Park, Clinton invoked Theodore Roosevelt and Perito Moreno, who had visited Patagonia together in 1912. He promised $1billion to help developing countries find alternative energy sources and praised his host, President Menem, for stating that developing countries should have emissions targets.[7] Argentina's backing was a coup. Historically Argentina had provided the intellectual leadership of the developing country movement and the first COP after Kyoto was being held in Buenos Aires.

Meanwhile a fierce debate raged between the Clinton administration and Congress over the economic implications for the US of adopting Kyoto. In July, the administration produced its analysis. Emissions trading, joint implementation and the Clean Development Mechanism would enable the US to buy its way out of the problem at minimal cost. Trading among industrialised countries would more than halve the costs of climate change policies.[8] Supplemented by the Clean Development Mechanism, trading might reduce costs by up to eighty-seven per cent of a domestic-only approach.[9] Overall the report estimated annual costs to the US of $7–12 billion, equivalent to 0.07–0.11 per cent of GDP, a fleabite on the back of the booming US economy.[10]

The assessment was received with considerable scepticism on Capitol Hill. Jim Sensenbrenner, chairman of the Committee on Science, held hearings and asked the Energy Information Administration, an independent agency within the Department of Energy, to offer a second opinion. In October, the EIA produced a more comprehensive and detailed analysis which suggested that the costs would be an order of magnitude higher than the administration claimed. It projected a reduction in 2010 GDP of $61–183 billion (if revenue from auctioning emissions permits was used to reduce social security taxes) and a range of $92–397 billion (if permit revenues were returned to taxpayers in a lump sum), implying a range of 0.65–4.2 per cent of GDP for the two approaches.*[11]

---

*   In 2004, the General Accounting Office analysed the factors that led to these dramatically different cost ranges. It found the Council of Economic Advisers used a model that generally assumed that the economy adjusts smoothly to new policies over the longer-term. By contrast, the Energy Information Agency model used a more comprehensive cost measure and was thus able to capture certain costs that the Council of Economic Advisers' model did not. Other differences included assumptions about international trading and the proportion of reductions that would be achieved domestically. General Accounting Office, 'Estimated Costs of the Kyoto Protocol' GAO-04-144R, 30th January 2004, p. 3.

Having a debate on the economics of global warming made the US exceptional. The UK, which had taken a pragmatic attitude to the climate change negotiations, did not examine the economic consequences of Kyoto. Few people were better placed to see what went on than Andrew Turnbull. Cabinet secretary and Britain's top civil servant under Tony Blair between 2002 and 2005, before that, Turnbull had been a Treasury highflyer, working in Number 10 for Margaret Thatcher in her last two years as prime minister, permanent secretary at the Department of the Environment from 1994 before returning to the Treasury in 1998 as permanent secretary. According to Turnbull, at no stage was anyone inside the British government prepared to step back and reappraise the issue. Thatcher's championing of global warming had settled the issue. Her reputation as a politician not afraid to challenge orthodoxy and her scientific mind continued to have a huge impact long after she'd gone. Rising global temperatures through the 1990s made carbon dioxide appear the villain of the piece and policies to deal with it looked like a good idea. But the Treasury never did any serious work on the economics.

As a policy disaster in the making, global warming reminds Turnbull of the poll tax. At the beginning, people went along with it because they thought it a small-scale, incremental policy. After it went wrong and helped bring about Thatcher's fall, they would say, 'It's not my fault it blew up, I wouldn't have done it if I'd known what happened subsequently.' The European dimension of global warming reinforced this tendency. Here was a policy where Britain wasn't being a foot-dragger. Since Thatcher's Royal Society speech in 1988, the UK had been in a lead position. The dash-to-gas allowed Britain to show off at little apparent cost. Only later would the costs emerge in terms of closed steel mills, distorted tax policies and unattainable targets for renewable energy.[12]

The Buenos Aires COP4 was held in the first two weeks of November 1998. It adopted the Buenos Aires Plan of Action to put flesh on the bones of the Protocol by the end of 2000. More importantly, it turned out to be the high point of the Clinton administration's campaign to get some meaningful participation from developing countries.

It began promisingly. On the conference's first day Maria Julia Alsogaray, Argentina's secretary of natural resources and sustainable development, told the conference that while Argentina did not bear historic responsibility for the climate change problem, it wished to belong to the group of countries which had responsibility for finding a solution. Developing countries too had some responsibility for climate change and an ethical duty to ensure sustainable development.[13]

Nine days later, Carlos Menem told delegates that at the next COP Argentina would make a commitment to cap its emissions for the period 2008 to 2012.[14] 'This is a major, major move,' Stuart Eizenstat said in Buenos Aires, 'truly historic.'[15] Environmentalists were also ecstatic. 'It is a major breakthrough,' Michael Oppenheimer of the Environmental Defence Fund said, describing Argentina's move as 'a significant first step' in satisfying the Senate's requirements.[16]

The next day, Kazakhstan announced that it wanted to join Argentina and voluntarily assume Annex I obligations, which would enable it to sell its surplus emissions as 'hot air' to America. It looked like the Americans were on a roll. Speculation had been mounting that the administration would build on the momentum of Argentina's announcement by signing the Protocol. Senator Byrd, co-sponsor of the Byrd-Hagel resolution, warned Clinton against 'making empty gestures that will only make the potential future approval of the Protocol by the Senate more difficult.'[17] From Buenos Aires, Senator Liebermann urged Clinton to sign. 'If we are not at the table, we cannot cajole or convince the developing nations to become part of the solution,' Liebermann said.[18]

The day after Menem's speech, Peter Burleigh, America's acting representative to the United Nations, signed the Kyoto Protocol in New York. Publicly Clinton said nothing. Instead a statement was put out on behalf of Vice President Gore. Signing Kyoto imposed no obligations on the US, the statement said. 'We will not submit the Protocol for ratification without the meaningful participation of key developing countries in efforts to address climate change.'[19]

The downbeat spin in Washington contrasted with the stir it created in Buenos Aires. 'I am not gilding the lily when I say there was near euphoria among the delegates here,' Eizenstat told the *New York Times*.[20] Lieberman said it gave America the credibility to be at the table. 'That means we can not only make sure it happens, but that it happens in the way that we prefer.'[21] Hagel dared Clinton to invite the Senate to ratify it. 'If this treaty is good enough to sign, it's good enough to be submitted to the Senate for an open, honest debate.'[22]

Clinton avoided battle on the Senate floor. Instead Buenos Aires marked the furthest extent of the Clinton administration's global warming diplomacy. Like Napoleon's defeat at Borodino, it was the start of a two-year retreat. Argentina and Kazakhstan could announce their intention to assume

Annex I obligations, but there was no mechanism in the Protocol for them formally to do so. Agreeing a mechanism required consensus. Consensus, or rather the lack of it, was like General Winter to the retreating French; not an outcome decided in pitched battle, but worn down through steady attrition. By the time the administration had signed the treaty, the battle was already lost, defeat being confirmed at the conference closing plenary two days later.

At the start of COP4, there was a battle on whether voluntary commitments should be on the conference agenda. Speaking on behalf of the G77 plus China, Indonesia said the issue had been deliberated at length, but no consensus had been reached and proposed the agenda be adopted without it. India recalled the debate at Kyoto which had rejected the idea of voluntary commitments. A number of OPEC members warned that such a discussion was bound to be divisive and could lead to the imposition of voluntary commitments. China said developed countries' 'luxury' emissions were rising and that voluntary commitments would create a new category of parties under the convention.

Speaking in favour were Australia, Japan, Canada, New Zealand and the EU, which recognised that the question of broadening commitments in the long-term was necessary and unavoidable. Of the non-Annex I nations, only Chile spoke in support. The agenda was adopted without the proposed item.[23]

Two days later, the conference discussed the adequacy of commitments of both Annex I and non-Annex I parties to attain the convention's objective. The first review had been three years earlier and had resulted in the Berlin Mandate. Article 4.2(d) of the convention required a second review not later than 31st December 1998 (and thereafter at regular intervals). The article, suggested by American negotiators, was meant to be a periodic spur; without extending commitments beyond the Annex I parties, it was numerically impossible to stabilise greenhouse gas concentrations and thus achieve the convention's objective.[24]

The G77 plus China said that there was consensus that existing commitments were inadequate, as developed countries were shirking their responsibilities. The issue was passed to a contact group which met over the weekend. This failed to produce agreement other than to remit four different drafts to another body, this time the Subsidiary Body on Implementation. The US and Australia noted that the IPCC's evaluation confirmed that developed country actions by themselves would be insufficient, while China interpreted this as an attempt to extract commitments from developing countries. On the Tuesday (the COP was due to finish at the end of the week), the Canadian co-chair of the contact group reported that they agreed that commitments were inadequate, but not on the reasons or on any actions that might be required.[25]

At the COP final plenary two days after America had signed the Protocol, Alsogaray reported that the parties had not been able to review the adequacy of commitments as required by the convention.

The issue was left for COP5 in October 1999 in Bonn.

As with COP4, settling the agenda was the first issue for COP5. The draft agenda included the Article 4.2(d) adequacy review. Again, the G77 plus China objected. This time it wanted the wording of the item changed from 'adequacy of commitments' to 'adequacy of their implementation', changing the sense and purpose of the review requirement in the convention. After what many had felt to be a difficult COP in Buenos Aires, delegations experienced, in the words of convention secretary Zammit Cutajar, an unexpected mood of optimism, a mood bought at the cost of not attempting to resolve divisive issues. On the final day of the COP, the conference president, Poland's Jan Szyszko, said no agreement had been reached to resolve the adequacy review, recorded China's amendment, and gavelled the decision, saying the item would be taken up at COP6.[26]

A similar fate befell Kazakhstan's attempt to join Annex I. While Argentina announced its adoption of voluntary greenhouse gas growth targets, it had backed down from trying to change its non-Annex I status.[27] In response to the EU's suggestion of agreeing to increasing global participation after the first 2008-2012 commitment period, China said it would not undertake commitments until it achieved 'medium development level'.[28] (By 2008, China's per capita carbon dioxide emissions were above the world average.[29] Reinstein recalls a comment by China in one of the last sessions of the INC negotiating the convention: 'China will always be a developing country,' which he interpreted not as a statement about China's economic aspirations but as a firewall against China being dragged into OECD-like commitments.)[30]

Although Kazakhstan's proposal to join Annex I was supported by a number of Annex I parties, several non-Annex I countries said they did not have enough information on whether Kazakhstan could fulfil its obligations. There was no consensus and the COP decided that the issue should be taken up by COP6.

So on it rolled. The US, supported by Canada, Australia and New Zealand, pressed for COP6 to be held in early 2001, after the American elections. The G77 plus China pushed for November; the decision going their way.

The Hague COP6 was held six days after the disputed presidential election and Florida's hanging chads. The American team at The Hague did not know whether Al Gore or George W. Bush, who had spoken against Kyoto in the election, would be taking office in January. The attempt to get some evidence of future commitments from non-Annex I countries was now all but over. The draft agenda was adopted except for the item on the second review of the adequacy of commitments. No consensus on the matter had been found by the end of the COP, the G77 plus China saying the topic was sensitive so it would be better not to discuss it further.[31]

Instead the American side had to contain a counter-attack from the EU which in American eyes amounted to an attempt to reopen the basis of the deal struck at Kyoto. They also had to contend with a noisy NGO participation that stormed a meeting with locked arms and refused to leave.[32] Something was thrown at Loy. Wiping cake from his face, Loy reminded everyone that the day was the anniversary of the assassination of President Kennedy, who had urged Americans not to be swayed by those 'confusing rhetoric with reality'.[33]

The air of unreality at The Hague started with the reading of some poems by the Dutch poet laureate.

> *He lost his way within a maze*
> *In search of silver and of gold –*
> *He searched a lifetime and he found*
> *He was where he'd been from of old*

Presumably it sounded better in Dutch. Much discussion revolved around sinks. Jan Pronk, the Dutch president of COP6, recalled lengthy debates about the definition of a sink, the definition of a forest and even the definition of a tree. When is a tree a tree? 'All this went on year after year, month after month, seminar after seminar, workshop after workshop, conference after conference. And during the conferences and negotiations themselves, day after day, hour after hour, night after night,' Pronk recounted.[34]

Since Kyoto, European politics had turned deep green. Helmut Kohl lost the 1998 federal elections and was replaced by a Red-Green coalition led by Gerhard Schröder, Merkel being succeeded by the Green Jürgen Trittin. He joined Dominique Voynet, the environment minister in Lionel Jospin's government and one of the founders of the Greens in France. Trit-

tin and Voynet constituted a Green motor at the heart of Europe. Instead
of defining the precise rules and mechanisms needed to implement Kyoto,
COP6 was to be Europe's hour when it cleansed Kyoto of its loopholes and
forced rich countries (i.e., America) to face up to their responsibilities and
cut their own emissions, rather than buy up poorer countries' emissions
allowances.

France held the EU's rotating presidency. President Chirac's speech to
the conference was a call to arms against the common enemy – America.
There was no doubt that global warning had set in, he said. Without action, there would be dreadful consequences – rising sea levels, floods, ex-
tinctions of plants and animals, storms, typhoons, cyclones, hurricanes,
the spread of deserts and the emergence of environmental refugees. 'That is
why, I can confirm to you here, Europe is resolved to act and has mobilised
to fight the greenhouse effect.'

While acknowledging President Clinton's personal commitment, Chirac reminded the conference that each American emits three times more
greenhouse gases than a Frenchman. 'It is in the Americans, in the first
place, that we place our hopes of effectively limiting greenhouse gas emissions on a global scale.' The bulk of efforts in meeting the Kyoto targets
should be through efforts to curb domestic and regional emissions. Flexibility mechanisms were a complement: 'They should definitely not be seen
as a means of escape.' For the first time, he declared, humanity was insti-
tuting a genuine instrument of global governance. 'If the South lacks the
capacity to act, the North all too often lacks the will.'[35]

Battle was joined over sinks such as forests and how they should be
counted in reducing countries' emissions. Doing so reopened the basis on
which the emissions numbers had been agreed. 'We went to Kyoto intend-
ing to accept a target of no reduction from 1990 levels, but we ended up
with a seven per cent reduction,' Loy explained a couple of months after
the conference. 'One of the ways we were able to justify that to ourselves
was that there was a provision for sinks.'[36] (It's also worth recalling that,
at Kyoto, the EU moved from its opening position of a fifteen per cent
cut to eight per cent, but on more generous accounting.) The same went
for America's ability to use the Protocol's flexibility mechanisms to meet
its target. 'We would not have signed it if they hadn't been in there,' Loy
commented.[37]

The treatment of sinks deadlocked the conference. John Prescott, the
most thoughtful and realistic of the Europeans according to Loy, tried to
broker a deal.[38] The deal fell apart after Voynet took it to other EU en-

vironment ministers. It led to a spectacular falling out between her and Prescott. Voynet accused the former seaman of behaving like an 'inveterate macho' after Prescott had complained that Voynet had scuppered a deal because she had got cold feet and was tired and exhausted. 'I did not say the lady was tired,' Prescott told the House of Commons. 'She constantly said it herself. She was too tired to take in all the complexities. I quoted her words.'[39]

Less than three weeks after COP6 flamed out, the Supreme Court declared George W. Bush the next president.

During the last three years of his presidency, Clinton was deeply engaged on global warming. His final State of the Union message in January 2000 described global warming as the greatest environmental challenge of the new century. 'If we fail to reduce the emission of greenhouse gases, deadly heat waves and droughts will become more frequent, coastal areas will flood, and economies will be disrupted. That is going to happen, unless we act,' Clinton warned.[40]

He seems to have believed it. In a conversation with President Jiang Zemin two years before Kyoto, Clinton told the Chinese leader that he didn't want to contain China:

> 'The biggest security threat China presents the United States is that you will insist on getting rich the same way we did.' And he looked at me, and I could tell he had never thought of that. And I said, 'You have to choose a different future, and we have to help. We have to support you. And that does not in any way let us off the hook. But it just means that we have to do this together.'[41]

At the White House global warming wonkfest in October 1997, where he recalled the conversation, Clinton showed an easy mastery of the policy implications across all its dimensions, ranging from the apparent paradox of more droughts and more floods, to policy mistakes in the 1970s that stopped gas-fired power stations (the federal government had grossly underestimated domestic natural gas reserves – his Democrat predecessor, Jimmy Carter, had a big hand in that), to it being better to recover waste heat from electricity generation and to encourage consumer conservation than to force electricity companies to change their power plants.

Of course, Clinton understood the politics better than anyone else in the room: 'Number one, we can't get to the green line unless there is a

The first two scientists to have quantified the possible effect of the Industrial Revolution on global temperatures, Sweden's Svante Arrhenius (above) and the Briton Guy Stewart Callendar (below), thought global warming would delay the return of a future ice age.
Above: *PA*; Below: *G.S. Callendar Archive, University of East Anglia*

A green movement took shape in Britain between the wars with the Kindred of the Kibbo Kift preaching a programme of pacifism, open-air education and nature-craft using symbols drawn from North American Indians, Nordic sagas and the Saxons (above left). Advocating social credit, the movement turned into the Green Shirts (above right) in the 1930s often clashing with Oswald Moseley's Black Shirts, who drew their example from the Nazis and included early proponents of organic farming (right). Above: *The Kibbo Kift Foundation*; Right: *Philip M. Coupland*

In 1951, President Truman asked William S. Paley of CBS to head his Materials Policy Commission – at the centre of the picture (above), with fellow commission members. Their report, *Resources for Freedom*, argued that technology, free trade and American capitalism were the solution.

Time & Life Pictures/Getty Images

In the 1960s, two forces emerged to challenge the post-war American economic order. First, the modern environmental movement was born with the publication of Rachel Carson's *Silent Spring* in 1962.

AP/Press Association Images

Second came the emergence of the developing world. Two Argentine exiles, Che Guevara (above) and the brilliant economist Raúl Prebisch (right), were the stars of the first session of the United Nations Conference on Trade and Development (UNCTAD) in 1964, which institutionalised the economic claims of developing nations.

UNCTAD

'Whatever mark we have made in the last five years clearly bears your stamp too,' Lyndon Johnson wrote to Barbara Ward, pictured (far right) with Lady Bird Johnson at a White House reception in June 1965. It fell to Ward to reconcile the seemingly irreconcilable claims of First World environmentalism and the Third World's desire to industrialise ahead of the 1972 UN conference on the environment in Stockholm.

Francis Miller/Time & Life Pictures/ Getty Images

The other star of Stockholm was Indira Gandhi, Prime Minister of India, seen here being greeted by conference secretary-general Maurice Strong.
UN Photo/Yutaka Nagata

(Above) The Catholic convert giving a book on Buddhist economics to the born again president – E.F. 'F
Schumacher presenting Jimmy Carter with a copy of *Small is Beautiful* in the White House on 22nd Ma
1977, two months after the new president had asked Americans to recognise America's limits.

Jimmy Carter Library

All smiles at the Venice G7 in June 1980 at which Carter (left) briefed fellow world leaders on the *Glo
2000* report. It was very different a year earlier at Tokyo – 'One of the worst days of my diplomatic l
Carter said – when German chancellor Helmut Schmidt (right) attacked Carter's energy policies and
friend, French president Giscard d'Estaing (centre), brokered a face-saving formula.

Daniel Simon/Gamma-Rapho/Getty Images

...ter's energy policies were also criticised by Ronald Reagan (above), who described himself as an environmentalist ...eart. In May 1973 Governor Reagan led a campaign to conserve the John Muir Wilderness from the proposed ...ns Sierra Highway in Sierra Nevada – seen here briefing the press in the mountains near Bishop, California.

Ronald Reagan Presidential Library

1977 Schmidt's predecessor, Willy Brandt (below right), announced he was launching a commission on ...ernational development – pictured with fellow commissioner and former British premier Ted Heath.

PA

...garet Thatcher (previous page) rejected the Brandt Report and embraced its successor, led by Norwegian ...e minister Gro Harlem Brundtland – pictured together on the steps of Number 10 the day the Brundtland ...rt was published, 27th April 1987.

Press Association Images

...ne 1988 Western leaders took note of the Brundtland Report and formally adopted sustainable ...opment at the Toronto G7, enthusiastically in the case of Thatcher (above left) and Canada's Brian ...oney (above right) – photographed with Reagan at a working lunch on 20th June. It put global warming ...on the international agenda.

George H.W. Bush (left, s[...]
was elected as the enviror[...]
president, seen here signi[...]
Clean Air Act Amendme[...]
1990, looked on by Bill [...]
the first environmentali[...]
head the EPA, and [...]
secretary Admiral [...]
Watkins — future protag[...]
in an administration [...]
down the middle over [...]
warming.

William K. Reilly

British soft power: to lobby Bush to go to Rio, Prince Charles dispatched the Royal Yacht Britannia to Braz[...]
arranged for Reilly to meet Brazilian president Fernando Collor — pictured below with wife Rosana, tog[...]
with Princess Diana later in the royal couple's state visit.

AP/Press Association Images

1992 Rio Earth Summit was an election year political disaster for the Bush administration. A paper written Reilly suggesting concessions to enable the US to sign the Biodiversity Convention was leaked mid summit, e Al Gore (seen above left with Reilly at Rio) and other leading Democrats openly attacked the administration.

William K. Reilly

...netheless, the United Nations Framework Convention on Climate Change that Bush (below) signed in Rio 3rd June 1992 remains the only global warming treaty ratified by the United States.

UN Photo

Germany's reward for undermining the US at Rio was to host the climate change convention's first Conference of the Parties (COP) in Berlin in March 1995, Chancellor Helmut Kohl (above) seen here proposing a toast to the delegates two days before the COP's successful conclusion.

AP/Press Association Images

At the beginning of the COP, Germany's environment minister, Angela Merkel (left), was elected COP president – pictured speaking at the conference's first session. The Berlin COP agreed the Berlin Mandate, which set in stone the division between North and South.

AP/Press Association Images

In October 1997, two months before Kyoto, President Clinton flew to Argentina to stand shoulder to shoulder with President Carlos Menem – seen together on the next page in Patagonia's Nahuel Huapi National Park – to seek a path around the Berlin Mandate.

William J. Clinton Presidential Library

Al Gore (above) spent only one day at the Kyoto COP in December 1997 – photographed shortly befc
detonating his bombshell instruction to the US delegation to show 'increased negotiating flexibility'.
UN Photo/Frank Leather

More than anyone else, the credit for obtaining agreement on the Kyoto Protocol belongs to Raúl
Estrada-Oyuela (below), the Argentine diplomat who presided over the climate change negotiations
and delivered the Berlin Mandate.

UN Photo/Frank Leather

2007 turned out to be the hottest year for the politics of global warming, when Al Gore together with the IPCC were awarded the Nobel Peace Prize (left to right: Dahe Qin, Sir John Houghton, Susan Solomon and Bob Watson).

Sir John Houghton

The year climaxed in December at Bali, but the strain told on the UN convention secretary Yvo de Boer (left), with UN secretary-general Ban Ki-moon and Indonesian president Susilo Bambang Yudhoyono looking on.

epa/Mast Irham

Glum faces at the December 2009 Copenhagen COP as the reality of failure dawns on Western lead (above, left to right: EU Commission President Jose Manuel Barroso, Germany's Angela Merkel, Swed premier Fredrik Reinfeldt, France's Nicolas Sarkozy, Barack Obama of the US and Britain's Gordon Brow with India and China maintaining steadfast opposition.

DPA/Press Association Images

The real business at Copenhagen was negotiated by South Africa's president Jacob Zuma, Brazil's Lula, Obama (all pictured below left), along with Chinese premier Wen Jiabao and India's Manmohan Sir (below right) – leaving the Europeans out in the cold.

AP/Press Association Images

global agreement that involves both the developing and the developed countries.'[42] In his post-Kyoto testimony, Eizenstat told the Senate Foreign Relations Committee that the problem of global warming could not be solved unless developing countries got on board. By around 2015, China would be the largest overall emitter of greenhouse gases and by 2025 the developing world would be emitting more greenhouse gases in total than the developed world.[43] He was right, but underestimated the speed at which it was happening. China overtook the US in 2007, eight years before Eizenstat predicted, and non-Annex I emissions overtook Annex I emissions in 2008, seventeen years before Eizenstat thought they would.[44]

Administration officials believed if they could come back with a reasonable regime that included the larger developing country emitters, they would be able to get the Senate to go along with it. To succeed, they needed to breach the new Berlin wall. In retrospect, Loy believes that agreeing the Berlin Mandate was a serious mistake. Rio had got it more right, but the Berlin Mandate had hardened the structure into a bifurcated regime.[45]

Although global warming was a priority towards the end of Clinton's presidency, it wasn't at the beginning. National prosperity, social progress and the longest period of economic growth in America's history topped the list of administration accomplishments in his final State of the Union message. Like Thatcher a decade before, who had championed the environment in her last two years in Downing Street, fixing the economy was what Clinton was elected to do. If Clinton had emulated Carter, more likely than not, he would also have been a one-term president.

A *New York Times* poll published on the first day of the Kyoto conference found that sixty-five per cent of those surveyed agreed that the US should take steps to cut its emissions regardless of what other countries did. Although fifty-seven per cent of respondents said environmental improvements must be made regardless of costs, when asked of the most important problem facing America only one per cent answered the environment.[46] Voters wanted symbolism and that's what Clinton gave them.

Yet the whole policy was based on a massive illusion. Through thick and thin, developing countries stated that the developed world had to take the lead in cutting carbon dioxide emissions. If America had met its Kyoto commitments through using the Kyoto flexibility mechanisms to the hilt, all it would have shown is that the super-rich America lives by its own rules and could buy other countries' emission reductions so it didn't have to cut its own. It is hard to believe that developing countries would have viewed that as a realistic basis for their participation in a regime to cap their emissions. The Europeans too had a point, except they were sharing the consequences of the collapse of communism within the EU bubble.

Ultimately Clinton's global warming policy failed. For sure, he managed the politics superbly and pulled out every stop to secure some measure of developing country involvement. At Buenos Aires, even the experienced Eizenstat got carried away when in reality the battle was over. But the longer-term legacy of his efforts was to perpetuate a myth that Kyoto would have been viable but for five hundred and thirty-seven votes in Florida.

In this respect Clinton's predecessor left a more durable legacy by risking isolation to exclude emissions targets and timetables from the 1992 climate change convention. As Clayton Yeutter sees it, the strong economy of the 1990s would have made it impossible for the US to have complied with any probable targets and timetables that might have emerged at Rio. Reasonable Americans might have argued about this in the early 1990s, but twenty years on President Bush's decision was, in Yeutter's view, clearly the right one.[47] What might someone who served at a similar level in the Clinton White House say? The final negotiating instructions to the American delegation in Kyoto were relayed over the speaker phone in the chief of staff's office. Erskine Bowles, who held the position at the time, told me he was unable to recall his impressions of the evolution of the policy with sufficient accuracy from that long ago.[48] Silence speaks volumes.

On 6th March 2001 Chuck Hagel and three other senators wrote to Clinton's successor to clarify the new administration's position on Kyoto. A week later, President Bush wrote back: 'I oppose the Kyoto Protocol because it exempts eighty per cent of the world, including major population centres such as China and India.'[49] Only later in the month did the implications finally sink in: Bush was not submitting Kyoto to the Senate. 'The President has been unequivocal,' a White House spokesman said. 'It is not in the United States' economic best interest.'[50]

It ignited a firestorm. 'The world is tottering on the brink of climate disaster,' Friends of the Earth raged.[51] The State Department was inundated with cables reporting the dismay of foreign governments. A more measured analysis was provided by MIT economics professor Henry Jacoby, who explained that Kyoto was two different things. 'It's the current text and numbers, and it's a process,' Jacoby said. 'The numbers are no longer going to work, but the process is going to go on.'[52] Viewed like that, Bush had little choice, as Senate ratification was about giving its consent to the text and numbers in the Protocol.

The White House was taken aback by the international reaction. On the eve of his first European trip in June, Bush had a second go and began to map out the beginnings of an alternative approach. Somewhat naively, chief of staff Andy Card told reporters that other nations would come to appreciate Bush's decision. 'The emperor of Kyoto was running around the stage for a long time naked,' he said, 'and it took President Bush to say, "He doesn't have any clothes on."'[53] Only in the fable does the boy get thanked for saying so.

'Breaking up is so very hard to do if you really love him,' the Walker Brothers sang in their sixties' hit. 'Oh baby, it's so hard to do.' It wasn't for Bush. His no to Kyoto was how the new president introduced himself to the world. Breaking up wasn't hard at all. That was what probably hurt the Europeans most of all.

The Europeans should have seen it coming. They had done little to assist the Clinton administration in securing developing world participation. The result was the outcome of the logic of the decision made by COP1 in Berlin six years earlier. To keep the G77 plus China in the process, the Berlin COP made a trade-off that increased the probability of losing the US further down the track. But the view the parties took then was if they hadn't agreed to the developing world's demands, there would have been no process at all.

Columbia University's Scott Barrett has criticised the Bush rejection for lessening the chances of adoption of a more viable approach than Kyoto. 'In rejecting the treaty in the way that he did – and, crucially, in doing so without offering an alternative – President Bush only reinforced the view that Kyoto had to be the only way forward; and he only made other signatories, especially members of the European Union, *more* determined to conclude the negotiations and bring the treaty into force.'[54] No one gets criticised for blaming Bush, but the idea that the world was willing to entertain an alternative to Kyoto was for the birds.

Four months later, the suspended COP6 resumed in Bonn. When it concluded, the EU environment commissioner, Sweden's Margot Wallström, commented, 'I think something has changed today in the balance of power between the US and the EU.'[55] What actually happened was rather different.

The threshold at which the Protocol came into force had been set to accommodate American non-ratification. America's exit gave the remaining members of the Umbrella Group, especially Japan, Canada, Australia and Russia, much more leverage because they could decide whether the treaty ever came into force. Ironically the EU conceded far more to them than they had refused the US the previous November at The Hague. COP7 at Marrakesh in November 2001 doubled Russia's sink allowances from seventeen to thirty-three mega tonnes of carbon dioxide. The Japanese delegation, over eighty strong, gained a reputation for intransigence. At one point, a delegate speaking for the G77 plus China responded to Japan's request with 'you must be joking'.[56] They weren't. They too gained concessions on sinks and significantly weakened the compliance regime, a negotiating objective they shared with the Canadians and Australians.

In 2002, Canada announced that it would unilaterally claim a further thirty percent for its exports of hydro-electricity to the US, prompting the *Globe and Mail* to comment: 'If a country like Canada can claim credits in violation of the agreement and get away with it, more deceitful ways of breaking with the agreement can easily be found by other countries.'[57] Canada, a midwife of sustainable development in the 1980s, had travelled a long way in the fourteen years since the Toronto conference had called for twenty per cent emissions cuts below 1990 levels.

Kyoto ended up with a compliance regime that gave Annex I countries a free pass if they left the regime altogether (as Canada would do) and no financial or other economic penalties for staying outside it. By carrying forward excess emissions and adding an extra thirty per cent of the over-emission to the next commitment period, the compliance regime created incentives for countries to exit and incentives for everyone to forgive the overshoot to keep them inside it. Indeed, at COP16 in Cancún in December 2010, Japan confirmed it would not participate in a second commitment period of the Kyoto Protocol. For the EU and the environmental NGOs, Kyoto had become too big to fail, enabling other large Annex I countries to punch holes in Kyoto with near impunity.

Kyoto's only rationale was as a proof of concept in which the developed countries in Annex I took the first step in reducing their greenhouse gas emissions, with the rest of the world following at some unspecified point in an unspecified manner. The numbers tell their own story. In 1998, Tom Wigley, a leading climate scientist, published a paper which attempted to estimate the implications of the Protocol for the climate at the end of the twenty-first century. The analysis used the IPCC's value for climate sensitivity of carbon dioxide of 2.5°C in its Second Assessment Report. Adhering to Kyoto would, Wigley estimated, lead to a reduction in global mean temperatures of 0.08–0.28°C, depending on what happened to emissions after 2010.[58] This reduction compares to a projected 2°C rise by 2100 according to the IPCC's IS92a scenario. If fully implemented, Kyoto was estimated to delay global warming by between four and fourteen years over the course of the twenty-first century. The impact of the Kyoto reductions accrued even more slowly on sea level rise. 'The prospects for stabilising sea level over coming centuries are remote, so it is not surprising that the Protocol has such minor effects,' Wigley wrote.[59]

At one level, Kyoto could be counted a success. In 2008, reported Annex I emissions of the Protocol's six greenhouse gases were 9.6 per cent below their level in 1990. However, including methane and four other greenhouse gases, as required by the Protocol, leads to a distorted picture because different gases remain in the atmosphere for different lengths of time. Wigley found that there was no single scaling factor to convert between carbon dioxide and methane emissions.[61] A further distortion is that reported emissions also include estimates from changes in land use and forestry. In his February 1998 testimony, Eizenstat explained that changes in accounting rules meant that for the US, reducing greenhouse gas emissions by seven per cent 'is quite close to the President's original proposal to return emissions to 1990 levels by 2008–12'.[62]

Stripping out reductions from land use changes and emissions of other greenhouse gases to focus on core carbon dioxide emissions results in a quite different picture. The 9.6 per cent Annex I reduction shrinks to 2.2 per cent. If the US is excluded, reported carbon dioxide emissions fell by 1,142.7 million tonnes, or 11.6 per cent. But this reduction masks two opposing trends. The 1,142.7 million-tonne reduction comprises a fall of 1,590.1 million tonnes from the former Communist economies of Central and Eastern Europe (Economies in Transition, or EIT parties, in Protocol parlance) partially offset by a 447.4 million-tonne rise in carbon dioxide emissions from the other Annex I countries. Other than the US, the largest absolute increases came from Turkey, Australia and Canada, which all increased their emissions at a faster rate than the US (110.1 per cent, 44.1 per cent and 25.9 per cent respectively compared to 16.1 per cent for the US). Japan notched up a 6.2 per cent increase. Even Norway, which in 2008 announced its intention to become carbon neutral by 2030, increased its reported emissions by 27.0 per cent.[63]

Disaggregating the numbers produces a similar picture for the EU. The reunified Germany reported a 203.6 million-tonne fall in carbon dioxide emissions, but ninety-nine per cent of this fall was offset by increases from the four EU members that increased emissions the most: Spain, despite its colossal investments in wind and solar farms (up 109.3 million tonnes, or 47.9 per cent); Italy (up 32.3 million tonnes, 7.4 per cent); Greece (up 26.9 million tonnes, 32.4 per cent) and the Netherlands (up 16.4m tonnes, 10.3 per cent).

Sweden, Denmark and France recorded small reductions (11.0 per cent, 3.9 per cent and 0.7 per cent respectively, amounting to 10.9 million tonnes in all). Overall, the 42.3 million-tonne reduction by the non-EIT members of the EU, including Germany, was more than accounted for by the UK's 54.4 million-tonne fall, stemming principally from its dash-to-gas.[64] The EU's reputation had been saved by UK electricity privatisation.

Overall, the collapse of communism has been by far and away the single biggest factor in delivering the Kyoto emissions reductions – a truly one-off, epochal event. But these reductions have been swamped by the dramatic economic growth of the developing world. Wigley's study indicated that Kyoto would shave 0.08–0.28°C off a two-degree rise over the current century. A joint IEA / OECD 2009 study found that global carbon dioxide emissions were rising much faster than Wigley had assumed. Such an emissions growth trend would be in line with the IPCC's worst case scenario in its 2007 Fourth Assessment Report, which projects average world temperatures rising by between 2.4°C to 6.4°C by 2100.[65] Taking the midpoint of this rise would imply Kyoto delaying global warming by between twenty-two months and a little over six years over the course of this century.

Not that miracles don't happen. COP7 at Marrakesh agreed to permit Kazakhstan to become an Annex I party to the Protocol, but not to the convention. Because it had made no declaration when the Protocol was adopted, Kazakhstan does not have an emissions target listed – and no hot air to sell.[66] Like the soul of an unbaptised infant in Catholic theology, Kazakhstan exists in a special state of climate change limbo all on its own.

20
TURNING UP THE HEAT

The scientists tell us the 1990s were the hottest decade of the entire millennium.

President Clinton, Address before a Joint Session of the Congress on the State of the Union, 27th January 2000

In holding scientific research and discovery in respect, as we should, we must also be alert to the equal and opposite danger that public policy could itself become the captive of a scientific-technological elite.

President Eisenhower, Farewell Address, 17th January 1961

Climatically, Kyoto was nigh on perfectly timed. According to one widely used global temperature series, February 1998 recorded the highest ever average global temperature in the instrumental record. 1998 was the warmest year so recorded.[1]

The revised HadCRUT3 temperature series records a rise of slightly less than half a degree centigrade (0.496°C) from 1900 to 2000. Average observed temperature rose by 0.346°C from 1900 to 1944. Then, for almost a third of century, recorded average temperatures fell; the HadCRUT3 value for 1976 is actually lower than for 1900. It then rose by 0.526°C to 2000.

Put another way, over one hundred per cent of the recorded increase in average global temperature in the twentieth century occurred in its last quarter.

So perhaps it's not surprising that alarm about global warming rose through the 1990s. Nonetheless, the multi-decadal fall in temperatures before 1976 required some kind of explanation, particularly to bolster the credibility of computer predictions of future temperature increase.

The IPCC sought to provide an answer to this conundrum in its Second Assessment Report. Doing so was important. If the climate models cited by the IPCC were unable to reproduce the broad outlines of the changes in global average temperatures, why should governments place much confidence in their ability to predict the future? Just because computer models could reproduce passable versions of the twentieth-century temperature record does not mean they will accurately foretell the future. But if they couldn't reproduce the past, why should anyone have faith in them?

The Second Assessment Report claimed to have solved the puzzle. Including an assumption about the effects of sulphate aerosols enabled computer models to account for the thirty-year decline in observed temperatures from around 1944.[2] It also implied a higher value for the climate sensitivity of carbon dioxide. Computer simulations without aerosol forcing produced a best fit of a 1.5°C rise from a doubling of carbon dioxide in the atmosphere. Including sulphate aerosols resulted in the 4.5°C assumption providing the best fit.[3]

How can we be sure that the assumption about sulphate aerosols wasn't a case of adding epicycles? The Working Group I report recognised some shortcomings in knowledge. While there was a body of observations on aerosols, 'The sensitivity of the optical properties to the size distribution of the particles, as well as to their chemical composition, made it difficult to relate the aerosol forcing in a simple manner.'[4] Additionally the global impact of aerosols on the thickness and extent of cloud cover was 'recognised but could not be quantified'.[5]

There was a larger issue the report was silent on – the validity of relying on computer models. From the Second Assessment Report onwards, the IPCC used the same language to describe computer model results as for empirical evidence derived from experiments on nature – 'experiments with GCMs' (general circulation models); 'model experiments'; 'recent multi-century model experiments'; 'this hypothesis [dismissing the suppression of the greenhouse gas signature being masked by sulphate aerosols] is not supported by recent GCM experiments'.[6] Computer models thus attained an independent reality in the minds of climate scientists.

The Second Assessment Report noted that GCMs had to be calibrated by introducing systematic 'flux adjustments' to compensate for model errors.[7] In a post-Kyoto analysis, three distinguished MIT professors wrote that computer models were based on incomplete knowledge about the key factors that influence climate. 'Today's climate models cannot reproduce the succession of ice ages and warm periods over the last two hundred and fifty thousand years, let alone the smaller climatic fluctuations observed over the last century.'[8] Canadian mathematician Christopher Essex has described climate models as intricate pastiches to artfully simulate climatological phenomena in the absence of a comprehensive physical theory. Essex argued that climate models' dependence on *ad hoc* constructions, known as parameterisations, meant that climate models could only represent the current climate regime where these *ad hoc* invariants hold.[9] Their values cannot be empirically validated for climate which had not happened.

A further challenge in trying to detect human impact on the climate was trying to define the envelope of natural variability, a problem that the climatologist Hubert Lamb believed to be practically insoluble. On the basis that natural variability plus anthropogenic forcing equals the instrumental record, the Second Assessment Report recounts naive attempts by climate scientists to calculate a value for natural variability by subtracting the assumed temperature changes in response to greenhouse gas forcing. To work out by how much extra carbon dioxide would warm the atmosphere, you need to know the amount of natural variability. To work out the amount of natural variability, you need to know by how much higher levels of carbon dioxide have been warming the atmosphere. As the IPCC noted, deriving an estimate for natural variability this way 'depends critically' on the accuracy of the models' assumption of the climate sensitivity of carbon dioxide and other greenhouse gases.[10] The exercise risked toppling down the vortex of a circular argument.

In the absence of empirical data to fill critical assumptions, treating computer model results as *de facto* experimental evidence indicated a collective IPCC mindset that risked loss of contact with reality. After the IPCC Fourth Assessment Report, Bert Bolin wrote of new results from a 'much richer set of experiments with global climate models'.[11] Commenting on a critical analysis by dissenting scientists, Bolin wrote: 'The statement in their report that "computer simulations … can never be decisive as supporting evidence" is of course formally correct.' Relying on them was justified because the IPCC's conclusions were 'still very plausible, being based on the wide variety of model experiments'.[12]

This sort of thinking was something that shocked Professor Michael Kelly, a Cambridge University physicist and panellist in one of the 2010 Climategate investigations into the University of East Anglia's Climatic Research Unit. 'I take real exception to having simulation runs described as experiments (without at least the qualification of "computer" experiments),' he emailed a colleague:

> It does a disservice to centuries of real experimentation and allows simulations output to be considered as real data. This last is a very serious matter, as it can lead to the idea that 'real data' might be wrong simply because it disagrees with the models! That is turning centuries of science on its head.[13]

The question the world most wanted the IPCC to answer was also the most difficult to give an unambiguous response: Were humans warming the planet and, if they were, by how much? The issue was covered in Chapter Eight of the Working Group I report. Statements on whether man-made global warming was actually happening are 'inherently probabilistic in nature. They do not have simple "yes-or-no" answers'.[14]

This should matter less for politicians than scientists, the IPCC suggested. A distinction should be drawn, the report argued, between 'practically meaningful' i.e., what policy should be based on, and what was 'statistically unambiguous attribution' to scientists.

> While a scientist might require decades in order to reduce the risk of making an erroneous decision on climate change attribution to an acceptably low level (say one-five per cent), a policymaker must often make decisions without the benefit of waiting decades for near statistical certainty.[15]

The report also sought to pre-empt counter-arguments based on scientific uncertainty.

> The gradual emergence of an anthropogenic climate signal from the background noise of natural variability guarantees that any initial pronouncement that a change in the climate has been detected and attributed to specific causes will be questioned by some scientists.[16]

The answer to the difficult question of when detection and attribution of human-induced climate change was likely to occur 'must be subjective'.[17]

Discussion on the Second Assessment Report's top-line conclusion took a day and a half. Two of the Chapter Eight lead authors, Ben Santer and Tom Wigley, argued for a formulation saying that the balance of evidence pointed to an 'appreciable human influence' on global climate.[18] As chair, Bolin proposed 'discernible' instead of 'appreciable'.

> There were no objections to this proposal which better emphasised the uncertainty. Even though the precise meaning of the word 'discernible' was still somewhat unclear, to my mind it expressed considerable uncertainty as well as the common view that it was impossible to provide a more precise measure.[19]

Interviewed during the Kyoto conference, Bolin went further. Global warming was not something 'which you can prove', going on to say: 'You try to collect evidence and thereby a picture emerges.'[20]

When published in June 1996, the Second Assessment Report ignited a row about the final text of Chapter Eight of the Working Group I report.

Frederick Seitz, one of America's foremost physicists and a former president of the National Academy of Sciences, wrote in the *Wall Street Journal* that in more than sixty years as a member of the American scientific community, he had never witnessed a 'more disturbing corruption of the peer-review process'. After an IPCC meeting in Madrid the previous November, Seitz claimed that more than fifteen sections of Chapter Eight had been changed or deleted, including the sentence: 'None of the studies above has shown clear evidence that we can attribute the observed [climate] changes to the specific cause of increases in greenhouse gases.'[21]

Santer, as lead author of the Chapter, replied two weeks later in a letter co-signed with forty other scientists. They denied any procedural impropriety but admitted the draft had been changed at the behest of governments. 'The changes made after the Madrid meeting were in response to written review comments received in October and November 1995 from governments,' as well as from individual scientists and NGOs. Conceding that deletions had been made, the letter implied that they didn't matter: 'The basic content of these particular sentences has not been deleted.'[22] If so, why did the government reviewers insist on changing the text?

It is easy to see why the changes were politically necessary. The IPCC's headline claim to have detected a discernible human influence on global climate would have been hard to square with the statement that no study had shown clear evidence that changes in the climate could be attributed to increases in greenhouse gases. A deputy assistant secretary at the US State Department, Day Mount, wrote to Sir John Houghton, chairman of the IPCC Working Group I, on 15th November: 'It is essential … that chapter authors be prevailed upon to modify their text in an appropriate manner following discussion in Madrid.'[23]

Santer and his fellow scientists were correct in suggesting that acceding to political pressure conformed to IPCC principles and procedures. In addition to nominating lead authors, governments effectively had the final say on what the IPCC published. Bolin had drafted the principles and procedures adopted by the IPCC in June 1993 for the Second Assessment Report. 'Review is an essential part of the IPCC process,' they stated. 'Since the IPCC is an intergovernmental body, review of IPCC documents should involve both peer review by experts and review by governments.'[24] Advertised as summarising scientific knowledge, these procedures made IPCC reports politico-scientific documents in which scientific integrity took second place to political expediency in global warming's hierarchy of needs.

This was made clear in a 1997 article co-authored by Stephen Schneider, who regularly acted as a spear-carrier for the global warming consensus. The Second Assessment Report, he wrote, 'was fraught with political significance' because it was published shortly before COP2 in Geneva at which the Clinton administration announced its support for binding emissions targets.[25] Rejecting the implication that rules had been broken, Schneider conceded that Seitz's attack had 'demonstrated that a hybrid science/policy organisation like the IPCC needs better, more explicit rules of procedure'.[26]

Addressing the scientific issues underlying Seitz's criticism, Schneider agreed with long-time critics such as Pat Michaels that direct observational evidence of global warming effects were not well-matched to climate predictions of one degree Celsius compared to the half degree observed in the twentieth century.[27] While critics put the rise down to natural variability, doing so without characterising the probability was, Schneider asserted, 'a scientifically meaningless claim'. This is an odd position, as the 'null hypothesis', one where there is no statistical relationship between two phenomena, does not need to be explained. Odd, too, is Schneider's criticism, given Bolin's choice of 'discernible' to describe human influence on the global climate *because* of its imprecision. Schneider's reasoning implies that the IPCC's conclusion is also scientifically meaningless.

What, Schneider asked, is the probability that a half-degree warming trend was a natural accident? The answer could not be found in the thermometer record alone as it only stretched back a century. Doing so would be like trying to determine the probability of 'heads' by flipping a coin once. Climate scientists had to look at proxy records of climate change such as tree ring widths, deposits left by glaciers and ice cores. The proxy records, Schneider thought, suggested that a half-degree Celsius warming was not unprecedented, but neither was it common. 'In my judgement,' Schneider wrote, 'this circumstantial evidence implies that a global surface warming of half a degree has about an eighty to ninety per cent likelihood of *not* being caused by the natural variability of the system.'[28]

It was a bold claim. At a National Academy of Sciences hearing nine years later, a group of paleo-climatologists were asked by a member of the panel whether the science was such that they could determine the average century-scale temperature one thousand years ago within half a degree Celsius. Every presenter said 'no' — apart from one, who claimed to know the average century-scale temperature one millennia ago to within 0.2^{0}C.[29]

Schneider's probability claim underlines the importance of the pre-thermometer climate record in estimating the probability of whether mankind was causing the planet to warm which, he believed, computer models by themselves could not. It is also important in the history of the evolution of the scientific consensus on global warming. Before the scientific consensus claimed that the pre-thermometer record was unimportant when it had become discredited, it had claimed it was important.

Until the IPCC turned its attention to the pre-thermometer climate record, the widely accepted view was of considerable climatic variability, with a Medieval Warm Period starting around the turn of the first millennium, followed by falling temperatures and a Little Ice Age in the seventeenth century, followed by an erratic warming interspersed by reversions to colder conditions before a warming in the twentieth century.

Hubert Lamb believed that the Medieval Warm Period, which was well documented in Europe, extended across the northern hemisphere. Lamb cited a Viking report of a cousin of Erik the Red swimming two miles across a fjord in Greenland, deducing that water temperatures were at least four degrees Celsius warmer than in the second half of the twentieth century.[30] Tree ring records from California indicated, in Lamb's words, a sharp maximum of warmth, much as in Europe, between 1100 and 1300.[31]

Warmer temperatures at more northerly latitudes coincided with a 'moisture optimum' in the Lake Chad basin, with a maximum occurrence of the pollen of monsoon zone flora. Population estimates for the Indian sub-continent also suggested sequences that roughly paralleled temperature trends in higher latitudes, falling temperatures there being mirrored in population declines in the sub-continent, Lamb thought.[32]

The IPCC's re-writing of the pre-thermometer climate record began in the Second Assessment Report. 'Based on the incomplete evidence available, it is unlikely that global mean temperatures have varied by more than 1°C in a century' since the end of the transition from the last ice age.[33] At that stage, revisionism was sporadic. The report also presented evidence that conflicted with this, supporting the views Lamb had expressed in his last book. Recent evidence from ice cores drilled through the Greenland ice sheet indicated that 'changes in climate may often have been quite rapid and large, and not associated with any known external forcings'.[34] It also contained a warning that turned out to be prescient: 'Because the high quality of much-needed long-time series of observations is often compromised, special care is required in interpretation,' a warning the authors of the Third Assessment Report should have heeded.[35]

In 1995, David Deming of the University of Oklahoma published a study inferring temperature records from boreholes which suggested North America had warmed somewhat since 1850.[36] As Deming later recalled, it gave him credibility within the community of scientists working on climate change. A major person working in the area emailed him: 'We have to get rid of the Medieval Warm Period.'[37]

Fred Pearce, the British environmental journalist and author, discovered in 1996 that Tim Barnett of San Diego's Scripps Institution of Oceanography had teamed up with Phil Jones of University of East Anglia's Climatic Research Unit to form a small group to mine paleo-climate records for signs of global warming and to summarise their research in the IPCC's next assessment report. 'What we hope is that the current patterns of temperature change prove distinctive, quite different from the patterns of natural variability in the past,' Barnett told Pearce.[38]

How could people be persuaded to believe that current temperatures were unnaturally high, when it was it widely believed that temperatures had been higher several centuries before the start of the Industrial Revolution?

There was a way.

In 1912, fragments of the lower jaw of an orangutan, a human skull and a chimpanzee tooth were recovered from a quarry in the south-east of England. The bones, which had been stained with iron solution and acid, were taken to the British Museum. Man's evolutionary missing link had been found. In the teeth of entrenched opposition from the paleontological establishment, an anatomist correctly identified Piltdown Man as a hoax, a finding which took a further thirty years to be definitively accepted.

Tree rings from high altitude bristle cone pines would supply the raw evidence. In 1998, a paper written by a post-doctoral academic, Michael Mann, together with Raymond Bradley and Malcolm Hughes, based on Mann's Ph.D. thesis, was published in *Nature*. It presented a new temperature reconstruction of the Northern Hemisphere going back six hundred years to 1400. The following year Mann (the sole expert who said that he could know the average global temperature to within 0.2°C) and his co-authors published a second paper, extending the series a further four hundred years to 1000.

The picture it presented was of a stable climatic regime for the northern hemisphere, which lasted nine centuries, followed by unprecedented variability in the twentieth century, with the final decade averaging warmer temperatures than any time in the previous nine hundred and ninety years. The Medieval Warm Period had disappeared along with the Little Ice Age. The chart showed a long smooth line of low temperature variability trending downwards – in a 2007 Australian radio interview, Hughes claimed that the late nineteenth century was 'one of the coolest, if not the coolest of the last several thousand years' – followed by a sharp upward movement from around the beginning of the twentieth century.[39]

The Hockey Stick gave the strong impression that the twentieth-century warming was anomalous. Equally the Medieval Warm Period and the Little Ice Age no longer needed to be explained or put within the envelope of natural variability because now they hadn't happened. If Mann's reconstruction was robust, it would help answer Lamb's objection of the impossibility of defining a figure for natural variability and enable the IPCC to move decisively beyond the equivocal conclusion of the First Assessment Report – that the observed warming in the twentieth century had been within the bounds of natural variability.[40]

There was one problem. It was too good to be true.

The series of tree rings which generated the hockey stick shape had been selected by a researcher, Donald Graybill, for an earlier study into the possible effects of carbon dioxide fertilisation. Graybill selected samples from bristlecone and closely related foxtail pines in the western United States for 'cambial dieback', where the bark had died around most of the circumference of the tree. Graybill and fellow researcher Sherwood Idso reported anomalously high twentieth-century growth for these compared to full bark trees unrelated to temperature data from nearby weather stations, a fact known to Mann and his co-authors.[41] Self-evidently they would make highly unreliable temperature proxies.

Their inclusion by Mann and his associates in their multi-proxy temperature reconstruction needed an additional step. To put measurements from different proxy series on a common basis to be statistically analysed, the data are standardised using a mean and standard deviation of the whole timespan of the series. At an early stage in the computational sequence, Mann used an algorithm derived from only the post-1901 portion of the data.[42] The effect was similar to having a Google search algorithm to give hockey stick-shaped series the highest ranking in the analysis.

Did Mann know what he was doing?

He had graduated from Berkeley with a degree in applied mathematics and physics in 1989. Adopting this non-conventional approach to standardising proxy data would have required a conscious decision. To get the hockey stick from the data, Mann needed both the algorithm and Graybill's tree ring data.

Even if the algorithm had been selected erroneously, Mann had reason to know that producing a hockey stick depended on using the anomalous bristlecone ring series. Inside his directory of North American proxy data,

Mann had a folder, BACKTO_1400-CENSORED, containing the North American data excluding all sixteen of Graybill's series from the North American data. When the numbers from the CENSORED folder were run, the hockey stick disappeared.[43] If Mann hadn't realised that his algorithm searched for hockey sticks, removing the Graybill series should have alerted him to the flaw in his method and meant that Mann's public claims of robustness for the Hockey Stick were contradicted by what he'd found but buried in his CENSORED folder.

In 1998, Mann was nominated a lead author of the critical Chapter Two ('Observed Climate Variability and Change') of the Working Group I contribution to the Third Assessment Report, a signal achievement for someone only awarded his Ph.D. that year. The following year, he was appointed assistant professor at the University of Virginia. In 2000, the Hockey Stick got the highest possible political endorsement. In his final State of the Union message, President Clinton told Americans that the 1990s were the hottest decade of the entire millennium. Two years later, *Scientific American* named Mann one of fifty leading visionaries in science and technology.

Mann and his Hockey Stick didn't have the entire field to himself. Competition came from Keith Briffa of the University of East Anglia's Climatic Research Unit, who published a proxy temperature reconstruction within a couple of months of Mann's first effort. Thanks to the Climategate emails released on the internet in November 2009, we now know how much tension this caused and the way the IPCC process resolved the issue in favour of Mann's Hockey Stick.

Briffa wrote a paper for *Science* comparing the two temperature reconstructions. After he'd sent a draft to Mann, in April 1999 Mann contacted the *Science* editor. 'Better that nothing appear, than something unacceptable to us,' he emailed, copying in Raymond Bradley, Mann's co-author. Privately, Bradley immediately dissociated himself from Mann's remarks. 'As though we are the gatekeepers of all that is acceptable in the world of paleoclimatology seems amazingly arrogant,' Bradley emailed Briffa.[44]

After Briffa's paper was published, Mann tried to patch things up. 'Thanks for all the hard work,' he emailed colleagues in May.[45] The sentiment didn't go down well with Bradley. 'Excuse me while I puke,' Bradley emailed Briffa.[46]

John Christy, who was also a Chapter Two lead author, recalled that the Hockey Stick featured prominently in IPCC meetings from 1999, telling the House Science, Space and Technology Committee in March 2011:

those not familiar with issues regarding reconstructions of this type (and even many who should have been) were truly enamoured by its depiction of temperature and sincerely wanted to believe it was the truth. Scepticism was virtually non-existent.[47]

When the chapter lead authors met in Tanzania at the beginning of September, they were shown Mann's Hockey Stick and Briffa's reconstruction, which showed a sharp cooling trend after 1960.[48] The decline was more than a presentational problem. If tree ring growth declined when temperatures rose, what could be reliably inferred from them? And if the tree rings hadn't responded to warming in the second half of the twentieth century, how could we know that they hadn't done the same thing in response to possible medieval warmth?[49]

In a follow-up email on 22nd September, IPCC coordinating author Chris Folland of the UK government's Met Office said that a proxy diagram of temperature change was a 'clear favourite' for inclusion in the summary for policymakers. However, Briffa's version 'somewhat contradicts' Mann's and 'dilutes the message rather significantly', adding: 'We want the truth. Mike [Mann] thinks it lies nearer his result (which seems in accord with what we know about worldwide mountain glaciers and, less clearly, suspect about solar variations).'[50]

The same day, Briffa emailed acknowledging the pressure to present

> a nice tidy story as regards 'apparent unprecedented warming in a thousand years or more in the proxy data' but in reality the situation is not quite so simple.[51]

Briffa said he did not believe global mean annual temperatures had cooled progressively over thousands of years:

> I contend that there is strong evidence for major changes in climate over the Holocene [the current geological epoch] (not Milankovich [climate changes induced by changes in the Earth's orbit, tilt etc.]) that require explanation and that could represent part of the current or future variability of our climate.[52]

The same day, Mann said he would be happy to add back Briffa's temperature reconstruction. Including it risked giving 'the sceptics' a field day 'casting doubt on our ability to understand the factors that influence these estimates and, thus, can undermine faith in the paleo-estimates', unless there is a comment that 'something else' was responsible for the discrepancies.[53]

Briffa hurriedly re-did his reconstruction. He sent it to Mann at the beginning of October 1999, but the new version produced a larger post-1960 decline.[54]

When the diagram was presented at the next lead author meeting in Auckland, New Zealand in February 2000, Briffa's 'disagreeable curve' was not the same any more. It had been truncated around 1960; as Christy testified in 2011, 'No one seemed to be alarmed (or in my case aware) that this had been done.'[55] And that is how the IPCC decided to present it in the Third Assessment Report, without noting the data deletion.[56]

Star billing went to Mann's Hockey Stick. A picture is worth a thousand words and the Hockey Stick appeared twice in the synthesis report, twice more in a diagram combining past and future temperature change and on the third page of the Working Group I Summary for Policy Makers.[57] The text placed the Hockey Stick into the context of progress since the Second Assessment Report. Working Group I's contribution claimed that additional data from new studies of current and paleo-climates, together with 'more rigorous evaluation of their quality', had led to greater understanding of climate change.[58] Computer models suggested that it was 'very unlikely' (a term indicating a less than ten per cent chance) that the rise in observed temperatures could be explained by internal variability alone and the thousand-year temperature reconstructions indicated that this warming was unusual and unlikely (a ten to thirty-three per cent chance) to be entirely natural.[59]

This opinion was translated to the front of the four-hundred-page synthesis report to answer the question: What is the evidence for, and causes of, changes in the Earth's climate since the pre-industrial era? 'The Earth's climate system has demonstrably changed on both global and regional scales since the pre-industrial era, with some of these changes attributable to human activities,' it stated in big, bold, blue letters.[60]

The Hockey Stick had given the IPCC more than the single coin toss Schneider said was necessary to establish the probability of whether man-made global warming was real.

21
QUIS CUSTODIET?

New analyses of proxy data for the Northern Hemisphere indicate that the increase in temperature in the twentieth century is likely to have been the largest of any century during the past one thousand years. It is also likely that, in the Northern Hemisphere, the 1990s was the warmest decade and 1998 the warmest year.

IPCC – Third Assessment Report (2001)[1]

Obfuscation, denial and a cover-up that blew spectacularly on the eve of the most important climate change negotiations since Kyoto – the events following publication of the Third Assessment Report are the most astonishing in the science of global warming. Leading scientists and science academies and societies had to decide: were they to be guardians of scientific orthodoxy or upholders of scientific standards? They could not be both.

It took four decades for the scientific establishment to accept the truth about the bones known as Piltdown Man. During that time, hundreds of scientific papers were devoted to the concoction – nearly as many as to all legitimate specimens in the fossil record put together.[2]

That episode is a corrective to what the American physicist and philosopher Thomas Kuhn described as the persistent tendency of scientists to make the history of science appear as a linear, cumulative growth of knowledge. Combined with the generally unhistorical air of science writing, the impression was created that 'science has reached its present state by a series of individual discoveries and inventions that, when gathered together, constitute the modern body of technical knowledge'.[3]

Kuhn's 1962 classic *The Structure of Scientific Revolutions* rejected this. 'Cumulative acquisition of unanticipated novelties proves to be an almost non-existent exception to the rule of scientific development,' Kuhn argued.[4] He proposed instead a succession of incompatible paradigms. Scientists develop specialised vocabulary and skills and a refinement of concepts increasingly removed from commonsense prototypes. Increased professionalisation, Kuhn thought, leads to 'an immense restriction of the scientists' vision and to a considerable resistance to paradigm change'.[5]

An established paradigm gives scientists the rules and the tools so they can focus on solving problems, elucidating and extending the paradigm, and provides a textbook framework to initiate younger scientists into the field. Scientists were not particularly adept at the kind of thinking needed to analyse a problem from first principles. 'Though many scientists talk easily and well about the particular individual hypotheses that underlie a concrete piece of current research, they are little better than laymen at characterising the established bases of their field, its legitimate problems and methods,' Kuhn wrote.[6]

The pre-revolutionary period before the breakdown of a paradigm is marked by 'pronounced professional insecurity' caused by the persistent failure of the puzzles of normal science to come out as they should.[7] Kuhn recounts examples – the scandalous state of astronomy before Copernicus, Newton's theory of light and colour, Lavoisier's demolition of the phlogiston theory of combustion, Maxwell's electro-magnetic theories replacing theories of ether in the nineteenth century, which in turn created a paradigm crisis and Einstein's special theory of relativity in 1905.

As with a political revolution forcing a choice between two antagonistic views of politics outside the normal framework of politics, so the choice between competing paradigms in science proves to be a choice between 'incompatible modes of community life', which cannot be decided by the evaluative procedures characteristic of normal science.[8] With global warming, the link between science and politics is more than an analogy – global warming is a political idea as well as a scientific one. The science provides the feedstock for a political programme; in turn, politics funds and helps propagate the science. The relationship is so deeply symbiotic that the two cannot be separated.

The risks inherent in such a situation were raised by President Eisenhower in his Farewell Address. Together with the military-industrial complex, Eisenhower identified a 'scientific-technological elite' as purveyors of miracle cures capturing government policy in warning against the recurrent temptation of believing that 'some spectacular and costly action' might offer a 'miraculous solution' to all current difficulties.[9] Eisenhower was dismayed at the extent of government funding of scientific research. 'A government contract becomes virtually a substitute for intellectual curiosity.' The solitary inventor, 'tinkering in his shop', was overshadowed by task forces of scientists. 'The prospect of domination of the nation's scholars by Federal employment, project allocations, and the power of money is ever present and is gravely to be regarded,' Eisenhower warned.[10]

Perhaps it wouldn't have surprised Eisenhower that the man who demonstrated that the Hockey Stick was wrong wasn't a scientist employed by government or a tenured university academic. In fact, he wasn't even a scientist, more the solitary tinkerer of Eisenhower's imagining.

In 2003, Stephen McIntyre was a Canadian businessman involved in financing speculative mineral prospecting with time on his hands. A prize-winning mathematician from Toronto University, McIntyre's interest in global warming had been aroused by the claim that 1998 was the warmest year of the millennium.

How could they know?

A claim by Mann's co-author Malcolm Hughes caught McIntyre's eye. Attempting to explain the 'weaker correlation' – in fact a negative correlation, with tree widths shrinking and temperatures rising after 1960 – Hughes said it meant past climate reconstructions were 'better than we thought they were'. Apparently, Hughes said, 'we underestimated the differences between the present century and past centuries'.[11] The breakdown of a correlation led climate scientists to increase their confidence in its reliability? 'I could hardly believe that this sort of thing passed as science,' McIntyre recalled seven years later.[12]

He emailed Mann asking for data sets of the one hundred and twelve proxies used in his 1998 paper. Mann replied almost immediately. He'd forgotten the exact location and would ask a colleague to follow up.[13] It turned out the data had not been archived in a single location and the time taken to retrieve it suggested that no one had checked the data before the IPCC showcased the Hockey Stick in the Third Assessment Report.

McIntyre embarked on a painstaking forensic examination of the whole data set and compared it with the original data where he could. The data were full of errors – unjustified truncations, copying of values from one series to another, unjustified filling in of missing numbers, mis-copying of some series to a year earlier and use of obsolete data.[14]

McIntyre teamed up with fellow Canadian Ross McKitrick, an environmental economist at the University of Guelph. Their first paper in September 2003 concluded that substantially improved quality control to Mann's dataset yielded a temperature index in which the late twentieth century is 'unexceptional compared to previous centuries'. The extent of the errors in Mann's work meant that indexes computed from it were 'unreliable and cannot be used for comparisons between current and past climates'.[15]

The political world began to notice. The US Senate was debating the McCain-Liebermann cap-and-trade bill. McIntyre and McKitrick did a briefing on Capitol Hill.

Replication of the Hockey Stick still eluded McIntyre. He continued to press Mann for details of his computer code. 'I am far too busy to be answering the same question over and over for you again,' Mann replied in November 2003, 'so this will be our final email exchange.'[16] Thwarted, McIntyre sifted through Mann's website for clues. He found a fragment of computer code. From it, McIntyre unlocked the algorithm Mann used to standardise the various proxy data.

It became apparent to McIntyre and McKitrick that the algorithm systematically over-weighted hockey stick-shaped series, generating hockey stick results if any happened to be present. They performed a test by running statistically trendless 'red noise', simulating data from trees subject to random climate fluctuations. In ten thousand repetitions, McIntyre and McKitrick found that a conventional standardising algorithm almost never yielded a hockey stick shape as the pre-dominant pattern. Running the same data through Mann's algorithm produced a pre-dominant hockey stick shape over ninety-nine per cent of the time.[17]

They ran the data from his CENSORED folder. Without the Graybill series, there was no hockey stick.

In January 2004, McIntyre and McKitrick submitted a paper to *Nature*, the journal that had published Mann's 1998 paper. The draft was sent to Mann for comments. The process was underway. They were given two weeks to revise and resubmit in the light of reviewer comments.

Then in March, the journal's editor Rosalind Cotter told them to cut the manuscript substantially.[18] A condensed version was submitted. Months passed. In August, Cotter emailed McIntyre to say she wouldn't publish the piece. Evidently the paper was too hot for *Nature* – its mission 'to serve scientists through prompt publication of significant advances in any branch of science, and to provide a forum for the reporting and discussion of news and issues concerning science'.[19] In the interim, it carried a *Corrigendum* to Mann's 1998 paper. 'None of these errors affect our previously published results,' it erroneously claimed.[20]

Blocked by *Nature*, McIntyre and McKitrick put the entire record of their submission, together with referee reports, on the web. A revised version was published by *Geophysical Research Letters* in February 2005. When Berkeley physicist Richard Muller read about Mann's algorithm producing hockey sticks from red noise tests, it hit him like a bombshell. 'Suddenly the hockey stick, the poster-child of the global warming community, turns out to be an artefact of poor mathematics,' Muller wrote.[21] Bert Bolin was dismissive. 'Their analysis is hardly more reliable than the one published by Mann *et al.*'[22] Bolin had picked up the wrong end of the stick. McIntyre had not claimed to have made an alternative temperature reconstruction to Mann's, only that Mann's reconstruction depended on unreliable data and statistical methods.

Seeing that a climate journal edited by Stephen Schneider was in the process of reviewing one of Mann's papers, McIntyre contacted him. Invited to become one of Mann's referees, McIntyre asked Schneider to obtain Mann's supporting calculations and source code. Phil Jones emailed Schneider pleading with him not to. It would be setting 'a VERY dangerous precedent', Jones told Schneider.[23] 'In trying to be scrupulously fair, Steve, you've opened up a whole can of worms.'[24]

Separately McIntyre had written to the National Science Foundation, which had financed Mann's work. Although Schneider agreed that data should be made available, Schneider and the NSF drew the line at computer code. For both, it was 'an intellectual property issue', as Schneider put it.[25] 'The passing of time and evolving new knowledge about Earth's climate will eventually tell the full story of changing climate,' the director of the paleo-climate programme at the National Science Foundation, David Verado, emailed in 2003, which begs the question why the taxpayer was funding the research in the first place.[26]

Asserting intellectual property rights was also popular with British climate scientists. In 2005, an Australian climatologist asked Phil Jones of the University of East Anglia's Climatic Research Unit for the underlying data used to compile its global temperature series. Jones refused. 'We have twenty-five or so years invested in the work. Why should I make the data available to you, when your aim is to try and find something wrong with it. There is IPR to consider.'[27] A British government minister blocked a Freedom of Information request on similar grounds: 'Intellectual property rights must also be considered.'[28]

Why? Are scientific data and methodologies like the recipe for Coca Cola?

Intellectual property is fundamentally different from physical property. As Alan Greenspan observed, someone's use of an idea does not make that idea unavailable to others at the same time.[29] The sole economic function in establishing intellectual property rights is to provide temporary protection from commercial exploitation by third parties, so innovation can be rewarded and incentivised.

The effect of applying the concept of intellectual property rights in pure scientific research is to attack the roots of science. 'Verification, or checking, or confirmation, is basic to every scientific enterprise, and also to every enterprise in daily life in which it is important to be sure that we are making no mistake,' Bridgman wrote in 1959. 'The meaning of truth is to be found in the operations by which truth is "verified."'[30]

Mann wasn't budging. 'These contrarians are pathetic, because there's no scientific validity to their arguments whatsoever,' he told an interviewer in the spring of 2005.[31] The controversy spilled over onto the front page of the *Wall Street Journal*, where Mann described it as a battle of 'truth versus disinformation'.[32] German climate scientist Hans von Storch, who had also produced findings that suggested Mann had underestimated past temperature variability, told the paper he had come under pressure from colleagues. There was a tendency in climate science, von Storch said, to 'use filters and make only comments that are politically correct'. A supporter of Mann claimed his critics were on 'some kind of witch hunt'.[33]

It was a meme that would spread rapidly from Mann's partisans to the scientific establishment and then to politicians, turning a cover-up into a point of high principle. 'Giving them the algorithm would be giving in to the intimidation tactics that these people are engaged in,' Mann said.[34] With this statement, Mann had thrown down the gauntlet. It was picked up by Joe Barton, the Republican chairman of the House of Representatives Committee on Energy and Commerce.

Barton decided to launch an investigation. In June, he wrote to Mann, Bradley and Hughes for details of their work, financial support and asking Mann to provide the exact computer code used to generate his results.

Quis custodiet ipsos custodes? – Who watches the watchmen?

Barton's intervention unleashed a storm. It was as if the separation of church and state had been repealed. Fellow Republican Sherwood Boehlert, chairman of the House Committee on Science, wrote to Barton, calling his investigation an illegitimate attempt to intimidate a prominent scientist. It would set a 'truly chilling' precedent. Scientific research must operate outside the political realm. 'Your enquiry seeks to erase that line between science and politics,' Boehlert wrote.[35]

Democrat Henry Waxman, chair of the Energy and Commerce Subcommittee on Health and the Environment from 1979 until 1995, wrote to Barton complaining of his 'dubious investigation', which looked like 'a transparent effort to bully and harass climate change experts' who had produced 'highly regarded research'.[36]

Scientists weighed in, too. Alan Leshner expressed the deep concern of the American Association for the Advancement of Science (AAAS). That the Hockey Stick formed part of the basis of the IPCC's conclusions was a reflection of it 'passing muster' in the IPCC peer review process, Leshner wrote.[37] Twenty scientists, including James Hansen and John Holdren (a past and future White House science adviser), also expressed their deep concern. At the same time, they began downgrading the importance of the Hockey Stick. It was not an essential element but merely 'a useful *illustration* of our understanding'.[38]

In a joint letter, the presidents of the American Geophysical Union (AGU) and the American Meteorological Society (AMS) claimed that the prospect for scientists having to defend unpopular results in the political arena could well undermine scientific progress and produce 'tainted results'.[39] The editors of *Nature* accused Barton of cherry-picking selected information on the Hockey Stick. 'Science is, by its very nature, a process open to the questioning and overthrowing of currently accepted ideas, and the detail of Mann and his colleagues' work has been debated within the climate community,' the editorial ran, without disclosing that the journal had declined to publish criticisms of Mann's work in its own pages.[40]

'My research has been subject to intensive peer review,' Mann wrote in response to Barton.[41] Leshner of the AAAS agreed. The Hockey Stick had been subject to 'multiple levels of scientific peer review' to achieve publication, then 'multiple layers of the IPCC process itself'.[42] The presidents of the AGU and AMS called on Congress to respect peer review, 'this time-tested process of scientific quality control'.[43]

The issue not mentioned was why peer review had failed to uncover even a fraction of the problems McIntyre had found. The letters from the presidents of the AAAS, the AGU and the AMS demonstrated a stunning lack of intellectual curiosity – wasn't anyone interested in getting to the bottom of the controversy and finding out for themselves?

To the British philosopher Roger Scruton, the answer would be self-evident. The strategy of inventing experts backed up by the apparatus of scholarship, research and peer review goes back to the beginnings of the modern university in the Christian and Muslim communities of the Middle Ages. Theology was their foundational discipline and an entirely phoney one:

> The purpose of theology has been to generate experts about a topic on which there are no experts, namely God. Built into every version of theology are the foregone conclusions of a faith: conclusions that are not to be questioned but only surrounded with fictitious scholarship and secured against disproof.[44]

The dispute had escalated beyond Mann and the Hockey Stick. Ultimately it was a question of trust. Should society defer to the collective wisdom of experts or withhold scientific status to statements that cannot be independently verified, the method by which science had escaped the gravitational pull of medieval scholasticism?

In his reply to Barton's letter, Mann tried to finesse the issue. The key to replication was unfettered access to all the underlying data and the methodologies. And the code, which was the only way of verifying the actual methodology he had used? 'My computer program is a private piece of intellectual property, as the National Science Foundation and its lawyers recognised.'[45]

In a sense, the person at the centre of the dispute was not Michael Mann, but Stephen McIntyre. It was McIntyre's insistence on seeing for himself how tree ring data were used to represent a temperature reconstruction that completely revised previous understanding that had led to this clash. 'Your statement that you have verified something is indifferent to me unless I believe that I could make the verification also,' Bridgman wrote.[46] Half a century on, Schneider described McIntyre as a 'serial abuser of legalistic attacks' for insisting on seeing Mann's computer code.[47] Something had happened to scientific standards in the intervening years.

Ralph Cicerone, president of the National Academy of Sciences (NAS), also wrote to Barton. A former research chemist at the Scripps Institution of Oceanography, now a seasoned Washington insider, Cicerone suggested that the National Academy of Sciences create an independent expert panel to conduct an assessment 'according to our standard rigorous study process' to assess Mann's area of research. 'Please let us know if we can help,' Cicerone offered.[48]

Barton wasn't biting. 'We can't evaluate the idea without having seen it, and maybe it's a darned fine one,' committee spokesman, Larry Neal, told the *Washington Post*, 'but an offer that says "Please just go away and leave the science to us, ahem, very intelligent professionals," is likely to get the response it deserves.'[49]

Boehlert accepted Cicerone's offer on behalf of the House Science Committee which in turn empanelled a National Research Council (NRC) chaired by Gerald North, an atmospheric physicist from Texas A&M University. North had no doubt as to the significance of the Hockey Stick. 'The planet has been cooling slowly until one hundred and twenty years ago, when, bam! It jumps up,' North told *Science* in 2000. 'We've been breaking our backs on [greenhouse] detection, but I found the one-thousand-year records more convincing than any of our detection studies.'[50]

Boehlert asked the NAS to examine three issues, specifically mentioning Mann's work, the validity of criticisms of it and whether the information needed to replicate his work had been made available.[51] Something got lost in translation. The panel's terms of reference were re-written, dropping any reference to Mann's work.

Meanwhile Barton and Ed Whitfield, chairman of the Subcommittee on Oversight and Investigations of the Energy and Commerce Committee, announced the formation of a second panel, led by Edward Wegman, a former chairman of the NAS Committee on Applied and Theoretical Statistics and a Fellow of the Royal Statistical Society, to perform an independent verification of McIntyre and McKitrick's critique of Mann's Hockey Stick papers.

In public, leading IPCC figures continued to promote the Hockey Stick. Giving evidence to a House of Lords enquiry in January 2005, Sir John Houghton, who had led Working Group I from 1988 to 2002, asserted that the increase in twentieth-century temperature had been 'phenomenal' compared with any variation over the whole millennium.[52]

Privately, some of the leading figures in the IPCC were less sure. The previous October, Tom Wigley, a lead author on the Second Assessment Report and a former director of the University of East Anglia's Climatic Research Unit, emailed Phil Jones to express his doubts. Replying, Jones certainly believed that the picture of unprecedented twentieth-century warmth was true. There was 'no way' that the Medieval Warm Period was as warm as the last twenty years had been, Jones replied. Similarly there was 'no way' a whole decade during the Little Ice Age was more than $1\,^\circ$C on a global basis cooler than the global average from 1961 to 1990.

How could he know? These claims weren't something Jones could objectively demonstrate: 'This is all gut feeling, no science, but years of experience.'[53]

In July, Houghton addressed the Senate Energy and Natural Resources Committee. On the basis of two unpublished papers by two of Mann's colleagues, Caspar Ammann and Eugene Wahl, Houghton claimed 'the assertions by McIntyre and McKitrick have been shown to be largely false'.[54] Concluding his prepared remarks, Houghton said he was optimistic that action to save the world from global warming would be taken. 'As a Christian, I believe God is committed to his creation and that we have a God-given task of being good stewards of creation – a task that we do not have to accomplish on our own because God is there to help us with it.'[55]

The reality of Cicerone's 'standard rigorous study process' turned out much as Barton expected. The NRC panel 'just kind of winged it', North told a Texas A&M seminar in 2006 – 'that's what you do in that kind of expert panel'.[56] The panel recommended strip-bark samples, i.e., Graybill's bristlecones (and foxtails) not be used as proxies in temperature reconstructions. Yet it presented four other temperature reconstructions without checking whether they also used bristlecones (they did).

At the beginning of March 2006, the panel held public hearings. One of the highlights was a presentation by paleo-climatologist Rosanne D'Arrigo. It included a mom-and-apple-pie rendition of the 'seek and ye shall find' principle, with a slide headlined 'Cherry picking'. You have to pick cherries if you want to make cherry pie, an astonished McIntyre recorded in a contemporaneous posting.[57] D'Arrigo was as good as her word. For one of her temperature reconstructions, she had used ten out of thirty-six chronologies that had been sampled, retaining only the most 'temperature-influenced' ones and binning the rest. 'If we get a good climatic story from a chronology, we write a paper using it. That is our funded mission,' D'Arrigo's co-author, Gordon Jacoby, wrote to Schneider in his capacity as editor of *Climatic Change*.[58]

Having smelled a rat, North's panel held its nose. Cherry-picking had become so endemic in paleo-climatology that the practitioners could no longer see – or smell – anything wrong with it. Jan Esper, another tree ring researcher, had written three years before that reducing the number of series could enhance a 'desired signal'. 'The ability to pick and choose which samples to use is an advantage unique to dendroclimatology,' Esper and four others wrote in a peer-reviewed paper.[59] Esper's reconstruction was one of the temperature reconstructions included in the panel's final report.

D'Arrigo wasn't finished. Like Briffa's, her temperature reconstruction had a decline during the late twentieth century. Panellist Kurt Cuffey of Berkeley picked up on it. 'Oh, that's the "Divergence Problem,"' D'Arrigo responded. Cuffey probed further. How could you rely on these proxies to register past warm periods if they weren't picking up modern warmth? The matter was being studied, D'Arrigo replied.[60]

Sitting in the audience, Richard Alley, a glaciologist at Penn State University, noticed the worried look of the panel. He urgently emailed Keith Briffa. The panel's reaction suggested that 'they now have serious doubts about tree-rings as paleo-thermometers' which Alley shared – 'at least until someone shows me why this divergence really doesn't matter'.[61]

The NRC report, published in June, was nuanced and in places surreal. The panel concluded that it could be stated 'with a high level of confidence' that the global mean surface temperature during the last few decades of the twentieth century was higher than any comparable period during the preceding four centuries.[62] It had less confidence in temperature reconstructions for the prior seven centuries back to AD 900.[63]

A technical chapter reported McIntyre and McKitrick's production of hockey sticks from trendless 'red noise' using Mann's standardisation procedures. Mann's results, the report said, were 'strongly dependent' on his statistical methodology. 'Such issues of robustness need to be taken into account in estimates of statistical uncertainties,' the report stated – the closest the NRC came to criticising Mann's methods.[64]

The panel entered a caveat about its lower confidence in the period before 1600. It had even less confidence in the Hockey Stick's headline claim that the 1990s was likely to have been the warmest decade and 1998 the warmest year in at least a millennium.[65] However, it declared that surface temperature reconstructions were no longer considered 'primary evidence'.[66] Instead climate model simulations showed that 'estimated temperature variation' in the two thousand years before the Industrial Revolution could be plausibly explained by estimated variations in solar radiation and volcanic activities.[67]

How could the panel be so sure of the reliability of these estimates? They couldn't.

Data for natural forcings such as changes in solar radiation and volcanoes came largely from the same sources as the proxy evidence for surface temperature variations.[68] 'These reconstructions are typically associated with as much uncertainty as reconstructions of surface temperature,' the report explained.[69]

The *New York Times* reported the Hockey Stick had been endorsed 'with a few reservations'.[70] Mann professed himself 'very happy'.[71] Asked about Mann and his co-authors' work, North replied, 'We roughly agree with the substance of their findings.' But Kurt Cuffey said the prominence the IPCC had given the Hockey Stick 'sent a very misleading message about how resolved this part of the scientific research was'. Statistician Peter Bloomfield commented that he'd seen 'nothing that spoke to me of any manipulation'.[72]

Cicerone penned the report's opening sentence: 'Our understanding of climate and how it has varied over time is advancing rapidly as new data are acquired and new investigative instruments and methods are employed' – a sentiment that conforms to the narrative of a linear, cumulative advance of scientific knowledge.[73] As far as the development of theories went, Kuhn argued that this view was not supported by the history of science.

Empirical evidence should be different. Previously accepted facts about the Medieval Warm Period and the Little Ice Age gave way to new facts to fit an agenda-driven science.

Three weeks after the NRC reported, Barton released the Wegman report. Its language was as sharp as the NRC's was nuanced. Mann's work was 'somewhat obscure and incomplete'. McIntyre and McKitrick's criticisms were 'valid and compelling'.[74] There was no evidence that Mann or any of the other authors in paleo-climatology studies had 'significant interactions with mainstream statisticians'.[75]

The isolation of the paleo-climate community was reinforced by a dense social network of authors and over-reliance on peer review 'which was not necessarily independent'.[76] Politicisation of their work meant that the paleo-climate community could hardly reassess their public positions without losing credibility. Mann's claim that the 1990s was the hottest decade of the millennium and that 1998 was the hottest year of the millennium 'cannot be supported by his analysis'.[77]

At a congressional subcommittee hearing on 19th July, first Wegman then North were questioned on their reports.

Barton asked North whether he disputed Wegman's conclusions or methodology. 'No, we don't. We don't disagree with their criticism. In fact, pretty much the same thing is said in our report,' North replied. This didn't mean the conclusions were false – 'It happens all the time in science,' North added.[78]

Asked for his opinion on Mann's statistical methodology, Bloomfield said that some of the choices had been 'appropriate. We had much the same misgivings about his work that was documented at much greater length by Dr Wegman.'[79]

Holed beneath the water line, the SS Hockey Stick was listing badly.

Privately, leading climate scientists recognised it had never been seaworthy. In his exchange with Jones in October 2004, Wigley said he had read McIntyre and McKitrick's paper. 'A lot of it seems valid to me. At the very least MBH [Mann, Bradley & Hughes] is a very sloppy piece of work – an opinion I have held for some time.'[80]

The public line was denial. Asked in 2005 whether it had been unwise for the IPCC to have given so much prominence to the Hockey Stick, the IPCC chair Rajendra Pachauri replied:

> No. It is no exaggeration and it doesn't contradict the rest of the IPCC assessment. Of course you can always argue about details. But we assess all the available literature, and we found the hockey stick was consistent with that.[81]

The authors of the Fourth Assessment Report continued to tiptoe away from it. In May 2006, Mann emailed Briffa. It was 'an absolute travesty' that the Hockey Stick was being relegated.[82] Both found it convenient to blame Susan Solomon, Working Group I co-chair. Briffa complained that 'much had to be removed'. He had been 'particularly unhappy' that he could not get the statement into the Summary for Policy Makers. 'I tried my best but we were basically railroaded by Susan,' Briffa wrote.[83]

Some climate scientists argued that even if the Hockey Stick failed, it didn't matter. In 2005 Stefan Rahmstorf, a partisan of Mann's at the Potsdam Institute for Climate Impact Research, wrote that even if the Hockey Stick was wrong it would 'tell us nothing about anthropogenic climate change' because it post-dated the 1995 Second Assessment Report's verdict that the balance of evidence suggested a 'discernible' human influence on the climate.[84] If so, why have any more IPCC reports?

Such revisionism needs to be set against the context of what prominent climate scientists had been saying previously. For Schneider, the one-thousand-year record did matter. Otherwise scientists could only gauge the probability that climate change in the twentieth century was natural or anthropogenic based on a single coin toss. For Gerald North, the Hockey Stick had been, bam! – the temperature jumps up.

Alternative temperatures reconstructions, telling essentially the same story, were therefore pressed into service. It was like someone was looking for sixes from rolling dice – use an algorithm that gave greater significance to series with high numbers of sixes (Mann's technique). It still left two others: pre-selecting runs that had a high number of sixes (bristlecones and foxtails were essential to most reconstructions) and through truncations and interpolations to create runs with higher numbers of sixes. According to McIntyre, 'The active ingredients in the twentieth-century anomaly remain the same old whores: bristlecones, foxtails, Yamal' – a narrow selection of tree rings from the Siberian Yamal peninsula. 'They keep trotting them out in new costumes,' McIntyre blogged in 2007.[85]

The one seen by more people than any other turned out to be a cross-dressed version, Mann's original dolled up in an entirely different set of clothes – starring in the most famous climate change movie of all time.

22
CLIMATEGATE

O, That this too too solid flesh would melt,
Thaw, and resolve itself into a dew.

Hamlet

Over Memorial Day weekend at the end of May 2006, four cinemas screened a movie.

'You look at that river gently flowing by … It's quiet. It's peaceful. And all of a sudden, it's a gear shift inside you. And it's like taking a deep breath and saying, "Oh yeah, I forgot about this."'

Cut to a lecture theatre.

'I used to be the next President of the United States.'

Pause.

Deadpan: 'I don't find that particularly funny.'

Smile.

Audience applause.[1]

A week later, *An Inconvenient Truth* moved into the top-ten grossing movies playing that weekend. By mid July, it overtook *The Da Vinci Code*. At the end of the year, it had grossed nearly $50 million and won two Oscars.[2] (Michael Moore's *Fahrenheit 9/11*, released in 2004, grossed $222 million worldwide, receiving a twenty-minute standing ovation at the Cannes Film Festival – but no Academy Awards.)[3]

An Inconvenient Truth was the cinematic sequel to *Earth in the Balance*, fusing Gore's search for the meaning of life and saving the environment. He recalls listening to Roger Revelle as a student ('I just soaked it up'); his six-year-old son's near fatal car accident ('It just changed everything for me. How should I spend my time on this Earth?'); a tobacco farming family, losing sister Nancy to lung cancer ('It's just human nature to take time to connect the dots. I know that. But I also know that there can be a day of reckoning'); the 2000 election ('a hard blow … It brought into clear focus the mission that I had been pursuing for all these years'); and the ultimate meaning of what Revelle had told him ('It's almost as if a window was opened through which the future was very clearly visible. "See that?" he said, "see that? That's the future in which you are going to live your life"').[4]

After the biopic segments, ice took up a large part of the movie.

The melting of the Greenland ice sheet could shut down the Gulf Stream and plunge Europe into an ice age. Viewers were left in the dark about when this might happen. In his 2007 book, Bert Bolin acknowledged that the rim of the Greenland ice sheet was melting faster than a few decades earlier, but snow was still accumulating over the ice sheet plateau. 'At some point, probably more than centuries into the future, a situation of no return may be reached and the ice sheet might disappear in a matter of a millennium or more.' *An Inconvenient Truth* was 'not always adequately founded in the basic scientific knowledge that is available,' Bolin wrote.[6] It created the impression that the ice ages were caused by variations in atmospheric carbon dioxide, 'which of course is wrong'.[7]

Gore visited Antarctica. The ice has stories to tell us. 'Right here is where the US Congress passed the Clean Air Act.'[8] Wrong again. Eric Steig, an isotope geologist, wrote, 'You can't see dust and aerosols at all in Antarctic cores — not with the naked eye.'[9]

Ice cores can measure the different isotopes of oxygen and figure out a 'very precise thermometer', Gore explains. 'They can count back year by year the same way a forester reads tree rings. And they constructed a thermometer of the temperature,' as a graph with a remarkable similarity to Mann's Hockey Stick flashed up on a seventy-foot digital screen. 'The so-called sceptics will sometimes say, "Oh, this whole thing is a cyclical phenomenon. There was a medieval warming period, after all,"' Gore continued. 'But compared to what's going on now, there's just no comparison.'[10]

Gore's ice core temperature graph looked like Mann's Hockey Stick because it was Mann's Hockey Stick.[11]

In February 2007, the IPCC started to release its Fourth Assessment Report. The attribution of rising temperatures to human activity was upgraded a further notch: 'Most of the observed increase in global average temperatures since the mid twentieth century is *very likely* due to the observed increase in anthropogenic GHG [greenhouse gas] concentrations' – 'very likely' meaning a higher than ninety per cent chance of being correct.[12]

In October, Gore and the IPCC were jointly awarded the 2007 Nobel Peace Prize for their role in creating 'an ever-broader informed consensus about the connection between human activities and global warming'.[13] The timing was propitious. In December, negotiators were to meet in Bali and adopt the Bali Road Map with a deadline of agreeing a follow-on deal to the Kyoto Protocol in Copenhagen in December 2009.

A month before Copenhagen, over a thousand emails to and from scientists at the UEA's Climatic Research Unit, together with three thousand other documents, found their way onto the internet. It was soon dubbed Climategate.

The origins of Climategate lay in the IPCC's attempt to quarantine the Hockey Stick without repudiating it. Doing so meant subverting IPCC principles. All parts of the IPCC assessment process, Sir John Houghton wrote in 2002

> need to be completely open and transparent. IPCC documents including early drafts and review comments have been freely and widely available – adding much to the credibility of the process and its conclusions.[14]

The aim of IPCC reports is to summarise the latest science. The IPCC was therefore duty bound to report McIntyre and McKitrick's critique of the Hockey Stick – unless they could find a more recent study that sidelined their conclusions. So that's what they set out to do.

They consulted two unpublished papers by Caspar Ammann and Eugene Wahl. After a couple of attempts, the first paper was turned down by *Geophysical Research Letters*. Stephen Schneider facilitated provisional acceptance of the second in *Climatic Change* to meet the IPCC deadline. The published (and reviewed) version had verification statistics that corroborate McIntyre and McKitrick's critique, but fell outside the IPCC's deadline. So the final IPCC text claimed McIntyre and McKitrick were unable to reproduce Mann's results (they could, using Mann's algorithm) but that Wahl and Ammann could when using Mann's original methods (without mentioning that Wahl and Ammann's published paper reported that the reconstruction failed a verification test).[15]

As an IPCC reviewer, McIntyre prodded the lead authors to show the decline on the Briffa temperature reconstruction. Don't stop in 1960 – 'then comment and deal with the "divergence problem" if you need to.'[16]

When published, the comment was there, but the decline wasn't.

After publication, McIntyre wanted to see how his comments had been handled. Rejected, still considered inappropriate to show the recent section of Briffa's reconstruction, was the editorial response.[17] The trail led back to the UK and to the Chapter Six review editor, John Mitchell of the Met Office.

On 21st June 2007, David Holland, a semi-retired engineer, submitted a Freedom of Information Act request to Department for Environment, Food and Rural Affairs (Defra), the UK government department responsible for oversight of the IPCC review records. He followed in January 2008 with requests to the Met Office.

The story Holland was told kept changing. First; Mitchell's records had been deleted; then, Mitchell's involvement in the IPCC had been in a personal capacity; finally, release of Mitchell's emails would prejudice relations between the UK and an international organisation and that the IPCC – contrary to its policy of openness and transparency – refused to waive confidentiality.[18]

In May, Holland sent Freedom of Information requests to Reading and Oxford universities and to the University of East Anglia about the change in the deadline for the Wahl and Ammann paper. Within two days, Phil Jones emailed Mann:

> Mike, Can you delete any emails you may have had with Keith re AR4 [the Fourth Assessment Report]? Keith will do likewise … Can you also email Gene [Wahl] and get him to do the same? I don't have his new email address … We will be getting Caspar to do likewise.[19]

Mann forwarded the email to Wahl, who told a Department of Commerce investigation that he 'believes he deleted the referenced emails at that time'.[20]

On the morning of 17th November 2009 someone tried to upload 160MB of data from the CRU server onto the RealClimate website. They must have had a sense of humour – RealClimate was established with a mission to fight McIntyre in the blogosphere Hockey Stick wars. Later that day, an anonymous poster, FOIA, appeared on the climate sceptic Air Vent website.

> We feel that climate science is, in the current situation, too important to be kept under wraps. We hereby release a random selection of correspondence, code, and documents.[21]

The blogosphere lit up. The mainstream media was slower, apparently queasy at publishing private emails and unsure whether they were genuine. Three days later, the University of East Anglia confirmed they were.

It is hard to conceive of a less favourable run-up to the Copenhagen climate change negotiations. The CRU's initial reaction of going to ground only made it worse. The Met Office's Vicky Pope was left branding the release of the emails 'a shallow and transparent attempt to discredit the robust science undertaken by some of the world's most respected scientists'.[22] George Monbiot in the *Guardian* thought otherwise. 'Confronted with crisis, most of the environmentalists I know have gone into denial,' Monbiot wrote.[23] 'There is a word for the apparent repeated attempts to prevent disclosure revealed in these emails: unscientific.'[24]

Two prominent climate scientists agreed. 'The whole concept of "we're the experts, trust us" has clearly gone by the wayside with these emails,' Judith Curry of Georgia's Institute of Technology, told Andrew Revkin of the *New York Times*.[25] Mike Hulme of the University of East Anglia told Revkin that 'the IPCC itself, through its structural tendency to politicise climate change science, has perhaps helped foster a more authoritarian and exclusive form of knowledge production'.[26]

The following weekend, the *Sunday Times* carried a story that the University of East Anglia had thrown away records from which the temperature reconstructions had been derived. The original numbers had been dumped to save space. Roger Pielke Jr of Colorado University discovered the loss when he asked for the original records. 'The CRU is basically saying, "Trust us,"' Pielke said.[27]

The disclosure fed speculation that the CRU had been fiddling its surface temperature reconstruction, one of the three principal ones used in climate studies derived mainly from the Global Historical Climatology Network.* There was another explanation. Proper record keeping was hardly one of the CRU's strengths. In 2002, historian James Fleming, writing a short biography of Guy Stewart Callendar, was shocked to find that Callendar's papers at the CRU hadn't been stored properly. As a result, the CRU agreed to loan the papers to Colby College, Maine, where they were organised into archive boxes.[28]

In December, the Met Office wrote to seventy scientists at British universities asking them to collect signatures for a statement to 'defend our profession against this unprecedented attack'. Over one thousand, seven hundred scientists signed.[29]

> The evidence and the science are deep and extensive. They come
> from decades of painstaking and meticulous research, by many

---

*   The Global Historical Climatology Network (GHCN) contains eight thousand series whereas the CRU only uses two thousand. Despite the importance of global warming and therefore the monitoring of temperature trends, by 2005, the GHCN sample size has fallen by over seventy-five per cent from its peak in 1975 to less than any time since 1919. Ross McKitrick, 'A Critical Review of Global Surface Temperature Data Products' (unpublished, 2010) http://papers.ssrn.com/sol3/papers.cfm?abstract_id=1653928

thousands of scientists across the world who adhere to the highest levels of professional integrity. That research has been subject to peer review and publication, providing traceability of the evidence and support for the scientific method.[30]

It all looked somewhat desperate. 'The response has been absolutely spontaneous,' Julia Slingo, the Met's chief scientist improbably claimed. An anonymous scientist spoke of being put under pressure to sign. 'The Met Office is a major employer of scientists and has long had a policy of only appointing and working with those who subscribe to their views on man-made global warming.'[31]

At the beginning of December, the University of East Anglia announced it was establishing an independent review into the CRU emails headed by Sir Muir Russell, a retired civil servant. Meanwhile the House of Commons Science and Technology Committee started an inquiry of its own. It became clear that the Met Office's December statement on behalf of the UK science community was not universal. The Royal Society of Chemistry argued that the nature of science dictated that research be transparent and robust enough to survive scrutiny. 'A lack of willingness to disseminate scientific information may infer that the scientific results or methods are not robust enough to face scrutiny, even if this conjecture is not well founded.'[32]

The Royal Statistical Society argued for publication of data. 'Science progresses as an ongoing debate and not by a series of authoritative and oracular pronouncements.'[33] Commercial exploitation was not a valid reason to withhold data. If a company is granted a patent, the details of the invention must be revealed – 'it cannot justifiably seek reimbursement for that knowledge and not make it available'.[34] All parties needed to have access to the facts. 'It is well understood, for example, that peer review cannot guarantee that what is published is "correct."'[35]

The Institute of Physics was concerned about the integrity of scientific research. The emails constituted '*prima facie* evidence of determined and co-ordinated refusals to comply with honourable scientific traditions and freedom of information law'.[36] A wider inquiry into the integrity of the scientific process in the CRU's field of research was needed, the Institute argued.

Of all the congressional and parliamentary hearings on global warming, the Science and Technology Committee's hearing on 1st March 2010 was the most important since Hansen's appearance in 1988. The inquiry had been prompted by Labour's Graham Stringer. By the time it began, it was on a compressed timetable ahead of the May 2010 general election, with a single extended hearing.[37] The hearing didn't resolve the scientific issues. Its importance was in raising a question mark over apparently settled science.

It was also Phil Jones' first public appearance since the story broke. Fleet Street's parliamentary sketch-writers reported from the packed committee room. For the *Guardian's* Simon Hoggart, Jones brought back memories of the weapons scientist David Kelly shortly before his suicide in the run-up to the Iraq war. 'The resemblance was disturbing and painful,' Hoggart wrote.[38] Jones looked 'taut, nervous, often miserable. At times his hands shook'.[39] His low spot, Hoggart thought, came when Stringer, with a Ph.D. in chemistry, asked Jones about not making data available because all they'd do is find something wrong with it. 'Yes, I have obviously written some very awful emails.'[40]

Jones' appearance hadn't been made easier by the committee's first witness. 'With the aggression of someone who used to go eyeball to eyeball with Margaret Thatcher,' Hoggart wrote that former chancellor Nigel Lawson

> spoke with dripping contempt. 'Proper scientists, scientists with integrity, wish to reveal their data and all their methods. They do not require freedom of information requests!'[41]

According to the *Telegraph's* Andrew Gimson: 'One hammer blow followed another, culminating in the crushing accusation from Lord Lawson that for the period before 1421, the scientists "relied on one single pine tree" to establish how hot the world was, "which was more than it [the pine tree] could bear."'*[42]

Professor Edward Acton, the university's vice chancellor, provided Quentin Letts with comic relief, a younger version of Professor Calculus from the Tintin books, Letts wrote in the *Daily Mail*, nodding and beaming at everything Jones said,

> his eyeballs bulged with admiration for the climate change supremo. His eyes were pulled so wide in wonderment they must have nearly

---

* It was actually worse than Lawson implied. Mann interpolated values for the first five years (1400–1404) of the Gaspé series, the only series going back to the fifteenth century because there were zero trees for this period. Stephen McIntyre & Ross McKitrick, 'Corrections to the Mann et al. (1998) Proxy Data base and Northern Hemispheric Average Temperature Series' in *Energy & Environment* Vol. 14, No. 6 (2003), Table 5.

split down the seams like banana skins. Others, watching the tremulous Professor Jones, will have been less impressed. He may be right about man-made climate change. But you do rather hope that politicians sought second, third, even twentieth opinions before swallowing his theories and trying to change the world's industrial output.[43]

More than a year later, what surprised Stringer most about the hearing was Jones' 'astonishing' admission that his temperature series wasn't reproducible. Although the data-sets remain available, the computer programs had changed. Scientists – and Jones himself – couldn't reproduce his graph.[44] 'That is just a fact of life in climate sciences,' Jones had told the committee.[45]

23
STATE OF DENIAL

Q. So you are not prepared to comment on whether the events at CRU
undermine the IPCC or not?
A. If we take Chapter Six ... This is the most robust peer review process
that you will see in any area of science.
Professor Julia Slingo, Chief Scientist, the Met Office
(1st March 2010)[1]

After the sketchwriters left, the MPs cross-questioned a trio of government scientists – Sir John Beddington, the government's chief scientific adviser, the Met Office's Julia Slingo and Bob Watson, who had moved from the White House, via the World Bank and chairing the IPCC, to Whitehall as Defra's chief scientific adviser.

Before the hearing, Beddington had sent the committee a memorandum. 'The integrity of British science is of the highest order,' he wrote. Certainly the British government had a big exposure to climate change science. Of the nineteen countries that sent and paid the fifty-one lead authors of the four key chapters of the Fourth Assessment Report, the US and the UK provided eighteen, an analysis by David Holland shows. Together they provided half the review editors and one third of the authors of the summaries for policymakers. '[The] IPCC, which has a tiny budget, is dominated by the hugely funded climate research organizations of the USA and the UK,' Holland concluded.[2]

Climategate heaved a large rock into this pond. Had it damaged the image of UK science, one MP asked?

'No, I do not think UK science has been damaged,' Beddington replied.[3]

Did the emails give him any cause for concern?

Yes. 'I think some of the wording is unfortunate.'[4]

Had the events at the CRU undermined the IPCC? Slingo told MPs they should remember that the IPCC peer review process was 'much greater than any other science ever receives'.[5]

Didn't the Hockey Stick and the fact McIntyre had been in a tiny minority give her some cause for worry about peer review, Stringer asked?

'Not at all, no,' Slingo replied. 'The controversy around the original methods of Mann *et al* has been fully addressed in the peer review literature and I think those issues are now largely resolved.'[6]

In some ways, Slingo's answer was the most extraordinary of the day. True, the Wegman report had endorsed McIntyre's critique of Mann's handling of statistics and orally Gerald North had agreed with Wegman's findings. So in that sense, Slingo was correct to have said the issue had been resolved. But the version furnished by the IPCC in the Fourth Assessment Report – the most robust peer review process in any area of science, Slingo claimed – was a falsification, being silent on Wegman, relying instead on a paper that hadn't been published, requiring a retroactive change in IPCC rules, the published and peer-reviewed version of which contained verification statistics that corroborated McIntyre.

Scientists' power in debates on global warming derives from their monopoly in the presentation of scientific matters. Underpinning the idea of global warming is that scientists should be trusted to represent the science in a balanced and objective way. At issue in this exchange was not scientific knowledge itself, but the process of documenting and agreeing it. Here, Britain's most powerful climate scientist was presenting her interpretation of a process which scientist and non-scientist alike could see was so detached from reality as to be a fairy tale.

Watson downplayed the importance of the Hockey Stick. The Third Assessment Report's hit single, '1998 – the hottest year of a thousand years', had been superseded by the not-as-catchy 'Model that heat'. 'A lot was made of the Hockey Stick, but a much more important issue is what has happened in the last half-century,' Watson told the committee.[7] The evidence for attributing cause and effect was derived from 'theoretical modelling' by trying to explain observed changes in the climate.[8]

The biggest question mark raised by Climategate was the evidence of intent to delete emails subject to a Freedom of Information request. What information did top climate scientists want to suppress, to the extent of breaking the law to do so? A cover-up had brought down President Nixon. Jones was luckier. By the time it had come to light, prosecution was time-barred.

Earlier in the session, Stringer charged that the university was attempting to dodge allegations of malpractice, in particular by deleting emails. 'It is hard to imagine a more clear-cut or cogent *prima facie* piece of evidence, is it not, and yet you have taken the opposite view?' he challenged Acton.[9] 'To my mind there is *prima facie* evidence,' Acton replied. 'Why else did I set up the Muir Russell independent review?'[10]

Russell, the former civil servant, took a different view. 'The Prime Minister doesn't want the truth, he wants something he can tell Parliament,' Yes Minister's Sir Humphrey Appleby says.[11] 'I wasn't going to put the review into the position of making the sort of quasi-judicial prosecutorial investigative judgement,' Russell told the committee in October 2010.[12] To have done so would be 'alleging that there might have been an offence, and that really wasn't the thing that my inquiry was set up to do … If we ducked or avoided, I plead guilty to that', Russell added.[13]

Russell recognised that the tactic of the Fourth Assessment Report's Chapter Six to distance the IPCC from the Hockey Stick without disowning it involved a degree of subterfuge. The second order draft of the Chapter cited Wahl and Ammann's work to refute McIntyre and McKitrick. This provoked the US government reviewer: the reference to Wahl and Ammann should be deleted; it did not comply with Working Group I deadlines and substantial changes subsequently made to the paper, including the insertion of tables of statistical verification tests, showed Mann's reconstruction had failed.[14] The comment elicited a tart response: 'Rejected – the citation is allowed under current rules.'[15] Russell took the view that the ends justified the means. 'We are trying to get to the big issue end point,' he told MPs. 'We are really just saying, be all this as it may, that the end point seems to us to be a sensible place.'[16]

Meanwhile the UEA had commissioned a second panel under Lord Oxburgh, an eminent geologist and prominent advocate of alternative energy. At the March hearing, Acton told the committee its purpose was to 'reassess the science and make sure there is nothing wrong'.[17] In October, five months after he had submitted his report, Oxburgh told the committee that what Acton had told them was 'inaccurate'.[18] Instead Oxburgh decided to focus on the honesty of the scientists and the integrity of the researchers, in doing so, taking care to tiptoe around the elephant in the room – the practice of deleting emails in response to Freedom of Information requests. Honesty was one thing, what about competence? Liberal Democrat Roger Williams pointed out that a scientist could be honest but incompetent and honest but misled. 'That is a complicated question,' Oxburgh replied.[19]

The five-page Oxburgh report, written in around three weeks, found no evidence of deliberate scientific malpractice.[20] Nor did it find anything to alter the overall results of the CRU's instrumental temperature reconstruction.[21] But Stringer found the report 'quietly devastating'.[22] It remarked on the 'inappropriate statistical tools' used by some other paleo-climatologist groups and their potential for producing misleading results, 'presumably by accident rather than design'. The potential for misleading results arising from selection bias was 'very great'. It reiterated criticisms made in the 2006 Wegman report:

> It is regrettable that so few professional statisticians have been
> involved in this work because it is fundamentally statistical. Under
> such circumstances there must be an obligation on researchers to
> document the judgemental decisions they have made so that the
> work can in principle be replicated by others.[24]

The Oxburgh report described as 'regrettable' the practice of the IPCC to
neglect to highlight the divergence issue (it had been the decision of CRU's
Briffa to underplay the divergence).[25] Muir Russell agreed, describing the
truncation as 'misleading'.[26]

By a three to one vote (Stringer being the dissenter), the House of Commons committee found no reason to challenge the scientific consensus on
global warming.[27] However it criticised the withholding of data and codes,
a practice it called problematic 'because climate science is a matter of global
importance and of public interest, and therefore the quality and transparency of the science should be irreproachable'.[28]

At a press conference, committee chair Phil Willis went further, calling it reprehensible. 'That practice needs to change and needs to change
quickly,' he said.[29] As for Jones, there was no reason why he should not
resume his post as CRU director: 'He was certainly not co-operative with
those seeking data, but that was true of all the climate scientists.'[30]

Some climate scientists spoke out against the committee's emphasis on
disclosure. Oxford University's Myles Allen said climate scientists had used
their professional judgement to distinguish between professional scientists
and activists and members of the public. 'The big implication in all this
for science is that the [FOI Act] is taking away our liberty to use our own
judgement to decide who we spend time responding to.'[31]

The committee argued that Jones had brought the FOI requests on himself by his failure to respond helpfully to data requests, which was bound
to be viewed with suspicion.[32] Had all the available raw data been available
online from an early stage, these kinds of unfortunate email exchanges
would not have occurred, the committee concluded. One of those was an
email from Mann to a colleague at the CRU in 2003 – the subject: 'Reconstruction errors':

> I'm providing these for your own personal use, since you're a trusted
> colleague. So please don't pass this along to others without checking
> w/ me first. This is the sort of 'dirty laundry' one doesn't want to
> fall into the hands of those who might potentially try to distort
> things...[34]

Jones had told the committee that the published emails represented one tenth of one per cent of his output, implying one million emails. 'Further suspicion could have been allayed by releasing all the emails,' the committee thought.[35]

After the general election, it fell to David Cameron's Coalition government to respond to the committee's report. The Climategate emails did not provide evidence to discredit evidence of global warming; the rigour and honesty of the scientists were not in doubt; the peer review process had not been subverted or the IPCC process misused.[36] Openness and transparency should be the presumption, but there were good reasons for not making data available immediately or, indeed, at all. Scientists might not be legally allowed to give out data; commercial rights should be respected; there might be 'security considerations'.[37]

The Coalition's arguments highlighted the contradictory nature of 'state science'. The advance of scientific knowledge is based on destructive challenge. Because it is always possible to achieve agreement between a theory and observational evidence, Popper argued that the supreme rule for deciding on the subsidiary rules of empirical science was specifying that they do not protect any statement in science against falsification.[38] The general attitude of promoting a search for falsifying instances was, according to the American philosopher of science John Losee, the most important in the history of science, typified by the eighteenth-century astronomer William Herschel's view that the scientist must assume the role of antagonist against his own theories, a theory's worth being proved only by its ability to withstand such attacks.[39]

Barriers preventing such attacks are barriers to science. By carving out exemptions for the publication of data and code, the government was inviting scientists to find ways of subverting Popper's supreme rule. If the government's interest had been in genuine scientific knowledge, it would have stipulated that it would only fund research based on data and methods which are freely available. That such a course would have been unthinkable for a government fully signed up to global warming illustrates the incompatibility between the presentational constraints of state science and the epistemological requirements of the real thing.

In January 2010, HRH the Prince of Wales visited the CRU. Its patron for nearly twenty years, the prince was briefed by Jones and discussed 'the appalling treatment they had endured'.[40]

The CRU's refusal to disclose data was raised during Acton's second appearance before the Science and Technology Committee. He spoke of his keenness to become an exemplar on disclosure and freedom of information. 'I want my university to be whiter than white on it,' Acton averred.[41] Even as he was speaking, Acton's university was engaged in a fourteen-month battle before the Information Commissioner to prevent Professor Jonathan Jones, a physics lecturer at Oxford University, being copied data the CRU had given Georgia Tech.

The Oxford Jones had first requested the data in July 2009. The university refused. In October an internal inquiry upheld the refusal. In December, Jones complained to the Information Commissioner which started its analysis of the case in March 2010. The UEA used every conceivable excuse – including mutually incompatible ones, such as the information was already in the public domain but disclosure might adversely affect Britain's international relations.

On 23rd June 2011 the Information Commissioner ruled that UEA had been in breach of the Freedom of Information Act. Subject to appeal, the university was given thirty-five days to comply or face the prospect of being held in contempt of court.[42]

Meanwhile, the IPCC's standing was dealt a further blow in January 2010 with media uproar about its claim, recycled from a WWF report that the Himalayan glaciers could disappear by 2035 – centuries earlier than the most pessimistic forecasts. A second claim, that fifty-five per cent of the Netherlands lay below sea level (the correct figure being twenty-six per cent), led to a storm in the Dutch media. The Dutch legislature stated that the previously accepted reliability of the IPCC was now at issue and instructed the government to carry out a review.[43]

The Netherlands Environmental Assessment Agency published a report in July. It focused on the Working Group II report on impacts. Seven of the thirty-two conclusions in the summaries could not be traced to the main report.[44] It also found that the Working Group II summary focused only on potential negative impacts of climate change, rather than presenting policymakers with a complete picture.[45]

Such was the damage to the IPCC's credibility that in March 2010 the UN secretary-general and chair of the IPCC asked the InterAcademy Council (IAC) to review IPCC procedures and management. The panel, chaired by an economist, Princeton's Harold Shapiro, delivered a carefully worded report. Scientific debates always involve controversy, Shapiro wrote, describing climate science as 'a collective learning process'.[46] In Shapiro's judgement, whether the IPCC remained 'a very valuable resource' was conditional on it highlighting 'both what we believe we know and what we believe is still unknown' – a fine-grained description of the epistemological issues at the heart of the debate on the science of global warming.[47]

The IAC also highlighted the problematic relationship between science and politics. Although scientists determined the summaries for policymakers, the final wording was negotiated with government representatives 'for clarity of message and relevance to policy'.[48] At the same time, the panel warned that 'straying into advocacy' could only harm the IPCC's credibility.[49] When chapter lead authors are sitting next to their government representatives, it could put the author in the position of either supporting a government position at odds with the working group report or opposing their government. 'This may be most awkward when authors are also government employees,' the panel suggested.[50]

The effect of dependence on government patronage for policy-driven research can be seen in Penn State's investigation into allegations of misconduct by Michael Mann following the Climategate emails. The report exonerated Mann and showered him with praise. Since 1998, Mann had received research funding from two government agencies. In a description of Mann's work and conduct on the Hockey Stick that the *Atlantic*'s Clive Crook said defied parody, both agencies had an

> exceedingly rigorous review process that represents an almost insurmountable barrier to anyone who proposes research that does not meet the highest prevailing standards, both in terms of scientific/technical quality and ethical considerations.[51]

Success in getting funding 'clearly places Dr Mann among the most respected scientists in his field'.[52] The committee found only one ground for criticism of Mann's conduct. Sharing someone else's manuscripts without their permission had been 'careless and inappropriate'.[53]

Nearly five decades after President Eisenhower had spoken of the baleful prospect of the domination of America's scholars by federal employment, the investigatory criterion used by Penn State provides evidence of his prescience. There was another consequence of taxpayer-funded science. Since James Hansen's 1988 testimony, the single individual who has had the most impact on the course of the debate on the science of global warming was not drawn from the legion of government scientists, but the solitary Stephen McIntyre.

Dissenters such as Richard Lindzen, who disagree with the consensus about the physical processes and likely effect on atmospheric temperatures of rising levels of carbon dioxide, were sidelined. Unlike them, McIntyre's disagreement was not about the physical mechanisms of global warming.

His work focused on the methodological and procedural mistakes under-pinning the findings adopted by the consensus. His demonstration that Mann's one-thousand-year temperature record was flawed forced the IPCC to change direction. Thus the 2007 Fourth Assessment Report retreated from the 2001 Third Assessment Report to a position closer to the 1995 Second Assessment Report – a shift from empirical evidence derived (by flawed means) from nature to justification based on theoretical computer modelling.

The impact of McIntyre's work in undermining public confidence in the scientific consensus was magnified by the reaction of the IPCC and the national scientific elites, particularly those in Britain and America. Rather than acknowledge there had been a problem, the IPCC embarked on a strategy of denial. So the Fourth Assessment Report was stitched up to avoid undermining the credibility of the IPCC's previous pronouncements, an exercise in which the British side took the lead.

It turned out to be a disastrous misjudgement. When the cover-up was blown open with the release of the Climategate emails, more than climate scientists' credibility was called into question. Their integrity was, too.

24
TIME'S WINGÈD CHARIOT

And yonder all before us lie
Deserts of vast eternity.

Andrew Marvell

Anyone who believes in indefinite growth of anything physical on a
physically finite planet is either a madman or an economist.

Kenneth Boulding

Time. The measurable aspects of science and civilised life of the more fundamental passage of nature, A.N. Whitehead defined it.[1]

Time Present could play tricks. 'Global warming is happening' as a statement of physical reality in the one hundredth of a second that constitutes the psychological present is not verifiable. The most that can be said is global warming *has* happened between two dates in the past.*

Time Past tripped up climate scientists, intent on re-writing climate history.

Time Future poses an insuperable problem. We cannot know it until it has happened. The expected impacts of global warming occur at a glacial speed compared to the quick march of human cohorts across the plain of terrestrial existence. The differential tempo led advocates of action on global warming to speed it up to accommodate it to humanity's timescales, the IPCC notoriously bringing forward a melting of the Himalayan glaciers by over three centuries.[2]

Ancient civilisations moved so slowly as to be barely perceptible to the modern eye. The Egypt of the Pharaohs lasted around twenty-six centuries. In one hundred and twenty paces, the British Museum's Egypt gallery traverses more than two thousand years of artefacts bearing the stamp of a way of life that barely changed over centuries and millennia.

Adjacent galleries portray the explosive growth of a younger civilisation. Ancient Greece developed from its archaic to its classical period in a couple of centuries. Small, unstable city states, dialogue with other cultures and a culture that prized innovation gave Greek civilisation a dynamism

---

* It is not possible to verify whether the global temperature anomaly now is higher or lower than it was one hundredth of a second before. By contrast, the velocity of a moving object can be determined now, a concept that defeated the ancient Greeks but was solved by Galileo.

that made it impossible to know where it was going next. The accuracy of long-range forecasts – or prophecy as it was once called – depends on the assumption that societies don't change; a valid assumption in the case of the Egypt of the Pharaohs but invalid for ancient Greece, or our own.

It fell to economists to systematically bring together the geophysical and human timescales. In doing so, they risked the mockery of nature and of future generations because it depends on assumptions of determinism and causality for the global climate system and the development of human civilisation.

'Time is the ultimate constraint on mortals,' British economist Charles Goodhart has written.[3] 'If time were unlimited and costless, wealth could always be augmented by more work.'[4]

Time is money. It plays a central role in the Austrian school of economics' theory of capital. The time from production of intermediate goods to the final sale to a consumer is a factor that accumulates in the cost schedule of consumer goods. It's a small step from this nineteenth-century insight to valuing capital investments as a discounted stream of expected returns underpinning modern financial theory as a way of recognising the cost of time.

The practical consequences of not including the value of time can be seen in the economies of the pre-1990 Soviet bloc. As disciples of Marx's labour theory of value, capital had no value other than the labour embodied in it. Time was excluded. As a result, communist economies squandered capital on a colossal scale, destroying their economies in the process.

The middle years of the first decade of the twenty-first century saw concern about global warming reach a fever pitch. Participants at the January 2007 Davos World Economic Forum voted climate change the issue with the greatest global impact in the coming years.

Twenty months later, Lehman Brothers filed for bankruptcy. The world was condemned to a different future. 'A fall in the pit, a gain in your wit,' China's premier Wen Jiabao told the 2009 Davos Forum, 'Shaping the Post-Crisis World'.[5]

Why had none of you predicted it, the Queen asked an economist in 2009? Like natural scientists, economists are – or were – believed to be gifted with special powers to pierce through the inscrutable character of the future. Unlike them, economists have a reputation for arguing with each other. Whereas the history of the natural sciences is characterised by successions of dominant paradigms, economics is typified by clashing schools – classical economists against Keynesians, neo-Keynesian against neo-classical schools, Austrians and Marxists and neo-Marxists.

Schumpeter explained why he thought economists were so disputatious compared to scientists. Arguing was endemic in economics. 'Nature harbours secrets into which it is exciting to probe; economic life is the sum total of the most common and drab experiences,' he wrote. 'Social problems interest the scholarly mind primarily from a philosophical and political standpoint.'[6] An economist needed to have a vision designed to give expression to certain facts of the world in which we live and different visions give rise to different interpretations of economic processes. Keynes was the pre-eminent example, a vision derived from the special characteristics of England's 'ageing capitalism' as seen by an English intellectual, Schumpeter thought.[7]

British-born economist Kenneth Boulding had vision in abundance. Economics was too narrow to understand what it was trying to describe, Boulding, the founder of evolutionary economics, argued. What was needed was an approach that unified natural and social sciences: systems science or systems analysis. Boulding's brilliance was recognised by Keynes, who published a paper of his in 1931, when Boulding graduated from Oxford. Boulding then settled in the US. In 1949, he became the second winner of the American Economic Association Bates Medal awarded to the most distinguished young economist, the first being Paul Samuelson and Milton Friedman the third.

With his white shoulder-length hair and Liverpudlian accent, Boulding became something of a visionary and guru in later life. 'Does man have any responsibility for the preservation of a decent balance in nature, for the preservation of rare species, or even for the indefinite continuance of his race?' he asked four years before *Silent Spring* popularised ecological issues.[8] A committed pacifist, in 1965 Boulding helped organise the first anti-Vietnam War teach-in. The following year, Boulding was the star at a Resources For Freedom forum in Washington, DC, when he picked up Adalai Stevenson's Spaceship Earth and spoke of the open 'cowboy economy', and the closed economy of the spaceman.[9] 'The shadow of the future spaceship, indeed, is already falling over our spendthrift merriment,' Boulding warned. 'Oddly enough, it seems to be in pollution rather than exhaustion that the problem is first becoming salient.'[10]

This raised a further question. Why conserve, Boulding asked? What has posterity ever done for me? Unless the individual identified with some inter-generational community, 'conservation is obviously "irrational"'.[11] Even if it were conceded that posterity is relevant to present problems, 'we still face the question of time-discounting' – that is, the price put on the value of time, 'and the closely related question of uncertainty discount-ing'.[12] It could be argued that the ethical thing to do is not to discount the future at all – this would be the approach taken by the British government's Stern Review forty years later – that putting a cost on time was 'mainly the result of myopia' and was 'an illusion which the moral man should not tolerate'.[13]

Such reasoning did not satisfy Boulding. Time-discounting might be 'a very popular illusion' but it had to be taken into consideration in the formulation of policies.[14] So conservationist policies almost always had to be sold under some other pretext which seemed more pressing, Boulding told the forum.[15]

Of recent economists, Yale's William Nordhaus – 'about the most rea-sonable person I know', according to fellow economist Jeffrey Sachs – has the longest professional interest in the economics of global warming.[16] As the first environmental wave was cresting in the early 1970s, Nordhaus wrote an eviscerating critique of Jay W. Forrester's 'World Dynamics' mod-el used in the Club of Rome's *The Limits to Growth*. 'Can we treat seri-ously Forrester's (or anybody's) predictions in economics and social science for the next one hundred and thirty years?' Nordhaus asked in his review, 'Measurement without Data'.[17] Forrester's lack of humility in predicting the future was not warranted when placed beside economists of great stat-ure who had also got the future badly wrong, Nordhaus wrote. Marx had predicted the immiserisation of the working class under capitalism; Keynes guessed that capital would have no net productivity in 1973; Galbraith, that scarcity was obsolete. 'And now, without the scarcest reference to eco-nomic or empirical data, Forrester predicts that the world's standard of living will peak in 1990 and then decline. *Sic transit Gloria*.'[18]

In 1979, Nordhaus was one of the first professional economists to raise the issue of global warming. There was 'widespread evidence' that combus-tion of fossil fuels, in causing the build-up of atmospheric carbon dioxide, 'will be the first man-made environmental problem of global significance'.[19] But the conclusions he drew were tentative and circumspect. Climatolo-gists thought that a 0.6°C rise over the previous hundred years had led to major, but not catastrophic, results. Such temperature changes were 'rather trivial', according to Nordhaus. 'Mean temperature changes of this size are not economically significant.'[20] He qualified his recommendation about the desirability of policies to slow down the consumption of fossil fuels as *deeply unsatisfactory, from both an empirical and a theoretical point of view.* I am not certain that I have even judged the direction in the desired movement in carbon dioxide correctly, to say nothing of the absolute levels.'[21]

Nordhaus also grappled with the problem of future time. In a 2007 paper, he challenged economists' assumption that generations living many years from now would have the same tastes and preferences as people today, when they would be consuming goods and services largely unimagined in a vastly different world. Future generations might come to love the altered landscape of a warmer world. Perhaps, Nordhaus suggested, economists should incorporate uncertainty about future preferences, an approach that was 'largely uncharted territory' in economic growth theory.[22]

From the late 1980s, more economists became interested in global warming. In 1991, *The Economic Journal* carried a special issue on the subject. The American economist William Cline, a specialist in trade and capital flows, endorsed the science. 'Overall, greenhouse science holds up well to scrutiny,' Cline wrote. 'Its logic and physics are compelling. Although warming to date is less than predicted, the shortfall is within the range of natural variability.'[23] The principal shortcoming in the scientific and policy debate, Cline thought, had been the failure to extend the time horizon of the analysis to two hundred and fifty to three hundred years. 'For purposes of planetary management, a horizon of thirty-five years is woefully inadequate.'[24]

In his contribution, Nordhaus wrote that climate change was likely to produce a combination of gains and losses – 'with no strong presumption of substantial net economic losses'.[25] This wasn't an argument in favour of climate change or a laissez-faire attitude, but rather for a careful weighing of costs and damages 'if we are to preserve our precious time and resources for the most important threats to our health and happiness'.[26]

The vast majority of economists expressing a view followed Cline in taking the consensus on the science as given and not to be questioned. As Nordhaus put it in a 2007 seminar, 'We social scientists are downstream: we collect the debris from science as it comes by us, the good models, the bad models, the good studies and the bad studies.'[27] This attitude of uncritical acceptance came under sustained challenge in a series of papers and articles by David Henderson, the former OECD chief economist. Henderson argued that it was 'unnecessary and imprudent' for economists to arrive at such confident and sweeping conclusions.[28] There was 'pervasive uncertainty' and 'sheer lack of knowledge' in relation to the climate system. It was 'misleading' to speak in general terms of 'the science' in a way that suggested there were 'no significant doubts, queries or gaps'.[29] A study of the contribution of Working Group I to the Fourth Assessment Report found that the terms 'uncertain' and 'uncertainties' appeared more than one thousand, three hundred times.[30]

As the rhetoric of alarmism ratcheted up in the first decade of the new century, Henderson criticised received opinion as 'seriously over-presumptive' characterised by a 'lack of awareness of today's prevailing over-statement, over-confidence, and ingrained bias'.[31] The IPCC assessment reports, Henderson cautioned, were far from being models of 'rigour, inclusiveness, and impartiality'.[32] Economists were inadvertent in ignoring issues of professional conduct that had come to light over the Hockey Stick. The strong commitment to the official consensus led its upholders to react to any form of criticism or dissent as undermining established science, non-subscribers being portrayed as members of a 'denial lobby' and treated as Thought Criminals.[33]

Should economists, as Nordhaus suggested, simply take whatever natural scientists decided to float down the river or follow Henderson and, as he put it, exhibit the lack of credulity economists would deploy in analysing any other policy issue? Economists should be in a better position than others to make their own assessment of the science because much of it is about statistics and modelling.

To Australian economist Ross Garnaut, the answer was a no-brainer. 'The outsider to climate science has no rational choice but to accept that, on a balance of probabilities, the mainstream science is right in pointing to high risks from unmitigated climate change,' Garnaut wrote in his 2008 government review for the states and Commonwealth of Australia.[34]

Canadian economist Ross McKitrick is critical of the credulity of professional economists in accepting the claims of climate scientists when they are generally better trained and equipped in the handling of statistics. 'The typical economist has way more training in data analysis than a typical climatologist,' McKitrick told the author. 'Once they start reading climate papers they start spotting errors all over the place.'[35]

In a 1939 review 'Professor Tinbergen's Method,' Keynes wrote a scathing attack on the shortcomings of multiple correlation analysis to quantify the effect of a single factor. Suppose a model takes account of three factors. It is not enough, Keynes argued, that these should be causal factors: 'There must be no other significant factor.' If there were 'then the method is not able to discover the relative quantitative importance of the first three'.[36] For carbon dioxide to be the only possible explanation for heightened global temperatures, as a matter of logic, scientists must first be able to quantify every single feature of the changing climate. Yet large-scale changes in the climate, such as the causes and timing of ice ages, are still not well understood.

Economics should be central to deciding what, if anything, to do about global warming. Yet only the US had conducted an economic appraisal ahead of the Rio Earth Summit. No official economic analysis had preceded the Kyoto Protocol – a conceptual disaster, according to Nordhaus, lacking political, economic, or environmental coherence.[37] Instead, the policy debate was framed as a binary question: *Is global warming happening? Scientists tell us it is, so we must do something*. That 'something' – attempting to return the developed world to the emissions level at the beginning of the 1990s – was about symbolism, not economic rationality.

Not until 2005 did any national body outside the US begin to consider the economic dimension. Early that year, the House of Lords Economic Affairs Select Committee held hearings on the economics of climate change. The committee included two former Conservative chancellors (Nigel Lawson and Norman Lamont), a former governor of the Bank of England (Robin Leigh-Pemberton) and economist and Labour peer Richard Layard.

When they cross-examined a senior Treasury official, it emerged that the Treasury had not conducted any appraisal of the economic costs and benefits of global warming to the British economy.[38] Earlier, American economist Robert Mendelsohn had told the committee that global warming would be beneficial for regions such as the UK that were 'too cold'.[39]

Neither had the Treasury conducted an economic appraisal of the costs of meeting the UK's target for a sixty per cent cut in carbon dioxide emissions by 2050. 'The target was quite consciously introduced over a very long period because we understand the costs of making these changes are much smaller if they are planned over substantial periods of time,' Paul Johnson, the Treasury's chief micro-economist, said.[40] It had left the economic analysis to the IPCC, with some input from Defra. Lawson expressed astonishment. 'In my time at the Treasury as Chancellor it would have been unthinkable for the Treasury not to spend quite a lot of time on a serious economic analysis of an issue as important as this.'[41]

The committee's chairman Lord Wakeham, a former Conservative energy secretary, was determined to get a united report and restricted discussion on the science to avoid splitting the cross-party committee. Wakeham was dismayed by what he saw of the IPCC, a 'magic circle' creating certainties out of massive uncertainties. 'Wickedly bad' was his verdict on the IPCC's process, an institution he thought intent on its self-perpetuation.[42]

It was evident to the committee that the IPCC was prone to deep-seated politicisation. In his evidence, environmental economist Richard Tol of the University of Hamburg said that, although he had been involved in the Third Assessment Report, he had not been nominated by the German government to work on the Fourth. German government policy meant only those with close connections to the Greens would be nominated to Working Groups II (on the impacts of climate change) and III (on policy responses). 'Things have become more and more politicised,' Tol observed.[43]

In its report published at the beginning of July 2005, the committee criticised the Blair government's lack of candour. The costs of its decarbonisation policies were 'unhelpfully vague'. Its claim that costs prior to 2020 were 'negligible' was 'wildly optimistic'.[44] It called on the Treasury to be 'more active', concluding that unless it was 'we do not see how the Government can argue that it has adequately appraised its long-term climate targets in terms of likely costs and benefits'.[45]

25
STERN REVIEW

If we don't act, the overall costs and risks of climate change will be equivalent to losing at least five per cent of global GDP each year, now and forever.

Nicholas Stern[1]

Forecasts tell you little about the future but a lot about the forecaster.

Warren Buffett

Be careful what you wish for.

Two weeks after the Lords committee reported, Chancellor Gordon Brown announced that Sir Nicholas Stern would lead a major review on the economics of climate change.

Stern had been appointed to the Treasury to head the Government Economic Service in 2003. He had come to Treasury with very fixed ideas about taxation, but Brown wasn't interested. He had enjoyed relatively short spells at his previous employers, the World Bank and the European Bank for Reconstruction and Development. He didn't seem to have much else to offer and was shunted off to work on Tony Blair's Africa Initiative.

Global warming was Stern's lucky number. Other economists had thought longer and harder about the economics of global warming; none would rival Stern's public impact or attain his status as a global warming guru. Stern's academic background was in development economics. His advocacy of more aid flows and central planning brought him into conflict with the free-market economist Peter Bauer. 'Preoccupation with the analysis of market failure and the theory of corrective intervention is a notable feature of development economics,' Bauer wrote in a 1984 riposte to Stern.[2]

To these was added certainty about the science of global warming. Asked in 2009 about the possibility that 'the science' might be wrong – ten years into a period of no statistical rise in observed global temperatures – Stern answered, 'It's very, very remote.' Less than one in a hundred? 'Oh, much, much less.'[3]

Nonetheless Stern's grasp of the science was poor. In the same interview, Stern stated that the greenhouse effect could be observed experimentally in greenhouses – 'and most people have observed the greenhouse effect themselves in greenhouses. Yes?'[4] No. In a greenhouse, rising warm air is prevented by glass from escaping – a convection effect. The physics of the atmospheric (so-called) greenhouse effect are entirely different: the absorption by water and carbon dioxide molecules of long-wave radiation from the Earth's surface – a radiation effect.*

In arguing that humans could not adapt to a warmer world, Stern asserted that the risk was of a rise in temperature greater than any since the end of the last ice age 'ten or twelve million years ago'.[5] In fact, the last glaciation ended, and the current inter-glacial began, around eleven thousand, five hundred years ago. (The oldest Palaeolithic cave paintings in central and southern France are thought to date back twenty-three thousand years ago.)[†]

Science – or 'The Science' – was the occasion of Stern's first skirmish with fellow economists. Henderson assembled a team that included two members of the Lords Economic Affairs Committee (Nigel Lawson and Robert Skidelsky), McKitrick and five other economists. Stern had made a 'premature and injudicious choice' in basing the review on 'an unbalanced and technically defective account of 'the science', they wrote.[6] His use of the Hockey Stick created a misleading impression of a dramatic departure from a stable thousand-year norm. 'By taking as given hypotheses that remain uncertain, assertions that are debatable or mistaken, and processes of inquiry that are at fault, the Review has put itself on a path that can lead to no useful outcome,' Henderson and his colleagues argued.[7]

In a swift rebuttal, Stern gave no quarter. 'This is not a theory that is fraying at the edges,' he wrote.[8] Falling into Professor Tinbergen's trap, Stern argued that unless the role of anthropogenic greenhouse gas emissions was recognised the temperature increase of the previous forty or fifty years 'cannot convincingly be explained' by climate models.[9] 'In fact, the latest science suggests that the risks could be substantially greater than previously seen,' a claim that was not based on any real world evidence.[10]

The Stern Review was published in October 2006. For the first time outside the US, public debate about global warming shifted to its eco-

---

* Stern was in good company in mis-ascribing the effect of convection to radiation. In a primer on global warming, Sir John Houghton, the first chair of the IPCC's Working Group I, wrote of glass in a greenhouse as having 'somewhat similar' properties to the atmosphere in absorbing radiation which is re-emitted back into the greenhouse, the glass acting as a 'radiation blanket'. *Global Warming: The Complete Briefing* (1994), p. 21.

† Of the many interglacials of the Quaternary Period (there have been at least nine), the current one is but the most recent. Its maximum period of warmth is now passed – in North West Europe, some five to seven thousand years ago.

nomic consequences – in apocalyptic terms. Failure to act could create economic and social disruption on a scale associated with the First and Second World Wars and the Great Depression of the 1930s.[11] The costs and risks of climate change would be equivalent to losing at least five per cent of global GDP every year 'now and forever'. If a wider range of risks and impacts was taken into account, 'The estimate of damage could rise to twenty per cent of GDP or more.'[12] These were eye-popping numbers.

How had he done it?

As with other cost-benefit analyses of global warming, the Stern Review used a model to integrate physical impacts and a range of economic scenarios and variables to derive a social cost of carbon dioxide. The PAGE integrated assessment model used by Stern and his team had been developed by Chris Hope, a Cambridge academic. Although the details differed, it shared the economic and utilitarian principles of the other two widely cited models, Nordhaus's DICE and Tol's FUND models.

PAGE used a time horizon stretching out to 2200 – a compromise between natural scientists who wanted to go out to 2400 or 2500, and economists who, as Hope put it, were unhappy to go beyond 2050, knowing that economic models were lucky to hold up much beyond five to ten years. But if the modelling stopped before 2050, it would be too early to show benefits from capping greenhouse gas emissions.[13]

The review team was especially attracted to PAGE's ability to handle uncertainty, using a variant of Monte Carlo probability analysis, with ten thousand to one hundred thousand model runs to derive a single result. The model incorporated the possibility of catastrophic climatic events, such as the melting of the West Antarctic ice sheet occurring *before* 2200 based on some work by Hans Joachim Schellnhuber and Stefan Rahmstorf of the Potsdam Institute. In Hope's words, these were 'just slightly more than illustrative' – the evidence base for them being 'very thin'.[14]

The single largest impact on estimating a value for the social cost of carbon is the climate sensitivity of carbon dioxide.[15] The Review took a triangular distribution ranging from 1.5°C to 4.5°C, with 2.5°C as the most likely value. The Review also ran a 'high climate' scenario to demonstrate a sizeable probability that the climate sensitivity of carbon dioxide was higher than previously thought.[16]

The second most important input was the pure time preference rate; in layman's terms, the cost of time. Stern rejected the approach used by economists such as Nordhaus to derive the cost of time from market data, such as from bond yields, returns on investment and the amount people saved from their incomes. For Stern, it wasn't a question of what the pure time preference rate *is*, but what it *ought* to be. 'We take a simple approach in this Review: if a future generation will be present, we suppose that it has the same claim on our ethical attention as the current one.'[17]

The distinction has profound implications for what the Review was about. Was it about economics or was it, above all, about ethics? 'If you care little about future generations you will care little about climate change,' Stern argued, a position which did not have 'much foundation in ethics and which many would find unacceptable.'[18] By the same token, it could be said; if you care little about the present, you will care a lot about climate change. There is a way of balancing the two. The discount rate, embodying the cost of time, is the mathematical bridge linking the present and the future.

At the heart of the Stern Review is an ethical argument, one that Stern articulated in almost identical terms as Boulding had suggested – but rejected – forty years earlier. Stern quoted Frank Ramsey, the brilliant young Cambridge mathematician and philosopher who, in the 1920s, described pure time discounting as 'ethically indefensible' and Oxford economist Roy Harrod, who called it a 'human infirmity' and 'a polite expression for rapacity and the conquest of reason by passion'.[19]

These views neglect mortality as the most certain fact of an individual's existence. Stern did recognise the relationship between an individual's mortality and the cost of time. 'The allocation an individual makes in her own lifetime may well reflect the possibility of her death and the probability that she will survive a hundred years may indeed be very small,' Stern conceded.[20] Individuals' preferences had 'only limited relevance for the long-run ethical question associated with climate change', Stern argued.[21] The Review was thus couched firmly within a collectivist perspective – what matters is the welfare of the anthill, not the individual ant. In his modelling, Stern used a pure rate of time preference of 0.1 per cent a year to reflect the possibility of humanity being wiped out, implying an almost ten per cent chance of the extinction of *homo sapiens* before 2100.[22]

There was a downside to Stern's ethics – his treatment of the world's poor and the transfer of wealth from them to the richer generations of tomorrow. Sir Partha Dasgupta, Frank Ramsey Professor of Economics at Cambridge, criticised Stern for taking a very inegalitarian attitude to the distribution of wellbeing when futurity was not at issue. The ethical parameter Stern had adopted to reflect inequality and risk in human wellbeing was, Dasgupta wrote, 'deeply unsatisfactory'.[23] Overall, Stern's assumptions would require the current generation to save 97.5 cents of every dollar it produced – 'so patently absurd that we must reject it out of hand'.[24] Economists had taken the threat of climate change seriously, Dasgupta concluded, 'but the cause is not served when parameter values are so chosen that they yield desired answers'.[25]

For Stern, it was all about the future. It was difficult to assess the impacts over a very long time period because future generations 'are not fully represented in current discussions'.[26]

Who should then represent them and who knows what they will think?

The implication is Stern and like-minded successors, in a dynasty of economic Pharaohs, presiding over the global economy for decades and centuries ahead. In a 2007 critique, Nordhaus wrote of Stern, stoking the dying embers of the British Empire, to apply colonial-style Government House utilitarianism from 'the lofty vantage point of world social planner'.[27]

Nordhaus also solved the puzzle of how Stern had derived his numbers. By using his DICE model, he could convert a one per cent reduction in output over the next century to a 14.4 per cent reduction 'now and forever'. On Stern's methodology, more than half the estimated damages 'now and forever' occur after 2800. 'The large damages from global warming reflect large and speculative damages in the far-distant future magnified into a large current value by a near-zero time discount rate,' Nordhaus wrote.[28]

Having answered the 'How?' what of the 'Why?'

Just as with the British government's assessment of weapons of mass destruction, Nordhaus suggested the Stern Review should be read primarily as 'a document that is political in nature and has advocacy as its purpose'.[29] Was this overly harsh? An answer can be found in the Review. 'Much of public policy is actually about changing attitudes,' Stern wrote, in an authentic expression of the Blair-era style of governance as PR.[30]

Thus there is nothing in the Review that might put a question mark over whether Kyoto was a good deal for Britain or for the world. Despite mounting evidence to the contrary, Stern argued that countries would meet their Kyoto obligations. 'Governments make and respect international obligations because they are in line with perceptions of responsible and collaborative behaviour,' Stern wrote, 'and because domestic public opinion supports both the objectives and mechanisms for achieving them' – a finding contradicted by Scott Barrett's authoritative analysis.[31]

Neither did Stern examine what the costs and benefits of global warming might be for Britain. If a warmer climate benefited Britain, then cutting emissions is a lose-lose proposition.

Stern was dismissive of adaptation. 'An inherent difficulty for long-term adaptation decisions is uncertainty, due to limitations in our scientific knowledge of a highly complex climate system,' Stern wrote.[32] While uncertainty was an impediment to adaptation, the same lack of knowledge wasn't a barrier to governments. 'There speaks the true bureaucrat' was Nigel Lawson's stinging comment on Stern's presumption of the superiority of government wisdom.[33]

By presenting an ethical argument – that future generations should have as much weight as the present – in the garb of an economic cost-benefit analysis, the Stern Review was mis-sold by its author and by its sponsoring government. 'Tackling climate change is the pro-growth strategy,' the review claimed.[34] 'In broad brush terms,' the review stated, 'spending somewhere in the region of one per cent of gross world product forever could prevent the world losing the equivalent of five to twenty per cent of gross world product forever.'[35]

There's something morally suspect about a proposition couched in terms of making you better off financially and morally. Ethics come into play when following financial self-interest leads to a morally bad outcome. On the other hand, ethics are cheapened when used in support of someone's supposed material self-interest. If Stern had had the courage of his (moral) convictions, he should have made the case that taking action against global warming is costly and would hurt financially, but that the current generation had a moral duty to later generations.

How long would the pain last? Deep in the Review are two charts showing the costs of stabilising emissions at Stern's target of 550 ppm of carbon dioxide equivalent. On the assumption that this would cost one per cent of Gross World Product (GWP), the chart showed a break-even point around 2080; if the cost was four percent of GWP, the benefits would not exceed the costs until around 2120.[36] The midpoint of the two implies there being no net benefit during the twenty-first century. A young person's great-grandchildren might conceivably benefit, but not their children or grandchildren.

For countries committed to cap their emissions, the break-even point – assuming there is one – would be pushed into the twenty-second century and probably beyond. Stern reckoned that non-Annex I parties were likely to be responsible for over three quarters of the rise in energy related carbon dioxide emissions.[37] Agriculture and changes in land use alone accounted for forty-one per cent of emissions, with Indonesia and Brazil accounting for half these.[38]

Since the 1995 Berlin Mandate, the world community had been locked on a course that excluded non-Annex I parties from emissions caps. While

endorsing Kyoto, Stern did not analyse the emission cuts required by Annex I countries to meet his 550 ppm stabilisation target or the impact on
their economies. For citizens of Annex I countries, the prospect of action
on climate change ever producing a net benefit was very remote, even if
Stern's assumptions on the science turned out to be right.

26
SELLING SALVATION

'Solutions' are at hand, given wise collective decisions and actions. It is the combination of alarmist visions with confidently radical collectivist prescriptions for the world as a whole which characterises global Salvationism.

David Henderson, 2004[1]

On 30th October 2006, flanked by Tony Blair and Gordon Brown, Stern launched his Review. Blair spoke first. Within seconds, the hyperbole was in full flow. If the science was right, the consequences for the planet were literally disastrous – not in some science fiction future many years ahead, 'but in our own lifetime'.[2]

The Review was the most important report on the future produced by the government, Blair said. 'We know it is happening. We know the consequences for the planet.' Stern showed the economic benefits of strong early action easily outweighed the costs. 'For every £1 we invest now, we can save at least £5 and possibly much more by acting now.' Investment to prevent it 'will pay us back many times over'.[3]

Blair spoke for less than ten minutes.

Brown then took the stage – for an interminable sixteen. Nothing was too small to escape mention. A rainforest initiative with Brazil, Papua New Guinea and Costa Rica. A plug for biofuels. 'I'm determined that we use biofuels from palm and rape oil, to soya and sugar and eventually cellulosic biofuels,' he said, announcing that Al Gore was joining Alan Greenspan as his personal adviser. 'Environmental policy is economic policy,' Brown insisted.[4]

It was also about politics. As Bagehot in the *Economist* noted, thanks to the Conservatives' new leader David Cameron putting green issues at the heart of his attempt to re-brand the Conservative party, 'Stern has acquired a significance for British politics that Mr Brown would almost certainly not have predicted.'[5]

Blair's spin won.

'Blair: World needs to act on climate change now,' read the headline in the next day's *Daily Mail*. Stern's calculation of spending one per cent of GDP to save potential costs of five to twenty per cent of GDP were 'certainly compelling', *The Times* said in its leader.[6] Given the risk of 'something really catastrophic', like the melting of the Greenland ice sheet, 'the costs are not huge. The dangers are', the *Economist* concluded.[7]

To the *Daily Telegraph*, Stern's pinning a price tag on global warming was 'invaluable'.[8] According to the *Financial Times*, the economic benefits of action would eventually far outweigh the costs by as much as $2.5 trillion a year, although the paper didn't say when that might be. How convincingly had the review made its case, asked the *FT*'s lead economic commentator Martin Wolf? 'Sufficiently so,' he wrote, putting his finger on the issue of the discount rate. 'The review argues, sensibly, that there is no reason why the welfare of our generations should be intrinsically more important than those of our grandchildren,' Wolf thought.[9]

There was some isolated dissent. To economist and energy expert Dieter Helm, the one per cent cost of action seemed a 'terribly low' estimate and hard to square with the 'substantial lifestyle changes that many environmentalists argue are necessary and the scale of the taxes that appear necessary'.[10]

Most scathing was the *Daily Mail*. Even if Stern was right, on its own, Britain could do precious little about it. 'But never fear – Superman is here, in the shape of our posturing prime minister,' the paper said. Calling him deluded, 'anyone listening to him yesterday would think he could save the world single-handedly'.[11] To Nigel Lawson, the near universal and credulous acceptance of the Stern Review was the result of two things coming together: 'The ever-present media appetite for alarmism and the uncritical respect accorded by the innumerate majority to anything with numbers in it, however dubious.'[12]

The real target was overseas. The Review would be used as 'a vehicle to take on the doubters internationally' and enable Tony Blair to persuade a sceptical George Bush, a Whitehall source told the *Financial Times*.[13]

There was a great deal more scepticism and suspicion on the other side of the Atlantic. The *Washington Post*'s economic commentator Robert Samuelson dismissed the review as 'a masterpiece of misleading public relations'.[14] Stern's headlined conclusions were 'intellectual fictions' fabricated to justify an aggressive anti-global warming agenda, Samuelson argued. 'Anyone serious about global warming must focus on technological progress – and not just assume it,' as Stern had done. 'Otherwise, our practical choices are all bad: costly mandates and controls that harm the economy, or costly mandates and controls that barely affect greenhouse gases. Or, possibly, both,' Samuelson concluded.[15]

The widespread acceptance of the Stern Review revealed a paradox. The politics of the moment demanded a call for action which collectively the governments of the world wouldn't sign up to and politicians were not capable of delivering. On the other hand, most mainstream economic analysis pointed to an optimal path of a gradually tightening of greenhouse gas emissions, a more achievable goal, but one that did not satisfy the apocalyptic temper of the times. William Nordhaus's DICE model suggested a social cost of carbon of $35 a ton in 2015 rising to $206 a ton at the end of the century.[16] By contrast, the Stern Review estimate of the current social cost of carbon at $350 a ton was ten times higher.[17]

The snow lay thick on the ground when Stern met his economist peers at Yale in February 2007. The Yale symposium on the Stern Review was a 'really serious occasion', Chris Hope recalled. The US was engaging with Stern intellectually rather than politically and had rolled out its big guns. With several hundred people in the hall, it was the first time in fifteen years Hope felt the need to rehearse a presentation word for word.[18]

Chaired by Ernesto Zedillo, the former president of Mexico, symposium participants included Jeffrey Sachs, Scott Barrett, Robert Mendelsohn, William Cline and Nordhaus. Each offered penetrating comments. Of them, Sachs, Cline and Barrett were most sympathetic to Stern's conclusions. Sachs went furthest. By 2010, the world would have agreed a post-Kyoto target to stabilise atmospheric carbon dioxide at 500 ppm. 'It will take two years to ratify, and go into effect January 1st 2013,' Sachs predicted.[19]

Although Cline thought the Review 'very much on the right track', he laid bare the questionable mechanics of how Stern had arrived at his conclusions.[20] Stern had to modify his zero cost of time assumption by factoring in a small allowance for mankind's self-implosion, otherwise the Review's use of an infinite time horizon 'simply explodes'.[21] Putting Stern's welfare equation into a spreadsheet would show that ninety-three per cent of all future welfare occurs after 2200. In Cline's view, Stern probably should not have extrapolated the damage rate into the infinite future.[22] 'The combination of near-zero pure time preference with an infinite horizon probably balloons the value of damage avoided unreasonably,' Cline told the symposium.[23]

Welcoming the decisive role of ethics in Stern's analysis, Barrett disagreed with Stern's conclusion that the case for 'strong, early action' was clear cut. 'I am not saying his conclusions are wrong; I am saying that other conclusions can be supported.'[24]

Others were more critical. Mendelsohn said the review was not an economic analysis. It had merely asserted that 550 ppm was the least cost option without comparing it against alternatives other than doing nothing at all. It was like saying: 'I have a great policy for educating children and look, it is better than closing all schools.'

Stern had ignored the environmental damage implied by his proposals; one plan involved a combination of two million windmills, ten million hectares (24.7 million acres) of solar cells and five hundred million hectares of biofuel (1.2 billion acres) – more than ten times the surface area of California and more than forty times California's 2007 farm acreage.[25] Taking away that amount of cropland for renewable energy would very likely have a much larger impact on agriculture than climate change, Mendelsohn suggested. 'One can look at the Stern Review as a fairly complete argument why aggressive near term abatement does not make sense.'[26]

Nordhaus was particularly critical of Stern's central assertion that the cost of climate change was the equivalent of a twenty per cent cut in per capita consumption 'now and forever'. Stern's formulation inflicted 'cruel and unusual punishment' on the English language because the Review's 'now' didn't mean 'today'. A 'distant rumble' of a three per cent consumption loss in 2100 on Stern's extreme-extreme-extreme case was exaggerated by a factor of one thousand per cent, not because of the estimates of the damages, but primarily through discounting.[27]

When it came to his response, Stern made a partial concession. Although the 'now and forever' language was accurate, 'Perhaps it wasn't particularly felicitous, and on reflection, we might have used some other wording.'[28] Grudging, perhaps. Belated, certainly. But collectively, economists acquitted themselves far better than had the natural scientists with their cover-up of the Hockey Stick. And, unlike the author of the Hockey Stick, Stern on this occasion was prepared to reason and debate with his critics.

In a subsequently published postscript to the Review, Stern gave further ground. 'Ethical positions cannot be dictated by policy analysts,' he wrote.[29] For the first time, Stern provided numbers that demonstrated the huge sensitivity of his conclusions to the discount rates assumed – an increase in the discount rate from 1.4 per cent to 3.5 per cent would reduce the estimates of the economic cost of greenhouse gas emissions from five per cent to 1.4 per cent of world GDP.[30] At this higher, but still modest discount rate, Stern's clarion call for immediate and drastic action simply evaporated.

Stern's methods had not withstood scrutiny, but his call to action based on catastrophist assessments remained fashionable. In a July 2008 paper, Harvard economist Martin Weitzman argued that Stern was right, but for the wrong reasons. Stern's cost benefit analysis was completely flawed. Moreover, the use of cost benefit analysis was inappropriate for an issue such as climate change.

Based on a survey of twenty-two studies on the climate sensitivity of carbon dioxide, Weitzman focused on the fifteen per cent of cases in which temperature increases substantially greater than 4.5°C 'cannot be excluded'. Weitzman super-imposed 'the non-zero probability' of greenhouse gas self-amplification, such as methane-out-gassing precipitating a cataclysmic runaway-positive feedback warming. If temperatures rose by around 10–20°C, there could exist 'truly terrifying' consequences such as the disintegration of the Greenland and at least part of the Western Antarctic ice sheets – 'horrifying examples of climate-change mega-disasters [that] are incontrovertibly possible on a time scale of centuries', Weitzman wrote.[31]

From small probabilities of huge climate impacts occurring at some indefinite point in the remote future, Weitzman conjured up 'fat tails' – low probability, high impact events – conjoining with fat tails begetting yet fatter tails.[32] Unlike traditional 'thin-tailed' cost benefit analysis, Weitzman acknowledged that it was 'much more frustrating and much more subjective – and it looks much less conclusive – because it requires some form of speculation (masquerading as an "assessment")'.[33]

Weitzman's analysis gained extra currency following the bankruptcy of Lehman Brothers and the near collapse of the West's banking system. All of a sudden, risks which financial models suggested were extremely remote became fat-tailed risk events. Even before the banking crisis struck, Martin Wolf in the *Financial Times* was strongly influenced by the fat-tail analysis: 'Above all,' Wolf wrote, 'I find persuasive the argument of Professor Martin Weitzman of Harvard University that it is worth paying a great deal to eliminate the risk of catastrophe.'[34]

The trouble was no amount of money could completely eliminate the risk of climate catastrophe. If climatic 'tipping points' exist, no one can be sure at what point they tip. Even if emissions fell to zero, past emissions would mean that the world is 'committed' to many decades of further warming.

Weitzman himself drew a different conclusion. The existence of fat-tailed potential catastrophes meant paying more attention to how fat the bad tail might be. If thought to be fat, it meant being much more open to drastic action, including 'serious mitigation' (emissions cuts) and possibly using geo-engineering technology to slim down the fat tail fast.[35]

Lawson for one believes Weitzman's position to be absurd.

> In a world of inevitably finite resources, we cannot possibly spend large sums on guarding against any and every possible eventuality

> … The fact that a theoretical future danger might be devastating is
> not enough to justify substantial expenditure of resources here and
> now, particularly since there are many other such dangers wholly
> unconnected with global warming.[36]

Weitzman's fat-tails mark an important milestone in the development – or
more accurately, the disintegration – of the idea of global warming and its
call to cut carbon dioxide emissions. The assumption that there is some kind
of stable, quantifiable relationship relating the amount of carbon dioxide in
the atmosphere to global temperatures and thence the impacts on societies
and the environment provides a quantified rationale for preventative action.

Under the fat-tail analysis, there is no level of emissions reduction that
can completely remove the risk of catastrophe over the indefinite future.
Even in its own terms, a policy of doing nothing becomes a rational response, as it is no longer possible to quantify the avoided costs and risks
that emission cuts are meant to be buying.

Catastrophic events occur. As readers of Asterix and Obelix know, the
only thing the Gauls feared was the sky falling on their heads. And it seems
that it did – a massive comet struck Southern Bavaria sometime in the
third and fourth centuries BC, scarring the culture of the Celts. To live life
under the shadow of the possibility of another such event suggests a somewhat morbid sensibility. *You only live once*, as they say.

The optimal economic response points in the direction of abandoning
policies that retard economic growth, specifically those purportedly designed to slow down or arrest global warming. What constitutes a natural
catastrophe to one society might be a minor inconvenience to a richer
one. Bert Bolin wrote in 2007 that the IPCC was not yet able to tell from
climate models which countries would be most affected. 'The issue could
thus not then be resolved adequately beyond the obvious conclusions that
poor countries were more vulnerable than rich ones and less able to protect
themselves.'[37] Bolin had stumbled on the insight that Frédéric Bastiat had
derived when he asked why mid nineteenth-century Europe no longer suffered from famines. The answer? Rising prosperity.

No one knows what the climate of the future will be. Still less can we have
any idea how societies of the future will respond to these unknown changes.
But history shows that wealth insulates societies from nature and that wealthier
societies are better equipped to overcome natural disasters than poor ones.

Whether the cause is natural, man-made or some combination of the
two – the answer is the same. Economic growth.

27
CUCUMBERS INTO SUNBEAMS

America is addicted to oil ... By applying the talent and technology of America, this country can dramatically improve our environment, move beyond a petroleum-based economy and make our dependence on Middle Eastern oil a thing of the past.

George W. Bush, 31st January 2006[1]

We will harness ... the soil to fuel our cars.

Barack Obama, 20th January 2008

Economists assumed governments would adopt optimal policies to reduce greenhouse gas emissions at the lowest possible cost. What actually transpired bore greater resemblance to what Gulliver witnessed on his travels.

At the grand academy of Lagado, Gulliver saw a professor working to extract sunbeams from cucumbers. In another eight years, he should be able to warm the governor's garden. Would Gulliver give him something to encourage him in his ingenuity? Gulliver's master had given him money for this very purpose 'because he knew their practice of begging from all who go to see them'. (In the age of global warming, tendering financial inducements would be obligatory to encourage renewable energy.)

A second professor was engaged in a project to return human excrement to its original state as food. (Recycling human effluent was a particular fixation during the first environmental wave.) A third was contriving a method of building houses starting at the roof and working downwards. (New houses in England have small windows to reduce their carbon footprint.)

But it was the political school where the professors appeared wholly out of their senses – 'a scene which never fails to make me melancholy', Gulliver says. Economists urged politicians to set a mechanism to price carbon dioxide emissions and let the market find the most efficient means. But politicians couldn't stop themselves from prescribing what people and businesses should do – irrespective of the cost per ton of carbon dioxide saved or whether it actually reduced emissions. European politicians were especially partial to wind farms, producing some of the world's most expensive electricity (solar power, which German politicians favoured most of all, was even more costly).

Neither could politicians evade the global logic of global warming. Without a global agreement, unilateral action was pointless. Governments committed to massively costly renewable energy programmes thus had incentives to inflate the prospects for successive rounds of international climate change negotiations. Living under its Kyoto bubble, politicians in the European Union would point to the faintest possibility of a son-of-Kyoto at the end of the rainbow. In 2006, California's politicians passed a state-wide cap on greenhouse gas emissions, inviting competing states to help themselves to some of California's GDP.

The global warming policy spectrum ranged from petty infringements of personal freedom, such as the ban on incandescent light bulbs in the EU, Australia and Canada, to policies harming the world's poorest and damaging the environment. When the EU leaders discussed the light bulb ban in 2007, Angela Merkel complained that the green replacements weren't as good as the old ones. 'Most of the light bulbs in my flat are energy-saving bulbs,' Merkel said. 'They're not yet quite bright enough. When I'm looking for something I've dropped on the carpet, I have a bit of a problem.'[2] Merkel wasn't alone. In the UK, the prospect of withdrawal of high-wattage incandescent bulbs from supermarkets sparked a stampede.

Further along the spectrum were attempts to create markets for permission to emit carbon dioxide. Government-planned markets are inherently problematic. As Martin Wolf has written, 'Wherever there is a gap between the market value of something and an official price or the price government is prepared to allow, there is an incentive to cheat and bribe.'[3] Because it does not cost anything to emit carbon dioxide, when politicians legislate a value on it, they created a universe of opportunities for fraud and organised crime.

The EU's Emissions Trading Scheme (ETS) is the most ambitious and complex cap-and-trade scheme – a Common Agricultural Policy for the atmosphere, a sort of Gosplan meets Milton Friedman. The largest ETS scam is carousel trading. Fraudsters buy carbon credits in one country without paying VAT, then sell them in another with VAT, pocketing the difference, costing European taxpayers an estimated €5 billion. According to Europol, up to ninety per cent of all 2009 trades could have been carousel trading.[4]

Analysts at investment bank UBS reckoned that in 2012 the ETS will cost consumers €18 billion, but will have only reduced power sector emissions by between one and three per cent since its inception. By 2025, the cumulative windfall to electricity producers could total €210 billion.[5] The ETS also pumps billions of euros to countries not subject to emissions caps via the Kyoto Protocol's Clean Development Mechanism, which failed for the reasons Raùl Estrada anticipated in his 1998 critique.

South Korea turned out to be the biggest winner of the CDM jackpot, scooping eighteen per cent of all the credits issued worldwide. The French owner of a factory in Onsan was expected to reap more money than the whole of Africa. 'We didn't make the rules of the game,' an executive of Rhodia SA told the *Wall Street Journal*.[6] Rhodia could expect to earn more than $1 billion over seven years from destroying laughing gas, but the real joke was on European consumers and taxpayers. 'It's good business, because the Western world is basically desperate,' a consultant explained, as it needed to buy emission reductions credits.[7]

Biofuels are at the most harmful end of the policy spectrum. When more than three quarters of the three-year increase in world corn production is diverted to non-food use, economics predicts that the price of corn will move in one direction: up. Between January 2002 and June 2008, food commodity prices more than doubled, with nearly half that increase occurring in the eighteen months from January 2007.[8]

An internal World Bank paper estimated that most of the seventy to seventy-five per cent increase in food prices not accounted for by higher energy costs and the fall in the dollar was 'due to biofuels and the related consequences of low grain stocks, large land use shifts, speculative activity and export bans'.[9] In March 2008, the director of the UN World Food Programme told the European Parliament that the shift to biofuels production has diverted lands out of the food chain. 'In the short term, the world's poorest are hit hard.'[10]

Spiralling food prices led to rioting across the globe. In Haiti, the government fell. Rioting spread across vulnerable Muslim countries, including Egypt, Yemen, Mauritania and Bangladesh. There were street protests in Italy at the price of pasta, although the government in Rome didn't fall.

Global warming was predicted to raise food prices and create instability in vulnerable parts of the world. 'Warming of a few °C is projected to increase food prices globally, and may increase the risk of hunger in vulnerable populations,' the IPCC warned in 2001.[11] Temperatures overall hadn't risen in the first decade of the new century, but food prices and hunger did. The cause was global warming policies – in a brutal form of the Global Warming Policy Paradox (GWPP).

Global warming policies damage the environment. Rising global temperatures were also predicted to harm ecosystems and reduce biodiversity. Cutting down tropical rain forests to turn into palm oil plantations certainly does destroy wildlife habitat and reduce biodiversity. The GWPP is not an accident or down to bad luck. It is an inescapable outcome of the economic and political dimensions of the global warming idea.

Some of the most vociferous proponents of the global warming orthodoxy, including leading scientists and a large number of NGOs such as Greenpeace, Friends of the Earth, Oxfam and the WWF, reject mainstream economics and dismiss concerns about costs. The catastrophist conclusions of the Stern Review reduce the near-term costs of cutting carbon dioxide emissions relative to the potential gains (in terms of losses avoided) in a far distant future. To the extent such costs aren't accorded their due weight, harmful policies will be adopted.

Hyping global warming as a planetary catastrophe and driven by a deep-seated hostility to fossil fuels, NGOs shared responsibility for the ensuing policy insanities. Having campaigned tirelessly for bio-energy, in 2010 Greenpeace was caught out by the policies it had advocated. After an outcry at the destruction of Indonesian rainforest, Greenpeace UK's John Sauven denounced subsidised palm oil power stations as 'orang-utan incinerators'.[12] The plantations weren't 'sustainable'. According to Liz Bossley of energy consultants Consilience Advisory, 'While there is a food shortage in the world, there will always be a question mark over the use of land to grow plants for power generation.'[13]

The Royal Society for the Protection of Birds (RSPB) is a vociferous supporter of wind farms, although they kill eagles and other raptors. 'Switching to renewable energy now, rather than in ten or twenty years, is essential if we are to stabilise greenhouse gases … Wind power is the most advanced renewable technology,' the RSPB claims.[14] In similar vein, America's Audubon society 'strongly supports' wind farms, while acknowledging that its stance 'will not be without some impact' on birdlife.[15]

More concerned with fundamentally changing the economic basis of modern urban civilisation than preserving the countryside and wilderness-es, environmental NGOs ended up supporting the despoliation of rural areas and uplands with arrays of alien wind farms. It represented the negation of what their spiritual forebears stood for, transcendentalists such as Emerson and Thoreau and the trio of John Muir, Gifford Pinchot and Teddy Roosevelt. The attitude of environmental NGOs to the environment became that of the American major in the Vietnam War: it became necessary to destroy the village to save it.

'It all sounded so, well, intelligent,' *New York Times* columnist Thomas Friedman wrote in December 2009 on Denmark's renewable electricity.[16] While the Danes claim that thirty per cent of their electricity comes from renewables, on average, wind power – the largest one – provided less than ten per cent of the country's needs.[17]* According to Paul-Frederik Bach, who integrated wind power into the Danish grid, 'maintaining the myth of the successful integration of wind power may be good public relations, but refusing to face realities is self-deception'.[18]

Although Denmark installed around three thousand megawatts of wind power capacity and its Vestas wind turbine company became a world leader, it had not cracked the fundamental problem of generating electricity from wind. Wind farm electricity is unpredictable. Its output profile is different from the profile of electricity demand.

While onshore wind farms generate around one fifth of their theoretical capacity, during calm periods, output plunges. During one twenty-four-hour period, output from all Denmark's wind farms fell to less than one quarter of one per cent of capacity.[19] Too much wind at the wrong time – and surplus electricity has to be given away to neighbouring countries at spot prices close to or actually zero. When spot electricity prices are negative, Denmark *pays* other countries to take their surplus wind power.[20]

Germany made the largest commitment to renewables. In 2008, a combined wind and solar capacity of twenty-nine thousand, two hundred and eleven megawatts put Germany just ahead of the US, with twenty-five thousand, nine hundred megawatts.[21] A 2009 study by the University of Bochum described Germany's renewables experience as 'a cautionary tale of massively expensive environmental and energy policy that is devoid of economic and environmental benefits'.[22]

Its renewable regime was established in 1991, with generous feed-in tariffs, which in 2000 were extended for up to a further twenty years. Under it, the least efficient technologies receive the highest subsidy.† For producing a fraction of one per cent of Germany's electricity, solar power producers can expect to receive €53 billion in subsidies – two and a half times the €20.5 billion for wind power.[23] German feed-in subsidies run in parallel with the EU's Emissions Trading Scheme. Thus marginal reductions in German

---

* In reality, Denmark's electricity market is so tightly integrated into Germany's that, in practical terms, it is part of the German market. Wind power accounts for only seven percent of the combined market. Paul-Frederik Bach, *The Variability of Wind Power* (2010), p. 26.

† In 2005, solar received €54.53 per kWh – over six times the €8.53 per kWh for wind. Manuel Frondel, Nolan Ritter, Christoph M Schmidt, Colin Vance, *Economic Impacts from the Promotion of Renewable Technologies: The German Experience* (2009), Table 1.

emissions increase the quantity of tradable emissions certificates to electricity producers in other European countries. The principal beneficiaries turn out to be the coal-fired power stations of Italy's ENEL and Spain's Endesa.[24] Far from creating a German win-win, the Bochum study concluded that Germany's renewables programme 'imposes high costs without any of the alleged positive impacts on emissions reductions, employment, energy security, or technological innovation'.[25]

Spain, second after Germany in its commitment to solar power, took a different path. Rather than charge electricity users the full cost of renewables, electricity generators received a 'tariff deficit' credit from the government. By the end of 2012, they are projected to have accumulated €21 billion of IOUs from the government.[26] Aside from the dire fiscal consequences as Spain struggles to shrink its budget deficit, a 2009 study by Gabriel Calzada Alvarez of Madrid's Universidad Rey Juan Carlos put a price tag on green jobs: €570,000 per job since 2000. Each green job cost Spain 2.2 real jobs, Calzada estimated.[27]

America was not spared similar follies. California has its own cap-and-trade regime and, in 2005, seven states – Connecticut, Delaware, Maine, New Hampshire, New Jersey, New York and Vermont – formed the Regional Greenhouse Gas Initiative (Massachusetts under Governor Mitt Romney dropped out at the last moment, but re-joined under his successor).

Like H.J. Heinz, federal renewable and energy efficiency programmes come in fifty-seven varieties.[28] Some, like a $10 million tribal energy programme, date from the Carter-era 1975 Energy Policy and Conservation Act. Others came about as a result of Energy Policy Act of 2005 and the Energy Independence and Security Act passed two years later. With their help, American politicians developed a serious bioethanol habit, even though seventy-four to ninety-five per cent of its energy content comes from coal and other conventional energy sources. It promised them a double hit – a national security high and a global warming one. Bioethanol wasn't a fossil fuel, so it was green, and it didn't come from the Middle East, but pushed up food prices, stoking instability in the Middle East.

Bioethanol producers were enriched with tax credits, grants, loan guarantees and import controls. Most of all they benefited from the Energy Policy Act's renewable fuel standard which requires bioethanol – costing a multiple of conventional hydrocarbons – to be blended into transportation fuel; 13.95 billion gallons in 2010 rising to 36 billion gallons in 2022.[29]

Other than Australia, the US was the only developed nation not to ratify the Kyoto Protocol – and Australia did after John Howard lost the 2007 election. Some that ratified Kyoto treated it as little more than a statement of intent. Canada's finance minister John Manley suggested it would be all right to ratify but not comply. 'The bailiff isn't going to arrive to seize our property,' he remarked in November 2002.[30] And when Canada found Kyoto too burdensome, the Harper government decided to withdraw from it. For the US, Kyoto would have been a legal commitment that could have been litigated through the courts. The case of *Massachusetts v. EPA*, which the Bush administration lost in the Supreme Court, illustrates how judicial rulings can have unforeseen and potentially far-reaching effects.

The political debate in the US was also fundamentally different. In parliamentary systems, legislators are subject to strong party discipline. Even in Canada, with its federal system and hydrocarbon-rich provinces such as Alberta, the Prime Minister Jean Chrétien obtained every vote of his Liberal party caucus to ratify Kyoto. None of Canada's major parties challenged the scientific rationale for action.[31]

In the US, there was a debate.* In July 2003, Senator James Inhofe of Oklahoma, chair of the Senate Committee on Environment and Public Works, directly attacked the scientific consensus. 'If the relationship between public policy and science is distorted for political ends,' Inhofe argued, 'the result is flawed policy that hurts the environment, the economy and the people we serve.'[32] He ridiculed science writer David Appell for claiming global warming would create greater chaos than the two world wars, and cited political scientist Aaron Wildasky's description of global warming as the mother of all environmental scares. 'Much of the debate over global warming is predicated on fear, rather than science,' Inhofe said. 'After studying the issue over the last several years, I believe that the balance of the evidence offers strong proof that natural variability is the overwhelming factor influencing climate.'[33] Concluding, Inhofe asked: 'Could it be that man-made global warming is the greatest hoax ever perpetrated on the American people? It sure sounds like it.'[34]

At the beginning of the nineties, corporate America responded to the rising wave of environmentalism in much the same way as big business elsewhere: it rode it. Coca Cola's Don Keough provided Maurice Strong with some top marketing and public relations executives for the 1992 Rio Earth Sum-

---

* In Australia, political argument between the parties broke out in 2009 after opposition leader Malcolm Turnbull, who supported the Rudd government's climate change policies, was deposed and replaced by sceptic Tony Abbott.

mit. Strong was thrilled. 'Since no organisation has a more sophisticated capacity for marketing, this was a gift indeed,' Strong wrote. 'Thus were our key messages promulgated throughout the world.'[35]

Strong asked Swiss industrialist Stephan Schmidheiny to mobilise business support. Schmidheiny set up the Business Council for Sustainable Development. It produced a business manifesto, *Changing Course*, co-signed by forty-seven chairmen and CEOs, including two from oil companies (Chevron and Shell) and three auto manufacturers (Volkswagen, Nissan and Mitsubishi). The largest number was from US corporations.*

Changing Course could have been vintage 1972 Barbara Ward in arguing that environmental degradation and rich countries' over-consumption prevented the development of poorer ones. 'These two sets of alarming trends – environment and development – cannot be separated.'[36] The world was moving on. 'The national income of Japan's one hundred and twenty million people is about to overtake the combined incomes of the 3.8 billion people in the developing world,' the authors of *Changing Course* wrote, just as Japan was entering two lost decades at the end of which, by one measure, it had been over-taken by China as the world's second largest economy.[37]

Global warming was acknowledged as politically the most difficult issue. 'We cannot return to the lower energy scenarios of the past nor change our energy systems drastically,' i.e., little change of course in *Changing Course*.[38] 'We foresee a gradual shift to a more sustainable mix of energy sources,' – hardly a ringing endorsement of the prospects for a post-fossil fuel economy.[39]

After Rio, a split began to develop within the US business community and with the rest of the world. Leading the challenge was the Global Climate Coalition, comprising oil companies, automakers, utilities and trade associations such as the US Chamber of Commerce.

Formed in 1989 in response to James Hansen's testimony, initially it had a watching brief. That changed after the 1992 presidential election. To win support for Al Gore's BTU tax, the Clinton administration did a deal with Senator Robert Byrd – a cut in taxes on coal in exchange for higher taxes on oil. According to William O'Keefe, who led the Global Climate Coalition, it fostered the perception that the new administration was deeply hostile to the use of liquid petroleum products.[40]

---

* They were Kenneth Derr of Chevron, Maurice Greenberg of AIG, Charles Harper of Conagra, Allen Johnson, retired chairman of 3M, Samuel Johnson of SC Johnson, Frank Popoff of Dow Chemical, former EPA Administrator, William Ruckelshaus, of Browning-Ferris, Paul O'Neill of ALCOA and treasury secretary under George W. Bush, and Edgar Woolard of DuPont.

In the run-up to Kyoto, there was a twin-track campaign highlighting the economic consequences of capping carbon dioxide emissions. The first was an advertising campaign through the summer of 1997: 'The UN Climate Treaty isn't Global ... and it won't work.'[41] The second focused on the Congress and the Senate in particular. Byrd asked the coalition to help find co-sponsors for what became the Byrd-Hagel resolution, ending up with sixty-four. 'We communicated a lot with members of the Congress to support the resolution,' O'Keefe recalled.[42]

The ninety-five to zero vote in favour of Byrd-Hagel was the coalition's high point. Environmental NGOs battered its members with shareholder proxy campaigns and membership haemorrhaged. Before Kyoto, BP broke ranks and quit. In 1999, Ford Motor Company left. Ford chairman, life-long environmentalist William Ford, told a Greenpeace business conference the following year, 'I expect to preside over the demise of the internal combustion engine.'[43] Shell, Texaco and Daimler Chrysler also left and it was disbanded in 2002.

The coalition was advised by Don Pearlman, a Washington attorney with a wide range of clients, including OPEC members. Pearlman had a reputation for his ferocious intelligence and unrivalled knowledge of the labyrinthine negotiating texts spawned by the Rio Convention. 'I respected how well he did his job,' Bob Watson, IPCC chairman at the time, told the author.[44] Helping bring about Watson's ouster turned out to be the coalition's parting shot. There was considerable opposition to Watson's reappointment within the US business community. The incoming Bush administration was persuaded that, in O'Keefe's words, Watson was 'too much of an advocate'.[45]

Watson won some votes, but lost those of Asia, Africa and Eastern Europe. The US had already announced its support for India's Rajendra Pachauri. The choice would have unexpected consequences. By turns aggressive and dismissive, Pachauri's reaction to widely publicised mistakes in the Fourth Assessment Report did little to enhance the IPCC's battered credibility.

In the mythology of global warming, fossil fuel firms prevented the US from joining the EU and other developed nations in leading the world to a virtuous low carbon future. There was a simpler explanation. There were never enough votes in the Senate for a simple majority, let alone the sixty votes needed to avoid a filibuster, to pass cap-and-trade. In 2003, the McCain Lieberman Climate Stewardship Act was defeated fifty-five to forty-three. By voice vote two years later, the Senate passed a resolution calling on Congress to enact a comprehensive and mandatory market-based scheme to stop or slow the growth of greenhouse gas emissions without inflicting 'significant harm' on the economy.[46] It was a hollow statement. An amendment to the Energy Bill, calling for voluntary action sponsored by Chuck Hagel, was carried by sixty votes to twenty-nine. A competing one sponsored by McCain and Lieberman that called for mandatory caps went down by thirty-eight to sixty votes.

Two years later, the Senate debated another cap-and-trade proposal, this time targeting a sixty-three per cent reduction by 2050 (similar to the UK's Climate Change Bill). The legislation never made it out of committee.

By then, an alternative path had opened up. In a five to four judgement, the Supreme Court required the EPA to regulate greenhouse gas emissions under the 1972 Clean Air Act. 'Perhaps the most important decision ever handed down in the annals of environmental law,' Lisa Jackson, EPA administrator in the Obama administration has called *Massachusetts v. EPA*.[47] It was also perhaps the most stupid. The Court might as well have instructed King Canute to reverse the incoming tide.

While there is a clear rationale to regulating what comes out of automobile tail pipes to reduce local air pollution, global warming is a global phenomenon. In the Court's opinion, because US motor vehicles accounted for six per cent of global emissions of carbon dioxide (four per cent of global greenhouse gas emissions, as the Chief Justice wrote in his dissent), they made a 'meaningful contribution' to greenhouse gas concentrations.[48] 'While it may be true that regulating motor vehicle emissions will not by itself *reverse* global warming, it by no means follows that we lack jurisdiction to decide whether EPA has a duty to take steps to *slow* or *reduce* it.'[49]

Having the jurisdiction is one thing. Having the means is something else. Even if EPA regulations reduced fuel burn by fifteen per cent from 2016, and assuming US vehicle emissions remain at the same percentage of global emissions for a hundred years, it would delay the full effect of a century's worth of global warming by ten months, from 1st January 2116 to 25th October 2116.*† This assumes people don't change their behaviour. If, in response to finding that a tank of gas taking them farther, Americans decided to drive more miles, the smaller the effect will be on emissions. If they don't, lower demand for oil will mean lower oil prices, making it cheaper for drivers elsewhere in the world to use their cars more and emit more carbon dioxide.

---

*   EPA regulations for new vehicles project average light vehicle emissions of 295g of CO_2 for the 2012 model year falling to 250g per mile for the 2016 model year. *EPA and NHTSA Finalize Historic National Program to Reduce Greenhouse Gases and Improve Fuel Economy for Cars and Trucks* (April 2010), p. 4.

†   On the (more correct) basis of the Chief Justice Robert's dissenting opinion that US motor vehicles account for four per cent of global greenhouse gas emissions, the full effect would be postponed by less than seven months.

Massachusetts v. EPA revolved around whether the EPA's refusal to regulate gas emissions presented a risk of harm to Massachusetts that was both 'actual' and 'imminent'.[50] In the opinion of the Chief Justice, arriving at such a conclusion required such an attenuated chain of causation that it went to the very outer limit of the law.[51]

To demonstrate injury to Massachusetts, the Court cited a report by the National Research Council that identified a number of environmental changes that, in the Court's opinion, had 'already inflicted significant harms'. These included the retreat of mountain glaciers, reduction in snow cover extent, earlier spring melting (harmful to the Commonwealth of Massachusetts?) and accelerating sea level rise.[52]* A 10–20cm rise in sea levels during the twentieth as a result of global warming, had already begun to 'swallow' Massachusetts' coast land, the Court asserted.

In his dissent, Chief Justice Roberts described this as 'pure conjecture'.[53] Boston's rising sea level had been caused by land subsidence. The anticipated sea level rise over the course of the twenty-first century could be less than the margin of error of the model used to estimate the elevation of coastal land. 'It is difficult to put much stock in the predicted loss of land.'[54]

Should carbon dioxide – without which there would be no plant life and only single celled life-forms and funguses – be defined as a pollutant, as defined by the Clean Air Act? For the Court, the matter was straightforward: carbon dioxide is a physical and chemical substance emitted into the ambient air. By the same definition, so is the most important greenhouse gas in the Earth's atmosphere – water vapour.

On 7th December 2009 – the opening day of the Copenhagen climate conference – the Obama administration announced its endangerment finding on carbon dioxide and other greenhouse gases, as required by the Supreme Court. 'This administration will not ignore science or the law any longer,' Lisa Jackson said. The EPA was now 'authorised and obligated' to reduce greenhouse gas emissions under the Clean Air Act.[55]

As president-elect, Barack Obama videotaped some remarks on climate change. A federal cap-and-trade system would cut emissions by eighty per cent by 2050. Not only would this save the planet, 'it will also help us transform our industries and steer our country out of this economic crisis'.[56] With its upside down economics, the speaker might have been one of the professors of the political school of the grand academy of Lagado.

---

*   Nowhere in the Court's opinion is there any discussion of the potential benefits of longer growing seasons and stronger plant growth that might arise from having more carbon dioxide in the atmosphere.

28
Hugging Huskies

There is money to be made and there are jobs to be created. To do that we must meet the challenge of Kyoto.

Tony Blair, 14th December 1997[1]

I want us to be the greenest government ever.

David Cameron, 14th May 2010[2]

Concluding his visit to the academy, Gulliver relates that he had seen nothing to invite a longer continuance. He began thinking of returning to England. For a traveller wearying of the policy follies of global warming, England could offer little respite.

From 2002, a Renewables Obligation was imposed on energy companies, costing energy consumers £7.3 billion to March 2011.[3] It proved a spectacularly inefficient way of reducing carbon dioxide emissions, costing up to £481 per tonne of carbon dioxide displaced from gas-fired power stations – nearly twenty times more than the £25 per tonne estimate used by the government.[4]

Harming the many, the obligation was highly lucrative for the few – wind farm developers and some of Britain's largest landowners. The development of off-shore wind farms would result in a windfall to one of the largest – £38 million a year to the Royal Family according to one newspaper report, as the seabed within Britain's territorial waters is owned by the Crown Estate.[5] Nonetheless, in 2011 Prince Philip told a wind farm developer that wind farms were absolutely useless, completely reliant on subsidy and an absolute disgrace. 'You don't believe in fairy tales, do you?' the Duke asked Mr Wilmar of Infinergy, who expressed surprise at the Duke's 'very frank' views.[6]

Earlier that year, a senior executive of a German-owned utility confirmed to the author that the Duke was right: the only economic function of wind farms was to collect tax revenues. Seen that way, wind farms are a throwback to a distant era. Tax farms were used before the English Civil War. In 1641, Parliament passed a bill confiscating the estates of some of the biggest tax farmers, later commuted to a heavy fine. They were no more popular in pre-revolutionary France; Lavoisier was guillotined for the same crime.

In June 2008, the House of Commons debated the Climate Change Bill to write into law the government's target for a sixty per cent cut in carbon dioxide emissions by 2050, something no other country was doing. In his third term, Tony Blair had come under pressure from 'The Big Ask Campaign', spearheaded by Friends of the Earth, for legislation to mandate year-on-year cuts in emissions.

The decisive pressure came from the new approach of the Conservative opposition under David Cameron. Green issues were central to Cameron's re-branding of the Conservative Party. The shift began after the 2005 election during Oliver Letwin's tenure as shadow Defra secretary. In October, Letwin and his Liberal Democrat counterpart, Norman Baker, issued a joint letter urging 'independent verification' of 'year on year carbon reduction requirements'.

One of the progenitors of the poll tax in the 1980s, Letwin was also David Cameron's chief policy adviser in his campaign for the Conservative Party leadership. On a visit to the Eden Project in Cornwall at the end of that month, Cameron declared: 'With global poverty and terrorism, climate change is one of the three greatest challenges facing mankind today.' The Conservatives should 'show real leadership on this vital issue' and committed the party to annual targets underpinned by a statutory framework if he won.[7]

Once elected, Cameron consistently outbid Labour on commitments to rapid decarbonisation. In March 2006, he criticised Gordon Brown: 'In a carbon-conscious world, we have got a fossil fuel Chancellor.'[8] A month later, he flew to Norway to be filmed hugging a huskie and inspecting a re-treating glacier, a trip that helped define his leadership.

In August, a letter from a cross-party group of MPs called for a bill setting annual targets to be introduced in the next parliamentary session. In a coordinated move, Cameron urged cuts in emissions of at least sixty per cent by 2050, without any apparent attempt to estimate the cost.[9] Certainly no cost estimates were made public.

Labour felt obliged to respond. It committed to a Climate Change Bill in the Queen's Speech of November 2006. Again, Cameron upped the stakes. 'I hope that it will be a proper bill, and not a watered-down bill,' he said. 'Government have got to give a lead by setting a proper framework; that must mean an independent body with annual targets and an annual report from Government on its progress.'[10] This was much more interventionist than Blair, who in February 2007 warned of the impracticality of annual targets. The bidding war was now in full swing.

The bill was introduced in the Lords in November 2007. There was little real debate. It passed its Third Reading without a division on 31st March 2008 and reached the Commons with a strong cross-party consensus behind it, where there were only a handful of dissenters. The most long-standing of them was Andrew Tyrie, Conservative MP for Chichester. He had been sceptical about the economics of rapid decarbonisation since early 1990 when, as John Major's advisor in the Treasury, he had been involved in an inter-departmental working group, chaired by the deputy chief economic advisor, John Odling Smee. In 2005 and 2006, Tyrie tried to dissuade the front bench from making expensive commitments to legislate on carbon reduction, to little avail.

Tyrie was determined to register his dissent and pressed ahead with opposition at the bill's Second Reading by ensuring there was a division. But he was able to rally the bare minimum needed to force a vote. No other country would be foolish enough to consider such a measure, he said in the debate: 'Although UK emissions will fall, they will reappear, probably at even higher levels, as the industries that we close down with our higher costs base reopen in China and elsewhere.'[11] The bill would give China every incentive to delay an international agreement. 'Why should they rush to agree anything when they can acquire our industrial base and those of other countries silly enough to go it alone?' Tyrie enquired.[12]

The all-party consensus resumed as soon as Tyrie sat down. Labour's Desmond Turner said Tyrie was a member of the Flat Earth Society. 'The issue is not counting beans but the survival of the species,' Turner declared.[13]

Shortly before the debate, Peter Lilley obtained a copy of the bill's regulatory impact statement. He was stunned. At first, he thought he had been reading the figures back to front. At best, the benefits might exceed the costs by £52 billion; at worst, the costs would be £95 billion greater than the benefits – and those excluded transitional costs of up to one per cent of GDP until 2020 and the leakage of carbon-intensive business abroad.[14] It exposed the black hole at the heart of the bill. It was probably the most expensive legislation ever put before Parliament.

Lilley intervened when the junior environment minister, Phil Woolas, who subsequently became the first MP to be disqualified by an election court for lying about his opponent, claimed the benefits would exceed the costs. 'He makes an interesting point and we will be able to debate it,' the minister replied. 'It is not a fundamental principle.'[15] The cost estimates were not debated then and the bill went through the whole of its Commons committee stage without any discussion of its supposed costs and benefits.

The whips on both sides packed the debate and told any doubters to abstain rather than force a division. Pressure was brought to bear on the remaining dissenters. At both Second and Third Reading, just five MPs voted against the bill, including the two tellers for the noes. In addition to Tyrie and Lilley, Christopher Chope, Philip Davies, and Ann Widdecombe constituted the entire complement of dissenters. At the Third Reading, the Whips packed the debate, so that Tyrie, the leading dissenter, was not called to speak.

During passage of the bill, the 2050 target was raised from sixty per cent to eighty per cent. Given that the target has a base year of 1990, and using reasonable growth assumptions, an eighty per cent reduction is equivalent to about ninety per cent on levels that would have been achieved in 2050; in other words, almost total decarbonisation.[16]

The eighty per cent target required a new regulatory impact assessment. The government produced a new estimate in March 2009. The benefits of cutting emissions had risen nearly tenfold from those estimated when the bill was presented to Parliament – to £1,020 billion. Lilley wrote to Ed Miliband, the new climate change secretary, a Cabinet post created six months earlier, asking him to confirm that the cost of the Climate Change Act amounted to £16,000 to £20,000 for every UK household.[17]

Miliband replied a month later. Climate change was a potential public health catastrophe. The new estimates were predicated on a global agreement to cap emissions. 'Showing leadership through the Climate Change Act, the UK will help to drive a global deal,' Miliband wrote, a claim that would be put to the test less than eight months later at Copenhagen.[18]

The impact statement had been frank about the consequences of not reaching agreement. 'The UK continuing to act while the rest of the world does not, would result in a large net cost for the UK,' as the benefits of UK action would be distributed around the world, but the UK would bear all the costs.[19] In his letter, Miliband rejected Lilley's claim of the cost of the legislation to UK households and distorted what the impact statement said. 'The impact statement shows that the benefits to UK society of successful action on climate change will be far higher than the costs,' Miliband claimed.[20]

He was wrong. The impact assessment's £1,000 billion estimate was of the benefits to the world of UK action within the context of an international agreement to cap emissions, not the benefits to the UK. The study had not examined the possible local effects of global warming on Britain, which it is quite plausible to believe might be beneficial to the UK even if it was harmful to the rest of the world.

Miliband should have known that what he had written was untrue. As the responsible minister, six weeks before writing to Lilley, he had certified that he had read the one-hundred-and-twenty-six-page document and that it represented a 'reasonable view' of the costs and benefits of the legislation.[21]

Subsequently Lilley raised the matter with Ed Davey, Miliband's successor but one as climate secretary. 'We are not aware of evidence that would have allowed us to have made a reliable estimate of the distribution of those benefits, including the UK,' Davey replied in April 2012.[22]

Just as the British government became a climate change outrider, Britain's largest oil company adopted the opposite strategy to its American peers. In May 1997, three weeks after Tony Blair's election, BP chief executive John Browne signalled the new strategy in a speech at Stanford. While all science is provisional, Browne declared, 'It falls to us to begin to take precautionary action now.'[23] 'We came out of denial,' he said of the speech on its tenth anniversary. Other companies had followed, 'But the old church is now a pretty small place.'[24]

Five months later, Browne addressed the second annual Greenpeace business conference. BP's close relationship with Greenpeace was evidence of the deepening relationship between the environmental movement and business. 'We support that effort, which can only be beneficial,' Browne said.[25] BP hired Tom Burke, formerly of Friends of the Earth, as its environmental adviser. Burke is at the nexus of green power in Britain, with its overlapping circles of NGOs (Burke had also been director of the Green Alliance for nine years), government (special adviser to three Conservative environment secretaries), academia (visiting professor at Imperial and University Colleges, London), and business (later moving from BP to be Rio Tinto's environmental policy adviser).

At the 1998 Davos World Economic Forum a month after Kyoto had been agreed, Browne made an impassioned plea for other companies to support it. When he'd finished, the Global Climate Coalition's O'Keefe got up. The US petroleum industry would not support Kyoto and the US would not ratify it, O'Keefe said. Browne turned his back on him. A London colleague called to say that he had never seen Browne so angry.[26]

The following year, Browne was at the UN headquarters in New York to receive an Earth Day award. 'People want large and successful corporations to use their skills and their know-how to address the environmental agenda,' he told the ceremony.[27]

After acquiring three oil companies (Amoco in 1998; ARCO in 1999; and Burmah Castrol in 2000), BP adopted the tagline 'Beyond Petroleum

2001.' Apparently BP was no longer an oil company. It was now an energy company. Extensive internal polling after the Amoco merger showed that sixty per cent of BP staff saw addressing the environmental issue as the single most important issue in defining the quality of the company they worked for.[28] Safety did not top the list. Perhaps it was a warning of what was to come.

Not so Exxon Mobil. It was an oil company and continued to behave like one. After the demise of the Global Climate Coalition, Exxon Mobil continued to support groups that challenged the science and economics of global warming. In its 2005 Corporate Citizenship Report, Exxon Mobil described the IPCC's conclusions on the attribution of recent warming to increases in greenhouse gases as relying on expert judgement rather than objective, reproducible statistical methods.[29]

This provoked an irate letter from the Royal Society's Bob Ward accusing Exxon Mobil of being 'very misleading'.[30] The IPCC's 'expert judgement' was, Ward wrote, based on objective and quantitative analyses. Despite Ward's protestations, at issue was not whether the IPCC's conclusions were based on subjective judgement, which was clearly the case, but the scientific standing of such judgements. Even so, there is quite a lot of make-believe in the Royal Society's characterisation of the IPCC's conclusions, especially as it relates to the IPCC's Summary for Policy Makers. Britain's former top civil servant Andrew Turnbull said they would be more accurately described as a summary *by* policymakers, not for policymakers:

> The scientists prepare a draft but this is redrafted in a conclave of representatives from the member Governments, mostly officials from environment departments fighting to get their ministers' views reflected.[31]*

Ward went on to express concern about Exxon Mobil's support for sceptic organisations that were 'misinforming' the public on the science.[32] According to the *Washington Post*, the 'testiest moment' at Exxon Mobil's 2006 annual shareholder meeting came when chief executive Rex Tillerson was questioned about the company's sceptical stance in the face of a growing scientific consensus. 'Scientific consensus' was an 'oxymoron', Tillerson replied.[33]

---

* Regarding the summaries for policymakers in the Third Assessment Report, the Royal Society had stated in March 2005: 'Each sentence of which was agreed sentence by sentence at meetings of the governments from member countries of the IPCC.' The Royal Society, *A guide to facts and fictions about climate change* (March 2005).

By then, Exxon Mobil was preparing to change its posture. It wasn't in business to be on the losing side in a battle of ideas. In 2005, it decided to cease funding groups such as the Competitive Enterprise Institute, one of the most effective sceptic organisations. 'The fact that we were supporters of some of those groups had become a real distraction to the issue at hand, which is how do we produce the energy the world needs without more greenhouse gas emissions,' Kenneth Cohen, the company's VP for public affairs, told journalists in February 2007.[34] According to the Natural Resources Defense Council's Dan Lashof, 'They found that it was untenable to be in a position of casting doubt on whether global warming is happening and whether pollution is responsible for that.'[35] The episode is evidence refuting the widely held belief that fossil fuel companies are to blame for America not signing up to binding emissions controls.

BP and Exxon Mobil disagreed on virtually every other aspect of global warming. BP's Browne supported Kyoto; Exxon Mobil's Tillerson argued that every nation would need to participate ('developed nations cannot go it alone').[36] Browne supported emissions trading ('one of the most promising of all the options').[37] Tillerson thought it would result in volatile prices for emissions allowances, create economic inefficiencies and invite market manipulation. Instead Tillerson supported a revenue-neutral carbon tax.[38]

They differed on investment strategy. BP made a big bet on solar. In 1998, Al Gore opened BP's first solar manufacturing facility in the US. The next year, BP bought Solarex to become the world's largest solar energy company.[39] BP's solar capacity increased from just over twenty megawatts in 1997 to two hundred in 2006; in 2007, Browne said that he anticipated this would rise to over seven hundred megawatts. 'We plan to invest at $1 billion per annum in alternative energy sources such as these,' Browne pledged.[40]

Four years later, BP announced the complete closure of the business. 'We have realised that we simply can't make any money from solar,' the company told the *Financial Times* in December 2011.[41]

Exxon Mobil stuck closer to its hydrocarbon DNA. In July 2009 it signed a deal with Synthetic Genomics of La Jolla, California, to research and develop biofuels derived from algae by using sunlight to convert carbon dioxide into oils and long-chain hydrocarbons.[42] Later in 2009, it deepened its commitment to extracting hydrocarbons from shale rock with the acquisition of XTO Energy.

What explains the different responses of the two? Leadership doubtless played a part. But perhaps the most important is the different political environment the two operated in. No American oil company has as intimate relationship with the US federal government as BP's with the British government. Ever since 1913, when Winston Churchill took a controlling stake in BP's original predecessor, the interests of BP and the British state were seen in Whitehall as virtually indistinguishable.

In the 2000s, BP was Blair Petroleum. One of Blair's top aides, Anji Hunter, left Downing Street to work for Browne. It would have been unthinkable for BP to have opposed Kyoto and the policy of the British government. For a time, being ahead of the curve on climate change appeared commercially smart.

Investors thought so, too.

Aggressive cost cutting – necessary to compensate for BP's green investments that yielded no return – helped propel BP's share price upwards. From the date of Browne's Stanford speech in May 1997 to 20th April 2010, BP's share price rose from 359.5p ($5.84) to 655.4p ($10.00) – a seventy-one per cent increase in dollar terms, compared to a thirty per cent increase in Exxon Mobil's stock price. After the markets closed on 20th April, there was an explosion on the Deepwater Horizon drilling rig in the Gulf of Mexico.

It was BP's third – and most serious – accident caused by safety shortfalls, the first being an explosion at BP's Texas City refinery (2005) and then a ruptured pipeline spewed oil across Alaska's North Slope (2006).

Six months after the Deepwater Horizon explosion, BP's share price closed at 377.2p ($5.95), giving up ninety-seven per cent of the dollar gain it had made since Browne's Stanford speech.

29
DANGEROUS CLIMATE CHANGE

I'm more worried about global warming than I am of any major military conflict.

Chief UN weapons inspector Hans Blix, 13th March 2003[1]

The world has already reached the level of dangerous concentrations of carbon dioxide in the atmosphere and immediate and very deep cuts in the pollution are needed if humanity is to survive.

Rajendra Pachauri, chairman of the IPCC, January 2005[2]

The prodigious expenditure of effort and resources corralled by governments trying to cut emissions of carbon dioxide yielded puny results. Unable to make good on their promises to cut carbon dioxide emissions, and as global temperatures remained more or less flat, the rhetoric of alarm was ratcheted up.

In 2000, Annex I carbon dioxide emissions were 538 million tonnes lower than in 1990 – a fall of 3.6 per cent. Emissions from the ex-Communist countries of the Soviet bloc more than accounted for this – down 1,752 million tonnes – or forty-four per cent (a figure which excludes the former East Germany).[3] The collapse of communism turned out to be the most effective decarbonisation policy of all time.

In 2007, Annex I carbon dioxide emissions were 593 million tonnes higher than 2000 – a rise of four per cent. The onset of the global recession cut Annex I emissions by 1,3650 million tonnes (a nine per cent fall) – the second most effective global warming policy.[4] Virtually all this was offset by increased non-Annex I emissions. The net effect of the worst global recession since the 1930s was a reduction of less than twelve million tonnes of carbon dioxide.[5]

Kyoto's bifurcation between 'rich' North and 'poor' South actually helped push up emissions. According to Dieter Helm, part of Britain's apparent reduction in emissions came about through de-industrialising. 'Driving up our energy prices drives energy-intensive production overseas,' Helm wrote in February 2012.[6] This led to higher emissions. In the three years to 2009, non-Annex I countries emitted fifty-seven per cent more carbon dioxide (642g) to generate one kWh of electricity than Annex I nations (408g). And the trends were diverging. While Annex I countries were reducing the carbon-intensity of electricity production – emissions per kWh fell by eight per cent between 2000 and 2009 – non-Annex I countries increased their emissions per kWh by 3.5 per cent.[7]

Doing nothing would have been more rational than what governments actually did. Rationality was not the yardstick. During the middle years of the first decade of the new century, climate change became *dangerous* climate change.

To UN weapons inspector Hans Blix, climate change presented a bigger risk than a major war.[8] In his 2005 valedictory address as president of the Royal Society, Lord May, a zoologist, compared climate change to weapons of mass destruction.[9] To Sir Richard Mottram, a former permanent secretary at Britain's Ministry of Defence and chairman of the Joint Intelligence Committee, 'Climate change is a vastly greater threat to civilisation than terrorism.'[10]* In January 2004, Sir David King, Tony Blair's chief scientific adviser, described climate change as a more serious threat than terrorism.[11] Eighteen months later, suicide bombers killed fifty-two people and injured seven hundred on the London Underground and on a double-decker bus.

These are all examples of climate change derangement syndrome: otherwise perfectly sane people making statements that in any other context would be regarded as absurd. According to John Ashton, the UK's first climate change envoy, 'There is every reason to believe that as the twenty-first century unfolds, the security story will be bound together with climate change.'[12] The Foreign Office was given the strategic goal to create the right political conditions to reach international agreement on tackling global warming. It was going to do this by persuading world political leaders that 'a stable climate is essential for their national security and prosperity' – similar language to Tony Blair's justification of the Iraq War.[13] It was downgraded after Labour lost the May 2010 election and William Hague became foreign secretary.

James Lee of American University's Inventory of Conflict and Environment Project predicted that people would respond to climate change 'by building bomb shelters and buying guns'. The prospect of war between the US and Canada over rights to the Northwest Passage was not farfetched,

---

* For a semi-anonymous civil servant, Mottram shot to national fame for telling a fellow civil servant: 'We're all fucked. I'm fucked, you're fucked, the whole department's fucked. It's been the biggest cock-up and we are all completely fucked.' He wasn't talking about climate change but the resignations of his department's senior media handlers. David Graves and George Jones, 'Sixsmith stands by story as infighting continues' in the *Daily Telegraph*, 25th February 2002.

Lee wrote in the *Washington Post*. 'Anyone convinced that the United States and Canada could never come to blows has forgotten the war of 1812.'[14] When the article appeared in January 2009, Americans were too busy buying record numbers of snow blowers to cope with that winter's heavy snowfalls to be worrying about invasion from the north.

A 2003 study for the Pentagon hyped up the threat to 'dramatise the impact' of global warming.[15] There was too much 'Imagining the Unthinkable' – the study's subtitle – and a dearth of 'Recognising the Obvious'. Abrupt climate change 'could potentially de-stabilise the geo-political environment, leading to skirmishes, battles and even war due to resource constraints'.[16] Drawing on archaeological and ethnographical data from pre-industrial eras, it offered a doom-laden, neo-Malthusian prognosis of resource shortages leading to war. 'Humans fight when they outstrip the carrying capacity of their natural environment. Every time there is a choice between starving and raiding, humans raid.'[17]

The Pentagon's 2010 Quadrennial Defense Review stated that 'climate change and energy are two key issues that will play a significant role in shaping the future security environment'.[18] Intelligence assessments indicated that climate change could have 'significant geopolitical impacts' around the world by acting as an 'accelerant' of instability and conflict.[19]

So to flood and drought, famine and pestilence was added the spectre of resource wars. Just as predictions of food shortages become self-fulfilling, threats to the international system and world peace are more likely to come about because of global warming policies than global warming itself. In potentially the most destructive example of the Global Warming Policy Paradox, global warming policies risk undermining the international trading system and the economic structure of mutual advantage that would render a resource war a self-defeating strategy.

Digging around ancient burial sites for potential causes of war in the twenty-first century, the lessons from the single most important event of the twentieth century were lost. In an open global trading system, wars of conquest are economically insane. The Second World War was a struggle for control of territory and resources, Gerhard Weinberg, one of the conflict's foremost historians, has written.[20]

Germany and Japan didn't need to control a resource to benefit from it. The post-war performance of the German and Japanese economies disproved the efficacy of militarist/economic resource war theories of conquest and national survival. Neither country needed to conquer to obtain resources to prosper. Both performed incommensurately better as part of the international trading system than they had in attempting to overturn the world order.

Thus the first lesson is economic. Trade is based on voluntary exchange, in which both sides have an incentive to maintain the exchange. The gains from trade are greater than those from plunder. The plunderer, in the act of expropriation, destroys the incentive of the people who are plundered to keep producing. After the Nazi-Soviet Pact of 1939, the two totalitarian regimes agreed to deepen economic ties. For around a year, the Soviet Union accounted for the bulk of German overseas trade, supplying critical war materials that the Nazi war machine then used against the Soviet Union. Indeed, Germany obtained more from the Soviet Union through trade than it did from pillage.

The second lesson is geo-strategic. Power is not based on control of resources, but the ability of an economy to add value to those resources. The Allies paid for their war supplies. Where they could, the Axis plundered.

The third is political. A country can't invade and then trade. An economic policy based on conquest will result in the exclusion of that country from the international trading system. Conquering countries to get hold of primary resources – food, minerals or energy – with the idea of re-exporting them in manufactured goods is self-evidently absurd.

These incentives and penalties pre-suppose an international trading system. Countries which are part of it enjoy the benefits of membership. Those which are not, do not. Its existence therefore constitutes a powerful incentive for good behaviour and for states to resolve their differences peaceably.

The post-war trading system was the product of one of the greatest acts of statesmanship in history. It was conceived by the US during the Second World War. Cordell Hull, President Roosevelt's secretary of state, was determined that the disasters of protectionism, which he saw had imperilled peace and prosperity, would not be repeated. American leadership had to overcome stiff opposition from Britain, which wanted to keep imperial preference, and protectionist interests at home, to incorporate America's former enemies into an expanding international trading system.

If Roosevelt and Hull were right about the link between peace, prosperity and an open trading system, global warming policies that fragment global markets undermine world peace. At an EU summit in March 2008, the EU threatened the US and China with trade sanctions if they didn't commit to ambitious cuts in greenhouse gases. Should international negotiations fail, 'appropriate measures' could be taken to protect European industry, European leaders declared.[21] France's President Sarkozy went further. A mechanism was needed to 'allow us to strike against the imports of countries that don't play by the rules of the game on environmental protection'.[22]

The EU's 2008 Climate Action and Renewable Energy Package provides one. In the absence of an effective international agreement, the European Commission is to bring forward proposals for green tariffs equivalent to the price of emissions credits under the Emissions Trading Scheme, even though the EU allocated credits worth tens of billions of euros for free. In 2012, EU plans to extend its Emissions Trading Scheme to non-EU airlines drew threats of retaliation from China. The continent which started the Second World War hadn't learnt its lessons.

On 18th November 2004, UN secretary-general Kofi Annan received the Russian Federation's instrument of ratification. Ninety days later, on 16th February 2005, the Kyoto Protocol came into force. The EU had traded Russia's membership of the World Trade Organisation, ironically swallowing the continuation of energy subsidies for Russian businesses, for its desire for Kyoto to take effect.

Russia's ratification unleashed a wave of climate change alarmism. Finding a successor to Kyoto became the focus of international climate change negotiations. The thirty-four months to the Bali conference in December 2007 marked the most febrile phase of the fever. The UN Environment Programme's Klaus Töpfer spoke of a terrifying vision of a 'planet spinning out of control'. Global temperatures could rise by 5.8°C by the end of the century, Töpfer said, a recently published report in *Nature* claiming the rise might be even higher as early as the middle of the century.[23]

Kyoto going live isolated two non-ratifiers – George W. Bush and Australia's John Howard. 'Until such time as the major polluters of the world, including the United States and China, are made part of the Kyoto regime, it is next to useless and indeed, harmful, for a country such as Australia to sign the Kyoto Protocol,' a defiant Howard told the Australian Parliament.[24] 'The more I studied it, the more I became convinced that Kyoto was very Eurocentric,' Howard told the author in 2011, down to the choice of the 1990 base year. The collapse of the command economies meant that the progressive Left had to find other causes to fight, climate change fitting the bill, becoming a substitute religion.[25]

Unlike Australia, US participation in a son-of-Kyoto was essential. The UK held the presidency of the G8 in 2005 and between July and December also the EU presidency. The opportunity for Tony Blair's brand of messianic Salvationism was irresistible.

Before Russian ratification, Blair focused his efforts on Putin. In July 2004, the Russian Academy hosted a seminar in Moscow on climate change and Kyoto with a British delegation led by Sir David King. It was an ill-tempered affair. At a press conference, Andrei Illarionov, Putin's principal economics adviser, denounced the British and singled out King. 'At least four times during the course of the seminar ugly scenes were staged that prevented the seminar from proceeding normally.'[26]

By this stage, Illarionov was on the losing side inside the Kremlin. Illarionov criticised Putin's decision to ratify Kyoto as 'motivated purely by politics – not by science or economics'.[27]

Having squared Putin, Blair switched his focus. 'To describe George as a sceptic on climate change would be an understatement,' Blair wrote in his memoirs. 'As time progressed he shifted his thinking, but did so too slowly – a quality of conservatives I don't admire.'[28] As Paula Dobriansky, under-secretary of state for democracy and global affairs, put it, Blair and Bush had a 'vibrant and active exchange' during the British G8 presidency.[29]

Despite Blair's characterisation, Bush showed a stronger grasp of the problem than Blair. His administration's policy was a determined, cogent and well-developed effort to press the reset button on the two components of the international climate change negotiations that were visibly failing – its heavy reliance on emissions reductions and the Annex I bifurcation. What Blair and other world leaders achieved was to push Bush – against his better instincts – into accepting the principle of Kyoto-style emissions caps.

Bush's attempt to bridge the Annex I bifurcation was taken forward by his successor. It was defeated at Copenhagen. But the policy Bush inherited had come to a dead end. He had to try something different. To have carried on where Clinton had left off would have meant falling into Einstein's definition of insanity – doing the same thing over and over again expecting a different result.

The Bush reset began with a speech in June 2001, just before his first trip as president to Europe. 'America's unwillingness to embrace a flawed treaty should not be read by our friends and allies as any abdication of responsibility,' Bush said. 'To the contrary, my administration is committed to a leadership role on the issue of climate change.'[30] He pledged to work within the UN framework – and elsewhere – to develop an 'effective and science-based' response to global warming. He also spoke of the uncertainties:

We do not know how much effect natural fluctuations in climate may have had on warming. We do not know how much our climate could, or will change in the future. We do not know how fast change will occur, or even how some of our actions could impact it.[31]

From May 2001, Paula Dobriansky was responsible for leading the US team in the climate change negotiations, filling the post previously occupied by Tim Wirth and Frank Loy. On taking up her position, Dobriansky talked to both, the latter being particularly engaged (the two had previously worked together and had the same special assistant, Nigel Purvis, at the State Department). There had been questioning of the science at Cabinet-level meetings at the White House. So the National Academy of Sciences was brought in. Working closely with Dobriansky in the State Department, it assessed all types of issues relevant to climate change and ended up restating the consensus view.[32]

The initial phase came to an end on 9/11, when the focus switched to counter-terrorism. Subsequently a two-pronged strategy was developed: prioritising technological solutions and developing complementary diplomatic avenues to those established under the UN climate change convention. By 2007, the Bush administration had spent $37 billion on climate science, technology and incentive programmes.[33] In parallel, it developed a series of international initiatives, including the Asia-Pacific Partnership on Clean Development and Climate, and collaboration on projects such as carbon sequestration and the development of hydrogen fuel-cell technology. It culminated in May 2007 with the inception of the Major Economies forum to bring together the world's largest emitters.

American negotiators were frustrated at the incapacity of the UN process to produce results – 'very challenging', as Dobriansky called it.[34] Indeed, the Major Economies initiative was similar to that set out in a June 2007 article by Todd Stern, a former Clinton administration official and later Obama's climate envoy, and William Antholis of the Brookings Institution. They called for an ecological E8 of world leaders, half from the developed world, and half from developing nations.

In September, Boyden Gray, America's ambassador to the EU, wrote in the *Financial Times* of the 'sclerotic UN process' hobbled by the participation of nearly two hundred countries. It had been US leadership of a small group of major countries that had driven through the Montreal Protocol and delivered ten times the greenhouse gas reduction of Kyoto, Gray reminded suspicious Europeans.[35]

However, the differences between the Montreal and Kyoto protocols were substantive as well as procedural. When the Montreal Protocol was concluded, there were ready substitutes for CFCs and the main emitters of ozone-depleting substances were the industrialised nations. Attempting to repeat the success of the Montreal process pre-supposed that the principal emitters of carbon dioxide were willing and able to cut their emissions. With China adding new coal-fired power stations by the week and rapidly overhauling the US as the number one producer of carbon dioxide, the big question was: supposing China was not willing?

For Tony Blair, the obstacle wasn't China and the other large emerging economies. It was President Bush. 2005 was the year to heighten the pressure ahead of July's Gleneagles G8.

At the beginning of February, the British hosted a three-day conference, 'Avoiding Dangerous Climate Change', at the Met Office's headquarters in Exeter. There were two ghosts at the party: Izrael and Illarionov. 'Anyone who is frightened about the prospect of global warming is welcome to come and live in Siberia,' Illarionov told a journalist.[36]

Other participants stuck to the script. Chris Rapley, director of the British Antarctic Survey, was alarmed by the melting of the West Antarctic ice sheet.* Antarctica was no longer the 'slumbering giant' of the Third Assessment Report: 'I would say that this is now an awakened giant.'[37] Bill Hare of the Potsdam Institute told delegates that the 3°C increase expected by 2100 would kill off all the frogs and spiders in South Africa's Kruger National Park and leave more than 3.3 billion people living in countries suffering large crop losses.[38] Lord Oxburgh, chairman of Shell's UK holding company, warned that unless governments took urgent action there 'will be a disaster'.[39]

Was the amount of carbon dioxide in the atmosphere reaching danger level? The previous month, Rajendra Pachauri was unequivocal. Carbon dioxide concentrations had already reached dangerous levels and called for immediate and 'very deep' cuts in the pollution if humanity is to 'survive', he told a UN conference in Mauritius.[40]

Collectively the scientists and assorted experts gathered in Exeter to talk about avoiding dangerous climate change weren't so obliging. 'That's a value

---

* It was hearing from the British Antarctic Survey about the ozone layer that had persuaded Margaret Thatcher to throw her support behind international efforts to cut emissions of CFCs and other ozone-depleting substances.

judgement to be made by policymakers,' said Bert Metz of the Netherlands Environmental Assessment Agency.[41] The conference concluded that the risks of global warming were 'more serious' than previously thought. 'Avoiding more serious climate change' didn't have quite the same ring. In 2006, Nicholas Stern would be more reliably on-message with forecasts of catastrophes, generating many times the PR impact of the Exeter conference.

Writing in the *Times of India* later that month, Swaminathan 'Swami' Aiyar sounded a note of caution. The best scientific assessment says global warming is happening, 'yet never in history have scientists accurately predicted what will happen one hundred years later'.[42] He had nearly been convinced by photos of the rapid retreat of an Andean glacier publicised by Greenpeace. When Swami visited it, he found others had shown little movement and one glacier had advanced. Greenpeace and other ecological groups had well-intentioned people with high ideals. But as crusaders, 'they want to win by any means, honest or not. I do not like being taken for a ride, by idealists or anyone else'.[43]

A month before the Gleneagles G8, the national science academies of the G8 nations plus those of Brazil, China and India issued a joint statement:

> The scientific understanding of climate change was sufficiently clear
> to justify taking prompt action to reduce net global greenhouse gas
> emissions.[44]

The academies told the G8 leaders that they should 'acknowledge that the threat of climate change is clear and increasing'.[45] At the beginning of July, the Royal Society published a sixty-page report saying that increased levels of carbon dioxide would cause the oceans to acidify.

Bush was being set up in a pincer movement between the science and the threat of G8 isolation. Although he acknowledged the threat of global warming, he qualified it by reference to the scientific uncertainties, an escape hatch the science academies were trying to close off. 'Tony Blair is contemplating an unprecedented rift with the US over climate change at the G8 summit next week, which will lead to a final communiqué agreed by seven countries with President George Bush left out on a limb,' the *Guardian* reported.[46] France and Germany preferred an unprecedented split communiqué to a weak one.

According to the report, the US objected to drafting that described climate change as a serious and long-term challenge – wording that got into the final communiqué – and that which said there was strong evidence that 'significant' global warming was occurring with human activity contributing to it – wording that did not. The US made a significant concession in accepting that 'we know enough to act now' to justify action to stop and then reverse the growth of greenhouse gases.[47] Inch by inch, the Bush administration was being cornered into accepting the principle of emissions caps.

If 1988 was global warming's *annus mirabilis*, 2007 was the *ne plus ultra*, with a concatenation of events culminating in Bali at the year's end. Australia's voters obliged, voting out the other Kyoto hold-out. Nature was unbiddable. Observed global temperatures stubbornly showed no discernible upward trend since the turn of the century.

At the beginning of February 2007, the IPCC released a twenty-page summary of its Fourth Assessment Report. It declared global warming 'unequivocal' and human activity its main driver. Compared to the 2001 Third Assessment Report, the IPCC raised its confidence level in its projections from 'likely' (meaning sixty-six to ninety percent) to 'very likely' (better than ninety per cent), although there exists no empirical means of verifying either the forecasts or the confidence levels surrounding them.

'February 2nd will be remembered as the date when uncertainty was removed as to whether humans had anything to do with climate change on this planet,' Achim Steiner, Töpfer's successor at UNEP, claimed. 'The evidence is on the table.'[48] In reality, the 'evidence' was the product of three days and nights of wrangling between teams of government officials from more than a hundred countries and the report's lead authors, the *New York Times* reported.[49]

A month later, the EU agreed a 2020 package to cut emissions to eighty per cent of 1990 levels by 2020 and to derive twenty per cent of its energy from renewable sources by the same year. 'We can avoid what could well be a human calamity,' said Angela Merkel, chair of the two-day summit.[50]

Groundbreaking, bold and ambitious, Blair described the deal.[51] That was certainly true for Britain and came as a surprise to the rest of the British government. They thought Blair was committing Britain to deriving fifteen per cent of its *electricity* production from renewables, the maximum amount thought possible. Instead Blair committed Britain to fifteen per cent of its total *energy* production, including home heating and transport, from renewables. Sometimes important details slipped Blair when he was after the big picture. He had not known whether the forty-five-minute readiness-for-use claim in the intelligence dossier on Iraqi weapons of mass destruction applied to battlefield or strategic weapons.[52] Had Blair made a similar slip at his final EU summit as PM? In 2011, Tony Blair's office told BBC's *Panorama* that the decision hadn't been a gaffe but a decision to protect the environment and help energy security.[53]

On 24th September, the UN convened a high-level meeting in New York. Bush gave it a miss. Arnold Schwarzenegger took centre stage. California was pushing the US beyond debate and doubt to action. The responsibility of all nations was 'action – action, action, action'.[54] The pressure was piling up on Bush, as Britain's environment minister Hilary Benn made clear. The US had to end its opposition to mandatory caps on emissions. 'It is inconceivable that dangerous climate change can be avoided without this happening,' Benn said.[55]

Among the eighty heads of state and governments, there was a lone dissenting voice – Václav Klaus, president of the Czech Republic. 'The risk is too small, the costs of eliminating it are too high and the application of a fundamentalistically [sic] interpreted "precautionary principle" is a wrong strategy,' Klaus told the conference.[56] Mingling with other world leaders, several congratulated Klaus for speaking out and said how much they agreed with him.[57]

In the debates on global warming and environmentalism, Klaus is the anti-Gore. The two are a study in contrasts: Gore, the Southern Baptist preacher invoking the terrors of the Earth if mankind did not repent from its breach with nature, in Bali beseeching delegates to find grace and feel joy; the other, speaking in gentler cadences and the precision of a former econometrician, the central European who had learnt the value of freedom and classical liberalism from its absence in post-war Czechoslovakia.

No other world leader challenged Gore. They first crossed swords in a televised debate in February 1992 during the run-up to the Rio Earth Summit. 'I disagreed with almost everything he was saying at that time,' Klaus wrote later.[58] Subsequently Klaus described a lecture by Gore as 'utterly absurd' and 'scaremongering'.[59]

More than his disagreement with the scientific consensus and the economics of the proposed solution, Klaus's opposition is philosophical. At stake was human freedom. 'If we take the reasoning of the environmentalists seriously, we find that theirs is an anti-human ideology,' Klaus wrote in 2008. 'It sees the fundamental cause of the world's problems in the very existence of *homo sapiens*.'[60] Socialism was no longer the greatest threat to freedom, democracy and the market economy, Klaus argued. It was 'the ambitious, arrogant, unscrupulous ideology of environmentalism'.[61]

Three days after the UN conference, the US hosted a meeting of the sixteen country Major Economies grouping, including seven non-Annex I nations. 'We've come together today because we agree that climate change is a real problem and that human beings are contributing to it,' secretary of state Condoleezza Rice told the gathering.[62] The next morning, President Bush came to the State Department to address the delegates. He looked exhausted, stumbling over the names of the key people in the forthcoming climate conference in Bali. A new approach was needed, Bush said. It should involve the world's largest greenhouse gas emitters, developed and developing nations alike:

> We will set a long-term goal for reducing global greenhouse gas emissions. By setting this goal, we acknowledge there is a problem. And by setting this goal, we commit ourselves to doing something about it.[63]

His pledge was a substantial concession. It didn't earn him any applause from the delegates.

What did was Bush's assurance that the US would advance negotiations under the UN climate change convention. Delegates applauded for opposite reasons. The Europeans were wedded to belief in the efficacy of multilateral institutions. At the UN conference, Angela Merkel had spoken of the centrality of the UN process and called for global emissions to be halved by 2050 – seemingly oblivious that the UN process was incapable of delivering such commitments.[64] Non-Annex I delegates applauded because the UN process provided them with the surest guarantee of not having to control their emissions while minimising any political fall-out.

On 12th October, the Norwegian Nobel Committee announced it was awarding the 2007 Nobel Peace Prize jointly to the IPCC and Al Gore. The committee wanted to

> contribute to a sharper focus on the processes and decisions that appear to be necessary to protect the world's future climate, and thereby to reduce the threat to the security of mankind.[65]

A month later in Valencia, Spain, UN secretary-general Ban Ki-moon launched the IPCC's Fourth Assessment Report. 'Already, it has set the stage for a real breakthrough,' Ban said. At the UN meeting in September, political leaders had been clear: 'We cannot afford to leave Bali without such a breakthrough.'[66]

On 24th November, Australians went to the polls and delivered their Bali breakthrough. Climate change was a 'perfect storm', according to Howard.[67] It hadn't been much of a political issue until 2006. There was a long drought and an early start to the bush fire season. The Stern Review generated a lot of publicity. So did Al Gore's *An Inconvenient Truth*, which Howard thought 'spiced with attacks' on the Bush administration.[68]

Howard tried to adjust to the new political climate in a January 2007 speech. Describing himself as a 'climate-change realist', Howard said he accepted the broad theory about global warming. 'I am skeptical about a lot of the more gloomy projections,' he told the National Press Club in Canberra.[69]

Howard was not going to surf the climate change wave like Labor's Kevin Rudd. He rejected Rudd's claim that climate change was the overwhelming moral challenge facing Australians. 'It de-legitimises other challenges over which we do have significant and immediate control.' Neither should Australia set a target based on the needs of other countries. 'I will not sub-contract our climate change policy to the European Union,' Howard said, rejecting Labor's call for a sixty per cent cut in Australia's emissions by 2050.[70] Looking back four years on, Howard though the politics of global warming contributed to his defeat; it was a case of 'John Howard didn't seem that interested' when the issue had come to dominate Australian politics.[71]

Ten days after taking office, Kevin Rudd flew to Bali and handed Ban Ki-moon Australia's instrument ratifying Kyoto. Moments later, he addressed the conference and 'all people of goodwill committed to the future of our planet'. Climate change was the defining challenge of the age, Rudd said. It was imperative for the conference to agree to work together on a global emissions goal, one that recognised the core reality: 'We must avoid dangerous climate change.'[72]

30
BALI

*This is a historic moment, long in the making ... Now, finally, we are
gathered together in Bali to address the defining challenge of our age.*

UN secretary-general Ban Ki-moon[1]

There is no doubt that the fate of our civilisation hangs in the balance.

The Prince of Wales[2]

As Berlin was to Kyoto, so Bali was to Copenhagen.

Twelve years on, the climate change negotiations had accreted multiple layers of complexity. The Berlin Mandate had been relatively straightforward, covering three pages. Bali was the thirteenth meeting under the UNFCCC (COP13) *and* the third conference of the parties serving as the meeting of the parties to the Kyoto Protocol (COP/MOP3). The world's largest economy was a party to the convention but not the Protocol, so the COP/MOP had to decide how to manage this fissure.* In addition, there were meetings of subsidiary bodies, dozens of contact groups (a way to get around UN rules that permit no more than two meetings at the same time) and informal consultations. The resulting Bali Road Map was not defined in a single document; rather it set up a series of processes with the aim of agreeing a comprehensive regime in December 2009 at Copenhagen.

The degree of complexity was in inverse relation to the probability of reaching an effective agreement. It all pointed to the essential unreality of attempting to create a global regime to regulate the quantity of ubiquitous, naturally occurring gases.

Carbon dioxide is released into the atmosphere not only from burning fossil fuel (which along with cement production accounts for seventy-five per cent of the increase in atmospheric carbon dioxide).[3] Carbon dioxide is also released from burning wood and animal dung (providing a source of heat for millions in the developing world) and through bacteria breaking down organic matter. It is absorbed by growing vegetation and by the oceans. The IPCC estimated that the remaining twenty-five per cent came

---

* It agreed on a twin-track approach, establishing a new Ad Hoc Working Group on Long-Term Cooperative Action under the convention in addition to an existing Ad Hoc Working Group on Further Commitments for Annex I Parties, under the Protocol.

from deforestation, turning grassland into cropland and changing agricultural practices.

Methane, the second most important 'man-made' greenhouse gas, is released from fossil fuel production, but also by farm animals and rice paddy fields. In the Fourth Assessment Report, the IPCC thought it 'very likely' that observed increases in nitrous oxide had been driven by increased fertiliser use and more intensive agricultural practices, as well as fossil fuel combustion.[4]

Agreement to slow down global warming would require regulating not only energy production but also agriculture and land use. The regime would need to last decades and even centuries. For developing countries experiencing rapid industrialisation, still heavily reliant on agriculture, with food accounting for a high proportion of household budgets, that included countries which were custodians of the vast majority of the world's tropical forests, the logic of such an agreement was not an enticing prospect.

Yet for the true believers, Bali carried a huge burden of expectation. It was going to change the course of history. 'It is our chance to usher a new age of green economics and truly sustainable development,' Ban Ki-moon told the conference.[5] One hundred and fifty corporate CEOs put their names to the Bali Communiqué organised by the Prince of Wales. It called for global emissions to be more than halved by 2050, a proposition supported by brands such as GE, DuPont, Shell UK, Coca Cola, Nike, Nestlé, British Airways, NewsCorp, Nokia, Volkswagen and Tesco. The shift to a low carbon economy would create significant business opportunities worth billions of dollars.[6]

To Al Gore, these were the foothills. The greatest opportunity of solving the 'climate crisis' was not new technology and sustainable development. It was in finding 'the moral authority' to solve all the other crises and unleashing 'the moral imagination' of humankind.* 'We are one people on one planet. We have one future. One destiny,' Gore told the packed hall. They should feel privileged 'to be alive at a moment when a relatively small group of people could control the destiny of all generations to come'.

The proximate obstacle to the realisation of this vision was not a Lockean argument in favour of freedom and popular sovereignty. Neither was it doubts

---

* Gore's speech at the Bali conference on 13th December 2007 is one of the most significant he made on this or any other subject. At the time of writing there is no transcript on Gore's website at http://blog.algore.com/2007/12/ but there are a number of websites with video of the speech and a fairly complete transcript, from which the quotes used in this chapter have been checked, can be found at http://www.irregulartimes.com/gorebalispeech.html

over the science or the machinations of shadowy vested interests undermining the consensus and somehow preventing governments from acting.

If capping carbon dioxide emissions really was 'the pro-growth strategy', as the one hundred and fifty corporate leaders asserted, why had the G77 plus China been so hostile to acquiring anything that appeared like Annex I-style obligations right from the start of the climate change negotiations? The blanket exemption of non-Annex I countries had been the principal cause of America's non-ratification of the Kyoto Protocol. Without extending emissions caps to the major emerging economies, Annex I countries would face deeper emissions cuts and higher carbon prices. As long as the price of carbon in the rest of the world was zero, even more economic activity would be diverted from them to non-Annex I countries.

With the US intent on getting developing world commitments onto the table, the outcome was a real world test of the concept of sustainable development. Did sustainable development have any genuine content or was it a masterstroke of branding to buy Third World acquiescence for First World environmentalism, as long as it was lubricated with copious aid flows and did not constrain their economic aspirations?

The dynamics between the three key players – the US, the EU and the G77 plus China – were almost unchanged from Kyoto. Bali was the last chance for the Bush administration to overcome the original sin of the climate change negotiations so that a future agreement should contain bankable commitments from key members of the G77 plus China. Conversely, the objective for the G77 plus China was, as far as possible, to avoid assuming such commitments and to deflect attention from this by playing up the alleged inadequacy of the Annex I nations meeting their obligations.

In this, the G77 plus China was aided and abetted by the EU, together with the usual supporting cast of assorted NGOs and scientists proclaiming the end of the world if the US did not commit to drastic emissions cuts. Then there was Al Gore, who reprised the role he had played in Kyoto in making a dramatic appearance to under-cut US negotiators.

Unlike Kyoto, Bali was to be the beginning of a process leading to an agreement on emissions caps two years later. However the EU decided it wanted to start at the end, by negotiating the overall quantum of emissions cuts. The EU wanted to corner the US into a putting a number on its emissions cut right away. The Bali conference would be meaningless if it did not set clear targets, in the words of Sigmar Gabriel, the German environment minister.[7]

Based, it was said, on the Fourth Assessment Report, the EU demanded agreement that global emissions be cut by twenty-five to forty per cent below 1990 levels by 2020. The IPCC was not meant to give explicit policy advice. At the February 2007 launch of the summary, Susan Solomon, the American Working Group I co-chair, refused to be drawn on its policy implications. 'It would be a much better service for me to keep my personal opinions separate than what I can actually offer the world as a scientist,' she had told a press conference. 'People are going to have to make their own judgement.'[8]

Politicians sought the cover provided by what scientists said should be done. The latter obliged with the Bali Declaration. Signed by more than two hundred scientists, the declaration said that a new climate treaty should limit temperature increases to no more than 2°C above pre-industrial temperatures, a number already adopted by the European Union. A 'fair and effective' agreement, in the opinion of the scientists, would require greenhouse gas emissions in 2050 to be no more than half their 1990 level.[9]

Unwisely, the UN's Yvo de Boer aligned the secretariat with the EU by circulating a four-page text containing the twenty-five to forty per cent figure. Its preamble cited the 'unequivocal scientific evidence' that required Annex I nations to cut their emissions by this magnitude, although there was no evidence as such, only computer simulations based on a series of unverifiable assumptions.[10] Defining the emissions caps upfront was dismissed by Harlan Watson of the US negotiating team. 'In our view that pre-judges the outcome of the negotiations over the next two years.'[11] In this, the US had the support of Canada, Japan and Russia.[12] De Boer disagreed. It would be a 'critical issue' for the negotiations.[13]

By trying to turn Bali into a showdown with the US over the quantum of emissions reductions, the EU was repeating the mistake of Kyoto. The critical issue was not the quantum of emissions reductions, but the extent to which non-Annex I nations would be subject to them. A treaty that didn't include commitments for China and the other large non-Annex I economies would be dead on arrival in the Senate. Were the EU and the secretariat trying to disprove Einstein's definition of insanity?

In part, the EU's negotiating obtuseness reflected its immense institutional inertia in having obtained agreement among its twenty-seven member states. In part, it was because lead responsibility lay with member states' environment ministries and the European environment commissioner who saw their principal constituency as environmental NGOs. Then there was the superficially attractive narrative that framed President Bush, who would be leaving the White House in thirteen months, as the principal obstacle to reaching agreement.

In a lightning visit, Bush's opponent in the 2004 election endorsed the EU narrative by attacking the Bush administration for undermining attempts to agree stringent emissions caps. Global momentum would make emissions caps a reality whatever the opposition of Bush or from Congress. 'This is going to happen,' Kerry told reporters. 'It's going to happen, because it has to.'[14]

By contrast with the EU's environment ministry-led approach, the US negotiating position was the product of an inter-agency process convened by the National Security Council and involved the Departments of Agriculture, Commerce, Defense, Energy, Justice, State, and Treasury, the White House Council on Environmental Quality, the National Economic Council and the EPA. The State Department led the negotiations, institutionally vastly more experienced in international diplomacy than Europe's environment ministries.

Before heading to Bali, Dobriansky and her team in the State Department met negotiators who had served in the Bush I and Clinton administrations. Several from the Clinton administration emphasised the importance of obtaining high-level commitments from non-Annex I parties. This, they argued, needed to be set forth in Bali. One former senior State Department official asked for a private meeting with Dobriansky to give her some insights before Bali. 'Very helpful, very useful,' Dobriansky recalled.[15]

Thus there was a consensus among current and former executive branch policymakers of both parties. Furthermore, the US had reached agreement on a text with key parties prior to Bali, according to Dobriansky.[16] Yet what transpired in the Bali conference hall suggested something rather different and made the denouement at Bali the most dramatic of all the COPs before Copenhagen.

Snow lay thick on the ground in Kyoto ten years before, and snow would fall on the delegates in Copenhagen two years later. Lying eight degrees south of the equator, Bali was better located for a December meeting on global warming. It drew nearly eleven thousand participants. They included more than three thousand, five hundred government officials, outnumbered by five thousand, eight hundred representatives of NGOs, UN bodies and agencies and nearly one thousand, five hundred accredited members of the media.[17]

The Indonesian government brought some welcome colour. COP President Rachmat Witoelar and others on the conference platform wore tropical shirts. Indonesian President Susilo Bambang Yudhoyono wrote a song for the occasion – its lyrics a marked improvement on the Dutch poet laureate's efforts at The Hague in 2000:

Mother Earth is getting warmer
Climate change is tragedy for all
Together we must find answers
Don't let it destroy our life

Ill-at-ease government leaders and ministers were invited to sing the chorus as a video of smiling children, burning forests and trees uprooted by storms was beamed into the hall:

We all gather in Bali
We all gather in Bali
We want to save our planet
We want to save our planet
We are all united here in Bali
For a better life, a better world
For you and me[18]

The Indonesians also broadened the talks beyond environment ministers to bring in trade and finance ministers. These included talks aimed at removing trade barriers and tariffs on environmental goods and services. There was little doubt about the geopolitical orientation of the conference chair as a leading member of the G77. In 1955, Sukharno, Indonesia's first president, hosted the Bandung Conference, the first major Asian/African conference, and in 1961 founded the Non-Aligned Movement together with Tito (Yugoslavia), Nasser (Egypt), Nehru (India) and Nkrumah (Ghana).

'We are all united here in Bali,' the chorus sang.

Up to a point. The delegates were united in their determination to present the outcome of the COP as a success, a sentiment which the G77 plus China used to isolate the United States in the COP's final minutes.

The underlying motivations of the key players can be assessed by their responses to attempts at Bali to find breaches in the Berlin Wall separating the Annex I parties from the rest. There was a renewed effort on voluntary commitment, which China and the G77 had chased off the agenda at Buenos Aires in 1998. At Bali, it was Belarus' proposal to 'legitimise' its participation in Kyoto's first commitment period, supported by Russia and the Ukraine. It sank without trace.

On the conference's third day, there was discussion of a long-standing Russian proposal to enable developing countries to take on voluntary emission limits. It attracted the support of the EU and other Annex I parties. India and Saudi Arabia voiced their opposition.[19]

There had been ongoing discussion about how to carry out a review of the Protocol. The fifty-four-member African Group and China warned against 'undermining the Protocol', even though it specifically required the review. India went further, wanting to rule out new commitments for developing countries.[20]

At the beginning of the conference's second week, there was another meeting on the review. Annex I parties wanted it to focus on the effectiveness of meeting the Protocol's objective. Growth of non-Annex I emissions would inevitably call into question the Annex I bifurcation. Russia, Canada and Australia wanted to establish a working group.* They were opposed by South Africa, China, India and Saudi Arabia. Joined by the EU, the three Annex I parties then proposed requesting proposals on how to amend the Annexes to the Protocol, i.e., to provide some form of graduation mechanism. They were opposed by a solid phalanx of China, India and Saudi Arabia.[21]

The consistent pattern of opposition by the G77 plus China provides context for their public statements in front of the cameras. At the high-level segment a couple of days later, the US restated President Bush's position that a future agreement should include a long-term global emissions goal and national plans with measurable mid-term goals. In front of the TV cameras, South Africa declared that it would take serious mitigation actions (i.e., limits on greenhouse gas emissions) that were measurable, reportable and verifiable.[22] If made in good faith, why had South Africa – with China and India – acted to block discussion that might result in a developing nation becoming an Annex I party or acquiring similar obligations? It was a question that would hang over the climactic events during the COP's grand finale.

Before that came the conference highlight. The hall was packed and security tight. Many delegates were forced to watch the proceedings on TV. For a time, Rajendra Pachauri was locked out of the hall.[23]

'Fresh from receiving the Nobel Peace Prize in Oslo alongside the IPCC, Academy-award winner, best-selling author, former Vice President, Senator and Congressman from the United States of America and climate change's single most effective messenger to the world, I present to you Al Gore,' Cathy Zoi – an employee of Gore's Alliance for Climate Protection – told the cheering hall as Gore strode across the platform.

'We, the human species, face a planetary emergency,' Gore intoned. 'That phrase still sounds shrill to some ears but it is deadly accurate as a description of the situation that we now confront.' He spoke of his shock as

---

*   The US was not present, as it was not a party to the Protocol.

scientists had repeatedly brought forward estimates for the date when the entire north polar ice cap would disappear. Years ago, they had thought it might be gone towards the end of the twenty-first century. Only three years ago, they thought it could happen by 2050. 'Now, this week, they tell us it could completely disappear in as little as five to seven years.'

He compared people who believed in the threat of climate change, but did nothing about it, to victims of Nazi death squads.

> 'First they came for the Jews, and I was not a Jew, so I said nothing. Then, they came for the Gypsies, and I was not a Gypsy, so I said nothing,' and he listed several other groups, and with each one he said nothing. Then, he said, they came for me.

Those who thought that the climate crisis would only affect their grandchildren – and, as the crisis got closer to them, their children – were wrong. It would get them too. 'It is affecting us in the present generation, and it is up to us in this generation to solve this crisis.' Quoting Churchill, most world leaders were like the appeasers of the 1930s and 'decided only to be undecided, resolved to be irresolute, adamant for drift, solid for fluidity'.

Speaking ten years and four days after his appearance at the Kyoto conference where he had publicly instructed American negotiators to make concessions, Gore dropped a second COP bombshell. 'I am not an official of the United States and I am not bound by the diplomatic niceties. So I am going to speak an inconvenient truth.' His voice tightened as he wiped sweat from his face. 'My own country, the United States, is principally responsible for obstructing progress here in Bali.' The hall went wild with applause and cheering. There were others, Gore said, who could also help move the process forward, but they weren't named – and would the audience have cared? They had just heard what it was convenient to believe.

Those who had just applauded his 'diplomatic truth' had two choices. They could direct their anger and frustration at the United States. Or they could decide to move forward without the US; do all of the difficult work and save a large, blank space in the document and footnote it: 'This document is incomplete, but we are going to move forward anyway.'

The negotiations would culminate in Copenhagen in two years' time. 'Over the next two years the United States is going to be somewhere it is not now,' Gore told the delegates. 'You must anticipate that.' He could not guarantee that the next president would have the position he assumed – 'but I can tell you that I believe it is quite likely'.

Gore spelt out the issues that needed to be decided in Bali. Targets and timetables, of course, together with that blank space for the next president of the United States to ink in; a plan for a fully-funded, ambitious adaptation fund (not a tough sell in a hall packed with delegates from countries who expected to be its beneficiaries); and a deforestation plan ('it is difficult to forge such an agreement here') – and not a word on the single biggest lesson from the Kyoto Protocol: its failure even to contemplate the prospect of major developing economies eventually being subject to a global agreement to limit their emissions.

A global agreement was not going to work unless it included the world's largest economies. Rather than use his standing to highlight the hole in the heart of the climate change treaties, Gore chose to isolate the US and the Bush administration as it attempted to fill the hole that the Clinton-Gore administration had bequeathed it. 'We have everything we need,' Gore bellowed, 'save political will. But political will is a renewable resource.'

It was scarcely Gore's finest hour.

New Scientist environment blogger Catherine Brahic described what happened next:

> The audience rises to its feet, cheers, whoops some more, Gore makes his way down the aisle, drenched in sweat, shakes the hands that are reaching towards him. The last one he shakes is that of a grinning government representative sitting just behind me – he's from China. I ask him if political will really is a renewable resource. 'We will see,' he smiles.[24]

China's answer came two days later. Ministers and officials had wrangled for much of the day over the precise wording that might – or might not – provide a basis for some form of construction to bridge the gaping divide in the climate treaties. A smaller group met until the early hours of Saturday morning, reaching apparent agreement on the most contentious issues.

Shortly after 8am, Rachmat Witoelar gavelled the resumed session to order. Even minor changes to the text would compromise the meeting's ability to come to an agreement, Witoelar warned.[25] He invited the COP to adopt the draft text. Portugal, on behalf of the EU, supported the text and called for all parties to do the same. Witoelar scanned the hall. 'India, please come forward.'

At a small meeting mandated by Witoelar, the Indian delegate explained, the G77 plus China had agreed a modification of the text in respect of the scope of possible obligations placed on developing country parties: nationally appropriate mitigation actions by developing country parties in the context of sustainable development, supported by technology, financing and capacity building, in a measurable, reportable and verifiable manner. The language hid a shift in emphasis. Measurable, reportable and verifiable now applied to what developed nations were to do for developing ones, de-emphasising the accountability of developing countries in meeting their mitigation commitments. 'Mr President, this is our preference,' the Indian delegate's politeness indicating the strength of the hand India and its allies were playing.

Not so the Chinese delegation, whose intervention let the cat out of the bag. It was wrong to ask the meeting to adopt a text when the other meeting, convened by the Indonesian foreign minister and other members of the G77 plus China, was discussing this very matter. 'At this moment, we cannot adopt this decision.'

Witoelar suspended the session.

When it resumed, the Chinese delegation intervened again. The Indonesian foreign minister was still in consultations. It was therefore still inappropriate for the matter to be discussed. A second member of the delegation took the microphone. In English, he accused the secretariat of intentionally holding the session in the hall when he knew that the G77 was still meeting the Indonesian foreign minister. To applause, he demanded apologies from the secretariat.

'Yes, I have been offended,' the microphone picked up de Boer telling Witoelar. 'This is a process I was not aware of.'

Pakistan, on behalf of the G77, asked for a further suspension while negotiations continued outside the hall.

Witoelar began the resumed session with an apology; as chair of the conference, he had not been without faults. But he had brought heavy reinforcements. 'I come before you very reluctantly,' Ban Ki-moon told the delegates. 'Frankly I'm disappointed at the lack of progress.' Everyone (i.e., the US) should be ready to make compromises. 'No one leaves this chamber fully satisfied.'

Witoelar made another apology, asking for delegates' understanding and forgiveness for any unintentional mistakes (i.e., that the G77 plus China stitch-up had become public in such an embarrassing manner). The apology wasn't enough for the Chinese delegation, who wanted to know from the executive secretary why China had needed to make two speeches on a point of order earlier in the day.

Yvo de Boer switched on his microphone. The words didn't come easily; two or three at a time before trailing off. Then a complete sentence. 'The secretariat was not aware that parallel meetings were taking place and was not aware that text was being negotiated elsewhere.' He switched off his microphone, closed his light blue UN folder and left the platform. China had made its point.

Take two. India took the floor. The G77 plus China had accepted 'somewhat different' language and read out the text again.* 'This is our preference.'

Portugal expressed the EU's support. Cheering and applause filled the hall.

Now it was the turn of the US. Dobriansky explained that the US had come to Bali with the hope of agreeing a strong statement about common global responsibility to address climate change, recognising differences among national circumstances. However, the formulation proposed by India was not one the US could accept as it represented a change in the balance that the parties had been working towards.

She was met with boos and catcalls.

Japan, in a series of circumlocutions, avoided explicitly accepting or rejecting the proposal.

To applause and cheers, South Africa's Marthinus van Schalkwyk said that the suggestion that developing countries were not willing to assume their full responsibilities was 'most unwelcome and without any basis'. They were saying voluntarily they were willing to commit to measurable, verifiable mitigation actions. 'It has not happened before.' The US should reconsider its position.

Brazil said the text was a balanced and fair basis.

More cheering.

US-born Kevin Conrad for Papua New Guinea unleashed more. The US should either lead or get out of the way, conference-speak for the US to do the opposite and fall into line and accede to the position of China, India and the rest of the G77.

The US was isolated.

Dobriansky indicated she wished to speak again. 'We've listened very closely to many of our colleagues here,' she said. The US had come to Bali 'very committed' to developing a long-term, global greenhouse gas emission goal. It was also committed to giving very serious consideration to the views of Japan, Canada and the EU, to lead to a halving of global emis-

---

* It was adopted as 1 (b) (ii) of the Bali Action Plan. The placement of the word 'enabled' differed from the version read out in the morning session, but the two versions were functionally identical.

sions by 2050. It had sought agreement on the principle that commitments should be measurable, reportable and verifiable, including emission reduction or limitation objectives in a way that ensures comparability between countries' different circumstances. 'We have all come a long way here,' Dobriansky continued. The US just wanted to ensure that everyone acted together – 'we will go forward and join consensus'.

Later that day, the White House released a statement welcoming the outcome of the talks. Many features of the decision were 'quite positive'. But it also had 'serious concerns'. The negotiations needed to proceed on the basis that emissions cuts solely by developed countries would be insufficient.

> It is essential that the major developed and developing countries be prepared to negotiate commitments, consistent with their national circumstances, that will make a due contribution to the reduction of global emissions.[26]

Had Dobriansky been right to reverse her position and join the consensus? The result, as she indicated, fell short of what the US was seeking. In particular, there was no explicit recognition of the need to limit the rise or to reduce developing counties' emissions. The effect of the Berlin Mandate had been to preclude any discussion of emissions limitations for non-Annex I countries. In this respect, Bali was a breakthrough. The principle of developing countries taking on commitments to limit or reduce their emissions was on the table.

No power on Earth was strong enough to compel China, India and the other major developing economies to accept commitments on emission reductions against their will. What Bali achieved was keeping the option on the table that they might do so voluntarily, avoiding a second Kyoto and an almost certain Senate rejection. If Dobriansky had not acceded, the US would have been blamed a second time for derailing the climate change negotiations. It was a gutsy call and a class performance.

The Bush administration would bequeath its successor a viable negotiating framework. At Copenhagen two years later, the world would discover just how far leading developing countries were willing to go.

On 15th September 2008 Lehman Brothers filed for bankruptcy protection.

The impact on the Second Environmental Wave was similar to the Egyptian army smashing through the Bar Lev Line on the First. After Lehman, the language and the rhetoric were the same, but the intensity had gone. Saving the planet became less important than rescuing the banking system and staving off global economic collapse.

There was an additional effect. The West, specifically its governments, which seemed, or presumed, to have the answers to the world's problems, were suddenly exposed.

They didn't.

31
SHOWDOWN IN COPENHAGEN

*If we are willing to work for it, and fight for it, and believe in it, then
I am absolutely certain that, generations from now, we will be able to
look back and tell our children ... this was the moment when the rise of
the oceans began to slow and our planet began to heal...*

Barack Obama, 3rd June 2008[1]

*President Obama, acting the way he did, definitely eliminated any
differences between him and the Bush presidency.*

Lumumba Di-Aping of Sudan on behalf of the G77,
19th December 2009[2]

According to the Met Office, 2008 was the tenth warmest of the last one
hundred and fifty-eight years. As recently as the 1970s or 1980s, globally
2008 would have been considered warm, observed climate scientist Myles
Allen of Oxford University, 'but a scorcher for our Victorian ancestors'.[3]

Evidently the Victorians were made of sterner stuff. Without global
warming, many parts of the world would have experienced arctic conditions. 2008 began with China's worst winter for half a century. Heavy snow
closed the Chinese steel industry and killed one hundred and twenty-nine
people. For the first time in living memory, snow settled in Baghdad.

For Britain and other parts of Northern Europe, the summer was
marked by the lack of direct sunshine and South America was experiencing a particularly cold winter. Australian skiers had one of their best
seasons, with snow depths around twice the previous ski season. In the
spring, it snowed in sub-tropical southern Brazil – 'If snow is rare, to
get accumulation is astonishing,' the Metsul Brazilian weather centre reported – and in October, Sydney had early summer snow.[4] As Parliament
debated the Climate Change Act, London had its first October snowfall
since 1934. The tenth warmest year on record closed with freak snow
storms in Southern California and up to eight inches of snow fell in Las
Vegas, a record for the most snow in the month of December since official records began in 1937.[5]

Disbelief about the exceptional warmth of 2008 extended to American consumers, who bought record numbers of snow blowers. Sales of the
machines were up 'high double digits' over the previous year, one chain re-

ported, particularly among the heavier-duty big-ticket models, spurred by December weather that broke more than two thousand snowfall records.[6]

'When climate scientists like me explain to people what we do for a living we are increasingly asked whether we "believe in climate change,"' Vicky Pope, the Met Office's head of climate change advice, wrote in February 2009.[7] To Pope's dismay, a November 2008 poll for *The Times* found that only forty-one per cent of those surveyed accepted as an established fact that global warming was taking place and was largely man-made. Only twenty-eight per cent believed that global warming was happening and that it was 'far and away the most serious problem we face as a country and internationally'. Awareness of the scale of the problem resulted in people taking refuge in denial, Pope explained.[8]

On a pre-inaugural whistle-stop tour in January 2009, Barack Obama spoke of the dangers of a planet 'warming from our unsustainable dependence on oil'.[9] A poll suggested the view was held by a minority of his fellow citizens. Forty-one per cent of Americans blamed global warming on human activity, compared to forty-four per cent who thought long-term planetary trends were the cause. The numbers were a sharp reversal from a similar Rasmussen poll taken in July 2006, when forty-seven percent blamed global warming on human activity compared to thirty-four percent who viewed long-term planetary trends as the culprit.[10] A Pew poll suggested that Americans did not view global warming as a priority, the issue coming twentieth out of twenty (down from eighteenth in a January 2007 poll).[11]

In July 2009, President Obama joined other leaders for his first G8 summit. The venue had been switched to L'Aquila in central Italy after it had been struck by a severe earthquake. Since the previous G8, a financial earthquake had hit the global economy. Now the financial crisis was yoked together with climate change and the elimination of poverty in an all-encompassing megacrisis, the G8 leaders stating their determination to tackle these 'interlinked challenges' with what they hopefully called a 'green recovery'.[12] 'A shift towards green growth will provide an important contribution to the economic and financial crisis recovery,' the G8 claimed.[13]

Recognising the 'broad scientific view' that the average global temperature should not rise more than 2°C above pre-industrial levels, the G8 wanted 'to share' the goal of cutting global emissions by at least fifty per cent by 2050. Global emissions would have to peak 'as soon as possible'. It would imply that developed countries would have to cut their emissions by eighty per cent or more.[14]

On the summit's second day, a meeting of the Major Economies Forum indicated limited willingness to share the G8's self-imposed burden. Affirming the 2°C goal, the Major Economies leaders – which included Brazil, China, India and South Africa – agreed on work to 'identify a plan for substantially reducing global emissions' by 2050. However, its declaration avoided reference to any emissions reduction target.[15]

Speaking on behalf of the G8, Silvio Berlusconi stated that 'the active agreement of all major emitting countries through quantitative mitigation action was regarded by the G8 as an indispensable condition to tackling climate change'.[16] Nonetheless, the G8 praised the Forum's 'constructive contribution' and looked forward to a global, wide-ranging and ambitious post-2012 agreement in Copenhagen.[17]

As in 2007 and the lead up to Bali, there was a steady drum-beat to the COP in December. In September, Ban Ki-moon hosted a climate change summit at the UN attended by more than a hundred world leaders. None was as dedicated as Britain's Gordon Brown, one of the first leaders to say he would be attending the COP.

In October, Brown hosted a meeting of leaders' representatives of the Major Economies Forum at Lancaster House. There were less than fifty days to reach an agreement and avoid catastrophe, Brown declared. 'In just twenty-five years the glaciers in the Himalayas, which provide water for three quarters of a billion people could disappear entirely,' Brown told them, recycling a discredited IPCC claim.[18] 'Failure to avoid the worst effects of climate change could lead to global GDP being up to twenty per cent lower than it would otherwise be,' Brown said, repeating the most alarmist claim of the Stern Review, one that had collapsed under critical scrutiny, '[a]nd that is an economic cost greater than the losses caused by two world wars and the Great Depression.'[19] Developed countries had to come forward with offers of finance, Brown said. He had been working on a $100 billion per year package in 'predictable public and private funding by 2020'.[20]

There was a fragility that hadn't been apparent two years earlier. It was evidenced in the shrill reaction to the fall-out from the release of the Climategate emails in November. Writing in *The Times*, former chancellor Nigel Lawson slammed the integrity of the scientific evidence deployed by the IPCC to base far-reaching and hugely expensive policy decisions. 'The reputation of British science has been seriously tarnished,' Lawson wrote.[21]

Climate secretary Ed Miliband branded Lawson and other sceptics 'climate saboteurs'. He accused them of being 'dangerous and deceitful' for misusing data and misleading people in an attempt to derail the Copenhagen conference.[22] Brown then weighed in. 'With only days to go before Copenhagen we mustn't be distracted by the behind-times, anti-science, flat-earth climate sceptics,' Brown told the *Guardian*. 'We know the science. We know what we must do.'[23]

It was delusory to believe a small group of climate sceptics might sway governments' assessment of their national interest and swing the outcome at Copenhagen. The bluster betrayed insecurity. The air was coming out of the balloon.

Still more dramatic were political developments in Australia. At Bali, Kevin Rudd had been the COP hero. By a single vote in a 1st December party caucus ballot, the opposition Liberals ditched Malcolm Turnbull and his policy of cooperating with Labor to pass Rudd's emissions trading scheme. In came Tony Abbott. Two months before, Abbott had described climate change as 'absolute crap' – something the newly elected leader now described as 'a bit of hyperbole'.[24] The next day, the Australian Senate voted down the ETS for the second time. If Rudd had the courage of his convictions on the ETS, he could have called a double dissolution and fought an election on climate change. He blinked. Rudd's hold on power was slipping, a victim of climate change.

Copenhagen provoked millennial expectations among some of the committed. Tom Burke, NGO leader, government adviser, corporate environmental guru and academic extraordinaire, boldly declared 2009 the most important year in human history.[25] The World Council of Churches asked churches around the world to ring their bells on the Sunday midway through the conference. Bill McKibben, a leading environmental activist and Sunday school teacher, spoke of the special role of churches. 'Where I live, in the United States, before we had radio when somebody's house caught fire, we rang the church bells so that everybody would know and come out to do something about it,' McKibben explained. 'Well, something's on fire now.'[26]

In Britain, Christian, Jewish, Muslim, Hindu, Sikh, Buddhist, Bahá'í, Jain and Zoroastrian faith leaders put their names to a joint statement overseen by Ed Miliband and filmed by the Foreign Office for worldwide distribution. Tackling the causes of global warming was an unequivocal moral imperative, the statement declared.[27]

Two days before the conference, more than twenty of Britain's church leaders painted their hands blue and called for an ambitious deal in Copenhagen. Addressing an ecumenical service in Westminster City Hall, the

Archbishop of Canterbury provided some perspective. 'It looks in the last few decades particularly and perhaps the last few millennia as if the human race has on the whole not been very good news for the rest of creation,' Rowan Williams told the congregation.[28]

From the spiritual to the temporal, Copenhagen would test the willingness of developing countries to accept the idea that cutting greenhouse gas emissions would boost their economies. If the notion of a green recovery was widely believed, countries would be falling over themselves to outbid each other with offers to cut their emissions. In the event, although President Obama talked the talk, only the EU walked the walk, offering to up their twenty per cent emissions cut to thirty per cent if others followed. None did.

The environmentalist agenda made inroads in developing nations. Unlike the West, especially Western Europe, economic considerations were paramount. The refusal of developing countries to subscribe claims about the benefits of 'green growth' set the scene for a confrontation between Western environmentalism and the Third World's growth ambitions. Copenhagen thus brought the series of UN environmental conferences full circle.

Separated by thirty-seven years, Stockholm and Copenhagen shared similar symbolic actions. Nixon's EPA announced its DDT ban and Obama's EPA issued its finding that carbon dioxide was dangerous. There is the role of environmental NGOs; introduced by Maurice Strong at Stockholm as messaging propagators, but drastically curtailed in Copenhagen's Bella Center as the conference teetered on the brink of chaos.

Then there are the roles of India and China. For Strong, both were crucial. He had courted Indira Gandhi, who delivered the conference keynote address. Did her warning that the welfare of men came before the preservation of beasts still reflect developing country attitudes? Copenhagen would provide the answer.

In 1972, China was groping to find its place in the world. Strong had coached its delegation so the Stockholm Declaration could be adopted by consensus. In 2009, China was the world's second largest economy. Its diplomats were confident and highly proficient in navigating their way around the climate change negotiations. At Copenhagen's climactic moment, China fielded a mid-level official in face-to-face negotiations with the president and other world leaders which determined the outcome.

The accommodation between environmentalism and the developing world – hammered out in the Founex formula by Maurice Strong and Barbara Ward in 1971 – was based on a non-binding aspiration by developing countries not to emulate the developed world's path of industrialisation. If their development path deviated from the one preferred by environmentalists – Barbara Ward and Fritz Schumacher in the 1970s and their successors such as Al Gore and Prince Charles today – each developing country could decide for itself its trade-off between economic growth and environmental objectives.*

The Founex formulation was not written into the international climate change agreements, but it permeated their every pore. There are innumerable references to 'sustainable development' from the preamble of the 1992 convention to the critical paragraph 1 (b) (ii) of the Bali Action Plan on nationally appropriate mitigation actions by developing countries 'in the context of sustainable development.'

Although the use of the words 'sustainable' and 'sustainability' became *de rigueur* in the West by companies and governments, for developing countries, the meaning of sustainable development is about environmental policies not constraining human needs and aspirations and the Brundtland Report giving overriding priority to the world's poor. The texts do not define what is meant by sustainable development, but it is clear from them that the concept chiefly applies to developing countries. There is no mention, for example, of sustainable development in the corresponding paragraph 1 (b) (i) of the Bali Action Plan with respect to developed country parties.

For the West to prevail at Copenhagen, the large emerging economies, principally China and India, but also Brazil, Indonesia, Mexico, South Africa and South Korea, would have to agree to at least one of two propositions: first, that they no longer considered themselves to be poor or developing nations; second, that the threat posed to them by global warming was so grave that it overrode the condition accepted by Strong to gain Third World participation at the Stockholm conference – that environmental protection would not fetter their development ambitions.

This made the Copenhagen conference unlike its predecessors and something international conferences try and avoid. The logic of global warming – the harm caused by an extra tonne of carbon dioxide in the atmosphere was the same irrespective of how it got there or who put it there – and the economic priorities of developing countries made confrontation inescapable. It permitted only a binary outcome. One side would win; the other would lose.

---

* The third part of the Founex formula related to money. The principle was uncontroversial, but there were always disputes over the amount, who would get it and who would control it.

The alignment of the main blocs at Copenhagen was also different. In Rio, Kyoto and Bali, the US and the EU had clashed. For the first time, they pitched camp on the same ground. There was EU grumbling about the scale of the US cut – four per cent below their 1990 levels by 2020 compared to the EU's twenty per cent. But both believed a credible agreement had to involve the major emitting nations.

American negotiators came to Copenhagen determined to apply the lessons from the failure of Kyoto. They didn't want an agreement they couldn't get through the Senate and warned that Obama wasn't going to arrive in Copenhagen and act as a *deus ex machina*, as Gore had done. 'We don't want to promise something we don't have,' chief negotiator Todd Stern told reporters.[29]

Congressional Democrats were as supportive to the American position in Copenhagen as they had been hostile at Bali, despite it being identical. 'The concerns that kept us out of Kyoto back in 1997 are still with us today,' Senator Kerry told the conference. 'To pass a bill, we must be able to assure a senator from Ohio that steelworkers in his state won't lose their jobs to India and China because those countries are not participating in a way that is measurable, reportable and verifiable.'[30]

Gore made the same point. Obligations applied to one part of the world but not to another part could heighten people's fears about their economic circumstances. 'I would ask for an understanding of the difficulty that goes for elected officials.'[31]

On the other hand, divisions within the EU were more visible. Britain and France wanted to raise the EU's offer to a thirty per cent cut. 'Because of the economic recession, a thirty per cent cut is much more like a twenty per cent cut two years ago,' Britain's foreign secretary, David Miliband, explained from Brussels.[32] At least the recession was helping save the planet. Speaking for coal-dependent central and eastern European states, Poland's Mikolaj Dowgielewicz, minister for European affairs, was having nothing of it. 'The conditions for that are non-existent.'[33]

Arrayed on the other side were the G77 plus China, along with the usual assortment of NGOs. Sudan, China's principal ally in Africa, spoke for the bloc. Its core was formed by Brazil, South Africa, India and China – the BASIC nations, the last two constituting the bloc's inner core.

Before the conference, China announced that it would cut its carbon-intensity by forty to forty-five per cent in 2020 compared to 2005, a move which unsettled India. At a November meeting in Beijing, the BASIC group reiterated its non-negotiable position. A relieved Jairam Ramesh,

India's environment minister, expressed confidence that China would not 'ditch us'. Should industrialised countries seek to override them, the BA-SIC four would stage a collective walk-out.[34]

Both sides knew the other's strategy. The aim of the US was to peel off as many members of the G77 as possible and leave China isolated. Its big bazooka was the third part of the Founex formula: money, huge amounts of it, targeted at the African nations.

Halfway through the conference, China's vice foreign minister, He Ya-fei, told the *Financial Times* that China would not be the fall guy if there were a fiasco. 'I know people will say if there is no deal that China is to blame,' he said. 'This is a trick played by the developed countries.'[35]

The rest of what went on at Copenhagen was noise. It was fractious, at times farcical – the largest gathering of world leaders outside the UN in New York – but such were the tensions between them, no team photo.

There was the usual PR hoopla of climate conferences, but more so. The Nepalese Cabinet was helicoptered to a remote plateau in the Himalayas. They took part in a traditional Sherpa prayer ceremony before approving the speech that Nepal's PM would deliver in Copenhagen. Sonoma County, California, despatched a seven-person delegation at a cost of $225,000. 'This is a Disneyland for policy wonks,' exclaimed Gary Gero of the Los Angeles-based Climate Action Reserve.[36]

Coca Cola was the most visible brand in Copenhagen, its logo and 'Ho-penhagen' splashed across city billboards. More than forty thousand people came, but the lines to enter the conference were a lot longer than at Disney. On the first day, a snag in credentialing left more than a thousand delegates shivering outside the fifteen-thousand-capacity Bella Center for nine hours. Less remarked was the bitter cold. Climate change conferences were irony-free zones when it came to adverse weather events like heavy snowfall.

'Maybe I'm naïve, but I'm feeling optimistic about the climate talks starting in Copenhagen,' economist Paul Krugman wrote in the *New York Times*.[37] So was the White House. Pointing to signs of progress toward a 'meaningful' agreement, the president's trip was rescheduled to the end of the conference.[38] Gordon Brown wrote that Copenhagen was poised to achieve 'a profound historical transformation: reversing the road we have travelled for 200 years'.[39] Quite why it should make sense to turn the clock back to the beginning of the nineteenth century, Brown didn't say.

It was different on the ground. The COP's opening was pushed off balance by the furore of the Climategate emails. 'It's an eleventh-hour smear campaign,' Hockey Stick author Michael Mann said, adding, 'I've done nothing wrong; I have nothing to hide.'[40] The National Oceanic and Atmospheric Administration's James Overland complained: 'It has sucked up all the oxygen.' IPCC vice-chairman Jean-Pascal van Ypersele agreed: 'We are spending lots of useless time discussing this.'[41]

Saudi Arabia's Mohammad al-Sabban called for an independent inquiry. The 'level of trust' had been shaken, 'especially now that we are about to conclude an agreement that … is going to mean sacrifices for our economies'.[42] The IPCC's Pachauri went on the offensive. 'The only debate is who is behind it, I think we should catch the culprits.' Climategate was an attempt to tarnish the IPCC. 'The Fourth Assessment Report is completely objective, totally unbiased and solid in its scientific assessment,' Pachauri claimed.[43]

Striking a markedly less belligerent note, the UN's Yvo de Boer conceded the emails looked 'very bad' and were fuelling scepticism, but media scrutiny was not unwelcome:

> It's very good that what is happening is being scrutinised in the media because this process has to be based on solid science. If quality and integrity is being questioned, that has to be examined.[44]

Pachauri's bravado didn't last. As well as the inquiry mandated by the Dutch Parliament, Pachauri and Ban Ki-moon subsequently asked the InterAcademy Council to investigate the IPCC.

CEOs of Western corporations flocked to Copenhagen. 'Not one single Indian CEO is here, and do you know why? Because they do not consider Copenhagen to be the most important event in one hundred years,' a participant observed. De Boer was blunt. 'Basically you're not playing any role in a serious way.'[45]

Five thousand miles away, Exxon Mobil demonstrated its seriousness – a $41 billion deal to acquire shale gas and fracking corporation XTO Energy. It was the largest energy sector transaction in four years and Exxon's largest since it bought Mobil Corp in 1999. 'This is not a near-term decision,' said CEO Rex Tillerson. 'This is about the next ten, twenty, thirty years.' Combined with XTO's holdings, Exxon Mobil would control about eight million acres of land on top of unconventional natural gas.[46]

The quantum expansion of natural gas reserves unlocked by fracking gas shale presents the prospect of cheap, abundant energy. No one in Copenhagen seemed to notice. 'As politicians dither and debate,' the *Daily Telegraph*'s Damian Reece wrote, 'the market has taken another decisive step in dictating where the world's energy dollars are invested, whether campaigners like it or not.'[47] For those professionally engaged in worrying about global warming, shale gas was not part of the plan. It wasn't 'clean' energy. Of the three paths to large-scale emission reductions, the collapse in Soviet communism was unrepeatable and the 2008–2009 global recession undesirable. Only Britain's dash-to-gas – replacing coal with gas-fired power stations – required no government subsidies or artificial price support.

No big climate conference could do without Al Gore or the Prince of Wales. Both were in Copenhagen. Prince Charles garnered the better press with his plea to slow down tropical deforestation. 'The quickest and most cost-effective way to buy time in the battle against catastrophic climate change is to find a way to make the trees worth more alive than dead,' he told the conference.[48]

Although not entirely eschewing the histrionics of his Bali performance ('the future of our civilisation is threatened as never before'), Gore was low key. His role was subsidiary, more of a John the Baptist preparing the way for He who would be flying in on Air Force One. Even so, Gore managed to land himself in hot water over his Arctic ice prediction. The date for the 'possibility' of an ice-free Arctic ocean 'for a short period in summer' had been pushed back to 'perhaps as early as 2015' (at Bali, the forecast had been as early as 2012 to 2014).[49] This time, Gore was swiftly rebutted. Wieslaw Maslowski, a climatologist at the US Naval Postgraduate School in California, said that it misrepresented the information he'd given Gore's office. 'Why would you take anything Al Gore said seriously?' MIT's Richard Lindzen asked. All Gore had done was extrapolate from 2007, when there was a big retreat in the sea ice, and got zero, Lindzen explained.[50]

Kyoto took place towards the end of a decade of rising temperatures. Coming near the end of a trendless temperature chart, Copenhagen was more of a challenge. The Met Office did the next best thing. 2010 was 'more likely than not' to be the world's warmest year on record and man-made climate change would be a factor. 'If 2010 turns out to be the hottest year on record it might go some way to exploding the myth, spread by the climate conspiracy theorists, that we're experiencing global cooling,' Greenpeace's Ben Stewart said. 'In reality the world is getting hotter, possibly a lot hotter, and humans are causing it.'[51]

The trio of Venezuela's Hugo Chavez, Zimbabwe's Robert Mugabe and Bolivia's Evo Morales entertained the conference with their denunciations of capitalism as the cause of climate change. 'When these capitalist gods of carbon burp and belch their dangerous emissions, it's we, the lesser mortals of the developing sphere who gasp and sink and eventually die,' declared Mugabe, the octogenarian Marxist who had destroyed Zimbabwe's economy. 'A ghost is stalking the streets of Copenhagen' Chavez told the conference. 'Capitalism is that ghost,' provoking wild applause from the representatives of civil society, aka the environmental NGOs, who seemed not to know that the collapse of Soviet communism accomplished more for the environment than any other event in history.[52]

The violence of some of the language in the conference hall was reflected outside. Three hundred youths shrouded in black threw bricks and smashed windows as around thirty thousand people demonstrated in central Copenhagen. Police made nine hundred and sixty-eight arrests.[53]

NGOs stoked the anger with inflammatory rhetoric. 'Each year three hundred thousand people are dying because of climate change,' Kumi Naidoo of Greenpeace said at a rally.[54] But they had little purchase over the governments of India, China and others in the developing world. So the story they spun at the end of Copenhagen – widely taken up by the media – was to blame the rich nations for blocking progress. 'Rich countries have condemned millions of the world's poorest people to hunger, suffering and loss of life,' stormed Nnimmo Basey of Friends of the Earth. 'The blame for this disastrous outcome is squarely on the developed nations.'[55]

As a description of the showdown at Copenhagen, it was pure NGO fantasy. Nor was Copenhagen a confrontation between capitalism and socialism. It was a battle between the West that had signed on to the environmentalist agenda and the largest emerging economies asserting their right to a prosperous future.

It mostly took place away from the media behind closed doors. From time to time, the clash spilled out into the open. It didn't need a codebreaker to decipher the positions of the main protagonists, which were clearly signalled in speeches in the conference hall.

There was a clear victor. Equally clearly, there was a side that lost more comprehensively than at any international conference in modern history where the outcome had not been decided beforehand by force of arms.

32
Never Again

If by the end of next week we have not got an ambitious agreement, it will be an indictment of our generation.

Gordon Brown, 7th December 2009[1]

How are we going to look on Friday or Saturday if there are more than a hundred heads of state and government from all over the world and that what we say to the world is it was not possible to come to an agreement?

José Manuel Barroso, 14th December 2009[2]

Battle was joined on the second day. The *Guardian* leaked what quickly became known as the 'Danish text', a negotiating draft circulated by the Danes as COP president.

Sudan's Lumumba Di-Aping claimed the draft destroyed the Kyoto Protocol and the UN. 'It sets new obligations for developing countries,' Di-Aping charged. 'It does away with two years of negotiations.'[3] Oxfam's Antonio Hill said the draft was a backward step. 'It tries to put constraints on [emissions in] developing countries when none were negotiated in earlier UN climate talks.' Andy Atkins for Friends of the Earth called the text profoundly destructive: 'It violates the principles of UN negotiations.'[4]

In part, the vehemence was synthetic. 'Some changes, but nothing earth-shattering,' a veteran developing country negotiator told the *Earth News Bulletin*.[5] For India and China, the thirteen-page document contained two highly objectionable features.

The first was substantive. The parties were to agree that global emissions should peak 'as soon as possible,' with 2020 in square brackets as the backstop year and that *global* emissions should be cut by fifty per cent by 2050 (compared to 1990) and by an unspecified X per cent by 2020.[6] It set out a vision of long-term cooperative action, under which all parties, except the least developed nations, would have been obliged to take some form of mitigation action, i.e., be subject to limit or reductions in their greenhouse gas emissions.

Developing countries would undertake to reduce their collective emissions compared to business as usual (here the text provided a Y) to peak at a specified date and decline thereafter. On Attachment B, each developing country was to list its proposed actions together with the quantified emissions outcome expected from each action. Attachment B would morph into Appendix II of the Copenhagen Accord, in the process losing its essential feature – quantification.

Their second objection was procedural. The Danish text attempted to bring together in one agreement the two post-Bali streams, the first under the convention and the second under the Kyoto Protocol. The latter enshrined the Berlin Mandate and provided the best defence against the threat of quantified mitigation targets.

It also had the benefit of keeping the eyes of the world on the performance of Annex I parties in meeting their Kyoto obligations. 'You will find a huge gap if you make a comparison between their pledges and the actions they have taken so far,' China's envoy Yu Qintai observed on the conference's third day. 'We have no lack of legal documents, but a lack of sincerity for taking action.'[7]

It was in the interests of India and China to frustrate post-Bali discussions. Even the EU, wedded as it was to Kyoto, recognised its insufficiency. On the conference's first day, Sweden, speaking for the bloc, stated that Kyoto alone could not achieve the goal of having emissions peak by 2020 and halve them by 2050 to meet the 2°C limit.[8] When discussed two days later, India, China and Saudi Arabia opposed a new protocol, with China urging focus on countries implementing their existing Kyoto commitments.

In an attempt to close down this avenue, the formal discussions on future cooperation under the convention produced an unworkable outcome. 'The negotiating text evolved into the most complex document in the history of the UNFCCC, with nearly two hundred pages reflecting various proposals by all UNFCCC parties and thousands of brackets indicating areas of disagreement,' the authoritative *Earth News Bulletin* reported.[9]

Seemingly arcane arguments over whether Copenhagen should produce a unified document or two separate ones in reality were a fight to determine the future of the climate change regime. A unified approach, reflected in the Danish text, would have demolished the Berlin Wall. Two documents meant primacy for the Kyoto Protocol. Because the US was not a party to the Protocol, the first agreement would probably be the last as it would most likely be dead-on-arrival in the United States Senate.

So the G77 plus China lined up foursquare behind Kyoto. 'The death of the Kyoto Protocol would be the death of Africa,' declared Ethiopia's PM Meles Zenawi, speaking for the fifty-three-nation African Union. 'I have been assured of China's support and India will probably take the same position.'[10] Surprisingly, Ban Ki-moon lent the neutrality of his office to the two documents camp.* Until there was a legally binding treaty, 'The Kyoto Protocol remains the only legally-binding instrument that captures reduction commitments,' Ban told the conference. 'As such it must be maintained.'[11]

On the conference's fourth day, a second front opened, with a skirmish between the US and China over money. China argued that countries like the US had a duty to pay out billions of dollars in compensation to poorer, developing countries. US negotiator Jonathan Pershing rejected China's demand. 'If you think about what will be prioritised in terms of the needs of the ... poorest countries, the countries that are hardest hit, I wouldn't start with China.'[12]

The spat got personal. Responding to a comment by Todd Stern that China was too prosperous to be a recipient of US climate funding, He Yafei expressed shock. 'I don't want to say the gentleman [Stern] is ignorant ... but I think he lacked common sense ... or he's extremely irresponsible,' He told a press conference. (Stern later described his comment as 'a bit unfortunate', but the position remained the same).[13]

At stake was one of the key principles of the climate change negotiations. 'Common but differentiated responsibilities' runs through the texts as frequently as 'sustainable development'. Indeed, 'common but differentiated responsibilities' is mentioned on the first page of the text of the convention and 'sustainable social and economic development' on the third. Yet the West and the developing world had a profoundly different understanding as to what it implied.

Western negotiators emphasised the 'common' part of the formulation and interpreted responsibilities to mean forward-looking obligations, an interpretation supported in the convention which goes on immediately to speak of countries' 'respective capabilities and their social and economic conditions.' As the West is richer, it is more capable of taking action. As developing countries become wealthier, they too can assume greater responsibilities.

Developing nations emphasised 'differentiated'. For them, responsibility is historic – the nations who had been responsible for increasing the amount of carbon dioxide in the atmosphere are the ones obliged to take action. Developing nations could also point to the convention. Its third paragraph states:

---

* Before becoming UN Secretary-General, Ban Ki-moon had been South Korea's foreign minister, a country which was a major beneficiary of Kyoto in being a highly industrialised non-Annex I nation.

the largest share of historical and current global emissions of greenhouse gases has originated in developed countries, that per capita emissions in developing countries are still relatively low and that the share of global emissions originating in developing countries will grow to meet their social and development needs.[14]

At a meeting with journalists in Copenhagen, China's He Yafei argued that history was the basis on which the negotiations could move forward:

> For developed countries, they have to face the history squarely. The obligations for developed countries to live up to their commitments in emission reduction and the provision of funds and technology transfer, is an obligation they have undertaken … The key, the prerequisite, for a successful Copenhagen conference, is that developed countries need to live up to their responsibilities.[15]

On America's denial of China's eligibility for climate change funding, it was as if

> all of us are sitting for dinner, we finish the main course, and then comes the dessert. The poor man walks in and sits down and has dessert. And we say right, you have to pay for the meal.[16]

Was China like the poor guy being slapped with the bill?

> We still have over one hundred and fifty million people under the poverty line, according to UN standards. If you care to go into the interior parts of China, the south-western parts of China, you will see lots of poverty. So poverty reduction – to provide a better life for Chinese people – is and will be the priority for the Chinese government.[17]

Whatever the outcome of Copenhagen, He warned, it should not be done at the expense of the rights to development by developing countries.

Yet the US and the EU and other Western nations were adamant that in some way or another, developing countries would have to limit and then reverse the growth of their greenhouse gas emissions. Was there any way of bridging the divide, perhaps with 'green growth'? Takers for that proposition were hard to come by.

As each day passed, expectations were downgraded. Before the start of the COP, the possibility of Copenhagen producing a treaty text was replaced with the aim of a strong political declaration with a firm timetable to a treaty before 2010 was out.

On 15th December, Pope Benedict XVI sent a World Peace Day plea. 'It is indeed important to recognise, among the causes of the current ecological crisis, the historic responsibility of the industrialised countries.'[18]

The next day, Connie Hedegaard, Denmark's environment minister, resigned as COP president. Her handling of the conference had not been a success. In 2010, she was appointed the EU's first climate change commissioner, where she endeavoured to start a trade war with China by extending the EU Emissions Trading Scheme to international airlines.

Danish Prime Minister Lars Løkke Rasmussen took over. His debut as COP president was peppered with hostile interventions challenging the status of the texts proposed by the Danish presidency. It was an issue of 'trust between the host country and parties', China said, noting that the process had not been transparent.[19]

That afternoon, the working group on long-term cooperative action under the convention held its closing plenary. It was chaired by the convention's first and longest serving executive secretary, Michael Zammit Cutajar. So many changes had been suggested that it would not be possible to prepare texts in time for the COP plenary two days later, Zammit Cutajar said. His proposal that the entire package be adopted as 'unfinished business' was accepted.[20]

If this group wasn't going to produce a text, who was?

A day later, with world leaders gathering in Copenhagen, Angela Merkel voiced her fears. 'The news reaching us is not good.'[21] A sense of foreboding spread through the delegations. 'There are more than one hundred and thirty leaders here. If they cannot seal a deal, who can?' asked Ban Ki-moon.[22] 'I believe in God. I believe in miracles,' Brazil's President Lula declared the next day.[23]

The outside world had little inkling how badly things were going. The Danes ensured that the country delegations were hermetically sealed from the NGOs and the media. According to ITN's Jon Snow, covering the conference for Channel 4 News, tight security made it very difficult to doorstep conference participants. So the media relied on NGOs, who didn't know either, and Yvo de Boer, whose press briefings seemed perpetually upbeat.[24]

The West had one more card to play. 'It was unforgettable political theatre,' reported the *Independent*'s Michael McCarthy. 'Like a poker player with a sudden new bet, the power-dressed Mrs Clinton changed the game instantly as she pulled her gigantic sum out of the US back pocket.'[25] The

United States, announced Clinton, was willing to work with other countries towards a goal of mobilising $100 billion a year by 2020 – conditional on all major economies standing behind 'meaningful mitigation actions'.[26]

The message was clear – and it wasn't subtle: an extra $100 billion a year for Africa if China capitulated; not a cent if it didn't. In any case, it was made up of funny money – 'public and private, bilateral and multilateral, including alternative sources of finance', Clinton said in her speech. As an administration official explained, 'The private sector is going to be the engine that drives all this.' In other words, flows which in all likelihood would be happening anyway, so much of it wouldn't be additional money. 'A lot of this is not aid in the traditional sense of aid,' the official said. How could it be otherwise, given that the West's public finances had been shot to pieces? Republican congressional leaders said they would introduce a 'disapproval resolution'. Republican House leader John Boehner commented, 'The administration wants to give billions in US taxpayer dollars we don't have to other countries.'[29]

On the last Thursday of the COP, there was a high-level segment for speeches by world leaders. Gordon Brown, the son of a Presbyterian minister, was biblical. 'Hurricanes, floods, typhoons and droughts that were once all regarded as the acts of an invisible god are now revealed to be also the visible acts of man,' Brown said.[30] His talks during the week had convinced him that while reaching agreement was difficult, there was, 'no insurmountable [sic] wall of division' that prevented agreement.

Where Brown was declamatory, Angela Merkel, the daughter of a Protestant pastor, was earnest, more of a 'let's all hold hands' homily than a sermon. 'We need to help each other. But we also need to stand ready to change our way of living, our lifestyle.'[31] Renewable energy was 'so important'. Germany and the European Union were ready and willing to 'open their arms' to take the negotiations forward and reach agreement so that world leaders could face the world on Friday and be able to say they had got the message: 'Life cannot go on as it was. The world needs to change.'

Jabbing the air, French President Nicolas Sarkozy harangued delegates. 'A failure in Copenhagen would be a catastrophe for each and every one of us,' he said.[32] Much of it was directed against China. 'Who could dare to say they should be against giving money to the poorest countries?' He was crude. If there wasn't an agreement, 'Let me say to my African friends, you'll be the first to suffer from it.' Without naming them, he dared the Chinese to come to the podium. 'Who would dare say that the poor countries of Asia should be treated the same way as Brazil and China, the giants of tomorrow?' He railed: '*Mes chers amis*, time is short. Let's stop posturing.' It was pretty desperate.

Even as the Europeans spoke of the perils and dangers of climate change, a rumble from Europe's periphery betokened a real crisis. During the conference's first week, credit rating agency Fitch had cut Greece's rating to BBB+ with negative outlook the day after Standard & Poor's said it was considering downgrading Greece.[33]

The conference's Big Three – the leaders of the US, China and India – were slated to speak the following day. Before then, Queen Margrethe II hosted a dinner. Sarkozy had called for the leaders to negotiate the agreement after the gala dinner, so the outcome could be presented to the world on Friday, the COP's last day.

During the dinner, Wen Jiabao picked up a rumour that he hadn't been invited. Annoyed at the perceived snub, Wen repaired to his hotel, sending He Yafei in his place. It meant that China was represented by someone who knew the negotiating texts better than any of the leaders in the room.

As daylight broke on Friday morning, Air Force One touched down at Copenhagen's Kastrup airport. It was cold and windy and started to snow as Obama stepped into his limo – his second trip to Scandinavia in a week. The first was to Oslo to pick up his Nobel Peace Prize. It was also his second trip to Copenhagen in three months, having flown there to support Chicago's losing bid for the 2016 Olympics. This time Obama was prepared for failure and armed with a draft statement prepared by Jonathan Pershing for that eventuality.[34]

To Jon Snow, it seemed as if the drama that tumultuous day centred on the schedule of the president's plane.[35] Obama hadn't planned to stay long. A snowstorm was forecast to hit the eastern seaboard, bringing forward his return flight.

The next twelve hours were not only to be the end point of two years of negotiations since Bali to agree a successor to the Kyoto Protocol. For the first time, the international community was to come together to agree a comprehensive, global approach. 'Kyoto was a treaty that aimed at making a point, but less successful at making a policy,' Blair told a meeting at the conference, 'Copenhagen is where we need to make a policy.'[36] 18th December 2009 was thus the culmination of nineteen years of climate change negotiations since the UN General Assembly adopted the resolution establishing the Intergovernmental Negotiating Committee for a Framework Convention on Climate Change nineteen years before – on 21st December 1990.

The speeches of the Big Three delineated the gulf separating the West and the world's major emerging economies. President Obama used his not to persuade, but to lecture. In similar language used to justify the Iraq War, climate change posed a 'grave and growing danger'.[37] America was taking action to cut its emissions not only to meet its global responsibilities, but also because it was in America's self-interest. America would proceed to a 'clean energy' economy, no matter what happened in Copenhagen. It was essential to America's national security to reduce its dependence on foreign oil, an argument used to domestic audiences, which jarred with an international one comprising America's trade partners and oil exporters.

Any agreement must have a mechanism to assess compliance. 'Without such accountability, any agreement would be empty words on a page,' he said. 'It would be a hollow victory.'[38] This was aimed at China, which had been resisting pressure to accept some form of verification. By then, it had signalled it was ready to concede – in a way that made the entire issue moot.

With time running short, 'The question is whether we will move forward together or split apart, whether we prefer posturing to action.'[39] He left a sting in the tail. 'We have charted our course. We have made our commitment,' he concluded.[40] The message was stark: take it or leave it.

To those who hoped Obama would rescue the conference by making some grand offer, it was a terrible letdown. At no point in his remarks had the president mentioned the goal – so dear to the Europeans – of limiting the increase in global temperatures to 2°C, which Obama and other members of the G8 had affirmed at L'Aquila in July.

The reaction in the Tycho Brahe conference hall was as chilly as the weather outside. Suddenly the realisation dawned on the NGOs – and from them to the world beyond – that Copenhagen was heading for disaster and Obama was doing nothing to stop it. In truth, there was nothing he could have done to have turned the conference around.

Every inch undisputable Third World authenticity in a dark Nehru jacket and blue turban, India's Manmohan Singh recognised the sensibilities of Western environmentalism. He praised the 'valiant efforts' to build a global consensus on 'highly complex issues'.[41] The vast majority of countries did not support any renegotiation or dilution of the principles and provisions of the climate change convention and in particular the principle of equity enshrined in 'common but differentiated responsibilities and respective capabilities'.

More action should be expected than at the time of the Rio treaty and the Kyoto Protocol. That meant adhering to the Bali mandate for future discussions – a clear signal that agreement wasn't going to be reached at

Copenhagen. Kyoto should stand and the parties to it should deliver on their 'solemn commitments'. India, entirely voluntarily, had made a pledge to reduce the emissions intensity of its economic growth by around twenty per cent by 2020. India would deliver this goal regardless of the outcome of Copenhagen.

Speaking deliberately, Singh told the conference that any agreement on climate change must respect the need for development and growth in developing countries. Every citizen had an equal right of entitlement to the global atmospheric space, Singh concluded.

The growth of developing country emissions was now the single largest driver of global emissions. India's position was incompatible with Western demands for a global limit on carbon dioxide emissions and setting a date when emissions would peak and then decline. If the computer models relied on by the IPCC were to be believed, the 2°C aim could be consigned to history.

Like Obama and Singh, Wen Jiabao did not mention the 2°C goal in his speech, half of which was taken up with telling the conference what China had already done. In modernising its economy, China had scrapped heavily polluting steel, cement and coke-making plants. It was investing in renewable energy and had planted the world's largest acreage of man-made forests. It had reduced its carbon dioxide intensity by forty-six per cent in fifteen years and aimed to do so again.

'Dear colleagues,' Wen continued, the principle of 'common but differentiated responsibilities' was the 'core and bedrock' of international cooperation on climate change. 'It must not be compromised,' Wen stated.[42] Developed countries had accounted for eighty per cent of total carbon dioxide emissions since the Industrial Revolution:

> If we all agree that carbon dioxide emissions are the direct cause of climate change, then it is all too clear who should take the primary responsibility. Developing countries only started industrialisation a few decades ago and many of their people still live in abject poverty today. It is totally unjustified to ask them to undertake emission reduction targets beyond their due obligations and capabilities in disregard of historical responsibilities, per capita emissions and different levels of development.[43]

Wen criticised the West for its failure to honour its commitments. A one-thousand-mile journey starts with the first step, yet emissions from many developed countries had increased. It was more important to focus attention on achieving promised reductions in the short-term than setting long-term goals, Wen argued.

Like India, China's carbon-intensity reduction was its own affair and not linked to any other country's target. The formulation used by both leaders conveyed a clear message. India and China were not going be parties to an agreement which specified global emissions caps or dates by when emissions should peak.

Gordon Brown called Copenhagen 'the most important conference since the Second World War'.[44] The decisive confrontation took place at a four-and-a-half-hour meeting that afternoon in the Bella Center's Arne Jacobsen room.

Present were the conference Big Three – Obama, Singh and He Yafei for China; the European Big Three – Merkel, Sarkozy and Brown. The other two BASIC countries were there – South Africa's Zuma and Brazil's Lula, plus an assortment of other leaders, including Ethiopia's Meles Zenawi representing Africa, the Maldives' Mohamed Nasheed for the small island states, Mexico's Felipe Calderón (host of the next COP), Australia's Kevin Rudd (climate change's golden boy), and Norway's Jens Stoltenberg (after Canada's loss of interest, representing the original conscience of global warming) – twenty-five countries in a summit chaired by Denmark's Rasmussen. With them were Ban Ki-moon, other senior UN officials and leaders' advisers. Altogether there were fifty to sixty people in the room.[45]

The leaders spent their time working on a draft that resembles an evolved version of the controversial Danish text based on the framework of a global cap – a reduction of 'X' by 2020 and 'Y' by 2050. A 1.2-gigabyte sound recording of the meeting found its way to *Der Spiegel*, which in May 2010 published an account of the meeting.*

Rasmussen asked if there were any major objections. 'We just have to go,' Merkel responded. 'And if we do not agree today then we have to say within four weeks because we cannot go over and say nice things but X and Y please wait one year or so.'[46]

He Yafei said the meeting needed to go through the draft line by line, comment by comment (death by square bracket, the fate that had befallen Zammit Cutajar's text).

An Indian representative spoke in support of China: 'We have all along been saying "don't prejudge options,"' provoking Merkel to retort, 'Then you don't want legally binding.' To which the Indian responded: 'Why do

---

*   Excerpts from the recording can be streamed at http://www.spiegel.de/international/
     world/0,1518,692861,00.html

you prejudge options? All along you have said don't prejudge options. This is not fair.'

He Yafei expressed surprise the numbers were still there: 'We have made our objections very clear this morning.'

Gordon Brown intervened. 'We are trying to cut emissions by 2020 and 2050. That is the only way we can justify being here. It is the only way we can justify the public money that is being spent to do so' – an observation that must have struck the Chinese and Indians as otiose.

It was also a misreading of their goal. The duo's strategic objective consisted of destroying any prospect that their economies would be subject to international emissions controls – now and at any point in the future.

That was clear when China vetoed the inclusion of a target by industrialised countries of eighty per cent cut by 2050. 'Why can't we even mention our targets?' demanded Merkel, recorded Mark Lynas, an environmental activist advising Nasheed of the Maldives.[47] At this point, according to Lynas, Rudd started banging his microphone and a Brazilian representative asked why rich countries should not even announce a unilateral cut. When the Chinese delegate said 'no', Merkel threw up her hands.

Merkel had one more go. 'Let us suppose a one hundred per cent reduction, that is, no CO_2 in the developed countries any more. Even then, with the two degrees, you have to reduce carbon emissions in the developing countries. That is the truth.'

China fully understood the logic of the two degree target. 'Thank you for all these suggestions,' He responded. 'We have said very clearly that we must not accept the fifty per cent reductions. We cannot accept it.'

A lit fuse reached the gunpowder. Sarkozy exploded. Speaking in French, he angrily declared China's position 'absolutely unacceptable' before accusing China of hypocrisy. Poor countries would not be getting the money promised them because of China's refusal to shoulder responsibility for the fifty per cent.

Then President Obama spoke.

Unlike his French colleague, the American was clinical, almost detached. The politics meant that the financing commitments had to be linked to adoption of the targets. 'In order for us to mobilise the political will within each of our own countries to not only engage in substantial mitigation efforts ourselves, which are very difficult, but also then to channel some of the resources from our countries, is a very heavy lift,' Obama said. 'If there is no sense of mutuality in this process, it is going to be difficult for us ever to move forward in a significant way.'

In the conference hall earlier in the day, Obama had been a unilateralist. Now, behind closed doors, Obama was a multilateralist. He could read the polls as well as anyone. A Gallup survey two days earlier suggested that a majority of Americans would support him on a climate pact, but that eighty-five per cent of Americans wanted the economy, not global warming, to be the focus.[48] By linking economic issues to tackling climate change, poll-driven talk of green growth was for domestic consumption, not an argument to be used with India and China.

An AP Stanford University poll suggested how much or, rather, how little Americans were willing to pay. While three quarters of respondents said they would support action to address climate change, fifty-nine per cent said they wouldn't support any action if it increased their electricity bills by $10 a month.[49]

Obama then expressed irritation at Wen Jiabao's absence. 'I am very respectful of the Chinese here,' Obama said, addressing He Yafei, 'but I also know there is a premier here who is making a series of political decisions. I know he is giving you instructions.'

That rebuke was as nothing as to what the president said next. Obama turned to Sarkozy. 'Nicolas, we are not staying until tomorrow,' he said. 'I'm just letting you know, because all of us obviously have extraordinarily important other business to attend to.'

He Yafei reacted coolly, as well he might, for Obama had just told him all he needed to know. Obama wanted an agreement. 'I am saying that, confident that, I think China is as desirous of an agreement as we are,' Obama had told the meeting. Saving face was Obama's objective. Any agreement would do.

Now the Europeans were not only isolated. They had been crushed. For them, climate change was an existential issue. There could be no more important business than saving the planet. Obama wanted a deal with China and India more than he was willing to use the collapse of the talks to try to isolate the duo and force them to concede.

'I heard President Sarkozy talk about hypocrisy,' He Yafei said in his perfect English. 'I think I'm trying to avoid such words myself.'

He then asked for the meeting to be suspended for a few minutes for some consultations. It was around 4pm.

The meeting did not reconvene.

According to the conference schedule, the closing plenary was meant to have started at 3pm and be over by 6pm. An hour after it was due to have started, there was still no agreement. The explanation was simple: there was no agreement because there was no agreement.

Events then took a bizarre turn. In an account given to journalists travelling back with the president on Air Force One, Obama wanted one more try. He decided to meet directly with the leaders of the BASIC group. The president's advance team was told that Singh was already at the airport; the Brazilians didn't want to meet without the Indians there. Zuma, according to this account, also cried off. 'If they're not coming, I can't do this.'[50] Wen's team then came on the line to say the Chinese were ready to meet Obama.

Obama's team then went to find a room for the meeting, only to find they could not get in. 'We've now figured out why we can't get into that room: because that room has Wen, Lula, Singh and Zuma,' the official said. 'They're all having a meeting.'[51]

Obama decided to go in.

'Mr Premier, are you ready to see me? Are you ready? Mr Premier, are you ready to see me? Are you ready?' Obama cried.[52]

'I'm going to sit by my friend Lula,' as an aide to the Brazilian president gave up his chair.[53]

They spent eighty minutes working on a text. The outcome was the Copenhagen Accord.

'I don't think anything like this has ever happened, and I'm not sure whether something like this will ever happen again,' Yvo de Boer commented in what must be the understatement of the conference.[54] Speaking to journalists in Berlin, Merkel swore she would not risk the same humiliation again.[55]

She was as good as her word. Of the European leaders, only Norway's Jens Stoltenberg attended the next COP in Cancún.

33
AFTERMATH

Nothing except a battle lost can be half so melancholy as a battle won.

Duke of Wellington, 1815

The first requirement of statesmanship is a sense of reality – Disraeli rather than Gladstone; Bismarck rather than Napoleon III; Nixon rather than Carter. At Copenhagen, the Europeans did not comprehend the entrenched positions of China and India. Barack Obama did. Having concluded an agreement with the BASIC Four, Obama did what many advise American presidents finding themselves in intractable overseas entanglements. He declared victory and left.

At 10.30pm, Obama held a press conference to announce a 'meaningful and unprecedented breakthrough'.[1] It was, the president claimed, the first time in history all major economies had come together to take action on climate change. 'OK, thank you very much everybody, we'll see some of you on the plane.'[2]

It was over. Obama couldn't get out of Copenhagen fast enough. He had, as he'd told the Europeans, more important business to attend to.

On the flight back, the president secured the sixtieth Senate vote for his healthcare legislation. 'After a nearly century-long struggle, we are on the cusp of making healthcare reform a reality in the United States of America,' Obama exulted.[3]

Climate change was a priority for Obama. It just wasn't the most important. In his June 2008 speech on winning the Democratic nomination, the first thing people would be telling their children wasn't about the slowing of the rise of the oceans and the healing of the planet. It would be about when America started providing care for the sick.[4]

There was one breakthrough. Malta became the first non-Annex I party to attain Annex I status in the history of the convention.* If it was a miracle, it wasn't a divine agent but Malta's Zammit Cutajar to whom the credit belonged.

China spoke of a 'positive' result, though not of a breakthrough. 'All should be happy.'[5] Happiness was in short supply in the Bella Center. Jon

---

* To date, Malta is the only developing country to have graduated to Annex I. Croatia, the Czech Republic, Slovakia and Slovenia were the products of parties to the convention that had split. The other addition to the original list was the Principality of Liechtenstein.

Snow saw eager young men and women in NGO T-shirts in tears. Copenhagen ended 'more dramatically badly than any conference I've ever been to', Snow – who had covered every major summit from the Reagan-Gorbachev meetings – recalled. It was meant to have been the great moment. 'This was going to be it.' Instead it turned out to be the moment when all the wind went out of the climate change negotiations.[6]

Denmark's Rasmussen had the thankless task of trying to get the Accord approved by the COP plenary. The session started at 3am on Saturday. It was a rocky ride, lasting nearly thirteen hours. Tuvalu, one of the most vocal small island states, could not accept the Accord, despite the offer of financing. To do so would 'betray our people and sell our future, our future is not for sale'.[7] Saudi Arabia's delegate declared Copenhagen 'the worst COP plenary' he had ever attended. It was evident there was no consensus and the parties were simply restating their positions.[8]

Speaking for the G77, Lumumba Di-Aping compared the proposed deal to the Holocaust. '[This] is asking Africa to sign a suicide pact, an incineration pact in order to maintain the economic dependence of a few countries. It's a solution based on values that funnelled six million people in Europe into furnaces.'[9]

Di-Aping's remarks were immediately condemned by the UK, Norway, the EU and others. They hadn't objected when Gore made the comparison at Bali two years earlier or when the world's most famous climate scientist, James Hansen, called coal trains 'death trains'.[10]

The NGOs went into over-drive, demonstrating how they had lost the plot. 'By delaying action, rich countries have condemned millions of the world's poorest people to hunger, suffering and loss of life,' said Nnimmo Basey, chair of Friends of the Earth. 'The blame for this disastrous outcome is squarely on the developed nations.'[11] Kumi Naidoo for Friends of the Earth denounced the Accord as a 'betrayal of the poor' and blamed the conference failure on racism. Why was there such a lack of urgency? 'Is it because of the colour of their skin' of those in the front line of climate change, Naidoo asked?[12] It was a question better addressed to Beijing and New Delhi rather than Berlin and Paris.

As the plenary session wore on, Ethiopia, on behalf of the African Union, supported the Accord. Tuvalu then backtracked and decided to betray its future, suggesting that it be adopted as a 'miscellaneous document' of the COP. The UK proposed adopting the document as a COP decision. Opposition from Bolivia, Cuba and Venezuela and two or three others prevented consensus. At 10.35 on Saturday morning, it was proposed that the COP 'take note' of the Copenhagen Accord. Parties could signify their (non-legally binding) support for the Accord by being listed in an appendix.

Hours of procedural wrangling followed. Late on Saturday morning, the COP finally decided to 'take note' of the Accord. 'You sealed a deal,' Ban Ki-moon told exhausted delegates – only they hadn't.[13] 'We will try to have a legally binding treaty as soon as possible in 2010,' Ban promised reporters.[14]

There wasn't a treaty in 2010. Or in 2011.

The institutional gulf in the Accord separating Annex I nations from the rest was laid bare in the respective appendices for both groups. Appendix I listed each Annex I party's quantified emissions target for 2020. In Appendix II, there was a list for *unquantified* mitigation actions by developing country parties. In Attachment B of the Danish Text, there had been an additional column for the quantified impact of each action in units of millions of tons of CO_2 equivalent. In Appendix II of the Accord, it had disappeared. Obama's warning that it would be a hollow victory unless developing country commitments were 'measurable, reportable and verifiable' turned out to be exactly that. The actions might be reportable and even verifiable, but they were no longer measurable.

Out too went any specified year when global and national emissions should peak. The Accord's aim was to achieve a peak as soon as possible

> recognising that the time frame for peaking will be longer in developing countries and bearing in mind that social and economic development and poverty eradication are the first and overriding priorities of developing countries and that a low-emission development strategy is indispensable for sustainable development.[15]

There was just enough in the Accord to keep the whole negotiating process going indefinitely and provide cover for European governments to continue with their global warming policies. Everything could go on much as before. And, if the scientists and the IPCC were right, it would mean unabated global warming.

Angela Merkel put on a brave face. 'It is a first step toward a new world climate order, nothing more but also nothing less,' she told the *Bild am Sonntag*.[16] What was needed, Merkel thought, was 'a UN environment organisation that could control the implementation of the climate process.'[17] Quite how that could come about, she didn't say.

Nicolas Sarkozy was closer to the mark. The deal was the only one that could be reached after the summit had revealed deep rifts. The UN process of moving forward by consensus of one hundred countries was not workable. Although China was a permanent member of the UN Security Council, if India were too, 'it would be far easier to get her to shoulder a greater proportion of her responsibilities', Sarkozy said. 'Seeing a system like this makes it blindingly obvious.'[18]

More likely, Sarkozy's explanation had it the wrong way round. Given the opprobrium heaped on those viewed as being on the wrong side of the argument about global warming, the UN negotiating forum was ideal for China and India. Fundamental disagreements could be masked as procedural objections and proxies could make arguments on their behalf. If the world's major economies were genuinely agreed on a way forward, it is hard to believe that the rest of the world would not have followed, as happened with ozone-depleting substances and the Montreal Protocol. The fundamental reality at Copenhagen was the failure of the West to get its way.

Some found it hard to come to terms with. Gordon Brown and Ed Miliband decided to pick a quarrel with the world's second largest economy. Writing in the *Guardian* on the Monday after the conference, Miliband accused China of vetoing quantified caps. 'We will make clear to those countries holding out against a binding treaty that we will not allow them to block global progress,' Miliband threatened. The process had been hijacked, presenting a 'farcical picture'.[19] There needed to be major reform in the way climate change negotiations were conducted.

'Such an attack was made in order to shirk the obligations of developed countries to their developing counterparts and foment discord among developing countries,' a spokeswoman for China's foreign ministry said.[20] The next day, Brown took up the cudgels. 'Never again should we face the deadlock that threatened to pull down those talks,' Brown thundered in sub-Palmerstonian vein. 'Never again should we let a global deal to move towards a greener future be held to ransom by only a handful of countries.'[21] How was Britain going to take on China? Send a gunboat up the Yangtze? Brown didn't say.

Meanwhile in Beijing, French premier François Fillon arrived with a delegation of ministers and business leaders. 'Even though it is our first meeting in person, I feel like we are friends,' Wen told Fillon. 'Our two countries' partnership is unmatched,' Fillon replied. The two signed agreements on aviation and nuclear cooperation.[22] A source said the French would leave China with €6.3 billion of signed contracts.[23]

Nonetheless, China remained sensitive about its role at Copenhagen. The same day, Wen declared that China had played an 'important constructive' part at the climate conference.[24] Maintaining China's climate alliance with India was vital. At a meeting with Manmohan Singh, the Chinese premier gave an assurance that China 'would like to pursue relations with India on the basis of equality', according to India's foreign minister Nirupama Rao.[25] Global warming had brought together these two long-standing Asian rivals into an alliance to protect their common interests against the West.

'It is easy to discern China's fingerprints all over the international climate change fiasco,' wrote John Tkacik, a former chief China analyst at the State Department's Bureau of Intelligence and Research.[26] If his intelligence briefers had been reading the Chinese press, Obama would have seen it coming. In a September article in Beijing's *Science Times*, Ding Zhongli, China's top paleo-climatologist and VP of the Chinese Academy of Sciences, had written that 'the idea that there is significant correlation between temperature increases and concentrations of atmospheric carbon dioxide lacks reliable evidence in science'.[27] Given the deep scepticism of the Chinese Academy of Science's senior climatologist, Tkacik wrote, 'It is clear that no one in the Chinese politburo is truly anxious about the climatic consequences of global warming.'[28]

In New Delhi, the opposition Communist Party of India (Marxist), known by its initials CPM, accused the Singh government of being too soft and making pre-summit concessions which enabled the US to undermine the Kyoto Protocol. 'The CPM had warned the government that unilateral concessions before the negotiations, and without conditional linkages to deep cuts by developed countries, will not yield results. This is indeed what has happened.'[29]

As for the Indian government, in a March 2010 interview in the *Wall Street Journal*, environment minister Jairam Ramesh described himself as a climate agnostic. Ramesh, who headed India's delegation at Bali and addressed the Copenhagen conference, said the climate negotiations were in a 'complete quagmire' and heading nowhere.[30] 'In many parts of India people are dying because of excess pesticides in the water, or arsenic in the water,' according to Ramesh. 'That's more important and more urgent than climate change.' The other BASIC nations shared the same perspective. They had bonded 'very well' at Copenhagen. 'We are united in our desire not to have a binding agreement thrust upon us which will constrict our developmental options,' Ramesh said.[31]

China could even claim the support of the weather. The first week of 2010 saw Beijing temperatures plunge to -18°C as a blizzard dumped the heaviest snow fall in a single January day since 1951. For two months beforehand, China had experienced widespread gas shortages as demand rose because of the unusually cold weather. In Seoul, more than ten inches of snow fell on the Korean capital – the greatest amount since records began in 1937.[32] In Mongolia, temperatures fell to -50°C. Ferocious winter conditions killed almost ten million sheep, cattle, goats, horses and camel – a fifth of the country's total.[33]

In Washington, Senator Inhofe's grandchildren built an igloo with a sign saying 'Al Gore's New Home'. 'This isn't a good old-fashioned winter for the District of Columbia, not unless you're remembering the last ice age. And it doesn't disprove global warming,' wrote Bill McKibben, the Copenhagen bell-ringer, in the *Washington Post* in February. 'Instead, the weird and disruptive weather patterns around the world are pretty much exactly what you'd expect as the planet warms,' McKibben rationalised.[34]

Whether or not global warming caused the heavy snowfall, McKibben's claim that more snow was exactly what was expected contradicted one of the most famous predictions in the history of global warming. Within a few years, winter snowfall will become 'a very rare and exciting event', David Viner, of the University of East Anglia's Climatic Research Unit told the *Independent* in March 2000. 'Children just aren't going to know what snow is,' Viner forecast.[35]

Mongolian nomadic herdsmen had a name for the harsh winter – *dzud*, meaning 'white death'.[36] Writing three days after McKibben, the *New York Times'* Thomas Friedman coined his own. Avoid the term 'global warming', Friedman advised. 'I prefer the term global weirding.' As global temperatures rise, the weather gets weird, Friedman asserted.

Global weirding even found its way onto the website of the National Oceanic and Atmospheric Administration (NOAA). 'Global warming or global weirding?' Don't draw long-term, large-scale conclusions from short-term local weather patterns, was NOAA's careful answer.[37]

The scientists at NOAA had good reason to be cautious. As a scientific concept, global weirding is, well, weird. Following Popper's criterion of falsifiability, the more a theory states that certain things cannot happen, the stronger the theory is. The problem with global weirding is that it doesn't preclude anything – rather it suggests the opposite. Anything could happen.

And how is weirdness measured? In Britain in 1975, near the start of a three-decade rise in global average temperatures in a record-breaking hot summer, the weather suddenly turned cold in the first week of June. Derbyshire was playing Lancashire in a county cricket championship match at Buxton. It started to rain, then snow. 'When I went out to inspect the wicket, the snow was level with the top of my boots. I'd never seen anything like it,' recalled umpire Dickie Bird.[38] Is summer snow in Buxton more or less 'weird' than winter snow in Washington?

Despite this, global weirding captures a reality that changes in global average temperature do not. We only experience local temperature and local weather. No one experiences a global average temperature – a statistical artefact created by climate scientists. As measured by global average temperature, 2010 was one of the warmest years on record. Yet what was experienced by Mongolian nomads, the inhabitants of Beijing or Senator Inhofe's grandchildren in their igloo was quite different. If climate scientists had not been pre-disposed to worry about global warming, would anyone have noticed that 2010 was statistically one of the warmest years on record?

The lack of observed warming during the first decade of the new century began to create a stir among climate scientists. In May 2009, Phil Jones, Britain's best known climate scientist, reassured a colleague in a government funding agency. 'Bottom line – the no upward trend has to continue for a total of fifteen years before we get worried,' Jones wrote – giving himself more time by dating the fifteen years from 2004/05, and not 1998, as that was an El Niño year.[39] It was as if a doctor was dismayed rather than pleased to find a patient's disease hadn't progressed as fast as he had anticipated. In such a situation, most people would find themselves another doctor.

While climate scientists might be over-committed to the idea of climate warming, political leaders most over-invested in global warming turned out to be Copenhagen's biggest political casualties. No politician had toiled as hard as Gordon Brown. Trailing in the polls, a breakthrough at Copenhagen was Brown's last chance of pulling around his electoral fortunes, even though, when talking climate change, it often sounded like a foreign language Brown hadn't mastered. In the May 2010 election, Brown led Labour to its worst defeat since 1983.

For Australia's Kevin Rudd, Copenhagen was, in the words of opposition leader Tony Abbott, 'an unmitigated disaster'.[40] Before the 2007 election, Rudd had described climate change as 'the greatest moral, economic and environmental challenge of our generation'.[41] He then upped the stakes. Rudd dismissed opposition arguments to delay introducing cap-and-trade legislation until the outcome of Copenhagen was clear. 'The argument that we must not act until others do is an argument that has been used by political cowards since time immemorial,' Rudd said in November

2009. 'There are two stark choices – action or inaction. The resolve of the Australian Government is clear – we choose action, and we do so because Australia's fundamental economic and environmental interests lie in action,' Rudd declared.[42]

An RAAF plane was put on standby to fly Rudd to Copenhagen at short notice. A provisional delegate list numbered one hundred and fourteen Australians, including Rudd's official photographer, compared to a seventy-one-strong UK delegation.[43]

In April 2010, Rudd did an about-turn. Blaming the opposition and the pace of international negotiations, he announced a delay of his Carbon Pollution Reduction Scheme until the end of 2012. Two months later, the Labor caucus heaved Rudd out of office and replaced him with his deputy Julia Gillard, whom Rudd also blamed for his decision to postpone the plan.

Global warming played a part in Rudd's downfall, according to his predecessor John Howard. It hurt him personally: one moment he had been saying it was the greatest moral challenge, then he was putting it off for two years, precipitating the sharp fall in his poll ratings.[44]

The biggest casualty of Copenhagen was the West's standing in the world. It had declared global warming the most serious issue of the age. The US and the EU had come together and pushed hard for a comprehensive agreement covering all the major economies. The build-up of pressure going into the conference was immense.

However, the West misunderstood the contingent nature of the Third World's participation in international environmental negotiations. Western politicians talked a story that the world's poor would be hardest hit by global warming. But the nations with the largest numbers of poor people had priorities that conflicted with what the West wanted. Its leaders understood better than their colleagues in the West what Bastiat had found in the nineteenth century – the best defence against capricious nature is wealth.

In this regard, it is striking how little had changed since 1972 and the Stockholm conference. There was some movement. The language of environmentalism made inroads. China committed to huge investments in renewable energy. Brazil moved from the outright hostility of its military rulers. Even so, Brazil stuck by China and India. When he got home from Copenhagen, Lula pointed the finger: 'The United States is proposing a reduction of four percent from the date fixed by the Kyoto Protocol. That is too little,' Lula said on his weekly radio show *Coffee with the President*.[45]

At the same time, the power of the idea of global warming meant China and India couldn't simply say 'no'. So they fought the West by other means and played for time: fielding high calibre negotiators with a mastery of the conference texts and procedures; holding on to ground taken in previous rounds for as long as possible, especially the Berlin Mandate; using proxies to articulate their arguments and, most of all, maintaining the cohesiveness of the G77, despite the disparate interests of the small islands states and Africa from those of China and India. Throughout, they were aided by NGOs for whom blaming the West was encoded in their DNA.

In the end China and India succeeded. If there was going to be an agreement, it would have happened at Copenhagen. The Durban COP in December 2011 demonstrated the enormity of their victory at Copenhagen. Canada, Russia and Japan had already announced they would not enter into a second commitment period under the Kyoto Protocol. In setting the goal of reaching agreement to cover the period from 2020, the Durban Platform confirmed the failure of the Bali Road Map to reach its intended destination. There would be a gap between 2012 – the end of the first commitment period under the Kyoto Protocol – and the start of a first commitment period of a yet to be negotiated treaty.

The Durban Platform had a glaringly obvious credibility problem. If negotiating a legally binding agreement to cover the period after 2012 was too difficult, why would it be any easier to negotiate one for the period after 2020?

The scale of the challenge was made apparent immediately after the COP when Canada announced its withdrawal from the Kyoto Protocol. Environment minister Peter Kent said quitting the Protocol would save Canadians $13.6 billion it would otherwise have to spend on buying emissions credits from other countries.[46]

Canada's repudiation of Kyoto – inconceivable two years before at Copenhagen – made the prospect of a new treaty even less plausible. It strengthened China and India's ability to resist pressure to cap their emissions. In public, they could hardly welcome Canada's move, so they did the next best thing. 'Any attempt by developed countries to casually set aside their existing legal commitments while calling for a new legally-binding agreement seriously questions their credibility and sincerity in responding to the climate crisis,' a February 2012 statement on behalf of the BASIC Four said.[47]

The long-standing position of China, India and the rest of the G77 was that developed nations must first demonstrate their commitment by actually cutting their emissions, the only interpretation of Kyoto that makes any sense. The US had not ratified Kyoto and now Canada had repudiated it, ostensibly because it did not cover developing nations. The result was to leave the climate negotiations in an unconsummated equilibrium with the potential to last indefinitely.

It left the EU to negotiate with itself and with Norway and Switzerland over the emissions cuts for a second Kyoto commitment period. Outside this hard-core, there remained a handful of unilateralists. At enormous political cost, the Australians under Julia Gillard passed a carbon tax. In the US, California is a staunch climate change unilateralist. The three branches of the federal government are split between multilateralists and unilateralists. Cap-and-trade legislation was unable to make it through the Senate and had no chance after the 2010 mid-term elections, when Republicans took control of the House of Representatives. In its five to four decision on *Massachusetts v. EPA*, the Supreme Court endorsed unilateralism. Within the executive branch, the EPA under its administrator Lisa Jackson has adopted a hard-line unilateralist position. Obama's position depended on the audience. In public, he was a unilateralist. Negotiating with India and China, he morphed into a multilateralist.

At the conclusion of the Copenhagen conference, Ban Ki-moon hailed the Copenhagen Accord as an 'essential beginning'.[48] At Bali two years earlier, Copenhagen was to be the final destination on the Bali Road Map.

'Pathwalker, there is no path,' Gore told the delegates at Bali in words that were more prophetic about the climate change negotiations than he'd hoped. Like the Voyager spacecraft after a multi-decade planetary tour, perhaps the fate of the COPs and the MOPs and their subsidiary bodies is to leave the solar system and journey into outer space.

34
REFLECTIONS

It is by solidity of criticism more than by the plenitude of erudition, that the study of history strengthens, and straightens, and extends the mind ... Be more severe to ideas than to actions; do not overlook the strength of the bad cause or the weakness of the good.

Lord Acton, 1895 Inaugural Lecture

For most cities which were great once are small today; and those which used to be small were great in my own time. Knowing, therefore, that human prosperity never abides long in the same place, I shall pay attention to both alike.

Herodotus[1]

On 4th February 2010, Stephen Schneider gave one of his last lectures at Stanford, where he was professor of interdisciplinary environmental studies and of biology. Six months later, he died at the age of sixty-five. 'No one, and I mean no one, had a broader and deeper understanding of the climate issue than Stephen,' Michael Oppenheimer, Princeton professor of geosciences, told the *Washington Post*. 'More than anyone else, he helped shape the way the public and experts thought about this problem – from the basic physics of the problem, to the impact of human beings on nature's ecosystems, to developing policy.'[2]

Schneider's lecture showed why. He mixed a conversational style with an easy authority. No one could doubt who was the smartest person in the room. In ninety minutes, Schneider – who had been involved with the IPCC since 1988 – addressed issues rarely, if ever, ventured by other leading proponents of global warming. For this reason, Schneider's talk can claim to be the most important presentation by a climate scientist since James Hansen's congressional testimony.

Thomas Kuhn thought scientists were little better than laymen at characterising the established bases of their field.[3] Schneider made a similar point. 'Very few people learn about the basic philosophy of science and how it works.'[4] Universities were handing out a Ph.D. in science with no 'Ph' in it. 'OK guys, now we're doing epistemology,' Schneider would tell his freshmen class – and spoke of his frustration that many of his colleagues did not study it.

Other climate scientists showed how they could have benefited from attending Schneider's class. One such was Kevin Trenberth, a senior physicist at Boulder, Colorado's National Centre for Atmospheric Research, IPCC lead chapter author and one of the world's most cited geophysicists.[5] Trenberth's foray had been provoked by a Climategate email of his that had gone viral.

Responding to Schneider's request for help in rebutting a BBC report suggesting that there had been no warming since 1998, Trenberth emailed Schneider and Michael Mann. 'The fact is that we can't account for the lack of warming at the moment and it is a travesty that we can't.' People in Boulder were asking where the heck global warming was. The previous two days had smashed all previous cold records. 'This is January weather,' Trenberth wrote on 12th October 2009.[6]

In a January 2011 paper to the American Meteorological Society in tribute to Schneider, Trenberth argued that the null hypothesis test should be stood on its head. For there to be a relationship between two variables, the null hypothesis – that there is no relationship – should first be shown to be false.

Trenberth took the opinion expressed by the IPCC as foundational truth. Because the Fourth Assessment Report had declared global warming 'unequivocal' and 'very likely' due to human activities, 'the null hypothesis should now be reversed, thereby placing the burden of proof on showing that there is no human influence'.[7]

It is an axiom of the null hypothesis that it cannot be proven. By reversing the test, Trenberth set critics an impossible task. Even so, he misspecified the problem. It is not whether humans might influence the climate, but by how much. Here Trenberth's viral email pointed to the real difficulty. It wasn't so much a travesty that Trenberth and other climate scientists were unable to reconcile rising carbon dioxide concentrations and flat global temperatures, for Trenberth might have been on a fool's errand. 'For small changes in climate associated with tenths of a degree, there is no need for any external cause,' Richard Lindzen wrote in 2009. 'The earth is never exactly in equilibrium.'[8]

Schneider was too smart to make such elementary mistakes on the null hypothesis and knew the obstacles he had to navigate around. Science subject to test by falsification should be distinguished from system science. 'Is the science of anthropogenic climate change settled?' he asked. It was a dumb question, which the class fell for. Why? 'Climate science is not like test tube science. You don't falsify. Eventually you do, but not right away,' Schneider explained. 'It's system science.'

Schneider characterised system science as built on a base of well-established components, then a layer of competing explanations and finally a layer of what he called speculative components. 'Every single complicated system science, whether we're talking climate science, healthcare, security, education, always is going to be in this category,' Schneider said, illustrating the convergence of natural science with economics and social sciences.

The convergence enables scientists to stake their claim to formulating government policy, traditionally the province of the social sciences, enhanced by its reputation as a hard science, even though system science was diluting it. Now natural scientists were trading the rigour of knowledge derived from experimentation and falsifiability for a lead role in determining public policy.

'Opinion' perhaps better describes its output. 'Knowledge' implies what is known whereas opinion indicates a statement of belief. In the physical sciences, what is determinative is not what scientists think or believe, but what can be demonstrated by formulating hypotheses and testing them against nature.

In forsaking falsifiability, climate scientists kept a problematic feature of scientific practice – the strong collective tendency to operate within an unquestioned, dominant paradigm. Whereas arguments between economists of different schools of economic thought (and often within them) created scepticism about any claim made by an economist, the adherence of scientists to a dominant paradigm creates the opposite impression.

This makes even more problematic the form of system science falsification permitted by Schneider. 'We do not falsify by single experiments. We falsify on the basis of accumulated numbers of papers and numbers of bits of information.' Determining the relative credibility of each was not simple. It took assessment groups like the US National Academy of Sciences, with their multiple disciplines arguing out the relative merits of various competing or speculative components. Yet the process described by Schneider could be applied to any field of learning. The process of institutional oversight, peer review of papers and so forth, sometimes mistakenly described as the scientific method, is not unique to science.*

Schneider returned to the subject of falsifiability towards the end of his lecture. 'There are still some people who think [climate science] operates

---

* An example is provided by Naomi Oreskes, historian of science and co-author of *Merchants of Doubt: How a Handful of Scientists Obscured the Truth on Issues from Tobacco Smoke to Global Warming* (2010). In an interview on Australian radio, Oreskes said: 'Well, of course, no one can ever say, a hundred per cent, that any particular individual piece of science is correct, but that's what the scientific process is all about. And over the past four hundred years, scientists have developed mechanisms for evaluating scientific work, and the most important mechanism is peer review.' *The World Today*, 19th October 2010.

on the basis of falsification.' In the case of system science it does – by 'community action over decades'. Thus the 'scientific community' is accorded the determinative role formerly given to experiments conducted on nature.

What defined this community? By scientific community, 'I'm talking about those people who actually do the work,' not non-climate scientists who drop in opinions from the outside. The release of the Climategate emails had made scientists 'very, very angry about their critics', Schneider said. The critics almost never showed up at scientific meetings.

> They just write blogs and screeds and do 'audits' without really being members of the community. So they're not welcome. That's absolutely true because they're not part of the debate. That's cultural. That's not a matter of who's right and who's wrong.

Climate science, Schneider continued, gave plenty of scope for those with ideological agendas to fasten on to particular elements to prosecute their case. Their arguments might be technically correct, but they would neglect others in what Schneider called 'selective inattention to inconvenient components'. Schneider dubbed this 'courtroom epistemology'; in other words: 'It's not my job to make my opponent's case.' Scientists, Schneider went on, would view that as an 'immoral philosophy'. Schneider was more robust. 'I don't agree with that because if I were accused of something, I don't want my lawyer dwelling on abstractions of truth. I want him to get me off.'

Schneider was particularly exercised by the role of the media. In reporting both sides of the debate, the media presented a spurious balance of the extreme ends of the bell curve of the possible outcomes of global warming.

> It is inconceivable that debate polarised between 'end of the world' and 'good for you' – which for me are the lowest probability outcomes – can possibly be properly communicated through that kind of advocacy dichotomy.

The job of climate scientists was to evaluate risk and the role of 'the community' was to winnow out the relative probabilities. For the media not to report the middle of the bell curve was to 'miscommunicate' the nature of science.

This, Schneider suggested, raised a further question: can democracy survive complexity? The media focus on points of contention and its alleged neglect of the mainstream view had created public confusion about the science. This, Schneider argued, led to policy paralysis.

The view that public confusion about the science – sowed by malign fossil fuel interests – stalled global action is only plausible if the history of global warming is ignored. The 1992 climate change convention had written the scientific consensus into a treaty signed by over one hundred and sixty-five nations. It had been swiftly and unanimously ratified by the United States Senate. The most consistent finding of opinion surveys is not scepticism about the science, but that tackling climate change came way down the list of voters' concerns. It was a convenient community myth to blame the West, when the true block on global action was the refusal of India and China. But then, what pull do climate scientists – or NGOs for that matter – have in New Delhi and Beijing?

Schneider's second problematic claim was to suppose that nature would conform to a bell curve of climate scientists' expectations of the future. In an unusually candid description, Schneider characterised scientific judgement as an objective set of issues with subjectivity buried when it's about the future, because there's no data about the future. In projecting the future, 'It's always subjective by definition.'*

In 1957, the scientists Hans Suess and Roger Revelle wrote of human beings carrying out a large-scale geophysical experiment by increasing the amount of carbon dioxide in the atmosphere. It is bad scientific practice to prejudge the outcome of a unique experiment. The laws of physics can't be used beforehand to determine the climate sensitivity of carbon dioxide, so no one knows if the climate sensitivity assumed by the IPCC will turn out to have been correct.[†]

Global warming involved a second experiment – not a geophysical one, but a political experiment of a scale and ambition surpassing anything before

---

*   'Buried' is the right word to use about the IPCC's handling of subjectivity. It does not appear in any of the summaries for policymakers in the IPCC's 2007 Fourth Assessment Report. Neither does it appear in the crucial Chapter Nine on understanding and attributing climate change, but is buried in the chapter's supplementary material.

[†]   In its 2007 Fourth Assessment Report, the IPCC acknowledged that observational uncertainty, uncertainty about external influences on the climate ('forcing uncertainty') and internal climate variability affect the width of probable outcomes ('the prior distribution'). The prior distribution used in the calculations, the IPCC authors wrote, 'indicates that little is known, a priori, about the parameters of interest except that they are bounded below and above. Even so, the choice of prior bounds can be subjective'. Hegerl, G.C., F.W. Zwiers, P. Braconnot, N.P. Gillett, Y. Luo, J.A. Marengo Orsini, N. Nicholls, J.E. Penner and P.A. Stott, '2007: Understanding and Attributing Climate Change' in *Climate Change 2007: The Physical Science Basis. Contribution of Working Group I to the Fourth Assessment Report of the Intergovernmental Panel on Climate Change*, Appendix 9.B, SM.9–3.

it. Because fossil fuels are the principal source of energy of industrial civilisation, attempts to decarbonise society affect virtually every facet of government policy: energy policy, but also economic policy, land use planning and housing, transportation, agriculture, industrial policy and international relations – successive G8 summits and the largest gatherings of world leaders were devoted to solving global warming. Never has the impact of scientists on how societies are governed been as great. During the age of global warming, the West came closest to realising Francis Bacon's ideal of a republic governed by a body of scientists that he made nearly five centuries ago.

For leading scientists, the political elevation of science was its due. In April 2010, the presidents of the Royal Society and the National Academy of Science, Martin Rees and Ralph Cicerone, wrote: 'Our academies will provide the scientific backdrop for the political and business leaders who must create effective policies to steer the world toward a low-carbon economy,' seemingly oblivious to the fact that at Copenhagen four months earlier, the world had failed to agree steps to decarbonise their economies.[9]

No one questioned the role scientists had acquired. Based on their collective record, natural scientists would be among the very last people to involve in government policy. During the First Environmental Wave of the late 1960s and early 1970s, they had predicted the imminent collapse of civilisation and called for the abandonment of economic policies designed to satisfy humanity's material needs and generate rising prosperity. Their dire predictions turned out to be completely wrong and their recommendations disastrous – had any government been foolish enough to have acted on them.

And so it proved in the era of global warming. Across every dimension, global warming policy has been a costly fiasco. Unsustainable commitments to solar and wind energy in Germany and Spain; the morally abhorrent diversion by rich countries of resources from growing food into making biofuels; the collapse of the EU's carbon market; the transformation of the UK's liberalised energy market producing some of the cheapest electricity in Europe to become Europe's most expensive electricity producer; the scandals associated with the Clean Development Mechanism; the destruction of tropical rainforests to make way for palm oil plantations – all provide material for students of policy folly.

After the West pushed its demands to breaking point, global warming has been a story of defeat and retreat. Its failure at Copenhagen is a milestone in the deterioration of the West's prestige and the ascendance of China and India.

The implications of Copenhagen on the efficacy of global warming policies are nothing short of disastrous. Whatever the predictive merits of the science, the absence of a regime capping global greenhouse gas emissions rendered the West's global warming policies completely pointless. The results of global warming's political experiment already provide a definitive verdict: global warming policies have made the world unambiguously worse off, a conclusion which holds irrespective of the outcome of the geophysical experiment.

In addition to the higher cost of producing electricity from renewables (their capital costs alone are estimated to total $160 billion a year before the 2008 recession) over the most efficient conventional means – there are hidden costs.[10] Energy accounts for a higher proportion of poorer household spending, so those on lower incomes are disproportionately hit by higher energy prices. For social democrats such as Tony Crosland in the 1970s, concerns about the welfare of the working class and poverty reduction trumped the claims of environmentalism, the opposite of the situation today.

Then there are the opportunity costs of global warming policies – the valuable activities that the world has foregone. These include the innovation and productivity boost from Silicon Valley venture capital dollars diverted into green tech investments. Because alternative energy projects depend on government support, entrepreneurs and energy utility executives are turned into government lobbyists maximising their take from global warming policies.

Perhaps the biggest casualty is science. The rapid growth of climate science was not for the sake of pure knowledge, but because it is the leading branch of global therapeutics. Scientific knowledge can be of immense therapeutic benefit. Medicine is the outstanding example. The desire on the part of the physician or medical researcher to cure the sick is one of the finest of all human qualities. A similar motive drove Schneider, whose decision to become a climate scientist was, he once said, 'a marriage of convenience and deep conviction' – a decision he had made on Earth Day 1970 at the age of twenty-five to devote himself to the environment.[11]

In medicine what matters is not the motive of the practitioner but the efficacy of the therapy. A century ago, Professor Lawrence Henderson of Harvard drew attention to the remarkable advances in medical science, technology and therapy. 1912, Henderson claimed, marked a 'Great Divide' when 'for the first time in human history, a random patient with a random disease consulting a doctor chosen at random stands a better than fifty-fifty chance of benefiting from the encounter'.[12]

In his book *The Role of Medicine: Dream, Mirage or Nemesis?* medical historian and demographer Thomas McKeown wrote that 'the notion that treatment of disease may be useless, unpleasant, and even dangerous has been expressed frequently and vehemently, particularly in French literature', notably by Montaigne, Molière and Proust.[13] 'Remarkably, considering the eminence of the critics, such views had little effect on medicine or the public's estimate of it,' McKeown observed.

'The fashionable doctors ... stood as they do now, in admiration of their own science. As now, they talked as if illness and death were mastered ... The learned, magic, meaningless words, the grave looks at each other, the artful hesitation between one worthless formula and another – all are there,' Nancy Mitford wrote in her biography of Louis XIV.[14]

McKeown argued that

> patients have been and continue to be exposed to pain and injury from misguided attempts to do them good. Suffering is marginally more tolerable when inflicted with the best of intentions, and the death of Charles II under treatment by his doctors was much more cruel than that of his father at the hands of his executioner.[15]

When did reputable doctors retrospectively become quacks and when did clinical interventions, based on the medical science of the day, become of net benefit to patients? Even with the benefit of hindsight, it's hard to know. One answer is certainly wrong – at doctors' evaluation of their own abilities. Good intentions and strength of belief are highly misleading indicators of the quality of scientific knowledge. Physicians had been swearing the Hippocratic Oath to do no harm for twenty-three centuries prior to Henderson's Great Divide.

A tiny minority of climate scientists scrupulously avoided lending their voices to policy pronouncements. The vast majority saw it as part of their vocation. In the Fourth Assessment Report's chapter on climate change and sustainable development, the Working Group II authors said that the 'real message' from the IPCC's estimates of future global average temperatures was that

> no threshold associated with any subjective judgement of what might constitute 'dangerous' climate change can be guaranteed by anything but the most stringent mitigation interventions, at least not on the basis of current knowledge.[16]

Despite uncertainties acknowledged by the authors, there can be no mistaking the therapy these doctors believed necessary – 'on the basis of current knowledge'.

How can we know whether current knowledge on climate science is correct? In a video in the run up to the Copenhagen climate conference, Schneider made the comparison with tobacco smoking and lung cancer.

> We to this day do not know the precise mechanism whereby smoking causes lung cancer, but the statistics are so overwhelming that it would be irresponsible not to act. It's the same in climate.[17]

Al Gore also made the link. It's human nature to take time to connect the dots, Gore says in *An Inconvenient Truth* of his sister's death from lung cancer.

Leading climate scientists have invoked the American tobacco industry's denial of the link between smoking and lung cancer.* The attacks on climate science ahead of the Copenhagen conference mirrored the earlier tactics of the tobacco industry, according to IPCC vice-chair Jean-Pascal van Yperselethe.[18] Five years before, Robert May, president of the Royal Society at the time and previously the British government's chief scientific adviser, accused those questioning the science of using tactics 'reminiscent of the tobacco lobby's attempts to persuade us that smoking does not cause lung cancer'.[19]

David King, May's successor as chief scientific adviser, mounted a similar argument after the collapse of the Copenhagen conference.

> When paid lobbyists try to discredit the scientific theory that smoking causes lung cancer, they used the argument that it wasn't a proven fact. Well it wasn't then, and nor will it ever be, but would you now bet against it? ... And in the case of climate change, the scientific probability that the world is warming, and that humans are the chief cause, is overwhelming.[20]

---

*   Notoriously the US tobacco industry ran an advertising campaign in the 1950s claiming that its customers' health was the industry's overriding concern. The response of the UK industry was different. After the industry's chief statistician was sacked for saying he would resign unless the tobacco industry accepted that smoking caused lung cancer, he was reinstated six weeks later and the industry agreed not to say anything to imply that smoking did not cause lung cancer. Conrad Keating, *Smoking Kills: The Revolutionary Life of Richard Doll* (2009), pp. 183–6.

King made the comment in 2010 – at the end of a decade which showed no statistical trend in average global temperatures.

The clear implication is that the relationship between rising levels of carbon dioxide in the atmosphere and changes in global temperature is as solidly founded as that between tobacco smoking and lung cancer. There is little dispute that tobacco smoking is, in the words of Eric Feldman and Ronald Bayer, authors of *Unfiltered: Conflicts over Tobacco Policy and Public Health*, 'the single most important preventable source of morbidity and mortality in advanced industrial societies'.[21]

The parallel with smoking and lung cancer is a potent advocacy tool to discredit opponents. Global warming was an idea in search of evidence, reversing Popper's formulation that a theory must allow us to *explain* the observations that created the problem.[22] Here, the theory preceded the observations: speculation that rising levels of carbon dioxide would lead to rising global temperatures led concerned scientists – many of whom were worried about the possibly deleterious consequences on the environment if such a rise were to occur – to seek evidence for it.

Superficially, the most compelling evidence for global warming was derived from temperature reconstructions that purported to show that the rise in temperatures during the twentieth century was unprecedented and way outside the bounds of natural variability. After the Hockey Stick was discredited, the IPCC changed tack. Now the principal evidence was the ability of computer models to replicate global temperature trends over the second half of the twentieth century. The rise in average global temperature could only be explained by the rise in carbon dioxide (although the computer models used assumptions about cooling induced by sulphate aerosols that were little more than guesswork).* Secondary evidence was also adduced, including glacier retreat, arctic sea ice extent, the number of polar bears, extreme weather events and sometimes lurid forecasts of what the world was going to look like, amplified and often distorted by NGOs who shared scientists' concern about the environment.

In terms of Schneider's 'courtroom epistemology', carbon dioxide was in the dock from the start. To change the metaphor, the disease pathway

---

*   According to Richard Lindzen, 'The models focus on aerosols and solar variability, and generally assume that natural internal variability is accurately included and accounted for. That models each use different assumptions for aerosols and solar variability makes clear that these are simply adjustable parameters.' Richard S. Lindzen, 'Response to the critique of my lecture in the House of Commons on 22nd February 2012', 12th April 2012 http://thegwpf.org/the-climate-record/5437-richard-lindzen-response-to-the-critique-of-my-house-of-commons-lecture.html had been found before evidence of disease – the opposite of the case with lung cancer.

Until the 1920s, cancer of the lung was considered rare. Death rates from infectious diseases such as tuberculosis, typhus and cholera had fallen steadily during the nineteenth century. As deaths from infectious epidemics fell, lung cancer rates climbed. In Britain, lung cancer rose by one thousand, five hundred per cent between 1922 and 1947 and overtook the declining death rate from tuberculosis. 'By the late 1940s,' according to the medical historian Conrad Keating, 'Britain had the highest lung cancer rates in the world, and the reasons for this were completely unknown.'[23]

In 1947, the Ministry of Health wrote to the Medical Research Council. At a meeting of thirteen leading researchers, various hypotheses were put forward. These included proximity to gas works, tar on roads, vehicle exhaust fumes and cigarette smoking. 'There was no consensus of opinion.'[24]

The task of finding the cause was given to Austin Bradford Hill (a pipe smoker) and Richard Doll (who smoked a pipe and non-tipped cigarettes). 'I was not antagonistic to tobacco when, in 1947, I began to study its effects,' Doll wrote in 1999.[25] 'Originally Doll thought the increase in motor cars and the tarring of roads were likely to be responsible for the epidemic,' Keating wrote in his biography of Doll. 'Hill, typically, was reported to have entered the study "with an open mind."'[26]

The survey questionnaire designed by Hill and Doll was 'no frontal attack on smoking, which formed one section out of nine – eleven questions out of nearly fifty', others being on social class, diet, electric or gas cookers, whether those surveyed lived near a gas works.[27] After the study had been extended for a year, Hill and Doll's analysis started to reveal evidence neither had anticipated. In October 1949, Doll wrote to the Medical Research Council of a 'real association between smoking and cancer of the lung'.[28] It was only then that Doll quit smoking. 'That so many diseases – major and minor – should be related to smoking is one of the most astonishing findings of medical research in this century,' Doll wrote fifty years later.[29]

Coincidentally in 1948 Ernst Wynder, a summer student at New York University, decided to conduct a case-control study on smoking and lung cancer. In February 1949, Wynder presented the results of his study to the national meeting of the American Cancer Society. They aroused little interest. In May 1950 Wynder and his supervisor, Evert Graham, published a paper in the *Journal of the American Medical Association*. It concluded: 'Smoking, especially in the form of cigarettes, plays an important role in the aetiology of lung cancer.'[30]

Two studies – completely independent of one another – came to the same conclusion. The two teams were not part of a community, comparing notes as part of a collective endeavour. In the case of the Englishmen, both were rigorous in separating scientific research from policy. Doll, a committed communist for much of his life, never permitted his personal political views to cross over into his work as a scientist. Doll had an ideological immune system and scrupulously followed what Hill had taught him: 'If you were going to contribute to a subject it was very important to separate the presentation of evidence from the discussion of what should be done on the basis of that evidence.'[31] A scientist was an expert witness, not a policy advocate.

Doll was acutely conscious of the susceptibility of epidemiological evidence to distortion: 'The only safeguard is always to suspect the influence of bias, consider every way it could have entered the study and then test to see if it has.'[32] According to Keating, 'In nearly every way Doll embodied Charles Darwin's definition of a value-free experimenter. "A scientific man ought to have no wishes, no affections – a mere heart of stone."'[33] Doll was thus an exemplar of the scientific method that Gore vehemently denounced in *Earth in the Balance*, guilty of man's breach with nature and contributing to the evils perpetrated by Hitler and Stalin.

For his part, Doll was critical of claims – inspired by Rachel Carson and *Silent Spring* – made by the US environmental movement that the widespread use of chemicals and other forms of industrial pollution were causing a cancer epidemic. A 1981 paper written with Richard Peto concluded: 'Were it not for the effects of tobacco, total US death rates would be decreasing substantially more rapidly than they already are.'[34] Indeed Keating makes the case that US environmentalists helped Big Tobacco off the hook:

> The claim that twenty per cent of cancers were a result of the actions of a rapacious chemical industry created an apologia for Big Tobacco ... In 1980-81 the American cigarette industry had a record year ... Commenting on this, the Chairman of the largest American cigarette manufacturer was reported as saying that he thought the 'cancer problem' was no longer hitting sales as hard as before because 'so many things have been linked to cancer' that people might be getting sceptical.[35]

The implication is inescapable. Environmentalism cost lives.

With global warming, there is an additional layer of opaque uncertainty – the extent to which climate science is subject to a paradigm in the sense

Kuhn wrote about in *The Structure of Scientific Revolutions*. 'Current scientific knowledge' views large-scale changes in the Earth's climate, whether natural or man-made, through the prism of a paradigm of CO_2-induced climate change. Accordingly changes in concentrations of carbon dioxide are assumed by climate scientists to play a major role in the succession of glacial cycles.*

'The proponents of competing paradigms are always to some extents at cross-purposes,' Kuhn wrote. 'They are bound partly to talk through each other in a battle that cannot be resolved by proofs.'[36] Thus debates between scientists are not going to settle the issue. Neither would counting the number of scientists for or against the prevailing consensus resolve the matter. The existence of consensus might only constitute evidence of a paradigm's hold on the minds of contemporary scientists.

However there is an indicator that provides a rough and ready litmus test. Popper's search for a principle to distinguish science from pseudo-science was sparked by the contrast between Einstein's theory of relativity and Marx's theory of history, Freud's psycho-analysis and Alfred Adler's 'individual psychology'. Einstein's theory was supported by passing the severe test conducted by Eddington, a test it could have failed. By contrast, subscribers to the theories of Marx, Freud and Adler found confirmatory evidence wherever they looked. Their theories seemed to explain practically everything within the fields to which they referred. Whatever happened always confirmed it. 'It was rather that I felt that these three other theories, though posing as science, had in fact more in common with primitive myths than with science; that they resembled astrology rather than astronomy,' Popper wrote.[37]

Common to the three, Popper noted, was their treatment of unbelievers – or, to use the terminology of global warming, sceptics and deniers.

---

* For example, Brian Hoskins, J. Mitchell, T. Palmer, K. Shine & E. Wolff wrote that the termination of the most recent glaciation, with a small initial rise in temperatures followed by several thousand years in which temperatures and CO_2 rose together, 'is entirely consistent with the role of CO_2 as an amplifier of an otherwise small external forcing' (*A critique of the scientific content of Richard Lindzen's Seminar in London, 22nd February 2012*). In response, Lindzen wrote: 'The notion that the small changes in globally and annually averaged insolation are the crucial driver is implausible to say the least, but it stems from the current simplistic view of climate consisting in a single variable (globally averaged temperature anomaly) forced by some globally averaged radiative forcing – an idea that permeates the critics' discussion.' Richard S. Lindzen, 'Response to the critique of my lecture in the House of Commons on 22nd February 2012' 12th April 2012 http://thegwpf.org/the-climate-record/5437-richard-lindzen-response-to-the-critique-of-my-house-of-commons-lecture.html

Their defiance in the face of manifest truth had a ready explanation, for, as we've already seen,

> unbelievers were clearly people who did not want to see the manifest truth; who refused to see it, either because it was against their class interest, or because of their repressions which were still 'un-analysed' and crying out for treatment.[38]

Attempts to settle a dispute by pointing to the other side's motives are the stock in-trade of the political campaigner. In framing the argument on global warming in terms of scientific truth versus the false consciousness promoted by special interests, proponents of the idea of global warming inadvertently proclaim their adherence to a pseudo-science.

The argument that the public became confused about the science because of the activities of malign special interests (i.e., fossil fuel companies) is so ubiquitous as to be an intrinsic component in the morphology of global warming. It has been articulated by leading scientists (Michael Mann has written an entire book blaming the shortcomings of the Hockey Stick on special interests), politicians (Gordon Brown and Kevin Rudd, as well as Al Gore), and environmental NGOs. In 2012, William Nordhaus compared the 'distortion' of climate science to the activities of tobacco companies. 'Scientists, citizens, and our leaders will need to be extremely vigilant to prevent pollution of the scientific process by the merchants of doubt,' Nordhaus wrote, criticising global warming sceptics.[39]

It is also unhistorical. Despite the opposition of tobacco farmers and cigarette manufacturers, governments ran extensive anti-smoking campaigns and adopted other preventive measures, including vertiginously high taxes on tobacco. 'By the close of the twentieth century, anti-tobacco advocates, public health officials, physicians' groups, and international organisations, separately and in concert, had succeeded in putting tobacco control on the policy agenda of every industrialised democracy,' Feldman and Bayer wrote.[40] Thanks to them, cigarette smoking has fallen in the Western world. As predicted by Doll, after a lag, lung cancer rates fell too.

Even the most ingenious maker of conspiracy theories would be hard pressed to forge a chain of causality linking the activities of Western fossil fuel companies to the refusal of India and China to accede to the West's demands for a global cap on greenhouse gas emissions, especially as the Third World's resistance to the claims of Western environmentalism had been adopted in the early 1970s – a decade and a half before the arrival of global warming in world politics in 1988.

So we come to the final paradox of global warming. The science is weak, but the idea is strong. The science is inherently weak because it is not capable of being falsified in the here and now. Voluminous evidence is itself testament to its weakness, for the same reasons Popper noted with respect to the trio of pseudo-sciences prevalent in Vienna in the 1920s.

Predictions that global warming will be harmful or dangerous are future statements which cannot be verified. By default, computer models have been used to guide governments, but they too depend on unverified assumptions about the cooling effect of aerosols.* But these models have failed to capture the amplitude of natural variability or to predict the absence of a clear trend in average global temperatures during the twenty-first century in what could be called Trenberth's Travesty.[†]

Bias in the IPCC is endemic, from language of the expected signal of global warming emerging in the future, the cover-up of flaws in the Hockey Stick, its politicisation through government selection of lead authors and their control over what the IPCC says, to its infiltration by NGOs. 'Despite the numbers of persons involved, and the lengthy formal review procedures, the preparation of the IPCC Assessment Reports is far from being a model of rigour, inclusiveness and impartiality,' David Henderson wrote in a critique of the IPCC.[41]

After the Fourth Assessment Report was found to be full of errors, Working Group II co-chair Martin Parry wrote to colleagues characterising it as a 'clamour without substance' fed by critics and sceptics, at the same time defending the inclusion of NGO literature in IPCC output.[42] Bob Watson, the IPCC's second chairman, thought otherwise. 'The mistakes all appear to have gone in the direction of making it seem like climate change is more serious by overstating the impact. That is worrying,' Watson said. 'The IPCC needs to look at this trend in the errors and ask why it happened.'[43]

Yet global warming's success in colonising the Western mind and in changing government policies has no precedent. It dominated the international agenda from the 1992 Rio Earth Summit until the 2008 banking crisis and the West's defeat at Copenhagen a year later. The prospect of

---

*   'There are considerable uncertainties in estimating the impact of aerosols on climate,' according to Hoskins et al., who go on to say that 'uncertain' does not mean 'unknown' or that the cooling effect of aerosols is zero. Brian Hoskins, J. Mitchell, T. Palmer, K. Shine & E. Wolff, *A critique of the scientific content of Richard Lindzen's Seminar in London, 22nd February 2012* (undated).

†   According to Lindzen, 'The assumption that the models adequately represent natural internal variability is seriously mistaken.' Richard S. Lindzen, 'Response to the critique of my lecture in the House of Commons on 22nd February 2012'.

planetary salvation inflated the science so it became too big to fail, justifying the anti-scientific practice of withholding data and methods from potential critics and de-legitimising critical argument.* 'What is called objectivity consists solely in the critical approach,' Popper wrote.[44]

The credibility of global warming rested on the prestige of science – the branch of knowledge that had advanced further and faster than any other in human history. Underneath though, the nature of science was changing. It is hard to see a scientist such as Percy W. Bridgman in the middle of the twentieth century accepting with equanimity unverifiable future statements as science. Without the possibility of verification, Bridgman wrote, truth becomes meaningless.[45] Apply his criterion to the output of the IPCC, and there wouldn't be much science left to furnish the basis of an immensely costly call to action.

This change was accompanied by a highly expansive view of the social role of scientists as uniquely capable of identifying and devising solutions to the problems threatening the survival of humanity and the planet. To this, scientists brought their cultural aversion to learning from the past. For them, history is not so much a closed book as irrelevant to the problems of the future. So they didn't ask why previous predictions of imminent catastrophes, from Malthus and Jevons in the nineteenth century to the limits to growth debates of the early 1970s, were all wrong.

True to form, in 2012 the Royal Society produced the latest in the series of doomsday predictions. Unsurprisingly *People and the Planet* argued there were too many of the former for the latter.

> Over the next thirty to forty years the confluence of the challenges described in this report provides the opportunity to move towards a sustainable economy and a better world for the majority of humanity, or alternatively the risk of social, economic and environmental failures and catastrophes on a scale never imagined.[46]

The last claim was untrue. Such catastrophes had been imagined. Exactly forty years earlier, Julian Huxley, winner of the Royal Society's Darwin Medal, together with four other Fellows of the Royal Society and twenty-

---

* Hill and Doll's findings on tobacco and lung cancer were fiercely attacked by R.A. Fisher, the leading geneticist and statistician of the period (Fisher formulated the null hypothesis test), who demanded to see the underlying data. Hill and Doll passed two data sets to Fisher. Conrad Keating, *Smoking Kills: The Revolutionary Life of Richard Doll* (2009), p. 191.

nine eminent scientists and experts, predicted the collapse of industrial civilisation in famine, epidemic and war within the lifetimes of people then living. 'On a planet with finite resources there are limits to growth,' the Royal Society stated, repeating the message of the Club of Rome's *The Limits to Growth*, also from 1972, and making the same error.[47]

When it comes to learning from their mistakes, collectively scientists vie with the Bourbons.

In believing scientists and politicians can solve the problems of a far distant future, the tangible needs of the present are neglected. We cannot know what the future holds. It is like walking into a dense fog armed with a flashlight and one's wits, picking out objects which we only know for sure what they are when nearly upon them.

No one knows what the Earth's climate will be at the end of the century. Based on history, it is possible to hazard a prediction of a different kind. Before the end of the century, the Western mind will conceive another environmental crisis necessitating the ending of the modern industrial economy, the only form of economic arrangements that has lifted mankind to undreamt of prosperity.

The big question is whether the Western mind will be sovereign at the century's end and the West remain the core of the world economy or relegated to its periphery – something only the passing of the present century can answer.

NOTES

1
THE IDEA

1. Ludwig von Mises, *Socialism* (1981), p. 461.
2. Karl Popper, *The Myth of the Framework* (1994), pp. ix–x.
3. From two hundred and eighty parts per million (that is 0.028 %) before industrialisation to three hundred and seventy-nine ppm in 2005 (0.0379 %) according to the Intergovernmental Panel on Climate Change (IPCC), *Climate Change 2007: Synthesis Report Summary for Policymakers* (2007), p. 37.
4. IPCC, *Climate Change 2007: Synthesis Report Summary for Policymakers* (2007), p. 39.
5. A.N. Whitehead, *Science and the Modern World* (1967), p. viii.
6. Barbara Ward and René Dubos, *Only One Earth* (1974), p. 66.
7. Speech by HRH The Prince of Wales at The Prince's Foundation for the Built Environment conference 2009 titled 'Globalisation from the Bottom Up', 5th February 2009, http://princeofwales.gov.uk/speechesandarticles/
8. Peter Raven, 2002 AAAS Presidential Address, Science, *Sustainability, and the Human Prospect* http://www.sciencemag.org/cgi/content/full/297/5583/954
9. 'Human consumption: Flying in the face of logic', *Guardian*, 16th July 2008.
10. Paul Ehrlich & Anne Ehrlich (2008), *The Dominant Animal: Human Evolution and the Environment*, p. 3.
11. Bjorn Lomborg, *The Skeptical Environmentalist* (2001), p. xix.
12. Nina Mazar & Chen-Bo Zhong, 'Do Green Products Make Us Better People,' *Psychological Science*, April 2010 Vol. 21 No. 4, pp. 494–8.
13. A.N. Whitehead, *An Introduction to Mathematics* (1911), p. 61.

2
PROMETHEAN REVOLUTION

1. Ronald H. Coase, 'The Problem of Social Cost', *Journal of Law and Economics* (1960).
2. Paolo Rossi, *Francis Bacon: From Magic to Science*, translated by Sacha Rabinovitch (1968), p. xiii.
3. William Rawley, *The Life of the Right Honourable Francis Bacon*, Vol. 1 of the Complete Works (1730), p. 5.
4. Quoted in Benjamin Farrington, *Philosopher of Industrial Science* (1951), p. 64.

5. Francis Bacon, *Novum Organum*, p. 129.
6. Quoted in Farrington op. cit., p. 54.
7. Francis Bacon, *The Moral and Historical Works of Lord Bacon*, ed. Joseph Devey (1874), p. 297.
8. Karl Marx, *Capital* (1961), p. 136.
9. Karl Popper, *The Myth of the Framework* (1994), p. 198 (emphasis in the original).
10. ibid., p. 193.
11. A.N. Whitehead, *Science and the Modern World* (1967), p. 12.
12. ibid.
13. Popper, *The Myth of the Framework* (1994), p. 203.
14. Kevin Rudd, Address to the Lowry Institute, 6th November 2009.
15. Popper, *Conjectures and Refutations* (2002), p. 45.
16. Popper, *The Myth of the Framework* (1994), p. xiii.
17. ibid., p. 110.
18. Thomas L Friedman, Our One-Party Democracy, *New York Times*, 9th September 2009.
19. Martin Wolf, *Why Globalisation Works* (2004), p. 41.
20. Paolo Rossi, *Francis Bacon: From Magic to Science*, translated by Sacha Rabinovitch (1968), p. xi.
21. Thomas Malthus, *An Essay on the Principle of Population* (1798).
22. Malthus, *An Essay on the Principle of Population* (1798).
23. ibid.
24. ibid.
25. Geoffey Gilbert (ed.), *TR Malthus Critical Responses* (1998), Vol. 3, p. 178.
26. www.ons.gov.uk/census/census-history/index.html
27. B.R. Mitchell, *International Historical Statistics Europe 1750–2000* (2003), Table A1.
28. Sam Peltzman, 'Mortality Inequality', *Journal of Economic Perspectives*, Vol. 23, No. 4 (2009), pp. 175–90.
29. Mitchell, *International Historical Statistics Europe 1750–2000* (2003), Tables B4 & B5.
30. ibid., Table H2.
31. ibid., Tables D1 & D2.
32. Malthus, *An Essay on the Principle of Population* (1798).
33. Maurice Strong, *Where on Earth are We Going?* (2001), p. 7.
34. Strong, *Where on Earth are We Going?* (2001), p. 21.
35. ibid., p. 22.
36. Charles Darwin, *Autobiography* (2010), p. 82.
37. Ronald Findlay in *The New Palgrave Dictionary of Economics*, ed. John Eatwell et al (1998), Vol. 1, p. 514.

3
ANTECEDENTS

1. Geoffrey Gilbert (ed.), *TR Malthus Critical Responses* (1998), Vol. 3, p. 50.
2. W. Stanley Jevons, *The Coal Question* (1865).
3. Joseph A Schumpeter, *History of Economic Analysis* (1994), p. 826.
4. Harro Maas, *William Stanley Jevons and the Making of Modern Economics* (2005), p. 33.
5. W. Stanley Jevons, *The Coal Question* (1865), p. 149.
6. ibid., p. 150.
7. ibid., p. 154.
8. ibid., p. vii.
9. ibid., p. viii.
10. ibid., p. xix.
11. ibid., pp. 154–5.
12. ibid., p. 345.
13. ibid., p. 344.
14. ibid., p. 349.
15. Ronald L. Meek, *Marx and Engels on Malthus* (1953), p. 24.
16. Meek, *Marx and Engels on Malthus* (1953), p. 69.
17. Gilbert (ed.), *TR Malthus Critical Responses* (1998), Vol. III, p. 50.
18. Meek, *Marx and Engels on Malthus* (1953), p. 63.
19. Jevons, *The Coal Question* (1865), p. 117.
20. ibid., p. 117.
21. ibid., p. 119.
22. ibid., p. 141.
23. ibid., p. 141.
24. ibid., p. 144.
25. Ian Byatt, *The British Electrical Industry 1875–1914: The economic returns to new technology* (1979), p. 1.
26. Meek, *Marx and Engels on Malthus* (1953), p. 82.
27. Schumpeter, *History of Economic Analysis* (1994), p. 500.
28. Gilbert (ed.), *TR Malthus Critical Responses* (1998), Vol. 3, p. 191.
29. ibid., p. 191.
30. http://www.bom.gov.au/climate/drought/livedrought.shtml
31. Gilbert (ed.), *TR Malthus Critical Responses* (1998), Vol. 3, p. 178.
32. Meek, *Marx and Engels on Malthus* (1953), p. 110.
33. John Cunningham Wood (ed.), *William Stanley Jevons: Critical Assessments* (1988), Vol. 3, p. 49.
34. B.R. Mitchell, *International Historical Statistics Europe 1750–2000* (2003), Table D2.

35. Jevons, *The Coal Question* (1865), p. 215.
36. Wood (ed.), *William Stanley Jevons: Critical Assessments* (1988), Vol. 1, p. 65.
37. ibid.
38. ibid.
39. http://www.columbia.edu/~jeh1/mailings/2007/20071219_DearPrimeMinister.pdf
40. William H. Brock, *The Fontana History of Chemistry* (1992), pp.103–4.
41. A.N. Whitehead, *Science and the Modern World* (1967), p. 99.
42. Thomas S. Kuhn, *The Structure of Scientific Revolutions* (1996), p. 139.
43. ibid., p. 96.
44. Brock, *The Fontana History of Chemistry* (1992), p. 84.
45. ibid., pp. 111–12.
46. James Rodger Fleming, *The Callendar Effect* (2007), p. 66.
47. ibid.
48. Quoted in Mike Hulme, 'On the origin of "the greenhouse effect": John Tyndall's 1859 interrogation of nature', *Weather*, Royal Meteorological Society (May 2009), Vol. 64, No. 5, p. 121.
49. ibid.
50. ibid., p. 122.
51. Spencer R. Weart, 'The idea of anthropogenic global climate change in the twentieth century,' *Wiley Interdisciplinary Reviews: Climate Change*, Vol. 1, No. 1 (January/February 2010), p. 68.

4
FIRST STIRRINGS

1. 'The Changing Arctic,' *Washington Post*, 2nd November 1922.
2. http://www.ncdc.noaa.gov/oa/climate/research/cag3/na.html
3. http://www.crh.noaa.gov/arx/events/heatwave36.php
4. http://www.nasa.gov/centers/goddard/news/topstory/2004/0319dustbowl.html
5. Gordon Manley, 'Central England temperatures: monthly means 1659 to 1973', *Quarterly Journal of the Royal Meteorological Society* (1974), 100, pp. 389–405.
6. O. E. Tveito, E. Førland, R. Heino, I. Hanssen-Bauer, H. Alexandersson, B. Dahlström, A. Drebs, C. Kern-Hansen, T. Jónsson, E. Vaarby Laursen, Y. Westman, *Nordic Temperature Maps*, NordKlim (2000), Fig 20.
7. James Rodger Fleming, *The Callendar Effect* (2007), p. 65.
8. ibid., p. 68.
9. ibid., p. 72.

10. ibid., p. 50.

11. Theodore Roosevelt, *An Autobiography* (1913), p. 94.

12. ibid., p. 47.

13. Henry David Thoreau, *Walden and Civil Disobedience* (1986), p. 47.

14. Roosevelt, *An Autobiography* (1913), p. 95.

15. Thoreau, *Walden and Civil Disobedience* (1986), p. 184.

16. Paul Brooks, *Speaking for Nature* (1980), p. 113.

17. Roosevelt, *An Autobiography* (1913), p. 435.

18. ibid., p. 434.

19. ibid., p. 410.

20. ibid., p. 423.

21. Robert Bradley, *Capitalism at Work: Business, Government, and Energy* (2009), pp. 205–6.

22. Roosevelt, *An Autobiography* (1913), p. 424.

23. ibid., p. 425.

24. *The International Petroleum Cartel*, Staff Report to the Federal Trade Commission, released through Subcommittee on Monopoly of Select Committee on Small Business, U.S. Senate, 83rd Cong., 2nd session (Washington, DC, 1952), 'Development of Joint Control over Foreign Oil,' pp. 37–46.

25. Robert Bradley, *Capitalism at Work: Business, Government, and Energy* (2009), pp. 206–7.

26. ibid., p. 206.

27. Annual Message to Congress, December 6, 1923, http://www.presidency.ucsb.edu/ws/index.php?pid=29564

28. Anna Bramwell, *Ecology in the 20th Century* (1989), p. 162.

29. ibid., p. 200.

30. ibid., p. 173.

31. ibid., pp. 39–40.

32. ibid., p. 107.

33. T.S. Eliot, *Christianity and Culture* (1988), p. 26.

34. Stanley Baldwin, *On England, and Other Addresses* (1938), pp. 6–7.

35. Peter Hall, Harry Gracey, Roy Drewett & Ray Thomas, *The Containment of Urban England* (1973), p. 102.

36. ibid., p. 628.

37. George Orwell, *The Lion and Unicorn: Socialism and the English Genius* (1941), included in *Essays* (2002), p. 292.

38. Cecil Palmer, 'Do We Agree? A Debate Between G. K. Chesterton And Bernard Shaw with Hilaire Belloc in the Chair' (1928) http://www.cse.dmu.ac.uk/~mward/gkc/books/debate.txt

39. George Orwell, *The Collected Essays, Journalism and Letters of George Orwell*, from *In Front of Your Nose*, Vol. 4 (1968), pp. 162–3.

40. Orwell, *The Collected Essays, Journalism and Letters of George Orwell*, p. 189.
41. http://www.kibbokift.org/jhbio.html
42. John Maynard Keynes, *The General Theory of Employment, Interest and Money* (1973), p. 371.
43. Rolf Gardiner & Heinz Rocholl (ed.), *Britain and Germany: A Frank Discussion Instigated by Members of the Younger Generation* (1928), p. 19.
44. ibid., p.124.
45. Bramwell, *Ecology in the 20ᵗʰ Century* (1989), p. 165.
46. ibid., p. 118.
47. Quoted from Henry Williamson, *Phoenix Generation*, cited in Anna Bramwell, *Ecology in the 20ᵗʰ Century* (1989), p. 142.
48. ibid., p. 164.
49. ibid., p. 110.
50. ibid., p. 110.
51. ibid., p. 217.
52. http://www.soilassociation.org/Aboutus/Ourhistory/tabid/70/Default.aspx
53. Gardiner & Rocholl (ed.), *Britain and Germany: A Frank Discussion Instigated by Members of the Younger Generation* (1928), p. 123.
54. ibid., p. 129.
55. Bramwell, *Ecology in the 20ᵗʰ Century* (1989), pp. 198–200.

5
TURNING POINT

1. James Rodger Fleming, *Historical Perspectives on Climate Change* (1998), p. 125.
2. Al Gore, 'Rachel Carson and Silent Spring' in Peter Matthiessen (ed.), *Courage for the Earth* (2007), p. 63.
3. Fleming, *The Callendar Effect* (2007), p. 72.
4. ibid., p. 31 & p. 78.
5. Harry S. Truman, Letter to William S. Paley on the Creation of the President's Materials Policy Commission, 22ⁿᵈ January 1951 http://www.presidency.ucsb.edu/ws/print.php?pid=13876
6. *Resources for Freedom*, A Report to the President by The President's Materials Policy Commission, Washington (1952), Vol. 1, *Foundations for Growth*, p. 1.
7. *Resources for Freedom* (1952), Vol. 1, *Foundations for Growth*, p. 21.
8. ibid.
9. ibid.
10. ibid., p. 3.
11. ibid.

12. ibid., p. 20.
13. ibid., p. 3.
14. ibid., p. 77.
15. ibid., p. 107.
16. Statement of Charles G. Groat, Director USGS, before the subcommittee on Energy and Mineral Resources Committee on Resources US House of Representatives 'The Role of Strategic and Critical Minerals in Our National and Economic Security', 17th July 2003 http://www.usgs.gov/congressional/hearings/testimony_17july03.asp
17. *Resources for Freedom* (1952), Vol. 4, *The Promise of Technology*, p. 23.
18. Gary Kroll, 'Rachel Carson's *The Sea Around Us*, Ocean-Centrism, and a Nascent Ocean Ethic' in Lisa H. Sideris & Kathleen Dean Moore, *Rachel Carson: Legacy and Challenge* (2008), p. 119.
19. Paul Brooks, *Speaking for Nature* (1980), pp. 276–7.
20. Brooks, *Speaking for Nature* (1980), p. 278; Linda Lear, *Rachel Carson Witness for Nature* (1999), p. 90.
21. Brooks, *The House of Life – Rachel Carson at Work* (1972), p. 299.
22. John F. Kennedy, 'Address Before the 18th General Assembly of the United Nations,' 20th September 1963 http://www.jfklibrary.org/Historical+Resources/Archives/Reference+Desk/Speeches/JFK/003POF03_18thGeneralAssembly09201963.htm
23. Lisa H. Sideris, 'The Ecological Body: Rachel Carson, *Silent Spring*, and Breast Cancer' in Lisa H. Sideris & Kathleen Dean Moore, *Rachel Carson: Legacy and Challenge* (2008), p. 142.
24. Frank Graham Jr, 'Rachel Carson', in the *EPA Journal* (1978), http://www.epa.gov/history/topics/perspect/carson.htm
25. Brooks, *The House of Life – Rachel Carson at Work* (1972), p. 299.
26. Henry David Thoreau, *Walden and Civil Disobedience* (1986), pp. 362–3.
27. Rachel Carson, *Silent Spring* (2000), p. 22.
28. ibid.
29. ibid., p. 41.
30. ibid., p. 42.
31. ibid., p. 43.
32. ibid., pp. 100–1.
33. ibid., p. 211.
34. ibid., p. 195.
35. ibid., p. 212.
36. ibid., p. 193.
37. ibid., p. 24.
38. ibid.
39. Linda Lear, *Rachel Carson Witness for Nature* (1999), p. 429.
40. Chris J. Magoc, *Environmental Issues in American History* (2006), p. 227.

41. Carson, *Silent Spring* (2000), p. 121.
42. ibid., p. 161.
43. ibid., p. 164.
44. H. Patricia Hynes, *The Recurring Silent Spring* (1989), p. 115.
45. Brooks, *The House of Life – Rachel Carson at Work* (1972), p. 316.
46. Sideris, 'The Ecological Body: Rachel Carson, *Silent Spring*, and Breast Cancer' in Sideris & Moore, *Rachel Carson: Legacy and Challenge* (2008), p. 137.
47. Lear, *Rachel Carson Witness for Nature* (1999), p. 450.
48. Brooks, *The House of Life – Rachel Carson at Work* (1972), p. 325.
49. Friedrich Nietzsche, *On the Genealogy of Morals*, Third Essay, Section 25.
50. http://motherjones.com/politics/1997/01/stephen-jay-gould?page=1
51. Brooks, *The House of Life – Rachel Carson at Work* (1972), p. 319.
52. Carson, *The Sea Around Us* (1989), p. 15.
53. Wilfred Beckerman, *In Defence of Economic Growth* (1976), p. 265.

6
SPACESHIP EARTH

1. Edgar J. Dosman, *The Life and Times of Raúl Prebisch* (2008), p. 129.
2. Raúl Prebisch, *Power, Principle and the Ethics of Development* (2006), p. 54.
3. Dosman, *The Life and Times of Raúl Prebisch* (2008), pp. 248–9.
4. ibid., p. 249.
5. J.T. Cuddington, 'Long-Run Trends In 26 Primary Commodity Prices – A Disaggregated Look at the Prebisch-Singer Hypothesis' in *Journal of Development Economics* 39 (2) (1992), pp. 207–27.
6. http://www.bartleby.com/73/477.html
7. Kenneth Boulding, 'The Economics of the coming Spaceship Earth' in Henry Jarret (ed.), *Environmental Quality In a Growing Economy – Essays from the Sixth RFF Forum* (1966), p. 3.
8. ibid., p. 9.
9. ibid., p. 10.
10. Barbara Ward, *Space Ship Earth* (1966), p. 22.
11. ibid., p. 24.
12. E.F. Schumacher, *Small is Beautiful* (1993), p. vii.
13. Barbara Wood, *Alias Papa: A Life of Fritz Schumacher* (1984), p. 241.
14. ibid., p. 222.
15. ibid., p. 236.
16. ibid., p. 244.
17. ibid., p. 248.
18. ibid.

19. Schumacher, *This I Believe* (2004), p. 8.

20. ibid., p. 131.

21. ibid., p. 41.

22. ibid., p. 42.

23. ibid., p. 44.

24. ibid., p. 43.

25. ibid., p. 44.

26. ibid., p. 129.

27. http://www.youtube.com/profile?user=Efssociety#p/u/6/RebfgHCfrmw

28. Wood, *Alias Papa: A Life of Fritz Schumacher* (1984), p. 353.

29. ibid., p. 320.

30. Schumacher, *Small is Beautiful* (1993), p. 131.

31. Norman Borlaug, 'Are We Really in Danger', *Observer*, 5th March 1972

32. 'Norman Borlaug, scientist who "saved 245m lives", dies aged 95', *The Times*, 14th September 2009.

33. Harry Cleaver, *American Economic Review*, Vol. 62, Issue 2 (1972), pp. 177–86.

34. Douglas Kellner (ed.), *Collected Papers of Herbert Marcuse*, Vol. 3, *The New Left and the 1960s* (2005), p. 173.

35. ibid., p. 174.

36. ibid., p. 173.

7
LIMITS TO GROWTH

1. Dennis L. Meadows et al, *The Limits to Growth: A Report for the Club of Rome's Project on the Predicament of Humanity* (1972), p. 197.

2. http://www.earthday.net/node/77

3. Richard Reeves, *President Nixon: Alone in the White House* (2001), p. 163.

4. http://www.presidency.ucsb.edu/ws/?pid=2921

5. Robert B. Semple Jr, *New York Times*, 23rd January 1970.

6. Reeves, *President Nixon: Alone in the White House* (2001), p. 163.

7. ibid., p. 238.

8. Lou Cannon, *Governor Reagan: His Rise to Power* (2003), p. 300.

9. Cannon, *Governor Reagan: His Rise to Power* (2003), p. 313.

10. Lisa H. Sideris, 'The Ecological Body: Rachel Carson, Silent Spring, and Breast Cancer' in Lisa H. Sideris & Kathleen Dean Moore (ed.), *Rachel Carson: Legacy and Challenge* (2008), p. 137.

11. Francis Sandbach, *Environment, Ideology & Policy* (1980), p. 19.

12. Wilfred Beckerman, *In Defence of Economic Growth* (1976), p. 247.

13. 'Pollution: Nuisance or Nemesis? A Report on the Control of Pollution' (1972), p. 7.

14. Beckerman, *In Defence of Economic Growth* (1976), p. 14.

15. Meadows et al, *The Limits to Growth: A Report for the Club of Rome's Project on the Predicament of Humanity* (1972), pp. 9–10.

16. ibid., p. 23.

17. ibid., p. 24.

18. ibid., p. 154.

19. ibid.

20. ibid., p. 147.

21. ibid., p. 155.

22. Beckerman, *In Defence of Economic Growth* (1976), p. 258.

23. Edward Goldsmith el al, *A Blueprint for Survival* (1972), p. 28.

24. ibid., p. 14.

25. ibid.

26. 'Pollution: Nuisance or Nemesis? A Report on the Control of Pollution' (1972), p. 3.

27. ibid., p. 9.

28. ibid., p. 80.

29. ibid.

30. Beckerman, *In Defence of Economic Growth* (1976), p. 14

31. ibid.

32. ibid., p. 35.

33. ibid., p. 163.

34. Anthony Crosland, *A Social Democratic Britain* (1971).

35. Beckerman, *In Defence of Economic Growth* (1976), p. 110.

36. http://unfccc.int/files/meetings/seminar/application/pdf/sem_pre_brazil.pdf

8
STOCKHOLM

1. Maurice Strong, 'Our common future – 15 years after the Stockholm conference' in World Media Institute, *TRIBUTE …to Barbara Ward: Lady of Global Concern* (1987), p. 79.

2. Maurice Strong, *Where on Earth are We Going?* (2001), p. 51.

3. ibid., p. 58.

4. ibid., p. 118.

5. ibid.

6. Strong, 'Our common future – 15 years after the Stockholm conference' in World Media Institute, *TRIBUTE …to Barbara Ward: Lady of Global Concern* (1987), p. 94.

7. Strong, *Where on Earth are We Going?* (2001), p. 156.

8. ibid., p. 86.

9. ibid., p. 190.

10. ibid., p. 125.

11. Paul Lewis, 'British Economist Dies' in *New York Times*, 1ˢᵗ June 1981.

12. Harold Wilson, *The Labour Government 1964–1970: A Personal Record* (1971), p. 499.

13. David Satterthwaite, *Barbara Ward and the Origins of Sustainable Development* (2006), p. 65.

14. 'Barbara Ward, British Economist, Dies', *New York Times*, 1ˢᵗ June 1981.

15. Satterthwaite, *Barbara Ward and the Origins of Sustainable Development* (2006), p. 46.

16. ibid., p. 16.

17. http://www.vatican.va/holy_father/paul_vi/encyclicals/documents/hf_p-vi_enc_26031967_populorum_en.html

18. Satterthwaite, *Barbara Ward and the Origins of Sustainable Development* (2006), p. 15.

19. Barbara Ward, *A New Creation? Reflections on the Environmental Issue*, first published by the Pontifical Commission Justice and Peace in Vatican City in 1973, in World Media Institute, *TRIBUTE …to Barbara Ward: Lady of Global Concern* (1987), p. 16.

20. ibid.

21. ibid., p. 15.

22. ibid., p. 31.

23. Barbara Ward, 'The End of an Epoch?' in *Economist*, 27ᵗʰ May 1972.

24. Barbara Ward, *Space Ship Earth* (1966), p. 3.

25. Barbara Ward and René Dubos, *Only One Earth – The Care and Maintenance of a Small Planet* (1974), p. 10.

26. ibid., p. 26.

27. ibid., p. 266.

28. ibid., p. 268.

29. ibid., p. 145.

30. ibid., p. 84.

31. ibid., p. 85.

32. Satterthwaite, *Barbara Ward and the Origins of Sustainable Development* (2006), p. 15.

33. Strong, *Where on Earth are We Going?* (2001), p. 125.

34. ibid., p. 128.

35. UNEP, *In Defence of the Earth: The basic texts on environment: Founex. Stockholm* (1981), p. 3.

36. ibid., p. 5.

37. ibid., p. 8.

38. 'UN secretary-general calls on all nations to meet crisis of a polluted planet' in *The Times*, 6ᵗʰ June 1972.

39. 'Delegates' bicycles vanish in Stockholm scramble' in *The Times*, 8th June 1972.
40. John McCormick, *The Global Environmental Movement: Reclaiming Paradise* (1989), p. 101.
41. http://www.mauricestrong.net/2008091028/video/video/unche.html
42. 'UN secretary-general calls on all nations to meet crisis of a polluted planet' in *The Times*, 6th June 1972.
43. http://www.mauricestrong.net/2008091028/video/video/unche.html
44. ibid.
45. 'Mrs Gandhi blames profits race for crisis' in *The Times*, 15th June 1972.
46. http://www.mauricestrong.net/2008091028/video/video/unche.html
47. McCormick, *The Global Environmental Movement: Reclaiming Paradise* (1989), p. 99.
48. '$100m fund proposed to carry on fight' in *The Times*, 16th June 1972
49. http://www.mauricestrong.net/20080626154/stockholm/stockholm/stockholm.html
50. UNEP, *In Defence of the Earth: The basic texts on environment: Founex. Stockholm* (1981), pp. 42–7.
51. ibid., p. 82.
52. *Guardian*, 1st June 1981.

9
BREAKING WAVE

1. Henry Kissinger, *Years of Upheaval* (2000), p. 857.
2. Jimmy Carter, Inaugural Address, 20th January 1977 http://www.presidency.ucsb.edu/ws/index.php?pid=6575
3. Uri Bar-Joseph, *The Watchman Fell Asleep: The Surprise of Yom Kippur and Its Sources* (2005), p. 226.
4. Francis Sandbach, *Environment, Ideology & Policy* (1980), p. 7.
5. ibid.
6. Kissinger, *Years of Upheaval* (2000), p. 854.
7. E.F. Schumacher, *This I Believe* (2004), p. 22.
8. ibid., p. 21.
9. ibid., p. 22.
10. John Dumbrell, *The Carter Presidency: A re-evaluation* (1993), p. 172.
11. Jimmy Carter, *Keeping Faith: Memoirs of a President* (1995), pp. 117–18.
12. Ed Richard B. Parker, *The October War* (2001), p. 7.
13. Kissinger, *Years of Upheaval* (2000), p. 872.
14. Ray Maghroori & Stephen Gorman, *The Yom Kippur War: A Case Study in Crisis Decision-Making in American Foreign Policy* (1981), p. 61.

15. ibid., p. 65.
16. Kissinger, *Years of Upheaval* (2000), p. 857.
17. Address to the Nation About Policies To Deal With the Energy Shortages, 7th November 1973 http://www.presidency.ucsb.edu/ws/print.php?pid=4034
18. US Energy Information Administration, MTTIMUS2, http://tonto.eia.doe. gov/dnav/pet/hist/LeafHandler.ashx?n=PET&s=MTTIMUS2&f=A
19. Kissinger, *Years of Upheaval* (2000), p. 885.
20. Prices are for Saudi Light from 1971-1974 and Imported Refiner Acquisition Cost (IRAC) from 1975 expressed in March 2009 dollars. US Energy Information Administration http://tonto.eia.doe.gov/country/timeline/oil_chronology.cfm
21. Kissinger, *Years of Upheaval* (2000), p. 897.
22. Yanek Mieczkowski, *Gerald Ford and the Challenges of the 1970s* (2005), pp. 209–10.
23. W. Carl Biven, *Jimmy Carter's Economy: Policy in an Age of Limits* (2002), p. 258.
24. Carter, *Keeping Faith: Memoirs of a President* (1995), pp. 102–3.
25. ibid., p. 121.
26. President Carter address on Energy Policy, 18th April 1977 http://www.pbs. org/wgbh/amex/carter/filmmore/ps_energy.html
27. ibid.
28. George Melloan & Joan Melloan, *The Carter Economy* (1978), p. 118
29. Environment Message to the Congress, 23rd May 1977 http://www.presidency. ucsb.edu/ws/index.php?pid=7561
30. President Carter, televised address of 15th July 1979 http://www.cartercenter. org/news/editorials_speeches/crisis_of_confidence.html
31. US Energy Information Administration, US Energy Consumption by Energy Source http://www.eia.doe.gov/cneaf/solar.renewables/page/trends/table1. html
32. Biven, *Jimmy Carter's Economy: Policy in an Age of Limits* (2002), p. 157.
33. Melloan & Melloan, *The Carter Economy* (1978), p. 143.
34. BP 'Statistical Review of World Energy 2012' http://www.bp.com/ sectiongenericarticle800.do?categoryId=9037130&contentId=7068669
35. Richard C. Thornton, *The Carter Years: Towards a New Global Order* (1991), p. 422.
36. Don Richardson (ed.), *Conversations with Carter* (1998), p. 173.
37. ibid., pp. 203–4.
38. Carter, *Keeping Faith: Memoirs of a President* (1995), p. 117.
39. ibid., p. 121.
40. 'Crisis of Confidence' by Jimmy Carter, 15th July 1979 http://www. cartercenter.org/news/editorials_speeches/crisis_of_confidence. html?printerFriendly=true

41. 'Crisis of Confidence' by Carter.
42. US Energy Information Administration, MTTIMUS2, http://tonto.eia.doe.gov/dnav/pet/hist/LeafHandler.ashx?n=PET&s=MTTIMUS2&f=A
43. Thornton, *The Carter Years: Towards a New Global Order* (1991), p. 421.
44. Biven, *Jimmy Carter's Economy: Policy in an Age of Limits* (2002), p. 259.
45. Gerald O. Barney, 'The Whole World in Our Hands' in *San Francisco Chronicle*, 31st December 2000.
46. Gerald O. Barney (study director), *The Global 2000 Report to the President: Entering the Twenty First Century* (1980), Vol. 1, p. 42.
47. Angus Maddison, *The World Economy: A Millennial Perspective* (2001), p. 125.
48. Barney, *The Global 2000 Report to the President: Entering the Twenty First Century* (1980), Vol. 1, p. 3.
49. ibid., p. 1.
50. ibid., p. iii.
51. ibid.,p. 32.
52. ibid., p. 42.
53. United Nations, Department of Economic and Social Affairs, *World Population Prospects: The 2006 Revision Highlights* (2007), Fig. 4.
54. Barney, *The Global 2000 Report to the President: Entering the Twenty First Century* (1980), Vol. 1, p. 17.
55. UN Food and Agriculture Organisation http://.fao.org/fileadmin/templates/ess/img/chartroom/72.gif
56. Barney, *The Global 2000 Report to the President: Entering the Twenty First Century* (1980), Vol. 1, p. 2.
57. BP 'Statistical Review of World Energy 2012' http://www.bp.com/sectiongenericarticle800.do?categoryId=9037130&contentId=7068669
58. Barney, *The Global 2000 Report to the President: Entering the Twenty First Century* (1980), Vol. 1, p. 36.
59. ibid., p. 37.
60. ibid., p. iv.
61. James Rodger Fleming, *Historical Perspectives on Climate Change* (1998), p. 132.
62. Kiron Skinner, Annelise Anderson & Martin Anderson, *Reagan In His Own Hand* (2001), p. 329.
63. Skinner, Anderson & Anderson, *Reagan In His Own Hand* (2001), p. 326 & p. 339.
64. ibid., p. 319.
65. ibid., p. 322–3.
66. ibid., p. 320.
67. US Energy Information Administration http://tonto.eia.doe.gov/country/timeline/oil_chronology.cfm
68. Barbara Ward, 'A New Creation? Reflections on the Environmental Issue' in

World Media Institute, *TRIBUTE … to Barbara Ward: Lady of Global Concern* (1987), pp. 14–15.

10
PUPATION

1. Mihajlo Mesarovic & Eduard Pestel, *Mankind at the Turning Point* (1975), p. ix.
2. ibid., pp. x–xi.
3. ibid., p. 123.
4. ibid., p. 149.
5. Anthony Tucker, 'Hang together or hang separately' in the *Guardian*, 24th March 1975.
6. Leonard Silk, 'Scholars Favor Global Growth' in *New York Times*, 13th April 1976.
7. ibid.
8. UNEP, *In Defence of the Earth: The basic texts on environment: Founex, Stockholm, Cocoyoc* (1981), p. 115.
9. ibid., p. 110.
10. ibid., p. 109.
11. ibid., p. 110.
12. ibid., p. 115.
13. Barbara Ward, 'A New Creation? Reflections on the Environmental Issue' in World Media Institute, *TRIBUTE … to Barbara Ward: Lady of Global Concern* (1987), p. 34.
14. UNEP, *In Defence of the Earth: The basic texts on environment: Founex, Stockholm, Cocoyoc* (1981), pp. 116–17.
15. Dinesh D'Souza, *Ronald Reagan: How an Ordinary Man Became an Extraordinary Leader* (1997), p. 230.
16. Independent Commission on International Development, *North-South: A Programme for Survival* (1980), p. 33.
17. ibid., pp. 19–20.
18. ibid., pp. 46–7.
19. ibid., p. 33.
20. ibid., p. 255.
21. Text of the Declaration of the Venice Economic Summit Meeting, *New York Times*, 24th June 1980.
22. Edgar J. Dosman (ed.), *Raúl Prebisch: Power, Principle, and the Ethics of Development* (2006), p. 57.
23. Margaret Thatcher, *The Downing Street Years* (1993), pp. 168–9.
24. Julian L. Simon & Herman Kahn (ed.), *The Resourceful Earth: A Response to Global 2000* (1984), p. 1.

25. David Henderson, 'Survival, Development and the Report of the Brandt Commission' in *The World Economy*, Vol. 3 No. 1 (June 1980), pp. 87–117.

26. ibid.

27. UN Resolution 38/161 (December 1983), para 8 (a).

28. World Commission on Environment and Development, *Our Common Future* (1990), p. 362.

29. Department of Public Information United Nations, *Year Book of the United Nations* 1983 Vol. 37, p. 771.

30. World Commission on Environment and Development, *Our Common Future* (1990), p. 4.

31. Gro Harlem Brundtland, Speech to UNEP, Nairobi, 8th June 1987 http://www.regjeringen.no/upload/SMK/Vedlegg/Taler%20og%20artikler%20av%20tidligere%20statsministre/Gro%20Harlem%20Brundtland/1987/Presentation_of_Our_Common_Future_to_UNEP.pdf

32. ibid.

33. World Commission on Environment and Development, *Our Common Future* (1990), p. 43.

34. Henderson, 'Survival, Development and the Report of the Brandt Commission' in *The World Economy*, Vol. 3 No. 1 (June 1980), pp. 87–117.

35. World Commission on Environment and Development, *Our Common Future* (1990), p. 44.

36. ibid.

37. ibid., p. 46.

38. ibid., p. 43.

39. ibid., p. 3.

40. Gro Harlem Brundtland, Speech to UNEP, Nairobi, 8th June 1987.

41. World Commission on Environment and Development, *Our Common Future* (1990), p. 76.

42. ibid., p. 44.

43. Brundtland, Speech to UNEP, Nairobi.

44. World Commission on Environment and Development, *Our Common Future* (1990), p. 8, p. 45 & p. 9.

45. Mikhail Gorbachev, *Memoirs* (1996), p. 205.

46. World Commission on Environment and Development, *Our Common Future* (1990), p. 181.

47. Statement by the UNEP/WMO/ICSU International Conference on the Assessment of the Role of Carbon Dioxide and of other Greenhouse Gases in Climate Variations And Associated Impacts Villach, Austria, 9–15th October 1985 http://www.icsu-scope.org/downloadpubs/scope29/statement.html

48. Bert Bolin, *A History of the Science and Politics of Climate Change: The Role of the Intergovernmental Panel on Climate Change* (2007), p. 40.

11
ANNUS MIRABILIS

1. http://www.pbs.org/wgbh/pages/frontline/hotpolitics/interviews/wirth.html
2. Hearing before the Committee on Energy and Natural Resources, United States Senate, 23rd June 1988.
3. http://www.g8.utoronto.ca/summit/1988toronto/communique.html#environment
4. Brian Mulroney, *Memoirs 1939–1993* (2007), p. 589.
5. http://www.g8.utoronto.ca/summit/1988toronto/communique.html#environment
6. Mulroney, *Memoirs 1939–1993* (2007), p. 591.
7. www.cmos.ca/ChangingAtmosphere1988e.pdf
8. http://cdiac.ornl.gov/ftp/trends/temp/jonescru/global.txt
9. Speech to the Royal Society, September 27 1988 http://www.margaretthatcher.org/speeches/displaydocument.asp?docid=107346
10. R.K. Pachauri and A. Reisinger (ed.), *Climate Change 2007: Synthesis Report* (2007), Table 3.1.
11. Bert Bolin, *A History of the Science and Politics of Climate Change: The Role of the Intergovernmental Panel on Climate Change* (2007), pp. 48–9 & p. 57.
12. ibid.
13. ibid., p. 118.
14. ibid.
15. James Hansen, 'Global Warming Twenty Years Later: Tipping Points Near' www.columbia.edu/~jeh1/2008/TwentyYearsLater_20080623.pdf
16. ibid.
17. Hansen, 'Statement of Dr James Hansen, Director, NASA Goddard Institute for Space Studies' in *Hearing before the Committee on Energy and Natural Resources United States Senate, One Hundredth Congress, First Session on the Greenhouse Effect and Global Climate Change* (1988), pp. 39–40.
18. Hansen's 1988 projections have been the subject of controversy in the climate change blogosphere. The data and conclusions here have been drawn from a 13th August 2010 post by John Christy: 'Is Jim Hansen's Global Temperature Skillful?' http://pielkeclimatesci.wordpress.com/2010/08/13/is-jim-hansens-global-temperature-skillful-guest-weblog-by-john-christy/; a 28th July 2008 post by Steve McIntyre on his Climate Audit blog: 'Hansen update' http://climateaudit.org/2008/07/28/hansen-update/; and Lucia Liljegren's 1st January 2008 post on her blackboard blog, 'Temperature Anomaly Compared to Hansen A, B, C: GISS Seems to Overpredict Warming' http://rankexploits.com/musings/2008/temperature-anomaly-compared-to-hansen-a-b-c-giss-seems-to-overpredict-warming/

19. Author interview with Sir Crispin Tickell, 14th January 2010.
20. http://www.g7.utoronto.ca/summit/1984london/communique.html
21. George Guise email to author, 31st March 2010.
22. Author interview with Sir Crispin Tickell, 14th January 2010.
23. ibid.
24. Speech to the Royal Society, 27th September 1988 http://www.margaretthatcher.org/speeches/displaydocument.asp?docid=107346
25. Nigel Lawson email to author, 23rd September 2010.
26. A.N. Whitehead, *Science and the Modern World* (1967), p. 10.
27. Karl Popper, *Conjectures and Refutations* (2002), p. 47.
28. Popper, *Conjectures and Refutations* (2002), p. 48.
29. Karl Popper, 'Science: Problems, Aims, Responsibilities' in *The Myth of the Framework*, ed. M.A. Notturno (2006), p. 94.

12
TWO SCIENTISTS

1. Richard Reeves, *President Kennedy* (1994), p. 555.
2. Karl Popper, *Conjectures and Refutations* (2002), p. 293.
3. P.W. Bridgman, *The Way Things Are* (1959), p. 69.
4. ibid., p. 239.
5. ibid., p. 62.
6. ibid., p. 70.
7. H.H. Lamb, *Climate History and the Modern World* (1982), p. 6.
8. ibid., p. 186.
9. ibid., pp. 188–9.
10. ibid., p. 52.
11. ibid., p. 12.
12. ibid., p. 14.
13. ibid., p. 330.
14. Bridgman, *The Way Things Are* (1959), p. 56.
15. Karl Popper, 'Science: Problems, Aims, Responsibilities' in *The Myth of the Framework* (1997), p. 110.
16. Bridgman, *The Way Things Are* (1959), p. 55.
17. ibid., p. 129.
18. ibid., p. 56.
19. Mike Hulme, *Why We Disagree About Climate Change* (2009), pp. 51–2.
20. ibid., p. 95.
21. 'Move to new planet, says Hawking', BBC News, 30th November 2006 http://news.bbc.co.uk/1/hi/uk/6158855.stm
22. Bridgman, *The Way Things Are* (1959), p. 129.

23. Hulme, *Why We Disagree About Climate Change* (2009), p. 77.

24. Popper, 'Science: Problems, Aims, Responsibilities', in *The Myth of the Framework*, ed. M.A. Notturno (2006), p. 93.

13
GREEN WARRIOR

1. Margaret Thatcher, 'Speech to Conservative Party Conference', 14th October 1988 http://www.margaretthatcher.org/document/107352

2. Laura Raun and Bruce, 'Green Revolution in International Relations: The growing awareness of a threat to the planet' in the *Financial Times*, 13th March 1989.

3. Bert Bolin, *A History of the Science and Politics of Climate Change: The Role of the Intergovernmental Panel on Climate Change* (2007), p. 55.

4. Declaration of The Hague http://www.nls.ac.in/CEERA/ceerafeb04/html/documents/lib_int_c1s2_hag_230300.htm

5. The Queen's Commonwealth Day message, *The Times*, 13th March 1989.

6. Al Gore, *Earth in the Balance* (1993), p. 8.

7. Michael Dukakis, 'A New Era of Greatness for America': Address Accepting the Presidential Nomination at the Democratic National Convention in Atlanta, 21st July 1988 http://www.presidency.ucsb.edu/ws/index.php?pid=25961

8. George H.W. Bush, Address Accepting the Presidential Nomination at the Republican National Convention in New Orleans, 18th August 1988.

9. Larry B. Stammer, 'Forty-Nation Environmental Panel Act Quickly on Global Warming, Baker Asks' in the *Los Angeles Times*, 31st January 1989.

10. Bolin, *A History of the Science and Politics of Climate Change: The Role of the Intergovernmental Panel on Climate Change* (2007), p. 54.

11. Philip Shabecoff, 'Joint Effort Urged to Guard Climate' in the *New York Times*, 31st January 1989.

12. Press Conference of François Mitterrand, President of the French Republic, On the Conclusion of the Fifteenth Summit of Industrialised Countries, 16th July 1989 http://www.g7.utoronto.ca/summit/1989paris/press_english.html

13. G7 Summit, Paris, 1989, para 40, http://www.g8.utoronto.ca/summit/1989paris/communique/environment.html

14. G7 Summit, Paris, 1989, para 1.

15. Gore, *Earth in the Balance* (1993), p. 172.

16. Judy Leep email to author on behalf of George Shultz, 26th October 2010.

17. Scott Barrett, *Environment and Statecraft: The Strategy of Environmental Treaty-Making* (2003), p. 230.

18. ibid., p. 239.

19. George Guise email to author, 23rd September 2010.

20. UN General Assembly, 'Protection of global climate for present and future generations of mankind' A/RES/43/53, 6th December 1988.
21. Data supplied to the UNFCCC shows EU-15 CO_2 emissions fell by 3,508Gg 1990-2000, with German emissions falling by 149,816 Gg and UK emissions by 38,095Gg over the period. Without this, EU-15 emissions would have risen 5.5 per cent over the decade. Figures extracted from Time series – Annex I, Total CO_2 Emissions without Land Use, Land-Use Change and Forestry http://unfccc.int/ghg_data/ghg_data_unfccc/time_series_annex_i/items/3814.php
22. Crispin Tickell email to author, 30th November 2010.
23. House of Commons debates, 23rd February 1989, *Hansard*, Col. 1143.
24. Raun and Bruce, 'Green Revolution in International Relations: The growing awareness of a threat to the planet' in the *Financial Times*, 13th March 1989.
25. UNFCCC, The Noordwijk Ministerial Declaration on Climate Change, November 1989 http://unfccc.int/resource/ccsites/senegal/fact/fs218.htm
26. UNFCCC figures extracted from Time series – Annex I, Total CO_2 Emissions without Land Use, Land-Use Change and Forestry http://unfccc.int/ghg_data/ghg_data_unfccc/time_series_annex_i/items/3814.php
27. Paul Montgomery, 'US and Japan refuse curbs on carbon dioxide' in the *New York Times*, 7th November 1989; UNFCCC figures extracted from Time series – Annex I, Total CO_2 Emissions without Land Use, Land-Use Change and Forestry http://unfccc.int/ghg_data/ghg_data_unfccc/time_series_annex_i/items/3814.php
28. Daniel Bodansky, 'Prologue to the Climate Change Convention' in Irving M. Mintzer & J. Amber Leonard (ed.), *Negotiating Climate Change: The Inside Story of the Rio Convention* (1994), p. 72.
29. Margaret Thatcher, Speech to United Nations General Assembly (Global Environment), 8th November 1989 http://www.margaretthatcher.org/document/107817
30. Speech to United Nations General Assembly (Global Environment), 8th November 1989 http://www.margaretthatcher.org/document/107817
31. Paul Lewis, 'Thatcher urges pact on climate' in the *New York Times*, 9th November 1989.
32. Note by Robert E. Grady, 11th November 1989, 'White House comment on Thatcher's UN speech (Bush "could easily have given it")', accessed via Thatcher Foundation http://www.margaretthatcher.org/document/110772
33. John Hunt, 'Market way sought to a greener world' in the *Financial Times*, 2nd May 1990.
34. Michael McCarthy, 'Whaling batters Norway's image' in *The Times*, 14th May 1990.
35. William Claiborne, 'Memo shows Canada supports US resistance to tighter pollution controls' in the *Washington Post*, 11th May 1990.

36. 'Pollution crackdown pledged Bouchard makes abrupt turnaround on global warming' in the *Toronto Star*, 17ᵗʰ May 1990.

37. UNFCCC figures extracted from Time series http://unfccc.int/ghg_data/ ghg_data_unfccc/time_series_annex_i/items/3814.php

38. Lead article, *Financial Times*, 18ᵗʰ May 1990.

39. Michael McCarthy, 'US fears over cost of global warming' in *The Times*, 16ᵗʰ May 1990.

40. The Bergen Conference and its proposals for addressing climate change, May 1990 http://unfccc.int/resource/ccsites/senegal/fact/fs220.htm

14
RUSH TO JUDGEMENT

1. Bert Bolin, *A History of the Science and Politics of Climate Change: The Role of the Intergovernmental Panel on Climate Change* (2007), p. 64.

2. ibid., p. 61.

3. ibid., pp. 61–2.

4. J.T. Houghton, G.J. Jenkins, J.J. Ephraums, *Climate Change: The IPCC Scientific Assessment* (1990), p. xii.

5. ibid., p. 199.

6. ibid., p. 233.

7. ibid., p. 243.

8. ibid.

9. ibid., p. 254.

10. ibid., p. xxiii.

11. ibid., p. xxv.

12. ibid., p. xi.

13. ibid., p. xxxix.

14. John Houghton, 'World climate needs concerted action' in the *Financial Times*, 10ᵗʰ November 2010.

15. Houghton, Jenkins, Ephraums, *Climate Change: The IPCC Scientific Assessment* (1990), p. xvii.

16. ibid., p. 202.

17. ibid., p. 48.

18. ibid., p. 78.

19. ibid., p. 79.

20. ibid., p. xxv.

21. ibid., p. 80.

22. ibid.

23. ibid., p. 80.

24. ibid., p. 73.

25. J.T. Houghton, *Global Warming: The Complete Briefing* (1994), p. 68.
26. ibid., p. 69.
27. Houghton, Jenkins, Ephraums, *Climate Change: The IPCC Scientific Assessment* (1990), p. 73.
28. ibid., p. 17.
29. ibid., p. xi.
30. P.D. Jones, D.E. Parker, T.J. Osborn, and K.R. Briffa (2010), 'Global and hemispheric temperature anomalies – land and marine instrumental records' in *Trends: A Compendium of Data on Global Change*, Carbon Dioxide Information Analysis Center, Oak Ridge National Laboratory, U.S. Department of Energy, Oak Ridge, Tenn., U.S.A. doi: 10.3334/CDIAC/cli.002 http://cdiac.ornl.gov/ftp/trends/temp/jonescru/global.txt
31. Sir John Houghton, interview with author, 10th May 2010.
32. Margaret Thatcher, Speech opening Hadley Centre for Climate Prediction and Research, 25th May 1990 http://www.margaretthatcher.org/document/108102
33. Marlise Simons, 'Scientists urging gas emissions cuts' in the *New York Times*, 5th November 1990.
34. Reuters News Service, 'Expert says warming could spur starvation' 25th October 1990.
35. Margaret Thatcher, Speech at Second World Climate Conference, 6th November 1990 http://www.margaretthatcher.org/document/108237
36. John Hunt, 'World climate conference: Thatcher urges swift action on global warming' in the *Financial Times*, 7th November 1990.
37. Marlise Simons, 'US view prevails at climate parley' in the *New York Times*, 8th November 1990.
38. Maurice Strong address to the Second World Climate Conference, November 1990, in J. Jäger and H.L. Ferguson (ed.), *Climate Change: Science, Impacts and Policy: Proceedings of the Second World Climate Conference* (1991), p. 434.
39. ibid., p. 519.
40. ibid., p. 522.
41. Thatcher's speech at Second World Climate Conference, 6th November 1990 http://www.margaretthatcher.org/document/108237
42. Nigel Hawkes, 'Is this really a scientist speaking?' in *The Times*, 8th November 1990.
43. Margaret Thatcher, *Statecraft*, London (2002), pp. 451–2.
44. Thatcher's speech at Second World Climate Conference, 6th November 1990 http://www.margaretthatcher.org/document/108237
45. ibid.
46. Bolin, *A History of the Science and Politics of Climate Change: The Role of the Intergovernmental Panel on Climate Change* (2007), p. 68.
47. Daniel Bodansky, 'Prologue to the Climate Change Convention' in Irving M. Mintzer & J. Amber Leonard (ed.), *Negotiating Climate Change: The Inside Story of the Rio Convention* (1994), p. 67.

15
A HOUSE DIVIDED

1. President George H.W. Bush, 'The President's News Conference With Prime Minister John Major of the United Kingdom at Camp David', 7ᵗʰ June 1992, *Administration of George Bush 1992*, p. 906.
2. Chandrashekhar Dasgupta, 'The Climate Change Negotiations' in Irving M. Mintzer & J. Amber Leonard (ed.), *Negotiating Climate Change: The Inside Story of the Rio Convention*, Cambridge (1994), p. 141.
3. Bob Grady interview with author, 15ᵗʰ March 2011.
4. William Reilly interview with author, 21ˢᵗ December 2010.
5. Reilly interview with author.
6. Michael Boskin interview with author, 20ᵗʰ December 2010.
7. Reilly interview with author.
8. President George H.W. Bush, Remarks on departure for the United Nations Conference on Environment and Development, 11ᵗʰ June 1992 http://bushlibrary.tamu.edu/research/public_papers.php?id=4412 &year=1992&month=6
9. Robert Watson interview with author, 6ᵗʰ December 2010.
10. D. Allan Bromley, *The President's Scientists: Reminiscences of a White House Science Adviser* (1994), p. 34 and p. 21.
11. ibid., p. 148.
12. John Sununu, interview with author, 12ᵗʰ November 2010.
13. Boskin interview with author, 20ᵗʰ December 2010.
14. John H. Sununu, interview with author, 11ᵗʰ November 2010.
15. Michael Boskin, Richard Schmalensee & John B. Taylor, *The Annual Report of the Council of Economic Advisers* (1990), p. 211.
16. Reilly interview with author.
17. Bromley, *The President's Scientists: Reminiscences of a White House Science Adviser* (1994), pp. 144–5.
18. Boskin interview with author.
19. Boskin, Schmalensee & Taylor, *The Annual Report of the Council of Economic Advisers* (1990), p. 212.
20. ibid., pp. 214–15.
21. ibid.
22. ibid., Table 6.2.
23. ibid., p. 222.
24. ibid., p. 223.
25. President George H.W. Bush, Remarks at the Opening Session of the White House Conference on Science and Economics Research Related to Global Change, 17ᵗʰ April 1990. http://www.presidency.ucsb.edu/ws/index.php?pid=18366&st=&st1

26. Michael Weisskopf, 'Bush says More Data on Warming Needed' in the *Washington Post*, 18th April 1990.

27. Bob Hepburn, 'Bouchard rebukes Bush for stalled pollution fight' in the *Toronto Star*, 18th April 1990.

28. Bert Bolin, *A History of the Science and Politics of Climate Change: The Role of the Intergovernmental Panel on Climate Change* (2007), p. 60.

29. Jerome Idaszak, 'Bush, critics clash on steps to combat climate change' in the *Chicago Sun-Times*, 18th April 1990.

30. Richard Benedetto, 'Europeans press US to act to prevent global warming' in *USA Today*, 18th April 1990.

31. Reilly interview with author.

32. Bush, Remarks at the Closing Session of the White House Conference on Science and Economics Research Related to Global Change, 18th April 1990.

33. Reilly interview with author.

34. Richard Benedetto, 'Bush does about-face at warming conference' in *USA Today*, 18th April 1990.

35. Philip Shabecoff, 'Bush Denies Putting off Action on Averting Global Climate Shift' in the *New York Times*, 19th April 1990.

36. Maurice Strong, *Where on Earth are We Going?* (2001), p. 190.

37. Bob Grady interview with author, 15th March 2011.

38. J. Jäger and H.L. Ferguson (ed.), *Climate Change: Science, Impacts and Policy: Proceedings of the Second World Climate Conference* (1991), p. 431.

39. 'North and South Hold Environment Hostage' in the *Seattle Times*, 3rd June 1992.

40. Strong, *Where on Earth are We Going?* (2001), p. 125 & David Lascelles and Christina Lamb, 'The Earth Summit: Compromise on aid cash eludes officials at Rio' in the *Financial Times*, 10th June 1992.

41. Dasgupta, 'The Climate Change Negotiations' in Irving M. Mintzer & J. Amber Leonard (ed.), *Negotiating Climate Change: The Inside Story of the Rio Convention* (1994), p. 141.

42. Jose Goldemberg, 'The Road to Rio' in Mintzer & Leonard (ed.), *Negotiating Climate Change: The Inside Story of the Rio Convention* (1994), p. 181.

43. José Goldemberg interview with author, 31st January 2010.

44. Goldemberg, 'The Road to Rio' in Mintzer & Leonard (ed.), *Negotiating Climate Change: The Inside Story of the Rio Convention* (1994), p. 176.

45. Goldemberg interview with author.

46. Jonathan Dimbleby, *The Prince of Wales: A Biography* (1994), p. 605.

47. Reilly interview with author.

48. Clayton Yeutter memorandum to author, 31st December 2010.

49. Yeutter memorandum to author.

50. Reilly interview with author.

51. Goldemberg, 'The Road to Rio' in Mintzer & Leonard (ed.), *Negotiating Climate Change: The Inside Story of the Rio Convention* (1994), p. 181.

52. Robert Reinstein email to author, 29th April 2011.

53. Michael Howard email to author, 26th April 2011.

54. Howard interview with author, 12th April 2010.

55. Reilly interview with author.

56. Christopher Marquis and Sam Dillon, 'Bush's US Seen as Environmental Outlaw' in *Miami Herald*, 3rd June 1992.

16
PRESIDENT BUSH GOES TO RIO

1. Clayton Yeutter memorandum to author, 31st December 2010.

2. Steve Fainaru, 'Rio becomes a City under siege as leaders meet at Summit' in the *Boston Globe*, 11th June 1992.

3. Clayton Yeutter memorandum to author.

4. William Reilly interview with author, 21st December 2010, and William Reilly email to author, 23rd December 2010.

5. Dianne Dumanowski and John Mashek, 'US is Isolated in Opposing Biodiversity Treaty' in the *Boston Globe*, 9th June 1992.

6. David Lascelles, 'Survey of the Earth Summit (10)' in the *Financial Times*, 2nd June 1992.

7. Dianne Dumanoski, 'US, in shift, Backs 2 keys points at Rio' in the *Boston Globe*, 11th June 1992.

8. Michael Weisskopf, '"Outsider" EPS Chief being Tested' in the *Washington Post*, 8th June 1992.

9. President George H.W. Bush, The President's News Conference with Prime Minister John Major at Camp David, 7th June 1992, *1992 Public Papers of the Presidents of the United States*, Books I and II, p. 908.

10. Paul Hoversten, 'Treaty for Rio eludes EPA chief' in *USA Today*, 8th June 1992.

11. Dianne Dumanowski and John Mashek, 'US is Isolated in Opposing Biodiversity Treaty' in the *Boston Globe*, 9th June 1992.

12. William Long, 'Brown finds Perfect Forum in Rio' in the *Los Angeles Times*, 7th June 1992.

13. Susan Benesch, 'Senators: Anti-US sentiment strong in Rio' in the *St Petersburg Times*, 7th June 1992.

14. 'Wirth: Bad PR taints US image' in the *Denver Post*, 10th June 1992.

15. Ann Devroy, 'White House scorns summit critics' in the *Washington Post*, 10th June 1992.

16. Associated Press, 'President tells Earth Summit: "I didn't come here to apologise"', 12th June 1992.

17. Eugene Robinson and Michael Weisskopf, 'Bonn Pushes Tough Stand on Warming' in the *Washington Post*, 9th June 1992.

18. Devroy, 'White House scorns summit critics' in the *Washington Post*, 10th June 1992.

19. Associated Press, 'President tells Earth Summit: "I didn't come here to apologise"', 12th June 1992.

20. UNFCCC figures extracted from Time series – Annex I, Total CO_2 Emissions without Land Use, Land-Use Change and Forestry http://unfccc.int/ghg_data/ghg_data_unfccc/time_series_annex_i/items/3814.php

21. 'As Population Grows, People will live "Like Rats", Cousteau says' in the *Los Angeles Times*, 6th June 1992.

22. Joel Achenbach, 'On the Fringe of Rio – Vikings, Vegetarians and Taoists at the Alternative Summit' in the *Washington Post*, 4th June 1992.

23. Maurice Strong, *Where on Earth are We Going?* (2001), p. 231.

24. Achenbach, 'On the Fringe of Rio – Vikings, Vegetarians and Taoists at the Alternative Summit' in the *Washington Post*, 4th June 1992, and 'Whalers backed' in *The Times*, 4th June 1992.

25. Fiona Godlee, 'Rio Diary: a fortnight at the earth summit' in *British Medical Journal* Vol. 305 (11th July 1992), p. 103.

26. *Financial Times*, 6th June 1992.

27. Vaclav Havel, 'Rio and the New Millennium' in the *New York Times*, 3rd June 1992.

28. Godlee, 'Rio Diary: a fortnight at the earth summit' in *British Medical Journal* Vol. 305 (11th July 1992), p. 103.

29. 'North and South Hold Environment Hostage' in the *Seattle Times*, 3rd June 1992.

30. José Goldemberg interview with author, 31st January 2010.

31. United Nations, *Agenda 21: Earth Summit – The United Nations Programme of Action from Rio* (1993), para 1.1.

32. Strong, *Where on Earth are We Going?* (2001), p. 210.

33. Clayton Yeutter memorandum to author.

34. John H. Sununu, interview with author, 11th November 2010.

35. Ed Meese interview with author, 11th March 2010.

36. Associated Press, 'US to Spend Extra to Save Forests', 1st June 1992.

37. William Reilly interview with author.

38. John Holusha, 'The Earth Summit Poll finds Scepticism in US about Earth Summit' in the *New York Times*, 11th June 1992.

39. Gwen Ifill, 'The Earth Summit: President, in Rio, defends his stand' in the *New York Times*, 13th June 1992.

40. Mitchell Locin, 'Clinton Downplays "Foreign Policy Vote" as a Factor' in the *Chicago Tribune*, 19th June 1992.

17
TWO PROTOCOLS

1. Maggie Farley, 'Gore vows flexibility in climate talks' in the *Los Angeles Times*, 8th December 1997.
2. Richard Benedick, *Morals and Myths: A Commentary on Global Climate Policy*, 109 WZB-Mitteilungen (2005).
3. Scott Barrett, *Environment and Statecraft: The Strategy of Environmental Treaty-Making* (2003), p. 360.
4. Al Gore, *Earth in the Balance* (1993), pp. 177–8.
5. Robert Reinstein, 'Ozone Protection and Global Climate Change: Is the Montreal Protocol a Good Model for Responding to Climate Change?' (Unpublished, 1996).
6. J.T. Houghton, L.G. Meira Filho, B.A. Callander, N. Harris, A. Kattenberg & K. Maskell (ed.), *Climate Change 1995: The Science of Climate Change: Contribution of WG1 to the Second Assessment Report of the Intergovernmental Panel on Climate Change* (1996), p. 5.
7. Cass R. Sunstein, 'Of Montreal and Kyoto: A Tale of Two Protocols' in *Harvard Environmental Law Review*, Vol. 31 (2007), p. 24.
8. ibid., p. 35.
9. ibid., fig. 3.
10. ibid., fig. 1.
11. ibid., fig. 2.
12. ibid., fig. 4.
13. ibid., p. 45.
14. ibid., pp. 45–6.
15. ibid., pp. 22–3.
16. UNFCCC figures extracted from Time series – Annex I, Total CO_2 Emissions without Land Use, Land-Use Change and Forestry http://unfccc.int/ghg_data/ghg_data_unfccc/time_series_annex_i/items/3814.php
17. Tim O'Riordan & Jill Jäger (ed.), *Politics of Climate Change: A European Perspective* (1996), p. 18.
18. Christiane Beuermann & Jill Jäger, 'Climate Change Politics in Germany: How long will any double dividend last?' in Tim O'Riordan & Jill Jäger (ed.), *Politics of Climate Change: A European Perspective* (1996), pp. 194–5.
19. UNFCCC figures extracted from Time series http://unfccc.int/ghg_data/ghg_data_unfccc/time_series_annex_i/items/3814.php
20. Dieter Helm, *Energy, the State, and the Market: British Energy Policy since 1979* (2003), p. 169.
21. UNFCCC figures extracted from Time series http://unfccc.int/ghg_data/ghg_data_unfccc/time_series_annex_i/items/3814.php

22. John H. Cushman, 'In Shift, US Will Seek Binding World Pact to Combat Global Warming' in the *New York Times*, 17ᵗʰ July 1997.

23. UN, *United Nations Framework Convention on Climate Change* (1992), Article 4 2 (f).

24. UNEP, *The Montreal Protocol on Substances that Deplete the Ozone Layer* (2000), Article 5.

25. Kevin A. Baumert, Timothy Herzog & Jonathan Pershing, *Navigating the Numbers Greenhouse Gas Data and International Climate Policy* (2005), Fig. 4.1.

26. GDP per head, US $, constant prices, constant PPPs, reference year 2000, extracted from OECD Statistics, http://stats.oecd.org/index.aspx?queryid=559

27. Joanna Depledge, *The Organisation of Global Negotiations: Constructing the Climate Change Regime* (2005), p. 28.

28. ibid., p. 92.

29. Farley, 'Gore vows flexibility in climate talks' in the *Los Angeles Times*, 8ᵗʰ December 1997.

30. Michael Grubb with Christiaan Vrolijk & Duncan Brack, *The Kyoto Protocol: A Guide and Assessment* (1999), p. xiii.

31. Timothy E. Wirth email to author, 25ᵗʰ March 2011.

32. Gore, *Earth in the Balance* (1993), p. 238.

18
CHINA SYNDROME

1. Leyla Boulton, 'China attacks proposed gas curbs' in the *Financial Times*, 6ᵗʰ December 1997.

2. Al Gore, 'Rachel Carson and Silent Spring' in Peter Matthiessen (ed.), *Courage for the Earth* (2007), p. 67.

3. Al Gore, *Earth in the Balance* (1993), p. 367.

4. ibid., p. xii & p. 39.

5. ibid., p. 328.

6. ibid., p. 79.

7. ibid., p. 127.

8. ibid., p. 213.

9. ibid., p. 232 & p. 228.

10. ibid., p. 230.

11. ibid., p. 253.

12. ibid., p. 257.

13. ibid., pp. 256–7.

14. Bill Clinton, *My Life* (2004), p. 414.

15. Robert Watson interview with author, 12ᵗʰ December 2010.

16. Gore, *Earth in the Balance* (1993), p. xiv.
17. John Cushman & David Sanger, 'Global Warming No Simple Fight' in the *New York Times*, 1ˢᵗ December 1997.
18. ibid.
19. Clinton, *My Life* (2004), pp. 493–4.
20. Dawn Erlandson, 'The Btu Tax Experience: What Happened and Why It Happened' in *Pace Environmental Law Review*, Vol. 12 (1994) pp. 175–6.
21. Clinton, *My Life* (2004), p. 522.
22. Bob Grady interview with author, 15ᵗʰ March 2011.
23. UNFCCC figures extracted from Time series http://unfccc.int/ghg_data/ghg_data_unfccc/time_series_annex_i/items/3814.php
24. S. Fred Singer, 'Clinton's Global Warming Action Plan: Just a Lot of Hot Air?' in the *Washington Times*, 23ʳᵈ March 1994.
25. IISD, *Earth Negotiations Bulletin*, 6ᵗʰ April 1995.
26. Raúl Estrada-Oyuela interview with author, 14ᵗʰ March 2011.
27. John Gummer interview with author, 8ᵗʰ April 2011.
28. Gummer interview with author.
29. Raúl Estrada-Oyuela, 'Copenhagen needs a lead negotiator' in *Nature*, Vol. 461, 22ⁿᵈ October 2009.
30. Joanna Depledge, *The Organisation of Global Negotiations: Constructing the Climate Change Regime* (2005), p. 94.
31. UN, 'The Berlin Mandate' in FCCC/CP/1995/7/Add.1, *Report of the Conference of the Parties in its First Session* (6ᵗʰ June 1995), Article II, 2 (b).
32. Amy Royden, *US Climate Change Policy Under President Clinton: A Look Back* (2002), http://digitalcommons.law.ggu.edu/ggulrev/vol32/iss4/3 pp. 425–6.
33. Raúl Estrada-Oyuela interview with author, 14ᵗʰ March 2011.
34. Raúl Estrada-Oyuela email to author, 22ⁿᵈ March 2011.
35. Raúl Estrada-Oyuela, 'Copenhagen needs a lead negotiator' in *Nature*, Vol. 461, 22ⁿᵈ October 2009.
36. Raúl Estrada-Oyuela interview with author.
37. Depledge, *The Organisation of Global Negotiations: Constructing the Climate Change Regime* (2005), p. 47.
38. ibid., p. 65.
39. ibid., p. 50.
40. ibid., Box 8.1.
41. UN, FCCC/CP/1996/15/Add.1, *Report of the Conference of the Parties on its Second Session* (29ᵗʰ October 1996), p. 72.
42. Raúl Estrada-Oyuela communication with author, 10ᵗʰ April 2011.
43. Taylor Branch, *The Clinton Tapes: Wrestling History with the President* (2009), p. 456.
44. Labour Party, *New Labour because Britain deserves better* (1997) http://www.labour-party.org.uk/manifestos/1997/1997-labour-manifesto.shtml

45. Chuck Hagel interview with author, 25th February 2011.

46. President William J. Clinton, 'Remarks at the National Geographic' 22nd October 1997, *1997 Public Papers of the Presidents of the United States*, Vol. II, pp. 1409–10.

47. Associated Press, 'Conference fiddles while the earth ends hottest year' 5th December 1997.

48. Charles Krauthammer, 'Global Warming Fundamentalists' in the *Washington Post*, 5th December 1997.

49. Fred Knapp, 'Hagel chides Gore's push for flexibility' in the *Lincoln Journal Star*, 9th December 1997.

50. Willis Witter, 'China rejects plea to reduce gases' in the *Washington Times*, 3rd December 1997.

51. Indira Lakshmanan, 'Kerry says cuts would benefit Mass' in the *Boston Globe*, 8th December 1997.

52. Gummer interview with author.

53. Heike Schröder, *Negotiating the Kyoto Protocol* (2001), pp. 77–9.

54. Bennett Roth, 'Political heat awaits Gore from all sides' in the *Houston Chronicle*, 2nd December 1997.

55. Willis Witter, 'Gore dares Congress to resist pact' in the *Washington Times*, 9th December 1997.

56. Richard Berke, 'Gore walks a political tightrope' in the *New York Times*, 9th December 1997.

57. Harlan L. Watson interview with author, 7th March 2011.

58. William Stevens, 'Gore, in Japan, signals that US may make some compromises' in the *New York Times*, 8th December 1997.

59. Watson interview with author.

60. Chuck Hagel interview with author, 25th February 2011.

61. Watson interview with author.

62. IISD, *Earth Negotiations Bulletin*, Vol. 12 No. 75, 10th December 1997.

63. Comments by Gene Sperling in 'Press Briefing by Gene Sperling, Assistant to the President for Economic Policy, Jim Steinberg, Deputy Assistant to the President for National Security Affairs, and Leon Fuerth, National Security Advisor for the Vice President' 11th December 1997 http://www.presidency.ucsb.edu/ws/?pid=48621

64. Joby Warrick, 'Climate Pact rescued in final hours' in the *Washington Post*, 13th December 1997.

65. Department of State, 'The Kyoto Protocol on Climate Change: A Fact Sheet released by the US Department of State' 15th January 1998 http://www.ait.org.tw/infousa/enus/government/forpolicy/kyoto.html

66. Raúl Estrada-Oyuela, 'First Approaches and Unanswered Questions' in José Goldemberg (ed.), *Issues & Options: The Clean Development Mechanism* (1998), p. 25.

67. ibid.
68. Alex Barnum, 'US works to bridge gap with Third World' in the *San Francisco Chronicle*, 3rd December 1997.
69. IISD, *Earth Negotiations Bulletin*, Vol. 12 No. 76, 10th December 1997, p. 13.
70. Watson interview with author.

19
THE MORNING AFTER

1. Bill Clinton, 'Address Before a Joint Session of the Congress on the State of the Union' 19th January 1999 http://www.presidency.ucsb.edu/ws/?pid=57577
2. Willis Witter, 'Gore dares Congress to resist pact' in the *Washington Times*, 9th December 1997.
3. Associated Press, 'Lott: Treaty faces "bleak prospects" in Senate' 10th December 1997.
4. John Godfrey, 'White House to hold off sending climate pact to Hill' in the *Washington Times*, 12th December 1997.
5. Frank Loy interview with author, 21st February 2011.
6. Loy interview with author.
7. President William J. Clinton, 'Remarks at the National Geographic' 22nd October 1997, *1997 Public Papers of the Presidents of the United States* Vol. II, Washington DC, p. 1400.
8. Council of Economic Advisers, *The Kyoto Protocol and the President's Policies to Address Climate Change: Administration Economic Analysis* (1998), p. 51.
9. ibid., p. 52.
10. ibid., Table 5.
11. Energy Information Administration, *What Does the Kyoto Protocol Mean to US Energy Markets and the US Economy? – A Briefing Paper on the Energy Information Administration's Analysis and Report* (1998) p.17. Estimated 2010 GDP of $9,425 billion is extracted from Energy Information Administration, *Impacts of the Kyoto Protocol on US Energy Markets and Economic Activity* (1998), p.xvii.
12. Andrew Turnbull interview with author, 7th April 2001.
13. IISD, *Earth Negotiations Bulletin*, Vol. 12 No. 97 (16th November 1998), p. 2.
14. ibid., p. 10.
15. William K. Stevens, 'Argentina Takes a Lead in Setting Goals on Greenhouse Gases' in the *New York Times*, 12th November 1998.
16. ibid.
17. John H. Cushman, 'Washington Skirmishes over Treaty on Warming' in the *New York Times*, 11th November 1998.
18. ibid.

19. Al Gore, 'Statement By Vice President Gore on the United States' Signing of the Kyoto Protocol' 12th November 1998 http://clinton4.nara.gov/CEQ/19981112-7936.html

20. John H. Cushman, 'US signs a Pact to Reduce Gases Tied to Warming' in the *New York Times*, 13th November 1998.

21. ibid.

22. ibid.

23. IISD, *Earth Negotiations Bulletin*, Vol. 12 No. 97 (16th November 1998), p. 3.

24. Robert Reinstein email to author, 3rd April 2011.

25. *Earth Negotiations Bulletin* (16th November 1998), pp. 7–8.

26. ibid., pp. 2–3.

27. ibid., p. 13.

28. ibid.

29. IEA, *CO2 Emissions From Fuel Combustion Highlights* (2010), Fig. 10.

30. Robert Reinstein email to author, 3rd April 2011.

31. *Earth Negotiations Bulletin* (27th November 2000), p. 3.

32. Amy Royden, *US Climate Change Policy Under President Clinton: A Look Back* (2002), p. 60.

33. *Earth Negotiations Bulletin* (27th November 2000), p. 19.

34. Jan Pronk, 'The Last Straw' The Hague, 13th February 2007 http://www.janpronk.nl/speeches/english/the-last-straw.html

35. Jacques Chirac, 'Speech By Mr. Jacques Chirac French President To The VIth Conference of the Parties to the United Nations Framework Convention on Climate Change The Hague' 20th November 2000 http://sovereignty.net/center/chirac.html

36. Mary H. Cooper, 'Global Warming Treaty' in *CQ Researcher*, Vol. 11, No. 3 (26th January 2001), p. 55.

37. Cooper, 'Global Warming Treaty' in *CQ Researcher*, Vol. 11, No. 3 (26th January 2001), p. 49.

38. Loy interview with author.

39. Andy McSmith, 'French anger at "macho" Prescott' in the *Daily Telegraph*, 28th November 2000.

40. Bill Clinton, 'Address Before Joint Session of the Congress on the State of the Union' in *Administration of William J. Clinton, 2000 Public Papers of the Presidents of the United States* (27th January 2000), p. 138.

41. Bill Clinton, 'Remarks During the White House Conference on Climate Change' 6th October 1997 http://www.presidency.ucsb.edu/ws/?pid=53351#axzz1Jc1NudR1

42. Clinton, 'Remarks During the White House Conference on Climate Change' 6th October 1997 http://www.presidency.ucsb.edu/ws/?pid=53351#axzz1Jc1NudR1

43. Stuart Eizenstat, Prepared Testimony On Kyoto Protocol (Delivered before Senate Foreign Relations Committee, 11th February 1998) http://www.iitap.iastate.edu/gcp/kyoto/protocol.html

44. IEA, *CO2 Emissions From Fuel Combustion Highlights* (2010), p. 7.
45. Frank Loy interview with author.
46. *New York Times*, 'Poll: Early action favoured' 1st December 1997.
47. Clayton Yeutter email to author, 28th March 2011.
48. Erskine Bowles email to author, 22nd March 2011.
49. George W. Bush, Text of a Letter from the President to Senators Hagel, Helms, Craig, and Roberts, 13th March 2001 http://www.whitehouse.gov/news/releases/2001/03/20010314.html
50. Douglas Jehl, 'US Going Empty-Handed to Meeting on Global Warming' in the *New York Times*, 29th March 2001.
51. Friends of the Earth, 'World Faces Climate Disaster As Bush Rats On Kyoto Treaty' 28th March 2001 http://www.foeeurope.org/press/28.03.01.htm
52. Andrew C. Revkin, 'Bush's Shift Could Doom Air Pact, Some Say' in the *New York Times*, 17th March 2001.
53. David E. Sanger, 'Bush Will Continue to Oppose Kyoto Pact on Global Warming' in the *New York Times*, 12th June 2001.
54. Scott Barrett, *Environment and Statecraft: The Strategy of Environmental Treaty-Making* (2003), p. 371.
55. *Earth Negotiations Bulletin* (30th July 2001), p. 14.
56. *Earth Negotiations Bulletin* (12th November 2001), p. 15.
57. Barrett, *Environment and Statecraft: The Strategy of Environmental Treaty-Making* (2003), p. 374.
58. T.M.L. Wigley, 'The Kyoto Protocol: CO_2, CH4 and climate implications' in *Geophysical Research Letters*, Vol. 25 (1998), p. 2287.
59. Wigley, 'The Kyoto Protocol: CO_2, CH4 and climate implications' in *Geophysical Research Letters*, Vol. 25 (1998), p. 2288.
60. Numbers derived from World Resources Institute, Climate Analysis Indicators Tool (CAIT UNFCCC) Version 4.0 (2011).
61. Wigley, 'The Kyoto Protocol: CO_2, CH4 and climate implications' in *Geophysical Research Letters*, Vol. 25 (1998), p. 2287.
62. Eizenstat, Prepared Testimony On Kyoto Protocol (Delivered before Senate Foreign Relations Committee, 11th February 1998) http://www.iitap.iastate.edu/gcp/kyoto/protocol.html
63. Elisabeth Rosenthal, 'A carbon-neutral Norway: Fine print in the plan' in the *New York Times*, 20th March 2008.
64. Numbers derived from World Resources Institute, Climate Analysis Indicators Tool (CAIT UNFCCC) Version 4.0 (2011).
65. IEA, *CO2 Emissions From Fuel Combustion Highlights* (2010), p. 8.
66. UNFCCC, 'Countries included in Annex B to the Kyoto Protocol and their emissions targets' http://unfccc.int/kyoto_protocol/items/3145.php

20
TURNING UP THE HEAT

1. P. Brohan, J.J. Kennedy, I. Harris, S.F.B. Tett and P.D. Jones, 2006: Uncertainty estimates in regional and global observed temperature changes: a new dataset from 1850. *J. Geophysical Research* 111, D12106 HadCRUT3 combined land and marine [sea surface temperature (SST) anomalies from HadSST2] http://www.cru.uea.ac.uk/cru/data/temperature/hadcrut3gl.txt

2. J.T. Houghton, L.G. Meira Filho, B.A. Callander, N. Harris, A. Kattenberg & K. Maskell (ed.), Climate Change 1995: The Science of Climate Change: Contribution of WG1 to the Second Assessment Report of the Intergovernmental Panel on Climate Change (1996), Fig. 16.

3. ibid.

4. ibid., p. 103.

5. ibid., p. 104.

6. ibid., p. 35, p. 411, p. 411 & p. 427.

7. ibid., p. 34.

8. Henry D. Jacoby, Ronald G. Prinn & Richard Schmalensee, 'Kyoto's Unfinished Business' in *Foreign Affairs*, July/August 1998 Vol. 77, No. 4, p. 57.

9. Christopher Essex, 'What do climate models tell us about global warming?' in *Pure and Applied Geophysics* Vol. 135, Issue: 1 (1991), pp. 125–6.

10. Houghton, Meira Filho, Callander, Harris, Kattenberg & Maskell (ed.), Climate Change 1995: The Science of Climate Change: Contribution of WG1 to the Second Assessment Report of the Intergovernmental Panel on Climate Change (1996), p. 418.

11. Bert Bolin, *A History of the Science and Politics of Climate Change: The Role of the Intergovernmental Panel on Climate Change* (2007), p. 196.

12. ibid., p. 197.

13. http://climateaudit.org/2010/06/22/kellys-comments/

14. Houghton, Meira Filho, Callander, Harris, Kattenberg & Maskell (ed.), Climate Change 1995: The Science of Climate Change: Contribution of WG1 to the Second Assessment Report of the Intergovernmental Panel on Climate Change (1996), p. 413.

15. ibid.

16. ibid., p. 438.

17. ibid., p. 439.

18. Bolin, *A History of the Science and Politics of Climate Change: The Role of the Intergovernmental Panel on Climate Change* (2007), pp. 112–13.

19. ibid., p. 113.

20. Associated Press, 'Chief scientist responsible for global warming' 1st December 1997.

21. Frederick Seitz, 'A Major Deception on Global Warming' in the *Wall Street*

Journal, 12th June 1996.

22. Benjamin D Santer, 'Letters to the Editor: No Deception in Global Warming Report' in the *Wall Street Journal*, 25th June 1996.

23. S. Fred Singer, Letter to IPCC (Working Group 1) Scientists, undated http://www.his.com/~sepp/Archive/controv/ipcccont/ipccflap.htm

24. IPCC, Report of the Ninth Session of the Intergovernmental Panel on Climate Change, 29–30th June 1993, Appendix G.

25. Paul N. Edwards & Stephen H. Schneider, 'Broad Consensus or "Scientific Cleansing"?' in *Ecofable/Ecoscience* 1:1 (1997), pp. 3–9.

26. ibid.

27. ibid.

28. ibid.

29. 'One observer's report on the NAS panel' 4th March 2006 http://climateaudit.org/2006/03/04/one-observers-report-on-the-nas-panel/

30. H.H. Lamb, *Climate History and the Modern World* (1982), p. 166.

31. ibid., p. 163.

32. ibid., p. 198.

33. Houghton, Meira Filho, Callander, Harris, Kattenberg & Maskell (ed.), Climate Change 1995: The Science of Climate Change: Contribution of WG1 to the Second Assessment Report of the Intergovernmental Panel on Climate Change (1996), p. 28.

34. ibid., p. 62.

35. ibid., p. 61.

36. A.W. Montford, *The Hockey Stick Illusion: Climategate and the Corruption of Science* (2010), p. 27.

37. ibid., p. 28.

38. Fred Pearce, *The Climate Files: The Battle for the Truth about Global Warming* (2010), p. 44.

39. ABC Radio National, 'In conversation' 5th April 2007 http://www.abc.net.au/rn/inconversation/stories/2007/1882479.htm

40. Lamb, *Climate History and the Modern World* (1982), p. 330.

41. Ross McKitrick, 'The Mann et al. Northern Hemisphere "Hockey Stick" Climate Index: A Tale of Due Diligence' in Patrick J. Michaels (ed.), *Shattered Consensus: The True State of Global Warming* (2005), p. 41.

42. ibid., p. 35.

43. ibid., pp. 42–3.

44. Raymond S. Bradley email to Keith Briffa, 19th April 1999.

45. Michael E. Mann email to Keith Briffa, 12th May 1999.

46. Raymond S. Bradley email to Keith Briffa, 14th May 1999.

47. John R. Christy, Testimony to a House Science, Space and Technology Committee, 31st March 2011, p. 5 http://science.house.gov/hearing/full-committee-hearing-climate-change

48. ibid.
49. Stephen McIntyre, 'Climategate: A Battlefield Perspective – Annotated Notes for Presentation to Heartland Conference, Chicago' 16th May 2010, p. 2 www.climateaudit.info/pdf/mcintyre-heartland_2010.pdf
50. Chris Folland email to Michael E. Mann and others, 22nd September 1999.
51. Keith Briffa email to Michael E. Mann and others, 22nd September 1999.
52. Briffa email to Mann and others.
53. Michael E. Mann email to Keith Briffa, 22nd September 1999.
54. Stephen McIntyre, 'IPCC and the "Trick"' 10th December 2009 http://climateaudit.org/2009/12/10/ipcc-and-the-trick/
55. Christy, Testimony to a House Science, Space and Technology Committee, 31st March 2011, p. 6 http://science.house.gov/hearing/full-committee-hearing-climate-change
56. J.T. Houghton, Y. Ding, D.J. Griggs, M. Noguer, P.J. van der Linden, X. Dai, K. Maskell, C.A. Johnson (ed.), *Climate Change 2001: The Scientific Basis* (2001), Fig. 2.21.
57. Robert T. Watson (ed.), *Climate Change 2001: Synthesis Report* (2001), Fig. 2–3, Fig. 5, Fig. 9–1b (appears on p. 34 and p. 140).
58. Houghton, Ding, Griggs, Noguer, van der Linden, Dai, Maskell, Johnson (eds), *Climate Change 2001: The Scientific Basis* (2001), p. 2.
59. ibid., p. 10.
60. Watson (ed.), *Climate Change 2001: Synthesis Report* (2001), p. 4.

21
QUIS CUSTODIET?

1. J.T. Houghton, Y. Ding, D.J. Griggs, M. Noguer, P.J. van der Linden, X. Dai, K. Maskell, C.A. Johnson (ed.), *Climate Change 2001: The Scientific Basis* (2001), p. 2.
2. J.S. Weiner, *The Piltdown Forgery* (2004), p. 186.
3. Thomas S. Kuhn, *The Structure of Scientific Revolutions* (1996), p. 140.
4. ibid., p. 96.
5. ibid., p. 64.
6. ibid., p. 47.
7. ibid., p. 68.
8. ibid., p. 94.
9. Dwight D. Eisenhower, Farewell Address, 17th January 1961 http://www.presidency.ucsb.edu/ws/?pid=12086
10. ibid.
11. *Science Daily*, 'Increased Snow Is Shortening Tree-Growing Season in Subarctic Siberia' 8th July 1999 http://www.sciencedaily.com/releases/1999/07/990707181851.htm

12. Stephen McIntyre, 'Climategate: A Battlefield Perspective – Annotated Notes for Presentation to Heartland Conference, Chicago' 16th May 2010, p. 10 www.climateaudit.info/pdf/mcintyre-heartland_2010.pdf

13. A.W. Montford, *The Hockey Stick Illusion: Climategate and the Corruption of Science* (2010), p. 72.

14. Stephen McIntyre & Ross McKitrick, 'Corrections to the Mann et al. (1998) Proxy Data Base and Northern Hemispheric Average Temperature Series' in *Energy & Environment* Vol. 14. No. 6 (2003), p. 753.

15. ibid., p. 766.

16. Montford, *The Hockey Stick Illusion: Climategate and the Corruption of Science* (2010), p. 106.

17. Ross McKitrick, 'What is the "Hockey Stick" Debate About?', 4th April 2005, p. 10.

18. Montford, *The Hockey Stick Illusion: Climategate and the Corruption of Science* (2010), p. 128.

19. *Nature* mission statement, http://www.nature.com/nature/about/index.html

20. Michael E. Mann, Raymond S. Bradley & Malcolm K. Hughes, 'Corrigendum: Global-scale temperature patterns and climate forcing over the past six centuries' in *Nature* 430, 105, 1st July 2004.

21. Richard A. Muller, 'Global Warming Bombshell' in *Technology Review*, 15th October 2004.

22. Bert Bolin, *A History of the Science and Politics of Climate Change: The Role of the Intergovernmental Panel on Climate Change* (2007) p. 167.

23. Montford, *The Hockey Stick Illusion: Climategate and the Corruption of Science* (2010), p. 434.

24. ibid., p. 435.

25. Stephen H. Schneider email to Ben Santer, 6th January 2009.

26. David Verado email to Stephen McIntyre, 17th December 2003, reproduced in Michael E. Mann letter to Joe Barton, 15th July 2005 www.realclimate.org/Mann_response_to_Barton.pdf

27. Email from Phil Jones, Climatic Research Unit, University of East Anglia to Warwick Hughes, 21st February 2005 http://www.climateaudit.org/correspondence/cru.correspondence.pdf

28. Letter from Phil Woolas MP to Tim Boswell MP, 8th January 2007. Cited in Holland (2008), p. 7.

29. Alan Greenspan, *The Age of Turbulence* (2007), p. 495.

30. P.W. Bridgman, *The Way Things Ares* (1959), p. 56.

31. David Appell, 'Behind the Hockey Stick' in *Scientific American*, March 2005, p. 35.

32. Antonio Regalado, 'In Climate Debate, the "Hockey Stick" Leads to a Face-Off' in the *Wall Street Journal*, 14th February 2005.

33. ibid.

34. ibid.

35. Sherwood Boehlert letter to Joe Barton, 14ᵗʰ July 2005 www.realclimate.org/Boehlert_letter_to_Barton.pdf

36. Henry Waxman letter to Joe Barton, 1ˢᵗ July 2005.

37. www.aaas.org/spp/cstc/docs/05-7-13_climatebarton.pdf

38. Michael Bender and others, letter to Joe Barton & Ed Whitfield, 15ᵗʰ July 2005 http://www.realclimate.org/index.php/archives/2005/07/barton-and-the-hockey-stick/

39. John Orcutt and Walter Lyons letter to Joe Barton, 8ᵗʰ August 2005 http://www.realclimate.org/index.php/archives/2005/07/barton-and-the-hockey-stick/

40. *Nature*, 'Climate of distrust' Vol. 436, No. 7047, 7ᵗʰ July 2005.

41. Mann letter to Joe Barton, 15ᵗʰ July 2005.

42. Alan Leshner letter to Joe Barton, 13ᵗʰ July 13 www.aaas.org/spp/cstc/docs/05-7-13_climatebarton.pdf

43. John Orcutt and Walter Lyons letter to Joe Barton, 8ᵗʰ August 2005 http://www.realclimate.org/index.php/archives/2005/07/barton-and-the-hockey-stick/

44. Roger Scruton, *The Uses of Pessimism* (2010), p. 170.

45. Mann letter to Joe Barton.

46. Bridgman, *The Way Things Are* (1959), p. 56.

47. Stephen H. Schneider, *Science As A Contact Sport* (2009), pp. 147–8.

48. Ralph J. Cicerone letter to Joe Barton, 15ᵗʰ July 2005 http://www.realclimate.org/index.php/archives/2005/07/barton-and-the-hockey-stick/

49. Juliet Eilperin, 'GOP Chairmen Face Off on Global Warming' in the *Washington Post*, 18ᵗʰ July 2005.

50. Richard A Kerr, 'Draft Report Affirms Human Influence' in *Science*, Vol. 288, 28th April 2000.

51. Montford, *The Hockey Stick Illusion: Climategate and the Corruption of Science* (2010), p. 229.

52. House of Lords Select Committee on Economic Affairs, *The Economics of Climate Change*, Vol. II (2005), pp. 16–17.

53. Phil Jones email to Tom Wigley, 21ˢᵗ October 2004.

54. J.T. Houghton, Testimony to the US Senate – Energy and Natural Resources Committee, 21ˢᵗ July 2005 http://ftp.resource.org/gpo.gov/hearings/109s/24631.txt

55. ibid.

56. Gerald R. North, Presentation to Dessler Seminar (2006) http://www.met.tamu.edu/people/faculty/dessler/NorthH264.mp4

57. Stephen McIntyre, 'D'Arrigo: Making Cherry Pie' 6ᵗʰ March 2006 http://climateaudit.org/2006/03/07/darrigo-making-cherry-pie/

58. Montford, *The Hockey Stick Illusion: Climategate and the Corruption of Science* (2010), p. 237.

59. ibid., p. 289.

60. Stephen McIntyre, 'Climategate: A Battlefield Perspective – Annotated Notes for Presentation to Heartland Conference, Chicago'.

61. Richard Alley email to Jonathan Overpeck & Keith Briffa, 8th March 2006

62. National Research Council, *Surface Temperature Reconstructions for the Last 2,000 Years* (2006), p. 3.

63. ibid.

64. ibid., p. 113.

65. ibid., p. 4.

66. ibid.

67. ibid.

68. ibid., p. 98.

69. ibid., p. 99.

70. Andrew Revkin, 'Panel Supports a Controversial Report on Global Warming' in the *New York Times*, 23rd June 2006.

71. Geoff Brumfiel, 'Academy affirms hockey-stick graph' in *Nature*, 441, 1032-1033 (29th June 2006) .

72. Brumfiel, 'Academy affirms hockey-stick graph' in *Nature*, 441, 1032-1033 & Revkin, 'Panel Supports a Controversial Report on Global Warming' in the *New York Times*.

73. National Research Council, *Surface Temperature Reconstructions for the Last 2,000 Years* (2006), p. vii.

74. Edward J. Wegman, David W. Scott & Yasmin H. Said, 'Ad Hoc Committee Report on the "Hockey Stick" Global Climate Reconstruction' July 2006, p. 4.

75. ibid.

76. ibid.

77. ibid.

78. Questions Surrounding The 'Hockey Stick' Temperature Studies: Implications For Climate Change Assessments Hearings Before The Subcommittee on Oversight and Investigations of The Committee on Energy and Commerce, House of Representatives, 19th and 27th July 2006, p. 74.

79. ibid.

80. Wigley email to Jones.

81. 'Climate change: Is the US Congress bullying experts?' in *Nature*, Vol. 436, No. 7047, 7th July 2005.

82. Michael E. Mann email to Keith Briffa.

83. Keith Briffa email to Michael E. Mann, 29th April 2007.

84. Stefan Rahmstorf, 'What If ... the "Hockey Stick" Were Wrong?' 27th January 2005 http://www.realclimate.org/index.php/archives/2005/01/what-if-the-hockey-stick-were-wrong/

85. Stephen McIntyre, 'Bürger Comment on Osborn and Briffa 2006' 30th June 2007 http://climateaudit.org/2007/06/30/burger-comment-on-osborn-and-briffa-2006/

22
CLIMATEGATE

1. *An Inconvenient Truth*, Participant Productions (2006).
2. http://www.boxofficemojo.com/movies/?page=main&id=inconvenienttruth.htm
3. http://www.boxofficemojo.com/movies/?id=fahrenheit911.htm
4. *An Inconvenient Truth.*
5. Bert Bolin, *A History of the Science and Politics of Climate Change: The Role of the Intergovernmental Panel on Climate Change* (2007), p. 208
6. ibid., p. 212.
7. ibid.
8. *An Inconvenient Truth.*
9. Eric Steig, 'Al Gore's movie' 10th May 2006 http://www.realclimate.org/index.php/archives/2006/05/al-gores-movie/
10. *An Inconvenient Truth.*
11. Stephen McIntyre, 'Gore Scientific "Adviser" says that he has no "responsibility" for AIT errors' 13th January 2008 http://climateaudit.org/2008/01/13/sticking-thermometers-in-places-they-dont-belong/
12. R.K. Pauchauri and A. Reisinger (ed.), *Climate Change 2007: Synthesis Report. Contribution of Working Groups I, II and III to the Fourth Assessment Report of the Intergovernmental Panel on Climate Change* (2007), p. 5.
13. The Norwegian Nobel Committee, 'The Nobel Peace Prize for 2007' 12th October 2007 http://nobelprize.org/nobel_prizes/peace/laureates/2007/press.html
14. J.T. Houghton, 'An Overview of the Intergovernmental Panel on Climate Change (IPCC) and Its Process of Science Assessment' in *Issues in Environmental Science and Technology*, No. 17, Royal Society of Chemistry (2002), p. 6.
15. Solomon, S., D. Qin, M. Manning, Z. Chen, M. Marquis, K.B. Averyt, M. Tignor and H.L. Miller (ed.), *Contribution of Working Group I to the Fourth Assessment Report of the Intergovernmental Panel on Climate Change* (2007), p. 466.
16. Stephen McIntyre, 'Climategate: A Battlefield Perspective – Annotated Notes for Presentation to Heartland Conference, Chicago' 16th May 2010, p. 15 www.climateaudit.info/pdf/mcintyre-heartland_2010.pdf
17. ibid.
18. Stuart Matthews letter to David Holland, 19th August 2008.
19. Phil Jones email to Michael Mann (Mann's response dated 29th May 2008.
20. Todd J. Zinser letter to Senator James Inhofe, 18th February 2011 http://www.environbusiness.com/News/2011.02.18_IG_to_Inhofe.pdf
21. Jeff Id, 'OK it's blown wide open' 19th November 2009 http://noconsensus.wordpress.com/2009/11/19/ok-its-blown-wide-open/

22. Andrew Revkin, 'Hacked E-Mail Data Prompts Calls for Changes in Climate Research' in the *New York Times*, 28th November 2009.

23. George Monbiot, 'Pretending the climate email leak isn't a crisis won't make it go away' in the *Guardian*, 25th November 2011.

24. ibid.

25. Revkin, 'Hacked E-Mail Data Prompts Calls for Changes in Climate Research' in the *New York Times*, 28th November 2009.

26. ibid.

27. Jonathan Leake, 'Climate change data dumped' in the *Sunday Times*, 29th November 2009.

28. James Rodger Fleming, *The Callendar Effect* (2007), p. 94.

29. Ben Webster, 'Top scientists rally to the defence of the Met Office' in *The Times*, 10th December 2009.

30. The Met Office, 'Statement from the UK science community' 10th December 2009 http://www.metoffice.gov.uk/news/releases/archive/2009/science-community-statement

31. Webster, 'Top scientists rally to the defence of the Met Office' in *The Times*, 10th December 2009.

32. House of Commons Science and Technology Committee, *The disclosure of climate data from the Climatic Research Unit at the University of East Anglia Eighth Report of Session 2009–10*, Volume II (2010), Ev 171.

33. ibid., Ev 186.

34. ibid.

35. ibid.

36. ibid., Ev 167–8.

37. Graham Stringer interview with author, 21st June 2011.

38. Simon Hoggart, 'The sight of another scientist being skewered makes for painful viewing' in the *Guardian*, 2nd March 2010.

39. ibid.

40. House of Commons Science and Technology Committee, *The disclosure of climate data from the Climatic Research Unit at the University of East Anglia Eighth Report of Session 2009–10*, Volume II (2010), Q103, Ev 29.

41. Hoggart, 'The sight of another scientist being skewered makes for painful viewing' in the *Guardian*, 2nd March 2010.

42. Andrew Gimson, 'On the trail of the lonesome pine' in the *Telegraph*, 2nd March 2010.

43. Quentin Letts, 'Lord Lawson labelled them climate alarmists' in the *Daily Mail*, 2nd March 2010.

44. Stringer interview with author.

45. House of Commons Science and Technology Committee, *The disclosure of climate data from the Climatic Research Unit at the University of East Anglia Eighth Report of Session 2009–10*, Volume II (2010), Q136, Ev 32.

23
STATE OF DENIAL

1. House of Commons Science and Technology Committee, *The disclosure of climate data from the Climatic Research Unit at the University of East Anglia Eighth Report of Session 2009–10*, Volume II (2010), Q 198, Ev 59.
2. David Holland (2008), *Submission to the Garnaut Review: Deficiencies in the IPCC Fourth Assessment Report of the Scientific Basis of Climate Change*, p. 4.
3. *The disclosure of climate data from the Climatic Research Unit at the University of East Anglia Eighth Report of Session 2009–10*, Volume II (2010), Q 194, Ev 59.
4. ibid., Q 195, Ev 59.
5. ibid., Q 198, Ev 59.
6. ibid., Q 207, Ev 60.
7. ibid.,Q 207, Ev 60.
8. ibid.
9. ibid., Q 130, Ev 31.
10. ibid.,Q 130, Ev 32.
11. http://www.jonathanlynn.com/tv/yes_minister_series/yes_minister_episode_quotes.htm
12. *The disclosure of climate data from the Climatic Research Unit at the University of East Anglia Eighth Report of Session 2009–10*, Volume II (2010), Q 85, Ev 13.
13. ibid.
14. Muir Russell et al., *The Independent Climate Change E-mails Review* (2010), pp. 78–9.
15. ibid.
16. *The disclosure of climate data from the Climatic Research Unit at the University of East Anglia Eighth Report of Session 2009–10*, Volume II (2010), Q 121, Ev 18.
17. ibid., Q 129, Ev 31.
18. ibid., Q 4, Ev 2.
19. ibid., Q 17, Ev 3.
20. Ronald Oxburgh et al., *Report of the International Panel set up by the University of East Anglia to examine the research of the Climatic Research Unit*, (2010), p. 5 www.uea.ac.uk/mac/comm/media/press/CRUstatements/SAP
21. ibid., p. 4.
22. Graham Stringer interview with author, 21st June 2011.
23. Oxburgh et al., *Report of the International Panel set up by the University of East Anglia to examine the research of the Climatic Research Unit*, (2010), p. 2.
24. ibid., p. 3.

25. ibid., p. 5.
26. Muir Russell, 'Emails Report Launch – Notes for MR Introduction' para 23 www.cce-review.org/pdf/MR%20Launch%20intro.pdf
27. *The disclosure of climate data from the Climatic Research Unit at the University of East Anglia Eighth Report of Session 2009–10, Report, together with formal minutes* (2010), para 137.
28. ibid., para 54.
29. James Renderson, 'Climate researchers' "secrecy" criticised – but MPs say science remains intact' in the *Guardian*, 31ˢᵗ March 2010.
30. Ben Webster, 'Climate-row professor Phil Jones should return to work, say MPs' in *The Times*, 31ˢᵗ March 2010.
31. Renderson, 'Climate researchers' "secrecy" criticised – but MPs say science remains intact'.
32. *The disclosure of climate data from the Climatic Research Unit at the University of East Anglia Eighth Report of Session 2009–10, Report, together with formal minutes* (2010), para 38.
33. ibid.
34. Michael E. Mann email to Tim Osborn, 31ˢᵗ July 2003.
35. *The disclosure of climate data from the Climatic Research Unit at the University of East Anglia Eighth Report of Session 2009–10, Report, together with formal minutes* (2010), para 38.
36. HMG, *Government Response to the House of Commons Science and Technology Committee 8th Report of Session 2009–10: The disclosure of climate data from the Climatic Research Unit at the University of East Anglia* (September 2010), Cm 7934, para 6.
37. ibid., Cm 7934, para 13.
38. Karl Popper, *The Logic of Scientific Discovery* (2009), p. 33.
39. John Losee, *A Historical Introduction to the Philosophy of Science* (1980), p. 120.
40. Prince Charles, 'A speech by HRH The Prince of Wales at the opening of Atmosphere, The Science Museum, London' 3ʳᵈ December 2010 http://www.princeofwales.gov.uk/speechesandarticles/a_speech_by_hrh_the_prince_of_wales_at_the_opening_of_atmosp_897061599.html
41. *The Reviews into the University of East Anglia's Climatic Research Unit's E-mails First Report of Session 2010–11*, Volume I (2011), Q 102 & 103, Ev 14.
42. Information Commissioner's Office, 'Decision Notice: FER0282488' 23ʳᵈ June 2011.
43. PBL Netherlands Environmental Assessment Agency, *Assessing an IPCC assessment: An analysis of statements on projected regional impacts in the 2007 report* (2010), p. 24.
44. ibid., p. 43.
45. ibid., p. 44.

46. Harold T. Shapiro et al., *Climate change assessments: Review of the processes and procedures of the IPCC* (2010), p. vii.
47. ibid., p. viii.
48. ibid., p. 8.
49. ibid., p. xv.
50. ibid., p. 23.
51. Clive Crook, 'Climategate and the Big Green Lie' in the *Atlantic*, 14th July 2010 http://www.theatlantic.com/politics/archive/2010/07/climategate-and-the-big-green-lie/59709/ and Pennsylvania State University Investigatory Committee, 'RA-1O Final Investigation Report Involving Dr Michael E. Mann' 4th June 2010, p. 15.
52. Pennsylvania State University Investigatory Committee, 'RA-1O Final Investigation Report Involving Dr Michael E. Mann' 4th June 2010, p. 16.
53. ibid., p. 19.

24
TIME'S WINGÈD CHARIOT

1. A.N. Whitehead, *Concept of Nature* (1971), p. 54.
2. Damian Carrington, 'IPCC officials admit mistake over melting Himalayan glaciers' in the *Guardian*, 20th January 2010.
3. C.A.E. Goodhart, *Money, Information and Uncertainty* (1989), p. 1.
4. ibid., p. 2.
5. Wen Jiabao, 'Strengthen Confidence and Work Together for a New Round of World Economic Growth' 28th January 2009 http://english.sina.com/china/2009/0128/214624.html
6. Joseph A. Schumpeter, *History of Economic Analysis* (1994), p. 53.
7. ibid., p. 42.
8. Nathan Keyfitz, *Kenneth Ewart Boulding* (1996), p. 7.
9. Kenneth E. Boulding 'The Economics of the coming Spaceship Earth' in Henry Jarrett (ed.), *Environmental Quality in a Growing Economy – Essays from the Sixth RFF Forum* (1966), p. 9.
10. ibid., pp. 12–13.
11. ibid., p. 10.
12. ibid., pp. 11–12.
13. ibid., p. 12.
14. ibid.
15. ibid.
16. Yale Center for the Study of Globalization, *Yale Symposium on the Stern Review* (2007), http://www.ycsg.yale.edu/climate/forms/FullText.pdf, p. 112.
17. William D. Nordhaus, 'World Dynamics: Measurement without Data' in *The Economic Journal*, Vol. 83 332 (1973), p. 1183.

18. ibid.
19. William D. Nordhaus, *The Efficient Use of Energy Resources* (1979), pp. xviii–xix.
20. Nordhaus, *The Efficient Use of Energy Resources* (1979), p. 131.
21. ibid., p. 142.
22. William D. Nordhaus, *The Stern Review on the Economics of Climate Change* (2007), http://nordhaus.econ.yale.edu/stern_050307.pdf, p. 19.
23. William Cline, 'Scientific Basis for the Greenhouse Effect' in *The Economic Journal*, Vol. 101 407 (1991), p. 913.
24. ibid.
25. William D. Nordhaus, 'To Slow or not to Slow: The Economics of the Greenhouse Effect' in *The Economic Journal*, Vol. 101 407 (1991), p. 933.
26. ibid.
27. *Yale Symposium on the Stern Review* (2007), p. 131.
28. David Henderson, 'Economists and Climate Science: A Critique' in *World Economics*, Vol. 10, No. 1 (2009), p. 66.
29. ibid., p. 67.
30. ibid.
31. Martin Weitzman, 'On Modelling and Interpreting the Economics of Catastrophic Climate Change' in *The Review of Economics and Statistics*, Vol. XCI, No. 1 (2009), p. 5.
32. David Henderson, 'Climate Science, Economics, and Policy' in *AIER Economic Bulletin*, Vol. XLIX (June 2009), p. 5.
33. ibid., p. 6.
34. Ross Garnaut, *The Garnaut Climate Change Review* (2008), p. xvii.
35. Ross McKitrick email to author, 26th October 2011.
36. J.M. Keynes, 'Professor Tinbergen's Method' in *The Economic Journal* 49 (September 1939), p. 560.
37. *Yale Symposium on the Stern Review*, (2007), pp. 131–2.
38. House of Lords Select Committee on Economic Affairs, *The Economics of Climate Change* (2005), Vol. II, Q 357.
39. *The Economics of Climate Change* (2005), Vol. II, p. 266.
40. ibid., Vol. II, Q 352.
41. ibid., Vol. II, Q 358.
42. John Wakeham interview with author, 7th June 2011.
43. House of Lords Select Committee on Economic Affairs, *The Economics of Climate Change* (2005), Vol. II, Q 226.
44. ibid., Vol. I, para 86.
45. ibid., Vol. I, para 94.

25
STERN REVIEW

1. Nicholas Stern, *The Economics of Climate Change: The Stern Review* (2007), p. xv.
2. P.T. Bauer, *Reality and Rhetoric – Studies in the Economics of Development* (1984), p. 147 .
3. Decca Aitkenhead, '"We're the first generation that has had the power to destroy the planet. Ignoring the risk can only be described as reckless"' in the *Guardian*, 30th March 2009.
4. ibid.
5. Yale Center for the Study of Globalization, *Yale Symposium on the Stern Review* (2007), http://www.ycsg.yale.edu/climate/forms/FullText.pdf, p. 8.
6. Ian Byatt, Ian Castles, David Henderson, Nigel Lawson, Ross McKitrick, Julian Morris, Alan Peacock, Colin Robinson and Robert Skidelsky, 'The Stern Review "Oxonia Papers": A Critique' http://webarchive.nationalarchives.gov. uk/+/http://www.hm-treasury.gov.uk/sternreview_backgroundtoreview.htm, p. 3.
7. ibid., p. 5.
8. Nicholas Stern, 'Reply to Byatt et al' in *World Economics*, Vol. 7, No. 2 (April–June 2006), p. 154.
9. ibid., p. 156.
10. ibid., p. 155.
11. Stern, *The Economics of Climate Change: The Stern Review* (2007), p. xv.
12. ibid.
13. Chris Hope interview with author, 27th October 2011.
14. Hope interview with author.
15. *Yale Symposium on the Stern Review* (2007).
16. Stern, *The Economics of Climate Change: The Stern Review* (2007), Box 6.1 and p. 4.
17. ibid., p. 35.
18. ibid., p. 54.
19. ibid., p. 35.
20. ibid., p. 54.
21. ibid.
22. ibid., p. 53.
23. Partha Dasgupta, 'Commentary: The Stern Review's Economics of Climate Change' in *National Institute Economic Review*, No. 199, January 2007, p. 6.
24. ibid.
25. ibid.
26. Stern, *The Economics of Climate Change: The Stern Review* (2007), p. 35.

27. William Nordhaus, *The Stern Review on the Economics of Climate Change* (2007) http://nordhaus.econ.yale.edu/stern_050307.pdf, pp. 14–15.

28. ibid., p. 25.

29. William Nordhaus, *A Question of Balance: Weighing the Options on Global Warming Policies* (2008), p. 167.

30. Stern, *The Economics of Climate Change: The Stern Review* (2007), p. 448.

31. ibid., p. 523.

32. ibid., p. 468.

33. Nigel Lawson, *An Appeal to Reason: A Cool Look at Global Warming* (2008), p. 44.

34. Stern, *The Economics of Climate Change: The Stern Review* (2007), p. 191.

35. ibid., p. 320.

36. ibid., Figs 13.1 & 13.2.

37. ibid., p. 193.

38. ibid., Box 7.1.

26
SELLING SALVATION

1. David Henderson, *The Role of Business in the Modern World* (2004), p. 82.

2. Royal Society, 'Stern Review on the Economics of Climate Change' 30th October 2006, http://royalsociety.tv/rsPlayer.aspx?presentationid=114

3. ibid.

4. ibid.

5. 'We're all green now. Up to a point' in the *Economist*, 2nd November 2006.

6. 'Stern Warning' in *The Times*, 31st October 2006.

7. 'Stern Warning, Economics of climate change' in the *Economist*, 4th November 2006.

8. 'Why governments can't save the planet' in the *Daily Telegraph*, 31st October 2006.

9. Martin Wolf, 'A compelling case for action to avoid a climatic catastrophe' in the *Financial Times*, 1st November 2006.

10. Scheherazade Daneshku, 'Change that is costing the Earth' in the *Financial Times*, 31st October 2006.

11. 'What planet are they on?' in the *Daily Mail*, 31st October 2006.

12. Nigel Lawson email to author, 2nd January 2012.

13. Christopher Adams, 'Warning of climate change catastrophe' in the *Financial Times*, 23rd October 2006.

14. Robert J. Samuelson, 'Greenhouse Guessing' in the *Washington Post*, 10th November 2006.

15. ibid.

16. William Nordhaus, *The Stern Review on the Economics of Climate Change* (2007), http://nordhaus.econ.yale.edu/stern_050307.pdf, p. 30.

17. ibid.

18. Chris Hope interview with author, 27th October 2011.

19. Yale Center for the Study of Globalization, *Yale Symposium on the Stern Review* (2007), http://www.ycsg.yale.edu/climate/forms/FullText.pdf, p. 116.

20. ibid., p. 86.

21. ibid., p. 81.

22. ibid., p. 82.

23. ibid., p. 83.

24. ibid., p. 104.

25. According to the US Department of Agriculture, California's total land area is 99,689,515 acres and its total farmland in 2007 was 25,364,695 acres http://www.ers.usda.gov/statefacts/ca.htm#FC

26. *Yale Symposium on the Stern Review* (2007), p. 100.

27. ibid., p. 73.

28. ibid., p. 124.

29. Nicholas Stern, *The Economics of Climate Change: The Stern Review* (2007), p. 664.

30. ibid., Table PA. 3.

31. Martin Weitzman, 'On Modelling and Interpreting the Economics of Catastrophic Climate Change' in *The Review of Economics and Statistics*, Vol. XCI, No. 1 (2009), p. 5.

32. ibid., p. 4.

33. ibid., p. 18.

34. Martin Wolf, 'Why obstacles to a deal on climate are mountainous' in the *Financial Times*, 8th July 2008.

35. Weitzman, 'On Modelling and Interpreting the Economics of Catastrophic Climate Change' in *The Review of Economics and Statistics*, Vol. XCI, No. 1 (2009), p. 18.

36. Nigel Lawson, *An Appeal to Reason: A Cool Look at Global Warming* (2008), p. 90.

37. Bert Bolin, *A History of the Science and Politics of Climate Change: The Role of the Intergovernmental Panel on Climate Change* (2007), p. 96.

27
CUCUMBERS INTO SUNBEAMS

1. George W. Bush, State of the Union Address, 31st January 2006 http://www.washingtonpost.com/wp-dyn/content/article/2006/01/31/AR2006013101468_pf.html

2. http://www.slate.com/id/2175313/

3. Martin Wolf, *Why Globalization Works* (2004), p. 74.

4. Per Lekander, Alberto Gandolfi & Patrick Hummel, 'Carbon price to collapse, €210 billion wasted' UBS Investment Research (17th November 2011), p. 16.

5. ibid., p. 15.

6. Charles Forelle, 'French Firm Cashes in Under UN Warming Programme' in the *Wall Street Journal*, 23rd July 2008.

7. ibid.

8. Donald Mitchell, *A Note on Rising Food Prices*, World Bank Policy Research Working Paper 4682 (July 2008), p. 2.

9. ibid., p. 17.

10. 'Rush for biofuels threatens starvation on a global scale' in *The Times*, 7th March 2008.

11. IPCC, *Climate Change 2001. Synthesis Report*, Cambridge (2001), p. 71.

12. Jonathan Leake, 'Scourge of the rainforests' in the *Sunday Times*, 11th April 2010.

13. ibid.

14. http://www.rspb.org.uk/ourwork/policy/windfarms/

15. http://policy.audubon.org/wind-power-overview-0

16. Thomas L. Friedman, 'The Copenhagen That Matters' in the *New York Times*, 23rd December 2009.

17. Paul-Frederik Bach, *The Variability of Wind Power* (2010), p. viii.

18. ibid., p. 32.

19. ibid., p. 2.

20. ibid., p. 5.

21. Manuel Frondel, Nolan Ritter, Christoph M Schmidt, Colin Vance, *Economic Impacts from the Promotion of Renewable Technologies: The German Experience* (2009), Fig. 3.

22. ibid., p. 20.

23. ibid., p. 11.

24. ibid., p. 15.

25. ibid., p. 19.

26. Ministerio de Industria, Turismo y Comercio, 'Energías renovables: situación y objectivos' (April 2010), p. 15.

27. John Constable, *The Green Mirage* (2011), p. 93.

28. Lynn J. Cunningham & Beth A. Roberts, *Renewable Energy and Energy Efficiency Incentives: A Summary of Federal Programs*, Congressional Research Service (22nd March 2011).

29. Brent D. Yacobucci. *Biofuels Incentives: A Summary of Federal Programs*, Congressional Research Service (1st July 2011), p. 1.

30. Kathryn Harrison, *The Road Not Taken: Climate Change Policy in Canada and the United States* (August 2006), p. 18.

31. ibid., p. 21.

32. James M. Inhofe, 'The Science of Climate Change' 28th July 2003 http://inhofe.senate.gov/pressreleases/climate.htm

33. Inhofe, 'The Science of Climate Change'.

34. ibid.

35. Maurice Strong, *Where on Earth are We Going?* (2001), p. 219.

36. Stephan Schmidheiny (with the Business Council for Sustainable Development), *Changing Course: A Global Perspective on Development and the Environment* (1992), p. 3.

37. Schmidheiny, *Changing Course: A Global Perspective on Development and the Environment* (1992), p. 2 & Andrew Monahan, 'China Overtakes Japan as World's No. 2 Economy' in the *Wall Street Journal*, 14th February 2011.

38. Schmidheiny, *Changing Course: A Global Perspective on Development and the Environment* (1992), p. 35.

39. ibid., p. 50.

40. William O'Keefe interview with author, 19th December 2011.

41. Sybille van den Hove, Marc Le Menestrel & Henri-Claude de Bettignies, 'The oil industry and climate change: strategies and ethical dilemmas' in *Climate Policy* 2 (2002), pp. 3–18.

42. ibid., pp. 3–18.

43. Michael McCarthy, 'Ford predicts end of car pollution' in the *Independent*, 6th October 2000.

44. Robert Watson interview with author, 6th December 2010.

45. van den Hove, Le Menestrel & de Bettignies, 'The oil industry and climate change: strategies and ethical dilemmas' in *Climate Policy* 2 (2002), pp. 3–18.

46. Environment News Service, 'U.S. Senate Takes Global Warming Seriously' 22nd June 2005 http://www.ens-newswire.com/ens/jun2005/2005-06-22-09.html

47. Lisa Jackson, 'Remarks to the 2nd Annual Governors' Global Climate Summit' as Prepared for delivery, 30th September 2009 http://yosemite.epa.gov/opa/admpress.nsf/12a744ff56dbff8585257590004750b6/dfb9d60add641fac852576410070a78d!OpenDocument

48. Supreme Court of the United States, Opinion of the Court, 549 US (2007), pp. 21–2.

49. ibid., p. 22.

50. ibid., p. 18.

51. ibid., pp. 13–14.

52. ibid., p. 18.

53. ibid., p. 8.

54. ibid.

55. Jackson, 'Remarks on the Endangerment Finding on Greenhouse Gases' as prepared for delivery, 7th December 2009 http://yosemite.epa.gov/opa/admpress.nsf/12a744ff56dbff8585257590004750b6/b6b7098bb1dfaf9a85257685005483d5!OpenDocument

56. Barack Obama, Videotaped Remarks to the Bi-Partisan Governors Global Climate Summit 18th November 2008 http://www.presidency.ucsb.edu/ws/index.php?pid=84875#ixzz1kH213nYG

28
HUGGING HUSKIES

1. Tony Blair, 'Facing up to a climate of change' in *The Times*, 4th December 1997.

2. James Renderson, 'Cameron: I want coalition to be the 'greenest government ever' guardian.co.uk, 14th May 2010.

3. *Hansard*, House of Lords Written Answers, WA128 (25th October 2011).

4. Defra, 'The Social Cost Of Carbon And The Shadow Price Of Carbon: What They Are, And How To Use Them In Economic Appraisal In The UK' (December 2007), p. 8.

5. Martin Delgado & Christopher Leake, 'Queen's £38m A Year Windfarm Windfall' in the *Mail on Sunday*, 24th October 2010.

6. Jonathan Wynne-Jones, 'Wind farms are useless, says Duke of Edinburgh' in the *Sunday Telegraph*, 20th November 2011.

7. http://conservativehome.blogs.com/toryleadership/files/CAMERON-ON-CLIMATE-CHANGE.pdf

8. *Hansard*, House of Commons Debates, 22nd March 2006, Col. 303–4.

9. 'Tories join calls for binding annual carbon targets' in *ENDS*, 7th September 2006. Caroline Lucas of the Greens, not at that time an MP, was also a signatory.

10. *Hansard*, House of Commons Debates, 15th November 2006, Col. 15.

11. *Hansard*, House of Commons, 9th June 2008, Col. 100.

12. ibid.

13. ibid., Col. 101.

14. Peter Lilley interview with author, 19th December 2011.

15. *Hansard*, House of Commons, 9th June 2008, Col. 38.

16. Andrew Turnbull, *The Really Inconvenient Truth, or, 'It Ain't Necessarily So'* (2011), p. 3.

17. Peter Lilley letter to Ed Miliband, 24th March 2009.

18. Ed Miliband letter to Peter Lilley, 23rd April 2009.

19. Department of Energy and Climate Change, *Climate Change Act 2008 Impact Assessment* (March 2009), Box 5.

20. Miliband letter to Lilley.

21. *Climate Change Act 2008 Impact Assessment* (March 2009), p. 4.

22. Ed Davey letter to Peter Lilley, 21st April 2012.

23. John Browne, 19th May 1997 http://www.bp.com/genericarticle.do?categoryId=98&contentId=2000427

24. John Browne, 26th April 2007 http://www.bp.com/genericarticle.do?category Id=98&contentId=7032698
25. John Browne, 7th October 1997 http://www.bp.com/genericarticle.do?catego ryId=98&contentId=2000305
26. William O'Keefe interview with author, 19th December 2011.
27. John Browne, 22nd April 1999 http://www.bp.com/genericarticle.do?categor yId=98&contentId=2000320
28. Browne, 22nd April 1999.
29. Exxon Mobil, *2005 Corporate Citizenship Report*, p. 23.
30. Bob Ward letter to Nick Thomas, 4th September 2006.
31. *Hansard*, House of Lords, 12th January 2012, Col. 280.
32. Ward letter to Thomas.
33. Steven Mufson, 'Exxon Mobil Warming Up To Global Climate Issue' in the *Washington Post*, 10th February 2007.
34. ibid.
35. ibid.
36. Rex Tillerson, 'Promoting energy investment and innovation to meet U.S. economic and environmental challenges' 1st October 2009 http://www. exxonmobil.com/Corporate/news_speeches_20091001_rwt.aspx
37. John Browne, 6th February 1998 http://www.bp.com/genericarticle.do?categ oryId=98&contentId=2000287
38. Tillerson, 'Promoting energy investment and innovation to meet U.S. economic and environmental challenges'
39. John Browne, 22nd April 1999.
40. John Browne, 26th April 2007.
41. Syliva Pfeifer & Pilita Clark, 'BP to close its unprofitable solar business' in the *Financial Times*, 21st December 2011.
42. Synthetic Genomics press release, 14th July 2009 http://www.syntheticgenomics. com/media/press/71409.html

29
DANGEROUS CLIMATE CHANGE

1. Hans Blix interview with John Norris, MTV, 13th March 2003 http://www. mtv.com/bands/i/iraq/news_feature_031203/index5.jhtml
2. Press Trust of India, 'Global warming has hit the danger point' 23rd January 2005.
3. UNFCCC, 'Time series Annex I – Total CO_2 Emissions without Land Use, Land-Use Change and Forestry (2011), http://unfccc.int/ghg_data/ghg_ data_unfccc/time_series_annex_i/items/3814.php
4. UNFCCC, 'Time series Annex I – Total CO_2 Emissions without Land Use, Land-Use Change and Forestry'.

5. International Energy Agency, *CO₂ Emissions From Fuel Combustion Highlights* (2011), p. 46.

6. Dieter Helm, 'Forget the Huhne hype about wind power' in *The Times*, 6th February 2012.

7. International Energy Agency, *CO₂ Emissions From Fuel Combustion Highlights* (2011), p. 109.

8. Hans Blix interview with John Norris.

9. Robert May, 'Threat to tomorrow's world' 30th November 2005 http://rsnr. royalsocietypublishing.org/content/60/1/109.full

10. Richard Mottram, 'Careful Science can help fight climate change' in the *Financial Times*, 29th July 2008.

11. David A. King, 'Climate Change Science: Adapt, Mitigate, or Ignore?' in *Science*, 9th January 2004, Vol. 303 No. 5655, pp. 176–7.

12. James R. Lee, 'Global Warming is just the Tip of the Iceberg' in the *Washington Post*, 4th January 2009

13. http://www.fco.gov.uk/en/fco-in-action/carbon/low-carbon/

14. Lee, 'Global Warming is just the Tip of the Iceberg'.

15. Peter Schwartz and Doug Randall, *An Abrupt Climate Change Scenario and Its Implications for United States National Security* (October 2003), p. 7.

16. ibid., p. 2.

17. ibid., p. 16.

18. Department of Defense, *Quadrennial Defense Review Report* (February 2010), p. 84.

19. ibid., p. 85.

20. Gerhard L. Weinberg, *A World at Arms* (1994), p. 2.

21. Paul Ames, 'European Union warns US, China over climate change, saying it could impose sanctions' Associated Press, 14th March 2008.

22. Ames, 'European Union warns US, China over climate change, saying it could impose sanctions'.

23. Klaus Töpfer, 'The Spectre at the Feast' 16th February 2005 http://www. unep.org/Documents.Multilingual/Default.asp?DocumentID=426&Article ID=4719&l=en

24. Australian Associated Press, 'Kyoto pact is useless and harmful: PM' 6th February 2005.

25. John Howard interview with author, 28th November 2011.

26. The Federal News Service, 'Remarks By Presidential Economic Adviser Andrei Illarionov at a Press Conference on Results of The Climate Change and Kyoto Protocol Seminar In Moscow' 8th July 2005 www.sysecol2.ethz.ch/Articles.../ Illarionov_Interv._9.Jul.04.pdf

27. Andrei Illarionov, 'Russian Ministers' decision to ratify Kyoto "motivated purely by politics" according to Putin's advisor' 30th September 2004 http://www. policynetwork.net/es/environment/media/russian-ministers%E2%80%99-

decision-ratify-kyoto-%E2%80%98motivated-purely-politics%E2%80%99-according-put

28. Tony Blair, *A Journey* (2010), p. 557.
29. Paula Dobriansky interview with author, 24th June 2011.
30. George W. Bush, 'President Bush Discusses Global Climate Change' 11th June 2001 http://georgewbush-whitehouse.archives.gov/news/releases/2001/06/20010611-2.html
31. Bush, 'President Bush Discusses Global Climate Change'.
32. Paula Dobriansky interview with author.
33. Harlan Watson, 'Testimony Before the Committee on Foreign Affairs Subcommittee on Asia, the Pacific, and the Global Environment United States House of Representatives Hearing on The Kyoto Protocol: An Update' (July 2007), p. 18.
34. Dobriansky interview with author.
35. Boyden Gray, 'Trust America on Climate Change' in the *Financial Times*, 26th September 2007.
36. Paul Brown, 'Climate conference hears degree of danger' in the *Guardian*, 3rd February 2005.
37. Geoffrey Lean, 'Apocalypse Now: How Mankind is Sleepwalking to the End of the Earth' in the *Independent on Sunday*, 6th February 2005.
38. Brown, 'Climate conference hears degree of danger'.
39. Lean, 'Apocalypse Now: How Mankind is Sleepwalking to the End of the Earth'.
40. Geoffrey Lean, 'Global Warming Approaching Point of No Return, Warns Leading Climate Expert' in the *Independent on Sunday*, 23rd January 2005.
41. Jenny Hogan, 'Alarm bells ring louder over climate change' in the *New Scientist*, 4th February 2005.
42. Swaminathan S. Anklesaria Aiyar, 'Global warming or global cooling' in the *Times of India*, 27th February 2005.
43. Aiyar, 'Global warming or global cooling'.
44. Joint science academies' statement: Global response to climate change (June 2005) http://royalsociety.org/policy/publications/2005/global-response-climate-change/
45. ibid.
46. Paul Brown, 'Blair may snub US on climate' in the *Guardian*, 1st July 2005.
47. ibid.
48. Elizabeth Rosenthal & Andrew Revkin, 'Science Panel Calls Global Warming "Unequivocal"' in the *New York Times*, 3rd February 2007.
49. Rosenthal & Revkin, 'Science Panel Calls Global Warming "Unequivocal"'.
50. BBC News, 'EU agrees renewable energy target' 9th March 2007 http://news.bbc.co.uk/go/pr/fr/-/1/hi/world/europe/6433503.stm
51. ibid.

52. Nicholas Watt, 'Weapons claim: the dossier, the PM, and the headlines' in the *Guardian*, 6th February 2004.

53. *Panorama*, 'What's Fuelling Your Energy Bill?' 7th November 2011.

54. Warren Hoge, 'UN Chief Urges Fast Action on Global Climate Change' in the *New York Times*, 24th September 2007.

55. ibid.

56. Václav Klaus, *Blue Planet in Green Shackles* (2008), pp. 108–9.

57. Václav Klaus remarks after delivering GWPF inaugural lecture, 21st October 2010.

58. Klaus, *Blue Planet in Green Shackles* (2008), p. 12.

59. ibid., p. 4.

60. ibid., p. 5.

61. ibid., p. 2.

62. Brian Knowlton, 'Climate Change Conference Opens' in the *New York Times*, 27th September 2007.

63. George W. Bush, 'President Bush Participates in Major Economies Meeting on Energy Security and Climate Change' 28th September 2007 http://georgewbush-whitehouse.archives.gov/news/releases/2007/09/20070928-2.html

64. Knowlton, 'Climate Change Conference Opens'.

65. Norwegian Nobel Committee, The Nobel Peace Prize 2007 Press Release 12th October 2007 http://www.nobelprize.org/nobel_prizes/peace/laureates/2007/press.html

66. Ban Ki-Moon, 'Address to the Intergovernmental Panel on Climate Change (IPCC) upon the release of its fourth assessment synthesis report' 17th November 2007 http://www.un.org/apps/news/infocus/sgspeeches/search_full.asp?statID=151#

67. John Howard interview with author.

68. Selina Mitchell & Cath Hart, 'Howard a climate convert' in *The Australian*, 26th January 2007.

69. ibid.

70. ibid.

71. John Howard interview with author.

72. Kevin Rudd, 'Prime Minister Kevin Rudd's Address To The UN Bali Conference On Climate Change' 12th December 2007 http://australianpolitics.com/2007/12/12/rudd-address-to-bali-climate-change-conference.html

30
BALI

1. Ban Ki-moon, Address to the High-Level Segment of the UN Climate Change Conference, 12th December 2007 http://www.un.org/apps/news/infocus/sgspeeches/search_full.asp?statID=161

2. Prince Charles, 'Bali offers a vital chance to take tough decisions' in the *Financial Times*, 29th November 2007.

3. K.L. Denman, G. Brasseur, A. Chidthaisong, P. Ciais, P.M. Cox, R.E. Dickinson, D. Hauglustaine, C. Heinze, E. Holland, D. Jacob, U. Lohmann, S Ramachandran, P.L. da Silva Dias, S.C. Wofsy and X. Zhang, '2007: Couplings Between Changes in the Climate System and Biogeochemistry' in *Climate Change 2007: The Physical Science Basis. Contribution of Working Group I to the Fourth Assessment Report of the Intergovernmental Panel on Climate Change,* Solomon, p. 512.

4. ibid., p. 502.

5. Ban Ki-moon, Address to the High-Level Segment of the UN Climate Change Conference.

6. The Princes of Wales's Corporate Leader Group on Climate Change www.princeofwales.gov.uk/content/.../Bali%20Communique.pdf

7. David Adam, 'Climate talks progressing despite US opposition to targets, Benn says' guardian.co.uk, 12th December 2007.

8. Elizabeth Rosenthal & Andrew Revkin, 'Science Panel Calls Global Warming "Unequivocal"' in the *New York Times*, 3rd February 2007.

9. Climate Change Research Centre at the University of New South Wales, '2007 Bali Climate Declaration by Scientists' http://www.climate.unsw.edu.au/news/2007/Bali.html

10. IISD, *Earth Negotiations Bulletin* Vol. 12 No. 349, 10th December 2007, p. 1.

11. David Adam, 'US balks at Bali carbon targets' guardian.co.uk, 11th December 2007.

12. IISD, *Earth Negotiations Bulletin* Vol. 12 No. 354, 18th December 2007, p. 15.

13. Adam, 'US balks at Bali carbon targets'.

14. David Adam, 'Kerry blasts Bush for resisting Bali climate goals' guardian.co.uk, 10th December 2007.

15. Paula Dobriansky interview with author, 29th September 2011.

16. Dobriansky interview with author.

17. *Earth Negotiations Bulletin*, Winnipeg, Manitoba, Vol. 12 No. 354, 18th December 2007, p. 1.

18. Alister Doyle, '"A better world, for you and me," in Bali' Reuters, 12th December 2007.

19. IISD, *Earth Negotiations Bulletin*, Vol. 12 No. 346, December 2007, p. 1.

20. ibid., Vol. 12 No. 347, 7th December 2007, p. 1.

21. ibid., Vol. 12 No. 350, 11th December 2007, p. 1.

22. ibid., Vol. 12 No. 352, 13th December 2007, p. 2.

23. ibid., Vol. 12 No. 353, 14th December 2007, p. 2.

24. Catherine Brahic, 'Al Gore tells Bali the inconvenient truth on US', in the *New Scientist*, 13th December 2007

25. The account and quotes presented here are drawn from a four part video posted on YouTube starting with 'Bali climate summit final plenary / part1' http://www.youtube.com/watch?v=fkubjGSBA9o&feature=related

26. Dana Perino, Office of the Press Secretary, 'Statement by the Press Secretary' 15th December 2007 http://georgewbush-whitehouse.archives.gov/news/releases/2007/12/print/20071215-1.html

31
SHOWDOWN IN COPENHAGEN

1. Barack Obama, 'Remarks in St Paul' in the *New York Times*, 3rd June 2008.

2. AFP, 'Climate deal "worst in history": G77' 19th December 2009.

3. Jack Lefley, 'Last 10 years have been warmest on record because of man-made climate change' in the *Daily Mail*, 16th December 2008.

4. http://icecap.us/images/uploads/RarelatewintersnowfallinBrazil.pdf

5. http://www.lasvegassun.com/news/2008/dec/17/rain-snow-moving-las-vegas-valley/

6. *Wall Street Journal*, 15th January 2009.

7. Vicky Pope, 'Scientists must rein in misleading climate change claims' in the *Guardian*, 11th February 2009

8. Ben Webster and Peter Riddell, 'Global warming is not our fault, say most voters in Times poll' in *The Times*, 14th November 2009

9. Remarks of President-Elect Barack Obama – Philadelphia, Pennsylvania, 17th January 2009 http://www.pic2009.org/pressroom/entry/remarks_of_president-elect_barack_obama_-_philadelphia_pennsylvania/

10. Rasmussen Poll (17th January 2009), *44% Say Global Warming Due To Planetary Trends, Not People* http://www.rasmussenreports.com:80/public_content/politics/issues2/articles/44_say_global_warming_due_to_planetary_trends_not_people

11. Economy, 'Jobs Trump All Other Policy Priorities', Pew Research Center, 22nd January 2009 http://people-press.org:80/report/485/economy-top-policy-priority

12. Group of Eight, 'Responsible Leadership for a Sustainable Future' paras 2 & 61 http://www.g8italia2009.it/static/G8_Allegato/G8_Declaration_08_07_09_final,0.pdf

13. ibid., para 60.

14. ibid., para 65.

15. White House, Office of the Press Secretary, 'Declaration of the Leaders The Major Economies Forum on Energy and Climate' 9th July 2009.

16. Silvio Berlusconi, 'Chair's summary' 10th July 2009 http://www.g8italia2009.it/static/G8_Allegato/Chair_Summary,1.pdf

17. Group of Eight, 'Responsible Leadership for a Sustainable Future' para 64.

18. Gordon Brown, 'PM's speech to the Major Economies Forum' 19th October 2009   http://www.docstoc.com/docs/22881299/Transcript-of-Gordon-Brown-Climate-Change-speech

19. ibid.

20. ibid.

21. Nigel Lawson, 'Copenhagen will fail – and quite right too' in *The Times*, 23rd November 2009.

22. John Vidal and Damian Carrington, 'Ed Miliband attacks Tory climate "saboteurs"' in the *Guardian*, 3rd December 2009.

23. Damian and Suzanne Goldenberg, 'Gordon Brown attacks "flat-earth" climate change sceptics' in the *Guardian*, 4th December 2009.

24. Michelle Grattan, 'We will have climate policy, Abbott says' in *The Age*, 2nd December 2009.

25. Tom Burke, 'The Future of Climate Policy' 18th June 2009 http://tomburke.co.uk/category/speech/

26. World Council of Churches, 'Churches to Ring the Alarm on Climate Change' 12th November 2009, http://www.oikoumene.org/en/news/news-management/eng/a/article/1634/churches-to-ring-the-alar.html

27. Archbishop of Canterbury press notice, 'Faith and Climate Change' 29th October 2009 http://www.archbishopofcanterbury.org/articles.php/770/faith-and-climate-change

28. Rowan Williams, 'Environment Service at Westminster Central Hall' 5th December 2009 http://www.archbishopofcanterbury.org/articles.php/852/environment-service-at-westminster-central-hall-london

29. Dina Cappiello and H. Josef Hebert, 'Analysis: Obama won't break new ground at summit' Associated Press, 16th December 2009.

30. Suzanne Goldenberg and Jonathan Watts, 'Kerry's promise of support in US Congress raises hopes for deal' in the *Guardian*, 7th December 2009.

31. Al Gore's speech at the Copenhagen on 15th December 2009 http://www.youtube.com/watch?v=KcUllhQ7C0Q

32. Fiona Harvey and Joshua Chaffin, 'EU raises stakes on emissions reductions' in the *Financial Times*, 7th December 2009.

33. Harvey and Chaffin, 'EU raises stakes on emissions reductions'.

34. 'India and climate-change negotiations: Back to basics' in the *Economist*, 5th December 2009.

35. Fiona Harvey, 'Beijing set to drop funding demand' in the *Financial Times*, 14th December 2009.

36. Margot Roosevelt, 'Californians flock to Copenhagen' in the *Los Angeles Times*, 16th December 2009.

37. Paul Krugman, 'An affordable truth' in the *The New York Times*, 7th December 2009.

38. Stephen Power, 'Obama, in Shift, Expects Climate Deal at Summit' in the *Wall Street Journal*, 5th December 2009.

39. Gordon Brown, 'Copenhagen must be a turning point' in the *Guardian*, 7th December 2009.

40. Amanda Debard, 'Climate-research furor might not stop US deal – Scientist decries "smear"; lawmakers want answers' in the *Washington Times*, 5th December 2009.

41. Ben Webster and Murad Ahmed, 'Climate scientists' email was hacked by professionals' in *The Times*, 7th December 2009.

42. Marlowe Hood, 'Copenhagen scientists, negotiators slam "Climategate"' AFP, 7th December 2009.

43. Hood, 'Copenhagen scientists, negotiators slam "Climategate"'.

44. Webster and Ahmed, 'Climate scientists' email was hacked by professionals'.

45. Jan M. Olsen, 'UN climate boss to CEOs: play a more serious role' AP, 11th December 2009.

46. Russell Gold, 'Exxon Bets Big on Gas With Deal for XTO' in *Wall Street Journal* online, 15th December 2009.

47. Damian Reece, 'While Copenhagen talks, Exxon bet $41bn on low-carbon gas' in the *Daily Telegraph*, 15th December 2009.

48. Prince of Wales, 'The eyes of the world are upon you' in the *Guardian*, 15th December 2009.

49. Al Gore's speech on 15th December 2009.

50. Hannah Devlin, 'Gore's Arctic claim unites scientist and sceptic alike' in *The Times*, 16th December 2009.

51. Ben Webster, '2010 will be the warmest year on record, predicts the Met Office' in *The Times*, 11th December 2009.

52. Anna Cuenca, 'Maverick trio scoff at the West at climate summit' in AFP, 16th December 2009.

53. '968 arrests at Copenhagen mass climate rally' in AFP, 12th December 2009.

54. 'Violence breaks out at Copenhagen climate protests' in AFP, 12th December 2009.

55. Richard Ingham, 'After gruelling summit, a contested deal emerges on climate' in AFP, 19th December 2009.

32
NEVER AGAIN

1. Gordon Brown, 'Copenhagen must be a turning point' in the *Guardian*, 7th December 2009.

2. Richard Ingham, 'Walkout heighten failure fear for climate marathon' AFP, 14th December 2009.

3. John Vidal, 'Rich nations accused of Copenhagen "power grab"' in the *Guardian*, 9ᵗʰ December 2009.

4. John Vidal and Dan Milmo, 'Copenhagen: Leaked draft deal widens rift between rich and poor nations' in the *Guardian*, 9ᵗʰ December 2009.

5. IISD, *Earth Negotiations Bulletin* Vol. 12 No. 450, 9ᵗʰ December 2009, p. 4.

6. Draft Copenhagen Agreement – the 'Danish Text' via http://www.guardian.co.uk/environment/2009/dec/08/copenhagen-climate-change

7. 'China Climate envoy criticises rich nations' AFP, 10ᵗʰ December 2009

8. IISD, *Earth Negotiations Bulletin* Vol. 12 No. 459, 22ⁿᵈ December 2009, p. 19.

9. ibid., p. 27.

10. '"Death of Kyoto would be the death of Africa": AU' AFP, 15ᵗʰ December 2009.

11. *Earth Negotiations Bulletin* Vol. 12 No. 456, 16ᵗʰ December 2009, p. 1

12. 'Battle of the texts looms at UN climate talks' AFP, 10ᵗʰ December 2009.

13. Brian Winter, 'China lashes out at US at climate conference' in *USA Today*, 12ᵗʰ December 2009.

14. '"Developed Countries Have Not Delivered": Chinese Vice Foreign Minister He Yafei on Climate Change' in the *Wall Street Journal* online, 13ᵗʰ December 2009.

15. ibid.

16. ibid.

17. ibid.

18. 'Rich nations have "historic responsibility" for environment: Pope' AFP, 15ᵗʰ December 2009.

19. *Earth Negotiations Bulletin* Vol. 12 No. 459, 22ⁿᵈ December 2009, p. 26.

20. ibid., p. 19.

21. 'Merkel says news from Copenhagen is "not good"' AFP, 17ᵗʰ December 2009.

22. Chris Otton, 'Little hope for last day of UN climate summit' AFP, 17ᵗʰ December 2009.

23. Michael Casey and Seth Borenstein, 'Obama, Wen offer no new emissions cuts at summit' AP, 18ᵗʰ December 2009.

24. Jon Snow interview with author, 27ᵗʰ March 2012.

25. Michael McCarthy, 'China holds the world to ransom' in the *Independent*, 18ᵗʰ December 2009.

26. Hillary Clinton, 'Remarks at the United Nations Framework Convention on Climate Change' 17ᵗʰ December 2009 http://www.state.gov/secretary/rm/2009a/12/133734.htm

27. ibid.

28. Stephen Power, Guy Chazan, Elizabeth Williamson and Jeffrey Bell, 'Showdown at Climate Talks; Obama Jets to Denmark, US Backs $100 billion Annual Aid to Clinch Carbon Deal' in the *Wall Street Journal* online, 18ᵗʰ December 2009.

29. Clinton, 'Remarks at the United Nations Framework Convention on Climate Change'.

30. Gordon Brown, Speech to COP 15, 17th December 2009 http://unfccc2.meta-fusion.com/kongresse/cop15_hls/templ/play.php?id_kongresssession=4155

31. Angela Merkel, Speech to COP 15, 17th December 2009, http://unfccc2.meta-fusion.com/kongresse/cop15_hls/templ/play.php?id_kongresssession=4172

32. Nicolas Sarkozy, Speech to COP 15, 17th December 2009 http://unfccc2.meta-fusion.com/kongresse/cop15_hls/templ/play.php?id_kongresssession=4180

33. Courtney Weaver, 'Greece rating cut deepens banks' gloom' in the *Financial Times*, 9th December 2009.

34. Jonathan Pershing speaking at the Center for Strategic and International Studies, Washington DC, 13th January 2010 http://csis.org/event/post-copenhagen-outlook

35. Jon Snow interview with author.

36. Jonathan Watts, 'Blair tells world to get moving as time runs short for deal' in the *Guardian*, 14th December 2009.

37. Barack Obama, 'Remarks by the President at the Morning Plenary Session of the United Nations Climate Change Conference' 18th December 2009.

38. ibid.

39. ibid.

40. ibid.

41. Manmohan Singh, Speech to the UNFCCC Plenary, Copenhagen, 18th December 2009 http://unfccc2.meta-fusion.com/kongresse/cop15_hls/templ/play.php?id_kongresssession=4277

42. Wen Jiabao, Speech to the UNFCCC Plenary, Copenhagen, 18th December 2009.

43. ibid.

44. Tobias Rapp, Christian Schwägerl and Gerald Traufetter, 'The Copenhagen Protocol: How China and India Sabotaged the UN Climate Summit' Spiegelonline, 5th May 2010.

45. Mark Lynas, 'How do I know China wrecked the Copenhagen deal? I was in the room' in the *Guardian*, 22nd December 2009.

46. This and other quotes from the meeting are taken from the streamed audio or text http://www.spiegel.de/international/world/0,1518,692861,00.html

47. Lynas, 'How do I know China wrecked the Copenhagen deal? I was in the room'.

48. Jim Tankersley, 'Dueling demands await Obama at talks' in the *Los Angeles Times*, 17th December 2009.

49. Dina Cappiello and H. Josef Hebert, 'Analysis: Obama won't break new ground at summit' Associated Press, 16th December 2009.

50. Stephen Collinson, 'Chaos greets new climate pact' AFP, 18th December 2009.

51. ibid.
52. ibid.
53. Charles Babington and Jenifer Loven, 'Obama raced clock, chaos and comedy for climate deal' AP, 19th December 2009.
54. ibid.
55. ibid.

33
AFTERMATH

1. Barack Obama, 'Remarks by the President during press availability in Copenhagen' 18th December 2009.
2. David Espo, 'Obama hails 60th Senate vote for health care' AP, 19th December 2009.
3. ibid.
4. Barack Obama, 'Remarks in St Paul' in the *New York Times*, 3rd June 2008.
5. Stephen Collinson, 'Chaos greets new climate pact' AFP, 19th December 2009.
6. Jon Snow interview with author, 27th March 2012.
7. IISD, *Earth Negotiations Bulletin* Vol.12 No. 459, 22nd December 2009, p. 8.
8. ibid.
9. John Vidal and Jonathan Watts, 'Copenhagen closes with weak deal that poor threaten to reject' guardian.co.uk, 19th December 2009.
10. *Earth Negotiations Bulletin* Vol. 12 No. 459, 22nd December 2009, p. 8 and James Hansen, 'Coal-fired power stations are death factories. Close them' in the *Observer*, 15th February 2009.
11. Richard Ingham, 'After gruelling summit, a contested deal emerges on climate' AFP, 19th December 2009.
12. Vidal and Watts, 'Copenhagen closes with weak deal that poor threaten to reject'.
13. Ban Ki-moon, 'Remarks to the UNFCCC COP-15 closing plenary' 19th December 2009 http://www.un.org/apps/news/infocus/sgspeeches/search_full.asp?statID=686
14. 'Copenhagen climate accord "essential beginning": Ban' AFP, 19th December 2009.
15. UNFCCC, 'Copenhagen Accord' (18th December 2009), para 2.
16. 'Merkel defends Copenhagen climate compromise' AFP, 20th December 2009.
17. 'Europe laments 'lack of ambition' in climate deal' AFP, 19th December 2009.
18. Nicolas Sarkozy, 'Press conference given by Nicolas Sarkozy after the Copenhagen summit' 18th December 2009 http://www.ambafrance-us.org/climate/press-conference-given-by-nicolas-sarkozy-after-the-copenhagen-summi/

19. Ed Miliband, 'The road from Copenhagen' in the *Guardian*, 21st December 2009.

20. 'China hits back at Britain in escalating climate talks row' in the *Guardian*, 21st December 2009.

21. Gordon Brown, 'Transcript of the PM's podcast on Copenhagen' 22nd December 2009 http://www.number10.gov.uk/Page21870

22. Benjamin Sportouch, 'France, China sign aviation, nuclear deals' AFP, 21st December 2009.

23. Benjamin Sportouch, '"Misunderstandings" with China are bygones: French PM' AFP, 21st December 2009.

24. 'China's role in Copenhagen "important and constructive": PM' AFP, 21st December 2009.

25. Simit Bhagat, 'Can't settle for less than Kyoto: PM' in the *Economic Times*, 20th December 2009.

26. John J. Tkacik Jr, 'China's imprints all over Copenhagen talks fiasco' in the *Washington Times*, 14th January 2010.

27. ibid.

28. ibid.

29. 'Opposition flays govt on climate "accord"' in the *Economic Times*, 21st December 2009.

30. Mary Kissel, 'Climate Change "Quagmire"' in the *Wall Street Journal*, 10th March 2010.

31. ibid.

32. Tania Branigan, 'Record snowfall brings Beijing and Seoul to a standstill' guardian.co.uk, 4th January 2010.

33. Tania Branigan, 'Mongolia: How the winter of "white death" devastated nomads' way of life' guardian.co.uk, 20th July 2010.

34. Bill McKibben, 'Washington's snowstorms, brought to you by global warming' in the *Washington Post*, 14th February 2010.

35. Charles Onians, 'Snowfalls are now just a thing of the past' in the *Guardian*, 20th March 2000.

36. Branigan, 'Mongolia: How the winter of "white death" devastated nomads' way of life'.

37. NOAA, 'The Facts About Snowstorms & Climate Change' http://www.noaa.gov/features/02_monitoring/snowstorms.html

38. Martin Williamson, 'Snow stopped play' in *Cricinfo*, 22nd May 2010 http://www.espncricinfo.com/magazine/content/story/462037.html

39. Phil Jones email to Mike Lockwood, 7th May 2009.

40. Sid Maher, 'Business calls for carbon plan rethink' in *The Australian*, 21st December 2009.

41. Kevin Rudd, 6th August 2007 http://www.youtube.com/watch?v=CqZvpRjGtGM

42. Kevin Rudd, 'The PM's address to the Lowy Institute' in *The Australian*, 6th November 2009.

43. Christian Kerr, 'Aussie footprint at 1817 tonnes, and counting' in The Australian, 11th December 2009.

44. John Howard interview with author, 28th November 2011.

45. 'Brazil points finger at US over climate failure' AFP, 21st December 2009.

46. BBC News, 'Canada to withdraw from Kyoto Protocol' 13th December 2011 http://www.bbc.co.uk/news/world-us-canada-16151310

47. PTI, 'BASIC countries slam Canada's withdrawal from Kyoto Protocol' 14th February 2012 http://ibnlive.in.com/generalnewsfeed/news/basic-countries-slam-canadas-withdrawal-from-kyoto-protocol/963616.html

48. 'Copenhagen climate accord "essential beginning": Ban'.

34
REFLECTIONS

1. Herodotus, *The Histories*, Book 1.

2. T. Rees Shapiro, 'Stephen H Schneider, climate expert, dies at sixty-five' in the *Washington Post*, 20th July 2010.

3. Thomas S. Kuhn, *The Structure of Scientific Revolutions* (1996), p. 47.

4. The account of and quotes from Stephen H Schneider's 'Climate Change: Is the Science "Settled"'' have been transcribed from http://www.youtube.com/watch?v=mmlHbt5jja4

5. NCAR, 'Dr Kevin Trenberth, Distinguished Senior Scientist' http://www.cgd.ucar.edu/cas/trenbert.html

6. Kevin Trenberth email to Michael Mann, 12th October 2009.

7. Kevin Trenberth, 'Communicating Climate Science and Thoughts on Climategate' (January 2011), p. 3.

8. Richard S. Lindzen, 'Resisting climate hysteria' in Quadrant Online (26th July 2009) http://www.quadrant.org.au/blogs/doomed-planet/2009/07/resisting-climate-hysteria

9. Martin Rees & Ralph Cicerone, 'What's happening to the climate is unprecedented' in the *Financial Times*, 9th April 2010.

10. Michael Liebreich, Chris Greenwood, Max von Bismarck & Anuradha Gurung, *Green Investing 2010: Policy Mechanisms to Bridge the Financing Gap*, World Economic Forum (January 2010), p. 6.

11. Douglas Martin, 'Stephen H. Schneider, climatologist, is dead at sixty-five' in the *New York Times*, 20th July 2010.

12. Theodore R. Marmor with the assistance of Jan S. Marmor, *The Politics of Medicare* (1970), p. 1.

13. Thomas McKeown, *The Role of Medicine: Dream, Mirage or Nemesis?* (1979), p. xi.

14. ibid., p. 177.

15. ibid.

16. Yohe, G.W., R.D. Lasco, Q.K. Ahmad, N.W. Arnell, S.J. Cohen, C. Hope, A.C. Janetos and R.T. Perez, '2007: Perspectives on climate change and sustainability' in *Climate Change 2007: Impacts, Adaptation and Vulnerability. Contribution of Working Group II to the Fourth Assessment Report of the Intergovernmental Panel on Climate Change*, p. 827.

17. Stephen H. Schneider, 'Stephen Schneider vs Sceptics' goodplanet.org (December 2009) http://www.youtube.com/watch?v=7rj1QcdEqU0

18. Damian Carrington, 'IPCC vice-chair: Attacks on climate science echo tobacco industry tactics' guardian.co.uk, 28th October 2010.

19. Robert May, 'Under-informed, over here' in the *Guardian*, 27th January 2005.

20. David King, 'Sir David King: IPCC runs against the spirit of science' in the *Daily Telegraph*, 6th February 2010.

21. Eric Feldman and Ronald Bayer, *Unfiltered: Conflicts over Tobacco Policy and Public Health* (2004), p. 4.

22. Karl Popper, *Conjectures and Refutations* (2002), p. 73.

23. Conrad Keating, *Smoking Kills: The Revolutionary Life of Richard Doll* (2009), p. ix.

24. ibid., p. 82.

25. ibid., p. 83.

26. ibid., pp. 83–4.

27. ibid., pp. 84–5.

28. ibid., p. 86.

29. ibid., pp. 446–7.

30. Ernst L. Wynder, 'Tobacco and Health: a Review of the History and Suggestions for Public Policy' in *Public Health Reports*, January-February 1988, Vol. 103, No. 1, p. 9.

31. Keating, *Smoking Kills: The Revolutionary Life of Richard Doll* (2009), p. 155.

32. ibid., pp. 93–4.

33. ibid., p. ix.

34. ibid., p. 372.

35. ibid.

36. Kuhn, *The Structure of Scientific Revolutions* (1996), p. 148.

37. Popper, *Conjectures and Refutations* (2002 edition), p. 45.

38. ibid.

39. William D. Nordhaus, 'Why the Global Warming Sceptics Are Wrong' in the *New York Review of Books*, 22nd March 2012.

40. Eric Feldman and Ronald Bayer, *Unfiltered: Conflicts over Tobacco Policy and Public Health* (2004), p. 1.

41. David Henderson, 'Governments and Climate Change Issues: The case for rethinking' in *World Economics*, Vol. 8, No. 2 (2007), pp. 183– 228.

42. Martin Parry letter to WGII authors, co-chairs and vice-chairs, 13th February 2010.
43. 'IPCC scientist dismisses furore over climate change report' in the *Daily Telegraph*, 15th February 2010.
44. Karl Popper, 'Science: Problems, Aims, Responsibilities' in *The Myth of the Framework*, (ed.) M.A. Notturno, (2006), p. 93.
45. P.W. Bridgman, *The Way Things Are* (1959), p. 239.
46. Royal Society, *People and the Planet* (2012), p. 105.
47. ibid., p. 63.

ACKNOWLEDGEMENTS

This book could not have been produced without the help of a large number of people. Global warming is a highly contentious subject and a history must be faithful both to evidence and to context. One sets sail in the knowledge of gales and squalls ahead. For this reason, I am grateful to those who agreed to be interviewed for it, particularly those who might not have been especially sympathetic to my point of view. All are identified in the text, so there is no need to list them again here. To each I provided a draft of wherever I quoted or cited what they had told me and gave them the opportunity to correct or alter it.

Global warming spans many disciplines. Rightly or wrongly, I took the view that while I might not know the right answer, I would know the right questions to ask and, one way or another, track down the right people to answer them. I am indebted to everyone who helped me in this – whether spending time answering my questions, providing leads, sourcing material or critically reviewing early drafts – Mark Banfield, Reinaldo Bellinello, Gordon Binder, Robert Bradley, Ian Byatt, Bob Carter, Jayant Chavda, John Constable, John Emsley, Guy Esnouf, Steve Hayward, Mike Hulme, Evelyne Joslain, William Kininmonth, Jürgen Krönig, Theodore Marmor, Julian Morris, Ross McKitrick, Neil O'Brien, Benny Peiser, Silvia Pondal Rios, Jeremy Rabkin, Bob Reinstein (especially for access to unpublished material), Andrew Riley of the Thatcher Foundation, Richard Ritchie, Ian Rowson, Jane Rundle, David Satterthwaite, Peter Snow, Tim Stone, Donald Sturrock, Max Telford, Michael Tooley, Gerald Traufetter, Andrew Turnbull, Harlan Watson and Nick Wood. Ian Tanner generously proofread the first draft.

Much time researching the book was spent in the library of the LSE, a rare institution retaining the belief in open access to knowledge. Photographs bring history alive. Two are sourced from the LSE, which holds the Kibbo Kift Foundation archives. Duke Blackwood and Steve Branch of the Ronald Reagan Presidential Library, John Keller of the William J. Clinton Presidential Library and Polly Nodine at the Jimmy Carter Library provided the photographs of their respective presidents and Patricia Powell in William Reilly's office provided the ones of him. Bridget Gillies of the University of East Anglia, Philip Coupland, Judge Smith facilitated approval of the inter-war years photos and Catherine Sibut-Pinote of UNCTAD provided those of Guevara and Prebisch.

Crispin Odey gave tremendous support and encouragement. Naim Attallah read an early draft of the first chapter – immediately committing to publishing the book. Without such an endorsement, it would not have been written. The rest of the team at Quartet Books showed similar confidence. In Gavin James Bower, I am fortunate to have had as editor a twice-published novelist, who while always respecting the writer's intent and expression, attended to the needs of the text, the result being a better book, and in Grace Pilkington tirelessly working to raise the book's profile.

I first heard David Henderson when he gave the Reith Lecture in the mid 1980s. When some two decades later I first met him, I was somewhat surprised to have him challenge me as to why I didn't believe in the triple bottom line. I soon learnt that a sense of humour is a prerequisite for the fields he was then interested in, one of which was global warming. The urge to write a book on the subject was sparked by conversations with him and the logic of its historical approach was refined and developed as a result of his criticisms and encouragement. The book profited immensely by drawing liberally from the deep well of his knowledge.

Age seems to confirm the veracity of clichés – and the one about a book being a third person in a marriage turns out to be true. This book has occupied half of my marriage to my wife Alice. Throughout she has always been supportive and tolerant of its excessive demands. To her the book is dedicated as some recompense – with love.

INDEX

DELINQUENCY

The Juvenile Offender in America Today

DELINQUENCY

The Juvenile Offender

in America Today

by Herbert A. Bloch

and Frank T. Flynn

Random House · New York

TO OUR WIVES,

Adeline Supove Bloch

and Elsie Gobel Flynn,

AND OUR CHILDREN

Contents

Part Three | TREATMENT AGENCIES

Part Four | PREVENTION

CHAPTER 17 *The Responsibility of Society* 511

List of Tables

List of Charts and Diagrams

Foreword

THERE IS no royal road to an understanding of the problems of delinquency, its causes and its treatment. Those who expect ready-made answers, simple formulas, and easy clichés may as well prepare themselves for disappointment. Our knowledge of human nature, particularly in its wayward expressions, is still meager and scanty despite notable progress in the fields of psychiatry, psychology, sociology, and social work during the past three decades. The best we can hope for is to put together what information we have and proceed to plan and develop our policies on the basis of the best tested evidence available. But let us not be deluded by false hopes and false illusions, expecting more than our limited knowledge for the present can provide.

It has been stated in another connection that anybody who has ever planted an ear of corn or a row of petunias fancies himself a horticultural expert. By the same token, all those who come into contact with children (and who among us does not?)—whether as parents, teachers, ministers, jurists, or police officials—frequently feel themselves especially qualified to speak with considerable authority on the problems of the waywardness of our youth. But let us exercise here a proper note of caution and restraint, and above all, let us not underestimate the role of the expert. The so-called common sense of the well-intentioned police official and the "good gray judge" is frequently little more than the cumulative bias and restrained cynicism developed over years of frustrating contacts with children who appear difficult, cantankerous, and unchangeable.

Nevertheless, during a period when constant "excursions and alarums" are being raised concerning the presumed rapid demoralization of our youth, it becomes important to exercise perhaps *more* than a reasonable restraint and to use only the tested knowledge that we have for the determination of intelligent public policy. In this field, possibly more than any other, we are exposed to hysterical points of view which all too often have little basis in fact. We have too long been exposed to the rabid outcries of aroused citizens and officials, abetted by a sensational press, which do little more than to distort further a picture which is already widely out of focus. The kaleidoscopic shifting of public attention from one scapegoat to another, whether it be the schools, the home, television or the comic books, may serve as a temporary catharsis for pent-up public feelings but it does not shed much light on the complex and deeply rooted disturbances which actually lie at the base of American delinquency.

The problems of youthful maladjustment and delinquency are largely a reflective phase of certain broad dislocations in the American social structure. In this field, since it concerns our youth, it behooves us, in Matthew Arnold's words, "to see life clearly and *to see it whole.*" As with the variety of other social disturbances that periodically appear on the American scene, we must recognize with Lawrence Frank that society, in effect, and not the individual himself, is the patient. Family life, in its profound effects in fashioning our young, serves as the vehicle through which these wider social tendencies are transmitted.

Despite the difficulties involved in assessing the enormous amount of diversified information, tested and untested hypotheses, truths and half-truths which abound in the field of delinquency investigation, some realistic and rational appraisal must be made if we are ever to move forward. For it is only in this way that a progressive and enlightened public policy in dealing with our wayward youth can be developed. Our public and private agencies dealing with maladjusted youth have a dual responsibility: to educate an impatient public to the subtle complexities of the problems of delinquency, and to establish public practices and goals in close conformity to the best facts we have. In this way, the wastefulness and futility of the perennial panaceas, ranging from excessive dependence upon recreational programs to curfews for minors and punishment for parents, may be placed in realistic focus.

Any public agency which attempts to set a course on the chartless seas of human motivation and the complexities of human misconduct must be intrepid and forward-looking. Yet, such undertakings must be launched. For it is only by attempting to assess in some *positive* fashion the varied discoveries made in research areas impinging upon the field of delinquency that we can hope to develop positive and progressive policies in delinquency treatment, prevention, and control. In this respect, our position is analogous to that of a physician who, though lacking complete certainty of the nature of a patient's illness, will nevertheless proceed to treat the patient on the basis of his best evidence, his best intuitions, and his best judgment.

It is heartening to note how much positive information has already been amassed—information which will afford us firmer ground upon which to launch policies of effective action. There are still many profound disagreements about the precise operation of the causal factors in delinquency, but there is a surprising amount of general agreement about the operation of certain broad causal processes. In this book we have tried to describe these areas of basic agreement, at the same time indicating the numerous dilemmas and unanswered questions with which the field of delinquency research still abounds. Serious consideration has also been paid to the inseminating pioneer researches which are enlarging our horizons and opening up new approaches in the study and treatment of delinquency. Particularly significant, it appears, are the recent disclosures in the typology of delinquency, indicating the correlations between delinquent types and specific socio-cultural and familial conditions, which the reader will find discussed in Chapter Seven and summarized in a coordinated chart in Chapter Eight. Further, since the pressing nature of the delinquency problem does not permit academic evasion, we have attempted to indicate clearly and forthrightly, in the concluding sections, those policies and procedures which are more likely to bring success in the diminution of delinquency.

Considerable care has been exercised in selecting whenever possible only those findings based on acceptable criteria of proof and confirmation. We have deliberately attempted to skirt opinion, regardless of how well-intentioned, unless it was based on evidence conforming to the requirements of recognized research procedures. This may not have been possible in every instance, but we were always mindful of these questions: (1) Did the research finding arise from a sufficient sample? (2) Did it tend to exclude subjective impressions and special biases of the investigator? (3) Was it representative of the individuals whom it attempted to study? (4) Could the results be compared with findings and observations obtained by independent investigators? The extensive, though necessarily selective, bibliography at the end of this volume will give some indication of the scope of the ground covered here. In addition, annotated lists of recommended further readings have been placed at the close of each chapter.

We have been distinctly mindful of that valiant band of men and 'women who have pioneered in this difficult area of human relations, as well as of those who, in the face of a frequently misunderstanding public opinion, are attempting to bring light upon an urgent problem —the innumerable researchers in public and private agencies, jurists, youth workers, institutional administrators, child psychiatrists, probation and social caseworkers. To this often-assailed group, we wish to pay particular tribute. We acknowledge with gratitude the kindness of all who helped in the arduous task of bringing this manuscript to completion. Special appreciation is expressed to Adeline Bloch for her unremitting cheerfulness and her tireless efforts in typing parts of the manuscript and in performing many bibliographical duties; to Susan Del Bloch for her splendid assistance in compiling special bibliographical materials on the meaning, extent, and causes of delinquency; and to Miriam Yudkowsky for her capable typing of a large part of the manuscript and her faithful performance of many other duties.

HERBERT A. BLOCH

FRANK T. FLYNN

Just two days before the galleys for this book were delivered, the shocking news of Frank Flynn's tragic and sudden death was received. To those of us who knew Frank Flynn and revered him as an associate and friend, his brilliant and perceptive mind, his warmth and great human compassion, and his dedicated devotion to the truth as he saw it will always be outstanding. The broad field of human relations in which he labored so strenuously, wisely, and well has lost a dedicated social worker, the impact of whose work will long be felt, a great teacher, and a brilliant social scientist.

Frank Flynn eagerly awaited the publication of this manuscript. The sections he wrote very likely represent the last distillate of his incisive thinking on one of the most pressing problems of our day. A book is never in itself a monument to a great and full life. In a small way nevertheless, this book may perhaps be considered a final landmark in a life replete with devotion to the service and good of others.

H. A. R.

January 29th, 1956.

Part One

THE MEANING
AND SCOPE OF
DELINQUENCY

Chapter 1

WHAT IS DELINQUENCY?*

Few problems on the American scene cause so much concern and widespread public interest as does the problem of youthful misbehavior and delinquency. The very fact of this widespread public concern reflects the rapidly changing character of American life and the confusion such a change betokens in social, moral, and legal standards. The American people have become increasingly restive concerning the problems of their youth, but what the nature of their dissatisfaction is, what has brought it about, what can be done about it, and how much they themselves are responsible for it, are questions the public is not quite so ready to face. The fact is that during a period of widespread social and economic change, particularly in such a complex social order as ours, the necessity of seeking new adjustments to the constant problems of the day becomes overwhelming.

All aspects of the American social structure have been affected by the tumultuous changes of the past half-century, but the emergent problems have become particularly acute in certain critical areas. Two

---

* The footnotes appearing in this and all subsequent chapters are stated, for the convenience of the reader, in abbreviated form. In the bibliographical index at the end of the volume, the complete source of reference material is given. At the end of each chapter, an annotated and descriptive listing of selected bibliographical materials, with complete reference to each source, is also provided.

of the most sensitive of such areas are the American family structure, rudely torn from its firm anchorage in tradition and custom fifty years ago, and the network of personal relationships profoundly rooted in the changing family pattern.

Youth, particularly, has felt this heavy impact. During a period of confusion about moral standards and about the vague, ill-defined limits of personal behavior, our young people are bewildered and at a loss to know what is expected of them, what their functions are, and how far they may go in achieving the poorly defined status of adulthood.[1] This transition from a relatively integrated society, where children "knew their places," and where the authority of the male parent as *pater familias* was generally conceded, has resulted in a profound uprooting of personal relationships which is difficult for the average person to envisage. Instead of the traditional family with its accepted rights and responsibilities, serving to promulgate basic character traits reflected in a myriad of social relationships, we have a variety of weakened "family types." This abandoning of customary prerogatives has created a social vacuum in which a variety of social institutions and agencies are attempting to assume the responsibilities that once were the exclusive concern of the family. If adults are confused about these things, how can one expect more of children?

In this confused setting we must attempt to determine the causal patterns of delinquency. History, if it does nothing more, at least offers assurance that even in some halcyon period of the past, where the definitions of right and wrong were more clearly articulated in a social structure revolving around a common framework of values, youth had its flings, its problems, and its difficulties of adjustment.

The difficulties involved in determining the causes of delinquency originate in the very ambiguous use of the term itself. Delinquency has come to mean all things to all men. It must be made extremely clear at the outset, therefore, that we can make no delineation of cause until we are aware of precisely what delinquency is. Delinquency, as the term is presently used in professional and official literature, may encompass almost any type of deviant youthful behavior.[2] Nor are we

---

[1] See Davis, "The Sociology of Parent-Youth Conflict"; Bloch, *Disorganization*, pp. 137-56.

[2] See Robison, *Can Delinquency Be Measured?*; Schwartz, "Statistics of Juvenile Delinquency in the United States," and Perlman, "The Meaning of Juvenile Delinquency Statistics."

aided by the arbitrary distinction between "adjudicated delinquents," who are those officially handled by the courts, and unofficial delinquents, who are the large number variously and unofficially handled by the courts, police departments, social welfare agencies, and special institutions. Even if we attempt to concentrate, as so often is suggested, wholly upon those officially adjudged delinquent by the courts, the problem of determining causes is hardly simplified. For, as many investigators have shown, it is largely a matter of jurisdictional accident and adventitious community practice whether a child falls into one category or the other.[3]

The Nature of Delinquency

It is important, therefore, to try to define the generic concept of delinquency. The legal definitions of this term are frequently as wide as the willingness of the community and the family to forego their responsibilities in certain areas of child care and rearing. During the past fifty years particularly, there has been a concerted movement to place in the hands of public agencies a number of authoritative functions that have traditionally been the exclusive concern of the family, the church, and the community. Nowhere is this better demonstrated than in the confused notion of delinquency that has developed along with our statutory codes. For example, unlike the criminal statutes defining the specific types of behavior that the community adjudges as criminal, there is little clarity (as will be shown) about the precise nature of the offenses legally considered delinquent. It seems that almost any of the innumerable common varieties of youthful misbehavior may be considered delinquent, depending upon family and social circumstances, community pressures, and the inclination of the court.

The concept of a "child" is a cultural definition, varying from society to society and from age to age. Although most states do not indicate the minimum age at which a young person shall be considered

---

[3] Robison, *Can Delinquency Be Measured?*, Ch. 1-3; Tappan, *Juvenile Delinquency*, pp. 3-30; Tappan, *Comparative Survey on Juvenile Delinquency*, pp. 1-8; Neumeyer, *Juvenile Delinquency in Modern Society*, pp. 16-18; Teeters and Reinemann, *The Challenge of Delinquency*, pp. 15-19; *Report of Sub-Committee on Prevention and Treatment of Juvenile Delinquency*, 1946; and Bloch, *Disorganization*, pp. 162-5.

a juvenile, it has become customary in most jurisdictions, and stipulated by statute in others, to consider seven years as the lower limit for juvenile court handling. This is an outgrowth of the common law conception in which a child below this age is held incapable of responsible intent in the commission of a felony. The upper age limits are extremely variable and are further confused by numerous differences in the statutory handling of age groups on the basis of sex differences and other considerations. Many states, for example, provide a higher age limit for girls than for boys. In addition, many municipalities have set down a broader definition of "juvenile" than the state courts. Further, there are special statutes (as in New York State) which, while not specifically labeled as juvenile delinquency measures, permit similar handling for groups between sixteen and twenty-one. (These special statutes will be discussed in some of the later chapters dealing with the juvenile courts.)

At the present time most of our jurisdictions (twenty-seven states, Alaska, Hawaii, and the District of Columbia) have established eighteen years as the upper age limit for legal consideration as a juvenile; six states (Delaware, Louisiana, Maine, Massachusetts, Missouri, and Kentucky) with some variations hold a person to be a juvenile up to the age of seventeen; and nine other jurisdictions (Connecticut, Georgia, Maryland, New York, North Carolina, Utah, Vermont, Puerto Rico, and the Virgin Islands) consider a person an adult when he is sixteen or older.[4] The federal government, in its own statutes, has set eighteen as the upper age limit for the handling of juveniles. This was the limit the National Probation and Parole Association decided upon in the model statute it recommended, the Standard Juvenile Act.[5]

Within this complicated maze of differential definition, varying treatment, and administrative differences, nothing is more confusing than the frequently contradictory statements of the experts themselves about what constitutes delinquency. Paradoxically, not only do legal authorities and other so-called experts disagree over the definition of delinquent behavior, but they have serious differences as to where delinquency under law begins and where it should end. The unprecedented growth of our society and the mobility of our population during the

---

[4] Rubin, "The Legal Character of Juvenile Delinquency," gives a comprehensive listing of these statutory variations.
[5] Rubin, "State Juvenile Court—A New Standard."

past half-century have resulted in a confusion of social standards. We have no clear definition of delinquency such as the British common law possesses: it regards delinquency simply as any act that, if committed by an adult, would be considered criminal.

There is a strong contrast between this clear, workable definition and the great variety of American statutory definitions, some of which we shall now briefly consider.

Variations in Statutory Definition and Administrative Practice: A "Legalistic Wilderness"

Despite the belief, still persisting among many citizens, that a juvenile delinquent is a child who has violated a criminal statute, the average legal coverage of the term includes a variety of such purely moral judgments as "willful disobedience" and "incorrigibility." In its broad designation, delinquency is *not* "junior crime." In certain areas, such as California and the District of Columbia, a substantive definition of delinquency is not even employed. This means, in effect, that where the community or the family find themselves unequal to the task of adequately supervising the child's behavior, the courts may step in. Under such circumstances, no "crime," in the usual sense, is committed.

When we refer to a *substantive* legal code—something conspicuously lacking in the juvenile court codes of this country—we are referring to carefully defined circumstances and situations in which the individual's *overt* act and his *culpable* intentions are jointly considered as evidences of lawbreaking. Except in a very limited degree, nothing of this sort occurs in our legal considerations of delinquent acts, either by juvenile court definition or by legally defined procedures for establishing guilt or innocence.

The New York code is rather typical. It begins with a straightforward recognition of the delinquent act as a form of criminal activity which may under certain circumstances be determined, if the court so chooses, by ordinary legal process. It states that a delinquent is a child "who violates any law or any municipal ordinance or who commits any act which, if committed by an adult, would be a serious crime, except any child fifteen years of age who commits any act which, if committed by an adult, would be a crime punishable by death or life sentence, unless an order removing the action to the children's court has been made and filed." [6] In addition, however, the New York statute includes children who are "incorrigible, ungovernable, or habitually disobedient," those who are "habitually truant," who desert their homes or places of abode without consent of parents or guardians, who associate "with immoral or vicious persons," frequent places "the existence of which is a violation of the law," habitually use obscene language, solicit alms in public places, or who so deport themselves as willfully to injure or endanger the morals or health of themselves or others.[7]

Our courts have upon occasion gone to ridiculous extremes in dealing with the wide varieties of youthful disorder we label as delinquent. According to Henry W. Thurston, a boy was sent to a reform school by a Chicago court at the turn of the century because he had, according to the court's charges, "burglariously, feloniously, and maliciously broken into his stepmother's pantry and had stolen a jar of jam." [8]

The New York State usage is fairly typical of the kind of coverage found in most other jurisdictions. In a survey of the wide range of circumstances covered by our courts in the handling of juvenile offenders, the Federal Children's Bureau lists no less than thirty-four separate conditions, the vast majority of which are forms of behavior which commonly typify normal adolescent protests against parental and adult authority.[9] How can we possibly classify under a common heading, in an attempt toward scientific and logical understanding, such activities as smoking cigarettes, patronizing a public poolroom, falling beyond the control of a parent or guardian, or engaging in sexual irregularities—just to mention a few? In view of the often capricious nature of the circumstances which bring many of these children before our courts and under which they find themselves charged, how can we adequately classify some children as delinquent and others as not? How does this type of behavior differ fundamentally from the normal behavior of the little-inhibited and nonneurotic child?

It is small wonder that the National Probation Association, recognizing this legal wilderness, has in virtual desperation declared that, since delinquency lacks substantive legal meaning, a delinquent child

---

[6] *New York State Penal Code*, Sec. 312-c, Subsec. c; and Sec. 312-f, Subsecs. a and b.

[7] *New York State Children's Court Act*, Article I, Sec. 2, Subsec. 2.

[8] Thurston, *Concerning Juvenile Delinquency*, p. 69.

[9] *Social Statistics*, 1945, p. 11.

might be adjudged to be any child over whom a children's court may exercise jurisdiction. This is reminiscent of the plight in which the clinical psychologists found themselves a few years ago, when they attempted to formulate an adequate definition of intelligence, based upon standard measuring instruments. In view of the wide variety of factors entering into the final intelligence-quotient score, certain psychologists tried to resolve their dilemma by defining intelligence as "that which the intelligence test tests"! By the same token, under our existing legal codes, any child becomes a delinquent who the courts decide may become a delinquent. This is a kind of circular reasoning, or meaningless logic, which is of little help in clarifying the problem.

A rose by any other name smells as sweet: almost any normal child under the exigency of certain critical circumstances might be thought of as a delinquent. Thus, in keeping with the tenuous limits of modern casework practice, a delinquent may be any child "whose occupation, behavior, environment, or associations are injurious to his welfare; who deserts his home or who is habitually disobedient or beyond the control of his parent or other custodian; who, being required by law to attend a school, willfully violates rules thereof or absents himself therefrom; or who violates any state law or municipal ordinance." [10] Where do we move in such a legal labyrinth, and how do we determine causes for such a multifarious set of conditions? To this confused state of affairs, Paul W. Tappan aptly applies the term "legal nihilism," and it becomes understandable that the National Probation Association recommends that the definition of delinquency be deleted from our juvenile court statutes.[11]

When delinquency is as loosely and broadly defined as has become customary and typical, there may be an inherent danger for the very children the laws are designed to protect. For the very act of exposing a child to the legal procedures of the court, irrespective of how altruistic and well-intentioned such procedures may be, may constitute a critical hazard and shattering experience in his life. Recognizing the accidental way in which a child may achieve delinquency status, we may feel justifiable concern over the part the children's courts themselves sometimes play in intensifying the very conditions of delinquency

[10] *Standard Juvenile Court Act*, p. 10.
[11] Tappan, *Comparative Survey on Juvenile Delinquency*, p. 3.

which they are attempting to ameliorate. For despite the fact that the courts are designed to protect the child's reputation and potential career, the bringing of a child to court does constitute a stigma, and often creates tensions in the child's life which produce further delinquency. This danger has already been clearly perceived by certain courts, one of which has stated (with considerable courage): "The judgment against a youth that he is delinquent is a serious reflection upon his character and habits. The stain against him is not removed merely because the statute says no judgment in this particular proceeding shall be deemed a conviction for crime or so considered. The stigma of conviction will reflect upon him for life. It hurts his self-respect. It may, at some inopportune, unfortunate moment, rise to destroy his opportunity for advancement and blast his ambition to build up a character and reputation entitling him to the esteem and respect of his fellow men." [12]

In modern times, in the face of the disastrous breakdown of customary controls over the child, our public authorities have been increasingly forced to assume functions of guardianship. Our courts have tended to reinforce their traditional right of *parens patriae*, or guardianship over minors, derived from the ancient chancery functions of the common-law courts. The length to which we have gone in establishing broad parental controls by the courts is cogently expressed in the following opinion: The law "is not for the punishment of offenders, but for the salvation of children, and points out the way by which the state undertakes to save, not particularly children of a special class, but all children under a certain age, whose salvation may become the duty of the state in the absence of proper parental care or disregard of it by wayward children. No child under the age of 16 years is excluded from its beneficent provisions. Its protecting arm is for all who have not attained to that age and who may need its protection." [13]

However laudable the intent of such a legal expression may be, it makes a legal definition of delinquency, for the purpose of studying causal processes, virtually untenable and worthless. At the same time, it should make it quite clear that a study of the causes of delinquency on the basis of officially handled court cases is of little value unless we take into account at the same time a wide variety of youthful misbe-

[12] *Jones et al.* vs. *Commonwealth*, 185 Va. 335, 38 S.E. 2nd 444, 1946.
[13] *Commonwealth* vs. *Fisher*, 213 Pa. 48, 62 Atl. 198, 1905.

haviors, the vast majority of which never find their way into our crowded courts, yet actually compose the bulk of this problem.

Delinquency and the Normal Behavior of Youth

In its generic meaning, delinquency may now be seen to include the following types of youthful deviants: (1) officially adjudicated delinquents, or those for whom the courts have made some official disposition; (2) unofficial delinquents, or those handled informally by the courts or some designated agency; (3) cases handled by the police, one of its bureaus, or some other law-enforcement agency; (4) children with special behavior problems or those giving evidence of antisocial practices, and treated by social welfare, casework, or other unofficial or nonpunitive agency; and (5) children presenting evidence of behavior problems or antisocial conduct, whether or not they are brought before official or unofficial agencies for handling and treatment.

In this spectrum of varying behavior, it should be recognized that a great many youths, although giving evidence of being guilty of much the same type of behavior which brings other children to the attention of the courts or some unofficial agency, are never detected and engage in activities which by generally accepted definition might properly make them fit subjects for treatment and handling as delinquents. In response to a questionnaire given to 340 college juniors and seniors during the period from 1943 to 1948, approximately 91 percent admitted that they had knowingly committed offenses against the law, both misdemeanors and felonies. This is particularly significant since the groups sampled came from considerably better-than-average middle-class homes. Women students were as glaringly delinquent in this respect as men, although the volume of major offenses which they admitted to was somewhat smaller than that for men. And in an extension of the study, which sampled groups of successful professional men and women, including a relatively high proportion of physicians and lawyers, it was found that percentages as great and even greater admitted to having committed in their youth the entire gamut of run-of-the-mill delinquencies, as well as more serious offenses.[14]

Professor Porterfield of the University of Texas gives even more striking confirmation of the prevalence of antisocial and illegal behavior

[14] Bloch, *Disorganization*, p. 260.

TABLE A: Offenses of College Students and Juvenile Delinquents*

	PERCENTAGE OF STUDENTS						PERCENTAGE OF JUVENILE COURT CASES CHARGED WITH THE OFFENSE	
	REPORTING THE OFFENSE			CHARGED WITH THE OFFENSE				
	PRE-COLLEGE		COLLEGE MEN	PRE-COLLEGE		COLLEGE MEN		
OFFENSES BY TYPES	MEN	WOMEN		MEN	WOMEN		BOYS	GIRLS
Vagabondage:								
Suspicious character	0.0	0.0	0.0	0.0	0.0	0.0	9.0	4.9
Vagrancy	4.0	0.0	4.0	0.0	0.0	0.0	0.3	0.0
Begging	5.5	0.0	3.0	0.0	0.0	0.0	0.5	0.0
Peddling, no license	5.5	0.0	5.0	0.0	0.0	0.0	0.2	0.0
Runaway, wandering	14.5	4.3	2.0	0.0	0.0	0.0	42.0	31.5
Stranded transiency	14.5	0.0	12.0	0.0	0.0	0.0	†	†
Truancy	42.5	34.3	28.0	0.0	0.0	0.0	1.0	1.1
Loafing in a pool hall	48.0	46.0	0.0	0.0	0.0	0.0	0.3	0.0
Percentage charged in court: Total:	....	....	....	0.0	0.0	0.0	53.3	37.5
Liquor violations:								
Illegal manufacture	8.0	0.0	0.0	0.0	0.0	0.0	0.2	0.0
Illegal possession	35.5	2.9	47.0	0.0	0.0	0.0	0.1	0.0
Buying as a minor	38.0	2.2	53.0	0.0	0.0	0.0	0.1	0.0
Drunkenness	39.0	2.9	43.0	0.5	0.0	0.0	0.8	1.1
Percentage charged in court: Total:	....	....	....	0.5	0.0	0.0	1.2	1.1
Theft:								
Automobile theft	0.5	0.0	0.0	0.0	0.0	0.0	0.9	0.5‡
Bicycle theft	0.5	0.0	0.0	0.0	0.0	0.0	2.5	0.0
Theft of tools, money	5.5	0.0	1.0	0.0	0.0	0.0	3.8	0.0
Burglary	7.5	0.0	4.0	0.0	0.0	0.0	7.0	0.0
Shoplifting	10.0	1.5	5.0	0.0	0.0	0.0	10.0	11.4
Miscellaneous, petty	23.0	8.8	11.0	0.0	0.0	0.0	2.7	4.1
Stealing melons, fruit	69.0	16.0	15.0	0.0	0.0	0.0	0.3	0.0
Percentage charged in court: Total:	....	....	....	0.0	0.0	0.0	27.2	16.0

Dishonesty (other than stealing):							
Forgery	2.5	5.1	1.0	0.0	0.0	0.2	1.6
False collection	8.0	2.2	10.0	0.0	0.0	0.2	0.0
Possessing stolen goods	20.0	3.6	14.0	0.0	0.0	1.4	0.0
Passing slugs, bad coins	24.0	0.0	14.0	0.0	0.0	0.1	0.0
Gambling	58.5	17.4	60.0	0.0	0.0	0.7	0.0
Percentage charged in court: Total:	....	....	....	0.0	0.0	2.6	1.6
Sex offenses:							
Attempt to rape	5.5	0.0	3.0	0.0	0.0	0.1	0.0
Indecent exposure	24.5	2.2	23.0	0.0	0.0	0.1	0.0
Extramarital coitus	58.5	0.7	59.0	0.0	0.0	0.5	11.4
Percentage charged in court: Total:	....	....	....	0.0	0.0	0.7	11.4
Other cases:							
Carrying concealed weapons	14.0	0.0	0.0	0.0	0.0	0.2	0.0
Homicide, murder	0.5	0.0	0.0	0.0	0.0	0.2	0.5§
Homicide, negligent	0.5	0.0	0.0	0.5	0.0	0.1	0.0
Incorrigible	0.0	0.0	0.0	0.0	0.0	1.4	10.3
Neglected, abused, etc.	0.0	0.0	0.0	0.0	0.0	0.1	12.0
Miscellaneous appearance in court				2.0	4.0	0.0	2.1
Percentage charged in court: Total:	....	....	....	2.5	4.0	2.0	24.9

* Porterfield, *Youth in Trouble*, p. 41. † See "runaway." ‡ As accomplice. § Self-defense.

among middle-class youths who are hardly ever apprehended on delinquent charges, either officially or unofficially. Considering the results of a preliminary study of over two thousand delinquents in the area of Fort Worth, Texas, he found that the offenses for which the delinquents were charged could be broken down into fifty-five categories, ranging from relatively trivial offenses of disturbing the peace to such serious charges as murder. Employing these categorical charges as a checksheet for 437 college students, both men and women, he found that all of them admitted to having committed one or more of the offenses listed.[15] It is worth noting that the number of offenses reported by these presumably economically and socially privileged young people yielded an average in excess of eleven offenses per youth, based upon the dubious factors of recollection and memory. An examination of the following chart gives a detailed breakdown of the character of these offenses. If the same offenses had been committed by the less fortunate contemporaries of these young people, the cases might very well have ended in the courts.

Whether a child becomes a delinquent or not will frequently depend upon the general attitudes of the community toward children and families with certain behavior problems, upon the character of the social agencies in the community, and, more specifically, upon the community's policies of referral for such children. Evidence of this has been seen by the United States Children's Bureau, in the findings of a study made to determine the extent of delinquency within the District of Columbia. Using as a composite index all cases handled in the courts and registered by all public agencies within the federal district, investigators found that whereas certain offenses, such as traffic violations, stealing, assaults, and acts of carelessness, were most frequently referred to the courts (to the extent of 99 percent in the case of traffic violations), large proportions of other characteristic juvenile offenses were handled by non-judicial agencies.[16] In fact, such commonplace offenses as truancy and running away rarely appeared in the courts, but were handled primarily by other public agencies. Furthermore, these findings do not include those children handled by the several private agencies, or by families themselves, interested friends, or neighbors.

[15] Porterfield, *Youth in Trouble*, pp. 38ff.
[16] Deardorff, "Central Registration of Delinquents."

So much depends upon varying community standards and policies that the problems of the adjudicated delinquent, the nonadjudicated delinquent, the neglected child, and the emotionally disturbed and "behavior problem" child are continually and widely overlapping. In many cases, the community reacts only if the child's behavior appears unusually dramatic or extremely bizarre—or, as is more likely, appears to be overwhelmingly dangerous to community standards, the child's interests, or the safety of others. But this is invariably a *relative* matter of community practice and standards. As the psychiatrist Marynia F. Farnham puts it in her study of adolescence, "Things have to get a great deal worse before anyone will broadcast an alarm. . . . No one is delinquent who merely cheats on his income tax or examination (unless caught), but anyone who steals an automobile or who holds up a bar or shoots his little brother is unquestionably so. So also is any girl who has an illegitimate child or has a career of sexual promiscuity even though she avoids pregnancy. So, too, are the chronic truants and the pilferers as well as the unmanageable and incorrigible youngsters who rebel against the intolerable homes in which every fundamental of human decency is violated. These are the problems that are recognized and cause consternation." [17]

If, however, these glaring affronts to social standards and convention are to be considered delinquency, how about the child who appears to be an incipient delinquent? Where do we place him? At what obscure point do ordinary youthful exuberance and excess of high spirits become the basis for a chronically dangerous delinquent pattern? "Is the precocious and adventurous child who has run away from home once, or several times, a delinquent? Is the one who reacts rebelliously in a home pervaded by an atmosphere of incessant hostility a delinquent? Is a daughter 'in bobby sox' who stays out later than her mother used to, who seems 'a little wild,' and causes her fearful family much anxiety, a delinquent? Is the boy who expresses a desire, thoroughly normal in a healthy maturing preadolescent, to emancipate himself emotionally and socially from his family and who behaves in a very independent fashion a delinquent? Is the youth who refuses to turn over his entire wage to his family? Is the girl who has become pregnant through ignorance, seduction, or curiosity?" [18]

[17] Farnham, *The Adolescent*, p. 147.
[18] Tappan, *Juvenile Delinquency*, p. 21.

It is clear that in order to comprehend the condition vaguely defined as delinquency, one must understand the so-called "behavior problem" child and the pre-delinquent, as well as the delinquent. Since we thus recognize that delinquency is merely one of a wide variety of youthful maladjustments, it is also apparent to us that a child's becoming a delinquent is largely determined by court standards and community practice. And since we are basically concerned with the *motivations* that cause children to protest and react against standards that the community and the family attempt to enforce, we must recognize that *common motivations may lead to a variety of outcomes for different children.* For example, a child whose deeply disturbed emotional state manifests itself in chronic physical assaults may be taken by its distressed middle-class parents to a child psychiatrist or, possibly, to a boarding school. The same emotional state in a slum child may result in his being brought summarily to the children's court. While the first child scarcely ever figures as a statistic in our compilation of data on delinquency, the second child may account for a prominent part of such data.

To quote another, and perhaps more common, example: A series of youthful flings by a group of high-school youths from comfortable economic circumstances may produce vigorous restraints through a voluntarily organized parents' council, while among underprivileged teen-age children such behavior becomes, as a matter of course, a problem for court action—and not infrequently, it should be added, becomes the subject matter of some sociologist's study of the "demoralizing" influence of the boys' gang upon delinquent behavior.

Since families that lose control of their children, or that lack resources for their care, or that are relatively indifferent about their upbringing, are apt to be found in communities which are themselves disorganized, it is reasonable to expect large numbers of officially adjudicated delinquents in certain families and certain communities. But the motivations which produce delinquency exist, in a sense, everywhere within American society. Consequently, if we are to analyze the causes of delinquency, we must look for motivations that cause children to become chronically maladjusted to conventional situations in the home, the streets, play-groups, and the school—situations in which we may reasonably expect them to conform to generally accepted standards of behavior.

Thus, in approaching the causes of delinquency, we must always reckon with the factors of *motivation, environmental opportunity,* and *community attitude.* Of these, *environmental opportunity* and *community attitude* are—in the words of the research scientist—the *dependent* variables, the results of the accidental presence of certain conditions. Motivation is the *independent* variable, the primary focus from which a variety of human behaviors may come.

In acknowledging that *motivation* is the basic problem, we must recognize that the motivation underlying the wide variety of youthful misbehavior encompassed by delinquency will include a gamut of children's disorders, ranging from the situation-caused protests of normal children (the "situational delinquents") to the deeply disturbed pathological cases.

For Further Reading

DAVIS, KINGSLEY, "The Sociology of Parent-Youth Conflict," in *American Sociological Review,* V (August 1940), pp. 523-35.

A comprehensive analysis of the focal points of tension in the American social structure that produce problems between parents and children.

ROBISON, SOPHIA M., *Can Delinquency Be Measured?* (New York, 1936).

A well-known, standard volume, describing the difficulty in arriving at a composite and uniform index for the measurement of delinquency.

SCHWARTZ, EDWARD E., "Statistics of Juvenile Delinquency in the U.S.," in *The Annals of the American Academy of Political and Social Science,* 261 (January 1949), pp. 9-20.

A searching investigation of the contradictory and conflicting sources of statistical information concerning delinquency in the United States.

TAPPAN, PAUL W., *Comparative Survey on Juvenile Delinquency, Part I: North America* (United Nations, Division of Social Welfare, New York, 1952).

An informative and comparative summary of the scope of delinquency in North America by a foremost legal and sociological authority in the field of delinquency.

National Probation and Parole Association, *A Standard Juvenile Court Act* (Revised Edition, New York, 1949).

A recommended uniform juvenile court act for the several states, based upon a comparative survey of state legislation and the emerging socio-legal conceptions concerning delinquency and its treatment.

PORTERFIELD, AUSTIN L., *Youth in Trouble* (Leo Potishman Foundation, Texas, 1946).

A statistical and descriptive analysis of the variety of maladjustments characteristic of contemporary youth on various socio-economic and cultural levels.

DEARDORFF, NEVA, "Central Registration of Delinquents," in *Probation,* 13 (June 1945), pp. 141-7.

A description of an attempt in an urban community to coördinate the registration of delinquents and illustrating the selective process whereby delinquencies are recorded in the average community.

Chapter 2

WHO ARE OUR DELINQUENTS?

Caveat: The Duplicity of Statistics

It is obvious, on the basis of what we have seen so far, that the ambiguous ways in which delinquency is defined and handled make it extremely difficult to measure and to categorize. Yet, it is of the utmost importance that we gain some conception of its dimensions as a problem and a critical understanding of the types of children and age groups involved. The questions "how much," "who," and "when" become indispensable to any adequate study of delinquency and its problems.

Nevertheless, it is well known that statistical data in the fields of crime and delinquency are notoriously unreliable and inadequate.[1] Thorsten Sellin, one of our most penetrating students of criminal statistics, has long pointed out the inadequacy of much of our criminal data, in that they fail to indicate clearly the kinds of discrepancies that exist and the serious shortcomings that must be overcome if we are ever to gain a reliable insight into the dimensions and scope of delinquency and criminal problems. As far back as 1931, the famous National Commission on Law Observance and Enforcement, better known as the Wickersham Commission, issued a solemn warning con-

---

[1] See Sellin, "The Uniform Criminal Statistics Act."

cerning the unreliability of our data in this field and their uncritical use and acceptance by the general public and the experts alike. In stressing the scrupulous care that must be exercised in both using and interpreting such data, the Commission wisely observed: "The eagerness with which the unsystematic, often inaccurate, and more often incomplete statistics available for this country are taken up by text writers, writers in the periodicals, newspaper writers, and public speakers, speaks for itself. . . . Actual data are the beginning of wisdom in such a subject, and no such data can be had for the country as a whole." [2]

Although some improvement has been made since this warning was issued, we must remain cautious in interpreting the data official and unofficial agencies give us, particularly in determining whether delinquency is increasing or decreasing and in what specific respects. Aside from the incomplete coverage that most of our official statistics provide, variations in the criteria as to whom to classify and in the kinds of statistical classifications employed create considerable confusion in attempts to set up *comparable* rates for urban-rural districts and for different sections of the country, as well as in the determination of trends for the country as a whole. Further, because of the public's sensational interest in delinquency and its problems and the tendency of the popular press to play up news items in this area, such questions as the size of the delinquency problem, its scope, and the groups affected all too frequently provide a Roman holiday for partisan political exploitation and for the public's appetite for the sensational.

The layman is hardly ever aware of the subtleties involved in statistical nuances. Only the trained statistician and the statistically sophisticated specialist recognize how easily the public can be duped by the mere change of a specific category. For example, as the criminologist Sutherland has shown, within the last two decades overcrowded conditions in Massachusetts penal institutions ordinarily housing major felons caused the legislature to change certain classifications of felonies to minor disorders and misdemeanors so that offenders in these categories could be remanded to other forms of custody. Here, though there was no actual change in the frequency of criminal behavior, the resulting statistical tabulation could have seemed to

[2] "Report on Criminal Statistics."

indicate a decrease in a serious form of criminal disorder. Comparable modifications of categories and statistical tabulations in the field of delinquency create one of the many pitfalls into which the understanding of the unwary public and its officialdom may fall. Frequently, therefore, an increase or decrease in a problem, created by the mere change of a statistical tabulation and classification, may appear to have occurred, when fundamentally there has been no substantial alteration.

The Sources of Juvenile Statistical Data: Their Questionable Accuracy

The sources, official and unofficial, from which we derive our information concerning delinquency themselves indicate the serious limitations under which we operate in attempting to determine a valid index of the character and volume of delinquency. Despite efforts since 1930 by the Federal Bureau of Investigation to develop a uniform system of crime reporting, we have no compulsory provision for reporting such data from the several states and local jurisdictions. Further, even the public agencies and authorities that *voluntarily* submit such information provide little assurance that their figures and classifications are reliably reported, despite the praiseworthy statistical safeguards set up by the F.B.I.

In all official reports issued by federal agencies about crime and delinquency, the data are overwhelmingly weighted in favor of the urban areas. Furthermore, since there are everywhere understandable precautions to safeguard young children from the burden of a police and court record, information concerning the actual incidence of delinquency frequently never reaches the official tabulating agency. Intake policies of juvenile courts commonly refer very young children or those with special behavioral difficulties to private agencies, with the result that jurisdictional areas differ in the character and volume of delinquency they report. Despite heartening improvements in the quality and accuracy of our information in the last ten years, the Federal Children's Bureau's latest report on juvenile court data specifically states that the information released is seriously handicapped by the following considerations: (1) communities vary widely in the organizational patterns of their childhood welfare services, thus limiting the type of data submitted, and (2) there are similar discrepancies in court policies as to the ages of children and types of cases handled.[3] Indeed, as the report warns, *there may be changes in policy concerning the reporting of age and type classifications for the same court during the same period for which data are ordinarily released to the Children's Bureau.* Since these reports by the Children's Bureau probably represent the best available official source of information, we can see how difficult it is to arrive at anything resembling a precise national measurement of delinquency and its manifestations.

The data ordinarily employed for determining the scope and nature of delinquency from year to year are obtained from both public and private sources. Not only are official reports unquestionably the most reliable sources of information, but they also provide some fairly reliable standards for comparing annual rates and for ascertaining the periodic rise or fall of delinquency. The Federal Children's Bureau began compiling these data in 1923 on a voluntary basis and in 1927 reorganized its reporting procedure by standardizing the form of the report sent in by local juvenile court jurisdictions. This resulted in the issuance of periodic summaries of juvenile court data in the supplement, *Social Statistics,* to the regular Children's Bureau publication, *The Child.* But—and this clearly indicates the statistical deficiency of these reports—at no time in the entire history of their existence did they cover more than 37 percent of the total child population, the maximum occurring in the last year (1945) of the publication of the series. In fact, when the series began in 1927, reports covered only 15 percent of the total child population.

But even with the improved method of reporting used in the successor to this earlier series, the latest report (1954) supplies data for only 586 courts in twenty-nine states, *covering only 29 percent of the entire child population.* It is significant to note that in this latest report such highly industrialized states as New York and Massachusetts are not represented. Obviously, such serious omissions of states that ordinarily have high rates of delinquency render much more difficult the task of arriving at a precise estimate of the extent and changes in volume of delinquency for the country as a whole. Further, the evaluation of comparative data for the various industrial sections of the

[3] *Juvenile Court Statistics, 1950-52.*

country and of rural-urban differences becomes even more hazardous.

In 1946 the Children's Bureau began a special effort to simplify and coördinate the reporting of juvenile court data, by relying for its information on a central agency in each state instead of attempting to obtain it from each of the local courts. The current series of reports, known as *Juvenile Court Statistics*, includes data on dependency and neglect as well as delinquency. The information for these reports is received from state departments of social welfare, responsible in most states for supervision of the states' delinquent charges, or from the central agency of the state's juvenile court system if such an official body exists. Much still remains to be done to develop an adequate and satisfactory reporting system. Even if every state could be prevailed upon to report its data regularly, the problem of how to obtain *complete* and *comparable* information from each area would still remain because of varying standards and jurisdictional procedures and because of the difficulty of obtaining the records of children handled by private agencies and unofficial resources.

As an illustration of existing discrepancies between officially reported delinquency and the large number of known delinquencies that are handled by private resources (ranging from family-arranged care to specially designated unofficial agencies), the experience in central registration of the District of Columbia Council of Social Agencies is particularly noteworthy. In 1943-44, the Federal Children's Bureau, in conjunction with the Council of Social Agencies of the District of Columbia, attempted an experiment in which the six public agencies of the district dealing with children's problems were requested to report to a central registry bureau each case handled. The significant fact disclosed by this accounting was that *less than half of the children known to be delinquent during that year were actually known to the juvenile court of the district.* This condition is typical of virtually all urban areas. In fact, with the wider range and greater number of the service agencies in our modern industrial areas, it is probable that the percentage of delinquency known to the courts in any large urban industrial area is considerably less than half. As a further commentary on the limited adequacy of even fairly satisfactory official data, the District of Columbia study revealed that a large number of delinquent children were handled by the police without any court referral and that many court cases were completely unknown to the police.[4] A similar experiment was undertaken in New York City between March 1, 1950, and March 1, 1951, with similar results. The total of 37,515 children registered as "delinquents" for that year—29,042 boys and 8,473 girls— was considerably in excess of the number that might have been anticipated that year on the basis of the regularly compiled court data of the area.

In addition to the Children's Bureau data, the Federal Bureau of Investigation has attempted to compile uniform crime data for all persons arrested and issues this information semi-annually in a publication, *Uniform Crime Reports for the United States*. Of the two types of information requested by the Federal Bureau—a broad summary report form on significant police activity and the so-called fingerprint arrest record—the latter is far more valuable as an index of crime and delinquency. The difficulties here, however, are that public policy varies as to the use of the fingerprint arrest record, particularly with young children. Moreover, the offenses recorded in this way are limited to municipal and state offenses, and do not reveal a wide variety of federal violations and institutional commitments. What is significant, however, is the close correspondence of the fingerprint arrest records of youths under twenty-one and the data on delinquency compiled by the Children's Bureau. Even though these sets of figures do not coincide, they tend to follow similar trend lines, affording us some corroboration of the overall increases and decreases in delinquency on a national level.

In addition to these prominent and most widely used official sources, we have periodic data compiled by the Bureau of the Census and the federal Department of Justice on institutional inmates, as well as a variety of reports issued by the state governments on institutional inmates and adjudication data for different types of courts. The probation departments of several of our juvenile courts also issue periodic reports, frequently quite adequate for local coverage but with very little comparative data for separate jurisdictions, the various states, and the country as a whole. In addition, there is a plethora of annual reports by private children's agencies on institutional or service care,

[4] Schwartz, "A Community Experiment in the Measurement of Juvenile Delinquency."

which provide little usable evidence for a long-range examination of the changing volume of delinquency locally, within the state, or nationally.

Nevertheless, despite these shortcomings, some estimates can be made of the volume of delinquency and, if proper precautions are exercised, some evaluation of the crucial problem of whether delinquency is rising or falling. But despite the formal classification of offenses the various public and private reports cover, they give us very little evidence concerning the changing *character* of delinquency. That is, we may be able to derive from them some sort of picture of rise or fall, but very little insight can be obtained into the kinds of children involved or their changing social and psychological backgrounds. For this information, we have to depend entirely on the significant researches of specialized investigators who, at best, can only deal with specific phases of the problem, limited samples, and delimited sections of urban or rural areas. Here, our best information comes from the work of scholars in the colleges and universities, or from investigators carrying on special research for foundations and the courts. The Federal Children's Bureau as well as many of our state agencies and commissions, which should be taking the lead in obtaining this information, have been woefully remiss. Only within the past five years has the Federal Children's Bureau recognized the need for going after this specialized information.

To summarize briefly, then, our difficulties in obtaining a precise index of the volume and changing rates of delinquency arise from: (1) our lack of uniform reporting and the absence of compulsory registration of delinquent offenses; (2) variations in court practice in the classification and handling of delinquents; (3) variations in community practice in the referral of delinquent and behavior-problem children; (4) institutional differences in the receiving of children for care, and their methods of reporting; and (5) differences in police administration for the handling and referral of delinquency charges brought to their attention.

As an example of the implications of this summary, refusal to admit because of overcrowding may be cited specifically under (4). Presiding Justice John Warren Hill of the New York City Domestic Relations Court, speaking before the Citizens' Conference on Juvenile Delinquency and Crime on September 15, 1954, made the statement that "hundreds of boys" who should be committed or investigated are being turned loose in New York City because the state is failing to provide enough room in training schools.[5]

The Volume of Delinquency: Is It on the Increase?

Although our meager and weighted evidence makes it extremely difficult to determine with any accuracy the long-range trend for delinquency, we have considerable reason to believe that there has been a general upward trend since the end of World War I. Although this rise over the last three and a half decades has not been precipitous, much of our evidence shows that at certain times (such as immediately after World War I and during several periods of the depression of the 1930's and World War II) the rise in delinquency for both sexes has been spectacular.

Despite variations appearing from year to year and difficult to assess properly because of changes in the number of official reporting agencies, annual estimates of delinquency for the country as a whole before World War II placed the volume at about 1 percent of our total youthful population between the ages of ten and sixteen years inclusive. According to estimates made before the war, the number of youths within this age category was approximately 17,000,000, which meant that the annual volume of court-handled or adjudicated delinquents during this period varied from 170,000 to 200,000 children. Lowell J. Carr estimated this to be the annual number of delinquent children passing through our courts during the period prior to World War II.[6] An examination of statistical tabulations from various sources for the period preceding World War II yielded an annual average figure of approximately 200,000 adjudicated delinquents for the same period.[7]

During World War II, our numbers of adjudicated delinquents rose precipitately, to record volumes for 1943 and 1945. If, for example, we establish 1940 as a base year for delinquency, calling its rate 100 percent, 1943 and 1945 attained the unprecedented level of 172 percent. For example, on the basis of data submitted by 206 courts to the Federal Children's Bureau for the period 1940-52, covering children

[5] New York Times, September 16, 1954.
[6] Carr, Delinquency Control, p. 37.
[7] Bloch, Disorganization, pp. 162-64.

aged ten to seventeen years inclusive, the numbers rose from 39,440 in 1940 to over 67,000 in 1943 and 1945. *What is particularly significant in this is the fact that the number of ten- to seventeen-year-old children for the country as a whole declined from 3 to 5 percent during the same period.* This means, therefore, that for the peak war years, on the basis of the evidence submitted by these reporting courts, the volume of delinquency increased by 72 percent while the number of children within the age category for the country as a whole *decreased* by 3 to 5 percent.

TABLE B

Juvenile Delinquency Cases (Ages 10-17), 1940-1952*

YEAR	JUVENILE DELINQUENCY CASES†		CHILD POPULATION OF U.S. (10-17 YEARS OF AGE)‡	
	NUMBER	PERCENTAGE (1940 = 100)	NUMBER	PERCENTAGE (1940 = 100)
1940.................	39,440	100	19,115,000	100
1941.................	44,173	112	18,893,000	99
1942.................	49,300	125	18,674,000	98
1943.................	67,837	172	18,481,000	97
1944.................	65,076	165	18,287,000	96
1945.................	67,837	172	18,089,000	95
1946.................	58,371	148	17,902,000	94
1947.................	51,642	131	17,776,000	93
1948.................	50,546	128	17,683,000	93
1949.................	53,061	135	17,586,000	92
1950.................	55,504	141	17,431,000	91
1951.................	58,961	149	17,746,000	93
1952.................	64,927	165	18,239,000	95
1955§.............	—	—	20,190,000	106
1960§.............	—	—	25,602,000	134

* *Juvenile Court Statistics, 1950-52,* p. 16.

† Data for 1946-52 based on cases disposed of by 206 courts serving about 12 percent of the child population of the United States; data for 1940-45 for these courts estimated by the Children's Bureau.

‡ Bureau of the Census, U.S. Department of Commerce. Data for 1940-49 are provisional revised estimates (unpublished).

§ These figures are projected estimates appearing in the original chart.

In its relation to war and postwar conditions, delinquency appears to follow a well-marked cyclical trend. Socio-economic upheavals, family separations and mobility, and cultural tensions produced by war tend to bring about an increase in delinquency, more marked among girls. The postwar transitional period, characterized by economic and socio-cultural trends toward societal readjustment, likewise appear to produce relatively high rates of delinquency, although the incidence of such disorders is usually not as high as during the more disorganized war years. Further, these rates reveal sectional differences and begin to show signs of abating as the trends toward stabilization begin to manifest themselves. With readjustment and the establishment of renewed stability, delinquency rates appear to decline appreciably, reverting to levels comparable to prewar conditions and reflecting the characteristic strains of a dynamic and expanding peacetime society. What is alarming about the present American situation is that these anticipated declines have not taken place according to the expected pattern and that, on the contrary, American delinquency has risen to proportions comparable to the peak war years with disquieting evidence that it may rise even higher. Although it may be argued that American society is undergoing a period of unusual strain with a virtual continuation of war conditions during the period of the so-called "cold war," the continuing high delinquency rates may perhaps be attributed in considerable degree to basic conditions of tension within the American social system itself.

Thus, after the expected decline for the period following World War II, the figures have again mounted, causing revision of many previous estimates. The total volume of delinquency declined rather rapidly for the years 1946-48, only to show an upward movement again for the period beginning in 1949. During 1952, for example, the last year for which official data are available from the Children's Bureau, the total volume was again assuming the same proportions that existed at the previous peak during the war years.

In comparison with 1 percent, which previously had often been employed as a crude index to measure the nation's annual volume of delinquency, the estimate for the year 1952 was 2 percent of all children between ten and seventeen, or a total annual volume of 385,000 children. If this be accepted with any credence, it means that our annual rate of delinquency has actually doubled since the period preceding

World War II. Thus, if we exclude from this percentage the estimated 0.8 percent, representing those delinquents that do not come to the attention of any court, we can assume that approximately twelve in every thousand children between the ages of seven and seventeen have been appearing before the juvenile courts because of delinquency ever since 1949. Actually, this provides only part of the picture. According to the estimates by the federal Children's Bureau for 1953, approximately one million teen-age youths are picked up by the police annually, although only about one-third of these are eventually brought before the courts. By 1960, according to the same report, it is possible that a million and a half children may be apprehended by the nation's police —truly a disturbing figure.

Some confirmation of the trend of delinquency comes from an independent source, the *Uniform Crime Reports* of the Federal Bureau of Investigation. This official publication does not report juvenile offenses, but it does report police arrests of youths under eighteen years of age for whom fingerprint arrest records have been filed. It should be emphasized that only some police jurisdictions actually fingerprint youthful offenders and that the majority of delinquents are not submitted to this process. Thus, the numbers reported by the F.B.I. are considerably less than the numbers passing through our juvenile courts. Despite this fact, the *trends* in the volume of offenses should appear the same. This is actually the case and the report by the F.B.I. on the fingerprint arrest records of juvenile offenders bears striking similarity to the upward and downward trends of juvenile delinquency during the past fifteen years.

The figures cited thus far, however, have been official figures dealing almost exclusively with adjudicated delinquents, i.e., children for whom formal petitions have been filed in our juvenile courts and for whom some official disposition is made. The large numbers of dependency and neglect cases are not included, nor those in which special proceedings may be instituted. Further, these figures do not include the large but undetermined numbers of children handled by the courts and other agencies in unofficial proceedings.

If dependency and neglect cases are incorporated within our totals, involving, for example, cases in which lack of adequate parental support and care or cruel treatment are in evidence—situations tantamount to or closely related to delinquency problems—or cases involving special proceedings, such problems as determination of custody and consent to marry, official estimates of delinquency would have to be increased by approximately 25 percent. During 1952, of the total volume of cases handled by the courts reporting to the Children's Bureau, only 75 percent were delinquency cases, while 19 percent were cases involving problems of dependency and neglect and 6 percent were cases in which special proceedings were involved. As Bertram M. Beck stated in a report for the Bureau of Public Affairs of the Community Service Society in October, 1951, it is futile to attempt to separate problems of delinquency in our juvenile courts from problems of dependency and neglect, since the two are so closely interrelated.

CHART I

Juvenile Delinquency Court Cases, Police Arrests of Children, and U.S. Child Population, 1940-49*

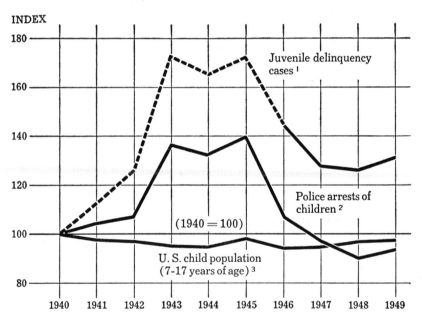

[1] Data for 1940-45 estimated by Children's Bureau; data for 1946-49 based on official and unofficial cases disposed of by 218 courts.

[2] Based on fingerprint records for children under 18 years of age reported in Uniform Crime Reports (annual bulletins), Federal Bureau of Investigation.

[3] Current Population Reports, Bureau of the Census, Series P-25, No. 41.

* Taken from *Juvenile Court Statistics, 1946-49*, p. 11.

CHART II

Types of Juvenile Court Cases Handled Officially and Unofficially*

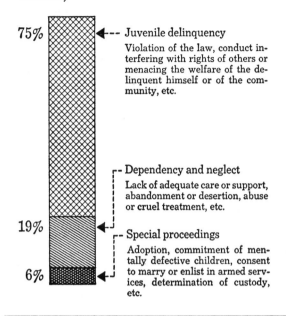

75% **◄--- Juvenile delinquency**
Violation of the law, conduct interfering with rights of others or menacing the welfare of the delinquent himself or of the community, etc.

Three-fourths of all juvenile court cases were delinquency cases

┌- Dependency and neglect
Lack of adequate care or support, abandonment or desertion, abuse or cruel treatment, etc.

19% **◄-┘ ┌-- Special proceedings**
Adoption, commitment of mentally defective children, consent to marry or enlist in armed services, determination of custody, etc.

6% **◄-┘**

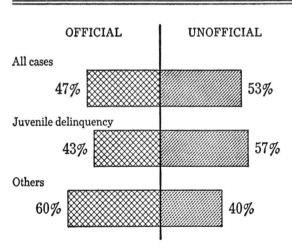

OFFICIAL | UNOFFICIAL

All cases
47% 53%

Juvenile delinquency
43% 57%

Others
60% 40%

More than half of all juvenile court cases were handled unofficially

A referral to a court can be a disturbing experience for a child. Many unofficial cases that do not require the formal judgment of a court might preferably be handled by other community agencies equipped to deal with such cases.

. . . . . without the filing of a petition for formal judicial hearing

1952 data

* *Juvenile Court Statistics, 1950-52, p. 2.*

If we can assume that the total volume of delinquency in the United States for 1952 was approximately 2 percent of all children between ten and seventeen, a total of 385,000 children, we should be able to anticipate what the potential problem may be, *if the present trend continues*. It must be stressed again that these estimates do not include dependency and neglect cases or children handled unofficially within different communities. Utilizing only the official estimates for adjudicated delinquents and the potential over-all increase in our youthful population within the next decade, we can gain some partial perspective. Thus, the possible amount of delinquency in 1960, based on the recorded total of 385,000 for 1952 and the estimated increase in the over-all child population, will be 539,000. This estimate is based upon the gradual secular trend for the past ten years. However, if we base our estimates on the far more precipitous rise during the last four recorded years (1948-52), the potential increase in delinquency appears unusually portentous. Thus, if the same secular trend continues as during the last four-year period (1948-52) for which data have been officially compiled, the volume of delinquency in 1960 will be approximately 6.75 percent *more* than the previously estimated volume, or a total of 575,382 delinquents. To appreciate fully the significance of this increase, one should take into consideration the official estimates of 200,000 frequently made before World War II. If these figures are at all tenable, we face a possible increase in delinquency of 238 percent as compared with the period directly preceding World War II.

However, considerable precaution must be exercised not to accept such estimates without qualification. We must remember, first, that far more districts now report delinquency than in the period before World War II, and second, that our information is probably far more complete today than it was even a decade ago. How much of this increase is attributable to more accurate and fuller statistical reporting and how much to actual changes in the make-up of our population, socio-cultural tensions on the American scene, and increased public awareness is a highly debatable, if not unanswerable, question. Nevertheless, while both of these sets of factors are likely to have played a part in producing the increase that now seems evident, it can be safely assumed that delinquency is far more prevalent today than it was twenty years ago. We can no longer afford reassuring ourselves that the increase in delinquency is almost wholly a consequence of our improved methods of gathering and compiling statistical data: although it is difficult to assess the exact size of the increase, we have sufficient evidence to substantiate the *fact* of such an increase. Thus it may not be entirely gratuitous to assert that the public, sensing the impact of the problem in many ways, may be more aware, in its statistical ignorance, of the growth of the problem than the expert has been willing to admit.

CHART III

Juvenile Delinquency Cases Are Rising*

An estimated 385,000 children (or about 2% of all children in the U. S. aged 10-17) were dealt with by juvenile courts in delinquency cases in 1952.

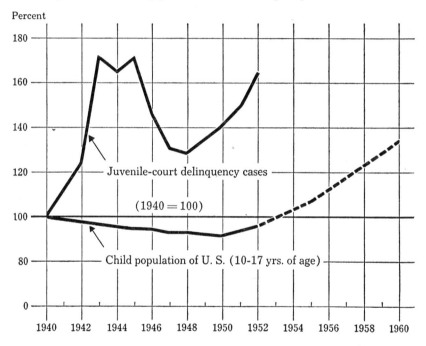

The increase in delinquency cases exceeds the increase in the child population.

By 1960, the child population 10-17 years of age (the predominant age group of delinquents) will be 40 percent higher than it was in 1952.

How will this population increase affect the future volume of delinquency?

* *Juvenile Court Statistics,* 1950-52, p. 3.

Age Levels of Delinquency

The age categories into which apprehended delinquents fall depend largely upon legal definition and customary practice. Since formal adjudication frequently does not take place until the antisocial behavior of the child brings him perilously close to the statutory dividing line between juvenile offenses and adult criminality, it is not surprising to find the chief cluster of ages falling within the two- to three-year age period directly preceding the statutory limitations for juvenile offenses. For example, in states where the juvenile courts have jurisdiction until the age of eighteen, approximately one-third of the delinquent boys and two-fifths of the delinquent girls are sixteen or seventeen. Where the division occurs at sixteen, the largest percentages of juvenile offenders are distributed in the fourteen- and fifteen-year-old age groups. Examination reveals that delinquency is primarily a matter of early adolescence, since the majority of these youthful offenders have had long prior histories of maladjustment and disorder within their families and communities before passing through the formal process of official court hearing and disposition.

Though the separation, according to age, between the juvenile and the adult offender is arbitrary at best, the various codes for the handling of offenders give greater latitude by far to juvenile than to adult courts and, with it, much wider scope in the possibilities of effective diagnosis and rehabilitation. For this reason, we are now in the midst of a pronounced trend to liberalize court procedures in the handling, disposition, and treatment of youthful offenders, in most cases the youngest (eighteen-to-twenty-one-year-old) category of so-called "adult" offenders. The Model Youth Authority Act, prepared by the American Law Institute and now adopted in various forms in seven of our states, is designed to permit greater scope in the handling and treatment of youthful offenders. California, which has taken the lead in the adoption of this model statute through the establishment of a State Youth Authority, utilizes procedures for offenders up to the age of twenty-one comparable to those employed in the juvenile courts, with corresponding flexibility in placement and handling of these offenders. New York State, with its confused and overlapping Youthful Offender Law and

Wayward Minor Act, originally designed to introduce greater flexibility in the handling of its sixteen- to twenty-one-year-old offenders, is undergoing a similar transition. Continuing study and a preliminary report, in November 1954, by the Subcommittee on Youth and the Family of The New York Temporary Commission on the Courts also aims to set up special youth courts for those falling outside the statutory age provisions of the regular juvenile courts.

Examination of the age-levels of children now brought before our courts shows that the median age of children involved in delinquency, as reported by 413 courts in 1949, was about fifteen and a half years.[8] In comparing the age levels of boys and girls at the time of their appearance in court, it was found in 1949 that the same median age of fifteen and a half years applied to both sexes and to unofficial as well as official cases. Although the large majority of cases in the preadolescent age groups are dealt with unofficially, far more of these boys than girls are brought before our courts for treatment and handling. The concentration of girls in the adolescent age grouping largely derives from the fact that at this age the young girl is particularly susceptible to sexual exploitation and demoralization; it is primarily for these charges, as compared to stealing and malicious mischief, the primary offenses for boys, that girls are apprehended and summarily dealt with. In all, official records have shown for some years that *the vast majority (about three-fourths) of the children involved in delinquency cases are fourteen years old or more.*[9] However, as we have said before, the official reports of the Children's Bureau remind us that in assessing the age-distribution of juvenile cases we must take into consideration the age level over which the juvenile court has jurisdiction. These official age levels are established by statutory regulation and vary from state to state.

In recent reports, the average age levels for both boys and girls brought before our courts still hover close to the fifteen-and-a-half-year-old age level, although the median age for boys in 1951 was 16.1 years as compared with a median of 15.6 years for girls.[10] The 1951 data conform to the established trend in showing the vast majority—eight

[8] *Juvenile Court Statistics, 1946-1949*, p. 4.
[9] *Juvenile Court Statistics, 1946-1949*, p. 4.
[10] *Juvenile Court Statistics, 1950-52*, pp. 4, 17

out of ten—of children brought before our courts as fourteen years old
or more.

Sex Composition

On the basis of the actual volume of boys and girls involved in delinquent activities, the general trend, as can be expected, is for far more
boys than girls to commit offenses. On the average, during the course
of the past two decades, boys were apprehended for offenses approximately 4.5 times more frequently than girls. This approximate ratio
has been maintained for some time according to the official records
of our courts. In reporting the numbers of boys and girls brought
before the juvenile courts, the Children's Bureau showed ratios of 4.7
boys to 1 girl in 1945 and 4.4 boys to 1 girl in 1946.[11] More recently
the ratio of boys to girls appears to have increased, the 1952 data
revealing that boys outnumber girls five to one in delinquency cases.[12]
It is far too early to say whether this indicates a trend. Since delinquency among girls has not shown the same rise as among boys during
the past ten years, and in some years and places has declined steeply,

CHART IV

Most Delinquent Children Brought to Court Were 14 Years of Age or Older*

Of every 10 boys

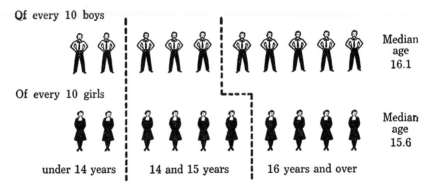

Median age 16.1

Of every 10 girls

Median age 15.6

under 14 years   14 and 15 years   16 years and over

The average age for boys was slightly higher than that for girls.   1951 data

* *Juvenile Court Statistics, 1950-52*, p. 4.
[11] *Social Statistics*, II, p. 11.
[12] *Juvenile Court Statistics, 1950-52*, p. 4.

it is possible that we may be witnessing a slow upward revision of the ratio, with an increasingly larger number of boys than girls becoming involved in delinquencies that bring them before the courts.

That in our particular culture we should find more male than female youngsters apprehended annually is not at all surprising. The role-definitions we apply to boys and girls in our culture are quite different, providing the boy with far more opportunity and incitement to enter delinquent activity. The socialization processes of boys and girls differ considerably, so that we have come to expect a certain amount of prankishness and misbehavior on the part of boys which we are hardly prepared to accept in girls. "Boys will be boys" is a maxim that clearly expresses the cultural tolerance of this form of behavior. Such permissive outlets for girls are regarded with considerable misgiving and disquiet, although in our to an extent male-dominated culture we are apt to show some slight regard for the so-called "tomboy."

In his comparative statistical studies of delinquent boys and girls, Elio D. Monachesi has pointed up rather effectively the suggestive quality of this tacit approval we give to boys' misbehavior as against that of girls.[13] As has been shown elsewhere, concern over the misbehavior of girls in our culture revolves about the loss of parental control (inviting possible sexual and other forms of molestation) and incipient

CHART V

*Boys Outnumber Girls About 5 to 1 in Delinquency Cases**

Boys are referred to courts mostly for stealing or malicious mischief. Such aggressive acts are more likely to come to a court's attention than are the behavior problems most frequently found among delinquent girls, such as ungovernable behavior, running away, and sex offenses.

1952 data

* *Juvenile Court Statistics, 1950-52*, p. 4.

[13] Monachesi, "Characteristics of Delinquents and Non-Delinquents"; Hathaway and Monachesi, eds., *Analyzing and Predicting Juvenile Delinquency with the MMPI*, especially Studies 1, 2, 5, and 6.

or actual forms of sexual laxity.[14] For this reason, our courts frequently are moved to act only in cases where the family has actually lost control over the girl or where there is definite evidence of sexual lapses. In the work done by and under the supervision of Monachesi, the Minnesota Multiphasic Personality Inventory, a test designed to indicate departures from normal emotional patterns, was employed to compare delinquent and nondelinquent boys and girls. Although not conclusive, Monachesi's results indicate emotional disturbance in a higher percentage of delinquent than of nondelinquent girls and of sample groups of both delinquent and nondelinquent boys. One of the implications, therefore, of Monachesi's statement that "the data presented . . . suggest that delinquency in females is more often the expression of personal inadequacies rather than a manifestation of cultural imperatives," [15] seems to be that the majority of girls will not engage in delinquent activities unless emotionally disturbed to begin with, whereas boys will do so under pressure of culture and environment. If this is true, the fact that it is mostly the emotionally disoriented girl who finds herself impelled into antisocial forms of behavior may explain the far greater percentages of boys engaged in delinquent activities.

The difference in public attitude toward boys' and girls' offenses can be seen in the disposal of such cases. According to data for 1951 supplied by the children's courts, 60 percent of the official cases were placed on probation, dismissed, or adjusted through referrals and other court facilities. A yet greater majority (86 percent) of unofficial cases were dismissed or "adjusted." *In the cases of the girls, however, commitments or referrals to agencies or institutions were far more frequent than for boys.*

We must exercise some precaution, however, in examining these consistently higher rates of delinquency for boys than for girls. Despite the indications the over-all rates give, a break-down of these differences into age categories reveals that in certain specific age categories the differences are not nearly so acute. For example, in the lowest age category, children under ten years of age, we find a vast preponderance of boys. But as we move up the age scale, toward the adolescent and post-adolescent levels, the numerical disparities seem to

[14] Bloch, *Disorganization*, pp. 169-70.
[15] Monachesi, "Characteristics of Delinquents and Non-Delinquents."

grow much smaller. Thus, in an earlier report on national data, the ratio of male to female delinquents in the category below ten years of age was 8.9 to 1; in the ten-to-eleven-year-old category, 9.9 to 1; in the twelve-to-thirteen-year-old category, 5.0 to 1; and in the fourteen-to-

CHART VI

Disposition of Official and Unofficial Cases*

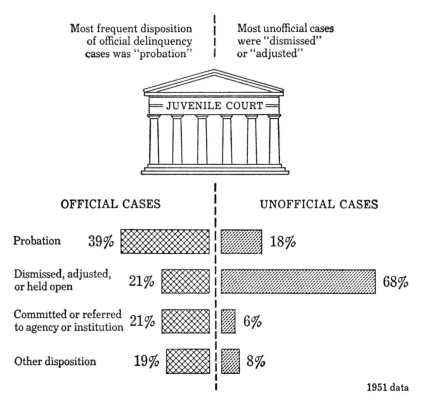

Most frequent disposition of official delinquency cases was "probation"

Most unofficial cases were "dismissed" or "adjusted"

JUVENILE COURT

OFFICIAL CASES | UNOFFICIAL CASES

Probation	39% / 18%
Dismissed, adjusted, or held open	21% / 68%
Committed or referred to agency or institution	21% / 6%
Other disposition	19% / 8%

1951 data

The disposition of boys' and girls' cases differed considerably. Dismissals or adjustments were higher for boys; commitments or referrals to agencies or institutions were more frequent for girls. This difference is attributable in part to the different reasons for which boys and girls are brought to court. Girls are usually referred because of sexual misconduct or related offenses. This is considered a more serious offense than stealing or malicious mischief, for which boys are most frequently referred.

---

* *Juvenile Court Statistics, 1950-52,* p. 6.

fifteen-year-old category, 4.1 to 1.[16] Although the F.B.I.'s arrest records are not directly comparable, these diminishing ratios are clearly established there too. In 1945, for example, F.B.I. arrest reports showed a ratio of 9.6 to 1 for sixteen-year-olds, 9.2 to 1 for seventeen-year-olds, and 3.8 to 1 for eighteen-year-olds. For the next six successive age groups, the reports indicate male-female ratios ranging between 2.6 and 3.2 to 1.[17] Much of the significance of these figures lies in the indication they give that as girls approach adolescence and the immediate post-adolescent years, the number of offenders, though still considerably less than that of boys, does increase significantly until, in the twenties, females make up from one-fourth to one-third of the entire offender group. Thus, although girls conform more than boys during the tempestuous years of early adolescence, their potentialities for disorder increase as they grow older. This may be due in part to our being more reluctant to prosecute adolescent girls than boys, except for cases of sexual intransigence, with the result that unrestrained anti-social behavior patterns "catch up" with girls in their late adolescent and post-adolescent years.

Types of Offenses Committed

The nature of a delinquent offense is largely a matter of cultural definition and a result of varying standards of community pressure and practice. Thus, the nature of juvenile offenses, their frequency, and their distribution reflect the community's awareness of what constitutes a serious delinquent disorder and its willingness to take cognizance, through official and unofficial action, of the kinds of youthful disorder existing within its ken. The differences noted above in the varying character and frequency of boys' and girls' offenses give some indication of the different values we apply to the expected behavior of the two sexes and the types of problems we hold to be particularly significant in youthful infractiousness. Nevertheless, despite variations in standards from community to community and despite the ambiguity with which delinquent behavior is generally defined, there is a discernible pattern in the character of the offenses most typical for the greater number of communities and the country at large.

[16] *Juvenile Court Statistics*, 1943, p. 16.
[17] *Uniform Crime Reports*, XVI, pp. 114-16.

Reports to the United States Children's Bureau, confirmed by most local surveys and studies, indicate that the primary offense among boys is stealing, followed by what the tenuous wording of the statutes describes as "general acts of carelessness or mischief." Among girls, the principal infractions are ungovernable behavior and sex offenses, in that order. Truancy, a common offense among both sexes, appears more frequently among girls than boys. This suggests that in the public mind unsupervised behavior, because of demoralization and the sexual dangers involved, emerges as a far more serious offense when engaged in by girls. Since it is reasonable to assume that boys play truant as often as girls, if not more so, the official data simply confirm the fact that girls are far more likely to be officially prosecuted for school absences than boys.

TABLE C

Reasons for Reference to Court in Boys' and in Girls' Cases Disposed of by 374 Courts: 1945*

REASONS FOR REFERENCE TO COURT	JUVENILE DELINQUENCY CASES					
	NUMBER			PERCENT		
	TOTAL	BOYS	GIRLS	TOTAL	BOYS	GIRLS
Total cases.................	122,851	101,240	21,611	. . .	. . .	. . .
Reasons for reference reported	111,939	92,671	19,268	100	100	100
Stealing...................	40,879	38,610	2,269	37	42	12
Act of carelessness or mischief	19,241	17,779	1,462	17	19	8
Traffic violation.............	9,852	9,659	193	9	10	1
Truancy...................	8,681	6,164	2,517	8	7	13
Running away..............	9,307	5,652	3,655	8	6	19
Being ungovernable..........	9,840	5,542	4,298	9	6	22
Sex offenses................	5,990	2,579	3,411	5	3	18
Injury to person.............	3,224	2,828	396	3	3	2
Other reason................	4,925	3,858	1,067	4	4	5
Reason for reference not reported...................	10,912	8,569	2,343	. . .	. . .	. . .

* *Social Statistics*, The Child, II, 11.

In the composite data compiled by official sources during the past ten years, stealing ordinarily appears first on the list of boys' offenses and fifth among girls' offenses.[18] Although it is very difficult to determine fluctuations over a period of years of ratios for boys and girls in specific offense categories, the primacy of pilfering and acts of carelessness among boys and of ungovernable behavior and sex offenses among girls seems well established. The fact that these sex-differentiated offense categories have consistently maintained their positions over a period of years illuminates American cultural values relating to differences in the role behavior of the sexes. There is little doubt that the average American community is far more prone to deal officially with boys than with girls for stealing, but is apt to be considerably less lenient toward girls in cases involving incipient or actual sexual offenses.

The most striking fact in this analysis is the vast number of serious property thefts committed by youths under twenty-one years of age—an overwhelming share of the total number of such thefts by individuals of all ages. The major proportion of our commitments to state penal institutions is of youths under twenty-one years of age—as high as 40 percent in most states. It has been estimated that in 1948-49, one-half of all automobile thefts, one-third of all burglaries, robberies, and other thefts, one in five of all rapes, and one in seven of all homicides were committed by youths under twenty-one years of age.[19]

These figures have shown very little prospect of diminishing during the past few years. In 1953, for example, the annual F.B.I. report revealed that arrests of juveniles (youngsters under eighteen years of age) rose by 7.9 percent for that year as compared with 1952, while adult arrests increased by only 1.9 percent.[20] As we compare the total number of juvenile arrests with the total volume of arrests for any given recent year, the percentages in themselves do not appear ominous until we break them down into the categories for which the arrests were made. Then, the picture changes drastically. Thus, in 1953, of the record number of arrests for that year (1,791,160) reported by 1,174 cities, 8.4 percent were of persons seventeen years of age or less and 14.7 percent of persons under twenty-one years of age. However, the

[18] See, for example, *Social Statistics*, II, p. 11.
[19] See Ellingston, *Protecting Our Children from Criminal Careers*.
[20] *Uniform Crime Reports*, 1953, p. 111.

vast majority of these arrests were for minor offenses, such as public intoxication and disorderly conduct, from which most youths would be excluded. The residue of hard-core major offenses, those which constitute the basic portion of our national crime problem, shows that the part played by youths under eighteen years of age is alarming. For example, 53.6 percent of the persons arrested for auto theft in 1953 were juveniles and, in fact, 29 *percent were not even old enough to get a regular driver's license in most states, where the required age is six-*

CHART VII

Persons Arrested Under 18 Years of Age for Crimes Against Property (Calendar Year 1954) *

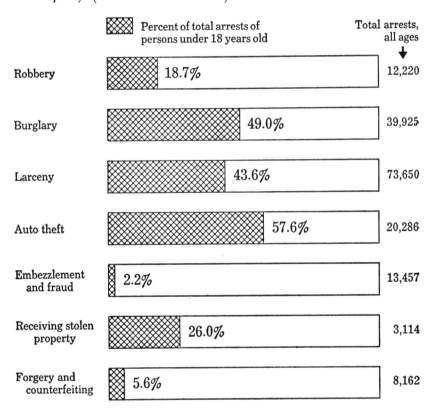

	Percent of total arrests of persons under 18 years old	Total arrests, all ages
Robbery	18.7%	12,220
Burglary	49.0%	39,925
Larceny	43.6%	73,650
Auto theft	57.6%	20,286
Embezzlement and fraud	2.2%	13,457
Receiving stolen property	26.0%	3,114
Forgery and counterfeiting	5.6%	8,162

1,389 cities . . . total population 38,642,183 (FBI chart)

* *Uniform Crime Reports*, XXV, p. 113.

teen. Nearly half (49.3 percent) of the persons arrested for burglary were not yet eighteen, and two-thirds of these were under sixteen years of age. This is where the true picture lies, for when we examine the major property and related offenses that constitute our principal burden of crime—offenses such as robbery, burglary, larceny, auto theft, and receiving stolen property—we find that youthful offenders under eighteen years of age have become what is possibly our greatest single threat to law-abiding security.

Minority Groups and Delinquency

Generally speaking, delinquency is a function of social marginality. Those groups that (1) cannot readily make ordinary socio-economic adjustments, (2) are employed largely in marginal and unskilled occupations, (3) are handicapped in their search for normal avenues of assimilation by powerful cultural barriers erected against them, and (4) find it difficult because of language, culture, and other reasons to identify with the predominant public culture, are the ones that annually yield the highest rates of delinquency. This is hardly new to the American scene. What is new is the fact that the focus of cultural discrimination tends to shift in the kaleidoscopic socio-cultural and ethnic pattern which constitutes the American social fabric.

Economically depressed, recently arrived immigrant groups and cultural "outsiders" have traditionally tended to produce high rates of delinquency. In the early part of the century, the ranks of delinquency were recruited largely from the children of foreign-born parents, irrespective of country of origin. In the history of the United States, contrary to popular impression, such early delinquents were not invariably the offspring of Southern and Eastern European immigrants. In the studies of successive waves of immigration to the United States from the middle of the nineteenth century, it can be found that the most recently arrived immigrant groups and those most rigorously excluded from participation in the common culture by virtue of language, ethnic background, and religion, were those most likely to produce relatively high annual quotas of delinquency. Two exceptions should be noted to this situation, however: (1) foreign-born children have rarely contributed a great deal to the delinquency problem, largely because, by virtue of language and family culture identification, they were not exposed so intensively to conflicting cultural standards and to outside influences tending to loosen family ties; (2) rates of delinquency have never appeared to be as high for children of immigrant parents whose cultural background, religion, and ethnic features to some extent resembled the prevailing American pattern.

Thus, whereas the problem of delinquency before 1930 was mainly a problem of the native-born child of foreign parentage, notably European, the problem has shifted, since the curtailment of immigration in 1924, to the new "migrants" and the new marginal groups on the American scene—the urban-drifting Negro, the Puerto Rican, and the Mexican. This shift, of course, does not indicate any tendency inherent in these groups toward youthful lawlessness. It is almost wholly a consequence of the barriers to adjustment on social, cultural, and economic levels placed in their way, the ecological concentration and cultural segregation they experience, and the development of a peculiar "delinquent subculture" (to be discussed later) into which many of their children, marginally excluded as they are, are inevitably drawn.

Statistics concerning the ethnic and cultural backgrounds of our juvenile offenders since the beginning of the century amply support these contentions. In 1930, for example, approximately two-fifths of our girl delinquents and one-half of our male delinquents were of foreign-born parentage. Today, the vast majority of offenders of both sexes, over 70 percent, are native-born of native-born parents. Negro rates of delinquency, however, have risen significantly, as have sectional rates for Spanish-speaking peoples, notably Puerto Ricans and Mexicans. Although comprising approximately 9.7 percent of the total population of the country, Negroes contribute 18 percent to the total delinquency rate, or almost twice as much as their percentage of the population would warrant.

In the case of Negroes, a unique problem exists for various reasons. First, in many parts of the country, despite the slow crumbling of vicious discriminatory patterns since the end of World War II, Negroes lack access to agencies and facilities available to white children. In a majority of the cases studied the first outside contact the Negro child has, as a consequence of delinquent or ungovernable behavior, is with the official agency of the court. Second, Negro children are commonly given institutional commitments at an early age for offenses for which white children are either dismissed or returned to their parents, or which are adjusted on an unofficial basis. Nevertheless, the strains of Negro family life during urban adjustment in the overcrowded sections of our large cities in which Negroes are segregated, coupled with lack of child supervision because both parents are working, provide a frequently occurring setting in which delinquency inevitably must flourish. Thus, Negro children figure about five times more often in the juvenile courts in New York City than white children, despite the marked disparity in obverse direction of their respective numbers in the total population of the city. In Los Angeles County, 4.2 percent of the juvenile population under eighteen was classified as Negro, according to a 1946 census, whereas 10.3 percent of all delinquent court cases involved Negro children. This heavy concentration of Negroes in our official data is carried forward in our findings on adult crime. In 1953, for example, according to the arrest records of the Federal Bureau of Investigation, 70.9 percent of all arrests in the 1,174 cities for which data were obtained were of members of the white race, while 26.9 percent of all arrests were of Negroes. In view of the fact that Negroes make up only approximately ten percent of the entire population of the United States, this volume of arrests represents a highly disproportionate ratio.[21]

Since crime and delinquency rates appear to be a function of cultural rejection, any barriers we place in the way of assimilation will tend to induce a continuing and increasing rate. That Negro children may be systematically and officially discriminated against in certain urban areas has been demonstrated by Axelrad in his study of Negro and white institutionalized delinquents.[22] In his examination of the case records of 300 institutionalized delinquents, 179 Negroes and 121 whites, he discovered that Negro children were consistently committed at earlier ages than white children and for less serious offenses. Such commitments were made on the basis of fewer previous court contacts and institutional records than the white children had had.

In the swiftly changing pattern of events on the American scene, the problem of the Negro delinquent may diminish in the face of the even more rapid rise of delinquency among our Spanish-speaking minorities. The enormous increase of delinquency among Puerto Rican children in New York City, the result of acutely demoralized conditions among

[21] *Uniform Crime Reports,* XXIV, p. 114.
[22] Axelrad, "Negro and White Institutionalized Delinquents."

people transplanted from tropical to urban slums in phenomenal numbers during the past two decades, is closely paralleled by similar conditions elsewhere. In Greater Los Angeles, where 13.9 percent of the juvenile population are of the Spanish-speaking minority group, primarily Mexican, 34.9 percent of all delinquents reported in 1947 were from this group—an estimated rise of 151 percent over the population norm. Houston, Texas, a southern city with few of the traditional immigrant patterns formerly characteristic of our Eastern seaboard industrial cities, faces an increasing delinquency problem with its unassimilated Spanish-speaking population. Of 4,287 delinquents reported during 1939-42, approximately 25 percent were Negro and 16.5 percent were Spanish-speaking, with the percentage of Spanish-speaking delinquents showing a consistent rise.

This is the inevitable price we pay for the social and cultural disenfranchisement of minority peoples, and the story can be duplicated in various parts of the country. The groups may change from time to time, but the effects of the cultural pattern of marginality remain largely the same.

Rural-Urban Differences

The majority of delinquencies still occur in large urban centers. This may not be entirely the result of the competitive conditions of city life, minority group pressures, overcrowded housing, industrial concentration, and the related problems of urban life, although, certainly, all of these play important roles. Apart from the incitements to delinquency that urban life provides, the large annual volume of delinquency in our cities is also the product of the character of police supervision and the presence of a wide variety of agencies and courts designed to deal with such problems. Many rural areas are not only conspicuously lacking in even some of the most fundamental child-care agencies, but they lack as well the most ordinary court facilities for the handling of delinquent children. Delinquent children in rural areas, therefore, are frequently either handled by the families, relatives, or friends, or by a minister or priest, or are treated by reprimand or quasi-official supervision by the local police. The result is that large numbers of children who would be officially identified as delinquents in urban areas and who thus would figure in our comparative statistics, find no place whatever in our comparative appraisals of rural and urban delinquent trends. Were the facts fully known, the percentage of rural juvenile offenses and offenders would probably be far higher than now emerges from our public data.

Nevertheless, annual delinquency statistics invariably show much smaller percentages for rural areas than for urban centers. Notwithstanding the lack of facilities for identification, apprehension, and disposition, it seems fairly conclusive even today that the conditions of rural life are such that delinquency is far less apt to occur. In the indexes for adult crime, the highest percentages of crime occur in our large cities of 100,000 or more in size. The ratios of delinquency and crime seem to decrease precipitously with the decrease in the size of the communities involved, though relatively high rates of delinquency are frequently found in the rural areas contiguous to our large industrial areas.

Two of the conditions that render it particularly difficult properly to assess the disparity in delinquency and crime rates between rural and urban areas are the increasing mobility of our population and the growing decentralization of industry. With the spread of industry into many former predominantly rural areas, and with the flow of industrial populations that such movements entail, the increase in delinquency becomes quite marked. Although it has become a sociological truism to observe that urban rates of delinquency and crime are three and a half to five times higher than rural rates, these differences might not be entirely tenable if all the facts were known. Very likely they will become less tenable as the mobility of our population and the industrialization of rural areas grow. Further, although certain offenses, because of their very nature, occur with far greater frequency in urban areas—e.g., larceny, burglary, and auto theft—this is not necessarily true for many personal offenses. In fact, rural rates for such offenses as rape, murder, and manslaughter, are often equally high and, in certain instances, markedly higher. In the case of sexual offenses among juveniles, although the point is extremely difficult to prove, it is dubious that urban rates are significantly higher than rural rates. Examination of local and regional evidence actually suggests that rural rates, in many instances, may be appreciably higher.

Despite the shortcomings in rural data, the fact remains that rural delinquency and crime have been climbing steadily during the past decade. According to a recent Federal Bureau of Investigation report, while the increase in offenses in urban areas for 1946 as compared to 1945 was 7.4 percent, the increase in rural areas for the same period was 14.1 percent, almost twice as much.[23] In its most recent report, the F.B.I. revealed that crime in rural areas has increased yearly since the publication of such tabulations began in 1944.[24] So far in this decade, crime in rural areas increased 9.6 percent in 1953 as compared with 1952, more than twice the increase in city crime. What is striking is that this type of year-to-year increase at a more rapid rate than corresponding urban increase appears to have occurred consistently during the past ten years. In fact, if we break down rates of crime for individual offenses, the only decrease during the year 1952-53 was in negligent manslaughter, which declined 5.5 percent. In view of the fact that this type of offense is related to overcongested traffic conditions, it is not surprising to note a decline in the less congested rural areas. On the other hand, we find substantial increases in all other types of crime, ranging from an 0.4 percent increase in murders to a 16.5 percent in-

TABLE D

Urban and Rural Rates per 100,000 of the Population for Leading Criminal Offenses, 1953 (Estimated Population) *

OFFENSES	*Urban Areas* (2,542 CITIES: TOTAL POPULATION, 76,811,320)	*Rural Areas* (TOTAL POPULATION: 39,917,306)
1) Larceny	939.3	268.6
2) Burglary	389.6	197.6
3) Auto Theft	185.2	59.8
4) Aggravated Assault	80.4	34.2
5) Robbery	60.9	18.6
6) Rape	11.2	12.0
7) Murder	4.6	4.6
8) Manslaughter	3.4	5.3

* Derived from data appearing in *Uniform Crime Reports*, XXIV, pp. 87-92.

[23] *Uniform Crime Reports*, XVIII, p. 79.
[24] *Uniform Crime Reports*, XXIV, p. 80.

crease in burglaries. Upward increments were similarly substantial in other categories.[25]

Rises in delinquency in rural areas during the same period seem to indicate the same general upward trend. Some comparisons of urban and rural rates for general criminal offenses may be obtained from the rates for leading crimes for the year 1953, shown in Table D.

Though urban delinquencies still outnumber rural ones by at least 3.5 to 1 and will probably continue to do so for an indefinite period, we can conclude that the increase in rural juvenile offenses is significant and that the upward trend may continue at a rate comparable to, and even greater than, urban rates. Further, in selected rural areas that are beginning to experience the impact of industrialization, the rates appear to be rising precipitously. That this is being borne home in many rural districts can be seen in the mounting public clamor in such regions for the establishment of special facilities and courts where this need was not apparent a scant two decades ago.

A Summarized Profile

Where do we now stand in evaluating the principal statistical characteristics through which we can identify the country's juvenile delinquents? Although the evidence appears contradictory and shifting and depends in large degree upon variations in statistical reporting and community and court practice, certain trends can be clearly discerned.

(1) Strong evidence indicates that the rates of delinquency have risen sharply since before World War II and are continuing to rise. It is likely that 2 percent of our children between the ages of ten to seventeen appear before our courts annually for delinquent offenses. Whether we may thus anticipate by 1960 a million and a half arrests for juvenile offenses annually is difficult to ascertain, although evidence indicates that this may not be entirely improbable.

(2) The median age for juvenile offenders is still about fifteen and a half, although more recent data suggest somewhat higher median ages for both boys and girls, with boys on the average about six months older than girls at the time of court adjudication.

(3) The sex ratio still is greater for boys by far—about 4.5 to 1—but we must take into account the differing cultural reasons for the appre-

---

[25] *Uniform Crime Reports*, XXIV, p. 80.

hension of girls and the ages at which they occur. The ratios certainly seem to shrink as the girls attain the eighteen-year-old level and in the six-year period beyond this age.

(4) The types of offenses for which boys and girls find themselves in trouble still appear to show the same trend that has been noted for years: boys are apprehended primarily for stealing and malicious mischief, and girls mainly for ungovernable behavior and sexual offenses. This is largely the result of differences in cultural attitudes toward the sexes.

(5) The alarming rise in the proclivity of our young people for serious offenses should be noted, as revealed in the recent findings that more than half our auto thefts and about half our burglaries are committed by youths under eighteen years of age.

(6) Delinquency still appears to be a function of minority group rejection. However, the focus has shifted from the native-born children of European immigrants, as in the first three decades of this century, to the children of our Negro, Puerto Rican, and Mexican minorities.

(7) Finally, although delinquency is still heavily concentrated in urban areas, the rate of rural delinquency is rising appreciably and appears to be accelerating more rapidly than in our cities.

With these over-all statistical lineaments of delinquency in mind, let us first look at some of the difficulties encountered in conducting a scientific inquiry into so complex a subject matter and examine what scholars can tell us about personality structure and organization. From there we shall move on to the more pressing problems of what specifically produces delinquency.

For Further Reading

SELLIN, THORSTEN, "The Uniform Criminal Statistics Act," in *Journal of Criminal Law and Criminology*, Vol. 40 (March-April, 1950), pp. 678-700.

> One of our foremost and ablest critics of contemporary crime and delinquency statistics recommends a specific form of legislation that may enable us to obtain an adequate grasp of this problem.

SCHWARTZ, EDWARD E., "A Community Experiment in the Measurement of Juvenile Delinquency," in *Yearbook of the National Probation and Parole Association* (1945), pp. 157-82.

A recommended procedure for the coördination of delinquency registration in a given urban area, indicating the variations in the identification of delinquents within the same area.

HATHAWAY, STARKE R., AND ELIO D. MONACHESI, EDS., *Analyzing and Predicting Juvenile Delinquency With the MMPI* (Minneapolis, 1953).

A series of challenging research projects employing the Minnesota Multiphasic Personality Inventory as a means of identifying selected personality and social characteristics of delinquents.

ELLINGSTON, JOHN R., *Protecting Our Children From Criminal Careers* (New York, 1948).

Basing his conclusions upon recent trends and statistical findings, the former executive secretary of the American Law Institute describes and recommends the adoption of the Model Youth Authority Act for the treatment of apprehended delinquents.

AXELRAD, SIDNEY, "Negro and White Institutionalized Delinquents," in *American Journal of Sociology*, 57 (1952), pp. 569-74.

A description of variations in commitment procedures in a large metropolitan community on the basis of racial differences.

Part Two | PRESSURES
TOWARD
DELINQUENCY

Chapter 3

THE SEARCH FOR THE ELUSIVE CAUSES

At the very outset, let us recognize that what we are actually searching for is a set of definitive principles by which we can begin to understand how different causal conditions tend to produce the wide variety of problems that occur in youthful maladjustment. What we are looking for is some workable hypothesis or theory, on the basis of which we may be able to comprehend a widely ranging and variable set of conditions. We begin with a relatively simple premise. We recognize, in the first place, that problems of youthful maladjustment assume a variety of forms and types, and that they appear in both similar and different forms on different socio-economic levels. Therefore, let us begin with the premise that *continuing* behavior which creates a series of tensions manifested in disturbances not only for the individual concerned but for those who come into daily immediate contact with him, such as his parents, siblings, teachers, and friends, provides the basis for any study of delinquent or youthful maladjustment patterns.

It is obviously impossible to develop a definition of normalcy and maladjustment which could suit the needs and demands of different social environments and different physical locales.[1] We must recognize

[1] See Wirth, "Ideological Aspects of Social Disorganization." The increasing convergence in view between psychiatrists and sociologists on this problem is summarized

that there is no common standard of adjustment to which we may expect all children to conform. The expectancies in a rigorously orthodox religious home differ greatly from the standards that can reasonably be expected from a child in a social, economic, and cultural setting in which the demands upon him are of another kind.[2] In fact, the characteristic behavior responses of a child, let us say, in a highly permissive and unconventional family atmosphere may produce a series of responses that would almost certainly be considered catastrophic in the old-fashioned patriarchal home.[3] As Folsom and Zimmerman have shown in their studies of changing family patterns on the American scene, we are producing a wide variety of family types in American culture, based fundamentally upon ecological and cultural differences, which in turn induce a series of behavior expectancies on the part of the child that are wholly indigenous to the peculiar social environment in which they are found.[4]

We are compelled, therefore, to regard maladjustment from the standpoint of the continuing types of tensions produced in different types of social milieux, remembering that the standards to which the child seeks adjustment are endlessly variable.

Here we have admittedly an open area for further discussion and analysis which appears to array the social scientist and the social psychologist on one side and the organically rooted psychiatrist on the other. There is still a remarkable tendency, despite the stimulating pioneer work of Harry Stack Sullivan, William Alanson White, and Karl Menninger to break away from the heavily freighted organic and Freudian orientations of traditional American psychiatry, to look for some type of universal standard of normalcy (largely based upon organic criteria, if they can ever be found), which may be employed as

in the *American Journal of Sociology*, 42 (May, 1937), pp. 773-877, in which representative psychiatrists and sociologists present their views, integrated in a general position by Dr. Herbert Blumer. See also Bloch, *Disorganization*, pp. 69-74.

[2] See Wiese and Becker, *Systematic Sociology*; also Wegrocki, "A Critique of Cultural and Statistical Concepts of Abnormality"; and Green, "Social Values and Psychotherapy."

[3] See Bossard, *The Sociology of Child Development*, pp. 283-310, 433-59; also Folsom, *The Family and Democratic Society*, pp. 326-64, and Bloch, *Disorganization*, pp. 89-91.

[4] Folsom, *The Family and Democratic Society*; Zimmerman, *The Family of Tomorrow: The Cultural Crisis and The Way Out*. Compare Davis and Dollard, *Children of Bondage*; Davis and Havighurst, "Social Class and Color Differences in Child-Rearing"; Green, "The Middle Class Child and Neurosis"; Havighurst and Taba, *Adolescent Character and Personality*.

critical elements in determining genetic standards of adjustment. Ironically, even when recognizing their limitations, many psychiatrists fail to see the far-reaching implications in the modern social psychiatric and anthropological movement away from Sigmund Freud's limited commentaries on social normalcy, social structure, and social organization in his *Totem and Taboo* and *Modern Civilization and Its Discontents*. Limitations of space and the objectives of this volume do not permit a lengthy analysis of the critical points of cleavage in this debate. However, from the standpoint of practical considerations in the handling of the variety of family types and methods of child-rearing in American culture, we cannot conceivably speak of definitive standards to which the child may adjust.

In analyzing causal patterns of delinquency, therefore, all we can do is to determine those common and culturally determined situations in which the expected standards of child behavior are so *continuously at variance* with the standards of the immediate groups and the family with which the child comes into contact as to constitute a serious threat to himself and the groups of which he is a part. Further, the tensions precipitated by the child's behavior will not only seriously impair the possibilities for his successful adjustment to the wider culture but will at the same time make it extremely difficult, if not impossible, for the members of his immediate social groupings to function in their expected and accustomed manner. In other words, the disruptive behavior of the child must be such that it will impair the efficiency of the functioning of the group—irrespective of how (within normal limits) that group regards its own standards—as well as the child's own capacity to make progressively successful adaptations to his environment.

What Is a Cause?

If we examine the enormous number and variety of studies that have been made of delinquency during the past three decades—and we have virtually been deluged with every conceivable type of study during this period—we find that either implicitly or explicitly the point of view which has just been stated is attaining recognition. Psychiatrists are not as prone, however, to recognize what has become evident as a commonplace fact to social scientists and social psychologists. We still find that psychiatrists, particularly those of the Freudian school, are apt to regard maladjustments as principally organically derived and to assume a generic or universal quality for all children, regardless of social class, or ethnic, economic, and cultural background. The way in which the concept of rejection is universally treated by psychiatrists is a case in point. There are as many varieties of rejection, all with differing impact, as there are differently structured and organized family types.

What most of these studies have attempted to do is to examine concomitant or associated factors recurring either in delinquency in general or in some one of its specialized types. Very few of the studies have attempted to standardize their findings on the basis of groups presenting common factors of socio-economic or cultural environments, let alone common problems of behavior. The majority of the studies undertaken in the field of delinquency have invariably dealt with some type of randomly drawn sample, based upon court findings, institutional populations, or groups in delinquency areas, and frequently based upon almost any type of youthful misbehavior the researcher regards as delinquent. Aside from the fact that the results of such pieces of research have for the most part been noncomparable, considerable confusion exists as to what constitutes a cause itself. It is for this reason that many competent students of delinquency and crime—including such able scholars as Walter C. Reckless and Negley K. Teeters—have regarded the search for causes with some dubiety and have frankly acknowledged that research interest should concentrate upon the problem of what constitutes delinquent or criminal behavior after it is already clearly recognized as an established behavior pattern. Although recognizing that many of our causal studies engage in what appear to be "will-o'-the-wisp" searches, the writers can hardly agree with such expressions of opinion. The complexity and the difficulties in this field should not dissuade us from pursuing our study of causal patterns, for the fact remains that, in the last resort, unless we comprehend the meaning of causal factors in delinquency we can never really come to grips with the problems of delinquency prevention and control.[5]

In the attempt to pursue their subject matters scientifically, the social sciences and psychology have tried to follow the fundamental pat-

[5] See Reckless, *The Crime Problem*, pp. ix, 7-19; Teeters and Reinemann, *The Challenge of Delinquency*, pp. 7-9, 212-14. Although the latter work seems to deny this thesis, many of the critical comments seem to imply the futility of a search for an adequate causal theory.

tern of causal thinking of the physical and the natural sciences. The history of these sciences has indicated that causes can be determined only on the basis of certain critical factors which ineluctably and inevitably will produce a certain consequence. All science however, as Lundberg has indicated, is conditional, i.e., it states that *if* certain stipulated conditions are found, *then* certain consequences will follow.[6] Like the present-day social scientists and psychologists, the early physical and biological scientists were baffled by the complexity of the problems and data with which they dealt. They discovered through painstaking effort, however, that by experimental method and the use of deductive logic based upon experiential check, it was possible to separate from a host of complex factors those which were most critical, or most directly instrumental, in producing a certain result. Before the law of falling bodies ultimately reduced the measured flight through space of heavy objects to the two basic constants of time and gravitational pull, a number of other factors were regarded as controlling such movement. However, the recurrent types of accelerated movement through space of heavy bodies in the same predictable manner always rested, in the last resort, upon the two critical factors of time and gravitation. When these two *critical factors* were finally separated from the wide variety of conditions which were once thought to operate, a causal theory was established which has stood the test of time and which has enabled us to make predictions about falling bodies of any type and under almost any conceivable circumstance.

This type of completely valid and accurate causal description is, of course, not possible at the present stage of development of the social sciences and may, in fact, never be possible to attain.[7] It does, however, represent a challenge and a model whereby we may attempt to make our own valid studies of causation, whether in delinquency, behavior disorder, or human waywardness. In the sciences dealing with human behavior, we are apt to feel overwhelmed by the complexity of the factors in even the simplest of human problems. For this reason, students of delinquency and crime have been inclined to feel that the time is not yet ripe for the development of adequate causal theories

[6] Lundberg, *Can Science Save Us?* pp. 33-4.

[7] See (among others) Chase, *The Proper Study of Mankind;* Chapin, *Experimental Designs in Sociological Research;* Lundberg, *Social Research* and his more recent *Can Science Save Us?;* Young, *Scientific Social Surveys and Research;* Greenwood, *Experimental Sociology;* and Goode and Hatt, *Methods in Social Research.*

because of present-day limitations of our state of knowledge. A commonplace rationalization of students of delinquency frequently has been to blame their unanswered problems on the psychologists who, they hold, have failed to provide these special areas with an efficient theory of personality. It is instructive to realize that early physical scientists were faced with similar problems and were prone to attribute their own difficulties in research to the presence of an overwhelming array of complex factors in the determination of any physical event. Read Bain, in a classic analysis, has indicated that complexity need not deter social scientists and psychologists in their search for causal processes, provided they gear their sights to the search for *critical and recurrent factors* in human problems.[8]

The problem, thus, is one of determining the *critical factors* producing a certain situation or a certain sequence of events. But the critical factors operating in a problem are not necessarily to be conceived as "causes" in a real sense. In fact, the philosophy of modern science has attempted to dispense with the term "cause." Moreover, as Albert K. Cohen has recently shown, factors in delinquency, usually present in intricate conglomerates, must be seen in their varying and configured impact upon a total situation before they can be recognized as causes. This requires the evaluation of cause in an organized theoretical view.[9] What we are looking for in most of the studies of human and physical happenings is an invariant relationship of certain *key* factors to a given set of conditions which, in the majority of instances in which these conditions occur, is always apt to be present. How can this relationship be discovered? In all scientific research, the procedures tend to be the same.

Fundamentally, there are two basic approaches, one, essentially a mass statistical approach to the problem, and the second, an approach based upon intensive and detailed studies of individual cases. The former can best be accomplished by drawing careful comparisons between selected groups or types of data, identical in all particulars except for the few factors we are attempting to measure. It is noteworthy that, despite the enormous number and variety of studies which have been undertaken in the field of delinquency, *very few have attempted to follow rigorously this basic tenet of statistically controlled scientific in-*

---

[8] Bain, "The Concept of Complexity in Sociology."
[9] Cohen, *Juvenile Delinquency and the Social Structure.*

vestigation.[10] Such ventures are not only very time-consuming—a limiting factor always present in a field such as delinquency where continuously pressing demands are made for immediate answers—but they depend upon the collection of evidence which is frequently very difficult to find. Not the least of the handicaps to this method is its high cost. The Gluecks' *Unraveling Juvenile Delinquency,* for example, falls into this category. If more investigations of this type could be carried out, we might more rapidly come close to some of the answers we are seeking. However, even in the case of such carefully controlled studies, certain rigorous precautions must be taken. It is not enough to make detailed, point-for-point comparisons. Such research must also relate directly to carefully framed hypothetical questions and postulates which the researchers raise. In the case of even such painstaking research as that developed by the Gluecks, theoretical questions and postulates were neither explicitly framed nor stated.

In the second approach, considered by certain students of delinquency the only effective method, the analyst devotes himself to the intensive study of individual case histories.[11] The procedure recommended in such case studies is to focus upon the manifold interrelationships between the developing personality and the environment, in both the formative and mature stages of the problem. *In this way, not only is the total complex of the individual's personal relationships assessed and studied, but each of the separate factors involved in the dynamic growth of the whole personality is evaluated according to its relative importance in the process.*

There are many variables in the personality of the delinquent and the delinquency-producing situation itself which the investigators may not readily discern and which themselves may constitute the critical factors involved in the delinquent act. The investigator may inadvertently focus upon conspicuous and seemingly important factors which, in the end, will reveal very little of the essential nature of delinquent behavior. Many ambitious studies have erred in this direction despite enormous expenditures of time and effort.

[10] See Chapin, *Experimental Designs in Sociological Research,* and Greenwood, *Experimental Sociology.*

[11] An interesting variation of this method is the comparative case technique of Lindesmith, derived from the sociologist Znaniecki and called "analytic induction." See Lindesmith, *Opiate Addiction,* Chapter I, and other writings; also Znaniecki, *The Method of Sociology,* pp. 232-45.

The Cambridge-Somerville Youth Study

What is in so many other respects one of the most commendable, painstaking, and honest pieces of investigation of the past ten years, the Cambridge-Somerville Youth Study, demonstrates that even competent and well-intentioned investigators are not above serious error in overlooking the essential meaning of the key factors in research.[12] It is unusual to find in the literature of this field a piece of research with so few pretensions and in which the intellectual integrity and probity of the research staff are so outstanding. The attempt made here was to determine whether or not in the case of a child with a delinquent record the sustained personal relationship and counselling of a friendly and interested adult will result in recognizable, concrete, and positive forms of adjustment. To test this hypothesis, the researchers went to considerable pains to compare relatively equivalent "controls" with the tested group, each of the two groups consisting of 325 boys.

Why, then, despite the attempt to make an adequate controlled comparison, could this project not reach a reliable conclusion in confirming or denying this hypothesis? The primary reason is that the *critical* factors to be tested were inherent in the basic assumptions of the research itself, and that these were *not* subjected to test; namely, the *character* of the relationship between the counselling adult and the delinquent child. As Professor Gordon W. Allport states in the preface to this work, "The initial hypothesis was a broad one: that the impact of personality upon personality, guided by good will and maturity of judgment, would have beneficial results. Although this hypothesis is certainly worth the testing, it is clear that, even if established, the bare statistics of success would not tell us *how* or *why* the change came about. The dynamics of the influence would have to be sought from an analysis of the case records—from a *post factum* reconstruction of the interplay of the two personalities at each stage of the relationship . . . To study the how and why of the change, . . . a deeper study of cause and effect would be needed." [13]

---

[12] Powers and Witmer, *An Experiment in the Prevention of Delinquency.*
[13] Powers and Witmer, *An Experiment in the Prevention of Delinquency*, pp. xi-xii.

Some Blind Alleys in the Search for Causes

A variety of false leads have been followed in attempting to determine the critical factors in the etiology of delinquency, i.e., in the search for an invariant relationship of key factors to stipulated types of youthful disorders. These research errors have taken three principal forms: (1) overemphasis of a given factor or set of factors (*particularism*); (2) searching for multiple causes in poorly selected samples for study (*multiple causal hypotheses*); or (3) attempting to locate a basic factor or a given situation as the prime determinant in either the chronological or emergent-patterned development of delinquency problems (searching for *primacy*).

The Particularistic Error

A classic error has arisen from the common tendency to overemphasize a single factor or set of factors, an error sociologists term the "particularistic fallacy." This frequently results from an apparent discovery which subsequently proves to be a commonplace, such as the overstress upon poor housing as a cause of delinquency. Also, like any other field of research, the study of delinquency has not been free of prevailing "winds of doctrine" and the cultish influences of a particular mode of research. Thus, the undue stress, i.e., the particularistic fallacy, is often also the consequence of a new or "fashionable" trend in research emphasis. In the 1920's and 1930's, for example, much interest was displayed in the so-called ecological school of delinquency research promoted by Clifford Shaw and his research associates at the University of Chicago. Closely related to what has been termed the "social disorganization" school of delinquency, this group laid special stress upon adverse influences of the urban environment. Sheldon Glueck has exposed with some penetration the fallacies of this type of thinking although he, as others, is attacking a position that has already passed · into the limbo of "lost causes." This view has been supplanted by the more realistic recognition that the understanding of delinquency may only be accomplished by (*a*) recognizing its distinctive forms, (*b*) relating such forms to a variety of different causal combinations, and (*c*) *relating such causal conditions to an explanatory causal theory.*

Without a demonstrable causal hypothesis, the relating of facts themselves serves little purpose.[14]

In general, however, the fallacy of particularism may be largely attributed to (1) the highly random nature of the samples of delinquents
used for a given study, and (2) the fact that either no controls or
inadequate controls were employed for purposes of comparison. As a
result, in late nineteenth and early twentieth century analyses of delinquency, it was common at one time to stress "bad companions," at
another, "inadequate schooling," and at still other times, "poor housing," "family discord," "early employment," or any one of the factors
which have come to be associated with delinquency. Incredible as it
may seem, certain judges of our juvenile courts, with striking and in-
genuous irony, have more recently gone so far as to profess the belief
that "deficiency in arithmetic study" or reading retardation in the public schools may operate as significant "symptomatic causes"! In passing,
it might be said that a current danger is the tendency to overstress the
psychiatric aspects of delinquency causation and treatment, in the common practice of regarding each delinquent as the result of some defect
of character or of some deep-seated emotional disturbance.

> Modern criminology received its first great impetus with the classical work
> of Lombroso and his disciple, Ferri, who as products of their age during
> the latter part of the nineteenth century, attempted to lay the basis for
> a fully scientific crimino-biological theory of crime. . . . The basis of
> crime was biological and innate, like Calvinistic predestination and
> damnation for those marked by certain stigmata. Not only were criminals
> conceived as possessing different physical characteristics, prognathic jaws,
> low foreheads, a peculiar helix of the ear, the nasal structure and other
> distinguishing features, but these were conceived as outer manifestations
> of innate psychological characteristics. This ready and over-simplified
> separation of the sheep from the goats suffered not only from a lack of
> knowledge of modern psychological and sociological factors, but from
> inadequacy in evaluation of comparative data, which is so important
> today. . . .

> The ingenuous nature of this and subsequent theories lay in the fact that
> their proponents sought to discover some magical touchstone, some al-
> chemist's miracle element, by which the knotty problem of criminality
> might be miraculously unraveled. Hence an entire series of such particu-
> laristic views was paraded before us, each to provide the answers to our

[14] See Glueck, *Crime and Correction: Selected Papers*, pp. 1-23.

questions and each soon to be supplanted by an equally spurious doctrine. Curiosity concerning the function of intelligence and its measurement arose during the First World War. The psychologist Goring in 1913 thought he had found the answer to the sphinxian riddle of criminality in low intelligence. Hot upon the chase, Goddard came along in 1919 and, through the much abused Kallikaks, sought to show that the basis of crime lay in feeble-mindedness. This trial balloon was soon pierced when, with a growing sophistication and temperateness, it was revealed by Herman Adler in 1918 that the intelligence scores of prisoners at Joliet Penitentiary yielded a higher average than a comparable sampling of representative groups in the United States Army. Under subsequent studies, the average intelligence of even selected officer groups suffered in comparison, a rating which apparently comes as no surprise to ex-GIs. The endocrine glands came in for their brief day, through the work of Berman, and Schlapp and Smith, heralding the day of "the new criminology," when for a brief moment we suspected that the judge's gavel might be replaced by the hypodermic syringe and the proper hormonic extract.

The discouraging quest for a unitary explanation finally led to the recent sociological emphasis upon (multiple) configurations of external (environmental) factors. We are still largely under the influence of this school of thought. . . .

At this point the circle has come full round. We have found ourselves on a theoretical merry-go-round whose spins and turns have largely been compelled by the dominant cultural interest at the moment.[15]

Not only was the failure to examine carefully the several *behavioral* components that entered into each generic condition a serious weakness of this approach but *an even more fundamental defect was the failure to relate specific generic conditions to the genetic growth of different personalities.* This means quite simply that each significant factor which has been uncovered conceals a great variety of separate behavior processes functioning differently in the life of each personality. Further, it suggests that the period during which such behavioral processes operate—in terms of their "frequency, duration, priority and intensity" as the criminologist Sutherland has put it—will play a vital part in revealing the causal process toward delinquency.

We must however, in all truth, pay some tribute to the value of particularistic studies of the past. Although highly limited and one-

---

[15] Bloch, "Social Change and the Delinquent Personality."

sided, they have nevertheless added to the growing insights of delinquency experts by (1) focusing attention upon factors which previously might have been overlooked, (2) compelling coördination of such insights with other accepted views, and (3) drawing the attention of the public to the multiple and changing conditions that tend to breed juvenile disorders. Since they did not attempt, any more than did other "lost causes" in delinquency research, to ally their findings with a comprehensive interpretation (or theoretical view), they were largely deficient in adding to our fundamental knowledge of delinquency. It must be stressed, practical considerations notwithstanding, that the uncovering of facts in itself is of little long-range value in attacking the problems of delinquency unless we can, at the same time, place those facts within an efficient theoretical framework. Although the uninformed layman may cavil at what he feels is an unwarranted intrusion of theory into a field which has already become obscured by a myriad cultish viewpoints, the fact remains that it is only through some comprehensive theoretical insight that we can interpret the facts that we have. A single case in point: Of what value is it to indicate the prevalence of substandard housing in the lives of many of our delinquents, while at the same time neglecting the fact that countless nondelinquent children are exposed to the same conditions? To account for such seeming contradictions, we must develop a viewpoint which will enable us to comprehend why delinquency results in one case, while in the other it does not. This is also true of the various other specialized factors that have appeared as symptomatic conditions of delinquency—bad companions, inadequate schooling, unwholesome recreation, broken families, economic deprivation, and the like.

Multiple Factor Hypotheses

A common practice of most early investigators was simply to collect a random sample of cases from the files of the courts or institutions, and to note the frequency with which certain factors recurred. The samples themselves were rarely homogeneous. Not only was the individual structuring of personality neglected, but a given sample frequently comprised the cases of children from different ethnic and racial groups, different economic levels, different educational backgrounds, and different homes, among the wide variety of differentiating factors. *It cannot*

Stscherbaw)

SPEECH RATING SHEET

Name of Speaker: *Stacherbon*   Time: 3:24   Grade: 90

Criteria	Exc.	Good	Fair	Poor	Comments
Idea		O.K.			Still need to clar
Organization		✗	✗		your specific p
Support		✗	✗		sentence. ~~~~
Logical Develop.			✗		you need to s
Use of Language		✗			each point as you
Interest		✗			it. Give source
Eye Contact	✗	✗			definition. Good direct del
Posture		✗			especially duri
Gestures			✗ ✗		first part of the
Voice	✗				you demonst
Rate		✗			more confiden
Enthusiasm	✗	✗			time but ne

work some
on supporte
points at pro
time. we m
more outlin
Lets discuss t
class next tim

be repeated sufficiently that sound scientific research in this field as in all others rests upon carefully controlled comparisons, based upon populations which are identical (or as nearly so as we can find them) in all respects other than the given factor or condition we are testing. Even when comparisons were attempted with other groups, it was rare to find groups that were directly comparable on the basis of common mental and psychological components, or such sociological factors as common income standards, family structure and organization, schooling, cultural levels, religious affiliations, and the many other factors that must be taken into consideration in careful scientific analysis. Certain social scientists have had recourse to such multiple factor theories as a kind of desperate "last ditch" stand, seeking to find "refuge in numbers," i.e., a multiplicity of causal conditions, in view of the apparent failure to unravel the complicated skeins of delinquency causation. In fact, this view is still held by many so-called experts who, in stating that there is no single cause of delinquency, feel that the dependence upon multiple factors is sufficient to provide an adequate explanation of delinquency.

The results of these multiple factor studies were historically significant in that they dramatized for the public the kind of corruptive and diversified environmental conditions that provide a setting for delinquency. They did little, however, to indicate the precise nature of the causal patterns that are most likely to produce specific types of youthful maladjustment, of which delinquency is but one. On the spurious assumption that the sample under investigation, drawn from court records, institutional cases, or social case work files, represented an adequate picture of delinquency (which it did not), studies from 1910 to 1930 revealed an endless repetition of the same types of factors operating in numerous samples, although these factors differed widely in their frequency of occurrence and, in some instances, were actually contradictory. For example, in 1927 Shideler assessed a number of such studies and discovered that "broken homes" as a causative factor varied from 40 percent in some studies to 70 percent in others. Somewhat later, Shaw and McKay suggested that this factor was considerably overstressed, figuring as an important condition primarily in the cases of children under ten years of age. The difficulty in assessing each contributory factor makes it virtually impossible to agree on how much each factor should be weighted in the causal conditions producing delinquency. What appears to us now as a kind of superficiality or naïveté was due to several things: (1) there was little agreement on the characteristics constituting delinquency, resulting in heterogeneous sampling of youthful offenders from the chronic truant to the seriously pathologically disturbed child; (2) there was little effort to compare delinquent and nondelinquent children from *comparable* socio-economic and cultural backgrounds; and (3) there was virtually no recognition that any one factor must be seen in relationship to the other factors involved. Thus, all kinds of combinations of factors are possible; the assumption that delinquency is created out of a set of conditions where "bad housing" constitutes 40 percent of the cause, "poor companions" 20 percent, "economic deprivation" another 12 percent, etc., etc., is naïve, to say the least. It is perhaps even more significant that these studies have conspicuously overlooked a very fundamental consideration, *viz.*, that not all individuals exposed to the same adverse conditions become delinquent or even seriously maladjusted. In fact, the vast majority, as we know, do not.

In a classic study of 4,000 delinquent boys in Chicago and Boston, Dr. William Healy indicated the fatuousness of this type of research by revealing the well-nigh innumerable combinations of the several supposed contributory factors producing any of the more common types of recognized delinquency. Broadly classifying the major statistical factors arising with great frequency into the three major categories of (1) antecedent factors, (2) the mental states of the delinquent, and (3) the delinquent offense, he found that virtually any combination of background factors in conjunction with any of the statistically revealed mental states might produce any type of delinquency.[16] The limited assumptions upon which this type of research is premised would, in effect, permit an almost unlimited number of permutations and combinations of significant contributory factors explaining major forms of delinquency, as the chart on page 69 reveals.

Recognizing the failure of this type of statistically unregulated and undifferentiated study, Healy took on the task of stressing the importance of intensive study of the individual delinquent. This work, probably more than any other, led to the inseminating collaboration of the psychiatric (individual) and the sociological (environmental) approaches to the study of delinquent disorders. The new insight has ushered in

[16] Healy, *The Individual Delinquent.*

the fruitful coöperation of the multidisciplinary approaches in which the sociologist, clinical psychologist, psychiatrist, social case worker, and statistician join their efforts.

The anthropologist and biologist Ashley Montagu has made a trenchant observation regarding research of the multiple factor type by remarking that almost any random collection of data—even about a group of cadavers prepared for dissection on the mortuary slabs of a medical school, as he ironically states—can be made to yield common

CHART VIII

Combination of Factors Entering into Differential Delinquent Behavior *

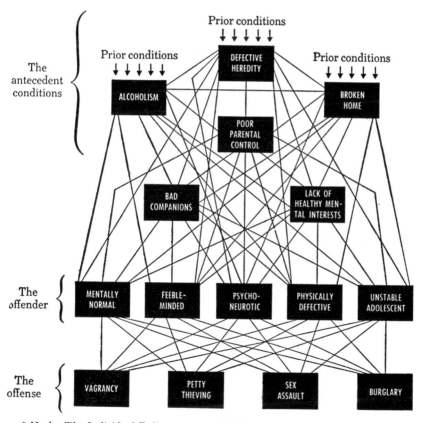

* Healy, *The Individual Delinquent*, pp. 164-65.

statistical characteristics. To impute the existence of a causal relationship between these statistical factors and the fact of the presence of the bodies on the slabs is valid only within the most restricted and tenuous limits. To regard factors of this type as sufficiently valid causes for the determination of individual problems of delinquency is, of course, a gross distortion of scientific logic.[17]

The recognition of these limitations has been instrumental in deflecting our research procedures in the direction of the remarkable pioneering work of Healy and Bronner in utilizing carefully drawn, controlled samples of identical twins and siblings, through dual case and point-for-point analysis, undertaken both on a group and a "paired" basis.[18] The conclusions to be drawn from their celebrated study, *New Light on Delinquency and Its Treatment*, are as valid today as they were when the study was first released. The results signify quite plainly that the mass approach and the individual approach are two entirely different types of operation. If we are to learn anything about the fundamental causes of delinquency, we must recognize that each personality is uniquely constituted at each phase of its development, and that each individual personality must be appraised in terms of the situational determinants and the distinctive conditioning and precipitating environmental influences which (*a*) set the pattern for habitual behavior and (*b*) determine whether or not delinquent behavior will result at any given time. It is a fallacy to believe that the so-called "accidental" factors entering into the complex behavior patterns we call delinquency cannot be scientifically studied. Just as fallacious is the assertion that the *uniquely* conditioned elements entering into delinquency preclude scientific analysis and verification because they do not follow statistically relevant causal sequences. Neither the uniqueness of an event nor its so-called "accidental" character place it beyond the sphere of scientific analysis. Accidental and unique factors are simply conditions which, for the present, we have not yet learned to understand. The physical sciences have amply demonstrated during their history that similar problems recurred—and were solved—after it had seemed hopeless to find explanations for what appeared to be unique and accidental occurrences. The acknowledgment of such elements as "accidents" is simply

[17] Montagu, "The Biologist Looks at Crime."
[18] Healy and Bronner, *New Light on Delinquency and Its Treatment*.

a confession of temporary ignorance, lack of research technique, or general retardation of the science.

Our recognition of the limitations of the frequently superficial and oversimplified multiple factor approaches suggests, in consequence, that youthful maladjustment may be envisaged only in terms of a number of fluid relationships between the personality and the environment. The multiplicity of factors found in certain social areas and among certain social groups provide, as Nathaniel Cantor has stated, a *sufficient* causal explanation, without getting at the heart of the matter in determining the *efficient* basis of causation.[19] The *sufficient* factors operating in any given situation are simply the *limiting* conditions under which a certain kind of behavior is more likely to take place. Actually, however, even such a likelihood of occurrence is also apt to be highly variable. A series of identical "demoralizing" conditions may exist in other cultures and other societies—such as in Southern Europe or Sicily—and may not, nevertheless, tend to produce maladjusted behavior or responses. Limiting conditions, such as poor housing, bad companions, deficient schooling, and poor medical history, simply set the stage within which delinquency *may* occur. They do not indicate when and under what conditions a given case of maladjustment leading to delinquency will take place. This is, of course, part of an age-old controversy in the determination of scientific causation revolving around the traditional Aristotelian view, in which class-factors have been stressed in the study of causes (*i.e.,* sufficient or limiting conditions), as compared to the functional views of Galileo, now generally adhered to in modern scientific methodology. The way in which these latter views have lately tended significantly to modify research procedures in psychology may be seen in the pioneering work of Kurt Lewin's A *Dynamic Theory of Personality.*

The false attribution of efficient cause to commonly recurrent statistical factors constitutes what the philosopher Alfred N. Whitehead refers to as "the fallacy of misplaced concreteness," the ever-present danger of confusing a setting or a series of strategically placed circumstances with the definitive causal relations that produce a specific effect.

The investigators have confused the search for the efficient causes of human behavior with the discovery of the limiting conditions, namely, the environmental setting and backgrounds of the individual. Broken

[19] Cantor, *Crime and Society,* pp. 57-64.

homes, slum areas, poor use of leisure time, and so on are factors frequently found in the lives of offenders. They do not explain why the offender commits crime. Given these conditions, behavior labeled criminal may follow. Will it? The answer depends upon the individual.[20]

We clearly acknowledge the difficulty in determining efficient causes. This difficulty, however, should not lead us to the common recourse of many investigators of simply adding further to the rapidly growing list of factors playing a part in stimulating delinquency, without giving us a clue as to how such factors are integrated with developing personalities. The affirmation that there is no *single* cause of delinquency—hence seeking refuge in what appears to be the inescapable necessity of multiple factor approaches—presents a vague hope and an even vainer illusion. The difficulty is thereby not resolved but actually increased.

The multiple factor approaches leave us with two conclusions: (1) An adequate comprehension of delinquency as a *mass problem*, located in specific segments of the social order, indicates that multiple factors in their combination must be related to a general theoretical view of *why delinquency should arise among certain groups and at certain times;* and (2) the proper understanding of individual delinquency may be accomplished only by the careful study of the developmental growth of each individual as he encounters specific situations resulting from a wide series of limiting background conditions.[21] An *environmental factor,* as Dr. Bernard Glueck has so well stated, *may never be accepted as a cause until it becomes a motive.* This is true of *any* factor, constitutional, environmental, or psychological. Such factors may be understood only in relation to the total functioning personality. The developmental process of each individual, with his own needs, emotions, perceptions, cognitions, attitudes, and intellectual characteristics, as they emerge in integrated form at each stage of his development, must be seen in respect to the peculiar complex of incitements and configuring circumstances that motivate the individual at a given time. The human personality is a highly complex functional entity which absorbs, modifies, and transforms impulses from without into new patterns of behavior.[22] Although this may seem to suggest primarily a "clinical approach" to the study of cause, it should be recognized (as so few psychiatrists rec-

[20] Cantor, *Crime and Society,* pp. 60-61.
[21] See Cohen, *Juvenile Delinquency and the Social Structure,* pp. 5-13.
[22] See Frank, "Structure and Growth."

ognize, for example) that research in the fields of sociology, social anthropology, and social psychology is today coming to be oriented almost wholly to a *functional*, rather than the older *structural*, view.

As Pauline V. Young has put it, the mere *addition* of factors to a problem obscures an understanding of its nature in terms of the interfunctioning of its several aspects into a dynamic and living whole.[23] The mixing together of potash, starch, mineral elements, water, and other necessary constituents does not constitute a potato, although such elements may be "abstracted" from the living plant. Nor do bad housing, poor companions, inadequate recreation, and the large host of "sociological horribilia" abstracted from the lives of individual delinquents in themselves constitute the nature of their delinquent acts. The problem is always: *How do they react to and interpret their immediate environments?*

It should be made clear, however, that the study of multiple factors in delinquency causation may still take a very definite place in the study and amelioration of the problems of delinquency. Though their limitations are recognized, multiple factor approaches may not be simply dismissed by mere casuistry or a wave of the hand. The recognition of personality differences in growth and their varying expressive forms does *not* mean that a consideration of multiple factors has no relevance whatsoever to an understanding of our problem. The varied perspectives with which we view human behavior may all provide significant insights, but *only* on certain levels and within strictly defined limitations or frames of reference. The fact that there are *"levels* of interpretation" as well as *"levels* of understanding" is frequently overlooked by research adversaries in this field. Explanation of a wide variety of contributory factors illustrates the limiting conditions under which delinquency is more likely to arise, though it will not indicate the precise combination of circumstances under which it must inevitably arise. In conclusion, therefore, the dictates of common sense are in accord with the principle that the kinds of explanation we seek in the understanding of delinquency will depend upon the level on which we intend to understand and the level on which we intend to operate. To the clinician, the study of the dynamic growth of the child in his relation to a particular milieu becomes paramount. On the other hand, for the social agency attempting to lessen the incidence of delinquency in a wide area, a study of

[23] Young, *Social Treatment in Probation and Delinquency*, pp. 147-48.

multiple factors within a causal and interpretive framework may serve a highly effective purpose. If this fundamental fact were clearly recognized, much of the aimless wrangling between the oft-times acrimonious schools of theorists might be cut short summarily.

The Search for Primacy

The subject of primacy is intriguing and difficult. Two things are involved: something that occurred in the past which may have been basic in producing a given problem, or something which is rooted in the personality *now* and which is the actuating source of the disorder. Thus, in more technical terminology, primacy refers to either (1) the primary factor in a chronological causal sequence which may have been basic in contributing toward delinquency, or (2) the basic syndrome, or combination of factors (personality, behavioral, or environmental, considered separately or in clustered arrangements), which is significant in producing a problem of behavioral maladjustment or delinquency.

Even if it were possible to identify the first in a series of factors in a chain, the problem itself may not be of undue significance in the handling of delinquency problems. To the clinical diagnostician, the recognition of a childhood trauma in the study of a character defect has its principal significance in that it may reveal the general behavioral imbalance and orientation of a given personality. Therapeutically, the problem is to better the general conditions of the personality or the precipitating conditions, so as to remove the underlying tensions provoking the delinquency. However, whereas traumatic experiences (a severe emotional shock to a child, for example), are often very dramatic and sudden and can be accordingly identified with relative ease, in the average individual changes in personality are gradual and subtle. Further, while a traumatic experience may appear to have been crucial, such experiences actually assume different forms, meanings, and dimensions for different individuals at different levels of growth. The ultimately predominant factor may *not* have been the traumatic experience, it may be discovered, but any one of a series of other factors which interacted with the personality at a subsequent stage of its development. Thus, while it may be possible to localize the significant impact of a trauma on several behavioral levels where traumatic experiences do not figure, the relationship of coinciding factors in a complex human situation makes it extremely difficult, if not impossible, to select predominant factors.

Gestalt psychologists have made it clear in theory and on the basis of considerable empirical evidence that the totality of the experience of the human individual must be taken into consideration when treating problems of motivation and perception. More recently, this perspective has become an important methodological research tool of social psychologists, social psychiatrists, anthropologists, and sociologists in the widely applied concept of the *"field-structured"* situation: in it, the human agent and the conditioning variables of the situation are envisaged as integrally related and constricted fields of force in which human behavior takes form. This concept signifies that any form of human behavior emerges in terms of a combination of dominant drives and the limiting conditions of the immediate situation reflecting the patterned effects of social and cultural determinants.[24]

According to this view, any form of human behavior is organized from specific elements: (*a*) the dominant drives at a given moment; and (*b*) the limitations which a given situation imposes upon the expression of these drives (technically known as "the field"). Implicit in these forces are the social and cultural determinants which have helped to fashion the situation in which the individual is striving to express himself. In this way, the "field-structured" view, while focusing upon dominant drives and the restrictions upon behavior imposed by the situation, tacitly recognizes at the same time the historic chain of events that has produced the present situation and the present motivation of the individual.

This does not necessarily mean that certain predominant factors may not be operating to produce a given problem of maladjustment or delinquency. It simply means that even if we select a given factor as primary, our understanding of delinquency is not furthered unless we assess this factor in relation to the entire complex of factors operating at a given time. Such factors operate in reciprocal fashion and are continually reinforcing or weakening each other. Thus, a personality

[24] See Lewin, *A Dynamic Theory of Personality*; Brown, *Psychology and the Social Order*, pp. 43-62, 469-502; Klein, "The Menninger Foundation Research on Perception and Personality, 1947-1952: A Review"; Klein, "A Clinical Perspective for Personality Research"; Blake and Ramsey, eds., *Perception: An Approach to Personality*, Chap. XII, "The Personal World Through Perception"; Klein and Schlesinger, "Perceptual Attitudes Toward Instability"; Klein, Schlesinger, and Meister, "The Effects of Personal Values on Perception."

trait, such as an ungovernable temper, may be modified or intensified by the action of a given parent. What we have in human behavior actually is not so much a basic or overwhelming condition but a series of continuous *action-reaction patterns*. Thus, the complex of situational factors operating at any given time functions as a totality, and the reciprocal functioning of these several elements makes it extremely difficult to select one without carefully considering not only the remaining factors *but the numerous ways in which they are patterned in their relationship to the factor which may appear dominant*.

This problem continually arises when the researcher attempts to assign relative weights to the several factors operative in any human situation. Whereas such weights may be assigned with some assurance in the laboratory procedures of the experimental psychologist, it becomes a hazardous enterprise to give weighted significance to factors in the actual background histories of juvenile offenders. It is obvious that the weights for the same types of factors differ radically from person to person, even though all may be operative to a certain degree. This is demonstrated by Shaw in the following hypothetical case.[25]

X is in prison for burglary. On examination, it is found that he is also a "constitutionally inferior psychopathic personality" and a habitual alcoholic. Further inquiry discloses that X and his parents have been long in dire poverty and that they reside in the vilest tenement house in a "delinquency area." Has X's criminality been caused by his "drunkenness," or have both the alcoholism and the misconduct been "caused" by his constitutional inadequacy, or did X's habitual imbibing of alcohol aggravate his original weak inhibitory capacity? Did X become a drunkard because he couldn't stand his family's miserable economic situation, or was the drunkenness the cause of that unhealthy economic status? All these behavioral sequences may have been in effect at different times in the life of X, as a series of vicious "action-reaction" mechanisms. But even aided by a close scrutiny of X's developmental history, it would be difficult to assign *primacy* to any of the factors involved.

The multiple action-reaction patterns that make up any human experience may frequently be viewed only as a configured whole which comprises, at the same time, a historical and experiential continuum. To wrench from its total context any single human factor, or any phase of the social complex in which it is expressed, distorts the entire picture

---

[25] Shaw, "Housing and Delinquency."

of the causal process and creates an almost wholly artificial representation of the problem sequence the researcher is investigating. The necessity of pursuing such studies remains imperative, although very little of our contemporary research has been able to probe the underlying nature of this problem. Let us consider briefly a case used by Pauline Young[26] from the standpoint of the kind of evidence many of our court records present, in order to appraise this difficulty further.

Henry Harrison, fourteen years of age, was arrested by a police officer for vagrancy. He was found roaming the streets of San Y. late at night. The arresting officer recognized Henry as a previous offender. The record shows that Henry was detained for a few days in Juvenile Hall upon his first offense about six months ago, but, upon being duly admonished, he was returned to his parents and the case dismissed.

The parents state that the boy has been running away persistently and staying away from home two days to two weeks at a time. He returns home only when he is desperately in need of food or clothing, or when he is ill. The last time, when apprehended by the police officer, he was in possession of new pants and small change for which the parents could give no account. He has grown thin and appears seriously undernourished. He also suffers from painful "skin eruptions."

Henry states that he ran away the first time because he was afraid of his father who came home drunk, beat up his mother, and kicked his brother. "I was arrested, but why wasn't Pop? They talked to me about staying home but I was afraid of being kicked in the stomach, like Alex was. Why didn't they give him a talking-to?"

The study of the family, made after Henry's first offense, is very brief. Mr. Harrison is thirty-nine years old. Mrs. Harrison is thirty-five. Henry is fourteen, and Alex is twelve years of age. They live in a five-room bungalow, well furnished, in a nice residential section of the city.

Mr. Harrison drinks heavily and is therefore unable to hold a job. When working, as a certified public accountant, he earns $75.00 a week. Has been out of steady work for nearly three years, during which time Mrs. Harrison's mother aided. There has been considerable conflict in the home, nagging and quarreling, and displays of temper, since Mr. H.'s loss of employment. Once Mr. H. came home so drunk that Mrs. H. had to run in the middle of the night to her mother's, taking Alex with her. Henry had already run away from home.

[26] Young, *Social Treatment in Probation and Delinquency*, 2nd ed., New York, 1952, p. 149. Partially reproduced here with permission of the publishers, McGraw-Hill Book Company, Inc.

What we have, in effect, is a type of "vicious circle" theory of delin-quency causation emerging in the ordinary attempt to investigate such a complex of causes. As the following diagram shows, we may begin at any point in the complex of problems and, moving clockwise or counterclockwise, present a fairly reasonable case to indicate what may have been the causal chain of events. More significant, however, is the fact that in the presentation of such a complex interrelationship of functioning factors, very little insight is gained in the distinction be-

CHART IX

*The "Vicious Circle" Concept of Causation**

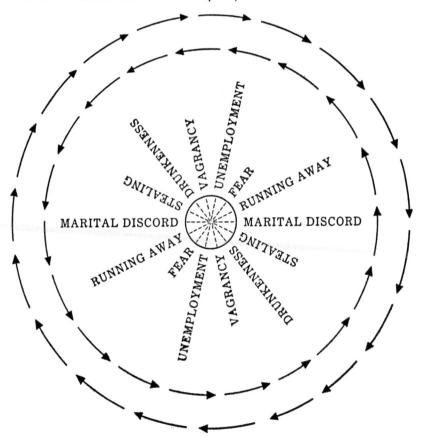

* Concept coined by Clifford R. Shaw; chart presented by Pauline V. Young, *Social Treatment in Probation and Delinquency*, p. 150.

tween mere behavioral symptoms and the underlying personality factors producing these conditions.

As in our discussion of multiple factors, this dilemma appears to come close to the heart of the problem of causation. We must learn to distinguish the precipitating factors operating to produce a given problem and the *several symptomatic forms of behavior indicative of personality tension and maladjustment,* as well as the underlying causal conditions revealed in such symptoms and behavioral traits. The "action-reaction" and "vicious circle" theories of delinquency and crime causation invariably confuse symptomatic patterns with underlying behavioral causes. However, this should not be construed to signify confirmation of the view that the proper method of evaluating causes and symptoms is by some arbitrary separation of personality traits and syndromes from behavioral forms and environmental conditions. The logical dictates of reason appear to suggest this expedient to many psychologists and psychiatrists. However, there is a specious and deceptive form of logic in such a ready-made dichotomy, as modern personality theory seems to indicate. *Motivation in human behavior is integrally related to a series of stimulating circumstances. The stimulating circumstance is as much a "part of the cause" as the motivational pattern and the personality orientation itself.*

Aside from the repeated demonstration of this fact in our experimental psychological laboratories, a brief examination of any human situation will reveal this to be true. A motive requires a given type of incitement to act upon it before it manifests itself in behavior. In a sense, motivation, as in the case of an attitude, must always have some outward focus in the situations the personality confronts. Without the opportunity of outward focus and some *defined* social situation—whether it be familial, that of a peer-age group, or some other commonly recurrent setting—the motivation itself remains purely latent. In a recent analysis of this postulate in psychological research, David Krech states: "Experimentally this means that we cannot talk about 'varying the stimulus conditions and holding motivation constant,' or 'varying motivations and holding knowledge constant.' Varying the stimulus conditions will vary [the organization of behavior] and therefore *all* of its attributes." [27]

To understand primacy in the only realistic sense, thus, is to recog-

[27] Krech, "Notes Towards a Psychological Theory of Personality."

nize that there are a number of underlying personality traits which, in combination, may lead to a number of different outcomes, dependent upon the situations to which the individual is exposed. Given personalities which, through accidents of rearing or because of constitutional difficulties, tend to produce the same or homologous types of motivational structure, it is reasonable to anticipate characteristic responses of *either* a social or antisocial nature. By the same token, given certain types of environmental pressure, it is reasonable, under limiting and stipulated conditions, to expect the emergence of motivational patterns which appear similar.[28] For these reasons, it would appear effective, at the present juncture in delinquency research, to learn to identify (1) motivational patterns on the basis of discoverable syndromes, i.e., patterns of behavioral traits, including constitutional and psychogenic factors when they can be discovered; and (2) clusters of situational and sociocultural determinants which may either promote the development of such patterns, or after disturbing traits have become imbedded in personality, serve as precipitating circumstances in encouraging antisocial behavior. If we pursue this road, not only may we be able to disclose those *suggestible* personality-types that are more prone to engage in illicit and antisocial acts, but we may at the same time sharpen our vision as to the *kinds* of deviant or antisocial acts to which such individuals are more liable. Further, we may be able to discern the kinds of situational components which, in combination, tend to produce broad personality types and their tendencies to various behavioral disorders. This research, thus far belated, is slowly coming to the fore and is manifested particularly in the work of Hewitt and Jenkins, A. J. Reiss, Jr., the Gluecks (in part), C. H. Growdon, and a few others. Although not related directly to the study of delinquency, certain recent developments in the experimental study of personality should prove of considerable value in giving us insight into these problems.

For Further Reading

BOSSARD, JAMES H. S., *The Sociology of Child Development* (New York, 1948).

[28] See Davis, *Children of Bondage.*

An analysis of the varieties of family structures on different socio-economic and cultural levels that produce differences in personality patterning among children.

ZIMMERMAN, CARL C., *The Family of Tomorrow: The Cultural Crisis and the Way Out* (New York, 1949).

Professor Zimmerman indicates the severe cultural strains upon modern family life and recommends certain means for safeguarding family life in a democracy.

GREEN, ARNOLD W., "The Middle Class Male Child and Neurosis," in *American Sociological Review*, 11 (1946), pp. 31-41.

In this well-known study, the author indicates the kinds of strains to which the middle class male child is exposed in a New England industrial community as contrasted with the children in factory workers' families.

HAVIGHURST, ROBERT J., AND HILDA TABA, *Adolescent Character and Personality* (New York, 1949).

A stimulating portrayal of the problems peculiar to the adolescent in American culture and their expression on various socio-cultural levels.

LUNDBERG, GEORGE A., *Can Science Save Us?* (New York, 1947).

A strong plea for the use of modern quantitative and scientific methods for the study of contemporary human problems by the leader of the quantitative school among American sociologists.

CHASE, STUART, *The Proper Study of Mankind* (New York, 1948).

A lucid and well-written popularized account of the progress made by the social sciences in this century, with recommendations for their wider application and use.

CHAPIN, F. STUART, *Experimental Designs in Sociological Research* (New York, 1948).

A carefully drawn statement of the meaning of adequate comparative controls in the study of social problems and demonstration of their use in several specialized studies.

YOUNG, PAULINE V., *Scientific Social Surveys and Research* (second edition, New York, 1949).

An interesting and informative review of some of the principal research procedures employed in modern sociology presented with an historical background for the several methodologies discussed.

GOODE, WILLIAM J., AND PAUL K. HATT, *Methods in Social Research* (New York, 1952).

A sound basic text dealing with the fundamental methods of modern social research and the logic of research planning.

GLUECK, SHELDON AND ELEANOR, *Unraveling Juvenile Delinquency* (New York, 1950).

In one of the most celebrated research ventures of the present day, this well-known research team makes a detailed controlled study of 500 delinquents and 500 nondelinquents in the Boston area.

POWERS, EDWIN, AND HELEN WITMER, *An Experiment in the Prevention of Delinquency* (New York, 1951).

A commendable and conscientious effort to test by means of a controlled sample the effectiveness of personal guidance in the lives of a selected group of delinquents in the Cambridge, Massachusetts, area.

HEALY, WILLIAM, AND AUGUSTA BRONNER, *New Light on Delinquency and Its Treatment* (New Haven, 1936).

This celebrated classic, conducted under the auspices of the Judge Baker Foundation of Boston, Massachusetts, and using comparative studies of siblings and twins, still remains one of the finest, if not the best, studies in the entire field of delinquency causation.

YOUNG, PAULINE V., *Social Treatment in Probation and Delinquency* (second edition, New York, 1952).

An interesting illustration of modern casework procedure in the field of probation and delinquency amply illustrated with applied casework materials.

Chapter 4

TRENDS IN PERSONALITY RESEARCH

The human personality consists of specific traits which appear in different and recurrent combinations in different individuals. Such traits may be the fundamental results of certain types of upbringing and family circumstances, reflecting the social, economic, and cultural conditions in which the individual and the family exist. For the purpose of our discussion, a trait may be considered any attribute or condition of the personality which contributes to the individual's social behavior and reactions. Further, the presence of combinations of traits may permit the individual to operate freely within his restricted environment or may impede his adaptation. Thus, traits of aggressiveness and hostility toward members of out-groups may facilitate the personality's active participation in a culturally approved competitive process, while absence of this combination of traits may serve as a distinctive handicap in adapting to the culture, relegating the individual to an inferior or secondary status.

The analysis of clusters of personality traits, giving us insight into motivational patterns in their relationships to constellations (or combinations) of situational factors, raises one of the most crucial problems in the entire area of human relations research, whether we are dealing with the normal personality or the abnormal or deviant personality. The configuration of social traits in personality finding expression in the motivation of the individual to different types of behavior inevitably brings us close to the problem of *how* the personality is organized. Students of delinquency and crime have frequently expressed the well-intentioned belief that if an adequate theory of personality could be devised, valid not only for specialized tests of the psychological laboratory but also for the functions of the human individual in his everyday living, then a truly scientific study of causation would automatically follow.

The Lack of an Inclusive Personality Theory

There is, as yet, no comprehensive, all-embracing theory of personality, sufficiently confirmed in empirical evidence and clinical fact, that will enable us to determine with any degree of completeness either the detailed or the over-all interpretations we require for adequate analysis of the causation of delinquency. The clinical interpretations thus far developed are either hypothetical statements applied to certain phases of abnormal behavior, viewed primarily from the perspective of the diagnostician in the consulting chamber, or all-embracing theories which lack the coherence of sound and proved scientific doctrine. This does not mean, however, that the search for valid hypotheses based upon demonstrated proof is not moving forward. Nor does it mean that work in the fields of delinquency may not be an important step in the development of an adequate personality theory. Instead of awaiting a scientific millennium, researchers in the field of delinquency causation may make a significant contribution to our growing knowledge of the mechanisms of personality. Research in this vital area is a reciprocal, two-way process; we cannot receive without giving.

The Situational Approach in the Study of Personality

Since any study of deviant or delinquent behavior always involves the reaction of a person within a given situation (what the psychologist and the sociologist are learning to call a *structured* situation), any theory of personality and the empirical evidence upon which it is based must be fairly comprehensive. An adequate view of personality involves *both* a constitutional emphasis and a recognition of the inter-relationships of personality factors and aspects of the social and physical environment. In short, inasmuch as it affects our understanding of delinquent behavior, the increasing stress on the *situational approach* appears to be the most promising development in personality research.

This approach begins with the assumption that there may be a functioning consistency to the behavior of the individual, resulting from the characteristic social and cultural experiences to which he has been exposed in the past. Such tendencies permit certain kinds of behavior to occur as the latent possibilities within the personality are exposed to different types of situations. That an individual may respond to situations on different cultural and social levels in apparent contradiction of a continuity of personality structure characteristic of his training, appears to be confirmed by careful investigation.[1] Moreover, the belief frequently held by both psychiatrists and sociologists that exposure to contradictory patterns must inevitably create tensions which frequently produce neurotic disorder or antisocial behavior is not fully in accord with the facts. The situational approach, in recognizing *latent* possibilities in behavior and the various alternatives for action available to each personality in a given situation, does much to dispel the traditional, unilateral view that psychological factors have predictable reactions in behavior, apart from the compulsive necessity of socially and culturally structured situations.[2]

The situational approach, embracing constitutional and psychogenic determinants in relation to social and cultural conditions, appears to be the only one which now offers genuine promise for delinquency research. Such determinants, constitutional and psychogenic, are reflected in specific types of patterned situations. The individual responds to situations and not to society and culture in the abstract. Moreover, he responds to them in terms of constitutional and psychological assets and liabilities—tension states, emotional effects, learning limitations, and the like—which operate in the form of integrated wholes in personality. Such an approach, necessarily, since it is essentially highly realistic,

[1] Benedict, "Continuities and Discontinuities in Culture Conditioning"; Dai, "Some Problems of Personality Development Among Negro Children"; Davis and Havighurst, "Social Class and Color Differences in Child-Rearing."

[2] Weinberg, *Society and Personality Disorders*, pp. 40-42.

as well as scientifically sound, depends upon two vital contingent considerations: (1) the need to coördinate our information from the various specialized disciplines dealing with human behavior—psychiatry, psychology, sociology, and anthropology; and (2) the development of integrated concepts that will enable us to bring these discrete findings into functioning conceptual units while permitting us to evaluate separately the relative strength of the component elements in any human tension situation.[3]

Implicit in this view is the current research procedure stipulating that human situations are characterized by states of equilibrium and disequilibrium. The conjunction of many factors operating at any given time produces human states tending toward *homeostasis*, the setting up of a balanced state of tension between the organism and the environment.[4] Within this complex of human and environmental forces operating at any given time is the recognition that a given tension state must be satisfied, and that the form the satisfaction will take depends upon the nature of the circumstances and the patterns of action available. At the same time, it does much to tell us why different forms of delinquency occur in different settings and why they are almost inevitable under certain environmental influences while under others they hardly arise at all.

The concept that personality is not wholly resident within the corporeal limits of the human body but must actually operate within the confines of a field of human action raises a whole series of new ideas in the understanding of human behavior.[5] Harry Stack Sullivan, in a series of studies whose full impact has not yet been felt, indicated clearly that the modern orientation of psychiatric studies in human behavior must proceed almost wholly from what he termed the "interpersonal" framework. This view is equivalent to the increasing emphasis of psychiatrists, psychologists, and sociologists on the "field-structured" or situational approach. If we are to utilize such new concepts effectively, however, we must begin to introduce and use more widely in research and analysis the important intellectual tools that the anthropologist and the modern social scientist have brought to the fore: the concepts of "family of orientation," social interaction, socialization,

[3] Murphy, "The Relationships of Culture and Personality."
[4] See Allport, *Personality*, p. 349.
[5] See Sullivan, "Multidisciplined Coordination of Interpersonal Data"; Sullivan, "The Study of Psychiatry"; and Sullivan, *Modern Conceptions of Psychiatry*.

cultural relativity, social roles, status, youth culture, and reinforcement in stimulus response learning.[6]

Sociological Tools for the Study of Personality

Foremost among the concepts increasingly engaging the attention of the specialists working in the area lying between personality and culture are the important tool ideas of *socialization, interaction, role, and status*. The modern concept of socialization is not only significant in the theory of the problems of personality; it is also becoming an invaluable research aid. Recognizing as it does constitutional limitations which may operate at the outset of the individual's career and which may directly affect his responses to others, it emphasizes the fact that the interactive process, as Sullivan so brilliantly perceived, produces a series of continuing and controlling effects upon the individual which enables him to adapt at certain cultural levels. *The process of socialization, thus, consists of the adaptive mechanisms the individual develops and which become part of the personality itself through the introjection (or internalizing) of standards and behaviors of individuals who have played a vital part in the characteristic forms of interaction he has been exposed to.* Particularly significant in this development is the recognition that acculturated personality types, i.e., types representative of different social groups, emerge within cultural settings, while at the same time individual variations occur within each one of these acculturated forms.

The task becomes one of identifying the situational determinants— as these emerge from family living on different social and cultural levels—that establish the specific types of subcultures to which the individual has been exposed. Allison Davis, John Dollard, August B. Hollingshead, R. J. Havighurst, and Kenneth Eells have shown with some conclusiveness the distinctive forms these cultural settings will take and the specific types of behavior expectancies on the part of children that such cultural settings will elicit.[7] A proper understanding of this fundamental research on personality functioning

[6] See Pollack and collaborators, *Social Science and Psychotherapy for Children.*

[7] The studies of the Committee on Human Development of the University of Chicago, with Robert J. Havighurst as chairman, are of considerable value in this respect, as is the recently inaugurated Yale Study on human maladjustment, neurosis, and psychosis in relation to different socio-cultural levels.

begins to shed light not only upon patterned personality characteristics that seem to be typical of certain types of children—Negro
children in the Deep South, Puerto Rican youths in Harlem, Italian children in certain urban settings, and other groups—but at the
same time reveals rather sharply why such groups are more prone to
delinquent behavior than others. Abram Kardiner's pioneer work,
through his technique of "psychodynamic projection," clearly illustrates the "basic personality structure" that different cultural settings
may produce in establishing combinations of psychological traits best
suited to certain types of social settings, personality types of "best fit,"
as he refers to them. Not only do we thereby obtain a trenchant
insight into problems of cultural relativity, but at the same time we
can begin to anticipate the kind of problems the individual will face
when transplanted from one setting to another.[8]

The concepts of *status* and *role* provide an effective bridge between
psychiatric-psychological and sociological understanding. Status refers
to the position an individual maintains with respect to certain *defined*
social relationships. Every society defines certain of its status positions
with some clarity, although not all societies make equally clear differences of status positions on their varying stratified levels nor among
their innumerable subgroups.[9] This latter is particularly true of a complex social order such as our own and is responsible for a vast volume
of deviant and antisocial behavior.[10] In some instances, the status of
individuals—what society may reasonably be expected to require of
them in a variety of conventionally defined situations—is made extremely specific and clear as, for example, with regard to sex and age
differentiations. Statuses fundamental to the group and, to a considerable degree, determined by biological factors, tend on the whole to be
well established in most societies. However, even within the defined
limitations of such *ascribed* statuses—to employ Ralph Linton's term—
varying definitions of interpretation may arise which will present focal
points of tension for individuals characterized by such ambiguities in
status position. For example, we have hardly defined with any clarity

[8] Kardiner *et al.*, *The Psychological Frontiers of Society*; Kardiner and Linton, *The Individual and His Society*.

[9] See Linton, *The Cultural Background of Personality*, pp. 76-82; Linton, *The Study of Man*, pp. 113-31.

[10] See Frank, *Society as the Patient*; Merton, "Social Structure and Anomie";
Parsons, "Age and Sex in the Social Structure of the United States"; Davis, "Mental
Hygiene and the Class Structure."

what we may expect from adolescents in respect to the asserted needs of growing adulthood, emancipation from the home, and the development of normal heterosexuality.[11] Nor, during the period of rapid social flux through which we are passing, have we been clear or consistent concerning the status of the woman who desires both marriage *and* a career, nor of the precise status of the old-age member of society, as recent geriatric studies so clearly demonstrate. (In fact, we have an indication of the significance of this view in the suggestion some researchers have made that the problem of "senescent psychosis" may not be the result of organic deterioration in itself, but may be induced largely by the failure to provide a useful place for the aged in our society.)[12]

Within the limitations determined by the relatively constricted ascribed statuses in our society, however, a large variety of choices are set up, in which the individual is relatively free to pursue his own objectives according to prescribed social mandates. These socially acceptable and defined objectives constitute the *achieved* statuses to which individuals may aspire and within which their behavior takes meaning. *The difficulty in reconciling the limitations of achievement for certain culturally and economically depressed groups in our society with the "popular success" ideology of our culture, and the corresponding tensions induced thereby, is a highly provocative source of both delinquent and criminal behavior.*[13]

Role, as contrasted with status, incorporates the dynamic forms of behavior available within the status-defined situation. The role, correspondingly, enables us to bring into play a study of the highly personalized tensions and motives of the individual which enable him either to accept the limitations of his status, grow restive under their restraints, or manifest those dangerous imbalances conducive to a variety of deviant behavior patterns. The study of role behavior on different social levels and within different subcultural settings provides a nexus for the conjoined operations of psychiatrists, psychologists, and sociologists. Kluckhohn and Murray have suggested a logical procedure for the evaluation of personality functioning on the basis of such coöperative

---

[11] See Williams, *Adolescence: Studies in Mental Hygiene*, pp. 102 ff.; Davis, "The Sociology of Parent-Youth Conflict"; and Bloch, *Disorganization*, pp. 137-41, 154-56.

[12] See Rothschild, "Senile Psychoses and Cerebral Arteriosclerosis."

[13] See Merton, "Social Structure and Anomie"; Bloch, "Structured Roles and Anomie."

study. Recognizing as their premise that every individual, in certain respects, is (a) like *all* other men, (b) like *some* other men, and (c) like *no* other man, the study of personality patterning may be broken down into the following categories: (1) constitutional determinants; (2) group-membership determinants; (3) interaction between constitutional and group-membership determinants; (4) role determinants; (5) situational determinants; and (6) interrelationships operative among all the determinants.[14]

The Striving of the Personality toward Self-Consistency

While recognizing all of the many elements that enter into the formation of personality, we must not overlook the fact that the developing personality reveals a considerable degree of self-consistency. Largely through the internalized standards, values, and behavior-images derived from the socialization process previously described, the individual tends to maintain a remarkable consistency when confronted by recurrent situations. Thus, although all of the above-mentioned determinants are significant in the development of personality, characteristic patterns of behavior on certain socio-cultural levels, involving appropriate constitutional and psychogenic factors, tend to coalesce into relatively consistent behavior types and personality forms. Each individual tends to have his own distinctive "style of life," in Alfred Adler's phrase.

Clinicians have long recognized the relative persistency of personal behavior in a variety of situations. The determination of such consistencies appears to be a logical and indispensable prerequisite for any completely valid study of delinquency. These consistent behavior forms, characteristic of the individual personality, indicate the reasons for the varying states of suggestibility of the individual to certain environmental situations. *For in the last resort, what constitutes delinquency? Why is it that the most innocent of situations seem to incite some individuals to extreme forms of behavior, violent and antisocial, while to others such situations remain innocuous and a simple matter of course? Conversely, why is it that a truly provocative situation leaves certain individuals unscathed but causes others to respond in antisocial fashion, to them, under the circumstances, the most "normal" of reactions? In*

[14] Kluckhohn, Murray, and Schneider, *Personality in Nature, Society, and Culture,* pp. 53-67.

this, it appears, lies the crux of the problem of delinquency. As Fritz Redl has shown in his study of a particularly deeply disturbed group of children, their consistent forms of response tend to make them react in the most violent of manners to the most innocuous situations.[15] Hence, if we understand how the significant determinants of behavior are organized within an individual into a certain pattern of suggestibility, we may be able to account for delinquent actions on his part as largely the result of a combination of this pattern of suggestibility with a chronic exposure to situations that tend to incite to antisocial forms of behavior.

This is the direction which the pioneer work of Healy and Bronner has taken, and which has been adapted by Bloch in his concept of the *psychogenetic pattern*.[16] This concept represents a crude but significant beginning in putting into some coherent form the conditioned effects of his developmental history upon the culturally oriented and organically vulnerable individual as they fall into a pattern and tend to impart consistency to his behavior.[17] For the present, such a conceptual framework can be envisaged only as a broad schematic outline which attempts to embrace the several psychological and environmental factors functioning conjointly to produce social and antisocial behavior. It has this validity, however: it suggests the kind of work which must eventually be done in close detail to piece together the various phases of personality development in their reaction to certain environmental stimuli.[18] Of even greater importance is the fact that it should begin to provide us with some perspective in the evaluation of the causal factors contributing to adjustment and maladjustment—constitutional, hereditary, social, and cultural—so that we can give proper weight to the functioning of these factors.

In the analysis of personality, we find that the early formative years, especially the first six years, are the most significant in developing certain socio-psychological needs and basic procedures for their fulfillment.[19] The primary needs, a resultant of the interplay of constitutional, cultural, and interpersonal factors arising from the cultural and family-

---

[15] Redl and Wineman, *Children Who Hate*, pp. 96-140.

[16] Healy and Bronner, *New Light on Delinquency and its Treatment*, pp. 1-13; Bloch, *Disorganization*, pp. 179-85.

[17] See Lecky, *Self-Consistency: A Theory of Personality*; Davis, *Human Society*, Chap. 9, pp. 238-41; and Bloch, "The Social Individual as a Primary Datum in Sociology."

[18] See Bloch, *Disorganization*, pp. 84-112, 179-82.

[19] See Bloch, *Disorganization*.

mediated methods of child-rearing, appear to emerge during the first two years of life. These deeply implanted needs, referred to as the "need phase" of the psychogenetic pattern, are partly derived from the feeding routines, handling and fondling, toilet training, and early sexual orientation which the psychiatrist has come to regard as the "organ learning" of the child. As the child develops his mechanisms of speech and his self-awareness—a parallel process—he begins to perceive the nature of these needs and the meaning of his relations to others. Through directed and accidental adjustments to his environment, occurring largely during the period from two to six years, he acquires the techniques of adjustment whereby these basic needs may be fulfilled. It is during this latter period as well that his conception of himself begins to come into sharper focus and to take shape and form. The organization of these needs, the methods of their fulfillment, and the resultant conception of self-awareness constitute the psychogenetic pattern of the developing personality. In the course of the individual's development, much of his striving in the successive environments to which he is exposed are efforts

CHART X

A Suggested Schema for the Causal Pattern of Delinquency*

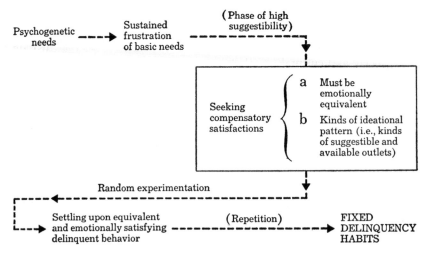

* Bloch, *Disorganization*, p. 180. Reproduced by permission of Alfred A. Knopf, Inc.

to satisfy the basic needs of the psychogenetic pattern and to fulfill the conception of the self.

One fact should be stressed in this brief analysis, however: there is nothing intrinsically "good" or "bad" in these early acquired need-traits of the personality. What may be "bad" in these basic needs and functions of the growing personality is the failure to provide adequate outlets for their satisfaction. Society is composed of an endless variety of individuals whose needs may be quite dissimilar and whose differences contribute to the rich diversification of social life. Society requires aggressive and enterprising individuals as well as it does the seclusive, retiring, and scholarly types. Danger to the individual occurs when inadequate outlets are provided for the types of needs and functions he has acquired. In the above diagram, this complex and rich organization of the personality is implied in the simple statement of the "psychogenetic needs."

Significant in the diagram is the emphasis it attempts to give to all phases of the human equation in delinquency. Recognizing at the outset that the psychogenetic structure is a composite of constitutional and psychogenic factors, it envisages the developing personality in terms of (*a*) family and socially implanted needs, and (*b*) methods for their satisfaction (the "functions" of the psychogenetic pattern). Secondly, it confirms the situational approach in its recognition of the fact that motivations and suggestibility toward delinquency arise from deprivation situations. Significant in the more recent analysis of delinquent histories are the high states of suggestibility characteristic of the early development of antisocial and delinquent practices, as evidenced in the marked conditions of emotionality, impetuousness, and impulsivity of our delinquent charges. Sustained frustration of basic needs and traits appears to produce suggestible states of mind in the adjusted as well as the maladjusted. *Suggestible patterns are released at such times in the behavioral outlets available within a given environment.* Those environments which provide, as the criminologist Sutherland repeatedly emphasized in his career, a *surplus* of suggestible outlets (*ideational patterns*) of an antisocial nature, will result in the individual's resorting to delinquent and criminal behavior. This is the basis of the well-known "differential association" theory in criminology.[20] The adventitious and highly accidental nature of much of our delinquency is thus strongly

[20] See Sutherland, *Principles of Criminology*, pp. 6-9.

underscored. Moreover, the *limited* function of certain stimulating circumstances in producing delinquency, whether they be organized recreational projects of a wholesome variety, motion pictures, comic books, or the prized association with peer-age groups, may be properly evaluated within this framework, since it indicates that the individual's response is inseparably associated with (1) *the degree of frustration or deprivation of the individual,* and (2) the *availability* of expressive forms of behavior in the environment.

For the present, however, such a conceptual scheme can only give us a general vista of the broad behavioral terrain within which delinquent activity may take place. It remains for us to develop the highly specialized pieces of research in the various behavior sciences and, showing their interrelations, to indicate the ways in which such a theory can be adequately confirmed. Promising beginnings have already been made. We will now turn to the various specialized areas of research in order to indicate the degree to which some of the questions concerning delinquency causation are being answered.

For Further Reading

DAVIS, ALLISON, AND ROBERT J. HAVIGHURST, "Social Class and Color Differences in Child-Rearing," in *American Sociological Review,* 11 (1946), pp. 698-710.

A penetrating exposure of the ways in which class and color differences function in early child-rearing practices and the possible effects which these may have upon subsequent personality structuring.

WEINBERG, S. KIRSON, *Society and Personality Disorders* (New York, 1952).

A noteworthy effort to organize the materials and appraise the ways in which social factors are related to a variety of behavioral, neurotic, and psychotic disorders.

SARGENT, S. STANSFELD, AND MARIAN W. SMITH, EDITORS, *Culture and Personality* (Viking Fund, New York, 1949).

A collection of informal papers by several experts in the field exploring the channels through which the interrelations between culture and personality must be studied.

SULLIVAN, HARRY STACK, *Modern Conceptions of Psychiatry* (The William Alanson White Psychiatric Foundation, Washington, D.C., 1945).

One of the few summarizations of the interpersonal approach to psychiatric problems formulated by the able pioneer in this area and critically departing from the former organically rooted and Freudian-centered views.

POLLACK, OTTO, *et al.*, *Social Science and Psychotherapy for Children* (Russell Sage Foundation, New York, 1952).

An interesting application of social science concepts to the field of psychotherapy with an effort to indicate how such concepts may be bridged.

KARDINER, ABRAM, *et al.*, *The Psychological Frontiers of Society* (New York, 1945).

A stimulating study of the application of modified Freudian concepts to social phenomena, demonstrating their use in the detailed investigation of selected preliterate and modern communities.

FRANK, LAWRENCE K., *Society as the Patient* (New Brunswick, New Jersey, 1948).

A collection of papers by the eminent writer in the field of social problems and mental health in which he stresses his theme that modern social processes manifest themselves in a variety of personal disorders.

KLUCKHOHN, CLYDE, HENRY A. MURRAY, AND DAVID M. SCHNEIDER, EDITORS, *Personality in Nature, Society, and Culture* (second edition, New York, 1953).

One of our foremost collections of essays and research dealing with the ways in which the human personality is shaped by constitutional, situational, social, class, and cultural determinants, and setting up a general theory for personality study.

REDL, FRITZ, AND DAVID WINEMAN, *Children Who Hate* (Glencoe, Illinois, 1951).

A dramatic description and analysis of the behavior of a small group of deeply emotionally disturbed children in an experimental treatment program in Detroit, Michigan.

BLOCH, HERBERT A., "The Social Individual as a Primary Datum in Sociology," in *American Sociological Review*, 8 (October 1943), pp. 499-512.

An effort to establish a sociological theory of personality with a recommended framework for the developmental study of personality growth.

Chapter **5**

THE PHYSICAL CONSTITUTION
OF DELINQUENTS

The Need for a Multidisciplinary Approach

In approaching the diversified areas of research which have played a part in disclosing the causes of delinquency, it will be helpful to examine them from certain specific categorical standpoints. There have been so many different types of research here that it is extremely difficult to develop an integrated or coherent point of view describing causal processes. Moreover, each specialized perspective—whether psychiatric, social, psychological, psychometric, sociological, genetic, or stemming from any of the specialized research instruments which have been employed—has revolved in its own delimited frame of reference, rendering it extremely difficult to relate the findings of one specialized area to the results in adjacent fields.

What the layman frequently fails to apprehend in approaching so difficult a problem as the causation of delinquency is the fact that whereas each of the separate fields of learning may help in a limited way, as a body they fail to give us the unified picture we desire. There is a popular feeling that if only the various specialists would coöperate and pool their findings, we would eventually have a perspective that would provide us with an adequate comprehensive view of what produces delinquency. The uninitiated person should recognize that coöperative research and the pooling of findings represent simply the merest preliminary beginnings toward understanding. A fruitful and encouraging beginning is already taking place in what is known as the multidisciplinary approach to the problems of human relations and motivation, i.e., a coördinated and coöperative attack upon these problems. What is overlooked, however, is the indispensable second step, which has hardly been touched upon in our studies of human behavior: the development of new conceptual frames of reference. This involves new tools of thought which, through systematic logic and directly related research evidence, will validate the discoveries that the new integrated concepts will reveal.[1]

An illustration of this emphasis can be seen by analogy in developments in the natural and physical sciences. Biochemistry, for example, does not simply "combine" biology and chemistry, but discovers new concepts and research procedures which apply neither to biology nor chemistry but rather to the new field of interest. In the same way, to understand the problems of human behavior within certain socioeconomic, cultural, and group contexts involves new mechanisms of thought and methods of verification which transcend the separate views of each field.

Nevertheless, to create some order out of the existing chaos, it should prove beneficial to recognize the differences in conceptual meaning and their implications for research of the following five categories of investigation: (1) constitutional; (2) psychogenic; (3) cultural; (4) social (or structural); and (5) situational.

The Major Research Areas

In speaking of *constitutional factors*, we are referring to organic factors present at birth, or shortly thereafter, and which, by their nature, appear to predispose the individual to maladjustment. In examining such data, we should make some effort to determine (1) the degree to which genetic, or hereditary, factors play a part in the creation of predispositions to antisocial behavior, (2) the degree to which such organic or constitutional factors may be modified, and (3) whether or not sig-

---

[1] See Murphy, "The Relationships of Culture and Personality."

nificant intervening factors of the environment must invariably be present before an organic predisposition manifests itself in maladjusted behavior.

In our reference to *psychogenic factor*, we deal with data concerning personality differentials arising in the course of the individual's psychological development, various characterological differences and emotional traits which, in manifesting themselves at different levels of the individual's career, may either persist in the form of malignant personality traits productive of personality disorder, or which at the time of their appearance may signalize the possibility of delinquent maladaptation.

These first two categories are well known to students of delinquency and others in the field of human development. The last three categories, however, are of a different nature, and not nearly as well known in their present usage to students of psychological and psychiatric problems. In referring to *cultural factors* as contributory to delinquency, we specify the value system of various groups which, either because they cannot be internalized effectively by the individual or because of the conflicts which such value systems present when brought up against the value standards of other groups, provide powerful stimulating circumstances to delinquent behavior. The child caught between divergent culture demands of his home and the community provides a classic example of this type of problem.

Social factors—frequently referred to as "structural" factors—present problems of still another type, and research evidence indicates the differing impact of such factors upon various children. Social factors refer to the individual's functioning social relationships with others, the ways in which he characteristically responds to and is reacted upon by other individuals within specific social settings. As an illustration of this category, we can point to children who come from *common* religious, ethnic, and economic backgrounds, but whose dissimilar patterns of family organization produce different types of problems for the oldest child as compared to the youngest, the girl as compared to the boy, the employed child as compared to the unemployed. Further, social relationships refer to the characteristic structural ties binding together the component units of a society—family, church, school, industry, etc. Such structural ties, in determining the various statuses of the individual in the social order, will govern to a large extent the way he reacts to others, the limitations to his mobility and aspirations, his freedom of choice, and the like.

Situational determinants are the appropriate conjunction of factors at a given time, which are sufficient to account for delinquent behavior under the duress of a situation. This category is very well known to all students of delinquent youth: a child may be prone to delinquency but may never actually commit an overt delinquent act because the strategic set of situations has never presented itself. (Lucien Bovet aptly terms these *potential* delinquents "the reserve troops of juvenile delinquency.")[2]

Each of these conceptual categories represents a different approach to the study of delinquency, and each suggests a different set of causal principles. We shall attempt to assess each category separately and then to coördinate them.

Constitutional and Organic Factors

Research on effects of organic and constitutional factors on delinquency is extremely varied and controversial. To understand the subject adequately we must move far afield, even into the traditional *argumentum in vacuo* of the hereditary *vs.* environmental antagonists. It appears to be generally conceded that this latter arbitrary separation serves no useful function in modern scientific analysis. If any fundamental distinction is to be made, it must be drawn between the structure of the body (including, of course, its internal components) and its several active and potential functions. Structure, the physical organization of the body, is largely determined by hereditary and congenital factors. Such factors may predispose the organism to an infinite variety of different behaviors. The fundamental problem is thus to determine whether certain bodily structures predispose individuals to certain types of behavior (functions) in certain social and cultural environments. In this way, *there is no valid separation between heredity and environment* since, in establishing the structural possibilities of behavior, hereditary factors from the very outset of life are exposed to limiting environmental conditions which shape them and give them expression, meaning, and form. Nevertheless, constitutional theorists, while frequently paying lip service to the futility of such an arbitrary dichotomy, often go on

---

[2] See Bovet, *Psychiatric Aspects of Juvenile Delinquency*, p. 20.

disavowing the same principle in presenting conclusions to their studies. Organic factors, because of the relative ease with which they may be studied and observed, have always seemed to exercise a peculiar fascination for students of delinquency and crime, both classic and modern.

Constitutional factors are the characteristic organic features that make up the physical structure of the body. That patterned arrangements of the various physical features of the organism play a part in predisposing the individual to certain forms of behavior, there can be no doubt, but precisely how these physical characteristics play their roles and under what conditions has never been adequately determined. Constitutional factors may range from physical limitations of the organism that make it more difficult for the individual to adjust (e.g., minor or gross bodily defects, endocrine malfunctioning, or defects of the nervous system that impair muscular or intellectual functioning) to the total body types (the somatotypes), which may have bearing on various forms of behavior. If physical characteristics both set the limits of human behavior and indicate some of the broad reactive patterns that the human individual will take, it seems reasonable to expect that certain inherited characteristics should be considered in attempting to understand the developmental growth of the individual.

Genetic Studies of Delinquent Behavior Patterns

In recognizing that physical characteristics are to a considerable degree innate or inborn, the result of genetic factors, scholars have attempted to discover the possible relationship between the hereditary background of the individual and the development of his delinquent traits. The research record of the past in this area has been misunderstood by many present-day students of delinquency and crime. It is still common to attribute to many early students of hereditary characteristics judgments concerning the necessary relationship between genetic constitution and delinquent behavior which they never actually made. In all fairness, one is led to wonder how many of our contemporary students have actually read these early accounts. To understand the problem adequately, we should be familiar with the distinction Professor Hankins made some years ago between the structural characteristics of the organism and its functional possibilities.[3]

[3] Hankins, "Organic Plasticity vs. Organic Responsiveness."

At birth, each child has a definite physical structure, which, however, can lend itself to a wide variety of forms of behavior. Physical structure, in its strictest meaning, indicates an enormous range of behavior potentials for any individual. If any doubt about this remains, the ethnographic studies made by anthropologists for the last forty years should put a complete end to it. It must be made clear to the uninitiated that in other cultures and societies individuals endowed with normal physical constitutions are capable of, and do develop, characteristic forms of behavior which, to us, may appear bizarre, strange, or even abnormal.[4] One has to be fully conversant with the remarkable range of modern anthropological literature to appreciate this fact fully. Even traits that were formerly considered to be universal and instinctive, such as forms of sexual experience, have often been found to be the results of cultural conditioning and learning.[5] Traits that we consider abnormal may constitute a normal pattern among peoples of different cultures, such as the universally expressed aggression and profound paranoid antipathies of the Alorese in the Netherlands East Indies.[6]

We should keep this in mind in contemplating the enormous range of potentials in behavior open to any given physical structure. However, we must also recognize that there are physical limitations in any culture, as *defined* by that culture, which may make it extremely difficult for some individuals to adjust. Marginal and subnormal intelligence, for example, are genuine handicaps in our own society, as are forms of muscular dystrophy and epilepsy. Here too, though, there are enormous divergences among different cultures. It is common, for example, in many of the cultures described by anthropologists to give epileptics high religious status; thus considerable prestige is accorded to an individual as the result of a physical condition which in our society constitutes a serious handicap.

For this reason, Bleuler has wisely counselled that in attempting to understand human behavior, we should not ask the question, "Is this organic or is it psychogenic?" but rather, "*To what extent* is the behavior in question organic and *to what extent* is it psychogenic?" However, it is not uncommon to find that certain students of human behav-

---

[4] See Benedict, *Patterns of Culture*; Mead, *Male and Female*, Chaps. 1-3; DuBois, *The People of Alor*; and Thomas, *Primitive Behavior*.

[5] See Mead, *Sex and Temperament in Three Primitive Societies*; Mead, "Anthropological Data on the Problem of Instinct."

[6] DuBois, *The People of Alor*.

ior and delinquency, while explicitly admitting the wisdom of this admonition, assume that forms of human behavior—*always a matter of social expression*—are a direct consequence of certain aspects of the physical structure itself.[7]

Early research into the relationship between heredity and human behavior reflected the peculiar intellectual atmosphere of the late nineteenth century. In an appraisal of the prevailing atmosphere of the period, two significant facts stand out: (1) it seemed apparent, without much further study, that certain biological family types and physical stocks of necessity would give rise to superior or to degenerate issue, and (2) modern scientific techniques in the appraisal of environmental effects were hardly known. Thus, it seemed perfectly natural in 1869 for Francis Galton, the father of modern eugenics, to assume that highly privileged families in Great Britain, with histories of illustrious ancestral lineage, considerable wealth, education, and position, would very likely not produce candidates for the bread line nor those who would grace with their presence the premises of Ludgate Prison; and to assert, naïvely, that such a felicitous state was due to their superior stock. The studies of hereditary genius by Galton and his contemporaries had a remarkable effect upon American students of family degeneracy, resulting in a spate of studies from 1887 to 1920, which attempted to show that deficient stock will tend to produce individuals with criminal traits, pathological tendencies, pauperism, low moral character, and the like. Virtually all of these studies tried to demonstrate that a high percentage of mental degeneracy, poverty, and crime was inevitable as a result of the genetic constituents of the families themselves. Thus, we have had a veritable torrent of studies, the fictitious names of the families involved having become household terms to generations of Americans—the Jukes, the Kallikaks, the Nam Family, the Pineys, the family of Sam Sixty, the Tribe of Ishmael, and many others.[8]

The forerunner and the most notable of all of these studies was that of the Jukes by Dugdale, in which he titillated his contemporaries by

---

[7] For example, this common logical fallacy appears in Bovet, *Psychiatric Aspects of Delinquency*, pp. 13-14, otherwise an informative analysis of the psychiatric aspects of delinquency.

[8] Dugdale, *The Jukes*; Estabrook, *The Jukes in 1915*; Goddard, *The Kallikak Family*; Davenport and Danielson, *The Hill Folk*; Estabrook and Davenport, *The Nam Family*; Kite, *The Pineys*; Kostir, *The Family of Sam Sixty*.

revealing that of the 1,200 descendants of this unhappy line, 140 were criminals (of whom 7 were murderers, 60 were thieves, and 50 were prostitutes), with such accompanying forms of deterioration as dependency, illegitimacy, poverty, and neglect amply swelling these numbers, and that they cost the State of New York approximately $1,300,000 during the short span of seventy-three years for which this sorry record was taken. Nevertheless, as Arthur E. Fink has affirmed: "Unread, misread, or wilfully distorted, [this study] has been used by hereditarians and environmentalists alike to assert and supposedly to prove their respective positions." [9] The fact remains that neither Dugdale nor his successors attempted to prove, or even to indicate, that environmental influence had no part to play in such records of family decadence. It is a fact, nevertheless, that the emphasis they placed upon their findings appeared to throw the weight of evidence overwhelmingly in favor of hereditary influence. Certainly this was the conclusion drawn by two generations of students and publicists of delinquency and crime.

It was relatively easy, therefore, for champions of eugenics to interlard their reports with data from such studies, which purported to show conclusively that criminality and delinquency were largely, if not entirely, the results of degenerative family stock. At no point in any of the studies cited was there the slightest attempt to appraise and measure scientifically the degrees to which adverse environmental influences and biological inheritance played their respective roles in producing the unhappy results that were surveyed. Carefully drawn comparative samples were *never* used in such studies. The criteria employed for the classification of behavior of persons both living and dead were largely based upon recollection and the most haphazard of hearsay evidence. The use of genetic behavioral studies was either neglected or unknown, and the study of emergent behavioral functions, so basic in the modern analysis of personality development, was entirely disregarded. All that these studies revealed was the untested and uncompared data of families exposed to every conceivable vicissitude of degenerative breeding and corruptive environment.

To overcome these handicaps, Henry H. Goddard made a more sophisticated attempt to study, under what he conceived to be partially controlled conditions, two family lines emanating from a common paternal ancestor, Martin Kallikak. Since the putative founder of the lines

[9] Fink, *Causes of Crime*, pp. 179-82.

had originally mated with a nameless barmaid, producing among the 480 descendants in this line a sizable quota of felons, alcoholics, and prostitutes, and then, in legitimate wedlock with a girl of good family, a long line of distinguished citizens, the case in favor of heredity seemed to be well established. But since the original misalliance was impossible to confirm and since no effort was made to establish controls whereby environmental influences could be clearly traced in *both* family lines, the study proved little other than that a certain percentage of feeble-mindedness was transmitted, the precise amount of which is unknown, and that children handicapped by both defective heredity and a deficient environment are apt to become dangerous social misfits.

A variation of such studies may be found in the work of the eminent trio of Italian criminologists whose influence has been so great, Garofalo, Ferri, and, especially, Cesare Lombroso, the founders of the so-called positivist school of criminology.[10] Lombroso, after exhaustive physical measurements of prisoners found in Italian and South European prisons but without the use of control groups, came to the conclusion that criminals were marked by well-defined physical and mental stigmata. Although this phase of his work has been overstressed by American criminologists, Lombroso was clearly aware of the significance of social factors in the production of delinquency and crime, and he stressed such factors strongly, especially in his later work. He did, however, indicate that constitutional characteristics exercised a predisposing and influential role in delinquent behavior, although they were not necessarily to be conceived as the ultimate determinants of crime and delinquency.

It is important to stress again some of the dangerous implications, militating against clarity of understanding, that such studies produce. Behavior in any form is the result of a complex set of adjustments to a given environment. What is particularly significant, and entirely omitted in such studies, is that developmental traits emerge at different stages of growth of the individual and *reflect the behavioral possibilities within a certain environment*. Further, these traits become integrated into the total complex of functioning behavior of the individual,

---

[10] Lombroso's classical work was first clearly articulated in his *Uomo Delinquente* (*Criminal Man*), published in 1876. Most of the data used by American students are found in *Crime: Its Causes and Remedies*, translated by Henry P. Horton.

thereby taking form and structure, and continue to manifest themselves in similar and different forms dependent upon the character of the social environment and the social situations to which the individual is progressively exposed. In specific detail, what we must recognize in each case is (1) *The underlying psychogenetic development of the individual* with its broad tendencies and habitual behavior mechanisms; (2) *the potentials of behavior at each level of maturity*, reflecting both the background tendencies of the individual and the emergent imperatives of the specific stage of growth; (3) *the integration of emergent traits with the entire ongoing flux of the total personality*, determining what weight and stress is to be accorded each new behavior pattern; and (4) *the limitations imposed upon the expression of behavior by different social environments and situations*. The entire trend of research and study in genetic psychology and the fundamental schools of psychiatry since this early period have emphasized these points. Yet the vestigial survivals of these early modes of study still arise to convince some students that there is more to the hereditary point of view than the average social scientist and psychiatrist are willing to admit. We have learned much from our modern techniques of study and we should be prepared consequently to acknowledge their effectiveness.

The Identical Twin Studies

If we are to learn anything effective about the influence of heredity upon behavior, the information must very likely come from the studies of monozygotic (identical) and dizygotic (fraternal) twins. The reason is perfectly apparent if we recognize the stress laid upon the need for adequate and effective "controls" for any form of scientific study. In the case of monozygotic twins, those born of a single fertilized ovum, we presume that the constitutional characteristics are identical. Consequently, any changes noted in behavior must be attributed to environmental influence. Dizygotic twins result from the fertilization of separate ova, and consequently they carry different sets of genetic factors, like any pair of siblings in the same family.

We still know very little, beyond reasonable conjecture, of the effects of birth trauma, variations in labor during delivery, and immediate postnatal effects upon children who may, nevertheless, be very much alike in physical constitution. The birth trauma is still frequently used as an abstraction to explain peculiarities in developmental patterns of growth which are difficult to account for in any other way.[11]

In examining studies of twins, however, we must be certain to recognize that subtle factors of the environment may operate differently even on identical twins, producing differences which, in particular instances, are quite distinct. Healy and Bronner, for example, reporting the behavior of two six-year-old identical twins, reared in the same household of parents of better than average economic circumstances, show how one child, a confirmed delinquent with deep-seated emotional problems, differed radically in personality structure from his brother who, presumably, was exposed to exactly the same environmental situation.[12] Although it appears relatively obvious that identical twins reared in different social environments may reveal considerable differences in intellectual performance and emotional functioning, which numerous monographs and the Bureau of Child Welfare of the University of Iowa have repeatedly reported, it is striking to note that even when reared in the same environment identical twins may display acute differences in behavior functioning, as William Blatz has shown, for example, in his study of the Dionne quintuplets.[13] In the studies of the developmental patterns of twins reared in the same and different environments we obviously lack the opportunities for highly detailed developmental observations and the application of the techniques for such observation and recording that we are beginning to employ with some success in our clinical and behavioral laboratories.[14]

Nevertheless, a number of studies on identical twins have attempted to show the powerful stimulus of common genetic determinants in producing identical forms of behavior. Johannes Lange has produced the classical study, *Crime and Destiny*, in which he has vainly attempted to demonstrate an invariant relationship between germinal factors and

[11] See Wetterdal, "Diagnosis for Children Delivered by Forceps"; Wile and Davis, "The Relation of Birth to Behavior"; Schroeder, "Behavior Difficulties in Children Associated with the Results of Birth Trauma"; Rosenow, "The Incidence of First Born Among Problem Children."
[12] Healy and Bronner, *New Light on Delinquency and Its Treatment*, pp. 95-8.
[13] Blatz, *The Five Sisters*.
[14] Among others, we are referring to the types of observational techniques under controlled and spontaneous conditions developed at Yale University under Professor Gesell. See, for example, Gesell and Ilg, *Infant and Child in the Culture of Today*; Gesell and Ilg, *The Child from Five to Ten*.

subsequent criminal behavior. M. F. Ashley Montagu, in assessing the various studies of twins and related patterns of behavior, has stated with unmistakable conviction that "there is not the slightest evidence to believe that anyone ever inherits a tendency to commit criminal acts. Crime is a social condition, not a biological condition." [15]

Ashley Montagu, in a summary of a number of studies on twins, has attempted to show how limited are the implications we can draw. In the following chart, it should be noted that although a relatively high percentage of *concordant* (or similar) behavior is found for identical twins, and a relatively high percentage of *discordant* (or dissimilar) behavior for dizygotic twins, a direct inference that genetic determinants have been primarily instrumental in producing such results is highly misleading. In such investigations, environmental factors that may account for both similar and dissimilar forms of behavior have *not* been precisely delineated. In other words, all we can say is that children of

TABLE E

Criminal Behavior of Twins *

AUTHOR	ONE-EGG TWINS (MONOZYGOTIC)		TWO-EGG TWINS (DIZYGOTIC)	
	CONCORDANT	DISCORDANT	CONCORDANT	DISCORDANT
Lange (1929).........	10	3	2	15
Legras (1932).........	4	0	0	5
Kranz (1936).........	20	12	23	20
Stumpfl (1936).......	11	7	7	12
Rosanoff (1934)......	25	12	5	23
TOTAL............	70	34	37	75
PERCENT.........	67.3	32.7	33.0	67.0

* Montagu, "The Biologist Looks at Crime." The works from which these data are drawn, primarily German, in which there is still a strong biological emphasis, are as follows: J. Lange, *Verbrechen und Schicksal* (Leipzig, 1929); A. M. Legras, *Psychose en Criminaliteit bij Tweelingen* (Utrecht, 1932); H. Kranz, *Lebensschicksal krimineller Zwillinge* (Berlin, 1936); F. Stumpfl, *Die Ursprünge des Verbrechens* (Leipzig, 1936); and A. J. Rosanoff *et al.*, "Criminality and Delinquency in Twins," *Journal of Criminal Law and Criminology* (January-February, 1934), pp. 923-24.

[15] Montagu, "The Biologist Looks at Crime."

common hereditary backgrounds have been shown to engage in common behavioral practices; but we cannot specify that such similarities *must* be due to genetic determinants. The same results could be shown for children genetically dissimilar who are exposed to strongly similar environmental pressures; in fact, the analysis of concordant behavior of dissimilar twins shows a considerably higher percentage than we should expect on genetic grounds.

Actually, although the above chart appears to be a rather convincing demonstration of the hereditary thesis, the facts, if they are to be in strict accordance with genetic theory, should reveal a much higher percentage of *concordant* behavior among the two-egg twins, if the theory is to be upheld. Reckless has stated, "If biological determination of destiny is correct, a discordant monozygotic (one-egg) twin set should be impossible, whereas discordant dizygotic (two-egg) sets should be frequent," the implications of which are strongly underscored by Ashley-Montagu in his affirmation that "[the] factor of environment has been virtually omitted from these studies of criminal behavior in twins." [16]

Rosanoff, Handy, and Rosanoff, in their study of 340 pairs of twins, purport to demonstrate "the existence of either pregerminal or germinal causative factors in adult criminality." [17] But unless there is some specification of the *degree* to which such factors have played a part in contributing to definite behavioral manifestations and their correlated criminal acts, as well as of the degree to which selected environmental factors have contributed, such a conclusion simply begs the question. A conclusion such as this comes close to asserting the most obvious of generalities, *viz.*, that heredity functions in the development of personality! The methodological weaknesses of many of the twin researches appear to have persisted since the early study by Charles Goring, the British investigator who claimed to show, although without sufficient basis, that siblings from delinquent families, even when separated, gave evidence of or continued in delinquent behavior. [18]

There can be little doubt that careful studies of the developmental characteristics of identical twins under the same and different environments can cast light on the behavior potentials of adjustment and maladjustment on the basis of constitutional inheritance. Thus far,

[16] Quoted in Teeters and Reinemann, *The Challenge of Delinquency*, p. 104.
[17] Rosanoff, Handy, and Rosanoff, "Criminality and Delinquency in Twins."
[18] Goring, *The English Convict.*

studies in delinquency that have attempted to reveal such snarled skeins of hereditary and environmental components have been singularly unsuccessful, largely because basic study in emergent psychological characteristics—on the emotional, intellectual, perceptive, cognitive, and motility levels—has thus far been carried forward only a very short distance. The crux of the problem, from which some day a partial answer may arise, is the need to observe emergent characteristics on the basis of early postnatal similarities and differences, and the functional expressive forms of behavior that manifest themselves in the course of normal maturation. The kind of observational techniques employed by Professor Gesell at Yale University, carefully detailed, day-by-day observation of various types of children, under both controlled and spontaneous conditions, is inapplicable in the study of children who are already delinquent or whose behavior patterns have already shown distinctive tendencies.

However, of this we can be fairly certain: common hereditary constitutional determinants of behavior produce physical responses of a similar character. These common response tendencies become meaningful only in specified person-to-person relationships and in conjunction with specific cultural meanings of particular groups and families. The fact remains, however, that even in the same family, the same environment, the same group, and the same culture, innumerable intervening conditions may arise which can alter the structure, form, and meaning of the responses of the individual. *The result is that emergent behavior patterns, even though arising from a common heredity and a common environment, may take considerably different forms.* Factors that may appear trivial or minor to the outward observer can loom up as enormously significant in the career of any individual. Sheerly accidental major and minor happenings in the lives of all individuals—illnesses, disappointments, frustrations, inhibitions in the expresson of aggression, lack of support by one's peers at a crucial moment, or a myriad of other situations—will continually emerge, *irrespective of common physical inheritance,* to accent in a different form significant behavior responses and to give a different meaning to the ongoing functions of personality.

Pathogenic Traits in Related and Unrelated Children

In recognizing that delinquent behavior traits are largely social and cultural products, and only indirectly biological, the recent significant work of Kallmann, Schilder, Bender, and others, in their studies of the development of pathogenic traits in unrelated children, siblings, and identical twins, should be carefully considered. Their work, especially that of the late Paul Schilder and the more recent findings of Lauretta Bender, deals primarily with the development of mental disorders in children. Since the position is generally accepted that many of these disorders are acquired rather than constitutional, the findings of these studies concerning hereditary and constitutional predispositions towards such disorders should undoubtedly shed significant light upon the entire area of human personality patterning.

Franz J. Kallmann has made two significant studies in which he has attempted to show the existence of a marked constitutional "taint" towards schizophrenia.[19] In the first, based on German hospital data for the years 1893 to 1902 and including 13,851 persons, he indicated that children with two schizophrenic parents would be expected to become schizophrenic in 68.1 cases out of 100. Further, the incidence of schizophrenia in these data appeared to show a definitely declining ratio as blood relationship declined, i.e., the more distant the blood relationship, the less the probability of acquiring the disorder.[20] However, Pastore, in an incisive critique of this work, holds that the results of this investigation are not scientifically tenable because of Kallman's unreliable diagnostic procedures, unsound statistical treatment of data, inadequate sampling procedure, and the presence of uncontrolled variables.[21] For example, the highly significant character of the relationship between children and their psychotic parents was examined neither genetically nor statistically.

In a more recent study by Kallman, based upon 794 twin index cases and their families taken from the records of New York State mental hospitals, the results appear to indicate clearly that the expectancy of schizophrenia diminishes as the blood relationship becomes more distant. For example, when one of a pair of identical twins was schizophrenic, 85.8 percent of the other twins would also be expected to be schizophrenic, with the incidence even higher (91.5 percent) if the twins were reared in the same environment.[22] Although Kallmann's figures seem to confirm the existence of a constitutional "taint" towards

[19] Kallmann, *The Genetics of Schizophrenia.*
[20] Kallmann, *The Genetics of Schizophrenia*, pp. 106-15.
[21] Pastore, "The Genetics of Schizophrenia."
[22] Kallman, *The Genetics of Schizophrenia*, pp. 207-9.

schizophrenia, when we examine the individual case records illustrating his findings, we find that (1) the environments to which identical twins were exposed were not nearly as dissimilar as Kallmann's emphasis would make them, (2) the relationships of twins reared with foster parents were taken for granted, as well as the periods in which they were placed in various homes, (3) the diagnoses of many cases were hardly adequate (a fact partially affirmed by Kallmann himself), and (4) environmental stresses in virtually all of the cases in themselves might have accounted for a high percentage of the disorders found. As Weinberg observes, the fact that both twins reacted in a schizophrenic or quasi-schizophrenic manner to adverse situations very likely shows that "the specificity of a schizophrenic reaction may be influenced if not determined by hereditary predispositions." Further, as with any presumed hereditary weakness toward general antisocial behavior, "since many predisposed individuals would not break down if they did not experience stress situations, the social experiences in effect are decisive in determining whether or not the breakdown will occur." [23]

Large as are the samples employed by psychiatrists and geneticists such as Kallmann, they have *limited* validity scientifically. To select a group of twin pairs revealing high rates of schizophrenia for both members of each pair is in itself no proof of a sound sample to test the given hypothesis. It is significant to recognize the innumerable variables which enter into the picture. Kallmann sees the end results and compiles these, but he avoids the very critical factors which might have provided a partial answer to the problem of germinal predisposition. *When were the twins separated? At what period of their lives? Under what conditions? For how long did they live with each parent? With both parents? How much schizophrenia existed in the family aside from the parents? To whom were the twins exposed and what was the character of the relationship after separation?* These, and countless other critical questions at the base of the problem, are left unanswered. What Kallman shows is simply a compilation of data on twins who come from schizophrenic parents and who, for varying periods of their lives, were exposed to schizoid environments to a greater or lesser degree. Even in his celebrated case of the Kaete and Lisa twins, he admits that *without knowing the schizoid state of one* he could *not* have diagnosed it in the other. In all reasonableness, we must exercise considerable

[23] Weinberg, *Society and Personality Disorders*, pp. 20, 21.

skepticism and scientific reserve in accepting conclusions drawn on so tenuous a basis.

The approaches developed by Dr. Paul Schilder and carried forward by Dr. Lauretta Bender appear unusually promising, however.[24] For example, the observation of children of psychotic and criminal parents in the Bellevue Children's Ward in order to detect *basic* motor differences in reactive tendencies has revealed disparities in motility (motor response patterns) and postural reflex reactions. The basic nature of this research is evidenced in the care which was taken to separate early physical and motor tendencies from the *socially meaningful* forms that the growth of such responses may take in environments rendered deficient by psychotic and criminal parents. Dr. Bender herself states that "a reactive psychosis may develop as a response to mental disease in the family"; further, that "it appears to be an expression both of constitutional weakness and of an emotional crisis in persons who show very deep or complex emotional relationships to the mentally sick members of the family."[25] The recognition of the strategic importance of the situational factor in producing personality distortions is clearly shown in the *character* of the identification of the child with the parent and *the stage at which it takes place.* However, although evidence is presented to indicate that constitutional factors are significant for a small number of children, particular stress is laid by Bender upon the deprivations imposed by the environment during the early formative years, particularly the lack of "normal environmental stimuli for growth, especially language development, in the early years."[26] This appears to be in accord with the findings of Piaget in his intensive studies of the child's social development.

In any final assessment of hereditary factors affecting delinquency, we must recognize the consensus that delinquent behavior in itself cannot be inherited. There is a growing belief, however, that early behavioral tendencies, of genetic origin, may be readily channeled by an adverse environment into various forms of delinquent behavior, although whether, as Bovet believes, these represent "character tendencies" is

---

[24] Bender, "Reactive Psychosis in Response to Mental Disease in the Family"; Bender, Kaiser, and Schilder, "Studies in Aggressiveness"; Bender, "Behavior Problems in the Children of Psychotic and Criminal Parents."
[25] Bender, "Behavior Problems in the Children of Psychotic and Criminal Parents."
[26] Bender, "Behavior Problems in the Children of Psychotic and Criminal Parents."

highly debatable.[27] Dr. Ben Karpman, in a general review of the literature, lays great stress upon the need for caution in accepting such a position in view of the limitations of our findings thus far. He indicates that similar constitutional components may be found in both delinquent and nondelinquent types. Karpman's critical evaluation appears to confirm the growing agreement that the interests of delinquency control and prevention might best be served by searching elsewhere, particularly in the environmental situations, for the crucial causes of delinquency.[28]

For Further Reading

BOVET, LUCIEN, *Psychiatric Aspects of Juvenile Delinquency* (World Health Organization, Geneva, 1951).

> A survey made by a well-known European psychiatrist to summarize the principal findings concerning psychiatry and delinquency, and indicating suggested relationships between organic factors and psychological disabilities.

MEAD, MARGARET, "Anthropological Data on the Problem of Instinct," in *Psychosomatic Medicine*, 4 (1942), pp. 396-97.

> A summary presenting some well-known anthropological findings on the ways in which traditional conceptions of human instincts are in the process of modification.

FINK, ARTHUR E., *Causes of Crime* (Philadelphia, 1938).

> A survey of the literature on the causes of crime with a cogent analysis of the several organic and constitutional theories.

LOMBROSO, CESARE, *Crime: Its Causes and Conditions* (New York, 1911), translated by Henry P. Horton.

> An English translation of the work of the Italian scholar associated with the so-called constitutional school of criminology, but which will indicate to the reader Lombroso's lively awareness of the significance of social factors in crime causation.

---

[27] Bovet, *Psychiatric Aspects of Juvenile Delinquency*, p. 25.
[28] Karpman, *Orthopsychiatry*, p. 169.

BLATZ, WILLIAM E., *The Five Sisters* (New York, 1938).

An interesting study of the variations in personal development of the Dionne quintuplets even under conditions of a similar environment.

ROSANOFF, AARON J., *et al.*, "Criminality and Delinquency in Twins," *Journal of Criminal Law and Criminology*, 24:5 (January-February, 1934), pp. 923-34.

A discussion of criminality and delinquency in identical and similar twins based upon studies to determine the presence of a predisposing genetic factor.

KALLMANN, FRANZ J., *The Genetics of Schizophrenia* (New York, 1938).

A carefully detailed study of schizophrenia among similar and identical twins and purporting to prove the existence of a constitutional predisposition to this disorder.

BENDER, LAURETTA, "Behavior Problems in the Children of Psychotic and Criminal Parents," *Genetic Psychology Monographs*, 19 (1937), pp. 229-338.

An impressive and cautious analysis of the manifestation of behavior disorders in children of psychotic and criminal parents studied at the Bellevue Clinic and indicating the significance of socially meaningful experience as applied to physical patterns of growth.

Chapter 6

BODILY RELATED FACTORS

Intelligence and Delinquency

Our perspectives have changed radically during the past twenty years regarding the function of intelligence in contributing toward delinquency. Until 1930, most of our studies appeared to confirm that delinquents were either defective in intelligence or borderline cases. Today, however, a considerable number of research conclusions seem to indicate that delinquents, by and large, do not differ radically in intellectual capacity from nondelinquent children coming from the same social and economic environments, although qualitative differences in the character of intelligence between delinquents and nondelinquents are beginning to be noted.[1]

In fact, it is interesting to note that many of the delinquency analysts who previously maintained the earlier position have actually reversed themselves. The lengthy history of study of intelligence in relation to delinquency and crime illustrates, at the same time, the defects which often surreptitiously creep into our conclusions when inadequate methods of investigation are employed, *particularly the misuse of statistical samples*. Unless this latter point is recognized, we would be led logically to believe that the cause of the shift in perspective is that the

[1] Glueck, *Unraveling Juvenile Delinquency*, pp. 198-214.

delinquent of today is a different type of youth from the one we examined twenty or more years ago. But unquestionably, our changes in perspective result from (1) the greater care observed today in the samples employed for study, (2) the considerable improvement in testing procedures and their administration during the past two decades, and (3) a greater awareness of the reasons for variations appearing in different jurisdictions, institutions, and geographical areas.[2]

Nevertheless, if the studies of a quarter of a century ago are valid in their revelation of high percentages of delinquents with subnormal intelligence, we have to accept the possibility that social and family conditions of the earlier period tended to accentuate such defects in producing delinquency. There is always the possibility that the nature of a psychological defect, whether of intelligence or some emotional disturbance, may be more conducive to a form of antisocial behavior at one time than another. Thus, for example, during one period and under certain social circumstances, defective intelligence or emotional imbalance may manifest themselves in either adjusted or maladjusted behavior, depending upon the pressures operating against the personality, the environmental opportunities, and the encouragement of certain forms of personal expression. In this sense, types of delinquents, as well as types of delinquency, may very readily vary from time to time. For example, there appears to be far greater likelihood today than twenty-five years ago that delinquents will manifest psychoneurotic tendencies. Similarly, mentally defective delinquents may have been more common in the 1920's and the 1930's than today. Some of the changes in the findings of our recent studies dealing with intelligence and delinquency may, in fact, be a result of the tendency of better conditions of schooling, special classes for retarded children, more careful guidance and early detection, etc., etc., to forestall delinquency among mentally defective children, with other types coming to the fore.

Even if defective intelligence and feeble-mindedness (both much abused terms) played a more significant role in contributing towards delinquency at the present time, how much could be attributed to heredity is doubtful. Although it is impossible to estimate exactly, very likely no more than 25 to 50 percent of all cases of feeble-mindedness are inherited.[3]

---

[2] Bloch, *Disorganization*, pp. 210-13.
[3] Bloch, *Disorganization*, pp. 513-15; Deutsch, *The Mentally Ill in America*, p. 369; *Report of the Division of Mental Deficiency*, pp. 33-34; *White House Conference on*

Lloyd Yepsen, for many years a penetrating student of the problems of mental deficiency, has stated: "We no longer believe that almost all mentally deficient persons are so because of heredity or neuropathic ancestry. We are aware that physical modifications may account for almost one-half of the subnormal individuals." [4] In calling such individuals the "seconds" of the human race, he indicates, in a listing of the occupations of fathers of children under five awaiting admission to a special institution for such defectives, the high percentages who come from professional and business classes.

The low-grade feeble-minded need not concern us here, since they are institutionalized and incapable of engaging in delinquent activity. Individuals of subnormal and low intelligence, however, are frequently more suggestible to environmental incitements and, in this way, may contribute towards the delinquency problem. On the other hand, they are likewise amenable to adequate controls and, if subjected to properly supervised environments, are capable of making perfectly good adjustments. It should be recalled as well that, in the majority of our courts, only those delinquents who evince an urgent need for psychiatric examination are so remanded, with the result that psychiatric studies frequently reveal a considerably higher percentage of mental defectiveness than would ordinarily appear if *all* delinquents passing through our courts were given such intensive examinations. For example, in 1947, of the 7,000 youths brought before the Cook County (Illinois) Juvenile Court, only 10 percent were given intensive psychiatric examinations and treatment. Such highly selective samples of course greatly distort our findings.

The recent voluminous research carried on in this particular area of delinquency study is proving quite conclusive. We have come a long way from the sententious judgment of Henry Goddard who, in his analysis of causal factors in 1921, stated that feeble-mindedness and low intelligence were direct incitements to delinquent behavior.[5] Healy and Bronner, in their significant study in 1926 of 4,000 delinquents in Chicago and Boston, found that only 63 percent of the cases they surveyed were of normal intelligence.[6] In the comparison of their results with the distribution of intelligence in normal populations, they concluded that

---

Child Health and Protection: Report of Sub-Committee on Growth and Development, pp. 220-25; Hall, "The Modern Approach to Mental Deficiency."

[4] Yepsen, "Where We Stand at Present in Care of Mentally Deficient."

[5] Goddard, *Juvenile Delinquency,* p. 22.

[6] Healy and Bronner, *Delinquents and Criminals,* pp. 151-74.

delinquency was apt to occur five to ten times more frequently among the mentally handicapped than among those who were normally endowed. For some time, their conclusions exercised a powerful influence upon many students of delinquency. However, in their more recent work, particularly in the study of 400 cases treated or investigated by the Judge Baker Guidance Clinic, including court delinquents, noncourt delinquents, and those with generic behavior problems productive of delinquency, they found a high percentage with considerably better than average intelligence, and a percentage of marginal and defective cases comparable to that in the ordinary population.[7] It is instructive to note that of the non-court delinquents, comprising 137 cases of whom 31 percent had better than average intelligence, a wide variety of commonplace and more serious delinquencies were practiced, ranging from the most frequent offense of "long record of stealing" to serious sexual misconduct.

Dr. David B. Rotman, for many years associated with the Cook County Juvenile Court as psychiatrist, has attempted to issue a final word on the dangers of attributing defective intelligence to delinquents by indicating that, with the exception of female sex delinquents, the groups he studied yielded distributions of approximately 2 to 5 percent for mental deficiency, a figure comparable to what we would expect in samples taken from nondelinquent groups.[8] Metfessel and Lovell, in their broad critical survey of the literature in this area, conclude that defective intelligence should be treated with considerable caution as a causal factor in delinquency, and that whereas some studies still show high expectancy rates for borderline cases, mental retardation may certainly not be considered a primary factor.[9] Weiss and Sampliner, in their study of 189 adolescents sixteen to twenty-one years of age who were first felony offenders, state that the distribution of intelligence for this group corresponds to that of normal populations.[10]

The previous emphasis upon defective intelligence in juvenile offenders is all the more striking in view of the consistent findings for many years of tested adult offender groups, who yield intelligence scores comparable to those for normal groups and, in some cases, somewhat higher than those for noncriminal groups. Herman Adler, for example, on the

[7] Healy and Bronner, *Treatment and What Happened Afterward*, pp. 602-3.
[8] Rotman, "Mental Characteristics of Delinquents."
[9] Metfessel and Lovell, "Recent Literature on Individual Correlates of Crime."
[10] Weiss and Sampliner, "A Study of Adolescent Felony Offenders."

basis of his study of Illinois prisoners, has shown that the general average of intelligence of inmate groups was higher than that for selected samples of enlisted and officer personnel in the United States Army at the end of World War I.[11] Although not bearing directly or exclusively on the problem of delinquency, Simon H. Tulchin's findings on the distribution of intelligence scores for native-born whites, foreign-born whites, and Negroes in the Illinois state penitentiary, reformatory, and army-drafted groups reveal a remarkable similarity in the distribution of intelligence scores for inmate populations (both reformatory and penitentiary) and army personnel.[12]

TABLE F

Comparison of Scores on the Army Alpha Intelligence Tests for Penitentiary and Reformatory Inmates, and Members of the Draft for the First World War, for Illinois (1920-26).

	INFERIOR SCORES (0-25)	AVERAGE SCORES (25-104)	SUPERIOR SCORES (105-212)	NUMBER OF CASES
Native-born whites				
Illinois State Penitentiary.....	9.2	73.9	16.9	3,199
Illinois State Reformatory.....	9.5	75.2	15.3	3,646
Illinois Army Draft..........	10.3	73.6	16.1	2,102
Foreign-born whites				
Illinois State Penitentiary.....	44.6	47.6	7.8	1,011
Illinois State Reformatory.....	25.3	64.6	10.1	336
Illinois Army Draft..........	44.2	50.3	5.5	728
Negroes				
Illinois State Penitentiary.....	41.6	56.2	2.2	1,302
Illinois State Reformatory.....	36.8	59.9	3.3	766
Illinois Army Draft..........	43.1	53.1	3.8	1,139

* Tulchin, *Intelligence and Crime*, pp. 19 ff. Reprinted by permission of The University of Chicago Press. Copyright 1939 by the University of Chicago.

[11] Adler and Worthington, "The Scope of the Problem of Delinquency and Crime as Related to Mental Deficency."
[12] Tulchin, *Intelligence and Crime.*

A slight discrepancy appears in the relatively higher rate of deficient scores for older Negroes as compared to the youthful (reformatory) Negro group, but this can be largely accounted for on the basis of the limited schooling of the older Negro age-groups. Murchison's studies of criminal intelligence, although indicating variations which may be reasonably explained on the basis of geographical differences, appear to be in substantial accord with these findings.[13]

As an indication of how recent studies have tended to reveal the declining incidence of low intelligence as a contributory factor to crime and delinquency, Sutherland's appraisal of 340 reports, in which he compares an early period (1910-14) with a later period (1925-28), shows a formidable decrease in the number of studies which stressed defective intelligence, from over 50 percent to approximately 20 percent.[14] Since the Sutherland appraisal, improvements in research methodology have gone even further in disclosing the decreasing significance of defective intelligence in contributing to delinquency.

What has been said so far about the intelligence findings of ordinary delinquents, however, does not appear to apply to female sex delinquents, who still yield high percentages of defective intelligence.[15] However, we can hardly attribute sexual delinquency to defective intelligence. The interrelated dynamics of emotional patterning, early maturity and sexual precocity, and environmental disorganization must be considered in assessing the causal factors that contribute to the demoralization of girls.[16]

We have already suggested in our analysis that the changes we have witnessed in the intellectual composition of our delinquent groups result largely from improved methodologies in studying delinquents and our greater care in assessing our samples and in the use of testing procedures. At the same time we must take into account the fact that changes in educational procedures for our young people in general and the prolongation of compulsory schooling have also very likely played a part in producing differences in our observed results. However, if we can accept the conclusion that delinquents, by and large, do not differ appreciably in intelligence from nondelinquents, a significant new problem is revealed concerning the *character* of intelligence for the two

[13] Murchison, *Criminal Intelligence.*
[14] Sutherland, *Principles of Criminology*, pp. 104-5.
[15] Goldberg, *Girls in the City Streets.*
[16] See Bloch, *Disorganization*, pp. 321-25, 382-96.

groups. At the present time, differences in the *kind* of intelligence displayed by delinquents and nondelinquents may prove of crucial interest. (It is a truism that progress in research and scientific analysis is paradoxically determined in the raising of new questions when the old ones are tentatively assessed. Poincaré, astute student of scientific method, suggested that a score of new problems press forward upon the heels of each dilemma resolved.)

The Gluecks have attempted to evaluate characteristic *qualitative* differences in the intelligence of delinquents and nondelinquents. In *Unraveling Juvenile Delinquency*, in which they compared 500 delinquents and 500 nondelinquents in the Boston area, they attempted to keep certain critical factors, such as environment, age, ethnic composition, and intelligence factors constant, with the result that they were in a position to determine any difference which may have existed in respect to such personality differentials as the *character* of intelligence and emotional patterning. On the basis of the Wechsler-Bellevue Scale, the test results indicated that delinquents average lower in verbal intelligence than nondelinquents, although the two groups resembled each other closely in performance intelligence.[17] As revealed by the five subtests of the Wechsler-Bellevue battery, delinquents show less aptitude in vocabulary, information, and comprehension, although they resemble nondelinquents in the average scores on similarities (recognition of comparisons), arithmetic reasoning, and memory span for digits. Although the resemblances in performance have been noted, some differences in the separate subtest scores were recorded, revealing, as we might expect, that delinquents are less successful in those tests requiring some degree of abstraction, concentration, and persistence. The Gluecks conclude that "the delinquents are, on the whole, somewhat superior in those intellectual tasks in which the approach to meaning is by direct physical relationship . . . with a minimum dependence on a structure of intermediary symbols," or, in other words, that they are more responsive to concrete realities than to abstractions.[18] This, it would appear, has a direct implication in the treatment of delinquents, suggesting that methods of retraining and rehabilitation should have less recourse to *formal* procedures and educational skills than to exposure to actual situations of a dynamic and strategically

[17] Glueck, *Unraveling Juvenile Delinquency*, p. 207.
[18] Glueck, *Unraveling Juvenile Delinquency*, p. 207.

conceived character. Various aspects of group dynamics are to be commended in this respect.

The results of the Rorschach Test, a projective device in which the
individual is asked to interpret a series of meaningless ink blots, to
which, theoretically, he imputes his own intellectual and emotional
tendencies, proved less conclusive in revealing sharp differences, although certain inferences can be drawn. Significant, for example, is the
finding that delinquents "have less potential capacity for genuine
objective interests, as opposed to having interests merely or predominantly for the sake of gaining prestige, earning money, having success,
procuring the attention, affection, or protection of others, and so on." [19]
Of greater importance, however, is the disclosure that *the intellectual
tendencies of delinquents are interwoven with emotional dynamics*, a
fact with which most modern research tends to be in fairly close
accord.[20] Although it is dubious that the delinquents in the Glueck
study are representative of delinquents in general, these findings are
nevertheless highly suggestive. The results tend to confirm the growing view that the personality patterning of recurrent delinquents imparts a distinctive emotional tone to their responses, affecting intellectual as well as behavioral functions, although the degree of such emotional stress is still to be determined.

The Endocrine Glands and Behavior

Powerful impulsions to behavior processes come from the functioning of the endocrine glands. Although considerable progress in the
understanding of the glands' functions, both as an interrelated system
and in the specific effects of each, has been gained since the excessive
claims of the 1920's, we are still very much in the dark concerning the
precise linkages operating between specific glandular functioning and
particular forms of behavior. The exaggerated and often ridiculous
claims of some of the early investigators into the relationship between
glandular dysfunctioning and delinquent tendencies, leading to the
dramatic belief that the glands provided the "chemistry of the soul,"
have been tempered by the more careful research of the past fifteen
years.

[19] Glueck, *Unraveling Juvenile Delinquency*, p. 214.
[20] Glueck, *Unraveling Juvenile Delinquency*, p. 214.

Only the most naïvely optimistic could have accepted with the slightest credulity such statements as that of M. G. Schlapp: "It would not surprise the writer if investigations were to reveal that a third of all present convicts were sufferers from emotional instability, which is to say gland or toxic disturbance." [21] For the untrained observer, this appears to have conjured up the rare but pleasing prospect of the judge's gavel being replaced by the hypodermic syringe and the use of hormonic counteragents to suppress the antisocial tendencies of prisoners brought before the bar of justice. Equally extravagant claims were made by Schlapp and Smith in their much heralded *The New Criminology*—special note should be taken of the title—in which Schlapp confirmed his previous findings that over one-third of 20,000 prison inmates he examined were glandularly imbalanced.[22] In further support of such extreme claims, Schlapp and Smith have described the murderer and the thief in glandular terms, stating that "the man capable of murder is disturbed in his glands, cells and nerve centers," and even more surprising, that "not until he has consummated his crime, does the emotional strain and excitement abate." [23] The latter should hardly surprise us, as Teeters states, since there is hardly one of us who does not show the results of hyperactive glandular excitation during periods of great strain and emotion, whether observing the ticker tape in a stockbroker's office or witnessing our favorite baseball team go down to defeat.[24]

No one can gainsay the extreme importance of glandular functioning in all phases of human behavior. However, the precise connection between the *hyper-* (over) and *hypo-* (under) activity of a given gland and its outcome in behavior is an extremely different matter. The modern endocrinologist is far more cautious in making claims that a *socially patterned form of behavior* is the direct outcome of a given form of glandular imbalance. To understand this properly, we must recognize that a given gland in itself does not activate a specific behavioral state. In the first place, the glands operate as a totally functioning and interrelated system. Second, the glands themselves are frequently affected by the environmental situation to which the personal-

[21] Schlapp, "Behavior and Gland Disease."

[22] Schlapp and Smith, *The New Criminology.* See also Bloch, *Disorganization,* p. 192.

[23] Schlapp and Smith, *The New Criminology,* p. 230.

[24] Teeters and Reinemann, *The Challenge of Delinquency,* pp. 97-98.

ity is exposed. Third, and possibly most important, is the fact that even if the person is strongly stimulated by a glandular process to engage in some form of activity, the social situation is the final determinant of the *form* which such behavior may actually take. Similar temperaments, directly resulting from our glandular functioning, do not necessarily induce similar forms of behavior. Extreme restlessness, high degrees of energy, ready irritability, volatility, and loss of temper, for example, do not necessarily imply that the individual so concerned will readily succumb to delinquent practices or will break the law. The social situation will always determine: (1) the form such activity will take, and (2) the character of the restraints the individual has learned to impose upon himself in the form of acquired inhibitions, *which in turn may actually alter the endocrine balance itself.*

There is considerable recent evidence to substantiate these points, particularly the latter. Rowe, for example, in studying the behavior of seventeen-year-old children suffering from various forms of endocrine malfunctioning, discovered that 18.3 percent gave evidence of behavioral disorders of a more or less serious nature, while 13 percent did not.[25] While appearing a rather significant difference, although *not* statistically reliable, the behavioral disorders to which Rowe refers are very much of the type that might readily have been processed by the environment, regardless of the biological motivation. Further, there appears to be reasonable evidence that many of the disturbed glandular states were heightened, if not directly caused, by environmental pressures, and were not the primary result of innate factors.

Gardner Murphy lays particular stress upon factors which affect the entire interrelated functioning of the endocrine system. Of primary importance, he points out, is the fact that endocrine functioning is a resultant of *effects* upon the nervous system, as well as of such seemingly unrelated factors as nutrition, health, and other aspects of the organic constitution.[26] Dr. James Halliday, from a completely different perspective, has indicated strongly the new orientation that studies of behavioral-organic functioning must take, in stressing the fact that the *entire organism* must adapt to changing conditions of the environment.[27] There is a significant implication here for diagnosis which is

---

[25] Rowe, "A Possible Endocrine Factor in the Behavior Problems of the Young."
[26] Murphy, *Personality: A Biosocial Approach to Origins and Structures,* pp. 92-101.
[27] Halliday, *Psychosocial Medicine,* esp. Chap. 1.

just beginning to make its impression upon the medical profession. Murphy, in summarizing considerable evidence, has stipulated: "To say, then, that this or that trait stems from this or that endocrine function is an abstraction of such a type as to be useful only when a great deal of valid evidence shows clearly the virtual irrelevance of other contributing functions; and such cases are rare." [28]

Actually, specific types of glandular functioning may be expressed in such a variety of ways as to deny emphatically a clean-cut one-to-one relationship between the activity of a given gland and a given behavior pattern. This is particularly well illustrated in the extreme cases of hyperthyroidism, manifested in Graves' disease, for example. The classical example of extreme imbalance in this disorder appears to be psychologically represented in such traits as hyperactivity, nervousness, general restlessness, and unremitting stress. At the opposite end of the pole, in those cases where we have hypothyroid (underactive) states, traits of a reverse order should tend to be common, and we do find occasional specimens of low pulse and respiratory rates and general indices of retarded living tempo. However, this to-be-expected antithesis does not work out as might be anticipated; we frequently find in such extreme cases of underactivity of the thyroid individuals who appear to manifest the same restlessness, the same nervousness, and the same hyperactivity as the excessive cases noted in Graves' disease. How do we account for this? It may well be, as psychologists have suggested, that activities which seem to contradict the endocrine economy of the organism take the form of compensatory mechanisms. This is apparently the case in the complex behavior processes that lead to delinquency. Many delinquents, by virtue of a series of complex psychological and environmental variables intervening between the original endocrine state of the organism and the eventual resultant in behavior, engage in various compensatory devices that appear to deny strongly the basal metabolic rates and the over- or under-functioning of the gland in question. As Murphy has stated: "Maybe there is something wrong with the way in which the relation of glands to personality has been stated." [29]

John Levy's study of problem children appears to illustrate this last point very well. In the investigation of a group of problem children

[28] Murphy, *Personality*, pp. 94-95.
[29] Murphy, *Personality*, p. 97.

characterized by hyperactivity, he found paradoxically that, in comparison with a group giving evidence of hypoactivity, the hyperactive group actually revealed a *lower* basal metabolism than the organically hypoactive group.[30] This is not evidenced in the lives of "problem" individuals only; we *all* learn through the experience of living to compensate frequently for the conditions imposed by our organic limitations. A strong tendency to engage energetically in too many activities at too strenuous a pace compels many of us to slow down and to use our energies more sparingly. Conversely, the highly lethargic and inactive individual will frequently feel impelled to bestir himself more energetically and to lead a more active and strenuous existence.

There are innumerable examples to illustrate the significance of personality organization and structure in repatterning endocrine outlets. Moreover, we are becoming increasingly and painfully aware of the degree to which a given endocrine state may be induced by environmental pressure and stress. Levy's study shows rather convincingly how personality functioning can alter the existent endocrine state. It is commonly found that a fright, prolonged distress, or a nervous shock can result in a hyperthyroid condition, a state produced by a complex alteration in the entire neuro-chemical system. In a study of sixty cases of Graves' disease, fifty-four of the cases revealed a history of sustained apprehensiveness *before* the clinical onset of hyperthyroidism. Further, despite the expectation that greater speed in tested psychological reactions might be anticipated with high basal metabolism rates, Steinberg has shown in his study of adolescent girls that the speed of reaction varied in inverse ratio to the basal metabolism.[31] Empirical evidence points to the conclusion that factors *outside* the endocrine system (directly linked to, and in many cases directly incited by, forces outside the body) must be considered when dealing with any organic factor.

In view of the significant organic changes of adolescence, a period closely linked to delinquent disorder, the challenges raised by endocrine functioning appear, on the surface, extremely impressive. Actually endocrine malfunctioning affords only a very partial and limited insight into certain forms of behavior disorder. Sexual maturation, although

---

[30] Levy, "A Quantitative Study of the Relationship between Basal Metabolic Rate and Children's Behavior Problems."

[31] Steinberg, "Relation between Basal Metabolic Rate and Mental Speed."

closely allied to the anterior pituitary gland, is a complex process involving many endocrine functions as well as other organs of the body. There is no single or unitary factor accounting for such complex changes that may enable us to isolate sources of maladjustment. In the relation between gonad development and social-sexual maturation, Stone and Barker have shown how the psychological orientation of girls after the onset of puberty is not the result of organic maturation alone, but is dependent upon the general psychological constitution of the personality and the requirements of a particular environment.[32] Girls of the same age and seemingly of the same level of maturity will reveal differences in the desire to retain their girlhood status or to press on rapidly toward womanhood.

The organic instability accompanying adolescence results in disproportionate forms of physical growth, emotional states, and environmentally structured attitudes. In other words, the particular stress experienced by the adolescent is far from being a glandular matter. The varied organic changes express themselves at different levels and in different forms: the growing boy or girl may be psychologically and socially advanced and at the same time organically retarded—a complex which in itself may prove disruptive and provoke behavior disorders— or be organically mature while psychologically and socially unprepared for his new status. Bayley and Jones, in the California Adolescent Study, show the priority of social considerations in inducing tensions among adolescent children; this predominating factor is frequently a fertile source of delinquent outbreaks where organic maturity has been delayed in specific respects.[33] *This means that the source of many behavior disorders during puberty is hardly the outcome of endocrine imbalance but primarily a result of the relationship between the children's patterned expectancies and their social settings.*

Our net conclusion, thus, must be that provocative sources of behavioral disorder, delinquent and otherwise, do not invariably result from glandular imbalance but rather from the way in which such forms of organic disequilibrium are channeled in relation to the structured needs of the personality and the environment. As Murphy has put it: "Per-

[32] Stone and Barker, "The Attitudes and Interests of Pre-Menarcheal and Post-Menarcheal Girls."

[33] Bayley and Jones, "Some Personality Characteristics of Boys with Retarded Skeletal Maturity."

sonality reflects not only the endocrine balance *but the socially ordered responses to this balance."* [34]

Bodily Types and Delinquency

A significant and perhaps ironic development of the past two decades in the fields of delinquency and criminology research has been the attempt to link various bodily types to delinquent behavior. Historically this purported connection is best known through the efforts of Cesare Lombroso (1836-1909) to prove that the "criminal type" is clearly marked both mentally and physiologically. Despite the fact that the Lombrosian theory of physical types and physiological determinism has lain dormant for some time, there is a singular effort to show the relationship between classified constitutional types, known as *somatotypes*, and the tendency to engage in deviant or delinquent behavior. The revival of this point of view is all the more surprising after the great forward strides made in psychiatry and sociology during the past two decades in disclosing the significant interpersonal processes that shape the formation of personality traits and the impressive role that situational determinants play in producing various types of behavior, delinquent and otherwise. As an indication of the stress currently placed on this view by some reputable scholars, the recent work of the Gluecks, long noted for their careful and detailed studies of delinquency, may be cited in that they attempt to assign to constitutional factors an instrumental role in the determination and prediction of delinquency.[35] In trying to establish correlations between constitutional determinants and behavioral processes, studies of this kind very often pay scant heed to the power, as dynamic elements in the processing of human behavior, of cultural values, group structures, family organization, personality patterning, the self-conceptions of the individual, and his role-playing tendencies under various conditions of social control.

The initial impetus for this recent development stems to a considerable degree from what appears to have been a reasonable assumption in the work of the psychiatrist Kretschmer.[36] As has been suggested

[34] Murphy, *Personality*, p. 101. (Italics ours.)
[35] Glueck, *Unraveling Juvenile Delinquency*, Chap. 15 (prepared by Dr. Carl C. Seltzer).
[36] Kretschmer, *Physique and Character*, trans. by W. H. Sprott from *Körperbau und Charakter*.

earlier, temperamental states (linked in part to the endocrine balance and other constitutional factors of the personality) may, under conditions of an adverse environment, lead the individual to engage in certain forms of unlawful conduct. Kretschmer's examination of mental patients in German hospitals suggested the possibility of classifying mentally deranged individuals into three basic types: (1) the *pyknic*, marked by rounded characteristics, stocky build, and fleshy smoothness of arms, limbs, and trunk; (2) the *asthenic*, long, angular, and lean, and characterized by prominent skeletal features; and (3) the *dysplastic*, possessing characteristics of the two previous types. Certain temperamental qualities, conducive to the manic-depressive state, appeared with relatively high frequency among the pyknic types, while schizophrenic tendencies appeared to be more pronounced in the asthenic category. The defects in Kretschmer's early research were soon made apparent by the difficulties involved in establishing such relationships generally and with clinical exactness, and in view of the very broad classifications employed. The dysplastic, for example, was such a tenuous category that, like the Procrustean bed of mythology, virtually all individuals could in some way be made to fit within its elastic limits.

Recognizing the limitations of this early typology, Dr. William H. Sheldon and his associates have attempted to develop adequate constitutional categories applicable to all individuals.[37] Professor Earnest Hooton has sought to discover through the study of a large sample of American prison inmates whether distinctive physical earmarks exist for such groups as compared with normal samples of the population.[38] In the celebrated Hooton study, 10,953 male prisoners in two widely separated states were compared with a "control" group of 909 white civilians and 1,067 Negroid subjects, drawn from a diverse sample of Nashville firemen, frequenters of public bath houses, patients at the Massachusetts General Hospital, and members of the Massachusetts militia. Although Hooton did not claim that he had discovered a specific type or series of "criminal" types, he has stipulated that certain physical characteristics emerged with greater frequency among the prison population than among his so-called normal samples. For example, such traits as thinner beards and less bodily hair, slight stature, eye folds, sloping and low foreheads, high narrow nasal roots

[37] Sheldon, Stevens, and Tucker, *The Varieties of Human Physique.*
[38] Hooton, *The American Criminal.*

and bridges, a roll helix to the ear, a marked overbite, and many other characteristics appear to occur with higher frequency among prison inmates. Because of the relatively high frequency of these traits, Hooton has attributed the behavioral characteristics of the "American criminal" to a form of "biological inferiority," in what appears to be a remarkable resurrection of the Lombrosian specter.

The mistakes in Hooton's position have been penetratingly exposed by a number of critics from different fields. Even the untrained reader should recognize the fallacies inherent in Hooton's use of "controlled" samples. (1) Hooton hardly compares criminality, as he implies, with noncriminality, but rather a group of prisoners in two institutional areas with a heterogeneous group of individuals assembled from various walks of life. In fact, statistically speaking, the differences *within* his so-called "normal" groups are considerably wider than the differences he claims to have shown between his criminal and noncriminal groups. The physical requirements for admission to the state militia and a municipal fire department, for example, are highly selective and would certainly mark off these groups considerably from the random sample of derelicts and patients he assembled. (2) Even a prison group can hardly be thought of as truly representative of either delinquents or criminals in general, as all students of crime and delinquency recognize. (3) Crime is a *social* phenomenon, hardly a biological trait as Hooton seems to imply. This is evidenced in changing conceptions of crime among different cultures, during different periods, and for different class levels. Is Hooton implying that a given physical constitution predisposes toward crime irrespective of the period and society in which it exists and the social class level on which an individual finds himself? There is not a shred of statistical or empirical evidence to support such a contention. As we have seen, only physical traits may be transmitted by heredity. Certainly, the gross bodily features of the organism, themselves the results of innumerable internal body mechanisms that have been affected by both intra-organic and external environments, can hardly be said to produce a certain form of behavior without our recognizing the wide range of specific determinants, *within* and *without* the organism, that contribute to behavior. (4) Finally, if Hooton's thesis of criminal "biological inferiority" is to be accepted, an inordinate number of citizens in the general population would fall within the biological limits he establishes for the "inferior" types and should tend, consequently, to engage in lawless behavior.

The extremism of this view can be seen in the fact that Hooton has even attempted to identify certain forms of criminality—forgery, murder, burglary, etc.—with specific social and physical types. Certainly, cross-sectional samples of offenders in various states hardly confirms the exaggerated view that the blonde, long-headed, pure Nordic type is "an easy leader in forgery and fraud, a strong second in burglary and larceny, and last or next to last in all crimes against persons." [39] Or that the brunet, round-headed Alpine type "ranks first in robbery but last in forgery and fraud," and similar allegations.[40] The misleading conclusions of Hooton's study, entirely divorced as they are from psychiatric, social psychological, anthropological, and sociological considerations, move us to paraphrase the frequently cited admonition: Any resemblance between Hooton's samples of American offenders and those of their traits he claims to have discovered are purely coincidental.

Dr. Sheldon and his associates, in a series of three studies, have attempted to overcome some of the technical difficulties earlier encountered in the classification of bodily types and to lay the basis for a new approach to personality study through what has been termed "constitutional psychiatry." [41] Instead of the broad Kretschmerian classification, Sheldon has contrived a series of bodily measurements covering the three major segments of the body—head and shoulders, torso, and limbs—by means of which individuals may be assigned specific index numbers corresponding to their general proportions. By use of these modern anthropometric (bodily measurement) devices, any person may be classified. Sheldon has set down three major prototypes to which all human beings correspond in varying degree: (1) the *endomorphic*, somewhat similar in form to the earlier pyknic classification of Kretschmer; (2) the *ectomorphic*, characterized by linearity, prominent skeletal structure, delicacy of body, small face, sharp nose, and fine hair; and (3) the *mesomorphic*, well-muscled and -proportioned, and predominantly characterized by heavy chest, prominently devel-

---

[39] Hooton, *Crime and the Man*, pp. 6-7.
[40] Hooton, *Crime and the Man*, pp. 250-78.
[41] Sheldon, Stevens, and Tucker, *The Varieties of Human Physique*; Sheldon, Stevens, and Tucker, *The Varieties of Temperament*; Sheldon, Hartl, and McDermott, *Varieties of Delinquent Behavior*.

oped arms, limbs, and connective tissue. By statistical correlation, Sheldon and his associates claim to have discovered distinctive temperamental patterns associated with each of these types. The typical endomorph, for example, corresponds to the *viscerotonic* type, relaxed, easy-going, and relatively free from tension; the ectomorph, a *cerebrotonic* type, appears to be distinguished by tendencies to introversion, avoidance of crowds, and characteristic allergies such as skin troubles and insomnia; the mesomorph, known as a *somotonic*, is marked by extroversion, a dynamic personality, self-assertion, and interest in strenuous pursuits.[42]

If it can be genuinely proved that temperamental states are as closely allied to physical states as Sheldon implies, a strong clue may be afforded to the behavioral potentials of certain types of individuals on the basis of physical and hereditary components. But even the most unyielding endocrinologists appear to demur at such an extreme suggestion.[43] Temperamental states, *under defined conditions of the environment and in terms of the patterned responses of others*, may tend to lead more consistently than not to situations which are destructive and antisocial. Individuals who are generally choleric have greater difficulty in getting along in most situations than those who are placid, but there is certainly no assurance that an easily triggered temper will lead to delinquent activity in even the most unwholesome of environments. In fact, the rigid and unpermissive discipline of a highly underprivileged environment may produce more compulsive tensions for the placid individual in many instances than for the individual who more readily may express his aggressive impulses, something that psychiatrists have been pointing out for some time. To assert, therefore, as Sheldon does in his last work, which deals explicitly with delinquency and bodily types, that "where essential inadequacy is present the inadequacy is well reflected in the observable structure of the organism," appears to deny the most basic assumptions of empirically related studies in psychology and sociology.[44] Such studies have specified how personality traits and behavior patterns are fashioned out of the peculiar orientation

[42] Sheldon, Stevens, and Tucker, *The Varieties of Temperament*.
[43] See, for example, the strictures of Dr. Louis Berman concerning this view in his critique of Sheldon's work in the *Saturday Review of Literature*, September 14, 1940, p. 17.
[44] Sheldon, Stevens, and Tucker, *Varieties of Delinquent Behavior*, p. 752.

of a unique personality within a given depriving or satisfying environment. The tenacity with which this uncritical view still persists may be seen in some of the more extreme recent writings (hardly scientific!) of European students of delinquency and crime, where the Lombrosian myth is still being sedulously followed. The Italian criminologist Flesch, for example, has recently stated that "association with bad company is not the *cause* of future criminal conduct, but the consequence of perverse constitutional tendencies which impel the individual toward [bad company] by virtue of elective affinity." [45]

There is really little conclusive evidence in the most recent work of Sheldon, a study of 200 young adults referred to the Hayden Goodwill Inn in South Boston, that the prevalence of certain constitutional types in this selective group might appear with equal regularity in cross-cultural samples taken from groups coming from *other* social contexts and ethnic backgrounds in *different* geographical areas. Further, the insufficiency of clinical psychological evidence of the derivation of antisocial behavioral traits of the delinquents surveyed leaves the issue of constitutional types and delinquency in even greater doubt. It might be instructive for the advocates of such views to familiarize themselves with the insights of the eminent French social scientist Émile Durkheim, who, in the analysis of other forms of pathological behavior, has demonstrated clearly that *the mere presence of a statistical relationship is no proof of a causal relationship.*[46] As he has demonstrated in illustrating shifting rates of such problems as suicide, for example, observable defects in behavior are the results of social and cultural conditioning, class and group membership, and the peculiar personality constitution of certain individuals.

In addition to the criticisms of the Sheldon view, there is considerable direct evidence contradicting such findings. In a comparative study of 4,000 boys in two delinquency areas by four scientists—a physician, a sociologist, a physical anthropologist, and a statistician—in which sixty-three anthropometric measurements were taken for each subject, as well as medical, neurological, social, and morphological data, no significant difference between white delinquents and nondelinquents were dis-

[45] Flesch, "Valor y limites del factor hereditario en la etiologia de la criminalidad."
[46] See Alpert, *Émile Durkheim and His Sociology.* Also, Durkheim, *The Rules of Sociological Method,* trans. by G. E. Simpson; Durkheim, *Le Suicide.*

covered, although some slight differences were shown for Negroid subjects.[47] Paradoxically, in the case of the Negroes sampled, fewer of the
so-called stigmata of crime existed among the Negro delinquents than
among the nondelinquents. In the carefully controlled study by Healy
and Bronner, in which 105 delinquents were compared with an equal
number of nondelinquent siblings, no significant differences in structural types were noted, although the delinquents did reveal a higher
percentage of physical defects.[48]

The Gluecks, in their comparative study of 500 delinquents and 500
nondelinquents in the Boston area, based upon the findings of Dr.
Carl C. Seltzer, have revealed that both absolutely and relatively the
delinquents in their sample were mesomorphic (muscular) in constitution, with a much higher proportion of all mesomorphic types than
the nondelinquents and a far lower proportion of ectomorphs (linear,
thin types). Ectomorphs, endomorphs (round, plump types), and
balanced types, they found, were decidedly subordinate among the
delinquents. The control group of nondelinquents contained no extreme predominance of any bodily type, although substantial numbers
of ectomorphs *and mesomorphs* were found, with the former predominating.[49] Since the Glueck study deals with a highly particularized
sample from which over-all generalizations can be made only with the
utmost caution, it is possible that a preferential factor of selection may
operate to produce relatively high yields of mesomorphic types. The
cultural premium within the subcultural milieu of the boys' gang upon
physical and athletic prowess and combative skill may tend to bring to
the fore many mesomorphic types who eventually find their way into
our courts.

The Gluecks, however, are cautious in attributing an undue significance to such constitutional factors, asserting merely that constitutional
endowment must be considered "along with the early influences surrounding the child in his home, school and neighborhood." [50] Professional opinion has been strident and emphatic in condemning particularly this aspect of the Glueck study, however. Referring to this recent

[47] The study was conducted by B. Boshes, S. Kobrin, E. Reynolds, and S. Rosen-
baum, and has been appraised by M. F. Ashley Montagu in "The Biologist Looks
at Crime."

[48] Healy and Bronner, *New Light on Delinquency and Its Treatment.*

[49] Glueck, *Unraveling Juvenile Delinquency,* Chap. 15.

[50] Glueck, *Unraveling Juvenile Delinquency,* p. 196.

investigation, Marshall Clinard has stated, "The emphasis on William H. Sheldon's somatotypes, which has been subject to severe criticism, not only does not add to a study of this type but weakens one's faith in the entire work." [51]

Physical Health and Defects of Delinquents

In appraising the physical health and defects of delinquents, it is extremely difficult, because of the pervasive conditions which these states imply, to isolate factors as having played instrumental roles in producing characteristic forms of misbehavior and delinquency. For example, the discovery of a physical defect or a particular physical condition, even in relatively high percentage, constitutes no indication in itself that the condition discovered is a basic or primary factor in producing delinquent disorder. Recognizing as we do that physical conditions of the organism, in relation to the structuring limitations of the environment, may produce a wide range of differing psychological effects, the fact remains that *a tendency toward deviant behavior is always contingent on the actual determinants present at a crucial period in the child's life.* There can be no question that certain physical handicaps, taking almost any conceivable form, may in conjunction with a peculiarly disadvantageous environment produce a series of behavior tendencies in the child which culminate in overt delinquent acts or other forms of youthful misbehavior. The physical condition in itself, however, is not directly instrumental, *but may have been strategically important only at a peculiar conjunction in the child's life.* To try to prove otherwise, as certain physiologists and psychiatrists have, without taking into account, both qualitatively and functionally, carefully documented genetic studies of various levels of growth, *does little more than confirm a difference* without proving a cause. [52]

Furthermore, differences in states of physical health, morbidity, defects, impairments, size, weight, and stature are far from uniform in the several studies that have been made. Thus, whether a given physical state appears before or after an actual behavioral disorder is, as the criminologist von Hentig shows, largely a matter of accident. [53] However, studies of physical health and defects have shown certain significant

---

[51] See Clinard's detailed criticism of the Gluecks' recent work in *Federal Probation,* 17 (March, 1953), pp. 50-51.
[52] See Michaels, "Psychobiologic Interpretations of Delinquency."
[53] von Hentig, *Crime.*

trends that may shed light upon the relative importance of such factors. Generally speaking, these studies may be summarized under the following headings: (1) differential health conditions; (2) differences in size and weight; and (3) factors of appearance and gross physical defects.

(1) *Differential Health Characteristics.* The findings on health conditions and physical defects among delinquents present a highly confused picture. Seldom, if ever, do we find studies in this area conducted on a carefully controlled comparative basis. The results, at best, may be considered suggestive rather than indicative of causal processes in health and delinquency. Certainly, the results thus far, meager as they appear when viewed on a sound scientific basis, give little evidence to enable us to link specific health conditions with problems of delinquency. We find, periodically, high rates of physical disability in the studies of delinquents, but such rates would not appear to be substantially higher than the over-all rates for children coming from the same economic areas and similar backgrounds. It is true, nevertheless, that even in areas of economic and social deprivation, the greater neglect often accompanying defective parental control of delinquent children is manifested by greater evidence of physical disability and higher morbidity (illness) rates, a result of malnutrition and parental indifference to or ignorance of active or incipient health disorders. In a survey of the health conditions of delinquents revealed in various studies, the following conclusions were drawn:

General surveys of the health and physical characteristics of delinquents indicate that the physical disabilities from which they suffer are due primarily to poverty and parental neglect rather than to heredity, although certain exceptional instances must be noted. Today, it is considered obligatory to give the delinquent child entering an institution a very careful medical examination and to follow up as carefully as possible any defects that examinations may reveal. It is extremely difficult to establish genuine statistical differences between the incidence of certain physical defects among the criminal and delinquent populations and selected samples from the normal population, although a great many statistical studies do reveal certain percentage differences. The inference many investigators make is that the delinquent population is to a small degree distinguished from the nondelinquent population by poor health and physical abnormalities.[54]

[54] Bloch, *Disorganization*, p. 202. A survey of many leading studies can be found in Sutherland, *Principles of Criminology*, Chap. 6.

As has been suggested, many studies do appear to reveal higher morbidity rates for delinquents than for nondelinquents. On the basis of this disparity, however, little is shown of the significance of this factor as contributory, directly or indirectly, to delinquency rates. Thurston, for example, has attempted to demonstrate that a considerable proportion of such morbidity, if it actually exists among delinquents as compared with nondelinquents, may be attributed to general conditions of poverty and neglect, and especially, the malnutrition that exists under such circumstances.[55] Such debilitating conditions of physical standards of health, however, are not typical of delinquent groups alone, as Thurston shows in revealing a study of New York City districts where an estimated 42 percent of the children living within so-called delinquency areas (although the majority themselves were *not* delinquent) suffered from malnutrition, as compared with an estimated 10 percent of the general population. Reckless and Smith, in an early work, estimated a comparatively higher rate of physical deficiencies among delinquents than among nondelinquents, although it is extremely dubious that such evidence today can be accepted as valid.[56] Slawson, on the basis of rather specialized samples, concluded that delinquents suffered from a higher rate of visual and auditory defects than nondelinquents.[57] Cyril Burt, in what has become a classic study, estimated that approximately 70 percent of the delinquents he surveyed suffered from physical defects, although very few of these defects were of a sufficiently serious nature to indicate that these delinquents were not normal.[58] In fact, despite the frequent reference to this study by delinquency specialists, Burt's general conclusion was that delinquents did not differ materially from nondelinquents in general health conditions.

Illustrating the obverse side of the coin, Healy and Bronner actually found more delinquents in good physical condition than average school children drawn from the population at large.[59] The Gluecks, in their early study of one thousand delinquents, found that of 967 boys examined by the Judge Baker Foundation Clinic, 56.7 percent were in sound physical condition, 30.2 percent were in fair health, and 13.1

[55] Thurston, *Concerning Juvenile Delinquency*, p. 26.
[56] Reckless and Smith, *Juvenile Delinquency*.
[57] Slawson, *The Delinquent Boy*, Chap. 5.
[58] Burt, *The Young Delinquent*, pp. 238-40.
[59] Healy and Bronner, *Treatment and What Happened Afterward*.

percent were classified as being in poor health.[60] As an indication of the fluctuating results in such investigations, the Gluecks, in their most recent study, now state: "Summarizing the findings of the medical examinations of the delinquents and non-delinquents, we see that the view that delinquents are in poorer health than non-delinquents receives no support. Very little, if any, difference exists between the physical conditions of the two groups as a whole." [61] Very few modern students of delinquency would take exception to this conclusion. In a critical appraisal of many studies on the health and physical characteristics of delinquents, Mihanovich has stated: "It may be safely concluded, in spite of the differences of opinion, that physical shortcomings are primarily accessory and aggravating influences in delinquency." [62]

In the matter of *early health* of delinquents, however, certain differences indicative of potential problems of maladjustment have been noted that are significant for further investigation. A connection between specific disorders and emotional disturbances has been revealed in some of the studies. Whereas, in the 500 matched delinquents and nondelinquents studied by the Gluecks, inquiry of the mothers and examination of the medical records revealed no striking differences in the over-all health conditions of delinquents and nondelinquents as infants and young children, differences *were* noted in the considerably higher percentage of the delinquent group giving evidence of emotionally linked disorders, such as enuresis (bed-wetting).[63] Hirsch, among others, has examined this factor and has shown that 32 percent of the delinquents he studied suffered from enuresis as compared with 26.1 percent in the nondelinquent population.[64] In the Hirsch findings, the difference in itself is not necessarily significant statistically; further, the percentage difference gives little indication of uncontrolled factors that would shed light upon related psychological, constitutional, and social forces which may have contributed to this difference. We must reiterate: The mere assertion of a difference is no indication of a causal significance. Such differences must be repeatedly shown for different groups under varying conditions, and the developmental process of

[60] Glueck, *One Thousand Juvenile Delinquents*, p. 101.
[61] Glueck, *Unraveling Juvenile Delinquency*, p. 181.
[62] Mihanovich, "Who Is the Juvenile Delinquent?"
[63] Glueck, *Unraveling Juvenile Delinquency*, p. 181.
[64] Hirsch, *Dynamic Causes of Juvenile Crime*, p. 103.

such a disorder must be plainly demonstrated before we can come to any conclusions concerning causal factors.

Michaels has attempted to do this in a series of provocative studies, although he has given very little evidence of the causative function which enuresis or its related psychological or organic factors may play in predisposing certain children towards delinquency and deviant behavior.[65] What Michaels' studies do indicate, however, and with painstaking clarity, is that physical differences of health do not tell us much about how delinquency is caused unless we isolate specific factors at given times in the lives of the individuals concerned, making certain that the causative conditions may not be attributed to any factors other than the physiological precipitant. Thus, in his careful analysis of an isolated condition such as enuresis—and this is the only way in which health factors can be adequately studied, instead of lumping them all together under the dubious category of "general health conditions"— he stresses the importance of the onset of such a condition, its *persistence* at different age levels, and its association with other psychobiological and social factors, although his studies are limited in giving adequate weight to the latter. Particularly significant in his investigations have been the disclosures that persistent enuresis is a condition closely related to *certain types* of delinquency, particularly the offenses of psychopathic and emotionally disturbed offenders. This is indicated by the character of the offenses committed by the latter—arson, for example.[66] Although he suggests that with a small percentage of offenders, this difficulty may have a constitutional origin, the statistical evidence offered hardly substantiates such a claim. The early appearance and persistence of enuresis, associated with dubious *post facto* diagnoses of mental states, afford a very insubstantial basis for the claim that enuresis is a chronic malady induced by an organic disorder. It may be, but such studies hardly afford adequate proof. Moreover, even if such chronic maladies have a long-standing history in the organic development of the individual, there is no certain proof

---

[65] Michaels and Steinberg, "Persistent Enuresis and Juvenile Delinquency"; Michaels and Goodman, "Incidence and Intercorrelations of Enuresis and Other Neuropathic Traits in So-Called Normal Children"; Michaels, "The Incidence of Enuresis and Age of Cessation in One Hundred Delinquents and One Hundred Sibling Controls"; Michaels, "Psychobiologic Interpretation of Delinquency"; Michaels, "Parallels Between Persistent Enuresis and Delinquency in the Psychopathic Personality."

[66] Michaels and Steinberg, "Persistent Enuresis and Juvenile Delinquency."

of their origin. Also, as Michaels himself indicates, they apply to a limited number of delinquents only: of 200 delinquents studied, 19 percent suffered from enuresis.[67] Not all of these gave evidence of persistent enuresis, however; more important, *the delinquents with a history of enuresis did not differ significantly in the severity of their delinquency from the delinquents with no enuresis.*

(2) *Size and Weight of Delinquents.* The evidence with respect to differences in size and weight is equally ambiguous and confusing. No clear-cut picture emerges of distinctive differences in size and weight for the various age levels of different types of delinquents, with the possible exception of differences previously noted for female sex offenders. The latter does not come as much of a surprise, particularly when we recognize the relatively high percentage of intellectually marginal and submarginal girls who appear before the courts on charges of sexual intransigence or closely linked charges. Although early sexual maturity is frequently combined with relatively high intellectual potential, the reverse is also found in a sizable proportion of cases. Terman, for example, in a study of gifted girls, discovered that almost one-half (48 percent) attained puberty before the age of thirteen, as contrasted with groups of normal girls, of whom only about 25 percent attained puberty before that age. The girl from an underprivileged environment, with low intelligence and early leanings towards sexual precocity, may, under certain circumstances, very readily become a sexual offender.[68]

Aside from inherent tendencies, of which gross size and weight may be manifestations, physical factors would have to be regarded from the standpoint of their psychological effects upon certain types of children. There is such a variety of significant factors, or dependent variables, involved that studies of the effects of size and weight upon psychological development would have to include (among other items) factors of racial or cultural difference, the intrinsic family circumstances surrounding individual delinquents, and the patterns of delinquency that exist in different areas. Small size, as Clifford Shaw has shown in some of his life-history studies of delinquents, can prove highly beneficial under limited conditions, whereas in a culture fostering masculine values and competitive sports, the boyful wish for physical prowess and

[67] Michaels and Steinberg, "Persistent Enuresis and Juvenile Delinquency."
[68] See, for example, Frazier, *The Negro Family in the United States*, Chaps. 13, 14, and 17, especially pp. 349-57; Frazier, *The Negro Family in Chicago.*

for the capacity to dominate others might place a premium on increased stature and the mesomorphic (muscular) characteristics of which the Gluecks speak.[69]

Slawson, for example, notes that delinquent boys may be either somewhat taller and stronger than normal children, or else conspicuously smaller.[70] Healy and Bronner, in their statistical analysis of 4,000 delinquent boys, suggest the same type of findings. It is to be doubted that the standard studies of weight and size of delinquents have any genuine scientific validity. But they can simply be taken to mean that, for countless unspecified psychological, cultural, and social reasons, delinquents in certain selected samples show slight distortions of normal distributions for weight and height. It is difficult to see the value of a finding which states that the taller stature of certain boys tends to elicit leadership qualities and hence may induce towards the leadership of a boys' gang. The obvious question is: How about the rest of the gang, and the greater part, who happen to be normal or smaller in stature? Children who dominate others in delinquent acts, and children who are pliant and readily follow others in delinquent activities, whether through fear, desire for prestige, the need to belong, or a variety of other reasons, are *all* delinquent. In fact, the crucial factor in determining the delinquent pattern of causation may be either the motivation towards leadership or the desire to be dominated; in both cases, the factors of size, stature, and weight may be associated closely or remotely with the entire complex of motivation.

The problem of size, weight, and stature in its relationship to the problems of human motivation may be clarified by the recent work of Dr. Norman C. Wetzel, the Cleveland pediatrician who has demonstrated that the normal growth patterns of children fall into what he believes to be seven hereditary types. However, even if the evidence is conclusive concerning such hereditary types, whether an individual becomes delinquent will depend in part upon the impact of his appearance in the interpersonal relations to which he is exposed, and secondly, upon his neuromuscular responses to the demands and expectancies of different groups. There is, as yet, no evidence in cross-cultural samples to show that any of these types, particularly with regard to weight and stature, fall into specific delinquent classifications. Further, as Wetzel

[69] Shaw, *The Natural History of a Delinquent Career.*
[70] Slawson, *The Delinquent Boy*, Chap. 5.

has shown, *even the hereditary types may be distorted in their expected growth patterns by glandular and emotional disturbances.* Consequently, it is difficult to see at present how size categories play a uniform role in delinquency, particularly in view of the considerable percentages of emotionally disturbed delinquents whose basic pathologies presumably contribute to modifying normal stages of growth. It seems fairly certain, in conclusion, that such factors as size and weight are always relative to (1) the personality constitution of the individual, (2) his orientation to others, and (3) the patterned behavior responses of different groups (including delinquent groups) to him.

(3) *Appearance and Gross Bodily Defects.* There can be little doubt that the physical appearance of the individual, especially some stigma or deficiency (such as deafness or poor vision), may play an important part in the development of adjusted or maladjusted behavior. How an individual learns to respond characteristically to certain types of situations will largely depend upon the character of his deficiency and the way he was reared. An unwholesome or repulsive appearance might, in certain circumstances, produce one type of effect, while the consequence of an auditory or visual difficulty might be quite different under the same conditions.

What constitutes a favorable appearance, standard good looks, beauty, or simply a pleasing or passable appearance is, to a considerable degree, determined by the culture. Frances MacGregor, in a sociocultural analysis of facial features and their effects upon different family groups, employing case samples, has indicated the kinds of compensatory psychological mechanisms induced by parents, siblings, and the individual himself, as a result of facial disfigurement. She also suggests the possible channels to psychotic, neurotic, and antisocial behavior such a socially centered situation may produce.[71] In a society such as ours, especially, in which a high premium is placed upon physical appearance, a fact attested to merely by the volume of the beautician's business and the heavy stress our commercial advertising places on the need for "glamor" for both sexes, the individual who suffers from a serious defect in appearance is virtually compelled to seek compensatory devices for a lack he sorely feels and of which the entire cultural atmosphere tends to remind him continuously, both directly and indirectly.

[71] MacGregor, "Some Psycho-Social Problems Associated with Facial Deformities."

Alfred Adler, in his concept of organic inferiority, has demonstrated the effects of these compensatory mechanisms in neurotic and antisocial behavior and has provided us with a cliché in the concept of the "inferiority complex," which he believed arose from organic inferiority.[72] Small stature in a society that prizes tall, husky "he-men" carries its own psychological handicaps. It is probably not entirely fortuitous that some of the world's greatest military leaders, from Hannibal to Napoleon and Pershing, were men of short stature. Some psychiatrists have felt that the defective appearance of certain individuals may be the principal factor in providing the disorientation leading to deviant behavior patterns. Banay cites physical disfigurement as the prominent contributory factor of a series of behavior disorders, of which crime is one.[73] Karl Menninger has even suggested that the most substantial form of therapy for certain disordered lives might come from the plastic surgeon, to whom the psychiatrist and the clinical psychologist would simply offer supplementary help—a suggestion which apparently has had some effect upon certain state penal agencies. By 1947, facial surgery had been performed upon 376 inmates released from Illinois' Statesville Penitentiary; according to a follow-up study of these cases, less than 1 percent had been guilty of parole violations as compared with a normal state parole violation rate of 17 percent. Generalizations from this type of experience must be made with considerable caution, however. The personality pattern of the individual, the character of his defect, and the implicit and explicit psychotherapy involved in singling him out for concentrated attention will all play significant contributory roles in his rehabilitation. Dr. Royal Grossman, commenting upon a case of this kind, has added a realistic note: "If he lives by society's conventions and laws for ten years, I'll know we have accomplished something." [74]

For the child, particularly the adolescent child, painfully aware of his ungainliness and the repulsiveness of his appearance to others, the character of the personality orientation and the painful trauma it involves are certainly not difficult to envisage. The criminologist Hans von Hentig, in an ingenious approach to the study of antisocial behavior, indicates quite clearly how an environment that strongly repels

---

[72] Adler, "A Study of Organ Inferiority and Its Physical Compensation"; Adler, *The Practise and Theory of Individual Psychology.*
[73] Banay, "Physical Disfigurement as a Factor in Delinquency and Crime."
[74] *Time*, April 11, 1949, p. 69.

the individual because of his physical defects and peculiarities may be vitally instrumental in bringing about incipient *and* developing forms of delinquency and crime.[75] The child may be safely cushioned by the precautionary efforts of his parents but may find the repellent tensions of his teen-age and school situation far too much to endure. Even under the best of circumstances, the insidious entry of subtle interpersonal factors may make it extremely difficult for the child to make a normal adjustment, and he may be forced, as Grossman has stated, to react in the only way he knows, by "hauling off and punching the wall when you are frustrated." Westlund and Palumbo have shown, for example, how both overt and covert rejection may operate in homes with crippled children, where the parents' sense of guilt is projected upon the child, intensifying his feeling of anxiety and providing a series of tensions that culminate in a variety of disorders.[76]

In confronting such gross physical defects and limitations in appearance, we must recognize that, in direct ratio to the character of the stress placed by the family and society upon certain physical standards, serious psychological liabilities are often imposed upon the child, provoking a wide variety of personality tensions and disorders. Whether his behavioral outlets become delinquent will depend upon the character of the resultant motivation, opportunities in the environment, and the need for identification with suitable models in his immediate surroundings.[77]

The "Constitutional" Psychopath

In the entire range of delinquent types, none presents as great difficulty in classification and treatment as the so-called psychopath. This peculiar type of personality, marked by emotional immaturity and incapacity to identify with others, is frequently regarded as a constitutional type whose characteristics have been acquired through either

[75] von Hentig, *The Criminal and His Victim*, Chap. 3.

[76] Westlund and Palumbo, "Parental Rejection of Crippled Children;" Wallace, "Physical Defects and Juvenile Delinquency."

[77] See Merton, *Social Theory and Social Structure*, Chap. 4, "Social Structure and Anomie." In the anthropological field, we find innumerable examples of how the cultural stress of a given physical accomplishment tends to produce *characteristic* neurotic tendencies among those who cannot meet the standards of such an emphasis, particularly when the alternatives are limited. See the illustrations presented by LaBarre, "The Cultural Basis of Emotions and Gestures."

heredity or congenital accident. Unlike the neurotic delinquent, whose disorder is based upon intense anxiety feelings, or the psychotic, who retreats into a world of his own private attitudes, the psychopath is marked by arrested characterological and emotional development and by what the social scientist calls "defective socialization."

The psychopathic classification, however, has suffered from the variations in symptomatological standards—frequently reflecting the diagnostician's own moral views—according to which individuals are placed in this category and from the fact that persons who are not amenable to ordinary forms of therapy are often included in it. No concept in the lexicon of modern psychiatry and psychotherapy is so fraught with confusion and contradiction. The diagnosis of psychopath is frequently nothing more than a reflection of the therapist's own inability to determine the causal process and exact classification of this type of deviant. Sutherland, for example, has shown that whereas more than 75 percent of the inmates of Illinois state prisons were classified as psychopathic, only about 10 percent were so diagnosed in New York and Massachusetts state institutions.[78] As an indication of how a shift in the cultural tide can alter our expectancies of behavior, Lemkau demonstrated that, in a survey of a district of Baltimore in 1933, 1.3 percent of the population were classified as psychopathic, while three years later, when employment figures had shifted upward, the figure had dropped to 0.52 percent.[79] Diagnoses of psychopaths in our state mental hospitals place the figure at about 2.6 percent, although it is extremely dubious whether such a percentage may be regarded with any degree of confidence.[80]

While sociologists have been primarily concerned with showing the relationship between psychopathic behavior and crime, without necessarily tracing the roots of the deviation in itself, psychiatrists have attempted to delineate with some precision in individual cases the causal processes that culminate in delinquent and criminal behavior patterns.[81] Although the psychopath's pattern of symptoms overlaps into adjacent pathological areas, certain distinctive traits in the symp-

---

[78] Sutherland, *Principles of Criminology*, p. 110.
[79] Lemkau, *Mental Hygiene and Public Health*, p. 335.
[80] *Patients in Mental Institutions*, 1946, p. 21.
[81] Alexander and Staub, *The Criminal, the Judge and the Public*, pp. 145-52; Fenichel, *The Psychoanalytic Theory of Neurosis*, pp. 117-39, 324-86, 466-92; Bromberg, *Crime and the Mind*, pp. 54-55. For sociological illustrations, see also Sutherland, *Principles of Criminology*, pp. 103-17; Burgess, "The Individual Delinquent as a Person."

tomatic picture appear to mark off such an individual quite clearly from others. Moreover, recent work by social psychologists and sociologists has indicated with some clarity the character of the interpersonal relationships which, if not causal to this condition, nevertheless strongly contribute to it.[82]

The psychopath appears to the untrained observer as an individual completely devoid of conscience and unable to identify himself with the feelings and attitudes of others. Lacking normal restraints, he is essentially impetuous and impulsive, seeking immediate gratification for his desires. Unlike the normal individual, or the neurotic who suffers excessively from guilt feelings, the psychopath gives little or no evidence of self-condemnation for offenses to others. Although he may display slight guilt in limited situations, he appears oblivious and insensitive to the feelings of others for the greater part. Since his relationships are contingent upon the capacity or willingness of others to be exploited, his human contacts in general are temporary, sporadic, and lacking in sustained interest.[83] Relationships which *are* sustained for any period of time result largely from his need to ensure himself a source of gratification for his impulses, as, for example, in the case of sex gratification.[84] Striking in this peculiar personality orientation is an occasional sense of shame (but no guilt, largely because of his incapacity to internalize the standards of others) and feelings of acute hostility, similar to those of the paranoid, directed against those who frustrate him. Irrespective of the causes, be they primarily constitutional or acquired, the sociologist regards such reactions in part as the outcome of *defective socialization,* or the inability to enact the roles of others and to internalize their attitudes.[85] This is clearly the case with the psychopath, who, though he does comprehend social reality and can distinguish between right and wrong, does so only on a cognitive or intellectual plane.[86] He is not necessarily feeble-minded; his intelligence may be normal or even superior. His judgments, however, are defective and warped, largely because he is so regressed in impulsivity and cannot entertain sustained human relationships.

[82] Gough, "Sociological Theory of Psychopathy."

[83] Karpman, "The Principles and Aims of Criminal Psychopathology."

[84] Karpman, "The Case of Walter Manson."

[85] This basic concept in the development of self has been classically stated by the eminent social theorist G. H. Mead, in *Mind, Self and Society,* edited by Charles W. Morris, pp. 135-226.

[86] Karpman, "The Case of Walter Manson."

This classical picture of the psychopath is frequently diagnostically confused with those of various other deviants, such as the neurotic who acts out his disorders in some form of delinquent activity, the self-centered and indulged personality, and the subcultural deviant.[87] But though the symptoms may in certain respects appear to be similar, the causal process is different in each instance. The current controversy over a putative physical basis for psychopathic behavior and the possibility of modifying the behavior of psychopaths very probably stems mainly from confused diagnoses.

Principally on the basis of whether the etiology of psychopathy is organic or acquired, psychiatrists and others differ as to the possibility of a successful therapy. Charnyak, Henderson, and Nielsen and Thompson, for example, regard psychopathy as a result of brain injury and find inacceptable the possibility of modifying such personality structures.[88] Karpman appears to follow a similar view, although he sees these character defects as having been fixed at so early an age that the personality structure becomes totally inflexible. Lindner and others, however, regard the possibility of altering psychopathic behavior patterns as perfectly feasible.[89]

What can we say about the causal process of this most difficult type of delinquent behavior? Although much has been written about the constitutional basis of psychopathic deviation, *careful examination of the evidence indicates that the attribution of such behavior to organic factors is almost wholly a negative inference.* The fact that significant relational factors during the early years of the child's life—*particularly the first three years*—could not be traced is no indication that such factors may not have been present and highly significant. Since, as Nielsen and Thompson have shown, the frontal lobes of the brain, specifically the anterior thalamus nucleus, exercise a controlling function in self-conception and self-restraint, it is possible that we may be dealing with *two* types of psychopathic behavior, one an organic type (which studies of recent prefrontal lobotomies may help us clarify) and the other an acquired type. Certainly the evidence is highly significant for

[87] Weinberg, *Society and Personality Disorders*, pp. 263-64.

[88] Charnyak, "Some Remarks on the Diagnosis of the Psychopathic Delinquent"; Henderson, *Psychopathic States*; Nielsen and Thompson, *The Engrammes of Psychiatry*, pp. 206-7.

[89] Lindner, *Rebel Without a Cause*.

both types. Eliasberg, Charnyak, Henderson, and Nielsen and Thompson have attempted to show that such conditions are largely due to brain damage, and that the damage is very closely linked to hereditary disorders.[90] On the other hand, studies by Schachtel and Levi, and others, indicate the greater likelihood that children deprived of intimate parental relations during early formative years—institutionally reared and nursery children, for example—may develop characteristics precluding normal empathy (sympathetic identification with others).[91] Such children definitely appear to give evidence of psychopathic traits, as Goldfarb likewise points out in his study of emotionally deprived children who were shifted into other families.[92] It should be noted that these children do not display the same characteristics as rejected children, who show intense emotional strivings, the entire causal development being quite different.

In further evidence of the possibility of the acquisition of psychopathic personality characteristics, particularly by the age of six, Anna Freud and Dorothy Burlingham have dramatically shown in their studies how the institutional child may suffer serious disadvantage in internalizing the attitudes of others who have been in intimate contact with him and thus may find himself unable to integrate the "moral values" of society.[93] Spitz, likewise, discovered marked developmental differences in the first few years of life between deprived institutional children and the illegitimate children of delinquent minors in a nursery where the mothers could devote considerable time to their children.[94] The latter remained normal, while the former gave definite evidence of significant developmental retardation.

Such evidence seems to confirm Weinberg's conclusion that "the psychopath develops within a matrix of distant and impersonal parent-child relationships, and especially amidst changing and emotionally depriving parent figures." [95] It seems surprising, therefore, to observe the easy assurance with which Bovet, in his recent report, appears to conclude, *purely on the basis of negative evidence*, that the psychopath

[90] Eliasberg, "Psychopathy or Neurosis."

[91] Schachtel and Levi, "Character Structure of Day Nursery Children as Seen through the Rorschach."

[92] Goldfarb, "Psychological Privation in Infancy and Subsequent Adjustment."

[93] Freud and Burlingham, *Infants without Families*, pp. 124-25.

[94] Spitz, "The Role of Ecological Factors in Emotional Development in Infancy."

[95] Weinberg, *Society and Personality Disorders*, p. 279.

is a true constitutional type.[96] The evidence for such a conclusion is highly dubious, to say the very least.

For Further Reading

TULCHIN, SIMON H., *Intelligence and Crime* (Chicago, 1939).

A workmanlike summary of some of the leading research that has been conducted in the study of intelligence and criminal behavior, suggesting the care with which such data must be interpreted.

SCHLAPP, MAX A., AND EDWARD H. SMITH, *The New Criminology* (New York, 1928).

A strong statement of the influence of the endocrine glands upon criminal behavior, much quoted and generally discredited.

HALLIDAY, JAMES L., *Psychosocial Medicine* (New York, 1948).

A significant book whose influence is still to be felt, by an eminent British physician and public health authority, indicating the close relationship between various forms of illness and social conditions.

HOOTON, E. A., *The American Criminal* (Cambridge, 1939).

An extreme neo-Lombrosian position in which inconclusive proof is offered to indicate that American "criminals" have certain physical characteristics.

SHELDON, W. H., EMIL M. HARTL, AND EUGENE MCDERMOTT, *Varieties of Delinquent Behavior* (New York, 1949).

A widely cited anthropometric study, strongly criticized by contemporary sociologists, in which the claim is advanced that delinquents may be classified into constitutional types.

MICHAELS, JOSEPH J., "Psychobiologic Interpretations of Delinquency," in *The American Journal of Orthopsychiatry*, 10 (July 1940), pp. 501-9.

An attempt to indicate the kind of connections which must be sought in establishing linkages between delinquent behavior and biological conditions.

[96] Bovet, *Psychiatric Aspects of Juvenile Delinquency*, pp. 21-26.

SUTHERLAND, E. H., *Principles of Criminology* (Philadelphia, 1947), Chap. 6.

A summary and critique by the former dean of American criminologists of much of our present information concerning biological factors and criminal behavior.

BANAY, RALPH S., "Physical Disfigurement as a Factor in Delinquency and Crime," in *Federal Probation* (January-March, 1943), pp. 20-24.

A description by the psychiatrist Ralph S. Banay of the effects bodily and facial deformities and asymmetry may exercise in producing delinquent behavior.

LINDNER, ROBERT M., *Rebel Without a Cause* (New York, 1944).

An analysis of the case record of a psychopathic offender, with an interpretation of the meaning of psychopathic behavior and a recorded account of rehabilitation through hypnotherapy.

Chapter 7

EMOTIONAL PRESSURES

In discussing causal patterns of delinquency, we must recognize that the emergence of certain psychological factors at critical junctures in the individual's career may play a very important part in the character of the adjustments he makes to his social environment. The presence of such psychological factors, extreme anxiety, the need to express aggressive impulses, feelings of resentment, and the like, may *readily*, under certain circumstances, lead to delinquent acts or, through a process of intensification and aggravation, may *eventually* result in such forms of behavior. *The emergence of a psychological condition, however, whether in the form of an attitude, a new set of values, or a novel emotional orientation, must be seen in relation to the entire developing pattern of the personality.* It is for this reason that we have stressed at the outset the need for an integrated understanding of the development and functioning of personality. Isolated personality traits may not be sufficient in themselves to predispose to delinquency. Only when incorporated within the total developing structure of the personality may they redirect the character of the individual's outlook and help to precipitate deviant forms of behavior.

It is at this point in the analysis of delinquent etiology that conflicts frequently arise between sociologists and psychiatrists as to the degree of importance to be attached to psychological factors as against environmental pressures. Actually, there is no essential basis for genuine dis-agreement if we keep in mind the *relative* significance of personality pressures on the one hand, and of environmental stimulus and provoca-tion on the other, and the intimate relationships between the two. Differences of opinion are largely caused by the failure to apprehend differences in *degrees* of emphasis. The psychiatrist is primarily con-cerned with the individual's personal development, the formation of his character traits and their interrelationships. The sociologist devotes him-self to those conditions of the environment which are most apt to evoke antisocial tendencies and behavior. Both recognize the importance of the continuing interrelationship of a specific kind of environment and a specific kind of individual. At best, this is a matter of stress.

We may, nevertheless, discern certain traits of character that are more apt than others, under certain environmental conditions, to result in delinquency. By the same token, we recognize, as Carr has shown, that certain external conditions, particularly when broken down into their functioning components—the home, the neighborhood, the school, the peer-age groups, etc.—are more apt to induce adverse psy-chological traits, as well as opportunities for their expression, than other environmental contexts.[1] The latter may be regarded as "risk environ-ments" for delinquency, just as specific psychological characteristics may present greater hazards in certain individuals. The conclusions of some studies stressing psychiatric factors at the expense of sociological condi-tions—and vice versa—are frequently the accidental results of the selec-tive samples studied—whether or not adequate psychiatric services are attached to a given court, the geographical and cultural areas surveyed, and the kind of factors certain investigators are searching for. For exam-ple, largely because of research trends and what can be best described as "intellectual cults," we frequently find a far greater emphasis upon psy-chiatric factors among European students than we do among American ones. We should add this admonition: It is becoming increasingly im-portant for the understanding and control of delinquency, that psy-chologists, psychiatrists, and sociologists work together as a team. This should be done not only for the obvious purpose of pooling separate findings, but also for the development of new concepts and new re-

[1] Carr, *Delinquency Control*, pp. 153-77. Carr refers to these as "community pressures."

search techniques and insights, so as to fit together formerly isolated areas in a congruent and deeper comprehension of human behavior.

To condense the broad areas that encompass the psychological characteristics playing a causal role in delinquency, we shall concentrate briefly upon what the major forms of research have disclosed in the following areas: (1) emotional conflict and instability; (2) anxiety patterns; (3) unsocialized aggression; (4) the "acting-out" neurotic; (5) the self-centered individual; and (6) the cultural deviant.[2]

Emotional Conflict and Instability

Although widespread disagreement exists about the functioning of organic and environmental factors in the lives of delinquents, there is considerable unanimity on the part of most investigators about the presence of emotionally disturbed states among delinquent offenders, particularly the persistent delinquent. The precise diagnosis of these emotional states, however, is another matter and raises several vital questions. An emotional state is a pervasive accompanying condition, whose outward appearance may take the form of considerable impetuousness, volatility, defiance of authority, and the like. It may also manifest itself in overwhelming displays of mood, with violent fluctuations between marked ebullience of spirit and deepest gloom. However, as we have seen earlier, the causes of symptomatic states that appear similar need not necessarily be the same, and conversely, many emotional states that appear different in their manifestations originate from quite similar sources.

Although the evidence hardly seems to support the assumption of many investigators, such as Aichhorn, Redl and Wineman, and others, that *all* delinquent states are accompanied by various degrees of emotional malfunctioning, there can be little doubt of extensive emotional disturbance in large numbers of our persistent delinquent offenders. In simplest terms, an emotional conflict originates when the individual's tendency to engage in some type of habitual or goal-directed behavior is thwarted by elements within the personality structure which impede such behavior. The internalizing of the conflict may be due to the in-

[2] Bloch, *Disorganization*, pp. 207-10; Weinberg, *Society and Personality Disorders*, pp. 281-92.

dividual's inability to gratify certain desires because of the incorporation of self-restraints, in the form of conscience, an internal censor, or a superego (to use Freudian terminology); or because he has been exposed, as Thorsten Sellin points out, to dual and conflicting standards in the environment (as in the case of children of immigrant parents) which appear to immobilize the individual for normal decisions and action.[3] August Aichhorn's study of "dissocial" and delinquent youth, which has exercised considerable influence upon trends of thinking both here and abroad, makes the premise that the censorious aspects of the individual's personality—his "superego"—have either (1) become identified with delinquent and antisocial elements, so that no genuine conflict or remorse may exist, or (2) incorporate only *phases* of antisocial conduct, with the result that the child is confused, guilt-laden, and remorseful.[4]

No one is ever exposed only to an environment entirely devoid of conventional elements. As a result, a variety of conflicting standards exert their influences upon the individual. The views of Mowrer and Lindesmith and Strauss, and even the relatively extreme position of Redl and Wineman, seem to suggest that the internalizing of behavior standards reflects a variety of different controls imposed upon the child, with the consequence that disturbed emotional states are subtle and highly individualized, although, as Lindesmith and Strauss suggest, they do appear to fall into discernible patterns.[5] Kobrin has recently illustrated this last point very well and has launched a significant empirical attack upon Aichhorn's former position, which postulated the capacity of certain children to incorporate personality elements almost wholly of an antisocial nature.[6] (Aichhorn accepted the Freudian view that all individuals acquire deeply implanted social inhibitions in relation to the groups they are most intimately identified with. Thus, a thoroughly delinquent child develops a delinquent "superego" (or conscience) reflecting the standards in his antisocial peer associates.)[7]

Kobrin suggests that this is an "ideal" type of delinquent never actually encountered. For example, in his investigation of the conflict of

[3] Sellin, *Culture Conflicts and Crime*.
[4] Aichhorn, *Wayward Youth*.
[5] Mowrer, *Personality Adjustment and Domestic Discord*; Lindesmith and Strauss, *Social Psychology*, pp. 329-52; Redl and Wineman, *Children Who Hate*.
[6] Kobrin, "The Conflict of Values in Delinquency Areas."
[7] Aichhorn, *Wayward Youth*, pp. 222-25.

value systems within so-called "delinquency areas," he shows with ample statistical evidence that virtually all children are exposed to both conventional and nonconventional standards, with the result that most of them incorporate an active and sympathetic understanding, if not positive motivation, toward antisocial behavior. The result, however, is that many children, even if they are disturbed emotionally, do not engage in delinquent activities, and that others, who are conventional in their early youth, eventually engage in criminal activities. More significant, perhaps, is his explanation of the defiance of many delinquent children, in which he indicates in contradistinction to the accepted Aichhorn view, that such children have internalized certain normal standards which they feel compelled to reject by strong emotional protests and defiance and hostility toward adult authority. Redl and Wineman give ample evidence of this tendency in their description of deeply disturbed "children who hate" and appear to imply the same contradictory motivational source presented by Kobrin. It has been shown by the anthropologist Kennedy that a thorough identification with antisocial standards apparently does not succeed in producing the emotional disquiet accompanying the exposure of normal children to the innumerable *conflicting* standards of conventional and unconventional behavior which even the most demoralized environment presents.[8]

Although researchers differ as to the precise source of emotional problems of this kind, the broad contradictory social patterns upon which these emotional states are based and their extensive presence among delinquents are largely agreed upon. What we require is a more precise demarcation of the differing patterns of emotional conflicts and traits to enable us to classify delinquents more thoroughly.[9] The recent Boston area study by the Gluecks, for example, based upon extended use of the Rorschach Test, revealed that the delinquents exceeded the nondelinquents significantly in such traits as assertiveness, defiance, resentfulness, and ambivalent attitudes toward authority—findings which seem to confirm Kobrin's hypothesis. The results also show greater evidence of traits of sadism and impulsiveness in delinquents. Nevertheless, it is significant to note that in the diagnosis of both groups for neurotic trends, the delinquents fared better than their nondelinquent controls, the results showing neuroticism among 24.6 percent of the

[8] Kennedy, *Criminal Tribes of the Bombay Presidency.*
[9] Hewitt and Jenkins, *Fundamental Patterns of Maladjustment.*

delinquents as compared with 35.8 percent in the nondelinquents. The seeming discrepancy in this last result has led Marshall Clinard to question strongly the Glueck findings and to suggest that the "nondelinquents" were, in a sense unrecognized by the Gluecks, *more* delinquent than the delinquent sample.[10]

Actually, this is not necessarily true, as Healy and Bronner's work seems to have indicated; such results may simply point to the extensiveness of disturbed emotional states among the majority of children in "delinquency areas," whether they become actually delinquent or not. The fact that some do not become delinquent may result from the character of the disturbance and, as is very likely, from a series of accidental factors in the environment. In comparing delinquents with their nondelinquent siblings, Healy and Bronner found that failure to engage in delinquent activities was due to (1) different emotional patterns because of accidents of birth and rearing; (2) the ability to find normal emotional outlets during periods of crisis; (3) bodily defects incapacitating the child for delinquent activities; and (4) lack of opportunity.[11] Of the 143 delinquents studied, however, 91.6 percent (131 cases) gave substantial evidence of emotional malfunctioning. Fifty-three cases gave evidence of feelings of rejection, insecurity, and being unloved; forty-five gave evidence of being thwarted in self-expression; sixty-two showed symptoms of inadequacy and feelings of inferiority; forty-three displayed broad patterns of emotional disturbance linked to family disharmony; and forty-three were marked by manifestations of sibling jealousy and rivalry. That these states are closely allied to forms of common wish-striving in delinquent children can be demonstrated in the relationship between such emotionally frustrated behavior and the basic wishes which, according to the sociologist W. I. Thomas, are those of all individuals—wishes for security, response, recognition, and new experience.

Support for the findings shown above comes from various quarters. Burt, pointing to 85 percent of his subjects who were emotionally impaired, concludes that emotional disturbance is the most general trait among delinquents.[12] Similar conclusions have been drawn by the Gluecks, John Slawson, L. J. Carr, and others.[13]

[10] See Clinard's excellent review of the Gluecks' recent work in *Federal Probation*, 17 (March, 1953), pp. 50-51.

[11] Healy and Bronner, *New Light upon Delinquency and Its Treatment*, p. 49.

[12] Burt, *The Young Delinquent*, pp. 491-92, 541.

[13] Glueck, *One Thousand Juvenile Delinquents*, pp. 102-6; Slawson, *The Delinquent Boy*, pp. 223 ff.; Carr, *Delinquency Control*, pp. 140-48.

The character of the child's early predispositions and his unique exposure to a particular environment has been more clearly illustrated in recent research by the differing forms such emotional states take. Although a given emotional state may not necessarily lead to a specific form of delinquency, or, in fact, to delinquency at all, there is nevertheless a close correlation between certain emotional states and types of delinquent acts. Hewitt and Jenkins examined 500 delinquents to discover whether they could find typical behavioral syndromes (patterns of symptoms) among these social deviants. This research disclosed three

CHART XI

*Emotional States Occurring in Conjunction with Delinquent Behavior**

Emotional States Occurring in
Conjunction with Delinquent
Behavior (Healy and Bronner)

The Wish-Patterns
(W. I. Thomas)

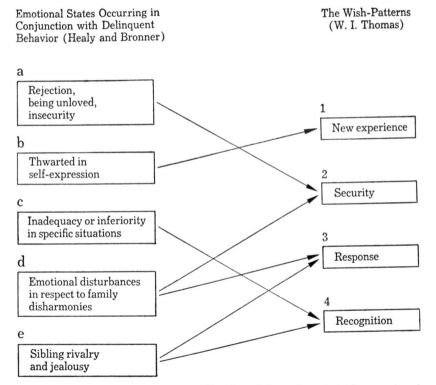

a
Rejection,
being unloved,
insecurity

b
Thwarted in
self-expression

c
Inadequacy or inferiority
in specific situations

d
Emotional disturbances
in respect to family
disharmonies

e
Sibling rivalry
and jealousy

1
New experience

2
Security

3
Response

4
Recognition

* From Bloch, *Disorganization*, p. 209, adapted from the principal categories of emotional disturbance found among the 143 delinquents studied by Healy and Bronner in *New Light on Delinquency and Its Treatment*, pp. 49, 128.

principal categories of maladjusted and delinquent children, characterized by: "(1) assaultive tendencies, temper displays, bullying, vengefulness, defiance of authority, etc.; (2) gang activities, coöperative stealing,
aggressive stealing, staying out late nights, truancy from school, etc.; (3)
sensitiveness, seclusiveness, shyness, awkwardness, jealousy, etc." [14] Although some criticism has been leveled against their methodology, the
results are highly suggestive. There can be little doubt that similarities
in emotional patterning emanate from certain environmental and personality constellations, and that such common disturbances may
strongly predispose towards characteristic delinquent acts. It is strongly
suggested that the examination of such relationships is the direction
much of our contemporary research should take.

Anxiety Patterns

Recognizing as we do that disturbed emotional states are at the bottom of considerable delinquency, the primary problem becomes one of
classifying these states with some precision, separating them, and then
attempting to determine what the personal and social factors are that
predispose to the creation of a given state. To pursue this problem adequately would take us far beyond the scope of this book. However, we
can at least begin to indicate the principal configurations that play a
part in producing definite and well-recognized emotional states whose
manifestations frequently lead to various types of delinquent acts. One
of the leading categories of emotional disturbance is the clearly marked
anxiety pattern. Since anxiety patterns are produced by specific types of
family and interpersonal factors, arising with particular frequency in
specific groups and classes, we can begin to pinpoint in part the sources
which, under certain conditions, may end in delinquent misbehavior.
However, it must be clearly understood at the start that not all anxiety
patterns emerge as well-defined delinquent acts.

Anxiety, in a profoundly real and tragic sense, is the protean disorder
of modern society, manifesting itself in a variety of behavior forms—
delinquent, neurotic, and even psychotic. Because of its ubiquity, it
may be regarded as a symbol of the modern age. The emotional disturbances we have discussed thus far, emerging in the lives of some of
our children as provocative stimuli to delinquent activity, have been

---

[14] Hewitt and Jenkins, *Fundamental Patterns of Maladjustment*, p. 26.

viewed up to this point as broad patterned effects upon the personality. Ultimately, however, they may be reduced to precise personality organizations reflecting specific kinds of interpersonal relationships. Personalities limited by certain anxiety states permit only a partial perspective and a limited ability to engage in normal and conventional activities. The extent to which anxiety patterns invade the personality, however, is variable, ranging from minor and episodic manifestations to sustained and deeply rooted states basic to neurotic and psychotic disorders.[15]

Although the layman readily comprehends fears with a realistic basis, he frequently has difficulty in understanding the anxiety patterns of the emotionally disturbed. Yet such persistent emotional unease lies at the root of most of our mental disorders and may account for an immeasurable portion of our less serious unsocial and antisocial behavior manifestations.[16] As Karl Menninger has said, in commenting upon the difficulty normal persons have in apprehending such states, "It is difficult for a free fish to understand the plight of a hooked one." And how can we describe an anxiety state? Its primary character is a *sustained apprehension,* for which there does not appear to be a realistic or commensurate reason, yet which pervades the entire system of personal reactions. Ordinary fears (those of soldiers in combat, for example) can be understood and realistically reacted to; the individual can meet and handle them realistically, even though he is subject to feelings of panic. This is hardly true of the intense panic that may result from a prolonged anxiety state in which, as with many disturbed delinquents, the ego organization is not equipped to tolerate or cope with the slightest frustration. In such cases, it is not uncommon for disturbed delinquents to become violently destructive in the face of even minor handicaps, adult reproofs or admonitions.[17]

Rollo May's study of such emotional states suggests their principal sources.[18] Although there are innumerable family and social contexts that may tend to induce states of mind of this sort, and although *certain cultural and social levels tend to accentuate and encourage them,* a general pattern marking the origin of this form of emotional disequilibrium is frequently discernible. In general, the anxiety pattern arises essentially from a series of jeopardizing situations or conceived

[15] Berg, *The Case Book of a Medical Psychologist,* p. 14.
[16] Berg, *The Case Book of a Medical Psychologist,* pp. 14-16.
[17] Redl and Wineman, *Children Who Hate,* pp. 76-78.
[18] May, *The Meaning of Anxiety.*

situational threats for which the individual is unable to organize a defense. It is difficult to see how such a state can originate until the child has developed a symbolic conception of himself, a conception of self-esteem, and a recognition of his status in relation to others, particularly his parents. May draws a sharp distinction between genuine fear, for which a comprehensible and actual reason exists, and the overwhelming sense of anxiety that arises out of the child's groping inadequacy in trying to cope with a series of intimately related and threatening situations upon which his entire emotional life seems to hang. Although such states may be induced in adulthood by a sequence of overpowering experiences, they are far more common and serious among individuals who from early childhood have developed an abiding sense of insecurity as an integral phase of the entire personality.[19] Although some anxiety responses may be directed principally toward particular persons or situations, they are usually a diffuse and invariant part of the entire range of the individual's responses to every situation he encounters. The anxiety-ridden person cannot seem to escape this compulsive affectivity; it always appears to be with him.

A chronic latent factor accompanying anxiety states is the pent-up hostility the individual is unable to release. This trait provides a clue to the generic origin of anxiety conditions. Anxiety-ridden individuals are *hostile* individuals—hostile to themselves, as Fromm has pointed out, as well as to others. Being threatened, without being able to defend oneself or to manipulate the threatening situation to one's own advantage, produces antagonism toward such situations and the key personalities (or their ideal surrogates) who have figured in them. Such delinquents' furious resentment of all adult authority, grounded in chronic distrust, becomes readily understandable under these circumstances. In view of the common findings that this aggression stems from ambivalent relationships (relationships upon which the child is emotionally deeply dependent and toward which, in consequence, he is inhibited or constrained in expressing hostility), the onset of anxiety increases the child's growing sense of insecurity and uncertainty.[20] As Adler has put it, such states tend to batten on themselves, with the result that the child learns to reject himself as he feels others have rejected him.[21]

---

[19] May, *The Meaning of Anxiety*, p. 197.
[20] Horney, *Our Inner Conflicts*, pp. 41-42.
[21] Adler, *The Case of Miss R.*, Chap. 1; Adler, *Problems of Neurosis*, Chaps. 2, 3.

Symonds has shown, however, that the necessary consequence of anxiety need not be negative.[22] Depending upon the family setting and the environment—and it is here that an underprivileged environment with its numerous opportunities for destructive outlets plays its dangerous role—constructive adjustments can be made through recreational opportunity, and competent, understanding, and intensive adult supervision. Symonds, and Davis and Havighurst, have shown in studies of adolescents how constructive adjustments may be made even under the stress of what appear to be extreme anxiety pressures.[23]

In coping with a deeply rooted anxiety state under adverse environmental conditions, however, the two most frequent reactions are total flight and avoidance of the tension-inducing situation or, as is common among delinquents, "ferocious attack and diffuse destruction" upon whatever and whoever is within immediate reach.[24] Significant in the behavior of such children are the mechanisms the ego contrives to fend off such stress, mechanisms so graphically described by Redl and Wineman, and characterized by hyperexcitability, extremely low tolerance to frustration, panic in the face of new situations, failure to learn from experience, inability to meet competitive challenge, and other forms of psychological retreat.[25] *Much of the hostility to adult authority, rendering the use of corrective therapy so difficult, is sustained as a means of retaining the illusion of adult perfidy.* The social and cultural setting may play a very significant role as well in providing a *group setting* for anxiety reactions. The economically and socially underprivileged child who has not learned to negotiate his hostility may find in escaping from the home supportive techniques supplied by his playmates who, *in common*, may vent their aggressive attitudes toward the community.

If a fundamental cause of anxiety patterns lies in the ambivalent tensions created in many children during early years, we must look to specific kinds of social relationship for the strong impetus to such disorganization. Although personality patterns of this type are frequently linked to middle class settings, as Arnold Green has attempted to show, there is ample evidence to indicate that various forms of family organization tending to encourage such conditions exist throughout the entire

[22] Symonds, *Adolescent Fantasy*, p. 174.
[23] Davis and Havighurst, *Father of the Man*, pp. 212-13.
[24] Redl and Wineman, *Children Who Hate*, p. 81.
[25] Redl and Wineman, *Children Who Hate*, Chap. 3.

social order.[26] The source of this ambivalence is found very often in family situations where, regardless of the particular cause involved, the mother has interests that remove her attention from the child at crucial periods, or where the network of family relationships is highly changeable and unpredictable.[27] The trauma frequently occasioned by violent transitions from overaffection to preoccupation with other interests by the parent, sibling rivalry, employment of the mother, and similar factors have all been shown to exercise a disorienting influence. Sullivan, Horney, Fromm, and May all add substance to this view by indicating the discouraging effect produced by conflicting demands upon the child.[28] This personal disorientation of the child may be further augmented by the extreme stress placed upon the need for the child to maintain an esteemed self-conception in the face of acute competitive pressures.[29] It is for this reason that middle class groups in our society have been thought of as particularly susceptible to anxiety pressures, as Green has shown in his comparative study of neurosis among middle class children as contrasted with the children of Polish immigrants in a New England community.

Geoffrey Gorer, although seeming to focus on middle class families rather than on the whole of American society, illustrates how the need to gain affection by demonstrating success in competition with his peers creates confusion in the child's mind.[30] Gorer believes this to be widespread in the entire American social structure, though more common in certain class groups. What we may be witnessing (perhaps a portent of future trends making the base of delinquent behavior wider than its former lower socio-economic class concentration) is the growth of a neurosis-based delinquency in middle class groups, as against the more characteristic and relatively undisturbed delinquents of the past. May, for example, found that of thirteen unwed mothers he studied those of low socio-economic levels did not give evidence of neurotic anxiety, while Lemkau, Tietze, and Cooper found that Negroes had more conduct problems but fewer neuroses than the white subjects they examined.[31] Hewitt and Jenkins found more cases of anxiety stress among

[26] Green, "The Middle Class Male Child and Neurosis."
[27] Jersild, Child Psychology; Ribble, "Anxiety in Infants."
[28] Fromm, "Individual and Social Origins of Neurosis."
[29] Green, "The Middle Class Male Child and Neurosis."
[30] Gorer, The American Character.
[31] May, The Meaning of Anxiety, pp. 344-45; Lemkau, Tietze, and Cooper, "Mental Hygiene Problems in an Urban District."

Jewish children than among Negro, *although Weinberg shows that when middle class Negro youths are included, the same strain toward anxiety is present.*[32]

It thus appears highly likely, that anxiety-induced emotional states may bring about a new stage in the development of delinquent patterns, and that such personal tensions are intimately associated with characteristic socio-economic and cultural conditions, as these are mediated through the influence of particular types of families.[33]

Unsocialized Aggression

The ambivalent patterns just described commonly result in the inability of the child to cope with a number of normal situations and, consequently, cause his behavior to be marked by persistent fear and distrust. The crux of his maladjustment frequently lies in the strong emotional dependence of the child on a parent or other adult. We have here some indication of the child's distorted socialization, a profound identification with others accompanied by a hostile uncertainty provoked by the child's lack of assurance as to the kind of response such emotionally contingent situations may evoke. With some youngsters, as Redl and Wineman have shown in their second volume on deeply disturbed children, the intense resentment experienced may take the form of excessive fears, phobias, and fantasies, or of simulated attacks upon the persons and property of others.[34] These reactions can prove so exhausting, so devastating and violently explosive, invading every segment of the child's ego, that this capacity to perceive and respond to the ordinary routines of living can be seriously impaired and consumed.[35] Or, in view of the conditioning family and social circumstances, the fear of retaliation for any form of aggression may be so great that the child deeply inhibits any such tendencies and becomes fearful and parasitic, as Davis and Dollard in their study of Negro children in the Deep South, as well as Redl and Wineman, have shown.[36]

---

[32] Weinberg, *Society and Personality Disorders*, p. 123.

[33] Recent reports of private agencies dealing with disturbed and delinquent children appear to confirm this possibility. See, for example, *Annual Report*, Hawthorne-Cedar Knolls School, 1949.

[34] Redl and Wineman, *Controls from Within*, pp. 282-89.

[35] Redl and Wineman, *Controls from Within*, p. 283.

[36] Redl and Wineman, *Controls from Within*, pp. 289-92; Davis and Dollard, *Children of Bondage*, pp. 68-96, 207-31, 293-94.

Normative psychological development is seriously impaired in those family situations and social settings in which the child has been afforded little or no opportunity for normal identification with either or both parents, particularly the mother. Hewitt and Jenkins, in their significant attempt to classify types of behavior patterns and their linkages to specific situational determinants, indicate three major types of maladjusted youth in their study: the unsocialized aggressive delinquent, the socialized delinquent, and the over-inhibited child.[37] The latter, according to their findings, frequently develops strong tendencies toward adolescent and adult neurosis, while the first two, particularly the unsocialized type, figure prominently in delinquency. It is probable that a considerable number of our habitual delinquents, and those who graduate into adult forms of criminality, originate within the unsocialized category. Since from their earliest years these individuals have failed to introject social patterns and have been provided with little or no opportunity for adequate identification with parents, they prove extremely resistant to reëducation and therapy. Successful corrective adjustments presuppose the capacity of the individual to react with some degree of empathetic understanding to the counsellor's or therapist's expressed willingness to extend assistance. Lacking this socialized basis for creating positive social relationships, prospects for rehabilitation are few. Hewitt and Jenkins describe the behavior characteristics of this type of delinquent as follows:

> The behavioral difficulties of this child, which have called the attention of other persons to him and resulted in his referral, center around his basically "mean" treatment of others. He is cruel, defiant, prone deliberately to destroy their property as well as to attack their persons violently. He is inevitably engaged in fighting and expresses little feeling of guilt or remorse.[38]

In their analysis of background factors, Hewitt and Jenkins attempt to show that a specific type of environmental configuration, especially the home setting, is primarily responsible for strongly aggressive and unsocialized attitudes. "It should be pointed out," they state, "that while the picture presented is one of generalized and continuous parental rejection, this condition not only begins at the time of the child's birth,

---

[37] Hewitt and Jenkins, *Fundamental Patterns of Maladjustment.*
[38] Hewitt and Jenkins, *Fundamental Patterns of Maladjustment*, p. 34.

or even earlier, but it is most noticeably expressed by the mother." [39]

Regarding these unsocialized traits, many students have placed constant emphasis on parental rejection as the basis for destructive tendencies, since the child later extends this rejection into feeling rejected by other adults and even by his peers. The theme of rejection, however, has recently been considerably broadened and clarified, and this effort must continue if we are to understand adequately the reasons for this rebelliousness. Rejection takes many forms, not only in specific interpersonal relations between parent and child, but on different cultural levels. The age at which it occurs, as Levy has suggested, and *the character of immediately ensuing relationships*, as well as those occurring later, must be carefully visualized.[40] Further, the character of other family relationships, other family members' expectancies with regard to the child's behavior, sibling rivalry, and the opportunity at the proper time to identify with strong models of social control, all play a vital part.

One of the truly effective differences which Eleanor and Sheldon Glueck show in their study is the high degree of emotional lability of their delinquents, as against the nondelinquent controls—43.5 percent and 18.5 percent respectively—which, as they point out, is closely associated with strongly rejective home conditions and parental control.[41] However, the character of outright rejection by a highly disorganized immigrant family in Boston is an extremely different affair from the unwilling and unpremeditated rejection of Negro children in the Deep South, as described by Davis and Dollard.[42] Moreover, these forms of rejection are considerably different in turn from the myriad subtle expressions taken by a similar interpersonal pattern in the middle class family, particularly when characterized by so malignant a process as maternal overprotection.[43]

The trends in research attempting to discriminate clearly between the various forms of rejection, as they operate within different interpersonal contexts and on different cultural levels, are very recent, having assumed really significant proportions only during the last fifteen years.

[39] Hewitt and Jenkins, *Fundamental Patterns of Maladjustment*, p. 36.
[40] Levy, "Maternal Overprotection and Rejection"; Levy, *Studies in Sibling Rivalry*.
[41] Glueck; *Unraveling Juvenile Delinquency*, p. 236.
[42] Davis and Dollard, *Children of Bondage*, Chaps. 2, 3, and 4.
[43] Levy, "Maternal Overprotection"; Newell, "The Psychodynamics of Maternal Rejection."

We are still on the threshold of this significant area of investigation. It is apparent that rejection may unleash rampant impulsiveness and destructive activity on the part of the child by reducing drastically his opportunity to develop acceptable controls through a socialized ego; however, the *emphases,* the *degrees* of difference, and the *different forms* that various family and cultural settings elicit and express, must be closely examined. Nevertheless, the basic syndrome and its broad causative conditions are clear, as Symonds has shown. "The rejected child is destined, on the average, to show those strong aggressive traits, to be hostile and antagonistic toward those with whom he must have dealings, and to develop tendencies which may lead to delinquency." [44]

Rosenheim's study of the character structure of the rejected child emphasizes the latter's inability to establish positive relations with others and his essentially unapproachable nature.[45] Moreover, despite differences within particular family contexts and social levels, in many of these studies certain common aspects emerge with striking frequency and clarity. Ruth Topping's case studies of aggressive delinquents, for example, although emphasizing their behavioral characteristics rather than their background factors, show the high incidence among such children of *early* rejection by parents, the deeply imbedded attitude that "nobody cares," and an acute desire for acceptance and affection.[46] Although Luton Ackerson does not attempt, as Hewitt and Jenkins have suggested, to isolate specific clusters of traits (or syndromes of behavior) for children presenting behavior problems, the demoralizing picture of vicious and immoral home conditions, and discord between parents (the invariable accompaniment of rejective patterns) is clearly evidenced statistically in his study of the interconnections among 162 separate trait items characteristic of delinquents.[47] To these conclusions, the recent Glueck study, *Unraveling Juvenile Delinquency,* despite its considerable methodological shortcomings, adds further emphasis and confirmation.

[44] Symonds, "A Study of Parental Acceptance and Rejection."
[45] Rosenheim, "Character Structure of a Rejected Child."
[46] Topping, "Case Studies of Aggressive Delinquents."
[47] Ackerson, *Children's Behavior Problems,* Vol. 2.

The "Acting-Out" Neurotic

The genuine neurotic is an anxiety-ridden person who reacts to the pressures of his environment and his inner tensions in terms of fantasy, autistic behavior (distorted social perspectives dictated by his frustrations), and removal from social contact. This type of personality structure does not necessarily concern us here in an analysis of delinquent types and causes. The acting-out neurotic, however, according to Weinberg, although seemingly an anomaly, is a somewhat different type of individual and *does* figure in the problem of delinquent behavior.[48] Technically, innerved by similar anxiety-prompted pressures, he should not resort to overt activity as a defense against his feelings of insecurity and uncertainty. Actually, however, certain children with well-marked neurotic traits do engage in overt predatory and antisocial acts and contribute to the widening pattern of delinquency.

On the basis of his external behavior, the youthful neurotic who expresses his tensions in terms of social protests appears to resemble the psychopathic personality we have previously discussed. However, the two represent distinct types, providing us with further evidence that common behavioral manifestations and symptoms frequently result from disparate and divergent personality structures and causal processes.[49] A frequent error of the untrained person in the field of delinquency study is to identify a common behavioral process as emerging from a common type of causal pattern. The fact that behavior *appears* similar, even though the causes may be quite different, results from our tendency to evaluate it on the basis of a single set of cultural standards, and from the existence of only limited environmental outlets for a variety of internal pressures. To the uninformed observer, the destructive child is destructive, no matter what inner meanings he may be venting in his destructive activity.

The differences between the neurotic and the psychopath are striking, however, regardless of the superficial resemblance of their outward behavior. The basic difference in personality structure renders the neurotically oriented delinquent more amenable to treatment than the inflexible and resistant psychopath. In the first place, the neurotic indi-

---

[48] Weinberg, *Society and Personality Disorders*, pp. 281-85.
[49] Bloch, *Disorganization*; pp. 100-3.

vidual has strong feelings of guilt and feels the need to be punished, while the psychopath most likely has no such conscience structure. Second, the neurotic, although strongly inhibited in establishing social contacts (as Hewitt and Jenkins have illustrated with their "over-inhibited child") and, as a direct expression of the neurotic disorder itself, lacking acquired facilities for establishing primary relations, may nevertheless under controlled and sympathetic conditions be able to establish psychological rapport with others. The psychopath tends to be almost completely unresponsive. Third, the hostility displayed toward his environment by the neurotic is a reaction to his own anxiety; the psychopath gives little or no evidence of anxiety feelings. Characteristic of the neurotic's temperament is his insularity, the isolation within which he immures himself as a result of his dual feelings of hostility and anxiety. The relations of the psychopath with others are based upon the pragmatic and expedient usages to which other individuals may be put, and it carries with it little identification of feeling and attitude.

In one sense, the behavior pattern of the neurotic constitutes a variation on the theme of rejection. As Szurek has shown, however, the psychodynamics of this developmental process are complicated and variable, although a definite basic pattern may be discerned.[50] The family backgrounds of such maladjusted children appear to reveal a profound conflict in the child's relationship to the family structure, particularly to the parents, where one parent, usually the mother, is permissive in her attitude toward the child while the father is strongly repressive, punitive, and hostile. In Greenacre's analysis of this peculiar family configuration, which is found with considerable frequency in *both lower and middle class contexts*, the attitude of the mother is ambiguous. While seemingly affectionate in many instances, the affection actually conceals a fundamental indifference and casualness toward the child.[51]

There are subtle overtones in this specious affection offered by the mother in her permissiveness, as against the hostile rejection by the father. Unlike the genuine neurotic who strives sedulously for the assurance of an affection that was *once* gained, this type of neurotic child, distrustful of the permissive mask for affection, desperately wants *some-*

---

[50] Szurek, "Genesis of Psychopathic Personality Trends."
[51] Greenacre, "Conscience in the Psychopath."

one to care. What arises out of this, on the basis of analyses by Mahler, Johnson, and others, is a highly contingent relationship to the mother on the part of the child, the emotional content of which is widely variable, with fluctuations in the generally repressive attitude maintained by the father.[52] Moreover, the research literature appears to confirm the conclusion that the antisocial activities of the child are not deterred by strong parental disapproval. On the contrary, *the child's predatory activities are frequently met with indifference or tacit approval.*

A significant theoretical question arises here, the eventual answer to which by proper research may do much not only to clarify different causal patterns in delinquency but also to illustrate fundamental differences in neurotic constitution. The genuine neurotic who does not act out his disquiet may differ from the delinquent type by virtue of his genuine feelings of guilt. The feelings render it difficult for him to engage in any form of direct action. The "neurotic" delinquent we have described may, however, be reacting to fear rather than to deeply entrenched guilt feelings. His delinquent reaction is far more likely to be compounded out of strong resentment toward the repressive father, as well as the need to assure himself of emotional response from the mother, whom he strongly distrusts. Further research must be done to determine whether the genuine guilt pattern that is often assumed is essentially basic to this type of situation. Adelaide Johnson's examination of adolescents with such disturbances gives reason to believe that a parent's permissive attitude toward the child's misconduct is not necessarily part of the same pattern as the characteristic relationship of strong emotional dependence entertained by the genuine neurotic.

If we can accept the repeatedly observed pattern of *permissiveness coupled with hostile repression and antagonism* as the ground plan for this disorder, variations in family relationships must be closely surveyed to discover the impact of these contradictory attitudes upon the child. Healy and Bronner, for example, imply that the beginnings of these attitudes toward children may be seen in the hostility and vengefulness that parents have for each other.[53] In such cases we can hardly treat the child without treating the parent. The relentless persecution of parent

---

[52] Mahler, "Ego Psychology Applied to Behavior Problems"; Johnson, "Sanctions for Superego Lacunae of Adolescents."
[53] Healy and Bronner, *New Light upon Delinquency and Its Treatment*, pp. 81-83.

by parent and the acrimony they express toward each other may often cause either or both of them tacitly to encourage the child to react destructively.

In addition to occurrences *within* the family, social pressures originating *outside* the family may accentuate the child's overtly expressed anxiety. The characteristic responses toward associates, teachers, and other adults may themselves become intimately interwoven with the entire developing life pattern. The attitude of others toward the genuine neurotic is apt to be quite different from that toward the acting-out neurotic. These differences in the reactions of others may play a very prominent part in fostering and continuing the delinquent behavior of the neurotically disturbed child.

The limitations of this study do not permit us to follow through the significant implications of this latter point. However, where neurotic behavior is more common, as among middle class families—as the recent Yale study on behavior disturbances in relation to class levels tends to show—the critical judgments of others to neurotic patterns should conceivably result in behavior forms and symptoms different from, say, those of families of low socio-economic status in which "tolerance" and even expectancy of destructive behavior are frequently found.

Egocentric Waywardness

Much of the waywardness of our youth, as we have seen, may be attributed to strong hostile impulses generated by unwholesome family patterns and the inability to identify oneself closely with others in effective, positive, primary relations. We have noted the various outcomes in behavioral patterns and symptoms and the basic personality types emerging with striking frequency in distinctive family settings. The development of normal social impulses and attitudes toward others, however, is a natural outcome of the maturing of emotional responses on different age levels. Ideally, the perfectly adjusted child is one whose emotional maturity, the capacity to exercise and control his emotions in accordance with the normal demands of a situation, keeps pace with his neuro-muscular, intellectual, and social growth.[54] In a sense, all disturbed children are emotionally retarded children. The retardation, as in the neurotic, may be due to inner conflicts or, as in the psychopath,

[54] Bloch, *Disorganization*, pp. 145-56; Williams, *Adolescence*, pp. 18-19, 102 ff.

to the nonemergence at an infantile level of the normal sequence of emotional patterning.

We have, on the other hand, the individual who has been seemingly arrested in emotional development at an extremely low level essentially as a result of the overprotection and overindulgence of the parent. Whereas, in the case of the psychopath, normal emotional growth appears never to have occurred, in the case of the egocentric the emotional development becomes fixed upon an extremely rudimentary level, roughly corresponding to the dependency of the preschool child. Freudians and neo-Freudians tend to regard such fixation as occurring prior to the latency or prepubescent period. The hostility displayed by these children is of a highly generic type, liable to run in different directions, and may be likened to that of the young child who has been thwarted in pursuit of his immediate gratifications. The thwarting of such a generalized pattern of hostility may assume a highly explosive and volatile character and, at the same time, renders the subject highly suggestible. The factor of suggestibility, thus, for this type of child and within certain types of environments, may play a particularly significant role in motivating the child to delinquent acts.

Lacking the anxiety-rooted hostility of the neurotic but externally similar to the psychopath in his demand for immediate gratification of his desires, this type of youth is represented by August Aichhorn as imperious, demanding, and stultified in the realistic appraisal of his status relative to others:

> This type of delinquency develops because the mother, or in some instances, the father, is not equal to the task of rearing the child. . . . Weighed down by cares for him, she worries continually about his welfare and cannot demand from him any postponement of renunciation of pleasure. She clears out of his way all disappointments and obstacles which the child must learn to face and overcome in later life and thus she robs the child of initiative.[55]

Characteristic family patterns of this type are found on various social levels, as has been shown in an analysis of adolescent tensions on the American scene.[56] Frankwood Williams has ably demonstrated the persistence of emotionally immature patterns in many aspects of adult life, and Luella Cole has illustrated the tenacious grip which such undevel-

[55] Aichhorn, *Wayward Youth*, p. 201.
[56] Bloch, *Disorganization*, pp. 134-42.

oped responses may have on the personality, thereby producing later effects similar to adult psychopathic behavior.[57] Levy, in his contrast of maternal overprotection with maternal rejection, indicates the chronic infantilism of this type of individual and his unwillingness to brook any interference with his impulsivity.[58] Marynia Farnham's analysis of such personalities gives added point to the fact that they are not amenable to normal control except on their own terms.

For this type of overindulged child, the school situation is apt to prove particularly frustrating and thwarting, with the result that truancy and parentally approved absenteeism are not uncommon. Chafing under the restraints of normal classroom discipline and unwilling to cope with the difficulties of formal classroom training except on his own limited terms, the child indulges in deportment frequently characterized by disruptive emotional displays that single him out for attack by teachers and peer associates alike.

The sources for this type of maladjustment are, in a sense, coextensive with society, though it is particularly concentrated in homes where the parents, either through defective psychological make-up, unsatisfactory marital ties, demoralized family relationships, or a combination of similar circumstances, are themselves emotionally incapable of handling the normal problems of child-rearing. Consequently, impaired emotional growth of this kind is found to recur regularly in broken homes in which the mother, as a result of individual disabilities and situational determinants mentioned above, lavishes excessive care upon the child. Likewise, with considerable regularity, such personalities are molded in families where the mother, because of difficulties with her husband, very often the husband of a second marriage, seeks in the child a compensatory outlet for her affections. The child thus frequently becomes a pawn in his mother's own frustrated and displaced craving for affection and security.

The Socialized Delinquent

The socialized delinquent is, in a sense, a *cultural deviant*. That is, his identification with the deviant standards of a subcultural group or

[57] Cole, *Psychology of Adolescence*, pp. 109-11.
[58] Levy, "Maternal Overprotection."

class marks him as different from others, although, in terms of the criteria for normal mental behavior, he may give very little evidence of genuine pathological tendencies. Havighurst, Davis, Hollingshead, Eells, and others, in the ground-breaking series of studies conducted under the auspices of the Committee on Human Development of the University of Chicago, have shown how the acquired patterns of lower socioeconomic class groups set children from these groups apart in the community and the classroom. Such children commonly earn the opprobrium of their teachers, for example, who regard their traits as pathological evidences of maladjustment rather than as socially patterned behavior traits.[59]

The sanctioned support the child receives from others of his own group, and the intimate personal relations he develops with them, may provide a substantial basis for emotional security, as Clifford Shaw has shown in an entire series of life histories of delinquents.[60] Nevertheless, because the type of behavior in which the child indulges is frequently so much at variance with commonly held standards, he may be regarded as abnormal and even psychopathic. Some psychiatrists, such as Kolb, have even tended to the extreme view of regarding all habitual criminals as psychopathic, with very little substantial justification.[61] Hewitt and Jenkins have shown in their study of the classified behavioral syndromes of 500 maladjusted children that the manifested disorders of this type of child bear some resemblance to those of the unsocialized aggressive deviant, although the former's depredations never appear to take as extreme a form as those of the latter.

For example, he, too, is deceptive and defiant toward authority. When possible, he avoids self incrimination by not accepting the blame for his own acts, and feels little guilt over his depredations. He may also be inclined to bully those weaker than himself; but in none of these traits does he approach the aggressiveness of the unsocialized child, and one senses even in their moderate display a quite different emotional pattern. Even more than the *unsocialized aggressive* child, he engages in petty stealing from home or school. But such behavior on his part would not appear to be motivated by a desire for revenge. He is also extremely

[59] Hollingshead, *Elmstown's Youth.*
[60] Shaw, *The Natural History of a Delinquent Career;* Shaw, *The Jack-Roller;* Shaw, *Brothers in Crime.*
[61] Kolb, "Types and Characteristics of Drug Addicts."

antagonistic toward school attendance, but expresses this antagonism in truancy rather than by "taking it out" on other persons.[62]

Albert J. Reiss, in a statistical study of major delinquency types and their social backgrounds, indicates the relatively high probability that such types may emerge eventually as mature and fairly well-adjusted adults.[63]

In their intensive statistical analysis of the situational determinants producing such deviants, Hewitt and Jenkins portray a general background of demoralized family and home life, poverty, and extreme community pressure towards delinquency. "The characteristics and habits of other persons in this home only serve to accentuate this picture of inadequacy and indifference." [64] One of the parents may be missing through death. Either no provision is made for responsible and continuing adult care of the child, or the responsibility may eventually devolve upon a stepparent, an "outsider" who is often indifferent to the needs and problem of the child. Further, there is a marked absence of supervision of the child, the mother, if living in the home, is likely to be employed, and there is little or no household routine in the ordinary sense. The parents themselves, when made aware of the illicit activities of their children, may shield them, or punish them in private to spare public embarrassment, or actually condone their misbehavior as "smart," as Shaw, Reiss, Sutherland, Hewitt and Jenkins, and many others have demonstrated.

If the conclusions drawn by some investigators in their studies of this type of child are valid, viz., that the child shows little or no evidence of emotional imbalance, such inferences are still open to serious question. Kobrin has shown that such children never *fully* identify themselves with one group as compared to another.[65] The socialization of the ego consists of the introjection of a number of varying traits and standards, many of which are not congruent and self-consistent. Such children are not only exposed to some normative standards, even in the most adverse of substandard homes, but are continually being exposed to contrasting standards in the wider community of the school and the neighborhood. The strong indictment expressed by them in furious out-

[62] Hewitt and Jenkins, *Fundamental Patterns of Maladjustment*, pp. 42-43.
[63] Reiss, "Social Correlates of Psychological Types of Delinquency."
[64] Hewitt and Jenkins, *Fundamental Patterns of Maladjustment*, p. 43.
[65] Kobrin, "The Conflict of Values in Delinquency Areas."

bursts and hostility toward others, even if shared by members of their groups in varying degrees, may nevertheless produce anxiety and guilt feelings, no matter how limited. The fact that so-called socialized delinquents, in raiding a school after hours, for example, typically engage in pathological extremes, as described by Kobrin, indicates the presence of certain sinister elements in personality regardless of the child's close identification with members of his own group. It seems highly likely, therefore, that although the prognosis for such children may be considerably better than for the other disturbed types described above, latent neurotic elements may be present in them which are not always recognized in the normative views assumed by many students of delinquency.

For Further Reading

SELLIN, THORSTEN, *Culture Conflicts and Crime* (New York, 1938).

The role culture conflicts play in producing crime, indicating the vast areas of research that still remain to be explored.

AICHHORN, AUGUST, *Wayward Youth* (New York, 1935).

A rewarding psychoanalytical account of the causes of certain forms of youthful misbehavior and delinquency with illuminating case illustrations of specific types.

KOBRIN, SOLOMON, "The Conflict of Values in Delinquency Areas," in *American Sociological Review*, 16 (October 1951), pp. 653-61.

A recent study of considerable significance illustrating the complex variations in standards acquired by children reared in delinquency areas and challenging the traditional view that certain delinquents identify themselves completely with a delinquent subculture.

HEWITT, LESTER E., AND RICHARD L. JENKINS, *Fundamental Patterns of Maladjustment: The Dynamics of Their Origin* (Springfield, Illinois, 1947).

A recent ground-breaking study, illustrative of the way in which much of our modern research in delinquency causation might profitably move, in which relationships are established between delinquent personality types, behavior traits, and social background.

REDL, FRITZ, AND DAVID WINEMAN, *Controls from Within* (Glencoe, Illinois, 1952).

The sequel to the authors' *Children Who Hate,* in which they attempt to analyze the personality structures of a selected group of emotionally disturbed children.

LEWIS, NOLAN, AND BERNARD PACELLA, EDITORS, *Modern Trends in Child Psychiatry* (New York, 1945).

An interesting series of papers that will provide the reader with a fund of information concerning some of the more recent developments in child psychiatry.

EISLER, K. R., EDITOR, *Searchlights on Delinquency* (New York, 1949).

A collection of articles and studies dealing with some of the recent psychiatric findings as applied to delinquent problems.

REISS, ALBERT J., JR., "Social Correlates of Psychological Types of Delinquency," in *American Sociological Review,* 17 (December, 1952), pp. 710-18.

One of the best of the recent psychosociological investigations of the causes of delinquency, based upon an extensive sample of delinquents in the Chicago area, and demonstrating the needed emphasis upon the relationships between delinquent types and a variety of causative social conditions.

Chapter **8**

THE PRESSURES OF
THE ENVIRONMENT

Environmental Deviation Pressures

To describe the variety of environmental influences contributing directly and indirectly to delinquency, we now turn to Lowell J. Carr's felicitous phrase, "community deviation pressures," used by him in describing the external forces and situations that tend to motivate children toward antisocial and maladjusted behavior.[1] So far we have concentrated on the variety of individual differences, constitutional and psychological, which may play a part in predisposing the child toward delinquent behavior. Delinquency, however, is an end product of a number of factors, both *within* the personality and *without*, which, in interaction, may cause activity that the community considers dangerous and antisocial.

In every neighborhood, and in every family, we find situations tending to encourage the child to make both bad and good adjustments. Even in the best of families, the well-intentioned father's preoccupation with business, for example, may cause him to neglect his active responsibility toward his child at a critical period in the child's life. However,

[1] Carr, *Delinquency Control*, Chap. 7.

ın such a situation the preponderance of wholesome social pressures, exerting their influence in encouraging the child to conform to the mandates of his society and his group, are likely to counteract the parent's lapse, unless the neglect was sustained and coupled with other unforeseen and unwholesome factors.

The behavior of any individual is a resultant of both internal and external pressures to conform as well as not to conform. In an age less hectic than ours, when social demands aimed at rigorous uniformity and when the control of children was largely the concern of the rural family, the strong social ties, aided by the equally strong support of the community, exercised powerful control to keep individuals within the bounds of customary and expected behavior. But today, in an industrial age, where much of human relationship has become mechanized and impersonal, where individuals move from place to place rapidly and often, and where each community struggles with a variety of incompatible social norms, it has become far more difficult to expect uniform standards of behavior that will satisfy everyone. Little wonder that, under such divergent and contradictory codes, some people tumble into the pitfalls of nonconformity which the very complexity of our patterns of social living have created.

In most communities, the pressures to conform are considerable. Muzafer Sherif, an eminent social psychologist, has pointed out, as William Graham Sumner did a half century ago, that all communities tend to develop common norms of behavior "which serve as focal points in the experience of the individual and subsequently as guides for his action." [2] Social psychologists have devised a theory, known impressively as the "J-curve hypothesis," which states that the presence of such pressures in the community tends to force most people to comply with the demands society makes upon them.[3] Nevertheless, certain individuals will tend to deviate from these norms, regardless of what the particular standard may be or how reasonable and sensible it may appear.

Why should there always be some persons who tend to veer away from social pressures? The answer is that all individuals are differently constituted, as we have attempted to show in the two previous sections, and that certain environments present so many incitements to deviation

---

[2] Sherif, *Psychology of Social Norms*, p. 85.
[3] Allport, "The J-Curve Hypothesis of Conforming Behavior."

that some people will almost inevitably succumb. Carr defines a deviation pressure as "any condition or situation that tends to block emotional satisfaction or to turn adjustment in an anti-social direction." [4] We must recognize that, for certain people, engaging in delinquent practices or other forms of maladjusted behavior is a normal response to an abnormal situation. People adapt, as we have seen, on the basis of the kinds of psychological pressures motivating them, and if, in the environment, the kinds of outlets that appear with highest frequency are those of an antisocial variety, it is natural for the individual to turn to these antisocial channels. *Maladjustment and antisocial behavior are both forms of adaptation to a difficult environment that limits the possibilities of release for the individual's psychological tensions.*

Carr has attempted to indicate the pressures towards nonconforming behavior in a provocative schematic device. Assuming, as we have learned, that *within* each individual personality there are both conforming and deviation pressures, and that the environment itself presents strong pressures toward conformity as well as toward nonconformity, whether an individual becomes delinquent or not will depend upon whether the positive (or conforming) factors outweigh the negative or deviation pressures. This is illustrated in the following diagram:[5]

$$CF \ (I \times E) - DF \ (I \times E) = \begin{cases} C \ D \\ or \\ D \ D \end{cases} \begin{array}{l} \longrightarrow \ CB \\ or \\ \longrightarrow \ DB \end{array}$$

We should note in the preceding diagram that *CF* (conforming factors), both internal and external, minus *DF* (deviation factors), also both internal and external, *equal CD*, a conformity differential (if conforming factors are greater) or *DD*, a deviation differential (if deviation factors are greater), which, respectively, lead to conforming behavior or deviant behavior. "Delinquency," according to Carr, "is the end term of an equation in which deviation factors exceed conformity factors." [6]

It is theoretically possible, on the basis of what we have already learned, to anticipate the volume and character of delinquency within certain areas. Some areas, which we will shortly examine, abound in pressures toward anti-social behavior. In fact, it is becoming possible

[4] Carr, *Delinquency Control*, p. 159.
[5] Carr, *Delinquency Control*, p. 160.
[6] Carr. *Delinquency Control*, p. 161.

through modern research techniques to evaluate these areas statistically.[7] Recognizing that certain individuals, because of their personality structures, are *more* vulnerable to delinquent behavior and therefore constitute greater risks, we may appraise their chances in an environment—including family, neighborhood, economic, and cultural factors —which is heavily weighted with adverse influences. This may be illustrated by the following chart:

CHART XII

*Vulnerability to Delinquent Behavior**

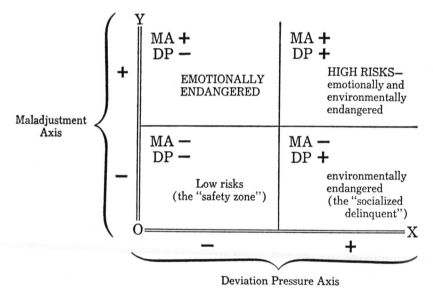

* Carr, *Delinquency Control*, p. 164. Reproduced by permission of Harper & Brothers.

In this chart, we note that the vertical axis, moving from O to Y, represents increased tendencies toward personality tensions. These tendencies may be determined on the basis of a variety of tests, such as, for example, the Haggerty-Olson-Wickman Rating Scale. The horizontal axis, moving from O to X, represents increased tendency toward adverse environmental situations. In dividing our diagram into four

[7] See Shaw, *Delinquency Areas*. Other composite measuring devices (indices) have been, and are being, worked out by statistical sociologists, including Calvin Schmid, Herbert A. Bloch, and others.

quadrants, we notice that *high* psychological pressure toward maladjustment but *low* community risks tends to produce emotionally disturbed, although not necessarily delinquent, children (upper left-hand quadrant). In the upper right-hand quadrant, we find those children with highly disturbed emotional states *and* exposure to a bad environment, leading to emotionally severely disturbed delinquent types. In the lower left-hand corner, we note the children who are least vulnerable to delinquency *or* maladjustment, children with little tendency toward psychological disturbances, living in an area with little environmental risk. In the lower right-hand corner, we have the "socialized delinquents" discussed in the preceding section, giving little evidence of deep-seated emotional disturbance but exposed to a highly dangerous neighborhood environment.

Our problem now turns to the question of what essentially are these environmental risks? They are basically those strongly adverse environmental pressures stemming from deviant homes, areas of culture conflict, deteriorated neighborhoods or delinquency areas, ill effects of certain peer-age associations, tensions produced by the school, the effects of demoralizing leisure activities and recreation, substandard economic conditions, and the impact of certain cultural values upon the child. Let us examine each of these in turn.

Deviant Homes

Though there is much disagreement about the countless factors that play a part in predisposing a child to delinquency, scholars and other researchers are agreed on the overwhelming significance of family life and the home in contributing to delinquent behavior. In view of the stress we have placed this far on the influence of the family in the early formative years and the vital effect of interpersonal relations on the personality during the first six years of life, this is certainly not difficult to apprehend. In the culmination of their ten years of intensive research on the causal factors of delinquency, Sheldon and Eleanor Glueck concluded that the character of the family situation had more to do with creating delinquency than residence in a slum area, or exposure to "conflicting cultures," or membership in a large family.[8] With the attempted prediction table for delinquency which they devised, based on four principal factors—discipline by the father,

[8] Glueck, *Unraveling Juvenile Delinquency,* Chap. XI.

supervision by the mother, affection by both parents for the child, and cohesiveness of the family group—they computed that the chances for delinquency were 98.1 out of 100, if these factors were unfavorable.[9] Nothing in the presumption of delinquency, according to the Gluecks, is as important as this so-called "under-the-roof" culture.[10]

None of this, of course, comes as a surprise to those working in the field of delinquency. However, the matter of family adequacy covers an extremely broad area, encompassing a number of special fields, each of which must be carefully surveyed in the light of tested evidence if we are to understand the importance of family life in shaping the career of the child. Judges and district attorneys fulminate at the so-called failure of the family in meeting the problems of adequate child adjustment and child-rearing. However, we must recognize that families themselves are frequently victimized by a number of circumstances either partially or wholly beyond their capacity to control or to modify. Consequently, instead of this widespread condemnation of the family for its failure to act effectively in correcting youthful disorders, we require considerable understanding of the inextricable web of circumstances and personalities which may render it almost impossible for the family to perform its functions satisfactorily.

Although the Gluecks appear perfectly explicit in accepting these facts, they fail to recognize their profound research implications, as sociologists are at pains to point out. Actually, the Glueck emphasis begs the essential research question of how certain types of destructive family relationships reflect, and are related to, the socio-economic and cultural conditions in which they are found. The Gluecks begin with the *fact* of an adverse family situation as a primary datum, when this is the very question to be investigated.

To meet its responsibilities effectively, the normal family should be characterized by a number of specific conditions. These conditions embrace "structural completeness, racial homogeneity, economic security, cultural conformity, moral conformity, physical and psychological normality, and functional adequacy." [11] In briefly assessing each of these factors, we must keep in mind that the aggravated malfunctioning of any of them may be sufficient to encourage a tendency toward delin-

[9] Glueck, *Unraveling Juvenile Delinquency*, p. 261.
[10] Glueck, *Unraveling Juvenile Delinquency*, p. 110.
[11] Carr, *Delinquency Control*, p. 166.

quency. *Structural completeness* refers to the unbroken home, the presence of both natural parents in the family setting. The broken family does not necessarily accompany delinquency, but it figures prominently in a number of cases. Although homes in which the parents are racially different can and do succeed, there are innumerable instances of the tensions this situation provokes, particularly in certain geographical areas, even in an America slowly tending to grow more enlightened about racial difference. *Economic security,* the foundation upon which the family can meet the physical, social, and psychological needs of its members adequately, is a basic bulwark against a variety of demoralizing situations to which the poverty-stricken family readily falls prey. Although the vast majority of underprivileged families do not produce delinquents and criminals, as the criminologist Hans von Hentig has repeatedly shown in his work, the *risk* of delinquency and crime is appreciably heightened when economic insecurity weakens the moral and social fiber of family life.[12] *Cultural conformity,* the sharing of common practices, attitudes, ideas, and values by parents and children, is a profound source of strength in building attitudes of emotional security; while *moral conformity* enhances the strength of the child's personality structure (the psychiatrist's superego) by providing community support for the child's disciplined social drives. *Psychological and physical normality,* the freedom of the home from impairment of its functions because of the handicapping presence of mentally or physically disabled individuals, is an equally strategic element in the development of normal childhood patterns.

Functional adequacy is likewise of enormous importance in shaping the child's career toward normal and responsible adulthood, but is not so readily understood. The satisfaction of the previous requirements refers to the family's culturally prescribed, social needs. They are functions that society hopefully expects each family to fulfill. To supplement these functions, however, the family is expected to satisfy the *individual* needs of its members, *i.e.,* the psychological needs, arising in interpersonal relationships, the satisfaction of which every child requires in order to develop normal patterns of emotional growth and social expectancy.[13] As Miriam Van Waters has shown in her analysis of the problems of modern family life and child-rearing, the two basic func-

[12] von Hentig, *Crime,* pp. 7-14 and Chap. 10.
[13] Bloch, *Disorganization,* pp. 595-96.

tions still remaining to the family are, first, satisfying the economic demands required to maintain the household and, second, *providing an atmosphere of emotional security in which to rear the child and to fortify him in his development of mature adult attitudes.*[14]

The research evidence upholding these basic principles is shown in a variety of supporting studies. It is significant, however, that studies of the effects of family life upon the child, not excepting the ambitious study of the Gluecks, still await more precise analysis and delineation of specific interpersonal and physical factors in child life for different types of groups and under varying cultural and economic conditions. All that we can indicate for the present are the general tendencies pointed to in now available research, which will very likely be augmented by future research evidence.

(*a*) *Broken Homes.* Technically speaking, a broken home is one in which a significant adult member, usually a parent, is missing because of death, desertion, or divorce. The effects of such broken homes vary among different groups and different children, at different age levels, and with difference of sex. Nevertheless, there is pronounced evidence that broken homes play a significant part in predisposing more children to delinquency than would be the case if this factor were not present.

However, any conclusions we draw must be qualified by knowledge of whether the father or the mother is removed from the household scene, and of the circumstances in which the removal took place, whether by death, desertion, or divorce. In effect, "without a certain amount of evaluation of the psychological atmosphere created by the broken home and the character of the individuals affected, it is virtually impossible to draw definite conclusions concerning this environmental factor."[15] Shideler, for example, estimated in an early study that from 40 to 70 percent of delinquents came from broken homes, as compared with an estimated 25 percent in the normal population who come from such homes. Healy and Bronner confirmed this finding to some extent by indicating that of the 4,000 delinquents they surveyed in Boston and Chicago, about half came from broken homes, with the greater incidence of this factor among delinquent girls.[16]

That the broken home is apt to be a more serious handicap for the

---

[14] Van Waters, *Parents on Probation.*
[15] Bloch, *Disorganization*, p. 194.
[16] Healy and Bronner, *Delinquents and Criminals*, pp. 121-25.

delinquent girl than for the delinquent boy is apparently borne out by several studies. The conclusion receives support from another quarter in the observed tendency of American culture patterns to exert stronger pressures for conformity in girls than in boys, as Monachesi has very ably suggested in his elaborate testing of male and female delinquents.[17] Mabel Elliott, in her studies of the Sleighton Farm girls at Darlington, Pennsylvania, and Mabel Ormsbee have both stressed the prevalence of broken homes among female delinquents.[18] A recent report by Reinemann of 220 Negro and white truants of both sexes appearing before the Philadelphia municipal court reveals that an extremely high percentage, 65 percent, had backgrounds in which broken home conditions existed.[19]

The need to see into the state of affairs in the broken home more clearly, to detect the underlying conditions of breakdown in interpersonal patterns for various levels of American culture and for different age groups, was first clearly demonstrated by Shaw and McKay.[20] It is here that a sociological perspective of the psychological discord produced by shattered homes is so important. We can draw some limited conclusions about the effects of broken homes on the lives of children if we bear in mind the precautions needed for an adequate assessment of the innumerable variables that enter into each family pattern of interpersonal relationships.

(1) Not *any* broken home will produce delinquency—only those homes with related deleterious conditions.

(2) Harmful effects on the child will depend largely on the general structural characteristics of the home and on which of the parents is removed from the scene.

(3) Girls, apparently, are likely to be more affected by the loss of a parent than boys are.

(4) The age at which the effects of the disintegration are experienced is likely to affect the behavior of the child. Male children at the age of ten show adverse effects in greater proportion than any other age groups. In general, the effects are more serious for children below ten and less serious for those above this age.[21]

[17] Monachesi, "Characteristics of Delinquents and Non-Delinquents."
[18] Elliott, *Correctional Education and the Delinquent Girl*, pp. 26-27; Ormsbee, *The Young Unemployed Girl*, pp. 58-60.
[19] Reinemann, "The Truant Before the Court."
[20] Shaw and McKay, "Social Factors in Juvenile Delinquency."
[21] Bloch, *Disorganization*, p. 195.

(b) *Immoral Homes.* Actually, in investigating home conditions that adversely affect the life of a child, investigators frequently group together several factors (often subjectively arrived at) which appear to them to be sufficient reasons for the breakdown of the child's personal relationships. From a research point of view, this is somewhat unfortunate, since we require rigorous, *uniform,* and well-defined frames of reference that will enable us to compare one group with another. For example, some investigators attempt to categorize homes on the basis of the "immoral" conditions presented by the environments. If a common, measurable, and operational definition of immorality could be devised, this might conceivably be helpful.

However, in appraising the great variety of investigations, we find that the term "immorality" has been used by different investigators in a variety of ways, being applied to homes where the child has been actively corrupted by criminal parents, poor and indigent homes, and homes marked by chronic inebriety and indifference to the child's welfare. Thus, Mabel Elliott, in employing a comprehensive definition of immorality, found that 56 percent of the girls at the Sleighton Farm came from such homes, while Healy and Bronner, using the term in a more restricted sense, estimated that only 21 percent came from such homes.[22]

Generally speaking, when homes fail because of reprehensible moral conditions, they do so because of neglect of those fundamental responsibilities in child-rearing that society attempts to exact from each family, namely, the proper exercise of its *permissive* and its *restrictive* functions. The neglect, indifference, and lack of concern of certain families in permitting children to engage in dangerous activities and associations constitute one phase of the problem. At the same time, each family has the responsibility of imposing its restrictive functions in such a way that the child's normal emotional development is not seriously jeopardized. Obviously, the exercise of these controls will vary on different socio-economic levels, *although the burden of neglect falls particularly heavily on the underprivileged and economically marginal groups.*

The research dealing with the so-called immoral home is actually concerned with a peculiar form of distorted and perverted *emotional atmosphere.* Our careful and prolonged investigation of this factor in many studies, and our attempts actually to measure it, reveal that "the

[22] Healy and Bronner, *Delinquents and Criminals,* pp. 126-27.

emotional atmosphere of the slum home may directly incite towards delinquency, whereas the atmosphere of the better-favored home may conduce towards delinquency by indirect means." [23] Since in appraising any home condition we look for those factors that impair the normal and expected relationships essential to the child's development, we can localize these faulty human relationships in certain types of homes. According to Coulter, disorganized homes may be classified into five principal categories: "(1) homes with criminal patterns; (2) homes in which there are unsatisfactory personal relations because of domination, favoritism, nonsolicitude, overseverity, neglect, jealousy, a stepparent, or other interfering relatives; (3) homes in which one parent has a physical or mental disability; (4) homes socially or morally maladjusted because of differences in race, religion, conventions and standards, or an immoral situation; (5) homes under economic pressures—unemployment, low income, homes in which mothers work out." [24]

(c) *Criminal Homes.* Recalling that vast numbers of our delinquents and maladjusted children come from homes where neither parents nor siblings are delinquent, the crushing impact of a home where criminality has actually been practiced is easy to envisage. Clifford Shaw has traced in detail the demoralizing effects of such an atmosphere on the child.[25] In Burt's classical study of vice and crime in England, he found five times as many delinquents from homes in which there was crime as in noncriminally patterned homes. The Gluecks found that 84.8 percent of the reformatory population of Massachusetts came from homes with other criminal members, and 86.7 percent of all delinquents surveyed came from such homes. The New York Crime Commission found that 83 percent of truants later charged with felonies had come from homes with criminal records.

In all homes where children are improperly reared the failure results from the loss of effective primary controls. Such primary controls are the characteristic forms of discipline and the emotionally charged relations between child and parent. In Burt's study of English delinquents, defective discipline was found 6.9 times more frequently in the homes of delinquents than in the homes of nondelinquents.[26] *It was four times more important than poverty in the creation of delinquency.*

[23] Bloch, *Disorganization*, p. 199.
[24] Coulter, "Family Disorganization as a Causal Factor in Delinquency and Crime.'
[25] Clifford Shaw, *Brothers in Crime.*
[26] Burt, *The Young Delinquent.*

There has been endless confirmation of these findings, as is evidenced in the predictive scale for delinquency recently devised by the Gluecks, in which the affective personal relationships between parents and children are the principal elements.[27] In their earlier study of one thousand delinquents, the significance of deteriorated relationships between parents and children were revealed by the fact that 70 percent of the delinquents surveyed came from homes characterized by "unsound disciplinary methods." [28]

Assessment of these findings in their various particulars has caused students, such as Coulter, to draw the following conclusions:

> The American home, so far as it fails, does so not through design or malignance, but through neglect, ignorance, and unwillingness to take the responsibility for directing its children. In few cases is the discipline vicious or criminal. In most cases it is inadequate and inconsistent. Our problem of delinquency is basically a problem of educating, directing, training, advising with and safeguarding parents, and of impressing upon them their continued responsibility. Give us better, more informed and responsible parents and we will guarantee a reduction of the problem of delinquency and crime.[29]

Cultural Conflict

The problem of cultural conflict in its relation to delinquency and crime in American life has been largely misunderstood. It is not to be doubted that the existence of conflicting cultural strains in American community life, resulting in different standards of behavior and imposing different types of control upon the same individuals, frequently produces personality tensions and behavior disorders. However, the general oversimplified view is that a prevailing set of cultural standards exists with considerable uniformity within a certain area and that these standards are at variance with the cultural practices of a given minority group or a group of families. As Sellin, Kobrin, Reiss, Barron, and others have indicated, the problem is hardly as simple as this.[30] A certain area may be the source of a variety of different cultural standards which, in turn, complement, support, contradict, or permit the peaceful

[27] Glueck, *Unraveling Juvenile Delinquency*, p. 261.
[28] Glueck, *One Thousand Juvenile Delinquents*, p. 82.
[29] Coulter, "Family Disorganization as a Causal Factor in Delinquency and Crime."
[30] See, for example, Barron, "Juvenile Delinquency and American Values."

coexistence of the cultural practices of different minority groups and families. The complexity of this problem and the wide variety of difficulties created for a certain area and for individuals from different minority groups, whose own standards may be highly contradictory, have hardly been adequately explored, as Thorsten Sellin has pointed out.[31]

Research evidence in the area of culture conflict is nonetheless entirely clear in a number of particulars. Individuals whose rearing, training, and values are quite different from the predominant standards of a particular area will, ordinarily, feel the impact of conflict and antagonism in both overt and subtle ways. More pertinent, perhaps, is the fact that such persons will experience difficulty in integrating these standards within their own personalities, with the result that they undergo personality tensions and conflict in varying degrees of intensity. As a secondary aspect, communities marked by cultural cleavages are apt to induce *expedient* forms of behavior, those most suitable to the individual's needs at a given moment irrespective of the social requirements of the larger community. These problems affect the lives of children in their formative years most acutely, before they have been able to develop a responsible sense of discrimination with regard to the conflicting demands of the community on the individual.

Cultural conflict, therefore, produces the dual problem of cultural *hybridism* and *marginality:* the individual falls between varying sets of cultural standards and values which impose a strain upon the integrated pattern of his personality. The implications of this culture conflict are very devious and complex, beginning with variations in early child-rearing, the introjection of home standards that openly conflict with the mores and standards of the outside world, and the feelings of guilt, rejection, shame, and loss of status that accompany the individual's attempted adjustments to conventional requirements outside the home. Clifford Shaw and his associates at the University of Chicago have given examples in their detailed case studies of the ways in which cultural differences play a significant part in encouraging the child to lawlessness, ranging from unwitting parental tolerance of the child's waywardness to the child's sense of inferiority the child experiences and tries to compensate for.[32] The English anthropologist Geoffrey Gorer has

---

[31] Sellin, *Culture Conflicts and Crime.*
[32] See, for example, Shaw, *The Jack-Roller*, pp. 42-53.

suggested that a broad base for lawlessness has been established throughout the entire range of American culture because successive generations have rejected the status of parental authority, which is frequently identified with an inferior immigrant culture.[33] In regulating the many problems of social control arising from this cultural heterogeneity, Americans have become the most overlegislated people in the world. Paradoxically, while this is a necessity, as studies by the National Law Institute have shown, it promotes further lawlessness at the same time.

There is considerable evidence to show that there is a close relationship between cultural diversity and high rates of crime and delinquency, although the precise causal processes linking the two can be ascertained only in relation to specific individuals and for specific cultural contexts. Nevertheless, successive studies have demonstrated that the highest incidence of delinquency appears originally to have occurred among the children of immigrants, themselves the prime focal targets for cultural diversity. The contemporary counterparts of this group today are Negro children, the children of Puerto Rican and Mexican immigrants, and rural-urban migrants, among all of whom relatively high delinquency rates obtain. Further, the wider the divergence of a group's cultural standards from the ones dominant in the American community in which it is situated, and the greater the obstacles placed in the way of cultural reconciliation, the greater the possibility of individual personality conflict, delinquency, and crime.[34] This problem, incidentally, is not restricted to American communities, as anthropologists have been pointing out recently in their studies of the rapid growth of critical points of tension in other parts of the globe.[35]

The significance of cultural difference and conflict in their effects on delinquency has been brought out by a variety of studies, giving both direct and indirect evidence. Probably the principal index is that problem rates in general tend to diminish in direct ratio to the degree of assimilation of the minority group. At the same time, the member of an out-group who remains assimilated to his *own* culture only seldom presents a problem of lawlessness and social disorder. Pauline V. Young has illustrated this well in her study of Russian Molokan children living in the Los Angeles area.[36] Here the younger children, born

[33] Gorer, *The American People.*
[34] Sellin, *Culture Conflicts and Crime.*
[35] See Kennedy, "The Colonial Crisis and the Future."
[36] Young, *Pilgrims of Russiantown.*

in the United States and exposed to outside cultural standards widely different from the peculiarly stringent requirements of this religious sect, showed an extremely high delinquency rate as against a negligible rate among children of the same group born abroad and thoroughly identified with their own culture. The foreign-born children, closely integrated with the parent culture, yielded a delinquency rate of 5 percent as against the phenomenally high rate of 78.3 percent for the nine-to-nineteen-year-old age group born in this country.

Further evidence, stressing psychological factors and dealing with native Negro children, illustrates the frustrations imposed by dual cultural pressures and the powerful aggressive tendencies that these frustrations may unleash.[37] The psychological disorientation promoted by conflicting cultural pressure is well evidenced in E. Franklin Frazier's studies of Negro family life in Harlem and Chicago, which clearly show the impact of *migration* on families recently removed from the rural South.

In reviewing the varied findings in this field, encompassing the broad dimensions of cultural conflict as a source of delinquent disorder, we may draw the following conclusions:

(1) Culture conflict always produces areas of community demoralization and declining social controls which—by incitement, imitation, and the learning process itself—render the child more liable to acquire delinquent behavior patterns.[38]

(2) Culture conflict erects barriers between family members of different generations. These barriers are accentuated by language and value differences, and among other results induce the breakdown of parental authority.

(3) The inability to identify oneself with varying cultures leads to confusion about guiding standards. This confusion is increased by the strain to achieve the superficial values of the dominant culture. Homes in which there is culture conflict are frequently marked by the children's contempt for the parents, who are identified with an "inferior" cultural group.

In analyzing cultural conflict in its relation to crime and delinquency, careful cognizance must also be taken of the *character* of the

[37] See, for example, Dai, "The Channelling of Negro Aggression by the Cultural Process."

[38] Sutherland, *Principles of Criminology,* pp. 6, 77-80.

cultural contexts involved, as well as the conditions under which the cultural groups intermingle and have contact. This is ordinarily neglected in most studies. For example, the value systems of the different cultural groups may be congruent enough to reconcile and even reinforce the various attitudes of the individuals involved in the different cultures. Likewise, the elements of the situation at a given time, *e.g.*, the *conditions* under which an alien group comes into contact with a dominant cultural group, may have great significance in the acceptance or rejection of the alien group. The variety of possibilities that may improve the effect of personality contact or heighten antagonism must always be carefully assessed in the light of the *kinds* of cultural values involved, the *points of tension* at which predominant values of both groups come into conflict, and the attitude of a group at a given time toward the acceptance or rejection of the members of an out-group.

The Deteriorated Neighborhood

The special branch of sociology known as *human ecology* (which deals with the distribution and concentration of populations in specific areas and the relationship of these population groups to the areas in which they are found) has long made us familiar with the impact of deteriorated neighborhoods on delinquency and other social problems.[39] One need hardly be an expert to recognize the close relationship between detrimental physical living conditions and the wide range of problems associated with them. Nevertheless, the particularized effects of certain aspects of these conditions and the reasons for their differing effects on human behavior raise some significant problems which much of the research has apparently neglected. What are the specific attributes of the physical environment in which the child lives that prove particularly hazardous to his behavior? At what phase of his life do these conditions play a significant part? To what degree can the child's family mediate and modify such adverse influences? Why do some children and not others succumb to neighborhoods characterized by poor housing, commercial invasion, and inadequate recreational outlets? What enables some families to maintain self-respect and control

[39] See Park, Burgess, and McKenzie, *The City*, particularly "The Ecological Approach to the Study of the Human Community"; also McKenzie, *The Metropolitan Community*; and McKenzie, "The Rise of Metropolitan Communities."

over their children in the most destructive of environments while others do not? These are only a few of the host of questions involved in any adequate study of the effects of neighborhood conditions, and yet they are the very ones that research hardly ever answers.

In any urban area, we can pinpoint with relative ease the districts most productive of delinquency and related social disorders. Typical is the study of a 333-acre Cleveland slum, containing 2.5 percent of the city's population, in which 6.8 percent of the total volume of delinquency is found, 21 percent of the murders, 26 percent of the houses of prostitution, and on which the city expends $1,750,000 yearly in excess of the total tax receipts for the area.[40] Although the original studies of the 1920's and the 1930's indicated that deteriorated areas were more commonly found next to the commercial and industrial centers of our cities, we know that they may be scattered throughout our metropolitan districts and even be found on the fringes of our cities.[41] They may also be found in rural districts and may there produce many of the same problems, though with lesser intensity than in major metropolitan districts or smaller cities. Ecological studies invariably reveal that deteriorated community areas of urban centers of industry and transportation are so-called "zones in transition"—areas lacking stability which are continually undergoing change under the encroachment of outside interests, frequently commercial and industrial. Within their miserably overcrowded and dangerously substandard housing proliferate delinquency, crime, sexual disorders, desertion, homelessness, and the like.

Clifford Shaw and his associates, in analyzing "delinquency areas," have demonstrated, through the application of varied techniques to these areas as well as the remaining zones of the city, that there is a statistical *gradient*, that is, a declining rate of delinquency from the center of the urban area to its periphery.[42] Considerable recent evidence indicates that such a gradient does not necessarily exist in American cities.[43] Bernard Lander, for example, in a recent (1954) study of 8,464 cases of juvenile delinquency in the metropolitan area of Baltimore, has demonstrated the inadequacy of the *gradient* concept

[40] Navin, Peattie, Stewart, *et al.*, *An Analysis of a Slum Area in Cleveland.*
[41] See, for example, Davie, "The Pattern of Urban Growth"; Hanes, *Case Study of Three Delinquency Areas.*
[42] Shaw and others, *Delinquency Areas.*
[43] See Davie, "The Pattern of Urban Growth."

in applying to this urban concentration. Although the concept of the gradient is not universally applicable, the highest rates of delinquency are nevertheless invariably found in these "zones of transition" and are commonly correlated with other high indices of social breakdown. By using the so-called social base map, Frederic M. Thrasher has shown graphically how in such districts, the juxtaposition of large and small business enterprises, deserted and abandoned dwellings, and a conglomerate of low-type commercial recreational establishments with correspondingly few wholesome recreational opportunities for growing youth, combine to produce an area of cultural discord and confusion.[44]

In themselves, however, the physical aspects of delinquency areas do not produce delinquency, no matter how they may augment such conditions. The vast majority of children residing in these areas do not become delinquents in the legal sense, nor even seriously maladjusted. Delinquency areas foster youthful misbehavior because of the character of the resident families and the nature of the circumstances that have brought them there, and *because of the opportunities these areas provide for illicit activity.* "Individuals who are forced to settle in such sections are already affected by the causal mechanisms productive of disorder; the disorganized nature of the community serves merely to intensify such latent capacities." [45]

How the specific institutions of a community of this kind serve to elicit these latent capacities has been well described by Carr, who suggests the basic causal mechanisms involved. Children who have been exposed to family conditions producing emotional disturbance and tension, or who, for a variety of family, developmental, and psychological reasons, are readily suggestible, may succumb to deviation pressures from the environment according to the *number, variety, continuity, direction,* and *intensity* of the disorganizing influences within the neighborhood.[46] Therefore, whether delinquency will occur at any given time, and whether it will be sustained as a continuing phase of the personality pattern, will basically depend upon whether the individual is "psychologically ready" for delinquent activity. If so, delinquency will occur if (1) he encounters adverse influences in the environment with sufficient frequency; (2) disorganizing influences make

[44] Thrasher, *Social Base Map, Local Neighborhood, New York City.*
[45] Bloch, *Disorganization,* p. 215.
[46] Carr, *Delinquency Control,* pp. 170-73.

themselves felt with sufficient variety to *continue* and *reinforce* the deviant trend; and if (3) the satisfactions these influences afford are pervasive and emotionally satisfying.

Therefore, it is a cardinal principle in delinquency control, which cannot be stressed often enough, to determine *when* the individual is psychologically vulnerable to the disorganizing influences of his environment. Since, under present conditions, it is virtually impossible to determine probabilities in each separate case, our best recourse is still to depend upon broad programs of recreation, parental education and guidance, and neighborhood rehabilitation, as means of forestalling delinquency on the part of the unknown vulnerable child; for there can be no doubt about one hard fact—that large numbers of these children live in such districts.

Peer-Age Groups and Associations

Although the mechanisms of neighborhood influences may be devious and indirect, the child's participation in the group activities of other children of his own age—the so-called *peer-age culture*—is a primary and direct factor in motivating many children toward delinquency. While it is regarded as a commonplace that the delinquent child rarely engages alone in his predatory activities, the significance of the close emotional tie with members of his own age group is only now beginning to be fully appreciated. (The "lone wolf" offender, although not uncommon, represents a peculiar type of specialized delinquency, one usually motivated by strongly disturbed emotional patterns or having a clearly psychopathological basis.)

Healy and Bronner have shown that 62 percent of the delinquents they studied carried on their activities in conjunction with companions or gang associates.[47] The significant fact is the extremely close association the youthful offender develops with other members of his group, manifested in the gang boys' code, and the profound emotional satisfaction these activities provide.[48]

The structure of the boys' gang and the stages through which its individual members pass in becoming welded into a closely knit and

[47] Healy and Bronner, *Delinquents and Criminals*, p. 179.
[48] Redl, "The Psychology of Gang Formation and the Treatment of Juvenile Delinquents."

well-integrated group have been carefully described by Thrasher in his study of 1,313 boys' gangs.[49] Although in deficient and unwholesome environments these associations assume a form that may prove dangerous to the boy and to the community, the motivations for such group patterns may be found on all social levels and in every area of American life. While the need for identification with the group may not be as intense in the middle class child as in the slum youth, pre-adolescent and adolescent groups seem to develop according to a specific pattern, described by Thrasher, beginning with spontaneous and random contacts and emerging in well-defined form, with specific structure, objectives, and leadership. Characteristic of all such peer-age groups are the intense feelings of loyalty they evoke and *the conflict and hostility they display toward outsiders.* This hostility is a channel already used by certain types of disturbed children for the expression of their aggressive tendencies, but *group* expression additionally affords the immunity of peer-age endorsement and protection. With the privileged child, the intense loyalty to his group does not necessarily lead to antisocial activities; with the underprivileged child, this intense concern with the group's status and *its conception of him* may automatically lead to predatory activities of a more or less serious nature.

It is not generally recognized that the strong impetus toward the formation of these groups, particularly among adolescents, is especially characteristic of American culture. Anthropologists such as Margaret Mead have shown that the storm and stress of adolescence, forcing young people to seek sanctuary in their own groups, is not necessarily typical of other parts of the world. Kingsley Davis, in his analysis of adolescent status in American society, has pointed out that the principal impetus toward the intense in-group loyalty of the teen-ager comes largely from the ambiguities the young person faces in the difficult transition from childhood to adulthood.[50] "Whatever the reasons," Newcomb has stated, "nearly all American investigators have agreed in stressing the eagerness with which most adolescents strive to conform to the standards of their own age groups." [51] In his study of adolescent behavior, Blos has shown the considerable power the group opinion of his peers exercises on the adolescent. He states that "the approval or

[49] Thrasher, *The Gang*, p. 57 ff.
[50] Davis, "Adolescence and the Social Structure."
[51] Newcomb, *Social Psychology*, p. 326.

disapproval of peers becomes progressively the most influential force in motivating adolescent conduct." [52] Virtually every investigator in the field of delinquency—the Gluecks, Healy and Bronner, Neumeyer, Cavan, and others—has attested to the significance of these group pressures in impelling the child's activity toward lawless patterns.

Thus, basically, the gang fulfills two important requirements for the delinquent boy. It provides (1) an ever-ready source of entertainment, recreation, and imaginative challenge; and (2) the elementary training in the skills required for successful predatory and unlawful activity. It is therefore both a recreational and an "educational" influence. However, in stressing these facts, we have not provided the entire picture. Recognizing that pressures toward peer-age activities are particularly powerful in American culture, we must discover the basic patterns in group association that support the child's impulsive tendencies to destructive activity and that enable him to compensate for the guilt feelings these activities may induce.

For the previously demoralized child, association with the illicit activites of the gang may constitute a normal transition in the process of growing up. However, the child who so far has had strongly conventional behavioral tendencies must receive different characteristic supports to enable him to engage in antisocial patterns. Fritz Redl has outlined the process by which specific interpersonal patterns and psychological qualities in the gang structure bring such variable supportive elements to the child's personality structure.[53] Moreover, as Hollingshead has intimated, identification with the gang may frequently be motivated by class feeling—the child's reaction against middle class standards from which he feels excluded—or, as Redl indicates, by his resentment of what he considers infringements upon his freedom by adults.[54]

The precise mechanisms involved in causing the child to identify himself closely with his peer-age group and those that free him from his inhibitions concerning illicit behavior reflect the powerful capacity of the in-group to provide a variety of sanctions to what may be highly individualized repressions and desires. By (1) demonstrating that the gang "can get away with murder," (2) providing psychological support

---

[52] Blos, *The Adolescent Personality.*
[53] Redl, "The Psychology of Gang Formation and the Treatment of Juvenile Delinquents"; Redl, "Group Emotion and Leadership."
[54] Hollingshead, *Elmstown's Youth*, pp. 204-23.

to the child's need for release from his tensions and uncertainties, and (3) offering "guilt insurance," by protecting the child with the group's *own* code of what is right and wrong, the gang associations provide a mighty bulwark for the child's ego and constant incitement to his uninhibited impulses. On the basis of these mechanisms, Redl has drawn the following conclusions:

> . . . "Gang psychology" enables the youngster to enjoy otherwise guilt-loaded or dangerous gratifications without the expense of guilt feeling and fear. It even offers him all the gratifications of "morality" at the same time: pride, moral indignation, the feeling of "being in the right" are still maintained, only they are carefully defined in terms of group code criteria.[55]

The School and Delinquency

By the time the child reaches school, his basic personality traits have already been formed, and many of the incipient and active tendencies to delinquency and waywardness have been well established. Moreover, even though the school can supervise the child for a major portion of his active day, it must contend with continuously operating factors in the community and the home, which may militate strongly against any effective procedure for the child's welfare that the school attempts to institute. The primary function of the school is still educational in the restricted sense: it imparts knowledge and intellectual and reasoning skills to enable the child to make practical adjustments to the type of world and community he will live in. Even in the recent trend toward "character education," the school is limited to certain types of formal procedures, usually applied in mass fashion, which may have but little value in helping a child overcome his emotional and behavioral difficulties.

School administrators, however, are becoming increasingly aware of the role of the school in accentuating delinquent traits originating outside the classroom, or even possibly in supplying the initial impetus toward active delinquency. Consequently, increasing recognition is now given the broader function of the school in studying, preventing, and assisting in the control of delinquency. Of this, Sampson G. Smith, an

---

[55] Redl, "The Psychology of Gang Formation and the Treatment of Juvenile Delinquents."

experienced school administrator, has said: "What a school does is determined by what a school believes its function to be."[56]

The school's primary contribution to delinquency arises from its presenting a series of frustrating situations to the child who already gives evidence of basic delinquent traits or possible trends toward maladjustment. Wickman has shown that teachers are often woefully deficient in understanding the dangerous behavioral symptoms manifesting themselves in the classroom. In rating their pupils, teachers tend to condemn outgoing or overt behavior as undesirable and to consider introverted and docile behavior the desired type of classroom deportment.[57] In either event, the reaction may be dangerous: in the first place, by intensifying what may be a malignant situation, and in the second, by failing to recognize a sinister latent tendency.

Children with emotional difficulties and delinquent tendencies manifest their disorders at an early stage of their formal schooling and are likely to continue their tensions throughout their limited school careers, as Kvaraceus, the Gluecks, Healy and Bronner, and others have demonstrated. With considerable uniformity the investigations of delinquents reveal consistent records of truancy, retardation, and antipathy toward school. Healy and Bronner have revealed that approximately 40 percent of the delinquents they investigated manifested an intense dislike of school, while an early Glueck study showed that approximately 25 percent gave evidence of a similar sentiment.[58] Of even greater significance in this respect is the Gluecks' recent investigation comparing delinquents and nondelinquents from similar environments; 88.5 percent of the delinquents showed marked dislike or indifference to school, as compared with 34.4 percent of the nondelinquents.[59] The reasons for such strong antipathy are highly revealing, *inability to learn, resentment of restriction and routine,* and *lack of interest* being offered, in that order, as the major reasons.

We must assume, therefore, that the schools early present deeply frustrating situations to many children with delinquent tendencies or with active delinquent disorders. This is probably best illustrated in the

---

[56] Smith, "The Schools and Delinquency."
[57] Wickman, *Children's Behavior and Teachers' Attitudes.*
[58] Healy and Bronner, *New Light on Delinquency and Its Treatment,* p. 62; Glueck, *One Thousand Juvenile Delinquents.*
[59] Glueck, *Unraveling Juvenile Delinquency,* p. 144.

records of truancy for delinquent children. With the delinquent child, truancy occurs early and persists throughout his school career, as against the later and intermittent truancy of the nondelinquent. This places a particular responsibility on the school since it is largely through truancy that most schools come to grips with the problem of delinquency. In a study by William C. Kvaraceus of 761 delinquent children referred to the Passaic Children's Bureau, it was found that 34 percent were truants, as compared to an over-all rate of 6.8 percent for the entire school population.[60] Actually, with a few notable exceptions, this rate for delinquents is lower than that found in most other investigations. Healy and Bronner report a truancy rate of 60 percent among delinquent children, while Fenton found that 52 percent of his delinquent cases were truants.[61] Bartlett, Nelson, and others also report high truancy rates in their studies of delinquents, while the New Jersey Juvenile Crime Commission, though reporting a rate of only 29 percent, estimates that if the records submitted for examination had been complete, the actual rate would have been in the vicinity of 66 percent.[62] According to the Gluecks, 94.8 percent of the delinquents in their most recent study "had truanted at one time or another during their school careers, while only 10.8 percent of the non-delinquents had truanted, and then only occasionally." [63]

The significance of truancy as a factor indicative of general social maladjustment, which is overlooked by the school until it is too late, is pointed up in one of the conclusions of the Passaic Children's Bureau study by Kvaraceus: *a third of the delinquents were known to have been truant prior to their referral for some misdemeanor.*[64] Irrespective of the individual motivations for truancy in the case of delinquents—and they are highly variable—it unquestionably arises mainly from their inability to countenance frustrating classroom situations and, because of emotional shortcomings, to develop a sense of responsible self-control in their relations to the school; the development of such an attitude of self-responsibility with regard to school functions is characteristic

[60] Kvaraceus, *Juvenile Delinquency and the School*, pp. 144-45.

[61] Healy and Bronner, *New Light on Delinquency*, p. 76; Fenton, *The Delinquent Boy and the Correctional School*, p. 66.

[62] Bartlett, "Personality Factors in Delinquency"; Nelson, *Prevailing Factors in Juvenile Delinquency in Brockton, Massachusetts*; *Justice and the Child in New Jersey*, p. 81.

[63] Glueck, *Unraveling Juvenile Delinquency*, p. 148.

[64] Kvaraceus, *Juvenile Delinquency and the School*, p. 155.

even of those children whose response to a normal school routine is considerably less than enthusiastic.

These emotional difficulties are highlighted in delinquent youngsters' characteristic record of failure, retardation, and subject-matter difficulties. It is too much to expect the already disturbed child to conform to the routines and regimen of the normal classroom. For the emotionally unimpaired child who suffers from learning difficulties, the impetus to delinquency can still be very real. The continual sense of frustration retardation gives at his school age-level and the failure to enlist his interest may bring about the same results. Failure to cope with a constantly irritating situation may release frustrated tendencies to aggression, the expression of which may find a ready outlet in the furtive freedom truancy and the examples set by truant companions offer, especially if the latter are emotionally disturbed children.

The unhappy record of persistent retardation of the delinquent child is painfully clear and appears to support these contentions. Kvaraceus accepts as an almost inevitable conclusion the fact that truancy and delinquency constitute an escape from conflict and failure in the classroom.[65] With regard to retardation, the early study of one thousand delinquents by the Gluecks shows that 84.5 percent of their cases had to repeat at least one year of school work, while Fenton reported that 47.5 percent of his group were retarded.[66] Mercer and Nelson, in separate studies, report rates of 56 and 57 percent respectively. The Gluecks' recent controlled study maintains that the mobility of the delinquents, placement in foster homes, and institutional commitments "do not completely account for the excessive repetition of grades, and marked backwardness in terms of achievement in relation to age and grade placements."[67] Virtually all the studies show high percentages of delinquents leaving school as soon as the mandatory age requirement in each state permits.

The dismal school records of delinquents, reflecting their generally frustrated reactions to the school situation, are further borne out in chronically poor levels of school performance. In the Passaic Children's Bureau study, "almost without exception, the delinquents were found to have received only failure or 'just passing' marks of P and M, the

[65] Kvaraceus, *Juvenile Delinquency and the School*, pp. 144-46.
[66] Glueck, *One Thousand Juvenile Delinquents*, pp. 87-88; Fenton, *The Delinquent Boy and the Correctional School*, p. 100.
[67] Glueck, *Unraveling Juvenile Delinquency*, p. 153.

two lowest marks on a five-point scale. . . ." [68] Percentagewise, over 98 percent fell into these categories as compared with approximately two-thirds of the nondelinquent children who received grades of "good" or better.

Additional light is shed on delinquents' maladjustment to school and their generally unstable mental state by their marked distaste for subject matter that demands strict logical reasoning, persistency of effort, and good memory. Although both delinquents and nondelinquents coming from similar environments show preference for manual training and a dislike for verbal discipline, delinquents' distaste for such studies as arithmetic, social studies, foreign languages, science, and commercial subjects were fairly well marked in the Glueck study.[69]

Reading deficiency has acquired some recent interest, as an early indication both of general maladjustment and delinquent trends. In view of the early stress upon reading skill as basic to the entire curriculum, reading is the first rigorous intellectual discipline that the maladjusted and potentially maladjusted child has to face. Emotionally disturbed children are very likely to react against such a discipline, and the resulting continuation of this basic deficiency will act as a chronic irritant and barrier to the child's entire subsequent educational program.

In effect, therefore, where the school contributes to delinquency, it does so largely by accentuating delinquent trends in children who are already predelinquent, actively delinquent, or emotionally disturbed. It has not been determined to what degree the school situation creates frustrations that render socially and economically deprived children, although otherwise balanced and integrated, susceptible to delinquency. Evidence indicates, however, that this is likely in a small percentage of cases.

Recreation and Delinquency

We have seen that, in general, delinquency manifests itself in two principal directions: through habitually violent and aggressive outlets under relatively controlled conditions and the refusal to conform to parental or other adult supervision (commonly classified in statutes as "ungovernable or unmanageable behavior"), or through the chronic

---

[68] Kvaraceus, *Juvenile Delinquency and the School*, p. 141.
[69] Glueck, *Unraveling Juvenile Delinquency*, p. 139.

abuse of leisure time in gang forays, petty thievery, and predatory neighborhood activities. That so much delinquency occurs in unsupervised free time has led many observers to believe that the misuse of leisure time is the principal cause of delinquency. In the well-known early Cleveland survey, Thurston came to the conclusion that 75 percent of the delinquents studied developed their behavioral difficulties through the habitual misuse of leisure time.[70] In a sense, this is less of a platitude than appears at first glance. It suggests that the innumerable opportunities for, and examples of, aggressive and lawless behavior in a "delinquency area" may readily provide children with delinquent tendencies living in such an area with the basis for habitual delinquent misconduct. The combination of motivation, provocation, and ample opportunity, *plus* lack of responsible adult supervision, may constitute a highly explosive and dangerous mixture.

Actually, however, statistically controlled research on the effects of different types of supervised and unsupervised recreation and leisure-time activities for different types of children has been extremely limited. The facts clearly reveal that not all children who have "habitually misused" their leisure, in the sense that this phrase is used by Thurston, become habitual or occasional delinquents, and that, conversely, many delinquents and nondelinquents who are exposed to well-organized civic recreational projects nevertheless either are seduced into or continue delinquent activity. The few fairly effective studies that have been undertaken in this field illustrate this point quite well, so that the utmost discretion is suggested in drawing conclusions that may appear flattering to civic bodies but that are hardly substantiated by the facts.

One of the most elaborate investigations undertaken in this field was the Chicago Recreation Commission study, launched under the chairmanship of the sociologist Ernest W. Burgess and carried out by Ethel Shanas.[71] Four well-defined "delinquency areas" and one control area were examined to determine the extent of participation of delinquent children in recreational programs and the variation in recreational preferences of delinquent and nondelinquent children. A total of 15,217 boys and 7,939 girls was examined during the course of the survey.

Although the study revealed that delinquents who attended recrea-

[70] Thurston, *Delinquency and Spare Time*, pp. 105-18.
[71] Shanas, *Recreation and Delinquency*.

tional projects committed fewer delinquencies than delinquents who did not participate, for what appears obvious reasons, it was *also* shown that delinquents spent more time in recreational projects *than nondelinquents*. The basically disturbed and maladjusted nature of the delinquent and the predelinquent has been interestingly demonstrated in this study by the character of the activities in which they engaged. Active delinquents and predelinquents *shunned* supervised activities, preferring active competitive sports and motion pictures. Moreover, their mobility from recreation center to center was considerably higher than that for nondelinquents. Since those who begin as nondelinquents in "delinquency areas" are not immune from the deviation pressures that create delinquency, it is interesting to note that the rate of later delinquency was three times as high for those who did *not* attend the original recreation centers as for those who did.

Can we claim even this meager triumph for organized recreation on the basis of the limited information we have? In view of our lack of evidence about the previous behavioral and familial histories of the nondelinquents who attended the recreation centers and those who did not, it is doubtful whether we can. Recent evidence provided by psychiatrists and group social workers makes it clear that habitual behavior mechanisms are not dissipated by exposure to organized leisure opportunities, but that these opportunities may, in fact, become the target for further aggression (as group social workers so well know) or serve as nothing more than painless interludes before the launching of further attacks on the community. The study by Frederic Thrasher has indicated how cautious we must be not to expect too much of even the best conceived recreational program. In a careful study of the functioning of a well-devised project, with adequate supervision and excellent physical facilities in an acutely disorganized area in New York City, he discovered that not only did this organization fail to make effective inroads on the rate of delinquency during four years of operation, but the incidence of delinquency was actually higher among members than nonmembers.[72] This was not necessarily a reflection on the organization or its program; it represented primarily the inability of one such agency to deal by *itself* with a problem of long standing.

Under the editorship of Arthur J. Todd, a voluminous five-volume research survey examined recreation carried on in Chicago during the

---

[72] Thrasher, "The Boys' Club and Juvenile Delinquency."

depression of the 1930's. Although conducted under the special circumstances of an economic depression, this report attempted to show that a paucity of adequate, supervised recreation and playground space is likely to foster delinquency.[73] A similar conclusion was drawn by Sullenger in a study conducted in Omaha some years before.[74] Although helpful, these surveys do not indicate the specific relationships that exist between behavioral patterns, adjusted and maladjusted, and specific types of recreation. Nevertheless, the evidence appears to show that the most successful recreation programs were those that were organized as phases of a wider program for community development.

We can draw certain limited conclusions from the evidence gathered thus far. The child with a lengthy history of delinquent activity, especially if it is accompanied by one of the common forms of psychological disability, may prove stubbornly resistant to corrective recreational programs. On the other hand, there can be little doubt of the deterrent value of these programs for an untold number of children in deprived areas whose circumstances dispose them to intermittent delinquent activity. There is no cynicism in stating that, aside from any therapeutic behavioral and psychological values that such programs may produce, periods of adult supervision obviously limit the time available for illicit behavior. This entire area is one in which a series of adequate studies of the *precise relationships* between developing personalities and the varied uses of leisure might prove of great benefit to the further study of delinquency.

The Mass Media of Communication and Delinquency

For the past two decades, the public has been particularly aroused about the possible dangers of popular media of communication such as motion pictures and radio, and, more recently, television and comic books, in their effects upon the young. Extreme claims and counter-claims have been made by both sides, frequently with very little substantive evidence to indicate the truth or falsity of one position or the other.

It is significant to note that those specially qualified to speak on the subject have been very cautious in making any positive statements about

[73] *Chicago Recreation Survey.*
[74] Sullenger, *Social Determinants of Juvenile Delinquency.*

the effects of these media on the demoralization of the young in general and on delinquency in particular. The loudest denunciatory outcries have come from civic leaders and those with only partial perspectives on the broad problem of delinquency, though the impact upon public opinion of this vociferous condemnation of motion pictures, radio and television programs, and comic books has been considerable.

Recently, the 83rd Congress, through a special subcommittee of the Senate Judiciary Committee, has been holding extensive hearings to determine the specific effects of these media on delinquency. Actually, however, the scope of the subcommittee's investigation has been far broader, taking into account the wide influence such channels of communication may have on much of our youthful population. Opinions from all quarters were heard—youth specialists of all kinds, mental health experts, leaders of civic and parents' organizations, religious leaders, radio and television executives, and comic book publishers—in an effort to determine what these media may be doing to our young. Although the subcommittee has not yet fully summarized its findings, we shall try to recapitulate here the principal conclusions that could be derived so far.

In analyzing the voluminous and detailed information it received, the subcommittee appears to have drawn the following tentative inferences. (1) Little, if anything, is actually known of the precise effects of the mass media on our youthful population, particularly with respect to possible incitement to delinquency. (2) Much of the present condemnation of these media, whether justified or not, is based on personal opinion and unbridled resentment, though there is also a considerable ground swell of general popular opinion against them. (3) The public should be given better information about the effect of these media on the developing mentality of children. (Witnesses of all shades of opinion repeatedly stressed the need for more adequate research and research subsidies.) (4) Given the tools of community action and an atmosphere of informed public opinion, alert citizens' groups might beneficially control radio and television programs and comic books. (5) It is likely, though not proved, that a demoralization of our youth in general, conceived in its broadest terms, results from its continual exposure to the spectacle of untrammelled sex and violence in our recreational media. (6) It would be dangerous to impose legal curbs or censorship on the mass media at this time, however warranted this may seem to be in some cases.[75] Certainly, the subcommittee, now under the chairmanship of Senator Estes Kefauver of Tennessee, should be commended for the objectivity of its report in so controversial a field.

It is important to appraise popular recreational media against the entire background of communication in a modern democratic society. Further, there are important side issues that inevitably arise in a discussion like this, such as the exposure of children to lurid journalism of the worst type (to which all children have access and which the Senate Subcommittee did not even examine), the question of pornography, the character of the literature children read apart from comic books, the exploitation of children by advertisers, the use of mailing lists obtained from comic book publishers and distributors to sell children items of a morally dubious and dangerous nature, and the impact of these media on popular audiences abroad.[76] These are only some of the significant questions that arise in discussions of the character of popular communication and recreation.

Americans have invariably been distrustful of any form of censorship, except when it is self-imposed and when it can be definitely proved that the censored matter is detrimental to the public welfare. This arises from the very nature of our democratic culture, composed as it is of a variety of minority groups with different customs and standards. However, no one cavils at censorship if it is shown that certain forms of entertainment, for example, are definitely injurious to the morals of young people. But it is most difficult to prove, either statistically or empirically, the danger of these forms of entertainment, at what stage in their lives children are affected, and precisely under what conditions these effects occur, regardless of how profound our suspicions may be. For radio, television, motion pictures, and comic books are but parts—and very intricate ones at that—of the interwoven

[75] This summary is based on a careful perusal of all the published hearings released thus far. For a good summarizing statement, see "Comic Books and Juvenile Delinquency."

[76] For example, a Communist magazine printed in East Germany, *U.S.A. im Wort und Bild* (*U.S.A. in Word and Picture*), caustically ridicules American comic books as an embodiment of American culture. Former ambassador to India Chester Bowles, in his recent book *Ambassador's Report* (p. 297), describes the horrified reaction of an Indian friend whose son had come into possession of an American comic book entitled *The Mongol Blood-Suckers*. See "Comic Books and Juvenile Delinquency." Experts in the field of public opinion have long shown how this becomes the basis for adverse stereotypes in public opinion.

fabric of society and the individual, and motivate individuals differently according to different needs, tensions, and attitudes. Each generation, we must remember, has been exposed to material which, in its day, was considered a serious threat to the moral and psychological well-being, of youth. While in our parents' and grandparents' day, it was the dime novel, the nineteenth century regarded with unconcealed suspicion the effect upon the young of the romantic novels of the period and the emerging novels of social criticism and realism, many of which are now accepted as major classics. Even today, when we examine some of our own juvenile classics, we have reason to believe that they may do much, under certain conditions, to disturb an emotionally distressed child. Even so celebrated a children's classic as Lewis Carroll's *Alice in Wonderland* is replete with accounts that may badly affect a disturbed youngster, giving expression to what many psychiatrists believe to be unrestrained sadism and cruelty. And under present conditions, when children can hardly be kept from reading in almost any daily newspaper lurid accounts—in all their licentious detail—of a variety of unsavory episodes, how can we clearly decide where to draw the line for reading material suitable for the young?

The very fact that certain children tend to select consistently the same types of recreational fare, be they in television programs, comic books, or other reading matter, is frequently indicative of some psychological disturbance in the child's make-up. Indeed, several witnesses before the Senate Subcommittee claimed that, since the child must be brought up in a world from which licentious sex experience and violence cannot be excluded, it would be foolhardy to insulate him completely from experiences he must inevitably encounter in some form as an adult. These critics, however, did not point out the significant difference there is between random and casual exposure to licentious and violent episodes as presented by the press, deplorable as this may be, and the entertainment media's studied cultivation of childish interests by deliberately contrived means—the process the psychiatrist Frederic Wertham refers to as "the seduction of the innocent." [77] The distinction is a basic one, and no society, particularly not a democracy, can be relieved of the duty of carefully guiding its children toward the eventual responsibility of making intelligent moral choices between what is wrong and what is individually and socially beneficial.

[77] Wertham, *The Seduction of the Innocent.*

What effect then can different types of recreational media have on differently constituted types of individuals? Theoretically, and on the basis of what substantiated evidence we have been able to gather so far, there are four types of effects we can expect, regardless of the medium in question. Since adverse effects depend on the given psychological constitution at a given time, the degree of suggestibility, the elements in a given situation, and the characteristic response-tendencies of the individual as a result of psychogenetic growth, the effect a given medium will have upon a child at a given time is likely to be one of the following.

(1) Depending upon the psychological constitution of the child and the immediate configuration of circumstances, the child may tend to *sublimate* his responses to the exciting and stimulating portrayal presented. In other words, he may be able to relieve many of his aggressive and antisocial tendencies vicariously by witnessing or reading about episodes of a violent or antisocial nature. (2) The entertainment experience the child is exposed to may merely *objectify* an experience completely alien to his own needs and background, or may simply stimulate and satisfy a curiosity that might otherwise not even have been aroused. In this respect, the entertainment medium has no other effect than that ordinarily taking place with an adult who witnesses, without apparent emotional disturbance, the strange and exotic tribal rite of a group of primitives. (3) In the case of a disturbed or delinquency-prone child, however, particularly in a highly suggestible state, the entertainment medium may intensify and activate a latent attitude toward a delinquent activity. Further, the content of the precipitating recreational experience might actually reinforce such a predisposing tendency by providing the child with information that may enable him to implement his antisocial tendency. Testifying before the Senate Subcommittee, Frederic Wertham stated: "I had no idea how one would go about stealing from a locker in Grand Central, but I have comic books which describe that in minute detail and I could go out now and do it." [78] (4) Even the child who is neither disturbed nor delinquency-prone may, in *critical periods of tension in his life*, become susceptible to influences of screen, radio, television, or comic books he might not have responded to if he had not been so exposed. Even the best adjusted of adults, however, may act embarrassingly, foolishly, or

[78] "Comic Books and Juvenile Delinquency."

even antisocially when going through critical periods of tension in their personal lives.

Of these four patterns of possible reaction, only the last two can be considered socially dangerous and injurious to the child's sense of restraint. Their greater danger also lies in the fact that children tend to lack the disciplined social inhibitions acquired by adults and the variety of alternative resources, personal and social, available to adults under tension.

Motion Pictures

From what has already been said, we can begin to anticipate the effects certain motion pictures might exercise upon certain types of children. To attempt to appraise these effects without considering the wide variety of differences among individual children and their different states of suggestibility would be nothing less than foolhardy. What we can do, however, and what has thus far been attempted, is to determine whether delinquents themselves may have been affected adversely by certain types of pictures.

The only comprehensive survey we have upon this subject is the ambitious Payne Fund Study, instituted a little over two decades ago under the sponsorship of the Motion Picture Council. This investigation included twelve separate studies dealing with various facets of the problem of the effects of motion pictures upon children. The study attempted to determine these effects upon delinquent and nondelinquent children of both sexes and utilized both questionnaires and case histories. Because of its heavy reliance on the statements of children themselves and its failure to employ adequate comparative controls, the study, although ambitious, gives little primary information of importance other than the attitudes of selected groups of children. Thus, it provides a limited insight into what certain groups of children, notably delinquent children, believe to have been the effects of motion pictures upon them.

In one of the principal volumes of the series, the study of Blumer and Hauser, it was revealed that of 368 male delinquents interviewed, only 10 percent believed that their delinquent activities could be directly attributed to motion pictures.[79] The fact that this percentage is so low

---

[79] Blumer and Hauser, *The Movies, Delinquency, and Crime.*

under the circumstances of the study may be regarded in itself as indicative of the limited part that motion pictures play in directly inciting to crime and delinquency. The general conclusion of this phase of the investigation, borne out by Blumer's companion study,[80] is the now widely accepted belief that only delinquency-prone and predisposed children are motivated to delinquency by such means. Blumer and Hauser suggest in their conclusion that the impression a film will make and its capacity to incite to action is a function of the total personality structure at a given time.[81]

With regard to the role of moving pictures as an instructional tool for children delinquent or strongly predisposed in that direction, the Blumer and Hauser study is far more specific and forthright. For example, 28 percent of the male delinquents indicated that the movies had taught them techniques of stealing, 21 percent claimed they had obtained knowledge of how to deceive the police, and 45 percent suggested that they were shown ways of obtaining "easy money" by the plots of pictures they had seen.[82] An actual confirmation of these statistics, suggestive as they appear to be, would require careful developmental studies of delinquent careers in action. Lacking corroborative evidence, we can only assume that moving pictures *may* have contributed to delinquent behavior for certain vulnerable children, while we keep reservations about the statements of others who claimed that they were adversely affected.

In the case of delinquent girls, of the 252 between the ages of fourteen and eighteen who were examined, 25 percent claimed that sexual relations with men were the direct outcome of seeing erotic scenes in the movies, 33 percent stated that they were encouraged to run away from home because of motion picture experiences, and 23 percent said that films were directly instrumental in bringing about the specific sex delinquency for which they were then institutionalized.[83] Because of the methods employed, and the character of the times and the conditions under which the study was made, we have reason to suspect the accuracy of these results without disclaiming the genuine possibility that certain girls may definitely have been affected adversely. This investigation, very likely the best we have to date, strongly underscores the

[80] Blumer, *Movies and Conduct.*
[81] Blumer and Hauser, *The Movies, Delinquency, and Crime,* p. 37.
[82] Blumer and Hauser, *The Movies, Delinquency, and Crime,* p. 71.
[83] Blumer and Hauser, *The Movies, Delinquency, and Crime,* p. 111.

need for research into this problem, with different methods, carefully controlled samples, and studies of developmental life histories.

In H. J. Forman's widely publicized popularization of the Payne Fund data, aspects of the effects of motion pictures were brought out which Blumer and Hauser had also strongly emphasized.[84] The setting up of false and artificial values for children in general, the low esthetic level of many of our films, their dubious moral quality, and their distorted sense of reality, all produce a dangerous and unrealistic attitude to which to expose youngsters, whether impressionable or not. Even though the precise effect of such spectacles has not yet been adequately measured, pictures based on these premises may well be laying the groundwork for a casual and more tolerant attitude toward the lowering of moral standards.

The fears inspired in the public by such a possibility have led certain religious groups, notably the well-known Catholic Legion of Decency, to classify certain films as objectionable and recommend non-attendance to church members. In some instances, this use of adverse publicity has been effective in curbing attendance. In other instances, attendance has possibly been increased by whetting the public curiosity as to the kind of film condemned. Different citizens' groups, including parent-teachers' organizations, community film councils, civic leagues, and women's clubs try, by a variety of information services, to alert parents and citizens to the unsuitability of many of our films for children. The Parents' Film Council and the Children's Film Library of the Motion Picture Association of America provide a valuable resource for information and guidance.

Television and Radio

Much of what has been said about motion pictures and youthful audiences and delinquency applies with equal force to television and radio. With the recent enormous increase in television reception in this country, there seems to have been a corresponding decrease in radio listening by youthful groups to programs other than musical broadcasts. It is likely, therefore, that radio will in the future figure far less prominently as a possible source of stimulation to juvenile disorders and maladjustments.

[84] Forman, *Our Movie Made Children.*

On the other hand, the more dramatic visual images of television and the ease of access to a variety of provocative programs makes the problem of television far more pressing. At the same time, when entertainment can enter into the family living room at the turn of a switch, it should render control and supervision by parents of what their children view much easier. A child's selection of certain types of programs is often highly indicative of his emotional state, while the clamorous protests of parents concerning the nature of the programs their children watch and the parents' inability to control the children's viewing habits are symptomatic of a dangerous loss of parental control in family life. At the same time, the indifference of many parents toward the viewing habits of their children is symptomatic of the failure to assume parental responsibility. Nevertheless, though the television set may be under direct parental control, the enormous psychological pressures by the child's peer-age associates and the telecaster, plus the ease with which programs can be turned on, makes modern television entertainment a formidable factor for good or for bad in American family life.

The growth of television facilities in this country has been phenomenal and, as with so many other modern technological innovations, the stunning impact of the problem has descended upon us before we could realize its implications. In 1946, there were only seven television stations in the United States, with an estimated viewing audience of a few thousand. Today we have more than 200 commercial television stations with an estimated 300 additional building permits already granted. The size of the modern television audience is shown in recent surveys revealing that there are approximately 25,000,000 television sets in the country today, and that they are located in homes housing approximately 80,000,000 people.[85] Significant in the growth of this audience is the great number of young children who spend considerable time watching television—as much time per week as that spent in school, according to one estimate. For example, in a survey made in 1953 in Chicago under the auspices of Northwestern University, more than 80 percent of the 4,000 elementary school children who were examined were regular television observers. Moreover, a high percentage of these children were in the highly impressionable lower age groups. A recent survey conducted by the United Parents' Association in New York

[85] *Hearings, Subcommittee to Investigate Juvenile Delinquency,* p. 3.

City revealed that children of five and six years of age are among the most persistent viewers of television, followed closely by children of elementary school age.

Several recent studies indicate that children of elementary school age devote anywhere from twenty-two to twenty-seven hours a week to watching television programs. Further, these same studies indicate that far from the decrease in television viewing that might have been ex· pected after the novelty of the medium had worn off, TV watching shows no sign of decreasing among children and, in fact, may be on the increase in some areas.[86]

As for the content of the programs, the emphasis upon acts or threats of violence is excessive. For example, in a monitored study of seven television stations in New York City by the National Association of Educational Broadcasters, during a single week in January, 1953, it was shown that 3,421 acts or threats of violence appeared on the programs of these stations—an average of 6.2 violent episodes an hour. During the so-called children's hour from five to seven p.m. each weekday, and on weekends from "sign on" until seven p.m., acts of violence appeared on an average of 15.2 times an hour, a rate approximately two and a half times the over-all rate for all programs. (This comparative rate of violence on children's programs may be still higher in view of the fact that the over-all average includes both children's and adult programs.) The Senate Subcommittee, in receiving this evidence, did recognize that a relatively high percentage of these acts or threats of violence were presented within a humorous context.

In attempting to estimate the effect of such programs, we have very little direct evidence other than the frequently conflicting opinions of so-called experts or evidence of a peripheral nature. Several years ago, for example, the American Bar Association organized a special committee, under the chairmanship of Arthur J. Freund, to study the effects of mass entertainment media upon law enforcement. It stated, among its conclusions, that "the vivid living portrayal of crime in the media has a profound impact on the mind of the juvenile, adolescent and impressionable, and grave harm has already resulted thereby to uncounted and perhaps uncountable members of our society." [87] However, it must be added that lawyers have not always been infallible in their

[86] *Hearings, Subcommittee to Investigate Juvenile Delinquency*, p. 4.
[87] Cited in *Hearings, Subcommittee to Investigate Juvenile Delinquency*, p. 7.

judgments on human nature and have been prone to render pontifical pronouncements in certain areas of human behavior in which sociologists and psychologists are far more cautious.

Some evidence of the effects television may have on children may be gained from two studies made some years ago which, while not dealing specifically with this medium, do concern themselves with related media. For example, Lucille Peterson and L. L. Thurston, in studying 4,000 school children to determine whether attitudes could be successfully modified by movies, discovered that substantial alterations of attitude took place after exposure to thirteen selected films. Tests were administered to these children to measure their attitudes toward specific areas, such as crime, punishment, and racial and nationality groups, both before and after the selected films were shown. Modifications of attitudes were noted even after more than eighteen months had elapsed from the initial showing of the films. It was likewise noted that the modified attitude became more deeply entrenched after repeated exposure to a given film content. Although it must be clearly recognized that an *expressed* attitude is quite different from its behavioral manifestation, such judgments are elements in the eventual transformation of behavior itself. Thus, if this investigation has broader validity, we may begin to exercise some concern regarding the eventual impact upon children who, night after night, watch television dramas that are replete with violence and whose general social and moral level is hardly uplifting.

In 1941 Mary Preston reported in the *Journal of Pediatrics* the results of a study of 200 school children with whom she had worked in a clinic. Of the 200 children, all of them physically and mentally normal, 116 were habitual viewers and listeners of movie and radio horror and crime programs. Among the several findings of her study, she showed far higher percentages of nervous and emotional disturbances among the movie- and radio-addicted children than among the others. For example, 76 percent of the addicted children showed more than average nervousness, as compared with 40 percent of the nonaddicted children. Also, 94 percent of the addicted children gave evidence of excessive fears, as compared with only 28 percent of the nonaddicted. Although this does not prove that movie, radio, or television crime and horror programs produce such adverse effects, it does suggest a close relationship between nervously predisposed children and entertainment of this type. Such viewing or listening appears to be symptomatic of emotional disturbances and very likely tends to intensify such conditions.

It is interesting to note, in conclusion, that the primary criticism of children's television programs originates with parents of the higher socio-economic levels. In the Communications Research Project of the National Council of Churches, released in 1954, under the direction of Everett C. Parker and David W. Barry, it was shown that parental attitudes toward children's television entertainment are conditioned by cultural, socio-economic, age, religious, and income factors, the more highly educated parents providing the greatest criticism. Yet, in over 3,500 households in New Haven, Connecticut, reported upon in this project, the majority of the parents interviewed (69 percent) generally approved the programs being offered their children. Although parents on all levels showed greater or lesser concern regarding the content of many of the programs, the predominant attitude seemed to be that the programs were generally entertaining and not necessarily detrimental to the mental health of the children. This would suggest, in any event, that unless a child becomes seriously impaired or otherwise involved in a behavioral difficulty, the average parent in at least one representative segment of the population is content to let well enough alone.

Comic Books

Very likely, of all the media of public entertainment for children, none has created the furor that the comic books have produced. More specifically, this refers primarily to comic books of the sensational crime and horror variety. In part this is a result of (1) the enormous growth of comic book publishing since 1940, allowing a longer period for their investigation by child experts, (2) the fact that for some time we have had a tradition concerning the examination of children's literature, and (3) the fact that a number of reports by specialists and psychiatrists have dealt exclusively with this issue.

The first of the present-day comic books was published in 1935 under the title *New Fun*, a sixty-four-page collection of original material printed in color. Shortly thereafter, *Action Comics* appeared (1938), and then *Superman Quarterly Magazine* (1939). In 1940, five years after the first appeared, there were at least 150 comic book titles published, grossing an annual revenue of over twenty million dollars. In 1950, approximately 300 comic books were published with an annual revenue of almost forty-one million dollars. Now there are over 650 comic books published annually with a gross annual income of approximately ninety million dollars. It is estimated that average monthly circulation increased from approximately 17 million copies in 1940 to about 68 million in 1953, about 400 percent in thirteen years. It is plain from these figures that young Americans in overwhelming numbers have become avid readers of the wild and bizarre antics of a wide variety of cartoon characters. It might be said in passing that not all of this interest is confined to youngsters.

It is interesting to note that with this phenomenal rise in the number of comic books since 1945, an increasing percentage each year has dealt almost exclusively with crime and horror material, conspicuously displaying sexually suggestive and sadistic drawings. In the words of the special Senate report on comic books and juvenile delinquency, "this increase of materials featuring brutality and violence is being offered to any child who has the 10-cent purchase price." [88] Also significant is the concentrated control of publication of these comic books, despite the large numbers annually being released. The 676 comic books now published are under the control of 111 corporations, but through interlocking ownership these comic books are actually published by 121 persons or families, with the exception of one corporation that has many stockholders.

The minimum issue of a comic book must be of at least 300,000 copies to make the venture profitable. On the estimate that there are 95,000 to 110,000 newsdealers in the country, this would mean that with a minimum issue each dealer would only have three copies as his share for distribution. Actually, however, press runs of 750,000 for a single issue are not uncommon. Frequently included in the bundles of comic books shipped by the wholesaler to the newsdealers are copies of sensational magazines, with such article titles as: "The Lady is a Man," "Sex Before Marriage," "I Sold Myself in the Marriage Racket," "Babes in Boyland," "Rica Rita—Pantie Model," "Sexie Tessie Up North," "Are Bosomy Beauties a Fad?" and similar edifying items. In its broad indictment of crime and horror comic books, and after analyzing in detail the content of such publications, the Senate Subcommittee came to the conclusion that these items "offer short courses in murder, mayhem,

---

[88] "Comic Books and Juvenile Delinquency."

robbery, rape, cannibalism, carnage, necrophilia, sex, sadism, masochism, and virtually every other form of crime, bestiality, and horror." [89] The studied techniques through which many of the comic books build up suspense by character, plot, and setting appear to epitomize for the child much of the tendency toward violence characteristic of our age. The coarse and brutal language serves to accentuate this nightmarish quality.

In appraising the effects of crime and horror comic books on the well-adjusted and normally law-abiding child, the majority opinion of reputable social scientists and psychologists clearly denies that such material may play a significant role in producing antisocial behavior. On the basis of our knowledge that there are no single causes of delinquency and that motivation toward delinquency involves a highly complex personality-situational configuration, we can only say that addiction to such material may act as a precipitating factor or, as a mere symptom, reveal the existence of a disturbed emotional state. Nevertheless, there are those who reject this point of view, despite the fact that the overwhelming majority of behavioral scientists who have expressed their opinions on the subject are frankly dubious about the adverse effects of comic book reading.

Frederic Wertham, the psychiatrist, who is regarded as the "leading crusader against comics," while claiming to reject the single factor theory of crime causation, nevertheless attributes a large proportion of juvenile crime to comic books.[90] Wertham's contentions, it should be noted, do not arise from any of the accepted research procedures ordinarily employed in the study of delinquency causation. Although he has declared that his conclusions are based on the study of thousands of children, none of this evidence has thus far been presented. The use of carefully drawn control groups, the *sine qua non* of any modern quantitative study of delinquency, has not been demonstrated by Wertham in his report on this problem, although he has claimed such a basis to his findings. In the absence of Wertham's presentation of acceptable evidence, we are forced to conclude that the cases he cites represent a limited and highly selective sample of disturbed children who either claim that they have been adversely affected or for whom, through psychiatric interpretation, such a claim may be made.

[89] "Comic Books and Juvenile Delinquency."
[90] Wertham, *Seduction of the Innocent*.

In an incisive attack upon those who have been making unwarranted or unsupported claims concerning the dangers inherent in comic books, Frederic M. Thrasher has illustrated the lack of acceptable research support for the extreme claims advanced.[91] Until recently, according to Thrasher, we have neither effectively proved or disproved the case against comic books. According to Thrasher, "it may be said that no acceptable evidence has been produced by Wertham or anyone else for the conclusion that the reading of comic magazines has, or has not, a significant relation to delinquent behavior." [92]

In its final appraisal of the voluminous data it has gathered, however, the Senate Subcommittee accepted the possibility that *emotionally disturbed* and *delinquency-prone* children may be adversely affected by such media. According to the Subcommittee, "There was substantial, although not unanimous, agreement among the experts that there may be detrimental and delinquency-producing effects upon both the emotionally disturbed child and the emotionally normal delinquent. Children of either type may gain suggestion, support, and sanction from reading crime and horror comics." [93] The reader should note that this conclusion refers only to the emotionally disturbed and delinquency-prone child. However, the Subcommittee voiced its concern for the welfare of the nation's youth as a whole who may be subverted by chronic exposure to meretricious and unwholesome recreational fare.

The interest of our young citizens would not be served by postponing all precautionary measures until the exact kind and degree of influence exerted by comic books upon children's behavior is fully determined through careful research. Sole responsibility for stimulating, formulating and carrying out such research cannot be assumed by parents' or citizens' groups. Rather it must also be assumed by the educational and social welfare agencies and organizations concerned.

In the meantime, the welfare of this nation's young makes it mandatory that all concerned unite in supporting sincere efforts of the industry to raise the standards of its products and in demanding adequate standards of decency and good taste. Nor should these united efforts be relaxed in the face of momentary gains. Continuing vigilance is essential in sustaining this effort.[94]

[91] Thrasher, "The Comics and Delinquency."
[92] Thrasher, "The Comics and Delinquency."
[93] "Comic Books and Juvenile Delinquency."
[94] "Comic Books and Juvenile Delinquency."

Substandard Economic Conditions

Poverty has invariably appeared to be associated with crime, delinquency, and other social disorders. However, for the vast majority of economically depressed groups, the truism, "to be poor but honest," has not been merely a figure of speech but a conclusion largely borne out by the facts. It appears that there are two essential questions to be answered here. In the first place, does a rapid decline of economic fortunes, or variability and uncertainty of economic position, tend to weaken the resistance of certain individuals to delinquency and crime, as von Hentig has suggested? [95] Secondly, are there certain invariable concomitants, or associated conditions of poverty, which in themselves tend to induce high yields of delinquency? Let us attempt to answer each of these queries in turn.

(1) Widespread changes in economic conditions, such as occur during a depression, have not tended to produce uniform results in matters of crime and delinquency. European criminologists, like Bonger and von Hentig, have tended to stress economic factors considerably in their studies of changing rates of delinquency and crime.[96]

The Dutch criminologist Bonger has shown rising rates of property offenses in England, Wales, France, and Germany, accompanying declines in earning and income levels of families. Similar conclusions have been drawn for Germany by von Hentig for the prolonged depression period in Germany after World War I. Neither of these writers, however, indicates that poverty or depressed economic conditions in themselves directly incite individuals to acts of lawlessness. Von Hentig, for example, merely points out that incentives to lawless activity are strengthened by the additional pressure economic strain imposes on the family and the individual.[97] Dorothy Swain Thomas's study of selected periods of economic crisis and prosperity in England indicates limited increases for certain types of offenses during periods of economic stress, although such rates are variable for different periods and for different types of offenses.[98]

[95] von Hentig, *Crime: Causes and Conditions*, pp. 225-26.
[96] Bonger, *Criminality and Economic Conditions*; von Hentig, *Crime: Causes and Conditions*, pp. 11, 225.
[97] von Hentig, *Crime: Causes and Conditions*, p. 11.
[98] Thomas, *Social Aspects of the Business Cycle*.

Studies in selected areas of the United States by Phelps and Winslow indicate higher rates of crime for dependent families and those on relief during the depression, although the figures are not high.[99] Whereas J. B. Maller, in a study of metropolitan New York, showed an increase in minor offenses during the depression of the 1930's, George B. Vold found no commensurate increase for the country as a whole.[100] A study of rural crime during the depression revealed a slight but not considerable over-all increase in youthful offenses, especially among lower middle class youths.[101]

Many of the foregoing studies are already dated; they were based on periods and special areas that do not apply to present conditions. The main drift of these studies, however, allows certain general conclusions. The factor of economic stress is always a relative condition, striking different families in different ways. Two points are worth noting: (1) Prolonged conditions of poverty do affect the complex of human relationships operating within a family, particularly with respect to the rearing of the child, by providing increased opportunity for impaired relationships to act adversely in community environments of great delinquency risk. (2) The economic factor is significant enough in American family life to produce drastic changes in human relationships for families whose economic basis of existence is suddenly transformed or modified. The resulting changes in attitude and motivation may prove an incitement to lawlessness for certain weakened families. As Cavan and Ranck have shown, however, some few families may be actually *strengthened* by economic adversity.[102]

(2) There is little doubt that the risks toward delinquency are considerably greater for children of families facing chronically depressed economic conditions. Aside from impairment to normal human functioning in such homes, the lives of both parents often show a background of neglect and poverty and the inevitable demoralizing situations brought about by poverty. In addition to the neglect and indifference toward children that poverty induces, when broken down into its component parts poverty implies a variety of specific situations danger-

[99] Phelps, "Cycle of Crime"; Winslow, "Relationship Between Employment and Crime Fluctuations as Shown by Massachusetts Statistics."

[100] Maller, "Juvenile Delinquency in New York City"; Vold, "The Amount and Nature of Crime."

[101] Bloch, "Economic Depression as a Factor in Rural Crime."

[102] Cavan and Ranck, *The Family and the Depression*, Chap. 7.

ous to the child: early employment in street trades, lack of organized routine in the home, child care by indifferent and irresponsible youthful siblings, overcrowding, lack of privacy, lack of parental supervision, and a host of other factors—any one of which, in itself, might prove hazardous to the youngster. In their early study, Breckenridge and Abbott showed that 75 percent of the delinquents appearing before the Cook County Court in Illinois came from homes described as "poor" or "very poor." [103] Because of differences in classification and the character of the sample employed, Healy and Bronner reported that only 27 percent of their cases (still a sizable percentage) came from economic conditions described as decidedly inferior.[104] In their analysis of the economic backgrounds of 925 families of delinquents, the Gluecks found that 76.3 percent came from either marginal or dependent homes, a result very similar to the findings of their earlier study of 500 criminal careers.[105] These studies also indicate the high percentage of such families on relief or receiving supplementary assistance of various kinds. Rarely is the income of such families derived from a single breadwinner, or even a few breadwinners, in the accustomed sense.

In their most recent controlled study, the Gluecks show that despite similarity of residence in underprivileged neighborhoods, the delinquents are economically less favored than the nondelinquents.[106] In addition to greater mobility, the delinquents' homes suffer more acutely from crowded conditions and a lack of cleanliness coupled with inadequate sanitary facilities. Further, a substantially greater proportion of delinquents belong to families on relief, with fewer breadwinners and more unskilled workers among them, and with a lower per capita income. The Gluecks likewise demonstrate that the families of delinquents reveal a far greater percentage of maternal and paternal backgrounds of poverty and dependency on relief for support. These backgrounds—*noted particularly among the families of delinquents' mothers* —thus contribute to a long-standing tradition of family demoralization.[107]

The vicissitudes to which delinquent children are exposed, after neglect in early child-rearing, are sufficient to invite and to aggravate

---

[103] Breckenridge and Abbott, *The Delinquent Child and the Home*, p. 72.
[104] Healy and Bronner, *Delinquents and Criminals*, p. 263.
[105] Glueck, *One Thousand Juvenile Delinquents*, p. 69.
[106] Glueck, *Unraveling Juvenile Delinquency*, p. 91.
[107] Glueck, *Unraveling Juvenile Delinquency*, pp. 93-94.

tendencies toward delinquency. The studies show, for example, that delinquency occurs three to ten times more frequently among children engaged in street trades than among those not so employed. As early as 1911, the Federal Children's Bureau disclosed that delinquency occurs four times more frequently among employed children than among unemployed. The substantiality of these hard facts has not changed appreciably since then.

As has been stated elsewhere, ". . . we must view poverty from the standpoint of those separate conditions it creates which disorganize the family process, particularly in their effects upon the child. Conditions of early child employment which, under certain aspects, are very likely to demoralize the child, or conditions of overcrowding in the home, or conditions which render it extremely difficult for the family to discharge its primary responsibilities of supervision, and other related factors in the *complex* of poverty, may have a direct bearing upon the waywardness of children." [108]

Environmental Factors: An Integrated View

We have now reviewed several of the specialized factors that operate as deviation pressures in motivating the individual toward delinquency. Concentration on such specialized pressures—family, economic, recreational, and the rest—makes it difficult for us to comprehend the problem of delinquency in its entirety. In our preoccupation with detail, we frequently lose sight of the grand plan, the major design. But is there a major design in delinquency? Is there an over-all picture or perspective that will enable us to gain an understanding of delinquency as a whole?

At the outset of our discussion, we attempted to provide some conception of causal processes in human behavior, how the personality operates. For example, we showed that for constitutional, social, and cultural reasons, certain behavioral tendencies are implanted within the child at an early age, usually by the time the child is six. The social and cultural forces operating in the life of the child affect his personal growth and development through the emotionally charged interpersonal relationships of the family environment. The characteristic behavior tendencies he develops as a result of these contacts cause him to

[108] Bloch, *Disorganization*, pp. 200-201.

respond more or less consistently to the recurrent conditions of his environment. We have shown that as the individual encounters sustained and disturbing frustrations in his later contacts with the environment, he tends to become highly suggestible, seeking outlets for his frustrated wish-drives. Whether he makes good or bad adjustments, whether he develops delinquent or nondelinquent habit patterns, will depend upon whether the social situations to which he is consistently exposed provide outlets that are socially endorsed or socially condemned during those suggestible periods when he is seeking release for his frustrated drives.

Of course, such a broad picture must, of necessity, be oversimplified. We have attempted to indicate, as well, that delinquents tend to fall into certain categories, although all categories, in their application to the endless diversity of human personality, tend to be self-defeating. However, for the clarification of our understanding and the organization of our research, we have shown that delinquents may fall into different categories, for example, the emotionally disturbed neurotic type; the aggressive, unsocialized delinquent; the seemingly undisturbed emotional type, the "socialized delinquent," and several others. However, whatever categories we devise, we must recognize the uniqueness of each child as well as the uniqueness of the social forces that have shaped him.

Nevertheless, when attempting to combine the factors we have analyzed, we find a remarkable similarity in the environmental patterns and designs that shape most of these children. We find striking resemblances in the configurations of similar family types, containing the same types of interpersonal patterns and tensions, fitting into common social and cultural contexts, and producing individuals with many like characteristics. We now stand on a new threshold of research in this area. Research today is attempting to "make the picture whole," to put together the several pieces of the jigsaw puzzle so as to present a complete picture. The recent research by Albert J. Reiss, Jr., to determine the social correlates of psychological types of delinquency, appears to be a significant step in this direction.[109]

An analysis of the court records of 1,110 white male juvenile delinquent probationers of the Cook County (Illinois) Juvenile Court for 1943 and 1944 revealed that the majority of these delinquents could

---

[109] Reiss, "Social Correlates of Psychological Types of Delinquency."

be classified into three major categories. Investigative data supplied by psychiatrists and social workers of the Institute for Juvenile Research disclosed three psychological types of delinquency: "(1) the relatively integrated delinquent; (2) the delinquent with markedly weak ego controls; (3) the delinquent with relatively defective superego controls." [110] It is not asserted, however, that these are the only classifications delinquents may fall into.

We have encountered the last two categories in our discussions of the various types of emotionally disturbed delinquents, of which the "acting-out" neurotic and the egocentric wayward child are examples (category 2 above); and the socialized delinquent, corresponding to category 3 above. The relatively integrated delinquent is a nonhabituated, intermittent delinquent, described by Reiss as "an adolescent with relatively integrated personal controls who in all probability will become a mature independent adult."

Significant in this report, however, are the comparatively well-defined social environmental patterns that accompany each type.[111]

(1) The *relatively integrated delinquent* generally comes from unsettled residential areas or areas productive of high delinquency rates, although his family is not excessively mobile. A family such as this is structurally intact; the parents maintain good marital relations and attempt to inculcate conventional moral ideals in their children through seemingly adequate techniques of supervision. The delinquent, however, is closely tied to his peer-age associates, although he gives evidence of good deportment in school, meets his age-level requirements, and, though he is a truant, is far less so than his more demoralized companions.

(2) The *defective superego delinquent*—our old acquaintance, the socialized delinquent—does not internalize the norms of conventional society and experiences little sense of guilt over his delinquent acts. Study of his personality structure reveals that he is closely identified with nonconventional social situations. Living in highly unstable semiresidential areas, the families of these children nevertheless move from these communities with relative infrequency. The families are large in size, with delinquent sibling members, and are characterized by a considerable degree of separation, divorce, desertion, and death of a

[110] Reiss, "Social Correlates of Psychological Types of Delinquency."
[111] Reiss, "Social Correlates of Psychological Types of Delinquency."

CHART 13 *Social Correlates of Three Major Psychological*

	1) THE RELATIVELY INTEGRATED DELINQUENT.
Personality Structure	Relatively integrated personal controls; will, in all probability, become a mature adult.
Residential Area Type	Less desirable residential areas, characterized by average or high delinquency rate; unstable & poor community controls.
FAMILY PATTERN — *Mobility*	Infrequent movement, mainly within same area.
Structure	Stable; good marital relations and conventional moral ideals; effective techniques of control over their children.
Orientation of Child	Close participation in peer–age culture.
EDUCATIONAL STATUS AND EXPERIENCE — *Extent of Schooling*	Generally leaves school at high school level, seeking employment in labor force where he is regularly employed. (Typical of low status class and income level). Grade level in keeping with age.
Truancy Record	Less often than other delinquent types.
General Deportment	Good. Scholarship pattern similar to other delinquent types.
OFFENSES — *Frequency***	Not significantly greater than other types.
*Types**	Burglary and larceny, especially automobiles. (Similar to defective superego type below.)
Group Character	One-time offender, or member of organized delinquent groups.
Average Age at Time of First Adjudication	15-16 years.
Recidivism	Less often than other two types. (Partially accounted for by higher initial age at time of adjudication?)

* Compare findings in Hewitt & Jenkins, *Fundamental Patterns of Maladjustment.*

Types of Delinquents

2) THE DEFECTIVE SUPEREGO DELINQUENT.	3) THE RELATIVELY WEAK EGO DELINQUENT.
Does not internalize conventional standards; oriented toward nonconventional groups and standards; little sense of guilt.	Insecure; highly aggressive and hostile; marked anxiety; considerable internal conflict; (frequently eldest child in small families.)
Areas of commerce, industry, rooming house and semi-residential.	Settled residential areas with adequate and conventional institutions.
Stable; infrequent movement.	High; both intra- and inter-community mobility.
Broken (separation, desertion, divorce, death); large number of siblings, many delinquent; parental conflict and hostility; lack of conventional moral ideas; ineffective control.	Unbroken; native-born parents. However, marked parental hostility and conflict, with little identification with conventional standards.
Usually member of gang; ready response to peer–age culture.	Not integrated to either family or peer–age group.
Generally does not complete grade school education; frequently found in elementary schools; overage in grade level.	Seldom leaves school; little employment, full or part-time.
High frequency.	High frequency.
Poor. Poor scholarship.	Poor. Average scholarship, although mostly on elementary grade level.
Not significantly greater than other types.	Not significantly greater than other types.
Burglary; characteristic offenses of organized delinquent groups.	Incorrigibility; destructiveness.
Readily suggestible to delinquent peer groups.	Least integrated toward peer–age culture.
Greatest frequency in very youthful age-category (12 years or less).	Tends to be in very youthful age-category (12 years or less).
Highest rate.	High, although not as high as category 2.

** Frequency of types of offenses in all three categories shows no appreciable difference. (Reiss, "Social Correlates of Psychological Types of Delinquency.")

parent. These children have school records that are uniformly poor in all respects, and they leave school for random, unskilled employment at the earliest opportunity. Of the three discussed, this type produces the highest rates of recidivism.

(3) The *relatively weak ego delinquent*—insecure, anxiety-ridden, and hostile—is found most often in stable and conventional residential areas. The families of these children are highly mobile and are marked by severe strains in marital relations and lacking concern for conventional standards. Delinquents frequently are the eldest children in small families. Their peer-age participation is limited, they are often "lone offenders," and while their scholarship is usually average, their school deportment is poor and they are often truant.

The chart on pages 226 and 227 summarizes the configurations of social and environmental traits found with considerable frequency for each of these delinquent types. Continuation of this kind of research should do much to help us not only to identify different types and the "typical" environments from which they come, but to help us develop an adequate prediction scale for the early detection of varieties of delinquency and recidivism.

Religion and Delinquency

Whenever the student of social maladjustment embarks on a study of the problem of religion and its effects on the human personality, whether beneficial or adverse, he finds himself operating in a highly delicate area where he is likely to offend the sensibilities of the religious and nonreligious alike. Still, the problem must be confronted honestly and forthrightly if we expect to find positive answers to the perplexing question of human waywardness.

An examination of the effects of religion on different individuals, and the specific relationship of religion to delinquency and crime, raises a number of highly complex issues relative to the nature of religious experience itself, the meaning of personality and human motivation, and the bearing of these factors on the totality of human experience and the social structure. These problems, which have harassed the minds of thinking men from the dawn of history, would take us far beyond the scope of this volume. Yet it is precisely on these topics that we have very limited empirical information. Those civic and religious authorities who are loudest in their fulminations against whoever seriously and sincerely questions the positive significance of formal religion as a deterrent to crime and delinquency frequently have little more to lend weight to their utterances than unsupported and unqualified opinion. It is difficult to stand up against the popular appeal of such leaders because of the deep roots of religion in our lives and the formal acceptance of religion as an essential phase of our total heritage. But empty response to the symbols of religion is one thing, while the deeply moving personal experience of religion that motivates people to lead better and ethical lives is another. Unfortunately, in this century, the two viewpoints are continually being confused.[112]

Certainly, the writers have the greatest respect for the enormous influence that religious training and institutions may exercise on the lives of modern men. This is far different, however, from making claims for the effectiveness of religious training and affiliation which, in the light of the best evidence available, remain unsupported by any facts gathered so far. Nor is the validity of the social effectiveness of religious affiliation and training strengthened further when supported by the untested opinion of even those seemingly well qualified to speak on the topic. When E. J. Cooley, one of our foremost early authorities on probation, states that "the most vital force in the upbuilding of the character of youth is the influence of religion and the church," we should listen with considerable respect to his seasoned judgment but must recognize that this assertion can be neither proved nor disproved.[113] This point of view is supported by virtually all writers in this field. As Murray and Flynn put it in their analysis of American social problems, "There is no scientific evidence regarding the effect of religion as such on crime." [114]

If we want to be entirely objective and scientific in our understanding of this complex human dilemma, we must remain alerted to the tendency of even the most respected institutions to arrogate to themselves credit for situations and human characteristics, both negative and positive, over which they may have had little effective control. It should be carefully noted that this does *not* mean that religious experi-

---

[112] Those interested in pursuing further the controversies in this area should refer to Coogan, "The Myth Mind in an Engineer's World," and the several rejoinders to this provocative article.
[113] Cooley, *Probation and Delinquency*, p. 14.
[114] Murray and Flynn, *Social Problems*, p. 471.

ence and training may not be one of the most significant forces, if not the most vital, in the social training of the individual.

Much of the difficulty in assessing the effectiveness of religious training is similar to that encountered in evaluating other institutional factors. What we are really studying in delinquency is the problem of human motivation and, as we have seen, motivation is a devious and complex affair involving a multitude of personality and environmental variables. The futility of mere correlation statistics in this area is pointed up by the tendency to establish relationships between such objective evidence as church attendance or religious affiliation and the extent of delinquency. For example, in eastern urban areas, with their high concentrations of Roman Catholics, it is not surprising to find positive correlations between such church membership and delinquency. When we gather statistics in rural areas, where there are high concentrations of Methodist and Baptist affiliations, we are likewise not surprised to find high positive correlations between Methodist-Baptist affiliation and delinquency rates. As the French sociologist Durkheim has shown, such simple correlations are meaningless without taking into account a wide variety of other variables, such as urban concentration, population differentials, economic conditions, age-levels, family structure, and ethnic composition. Nevertheless, many religious bodies are prone to employ the most superficial statistics of this type to prove or disprove a particular case.

Actually, the difficulty in this area lies in our trying to assess the effectiveness of an emotional experience unrelated to other factors in the lives of the individuals studied. Obviously, we first have to make a significant distinction between the formal outward shell of religion (including its ritualistic and ceremonial observances) and the kind of profound emotional experience closely related to many other aspects of the individual's total living experience. Then, we must examine the part the institutional patterns of religion play in the entire interwoven fabric of American social life.

If we consider the latter aspect carefully, as some able sociologists have done, we find a wide hiatus between, on the one hand, the major emphases in American life, focussing as they do principally upon economic considerations, and on the other, the functions of religious organizations.[115] As our society increases in specialization and complex-

---

[115] See, for example, Williams, *American Society*, Chaps. 6-8.

ity, we find increasingly that the major institutional patterns of oui social life tend to become dissociated from each other. In line with the value systems—such as the economic and the political—prevailing in our society, the crucial choices that each individual must make are often guided by considerations of expediency and likely immediate benefits. In effect, and simply stated, this means that many modern men tend to dissociate the formal aspects of their religious lives from the basic considerations of everyday living, despite the repeated lip service paid our religious responsibilities.

If we assume that motivation is the basis for any adequate study of delinquency, and that motivation is a highly complex affair, we must examine the character of religious participation and its claimed effects in deterring delinquency and crime. For the child, this participation is primarily formal, imposed as it is upon him for the most part by Sunday school attendance and religious worship in church and in the home. How effectively then do we reach delinquency-prone children by such means? Not very much so, if the discouraging evidence is correct. For, if such formal experience is to be effective as a delinquency deterrent, it must in the first place be psychologically meaningful and directly related to the critical experiences in the life of the child. Second, it must be psychologically reinforced by the child's primary group associations, the atmosphere provided by the home, the school, and a variety of direct community contacts. (For these reasons many religious groups favor the extension and promotion of parochial school education in which the school is intimately associated with the interrelated aspects of the child's social life.) Unless it is so reinforced, religious experience remains largely on an impersonal level with little or no direct relevance to the kind of moral choices the child faces. This appears to be substantiated by the best of our recent, although meager, evidence.

In his study of 761 delinquents in Passaic, New Jersey, W. C. Kvaraceus found that virtually all the children examined were affiliated with some church. Two-thirds were members of the Roman Catholic or Eastern Orthodox Churches, while apparently three-fourths attended church regularly or occasionally. In fact, only 6.8 percent claimed non-affiliation with any church, and only one-fourth claimed limited attendance at any church.[116] Yet all these children were delinquent. Studies

---

[116] Kvaraceus, *Juvenile Delinquency and the School*, pp. 101-3.

of prison and reformatory populations invariably show high percentages of inmates claiming membership in the major denominations. Indeed, in C. V. Dunn's study of twenty-seven penitentiaries and nineteen reform schools, 71.8 percent of the total population claimed membership in some organized religion, as contrasted at the time with 46.6 percent for the United States population as a whole.[117] Dunn stated that "there is no reliable evidence indicating whether religious affiliation, training or conviction does or does not aid in crime deterrence. . . . Indeed, we should first have to define carefully what was meant by the terms religion and crime." In most correctional institutions, inmates as matter of course indicate some religious preference or affiliation. Such affiliations, however, may be virtually meaningless. As Fathers Kolmer and Weir, chaplains at the Illinois State Penitentiary, have shown in their studies of inmates at Joliet, over 80 percent of the inmates registered as Catholic had not been practicing their religion.[118] Certainly this is no censure of organized religion as such. It simply means that the churches have encountered difficulty in coping with the seriously conflicting agencies of modern life that tend to neutralize or vitiate the fundamental tenets of religious teaching. It means further that the churches must develop a new dimension to their teaching, particularly for the young, and that they must learn to assume a wider community responsibility in reinforcing their teaching.

Nowhere has this been better illustrated than in the classic study by Hartshorne and May of the limited impression our formal moral teaching makes on the young.[119] In one sense, the findings of this celebrated study have never been seriously challenged. In the volume on *Studies in Deceit* especially, the authors attempted to determine precisely the effectiveness of various kinds of moral preachment and precept, as well as formal teaching, upon children. In attempting a general appraisal of differences in practicing moral behavior between children who attended Sunday school regularly and those who did not, Hartshorne and May actually found no essential differences. Further, as an interesting psychological commentary, they discovered that children exposed to a deliberately contrived form of moral education were more apt to cheat on examinations than those not given this special training. Para-

[117] Dunn, "The Church and Crime in the United States."
[118] Meyer, ed., *Crime and Religion*, p. 23.
[119] Hartshorne and May, *Studies in the Nature of Character*.

doxically, the tendency seemed to be that the more highly rated a child was on the "morality score," the more apt he was to resort to deceit. In attempting to measure the effectiveness of moral influences upon the child, with respect to the child's acceptance of moral judgments, the same authors found a correlation of +.55 between parents and children as compared with a correlation coefficient of +.002 between Sunday school teachers and children.

Motivation toward acceptable moral and social behavior, like any other type of motivation, depends upon the internalization of standards during the critical formative periods of childhood and is developed through close identification with parents, family members, and other significant primary-group figures. Much of this motivation is acquired unconsciously and depends in large degree upon behavioral examples rather than precept. In fact, church membership in certain instances may conceivably satisfy elements of the ego structure that are distinctly nonreligious, as in the case of individuals who join a church purely for social advancement. Effective church teaching reaches into the home and helps to articulate and broaden the child's sense of awareness of his moral responsibilities. Where the home has not provided such a moral basis, the task of organized religion must be conceived on a different basis, similar to the rehabilitative scope of other therapeutic agencies in the community. Certainly, in the latter case, neither preachment, exhortation, nor denunciation is sufficient.

Cultural Values and Delinquency

Any social problem, whether crime, divorce, excessive drinking, suicide, or delinquency, expresses something of the culture of which it is a part. Although delinquency is certainly not peculiar to America, the principal forms it assumes and its concentration in certain groups are direct reflections of the American social pattern. The offenses of delinquents constitute affronts to certain conventional standards of morality, propriety, and good taste which we associate with the basic patterns of American living. Although delinquency is no longer confined to lower economic class levels, it is still most frequent among depressed and marginal groups—in the main, those groups that appear to fall outside the general cultural stream.

In view of the heavier concentration of delinquency among certain groups, and the relative ease with which a delinquent tradition and a "delinquent way of life" develop among the children of depressed minorities, we can examine, as a factor in delinquency, the resistance of these groups to the acceptance of certain cultural standards. We frequently fail to recognize that the cultural standards of specific groups may differ considerably from the standards we assume to be universal for all Americans. Children immersed in one culture may be equipped with attitudes, points of view, and values that hinder or, in some cases, entirely prevent their successful adjustment to the larger community to which they belong. If a Negro child from the Deep South is suddenly removed to New York City or a Puerto Rican youngster is transplanted overnight from a tropical slum to a congested urban slum, the barriers his deeply rooted cultural training places in the way of his successful adjustment to the new environment may be greater than he can be reasonably expected to overcome.

Though it is the distinction and virtue of this democracy that we are a middle class country, bound and controlled mainly by middle class norms and standards, the recent work of Warner and Lunt has made us keenly aware of the differences in class structure in the United States and the distinctive value perspectives this involves for each class.[120] However, even if not reared in a middle class home, a child is judged and evaluated, and his opportunities for success gauged, largely on the basis of the prevalent middle class standard. Havighurst and Taba have shown in their study of the development of adolescent character and personality in American life how such differences of subcultural class factors function in giving the youth different expectancies, aspirations, and conceptions of success.[121] Teachers, public officials, and others, are continually asking non-middle class children to accept values, standards, and points of view which these children understand and appreciate but partially, if at all. Such children, as W. I. Thomas stated many years ago, are exposed to the "public culture" of American life but not its "private culture"—the outward symbols of our hopes, aspirations, and achievements, but not the deeply felt identifications and acceptances of the motives that contribute to the progress of American life. The indoctrination of such children—by the home, group,

---

[120] Warner and Lunt, *The Social Life of a Modern Community*; Warner and Lunt, *Democracy in Jonesville*.

[121] Havighurst and Taba, *Adolescent Character and Personality*.

or class—with values often running counter to the conventional pattern lays a fertile basis for variant codes of conduct, frequently delinquent. With ample support for her point of view in the well-documented research of E. W. Bakke on working class groups,[122] Margaret Mead describes this well in her analysis of the attitudes of working class children: "As class is an expression of economic success, then it follows that to belong as an adolescent in a class below others is a statement that one's parents have failed, that they did not make good. This is bad enough when they have not risen, unbearable if they have started to fall even lower. Deeper than our disapproval of any breaking of the ten commandments lies our conviction that failure to keep moving upward is an unforgivable sin." [123]

Significantly, the value standards of working class children and middle class children are quite widely separated: in effect, they express different philosophies of life, as Cohen, Allison Davis, Bakke, and others have demonstrated in their research.[124] Conspicuous in the working class outlook, and frequently internalized in the attitudes of working class children, are the intimate sharing with others, the lack of long-range goals, and the poorly articulated strivings for economic promotion and success. "Spend when you have it, charge it when you don't, and pay up back bills with whatever you can spare when you have it again," as Bakke summarizes it in his study.[125] Cohen has shown, in a comparative analysis of seventy-two working class children and forty-six middle class children, that differences in these value patterns are subtly absorbed by children and frequently become part of the adult way of life.[126]

The net result is that children from depressed minority groups (1) develop personality characteristics that are frequently quite different from those of more favorably placed children, and (2) are *reinforced* in these characteristics by an outlook deviating considerably from the conventionally accepted American pattern. This does not mean that such children must inevitably become delinquent, but it does mean that they are psychologically riper for delinquent roles and that their

[122] Bakke, *The Unemployed Worker.*
[123] Mead, *And Keep Your Powder Dry,* p. 197.
[124] See the review of this literature in Cohen, *Juvenile Delinquency and the Social Structure,* pp. 286 ff.
[125] Bakke, *The Unemployed Worker,* p. 24.
[126] Cohen, *Juvenile Delinquency and the Social Structure,* pp. 348 ff.

deviant cultural tradition will more readily tolerate group delinquent activities as a form of youthful adjustment. By virtue of a propitious cultural environment, these children are in a strategic position to become delinquent and, may we add, to enjoy their delinquency.

What we have said here points up the urgent necessity that all children be brought into the full bounty of American social life and values, or, to put it more simply, that American values be made *real* not only for certain favored children, but for our entire youth. The recalcitrance of many of our delinquents to reproof and admonishment by probation officers, police officials, and judges is unquestionably due very often to the dim grasp these delinquents have of the moral values that public functionaries try to convey. This lack of understanding results from either a failure in emotional rapport or from the kind of cultural disparity that actually makes it impossible for the child to understand what the counselling adult is trying to express, or from both of these causes.[127]

In summary, then, although many practical administrators may not sense it, this state of affairs sets one of the most difficult tasks of delinquency control in America, since, in effect, it requires reaching in some way the minds and emotions of delinquents in their most formative phases of development. The problem lies in reconciling the values stressed by American schools, churches, social agencies, and courts with the delinquent's private estimate of these values. Children, as May, Davis, Merton, and Havighurst have shown, absorb subtle emotional understanding of values from experiences they are deeply and closely involved in, regardless of any solemn public declarations made about what is best in American life for them and others.[128] The school and the church, tragically, and through no fault of their own, hardly touch these *felt* values of children in many cases. In addition, the values of different subgroups may help to strengthen the child's strong tendency to protest against what he considers, wrongly or rightly, as the hypocrisy and double-dealing of adults. To the socially and economically disenfranchised child, middle class values offer little comfort and have little relevance to a scale of living and aspiration quite different from what is perceived on safe adult, middle class levels. For such

---

[127] Barron, "Juvenile Delinquency and American Values."

[128] For a fuller exposition of this, see Chessman, *Cell 2455 Death Row*, esp. Chaps 6-11, the moving account of his own boyhood by a man sentenced to die in California's San Quentin Prison.

culturally deflected children, moving off in the slip stream of our stream-lined social order, delinquency is an answer and frequently, in their paradoxical search for status, a need.

For Further Reading

CARR, LOWELL J., *Delinquency Control* (revised edition, New York, 1950).

This volume still remains one of the better handbooks for information concerning primary factors conducing towards delinquency and for the practical implications it reveals for community control of this problem.

SHAW, CLIFFORD, *Delinquency Areas* (Chicago, 1929).

One of the original classics devoted to the ecological analysis of delinquency problems, with graphic descriptions of the demoralizing effects of disorganized areas in Chicago upon the young.

COULTER, CHARLES W., "Family Disorganization as a Causal Factor in Delinquency and Crime," in *Federal Probation*, 12 (September, 1948), pp. 13-17.

A statement concerning various types of family disorganization in their effects upon youthful maladjustment, valuable largely because of its emphasis of the interpersonal character of such breakdown and its change of focus from the frequently overemphasized physical features of the broken home.

SHAW, CLIFFORD, *Brothers in Crime* (Chicago, 1938).

An interesting series of comparative case studies of delinquent brothers in the same family, graphically illustrating the effects of intimate family contacts and a deteriorated neighborhood.

BARRON, MILTON L., "Juvenile Delinquency and American Values," in *American Sociological Review*, 16 (April, 1951), pp. 208-14.

In this study of certain significant American value systems, the author reveals the way in which they may contribute to the formation of delinquent practices among certain of our youth.

REDL, FRITZ, "The Psychology of Gang Formation and the Treatment of Juvenile Delinquents," in *The Psychoanalytic Study of the Child*, Vol. I (New York, 1945).

Unlike the standardized treatment of the gang process, the author reveals the way in which the youth's ego structure is maintained by gang participation.

KVARACEUS, WILLIAM C., *Juvenile Delinquency and the School* (Yonkers-on-Hudson, 1945).

> One of the few detailed investigations we have concerning the role of the school in contributing to and dealing with delinquent behavior, based upon the author's research among Passaic, New Jersey, school children.

SHANAS, ETHEL, *Recreation and Delinquency*, Chicago Recreation Commission (Chicago, 1942).

> A comprehensive survey undertaken by the Chicago Recreation Commission to determine the character of recreational participation by delinquents and nondelinquents in public community recreation projects and playgrounds.

"Comic Books and Juvenile Delinquency," *Interim Report of the Subcommittee to Investigate Juvenile Delinquency* (S. Res. 89 and S. Res. 190), (Washington, 1955).

> A good summarizing report of the investigation by the Senate Subcommittee under the chairmanship of Senator Estes Kefauver on the effects of comic books upon delinquent and nondelinquent children, impressive for its objectivity.

BLUMER, H., AND P. M. HAUSER, *The Movies, Delinquency and Crime* (New York, 1933).

> One of the few investigations available concerning the relationship of the motion pictures to delinquency and crime, and based upon questionnaires and case studies of delinquents of both sexes.

HARTSHORNE, HUGH, AND MARK A. MAY, *Studies in the Nature of Character*, 3 vols. (New York, 1928-30).

> A frequently-referred-to classical study in which the influence of various types of formal moral training and "character-building" are assessed to determine their effectiveness in the moral upbringing of our youth.

Part Three

TREATMENT AGENCIES

Chapter **9**

PRELIMINARY CONSIDERATIONS

It is clear from what has been said up to here that delinquency is a complex problem, not susceptible of easy solution. Consequently, the role of the treatment agencies in dealing with delinquency is especially important, and their capacity to deal with youngsters who get into difficulty is a matter of great concern to every community. In assessing the effectiveness of society's agencies for controlling delinquency, it is necessary to examine them for what their functions are supposed to be and how well they perform them.

While it is obvious that an evaluation of treatment agencies in this field is essentially concerned with identified delinquents, the community's responsibility for a total program to deal with the delinquency problem cannot be ignored. Therefore, before discussing the various specific agencies dealing with delinquents, such as the police, detention, the courts, and training schools, it seems desirable to consider briefly an over-all program containing the essential features of a broad community plan for activities. If the wider perspective is lost, no amount of focusing our view on specific agencies or programs will bring much insight to the basic problem.

According to the United States Children's Bureau, a complete program of community action would include the following:

(1) Strengthening of resources needed by all children.
(2) Protection of groups of children especially vulnerable to delinquency.
(3) Control of harmful influences in the community.
(4) Services for the delinquent child and the child with (other) behavior problems.[1]

A brief consideration of each of these recommendations will emphasize the importance of the relationship of the broad implications to specific fields of action.

"Strengthening of resources needed by all children" involves considerations affecting adequacy of income, home life, schooling, religious training, and recreation. In this area, incidentally, there is a great deal of confusion, brought on chiefly by the emphasis given to delinquency by many agencies and by those responsible for many programs whose concern is actually with all children and not especially with delinquent children. Often a housing or a recreational program is "sold" to the community on the grounds that it is preventing or "curing" delinquency, when actually it is doing a constructive and useful job simply by providing adequate housing and recreational facilities for children. In one community, a newly established boys' club reported an astounding 90 percent decrease in delinquency within one year, but later inquiry revealed that the statistics used were those of juvenile court cases. When the club began, the juvenile police officer assigned to the district referred virtually all cases of delinquency to the club. Because of this, the rosy statistical picture provided no real evidence of a decrease in delinquency *per se*. As would be expected, the condition described did not remain static very long; soon "delinquency" in the district was back to normal. At the other extreme are the agencies that boast of "never having had a child in court." If such statements contain any truth, the truth may indicate that the agencies or programs are not reaching the children in the community who are in need of the available resources. The point to keep in mind is that all children need decent home life in families that are economically and emotionally secure; they require education that takes into account their needs; they need opportunities for religious training; they need appropriate recreation and group activities. They need these things because they are children living in a democratic society, not because they are delinquent children. Considerations such as these do affect delinquency, in the broad sense that providing

[1] *Controlling Juvenile Delinquency*, p. 4.

the things that make for a normal, happy childhood inevitably influences the conduct patterns of children. But the case for making certain that children have the opportunity for normal growth and development is philosophically to be identified with our cultural and spiritual concern for children—not with delinquency as such.

"Protection of children especially vulnerable to delinquency" is an important but neglected function of our society. The vulnerable children are those who have mental and physical handicaps, who are living in extreme economic need, who have mothers who work, who are employed as child laborers, or who live in substandard, inadequate housing. It is quite true that many of the children in some of these categories are adequately provided for, but it is equally true that a significant number are not given the kind of care necessary for normal personality development. The mere fact that a child's mother is employed does not in itself indicate that the child is vulnerable to delinquency, but large numbers of children of working mothers are literally left to shift for themselves from the traditional school-closing hour until one or both parents return from work. This group—Agnes Meyer, noted Washington publisher, has aptly described them as "the latch-key children"— may well be without adult supervision for two to three hours each school day. It is difficult to place the blame here. Perhaps a mother would do better to remain at home to care for her children—but she may be widowed or divorced, or her husband may have deserted her. Or perhaps the wages of the husband and father are inadequate; despite improvements, a real living wage is not universal. Possibly the schools should do something about this, or possibly some other community agency should take up the slack. In any event, questions like these are largely unanswered, whether for the latch-key children or for any other disadvantaged group.

"Control of harmful influences in the community" is primarily, although not exclusively, the responsibility of the police. Although the term "harmful" involves a value-judgment, it is obvious that certain specific conditions are inimical to the welfare of children. Considerable attention has been paid to the widespread circulation of so-called harmful comic books; there has always been a smaller, perhaps more pernicious, distribution of pornographic literature; and the sale of intoxicants to children generally is condemned. These problems are far more difficult to control than is generally believed to be the case. For example, the use of fraudulent "proof-of-age" cards by teen-agers in buying liquor is relatively widespread; and in numerous instances there are pressures upon the police which make it very difficult to obtain convictions for violation of laws restricting sales of intoxicants.

"Services for delinquent children and other children with behavior problems" are the core of our concern with the juvenile offender in America today. While the services required by these children run the gamut from remedial reading classes in the schools to psychiatric child guidance clinics and family casework agencies, our chief interest here is in those treatment agencies specifically concerned with the delinquent child. These include such agencies as specialized programs in police departments, detention facilities, the courts, and training schools. In general, these agencies are distinguished by the fact that their attention is focused upon individual children. Children are frequently apprehended in groups or in so-called gangs, but once they are picked up it is necessary that they be recognized as individuals. It is axiomatic that in all cases treatment must be made based on the careful study and diagnosis of the individual needs of each child, and that treatment must be planned to deal with the specific causes of misbehavior so as to enable the child to develop the kind of personality necessary to cope with the demands of society. Treatment efforts must be coördinated with other constructive influences; if they are isolated they are bound to be ineffective.

The problems involved in providing resources for careful study and diagnosis, in making available necessary personnel for treatment of children who get into difficulty, and in supplying a coördinated, continuous program to deal with these children should not present an overwhelming task. Nevertheless, our society rarely has provided such facilities and resources. While there has been a great deal of attention devoted to the problem of juvenile delinquency, treatment agencies generally have not benefited from this concentrated concern. The search for the elusive panacea, the preoccupation with who is to blame for what, the shifting of responsibility from the home to the church to the school —all of these have had little real effect upon treatment agencies. Unquestionably, communities in recent years have been greatly aroused, concerned, and alarmed about juvenile delinquency, but there is no direct relationship between community concern on the one hand and provision of adequate treatment facilities on the other. Here and there some progress has been made, but in general it is completely out of proportion to the amount of alarm voiced by those who are ostensibly in positions of community leadership.

Why has progress in providing treatment facilities been so slow? Any analysis of this question should undertake to face some of the reality factors responsible for the great disparity between a community's intentions and its actual facilities. These factors may be grouped, rather arbitrarily, under four basic headings: (1) lack of knowledge, (2) confused public opinion, (3) absence of leadership, and (4) other obstacles in communities and agencies.

Lack of knowledge both of the causes of children's misbehavior and of how to treat existing difficulties is a specific reason for the lag between intention and action. The dynamics of human behavior are not yet completely understood; the term "mental hygiene" itself did not come into being until less than fifty years ago. It is also true that diagnostic skills generally are in advance of treatment abilities. As the preceding discussions of research studies have pointed out, there is little or no substantial evidence of the value of treatment as it is presently conceived. Even though the desirability of early treatment of difficulties is almost universally recognized, the simple fact is that youngsters who get into difficulty normally do not receive treatment help until long after their problems have been evident. When he is first referred to a juvenile court, a youngster may have been dealt with by the police four or five times, and inquiry by the juvenile court staff almost invariably brings out the fact that he was known as a problem in the schools several years before court referral. This fact points to one of the serious difficulties in present-day practice. Some children who present behavior problems in school do not become delinquent at a later period. Consequently, there is a real question as to whether we have the technical ability to identify children who are incipient delinquents at a point early enough to reach them with the treatment now available. If this raises questions in the minds of those whose hindsight tends to be better than their foresight, it may be countered by asking why some children fail to become delinquent when they present a series of problems that so often ultimately are identified with delinquent behavior. There seems to be some evidence that points to the possibility of recognizing the incipient delinquent, such as is presented in the Gluecks' *Unraveling Juvenile Delinquency*. Though we do not find this and other studies convincing, it is not suggested that research in this area is futile. Certainly it should be pursued to the utmost, even if, until now, various tests and projective techniques have not been validated thoroughly.

The confusion and conflict in public opinion has unfortunate results. Evidently the long road from private vengeance to public punishment to treatment has not been wide enough for all people to walk abreast. There are stragglers along the way, and the result is a confused public opinion in which the concept of fear is still relatively strong, and the notion of punishment, which has its origins deep in the Mosaic law, is a predominant factor even in today's discussions of this problem. While the "eye-for-an-eye" principle is rarely advocated at the present time, considerable attention is given to the deterrent effects of the "wood-shed" treatment, which is sometimes disguised as the so-called "shock therapy" of a brief jail term or even a sentence to a detention home. To a large extent this confusion accounts for the constant search for panaceas and the attempts to explain delinquency in terms of a monistic theory of causation. The recent attempts to blame parents for the delinquent acts of their children are typical of the current atmosphere. Advocacy of jail sentences for parents of delinquent children seems to have diminished in the past few years. Possibly the judges who utilized this device have become aware of the fact that thirty days in jail does not improve parent-child relationships, nor does it help the parent who has serious, difficult problems of his own.

The absence of intelligent leadership is a serious barrier to progress. Generally speaking, the legal profession, including that part of it which has direct contact with children who get into trouble, has contributed relatively little in the way of leadership which would stimulate and help formulate public opinion as to the need for adequate treatment resources. There are a few juvenile court judges who by force of their own personalities, and presumably because of deep underlying convictions about this problem, have had definite impact upon their own communities. But for the most part, these are exceptions to the general rule. It is generally recognized that service in a juvenile court is not likely to place one on the highroad to political success. Virtually no legal issues come before such a court, and to many persons prominent in the legal profession this type of experience is valueless or even tainted by misty-eyed idealism. A type of cultural lag operates here, attributable to some extent to the kind of education provided by law schools and emphasized by the reluctance with which judges accept assignment to the juvenile bench. One outstanding recent event may help to change this picture. Late in 1954, the National Probation and Parole Association received a substantial grant from the Ford Foundation which will enable the Association to make an appraisal of existing resources in a number of states. Another grant by the Babcock Foundation will assist the Association's Advisory Council of Judges to interpret probation needs to the community as a whole. This may well have a specific influence among developments in treatment resources, and it may provide the leadership which thus far the legal profession has failed to give in this important area.

Of course, the bar is not alone in its failure to exercise leadership in this field. The so-called leading citizens of most communities have failed to provide aggressive leadership. Although one could speculate indefinitely about the reasons for this, the basic cause may be that these community leaders lack adequate information about what the problem really is. Coupled with a basic fear of change, a typical reaction to many social problems, this lack of knowledge may well account for the inconsistency shown from time to time by prominent members of the community. For example, a luncheon club member, who proposed that several hundred dollars be set aside for youth activities, within the same hour inveighed bitterly against "the state's interference in children's work"—while condemning a proposal to provide expanded federal funds for child welfare services.

Certain other very real obstacles to improvement of treatment services exist. Only a few of these can be mentioned here, but some of them are discussed at greater length in subsequent chapters. Despite numerous and sincere efforts to change the situation, many families and many communities remain largely unaltered. Also, in effect, some communities tend to tolerate bad conditions and then insist on punishing the children who are the product of these conditions. As will be shown later, the structure of some of the specific treatment agencies makes it difficult to attract necessary personnel, and, above all, the salary situation throughout the country inevitably results in relatively few competent persons being attracted to these services.

This combination of absence of knowledge, conflict and confusion in public opinion, and lack of leadership, combined with the presence of other very real obstacles, tends to account in very large measure for the relatively slow progress in this field. The results, as far as treatment agencies are concerned, are underfinanced programs and overworked personnel. In the chapters that follow, various aspects of programs provided by the police, detention facilities, the courts, and the training schools will be considered. Without doubt, there have been some excellent improvements over the years in many of the agencies that fall within the categories mentioned. Nevertheless, the advances that have been made should not blind us to the reality facing most communities, namely, that despite occasional improvement in one or more of the categories to be considered, there is rarely found a uniform, continuous program of improvement extending through all the areas that deal with children in trouble. It is true that many communities are complacent about the programs as they now operate, but unfortunately there has been a tendency to conceal from the public the true shortcomings of some of the facilities under discussion. This clearly represents the failure of the administrators of these programs to make known their needs, or the failure of those responsible to pay attention to them. Often the result is that the agencies concerned present a façade that conceals the true situation from the public at large. Despite the presence here and there of adequate specialized juvenile control units in police departments, decent detention facilities, well-staffed juvenile courts, and training schools with dynamic programs, it is clear from all the evidence that these exist in relatively few places. Much more likely to be found are the undermanned specialized juvenile control unit, staffed by officers selected on some basis other than their ability to deal with youngsters in trouble; the detention facility that is merely a "cold storage" warehouse for children; the court that is overworked and undermanned; and the training school that is a junior prison. It should be emphasized that normally these conditions are not the deliberate intention or even the specific responsibility of any one person. On the contrary, most of those who are associated with these agencies are vitally concerned about the problems that beset them; but so overwhelming are the problems that little or nothing can be done about them. These conditions frequently put administrators and others responsible for such programs on the defensive, to the extent that the virtues of the programs are proclaimed and the faults ignored. Out of their own insecurity, the people responsible make statements which may sound well to the uninitiated, but which upon examination reveal gross inadequacies.

Altogether, this makes for a complex problem, and one that defies easy solution. Our examination of these treatment facilities should provide an adequate basis for forming critical judgments with respect to the programs under consideration. For this reason, special emphasis is placed on those areas that seem susceptible to early improvement. Nevertheless, one caution is required. Here, just as in all other complex social problems, complete reform cannot be expected overnight. Yet knowledge of the facts and their interrelationships must come before any real changes can take place.

For Further Reading

Controlling Juvenile Delinquency, U.S. Department of Labor, Children's Bureau, Pub. No. 301 (Washington, D.C., 1943).

A recommended plan for community action that provides an excellent framework for a practical analysis of the relationship between children's needs and the problem of juvenile delinquency. Its premises are vitally related to the basic theme of this section.

Recommended Standards for Services for Delinquent Children, U.S. Department of Health, Education, and Welfare, Children's Bureau (Washington, D.C., 1953).

This is a compendium of standards drawn from a variety of national agencies. Taken together, they provide acceptable criteria for many of the areas covered in this part of the book.

BECK, BERTRAM M., "Juvenile Delinquency," in *Social Work Year Book, 1954* (New York, 1954).

This is an unusually effective article by an able person, who was, when this was written, director of the Special Juvenile Delinquency Project associated with the Children's Bureau. The bibliography is excellent.

What's Happening to Delinquent Children in Your Town? U.S. Department of Labor, Children's Bureau (Washington, D.C., 1943).

An interesting popularized booklet that asks searching questions that every citizen should know about, and that every community should be able to answer.

Children and Youth at the Midcentury: Fact Finding Report, A Digest, Midcentury White House Conference on Children and Youth (Washington, D.C., 1950).

Taking the theme "For Every Child a Healthy Personality," this volume is a valuable summation of where we are in knowledge of human growth and development as well as a stimulating and provocative blueprint for social institutions.

Chapter **10**

THE ROLE OF THE POLICE

The police occupy a position of strategic importance in dealing with youngsters who get into trouble. The best estimates indicate that each year in the nation as a whole the police deal with well over 1,250,000 children who violate various state laws or municipal ordinances, or who in some way may be dealt with as juvenile delinquents. For a great variety of reasons, the police must exercise their own judgment as to which children will be referred to court. The juvenile courts, already overcrowded, simply cannot deal with all cases that come to the attention of the police, this in addition to the relatively trivial offenses handled by the police in summary fashion. According to federal Children's Bureau estimates, about three-fourths of the children dealt with by the police are not referred to court, although this proportion varies considerably from one jurisdiction to another.[1]

The Police as a Screening Agency

One of the most interesting issues in any discussion of the role of the police concerns their function as a screening agency. In effect, the police decide which children go to court and which children will be dealt with in some other fashion. In some jurisdictions, the police refer virtually

[1] *Some Facts about Juvenile Delinquency*, p. 5.

all children who have been involved in a delinquent act to the juvenile court; in other jurisdictions, only a relatively small proportion, 15 or 20 percent, are so referred. Even within one community, this is not necessarily a consistent pattern. A few years ago, one juvenile court reported a startling 40 percent one-year decrease in cases of delinquency, but inquiry disclosed the fact that the development of a new youth bureau in the police department was responsible for the drop. Instead of referring cases to the juvenile court, the bureau sent many children to other agencies or took responsibility for "adjusting" cases. In another community, an increase in the number of juvenile police officers resulted in larger numbers of referrals to the court and larger numbers officially dealt with by the police outside of the court, a jump in total cases obviously the reflection of increased police activity.

Likewise, there is no exact frame of reference that decides which youngsters are referred to the juvenile court or other agencies and which are dealt with by the police department itself. While it may be assumed that those who are brought to police attention for the more serious offenses in nearly all cases will be referred to court, relatively minor offenses are not so handled, though these offenses may be symptomatic of the need for serious attention on the part of a social agency, official or otherwise. Running away from home, for example, is considered by professional workers to be a symptom sufficiently serious to warrant careful examination of the circumstances surrounding the runaway; but in many police jurisdictions such cases are not referred to court unless the child repeatedly leaves his home. Despite the importance of the question, there is only one significant piece of research which gets into the important problem of the selective factors operating in the screening process through which some juvenile offenders are sent to court and others receive simple warnings. Dr. Nathan Goldman shows that the police base their reporting partly on the act of the offender and partly on the individual police officer's interpretation of the act and the degree of pressure applied by the community on the police. The attitudes of the community toward the offense and toward the offender and his family, as well as the police officer's private attitudes, his special experiences, and his own concern for status and prestige in the community, are important factors in determining whether a particular juvenile offender will be referred to the court.[2]

---

[2] Goldman, "Differential Selection of Juvenile Offenders for Court Appearance," especially pp. 185-89.

It is generally recognized that the responsibility of the police is to maintain the peace and to apprehend those who have broken the law. Within recent years, nevertheless, the functions of the police have been vastly expanded. Their responsibilities in the areas of licensing and the control of traffic are typical of this change. Unfortunately, the expansion of police responsibilities has not resulted in a corresponding increase in police personnel. Each new activity taken over by the police, with or without pressure from the public, generally means that personnel will be diverted from traditional functions to specialized duty.

The Police and Public Opinion

In recent years, the police have not had a good press, and in general police departments are waging an uphill fight to gain public confidence. Widespread revelations of graft in police departments; the general disregard for laws, indicated by the selective way in which Americans obey some laws and ignore others; allegations about police brutality; and the general prevalence of unsound personnel practices and administrative organization—all of these have created in the minds of the public a stereotype of the police which has resulted in underfinanced programs manned by frustrated personnel which make excellent targets for newspapers or other mediums of public information.

Unfortunately, many of the difficulties suggested really exist. When poor police morale exists, combined with the fact that only a relatively small proportion of major crimes are actually solved by the police— roughly one-fourth to one-third—the situation readily lends itself to truculence and defensiveness on the part of the police, and thence to unwillingness on the part of the public to support adequate police programs. Recognition of this dilemma is an important preface to any discussion of the operations of the police in connection with juveniles.

The police have many normal contacts with children through such activities as those dealing with missing persons, with truancy, with dance-hall supervision, with bicycle details, as well as in their regular operations on foot or in patrol cars. In addition, the trend in recent years has been toward the development of specialized police bureaus dealing with the juvenile problem. As the result of police activities in the sphere of juvenile delinquency, various questions have arisen concerning the appropriate functions of the police. Discussion of all of the various and complex programs that have arisen in this area is impossible, but it is possible to examine the more common patterns that have emerged.

Development of Specialized Juvenile Control Units

While the extent to which specialized juvenile control units have been developed in police departments in the country as a whole cannot be stated specifically, the most recent available statistics indicate that some degree of specialization is relatively widespread. A recent questionnaire study by the United States Children's Bureau, in coöperation with the International Association of Chiefs of Police, indicated the extent to which specialized units are used. Slightly less than one-half of the 502 urban areas with populations of 25,000 or more responded to the questionnaire. But the 247 reporting jurisdictions included 180 with juvenile specialists—less than 4 out of 10 of all jurisdictions, but over 7 out of 10 of those responding.[3] While these statistics are by no means conclusive, they demonstrate that numerous police departments consider it their responsibility to have a specialized program in this field.

Unfortunately, the statistics regarding the extent of specialization give us no indication of the quality of work being done, even though the Children's Bureau inquiry showed that 36 percent of the jurisdictions with juvenile specialists had special requirements for assignment to this work. Of the 109 jurisdictions reporting special requirements, for example, only 24 jurisdictions indicated that prerequisites included formal education over and above that required of police officers generally. As the report laconically states: "the nature of the requirements varies considerably." [4] Likewise, it is impossible to get an exact picture of the training programs provided for juvenile specialists after assignment. While some police departments have good general police training programs, and others may well have good in-service training programs for those assigned to juvenile work, no exact appraisal can be made. For example, in the Children's Bureau report a high proportion of jurisdictions report "assigned readings" as part of the in-service training program, but this kind of information is practically useless in any attempt to evaluate the quality of the personnel involved.

---

[3] *Police Services for Juveniles*, p. 67.
[4] *Police Services for Juveniles*, p. 79.

With some exceptions, the development of specialized juvenile control units throughout the country has been spotty with respect to both coverage and quality. There are some geographical differences, but the reasons for great variations in these programs cannot be attributed to geographical factors alone. For example, the Juvenile Bureau of the Chicago Police Department, which evolved from the assignment of so-called police probation officers to the Juvenile Court fifty years ago, had a relatively static existence from its beginning until a reorganization in 1950 doubled the size of the program. On the other hand, the police department of the Chicago Park District, an autonomous unit, created a Youth Bureau in 1946 which has become one of the outstanding units of its kind in the United States.

In examining the functions of the specialized juvenile control units, it is important to keep in mind that there is an astounding lack of similarity of functions from one community to another. This lack of uniformity even in a single department is graphically depicted by the numerous case stories in a study by Alfred J. Kahn, which, although perhaps unduly critical of the police, is the outstanding work of its kind.[5] As a result of this diversity and lack of correlation, it is necessary to generalize from the rather thin literature on the subject, including occasional annual reports.

Functions of Specialized Police Units

The special juvenile control units are variously named—juvenile aid bureau, youth bureau, and the like. Whatever the nomenclature, the services of these specialized units may be described under two general headings: (1) police services for allegedly delinquent or neglected children, and (2) preventive activities and related police programs. For the first of these categories, the chief problem is *how* the work is carried on, while for the second category, particularly in the so-called related police programs of a recreational character, often the question is whether the activity is a legitimate police function.

At the present time it is generally agreed that the method used by a police officer in his approach to a youngster in trouble may have seri-

---

[5] Kahn, *Police and Children*; see also Brennan, *The Prevention and Control of Juvenile Delinquency by Police Departments*, an interesting national survey of juvenile police activities, which likewise reveals great diversity among urban areas.

ous and definite implications. Whether a child is dealt with in a kindly and understanding manner, or is treated harshly and with abuse, may have lifelong results in terms of affecting his respect for law and order. Likewise, the success of the specialized police unit in sorting out the youngsters who are in need of further services from those who simply require a warning is likely to have significant consequences for the individual child's future. Kindliness and friendliness are of little value if the police lack sufficient sensitivity to select for appropriate referral children who need services that the police cannot provide. This problem is complicated seriously by the fact that in the vast majority of communities the police have the choice of merely warning a youngster in trouble or making a referral to the juvenile court. Referral to the court does not mean that there will be specific court action, or even a court hearing, since the problem may be adjusted at the intake desk with or without further inquiry. But it does mean that, because of overworked courts, a large number of children are dismissed with a warning either by the police or by the court staff, even though they need specific treatment from some appropriate agency.

In many communities, the problem described is accentuated by the absence of good public child welfare services and by the stringent intake policies of private agencies. It is necessary to face the fact that the great majority of voluntary agencies dealing with family and children's problems have intake policies which turn away many of these children who are in need of help, even if they are referred. Perhaps the most serious aspect of the problem is that even if intake policies were made flexible the private voluntary agencies could not possibly deal with all youngsters who get into difficulty. In 1954, the Chicago Police Department dealt with about 12,000 youngsters concerning whom an official record was made. Of this number, less than half were referred to the juvenile court. Those who are familiar with the situation confronting social agencies in communities such as Chicago, Los Angeles, Philadelphia, and New York know that the existing agencies could not absorb, even for exploration of the problems presented, the thousands of children involved.

The total effect of this situation is that many children who get into difficulty four or five times, because their offenses are relatively trivial, are dismissed with a warning to them and possibly to their parents, without further action being taken. When such a child gets into serious difficulty, it is not unlikely that those who know about the situation will raise the question of why the police did not refer the child to the juvenile court or to some other social agency. While the numerous and complex problems of the juvenile court will be examined in detail later, none is more serious than the lack of available personnel in relation to the numbers of children already being dealt with by the courts. Consequently, the police are faced with a dilemma which is not strictly speaking their own problem. On the one hand, they are expected not to refer large numbers of children to the court, and on the other hand, there is a paucity of resources available in other social agencies to which children might be referred.

It is important to emphasize this function of the police as a screening agency because the decisions made by the police with respect to referral to the courts, or to detention, or to other agencies, may be of the utmost importance in determining the ultimate welfare of a child. It is particularly unfortunate that, except for the rather simple criterion of the commission of a major offense, the police, even in specialized units, must rely largely upon common sense and instinct in determining which children should be sent to the court for official treatment. This is not to deny that many police officers, especially those in specialized units, exercise considerable skill and insight in making appropriate referrals. As a matter of fact, some of the police are extraordinarily competent in dealing with these questions. Nevertheless, in the absence of specific methods of selection for this type of important work and specific training for its responsibilities, one must be dubious about the total results.

The Police and Detention

The detention of juveniles presents a difficult decision for the police in many instances. There are relatively few specialized detention facilities that provide adequate programs, and jails continue to be used as places of detention for juveniles even though state laws frequently forbid such practices. Surveys and studies by the National Probation and Parole Association show with remarkable uniformity that many children are detained who do not require this form of treatment to insure their later presence in court. Too often detention means placing a child in "cold storage" for days or weeks or months, and once the decision has been made to place the child in detention his chances for staying there are relatively high. Obviously, it is a matter of convenience for the court and its staff to have a child located where he can be seen at the convenience of staff members; nevertheless, it is an all too frequent practice that children are detained sometimes for many weeks in order to obtain a psychological or psychiatric examination that could be provided on an out-patient basis. Thus the initial decision of the police in deciding whether detention should be used may have far-reaching effects upon the children involved.

The Police in the Treatment Role

While there is general agreement that specialized juvenile control units have responsibility for screening and for referral, there is considerable dispute as to the extent of their treatment responsibilities. On the one hand, it is urged that children who get into trouble present serious, unmet needs and that the police, acting in a treatment role, that is, dealing with the cases of individual delinquents, are simply filling a vacuum which would otherwise be intolerable. On the other hand, it is also urged that the police, because of the nature of their work, are not equipped to deal with youngsters on a treatment basis, and consequently this responsibility should be assumed by agencies properly staffed and equipped for such function. This represents a real problem, and the arguments made, simplified here for discussion's sake, have considerable merit on both sides of the question.

Undoubtedly, many juvenile control units exercise treatment functions on a somewhat limited scale, without recognizing that they are doing so. For example, one finds "unofficial probation" used by various police units, a youngster who has not been referred elsewhere being expected to report back to the police officer in charge of juvenile cases at periodic intervals, receiving friendly admonishment or even stern lectures with respect to his conduct. Naturally, a question arises here about the legal basis for police activities that resemble probation, since such children have not been adjudicated as delinquent in court. Yet the friendly intervention of the police in individual cases, extending far beyond screening and referral, may well be justified from the viewpoint of expediency. Despite the presence in the picture of councils of social agencies and other planning bodies, the fact remains that most communities simply do not provide adequate facilities for dealing with children who get into trouble. It may well be argued that the responsibilities of the police in the treatment area cannot be filled by those who do not possess requisite professional qualifications, particularly in the area of social casework, and it may be true also that blunders by unskilled, though interested, persons may cause serious damage to children. Yet it is altogether probable that children will not be harmed by the police any more than they are harmed by inadequate teachers or inadequate parents for that matter, and that some good may come from the situation.

A review of the salient facts concerned with this problem indicates that the burden of proof is upon the community agencies responsible for planning services for children. It has been suggested from time to time that police departments employ social workers either in a police or civilian capacity to deal with youngsters who get into trouble; but on the whole this proposal has not made very much headway, largely because of the structure of police departments generally. In a few instances, attempts have been made to get around this difficulty by providing some form of additional training, under departments of sociology or schools of social work, for police officers especially qualified by virtue of superior educational backgrounds. This seems to be an attempt to meet the problems involved on the basis of expediency and is for the most part a stopgap measure.

Nevertheless, the nub of the problem is that the functions of the police with respect to screening and referral require excellent diagnostic skills, and it is probable that even well-qualified members of juvenile control units should be content with dealing with individual case problems at the screening and referral levels, rather than engaging in treatment activities. In any event, the police should not be blamed for becoming involved in treatment roles, because they are simply responding to what seems to be an urgent and immediate need not otherwise being met in the community. The responsibility is that of the total community—not merely that of the police.

Police Philosophy Concerning Juvenile Offenders

Underlying police activities in this field is the type of philosophy that has been developed and accepted within a particular police department. If there is a harsh and punitive attitude toward youngsters, the presence of a specialized juvenile control unit within the department will not offset the damage that can be done by the other department members who are in day-to-day contact with children who get into difficulty. Consequently, it is extremely important that a sound philosophy, heavily imbued with protective attitudes toward children, determine the basic point of view of the entire police department, not merely of those who are especially assigned to juvenile work. Admittedly, this is very difficult to achieve, and unfortunately, the police often tend to react aggressively to the kinds of activity indulged in by delinquent children. In many ways they represent public opinion in the community, and acts of vandalism, for example, are likely to provoke an antagonistic reaction on the part of the police as well as other members of the community. When a gang of youngsters breaks into a schoolhouse, ransacks desks, tears up books and records, and splatters the walls with ink, the community becomes aroused, and so do the police. The question here is not whether the community or even the police should become aroused; rather it is the need to channel this concern into appropriate measures for dealing with the children in question, once they are apprehended. Vandalism of the kind described frequently brings the ire of the press down upon the heads of the police, who naturally become aroused and concerned. In such situations, the demands made upon the police in terms of objectivity are enormous, and the dilemma in which they find themselves is not to be treated lightly. Often they react in the "hard-boiled old fashioned" way.

As to the "old fashioned" way—Deutsch quotes the distinguished Milwaukee chief of police John W. Polcyn on this:

> The old methods of so-called stern justice and discipline—the strict and hard-boiled, gruff and growling youth-chasing policemen—have failed. The old police insistence on a pound of flesh for juvenile misconduct, bawling juveniles out and locking them up have not accomplished any favorable results. Rather they have developed fear and hatred toward the police among youth, and have, indeed, tended to increase juvenile crime.[6]

It is easy for the police to become antagonistic toward children and toward other agencies who deal with youngsters who get into trouble. For various reasons, arresting officers are frequently not informed of dis-

* Deutsch, The Trouble with Cops, p. 172.

positions of cases, and they rarely know the full circumstances surrounding the dispositions made by courts; and as a result, they may develop a frustrated, martyrdom-like attitude which takes the form of saying, "We knock ourselves out and endanger our lives apprehending some of these young hoodlums, and nothing ever gets done about it." If the police are going to develop progressive and intelligent attitudes toward juvenile offenders, it is obvious that agencies which deal with them have the responsibility of interpreting to the police the dispositions that are made. If the police are often ambivalent about delinquents, it may well be that they have not been kept informed and given reasonable interpretations of the functions of other agencies. Under the circumstances prevailing in most communities, the real wonder is that the attitudes of the police are as good as they are.

Police Preventive Activities

In addition to work with individual children, the police also have responsibilities for so-called prevention programs. These ordinarily take the form of control of harmful influences in the community, but in some instances the police have moved away from police work *per se* and have developed various athletic programs such as boys' clubs, summer camps, and other recreational activities. Presumably such programs arise from the notion that the police are thus seen by children in a role different from the traditional "ordering and forbidding" one; the provision of recreational activities in some police departments is believed to be an important public relations function, tending to show that the policeman is the child's friend and not his enemy.

There is no question at all concerning the responsibility of the police in supervision and control of the "danger spots" where children are likely to get into trouble. The poolroom of tradition, the candy store specializing in pornographic literature, the bar making illicit sales of liquor to minors—all of these are legitimate responsibilities of the police department. But in the development of specialized recreational activities many of the same issues arise that have been discussed previously with respect to individual treatment of children. The chief questions are of the ability of the police department to provide the kind of specialists equipped to do the job at hand, and of whether this is legitimately a police function. There is also the issue of whether the police department, already overburdened, should enter into activities which further deplete manpower. Careful consideration leads inevitably to a conclusion similar to that reached with respect to programs involving treatment of individual delinquents, namely, that generally speaking this is not a police function but rather a community responsibility that should be accepted by or diverted to agencies especially equipped to deal with this kind of problem. Mention should be made in passing that unquestionably some of the recreational-type programs began as the result of community pressures, especially identified with the desire of the police to "do something" about the delinquency problem. Presumably, in some instances, they originated in the desire of a particular police official for personal glory and publicity. But whatever the background, the fact remains that the police, in operating programs geared to their traditional responsibilities, have more than enough to do under normal conditions in most communities, and their thinly spread manpower might be utilized to better purposes if they confined themselves to activities within their own scope.

One of the unfortunate developments of recent years has been the increasing use of the patrol car and the virtual disappearance of the beat patrolman in most communities. While a complete review of this issue is not feasible here, it should be mentioned that the so-called old-fashioned beat patrolman tended to have a rather close contact with the immediate community that he patrolled on foot. There seems today to be a resurgence of interest in the function of the beat patrolman which might lead to improvement. Experiments with expanded use of foot patrolmen have been carried out in a number of communities. A current New York experiment—Operation 25—which involves a virtual saturation of one difficult police district with foot police, is being watched with interest, although its results are not yet certain.

There are numerous specific problems in police work with juveniles, problems involving the use of officers in uniform, the kinds of interrogation practiced, the use of marked automobiles for transporting juvenile offenders, and the like, but these need not be discussed here.[5] However, one issue, that of fingerprinting, deserves some attention because it is a subject of frequent controversy.[7]

[7] *Report on Role of Police.*

Fingerprinting and Related Problems

Perhaps the most pertinent argument against fingerprinting is the possibility of discrimination against a child who has been fingerprinted, either by the armed services or by the personnel departments of employers. On the other hand, to counter this argument, it is urged by some that fingerprints are becoming a commonplace, that they do not therefore constitute a psychological identification of the child with criminals generally, and that fingerprints are the only certain means of identification.

But if procedures for dealing with youngsters who get into difficulty are to be used to protect them as well as the community, it seems obvious that two important safeguards must be placed around fingerprinting: (1) fingerprints should never be taken unless there is a sound basis for using them, such as where they are needed to identify a child who refuses to reveal his name, or where they constitute vital evidence in a very serious crime; and (2) when fingerprints are taken and there is real evidence that the child whose prints were taken is not involved in a serious crime, the prints should be destroyed by official action.[8] When the arguments for and against are balanced it seems logical to follow at least these minimum safeguards. It seems clear that any other course will inevitably have untoward effects upon children who get into trouble. The same general principles apply to photographs, although their use is considerably less frequent than the use of fingerprints.

Training Juvenile Police Staff

The most important single development in training police officers for work with juveniles has been the Delinquency Control Institute operated under the direction of the School of Public Administration of the University of Southern California. This program began in 1946 after more than two years of intensive planning and research by police officials and various divisions of the university, including the schools of law, education, and social work. It operates on the basis of two twelve-

[8] *Police Services for Juveniles*, esp. pp. 27-31; see also Kenney and Pursuit, *Police Work with Juveniles*, pp. 102-103.

week sessions each year. Participating officers are limited to twenty for any one class, and they spend full time in residence at the university, where they are exposed to an intensive and varied curriculum, drawn from various parts of the university. Officers trained under this program have had an extremely significant impact, especially in California and other western states. Although police officers from other states may and do enroll in this program, there is a heavy concentration in California, which without question has the greatest incidence of specialized units when compared with all of the other states of the Union.

Students are carefully selected on the basis of academic and personal qualifications. Full scholarships are available, but an important feature is that the students are selected from police departments which keep them on full salary for the duration of the program. The latter is significant, because it indicates a definite interest on the part of the police departments in question, and it gives some assurance that the training actually will be used later.

The curriculum includes social treatment, aspects of delinquency control, special police techniques, conditioning factors in juvenile delinquency, administrative aspects of delinquency control, delinquency prevention techniques, techniques of learning and teaching, legal aspects of delinquency prevention, clinics in delinquency control, public speaking, growth and change, interviewing, and field work, which is provided for one day each week, generally in nearby juvenile bureaus.[9]

Since the inception of this program, the Delinquency Control Institute has been acclaimed the outstanding training facility in the entire United States, but despite this its extensive program has not been duplicated elsewhere, even though some universities, such as Louisville, Michigan State and Rutgers have police training programs. Obviously, the concentration of a program of this kind on the Pacific Coast has its limitations, and one of the great possibilities for the future lies in the development of a series of regional programs of a similar nature, perhaps embodying the basic curriculum content of the Delinquency Control Institute, but situated strategically in various parts of the country. In any twelve-week program, the cost of transportation is an important factor, and the obvious need for close coöperation between Institute staff and persons in the operating field means that while the Institute

[9] *Progress Report of the Delinquency Control Institute;* and Kenney and Pursuit, *Police Work with Juveniles.*

is known and used on the Pacific Coast, there is little identification with it in other parts of the country.

In 1949, the cost of operating the Delinquency Control Institute ranged from $450 to $600 for each student, excluding certain travel and subsistence allowances. Presumably, costs are higher now. While the Institute has been successful in obtaining foundation support, this seems to be a case in which there is need for financial support from the public treasury, logically from the federal government. The Police Academy of the Federal Bureau of Investigation already spends money for training local police officers, and an extension of such expenditures, using university facilities and staffs, would seem to be indicated. Although many police departments have training programs and even special training programs for juvenile police work, the fact is that the Delinquency Control Institute program seems to be far more intensive and extensive than anything offered by any single police department in the United States. When one considers the demands that are made upon the police, and the relatively inadequate police training provided, even for patrol duties, it becomes realistic to look for federal concern with this problem and some subvention of universities which have sufficiently varied resources to carry on a program similar to that of the Delinquency Control Institute.

It is increasingly clear that the role of the police in dealing with juvenile offenders against the law is becoming identified with the growth of specialized juvenile control units. Nevertheless, there are many unanswered questions, even though the case for a limited screening and referral function seems to be a strong one. Certainly the main concern of juvenile police work is to deal in an understanding and constructive way with those children who come to the attention of the police and to identify, locate and correct conditions which may lead to delinquency.

The great responsibilities involved in screening and referral, especially the need for superior diagnostic skills, suggest that only a vital concern with training will provide the appropriate background for improvement. If we persist in our naïve views about local autonomy, the road to improvement will be a long and hard one. But if we see the possibilities of help from federal funds for training juvenile police officers, we may move ahead rapidly. The police are the largest single agency dealing with children in trouble. Their importance cannot be overemphasized. Therefore, specialized units of adequate size and quality, under the leadership of competent commanding officers with prestige, can be described as a minimum essential for all police departments.

For Further Reading

Police Services for Juveniles, U.S. Department of Health, Education and Welfare, Children's Bureau, Pub. No. 344 (Washington, D.C., 1954).

> A summary of the proceedings of the Lansing Conference, jointly sponsored by the Bureau and the International Association of Chiefs of Police. This review of the most significant problems in this field is accompanied by the best analysis available to date of the extent of specialization by the police in juvenile problems.

KENNEY, JOHN P., AND DAN G. PURSUIT, *Police Work with Juveniles* (Springfield, Illinois, 1954).

> An extensive discussion of the responsibilities of the police in dealing with juveniles, containing a good summary of the police training program of the Delinquency Control Institute, University of Southern California.

KAHN, ALFRED J., *Police and Children: A Study of the Juvenile Aid Bureau of the New York City Police Department,* Citizens' Committee on Children of New York City, Inc. (New York, 1951).

> A careful, although perhaps overly critical, critique of the largest program of its kind. Its many case illustrations make it an interesting, provocative analysis.

Report on Role of Police, National Conference on Prevention and Control of Juvenile Delinquency (Washington, D.C., 1947).

> Discusses the arguments for and against many controversial police practices, such as photographing, fingerprinting, and the like. As in numerous conference reports, there is a dearth of definitive conclusions.

BRENNAN, JAMES J., *The Prevention and Control of Juvenile Delinquency by Police Departments* (New York, 1952).

> This is an interesting survey of actual programs operated by urban police departments by a man with long practical experience in juvenile bureau work.

Chapter 11

JUVENILE DETENTION

The detention of children who require temporary care either in secure custody or in some form of shelter, prior to court action or their return to another jurisdiction, is one of the most complex and difficult questions facing American communities today. As an examination of the multiple factors involved will demonstrate, this question cannot be solved easily, and there is no ready-made formula that can be applied to communities generally. In fact, the very persistence of the problem unquestionably demonstrates its perplexing ramifications, as well as the characteristic apathy and indifference on the part of those who should be concerned especially with its solution. This question involves such issues as the kinds of children detained, the type of facilities used, the manner in which they are used, their location, design and construction, and particularly, suitable personnel and program.

One of the unique features of the contemporary detention problem is the fact that only one agency, the privately supported National Probation and Parole Association, has been actively and consistently concerned with the problem during the past decade. The detention specialist of the Association, Mr. Sherwood Norman, is the only person in the United States who has devoted a substantial part of his professional career to a community-by-community study of this single problem. Unless otherwise indicated, the material in this chapter is drawn largely from the writings and addresses of Mr. Norman. Naturally, the responsibility for the interpretation of his materials is entirely that of the authors.

In the past, detention usually has been defined as the temporary care of a child removed from his own home pending investigation and action by the juvenile court; but in recent years a definite distinction has been made between detention *per se* and shelter care. Currently, *detention* is defined as the temporary care of children who require secure custody in physically restricted facilities prior to investigation and disposition; *shelter care* has essentially the same function, but it is reserved for those children, placed voluntarily or authoritatively, who do not require secure custody pending return to their own homes or placement for longer term care. The distinction is extremely important, because issues involving custody affect both the nature of the detention facility itself, and also the length of stay in the facility. The chief resemblance is that both are *temporary*; beyond that, detention and shelter care have little in common. Our chief concern in this chapter is with detention as secure custody, but in numerous aspects of the question the line between detention and shelter care is blurred, chiefly because practice has not caught up with the changed distinctions between the two.

Before considering some of the specific issues associated with secure detention of children in specialized facilities designed to a greater or lesser degree for that purpose only, it should be pointed out that large numbers of children actually are still detained in jails rather than in specialized facilities. According to best estimates, there are less than 200 specialized detention facilities in the entire United States, although there are at least 2,500 juvenile courts, which presumably have some kind of need for detention programs. While it is quite true that some communities do not use detention at all or use it very infrequently, there are many hundreds of jurisdictions in which the jail is the only resource when detention is considered necessary.

The Size of the Problem

One of the unfortunate aspects of the detention problem is that there are no exact statistics on its dimensions. We simply do not know either how many children are detained each year or in what kind of facilities they are placed. At least 50,000 children of juvenile court age, which is generally ten to seventeen years, are detained in jails, although some estimates place the number closer to 100,000. Including specialized detention facilities, the number detained probably ranges from 250,000 to 300,000 a year. In April, 1950, a one-day check by census enumerators showed 1,244 children under nineteen years of age in detention homes, and 6,681 in local jails and workhouses. Naturally, the latter number includes many seventeen- and eighteen-year-olds, so it is impossible to project these statistics to get a real picture of the size of the total problem.[1] Nevertheless, occasional studies enable us to grasp the magnitude of the problem of detention, as well as its diversity. For example, during 1952, more than 2,000 children were detained in jails in Virginia.[2] In the same year, about 1,200 children were detained in Connecticut, which has about two-thirds the population of Virginia, *but none of them were confined in jails.*

Some light on the size of the detention problem in one of our large states is provided by a careful recent study of detention by the California Committee on Temporary Child Care, under the direction of Sherwood Norman. Defining detention as "the temporary care of children who require custody in physically restricted facilities pending investigation and disposition," the Committee estimated that more than 35,000 youngsters up to age eighteen were detained in California in 1951. About three-fourths of these were held in thirty-three county "juvenile halls" (a term for a specialized detention facility used only in California), for periods ranging from an average of less than five days in one county to thirty days in another. Of the 35,000 children known to have been detained, *more than one-fourth were held in jails* for periods averaging over eleven days, and an additional unknown number were confined overnight in jails.[3] The *rate* of detention in California was nearly five times the rate in Connecticut, when population differences are considered.

Unquestionably, the detention problem is a major one, even if it is impossible to describe its exact statistical limits. Its importance is magnified by one simple fact: with relatively few exceptions, the facilities provided for the detention of children are a national disgrace.

[1] Unpublished data, Bureau of the Census, March, 1953, cited by Beck, "Juvenile Delinquency."

[2] *Virginia Welfare Bulletin* 31, p. 11.

[3] *California Children in Detention and Shelter Care.* A popularized version of this study was published as a Public Affairs pamphlet, *Care for Children in Trouble.*

In the discussion that follows, no attempt has been made to select "horrible examples" for criticism. As a matter of fact, much of the material used is from the published and unpublished surveys of the National Probation and Parole Association, and these surveys are *always* made upon request of public officials in the community studied. If anything, the National Probation and Parole Association studies reflect conditions better than average; in any event, the worst situations are not likely to be subject to professional "outside" scrutiny.

A Review of Detention Conditions

Although it is true that substantial improvements have been made in some communities, there is still a long way to go before adequate detention practices are universal. As Dr. George M. Lott aptly summarized it more than a decade ago, the numerous disadvantages in the detention picture include the prevalence of old-time penal practices, the use of hazardous, congregate detention, detention that is unduly prolonged, and the use of detention facilities as a dumping ground for a miscellany of problems.[4] This statement is equally true today.

Conditions in detention homes have been brought to the attention of the public repeatedly through popular media of interpretation. As recently as 1953, Flora R. Schreiber reported the picture in Utica, New York, as follows:

> The detention home . . . looks from the outside like an ordinary frame house. But inside I found children going "stir-crazy" behind bars. All their daylight hours were spent in a small room divided by a plywood board into a section for boys and a section for girls. There was absolutely nothing for the children to do but read comics or work puzzles.
>
> "It's not too bad for the first day," one boy said. "And the second day you can stand it. But after a week or two, when you have done all the puzzles and read all the funny books, it drives you nuts." [5]

The Schreiber article also points out that in Albuquerque, New Mexico, the city animal shelter operated on a budget of $15,000 a year, while the detention home received only $12,000 annually.

In another article, Albert Q. Maisel opened his grim story with the following description of conditions in Flint, Michigan, only ten years

---

[4] Lott, "The Juvenile Detention Home."
[5] Schreiber, "Our Forgotten Children."

ago. While the "shame of Flint" presumably has been eradicated, the scene described could be duplicated in many places even today:

Under the cold full moon the Juvenile Detention Home loomed dark and bleak against the sky. The investigator knocked on the door and waited, then knocked again, louder. From far down the gloomy halls came a shuffling sound. Then the door opened a crack. A suspicious night watchman peered out, a mop in his hand.

"We're closed for the night."

"I want to see the cell block."

"You seen it all day, didn't you?" the watchman growled.

"Never mind," the investigator replied. "Just open up."

Up the stairs the two men went, through the dim halls to the second floor rear. At an iron door they paused while the old man fumbled with the lock. Then the massive barrier swung open and they passed into a pitch-black corridor.

"Turn on the lights," said the investigator.

"Don't need to," answered the watchman. "Got my searchlight with me."

Again he fumbled. Then the light went on. Its beam fell on a steel-barred cell, then on another. At the third cell it paused, shining on the pale scared dirt-smudged face of an undersized eleven-year-old boy. Blinking into the glare, he stood like any adult thief or murderer, his small hands clutching the bars.

"Why aren't you asleep, son?" the visitor asked.

For answer the child just turned his head. The light followed—past the peeling plaster, the filthy toilet, the dripping washbasin, over the damp concrete floor. It settled on the double-deck iron bunks. The flat steel ribbons that served as springs were bare—no sign of mattress or bedding.

"Is he a delinquent?" asked the investigator.

"Well, no, not exactly," came the answer. "He's a dependent; his old man's still in the army; his mom is sick or something, I guess. It's hard to keep track of them all."

"But why keep him in here?"

"The matron put me in," the child answered. "Says I spit on a girl's hair in the playground." [6]

Because of muddled thinking, inadequate planning, and confusion as to the jurisdiction of various courts, many communities use jail detention even though specialized detention facilities with secure

[6] Albert Maisel, "America's Forgotten Children," *Woman's Home Companion,* January, 1947. Copyright, 1946, The Crowell-Collier Publishing Co.

custody are available. In one of the most objective, comprehensive reports made on this problem, Fred Gross reported that from 1938 to 1942, 319 juveniles were held in the Cook County jail (Chicago), and only 10 percent of these were held for less than five days. Perhaps the most spectacular case discovered by Gross involved a fourteen-year-old boy who was found guilty of petty larceny on two indictments—the value of the property being $2.00 in one case and $8.00 in the other. While hospitalized with pneumonia, this youngster was sentenced by the criminal court to two consecutive one-year terms in the county jail and assessed fines and costs totaling $300. This boy spent twenty-one days in jail awaiting court action, 666 days serving his sentences, and 200 days "working out" the fines and costs. He went into jail at the age of fourteen and came out at seventeen. Presumably the sentencing judge thought that this boy's formative, difficult adolescent years should be spent in acquiring good citizenship traits in a jail then notorious as a "school for thieves," [7] dominated by inmates, and without a single progressive program feature.

Unlike many spectacular reports of this kind, this one was not allowed to gather dust in an obscure file. A series of articles in the Chicago *Sun* (now *Sun-Times*) by Fletcher Wilson, a competent reporter, gave ample publicity to this disgraceful condition that existed in a county which had available secure custody in a juvenile detention facility, even though the detention home was generally regarded as being itself not much better than a jail. Even so, not much improvement resulted from the publicity.

Unquestionably, various journalistic efforts to shock communities into doing something about this grim question have produced some constructive results. For example, the Baton Rouge *Journal* did a scathing series that resulted in real improvement. Likewise, Seattle's scandalous jail detention of a decade ago was ended when a youngster was beaten to death by other boys; Seattle now has one of the best detention facilities in the country. Unfortunately in the great majority of states, apathy and indifference prevail. In the absence of a specific, simply stated formula for improvement, it is easy to understand why inertia is a logical concomitant. In other words, even when there is public indignation as the result of various exposés, the way to improvement is not always very clear. In effect, everybody agrees that something

[7] Gross, *Detention and Prosecution of Children*, pp. 66-67.

must be done about the problem, but nobody seems certain of precisely what should be done.

While professional surveys are couched in more diplomatic terms than articles in newspapers and popular magazines, they are equally depressing. The National Probation and Parole Association study of detention in Delaware in 1951 showed that nearly 700 children under juvenile court jurisdiction were admitted to places of detention during 1949. Slightly more than 200 were detained in jails, police lockups, and a workhouse. The other children were detained in the Detention Home for Juveniles, which was described as "still a fire hazard and improperly designed for modern detention care." The report noted: "It has been condemned by various grand juries over a period of fifteen years. Neither the staff nor the building is capable of handling the older, more aggressive youngsters." [8]

The Association's study of the detention problem in Michigan disclosed equally unsavory conditions. During 1950, 11,100 children under seventeen were admitted to various places of detention, with slightly more than 5,000 being held in Wayne County (Detroit) and almost 6,000 in the rest of the state. Although a majority of the children detained outside Wayne County were placed in shelter-type care, almost 3,000 were held in secure custody, more than 500 of these children were detained in county jails. In fact, only eleven Michigan counties did not use the jail at all for boys and girls under seventeen years of age. In sixty-three counties, the jail was the only place of secure custody available for children. The so-called specialized facilities also presented a dismal picture. As the report described them:

> Of the 20 counties which provide facilities for secure custody other than the county jail: two use lock-up rooms in county infirmaries for the aged; one uses locked and barred rooms in a hospital and another in the basement of the court house; 13 counties use lock-up rooms with bars or heavy screens obstructing the windows in county detention homes for children of all ages; Wayne County uses a large barred detention institution which was built in 1915 and is now obsolete. None of these facilities can be approved according to good standards of detention care.[9]

The two most recent nation-wide surveys were made by Florence Warner in 1932 and Sherwood Norman in 1945. The Warner survey

---

[8] Norman, *The Detention of Children in Delaware*, p. 6.
[9] Norman, *The Detention of Children in Michigan*, p. 5.

covered detention in 141 areas in thirty-eight states, and the report was depressing.[10]

The Norman survey examined sixty-eight different detention facilities in twenty-two states, allegedly the best available. The bleak conclusion of Mr. Norman's report was that no community at that time offered completely satisfactory detention facilities, although in many there were found some examples of good practice.[11]

Jail Detention

Despite general agreement that children should not be detained in jail, and although the majority of state laws contain certain restrictions or prohibitions on the use of jails for juveniles, jail detention is still relatively common. The rate of jail detention is problematical, and numerical estimates range from 50,000 to 100,000 children detained each year for varying periods of time in various kinds of jails. Variations in the rate of detention from one community to another are extreme, to say the least. One National Probation and Parole Association estimate suggests that if the rate for communities detaining the largest number of children were applied throughout the country, nearly 1,000,-000 children would be held in jail annually, and if the rate of those detaining the least number were applied it would be less than 40,000 a year. Virtually every study of the detention situation brings out this startling contrast, which cannot be explained on regional or cultural bases. Even counties close to one another in the same state will show wide variations, although all other factors present seem to indicate that there should be similarities. One community with 10,000 children of juvenile court age in the population may have no children in jail detention, and few in any other kind of detention; another community with the same child population may detain three or four children in jail each year; and still another similar community may detain sixty or seventy children in jail each year.

Another difficulty lies in the fact that the jail itself may be a "good" jail; but even in the good jails children are exposed to some contact with adults. Even when state law requires separate detention facilities for juveniles, the definition of what is a separate facility within a jail

[10] Warner, *Juvenile Detention in the United States.*
[11] Norman, *Detention for the Juvenile Court.* A revision of this standard work is now in progress.

is largely determined by the sheriff, normally the local law enforcement officer responsible for administration of county jails. The authors have visited jails, for example, in which the answer to the question of what separate detention facilities for juveniles were available was: "We use the women's cell." Then, to the inquiry about what happens when women are present in the jail, the answer usually was: "We do the best we can." There are even some jails that carry out the pretext of separate facilities for juveniles by placing mattresses for them on top of a block of cells—out of sight, but not out of sound.

This problem of jail detention of children is complicated by two factors: the jails tend to be the repositories for the flotsam and jetsam of any community; and the jails almost always contain a miscellaneous group of persons awaiting trial or disposition, and serving short sentences.

Although the jails have been the object of vigorous attack by reformers for many years, they are operated usually as entrenched local institutions, with little or no state supervision and control. Their outstanding characteristic is their ability to defy substantial improvement. Although the United States Bureau of Prisons of the Department of Justice did not publish its findings on jails in its most recent annual report, the consistent picture in recent years has been that only one-fourth of all the jails in the United States (excluding the so-called city and town lockups which are used for overnight detention only) are approved for federal prisoners. The Jail Inspection Service of the Bureau reviews conditions in the local jails because the jails (outside of New York City) are used on a *per diem* payment basis for detention of federal prisoners. As a matter of fact, the use of even one-fourth of the county jails for federal prisoners is no clear indication of their adequacy, because in the most recent year for which statistics were published only 14 percent of all jails were fully approved and the additional 11 percent were approved only for emergency purposes.[12]

There are many facets to the evaluation of jails by the federal Jail Inspection Service, but this review provides at least a crude picture of the condition of the jails at the present time. Unfortunately, many of the jails which cannot be used for federal prisoners—including white slavers, bank robbers, kidnappers, and the like—are used for the de-

---

[12] *Federal Prisons*, 1950, p. 92. In 1952, only about 750 of more than 3,000 county jails were authorized for federal use. (See *Federal Prisons*, 1952, p. 41.)

tention of children for varying periods of time, sometimes only overnight, but too often for days, weeks, and months.

While this is not the place to discuss the entire problem of the jails,[13] it is quite obvious that the situation in the jails at the present time makes it possible to state flatly that *a child of juvenile court age should not be detained in jail, except under very unusual circumstances, and then only on an overnight basis.* Realistically, there must be exceptions. Because the majority of states have an upper juvenile court age of eighteen, it is conceivable that a sturdy seventeen-year-old involved in a series of aggressive, assaultive robberies might be kept temporarily in a local jail if the community does not provide a secure detention facility. Nevertheless, if the youngster is to be dealt with by the juvenile court (waiver is provided in some of these situations), other arrangements for detention, when necessary, must be made at once.

These comments should not be interpreted to suggest that judges, prosecutors, chiefs of police, and sheriffs actually favor detention of children in jails. This has been demonstrated adequately by a 1951 survey financed by the Field Foundation and conducted by the Illinois Department of Public Welfare and the National Probation and Parole Association.[4] The study included extensive field visits in nineteen counties in southern Illinois, where 345 children were detained in jails during a period of eighteen months. Although about sixty key county officials were interviewed, only a few—actually two or three—made comments that could be interpreted as favorable to the use of the jail for detention purposes. Even these few statements applied to special kinds of cases, such as those in which an older child was involved and in which violence or attempted violence accompanied the delinquent act. This same study also proved that it is extremely difficult to get valid statistics with respect to the length of jail detention. Jail records on the whole are extremely inadequate, and in many instances the ages of those held in jail are not indicated. On the basis of a questionnaire study of other counties, the number of children detained in Illinois jails, excluding Cook County (Chicago), during the period January 1, 1950, to June 30, 1951, was estimated to be 2,000.[14]

There seems to be little point in berating the jails or adding to the voluminous rhetoric on the subject, since the case against them, partic-

[13] See Robinson, *Jails: Care and Treatment of Misdemeanant Prisoners in the United States.*

[14] Reed, *The Detention of Children in Illinois.*

ularly as facilities for juvenile detention, is so strong. Nevertheless, granting that the jails are totally inadequate as detention places for delinquent and dependent children, this still leaves many communities with a problem. What is an adequate substitute for the jail, especially when the number detained in a given jurisdiction may be relatively small—ten or twelve children a year? Unquestionably some reorganization of facilities is needed. There seems to be a strong case for removing children who must be detained in small communities from facilities under local jurisdiction to a regional or state facility. Real progress in this direction has been made by only three states—Connecticut, Rhode Island, and Utah. Connecticut, for example, uses three regional detention facilities which have completely replaced ninety-two town and village jails as detention places for children.

While the case for some other type of facility is very persuasive, the local jail has been able to resist change in an almost unbelievable manner. The discouraging picture of jail detention of children is pathetic indeed, but the tradition of local responsibility is strong, and the entrenched interests involved have been able to block progressive action in many sections of the country. Part of this problem lies in the almost reverential manner in which many people hold local institutions. There is a widely accepted stereotype which suggests that those institutions and agencies closest to the people, which operate at the "grass roots" level, are the best agencies of government. As a general proposition, this may be open to discussion, but in the area with which we are presently concerned or in the field of corrections as a whole, it is interesting to observe that the worst institutions, the jails, are operated by local government. The state institutions are better, and the federal correctional institutions are usually superior to either. In the field of detention, at least, the "grass roots" myth should have been exploded long ago.

Detention in Specialized Institutions

Specialized institutions for the detention of children may be grouped arbitrarily under the term "detention home." The generic term covers a great variety of agencies, ranging from one extreme to another in size, construction, personnel, and program. Although there are fewer than 200 specialized detention homes in the United States, examples of virtually any conceivable type of institution may be found. While the trend toward improvement of specialized detention facilities is clearly on the upswing, chiefly because of the efforts of the National Probation and Parole Association, it is important to face candidly the fact that the mere presence of a specialized detention facility in a community does not guarantee that children will receive adequate detention care.

Before considering the various kinds of specialized detention facilities found in the United States today, some attention should be given to the kinds of children found in detention homes. The great variety of problems presented by children in detention indicates in some measure the complexity of the total problem. Sherwood Norman has identified nine different groups of children frequently encountered in detention facilities:

1) Delinquents who have committed serious offenses or who have severe social problems.
2) Delinquents who have committed minor offenses or whose problems are less serious.
3) Children awaiting transfer to state training or industrial schools.
4) Runaways from institutions and from their own homes, including runaways from other communities.
5) Habitual school truants.
6) Mental defectives, delinquent and nondelinquent.
7) Material witnesses who are not themselves delinquent.
8) Uncared for children who represent the large dependent and neglected group.
9) Lost children needing emergency shelter, perhaps for only a few hours.

Mr. Norman adds: "Every boy and girl, from the delinquent who has committed serious offenses to the lost child, may have serious behavior and personality problems or may be comparatively normal. He may be only a few years old or may be a young adult. He may be overdeveloped physically and underdeveloped mentally, or the reverse. He may be kept in the institution part of an hour, or for days, weeks, possibly months if other facilities are inadequate." [15]

This enumeration gives some indication of the almost incredible difficulties that present themselves in planning for a detention program in any community. To any rational person, it is quite obvious that all of these children cannot be housed successfully in one institution.

[15] Norman, *Detention for the Juvenile Court*, p. 5.

Nevertheless, they are. An objective view of the problem leads inevitably to the conclusion that the chief goal must be twofold: (1) to minimize the problem of detention by eliminating detention entirely to the extent that this is possible; and (2) to develop a variety of facilities, even varied facilities and programs within one institution, which will tend to meet the specific needs of the children who must be detained.

It should be kept in mind that the use of specialized detention facilities for children is relatively recent. A Children's Protective Society Shelter was established in Boston as early as 1880, and the first detention facility connected with a juvenile court was established under private auspices in Chicago shortly after the turn of the century. The growth of specialized institutions thereafter was relatively rapid, although the developments of the past decade have accentuated this trend markedly. In 1946, there were fewer than 150 detention homes, but an increase since then has brought the number to nearly 200. Nevertheless, this number is far from satisfactory, because there are about 500 urban areas with populations of 25,000 and above and about 1,000 communities with populations of more than 10,000.

Although the problems of the specific kinds of facilities in use will be examined separately, there is one major consideration that should be borne in mind in any discussion of the detention problem. Those who have looked at this complex question seriously are in agreement that the cost of adequate detention care should roughly approximate, or perhaps even exceed, the cost of hospital care in a general hospital setting. According to recent estimates, the cost of general hospital care varies from about $14.00 a day to $20.00 a day, but the Norman studies have shown large numbers of detention facilities with costs closer to $2.00 or $3.00 a day. It seems fairly obvious that in the interest of getting children out of jails, many communities have developed detention facilities with little or no thought of the costs that an adequate program really involves. Consequently, many of the programs are understaffed, housed in substandard structures, and their facilities are lacking in manifest ways when tested against the general principles applicable to the field of child care.[16]

Even under ideal conditions, children who are in detention are tense, anxious, and insecure; furthermore, they are exposed to contamination and cross-infection with respect to attitudes. If the institution is re-

[16] Beck, "Juvenile Delinquency."

served solely for delinquents—and it should be—there is the added disadvantage, which is only beginning to be recognized, that children who are identified as delinquents by society, especially when they mingle in groups, are likely to develop self-identification as delinquents, which may predispose them to behave in the manner that the adult world expects of them. Even casual acquaintance with the case histories of delinquent children provides ample evidence of the identifications that develop.

It is equally obvious that specific methods of breaking the law are intensified by contacts made in institutions of this kind. The youngster apprehended while stealing a car because a police officer spotted a broken wind-vent may heed the simple advice of another child that there are numerous unlocked cars, many of them with the keys in the ignition switch. Or his horizons may be broadened: he may learn how to open wind-vents with a thin strip of steel and he may learn how to use a "jumper" to start a car when the ignition is locked. The child apprehended because the sound of breaking glass was noted by a passer-by may learn readily that the combination of heavy glued wrapping paper applied to a window and a dime-store glass cutter will make it possible to obtain entry to a store without making telltale sounds. While it is perfectly true that much of the argument for separate detention facilities for children has dealt with the danger of contamination from adults, and while the case for separation of children from adults is very strong on many grounds, the tendency to approach this question in a sentimental fashion has blinded many well-intentioned persons to the fact that transmission of attitudes, ideas, and techniques within peer-groups is both effective and frequent.

In view of the highly complex nature of the population of detention facilities, and in the light of the obstacles previously discussed, what then are the solutions that have been tried by various communities? These may be grouped arbitrarily under five main headings.

(1) *Boarding Homes.* Boarding homes have been used for detention purposes in a number of communities, and increasing attention is being paid to the feasibility of including them in a program, although they are identified chiefly with shelter care rather than secure custody. Boarding homes have been used extensively in Buffalo, New York, for the past quarter of a century. In the Buffalo plan, the number of boarding homes available has ranged from eight to ten, with one home

acting as a receiving home for boys, another as a receiving home for girls, and still another providing secure custody. These are subsidized boarding homes, and a flat sum is guaranteed the boarding parents, whether the facility is used or not. The number in detention at any one time is small, averaging about twenty, and the facilities are available only for children under sixteen years of age. While it is often overlooked in discussions of the Buffalo plan, reliance is placed on careful selection of boarding home parents, together with extensive supportive supervision. The staff includes a supervisor, caseworkers, and full-time teachers; limited medical and psychiatric services are available.

This kind of program has the obvious advantage of minimizing the glamour of delinquency, as well as diminishing the contagion and group aggressions that are found in large institutions. Nevertheless, it is not a cure-all, and it should be pointed out that Buffalo has had long experience in the use of foster home care for children generally. This program is feasible only when it is accompanied by careful screening done by well-trained workers. These conditions and safeguards are unquestionably responsible for the apparent success of the Buffalo program, but like many other devices and plans for dealing with delinquents, it does not represent a formula that may be used anywhere.[17] Probably it serves best to illustrate the point that many children now detained in secure facilities do not require custodial care accompanied by escape-proof devices.

Nevertheless, the Buffalo experience should be exploited to the utmost, especially in view of the substantial number of communities which have the problem of detention of a relatively small number of children for whom jail is obviously not a suitable place for detention. As a matter of fact, it is possible that many communities could go a long way toward solving the detention problem by combining careful screening at intake with the selection of subsidized supervised boarding homes of superior caliber. Like many other aspects of this question, there is little or no research to demonstrate the effectiveness of this kind of program.

In any event, it may well be a logical method to apply in a great many communities which are now without detention facilities of a specialized nature; adequate payments to subsidized boarding homes conceivably may result in attracting superior persons to this type of

[17] Lenz, "A Yardstick for Measuring Detention Homes."

work. While this issue of payment is tied in with the entire question of foster care of children, it should be observed in passing that the amounts of money traditionally paid for boarding care of children have been based on a subsistence level. Presumably more adequate payments, especially on a salary basis, would permit greater controls and more complete supervision, and do away with some of the customary dependence upon emotional identification with the children concerned which is utilized and even exploited by foster care agencies. For smaller communities generally, it is obviously logical that the first plan to be considered for specialized detention of children should be some form of subsidized boarding care. Supplemented by regional detention facilities affording security features, this may well be the answer for a great many communities.

(2) *Residence-Type Facilities.* Residence-type facilities are somewhat larger, dealing with as many as eight to ten children, in contrast with the three or four who are accommodated in the usual subsidized boarding home. Another distinguishing feature of the residence type is that the staff, frequently only a man and wife, is brought into the facility to operate it on a salaried basis. Although the National Conference on Prevention and Control of Juvenile Delinquency suggested that the residence-type facility offered a suitable place for a community to begin an acceptable detention program, and although one excellent illustration of this type of facility is given, the Conference report succinctly describes its inherent dangers:

> It is usually a synthetic boarding home of the idealized one big happy family type. It usually takes both boys and girls, often of a wide age range, and sometimes includes dependent as well as delinquent children. Usually the total number of children detained seems to call for a simple staff of a man and wife, and perhaps one assistant. Actually with the amount of maintenance work and administrative detail involved, it would be quite impossible to provide good supervision and program for boys and girls with a variety of problems and a wide age range, without more than doubling the staff.[18]

Probably the chief disadvantage to the residence-type detention home is that it is neither large enough to provide for suitable staff, with adequate relief and replacements, nor is it small enough to provide the personalized, individual care that could be available in an adequate

---

[18] *Report on Juvenile Detention,* p. 12.

subsidized boarding home. Because these programs lack adequate personnel, both in quality and numbers, there is little stimulation, and a great deal of the children's time is spent in routine cleaning duties, with play periods being occupied only by the "three C's"—cards, checkers, and comic books. Although it is theoretically possible that the numbers involved may make it feasible to develop the advantages of real group process, as well as careful observation of individual children, it is altogether likely that the usually unskilled staff simply cannot take advantage of such an opportunity. It is true that many such establishments lack the jail-like atmosphere of institutions housing larger numbers of children, but it is equally possible that they will become places for the "cold-storage" of children who wait day after day to learn what is to become of them. In the absence of adequate staff, these facilities enhance the restlessness and insecurity characteristic of children who are detained.

With occasional exceptions here and there, programs in the residence-type facility are not adequately financed. In addition to being seriously understaffed, and for the same lack of funds, the converted residence tends to be physically unsuitable for the minimum purpose of secure detention. With an adequately financed program and appropriate staff, together with realistic modifications in the physical surroundings themselves, and assuming appropriate supervision and careful screening of the children who are admitted, such a facility may well provide decent detention care. Generally, the conditions described are lacking, and the facilities themselves are only slightly better than the jails they have replaced.

(3) *The Small Institution.* Generally used for twelve to thirty children, the small institution departs from the residence-type home by becoming somewhat larger and less personalized. As a rule, the regimen bears little resemblance to family patterns of living. Like the other facilities described, quality may be expected to vary considerably from one institution to another, and the fact that a particular facility happens to be in the "small institution" category gives neither assurance of appropriateness nor guarantee of failure. Nevertheless, in terms of adequacy of standards, the small institution, which is likely to be found in communities of 100,000 to about 200,000, represents a real challenge to any community. Unless it is kept in mind that detention care is extremely expensive, and that suitable facilities are really difficult to develop, it is

easy to achieve a combination of factors that can produce disastrous results. Poor physical design, whether for new or remodeled structures, inadequate personnel, qualitatively or quantitatively, and inept intake controls are the chief hazards.

A description of one small institution serves to illustrate some of the inherent dangers that must be guarded against. Located in a Midwestern community of about 130,000, this detention facility began operating in 1923. For about twenty years it was supported and operated by a voluntary society, assisted by a subsidy of $1,000 a month from the county treasury. For a variety of reasons the institution finally was taken over entirely by the county and placed under the control of the judge responsible for juvenile court matters, with fiscal support being provided by the county board of supervisors. Although there had been some structural remodeling in 1923, including the construction of a small addition, the main part of the building was built in the 1860's and the two-story-and-basement frame structure had long since been condemned by the fire marshal. During a sixteen-month period a few years ago, 428 children were detained in this institution. The maximum number under care at any one time was twenty-five (although the rated capacity was twenty); the minimum number was two; and the number of children most frequently detained was eleven. There was no segregation by age or by type of child, and even segregation as to sex was incomplete. Those detained included a six-year-old dependent boy and a nine-year-old dependent girl, as well as a fifteen-year-old delinquent girl and a sixteen-year-old delinquent boy—both of whom were reported to present serious aggressive sex problems.

No isolation facilities were provided in the institution, and there was no way of insuring secure custody. As a result of this lack of security provisions, the number of children of juvenile court age detained in the county jail annually ranged from twenty to thirty-five during the several years preceding the survey. The staff itself consisted of a man and wife, but the man was employed elsewhere on a full-time job, so he was available evenings only. Intake policies were vague, and the institution was literally a dumping ground for dependency and neglect cases, as well as a convenient catchall for those above juvenile court age who had no other place to go. The equipment of the building was hopelessly inadequate, and there was no provision even for locker space for the children confined. As one would expect, the recreational features of the program were minimal and confined to the traditional cards, checkers, and comic books.[19]

This description does not represent an isolated instance; the conditions described are not at all unusual. Fortunately, communities here and there are gradually becoming aware of the fact that such a facility may well do a great deal more harm than good for children in trouble, and the trend toward their replacement by more suitable facilities seems rather definite.

Obviously, the same general principles of action that should be applied to other facilities for dealing with delinquents likewise should be imposed here. It is evident that the complacency about their detention facilities so characteristic of many communities must be shattered before real progress can be made. Merely getting children out of jails is not enough. One of the authors recently visited a small detention facility in one of the western states. The institution had a capacity of about sixteen, but at the time of the visit it housed only two boys, aged twelve and fourteen. This community had "removed its children from jail" by the simple expedient of erecting a modern county jail with excellent physical facilities and turning the old jail into a "detention home." As an added feature, in keeping with so-called modern standards, the bars were removed from the old jail, but the window spaces were filled in with glass brick. Ventilation was adequate, but the opaque brick made it impossible for the youngsters to see anything outside. And there was literally nothing to do inside. When the juvenile court worker asked the boys whether there was anything that he could do for them, the older one replied, "Sure, get us out of here and over into that new county jail so we can see something."

Clearly, the removal of children from jails is a necessity; but they must be taken from the jails into decent facilities, equipped to provide the kind of care children need.

(4) *Large Institutions.* The disadvantages of large institutions are widely known and well-established. As the National Conference on Prevention and Control of Juvenile Delinquency described the situation in 1946:

---

[19] Unpublished study, files of the National Probation and Parole Association, Midwestern Office. Another Midwestern study showed seven boys locked in a bare basement—to keep them segregated from the dependent children.

The basic disadvantage is that the relationship between a boy or girl and the adults in charge of him is bound to be impersonalized. This is a serious matter in detention, for the child's relation to authority is already at stake. The common results are that there is an unnatural amount of regimented routine, natural spontaneous activity is discouraged and organized program is not developed sufficiently to replace it; that delinquency is glamorized and conditions are ripe for delinquency contagion, for the development of youth-against-the-world atmosphere, and for spirals of aggression.[20]

The Conference recommended that the large institution be decentralized into small units, preferably dealing with twelve or fifteen children of like age and needs. It also pointed out that the partial subdivision of groups in a large institution is not enough, and that the units must be small and well-staffed, with the program of each unit specially set up to meet the particular needs of the group. Even with the best of facilities, the large institution presents clear-cut hazards in dealing with children even for a brief period of time. These hazards can be minimized only by reducing large institutions to reasonably small, homogeneous units. It has been argued with some merit that the breakup of the institution does not necessarily mean the creation of several smaller institutions scattered about a city; from the standpoint of efficiency and economy of management, there is no reason why virtually self-contained units could not be planned in one institution. Nevertheless, it must be borne in mind that this almost inevitably requires new construction, and that all the tinkering that has been done with institutions built thirty or forty years ago, before decent detention standards were developed and before there was any realization of the need for small homogeneous groups being dealt with independently of other groups, has not solved and cannot solve the problem of the large institution.

It is interesting that two large institutions—Youth House and the somewhat related Girls' Camp in New York City—even though they were handicapped by poor physical plants, have managed to provide reasonably adequate detention facilities, chiefly through the utilization of unusually well-qualified, trained personnel. Youth House, privately operated but supported by tax funds, came into being early in 1944 following a series of revelations and exposés of scandalous conditions

---

[20] *Report on Juvenile Detention*, p. 14.

in detention facilities operated by a private society.[21] Despite out-moded facilities, the emphasis upon psychiatrically oriented staff was strong enough to produce a permissive atmosphere that is considered relatively unique in modern detention annals. Under the competent leadership of Frank J. Cohen, Youth House went through a series of stages characterized first by experimentation, then by demonstration, and finally by the perfection of operating techniques. An essential part of its program, and one that proved invaluable to the children's courts of New York City, was the utilization of the detention period for study and observation. Accordingly, reports were made to the courts that were meaningful and useful in terms of understanding the children and helpful in determining appropriate disposition.[22]

(5) *The Detention-Study Home Combination.* What has been said about New York's Youth House may be interpreted incorrectly as giving blanket approval to the use of detention facilities as centers for observation and study of youngsters in difficulty. Actually, the case for a combination study and detention facility is highly dubious. The important distinction that must be kept in mind is between study and observation that takes place as a logical concomitant of detention, and the deliberate, planned use of a detention facility as a place for observation and study. Unquestionably, children who are caught in the traumatic experience of detention frequently display aggravated symptoms of the difficulties that beset them; consequently, it would be utterly unrealistic to protest that study and observation should not accompany the detention process. Nevertheless, if children are placed in detention for the specific purpose of having them observed and studied, an entirely different kind of institution would be required, with vastly different functions from those already ascribed to detention facilities. The danger here is that an incident attached to detention, namely, the opportunity for study and observation, can easily become the reason for detention, which is quite another matter.

Throughout this discussion of the detention problem, the importance of careful intake procedures has been stressed, and it is precisely at the point of intake that the entire detention process may well break down. Likewise, mention has been made of the dangers, largely psychological in nature, that surround all those connected with the detention process

---

[21] *The New York Times,* January 23, 1944. The private society, interestingly enough, was the Society for the Prevention of Cruelty to Children.

[22] Cohen, *Children in Trouble.*

if detention is considered a positive experience for the child. It seems eminently clear that if detention is used for the purpose of study and observation, there is an apparent pursuit of a legitimate objective, and ostensibly all concerned will be satisfied that the child belongs in detention.

Therefore, the cardinal point must be made that study and observation are merely incidental to detention and should never be used as objectives of detention. It is quite true that the combined functions represent an additional "selling point" to a community faced with the detention problem. Nevertheless, the results are easy to foresee if the suggested confusion develops. There is likely to be an increase in the rate of detention, and there may well be an increase in the average length of detention. Judges, unable to decide what to do in a complex situation, may refer the child to detention for study and observation and further report to the court. A continuance in detention for two or three weeks may ensue; afterward, the court receives a report from the "study center" on the child's IQ that could have been gotten from the school in the first place, or could have been obtained, in any event, with the child in an out-patient status. The fact that the child is being studied and observed gives an aura of social approval to the use of detention when otherwise there would be no justification for it.

These remarks do not constitute an objection to the development of badly needed centers for the study and observation of the behavior of disturbed children. Certainly it is also true that children who are committed by a court to a study center for emotionally disturbed children are in effect being detained. The key distinction lies in the fact that children in such a study home are there for a specific, legitimate purpose; and in an institution devoted to such a purpose they would not be involved with the run-of-the-mill detention cases. In the well-controlled study center, the intake determination rests primarily on the issue of whether the child needs residential care during a period of study and observation; in the case of detention, the important consideration is whether a child needs to be detained in secure custody or in shelter care pending disposition by the court or other agency concerned with his case.

The danger of mixed goals is emphasized by this example. Sherwood Norman, unquestionably the outstanding expert in this field, has made statements that, taken out of context, may seem to give complete approval to the combination detention-study home. For example, writing in the *California Youth Authority Quarterly*, Mr. Norman stated: "The child in need of detention is a child in need of clinical study and skilled observation. Thus a good detention home will serve as a short-term study home." [23]

The problem is that the phrase "in need of detention" in the foregoing quotation may readily be overlooked because of the seemingly desirable goal of providing an opportunity for short-term study of a child in a detention facility. In other words, if a child needs detention, then unquestionably appropriate studies of him should be made, and this period should be accompanied by skilled observation. Nevertheless, no child should be placed in detention solely because he needs study. If he is an emotionally disturbed youngster in need of residential clinical study, he should not be placed in a detention facility but in a study-home geared to the needs of emotionally disturbed children. The paucity of such resources is undeniably a fact that must be faced. But when such important resources are lacking, the problem cannot be solved by semantic gyrations in which the "Detention Home" becomes the "Child Study Center." Any realistic analysis of present-day concepts with respect to study and treatment homes for disturbed children demonstrates that the nature of the populations, the function of these institutions, and the programs themselves make them basically unsuited for combination with a detention facility.[24]

The examples given of various types of detention facilities offer ample evidence that the detention problem is not a simple one, and that it cannot be dealt with solely by condemnation of the indifference or apathy of communities that tolerate substandard facilities. Actually, this question of detention is highly technical, and relatively few persons have the knowledge necessary to plan and develop a suitable detention facility. Under existing circumstances, for the great majority of communities the only solution to the problem is to call in expert consultant service before decisions are made with respect to detention facilities.[25] While it is true that a few state departments of public welfare employ

[23] Norman, "New Goals for Juvenile Detention."

[24] Gula, "Study and Treatment Homes for Troubled Children." While the Gula article does not refer to detention as such, it describes study homes in such a way as to make it unmistakably clear that they should not be confused with detention homes.

[25] Norman, *The Design and Construction of Detention Homes for the Juvenile Court;* also, *The Construction and Design of Correctional Institutions,* especially Chap. 10, "The Planning and Construction of Juvenile Detention Homes."

child-welfare specialists with real awareness and understanding of detention problems, for most communities the only consultation service available is that of the National Probation and Parole Association. Recent developments in the United States Children's Bureau indicate that there is a strong possibility that the Bureau, by expanding its staff, may also be in a position to provide communities with badly needed consultation service on problems in this area.

Principles and Policies of Detention Care

While the complexities of detention make it impossible to undertake more than a cursory review of the principles and policies involved, certain essential principles and policies must be taken into account[26] in any evaluation. The separation of principles from policies is difficult, since the two merge at numerous points. It seems appropriate here to consider briefly such questions as what children need detention care and for what period of time, as well as what detention care is not or should not be in the light of its basic objectives. All of these issues and concepts, of course, must be seen as part of the basic philosophy of child welfare.

The only children who should be detained in secure custody are those who would be likely to run away or commit further offenses if they were left in their own homes, even under court supervision. Generally, these are children who are so disturbed following their apprehension or whose home and school relationships are so strained that temporary removal from home is indicated. Children in flight (usually identified as runaways) and children who are awaiting transfer to another institution also may require secure custody.

A 1923 publication of the United States Children's Bureau stated that detention "should be limited to children for whom it is absolutely necessary." The standards described are not especially helpful because they apply both to children who require shelter care and to those who require secure custody, which is confusing in a single statement of

[26] Although the principles described are drawn in large part from the writings of Sherwood Norman, some selection has been made, with some deliberate omission. For relatively brief, succinct statements applicable to principles of detention care, see Norman, *The Detention of Children in Delaware*, pp. 16-19, and Norman, *The Detention of Children in Michigan*, pp. 18-19.

standards. Nevertheless, they represent the considered judgment of the Bureau more than three decades ago, and therefore have some significance. According to the Bureau, the children to be detained are (1) children whose home conditions make immediate removal necessary; (2) children who are beyond the control of their parents or guardians, the runaways, and those whose parents cannot be relied upon to produce them in court; (3) children who have committed offenses so serious that their release pending the disposition of their cases would endanger public safety; (4) children who must be held as witnesses; and (5) children whose detention is necessary for purposes of observation and study and treatment by qualified experts.[27] Inclusion of the latter category seems scarcely defensible in the light of today's knowledge of the appropriate function of detention homes. The confusion of detention with observation and study, already discussed, is bad enough, but to utilize detention "for treatment by qualified experts" is utterly unrealistic.

Hugh P. Reed, a staff member of the National Probation and Parole Association, who has made numerous detention surveys, makes this clear statement: "The child who does need secure custody pending court disposition of his case is usually a rather seriously disturbed youngster, whether the symptoms shown are extreme aggressiveness, bizarre behavior, or a compulsion to run away from every situation in which he finds himself." [28] It is evident that Mr. Reed identifies only a special group—and a small group—as those for whom detention in secure custody is necessary.

It seems quite obvious that the length of stay of a child in detention facilities will vary from case to case, and that it depends to a large extent upon the speed with which the court arrives at a decision as to the disposition of the detained child. The relationship here is very clear. Sometimes the court is "on vacation"; at other times, the court may hear juvenile cases on Friday only; in some instances, weeks may be required before an overworked probation officer provides the information necessary for the court to act in the case. Presumably there will be a more extended length of stay when some form of clinical study takes place in the detention facility; as has been pointed out, this has its

[27] *Juvenile Court Standards*, pp. 3-4.
[28] Reed, *The Handling of the Neglected and Delinquent Child in Lincoln, Nebraska*, 1955, p. 32.

dangers. Recent National Probation and Parole Association surveys have suggested a three-day average length of stay when "custody only" is provided, and a two-weeks average when the children are studied clinically. This kind of standard, which evidently is not based upon objective research, is open to some question. The keynote in this very critical area is the development of good intake and referral policies, which will screen out those children who do not require secure custody and will make such necessary diagnostic and study facilities available either in appropriate residential centers or on an out-patient basis.

One of the most significant factors that emerged from the California study previously cited was the finding that of those detained about two-thirds were referred to probation departments for delinquent causes, and less than one-half of these ultimately received supervision on either a formal or an informal basis. Obviously, either many of these children were detained unnecessarily or a large number in need of probation services were released from detention without getting it. In any event, there is little to console us in this situation, with the exception of the single fact that the rate of detention increased less than the child population during the period 1945-51.[29]

It should be borne in mind that the statistics regarding length of stay may well be deceptive, especially if large numbers of children are held overnight who should have been released to their homes without detention. This can produce a rather low "average length of stay," which becomes virtually meaningless when measured against some other facility in which the majority of so-called "overnight" cases are eliminated without detention referral. It is equally true that detention after disposition by the court may not only disrupt statistics regarding average length of stay, but may damage the children held in a temporary care facility. In some states, the lack of resources for certain groups, such as mentally defective children, may result in detention for *months* after commitment to an institution.

Ray Studt, detention consultant for the California Youth Authority, has suggested certain criteria for determining length of care in detention. He takes issue with those who advocate a "short a time as possible" theory for length of detention and suggests that the length of a child's stay should be determined by a careful evaluation of what is happening to him. Mr. Studt makes the following points:

[29] *California Children in Detention and Shelter Care.*

1) Detention is pre-placement care.
2) As such it should be continued only long enough to insure the maximum possibility of success in the child's next placement.
3) Continuing detention after the child's readiness has been attained may destroy the results of the detention experience.
4) Terminating detention before such results have been achieved tends to make the child feel that he has "got away" with something.
5) Timing is an essential factor in making the detention experience a constructive part of the child's treatment.
6) Diagnostic skills are necessary to determine when a particular child has derived the maximum benefits from the detention experience.[30]

Another interesting development, and a relatively recent one, is the tendency for the period of detention to increase in communities in which new detention facilities have been established. This phenomenon has arisen not only when detention facilities for children are built to replace the jails formerly used for detention, but even when substandard detention facilities, measured by their physical aspects, are replaced by facilities that are considered adequate from the physical standpoint or even superior in design, construction, and equipment. While the relationship of total community facilities to the length of detention stay is unquestionably an important factor in any single community, it is a fact that there has been a gradual movement upward in the average length of stay in detention in many communities with newly established detention facilities replete with pastel colors, private rooms, and excellent recreational facilities, including rumpus rooms with television sets. Many experts in this field contend that detention under extremely favorable conditions may constitute a positive experience for the child, but it is the contention of the authors that detention cannot be a positive experience but at best is merely a neutral one. One suspects that the reason for increased length of stay is the false sense of security engenderd by the relatively lavish surroundings of some of the more recent detention facilities. In effect, the children are well cared for; they are well housed; and there is a false impression that because of these conditions, the urgent need for removal of all children from detention at the earliest possible moment has vanished. It is necessary to keep in mind that detention of any kind represents a disrupting experience in the life of a child. To regard detention as therapy is nothing more than

[30] Studt, *Functions of Detention—Principles, Operation*, pp. 7-8.

semantic acrobatics. Whatever the reason, any factor that tends to increase detention stay must be considered an undesirable development. This does not mean that detention facilities should not be attractive, well furnished, and pleasant. It is necessary to keep in mind that vigilance should not be relaxed, simply because comfortable, decent facilities are available to the child.

Good detention care is not punitive, and every aspect of building, program, and personnel must be geared to prevent emphasis on retaliation and vengeance as a feature of detention. Detention is not designed for extensive overnight use. In virtually all instances in which there is considerable use of detention facilities for overnight care, some administrative plan would be feasible that would make it possible to return most of the children to their homes in the first place. Detention care should not be confused with long-term care. While it is impossible to estimate the necessary length of detention in any given case, certainly the great majority of children should not be held for more than ten to fifteen days at the outside. The training features of the detention program are minimal at best, and the constantly changing group makes it virtually impossible to establish balance and equilibrium.

Detention homes should not be used for shelter care of dependent and neglected children who need to be removed from their homes. For them, more appropriate care may be given in open institutions or in boarding homes rather than in secure custody. It cannot be overemphasized that detention care is for children who present a real security risk or are a menace to themselves or others.

Detention care should provide service to the child, the court, and the community. The child should be given protection from himself and should be provided with activities that are meaningful while he is being helped by persons skilled in defining and understanding his problems. Detention care serves the court in providing custody for the more disturbed child, and at the same time providing the kind of insight into his total personality that can be gained through constant observation. Detention care serves the community by giving it further protection from aggressive, antisocial behavior, while helping to redirect the child's attitudes into positive channels. But to accomplish these objectives a basic casework principle is involved. Every feature of the program —personnel, activities, and the building—must demonstrate to the child that while his specific antisocial behavior is not approved by society, he is respected as a person and is not rejected. Therefore, the experience should have as much therapeutic value as possible for children at a critical time in their lives. To realize these objectives, certain conditions are necessary.

As Sherwood Norman puts it, "Objectives of this kind can be obtained only through the following requirements:

1) *An intake policy* which will assure extreme caution in the use of the home. . . .
2) *The best of physical care.*
3) *Custody* in a fireproof building which is neither prison-like nor with such flimsy security features that it offers an ever-present challenge to escape.
4) *A creative school and activities program* to prevent enforced idleness and destructive gossip, and to provide observation of the child's responses to this program.
5) *Guidance through casework* which will:
   a) Help the child to face the realities of his immediate situation. (Many children in detention develop various forms of duplicity and rationalizing, or make direct attempts to escape in order to avoid their predicament.)
   b) Assist the child and the supervisory staff to resolve disciplinary situations through casework and redirected activity rather than through punitive methods.
6) *Records* which have significance for the child's immediate treatment or future plans and which are summarized by professional personnel and given to the probation officer and the court who, in turn, should exchange information they may have so that the nature of the child's problems and type of treatment called for may be better understood." [31]

A strong case can be made for describing the principles of detention care of children in rather general terms applicable to all children. The White House Conference of 1940 defined the basic rights of childhood and the common needs of all children to include these things: *parents* to provide love, security, guidance, and companionship; *family life* which will respect the individual and induce him to respect the rights of others;

[31] Norman, *The Detention of Children in Delaware*, p. 19; Norman, "Standards and Goals for the Detention and Shelter of Children." The function of guidance through casework is stressed in Allaman, "Managing Misbehavior at the Detention Home."

dwellings which are clean, safe, and protecting; *health; protection* from accident, from evil influences, and from mistreatment; *education* and training through school, books, religion, play, recreation, and creative expression; *preparation for later life*—education in its broadest sense, education for living, for homemaking, and for the performance of civic duties.[32]

In commenting upon these rights of children, the National Conference on Prevention and Control of Juvenile Delinquency described these basic standards of child care as they apply to the detention problem as follows:

> For however short a time the detention home cares for a child it must not deny these basic rights. It must provide the best substitutes for the love and guidance of parents, for the mutual respect of the family; it must guarantee a clean, safe, protecting dwelling, health care, protection from evil influences and from mistreatment, education and training through a wide variety of media. There are at present children who remain in detention homes for months, denied every one of these things. What right have we to say that the child's parents have failed if, when authority steps in and removes him from his home to await court action, his basic rights are denied? [33]

In other words, the basic principles applicable to all children apply to children in all institutions, including children in institutions used for detention.[34]

A very succinct statement embodying clearly the basic principles of good detention practice appeared in a recent annual report of the executive director of Youth House. As the report put it:

> The focus and objectives of the Youth House operation have remained constant. At no time have we assumed, nor do we now suppose, that temporary detention can be viewed as a curative process. Our early assumption that much could be gained through positive relationship with the children in a temporary period of detention if the program was properly manipulated has been validated by our growing experience.
>
> We have moved a long distance from the days when temporary detention was thought of as the mere physical holding of the child in custody. We have found through our experience that many of the

[32] *Final Report*, pp. 63-72.
[33] *Report on Juvenile Detention*, p. 7.
[34] See Schulze, ed., *Creative Living in a Children's Institution*, especially Mrs. Schulze's "Introduction: Institutional Group Living in Fresh Perspective."

children who have been at Youth House have been helped toward a better adjustment in their life situations. . . . We have worked with the thought that most children, whatever their behavior, have the ability and strength to attain a useful and happy place in the community. To guide them and sustain them in that direction is the responsibility of society.[35]

Sound Planning for Detention Facilities

As surveys have demonstrated time and time again, the chief problem with respect to planning detention facilities is not the financing and construction of physical plant, or even budgeting for staff. Actually, these are only the final steps in a planning process which must include a careful evaluation of community facilities and resources and an estimate of the numbers and kinds of children to be detained. Only after this is it possible to project this information into specific planning for the type of facility needed, the staff, equipment, and budget. It is conceivable that detention care in a given community might be reduced considerably if the responsibility for determining when detention takes place is taken from the police and put in the hands of the probation department. Unfortunately, most probation departments are overworked and underfinanced, and the provision of twenty-four-hour service for this purpose may seem unrealistic in the light of existing probation department obligations. Likewise, the use of detention facilities for dependent and neglected children might well be reduced considerably if the appropriate child welfare agency in the community were able to provide minimum staffing on a twenty-four-hour basis.

Until serious efforts have been made to overcome the obstacles implicit in this situation, it is difficult to make a case for expansion of detention facilities as such. In other words, there is a very specific relationship between detention needs on the one hand and the provision of basic child welfare services on the other. When facilities are lacking, children remain in detention for weeks and for months *after* disposition by the court. In some states, they go on a "waiting list" for appropriate placement.

If the basic child welfare services are neglected, there is a strong probability that detention care will be used even when the opposite is

---

[35] Cohen, "Seventh Report of Executive Director."

clearly indicated. The problem is not confined to the entering process alone but extends throughout the entire period of detention. If foster-placement facilities, institutional or otherwise, are inadequate either in quality or number, children may be retained in detention for unduly long periods.

All these factors are minimum considerations to be dealt with in estimating the numbers of children to be provided for in detention facilities. Such estimates must be based upon an evaluation of what can be done about existing weak spots in the community's total welfare program for children, as well as provision of an insurance factor based on tight intake controls. It seems clear that the development of community support for any program should rest upon a careful consideration of these facts, and while a particular facility may represent a compromise between an ideal and that which can be accomplished in a relatively short period of time, there is no question but that long-term goals should be kept in mind.

The importance of qualified personnel should be obvious. In the absence of well-defined, accepted standards for personnel, the same basic principles should be applied to staff in detention facilities as to staff in any other phase of institutional work with children.[36]

The Control of Detention Intake

Both the police and the courts are involved in the question of intake control, one of the most critical issues in detention. A review of existing practices with respect to requests for detention by the police shows a completely illogical hit-and-miss pattern. In some communities virtually all children referred to the court are detained at the request of the police, while in other communities only two or three out of every hundred are so detained. The National Probation and Parole Association, after numerous surveys, is convinced that only 15 percent of children taken into custody by the police need secure detention; studies show that despite this 50 percent is common. Obviously the child in detention is conveniently accessible for the law enforcement officer charged with investigating a case. Likewise, when the court has assumed jurisdiction and it is decided to continue the child in detention instead of releasing

---

[36] See *Training Personnel for Work with Juvenile Delinquents*, especially Part III, Schulze and Meyer, "Training for Houseparents and Kindred Personnel in Institutions for Juvenile Delinquents."

him to the community, the fact that he is detained represents a convenient arrangement for the probation officer charged with getting appropriate information prior to court hearing. Nevertheless, the convenience of the police and the convenience of the probation staff are not at all important; what really is important is the welfare of the children concerned. As the previous review of detention facilities suggests, there is a strong case against unnecessary use of detention, even in the best of present-day facilities. Even when courts determine that a child should remain in detention until a hearing to determine disposition of the case, this should be a flexible, not a rigid arrangement, because detention may be justified at the time of the court hearing, but it may be unnecessary a few days later. Nevertheless, when a child is remanded to a detention facility and the case is continued two weeks, there is an almost universal tendency to keep the child in detention for two weeks, whether this is necessary or not. An overwhelming proportion of children detained ultimately are released to their homes; many of them should not have been detained at all, or only for a brief time. It should be emphasized that detention disrupts a child's normal routine and that, with rare exceptions, detention is a period of vegetation, not growth.

Paramount in any consideration of the control of admissions to detention facilities is the great importance of recognizing the need for centralizing the responsibility for intake in one agency. While proposals have been made that would designate various agencies to determine intake control, the case for centralization in the juvenile court is a strong one. The 1949 revision of the Standard Juvenile Court Act, prepared by a committee of the National Probation and Parole Association, provides for the jurisdiction of the juvenile court attaching from the time a child is taken into custody. In effect, this fixes responsibility upon one agency and one agency only.[37] This feature is important in protecting the civil rights of children. Too often, studies have shown children detained for many days on a "hold" order by the police. The detention of witnesses, often young children, who are held to testify against adults, while adults in the same cases are free on bail, strikes a discordant note. Probably a majority of such cases involve children who are alleged victims of sex attacks; they are not the sinners but the sinned against. Unless deten-

[37] A *Standard Juvenile Court Act*, rev. ed., p. 21. The same provision is found in the Children's Bureau 1923 *Juvenile Court Standards*, p. 3, a publication resulting from Children's Bureau-National Probation Association conferences.

tion is to become a travesty upon justice, it must be used only when the juvenile court determines that it is to be used. To make certain that the rights of children are protected, administrative controls must be defined clearly.

Juvenile Detention and State Responsibility

The question of who is responsible for organization and administration of detention facilities is one with many interesting sides. Even though it may be argued that detention is a local responsibility, it is evident that with few exceptions communities have failed to make provision for decent facilities. Probably communities with populations of 75,000 and upward can be expected to assume such obligations—but they seldom do. Likewise, it is probable that smaller communities cannot be expected to provide appropriate facilities. These statements do not suggest that citizen concern should be minimized; nevertheless, citizens need an appropriate vehicle through which their interest may be expressed. This leads inevitably to a discussion of the role of the state in dealing with the detention problem. This discussion omits reference to federal responsibilities in this area, since for some time at least it seems evident that federal activities will be confined to the consultation role, although the desirability of expanded federal action cannot be denied.

In view of the state's concern in matters of child welfare generally, the acceptance of state responsibility for juvenile detention does not necessarily constitute a revision of basic governmental policy. Nevertheless, state activity in this area has been at a minimum. Virtually all states operate training schools for delinquent children; they provide or supervise programs involving assistance to needy children; the majority of states provide various kinds of child welfare services originating in a division of the state welfare program; some states provide child guidance services and traveling clinics which visit rural areas—but very few states pay any attention to the problem of detention. This probably can be explained by the simple fact that the courts are local, organized usually on a county basis, and detention facilities generally have grown up under the aegis of the courts and are controlled by them. Attention has been called to the relatively few specialized detention facilities throughout the entire country and the prevalence of jail detention of children. The evidence seems to be very clear that, except for the larger communities, detention cannot be solved on a local or county basis. Even in communities with 100,000 or more population, the detention problem remains acute.

Theoretically there are three ways in which the states might take responsibility for dealing with the detention problem: (1) state supervision and inspection of detention facilities; (2) state subsidy to local communities that meet certain minimum standards; and (3) state control and operation of detention facilities.

In general, the states have power to inspect and to license child care facilities; detention facilities, therefore, in most states are subject to inspection by some agency of state government. In addition, many states have responsibility for inspection of jails, also used for detaining juveniles, together with the additional duty of enforcing state laws prohibiting jail detention of children. Note that a great deal of jail detention of juveniles is *illegal.* Nevertheless, state activities of this kind have been largely useless. Just as a fire inspector or a health officer may be in a legal position to close a detention home, a state child welfare agency may close an institution that does not meet certain minimum standards for child care. But a real dilemma is present here, simply because of the alternatives that must be faced. In general, closing a specialized detention facility, no matter how inadequate it may be, would result in returning children to jail detention. For the most part, therefore, the states have been content with "educational" efforts, designed to stimulate those responsible for facilities in the direction of improvement of services to children. On the whole, these efforts have been notoriously unsuccessful.

The use of a state subsidy to local communities has been tried here and there, but generally it has not been successful. Utah, which offered a *per diem* subsidy for each child detained, and Virginia, which was prepared to pay counties virtually all of the cost of detention care, found the experience disillusioning because of the apathy and indifference of the counties.

The only practical solution to the problem seems to be state control and operation of detention facilities. This has worked extraordinarily well in Connecticut, where four regional detention homes, operated in conjunction with Connecticut's state-wide juvenile court, have literally abolished jail detention of children in that state. Although Connecticut does not provide complete state control of the detention facilities, the pattern of regional facilities operated on a state-wide basis, and geared realistically to proved detention needs in the appropriate regions, seems to be the only feasible solution to this question.

State control and operation of detention facilities would ensure the use of reasonable standards, applicable both to the functions of the facilities and to intake procedures. Basing its estimates on the exhaustive studies by Sherwood Norman, the National Probation and Parole Association contends that not more than 15 percent of the children apprehended by the police need be detained, even on an overnight basis. But the proportion of children actually detained, varying greatly from one community to another, runs as high as 60 or 70 percent of children dealt with by the police. In effect, the absence of a reasonably uniform standard policy permits children who do not need detention to "clutter up" detention facilities, and thus makes already inadequate programs worse than they otherwise might be.

Illinois offers a good example of the need for some form of state operation of regional detention facilities. Late in 1954, in the 102 counties of the state, there were only three specialized detention facilities providing secure custody, with three more under construction. By the end of 1955, there will be ninety-six counties in Illinois without specialized detention facilities. In these counties, children either are not detained at all or are detained in jail. In the face of this evidence, to contend that this is a local problem that must be solved by local devices seems utterly unrealistic. Illinois had its first specialized facility more than fifty years ago. Even if present concern in the state about problems of detention should continue, those familiar with the local situation are convinced that it will be several decades before even one-tenth of the Illinois counties have detention facilities of a specialized nature.

It has been urged that intercounty coöperation could solve the detention problem, but the results thus far have not been encouraging. A few counties in a relatively few states have used specialized detention facilities of other counties, but there is nothing in the picture which suggests that any radical improvement will be made through coöperative efforts on the part of the counties themselves.

It seems clear that the state must intervene to the point of taking an active role in this problem. The regional detention home, state-operated and state-controlled, for children who require secure custody pending disposition by the court, coupled with the use of carefully selected boarding homes in the local community for those who do not require secure custody, seems to be the only formula that provides a rational an swer to this vexing question.

For Further Reading

California Children in Detention and Shelter Care, California Committee on Temporary Child Care (Sacramento, Calif., 1954).

A systematic and thorough examination of the detention problem in one of the major states. The study, under the direction of the foremost authority on detention in the United States, is a significant contribution because it relates facts to principles.

NORMAN, SHERWOOD AND HELEN, *Detention for the Juvenile Court: A Discussion of Principles and Practices*, second edition (New York, 1946; mimeographed).

A survey of existing practices, presumably the best available in 68 communities in 22 states. Practices are presented in the light of accepted principles of child care.

NORMAN, SHERWOOD, *Standards and Goals for the Detention and Shelter of Children. Part I: Detention* (New York, 1954).

This convenient résumé of standards and aims is based on the general content of the California Committee on Temporary Child Care Report. Its focus is clearly on what is essential for good detention.

Report on Juvenile Detention, National Conference on Prevention and Control of Juvenile Delinquency (Washington, D.C., 1947).

This is a good review of the detention problem that contains succinct descriptions of various types of detention facilities.

COHEN, FRANK J., *Children in Trouble* (New York, 1952).

This book describes the aims, objectives and philosophy of Youth House, New York City—one of the nation's most interesting experiments in detention.

SCHULZE, SUSANNE, ed., *Creative Living in a Children's Institution* (New York, 1951).

This is an unusually well-integrated series of articles dealing with the basic principles applicable to all children's institutions, including detention facilities. Mrs. Schulze's "Introduction: Institutional Group Living in Fresh Perspective," is a dynamic and realistic appraisal of goals.

Chapter **12**

THE JUVENILE COURT: BACKGROUND, PHILOSOPHY, AND STRUCTURE

The earlier discussion of the nature of delinquency[1] makes it evident that there are numerous and important questions that relate to the functions of the juvenile court itself. Note that throughout this discussion, the term "juvenile court" is used in its generic sense; in particular localities it may be identified as a children's court, a family court, or a domestic relations court. It does not refer to the adolescent's court, the wayward minor court, or the boys' court, all of which deal with youngsters above juvenile court age. Naturally, our concern here is chiefly with the juvenile court as it deals with delinquents, although some reference is made from time to time to dependent and neglected children.

With delinquency so vaguely defined, how and under what circumstances should the state step in and deal with children who misbehave? How far should the state go in interfering with, modifying, or abrogating the rights of parents with respect to their children? What are the assumptions and legal principles that underlie the treatment of delinquents under present juvenile court laws? How can the variations from

[1] Cf. Chap. 9.

juvenile court theory to juvenile court practice be explained and justified? When dealing with delinquents, is the juvenile court able to
function better as a court in the traditional sense or as a kind of social
agency? These are only a few of the questions that are answered in various ways by different people. Regarding them, there is little or no
consensus.

Therefore, before examining the origins, background, and current
status of the juvenile court movement in the United States, it is necessary to point out this lack of agreement as to the way juvenile court
functions should be defined and to make it clear that the differences
among so-called experts with respect to principles, philosophy, and practice are extreme and even contradictory. As an example, there is even
diversity of opinion as to whether the juvenile court is merely a special-
purpose court, or a social agency, or some combination of the two. The
vitality of some of these controversial subjects provides evidence that
many years will elapse before precise answers will be found for some of
the difficult questions that present themselves in a review of this
subject.

The attitudes taken toward the controversial aspects of juvenile court
functions unquestionably have effects upon practice in this field. In a
setting in which the traditional court features of the juvenile court are
emphasized and its social agency characteristics are deëmphasized, it is
altogether probable that the court will not order an inquiry made about,
or in any way take jurisdiction over, a child alleged to be delinquent,
until evidence at a hearing establishes the fact that the child actually is
delinquent and is therefore a proper subject for adjudication by the
court. In a different setting, in which stress is placed upon the social
agency features of the juvenile court, there is a probability that the court
may defer even a hearing until an investigation, or a social study made
prior to it, demonstrates that the child has a problem; when a hearing
is held, the court may assume jurisdiction simply because the child
presents a problem or perhaps a great many problems.

Actually, these conflicting points of view emerge from the nature of
juvenile court laws themselves. As was pointed out earlier, many juvenile court laws spell out delinquency in great detail but in extremely
nebulous terms; under some of these laws, virtually any child could be
called delinquent. The importance of this issue is underlined by the
fact that children under court jurisdiction may be subjected to various

forms of treatment presumably designed to protect them as well as to protect society. But the treatment itself may interfere with the rights of the parents, and, in the case of institutional commitment, it also may result in the child's loss of liberty for an indefinite period of time.

The juvenile court question today is surrounded by such issues as the methods by which courts take jurisdiction, the quality of personnel in the courts, and the adequacy of available treatment resources controlled by the courts or by other agencies. Any discussion of the qualifications of the probation personnel available to the courts for predisposition studies and for supervision of children placed on probation gets into specific, practical problems, not abstract, academic ones. Likewise, the qualifications of juvenile court judges, together with the issues involved in their selection and assignment, may be far more important than those in the traditional courts, where there are numerous time-tested safeguards. Certainly, the issue of whether the courts have available a variety of disposition resources realistically geared to the needs of children, or whether they must make a dismal choice between drab institutions and inadequate probationary supervision in unfavorable surroundings, is a crucial matter to the children involved. These important issues affecting today's juvenile courts are crucial ones for communities too because the juvenile court is inevitably the focal point for the community's efforts to deal with delinquent children.

Origins and Background

The first juvenile court in the United States began operations on July 1, 1899, as a branch of the Circuit Court of Cook County (Chicago), Illinois. The new court had many historical antecedents, so that it represented a logical culmination of many and diverse ways of giving special consideration to the status of childhood both in and out of the courts. The juvenile court of today can trace its backgrounds to the early English common law and to the development of chancery or equity jurisprudence. The distinction between these two forms of law should be kept in mind. The common law is unwritten law developed by judges on a case-by-case basis in their application of the customs of the country to individual situations. Usually the courts showed a tendency to be guided rather strictly by established precedents but, as numerous writers have pointed out, it does not necessarily follow that the common law was a fixed and rigid system of law. Chancery jurisdiction, on the other hand, arose from concern over the property of children. In the Wellesley case, decided in 1827, the doctrine was extended in a decision in which the welfare of children, rather than the protection of their property, was the main issue. Nevertheless, the chief emphasis in chancery cases even today is upon property.[2] In addition, the present-day juvenile court has profited from the differential treatment of children in specialized correctional institutions, as well as from the development of the concept of probation, which had its origins in the use of the suspended sentence.

Under the common law of England, which became the common law in nearly all the United States, the child under the age of seven was considered incapable of committing a felony or major crime; between the ages of seven and fourteen he was presumed to be incapable of committing a crime, although this presumption could be refuted; the child over fourteen was treated as an adult. Without doubt, the common law age distinctions as to criminal responsibility played a significant part in providing a legally accepted background for the modern juvenile court movement.

The other principal stream of law in which the juvenile court finds its origins is that of the chancery courts, through which the King's chancellor, acting for the Crown, made children wards of the state when necessary and placed them under the protection of the Crown. Such action was based on the doctrine of *parens patriae*, by which the King as father of his country was the ultimate father and protector of all his subjects; in the cases of children needing the protection of the Crown, the King stood *in loco parentis*.

Because juvenile courts today deal with delinquent, neglected, and dependent children, and because the status of these three groups is such that they may require the special protection of the state, it is occasionally said that the juvenile court represents merely an extension of chancery or equity jurisdiction. Actually, the evidence indicates that the legal roots of the juvenile court lie both in the special treatment of children under the criminal law and in the chancery courts.[3]

The development of specialized institutions for delinquent children

---

[2] See 2 Russell Chancery Reports I (1827), excerpted in Abbott, *The Child and the State*, I, pp. 15-29.

[3] Lou, *Juvenile Courts in the United States*, pp. 3-7; Schramm, "Philosophy of the Juvenile Court."

began in the early part of the eighteenth century, first in Rome, and then in Germany and England. In the United States, the first such institution was the House of Refuge which opened in New York City in 1825. Although it received public subsidy early, this institution was privately supported; it became the prototype for similar institutions founded in Boston, Philadelphia, and a number of other cities. These were the direct forerunners of the present-day state training schools, though the first state-supported and state-controlled institution was not opened until 1847 in Massachusetts. The early houses of refuge were roughly similar to the penitentiaries of the time, but they reflected the belief that in some fashion children should be differentiated from adults; and the segregation of child prisoners after disposition by the courts was characterized by lengthy hours of work and limited periods of formal education. As a result, like the penitentiaries, the early children's institutions soon became "busy prison factories," usually under the contract labor system. Nonetheless, some form of educational program persisted.

Another milestone in the process of separating children from adults in the eyes of the law began in 1869 when the Massachusetts legislature provided for a "visiting agent" whose duties included attendance at hearings on applications for the commitment of children to a reformatory. At these hearings, the agent was to appear "in behalf of the child." Under the statute a child could be placed out if the magistrate believed that the interests of the child would be served, and the visiting agent was charged with the responsibility of seeking out families with whom children could be placed.

A year later, in 1870, this act was extended. The visiting agent was placed under the supervision of the Board of State Charities, and he was required to appear in behalf of any child under sixteen in any case before a trial justice, police, or municipal court.[4] The Massachusetts Board of State Charities, which was created in 1863, was the first of the many supervisory boards that came into being when state after state built a multiplicity of institutions for the growing numbers of prisoners, the mentally ill, and various kinds of handicapped persons. This growth in numbers was relative, not absolute, and reflected in large part the increasing recognition of the needs of special classes and the growth of urbanization.

[4] Abbott, *The Child and the State*, II, pp. 366-368.

Also in 1870, Massachusetts provided for the separate trial of children's cases, and this action was followed soon by similar provisions in the statutes of New York, Rhode Island, and Indiana.

Probation in the form of suspension of sentence was a well-established legal tradition long before it was first adopted by statute in Massachusetts in 1878, in an act that applied to both adults and children. John Augustus, frequently referred to as the "father of probation" and as the "first probation officer," had provided a form of probation service in the Boston courts since about 1841. With long experience in probation services in the courts, Massachusetts was logically the first state to enact probation statutes for the criminal courts.

Commenting on the development of specialized institutions and the early modifications of the criminal law, Frederick B. Sussmann makes this statement:

> While these early laws embodied certain features of the juvenile court as we know it today, they nevertheless lack its basic concept, that children who break the law are not to be treated as criminals, but as wards of the state, in special need of care, protection and treatment. Children still, under these early enactments, were indicted and tried for the commission of a specific crime, and their trials were attended with all the formality and constitutional safeguards, such as trial by jury, which characterize the procedure in our adult criminal courts today.[5]

Likewise, Paul W. Tappan correctly points out the interrelationships that operated:

> The emergence of special provisions for the handling of juvenile delinquents reflects the co-ordination of several lines of historical development: probation, institutional treatment facilities, foster homes, social agency resources and punitive methods of the criminal court have been drawn together and instrumented through partially specialized children's courts. These various treatment modalities have each contributed something to the philosophy and method of the children's court; they have also each been modified somewhat by the evolving character of the court itself.[6]

As this cursory historical review indicates, the origins of the juvenile court are numerous and diverse; in a sense the court was a logical development in a step-by-step process that saw children singled out for specialized treatment in one form or another. To the specific develop-

[5] Sussmann, *Law of Juvenile Delinquency*, p. 12.
[6] Tappan, *Comparative Survey on Juvenile Delinquency*, p. 9.

ments that form the background of the juvenile court movement must be added the influence of the reformers in numerous fields. The nineteenth century witnessed the industrial revolution; and it also witnessed the revolution of ideas that brought the beginnings of protective legislation in the field of child labor, special care for the handicapped, the break-up of the almshouses, the growth of public education, the rise of the reformatory system, and many other developments. Together, these reforms showed that there was a growing acceptance of state responsibility for those in need of protection as well as an expansion of the area of interests to be protected.

The Juvenile Court of Cook County, the first in the United States and the first in the world, was established by an Act of the Illinois legislature approved April 21, 1899, and became operative on July 1 of that year. By this "Act to Regulate the Treatment and Control of Dependent, Neglected, and Delinquent Children" the legislature established a special court as a branch of the Circuit Court of Cook County; in the other counties of the state, similar jurisdiction was given to the county courts. The law defined a delinquent child simply as "Any child under the age of sixteen years who has violated any law of the state or any city or village ordinance." In addition, the act eliminated arrests of children by warrant, the use of indictment, and virtually all other features of criminal proceedings; and it provided a separate juvenile courtroom, separate records, and informal procedures. According to the act, the "care, custody and discipline of a child shall approximate as nearly as may be that which should be given by its parents. . . ."[7] The 1899 act gave the courts authority to appoint or designate "one or more discreet persons of good character" as probation officers, but it specifically prohibited their receiving compensation from the public treasury. Possibly this was to make the bill more palatable to the legislators; in any event, amendments in 1905 made it possible to pay probation officers.

The Illinois statute was the first one; other states soon followed suit. Within a decade, twenty-two states passed some form of juvenile court legislation, and many of these, including the New York law elsewhere cited,[8] tried to cover almost every conceivable kind of juvenile misbehavior.

[7] *Laws of Illinois*, 1899, p. 137.
[8] See Chap. 16, p. 466.

Although the Illinois act was finally passed without serious opposition, it represented the culmination of a decade of efforts by the leading reformers of that period. By 1891 Judge Harvey B. Hurd had drafted tentative juvenile court legislation, but there were disagreements among advocates of the measure as to the age limits, and numerous conferences and discussion failed to produce a unified front. Concerted action at last developed out of the considerable interest generated by the 1898 meeting of the Illinois State Conference of Charities, which was concerned chiefly with problems of children. After the Conference, the Board of State Charities asked the Chicago Bar Association to appoint a committee to make a study of the legal situation affecting children before the courts. Judge Hurd, who was appointed chairman, selected a committee that included various civic and sectarian groups. An acceptable bill was finally drafted, mainly through the efforts of Dr. Hastings H. Hart, director of the Illinois Children's Home and Aid Society, and then the Chicago Women's Club spearheaded a vigorous propaganda drive for the legislation.[9]

The rather simple definition in the original act was modified in 1907 by amendments which extended the jurisdiction of the newly created Juvenile Court to include a large number of situations and conditions that presumably were not violations of law or ordinance, and the upper age limit was raised to include boys under seventeen and girls under eighteen. By the amended definition, a delinquent child was one who

> . . . violates any law of this State; or is incorrigible, or knowingly associates with thieves, vicious or immoral persons; or without just cause and without consent of its parents, guardian or custodian absents itself from its home or place of abode, or is growing up in idleness or crime; or knowingly frequents a house of ill-repute; or knowingly frequents any policy shop or place where any gaming device is operated; or frequents any saloon or any dram shop where intoxicating liquors are sold; or patronizes or visits any public poolroom or bucket shop; or wanders about the street in the nighttime without being on any lawful business or lawful occupation; or habitually wanders about any railroad yards or tracks or jumps or attempts to jump onto any moving train; or enters any car or engine without lawful authority; or uses vile, obscene, vulgar, profane or

[9] Bowen, "The Early Days of the Juvenile Court"; Lathrop, "The Background of the Juvenile Court in Illinois"; Flynn, "Judge Merritt W. Pinckney and the Early Days of the Juvenile Court in Chicago."

indecent language in any public place or about any school house; or is guilty of indecent or lascivious conduct. . . .[10]

The 1907 amendments to the Illinois Juvenile Court Act are significant in that their loose and vague phraseology reflected both a pattern that had developed elsewhere and a conceptual framework that theoretically embraced many, many children. Inspection of the excerpt from the 1907 amendments reveals a very large number of situations in which subjective judgment unquestionably could be expected to play a great part. Obviously, there is no complete agreement as to what constitutes "vulgar language," and the same critique could be applied to "idleness," "frequents," "patronizes," and "habitually," to select a few. Although it is true that juvenile courts generally do not make use of them, the minutiae that appear in this and similar statutes have been widely and vehemently criticized as giving unwarranted powers to the courts. These attacks upon the juvenile court and the demands for curtailment of its powers are discussed later, but it must be admitted here that the reformers in the early days of the juvenile court movement may in their zeal have gone too far because they knew so little. It now seems perfectly clear that the knowledge of what causes delinquency and how it should be treated was at a primitive level at best, but at that time the problems seemed easy to solve. As Grace Abbott succinctly summarized the situation:

At that time little was known about the causes of delinquency and in consequence, little about treatment or prevention. It was believed that if children were separated from adult offenders and the judge dealt with the problems of "erring children" as a "wise and kind father"—as the statute creating the juvenile courts sometimes directed—wayward tendencies would be checked and delinquency and crime prevented or reduced. Under these laws the child offender was regarded not as a criminal but as a delinquent, "as misdirected and misguided and needing aid, encouragement, help, and assistance." . . . The challenging and seminal idea which was back of the juvenile court was that its function was to cure, rather than to punish, delinquency—a very much more difficult task.[11]

The reformers knew what they wanted: to remove children from the contamination of contacts with adults, to extend the protection of the

[10] *Laws of Illinois*, 1907, p. 70.
[11] Abbott, *The Child and the State*, II, pp. 331-332.

state to delinquent children as well as to neglected and dependent children, to provide help for those in trouble. These were the immediate goals, and their rationale was adequate for the times and for the persons involved. This was reform writ large, and the difficult and complex problems of administration of these laws were not envisaged clearly. If they thought about it at all, the early reformers would have no doubts or uncertainties about the caliber of judges who would be attracted to the juvenile court bench; and they had abundant faith in the power of voluntary efforts combined with private philanthropy and public authority. To them, the solution was as simple as the establishment of a separate detention facility—to get the children out of jails was the important thing! In any evaluation of the broad powers conferred upon juvenile courts, the climate of the times must be ranked as an important factor. When this legislation was tested in the higher courts, in state after state the decisions averred that children were no longer to be considered as criminals, that the juvenile courts were created to save children rather than to punish them, and that the state had a primary responsibility to protect children.

Two further significant factors deserve mention: the presence of aggressive civic support, and the honor and distinction for any judge assigned or elected to the juvenile court bench. In the early days of the Chicago Juvenile Court, for example, a self-organized Juvenile Court Committee raised funds for the salaries of probation officers, opened a detention home, and provided strong support for the court in its trying early years. In the same court, competent judges served in a climate that indicated that the juvenile court assignment was regarded as a mark of distinction and a civic responsibility. Judge Richard S. Tuthill, the first judge, was succeeded by the noted and capable Julian W. Mack, who later served on the United States Court of Appeals and whose writings on juvenile court legislation were the classics of that time. Judge Merritt W. Pinckney, while serving as presiding judge of the Circuit Court judges by election of his fellow judges, chose to occupy the Juvenile Court bench. A similar situation prevailed in many large cities. But in recent years, according to an official report of the Cook County court, a judge "at the insistence of his colleagues on the Circuit Court bench accepted, with reluctance, the Juvenile Court assignment." [12] Perhaps the atmosphere of aggressive civic ac-

---

[12] *Annual Message of William N. Erickson*, p. 245.

tivity and the presence of eminent judges lessened the potential dangers of the broad powers embodied in early juvenile court legislation.

By 1945 juvenile courts had been established in all the states. Nevertheless, there is actually no such thing as "a juvenile court system" in the United States today; in fact, there are hundreds, even thousands, of "systems." The specialized juvenile court, with a judge giving full time to the juvenile court, exists in less than fifty jurisdictions; in nearly 3,000 counties, the juvenile court is a branch or part of another court, which frequently has objectives and purposes altogether different from those of the juvenile court itself. In effect, this means that on a certain day of the week, or perhaps only as the occasion arises, a totally different court sits as the juvenile court. While some pretense may be kept up of recognizing the philosophical and other differences of the juvenile court, the functions of the juvenile court, all studies show, tend to be submerged in the normal routines of the court to which juvenile jurisdiction is assigned. Independent, specialized courts are rare; designated courts are the usual pattern; and a few juvenile courts are a special division of a family court or a court of domestic relations.

This miscellany of courts in 1954 dealt with about 475,000 delinquent children, according to United States Children's Bureau estimates. Although it is generally conceded that judges, whether full-time or part-time, need the help of qualified probation officers, more than half the counties in the United States in 1952 failed to provide probation services of any kind in the courts. There were about 1,700 juvenile probation officers, and about 2,000 other probation workers who dealt with both juvenile and adult cases.[13]

As early as 1920, Evelina Belden of the United States Children's Bureau studied the development of juvenile courts and evaluated them on the basis of features considered essential to the organization of a juvenile court, such as separate hearings, the use of informal or chancery procedure, regular probation service, separate detention of children, special court and probation records, and provision for mental and physical examinations. The report showed that only 16 percent of 2,034 courts from which information was obtained were able to meet the three critically basic criteria: separate hearings, regular probation service, and special court and probation records. According to this study, large cities had developed the special organization required for juvenile court work,

[13] *Some Facts about Juvenile Delinquency*, pp. 9-10.

but courts serving small communities were generally poorly equipped to serve the basic goals of juvenile court legislation.[14]

While conditions have tended to improve since 1920, the basic problems remain just about the same. As the National Conference on Prevention and Control of Delinquency reported in 1947: "Accepted in theory, standards outlined for juvenile courts more than 20 years ago are not uniformly put into practice. The courts in some communities are little more than legal entities without the social services and special facilities needed for the adequate handling of children's cases." [15]

Standards respecting juvenile courts, promulgated by the United States Children's Bureau and the National Probation and Parole Association at various times since 1923, have had indirect or direct impact upon legislation in about twenty states. Despite some progress, however, a great many states operate under laws unchanged for a half-century. Not only do less than half the counties in the United States provide probation services, but, as a review of recent directories of probation and parole officers in the United States published by the National Probation and Parole Association reveals, this is an alarmingly consistent pattern—in state after state, the populous, prosperous ones included, only about half the counties have probation service in juvenile cases. In Illinois, usually the sixth or seventh state in the nation in per capita income, a recent survey found only forty-three persons giving full time to juvenile probation work in 85 of the 101 counties outside of Cook County (Chicago).[16] Some of these conditions are understandable in terms of the conditions prevailing when the juvenile courts first were established, but it is difficult to accept the same situations in the light of present knowledge. Concerning the early days of the courts, Katherine Lenroot, former Chief of the United States Children's Bureau, summarily points up some of the contrasts that should make for real differences today:

> When the first juvenile courts were established professional training for social work had not yet been started; child guidance clinics had not been thought of; child-saving and child-caring work, chiefly under private auspices, emphasized the removal of children from undesirable surroundings, chiefly for care in institutions or free foster homes, rather than the

[14] Belden, *Courts in the United States Hearing Children's Cases,* pp. 10 ff.
[15] *Report on Juvenile Court Administration,* p. 2.
[16] *Children and Youth in Illinois,* p. 186.

strengthening and rebuilding of family life; and public outdoor relief was thought to be pauperizing and degrading.[17]

One can only comment: Things have changed a great deal, but not in the juvenile courts!

A breakdown by type of case shows that of about 475,000 children dealt with by juvenile courts annually, roughly 75 percent are delinquency cases, about 19 percent are in the dependency and neglect category, and about 6 percent are involved in special proceedings such as adoption, commitment of mentally defective children, and termination of custody in those juvenile courts having jurisdiction over such matters.[18] The manner in which these children are dealt with by the courts is a matter of vital importance to the affected children as well as to the community. Thus far, measured by any reasonable standard, the juvenile courts have failed to live up to the high expectations held by the early reformers. It is important, therefore, to examine the basic concepts and philosophy of the juvenile court as well as its legal and administrative structure to determine whether the failure to move ahead is the result of faulty theory or whether it is because of the almost inevitable lag which occurs when practice does not fully reflect the essential theories and principles under which practice is supposed to develop. Consequently, in the discussion that follows, wherever it is possible to do so an effort is made to distinguish between theory and practice in order that the one may not suffer from criticism of the other.

Basic Concepts and Philosophy

The basic philosophy of the juvenile court is identified clearly with the movement toward "individualized justice," which was characterized by the distinguished Dean Roscoe Pound as a reaction against the reliance upon rule and the distrust of judicial discretion that dominated nineteenth century jurisprudence.[19] Essentially, this individualization of justice involves a recognition of the individuality of the person before the court and some adaptation of the determinations of the court to accord with the individual and personal needs of the child before the

---

[17] Lenroot, "The Juvenile Court Today."
[18] *Juvenile Court Statistics, 1950-52*, p. 2.
[19] Pound, "The Juvenile Court in the Service State."

court.[20] Of course, the concept of individualization is not exclusively confined to juvenile courts; the extensive use of probation in adult criminal cases is ample proof of this.

As the most recent Children's Bureau statement of standards for juvenile courts aptly describes the situation, individualized justice is not easy to achieve.[21] According to the *Standards*, which were developed in coöperation with the National Probation and Parole Association and the National Council of Juvenile Court Judges, in order for a juvenile court to become fully effective and a fair tribunal operating for the general welfare, there must be:

1   A judge and a staff identified with and capable of carrying out a non-punitive and individualized service.
2   Sufficient facilities available in the court and the community to insure:
    (*a*) that the dispositions of the court are based on the best available knowledge of the needs of the child.
    (*b*) that the child, if he needs care and treatment, receives these through facilities adapted to his needs and from persons properly qualified and empowered to give them.
    (*c*) that the community receives adequate protection.
3   Procedures that are designed to insure that two objectives are kept constantly in mind, these being
    (*a*) the individualization of the child and his situation, and
    (*b*) the protection of the legal and constitutional rights of both parents and child.[22]

As the report points out, some courts meet all of these criteria, but others, especially those in rural areas, have not been able to find or to create the necessary facilities. Other courts have not grasped the concepts of nonpunitive justice, and some courts have not been able to keep a balance between individualization of the child on the one hand and protection of the legal and constitutional rights of both parents and child on the other.[23]

It is necessary at this point to recall that the juvenile court usually has jurisdiction over neglected and dependent children as well as delinquent children, and that its legal origin in the case of delinquent children comes from two streams of law—the extension of chancery or

[20] Schramm, "Philosophy of the Juvenile Court."
[21] *Standards for Specialized Courts Dealing with Children*, p. 1.
[22] *Standards for Specialized Courts Dealing with Children*, pp. 1-2.
[23] *Standards for Specialized Courts Dealing with Children*, p. 2.

equity jurisdiction and modifications of the common law applications to the criminal law. The review of early Illinois juvenile court legislation showed the extent of the extremely broad powers conferred upon the juvenile court by the legislature. But, in addition to understanding the specific statutes that have been enacted by the various legislatures, it is important to realize that in the final analysis the laws mean what the higher courts say they mean. In other words, one cannot rely upon the layman's interpretation of specific statutory provisions.

An important and interesting early decision that became virtually a ruling case and was cited in numerous subsequent decisions throughout the country was handed down by the Pennsylvania Supreme Court in *Commonwealth v. Fisher.* The opinion answered squarely the constitutional objection that the legislature had no power to enact a statute which would deprive a person of his liberty without "due process":

> To save a child from becoming a criminal, or from continuing in a career of crime, to end in maturer years in public punishment and disgrace, the legislatures surely may provide for the salvation of such a child, if its parents or guardian be unable or unwilling to do so, by bringing it into one of the courts of the state without any process at all, for the purpose of subjecting it to the state's guardianship and protection. . . . The act simply provides how children who ought to be saved may reach the court to be saved.

Respecting the attack on the statute's constitutionality (on the basis that no jury trial was provided), the Pennsylvania court held this opinion:

> Here again is the fallacy, that he was tried by the court for any offense. . . . there is no trial for any crime here, and the act is operative only when there is to be no trial. The very purpose of the act is to prevent a trial. . . .[24]

In sustaining the Illinois juvenile court law, the Supreme Court of that state concluded:

> "The purpose of this statute is to extend a protecting hand to unfortunate boys and girls, who, by reason of their own conduct, evil tendencies or improper environment, have proven that the best interests of society, the welfare of the State and their own good demand that the guardianship of the State be substituted for that of natural parents. To

[24] *Commonwealth v. Fisher,* 213 Pennsylvania 48 (1905).

accomplish that purpose the statute should be given a broad and liberal construction. . . ." But the court added this caution: ". . . the right of parents to the society of their offspring is inherent, and courts should not violate that right upon slight pretext nor unless it is clearly for the best interests of the child to do so." [25]

A review of pertinent legislation and decisions by the courts demonstrates without question that delinquent children dealt with by the juvenile court are not to be considered as criminals or treated as such in the sense that adults before the criminal courts may be proceeded against as criminals. The proceedings in juvenile courts are "in the interest of" or "on behalf of children," not proceedings against them. Nevertheless, the child who is alleged to be delinquent as compared with the person alleged to be a criminal loses certain rights and protections that are guaranteed to him under the criminal law. In keeping with Dean Pound's oft-quoted statement that the powers of the Star Chamber were a trifle in comparison with the powers of juvenile courts, numerous questions have been raised concerning the need to guard against abuses of its authority by the court.

This problem of protecting the child from abuses of authority by the juvenile court is magnified and complicated by some of today's confusion concerning the proper jurisdictional relationship between the juvenile court and the criminal court. In part, this confusion is due to the retention of punitive concepts by many of those associated with making, applying, and interpreting the laws, a serious threat to proper understanding of the basic philosophy of the juvenile court.

The Illinois situation provides an illustration of the confusion that can result when jurisdiction is divided between the juvenile courts and the criminal courts. While it is evident that its founders believed that the Illinois juvenile court had original jurisdiction in all children's cases, Supreme Court decisions held first that the juvenile court had concurrent jurisdiction with the criminal court, and then that the juvenile court actually exercised jurisdiction in so-called felony cases by permission of the state's attorney. In effect, the prosecutor decided which children would be dealt with by the juvenile court and which children would be proceeded against in the criminal court. In *People v. Fitzgerald*, 322 Illinois 54 (1926), the state Supreme Court held that the juvenile courts and criminal courts held concurrent jurisdiction in

[25] *Lindsay v. Lindsay*, 257 Illinois 328 (1913).

felony cases; and in *People* v. *Susie Lattimore*, 362 Illinois 206 (1935), it was held that the juvenile court was a court of limited jurisdiction and that the legislature was without authority to confer upon an inferior court the power to stay a court created by the state Constitution from proceeding with the trial of a cause, jurisdiction over which is especially granted to it by the Constitution. The court in the Lattimore case made this interesting comment: "It was not intended by the legislature that the juvenile court should be made a haven of refuge where a delinquent child of the age recognized by law as capable of committing a crime should be immune from punishment for violation of the criminal laws of the State, committed by such child subsequent to his or her being declared a delinquent child."

In commenting upon these decisions, Jerome S. Weiss describes the results of the decisions as "the development in the administration of laws concerning juvenile offenders in Illinois of a form of schizophrenia." In his scathing review of this troublesome question, Weiss points out that it is up to the state's attorney to decide whether the proceedings against a child should be criminal in nature (where the philosophy of punishment as a deterrent persists) or whether the proceeding will be in juvenile court (where the underlying philosophy is treatment and rehabilitation).[26] Because the Illinois Constitution sets the age of criminal responsibility at ten, all children under ten are presumed to lack criminal capacity. But, relying upon common law precedents, those between the ages of ten and fourteen can be prosecuted either as delinquents or criminals at the discretion of the state's attorney, with the presumption that they are incapable of committing crimes unless they know the difference between right and wrong. All children above the age of fourteen and under seventeen if boys and eighteen if girls may be prosecuted either as criminals or delinquents at the discretion of the state's attorney. One caution is necessary: This description applies only in the so-called felony cases which usually, though not always, involve more serious offenses. In Illinois, as in a great many other states, grand larceny, which is usually defined in dollar terms, is a felony. Consequently, a child who steals an article valued at $50.00 may be dealt with as an adult criminal, provided that he has attained the age of ten years. In practice, this is not done very often, especially with younger children, although tough-minded state's attorneys frequently resort to "drives" on

---

[26] Weiss, "Criminals or Delinquents?"

auto-theft or auto-tampering cases and other offenses which have relatively widespread public interest. While the Illinois situation is admittedly an unusual one, it may well provide a dangerous example to other states in which the hue and cry about delinquency is at a peak.

Another form of confusion that involves the juvenile court directly is described by Paul W. Tappan as follows:

> By the disinterest and default of others, children's care through courts as well as through social agencies generally has come into the hands of a group that is oriented rather completely to the philosophies of voluntary social work, with emphasis upon individualized diagnosis and therapy for emotionally unadjusted clients. The view has become very common that the nature of the child's delinquent behavior is unimportant except as a symptom of his underlying emotional problems, that jurisdiction should be predicated upon "the child's need for help," a need which itself is commonly inferred simply from his presence in court rather than from an act of delinquency. This implies that the juvenile court comes to be considered by some authorities as a very general tool in the armamentarium of child-welfare resources to help those youngsters who are in trouble—whether with their parents, school, neighbors or the police. It should be clearly understood, however, that among case-work and child-welfare authorities who are not associated with the courts it is the generally accepted view that the official and authoritarian agencies should be used only very rarely, when it is essential because of the type of problem presented.[27]

Unquestionably, the Tappan view, although an extreme one, is reflected increasingly in the literature of the juvenile court movement. Speaking of the social and legal aspects of the children's court, former Chief Justice Cobb of the Court of Domestic Relations of New York City made the following contentious statement of the problem in a talk before the Court of Domestic Relations, the Association of the Bar, and the County Lawyers' Association on February 6, 1945:

> Become legalistic for the occasion, the supporters of the unrestricted social processes in a court of law for children and their parents, have embraced the catch-words *parens patriae* and *chancery* as something equivalent to little or no legal restraint so that they may cast the beneficent safeguards of due process of law into the limbo of forgotten things. Nothing could be more fallacious. As we have seen, children must be

[27] Tappan, *Comparative Survey*, p. 2.

duly adjudicated before a children's court can assume authority. . . .

The appallingly perverted doctrine of *parens patriae*, so specious that it has wheedled the judiciary and even cast its spell over some courts of appeal, has in it the germ of case-work domination. It has led to the legal baptism by legislatures of youths up to voting age as children, and has made a rubber stamp in some states of the judicial function to the point that it has well nigh surrendered to social processes in the guise of "probation," instead of jealously protecting both child and parent from infringement of their constitutional rights and personal privileges. Both children and insane are wards of the state, but are they to be prejudged by determining them to be such without regard to forms of law? [28]

The recent Children's Bureau *Standards* in a restrained way un-questionably takes into account the implicit and explicit criticisms in the statements of Tappan, Cobb, and others. It is clearly stated that while a court must have reasonable discretion to act in the best interests of a child, certain principles "appear to be generally applicable even to the most progressive courts" and should be recognized. These include: (1) the conditions under which the State is empowered to intervene in the upbringing of a child should be specifically and clearly delineated in the statutes. (2) Both the child and his parents are entitled to know the basis on which the State seeks to intervene and on which it predi-cates its plan for the care and treatment of the child because they are entitled to rebut these bases directly or indirectly. There must be rules of evidence calculated to assure proceedings in accordance with due process of law. (3) The statute should authorize the court to take specific actions in relation to certain causes rather than allow the court unlimited discretion to make any disposition or to order any treatment that may be thought advisable. (4) In order to insure deci-sions affecting social planning for children being made on the basis of sound legal procedure, safeguards should be established for the protec-tion of the rights of parents and children.[29]

Despite the overwhelming approval by the courts of juvenile court statutes, the question still remains whether juvenile courts, by abandon-ing of traditional legal safeguards, actually pose a threat to the welfare of children brought before them. Those who deny this danger base their case chiefly upon the kind of reasoning followed in the Pennsylvania and Illinois Supreme Court decisions already cited, with particular emphasis

[28] Cited in Tappan, *Comparative Survey*, p. 120 (footnote 83).
[29] *Standards for Specialized Courts Dealing with Children*, pp. 6-8.

upon the premise that "guilt" is not an issue. In the 1920 Children's Bureau study referred to previously, Evelina Belden stated that the fundamental purpose of juvenile court procedure was "not to determine whether or not a child has committed a specific offense, but to discover whether he is in a condition requiring the special care of the State." [30]

On the other hand, Paul Tappan declares that the use of the equity or chancery character of the court is an "irrelevant identification of methods, whether the comparison is to ancient chancery, to modern equity, or to civil law." He further declares that it has been popular practice "to rationalize the abandonment, partial or complete, of even the most basic conceptions of due process of law: a specific charge; confrontation by one's adverse witnesses; right to counsel and appeal; rejection of prejudicial, irrelevant, and hearsay testimony; adjudication only upon proof or upon a plea of guilt." He takes issue with the presumption that because the state is determined to protect and save its wards, these children need no due process protection against injury. Exposure to court, jail detention, and a long period in a correctional school "with young thieves, muggers, and murderers—these can do no conceivable harm if the State's purpose be beneficent and the procedure be 'chancery'!" And as Tappan bitterly notes, "they become adult criminals, too, in thankless disregard of the State's good intentions as *parens patriae*." [31] This point of view regarding procedural safeguards is supported by the *Standards for Specialized Courts*, which makes this flat statement:

> It is not infrequently stated that the court is a court of equity and that its procedure is of a chancery or equity nature. This concept is sometimes urged as a justification for a looseness in procedures permitted neither in law nor equity. This concept is inaccurate. The founders of the juvenile court found precedents in chancery cases but juvenile courts were not actually derived from courts of chancery. Specialized children's courts are in fact statutory courts having jurisdiction over certain causes and as such have their own procedure adapted to the type of case heard. [32]

When all of the ramifications of this problem are taken into account, probably some kind of middle ground is desirable. While there are many who resent the legalistic emphasis that seems to be developing, there are

[30] Belden, *Courts in the United States Hearing Children's Cases*, p. 11.
[31] Tappan, *Juvenile Delinquency*, pp. 204-205.
[32] *Standards for Specialized Courts Dealing with Children*, p. 55.

others who are equally resentful of the summary manner in which courts in some instances have dealt with the rights of parents and the freedom of children. Bertram M. Beck, in an excellent analysis of the different points of view of the proper functions of the juvenile court, identifies three schools of thought: (1) that which places little emphasis upon legal aspects, but which emphasizes the social agency functions, including development of numerous services under the court; (2) that which limits the court to a finding of delinquency, with treatment in the hands of an administrative agency; and (3) that which confines the court's functions to conducting hearings and making dispositions in the light of facts produced at a hearing. It is the third point of view which seems to represent the "middle ground," and as Beck sees it, under it the court's activities would be curtailed, unofficial or informal handling of cases would be abolished, and most treatment services would be performed by other agencies (except those provided by the court's probation staff).[33]

Often overlooked in discussions of this problem is the fact that the great bulk of cases coming before the juvenile court involving allegations of delinquency are not contested. Although those trained in the law frequently argue that this may occur because neither the child nor his parents are certain of their rights before the court, observation leads to the conclusion that in nine cases out of ten the child did act in such a way as to bring him under the juvenile delinquency statute of the state and freely admits it. Even so, the one child in ten who does not belong in court or who denies the alleged act needs protection. Some writers have contended that the child is "protected" because the probation officer acts as "counsel" for the child.[34] This position is open to serious question. The probation officer, like the judge, ultimately may impose his own bias or his standards of culture and morals upon children who stand before the court.[35] Although it must be emphasized that juvenile courts must operate with informality and flexibility, and that proceedings with respect to children are nonadversary in nature, the key principle is that the rights of children and their parents must be protected.

[33] Beck, "Juvenile Delinquency."
[34] See, for example, Young, *Social Treatment in Probation and Delinquency*, pp. 182-184.
[35] See the letter by Judge Marion G. Woodward in *Social Service Review*, 18 (September, 1944), pp. 367-368.

Perhaps the final result of the current concern about protection of the rights of delinquent children before the juvenile court may be substantial modification of procedures—even to the point of making a clear distinction between the disposition process and the process of hearing to determine the right of the court to adjudicate in a given situation. In other words, the court would not act until it had first ascertained that the child was a suitable subject for adjudication. This would not be decided by a social investigation which might turn up the fact that the child, and perhaps his family, could be regarded as "a problem in the community," or even by a psychiatric determination that the child could be considered to be emotionally troubled or disturbed. Rather, the court would first ascertain that the child had committed a delinquent act. In all probability, this would have the virtue of confining juvenile court activities to a more restricted sphere and diverting to other agencies many of the child welfare functions and responsibilities now undertaken by juvenile courts. To the argument that the child may "need help with his problem," whether it is a question of getting along in school or one that involves a serious psychiatric disturbance, it might be replied that this kind of help should be made available by other community agencies, not by the juvenile court acting on an unproved hypothesis of delinquency.

On the other hand, if parents are resistive to treatment resources needed by the child from other community agencies, and thereby either the child or the community is endangered, then upon initiation by the appropriate agency the matter could become subject to adjudication in the juvenile court. But most cases would be dealt with in the realm of neglect rather than delinquency. Certainly it seems tenable to hold that the answer to the delicate and involved question of how to bring an erring child under the authority of the state in order to protect him and the community is neither the Star Chamber nor the criminal court, but rather the more careful, skillful, and protected use of a legal instrument that provides a logical framework for expression of the community's concern.

Structure, Organization, and Jurisdiction

The organization of juvenile courts, particularly with reference to their relationship to other courts, presents a strange and bewildering variety of patterns. It has been noted previously that the juvenile court may be a part of a court of general jurisdiction, such as a circuit, county, probate, common pleas, superior, district, quarter sessions, or municipal court. Whatever its name, whether juvenile court, children's court, or domestic relations court, it is usually organized as part of another court. Occasionally it may be independent of all other courts. With few exceptions, whether independent or otherwise, the court is organized on a county basis in conformity with our traditional governmental structure. Although the majority of rural jurisdictions are served by judges whose chief functions are in connection with another court, the practice in many large urban communities, even when the juvenile court is part of a court of general jurisdiction, is to assign a specific judge or judges on a more or less permanent basis to juvenile court work.

Whether a juvenile court should be organized separately or as a branch of a court of juvenile jurisdiction is a matter of some disagreement. Dean Roscoe Pound, for example, has consistently held that the status of juvenile courts is vastly enhanced by their identification with a court of general jurisdiction, and that there are dangers in this specialized court becoming a separate court. As he points out, there are cases in which children have been released from custody because the wrong judge acted or because the judge acted in the wrong court, which could not happen if the juvenile court were a branch of a court of general jurisdiction.[36] Adding weight to his contention is the fact that decisions on the constitutionality of juvenile court statutes made by the various supreme courts almost invariably have pointed to the fact that the creation of the juvenile court was simply an extension of the jurisdiction of another, well-established, and legally justified court. In the face of these arguments as to status and constitutionality, the creation by the legislature of the juvenile court as a completely new court does not seem especially strong. Nevertheless, when the juvenile court is a branch of another court, the customary rotation of judges seems indefensible from the standpoint of the problems with which they must deal. Similarly, the use of the part-time judge, who sits perhaps only two or three times a month as juvenile court judge, is equally indefensible and does not give any real assurance that the special needs of children coming before the court will be met adequately.

One proposal of considerable merit, which meets virtually all of the

[36] Pound, "The Juvenile Court and the Law."

objections to the practice of rotating judges and the use of occasional and part-time judges dealing with juvenile matters, is the creation of a new court on a state-wide basis. The state-administered and state-financed juvenile court systems now operating in three states—Utah, Connecticut, and Rhode Island—provide full-time judges and other court personnel selected for their special qualifications. The most recent revision of the National Probation and Parole Association's *Standard Juvenile Court Act* includes a plan for a state juvenile court. This action was based upon the approval of the following resolution introduced at the 1948 annual meeting of the Association:

> Whereas, although the law of every state in the Union provides for juvenile courts, large areas of most states are still without effective juvenile courts, and even when the need for an adequate separate juvenile court is recognized and the desire for its establishment prevails, it is impracticable to set up such courts in rural or less densely populated areas on a county basis because there is not sufficient volume of work to justify a full time qualified juvenile court judge, probation staff, clerical employees and detention facilities, with the attendant financial cost; and
>
> Whereas certain states, notably Utah, Connecticut and Rhode Island, have established and found effective the system of area or district courts to serve a combination of counties, towns and smaller cities within the borders of such area or district having a sufficient population and volume of work to justify an adequately staffed court and its attendant expense;
>
> Be It Resolved: That the plan of such area or district courts is commended and recommended.[37]

Because, in view of the irrefutable logic of the plan, the state juvenile court may well become the court of the future, some of its more important aspects deserve special consideration.

In the first place, the state juvenile courts now operating have made it feasible to provide full-time juvenile court judges rather than part-time, ex-officio judges. In Utah, the work of twenty-six ex-officio juvenile court judges was taken over by four full-time judges and one part-time judge; in Rhode Island, the twelve district court judges who acted ex-officio as juvenile court judges have been replaced by three special judges; in Connecticut, three special judges have replaced 169 town and city judges who heard juvenile court cases, only two of whom were juvenile court judges. Secondly, the state juvenile court plan provides

---

[37] *Standard Juvenile Court Act*, pp. 339-340.

complete service to the entire state, rather than to one or two metropolitan areas. This is a distinct advance, because under the present system only the metropolitan areas are served by judges who spend a relatively large part of their time in juvenile court work. According to Sol Rubin, with the exception of the three states with state-wide juvenile courts, there are only eighty counties with special judges in the 3,000 counties in forty-five states, and only one-half of these are full-time judges. As Rubin summarizes the picture, only 2 percent of all counties have full-time judges, and of these, one-third are not especially selected for juvenile court work.[38]

One important caution must be observed: The establishment of a state-wide juvenile court does not automatically deal with all of the questions that involve juvenile courts today. There still remain such issues as how judges should be selected, what their specific qualification and salaries should be, and problems involving probation personnel and other services available to the court. Nevertheless, the state-wide juvenile court unquestionably appears to provide the best framework for improvement. *Certainly, the dependence upon local autonomy and local fiscal support resting upon a county tax base has failed to produce results.*

Before examining several of the controversial areas in the field of juvenile court jurisdiction, it is desirable to review briefly the over-all pattern of jurisdiction now prevailing in the juvenile courts. No attempt is made here either to present all of the problems of jurisdiction, or to deal with many of the legal and other implications that are involved. In this area, extensive legal treatises would be required to deal with all of the basic questions. Consideration should, however, be given to the types of children who are dealt with by the courts, the offenses or conditions that make them subject to court adjudication, and their ages.

In general, juvenile courts have jurisdiction in the cases of delinquent children and usually in cases of dependent or neglected children. Often the distinctions between and among these groups of children are blurred, so that it is probable that a great many cases dealt with in one fashion in one court might conceivably be dealt with in another category in a different court. As was pointed out previously, about three-fourths of all cases dealt with by the juvenile courts are delinquency cases, with less than one out of five dependency or neglect cases, and only about one out of twenty in the several other categories over which some courts

---

[38] Rubin, "State Juvenile Court: A New Standard," pp. 103-107.

have jurisdiction. Both neglect and dependency tend to be rather loosely defined, the chief differences seeming to be that neglect involves a deliberate act on the part of a parent or other guardian, while dependency may exist solely because of the inability of a parent or other guardian to provide for a child. As a matter of fact, in many laws both neglect and dependency are defined in identically the same terms, although current opinion seems to lean heavily in the direction of making a more clear-cut distinction between these two.

There are some interesting questions involved here, including the issue of whether truancy, for example, should be considered a phase of delinquency or of neglect. It might be agreed that the use of delinquency proceedings smacks of placing the onus upon the child who is truant, while neglect proceedings would emphasize the failure of parents to fulfill the common law obligation to educate the child.

The problem of definition has certain important ramifications. For example, if distinctions are not properly made among delinquency, neglect, and dependency, it is conceivable that a dependent child may be committed to the same institution as delinquent children, and in fact this happens altogether too often. Also, it seems highly undesirable to clutter up the work of the court with dependency cases in which there is no obvious need for authoritative intervention by a court. As a matter of fact, the *Standard Juvenile Court Act*, while defining jurisdiction over children in relatively broad terms, is annotated in such a way as to exclude the standard dependency cases from the responsibility of the juvenile courts. According to the most recent revision (1949) of the *Act*, "It is generally agreed that the court should intervene only when there is need of authoritative action with respect to a child or the adults responsible for his care or condition. Cases of dependency without an element of neglect, or where no change of legal custody is involved, should be dealt with by administrative agencies without court action."

The confusion among these groups of children unquestionably has come about because of the historical association of the juvenile court with the chancery tradition. The tendency of the courts to exercise jurisdiction over dependent children even after the need for it passed was given considerable impetus by the fact that the early mother's pension statutes, now included in the Aid to Dependent Children program of the Social Security Act, actually were administered by the courts in a large number of states. The first mother's pension legislation was adopted in 1911 in Illinois, and the Illinois juvenile courts did not relinquish responsibility for it until 1941, six years after the passage of the Social Security Act. It should be remembered that at the time mother's pension functions were placed in the juvenile court there was no administrative agency in the community, other than the poor law agencies, to which the responsibility could have been given. But the overseers of the poor or the county commissioners charged with responsibility for the poor were generally in bad repute, while the juvenile court was still looked upon as the great reform agency and the hope of enlightened citizens.

The growth of public welfare agencies in recent years and the relatively acceptable status they occupy in the great majority of communities makes untenable the utilization of a court for what is obviously a purely administrative function, especially when the problem is one of dependency. Nevertheless, in some metropolitan communities, those associated with the courts have been "empire builders" and they are reluctant to divest themselves of responsibilities for any category of cases, once jurisdiction has been assumed. Numerous surveys by the National Probation and Parole Association attest to the fact that many courts are bogged down with responsibilities for which they have neither the facilities nor the manpower; yet most of these courts are reluctant to make their own task more manageable by diverting to appropriate administrative agencies cases that do not require court adjudication.

Other responsibilities placed by law in the juvenile courts vary considerably from one jurisdiction to another. The *Standard Juvenile Court Act* recommends that the court have jurisdiction in determining custody or guardianship of the person, in adoption cases, in termination of parental rights, in giving consent to the marriage of a child when required by law, and in proceedings involving the treatment or commitment of a mentally defective, mentally disordered, or emotionally disturbed child. The most recent review of jurisdiction in what might be called miscellaneous types of cases, although somewhat out-dated, showed that jurisdiction was included, in some sections of a state or the entire state, in certain classes of cases: divorce (two states), guardianship (nine states), adoption (ten states), custody questions (thirteen states), physically handicapped children of certain types (nine states), mentally defective or disordered children (nineteen states), and illegitimacy involving determination of paternity and support of child (eight states). Also, in several states the court had jurisdiction over material witnesses, the marriage of children of certain ages, and annulments of marriage.[39] This array of instances in which juvenile courts have been given jurisdiction in certain cases indicates rather clearly the way in which the court has been regarded as a general child-welfare agency. Nonetheless, it should be noted that a good case may be made for juvenile court jurisdiction in many of these categories whenever there are specific issues in dispute.

In about three-quarters of the states, the juvenile court has jurisdiction over adults charged with contributing to delinquency or with neglect, or in cases involving dependency of children, as well as the power to order parents or other legally responsible persons to contribute to the support of children within the court's jurisdiction. Obviously, when adult cases are tried before the juvenile court the adult should have all of the protections provided in any adult court. The case for dealing with adults charged with contributing to delinquency of children is an especially strong one, because the juvenile court presumably will protect the interests of the child while treating the adult in such a way as to provide him with all constitutional protections and guarantees. In recent years, juvenile courts have been especially active, even aggressively so, in punishing so-called delinquent parents. The tendency to blame parents for the delinquency of their children is not a new one, but in some areas it has been looked upon as a new panacea for "solving the delinquency problem." This is not the place for an excursion into the psychological and other factors that have caused this development, but this much needs to be said—the parents in question often are badly in need of help themselves, and the use of jail terms as "shock therapy" for them is calculated neither to help them nor to improve parent-child relationships.[40]

In 1950, the upper age limit of juvenile courts in boys' cases were as follows: eighteen years or higher in thirty-one states, parts of four others, and the District of Columbia; seventeen years in eight states and part of one other; and sixteen years in five states and in parts of five others.[41] Despite the fact that the United States Children's Bureau and the National Probation and Parole Association have been on record since

---

[39] Cosulich, *Juvenile Court Laws of the United States*, 2d ed., pp. 42-44.

[40] Alexander, "What's This about Punishing Parents?"; and *Parents and Delinquency*.

[41] Sussmann, *Law of Juvenile Delinquency*, p. 17.

1923 as favoring eighteen years as the standard for juvenile court jurisdiction, and even though in recent years some states with a lower age
limit have raised it to eighteen years and no state has lowered the age
limit, these recommendations should not necessarily be accepted un-
critically.

Even though the *Standard Juvenile Court* Act and the laws of many
states provide for transfer of cases to criminal courts in more serious
offenses, usually defined as felonies, the use of such waivers is relatively
infrequent. There is some possibility that the appearance in juvenile
court of older youngsters, especially those of sixteen and seventeen,
may constitute a long-run public relations problem for juvenile courts.
As a result of vague and, in most instances, false charges of "coddling
youthful toughs" in the juvenile courts, some judges in self-defense
may adopt a "get tough" policy or deal with such cases on the basis
of the offense rather than the offender. In either instance, free-handed
use of institutionalization is a likely result.

Even though questions may be raised about the age limit being
eighteen, it is difficult conscientiously to recommend the only practical
alternative currently available in the great majority of jurisdictions,
namely, the use of the criminal court. The failure of the vast majority
of communities to develop socialized procedures in the courts for those
between the juvenile court upper age limit and twenty-one years of age,
discussed elsewhere in this book, literally means making a choice between the informal, flexible, but sometimes sentimental dealing with the
more serious cases in a juvenile court and the use of harsh and punitive
measures in the criminal court. Naturally, the argument may be made
that the juvenile court need not be sentimental and that the criminal
court need not be harsh and punitive. Nevertheless, both extremes are
far too common. While it must be acknowledged that the extremes are
both undesirable and unnecessary—because there are realistic juvenile
courts and nonpunitive criminal courts—the danger here should not be
ignored. If the presence of the older youngsters who commit relatively
serious offenses affects the juvenile court in any way, it may be in the
direction of making the court a little more rigid, a little less informal,
and more and more inclined to adopt some of the attitudes of the
criminal court. Even though they cannot be measured objectively or
spelled out statistically, the implications for younger children dealt with
in such a court should be obvious.

In delinquency cases, juvenile courts deal with everything from the most trivial offenses to the most serious, including murder. In roughly half of the states, the original jurisdiction of the juvenile court is considered to be exclusive jurisdiction even in murder cases, but in others the jurisdiction is concurrent with that of the criminal court or must be relinquished entirely in certain kinds of cases of a more serious type, usually when the children are of specified ages.

Sussmann has prepared a chart showing a list of acts or conditions that are included in delinquency definitions or descriptions in the laws of the several states. Ranked in decreasing order of frequency, these are listed in their entirety as follows:

1. Violates any law or ordinance
2. Habitually truant
3. (Knowingly) associates with thieves, vicious or immoral persons
4. Incorrigible
5. Beyond control of parent or guardian
6. Growing up in idleness or crime
7. So deports self as to injure or endanger self or others
8. Absents self from home (without just cause and) without consent
9. Immoral or indecent conduct
10. (Habitually) uses vile, obscene or vulgar language (in public place)
11. (Knowingly) enters, visits house of ill repute
12. Patronizes, visits policy shop or gaming place
13. (Habitually) wanders about railroad yards or tracks
14. Jumps train or enters car or engine without authority
15. Patronizes saloon or dram house where intoxicating liquor is sold
16. Wanders streets at night, not on lawful business
17. Patronizes public poolroom or bucket shop
18. Immoral conduct around school (or in public place)
19. Engages in illegal occupation
20. In occupation or situation dangerous or injurious to self or others
21. Smokes cigarettes (or uses tobacco in any form)
22. Frequents place whose existence violates law
23. Is found in place for permitting which adult may be punished
24. Addicted to drugs
25. Disorderly
26. Begging
27. Uses intoxicating liquor
28. Makes indecent proposal
29. Loiters, sleeps in alleys, vagrant

30. Runs away from state or charity institution
31. Found on premises occupied or used for illegal purposes
32. Operates motor vehicle dangerously while under influence of liquor
33. Attempts to marry without consent, in violation of law
34. Given to sexual irregularities.[42]

The *Standard Juvenile Court Act* proposes a substitute for definitions of delinquency, namely, descriptions of cases over which the court is given jurisdiction. This same device is already employed in several states, and it is considered a desirable alternative to labeling the child as a delinquent, both because the court's jurisdiction is just as definite and because this device seems to be in accord with fundamental juvenile court philosophy.

Juvenile courts reporting to the United States Children's Bureau in 1952 handled 53 percent of all cases on an informal or unofficial basis and 57 percent of delinquency cases were so handled.[43] The use of informal methods, sometimes referred to as "unofficial probation" or "informal adjustment of cases," deserves close scrutiny. Usage varies considerably from one jurisdiction to another, but it is presumed that the development of such practices began at a time when there were no other community child welfare resources available. The courts, seeing children in need of help, decided to help them simply because there was no other place where they could obtain the required assistance, and court intervention by the use of a process of adjudication seemed unnecessary and even undesirable. Like many other social institutions, the development of unofficial handling of cases by juvenile courts has been surrounded with an aura that tends to conceal grave defects. Lou, a quarter of a century ago, hailed the practice as another step in the socialization of juvenile court procedures,[44] and many others have defended it as a way of avoiding "inflexibility" in court procedures. It has also been commended as a way of avoiding the "stigma" of official court action, or as a method of avoiding the potentially deleterious effects of "a court record."

It is important to distinguish between two kinds of so-called unofficial cases: (1) those dealt with on an informal, supervisory basis by the court staff, usually after some process of investigation, or the

---

[42] Sussmann, *Law of Juvenile Delinquency*, p. 20.
[43] *Juvenile Court Statistics, 1950-52*, p. 2. In 1953, 53 percent of all delinquency cases were dealt with unofficially. *Juvenile Court Statistics, 1953*, p. 2.
[44] Lou, *Juvenile Courts in the United States*, p. 127.

use of informal probation or supervision following an unofficial hearing before the court or its representative, in which the child or his parents may be warned; and (2) those in which referral is made informally to an appropriate social agency, either private or public, or when the whole matter is settled out of hand, simply by a conference among the affected persons. Although statistics on this score are quite unreliable, there is a strong presumption that most of the latter type are labeled as "dismissals" or "discharges."

In any event, while the exact extent of the use of informal supervision or unofficial probation is unknown, numerous theoretical and practical objections can be made to it. But many cases coming to the juvenile court may require the use of the conference method or appropriate referral on a voluntary basis, and it is difficult to quarrel with this practice.[45] The 1954 Children's Bureau *Standards for Specialized Courts Dealing with Children* recommends that informal adjustments be limited to the conference and referral type of activity.

As for the argument for "unofficial handling" that stresses avoidance of the stigma of court action, such stigma may result from the probation officer's investigation, whether the child appears in court or not. As to the question of the court appearance giving the child a "record," the answer seems to be one of setting up safeguards with respect to the use of such records in any other kind of proceeding. If this problem of unofficial handling is seen in proper perspective, it emerges as a kind of action highly susceptible to abuses. Whatever validity there may be to the criticisms of official juvenile court hearings before a judge, it is evident that the child dealt with unofficially is deprived of many of the rights observed in the usual court situation, however informal and flexible the official hearing may be.

The most appropriate answer to these problems consists of providing an adequate intake department that will make *decisions* leading directly to the filing of an appropriate petition in court, or to the referral and conference settlement of situations that may be dealt with safely outside of the court and that do not require court adjudication.

Probably this criticism of informal handling of cases should be tempered somewhat in its application to areas in which other child welfare services simply are not available. Nevertheless, the practical result in many communities seems to be that the retention of large

---

[45] *Standards for Specialized Courts Dealing with Children*, pp. 43-44.

numbers of unofficial cases—running up to 80 or 90 percent of all cases handled by a court in some instances—actually retards the development of adequate child welfare services in the community. As the chapter following demonstrates, juvenile court facilities and personnel are already strained beyond the breaking point. It seems utterly futile to condone a policy that results in large numbers of children being dealt with, sometimes for long periods, by a court staff that is already overworked, and the effect of which may be to deprive the children of the services they need badly.

As Tappan has aptly pointed out, if this were simply a question of sparing delinquents the label, a strong stand against unofficial handling of certain cases might be difficult to make, but in practice "too often it is the non-delinquent, better dealt with elsewhere, whom the court is trying to help." [46] It is a pathetic commentary upon today's juvenile courts that judges and other personnel persist in trying to retain what has become a vested interest in children who do not belong in the court and who were there in the first place only because a historical accident made the court a child welfare agency. In the face of developments in administrative agencies with responsibilities for child welfare problems, the persistence of so-called informal handling of cases by courts is illogical and inconsistent with their appropriate functions and actual facilities. To the children affected—denied the very help they need in many instances—it is even more pathetic that the very social instrument that was once hailed as a great reform now stands as a barrier to progress in meeting their basic needs.

For Further Reading

SUSSMANN, FREDERICK B., *Law of Juvenile Delinquency: The Laws of the Forty-Eight States* (New York, 1950).

An excellent compendium of information in this area, conveniently arranged, and expertly summarized.

TAPPAN, PAUL W., *Comparative Survey on Juvenile Delinquency, Part I: North America*. United Nations Department of Social Affairs, Division of Social Welfare (New York, 1952).

[46] Tappan, *Juvenile Delinquency*, p. 221.

An informative, comparative summary of the scope of delinquency problems by a foremost legal and sociological authority in this field.

A Standard Juvenile Court Act, National Probation and Parole Association, revised edition (New York, 1949).

A recommended uniform juvenile court act for the several states, based upon a comparative survey of progressive state legislation and the emerging socio-legal conceptions concerning delinquency and its treatment. Contains a discussion of each section, pointing up issues and problems.

Standards for Specialized Courts Dealing with Children, U.S. Department of Health, Education, and Welfare, Children's Bureau Pub. No. 346 (Washington, D.C., 1954).

Developed in coöperation with the National Probation and Parole Association and the National Council of Juvenile Court Judges, this statement is complementary to *A Standard Juvenile Court Act.* Taken together, they form an adequate basis for understanding virtually all issues facing juvenile courts today.

TAPPAN, PAUL W., *Juvenile Delinquency* (New York, 1949).

A widely-used standard textbook that emphasizes the legal aspects of delinquency.

RUBIN, SOL, "State Juvenile Court: A New Standard," in *Focus,* 30 (July, 1951), pp. 103-107.

This is a thorough examination of the case for the state-wide juvenile courts currently operating in Connecticut, Rhode Island, and Utah. The author is a discerning and astute commentator on the issues identified with the local character of the courts.

Chapter 13

THE JUVENILE COURT: OPERATIONS AND STAFF FUNCTIONS

At this point it seems reasonable to raise the question: How do juvenile courts actually function? In the light of their backgrounds and the somewhat vague basic concepts and philosophies ascribed to them, together with the somewhat inconsistent legal and administrative structure already described, it is more than difficult to make universally applicable statements. Similarities and differences from one court to another are hidden to a greater or lesser degree in the attitudes and administrative devices relied upon by court staffs. This is true not only with respect to state by state differences but also among courts operating in the same state. Observers are confused frequently by the vast gulf separating the operations of one court from another, even when ostensibly both are operating under identical laws.

As was pointed out previously, some children are dealt with by criminal courts, either because the criminal courts have original jurisdiction in certain kinds of cases, or because juvenile courts and criminal courts have concurrent or overlapping jurisdiction, or because juvenile courts under certain conditions waive cases to the criminal courts.

Except when otherwise noted, all references in this chapter are to delinquent children before the juvenile court.

Comparisons with the Criminal Courts

One way of getting some notion of general procedures in the juvenile court is by comparison with procedures in the criminal courts, which are likely to be more familiar than those of the juvenile courts. It must be understood that the comparisons that follow are extremely general and are not necessarily applicable in all cases. Nevertheless, they may provide a springboard for the discussion that follows.

Procedural Differences:
Juvenile Courts and Criminal Courts

JUVENILE COURTS	CRIMINAL COURTS
(1) Unless the child is already in custody, he is brought before the court by means of summons.	(1) Unless the person accused of crime is in custody, a warrant for his arrest is issued.
(2) A petition is filed on behalf of or in the interest of the child.	(2) The accused is proceeded against by indictment by a grand jury or an information filed by the prosecuting attorney.
(3) When required, detention is separate from adults or in a specialized institution or agency.	(3) The person charged is either detained in jail awaiting trial or is released by posting bond or on his own recognizance.
(4) A hearing is held to establish the child's need for state intervention to protect his interests.	(4) There is a trial on a specific charge to determine guilt, or the accused pleads guilty to the charge.
(5) Defense counsel is rarely used.	(5) An attorney, employed by the defendant or assigned by the court, defends the accused.
(6) Prosecuting attorneys almost never participate.	(6) A prosecutor invariably presents the case for the state.
(7) The hearing is private.	(7) The trial is public.
(8) In hearings, which are informal, both social and legal information are used, and the state may intervene if a preponderance of evidence indicates that it should.	(8) Trial is conducted under strict rules of evidence, and there must be proof of guilt beyond a reasonable doubt.

JUVENILE COURTS	CRIMINAL COURTS
(9) Juries are used rarely.	(9) The accused has the right to a jury trial.
(10) The social study is basic, and is sometimes used by the court before a hearing is held.	(10) Social investigation is not required, although it may follow determination of guilt.
(11) There is a disposition involving application of remedies or treatment.	(11) A sentence is pronounced, which often, though not always, takes the form of punishment meted out.
(12) The main emphasis is upon the need of the child for help and guidance.	(12) The chief emphasis is upon the protection of society, whether through punishment or isolation, or by efforts at rehabilitation through the use of institutional or non-institutional treatment.

It must be stressed that this summary is for illustrative purposes only, and it certainly does not apply in all cases. As a matter of fact, a number of reflections of criminal procedure are still found in many juvenile courts. In the majority of delinquency cases, complaints are filed by the police, and in the preliminary stages it is sometimes difficult to distinguish between a juvenile court hearing and a criminal court trial. Regardless of the semantics of the situation, the juvenile court has acquired a stigma that has rubbed off from the criminal courts. In some jurisdictions jury trials are used relatively frequently, and in a few courts prosecutors take an active and vigorous role. Delinquency itself often is defined in the language of the criminal code; and at the disposition stage, many judges utilize fines and short "sentences" to be "served" in a specialized detention facility or in a common jail.

The juvenile courts and the criminal courts have certain similarities: both require some form of hearing, social investigations or social studies are commonly used, and some form of disposition is made. A characteristic difference that almost always stands out is the utilization of a social study by the juvenile court in a substantial number of cases prior to the hearing. A final difference, and one that is almost always criticized by the opponents of "the socialized court," is the use of social information rather than legal evidence as the primary basis for the court's adjudication. Probably the chief characteristic that distinguishes the juvenile court is its informality, in contrast with the criminal court in which formal proceedings are used almost invariably. To the advocates of the juvenile court method, this informality has taken on the quality of an outstanding virtue; to its critics, informality is a plague and a cloak for illegal activities.

With these general comparisons in mind, it seems desirable to give specific attention to the pre-hearing process, the hearing itself, and the issues and problems associated with dispositions in the juvenile court.

The Pre-Hearing Process

Chronologically, the pre-hearing process actually gets under way when a youngster is apprehended by the police, or when a complaint is made about him by a social agency, parents, or other referring source.[1] Since the focus here is upon operations of the court, for practical purposes we will consider that the pre-hearing process starts at the point at which a complaint is received by a member of the juvenile court staff.

The Intake Process

All juvenile courts, large and small, utilize some form of intake procedure, whether it is organized as such and identified by that name or not. In the smaller courts, this may be a relatively informal process in which a staff member of the court, usually a probation officer, receives the complaint from the source of referral. In the larger courts, there may be a special intake department with a section identified as a "complaint desk." Regardless of the extent of the use of so-called informal handling of cases, previously discussed, the intake process invariably operates as a screening device. Even when the standards referred to earlier are operating, by which unofficial handling is restricted to those cases in which immediate referral is made to a social agency or in which adjustment by the conference device is utilized, a decision is made that states in effect that this is not a case for court action at this point. Naturally, the extent of screening at this early stage varies considerably from one jurisdiction to another and there are no well-developed or standardized criteria that seem to have anything like uniform application. In some courts, the petition process that leads to court action is begun in nearly all cases; in others, relatively few cases

---

[1] See "Procedural Differences," *supra*.

are so processed. There is general agreement that the complaint desk itself and the intake service of the court should be manned by workers who possess sound judgment and are able to utilize effectively the considerable discretion that must be exercised. Such workers must be able to operate under pressure of time, and they must be sensitive to the needs of children in addition to being fully aware of all available community facilities to which referral may be made. The selective use of community resources may be a relatively simple matter in a rural area; in a metropolitan community, where there may be scores and even hundreds of agencies, all of them with varying and changing policies with respect to intake, the responsibilities described call for skill, discernment, and up-to-date knowledge.

If it is decided that the indications are that a petition should be filed in order to bring the case before the court, certain prerequisites must be met. If the referring agency has not provided sufficient information to make adequate basis for determining whether a petition should be filed, it may be necessary at this early stage to conduct an investigation into the facts and circumstances that have been alleged to bring the child under the purview of the court. Because such an inquiry rarely is confined to legal facts and evidence, it tends to take on the manner and form of a comprehensive social study. It is this kind of social investigation that has been criticized so severely by many writers on the subject. Their chief concern appears to be with the almost inevitable result of the social investigation—the determination that the child, whether involved in a specific offense or not, presents problems. Those who agree with such criticisms logically favor some form of preliminary hearing before a judge (or his designated representative) in order to determine whether the child in fact should be before the court for adjudication. This point of view seems to have strongest validity when the complaint originates with the police, because unquestionably the need to bring in specific evidence of an offense will result in more careful preparation of cases and avoid captious referrals to the court.

Yet, even though about three-fourths of all complaints originate with the police, the problem of what to do with the remaining complaints, roughly one-fourth, still remains. Obviously, it is necessary for somebody to make an investigation of the facts as reported to the complaint department of the court, and this must be done either by the police or by a member of the probation staff. The activities of police departments, previously reviewed, do not lend encouragement to the view that these cases ought to be investigated by the police; therefore the probation department of the court normally will have to make appropriate inquiry. Nevertheless, in most courts there is a tendency to make the inquiry an unduly broad one, leading to the determination that the child has "a problem." The only solution that would meet the objections of the critics of the present situation would seem to be that of restricting the investigation at this stage to the facts alleged in the complaint made to the court. If, upon investigation, the facts reported initially do not warrant action by the court, the filing of a petition cannot be justified. Some may argue that, from a legal standpoint, the filing of a petition when a complaint is received, without additional investigation, should be the normal procedure, and that if the court finds insufficient cause to deal with the child from an adjudication standpoint, the court should then order an investigation of the facts, if it seems advisable, or dismiss the complaint as being unsupported by appropriate factual evidence.

Although most of the criticisms of the practice of making investigations before petitions are filed originate outside of the courts, they seem to have an inherent logic which would justify use of three standards as reasonable and appropriate. (1) In all cases that originate with the police, the report by the police should provide clear and sufficient evidence of violation of juvenile court law so as to make it appear probable that the child actually can be adjudicated by the court; in such cases, a petition should be filed. (2) All delinquency complaints originating outside the police, except those in which agencies rather than individuals are involved, should be subject to investigation by the probation staff, *but only as to the facts alleged*, before a petition is filed. (3) In all cases, before a complete social study of the child and his needs is made, there should be some type of hearing on a petition, whether it be called a preliminary hearing or some other name, which will determine that the court has the right to deal with the child before it.

This stand is supported to a large extent by statements made by the United States Children's Bureau in 1923 and in 1954. As the early *Juvenile Court Standards* recommends, "the judge, or a probation officer designated by him, should examine all complaints and after adequate investigation determine whether a petition should be filed or other formal action should be taken." [2] In its recent *Standards for Specialized Courts*, the Bureau makes this comment: "The social study should never be confused with the evidence necessary to substantiate the facts alleged in the petition." [3] Again, in the same *Standards*, reference is made to the social study as being an extremely important part of the court's procedure, and "on the basis of the study and other facts presented at the hearing, the court, having first made a finding regarding the facts alleged in the petition, makes appropriate disposition. . . ." [4]

When a petition is filed, it should be filed on behalf of or in the interest of a child and it should include at least the following information: (1) the facts alleged to bring the child within the jurisdiction of the court; (2) the name, age, and residence of the child; and (3) the names and residences of his parents, guardians, those having legal custody, or nearest known relative. [5]

If one accepts the criticisms of juvenile court procedures, logically the next step after a petition is filed would be some form of preliminary hearing, somewhat similar to arraignment before a magistrate in the criminal court system. In any event, if there is a preliminary hearing, the case may be continued and the child held in detention or released to his parents pending further court inquiry before disposition.

Whether the court utilizes a preliminary hearing or not, the next and very important process is that of the social study. In courts in which preliminary hearings are not used, when a child denies the incident which brought him to the attention of the court, there is a real question as to whether the social study should begin until the facts warranting the assumption of jurisdiction by the court have been ascertained. The importance of withholding the social study until determination of the court's right to act in the case of a child's denial or when there is reasonable doubt by the judge or probation officer that the child in fact was involved in the alleged offense cannot be overemphasized. As the recent Children's Bureau report points out, "a social study made by the court inevitably involves some intrusion of privacy, including

[2] *Juvenile Court Standards*, p. 3.
[3] *Standards for Specialized Courts Dealing with Children*, p. 50.
[4] *Standards for Specialized Courts Dealing with Children*, pp. 49-50
[5] *Standards for Specialized Courts Dealing with Children*, p. 48.

contacts with schools and neighbors, and results in some gossip about the child and his family." [6] One of the better courts in the nation is very clear in its point of view with respect to this question. The Juvenile Court for the State of Connecticut has commented: "Where a child has denied his delinquent act there should clearly be an adjudication of innocence or guilt before a widespread invasion of his personal privacy and that of his family is undertaken." [7]

The Social Study for the Court

The nature of the social study is derived largely from its essential functions, namely, to guide the court in its disposition of the situation and to offer a sound basis for a working plan that deals with the significant problems the child presents. Consequently, a social study generally inquires into and reports to the court on the child's social, emotional, mental, and physical development, and his relationships to his environment, including his home, school, church, and various positive and negative community influences. Focus is given to the child's relationships with other members of the family and to others with whom he is in close contact. As the *Standards for Specialized Courts* makes clear, the social study goes far beyond merely securing a mass of facts and clinical reports concerning the child and his family. Most important is the evaluation and interpretation of these facts in relation to the situation that faces the child and his family. As the *Standards* describes it: "the child's attitudes about the delinquent act in question are pertinent to the social study as they indicate his need for care and treatment, since the purpose of the social study is to determine the care or treatment needed and not to prove or disprove that a delinquent act has been committed." [8]

In view of the broad scope of the areas involved, information must be obtained from a number of sources, such as the child and his family, clinical reports, records of social agencies, and the information provided by schoolteachers and others who know the child. Because the report is to be used by the court it should go beyond merely pulling together the facts that may be available concerning a given child and his situation, and it should indicate diagnostically the treatment clues that

[6] *Standards for Specialized Courts Dealing with Children*, p. 50.
[7] Connecticut, *Annual Report of the Juvenile Court*, 1949, p. 4.
[8] *Standards for Specialized Courts Dealing with Children*, p. 51.

may be useful in developing an appropriate working plan for dealing with the child's problems. Consequently, in any good children's court one would expect to find not merely the bare bones of fact, but interpretation and judgment by a professional person on the meaning of the facts in relation to what should be done with the child. In other words, a good social study includes appropriate information about the child and his family, gathered from a variety of sources and brought together in a report that can be used by the court to determine appropriate disposition. Essentially, such a report should have a diagnostic tone. This means that the report should try to answer such questions as: (1) What is the matter here? (2) What has been done or is being done about it? and (3) What should be done about the problem or problems in light of existing resources?

Obviously, then, the focus is largely upon the personality of the youngster before the court and not upon the offense that he has committed. This does not mean that the offense and the attitude of the child, his parents, and the community toward it should not be taken into account, because in the case of serious assaultive acts, for example, there may be a need to consider isolation by way of institutionalization as an appropriate form of treatment of the child in question. (This does not imply that institutions should be used solely or even usually in such cases, or that the institutional role is chiefly one of isolation.) This point is often ignored in discussions of the problem because the social study deals with so many other facets of a child's life than the offense itself. Nevertheless, the question of whether a child at a given time may need restraint because he happens to be at that particular time a definite menace to himself or to others is an appropriate one for inclusion in a social study of a delinquent coming before the court.

In general, for the nation as a whole, the picture of social studies made for the juvenile courts is an extremely disheartening one. Although the National Probation and Parole Association and various individual probation departments have compiled guides for use of those making social studies, the results have not been encouraging, largely because the presence of a guide in itself does not guarantee the judgment that will be used in compiling the information suggested and in interpreting it in the best interests of child and community. It is generally believed that reports to the court should be uniform with respect to each report made to a given court, that is, that the information considered necessary and desirable should be included under appropriate headings and in a readily understood sequence. This helps to focus the attention of the worker upon the significant things that should be included and is a very great help to those juvenile court judges who actually try to read the social studies in cases coming before them. On the other hand, such a device, meritorious though it be in theory, tends to encourage a kind of drab uniformity of information, and the ultimate result in a great many courts is that the reports of social studies, outside of minor variations as to age and residence, contain almost identically the same information about each child. Consequently, the individual personality of a particular child does not stand out, and virtually the same things are said about him that are said about other children. This has a very serious aftermath—the tendency for courts to individualize only with respect to the offense which brought the child before the court in the first place. In such situations, the social study so laboriously compiled may be utterly worthless.

A review of hundreds of reports from a great variety of courts reveals an unhealthy combination of accumulated static information together with the inclusion of large amounts of useless data. For example, many courts use outlines which provide for some attention to "developmental history." It is not unusual to find a summary such as this: "Breast fed. Walked and talked at 1 year. No teething trouble, but some colic. Toilet training established at 2. Had whooping cough at 3, measles at 4, and chicken pox at 5." While some aspects of a specific study may suggest detailed exploration of some kinds of information, when early history is as typical as that described, the report with respect to developmental history should merely state "normal."

The trend in social casework today is to deal with information relating primarily to the "here and now" factors of a child's life, and it is axiomatic that in casework one begins with the child where he is.[9] Nevertheless, the majority of juvenile courts for many years in most areas have been outside the sphere of social work influence, and frequently the courts have an untrained, unskilled staff. The result is that the social studies made by probation officers for the purposes of the court's disposition of a delinquent child are reminiscent of the kind of information gathered by social caseworkers forty or fifty years ago. This

[9] See Chap. 14.

should not be interpreted as a blanket indictment of all juvenile courts. Some of them, provided with adequate personnel, do a superb job in making appropriate and necessary information available. Nevertheless, these courts are in the minority, and every important study of the past few years has brought out the fact that by and large the juvenile courts today are not staffed so as to provide the kind of information needed by the courts in disposing of the delicate and difficult problem situations brought before it.[10]

In addition to data gathered by members of the probation staff, other diagnostic facilities are available to some juvenile courts, usually in the form of clinical information provided by professional personnel such as physicians, psychiatrists, and psychologists, whether on the staff of the court, functioning as a separate clinic, or controlled by another agency. As a clinic "team" or individually, these professionals provide information and guidance to the court on the medical, psychiatric, and psychological aspects of children's behavior. The use of some form of clinical services for providing information to the courts began as early as 1909 in connection with the Cook County court, when private funds made it possible to provide a five-year demonstration clinic, known as the Juvenile Psychopathic Institute, under the direction of the famed Dr. William Healy. After the demonstration period, the clinic was supported by public funds, and it is the direct antecedent of the Institute for Juvenile Research of the Illinois Department of Public Welfare. As a matter of fact, the child guidance clinic as it is known today stemmed directly from the early clinics and services developed for juvenile courts,[11] not in adult psychiatry or pediatrics, its logical forerunners.

If the probation staff is expected to make recommendations to the court, it seems quite obvious that the information available from clinical sources should be included in the report to the court. But frequently clinical reports are made separately, and neither the probation officer responsible for the social investigation of the case nor those responsible for providing clinical data are aware of what the other person is doing. Occasionally, juvenile courts in metropolitan communities attempt to provide clinical examinations for all or most cases, but on the whole

---

[10] Kahn, *A Court for Children*, esp. Chap. VI, "The Case Study in the Probation Department."

[11] Gardner, "The Juvenile Court as a Child Care Institution."

this policy seems to be thoroughly impractical, and it is generally believed that such resources should be used selectively. An examination of one juvenile court's annual report showed this: by dividing psychiatric time available by the number of interviews reported statistically, it was determined that the average time spent in each interview was between seven and eight minutes. This represents a remarkable waste of expensive psychiatric time, because in so brief a period a psychiatrist is quite unlikely to make a diagnosis that will be meaningful to the court, unless he is dealing with a psychotic child.

Stress has been placed upon the critical problem area of the social study because of its central importance to the dispositions made by the court. When an adequate study of each child coming before the court is not available, the court is handicapped in making dispositions, and the children disposed of by the court may be dealt with very badly indeed.

The Juvenile Court Hearing

The hearing is a crucial point in the handling of any case for a juvenile court. At the hearing, decisions are made as to whether the court shall exercise jurisdiction over a child, or whether the case will be dismissed at that point; and as a result of the hearing, a disposition is made in all cases in which the court has accepted jurisdiction. *Standards for Specialized Courts* states that the hearing consists of two separate parts which may or may not be continuous.

1 The hearing of the evidence necessary to make a determination as to the court's jurisdiction and the facts alleged in the petition.
2 The hearing (if the court should find the child subject to its jurisdiction) of social evidence, including recommendations of the probation officer, culminating in disposition of the case.[12]

The separation of the hearing into two parts, continuous or otherwise, should not be interpreted to mean that the first part is concerned with a criminal charge as such. As was previously shown, the juvenile court foundations are solidly imbedded in the principle that the juvenile court, in dealing with delinquency, is not conducting a criminal trial. The provisions of A *Standard Juvenile Court Act* read as follows:

[12] *Standards for Specialized Courts Dealing with Children*, p. 53.

HEARING. All cases of children shall be dealt with by the court at separate hearings and without a jury. The hearings shall be conducted in an informal manner, and may be adjourned from time to time. Stenographic notes or other transcript of the hearings shall be required only if the court so orders. The general public shall be excluded and only such persons admitted as the judge shall find to have a direct interest in the case or in the work of the court. The presence of the child in court may be waived by the court at any stage of the proceedings.[13]

The use of noncriminal procedure in the juvenile courts is upheld in numerous important cases. One leading case,[14] which was decided in June, 1923, by the Supreme Court of Errors of Connecticut, dealt with virtually all constitutional objections that could be raised against noncriminal procedure in the juvenile courts. After citing cases from seventeen states and the District of Columbia, the court said that the fundamental principle of decision running through them all was that the inquiries conducted by juvenile courts were not criminal trials. Nevertheless, this does not mean that the court may with impunity gloss over issues of fact. As New York's highest court, the Court of Appeals, stated in 1933:

> When it is said that even in cases of law-breaking delinquency constitutional safeguards and the technical procedure of the criminal law may be disregarded, there is no implication that a purely socialized trial of a specific issue may properly or legally be had. The contrary is true. There must be a reasonably definite charge. The customary rules of evidence shown by long experience as essential to getting at the truth with reasonable certainty in civil trials must be adhered to. The finding of fact must rest on the preponderance of evidence adduced under those rules. Hearsay, opinion, trends of hostile neighborhood feeling, the hopes and fears of social workers are all sources of error and have no more place in children's courts than in any other court.[15]

The standards described and the meanings derived from the cases cited, together with the nature of the juvenile court itself, give some basis for assumptions regarding the conduct of hearings. At the same time, it is certain that no framework or set of rules and regulations

---

[13] *Standard Juvenile Court Act*, Sec. 17, p. 24.
[14] *Cinque* v. *Boyd*, 121 Atl. 678 (1923).
[15] *People* v. *Lewis* (Matter of Arthur Lewis), 260 N.Y. 171 (1933).

can eliminate the necessity for skilled, tactful, dispassionate, interested handling of the case by the judge and others attached to the court. As Judge Walter H. Beckham has remarked, the juvenile court is more a court of human relations than a court of law.[16]

The problem of conduct of hearings is especially acute in two widely different kinds of courts: the court held in a large metropolitan community, and the court which meets for only a few hours a month as part of another court. In both of these extremely different situations there are inherent dangers to the entire process of dealing with youngsters in trouble.

The large court may have an overcrowded docket, which makes for haste, and the hearing may lose any semblance of privacy because of the presence of a large number of court staff members, representatives of schools and social agencies, and the like. From the viewpoint of the child and his parents, there may seem to be a great deal of disorder and confusion resulting from the large number of persons on official business who are present in or about the courtroom. There may be long periods of waiting in an overcrowded room, and the child and his parents may be dealt with mechanically and even crudely by minor court attachés. The hearing room itself may be a very large courtroom which is unduly ornate or grimly dreary; the judge may conduct the hearing in a hurried, out-of-temper fashion; and the total effect upon the child and the parents may be negative. Because of time pressures and the apparent but unrealistic necessity for allocating only a few minutes for each case, children may be present during derogatory testimony about their parents by a probation officer or others that may destroy what remains of a normal parent-child relationship, and things told in confidence by interested persons may be repeated in open court.

In the part-time juvenile court, the conduct of hearings may closely resemble those in the criminal court, simply because the judge finds it far easier to remove his robe—if he does—than to eliminate the habits and attitudes that he carries from another court. While it is true that the judge in the small community may have a reasonably good working knowledge of the social conditions from which a child comes, it does not necessarily follow that he knows anything about the emotional life of children. Likewise, in the small community the judge is very close to

---

[16] Beckham, "Helpful Practices in Juvenile Court Hearings."

the public and in instances of serious acts of delinquency he may find it very difficult to be kindly, patient, and understanding.

It should be evident that in a court situation in which there is rarely a defense counsel and even more rarely a prosecuting attorney, the court in a sense acts in the different, and somewhat opposed, capacities of judge, prosecutor, and defender. This much seems obvious: unless the nature of the hearing is explained carefully and in meaningful terms to the child and his parents, there is very great danger that they will come away from the court situation far more confused, conflicted, and frustrated than they were before.[17]

Appeals

Although some laws contain no explicit provisions for appeals from juvenile court adjudication and others deny or limit the right of appeal, the right to appeal is available in one form or another in the majority of jurisdictions. As Sussmann suggests, appeals to higher tribunals are "of great importance" both in establishing fundamental legal principles in the operation of juvenile courts and in determining some limits to the exercise of their broad discretion.[18] Naturally, the right of appeal is inhibited by two factors: (1) appeals are expensive, both because of the fees of counsel and because, in many jurisdictions, costly printed briefs and transcripts must be filed; (2) many people are not fully cognizant of their rights concerning appeals because judges infrequently inform them and probation officers are reluctant to do so on the grounds that "it might cause trouble for the court."

If there is to be an appeal, there needs to be a record. Numerous authorities recommend verbatim recording of the hearing, particularly that part having to do with the determination of jurisdiction by the court. This may be done by a stenographer or stenotypist or through use of a mechanical recording device. The latter would seem to be far more economical, since appeals are rarely taken from juvenile court adjudication, and a legal record that includes a complete transcript is not necessary in all cases. If recording devices are used, the record may be filed, and, if an appeal is taken, the entire transcript will then be available to the higher court.

[17] Kahn, *A Court for Children*, Chap. V.
[18] Sussmann, *Law of Juvenile Delinquency*, p. 36.

Privacy of Records

One of the most disturbing questions that arises in many communities concerns the problem of juvenile court records, which should be private and also should be kept separate from records of criminal cases of adults or other kinds of cases. A number of states prohibit the publication in newspapers, without consent of the court, of the names or identity of children before the court, and juvenile court records are withheld from indiscriminate public inspection in about half the states. But, according to Cosulich, the laws are so written that, in most of the states prohibiting indiscriminate public inspection, the records may be inspected by the child's parents or other representatives. Only a few states explicitly extend privacy of court records to the social histories compiled by probation officers, so the degree to which these are privileged communications is in doubt in the great majority of states.[19]

The *Standard Juvenile Court Act* requires that the court's official records shall be open to inspection only by consent of the judge and only to persons having a legitimate interest in them. All information obtained in social records prepared in the discharge of official duty by any employee of the court shall be privileged and shall not be disclosed directly or indirectly to anyone other than the judge or other person entitled to receive such information, unless and until otherwise ordered by the judge. The Standard Act also states that "the name or picture of any child under the jurisdiction of the court shall not be made public by any newspaper, radio, or television station except as authorized by order of the court." The Act recommends that those violating these provisions shall be guilty of a misdemeanor and upon conviction may be punished by a fine not to exceed $500 or by imprisonment not exceeding one year or both fine and imprisonment.[20]

Obviously the purpose of these proposed restrictions is to prevent the demoralization that comes with widespread newspaper or other kinds of publicity, as well as to protect the kinds of confidential information frequently encountered in social records maintained by the court staff. Although attacked widely by newspapers as "secrecy," the restriction of information concerning children before the court appears to be

[19] Cosulich, *Juvenile Court Laws of the United States*, p. 74.
[20] *Standard Juvenile Court Act*, pp. 33-34.

in their own legitimate interest. Recently, there was violent opposition to a Nebraska bill that would provide the kind of safeguards described above. The protests stemmed chiefly from newspapers, some of which took the position that names and identities of children were published only when it was a second-offense situation, or when the child was a "repeater," or when a "serious crime" was involved. Actually, the case for allowing such decisions to be made by the court rather than the press seems conclusive. Presumably the judge is in a far better position to make this determination than anyone else, particularly when it seems safe to assume that self-serving interests may make the definitions of which cases should be publicized more and more elastic.

Dispositions by the Court

As discussed in this chapter, the problem of dispositions is viewed from a procedural standpoint, although the question of the quality of facilities available to the courts, discussed elsewhere, is of prime importance.[21] In general, following a hearing determining that the child may be dealt with by the juvenile court, a variety of dispositions are theoretically available to the court. These may be grouped under three broad headings: (1) discharge, or dismissal of the case; (2) probation; and (3) placement in an institution or foster home, either by referral to an appropriate agency or by specific commitment to a training school or similar institution.

The juvenile court has a great deal of discretion in determining the particular type of disposition used in a specific case, and under most laws it may adapt its treatment to the particular needs of an individual child. When commitment or placement is used, the statutes frequently refer to a "suitable" public or private institution or agency. When probation is used, the courts have wide latitude in setting the conditions of probation. In some instances, restitution is made a condition of probation; if used therapeutically, this may be desirable, but there is a tendency to use it as a punitive device and as a substitute for the fines imposed in adult criminal cases.[22]

The latest statistics collected by the United States Children's Bureau give some indication of the extent to which various kinds of dispositions

[21] See Chap. 14.
[22] See Sussmann, *Law of Juvenile Delinquency*, Chap. VI, "Disposition of Children's Cases."

are utilized. Nearly half of all cases, official and unofficial combined, result in dismissal with or without warning or in adjustment without further action; roughly one-fourth of all cases are disposed of by placing the children under supervision of probation officers; about 5 percent of delinquent children are committed to public institutions established for the purpose of dealing with delinquents, and another 5 percent are committed or referred to other public institutions, departments of public welfare, or private agencies and institutions. The high rate of cases dismissed or held open without further action presents some cause for concern, since more than one in five delinquent children described as "official cases" are dealt with in this fashion. Nearly four out of ten children in both official and unofficial categories combined are placed on probation under supervision of the court, and this makes the quality and caliber of probation services available to the court a matter of considerable importance.

Altogether, the statistics cited justify considerable concern on a number of counts. It is pretty well established that a large number of dismissals and discharges result from the "trivial nature of the offense," but one wonders what happens to children whose offense is symptomatic of underlying disturbances and who are dismissed without further action or referral of any kind. To a certain extent, the relationship of the court to other agencies in the community may determine whether appropriate referrals are made. The particular incident in which a child is involved may seem too trivial to warrant court action, but where the problems presented by the child and his family seem to be sufficiently serious to require further attention, unquestionably the court has some responsibility to refer the situation to a suitable agency. It might be argued that if there were strict adherence to the practice of deciding whether the case should be a court case in the first phase of the hearing process, it would be unlikely that "problems" presented by children and their families would be discovered. But the practical fact is that a great many of these situations involving dismissal occur *after* there has been a comprehensive social investigation by the court staff. With some exceptions, there is little or no relationship between the kind of offense committed by a child and the degree of pathology that may be involved in the child's or family's situation. This question is actually very similar to the problem discussed in connection with the police: What is the responsibility of official agencies in situations in which the trivial nature of an offense makes specific action seem unwarranted, but when even a cursory study reveals conditions that require at least the proffering of help from an appropriate agency? This whole issue, which cannot be resolved at this point because of the bewildering complexity of practice from one jurisdiction to another, underlines the crucial importance of an adequate intake service in the juvenile court.

One aspect of the disposition problem that deserves specific attention is the anomalous situation that occurs because the court's jurisdiction may continue during the minority of the child adjudicated as delinquent by the court. This may mean a long period of supervision by the court, even though the child was involved in a relatively minor offense. In other instances, a child may be committed to a training school for an indefinite period, often to the age of twenty-one, to be released at the discretion of the superintendent. While it is true that training schools under ideal conditions may be regarded as facilities that should be used selectively for treatment purposes, the simple fact of the matter is that a great many of them are junior prisons which offer only tenuous custody and little or no positive stimulation or reëducation. When disposed of by the court, the children committed to other agencies frequently pass out of the jurisdiction of the court; but in the training schools they may remain for a year, two years, or even three years. As far as the child is concerned this is a prison sentence. Frequently the courts reënforce this notion by the "one last chance" lecture. But the important point is that large numbers of children are sent to training schools for long periods of time for treatment that they do not receive in fact, while if adults were involved in the same offenses, the "punishment" meted out by a court might well be ten days or thirty days in jail. Without doubt, many criminal careers begin as a result of a rankling sense of injustice that comes to a child when he realizes that he is being "imprisoned" for many years for relatively trivial offenses.[23]

In making dispositions of children adjudicated as delinquent, the juvenile court has a great deal of power, and it should have an enormous sense of responsibility. There is some question as to whether the delicate balance between power and responsibility is achieved in many of our courts, but the dilemma of the courts is a real one. Faced with the need to provide treatment for delinquent children in accordance with individual requirements, the courts have few alterna-

---

[23] See Chap. 15, "Training Schools."

tives to choose from though they need a wide variety of facilities if they are to do a decent job. Unfortunately, the facilities are not available.

The Personnel of the Court

Up to this point, our concern with the juvenile court has been mainly with structure and function, as seen both in the law and in the practices that have developed in juvenile courts. While structure and function have a definite role in shaping any social instrument, the personnel and facilities, whether controlled by the court or outside of its jurisdiction, will determine in the last analysis what happens to children dealt with by this instrument, hailed a half century ago as the great reform movement. The Midcentury White House Conference went to the heart of the matter in this statement: "In the juvenile court . . . good personnel is of primary importance. Upon the judge and his staff rests the responsibility for the social procedures through which the spirit as well as the letter of the juvenile court law is carried out." [24]

But carrying out the spirit of the juvenile court law depends upon something more than the good intentions of staff. Juvenile courts deal with a variety of complex and delicate problems of human personalities, and skills of the highest order are required to deal with these problems. In addition, a court must be organized and administered so that it can operate effectively, and it must have resources within or outside the court available to make it possible to carry out realistic treatment goals. Therefore, it seems logical to look at the qualifications of judges and others who are responsible for the court process.

How well are the courts staffed? Are adequate diagnostic and treatment resources available to them? These issues are of such overriding importance that, even if one were to envisage an ideal juvenile court law, one that would meet every test, the law would not be effective unless implemented by appropriate personnel and facilities.

Juvenile Court Judges

In any discussion of the functions of the personnel of the juvenile court, the role of the judge emerges as the central and most important one. Not only does the judge have the power of making decisions that

---

[24] *Children and Youth at the Midcentury*, p. 153.

may well affect the entire lives of children and families with whom the court deals, but in addition he is an administrator, responsible for the direction and often the appointment of the other personnel of the court. He also is charged implicitly with a leadership function, because it is his duty to interpret to the community as a whole the needs of children who come before the court. It has been emphasized that no judge can be stronger than the staff and facilities available to him, but certainly it is also true that the presence of adequate staff and facilities and the absence of a suitable judge vitiates the juvenile court to the point at which it ceases to function effectively. What then are the qualifications of judges who serve in the juvenile court and how are they selected?

The *Standards for Specialized Courts* recommends that in addition to having legal training, being admitted to the bar in the state where he is to serve, and having some experience in the practice of law, the judge in the specialized court should be

1 Deeply concerned about the rights of people.
2 Keenly interested in the problems of children and families.
3 Sufficiently aware of the findings and processes of modern psychology, psychiatry, and social work to give due weight to the findings of these sciences and professions.
4 Able to evaluate evidence and situations objectively, uninfluenced by his own personal concepts of child care.
5 Eager to learn.
6 A good administrator, able to delegate administrative responsibility.
7 Able to conduct hearings in a kindly manner and to talk to children and adults sympathetically and on their level of understanding without loss of the essential dignity of the court.[25]

On the whole, these standards seem reasonable and desirable. They avoid the utilization of extreme virtues and characteristics which would require that a veritable paragon be obtained for the juvenile court post. There is no reference to a need to be a skilled child psychologist. A lawyer with a broad educational background, who has a decent, kindly regard for others, meets the minimum requirements adequately. Looking at the problem negatively, what is needed is to avoid the selection of judges who are emotionally immature and insecure persons, who are vain, egotistical, and authoritarian, or who cannot become sufficiently

[25] *Standards for Specialized Courts Dealing with Children*, p. 83.

detached to maintain an objective view of the situation or to rely upon professional staff for findings and recommendations appropriate to their own disciplines.

One positive virtue the juvenile court judge must have is a sense of altruism because, generally speaking, the work of the juvenile court judge is far more difficult and time-consuming than that of his confreres; it is far less lucrative than the practice of law; it is off the beaten track as far as other lawyers are concerned and therefore may lead him directly into political oblivion. To the layman, this latter statement may be surprising, but it should be remembered that a judge who spends most or all of his time in juvenile court work rarely has anything to do with other lawyers; and in a great many communities, the other lawyers do not know the work of juvenile court judges, simply because they themselves do not appear in juvenile court. Thus their own impressions and biases may lead them to believe that the juvenile court judge is inclined to be on the "soft and sentimental side." As Judge Alexander has pointed out, the volume of work is liable to be greater and the hours longer, and there is little or no chance to gain experience in the law, since there are relatively few legal problems that come before the juvenile court. He concludes that the juvenile court judge on a full time basis must be prepared to make financial and personal sacrifices.[26]

Above all factors required of the juvenile court judge, none is more important than his ability to deal with power without becoming arrogant and dictatorial. One of the most distinguished children's court justices, the Honorable Justine Wise Polier of the New York City court, made this statement a few years ago:

> Still another factor lies in the extent to which the judicial robe, whether worn or not, affects the man who wears it. As a member of that fraternity, I must admit that the power over other human beings that is given to every member of the judiciary in one way or another produces strange effects on many. I suppose humility is not the characteristic most likely to come to mind in describing members of the judiciary. Too often, instead, we find arrogance and self-righteousness, the need for preaching at people rather than human understanding, and impatience with the troubles of the many anonymous "little" people who come before the Court rather than an appreciation of the full possibilities of patient listening and earnest inquiry as to how their troubles or problems may be solved.

[26] Alexander, "Of Juvenile Court Justice and Judges."

All these factors that affect our judiciary generally have a special significance when we consider the problems that confront the Judge in the Children's Court. The Court is dealing with children, human beings in their formative years. To them the use or misuse of authority by the Court may have a special meaning. If, in using that authority, arrogance, indifference, impatience, lack of understanding are cloaked by the words of the Children's Court Acts that stress help rather than punishment, I am sure the children are among the first to detect the sham or lack of sincerity. Also, our Children's Courts deal almost exclusively with the children of the poor, and our whole procedure discourages appeal.[27]

In the light of the qualifications suggested, the actual methods used for selection of juvenile court judges fall far below what seems obviously to be required. Although there are no statistics showing the total proportion of all cases coming before juvenile courts that are dealt with by specialized judges, we know that such judges are few in number. Outside of the three states with state-wide juvenile courts, there are about forty counties with full-time judges serving in specialized juvenile courts and perhaps twenty other counties in which ex-officio judges serve full time in the juvenile court.[28] This means that in forty-five states there are about sixty counties in which judges devote full time to juvenile court work, and in about 2,900 counties juvenile courts are served by judges whose chief concern is with another court. A common misconception is that because the work in a children's court may take relatively little time, as far as courtroom work is concerned, it is economically feasible to have juvenile court judges devote part of their time to criminal court or civil court duties. This is far from the truth, because children's cases require diligent study and careful consideration, and there is need to spend a great deal of time on the administrative and other responsibilities previously mentioned.

The vast majority of judges in the United States are chosen by the traditional method of election, although some are appointed, usually by a governor and occasionally by a mayor. In view of the description of the juvenile court judges' functions already elaborated upon, it seems unnecessary to deal extensively with the rather obvious fact that the election device generally does not provide the right kind of judges for the juvenile court. The *Standard Juvenile Court Act* recommends a modification of the Missouri plan for selection of all judges which went

[27] Polier, *The Role of a Juvenile Court in 1948*, p. 9.
[28] Rubin, "State Juvenile Court."

into effect in 1941. It provides for appointment of judges by the governor from a list of three persons whose names are submitted by a panel with representation from the county welfare department, the bar association, and the board of education. This method is suggested for all counties with populations in excess of 100,000, but in counties with populations less than that the electors at a regular or special election are to determine whether a special judge of a juvenile court is to be appointed. If the electors approve affirmatively, the appointment by the governor from a list submitted by a panel would also be used. In the three state-wide juvenile courts, the method of appointment is as follows: in Utah, the judges are appointed by the public welfare commission; in Connecticut, the governor makes nominations to the general assembly; and in Rhode Island, the governor appoints with the advice and consent of the senate. In Rhode Island the term of the judge is ten years, and in Utah and Connecticut it is six years. These periods are sufficiently long for a person serving in the court to be able to gain a considerable amount of experience.

Referees

About one-third of the states make provision for the appointment of referees, who may or may not be lawyers but who normally make decisions on cases, subject to the approval of the judge of the juvenile court. Normally, provision is made for an appeal from any decision by the referee to the court itself. The system has many virtues, because it is probable that a referee will devote a considerable amount of time to juvenile cases and may in effect be able to pass on the great bulk of cases coming before a court. This makes available more time for the judge to deal effectively with the more difficult cases. The use of referees is especially desirable in the case of girls; in many of the larger courts, girls' cases are heard automatically before a woman referee. Naturally, the principles and policies discussed in connection with judges apply equally well to referees, especially when referees make decisions in a substantial proportion of cases coming before the court.

There is some question whether referees must have legal training, and many of the statements regarding standards for juvenile courts are silent on this point. Nevertheless, the *Standards for Specialized Courts* comes out flatly in favor of qualifications that include membership in the bar and some experience in the practice of law. It also states that while social work training is valuable it is no more essential to this position than to that of the judges.[29] Despite a considerable amount of evidence to the contrary, the authors are inclined to agree that legal training should be required for the referee, because he acts in the capacity of judge and his decisions may have far-reaching effects upon children.

The Probation Staff

Even a cursory examination of the relationship of probation staff to the operations of the court indicates the significant role played by the probation staff and leads inevitably to the conclusion that even the best-equipped judge cannot function adequately without the support of the skilled adjunctive services provided by a qualified staff of probation workers. The members of the probation staff, variously referred to as probation officers, probation workers, and probation counselors, directly affect the work of the court in two definite ways: they provide the social information required by a judge if he is to make an appropriate disposition of the cases of children who come before him; and they provide the supervisory services when children are disposed of through the use of probation. The authors believe that if the chief functions of probation workers are understood properly, nearly everything else relating to the probation staff becomes meaningful. Methods of appointment, qualifications, compensation, and training needs are discussed in the chapter following. Most of the areas mentioned depend directly upon answers to the question: What do probation workers do?

Probation staff members may carry on a great variety of functions, some of which have already been indicated. They may dispose of certain cases on the basis of authority delegated from the court, refer situations that seem not to require court action at point of intake, effect adjustments through the conference method, and collect funds, such as restitution payments. But their chief tasks are twofold: making social studies for the courts, and supervision of children placed on probation. As Walter Reckless briefly describes the work of probation officers, they should be in position to make "an adequate social study of the child and his background, so as to discover what his difficulties are, what

---

[29] *Standards for Specialized Courts Dealing with Children*, p. 85.

his needs are, and what form of social treatment will best meet his needs. . . . They should be in position to supervise juveniles who are placed on probation in their own homes." [30]

Some examination of these key functions of probation workers is desirable before getting into other important questions that affect probation staff, in order to shed some light on the issues and implications that are discussed in connection with other areas. The position is taken here that many of these other questions are directly related to the question of what the probation worker is supposed to do, and for that reason, some attempt is made to clear away the debris which surrounds the widespread public misunderstanding of the functions of probation workers. If there were wider public understanding of what probation workers are supposed to do and must do if the juvenile court is to function at all effectively, there would be much better public support for improvement in these vital services.

The Social Study Function of Probation Workers

If it be assumed that the juvenile court has the right to make decisions concerning a child who is properly before it, it is important to recognize that the principles and policies previously discussed, especially those that concern the individualization of treatment, cannot be accomplished unless the court is in the position to know the total situation affecting the child, not merely the offense which brought him before the court. Consequently, a social study or a social investigation is made by a member of the court staff, and the findings of this study are used in conjunction with information available from medical, psychological, and psychiatric resources, where these are utilized. Together, these reports make up the information concerning the child available to the court. While the content of the social study varies somewhat from one court to another, in general the tendency is to follow the pattern, if not the exact format, of a great many social agencies which have essentially the same task, namely, to identify as precisely as possible the nature and kind of problems presented in the individual case situation in order to determine what best may be done.

Most writers divide the social study into three component parts: study,

[30] Reckless, *The Crime Problem*, p. 208.

diagnosis, and treatment. This kind of division is somewhat suggestive of the process that goes on, but it should be emphasized that the entire process is a continuum and that the three phases described frequently go on simultaneously. That is, as facts are collected, there is some attempt at delineation of the specific information that will be brought together in an individual situation; as this information becomes more clear there is the beginning of classification or diagnosis of the facts; and, ideally, the development of relationship between the probation worker and the child and his family, which may begin early in the social study, is the first stage of treatment. Depending upon the ability of the worker and the readiness of the child or his family to establish the relationship in question, the treatment process may begin almost immediately.

The important thing here is to recognize that even the selective process that goes into fact-gathering requires a high order of skill on the part of the probation worker. There was a period thirty or forty years ago, when indiscriminate fact-gathering was a commonplace, and unfortunately this practice still persists to the present time in a good many places. In such situations, the probation worker, slavishly following an outline or guide, gathered information concerning virtually every aspect of the life of the child and his family. In building up a "life history," every detail that could be extracted from any informant was literally thrown into the case report. Modern thinking has changed this considerably, and disciplined selectivity at the fact-gathering stage is considered of the utmost importance.

But beyond the selection of facts is the necessity for interpretation of facts. An adequate interpretation demands considerable insight into the dynamics of human behavior as well as an awareness of one's own bias with respect to the problems presented by other people. While the need to replace subjective judgments by skilled, nonemotional evaluations is apparent immediately to anyone, the difficulties in achieving such a standard should be equally apparent. It should be recalled also that this discussion does not concern an abstract problem but rather children who are in trouble, children whose difficulties usually have been operating for some time. All studies demonstrate conclusively that as a rule youngsters who get into court were in some kind of difficulty several years before being acted upon officially by the court. This means often that habit patterns are fixed and that the behavior problems which are at the root of the difficulty—the offense being only a symptom— may be sufficiently complex as to defy clear-cut analysis.

What the court needs from the probation worker, as well as from medical and other sources of information, is a descriptive, diagnostic statement that will show the kinds of relationships the child has with his family and with others, the dynamics of the family background itself as it has an impact on the child, his ability to adjust to various situations, his capacity, and some indications as to his treatment needs.

To obtain this kind of information for the court, it is necessary to take into account both the strong inner drives of the individual and the demands of his social and economic setting. In other words, both the person and his environment are involved. The tools used in getting this information are the interview, which invariably includes the child as well as numerous collaterals, and the utilization of community resources. The child and his family may be known to other social welfare agencies in the community, and the school or neighborhood club may provide useful information.

The key point is that the type of social study described cannot represent a stereotype; since this is so, the understanding and skill of the worker are of prime importance.

The Supervision Function of Probation Workers

What has been said about the social study is equally true of the supervision of children placed on probation by the court. Not only must there be an intelligent, well-conceived plan of action, but there must be frequent and periodic contacts between the probation worker and the child and, in many cases, his family. Often the worker is dealing with a youngster who presents several serious problems; the child may be extremely resistive to any form of treatment; the family may be uncoöperative; the child may continue to make a poor school adjustment —in fact any one or more of a whole series of social and personality situations may either continue to operate or to develop in such a way as to make treatment very difficult.

When this disturbing picture is combined with a paucity of community resources which can be tapped for treatment purposes, then it is clear that there may well be serious difficulties in carrying out the treatment prescriptions of the court. Even though modern concepts emphasize the need to be selective in the areas that are to be treated as well as the need for realism in selection of such areas, the fact remains that children who have been a problem to themselves, to their families, and to the community for some years offer a serious and difficult challenge to any person attempting to deal with even a selected group of problems presented by a given child.

As a matter of fact, the position of the child as a delinquent, even though placed on probation by the court, may complicate problems that already exist, or bring new ones into being. For example, he may have had difficulty in making adjustments to school, and the attitude of his teachers toward him may be influenced negatively by his court appearance. This, in turn, may generate in the child more hostility toward the school and toward other authoritarian situations, with the result that he truants frequently or otherwise fails to get along in the school situation. The probation worker is not a lone operator, and whatever he does must be related to other facilities and resources within the total community.

Even this cursory description of the functions of the probation officer serves to highlight the fact that should now be obvious, namely, that this kind of work requires a number of attributes and skills not easily found. Implicit in what has been said is the fact that mistakes by the probation worker, resulting from lack of insight and skill, may have specific traumatic effects upon the child. The unskilled worker may overidentify with the child, tending to confirm him in his delinquency, or he may widen the breach between parent and child by interfering in areas that are the responsibilities of the parent and concerning which the parent has not demonstrated incompetence. Similarly, he may identify with the parents to the extent that he can be of no help at all to the child and, to an adolescent in revolt against authority and against his parents, this may mean literally being shut off from any real opportunity for obtaining help. After all, providing help is the foremost function of the worker, regardless of what task he is performing.

The Number of Probation Workers

There are about 4,000 juvenile probation workers in the United States, about half of whom work full time with juvenile cases, the other half dividing their time between juvenile and adult cases. In addition, there are an unknown number of part-time workers in both categories. These probation officers provide services to the courts in less than half of all of the counties in the United States. This does not mean that all courts without probation staff are without probation service of one kind or another, because, as will be discussed later, the judge may ask another individual or agency to provide the service required. On the whole, though, the picture is a disappointing one, because with the exception of the three states with state-wide juvenile courts, and a few states in which there is state-wide coverage through the services made available by staff members of an adult probation and parole program, it is clear that the characteristic unevenness of distribution of services must be regarded as something less than a tribute to our ability to organize governmental services efficiently and effectively.

Caseloads

When one looks at the problem of caseloads, the situation is unquestionably even more distressing than the estimate of numbers of workers shows. While it should be admitted that not enough research has gone into the question of what should be the appropriate work-load of a probation officer, both in social study and in supervision, common sense and observation, together with the pooling of opinions of informed persons in the field, lend adequate support to the standards recommended both by the United States Children's Bureau and the National Probation and Parole Association.[31] Both agencies agree upon fifty cases under supervision as an appropriate standard. The National Probation and Parole Association uses the term "work unit" in evaluating caseloads, assigning one unit to each case under active supervision and five units for each investigation case.

Despite widespread general agreement with these standards, and even though they have not been seriously challenged, the unpleasant fact is that in nearly all jurisdictions caseloads far exceed the standards described. Caseloads of one hundred or one hundred and fifty are not uncommon for workers doing supervision only, and for workers doing

---

[31] *Standards for Specialized Courts Dealing with Children*, p. 71; also Reed, *The Handling of the Neglected and Delinquent Child in Lincoln, Nebraska, 1955*, p. 26.

social studies for the court only caseloads of twenty to thirty, or 3 times the appropriate number, are common. Because the more usual, and even more economical, way to assign probation officers to their duties is to provide for a districting or zoning by geographical area, it is relatively common for a worker to do both comprehensive social investigations for the court and supervision of probationers.

Observation in court after court indicates that when the number of social studies required goes above the standard already suggested, supervision is seriously neglected. The usual result is that the worker, faced with deadline after deadline in preparing cases for the court, tends automatically to ignore his supervisory responsibilities until they are thrust upon him by the development of a crisis, such as a youngster being arrested by the police. This crisis-to-crisis planning is inevitable under the circumstances prevailing in the great majority of courts today. This situation is true only when an appropriate number of social studies are required; when that standard is exceeded, almost invariably the result is a series of stereotyped reports. Judging by the case reports presented to many of the courts, it becomes almost impossible to distinguish one child from another. This situation is especially devastating when it is recalled that the utilization of probation services is essential to adequate functioning of the juvenile court itself. The mere presence of a probation staff is no guarantee, and the qualifications of the probation staff make relatively little difference if the staff is unable to have adequate time to do the work required.

It seems evident that probation workers, who are expected to carry on a difficult and complex task, can be of very little practical use unless they have sufficient time to do the work required to individualize the children. Occasionally this situation is glossed over by suggesting that, like a physician, the skilled probation worker expediently selects on the basis of diagnostic tests those cases to which he gives considerable time. The analogy, while it has some merit, does not hold up entirely, because with heavy caseloads the work done is altogether too superficial to enable an accurate diagnosis of any kind being made. It may well be that the proper analogy is to first-aid work done by medical personnel on a battlefield; nevertheless, medical men would be the first to testify that first aid has only temporary results, and must be followed at the very earliest time possible by more permanent treatment. The difficulty with the probation staff situation, under caseloads as they are today, is that while some first-aid work is done, long-term treatment is neither planned nor accomplished.

This does not deny that under oppressive caseloads the more skilled workers can be expected to perform better than those who have less skill. Nevertheless, in the practical sense, with competition for workers what it is at present, the prospects are that skilled workers will not be enticed into a situation in which they cannot perform effectively simply because of the terrific demands upon their time. If they do accept employment in a court setting, they are quite likely to leave because of discouragement and their inability to get results when faced with so many problems and so little time with which to deal with them.

For Further Reading

KAHN, ALFRED J., *A Court for Children: A Study of the New York City Children's Court* (New York, 1953).

> This is a major study of the operations of a metropolitan community's juvenile court system. It points up especially staffing needs, and it reveals an unimpressive, uninspiring picture of the way children are treated in the courts.

ALEXANDER, PAUL W., "Of Juvenile Court Justice and Judges," in *National Probation and Parole Association Yearbook, 1947* (New York, 1948), pp. 187-205.

> A penetrating, candid, and factual account of the problems faced by juvenile court judges in comparison with their colleagues. The article gives considerable insight into the difficulties encountered in getting good judges on the juvenile court bench.

REED, HUGH P., *The Handling of Neglected and Delinquent Children in Lincoln, Nebraska, 1955* (New York, 1955).

> This recent survey of services for neglected and delinquent children provides both a current description of staffing problems in one community and a good review of the standards used by the National Probation and Parole Association in its recent court surveys.

GARDNER, GEORGE E., "The Juvenile Court as a Child Care Institution," in *Federal Probation*, 16 (June, 1952), pp. 8-12.

The author, director of the Judge Baker Guidance Clinic, Boston, and one of today's outstanding child psychiatrists, shows that child psychiatry originated in the juvenile court—not in adult psychiatry or pediatrics, its logical forerunners.

POLIER, JUSTINE WISE, *The Role of a Juvenile Court in 1948* (an address delivered at the annual meeting of the Illinois Children's Home and Aid Society, Chicago, Ill., January 30, 1948).

A searching and revealing statement on the significance of the helping role of the juvenile court judge by a distinguished children's court justice. Judge Polier makes a strong case against the misuse of authority.

Chapter **14**

THE JUVENILE COURT:
FACILITIES AND PROSPECTS

Although the discussion of operations and staffing in the previous chapter provides some indication of the sort of facilities required if juvenile courts are to function effectively, close scrutiny should be directed to the specific facilities needed, especially the probation staff and the other resources that in the final analysis determine the diagnostic and treatment limits of the court. The "right arm of the court," the probation staff is of paramount importance as the chief facility available to and controlled by the court. Consequently, the methods of appointment of probation workers, their compensation, qualifications, and training needs are examined. Also a matter of concern, because they affect the court's potential at every turn, are the other facilities and services, usually not controlled by the court, that determine ultimately the quality and variety of resources that juvenile courts can use. While a juvenile court cannot be efficient if it is saddled with a poor probation staff, it may have a good probation staff and still fall far short of fulfilling its basic responsibilities if the community fails to provide the varied and flexible tools needed for dealing with its problem children.

The Appointment of Probation Workers

Though there is almost universal agreement that probation workers should be chosen on the basis of particular qualifications and through some system of competitive merit examinations, in numerous courts the selection of personnel is complicated by the historical tradition that places upon the judge the responsibility for and the power of appointment. In the majority of jurisdictions, the probation officers are appointed by the court; consequently they are not subject to ordinary civil service procedures found today in most phases of government service. The legal situation is complicated somewhat by two higher court decisions which, while not in direct opposition to one another, produced findings that were different. In 1912, the Illinois Supreme Court in the famous Witter case held that the judicial power included the authority to select persons whose services may be required as assistance to the judge in the performance of judicial duties and the exercise of judicial power, even though the legislature in the legitimate exercise of its own power could prescribe reasonable qualifications which would exclude improper persons. In the same year, the New York Court of Appeals, the highest New York state court, corresponding to the Supreme Court elsewhere, after taking a look at the legislative history of the New York probation law, decided that the legislature had not intended to place the position of probation officer in the exempt class, and consequently probation officers were held subject to civil service at the discretion of the state civil service commission.[1] Even the Illinois decision, which has been followed generally, offers room for some leeway in interpretation. As Miss Breckinridge has suggested, a distinction may be made between the services rendered the judge before a determination is reached and the services given after the determination as to disposition has been made. As she pointed out, it is difficult to see the difference between the latter category of services and the services provided by heads of institutions to which delinquent children are committed, and no one has suggested that such officials be appointed by the court.[2]

---

[1] John Witter, Appellee v. The County Commissioners of Cook County et al., Appellants, 256 Illinois 616 (1912); Matter of Simons v. McGuire, 204 New York 253 (1912). These decisions are found conveniently in Sophinisba P. Breckenridge, Social Work and the Courts, pp. 41-52.
[2] Breckinridge, "Legal Problems of the Juvenile Court."

Although the numbers appointed under the several methods available cannot be estimated with any reasonable degree of accuracy, there are three kinds of appointments made in juvenile courts today: (1) appointments directly made by the judge with the recruitment and selection responsibility entirely in his hands; (2) appointment by the court with the use of an informal merit system which may be followed routinely, or with occasional exceptions, by the court, with a merit system committee or personnel advisory board being appointed by the court, or with the court utilizing the machinery of an existing merit system or civil service program, without being bound by it; and (3) appointments made under civil service regulations.

Personnel Practices

Whatever the appointment system followed, there is general agreement among those concerned with this field that the entire process of personnel management characteristic of other branches of public service should be followed, regardless of whether appointments are made by the judge or by some other body. This means that practices in the areas of recruitment, selection, advancement, retention, conditions of work, retirement, and separation should follow accepted personnel policies. In some jurisdictions, all of the practices of the so-called classified civil service are followed, with the single exception that the court is the appointing body.[3]

Many large courts have successfully used advisory committees of citizens to select eligible lists, but frequently other important areas of personnel administration are neglected. However, in many communities the presence of an advisory committee in connection with the selection of court personnel offers only a modicum of protection to the important function of getting good employees into this important service. Sometimes the advisory committee has a very limited function, such as submitting an eligible list to the court, which the court may use or disregard at will. At other times, eligible lists may be exhausted, and during an interim of several years the court may make direct appointments without resort to the advisory committee. In still other instances, such informal nonstatutory committees have little effective machinery

[3] White, *Introduction to the Study of Public Administration*; Klein. *Civil Service in Public Welfare.*

with which to operate; in some instances, for example, even the basic qualifications reported on application forms are not verified.

Many courts, following local or even state practices, impose residence requirements that may be a severe handicap in attracting good personnel. In New York, for example, where there is county civil service, residence restrictions prevent movement from one county to another, making positions in the probation field less attractive and restricting the appointment of probation workers not to the best available but to the best available in a particular county. The courts that have forged ahead in recent years have discarded or waived residence requirements; nationwide recruitment unquestionably has "paid off."

If the overriding importance of adequate personnel standards for juvenile court workers be granted, there is every reason to believe that, whatever the particular method of appointment followed, the standards should be consistent with those that have gradually been developed in the public social services generally, and should follow the general pattern of the merit systems that have been developed in numerous states as the result of requirements in the Social Security Act. The inevitable conclusion is that the courts have a long way to go before attaining desirable standards in this field. Naturally, good employee morale is an important and significant by-product of a good personnel system; where practices are inadequate or inconsistent, staff morale tends to be poor.

Salaries

The compensation paid to workers in this field compares favorably with other positions in the public social services, but some of the disadvantages frequently noted, such as lack of tenure and the absence of adequate retirement provisions and increment plans for continued service, tend to make it futile to attempt comparisons in terms of dollar amounts of salaries.

In early 1955, the National Probation and Parole Association recommended a minimum annual salary of $4,000, although the cost-of-living variations from one region to another necessarily make this amount a tentative standard only. At that time, positions in the federal probation service began at $4,205, and after a six-months probationary period, workers in the Wisconsin probation and parole program, which is governed by an excellent civil service system under the Wisconsin Bureau of Personnel, received $4,500 annually. These salaries are not munificent, and in most jurisdictions salaries are much lower. Without doubt, this means that many workers in the field engage in part-time or even full-time jobs in addition to their court work. Those who are heads of families in many instances must do this or leave the field entirely.

Some signs of improvement are present. The National Probation and Parole Association's *Focus* in January, 1955, indicated that a dozen courts were seeking workers, some with beginning salaries as high as $4,500; maximum salaries for the positions ranged to $6,800. Furthermore, the number of top administrative positions paying $9,000 and more is increasing.[4] Recent improvements in salary structure, if maintained, may have significant effects on recruitment, retention, and even professional preparation for this field.

Qualifications for Probation Personnel

Although there is no substantial disagreement as to the functions that should be performed by probation workers, especially the provision of comprehensive social studies to the court and supervision of children placed on probation, there is less harmony with respect to the backgrounds and qualifications necessary for the tasks in question. On one matter there is complete agreement, namely, that some form of formal training prior to entrance into probation work is highly desirable. But there is lack of agreement with respect to the specific form such training should take. Should this training be given at the undergraduate level? Should it be under the auspices of sociology or social work? Because the great majority of persons actually employed in the field are not trained in any formal fashion prior to their entering this work, the issue of what kind of formal training they should have has a slightly academic flavor. Nevertheless, in terms of their responsibilities, both explicitly and implicitly described in the discussion of the work of probation personnel, this issue, whether academic or not, is an important one.

The minimum standards suggested by the National Probation and Parole Association for personnel in this field are reproduced because they represent minimum qualifications at the entrance level and because these are standards that have been agreed upon by the Professional

---

[4] See "Salaries of Probation and Parole Officers in the United States, 1953-54."

Council of the Association, a group heavily weighted with practical administrators in this field. These are:

a. Personality: Emotional maturity, broad common sense, capacity to learn by experience, and interest in the welfare of human beings. The applicant must have good character, balanced personality, integrity, ability to work with others, and insight into the causes of human behavior, and a general knowledge of his community.
b. Education: A bachelor's degree from a college or university of recognized standing, with courses in the social sciences. Preferably he should have, in addition, professional training for probation work in an accredited graduate school of social work.
c. Experience: One year of paid, full-time experience under a trained supervisor in a social agency or similar agency of high standards, or one year of graduate work in a recognized school of social work in lieu thereof.[5]

It will be noted that the basic educational requirement describes as preferable "professional training in a graduate school of social work." Essentially, this is the chief area in dispute, although the preponderance of evidence seems to support this standard. There is no disagreement whatever with the other qualifications proposed by the Association. Recommended standards for case supervisors and directors are higher, with emphasis on leadership and administrative ability, and additional training and experience "as will enable them to give guidance to the workers and help them grow in professional skill and knowledge."

Probably the leading champion of the non-social-work school of thought in the past has been Walter C. Reckless, who based his case mainly upon two chief arguments: (1) that probation workers should have a good foundation in criminology and in corrections, this to be obtained through specially organized courses of a specific kind rather than generic social work training; and (2) that schools of social work, although ranked with departments of sociology as the best locale for students obtaining a basic underpinning in criminology, corrections, and social psychology, do not in fact make provision for appropriate courses in this area.[6] Even this position cannot be described as overwhelming opposition to social work training because the case is mainly one of expediency, namely, that schools of social work do not provide par-

[5] "Standards for Selection of Probation and Parole Officers."
[6] Reckless, "Training Probation and Parole Personnel."

ticularized courses in corrections. While this is not the place to develop the various reasons why curricula in schools of social work have moved so emphatically in the direction of generic rather than specific training, it should be observed that there is a growing conviction on the part of many social work educators that the pendulum should not swing much farther in the direction of generic training. This is seen especially in the area of field work, which is one of the extremely important curriculum facets, because some leading schools of social work have conceded that there is a necessity for providing opportunities for training in specialized settings of various kinds, including the correctional setting.[7]

It should be kept in mind that Reckless defines the functions of probation officers in such a way as to indicate rather clearly that basic social casework principles and methods are needed. On the whole, the belief that casework skills are required is not contested very often, but there are occasional challenges to this point of view from individuals as well as some educational developments that, taken together, make this subject worth additional exploration.[8]

Social Casework Skills and Probation Work

During the past decade there has been a rather definite increase in the number of universities and colleges offering what might be termed specialized curricula in corrections work. These are administered usually, though not always, by departments of sociology, and their chief function is to prepare students for the correctional field. For the most part, these programs operate on an undergraduate basis, and frequently they tend to be a one-man operation in that the specific content in the corrections field is taught by one faculty member, although students also take appropriate courses in sociology and related departments. Many of these specialized programs offer training at the graduate level as well, usually making it possible for a student to obtain a master's degree at the end of one year, in contrast with the master's degree in social work, which normally takes two years.

[7] See Studt and Chernin, "The Role of the School of Social Work in Educating and Training Personnel for Work with Juvenile Delinquents."
[8] See Blake, "Probation Is Not Casework"; but see also Meeker, "Probation Is Casework."

Specialized Curricula in Corrections

Although the content of the undergraduate and graduate programs in actual operation is difficult to ascertain, there are probably between fifteen and twenty of them in existence. A review of current curricula preparing students for law enforcement or corrections, compiled in 1953 by Professor Frank M. Boolson of Fresno State College, identified seventeen colleges or universities with corrections curricula of one kind or another. There were thirteen four-year programs and ten graduate programs, some institutions having both.[9]

The case for the development of specialized curricula in corrections, especially the kind of training provided at the undergraduate level, rests mainly on the fact that the great majority of employing agencies in this field neither require nor obtain workers with professional degrees in social work.[10] It is urged, therefore, that the reality is such that students who have received specialized training, even at the undergraduate level, will move into positions in the field far better equipped than those who have only a basic education in the social sciences, for example. The students not only receive exposure to conceptual content and the literature in several specialized courses in both juvenile and adult corrections, but in addition many of these programs provide some kind of field observation, through which students obtain some acquaintance with practices in the field. This often includes field trips, observation in juvenile courts, visits to training schools and to various kinds of adult correctional programs. In some instances, provision is made for a form of interneship in which a student is placed for a two or three month period, normally during a summer, for the purpose of getting practical experience in the field itself.

Although the fact that these programs are in operation and that most of them seem to be reasonably successful in placing students seems to make a case for their continuance, the case against them also seems relatively strong. In the first place, specialization at the undergraduate level runs counter to today's general trend in American higher education, which more and more has been emphasizing the importance of

[9] *Suggested College Curricula as Preparation for Correctional Service,* pp. 27-31.
[10] Reckless, "Training of the Correctional Worker."

broad, comprehensive preparation for life rather than narrow vocational specialization. The degree to which these programs try to straddle both is problematical; but in any case, in the colleges and universities of the highest standing the number of undergraduate hours available for specialization has been whittled down considerably in recent years. The most telling argument against the development of these specialized curricula, whether graduate or undergraduate, as they concern the juvenile court field, is that they have the almost universal flaw of failing to provide for the student's acquiring basic casework skills. The only major program of this kind that is casework-oriented is the University of Notre Dame's. The point made here is concerned specifically with probation services in the courts; in relation to other corrections fields, this argument is less conclusive. Its chief applicability is to areas in which casework is the chief skill required, but there are numerous positions in corrections in which casework skills are not required. However, from the previous discussion of the functions of probation workers, it seems clearly evident that their duties rest largely upon their knowledge of casework. The sixty graduate schools of social work in the United States and Canada offer ample proof of the fact that social work educators at the present time hold unanimously to the belief that casework skills cannot be communicated at the undergraduate level. Regardless of the curriculum emphasis of an individual school of social work, all schools are geared to the communication of basic casework skills, not to the exclusion of other areas, but to an extent that indicates the preëminence of casework concepts in virtually all phases of social work.

Casework Skills in the Juvenile Court Setting

All things considered, this subject cannot be conclusively decided without an understanding and awareness of what social casework is and what it attempts to do. Florence Hollis briefly defines social casework as "a method employed by social workers to help individuals find a solution to problems of social adjustment which they are unable to handle in a satisfactory way by their own efforts." [11] A more definitive statement has been made by Father Swithun Bowers, to whom social casework is "an art in which knowledge of the science of human relations and skill in relationship are used to mobilize capacities in the

[11] Hollis, "Social Casework."

individual and resources in the community appropriate for better adjustment between the client and all or any part of his total environment." [12]

A more descriptive definition has been formulated by Charlotte Towle, covering such questions as who casework clients are, why they seek help, and what the caseworker attempts to do in terms of treatment objectives. As Miss Towle, one of the outstanding educators in the area of social treatment, describes it: "The social caseworker deals with people who are experiencing some breakdown in their capacity to cope unaided with their own affairs. This breakdown may be due primarily to external forces beyond the control of the individual, or it may be partially, largely, or entirely due to factors within the individual; that is, he may himself have created his social dilemma. In either instance the caseworker deals with people who are in trouble and who, regardless of the source of difficulty, are prone to have disturbed feelings about it." The caseworker gives services which meet practical reality needs and takes action which modifies environmental stress and makes available opportunities in areas of deprivation and frustration. These very services, when oriented to feelings and to ways of responding, may ease anxieties, relieve discouragement, give new confidence, and enable the individual to manage his own affairs more competently.[13]

Enabling the individual to manage his own affairs more competently is the very heart and core of the casework process as it is conceived today. In effect, it rejects the "ordering, forbidding, and manipulating" methods frequently considered appropriate two or three decades ago, and at the same time it poses a problem involving the need for a far higher order of skill than older concepts seemed to make necessary. At the same time, as these definitions make clear, this does not mean that the social worker is or should pretend to be a "junior psychiatrist," but it does mean that many of the things he does in practice are related to dynamic psychology. It would be useful, therefore, to look at some of the concepts considered applicable in modern social work, particularly as they apply to the aspects of juvenile delinquency under consideration.

Obviously, in a field that is so rich in literature and so dynamic in content that it justifies the utilization of a considerable portion of a two-year period of graduate study, nothing but a cursory and even superficial review of some of the fundamental concepts should be

[12] Bowers, "The Nature and Definition of Social Casework."
[13] Towle, "Social Casework."

attempted here. Nevertheless, taken together with the functions that already have been described as being appropriate to probation workers, it is the utilization in practice of these concepts that makes the strong case for the use of social-work trained workers in this field.

Among the principles and concepts utilized in social casework are these:

1. *Behavior is purposeful, and it has a meaning for each individual.* Despite what seems to be a lack of logic, delinquent acts are essentially logical to the offender. Our knowledge of human nature is still too limited to permit complete understanding of all the motivations of behavior, including delinquent behavior. Nevertheless, it is known that mere exhortations or threats directed toward the offender are usually fruitless, and because they are so frequently not carried out, they may actually have a strong negative effect upon a person's behavior.

2. *The meaning of an experience to an individual must be understood.* In effect, this is a corollary to the first concept, and in its simplest terms it means that each person and his problems must be considered individually. What seem to be identical experiences—for example, when two youngsters steal an automobile—in fact are not identical experiences and usually have altogether different meanings and motivations for each person involved.

3. *The right of each person to self-determination must be respected.* This does not imply unrestricted license, or the right of any person to choose what he will do regardless of the consequences either individual or social. But it does mean that each offender must be helped to achieve socially acceptable objectives of his own choosing. Frequently this question involves a discussion of the authoritative setting in which probation work is practiced; but actually the controversial issue of how authority may be used in casework without vitiating or denying fundamental casework principles is not in fact a serious problem. Life imposes authoritative limits on all persons, including those dealt with in other social work settings. This does not ignore the fact that the omnipresent component of authority in this setting has implications for the worker as well as the person being helped, but many of these can be resolved if the worker himself is able to handle authority effectively, and particularly if he recognizes that it is authority that stems from society and the nature of the agency rather than from him as a person. After all, the question of whether casework can be done in the correctional setting

has been pretty well settled by the fact that it is done within the limits imposed by the very nature of the setting itself.[14]

4. *Growth and personal development come from within the individual and cannot be superimposed from outside.* Nevertheless, it is possible to stimulate, motivate, or strengthen this development through the help skilled caseworkers can provide, especially as they concentrate on strengths within a person and in his situation and not on weaknesses.

5. *The social work process includes the orderly, conscientious use of scientific method.* In effect, this is seen best through the continuing process of study, diagnosis, and treatment.

As Teeters and Reinemann have pointed out, these concepts recognize that fundamentally "casework is founded upon the respect for the individual as a unique personality and the recognition of his worth; equally, probation is based upon the idea of the dignity of every human being." [15] Unquestionably, the application of the concepts so briefly described here demands a considerable degree of insight into human personality as well as marked ability to develop relationships with other persons.[16] The utilization of these concepts cannot be expected from persons selected according to the standard suggested in the "discreet person of good character" of the statutes. On the other hand, it is imperative to point out that this review of these concepts does not justify the assumption that large numbers of persons capable of performing the tasks described are employed in juvenile court probation services. Actually, a relatively small proportion of those now engaged in this important work have the backgrounds and qualifications necessary to fulfill what seems generally agreed to be the basic objectives of probation work.

As Tappan suggests, a great deal of the difficulty in probation practice arises out of the fact that the field is inadequately professionalized. But he also holds out hope that some of the practices that have stood in the way of professionalization of probation work are beginning

---

[14] Slawson, "The Use of the Authoritative Approach in Social Casework in the Field of Delinquency"; Taber, "The Value of Casework to the Probationer"; Lippmann, "The Role of the Probation Officer in the Treatment of Delinquency in Children"; Pray, "The Principles of Social Case Work as Applied to Probation and Parole," and "The Place of Social Case Work in the Treatment of Delinquency"; Flynn, "Courts and Social Work." See especially Charlotte Towle's discussion of Pray's paper in *Social Service Review*, 19, pp. 244-246.

[15] Teeters and Reinemann, *The Challenge of Delinquency*, p. 420.

[16] Flynn, "Parole Supervision: A Case Analysis." See Appendix II.

to disappear, including the "old prejudice that social work is inconsistent with legal authority." [17] Richard A. Chappell takes a consistent stand on this and comments: "Although case-work techniques are essential, they are utilized fully in too few probation departments, both adult and juvenile." [18]

In an area in which Teeters and Reinemann, Tappan, and Chappell all agree on the importance of casework in its modern connotation as being an essential qualification for effective probation work, it may seem somewhat like redundant pursuit of the obvious to stress the importance of casework as a tool. But these eminent authorities are identified chiefly with disciplines distinct from social work. Teeters is a Temple University sociologist; Reinemann is Director of Probation, Municipal Court of Philadelphia; Tappan is a member of the sociology and law faculties of New York University who served for a time as chairman of the United States Board of Parole; and Chappell has recently returned to the private practice of law after long and distinguished service as chief of the Federal probation program and as member of the United States Board of Parole. Although their agreement with the need for utilization of basic social casework concepts in dealing with delinquents does not make the verdict unanimous by any means, their forceful declarations and opinions on the subject carry considerable weight.

Why So Few Social Workers in the Courts?

Despite the opinions on this subject of experts, it is possible to go from one juvenile court to another, even in metropolitan communities, without finding a single trained social worker on the staff. So, although a substantial body of opinion supports the need for social workers, the facts of the situation present quite another picture. Why do trained social workers in the juvenile courts represent only a very small fraction of total probation personnel? Many reasons might be advanced for this disparity between theory and practice, but the chief causes seem to be these:

(1) There are specific disadvantages, such as low salaries, persistence of inadequate personnel standards, failure to provide a total setting

[17] Tappan, *Juvenile Delinquency*, p. 335.

[18] Chappell and Turnbladh, "Probation: Case Work and Current Status." The "Current Status" section of the article was written by Mr. Turnbladh, executive director of the National Probation and Parole Association.

conducive to morale, and, sometimes, outright rejection of trained workers. The failure of the public social services to attract trained social workers is an unpleasant reality that applies to probation services even more than it does to a great many other aspects of public social work. The salary situation in the probation area is not attractive, even though it is reasonably competitive with other social work positions. In juvenile courts, employment and separation may depend entirely upon the whim or caprice of a judge, and while it is becoming less frequent, in some jurisdictions there is a rapid turnover of personnel with every change of judge. By and large, courts have not kept up with developments in personnel practices, so that the court setting frequently suffers competitive disadvantages even with other public social services. Merit systems, especially in the areas of child welfare, public assistance, and mental hygiene have succeeded in creating a climate that helps to attract and retain competent workers. Furthermore, in certain other fields, especially in child welfare, the issue of whether trained social workers are needed is rarely if ever raised as it is in the courts.

(2) The opportunities for professional growth and advancement tend to be negligible in comparison with many public agencies and nearly all private social agencies. For years most juvenile courts have been outside the main stream of social work influence, and consequently the standards of personnel management, particularly in the areas of supervision and consultation, are on a level characteristic of other areas of social work thirty or forty years ago. As a general rule, in probation services there is supervision only in the administrative, informational, or policy-serving sense, and not educational sense. In many courts, the functions of supervisors have not been well defined, and in consequence they do an inordinate amount of clerical work, leaving little or no time for the educational components of supervision. In effect, supervisors act as trouble-shooters, jumping from one crisis to another. Where psychiatric clinics exist and are utilized by courts, they tend to be isolated from the court staff; but in the great majority of private social work agencies, when psychiatric services are used, they are considered a force in the development of staff members through the use of the consultation process. To put it more directly, in the juvenile court the worker only occasionally may get to see a brief report from a psychiatrist; in the private child welfare agency, the worker frequently consults with the psychiatrist about a particularly difficult case.

(3) The corrections field, both juvenile and adult, is in disrepute. Many juvenile courts operate at a level low enough to justify the rejection of court experience by other agencies in evaluating personnel qualifications. In effect, this means that a worker may spend four or five years in a juvenile court and at best receive no credit for this experience; at worst he may find difficulty in obtaining suitable employment elsewhere because of his identification with an agency in which high caseloads combined with generally low standards have resulted in its formal or informal rejection by the social work community.

Taken together, these difficulties mean that social workers, who are, generally speaking, in a job market in which demand far exceeds supply, are reluctant to accept employment in courts in which standards are even better than average. It must be admitted that the rejection of the juvenile court by social workers is due in part to the fact that many of them are unaware of its potential values and others prefer the sheltered, even exotic existence available in other agency settings. This is a two-way street: not only are there factors in the juvenile courts which make it difficult to attract competent workers, even though salaries are commensurate with similar positions in the field; but also there is the persistent problem of the lack of interest on the part of trained social workers in going into this challenging, difficult, and complex field.

Two things seem to be certain. The juvenile courts must become completely realistic and provide conditions reasonably similar to those in other social work settings. And social workers should be more realistic in accepting the responsibilities inherent in work with courts. Both the court setting and the field of social work are involved here, and concessions must be made on both sides. The modifications in social casework practices suggested by the development of "aggressive casework," at best an unfortunate term, as envisaged and put into practice on the initiative of the New York City Youth Board, serve as a stimulus to those who believe that ultimately compromises will be made that will bring the services of qualified caseworkers to troubled children and families.[19]

This review of concepts and principles utilized in social casework

---

[19] See Chap. 16; "Pattern for Prevention"; and New York City Youth Board, News Notes, December, 1954.

makes no attempt to show specific areas of application, whether in the social study process or in supervision. This can be done only on a case-by-case basis, and only when awareness of a given situation is characterized by adequate breadth and depth. At the same time, the emphasis placed here upon the knowledge and skill required to do acceptable social casework either in the juvenile court or in any other setting should not be taken as an indication that this is a field in which technique and method reign supreme. Actually, certain personal attributes are prerequisite to training, and the majority of schools of social work are highly selective in their admission policies.

The Council on Social Work Education has suggested that these qualities, which are enhanced by training but are by no means provided through training, make a top-notch social worker: (1) a warm interest in people of all kinds and all ages, (2) faith in human beings, (3) ability to follow through, (4) ability to work with people, (5) a cheerful disposition, (6) intelligence, and (7) a broad perspective.[20] The possession of the qualities so briefly enumerated here makes it possible for some persons who have not had specialized training in social casework to do an effective job in the field. This does not mean that the possession of the personality characteristics described is enough in itself, nor does it mean that training is not necessary, but it is an unquestioned fact that some untrained workers operate in a thoroughly professional manner.

Obviously, the present situation in the courts demands relatively rapid solution of some kind. Only about 10 percent of those who occupy social work positions in courts serving children have had full social work training. But it is important to note that the 1950 Bureau of Labor Statistics survey showed that about three of five court workers had college degrees, while almost nine in ten had some college training.[21] Without glossing over the negative side of the picture, it is evident that by and large this is an educable group. In other words, these workers could profit considerably from well-organized staff development programs oriented to the job at hand.

[20] See *Careers in Social Work* and *Social Work as a Profession*. These pamphlets and other information about social work education, including fellowships, scholarships, and the most current listing of accredited graduate schools of social work, are available by writing to the Council on Social Work Education at 345 East 46th Street, New York 17, N.Y.

[21] *Social Workers in 1950.*

Staff Development Needs in the Juvenile Courts

Unfortunately, the courts as a whole have not taken advantage of the favorable situation presented by the relatively high educational attainments of court personnel. Since most courts are organized on a county basis, and since there are relatively few large courts, this should not be especially surprising as an over-all picture. But the same situation prevails in the metropolitan, specialized courts, in which excellent opportunities for staff development programs exist. Logically, it would be expecting too much for small counties with one or two workers to provide even rudimentary staff training programs; on the other hand, courts with staffs of fifty to one hundred, which have appropriate numbers and potential facilities, generally have not taken advantage of staff development opportunities. In the larger courts, the reason may be the apathy or indifference of judges or administrators of probation programs, or it may be simply that there is a lack of fiscal support, or there may well be a combination of the two reasons, since frequently these go hand in hand.

A realistic view of the situation seems to be this: neither now nor in the immediate future does there seem to be any prospect of filling very many available positions with graduates of schools of social work. Regardless of the current emphasis upon juvenile delinquency, with the concomitant interest in training, the facilities of schools of social work are not geared to provide large numbers of workers for this field. Social work is a highly competitive area, in which it is estimated that the supply-to-demand ratio is about one to three. Some of the conditions that make certain court positions unattractive, such as lack of tenure, heavy caseloads, and the like, may well remain for some time. Therefore, the reasonable approach seems to be (1) to recruit as many graduates of schools of social work as possible, recognizing that they will probably be a definite minority of all of those employed, regardless of improvements that may be made in the competitive position of juvenile courts; and (2) to embark upon a large-scale staff development program that will meet both the needs of newly recruited workers and those already on the job.

In its current usage, the term "staff development" goes far beyond mere in-service training. As it is used here, staff development refers to the entire process of communication to staff of the knowledge, skill, and ability appropriate to the functions performed, together with their integration at job level. Any comprehensive staff development program must include the following elements: (1) an orientation period for new workers, geared especially to getting them acquainted with the agency, its rules, procedures, and policies; (2) a continuous in-service training program, designed to meet the needs of workers at various levels, including administrative and supervisory personnel, attained through the organization of appropriate seminars or courses, together with heavy reliance upon the educational components of supervision; and (3) an educational leave program with provision for both part-time and full-time salaried leave for educational purposes.

Although this is not the place to spell out the content of such programs in detail, it should be observed that from a practical standpoint it is utterly impossible to develop an adequate staff development program, with component parts as described, in a small court with one or two probation workers. For smaller counties, at least, it is evident that some other device must be found. Even though larger juvenile courts are able theoretically to provide adequate training programs, the fact is that the great majority do not, and the presence of adequate staff development programs is a rarity. This, then, is a problem that affects both large and small courts. The number of workers dealing with delinquents is estimated to be close to 4,000—about 2,000 are concerned exclusively with children, and an additional 2,000 work with both juveniles and adults.[22] Therefore, because this is a neglected area and because so many workers are affected, there seems to be a strong case for trying to break the staff development bottleneck through the use of a realistic program that will meet at least minimum training needs.[23]

It is true that in some jurisdictions there have been training programs for public service employees under the direction of state departments of welfare or education; also, some state universities as well as other colleges and universities make available specific courses of value to workers in juvenile courts. Yet it is well established that the vast bulk of present-day court workers do not receive anything like consistent, uniform training of any sort. Although it may be thought that this is a

[22] *Probation and Parole Directory.*
[23] Meeker, "Training of Juvenile Court Probation Officers and Related Workers Who Cannot Attend Graduate School."

normal situation in the public social services, the fact of the matter is that certain other public programs have developed specific training methods, and consultants whose chief concern is with training have been used successfully for a long time in the federal-state public assistance program.

Since the passage of the Social Security Act in 1935 there have been federal training activities which have given help to public assistance agencies in the states. The reasoning behind this is that the expenditure of federal assistance grants by the states justifies the federal government's concern with training of the workers charged with responsibility for determining eligibility for public assistance and for providing various services to public assistance recipients. Federal training activities under the aegis of the U.S. Public Health Service also have taken place in connection with the development of mental hygiene programs under the National Mental Health Act of 1946. Particular stress has been placed upon the use of stipends to stimulate professional training in various phases of mental health work. Public child welfare programs have used training programs, also with considerable emphasis upon educational leave with stipends to encourage professional training. In the year ended August 31, 1953, 353 persons in 44 states completed a period of educational leave from state and local child welfare programs.[24] But child welfare service funds from federal sources are designed to meet problems of children in rural areas or other areas of special need, the definition of which is rather narrow. As far as delinquency is concerned, as the Senate Subcommittee to Investigate Juvenile Delinquency wryly remarked, the formula used is as unrealistic as an apportionment based on blonde girls or left-handed boys.[25]

A few state programs dealing with delinquents have participated in the child welfare educational leave programs under the Social Security Act. In Wisconsin, for example, where there is an omnibus Department of Welfare including a Division of Corrections, a few workers employed by the Bureau of Probation and Parole have been sent to schools of social work on child welfare stipends. But this avenue is open only to a few agencies, because such funds are available only to state agencies and not to local courts. There seems to be considerable interest in the development of similar training programs for juvenile court workers

[24] *Educational Leave in the Public Child Welfare Program*, 1953.
[25] *Interim Report*, 1954, Committee on the Judiciary, p. 30.

and others who deal with delinquent children, and several bills introduced into Congress make provision for stipends for these workers. A number of witnesses before the Hendrickson Subcommittee recommended the establishment of a National Institute of Juvenile Delinquency, with research, training, and technical aid functions.[26] Congressional approval of grants for educational leave would provide one answer, but not a complete answer, to the training problem posed, because many of the workers in question would not be eligible for admission to schools of social work. Even with relatively adequate stipends, it would be financially impossible or at least not feasible for married men with families to take advantage of such an opportunity.

As a way out of this dilemma, one of the present writers has elsewhere proposed that an intensive, full-time, three-months training program be organized for workers currently on the job. Possibly a small demonstration or pilot project should be developed first in order to ascertain on the basis of experience just what should be and can be included in an accelerated course. In any event, the proposed plan envisages the development of regional training programs, modeled after but not duplicating the kind of training program developed for juvenile police officers which has been notably successful at the University of Southern California's Delinquency Control Institute.[27] Such an undertaking probably would require federal support, and it should not be undertaken unless, within a limited period such as five years, there is a reasonable chance of meeting the training needs of at least half of those currently working in this field—roughly 2,000 staff members in undermanned agencies dealing with delinquents, but possibly 3,000 or 4,000 if the courts move in the direction of providing numbers of personnel commensurate with the task to be done.[28]

Unquestionably, this is a problem that will not be solved simply by wishful thinking. Individual courts should do their best to provide the most complete staff development program within their means, because nobody knows how long it will take for the need for the kind of program described here to make itself sufficiently felt to result in specific action by Congress. It is the conviction of the authors that the training needs of the juvenile courts can be established beyond question. There are

[26] *Interim Report,* pp. 13-14.
[27] See Chap. 10.
[28] See Flynn, "First Steps in Solving Training Needs of Court and Institutional Workers Who Treat Juvenile Delinquents."

literally hundreds of examples in the field of business in which it is clearly demonstrated that "training pays off." In business, the expenditures of funds by management for training purposes is a recognized phase of American industrial and commercial activity. Training is considered a normal business expenditure. In the light of the important functions performed by juvenile court workers and the skills that are vitally needed in dealing with extremely difficult situations, the absence of adequate staff development programs is disgraceful and scandalous. This is a problem that cannot be solved by stopgap measures such as occasional lectures and infrequent staff meetings that parade under the façade of in-service training. Until the majority of workers in this field have the minimum requisite skills to perform their tasks effectively, the question of a total training program is one that deserves careful and constant attention.

In any consideration of the problem of treating juvenile offenders, the juvenile court necessarily becomes a focal point. The quality of its probation staff is crucial in determining whether the courts can fulfill their mission. By affecting the quality of staff, dynamic training programs can be a significant instrument for improving one of the nation's vital services for youth.

Clinical Personnel in the Juvenile Courts

Although justifiable stress has been placed on both the role of the probation staff and its overwhelming importance in the work of the juvenile court, the advice and help of professional personnel from other disciplines also are required.

Especially important are the roles played by physicians, psychologists, and psychiatrists because the diagnostic information they provide may determine the line of action the court will take in any given situation. The following review of their functions is by no means definitive, merely suggesting the areas of responsibility customarily allocated to each discipline. They are discussed not in order of importance but in the order of frequency with which the courts usually have access to them.

Medical examination may reveal conditions previously unknown to the child's parents but having direct implications for treatment purposes. For example, a rheumatic heart condition that is uncovered may have specific effects upon a probation worker's plan for a child. It is not uncommon for probation staff members to recommend participation in group activities, including athletics; but when this is done without a physical examination to determine whether the child is capable of engaging in these activities, the court, through a staff member, may be responsible unwittingly for encouraging the youngster to undertake pursuits injurious to him.

Although most studies show that delinquents are at least as healthy as nondelinquents, and some studies even suggest that they are more robust, unquestionably there are children whose physical defects play an important role in their failure to make an adequate total adjustment to society. It may be thought that in this day and age school health examinations would provide an index as to a child's over-all condition as well as his specific treatment needs. But school medical programs tend to be partialized and related to specific conditions such as dental examinations and routine sight and hearing tests. Certainly, total planning by a court staff to meet the needs of children should take into account the state of their physical well-being. Even a routine physical examination may turn up clues extremely important in deciding the particular kind of program best suited to an individual child's needs.

Psychologists may play an important diagnostic and treatment role in cases of delinquents before the courts. It should be emphasized that psychologists with present-day training are equipped to go far beyond mere psychometric tests, and, even though the measurement of intelligence by individual testing may furnish important diagnostic clues as to treatment needs, the clinically trained psychologist is able to make further specific contributions to the total understanding of the child. He has available to him a great variety of tests which may give specific indications of what should be done in a given situation. It should be quite evident that the courts cannot rely very heavily on the diagnostic implications of a numerical intelligence quotient. The IQ may be meaningful, but more and more the conditions under which testing is done are being taken into account, and the IQ as a lone diagnostic tool has become increasingly suspect. Moreover, individual tests administered by the psychologist may have definite vocational implications. A youngster whose IQ is 80, as reported by the school on the basis of a series of group tests that are fairly consistent and show little variation over a period of time, may have mechanical aptitude far above average. The mere fact that a child has above-average mechanical aptitude may affect his school placement, and this in turn may influence his school adjustment. Since it is well established that many delinquent children have difficulties in adjusting to the school situation, in fact that a high proportion are truants, individualized tests that bring out the positive qualities and capacities of a child can have very important implications for his future adjustment. Test findings may suggest the desirability of a conference with school authorities; a different kind of school program may be decided upon; and a benign circle may swing into operation: the child becomes interested in school, he is less rebellious in attitude and demeanor, and as success seems to breed success, his involvement with useful activities lessens tensions—and delinquent behavior ceases since it is no longer a "necessary" way of life. It is recognized that this is an implicit criticism of the schools. Educators may protest that all children are placed in accordance with modern, scientific testing, and that placements are renewed from time to time or whenever symptoms of maladjustment appear. The fact is that the schools do a good job with the majority of children, but experience shows that some children are out of step with the schools because of inept placements or because the schools lack badly needed resources.[29]

Most psychologists would consider that their role is vastly oversimplified as described here, but from the standpoint of the courts even the low-level activities mentioned may be very useful. Without question, the interpretation of various psychological tests, especially those that give some index to personality, can have very great significance in helping the courts decide what disposition is appropriate. Well-trained psychologists can diagnose and deal with various kinds of disabilities, for example reading handicaps. In view of the importance of reading as a basic tool for learning, inability to read, regardless of the reason, may have serious effects upon a child's total adjustment to his school situation.

The psychiatrist plays a central role among the professional disciplines contributing to an understanding of children's behavior and misbehavior. The term "psychiatrist" is a canopy that covers a rather large number of variations in professional orientation, but essentially the child psychiatrist specializes in the diagnosis of the state of the emotional health or

[29] See Chap. 9.

well-being of the children examined, and in the treatment of malad-justments discovered. As was pointed out earlier,[30] children who manifest behavior disorders, including overt delinquent acts, are frequently the victims of emotional insecurity stemming from a variety of causes, in-cluding feelings of rejection, inferiority, and inadequacy. Most children have periods of insecurity, but the delinquent child may be reacting aggressively to a situation that a nondelinquent child will more or less take in stride. It is the psychiatrist's task to separate the normal from the abnormal, the reaction to growth and change that is within normal limits from that which is identified with a neurotic or even a psychotic condition. One child may respond to frustrated desires by submission, even unhealthy submission; another may react with belligerence and hostility against any form of authority—deprived, he strikes out, some-times by theft, by vandalism, or by setting fires.[31]

In the court's disposition process, psychiatric evaluations are particu-larly important. While it is perfectly true that a lay person may recog-nize that a delinquent child should be classified as "dull," such classifica-tions are inexact. Suppose the dullness of the youngster extends to the point of feeble-mindedness; this may in some instances mean that the appropriate disposition would be commitment to a school for defective children, rather than institutional or extramural treatment as a delin-quent *per se*. A psychologist is capable of dealing with most of these situations, but psychiatric evaluations are necessary when organic brain damage may be present, or when the child may be suffering from the aftereffects of a condition such as encephalitis.

The psychiatrist's functions are twofold: (1) to make meaningful diagnosis available to the court; and (2) to utilize treatment, usually psychotherapy, where indicated. In doing either of these things, he may work alone, or he may operate as the central figure in a team relation-ship with other disciplines, or he may function as a member of a team in a multidiscipline clinic situation in which there is some rotation of responsibility. Traditionally, the psychiatrist has been the dominant professional in a team relationship, although there is some evidence that the preëminence of the psychiatrist has diminished slightly in recent years.

[30] See Chap. 7.
[31] Gardner, "American Child Guidance Clinics."

Problems in Providing Clinic Services

Ideally, there is a strong case for the use of the clinic team functioning as a diagnostic and treatment aid to the court, a team consisting of one or more psychiatrists, psychologists, and psychiatric social workers. The psychiatric social worker is not a "junior psychiatrist" but does social casework as applied in the diagnosis and treatment of persons with social and personal maladjustment aggravated or caused by mental and emotional problems. Psychiatric social work is social work "undertaken in direct and responsible relation with psychiatry." [32] Relatively few juvenile courts have available the facilities of such a clinic, whether controlled by the court or separately organized and administered. Only ten or twelve clinics are attached directly to juvenile courts. But regardless of the numerical inadequacy of these services, their importance justifies some analysis of the problem of making these facilities available to the juvenile courts. Whether a part of the court or outside of it, however, clinical services available to the court are usually part-time, and, with some notable exceptions, complete clinical services of the kind suggested are rarely available. Where they exist in diluted form, especially when attached to a court, one usually finds a part-time psychiatrist or a part-time psychologist or both. Psychiatric social workers are rarely employed in court clinics, but they do function as part of the clinic team in the various kinds of noncourt child guidance clinics, under private or public auspices, that occasionally serve the courts.

The relatively high cost of professional personnel is one of the most serious complications in connection with provision of clinical services. While it is not inconceivable that court budgets could include provisions for services of psychologists and psychiatric social workers, the acute problem is highlighted in the area of psychiatry, chiefly because of the competition from private practice. Psychiatrists command high fees in private practice, and annual incomes of $25,000 and upward are relatively common. When psychiatrists provide service on a daily fee basis to various kinds of social agencies, the cost may well be from $75 to $100 daily. Relatively few courts, and only those in metropolitan areas, can afford to pay the going rate for psychiatric time. Most appropriating

---

[32] Knee, "Psychiatric Social Work."

bodies would regard with alarm the prospect of paying $8,000 or $10,000 a year to a psychiatrist for twelve to fifteen hours a week service. Therefore, even in courts with a large volume of business, it is usual to have very little psychiatric time available. Moreover, for perfectly understandable reasons, there is a tendency for the psychiatric time available to be utilized solely for diagnostic work. Frequently, this is a hurried process, not in keeping with the standards of good practice in psychiatry—not because the psychiatrists in question are culpable, but because they are quite likely to define their role as a screening one. Consequently, they attempt to cover as many cases as possible, recognizing that about all they can do is to rule out or to identify gross pathologies.

To a certain extent, this practice explains one public misconception about the use of psychiatric services in juvenile courts. When a mentally disturbed child goes berserk and commits serious assaults, even murder, it is fairly common for critics to point an accusing finger at the juvenile court and for the press to comment on the fact that the youngster in question was dealt with one or more times in the juvenile court and had been "studied" by juvenile court psychiatrists. The point should be made that the "studies" usually are very brief. Likewise, there are numerous cases in which serious disturbances are identified and brought to the attention of the court, but because of the lack of suitable disposition facilities or for other reasons, little if anything is done.

As a practical matter, it is apparent that there must be some selective use of clinical facilities when they are available at all. At their present stage of development, it is not reasonable to expect that all the larger juvenile courts, or even a majority of them, will be able to provide a full clinical staff to deal diagnostically with all of the children who come before the court. Large-scale clinical treatment programs seem out of the question. It should be observed also that, contrary to popular impression in some quarters, all delinquent children are not "sick children" in the sense that they need psychiatric care. Many of them are simply acting out conflicts and other difficulties that may have relatively minor impact upon their total personalities. If members of the probation staff had the qualifications to perform the tasks assigned them, in keeping with the standards that are implicit in the previous discussion of their work, it would be logical to expect them to use selectively the clinical facilities available to the courts. But it has been demonstrated that probation workers generally are not qualified in terms of the delicate responsibilities required, and it is very doubtful that the standards will be improved radically in the immediate future.

Therefore, it would be feasible for the screening to be done by members of a clinic staff such as psychiatric social workers or psychologists, thus winnowing out for psychiatric attention only those cases that seem to require psychiatric diagnosis. Inevitably this will mean that some children who are in need of psychiatric diagnosis will not get it, and the court may make unfortunate decisions in their cases because of the absence of appropriate information. Nevertheless, it is necessary to consider the situation as it exists: the great majority of these children do not get psychiatric attention anyway, and the services of qualified psychiatric social workers and psychologists cost only about one-fourth of what psychiatric services cost. The conclusion seems reasonable that wherever probation staff members have the professional qualifications that enable them to do a reasonably effective screening job, this might well be their responsibility. On the other hand, when workers do not possess these qualifications but supervisors do, the latter might make such decisions. Whenever the professional level of total staff does not promise effective screening, the use of either psychiatric social workers or psychologists, preferably working directly with psychiatrists, is recommended.

This problem of clinical services is a very difficult one to solve. Despite the very significant contributions to the entire field of child psychiatry of the clinics associated with the early juvenile courts, these facilities have not kept up with increasing needs. A great many courts are in the dubious position of having doubled or trebled their total caseloads without having added at all to the specialized services so clearly needed if adequate dispositions are to be made.

Until this point, the focus has been mainly on the problems associated with providing diagnostic services, but the dilemma of the courts with respect to treatment of children with emotional disturbances on an out-patient or in-patient basis is even more serious, when the relation between existing needs and present facilities is taken into account. Except for a few children's departments or divisions located in wings or wards of state hospitals, it is probable that the bed capacity of all institutional facilities for emotionally disturbed children does not exceed

1,500 or 1,800, whereas the need for such resources both for delinquent and nondelinquent children may well be forty to fifty times as great. Clinical facilities are not dispersed evenly throughout the country; they are congregated chiefly in metropolitan communities, with a heavy concentration on the Eastern seaboard. The plight of rural areas is especially serious, although a number of states provide some types of traveling clinics which ostensibly reach the rural areas. But the traveling clinics are months behind, even in their diagnostic studies, and relatively few children can receive treatment.

The picture has improved somewhat by the advances made by many communities under the provisions of the National Mental Health Act of 1946, but even the increases in trained personnel made possible because of the leadership of the National Institute of Mental Health of the U.S. Public Health Service and the availability of federal grants for training leave most communities far short of meeting total needs. This is not meant to disparage the improvements that have been made, but rather it is an attempt to appraise realistically some of the deficiencies present in the existing situation, deficiencies that may well be expected to continue for some time.

In view of the situation described, it is important to recognize the role that the professional clinical staff can play with respect to the other staff members. The device of integrating psychiatric information by utilizing lectures and seminar-type discussions for probation staff members, dealing with such areas as normal growth and development from the psychiatric point of view, conceivably would aid staff members. It would help them obtain a keener appreciation of the backgrounds and causative factors of personality disturbances and concurrently assist them in achieving some degree of selectivity in using the psychiatric resources available, meager though they may be. Although this may be a difficult decision to make, it is logical to suppose that clinical resources, already strained beyond the breaking point, might be used to greater advantage in improving the skills of probation staff members individually by consultation or in groups than by seeing routinely a relatively large proportion of the children coming before the court. Psychiatrists, psychologists, and psychiatric social workers could be very effective in interpreting to probation workers the vitally needed understanding of the reasons for children's behavior and misbehavior.

Administrative Organization of Court Services

The type of internal administrative organization of a juvenile court naturally depends to a large extent upon the size of the staff. In a small agency, intimate and informal contacts are normal and presumably they are effective; but in a large agency, the administrative methods, principles, and policies required for over-all efficiency of management should be in operation. The necessity for adequate personnel practices, previously discussed, underlines this point; and in general, the principles of organization common to a great variety of enterprises apply here. Obviously, there must be clear lines of authority through a rational chain of command, and there must be within the hierarchy of the agency methods of communication consistent with its needs. One would expect to find such devices as operating manuals, directives that are revised in accordance with current policies, staff conferences that permit ideas to flow both upward and downward, and many other similar practices.

In the absence of recent detailed studies, it is impossible to make definitive statements regarding the degree to which efficiency in operations through appropriate methods of administration is carried out in the larger courts. Nevertheless, observation suggests that top personnel, such as chief probation officers, often have been selected for talents other than executive ability, and that this has been accompanied by rather incomplete fulfillment of desirable administrative goals. In day-by-day operations this is reflected in numerous ways, such as inefficient use of time by workers who prepare long-hand reports to be copied later by typists or who type their own reports and case records rather than use efficient mechanical recording equipment. This example is suggestive merely and does not indicate the wide range of actual or potential inefficient practices in the larger courts.

Because of the dual responsibilities of the probation staff, there is some disagreement about whether probation workers responsible for social studies of children should also carry supervisory responsibilities in the cases of the same youngsters placed on probation, or whether the two functions should be separated. In favor of the former, it is urged that the close interrelationships among study, diagnosis, and treatment, together with the use of the relationship between child and worker, make a strong case for continuity of activity through one worker. Against this, the argument is advanced that some staff members may have a flair for investigative work but may be relatively ineffective in dealing with long-term relationships with children, and in addition that supervision will receive far more attention when it is given full time.

Probably the chief advantage of combining the study-supervision functions, in addition to their admitted interrelationship and the desirability of providing a continuum of experience for the child, is the fact that the worker who deals both with investigation and supervision can confine his operations to a relatively small district. It is strongly argued that the use of a small district, especially in metropolitan areas, lends itself to the development of knowledge of community resources useful both in the social study and in treatment, and that the worker's familiarity with the immediate community may reduce the amount of time spent in travel and make his day-by-day contacts more fruitful. Most agencies have combined rather than separated the two functions.

Time spent in court or awaiting appearance in court in connection with a particular case constitutes an unsolved problem. The usual practice is that the probation officer is available at the time of a court hearing to provide supplementary information when it is required by the judge. In a large court, this may involve a lengthy waiting period, because it is difficult to schedule cases exactly. If the court calendar on a given day contains thirty or forty cases, there is a chance that as many as fifteen or twenty probation officers will spend the entire morning in court waiting for their cases to be called. In the large courts, relatively little time is devoted to each case, and the worker is unable to schedule other interviews, dictating periods, or the like, since the court case in which he is interested may be called at almost any time. A few of the larger courts have dealt with this problem by scheduling cases so that a worker is required to be in court only one day each week. Since it is nearly universal practice for all cases to be heard during a morning session, this means that one-half day each week is devoted by the worker to court activities. In a few courts, the chief probation officer or some other person in a supervisory capacity represents the probation worker, but this practice has been criticized severely in some quarters on the grounds that the person representing the child before the court actually is too far removed from the immediate situation to make a significant contribution.

This dilemma is a serious one, and no easy answer is readily apparent. Probably the development of more adequate case histories, accompanied by significant diagnostic summary statements, would eliminate the need for the appearance of an individual probation worker in a number of cases, although it is generally considered desirable for the probation worker to be present if he so desires. The presence of the probation worker at the court hearing may represent the only friendly contact for a child during a very trying and difficult period, and whatever may be lost in terms of efficient management may be gained in terms of better relationships with the children involved.

In general, while there can be no excuse for slipshod, inefficient methods of operation, dedication to efficiency should never be allowed to interfere with the primary concern of the court staff—service to children in trouble. But actually the goals of efficient management and service to children are not incompatible, and it is no more realistic to use the excuse that the court is concerned with children as a basis for justifying inefficient methods of operation than it is to use efficient methods of operation as a reason for excusing inattention to the needs of children. Some rational compromise between these extremes is feasible.

Facilities Available Outside the Court

Although considerable stress has been placed upon the functions of the probation staff and others directly connected with the decision-making or disposition functions of the court, the court's role with respect to disposition in virtually all communities is affected by the pronounced unavailability of adequate facilities. This is true with respect to both institutional and noninstitutional resources, and the problem is particularly acute when the agencies are under private auspices, which usually can determine their own intake policies.

Institutional Facilities

In nearly all states there are one or more state training schools, and in some jurisdictions county or city training schools, which the courts are able to use either by direct commitment or by commitment to a central state, county, or municipal authority. (It should be noted that the *Standards for Specialized Courts Dealing with Children* avoids use of the word "commitment" because of the common confusion created about the rights and responsibilities of the courts, the parents, and the institution or agency receiving a child. The point has some validity, but the issues in question are not discussed here, and the term is in normal usage.) There are also various state or local noninstitutional facilities under public auspices which may be used by the courts. But whether the facilities are institutional or noninstitutional, the chief problem is the lack of diversity of resources. In effect, when disposition requires the use of these facilities, the court is forced to use them for a variety of children whose individual needs may not be met by the available programs. It is axiomatic that when delinquent children are subjected either to mass institutional treatment, or to routinized treatment by a community agency, the failure to meet the individual needs of the children may affect disastrously their future development.

The lack of diversified facilities supported by public funds is a serious problem, but in metropolitan communities it is dwarfed by the complex and perplexing situation presented by the multiplicity of privately controlled agencies, institutional or otherwise, that theoretically may be used by the court. Operated by private boards of directors, but usually supported in large measure by tax subsidies of one kind or another, these agencies determine their intake policies by defining their functions so as to include only children who meet certain specifications. While it might be an exaggeration to say that some of these facilities admit only "blond, blue-eyed boys," it is substantially true that intake controls may operate to exclude the very children who have the greatest needs and who appear in court in the largest numbers. In a great many large cities, by no means limited to the South, the problems faced by the juvenile courts in the disposition of Negro children are difficult and troublesome. It is not uncommon for a probation worker's summary to read something like this: "This boy cannot be accepted by Smithfield Village because he once ran away when placed there; his IQ is too low for admission to Rest Haven; being fifteen, he is too old for Half-Way House; therefore, since there are no other institutions accepting Negro boys, the only alternative is to place him on probation."

These problems are acute when reasonably normal children are concerned; they become almost insuperable when a child presents some special problem. In nearly all states, the mentally defective child who is also delinquent is seriously discriminated against; detention facility length-of-stay statistics demonstrate this because these unfortunate ones may wait many weeks or many months before being admitted to a state institution. These so-called "waiting list" cases, while not numerous, take up an enormous amount of probation-staff time, and they occupy space designed for temporary care, often when the space is badly needed for other children. Children with physical handicaps and those with emotional disturbances are likewise difficult to place, and often the courts in desperation "give up" and use probation as a last resort, even though such a plan is clearly contraindicated.

What is needed is the presence of a wide range of facilities adapted to the needs of children who come before the juvenile court and the selective use of a wide range of the various facilities that are available. When necessary, institutionalization should be used in a positive, therapeutic way and not on the grounds that a child has failed his "last chance." A child should never be removed from his home unless conditions obviously make it necessary for such drastic action to be taken but, when a child is removed, he should be placed in a facility that will meet his basic and essential needs in a constructive fashion. Unfortunately, the juvenile courts are far from attaining the reasonable goal of selective and positive use of treatment resources, and one of the vital reasons for this is the lack of suitable, flexible facilities.

Even though the courts have relatively few choices to make as to dispositions, it is evident that the court's relationships to other community agencies should be positive and constructive. Although this seems to be a trite remark, the pattern of relationships between the juvenile courts and other agencies frequently tends to be a stormy one. Both the courts and other community agencies are partially at fault. Sometimes the courts do not understand the carefully defined functions of other agencies, and occasionally the functions of agencies change without the courts being aware of it. This is equally true from the standpoint of the other agencies' views about the courts. They may not understand the functions of the court, and they may be unaware of its limitations, as to both personnel and available facilities. Some agencies in the community may look down upon the court because of the conviction that the court staff members have inferior professional qualifications when compared with the personnel of other agencies dealing with children's problems.

Here is an example of a case that may cause misunderstanding.

The court may deem it necessary to remove a delinquent adolescent boy from his home, but not from the community, and may refer the child to an agency which provides foster placement service. Placement agencies are aware of the fact that the foster-home placement of any adolescent is difficult, and it is nearly impossible to place a delinquent adolescent. There may ensue a long period of delay, perhaps weeks, during which the youngster is held in detention, and finally the agency reports to the court that it is unable to make a placement. In desperation, the court may commit to the training school. But the settlement house worker and the school counselor who have been interested in the youngster may take a dim view of the court's action because they believe that the boy does not belong in a state training school.

While there is no easy and immediate solution to the problems suggested, it is clear that the juvenile court has to do a public relations job of the first magnitude. It must take the leadership in informing the community of gaps in services and the need for various flexible facilities that will meet the disposition needs of the court; and its relationships with other agencies must be improved by the use of periodic conferences and particularly by written policy agreements. The truth of the matter is that neither the courts nor the other agencies are in a position that makes feasible their development as self-sufficient islands. All of the agencies concerned are interdependent, and their reliance upon one another should be based upon a common understanding of functions and a mutual and shared responsibility for the achievement of common goals.

The Use of Child Welfare Services

One of the most significant resources available to the courts, especially in rural areas, is the provision of child welfare services administered by the states in conjunction with the United States Children's Bureau under the federal-state program created by the Social Security Act of 1935 as amended. The child welfare services program exists for the purpose of "establishing, extending, and strengthening, especially in predominantly rural areas" and in areas of special need, public welfare services for the protection and care of homeless, dependent, and neglected children, and children in danger of becoming delinquent. By the end of 1953, about one-half of the counties of the United States had provided some form of child welfare services under the aegis of state or county departments of public welfare, and nearly 5,000 persons were employed full time in professional positions in the state and local child welfare programs, about one-fourth of them being paid for in whole or in part out of federal funds.[33] Many of these workers from time to time provide services to courts, chiefly in rural counties, and because large numbers of the smaller counties can not or will not provide probation services, child welfare personnel can fill this gap by assisting the courts in cases of dependent and neglected children. This program is not universally available, even in rural counties, but in many of the smaller juvenile courts it has proved to be a real asset, providing adequate social studies for the court and supplying casework treatment services where indicated.

It should not be assumed that the existence of these services automatically solves all problems. The personnel available are not distributed evenly in terms of court needs. Although a substantial proportion of child welfare workers have received graduate training in social work, not all of them are adapted to working with the difficult cases sometimes seen in the courts. Probation workers, when available, may resent the use of child welfare service personnel by the courts, even though this might mean a reduction of their own caseloads to manageable size. In some jurisdictions, a form of professional jealousy has developed. In one state, an association of probation workers protested vigorously to the state welfare director against the use of child welfare service staff in the courts—even in counties which did not have a probation staff—on the grounds that this was an infringement upon their territory. Nevertheless, this is a program that has expanded consistently in recent years. Its influence is being felt more and more, and when wisely used, it can provide an effective instrument for the courts.

State Aid to the Juvenile Courts

The states help juvenile courts in varied ways, such as making personnel available either for direct service or for consultation, performing a standard-setting function, providing financial assistance of some kind, and aiding in the compilation and interpretation of statistical data. Personnel may be provided either through the state child welfare pro-

[33] *Personnel in Public Child Welfare Programs: 1953*, pp. 1-3.

gram or through the services of an agency which has primary responsibility for correctional services to adults, such as a state-wide probation and parole system. Many of those who have examined this question, including child welfare administrators, believe that the chief role of the child welfare worker is to provide protective services, broadly defined, which in turn will make it possible for court staff to devote attention to the more seriously delinquent youngsters.

One of the most controversial aspects of the problem of state assistance to the courts occurs in connection with the provision of services by state-wide adult probation and parole agencies. The consensus seems to be that the use of personnel whose primary responsibility is in the area of adult corrections is unwise. It is urged that they do not have the skills required for work with children and that there is a danger of identification in the public mind of children before the juvenile courts and adult criminals. The issue of skills required is certainly debatable on theoretical grounds; it is open to question mainly because the skills required in correctional services for adults demand abilities of a very high order. But, from a practical standpoint, services for adults usually are implemented by personnel inferior in qualifications to those selected for work with juveniles. About one-third of the states are authorized to have combined adult probation and parole programs, and some of the agencies handling these programs are authorized to give services to juvenile courts upon request by the courts.

Recently an anomalous situation has developed, chiefly because of the situation in Wisconsin. There, the Bureau of Probation and Parole of the Division of Corrections, State Department of Public Welfare, was authorized by the legislature in June, 1955, to provide assistance to the courts upon request in cases of juveniles, and the high quality of services available in the Wisconsin program has been used elsewhere in an attempt to justify combined adult and juvenile probation activities. But certain unique features of the Wisconsin program are often overlooked in discussions of this question. Currently Wisconsin has an entrance standard that calls for completion of a two-year program in a graduate school of social work before employment by the Bureau; by administrative policy, workers in the larger jurisdictions specialize in juvenile cases wherever possible, thus avoiding the mixture of juvenile and adult cases; and in addition, the probation and parole program was for some years better staffed than the Department of Public Welfare's

Division of Youth and Community Services, which is responsible for the state child welfare program and which is considered the logical agency to assist the courts. Besides, it is altogether probable that the Bureau's functions in serving juvenile courts will be transferred ultimately to the child welfare program. Consequently, unless all the qualifications suggested are kept clearly in mind, Wisconsin should not be used as an example justifying the use of combined juvenile and adult correctional services.

Some states employ special training consultants in child welfare, whose services might be made available for staff development functions in various probation departments. An examination of policy manuals of the United States Children's Bureau indicates the feasibility of using federal child welfare service funds for one or more full-time consultants at the state level for staff development purposes in local probation programs. One authority has recommended that this function be given highest priority.[34] In Vermont and West Virginia, all or most of the juvenile probation service is given by state-appointed, state-paid workers; several states establish eligible lists for the appointment of local probation officers through competitive examinations; in New York, the Division of Probation of the State Department of Corrections has general supervision of probation administration throughout the state, including probation in the children's courts; in a few other states, the juvenile courts are required to make annual reports to the governor or to a state board or department.[35]

Another form of state aid to juvenile courts is provided by at least fifteen states, which authorize the appointment of citizens' advisory boards or committees to advise and coöperate with the courts. Because the advisory committees are appointed by the courts, and because the appointments are not mandatory, they may offer little or no help, or a great deal of help, depending upon the ability of the judge to use such a group effectively. Other state activities include the collection of statistical data from the courts, particularly since the 1946 revision of the Children's Bureau policy which resulted in the responsibility for reporting data from the courts being shifted to a state agency.[36]

This review of state aid and participation in the work of juvenile

[34] Meeker, *Training of Juvenile Court Probation Officers*, pp. 34-35.

[35] Sussmann, *Law of Juvenile Delinquency*, pp. 63-64; Cosulich, *Juvenile Court Laws of the United States*, pp. 101-107.

[36] Schwartz, "Statistics of Juvenile Delinquency in the United States."

courts suggests a great deal of activity, but actually there is a pronounced scarcity of information in this area. In fact, there is a real dearth of studies which would give a clear picture of the situation in the nation as a whole; and the current picture in any state is colored by the specific practices, personalities, and relationships that have developed. An examination of the law in a particular state may prove deceptive. For example, in Indiana for many years a state probation commission was responsible for establishing eligibility lists to be used in appointments of county probation department staffs. For a considerable period of time, the commission refused to release any information on the qualifications required for admission to the examinations held—on the dubious but interesting theory that if such information were available application forms would be "padded." A 1947 study showed that the commission admitted to examination many persons who did not qualify under commission rules, and that over a period of years virtually all probation officers who received temporary appointments pending examination passed the examination.[37]

Whatever the results of detailed studies that might be made in the future, the varieties of state aid to juvenile courts, with the possible exception of direct personal services, have not appreciably "solved the juvenile court problem." Whether this is because the aid proffered is inadequate, or whether it is because the local organization of the courts provides an insuperable barrier to "outside" help, is difficult to ascertain. In any event, the juvenile courts still need radical improvements.

Federal Aid

While it is impossible at present to forecast exactly what will happen, there are some prospects for federal aid that may have a direct impact upon juvenile courts. The considerable federal interest shown in the past several years may lead ultimately to specific new or enlarged programs. The activities of the Children's Bureau, the stimulation of the privately financed Special Juvenile Delinquency Project attached to the Bureau, the hearings and reports of the Senate Subcommittee to Investigate Juvenile Delinquency—all these have resulted in a burst of federal interest in the entire problem of juvenile delinquency. Along

[37] Indiana, *Report and Surveys of the State Penal and Correctional Survey Commission,* 1948, pp. 23-46.

with this, a great deal of concern has been expressed about the role of the courts.

The various activities of the United States Children's Bureau have been identified from time to time in this book, but it should be emphasized that since the Bureau was founded in 1912 it has had a definite concern with the problem of delinquency, based not only upon the Bureau's broad responsibility to investigate and report "on all matters pertaining to children," but also upon the specific inclusion of juvenile courts in the statute creating it.[38] All of the distinguished chiefs of the Bureau—Julia C. Lathrop, Grace Abbott, Katherine F. Lenroot, and Martha M. Eliot—gave high priority to this problem.

In 1955, Dr. Eliot was able to obtain additional funds from Congress, and a new Division of Juvenile Delinquency Service with an enlarged staff was created, enabling the Bureau to function more effectively in providing broad consultation services. The new Director of the division is Philip G. Green, formerly chief probation officer of the San Francisco Juvenile Court; William H. Sheridan, delinquency expert with the Bureau for a number of years, is Chief of the Technical Aid Branch; and Mrs. Elliot Studt, former faculty member of the School for Social Welfare, University of California (Berkeley), is chief of the Training Branch.

The Special Juvenile Delinquency Project, launched in July, 1952, was financed by foundations and individual donors, with the chief support coming from the Field Foundation. The project, housed in the offices of the Children's Bureau, has supplemented the Bureau's efforts with a threefold program: (1) the development of current materials on juvenile police services and training schools; (2) the formulation of goals and standards for action in such areas as institutions, juvenile police services, juvenile courts, and the training of personnel; and (3) the development of a broad campaign of public education to create public support for necessary improvements and services. Through a series of conferences and a number of lively and readable publications, the project has stimulated considerable interest both among those identified with the professional disciplines concerned with this field and in the lay community at large.

The Senate Subcommittee to Investigate Juvenile Delinquency,

[38] U.S. *Statutes* 79 (1912); see also *The Children's Bureau: Yesterday, Today and Tomorrow.*

created in 1953 under the chairmanship of Senator Robert C. Hendrickson, held public hearings in several large cities, covering numerous aspects of the delinquency problem and arousing considerable interest. On March 14, 1955, the Subcommittee released a voluminous report that dealt with various aspects of the juvenile delinquency problem and made broad recommendations for future improvement. The subcommittee, now under the chairmanship of Senator Estes Kefauver, continues to operate.

While it is unquestionably true that the increased tempo of federal interest is due to relatively widespread alarm at what seems to be a statistical rise in juvenile delinquency, the effects should be salutary. There is some cause for concern about the problem. Census Bureau estimates of a 40 percent increase from 1952 to 1960 in the child population of juvenile court age mean that all children's services will be faced with the impact of this increase. The need for services will be greater, even assuming no change in the incidence of the problems involved. Without a doubt, the juvenile courts will be inundated, and because existing services are clearly inadequate, the courts will be utterly incapable of dealing with the problems coming before them unless drastic improvements take place. Hopefully, federal leadership and federal aid may produce substantial changes for the better in the personnel situation, both quantitatively and qualitatively, by providing the kind of help and stimulation that will enable the states and the localities to take specific action to improve court services for children in trouble. Anything less than drastic improvement will not be enough.

The Effectiveness of Juvenile Courts

Generally, an appraisal of the effectiveness of any institution or agency rests upon a comparison of actual results with what reasonably may be expected. If this premise is accepted, the effectiveness of juvenile courts can be measured if it can be determined whether the courts are accomplishing what they are supposed to accomplish. Unfortunately, there is no clear-cut agreement as to what the courts are supposed to accomplish. In the beginning the juvenile court was a reasonable, civilized, and rational device that removed children from the often harsh, punitive, and rigid criminal courts and placed them in a setting that theoretically could be responsive to their needs. The juvenile court movement grew out of the reasonable conviction that child offenders should not be treated in the same manner as adults, and that the state, with a judge acting as a "wise and kind father," should extend its protection to children and "save" and "cure" them rather than punish them. But this sensible, realistic version of what juvenile courts were supposed to be has been embellished and extended, and in some quarters the juvenile court has taken on the reputation of being a panacea. In the minds of many unwise advocates of the expanded juvenile court, it would not only provide a practical and normal way of dealing with delinquent children but also act as a preventive of delinquency, in fact, a cure-all for delinquency. In other words, after having been saddled with numerous and extensive responsibilities in addition to its basic purpose, the juvenile court has been criticized severely for its alleged "failures."

Numerous studies have shown high rates of recidivism, and the well-publicized disclosures of "repeaters" in the juvenile courts, even in the "best" juvenile courts, have undermined public confidence in them. Recidivism should not be taken lightly; children who become delinquent again and again present a challenge to the community that cannot be ignored. Nevertheless, the juvenile court, with all its limitations, cannot be expected to assume full responsibility for a high recidivism rate, because in the last analysis the responsibility for treatment of delinquency rests with the total community, not with the juvenile court. Some of the early studies of recidivism had a shocking impact and were regarded as indictments of the juvenile courts. The Gluecks' five-year follow-up survey, which reported in 905 Boston juvenile cases that were *diagnosed* by the Judge Baker Clinic a "failure" rate of 88.2 percent, caused nation-wide consternation.[39]

Ignoring the difficult problems in the statistical measurement of "failure," with the need for long-term follow-up of individual cases and the necessity for arriving at specific definitions, it should be noted that later studies have reported less spectacular rates of failure. In any event, in view of the limited resources available to the court, it is easy to understand the reasons for high rates of failure. What happens is that the juvenile courts ultimately get many failures of the community; failure occurring after that is regarded as a failure of the court. This is both illogical and presumptuous. As Professor Harrison Allen Dobbs has observed, communities tend to use their juvenile courts as a scapegoat,

[39] Glueck, *One Thousand Juvenile Delinquents.*

and court workers are expected to redo completely and quickly what society has been undoing in children for a very long time. He adds, "It is doubtful if there is a single juvenile court in the country prepared to cure socially ill children with the precision and efficiency that characterizes the pediatrics ward of first-class hospitals." [40]

Probably the most realistic way of gauging the effectiveness of a social institution, particularly a complex agency such as the juvenile court, is to apply against it a reasonable set of standards that should be met if the court is supposed to fulfill its generally accepted functions. The National Probation and Parole Association has developed for a progressive juvenile court a series of eight standards against which any juvenile court may be measured. These are:

1. Exclusive jurisdiction over children. . . . Jurisdiction over adults in children's cases.
2. A judge chosen for his sympathetic understanding of children and parents.
3. Private friendly court hearings. . . . Informal noncriminal procedure.
4. A sufficient number of professionally trained probation workers, both men and women.
5. Facilities for physical examinations and for psychiatric study of problem children.
6. A well-equipped detention home or selected boarding homes for temporary care of children.
7. An efficient record and statistical system. . . . Adequate clerical help.
8. Coöperation with other agencies. . . . Community support through interpretation to the public.[41]

Examination reveals that these standards constitute a sound basis for determining whether a particular juvenile court is equipped to deal with children in trouble. None of the standards are exotic, and all are reasonable and feasible. But if they are to be implemented adequately there is need for far greater public understanding of the juvenile court problem than has been demonstrated thus far.

The Future of Juvenile Courts

The juvenile court movement has made great strides in this country; but it still has a long way to go before it can be safely assured of a

[40] Dobbs, "In Defense of Juvenile Courts."
[41] A *Yardstick for Measuring Juvenile Courts.*

permanent, well-defined position in the community's attempts to deal with delinquent youth. The juvenile court has been under attack from time to time, and in recent years its critics seem to have become more numerous and vociferous. Its constitutional position seems strong, but its public relations status is relatively weak. In many communities, the juvenile courts are under pressure to send the "worst" cases to the criminal courts; in some places, there is discussion about lowering the upper age limit of the juvenile court law, though no state has thus far done so.

Many of the attacks upon the court are based on complete or nearly complete misunderstanding of its true functions. But some of the attacks have been brought upon the courts by their own failure to move ahead with the times. Many of them tend to be sprawling and untidy; a high proportion of them are poorly staffed, both numerically and qualitatively; and in too many communities the court has become an isolated agency, no longer insulated from attack by the mantle of reform it once wore.

If the juvenile courts are to maintain the gains that have been made and to make needed improvements, it seems clear that they should assume a more limited role than they have tended to take on in the past. The demands for return to criminal procedures in handling youthful offenders have arisen from spectacular "failures" held to be the responsibility of the juvenile courts but about which the courts did little or nothing; underfinanced and overworked, they do little or nothing in a great many cases.

The answer to this problem lies in the courts. They must divest themselves of responsibilities that inherently belong elsewhere. If the juvenile courts persist in handling every truant, every mischievous child, every Halloween gate-lifter, and all dependency and neglect cases, then they must take the consequences of shoddy work with those youngsters who really need court attention. The juvenile courts themselves should insist upon a redefinition of their functions, which in turn should be supported by coöperative action of other responsible agencies. If the juvenile courts are successful in putting their own houses in order, the prospects for the future seem good; if they are unable to do so, the future will be bleak indeed.

For Further Reading

Training Personnel for Work with Juvenile Delinquents, U.S. Department of Health, Education, and Welfare, Children's Bureau Publ. No. 348 (Washington, D.C., 1954).

> This document, which is social work oriented, contains articles dealing with such questions as the roles of the schools of social work, the staff development needs of those who cannot attend graduate school, and the probable first steps needed to solve training needs of court workers.

MEEKER, BEN S., "Probation is Casework," in *Federal Probation*, 15 (June, 1948), pp. 51-54.

> This is a definitive statement which clearly presents the role of the probation worker as caseworker. It deals with nearly all the questions that have been raised as to the place of casework in the courts.

RECKLESS, WALTER C., "Training of the Correctional Worker," in Paul W. Tappan, ed., *Contemporary Correction* (New York, 1951), pp. 35-50.

> This article makes a strong case for the use of undergraduate training for the field of corrections; although the undergraduate curriculum is urged on a "for the time being" basis.

BOWERS, FATHER SWITHUN, "The Nature and Definition of Social Case work," in *Principles and Techniques in Social Casework* (New York, 1950).

> A scholarly review of the evolution of social casework, and an examination of the various definitions that have been developed.

TEETERS, NEGLEY K., AND JOHN OTTO REINEMANN, *The Challenge of Delinquency* (New York, 1950).

> An encyclopedic textbook in the field of delinquency, which features a very substantial emphasis upon historical backgrounds.

CHAPPELL, RICHARD A., AND WILL C. TURNBLADH, "Probation: Case Work and Current Status," in Paul W. Tappan, ed., *Contemporary Correction* (New York, 1951).

> A brief but informative discussion of current developments by the former Chief of Probation, Administrative Office of the U.S. Courts, and the present executive director of the National Probation and Parole Association.

Pattern for Prevention, New York City Youth Board (Nov. 10, 1953).

This is an exciting and challenging description of experimental modifications of social casework practices. Generally identified as "aggressive casework," particularly with those who resist services, this deviation from standard procedures, while not yet fully convincing, offers some interesting possibilities.

DOBBS, HARRISON ALLEN, "In Defense of Juvenile Courts," in *Federal Probation,* 13 (September, 1949), pp. 24-29.

A clear-cut appraisal of the juvenile court as a scapegoat of the community in its concern about delinquency. This is a thoughtful, discriminating analysis of the situation.

Chapter **15**

TRAINING SCHOOLS

While there is general agreement today that every community resource should be explored and exploited before delinquent children are committed to institutions, the training school still occupies a place of central importance in dealing with delinquents. The term "training school" is used here in its generic sense to include all institutions for training and reëducation to which delinquent children are committed, whether state, county, or municipally operated, whether privately controlled and managed under sectarian or nonsectarian auspices. Because state-owned and state-operated institutions are responsible for the largest number of children by far, most of the statements made here apply especially to state institutions. Generally excluded are specialized institutions for mentally defective and psychotic children; even though some children committed to specialized institutions are delinquent, they are committed chiefly because of their primary handicaps rather than for delinquency.

The training schools require more than passing attention for two reasons: (1) they are used for substantial numbers of children adjudicated as delinquent by the courts—about 40,000 were committed to training schools in 1951;[1] and (2) it is generally conceded that the training schools receive the "hard core" of delinquents, those who have failed

[1] *Some Facts about Juvenile Delinquency*, p. 7.

to make an adjustment through the help of existing community services. The training schools, then, represent an important phase of the correctional cycle. Because they receive a large number of children, and because these are generally the more difficult of all the youngsters who get into trouble, a review of the current status and special problems of the training schools and an evaluation of their potential role becomes a significant part of any examination of society's efforts to deal with juvenile offenders.

The interested person wants answers to a number of questions. What are the criteria used by the courts in selecting youngsters for institutional care? When children are committed to these institutions, how long do they stay and what happens to them? What are the functions and goals of these institutions, and to what extent are desirable aims achieved? Do the training schools resemble treatment centers in philosophy and general climate, or do they more nearly approximate junior prisons of a repressive, regimented type? What are the significant issues and unresolved problems in such areas as personnel, plant, and program? While definitive answers cannot be given for all of these, it is the purpose of this discussion of the role and function of the training school to indicate broadly the situation as it is today, to devote some attention to the general movement toward a treatment philosophy, and to analyze certain vexing specific problems that affect training schools.

There are no recent exact statistics on the numbers of children committed annually to training schools or resident in them at any one time. Nevertheless, reasonably close approximations may be made from available data. At first glance, the Children's Bureau estimate of 40,000 youngsters committed to training schools in 1951 seems to be relatively small in proportion to the 350,000 children dealt with by juvenile courts during the same year. But the cases of about half the children who came before the juvenile courts that year were dismissed, adjusted, or held open without further action. Of those remaining, about 95,000 were placed on probation, so that training school commitments were used in nearly one-fourth, about 23 percent, of all cases in which courts took action, and for every ten children placed on probation at least four were committed to training schools. During 1950, at any one time there were about 35,000 youngsters in training schools, and about 80,000 on probation. Latest available estimates show that there are about 22,000 youngsters in the 129 state training schools on the average day, and about 12,000 in various other institutions, including about thirty local public facilities and about sixty private institutions of various kinds receiving delinquent children from the courts. When commitment is used in nearly one-fourth of the cases in which courts take specific action of any kind, and when it is used nearly half as frequently as probation, the importance of the training school role seems demonstrated clearly. In addition to those committed by the courts, the training schools also receive an unknown but substantial number of returned violators, whose aftercare or parole adjustment has been unsuccessful.

About two-thirds of all boys and girls in training schools are in state-owned, state-operated institutions, of which twelve are coeducational; about 70 percent of these children are fifteen years of age or older, and about 70 percent of the total are boys. According to the best estimates, the average length of stay is slightly less than one year.[2]

The youngsters in training schools are regarded as the "hard core" of delinquent children (1) chiefly because they have not responded to other resources and because many, if not most, of them have "failed" in the community time and time again; or (2) because their conduct is considered reprehensible by the community, on account of either repeated minor offenses or one or more aggressive, assaultive major offenses; or (3) because of "bad home conditions." These children are the ones who are substantially out of conformity with the norms and demands of society; these are the ones whose controls are weak and whose impulses tend to be uninhibited; frequently these are the children who are at war with society and with every representative of authority; very often, despite the reluctance of the courts to do so, they are committed as a "last resort." The bulk of the committed youngsters go to state schools, which, except for occasional provisions with respect to psychotic and defective children, are unable to control their intake and must therefore accept those sent to them whether by the courts or by a central allocation agency! Whether they wish to do so or not, they must deal with the castoffs of the community. As Albert Deutsch has so aptly expressed it, these are "our rejected children."

What determines the selection of particular children for institutional treatment? Actually, one important criterion has already been suggested,

[2] *Some Facts about Juvenile Delinquency; Juvenile Court Statistics, 1950-52; State and National Correctional Institutions; Public Training Schools for Delinquent Children: Directory, May, 1955.*

namely, that the child has failed time and again when other methods have been tried. But this leads to an important issue: What was it that was tried before "failure" was admitted? As the review of probation services in the courts showed, the vast majority of jurisdictions do not have personnel and other facilities adequate in quantity or quality to deal with delinquent children. Often this means that the "last resort" is used when really not very much has been tried. It is axiomatic that training schools rarely get first offenders, except for those committing very serious offenses. Too often delinquent children placed on probation and subject only to nominal supervision receive little or no help with their problems. If, through a process of maturation, they do not again get into difficulty, or at least are not apprehended, they go on to become probation "successes." But if they get into difficulty again, even though this may happen because their basic problems are receiving little or no attention from anybody, they become candidates for training school placement. Observation suggests that failure on probation is the most common criterion for training school commitment.

A pattern of repeated offenses also may lead to commitment, often preceded by a series of court appearances, featured first by friendly cautions, then by stern admonitions, and, not quite finally, by angry threats, culminating in the "one last chance" routine. Sometimes a single major offense will be enough, such as causing serious injuries to another person, a stabbing, wrecking a stolen car, or extreme vandalism. In some of these situations, community pressures for "action" may be terrific; in others, the judge is convinced that temporary isolation of the offender is required; and in some others, the juvenile court judge decides to "teach him a lesson" or "deter others." Isolating criteria is not an easy task, because the judge's own reactions to a youngster's appearance and his demeanor—whether he is submissive or recalcitrant—may be an intangible, difficult to isolate, but determining factor. The absence of well-defined commitment criteria should not be considered solely a children's court phenomenon. The same situation prevails in the criminal courts; there are no well-established criteria regarding selection for probation or any other form of correctional treatment.

Unfavorable home conditions may affect commitment decisions. Understandably, the great majority of judges are reluctant to remove a child from his home. But even when this seems necessary because his difficulties are related specifically to his home situation, there is a disastrous lack of other community facilities for the delinquent child. Theoretically, the court has the right to remove a child from a home situation that may be the root of his difficulties, and theoretically the youngster may be placed in a community resource of a noninstitutional type. But, in the absence of noninstitutional community resources, the training school becomes virtually the only alternative available when home conditions demand the child's removal and when his delinquent conduct is a factor in the situation.

Careful consideration of this entire question leads to several important conclusions.

In the first place, court services for delinquent children who are allowed to remain in their own homes under supervision should be improved considerably. At the present time, probation services provided by the majority of courts are completely unrealistic.

In the second place, there has to be increasing recognition of the fact that offenses themselves are symptomatic and that the total needs of a child must determine the treatment applied. Offenses occasionally are so serious that temporary removal from the community seems required, but this should be treatment-oriented removal. Most children who commit very serious offenses are emotionally disturbed children who may require long-term residential treatment. Likewise, judges must learn that a child's surliness and belligerence in a court setting is symptomatic, frequently identifying a tense, anxious child.

In the third place, the importance of keeping children in the community, which, after all, is their natural habitat, should be understood so thoroughly by judges that they are willing to bend over backward in being tolerant of the home conditions of youngsters before the courts. There has been gradual recognition of the fact that a child's own home, even though it be a rather poor home measured from any standpoint, is the best place for him. In the past, courts have been prone to identify deficiencies in the home with the misconduct of youngsters, when in fact the relationship may not be as exact or direct as they believe it to be. The factors may be associated, but not often as cause and effect. If the home is inadequate, the courts ought to raise the question of whether it will be any more adequate a year later when the youngster returns from the training school. In any event, there is need to develop adequate alternatives in the community that may be used without resorting to institutional care. This point is extremely important, and a brief examination of one significant alternative to the training school is indicated.

Foster Homes for Delinquents

Any discussion about the use of community facilities for delinquents, especially foster homes, should be preceded by the candid acknowledgment that the issue is not one of avoiding the "evils" of the institution, but rather a factual recognition of an important principle generally accepted in child care today. Whether to use institutional or foster home care for a child who must be removed from his own home should be answered in relation to the needs of the child and the contribution that may be made by an institution or foster home to his development as a well-adjusted member of society. In other words, this is not the ancient issue of foster homes versus institutions, but rather the selective and discriminating use of each as a resource indicated by the particular needs of the youngsters in question. Also, it should be observed that the long-time absolute rejection of institutional care by many persons associated with social welfare has substantially disappeared, and, while in the broad field of foster care of dependent and neglected children the pendulum has swung over to greater use of foster homes than institutions, it is recognized that the problems of some children should be dealt with in institutions. According to 1950 census data, about 175,000 children were in foster homes and about 95,000 in institutions. In any event, the decision to use institutional care should not be one made by default, that is, where the institution is used because nothing else is available. Instead, there should be foster home resources in the community that could be used instead of institutional placement whenever this is indicated by a careful analysis of the needs of the particular child under consideration.

There are a great variety of foster homes—adoptive homes, boarding homes, free homes, work and wage homes, subsidized homes, group foster homes. For obvious reasons, not all of these facilities are available for delinquent children. Adoptive homes, and free homes, which in practice today are used pending the completion of adoption plans, are virtually ruled out for delinquents. In present-day usage, boarding homes normally are for temporary placements, either for long or short duration, and boarding parents are paid an amount supposedly equivalent to the cost of care of the foster children. Generally, in each case the agency making placement carries over-all responsibility for the child and for helping to preserve and strengthen his relationship with his own parents, and a child is not placed until a careful study and evaluation of a selected foster home is made in relationship to the physical and emotional needs of the child needing care. After placement, casework services are provided both for the foster family and the foster child. While boarding rates vary considerably from one place to another and from one agency to another, the average paid throughout the nation in 1951 was only $44.12 per month.[3] In view of the kinds of problems presented by delinquent children and the relatively low rates paid customarily for boarding care, foster home care does not seem to be a potentially useful resource.

Work and wage homes, which are survivals of the old indenture system of placing children, are used much less frequently, and a great many of the better agencies have virtually discontinued their use, chiefly because of difficulties in controlling the placement so as to avoid exploitation of the children. In part, this trend away from work and wage homes has been due also to urbanization, since most of the homes of this type are in rural areas. Partial, incomplete, and somewhat inconclusive studies from various sources indicate that homes of this kind have been used more often than other types of foster homes for delinquents, and that they are used particularly for those released from state training schools. One study indicates that about nine out of ten delinquent children reported on as being in foster family homes were in work or wage homes.[4]

The subsidized foster home is a boarding home for which the agency pays a fee-for-service in addition to the usual board rate; the agency may also guarantee payment for the care of a specific number of children even though the home is not used at all times. Similar in some ways to subsidized foster homes are group foster homes, which have not been used very often in most parts of the country. Somewhat higher than usual board payments are made for small groups of children living together in a family-like atmosphere. Ostensibly combining the advantages of individualized attention with group living, the large homes of this type resemble small institutions and may have some of their defects

[3] Hagan, "Foster Care for Children."
[4] *Children Served by Public Welfare Agencies and Institutions, 1945.*

without possessing very many of the virtues of institutions. Nevertheless, the subsidized boarding home and the group foster home offer the two main possibilities for foster placement of delinquents that deserve serious consideration.

Although more careful studies are needed, the evidence seems pretty conclusive that foster home placements of any kind are not a panacea.[5] Despite the early study by Healy and Bronner showing considerable success in the placement of delinquents in foster homes, later researches and studies suggest criteria for successful use of foster homes that are discouraging.[6] The criteria developed by Carl R. Rogers, which need not be repeated in detail here, include an age factor that unquestionably is unfavorable to the use of foster home care for delinquents, since Rogers concludes that age under nine years is optimum and over thirteen is unfavorable. Unfortunately, a large proportion of delinquents dealt with by the courts—roughly 8 out of 10—are in the latter category.[7] The Gluecks' study showed a success rate of only about 15 percent in placement cases, but only forty-one placement cases were included in the study, which is considered an inadequate number from which to draw conclusions.[8] Both observation and the various studies of foster home care suggest that extremely careful placements must be made, accompanied by adequate supervision of the placements. Comments by experts in the child care field tend to confirm the relatively poor prognosis suggested.

Despite the negative aspects of this rather cursory review of the use of foster home placements for delinquents, one significant observation should be made: Virtually all the studies that have been made and many of the observations relied upon have dealt with the traditional boarding home kind of foster care rather than the subsidized foster home or group foster home.

Although there has been a steady shift from free foster homes to boarding homes, communities are still relying heavily upon the emotional gratifications obtained by foster families in providing suitable,

[5] Gilpin, "Foster Home Care for Delinquent Children"; Williams, "Foster Homes for Juvenile Delinquents."

[6] Healy, Bronner, Baylor, and Murphy, *Reconstructing Behavior in Youth*, p. 48: the study concluded that about 85 percent of "normal children" who were labeled delinquent because they committed delinquent acts made satisfactory adjustments in foster homes and ceased to be delinquent.

[7] Rogers, *The Clinical Treatment of the Problem Child*, pp. 97-101.

[8] Glueck, *One Thousand Juvenile Delinquents*, Table XXVIII, p. 173.

decent homes for children who must receive care away from their own homes. This is borne out by the fact that the boarding rates paid are virtually at a subsistence level; also, a few agencies have demonstrated that even children with relatively severe personality disorders can be cared for adequately in carefully selected and supervised foster home placements if a high boarding rate with a substantial fee for service component is paid.

Therefore, despite the difficulties that must be acknowledged, the suitability of boarding home care for delinquent youngsters has not been disproved. Taking into account all the facts in the situation, the only sensible approach would be to experiment on a reasonably large scale with a relatively high payment to subsidized boarding homes, along with careful placement and equally careful supervision.

The Role of the Training School

When children must be removed from their homes, and when either their delinquent conduct is so serious that their presence in the community can no longer be tolerated or there are no suitable community facilities or institutional care is indicated in terms of their particular needs, delinquent youngsters are committed to training schools, normally for an indefinite or indeterminate period, not to exceed their minority. As the generic term "training" used here suggests, the present function of the training school is one of rehabilitation, reëducation, and treatment of a delinquent youngster so that he is able to return to the community able to adjust to its demands for conformity.

As a matter of fact, the names that have been used at various times to designate these institutions for delinquent children give some clue as to the role they were expected to play. As "houses of refuge" beginning in 1825 in New York City, the institutions were literally places of refuge from the prisons where children had been indiscriminately housed, established for children of the categories today called delinquent, dependent, and neglected. In keeping with the times, the early institutions emphasized hard work, stern discipline, and some education. Today they would be regarded as harsh, punitive, and despotic. As additional institutions were opened in various states, a new nomenclature developed and the institutions were referred to as "reform schools," and then "industrial schools," both terms indicating something of the nature of the programs, which variously stressed military training, country living, and learning a trade. In more recent years, it has been customary to use an innocuous name, usually associated with a person or place. For example, the Mississippi legislature changed the name of the Reformatory for Delinquent Negro Juveniles, established in 1942, to Oakley Training School. There are some inconsistencies in terminology even within a single state. Alabama has a state training school for girls and an industrial school for Negro children. The term "school," which has gained favor in the names of most institutions, is indicative of the modern concept of function, namely, that the training school is a specialized residential school for difficult children.

The early congregate institutions closely resembled prisons, but the development of the so-called cottage plan, featured by relatively small housing units, in a Massachusetts girls' institution in 1854 and an Ohio one for boys in 1856 changed the picture remarkably. With this innovation, virtually all of the succeeding institutions used some kind of cottage housing as opposed to congregate-type, although some of the cottages are so large as to demand considerable imagination in the use of such a word to describe them.[9]

It would be a pleasant task to report that, with changes in terminology, ostensibly consistent with transitions in function, and with changes in physical structure to make possible family-type living, training schools had become treatment-oriented and were fulfilling their generally accepted goal of social reëducation and preparation of children for return to the community. Unfortunately, all available evidence demonstrates that this goal is far from being achieved and that training schools, as they are presently operated, are able to fulfill the functions expected of them only in a partial, limited fashion. Granting the difficulty of making broad generalizations about so many and so varied and complex institutions, the brutal truth is that some of our modern training schools are best described as junior prisons, and that in a few of them conditions exist that would not be tolerated in an adult penal institution. This means that many youngsters committed by the courts to training schools are given little more than routine custodial care, too often accompanied by a combination of personal indignities and repeated exposures to contamination that result inevitably in their return

[9] Teeters and Reinemann, *The Challenge of Delinquency*, pp. 429-448; Bowler and Bloodgood, *Institutional Treatment of Delinquent Boys*, Part 1, pp. 1-9.

to the community with far less capacity to meet its demands upon them than they had before commitment. Naturally, some training schools are better than others, and in fact, some of them do not deserve at all the kind of criticism meted out here. In any case, without trying at this point to assess responsibility or to describe avenues to possible remedies, the picture is a grim one indeed.

While trends toward improvement will be noted later and although conditions are dynamic rather than static, the over-all problem is clearly shown by statements made in two White House Conference reports twenty years apart. In 1930, the White House Conference stated: "There are now in existence State institutions for delinquents which represent almost every stage in the development of principles and methods of treatment for children committed for institutional care." [10] The 1950 White House Conference reported on training schools as follows:

> Their programs represent several stages of development. Some persist in certain practices of the penal institutions from which they were separated over a century ago—mass treatment, repression, and physical punishment. Others which are not punitive nevertheless furnish little more than custodial care; they reflect the idea that the training school was primarily a place to which troublesome children can be removed. . . . Still other schools provide medical and mental health services, recreational and leisure-time activities, and educational, vocational, and spiritual guidance and training, and relate all of these elements in a well-integrated program. [11]

All available reports indicate that this last-mentioned group of schools is a distinct minority. Surveys and studies by public and private agencies, intensive reviews of the situation in individual states, reports by skilled observers, and periodic investigations concerning scandals that crop up from time to time in various states give an almost unrelieved picture of harsh, punitive treatment of children because of staff brutality or inept management, or utterly inadequate program, or some combination of these. A review of the more important studies and surveys is depressing and disheartening.

(It is recognized that some of the statements that follow may present a one-sided view of the situation, because some of the institutions

[10] *The Delinquent Child*, p. 298.
[11] *For Every Child a Healthy Personality*, pp. 154-155.

studied, although not all of them, may have been identified before the study as being among the worst institutions. In other words, their poor reputations may have provoked the studies. On the other hand, the reports quoted are factual, and even if only one side of the story is told, this does not mean necessarily that they are biased. The period covered is from 1937 to 1950, and that even the worst training schools could be so bad at this stage of development of child welfare principles and policies is dismaying.)

The Training School as Junior Prison

The Osborne Association, a highly respected agency, which has conducted numerous studies of adult correctional institutions, made a series of surveys of training schools during the period 1937-1942.[12] These were candid, factual, and down-to-earth descriptions of plant, personnel, and programs and their impact upon children. With only occasional though refreshing deviations from the pattern, they tell a sordid story. The Association came early to the general conclusion that the institutions did not have the facilities and the personnel to do their job well. After looking at thirteen schools in seven West North Central states, it was concluded that "although partisan politics and patronage, with their immeasurably detrimental effects, were a negligible factor in four of the thirteen schools, they dominated the management of five and were influential in the administration of the remaining four." In some institutions there was modern, fireproof housing "but unfortunately, more than one-half of all the children in the training schools of this area were living in buildings where there is constant danger of death by fire." And the Association added that it was a "shocking fact that in 1937, in institutions for juveniles, we found such punishments as whipping, wearing handcuffs, being shackled to the bed at night, working in shackles and leg chains, cold tubbings, confinement in strait jackets, and long hours of standing rigidly at attention." [13]

At the Kansas State Industrial School for Boys, Topeka, the disciplinarian carried a blackjack and all the officers were permitted to inflict corporal punishment, resulting in a "government by fists." At the Missouri Training School for Boys, Boonville, the youngsters had

---

[12] *Handbooks of American Institutions for Delinquent Juveniles.*
[13] *Handbook of American Institutions for Delinquent Juveniles,* I, pp. 1-2.

shaved heads, prison uniforms were worn, and numbers were used instead of names. At that institution the chief occupation was quarry work, crushing stone for a commercial firm. At the Nebraska State Industrial School, Kearney, fire hazards were considered appalling due to the type of construction and deterioration of the buildings; because of administrative negligence, the school failed to install fire escapes for months after they were purchased, permitted defective electric wiring to go unrepaired, allowed exits to be blocked, and required that boys be locked in the dormitories at night. The South Dakota Training School, Plankinton, housing both boys and girls, was described as an "old-time reform school, housed in shabby buildings, animated by a punitive spirit, and employing regimentation, fear and shame as the instruments of 'reformation.' " [14]

In its Kentucky and Tennessee survey, Ormsby Village, officially the Louisville and Jefferson County Children's Home, was consistently praised, but the five others did not come off very well. The Association reported that "Inadequate appropriations, poor and neglected physical plants, insufficient and untrained personnel and, most important of all, political interference have contributed their share to the present state in which most of these institutions now find themselves." The State Training and Agricultural School for Colored Boys, Pikeville, Tennessee, with an average daily population of about 300, had a library with exactly eight books, including Chaucer's *Prologue*. The Association regarded the school as the most desolate and forbidding of all those seen, and on the basis of its lonely, isolated, and inaccessible mountain-top location and a plant valued at not more than $25,000 exclusive of the powerhouse, recommended that the institution be abandoned. The Pikeville institution is still in operation. [15]

In 1940, at the Washington State Training School for Boys, Chehalis, the youngsters were marched to and from the dining room with arms folded, and strict silence was required throughout the meal hour. Despite the statement of the superintendent that the institution was using "the most modern concepts of child guidance," the leather strap was used for punishment because "boys must realize that the school is the authority." The use of cadets or monitors, punishment by requiring youngsters to do the "deep-knee bends," and long periods of standing at

---

[14] *Handbook of American Institutions for Delinquent Juveniles*, I, pp. 109 ff., 405.
[15] *Handbook of American Institutions for Delinquent Juveniles*, II, pp. 40, 194-197.

attention were also found in this "modern" institution.[16] Since the survey, "reforms" have affected the Chehalis institution. According to the 1953 Biennial Report of the Washington Department of Public Institutions (p. 10), ". . . the strap has been eliminated as a means of discipline." It is of more than passing interest to note that a resolution against corporal punishment was hotly debated at the Training Schools section of the National Conference on the Prevention and Control of Juvenile Delinquency, called by the Attorney General in 1946. The resolution passed by a vote of 20 to 5, but it is reliably reported that many who spoke against the resolution were from the "better" training schools.[17]

In 1946, the National Conference on Prevention and Control of Juvenile Delinquency made this statement about discipline:

> Among the disciplinary practices in training schools that have been reported by qualified and reliable observers in recent years are the following: whipping or spanking with sticks, wire coat hangers, paddles, straps; striking about the face and head with fists and sticks; handcuffing to the bed at night; use of shackles and leg chains; shaving of the head; cold tubbings; "standing on the line" in a rigid position for hours at a time; confinement in dark cells and dungeon-like basement rooms; silence rules; knee bends; a modified lockstep in marching formations; permitting boy monitors to discipline other boys, including corporal punishment.[18]

Probably the most vivid and spectacular account of how children are treated in some state training schools was made in 1950 by Albert Deutsch.[19] As Deutsch was not hampered by the protocol of either government agencies or private associations, he was able to combine his ability as an astute and scholarly observer with his talents as a competent journalist and he succeeded in focusing national attention on the training schools. As Deutsch states in his Introduction:

> The facts, as I found them, shook me profoundly. They added up, in my eyes, to a black record of human tragedy, of social and economic waste, of gross brutality, crass stupidity, totalitarian regimentation in institutions

[16] *Handbook of American Institutions for Delinquent Juveniles*, III, pp. 384-386.
[17] MacCormick, Austin H., "Preface," in Deutsch, *Our Rejected Children*.
[18] *Report on Institutional Treatment of Delinquent Juveniles*, pp. 36-37.
[19] Deutsch, *Our Rejected Children*, an elaboration of a series of articles that first appeared in the newspaper *PM* and a dramatic piece in the *Woman's Home Companion*, March, 1948, called "Is This Reform?"

and a corroding monotony even deadlier than physical violence. . . . I did find a few institutions that were good. Some institutions were advanced in some parts of a program but terribly backward in others. The good, I felt, was what one had a right to expect in institutions for child care in a rich and civilized community. The bad was inexcusable. The very bad was intolerable.[20]

In *Our Rejected Children*, Deutsch reports on fourteen state training schools for delinquent boys and girls in nine states and the District of Columbia. These were schools ostensibly above average—the states were among the wealthiest, measured by virtually any index. His interesting chapter "The Semantics of Reform" gives a good review of the practices of long ago that still flourish under modern names. Disciplinary or punishment barracks were called "adjustment cottages"; guards were "supervisors"; caretakers and custodians were "cottage parents"; whips, paddles, blackjacks, and straps were "tools of control"; isolation or solitary cells were "meditation rooms"; and children saving expense by working in industrial or farm pursuits or kitchen drudgery were in "vocational rehabilitation." [21] Deutsch reports that in nearly all the institutions he visited "an excessive and almost fanatic emphasis was placed upon the outward cleanliness. Signs of vigorous brushing, scrubbing and polishing of floors, walls and furniture are everywhere in evidence." But he saw hundreds of boys who wore no underwear because the state "felt too poor to provide it." [22]

Deutsch's review of conditions is an alarming indictment, not so much of training school administrators as of the public whose apathy and lack of interest make it feasible for legislators to ignore a vital problem. His story is a monotonous one—the Illinois "fire-hose and burlap brigade"; Ohio's Lancaster, a "big institutional slum" crowded with ragged urchins; and Missouri's Boonville, "a study in sadism." But Minnesota's Red Wing under Superintendent R. E. Farrell fares well, and so does Michigan's Lansing, where an experienced, able administrator, John B. Costello, had transformed a "hellhole" into a "haven." Just so long as there are some good institutions, the threat of inevitability is absent. If some can be effective, others can too. In fact,

[20] Deutsch, *Our Rejected Children*, pp. xix-xx.
[21] Deutsch, *Our Rejected Children*, p. 15.
[22] Deutsch, *Our Rejected Children*, p. 150.

if the best practices found in various places were combined in one institution, that training school might well demonstrate that "it can be done," and that children in trouble can get the help they need.

Many of the institutions adversely mentioned here have improved radically, and references to them are valid only for the time indicated. What may be found in one year may be utterly different from the next. This is a shifting scene. For a variety of reasons, especially political upheavals, the picture is difficult to keep in focus. There were a number of major scandals and investigations affecting these institutions during 1944-49: Delaware's Ferris School (1944), Iowa's School at Eldora (1945), Pennsylvania's Morganza (1948), Illinois' St. Charles (1948), Wisconsin's Waukesha (1948-49), Missouri's Boonville (1949), and Colorado's Golden (1949). In nearly all the places mentioned, reforms took place. But increasingly it is becoming evident that the problem is not how to get reforms but how to keep them.

Issues Concerning Personnel, Program, and Plant

Because of the confusions regarding functions of training schools already referred to, and because there are real and understandable differences of opinion about the best methods to carry out agreed-upon objectives, significant issues relating to personnel, program, and plant have emerged, not all of which can be discussed here.[23] Moreover, this is a field in which the standards agreed upon by various organizations interested in the question and by recognized leaders in the field are met in practice very rarely.

Consequently, summary treatment of some of these questions may create a false impression. One example of this should suffice. It is generally agreed that all staff members should be selected on the basis of merit, that they should have tenure, opportunity for advancement, and compensation equal to that paid in the community to persons with similar training, experience, and responsibilities. That this agreement is general may be demonstrated by the fact that statements similar to this one have been made by the National Conference on Prevention and Control of Juvenile Delinquency, the American Legion, the American Psychiatric Association, the Berkshire International Conference on

[23] See Costello, "Institutions for Juvenile Delinquents"; Costello's article is conveniently found in Tappan, ed., *Contemporary Correction*, pp. 346-358.

Training Schools, the Midcentury White House Conference on Children and Youth, and the National Probation and Parole Association.[24] But regardless of this agreement, the reality is altogether different. While there seems to be some improvement both in selection and personnel policies, the use of a merit basis for all or most employees is far from common. Similarly, there is widespread agreement that when specialized staff members are required, they should meet the standards of their particular specialization. Social workers should be graduates of accredited schools of social work, psychologists should be diplomates of the American Board of Examiners in Clinical Psychology, and nurses should be registered nurses. Unfortunately, these standards are not often fulfilled.

One issue that has developed gradually is the highly interesting and controversial question of qualifications of so-called cottage personnel, who number about 3,500 persons and represent about 60 percent of all training school staff. As the cottage plan itself developed, there was a natural tendency to copy standards characteristic of the other kinds of child-care institutions, for after all, in the best circles the training school was considered to be a child-care institution. Generally, this meant the employment of "cottage parents," whose functions frequently were identified with father and mother roles. Carrying this to extreme, it was often thought that they transformed the cottage into "one big happy family." But from a practical viewpoint, very few houseparents have specialized training for their work, and their educational backgrounds, unlike those of the probation officers previously discussed, leave a great deal to be desired. Recent data available from the Children's Bureau show that fewer than one of ten cottage personnel has a college degree, four of nine have had some high school, and two of nine have not gone beyond elementary school.[25] But what is the role of the houseparents, so lacking in specialized training and even in general education? As Schulze and Mayer, in the outstanding statement of the problem that has thus far appeared, succinctly put it, the houseparent's job in an institution for delinquents is composed of five major parts, all of which are equally important: (1) consistent provision of protection and control; (2) purposeful organization of everyday living; (3) creating a "we" feeling in the group; (4) develop-

---

[24] *Recommended Standards for Services for Delinquent Children*, pp. 15-16.
[25] *Training Personnel for Work with Juvenile Delinquents*, p. xi.

ment of a relationship to the individual; (5) integration of the house-parent's job with the various other services of the institution.[26] But in reality very few houseparents meet the standards of personality and maturity required by the functions described. Carrying out the "mother and father" notion, married couples are often employed. But large numbers are beyond the age of fifty before joining the staff of a training school; frequently they represent failures to a certain extent rather than successes; and, if personal observations are valid, the wife in the married-couple team is the dominant, even aggressive one, and the husband is on the indolent side, carrying out his "outside" assignments such as supervising work details, or marching groups of children from place to place, in a perfunctory, listless, uninterested fashion. With the coming of the eight-hour day for state employees, the married couple as cottage parents has become something of a luxury. Nevertheless, even the underpaid, poorly equipped cottage parents employed are required in relatively large numbers under present conditions. Generally, in the eight-hour-day and forty-hour-week states, each cottage may require two sets of cottage parents, covering the sixteen-hour waking period, and a night supervisor, together with enough relief personnel to provide for two days off each week, in addition to vacation time and sick leave. As Schulze and Mayer have commented, "The fact is that many of these people are simply employees who work on an eight-hour shift."[27]

The employment of men and women as cottage supervisors is still recommended in reputable quarters as a desirable standard, because it affords an opportunity for children to learn with adults of both sexes; and the Children's Bureau recent *Tentative Standards for Training Schools* recommends the use of both men and women as cottage parents.[28] But this is beginning to be questioned in some quarters. For example, Ernst Papanek, Executive Director of Wiltwyck School for Boys, one of the outstanding private institutions of its kind in the United States, states flatly, "At the training school the leaders of the group are counselors or educators, not 'parents,' cottage parents or the like. . . ."[29] This does not mean that institutions for boys should be "for males only" and that girls' training schools should have a staff comprising only females. The experience of some of California's forestry

---

[26] Schulze and Mayer, "Training for Houseparents and Kindred Personnel."
[27] Schulze and Mayer, "Training for Houseparents and Kindred Personnel."
[28] *Tentative Standards for Training Schools, 1954*, p. 54.
[29] Papanek, "The Training School: Its Program and Leadership."

camps suggests that the use of the counselor, perhaps of the "athletic-coach" type, may be a solution in institutions for boys. In any event, women in various capacities can and should be used, including dietitians, nurses, social workers, and classroom and craft teachers. Certainly, bold experimental approaches to this problem are needed. Institutions are not and cannot be "one big happy family," and in so many of them the presence of the traditional houseparents simply reflects the thinking of the past.

Of key importance in any training school program geared to meet the needs of the children is the over-all education program. Many of those committed by the courts not only have behavior difficulties but also are usually retarded academically and have considerable resistance to school work in the traditional sense.[30] Therefore, virtually all accepted standards describe instructional programs geared to meet the total needs of the child, with some emphasis upon the qualifications of teachers, which should be not less than those of special teachers in public day schools.

Many of the better institutions place considerable stress upon vocational training as part of the educational program, usually not in the sense of teaching youngsters trades, but rather giving them vestibule training and exposure to a variety of practical learning opportunities that may carry over into community life. A well-integrated program includes shopwork, with the academic courses being related as closely as possible to practical shop situations.

Despite this general agreement with respect to educational policies, the fact is that large numbers of state training schools are located in the open country, and many of them have a long-standing tradition of farming activities. Perhaps the widespread use of farming was justified when a relatively large number of children were received from rural areas. But in the present mechanized state of agriculture, economical farming operations are almost by definition large-scale operations; and although no nation-wide data are available, it is reasonably certain that the large majority of children in training schools come from urban areas. Consequently, even the best mechanized farming instruction will have little or no carry-over value to the normal civilian life of these children. While it is possible to extol such virtues of farming as giving youngsters an opportunity to "get close to the land," to "enjoy pure

[30] See Costello, "Institutions for Juvenile Delinquents."

air and sunshine," the reality is that farming is often sheer drudgery to urban youngsters. A clear-cut distinction must be made between farming as a training device and farming as employment. Unquestionably, various forms of farming can have useful results if the training motivation is uppermost. Nevertheless, the situation usually is that the school's farm production is the goal and that training values are incidental.

Many state training schools do not publish annual reports; of those that do, a high proportion stress the value of the farm crops and other types of farming production. For example, according to the report of the Board of Trustees of Mississippi's Oakley Training School for 1949-1951, the value of crops and live stock produced during 1950 was $14,629.34. In commenting upon staff needs, the report stated that the Board of Trustees was aiming toward the goal of having a well-trained practical farmer. At the bottom of the listing of goals appeared: "trained school teachers to teach the basic tools of learning." The example emphasizes the point made, but it does not discredit the management of the School, which is doing a capable job under severe fiscal handicaps.

Presumably training school superintendents are mindful of the fact that many members of the legislature and of legislative budget committees are from rural areas. Unquestionably there is pressure, hidden or otherwise, for the training school to make a good showing with respect to farm production in relation to the number of acres under cultivation or the number of head of livestock. If farming operations are to be used at all, they should be used for selected children and based on the needs of the youngsters, not on requirements for production of food crops for the training school or other state institutions. One of two things seems certain here: either virtues are being ascribed to the farm production program which are really nonexistent, because the primary goal is production, or a good cost-accounting study would reveal that the farming operations themselves are an expensive luxury. In one Mid-western state, nearly one-fourth of the population of the training school for boys is assigned to farming activities on a permanent, nonemergency basis, despite the fact that 90 percent of the youngsters are from urban areas. At that institution, where numerous tradesmen are employed under union rules, boys are not allowed to make even minor repairs to a fence. If an employee discovers a fence rail that requires a couple of nails, the procedure is for the head farmer to prepare an order for the carpenter shop in quadruplicate; the motor pool dispatcher, upon request from the carpenter shop, sends a pickup truck which takes a carpenter to fix the fence and later returns him to the shop.

Of course, there are those who defend the use of training school boys in farming operations. The usual rationale is that it "helps pay their own way." But the fact is that delinquent children are not committed to training schools to "help pay their own way." Presumably they are committed for treatment—the only test that deserves to be applied. It should be noted that forestry camps may also provide rather heavy doses of hard work, but the training functions and the opportunity for group living can be emphasized in a forestry camp setting, because the incentive of producing cash crops does not exist. Forestry camp programs are usually intended for conservation and fire protection purposes. If they were destined to become forest mining operations, through which thousands of acres of timberland would be prepared for market, the same objections would apply that have been advanced in connection with farming operations.

The issues with respect to training school plants include problems such as type of construction, location, size of housing units, use of central dining facilities, and a great many others. But in terms of training school objectives, one serious issue is that of size. Both the Children's Bureau,[31] and the American Psychiatric Association recommend that a single institution should provide for not more than 150 boys or girls.[32] But a conference on training school standards held in November, 1952, under the auspices of the Children's Bureau decided on 200 as the maximum number of children to be accommodated in any one school.[33] In any event, reality does not square with these standards even if the 200 standard is used, because nearly half of all state training schools have authorized capacities in excess of 200.

The implications of the situation are both obvious and serious. Training schools receive a variety of children who present a great many problems. Unquestionably some of them need intensive treatment, and in any case a group-living situation must be kept as informal as possible. It is axiomatic that as the number of youngsters dealt with increases,

---

[31] *Recommended Standards for Services for Delinquent Children*, p. 11.
[32] *Guide to Planning*.
[33] *Tentative Standards for Training Schools*, p. 23; see also Davidoff and Noetzel, *The Child Guidance Approach to Juvenile Delinquency*, p. 158.

the greater the extent of regimentation. Since the majority of training schools are open institutions, constant surveillance by the staff tends to be used as a substitute for walls and fences. As the number of children increases, surveillance becomes more difficult, and the need to keep track of the youngsters to avoid runaways results in formal group controls, including marching in a body and frequent "counts." In some schools, youngsters are counted every time there is a change in activity; this both disrupts a normal routine and helps to increase resistance, hostility, and tension instead of lessening them. Most serious of all is the predilection toward mass activities, when the need is for small groupings of youngsters around homogeneous interests and pursuits.

As regimentation increases so do the number of rules and the violations of rules and regulations. Inevitably, this means some form of penalty for infraction of rules, and even if the abuses of corporal punishment and the humiliations so often practiced are avoided, the mildest form of penalty takes the form of deprivation of privileges. In many cases these are rights rather than privileges, and a youngster may be kept out of a program activity that is beneficial to him. Rather than conducing to reëducation, the "lost privilege" status of a child stimulates an increase in his hostility toward all those in authority.

The case for the larger institution is that its population is sufficient to warrant special services and facilities that could not be made available in a smaller facility because of prohibitive cost. This argument has some merit, but not a great deal, because the cost of training school care is going to be very high in any case, whether the institution is large and well-equipped, small and well-equipped, or large or small without proper specialized staff and facilities. No attempt is made in this chapter to discuss the vexing problem of costs. Accounting methods vary greatly, so cost comparisons from one state to another are futile; besides, most states have abandoned the practice of publishing cost-of-care statistics. But the ratio of children to staff is under 3 to 1, many estimates placing it at about 2.5 to 1. Even in "poor" states, per capita costs are above $1,000 annually, without counting capital expenditures. Several large institutions are known to show per capita costs of between $3,000 and $4,000 a year.

The best argument for the small facility, in addition to the informal day-by-day contacts of staff with children and the avoidance of regimentation, is the possibility of classifying children on the basis of their needs and separating them accordingly. Every study of training schools shows a complex and heterogeneous child population, with wide age spans, with a great variety of backgrounds, and with diverse needs. If treatment goals are to be attained, this heterogeneous group must be broken down into relatively more homogeneous smaller groups, and a particularized setting must be provided that will meet the special needs of youngsters, separated according to their treatment requirements by competent professional workers skilled in diagnosis. Although it is true that a physical plant with a total capacity of 400 or 500 children could be devised with self-contained, separate units, this is considered impractical.

A better plan would be to break up the training school and divert its population into a series of facilities designed to serve the needs of at least four groups in the training school populations: (1) those with severe emotional disturbances who unquestionably require psychiatric treatment; (2) those who may be in need of some form of intensive treatment, but who, under existing conditions and available personnel, will not be those considered most in need of it, that is, those whose problems are complex but for whom intensive individual therapy simply is not available; (3) youngsters with urban backgrounds who may present complex problems and unfortunate habit behavior problems, but whose needs may be met in a stable institutional setting; and (4) youngsters presenting essentially the same kinds of problems as those just described but who have rural or small-town backgrounds and who probably should not be exposed to the more sophisticated attitudes of those from metropolitan centers, whose antisocial activities, viewed as expression of their maladjustment, are more likely to be of a more serious nature. Under these conditions, the case is strong for some kind of central diagnostic facility with allocation and transfer powers among a number of small facilities.[34]

This review of some of the central problems in the areas of personnel, program, and plant both implicitly and explicitly shows that the provision of institutional training facilities in any state is not easily accomplished if basic treatment goals are kept in the forefront. Although a more detailed critique in each of the three important areas discussed would reveal considerably more in the way of supporting evidence for

[34] A blueprint for coördination in one state is seen in "Coordination of the Program of Institutional Care of Juvenile Delinquents."

such a statement, it is believed that the problems entailed in the provision of adequate houseparents, suitable, well-rounded programs without undue emphasis on any single aspect, particularly farming, and the development of small institutions or facilities designed to deal with relatively homogeneous groups makes a clear case for really intensive, careful planning for institutions used for training purposes. Standards have been developed; they can be applied; and the issue of whether these institutions are to be treatment centers for boys and girls or junior prisons will be resolved only as the states begin to face up to their responsibilities in the light of accepted standards.

Toward a Treatment Philosophy

Any statement about the working philosophy of training schools must be conditioned by such factors as diversities in practice, the partial or incomplete acceptance by some of goals held basic and essential by others, and above all by the bias of the sources depended upon for providing guidance. Nevertheless, it is still possible to develop something like a working framework that provides an over-all, comprehensive standard or frame of reference. In discussing a philosophy geared to today's needs, reliance should be placed upon the best thinking of the experts on the subject and not upon a mere description of composite practices.

In this discussion, a great deal of reliance is placed upon three main sources. (1) Dr. George E. Gardner's paper presented to the Berkshire International Forum, June 23, 1951, entitled "The Institution as Therapist." Part of a symposium on "The Responsibilities of the Community and Institution in the Treatment of Juvenile Delinquents," the paper attempts to formulate the general principles and fundamental attitudes basic to the development of an appropriate emotional climate within an institution. Dr. Gardner is the director of the Judge Baker Guidance Center, Boston, Massachusetts, and the paper is considered a landmark. It was published in *The Child*, January, 1952. (2) The statement "A Philosophy for Training Schools" that appears in the U.S. Children's Bureau publication, *Tentative Standards for Training Schools*. This statement was prepared at the request of the November, 1952, Conference on Training School Standards, in which numerous training school superintendents participated. Unlike other parts of the document referred to elsewhere in this chapter, this statement was written by Children's Bureau and Special Juvenile Delinquency Project staff members, and was not available for discussion at the conference. Utilizing the Gardner paper freely, the "Statement" is an exceptionally useful, brief recapitulation of philosophical concepts. (3) The analysis entitled "The Role of the Training School" which is part of a recent survey by the Government Consulting Service, Institute of Local and State Government, University of Pennsylvania. The survey, called "Summary Report: Survey of Pennsylvania Training Schools for Juvenile Delinquents" (Philadelphia, June, 1954; mimeographed) is one of the most objective, comprehensive studies made of this difficult subject. Mr. Charles P. Cella, Jr., director, and Mr. Norman V. Lourie, special consultant for the study, were responsible chiefly for the section identified. Mr. Lourie, who is Executive Director of the Philadelphia Association for Jewish Children, is on leave (1955-56) from the Association while serving as Deputy Director, Department of Public Welfare, State of Pennsylvania.

Because the statements made here represent a synthesis drawn from these sources and from the writers' own beliefs and convictions, individual statements, whether quoted or paraphrased, are not always identified separately. The writers naturally take full responsibility for the synthesis and if the intent of the several documents is misinterpreted or in any way strained it is their sole responsibility.

In the treatment of delinquent youngsters in training schools, there is a marked lag between theory and practice. Just as with adult correctional institutions, a great many present-day training school facilities have not been touched at all by the formulations that appear in the best statements to be found in the literature; others have been affected only partially; and a few have rejected modern concepts as completely unproved, unsound, and illogical. But here and there may be observed signs of acceptance of realistic treatment goals and strivings toward their fulfillment. Even though agreement on what particular program facets make for treatment is by no means universal, there is substantial acceptance of treatment responsibility at one level or another by those charged with the administration of training schools.

Any detailed consideration of treatment philosophy must be prefaced by recognizing the probable diversity of goals implicit in the different outlooks of the institution, the community, and the children themselves. Institutional goals may range all the way from the relatively simple one of providing routine physical care in decent, safe surroundings to the more complex one of developing a therapeutic setting that will enable the child to change his fundamental ways of reacting to situations. The community, thoroughly annoyed with his troublesome wrongdoing, may expect the institution merely to retain the child for a reasonable period of time, isolating him to avoid further depredations; or it may expect the institution, through whatever devices are available, to change him for the better, so that he will return at least conforming, and preferably changed for the better. But to the child himself, the use of the institution almost invariably connotes punishment—he is "sent there" in retaliation for his wrongdoing; to him it may be a question of "doing time," and his chief reaction may be disgust with himself and frustration at being caught. This is likely to be the point of view of the youngster committed by the court, regardless of the aims, desires, and attitudes of the institution and community. It is important for us to reckon with this attitude, and no honest consideration of this subject can escape this unpleasant but realistic handicap to change.

In addition to the determined goal or goals of the training school, whether compartmentalized or integrated, the treatment role itself is found to be affected by the kinds of problems, emotional and otherwise, seen in youngsters who are found in training school populations. As Dr. Gardner observes, probably 90 percent of delinquency cases represent overt acts of hostility and aggressiveness: children break and enter, steal, assult, damage, persistently truant from school, and in general resent the authority of the community and the home. He stresses that the "chief and nuclear personality defects" in these boys and girls are brought about by (1) their concept of the external world and the human beings in it, and (2) their concept of self. To them, the outside environment is at all points aggressive, destructive, and primitive. As far as these youngsters are concerned, they are living in a predatory world, and they are sensitized to the hostility of others, expressed or unexpressed. Delinquents have been deprived of the corrective emotional experiences coming from the status of being "genuinely wanted and unconditionally loved."

In their study of 500 training school delinquents compared with 500 nondelinquents, the Gluecks found that delinquent children were distinguished by their inability to control rebellious, aggressive, and hostile feelings which were expressed in antisocial acts.[35] Dr. Donald A. Bloch, Chief of the Children's Psychiatric Service in the National Institute of Mental Health of the U.S. Public Health Service, reënforces the picture of the delinquent already suggested by observing that delinquents, because of their distorted notions about the real nature of other people, are constantly on the lookout to defend against any intimacy of relationship; delinquents need to prove that every one else should be catalogued as "a crook, a sucker, or a rejecting figure." [36] The implications of this are important: all who behave toward them in a depriving, rejecting fashion help to confirm and strengthen this attitude.

It may be argued that this description of the training school youngster reflects uncompromising acceptance of "the psychiatric point of view" with respect to delinquency. Actually, no attempt has been made at this point to examine or to discuss the "causes of delinquency" from a psychiatric point of view.[37] Even though the acceptance or nonacceptance of psychiatric theories of causation may have an important bearing upon training school programs, the chief concern here is with the symptoms actually presented by training school youngsters. Remember that this discussion is not about delinquents as a whole. It has been stated previously that not all delinquent youngsters are "sick" children; many children are sent to training schools solely because the community does not know what to do with them, not because they present the classical picture described here in a relatively oversimplified fashion. As a matter of fact, there is some possibility that the character of training school delinquents may have undergone some change in recent years, although this is by no means conclusively proved.

There is a possibility that the identification of a greater proportion of seriously disturbed children in the training school population may represent an improvement in diagnostic tools. Even the possibility should be acknowledged that the traditional vicious circle has been set up, through which we see every child as unloved, unwanted, and frustrated from infancy, simply because he happens now to be an identified delinquent. But as Herschel Alt makes clear, even though no definitive studies have

[35] Glueck, *Unraveling Juvenile Delinquency.*

[36] Bloch, "Some Concepts in the Treatment of Delinquency," pp. 49-55; quotation at p. 51.

[37] This is done elsewhere; see Chap. 7, pp. 151 ff. See, for example, the comparison made between certain psychiatrically oriented concepts of Healy and Bronner with the wish-patterns of the distinguished sociologist W. I. Thomas in Chap. 7, p. 157.

been made, the experience of those in the field combined with the rather limited analyses of diagnostic studies justify the opinion that there has been a change. Some decades ago, the delinquent was identified usually as a child from a broken home, reared in a disorganized, slum community, and deprived of normal opportunities for emotional and social growth. His milieu was characterized by inadequate family life and substandard educational and recreational opportunities. In other words, while he was regarded as a product of social forces, he was considered relatively normal—reacting normally to an abnormal situation.[38]

The important thing to recognize about youngsters who see themselves as predatory inhabitants of a predatory world, regardless of what causes them to behave as they do, is that, as Dr. Gardner puts it, "punishing an individual who has this self-concept not only will not alter the concept itself, but on the contrary will go far in confirming within the child the very attitude which is the motivation and source of power for his antisocial behavior." Dr. Gardner points out that although psychiatry is only now beginning to "envision dimly" how a delinquent arrives at such a concept of self, this concept is very prevalent. Sociologists for years have been aware of the importance of the concept of self, and in fact, they were among the first to question what happens to youngsters when they are dealt with by official agencies such as the police, detention homes, and the courts; the point is that the concept of self is important and it is not a "new formulation, peculiar to psychiatrists."

But if punishment is not a solution, then what is? If in fact we are dealing with personality disturbances, it seems obvious that the real need here is for individual psychotherapy. Dr. Gardner dismisses this as "a practical impossibility," but he makes a strong case for the use of the institution itself, whether or not there are specialized professional therapists available. He identifies four components of the therapeutic process: (1) the establishment of the optimal treatment relationship, which is noncombative and nonaggressive, accepting and permissive within limits; (2) self-awareness and self-insight as to an individual's underlying motives for behaving as he does—which group living in a correctional institution may stimulate; (3) the interpretation of behavior patterns by making clear repeatedly to a youngster just what he seems to be trying to do; this is done knowingly or unwittingly by the child's asso-

---

[38] See Alt, "The Training School and Residential Treatment."

ciates and staff members all the time; (4) a trial-and-error learning process, which is stimulated and promoted by a variety of program devices whether educational, religious, social, athletic, or vocational.

This view of the institution as therapist takes on overwhelming importance in relation to the oft-repeated notion that therapy can operate only when accompanied by the ministrations of a skilled specialist. The truth of the matter is that there are three kinds of treatment theoretically available: institutional treatment, individual therapy, and group therapy. For the vast majority of training school children institutional treatment is the only form of treatment really available to them. One state training school has described these three kinds of therapy realistically as follows:

Institutional therapy has been defined as a positive emotional experience gained by an individual boy through association with elders at the institution, including houseparents, work supervisors, custodians, and administrative officials. Casual relationships with professional therapists would also aid in effecting this type of therapy. Patterns of conduct in an institution are dictated by the mores of the society from which the individual comes. In an institution, because of the intensified nature of its living, closer relationships between individuals result and the lines for acceptable conduct are more clearly defined. Not only through the establishment of more clear-cut patterns of conduct, but also through the help of warm and meaningful relationships and acquaintanceships, boys are aided through institutional therapy in formulating controls so necessary for living together with others.

Individual therapy has been defined as the emotional experience a boy has in his relationship with one person—a professional person especially trained to provide help and understanding. This type of therapy is conducted by the psychiatrist, the psychologist, and the caseworker, the latter being commonly referred to in the institution as counselor. Through their own knowledge of the boy and of his problems, and of the causes for his problems, and through the close relationship they develop with him they are able, within the limits of present-day knowledge, to execute skills in the change and movement necessary in the boy's development. Their work constantly requires the use of diagnostic and treatment techniques. In order to help a boy they need fully to understand him.

Group therapy has been defined as a specific type of scientifically oriented relationships between a limited group and a professional therapist. Such a therapist needs to be specially trained and needs to have developed certain techniques whereby it is possible for him to affect movement within individuals conforming to set group standards.[39]

In commenting on institutional treatment, which is the only kind that will be available to most children for a long time to come, it should be obvious that the role of the staff member is paramount, and that the key to establishing the basic therapeutic atmosphere lies in the careful selection of personnel. In any training school situation, there are bound to be necessary restrictions, and it is only staff members who really accept children who can cope with the apparent punishment associated by youngsters with institutional restrictions of any kind. Admittedly, as the Children's Bureau notes, an enumeration of all the qualities desirable for an institutional staff member is likely to sound like a description of "an emotional superman," but it should be possible to weed out the "emotionally crippled" and to insist on training appropriate for the post to be filled. This means that from top to bottom the staff members must be warm, friendly, supporting, and sufficiently secure to be able to provide a climate of security for others. As Cella and Lourie suggest, the overt delinquent act, its incidence and severity are determined socially, but its dynamics are psychologically determined. Therefore, there is need for a "healthful environment which can be provided with accepting, non-punitive adults, stable relationships and enriched programs of living, play and work experience." We cannot heal and punish, cure and condemn, build up and destroy at one and the same time.

Standards for Training Schools

Consistent with the foregoing discussion and predicated upon essentially the same over-all conception of the dynamics of behavior are a series of twelve standards used as the theoretical and philosophical framework for the 1954 "Survey of Pennsylvania Training Schools for Juvenile Delinquents." These generalized precepts provide a sound basis for an evaluation of training school operations. The standards do not bear such a title in the original document; instead, they appear as divisional headings. As listed here, the order has been revised considerably, not because reorganization improves them, but because it was considered advisable to use them in the sequence that seemed most

[39] "Annual Report, 1949 to 1950, Illinois State Training School for Boys."

logical for this chapter. The "Survey" was given limited distribution and is not readily available.

1. *Commitment and orientation should reflect the children's special needs.* When training schools are used as dumping grounds, none of the children thrust upon them can be served well. One institution can absorb and treat different types of children, different ages, and even different sexes, but there must be an adequate diagnostic work-up to enable the school to know the child's particular needs. Proper orientation, and the planned easing of a child into the program, both test the diagnosis made and enable the child to adjust to a setting that may be frightening and threatening to him, despite his outward sullen or rebellious demeanor.

2. *Diagnosis and classification are recurrent tasks.* The child's progress should be marked and measured by recurrent reviews and, whenever necessary, his program should be changed. This can happen realistically only when his daily life is seen by every staff member as a significant element in the treatment process. Concomitant with this is the need to let the youngster know that he is in the hands of adults who are concerned about him from a treatment standpoint. Only then can he participate in his own rehabilitation.

3. *The individual child is the proper focal point of the training school program.* The program of the training school is geared essentially to relationships among children and between children and adults. All institutional facilities—classroom, work assignments, vocational training, religious, recreational, athletic, and other activities—are primarily mediums for relationships. Treatment must involve total control and directing of care through the penetration of each service, with a common point of view concerning the individual and the integration of facilities on his behalf.

4. *The total program objective should be to prepare the child for return to the community.* The institution must contain the essential features of healthy, normal life, if children are to return to the community and to family living. This requires reduction of isolation from the community, elimination of artificiality, and avoidance of undue use of the child to serve institutional needs. But regardless of what is done with the child in the institution, work must be done in the community with the child's family so that the child will find strength to support his gains.

5. *Program planning must be organized on a continuing and comprehensive basis.* All departments or units of the program must participate in the joint goal of service to individual children. But this cannot depend upon chance and happenstance. Program planning and development in training schools should be the central responsibility of one person or unit so that there is constant evaluation, study, and development of the program.

6. *The home life program should engender rich relationships with adults.* Training school children must be exposed to satisfying relationships, constructive experiences, and varied activities that make possible a sense of accomplishment and gratification. Because these children are often unable to face the demands of reality living, opportunities for processed or diluted living experiences and relationships must be made available by the resident staff. The most significant role is played by the houseparents, who must be part of a treatment team and who should have a clinical orientation, because on their skill ultimately depends the quality of services and treatment in any institution.

7. *The academic program should be geared to the special needs of problem children.* Because most disturbed children have school problems, great care is called for in gearing the academic program to the child's readiness for learning. School progress has meaning for the future of these children, and it may serve to reduce their sense of difference from other children. Therefore, individualized instruction is required at the level of the child's ability, no matter how low it may be. It must be provided at a pace suitable for each child, but above all it must be based upon an understanding of his emotional needs so that the team approach is maintained.

8. *The vocational program should teach healthy work habits and attitudes.* Disturbed children must be helped to utilize all possible opportunities for building their smashed or nonexistent self-esteem, to give them a sense of mastery of themselves and their capacities, as well as to help them to move into the community with usable skills. Because pre-occupational training involves bodily movement, outdoor activity, and participation in work with adults, through it upset children can find an outlet for anxiety and relief from inner loneliness. Paramount is the need for using the work for the children, not children for the work.

9. *The recreational program should contribute to personality development.* When integrated into the total treatment plan, recreational ac-

tivities provide a variegated and flexible instrument which can help children develop a genuinely constructive spirit as part of a group. Properly organized and staffed, a positive recreational plan can counteract destructive gang spirit, and teach children that leisure time, instead of being a boring void, can be occupied enjoyably.

10. *The religious program is an integral part of positive treatment.* As a force for ultimate good, religious programs have an essential and central role in training schools. In addition to promoting his own spiritual growth, a connection with a religious program of his own faith conveys to the youngster a valuable sense of belonging to a larger community of people, which may be vital to a child who has little inner security himself. Religion sometimes offers a child a positive identification with his parents' beliefs; for most of these children, any constructive feeling about their parents is valuable.

11. *The discipline policy should be aimed toward the development of self-control.* Discipline should be motivated by concern for the child, instead of providing emotional outlets for adults. Children need a framework of controls. The delinquent child especially must develop an inner sense of self-discipline which he will take with him into the community. When children feel that adults basically like and accept them, discipline can carry conviction for them which eventually they will acknowledge. The child's deep-seated realization of his own need for help and correction is the basis for treatment.

12. *Release and after-care must concentrate on child, family, and community.* Because children and parents are interlocking contributors and participants in the creation of problems, a "family centered" treatment concept is justified. Work with parents must be concurrent with the treatment program for the child who is being prepared for a new attempt to join the stream of normal existence. Release planning involves the need for determining the optimum point of readiness for the child's return to the community, and the failure to identify this may permit him to slip into a plateau of institutionalization which makes movement toward release as well as later adjustment more difficult. Especially important is the need to develop gradual movement away from a full-time institutional program through progressively longer visits to the family. If a different community placement, such as a group foster home, is indicated, there must be a bridge from one setting to the other. In any event, there will be need for sustained, intensive after-care

supervision by a trained caseworker in a rehabilitative relationship that is continuous with the institution's clinical approach. Some children will not readjust immediately in the community, but their return to the institution should not be considered complete regression, for often "failure" is a part of the testing-out process.

Special Training School Problems

These are standards that contain implicit as well as explicit goals. In this brief review are encompassed many aspirations only partly attained here and there and almost never fulfilled. Yet these are the standards that must be met if training schools are to become a useful resource in treating delinquent youngsters.

In the foregoing brief summary, many acute problems were barely touched upon; others were glossed over entirely. To illustrate the ramifications of some of the training school issues, as well as to come to grips with two important, troublesome questions that affect these institutions, attention is given to the perennial problem of runaways, and to the perplexing, baffling difficulties inherent in the attempts to evaluate training school results.

The Problem of Runaways

Nearly all state training schools are operated as open institutions, that is, they are not enclosed by escape-proof walls. Although many of these open institutions have limited security features, such as a "security cottage" or a few rooms designed for security purposes, virtually all have a runaway problem. The number of runaways varies from season to season, and fluctuates as the staff members are careful or careless in their supervision of youngsters and as the total program reaches high and low activity levels. Some training schools, threatened by adverse publicity about "escapes," have resorted to the use of a "security" fence enclosing a segment of the campus, but adolescent youngsters of average agility find no difficulty in surmounting the supposedly substantial barrier of an industrial-type fence; in fact, a fence may turn out to be a stimulating challenge.

The fact that there are runaways is a matter of grave concern, and the problem cannot be dismissed lightly. Nevertheless, it is easy to exaggerate its importance. After all, youngsters have run away from their own homes—even reasonably adequate ones—and from foster homes. But training school runaways, especially boys, are looked upon in a different light. They are considered predatory and aggressive, and even though a girl who runs away is likely to get involved in serious difficulties, it is the boy who "causes all the trouble." The youngster who runs away may be exhibiting traits of self-determination and ability to mobilize himself that may indicate a real potential for treatment. Nevertheless, when a boy runs away, not only does he remove himself from an environment designed to treat him, but also he emerges into one in which he may become a potential menace. In his flight, he may steal a car, and his need for money may drive him to burglary, robbery, and assault. Thus he may be plunged deeper into conflict with society, even though the incident which precipitated his departure may have been fear of another boy or a group of boys, fear of an adult supervisor, or merely an easy opportunity to depart from a situation that had become monotonous and distasteful.

In many areas, runaways from state schools have received extensive publicity, which often leads to two untoward results. (1) Adverse public opinion regarding the institution may develop, which in turn may retard improvements in personnel and program. But actually, these improvements may be the best way to reduce the number of runaways. Thus a vicious circle is created. (2) The institution affected by damaging publicity may be pushed into an emphasis on security that interferes with the development of an adequate program.

Unquestionably, newspapers have the right to publish information about runaways. In most metropolitan areas, the problem is not regarded as sufficiently newsworthy to warrant front-page and headline attention. During 1950, one private institution in the East, which is highly regarded, rightly or wrongly, averaged almost one runaway a day, ignored for the most part by the metropolitan press. Probably this training school would be less well accepted if newspaper readers, with monotonous regularity, were confronted with prominently placed stories about "escapes" and "more escapes."

Lack of public confidence in training schools may stem directly from feature stories about "vicious young hoodlums on a rampage." Legislators are readily affected by public opinion, and reduced training school appropriations may ensue—or thousands of dollars may be allocated for a "security fence" and even for mounted perimeter guards, very likely at the expense of more adequate treatment staff.

Whatever happens to training school budgets, whether they are reduced or remain the same or are increased, the public's anxiety about escapes is quite likely to be reflected in increased security emphasis. One common result of the security emphasis is restricted movement of youngsters within the institutional campus. Those assigned to details and to school are marched to a central location, grouped, and taken to their assigned places, all under the watchful eyes of supervisors. This means more regimentation than is necessary, and it is axiomatic that movement by groups inevitably results in rigid scheduling of program activities; in turn, this makes difficult the development of flexible, individually arranged programs. In one training school, an excellent hobby program, conducted evenings by volunteers from the staff, was discontinued when security regulations were tightened after widespread newspaper publicity about escapes. Revised regulations were introduced. Boys for each evening hobby group were called for at their respective cottages, conducted under supervision to the gym or school building, and later returned under supervision to the cottages. The volunteer program disintegrated rapidly—and so would a Boy Scout program in any community if a scoutmaster had to provide escort service by calling for and returning each boy in his troop. Although no boys had run away under the previous plan, which permitted youngsters to go individually to their respective hobby groups and return the same way, the prospect of a front-page story if a boy ran away while on his unsupervised way to the Stamp Club was a formidable danger. The early evening hours are usually the most difficult and least constructive part of any training school program.

As a result of public concern of predatory youngsters "on the loose," some states have moved in the direction of "security units" within an existing institution, or have put into operation separate security institutions. This raises such questions as whether this may lead to the development of "little prisons" for delinquent youngsters on the one hand, or the development of counterparts of the prison "hole" on the other. In a populous state, a reasonably good case may be made for the development of a small, specialized secure institution for temporary treatment of carefully selected youngsters. But it is difficult to avoid the emergence of a "little Alcatraz" with its concomitant stigma. Similarly, the use of security cells, by whatever name they are called, creates difficult problems of control. Too often they become "punishment" cells, where disciplinary problems and returned runaways are housed for unduly long periods.

The runaway problem is a serious one that affects almost every aspect of the program. Unless it is dealt with in a rational manner, the training schools cannot develop into a solid treatment resource.

The Problem of Evaluating Training School Results

The problems of training schools are varied and complex, in part because they are the institutions of last resort for the most persistent offenders and in part because they are used chiefly when all community agencies have been tried without success. It is true that an occasional first offender is received by training schools, and that some commitments are made because there are no other resources available, but in the main the term "delinquency" and "incorrigibility" conceal a history of multiple offenses resulting in numerous arrests, detention home or jail experiences, and court appearances. Some form of supervision in the community has been attempted in most cases, but commitment comes after these efforts have failed, often repeatedly.

It is not surprising, therefore, that follow-up studies of those released from training schools show a very high proportion of so-called failures, as measured by parole or after-care violations, arrests, convictions, and commitment to adult correctional institutions. These studies cannot be summarized briefly, and they do not lend themselves to comparisons with one another. While the number of these studies is not very great, on the whole there is good evidence that the recidivism rate is very high. Various studies of juvenile court and training school children report 60, 70, and even 80 percent of them as "failures" at some later point, usually five years or more after adjudication or release.[40]

[40] Healy and Bronner, *Delinquents and Criminals—Their Making and Unmaking*; and Glueck, *Juvenile Delinquents Grown Up*. See also Larkins, "A Study of the Adjustment of Negro Boys Discharged from Morrison Training School," described by the author as "a definite understatement of conditions" which showed that over three-fifths (63 percent) of the boys released appeared before courts other than juvenile courts subsequent to their training school experience. See Black and Glick, *Recidivism at the Hawthorne-Cedar Knolls School*, which shows a high success rate. But compare Mary E. Macdonald's review of this study in *The Social Service Review*, 17 (March, 1953), pp. 106-108, which raises some significant methodological questions about the study.

This situation has a number of interesting implications. It has been pointed out repeatedly that the rate of success of any form of treatment must be viewed in the light of what is reasonable to expect. There is reasonable expectancy of a high rate of success in the treatment of some kinds of physical illness and disabling conditions; with others, a low rate of successful outcome is expected; and in a few instances, a "success" rate of even five or six per hundred would be considered phenomenally high. Likewise, it is axiomatic that early treatment is more likely to succeed than treatment in the advanced stages of an illness. When delinquent behavior is considered, there are practically no norms to use as a guide. Very little research has been done in this area; and one is forced to suspend judgment as to whether 20, 30 or 40 percent success is high or low. This stand is strengthened by the fact that the training school receives those who are in the "advanced stages," as measured by the persistence of symptomatic delinquent behavior.

High rates of failure are alarming; whether they are higher or lower than should be expected never justifies complacency about the situation. The evidence of the cumulative failure of society's devices for dealing with young offenders makes a strong case for better conditions in local communities. Like the juvenile court delinquent population, the training school population does not reflect proportional representation of the state, or of any county or city. Sometimes this is because some judges use commitment more often than others. But some areas are unquestionably substandard, and presumably they produce far more than their share of delinquents. In such communities the problems are numerous and the needs are great. The needs cover the gamut—good family life, adequate living conditions, suitable schools, child guidance clinics, and well-staffed recreational and social agencies.

That the training school failure rates are high argues for better community prevention and treatment services in order to reduce the numbers who fail to respond to efforts within the community. When communities are better places to live in and when they offer better preventive and treatment facilities, the training schools may still have to contend with the failures of the community. It is to be hoped that they will not continue to be used as a place for failures, but will instead be used as treatment centers, where the population can be dealt with before it is "too late." In other words, the day may come when training schools will be used constructively, rather than as places of last resort.

As long as the institution is the depository for those who fail to respond to community efforts, it is only reasonable to expect that the rate of recidivism will be high—but it is a cumulative rate, and not one which should be charged exclusively to the training school. A youngster released from a training school still is a community responsibility, and the quality of resources available, including the quality of specific after-care services, may determine the outcome. It must be remembered that practically all those who leave the training schools return to essentially the same community conditions they left, and in nearly all cases the after-care supervisory services are of no better quality than the quality of supervision employed before commitment. Supervisory services, before and after commitment, are rarely adequate in quality or quantity, and they offer only a feeble barrier against adverse circumstances in the home and community. This helps to explain why the studies showing high rates of failure may show rates equally high in a "good" school in one state and a "poor" school in another state, or in a "good" administration of one school and a "poor" administration of the same school.

This does not justify the conclusion that "It doesn't make any difference what is done at a training school—the results are the same." The case for nonpunitive, treatment-oriented programs for youngsters in training schools needs to be made on a basis altogether outside the question of rate of success or failure. Common decency demands that those committed to the state's care be treated with humane consideration, that their physical, educational, social, and spiritual needs be met on a basis consistent with their dignity as human beings. That kindly decent standards of care produces fewer recidivists has not been proved; but neither has it been proved that they produce more recidivists. But whether fewer failures are produced or not, nobody in good conscience can favor the use of harsh, suppressive tactics and a punitive philosophy, or favor the abandonment of attempts to staff these institutions with the finest and most skilled persons who can be found.

The nonpunitive approach has often been called a "treatment" approach or even an "individualized treatment" approach to the question. Actually, the term "treatment" means an attempt to gear the institutional program to the needs of those committed. It does not mean "individualized treatment" in the accepted clinical sense of intensive therapy over a period of time by a qualified therapist, whether psychiatrist, clinical psychologist, or psychiatric social worker. Most "good" institutions try to devise a program within available facilities that takes into account the needs of the individuals. No training school has a program of "individualized treatment" which reaches more than a handful of the population. The fact that an institution has a staff with a relatively high number of social workers—even one for each forty or fifty youngsters in the average daily population—does not guarantee individualized treatment. The institution with an average daily population of 400 often serves 800 different youngsters a year. Much time necessarily is consumed by intake work, staffing cases, conferring with cottage parents, and handling minor or major crises as they occur. Intensive treatment, for practical purposes, may be defined tentatively in terms of treatment for one hour a week with an appropriate therapist. Using this yardstick, and taking into account the various other responsibilities of the specialists, a few children—two or three—may be given intensive treatment by each social worker; a clinical psychologist may deal with three or four intensively; and a psychiatrist may treat four or five intensively. Applying this standard to present optimum training school staff, this would mean that about forty to forty-five youngsters could receive intensive treatment at any one time, about 10 percent of the average daily population in an institution designed for 400 and staffed by ten social workers, three clinical psychologists, and a full-time psychiatrist.

The influence of these services on success and failure cannot be measured now. Measurements by any known statistical device may be virtually meaningless, because, for obvious reasons, "intensive treatment" is often reserved for the most difficult, most troublesome children, and its effectiveness may reside in better institutional adjustment, which may or may not carry over into the community. This can be defended on the ground that the first task of the institution is to get those having difficulty adjusting to the program stabilized sufficiently so that the total program will have some chance of becoming a positive force in their reëducation.

The blunt fact is that no study exists that either proves or disproves the contention that "individualized treatment" services in an institution will reduce the rate of failures. Services have never been adequate in quantity or quality in any public institution to provide treatment for all those committed, and no substantial follow-up study has been made of a state training school group given "individualized treatment" that was selected as a representative sample of the institutional population—the only fair test. Even then, demonstration of usefulness would be difficult; the kind and quality of after-care services and family and community conditions all affect statistical success and failure. Furthermore, often real improvement in individuals is as difficult to measure as it is to assign causal factors for it. Many persons who appear as statistical failures may have been stabilized by one experience or another, including the training school, so that their later failures involve less damage to society than would otherwise have been the case. These intangibles are difficult if not impossible to measure, but they make it necessary to be very cautious in interpreting statistics of success and failure.

For Further Reading

HAGAN, HELEN R., "Foster Care for Children," in *Social Work Year Book, 1954*, (New York, 1954), pp. 225-232.

> This is an excellent review of the foster care situation, and despite the summary nature of the article, the vital issues of foster care are given adequate emphasis.

BOWLER, ALIDA C., AND RUTH S. BLOODGOOD, *Institutional Treatment of Delinquent Boys, Part 1*, U.S. Department of Labor, Children's Bureau Pub. No. 228 (Washington, D.C., 1935).

> This pioneer study of a number of training schools is a forthright, factual appraisal, accompanied by an excellent historical summary.

Handbook of American Institutions for Delinquent Juveniles, The Osborn Association, Vols. I-IV (1938-1943).

> These are thoroughly professional surveys of numerous training schools, many being done by Austin MacCormick. Together they represent an amazing indictment of society's treatment of delinquent children.

Report on Institutional Treatment of Delinquent Juveniles, National Conference on Prevention and Control of Juvenile Delinquency (Washington, D.C., 1947).

> This is a compact and worth-while analysis of many of the complex problems facing training schools.

DEUTSCH, ALBERT, *Our Rejected Children* (Boston, 1950).

> A vivid and dramatic account of how children are treated in training schools in states that rank high in wealth. As a scholar-journalist who pulls no punches, the author depicts a truly shocking situation.

SCHULZE, SUSANNE, AND MORRIS FRITZ MAYER, "Training for House Parents and Kindred Personnel in Institutions for Juvenile Delinquents," in *Training Personnel for Work with Juvenile Delinquents,* U.S. Children's Bureau (Washington, D.C., 1954).

> This paper discusses the functions of houseparents and outlines a suggested program of training. Its clearcut and direct analysis of the problem makes it the best statement of its kind that has been published until now.

Tentative Standards for Training Schools, 1954, U.S. Children's Bureau Pub. No. 351 (Washington, D.C., 1954).

> The report of the Bureau's November 1952 Conference on Training School Standards, amplified by an excellent statement entitled "A Philosophy for Training Schools."

GARDNER, GEORGE E., M.D., "The Institution as Therapist," in *The Child,* January, 1952, pp. 70-72.

> Written by the distinguished director of the Judge Baker Guidance Center, Boston, this is undoubtedly the best single paper on the subject.

"Summary Report: Survey of Pennsylvania Training Schools for Juvenile Delinquents," Government Consulting Service, Institute of Local and State Government, University of Pennsylvania (Philadelphia, June, 1954; mimeographed).

> Directed by Charles P. Cella, Jr., with Norman V. Lourie as special consultant, this is one of the most objective and comprehensive studies of the training school problem in a particular state.

COSTELLO, JOHN B., "Institutions for Juvenile Delinquents," in *The Annals,* 261 (January, 1949), pp. 166-78.

> A highly competent and succinct review of the problem by an experienced administrator who has a capacity for clear organization and honest, direct handling of difficult topics.

Chapter **16**

TREATMENT OF YOUTHFUL
OFFENDERS

The anomalies, inconsistencies, and paradoxical differences in the operations of the various kinds of agencies responsible for the treatment of offenders of juvenile court age have been described. But the treatment of juvenile delinquents is a coherent and systematic unity that has a discernible and rational conceptual framework in comparison with the situation affecting those beyond juvenile court age, usually referred to as "youthful offenders." To those who consider the handling of juvenile delinquents an untidy affair, the treatment of the older youthful offenders will seem like chaos unrefined and unrestrained.

Allusions have been made earlier to the conflicts in public opinion reflected even in the handling by juvenile courts of older youngsters who commit more serious offenses. But those beyond juvenile court age, or removed from juvenile court jurisdiction because of the gravity of their offenses, are legally labeled youthful criminals, not children in need of the protection of the state. For the most part, they are dealt with under criminal statutes, whether modified a great deal, or slightly, or not at all. Generally, youthful offenders are between the upper juvenile court age limit and twenty-one years of age; they may be treated simply as adults or as persons who by reason of youth are subject to some modifications in handling by the courts and, in some instances, by treatment agencies.

The older juvenile offender dealt with as an adult is subject to the same general treatment given to all criminals. When he is arrested by the police, the traditional pattern of police handling of adult criminals is employed. Normally, he is not accorded any of the protections given to juveniles; he is arrested, fingerprinted, "booked," and detained in a police lockup or jail unless released on bail. Unlike most youngsters of juvenile court age, he is subject to public exposure because his name, address, and the charge against him indicated on the "police blotter" may be published in newspapers and his picture may be used with impunity. In other words, to all intents and purposes he is an adult, and with some exceptions, he is so regarded in the pre-trial process. Although some "leniency" may be shown by a court because of age, his status in the courts usually is governed by all the traditional criminal court practices.[1]

If found guilty, he is treated as an adult, whether placed on probation, fined, or given a short jail sentence or a longer sentence in a major penal institution. Although his special needs as an older adolescent youth may be taken into account if he is placed on probation, which supposedly is synonymous with individualized treatment, this does not occur if he is given a brief jail term. With occasional and rare exceptions, he literally is thrown in with the rest of the prisoners and is subjected to the demoralizing, debilitating regimen characteristic of most of the jails of the country.

If convicted of a major crime, he may be sentenced to a major correctional institution for a definite or indefinite (indeterminate) term in a prison housing large numbers of prisoners of all ages and types. Prisons receive persons convicted of major crimes or felonies. Although these are defined differently from state to state, such offenses as murder, assault with intent to kill, armed robbery, burglary, auto theft, and rape are invariably felonies. But one caution is important: the term "convicted" is crucial. For various reasons, the original charge is often reduced, for example, from burglary to petty theft, so that the conviction may be for a misdemeanor, or minor offense, usually making the misdemeanant ineligible for prison—but eligible for a jail term up to

[1] For a comparison between juvenile court and criminal court processes see Chap. 13

one year, which may be exceeded if fines are also imposed. As a working definition, a felony may be described as an offense punishable under law by one year or more in a state penal institution.

In some states, depending upon whether he was previously convicted of a felony, the youthful offender may be sentenced to a reformatory. A reformatory is an adult penal institution, not to be confused with a training school, sometimes referred to as a "reform school." The latter is for youngsters who are of juvenile court age at the time of commitment and who are dealt with under juvenile court law. The reformatory normally receives prisoners convicted of felonies, and it is usually the junior counterpart of the prison. With occasional exceptions, the reformatories receive prisoners who are between the upper age limit of juvenile court jurisdiction and a maximum age ranging from twenty-five to thirty, which is the most common age specified in the statutes establishing them. Practically, they are just like any other prisons; as a matter of fact, personal observation suggests that most reformatories are more security conscious, "tougher" as to disciplinary procedures, and more regimented and tense than the prisons, which have populations composed of older, more stable and mature offenders.

This is an interesting phenomenon. The first reformatory in this country was opened in 1877 at Elmira, New York, and it was speedily copied in many other states. Dedicated to the isolation and separation of those deemed reformable from the older, more mature, and allegedly more sophisticated criminals, it was restricted usually to so-called first felony offenders—which is often a misnomer, since a first offender may have been involved in dozens of serious crimes before being apprehended. Actually, the reformatories contain the most aggressive, most potentially dangerous prisoners of all, and their separation from the older prisoners to a certain extent involves their removal from a reasonably stabilizing influence. Obviously, fear of contamination was the rationale, although, psychologically, contamination by members of a peer group logically may be expected to have more deep-seated and longer-lasting influence.

This description is not intended to be cynical or in any way derogatory of the improvements that have been made in adult correctional institutions; in recent years, there has been substantial expansion of minimum security (unwalled) facilities. But those concerned with the treatment of adult prisoners are fully cognizant of the fact that reforms have come slowly and spasmodically, and it is evident that adult penal institutions with populations of several thousand can at best provide mass treatment only, with little or no individualization.[2]

Beginnings have been made in modifying some of the traditional criminal law processes with respect to those over juvenile court age but under twenty-one years of age, and in a few instances the modifications have extended to those two or three years older. Although the entire process of corrections from the time of arrest to the point of ultimate freedom logically should be considered as a continuum, the changes that have been made thus far have appeared separately, in the courts and in institutional treatment. Specialized courts for youth have been developed in some jurisdictions under various names such as "boys' court," "wayward minors' court," "youthful offenders' court," and "adolescents' court." These have pioneered in what, for lack of a better term, might be called quasi-criminal methods of dealing with older juveniles who offend against the law. In addition, the "youth authority movement," which is not very well understood in some quarters, modifies the disposition powers of the court by requiring commitment to a central authority rather than to a specific institution, and at the same time places upon the authority the responsibility for developing what is supposed to be an integrated program of institutional and other facilities designed for the individualized treatment of those committed.

The courts for youthful offenders and the youth authority movement require somewhat detailed consideration. Both are important because to a certain extent they represent a break with the traditional methods of dealing with youthful offenders and because there is increasing interest in the specialized handling of this very difficult group. To provide adequate correctional measures is a complex task and a difficult challenge.

All that has been said earlier about the nature and causes of delinquency and the difficult problems of developing adequate treatment programs for delinquents applies with equal if not greater force to the older youthful offender. From the standpoint of society, he is generally a more dangerous person and a more complex one. While youthful offenders are not simply "grown-up delinquents," they are often "graduates" of specialized treatment facilities designed for delinquents; they have been in juvenile court, often not once but many times; and many

[2] Barnes and Teeters, *New Horizons in Criminology*; Tappan, ed., *Contemporary Correction*; *Federal Prisons: 1954*; Sellin, ed., "Prisons in Transformation"; Oswald, "Correctional Treatment."

of them have been in training schools, sometimes more than once. Most important of all is the disturbing fact that they contribute far more than their proportionate share to the crime problem.

Youth and Crime

According to the Federal Bureau of Investigation, only 9.7 percent of all persons arrested in 1954 were under eighteen years of age, and just 16 percent of all arrested persons were under twenty-one years of age. (There is some under-reporting here; in many jurisdictions, the fingerprints of those under eighteen are not taken routinely, and fingerprints are the basis for the data cited.) The great majority of all arrests in all age brackets were for minor offenses, including intoxication and disorderly conduct, from which most youths are excluded. But the residue of serious offenses, which constitutes the core of the nation's crime problem, provides youthful offenders with an alarming role. They are our greatest single threat to law-abiding security. These youths—under 10 percent of all persons arrested—were responsible for about 58 percent of all auto theft cases, 49 percent of burglaries, nearly 7 percent of aggravated assaults, and over 4 percent of nonnegligent homicides.[3] The heart of the matter is that the under-eighteen age groups are involved in a relatively high proportion of serious offenses. Whatever the extent of the exaggerations and the "viewing with alarm" attitudes about the delinquency problem, the youthful offender makes a real contribution to crime, as a review of some of the more specific statistical data available makes clear.

The grim picture of the relationship of youth to crime is seen from New York State statistics, which show that of all adults arrested and charged with felony offenses in 1953, 8,411 or 26.7 percent were sixteen to twenty-one years of age.[4] Boys in this age group, although they comprise only 4 percent of the state's adult population, are responsible for about one-fourth of the arrests for major crimes. The situation respecting younger boys, aged sixteen, seventeen, and eighteen years, is still more striking. (In New York State, which is one of the few states with a very low juvenile court upper age limit, an adult is defined as any person 16 years of age or older.) Representing only 2.4 percent of the

[3] *Uniform Crime Reports*, XXIV, pp. 112-14.
[4] *Correction*, 19, p. 14.

state's adult population, 5,569 or 17.7 percent of all adults arrested and charged with major crimes in the state in 1953 were youths in this age group.[5] Youths sixteen, seventeen, and eighteen years of age ranked high in crimes of violence and property offences. This group accounted for 53.9 percent of arrests for auto theft; 35.0 percent of burglary arrests; 25.0 percent for rape; 21.7 percent for possession of dangerous weapons; 18.3 percent for robbery; 15.4 percent for grand larceny other than auto theft; and 8.4 percent of arrests for felonious assault.[6]

The Community Service Society study cites police department figures and court case statistics for New York City that show a pattern similar to that of the state: the age group sixteen to twenty-one is responsible for a gravely disproportionate amount of serious crime. This age group appeared in arrest statistics in 68.1 percent of auto theft cases, 44.2 percent of burglary arrests, 31.6 percent of robbery cases, and 34.4 percent of Sullivan Law violations (the New York firearms act). Significant is the role played by younger members of the sixteen to twenty-one age group as demonstrated by the following table:

With all the inadequacies of gross arrest statistics, the situation is clearly bad enough to justify alarm. Even with varied arrest practices in "suspicion" and "investigation" cases, and differences in police reporting of cases involving younger offenders, it seems safe to conclude that

TABLE G

Age Groups Ranked According to Numbers Arrested for Types of Major Crime in New York City, 1953.*

AGES	RANKS FOR EACH TYPE OF CRIME			
	AUTO THEFT	BURGLARY	ROBBERY	SULLIVAN LAW VIOLATIONS
16..............	1	1	5	1
17..............	2	2	4	3
18..............	3	3	2	2
19..............	4	4	1	4
20..............	5	5	3	5

* *Justice for Youth*, p. 120. (Adapted from data available in *Annual Report of the Police Department, City of New York, 1953*. Table title changed slightly here.)

[5] *Justice for Youth: The Courts for Wayward Youth in New York City*, p. 119.
[6] *Correction*, 19, p. 15.

youthful offenders are the nation's number one crime problem. Disposition statistics, which more directly relate the criminal and the crime than do arrest statistics, give support to this statement. Unfortunately, not many states collect and publish good disposition statistics, and the Bureau of the Census, after years of trying, finally in 1945 gave up its attempt to get nation-wide data from courts, at a time when only twenty-five states were making reports, most of them incomplete and inconclusive.

The California data are significant. During 1953, all dispositions of felony arrests reported to the State Department of Justice totaled more than 66,000. Nearly 16,000 were disposed of by release; over 6,000 were turned over to other jurisdictions; and misdemeanor complaints were filed in 7,000 cases. There were about 26,000 felony complaints filed, and over 11,000 were disposed of by being "turned over for juvenile handling." Thus, ignoring those released and those turned over to other jurisdictions, *over one-fourth of all felony arrests resulted in juvenile court cases.* An additional, unknown number of these involving youths under 21 were proceeded against under felony or misdemeanor complaints. In California, it will be recalled, juvenile court jurisdiction extends to the age of twenty-one, but there is concurrent jurisdiction with adult courts between the ages of eighteen and twenty-one.[7]

The Community Service Society report contains an excellent statement on the over-all relationships of youth and crime that provides a realistic springboard for the discussion that follows.

> The number and nature of the crimes committed by youths make for a major social problem that must be met swiftly and effectively. We cannot lull ourselves any longer with careless assumptions that the high rates of serious crime by youths are transitory, for they have shown no inclination to diminish over a period of years. But we must also guard ourselves against the other extreme of becoming overwhelmed by the magnitude of the problem and striking out impulsively, vengefully, and without avail. While punishment of young offenders may be effective if used with discretion and control, indiscriminate punishment proves all too often to be more in the nature of relief and satisfaction to the chastiser than cure for the chastised. In some instances recidivism is the boomerang of punishment randomly imposed without regard for the character and circumstances of the individual offenders.

[7] *Crime in California, 1953*, table 6, p. 16.

The very gravity of the problem calls for a comprehensive program in which vigorous action is planned, controlled, and calculated to reduce crime among our youths. The courts, of course, are institutions of very great importance in any community program to deal with youth crime and they must be sufficiently well organized to deal with young offenders justly, evenly, and with a view toward possible rehabilitation.[8]

Because they represent a serious problem from the standpoint of their numbers, their complexity, and the kinds of offenses they commit, there have been various attempts to sort out youthful offenders for some form of specialized handling. Unquestionably, society's motives in this are pretty well mixed up. On the one hand, it is recognized that this group constitutes a threat to the welfare and security of the community, but on the other hand it is known that often they are dominated by acute adolescent conflicts. Usually, specialized treatment has been reserved for those under twenty-one, who are legally minors with specific civil disabilities, including inability to make binding contracts except for legally defined necessaries. They are not men and women, but older boys and girls whose persistent and even dangerous behavior logically requires that they be given some special form of attention.

These special programs for dealing with youthful offenders require analysis, even though they do not fit into neat compartments. These programs are not numerous, but they have an importance and significance for the future that extend far beyond their numbers. Because of the overwhelming difficulties encountered in trying to view the picture as a whole, the discussion is broken into two segments, dealing with (1) the specialized courts for youth, and (2) the youth authority movement.

Specialized Courts for Youthful Offenders

Because of variations in upper age limits in juvenile court laws, some youngsters dealt with by the courts as adult criminals in certain jurisdictions would be handled as juvenile delinquents elsewhere.[9] In seven states, including New York, the youth who has reached his sixteenth birthday is no longer a delinquent; in twenty-eight states he may be

---

[8] *Justice for Youth*, p. 121.
[9] Puttkammer, *Administration of Criminal Law*.

considered a delinquent until he is eighteen, or even older. Thus, in some places, the efforts to obtain youth courts may substitute for attempts to raise the juvenile court age limit. In other places, there is a clear-cut recognition of the desirability of establishing special socialized procedures for those beyond juvenile court age, as demonstrated by the Boys' Court in Chicago, the Wayward Minor Court in Detroit, and branches of the Philadelphia Municipal Court, which have jurisdiction in certain cases between the ages of seventeen and twenty-one. But whether they substitute for expanded juvenile courts or function as socialized criminal courts for older adolescents and young people, they may provide a pattern for bridging the gap between the juvenile court with its doctrine of *parens patriae* and the criminal court, which too often operates on the dubious theory of *lex talionis*. For youthful offenders —neither the children who require the state's protection nor the so-called completely responsible adult punished on an "eye-for-an-eye" basis—perhaps the expansion of youth courts will provide a measure of individualized justice that may exert a benign influence in this entire area of criminal law. The administration of criminal justice in this nation leaves a great deal to be desired; individualized justice is still a goal dimly seen.

The first youth court was the Boys' Court, established March 16, 1914, as a branch of the Municipal Court of Chicago. It was followed in 1915 by the awkwardly named Boys' and Men's and Girls' and Women's Misdemeanants' Divisions of the Municipal Court of Philadelphia, with jurisdiction over certain offenders under twenty-one. New York in 1923 passed a Wayward Minor Act, and Michigan in 1927 created a Wayward Minor Act, applicable to Wayne County (Detroit), which gave the Juvenile Court in the Probate Court jurisdiction over some offenders aged seventeen to twenty-one. Two general kinds of jurisdiction are involved: (1) that over those committing misdemeanors (or felonies "reduced" to misdemeanors); and (2) that over so-called wayward, incorrigible, ungovernable youngsters, above juvenile court age but below twenty-one.

Although the youth courts identified were started in an atmosphere of great hope, they have generally lacked the facilities necessary for effective work. They separate older boys and girls in court from men and women—and from children—but they do little else. The auxiliary services provided by probation staff and clinical personnel are woefully inadequate, even when measured against the limited services and resources provided by juvenile courts.[10]

The Chicago Boys' Court is a good example of hopes unfulfilled. About 5,000 youthful offenders between the ages of seventeen and twenty-one appear before this court each year on charges of violating municipal ordinances (excluding traffic offenses) or state laws.[11] After preliminary interviews by one of two social workers, the evidence in the case is heard before the court acting as examining magistrate, the case being prosecuted by an Assistant City Prosecutor in city cases, or an Assistant State's Attorney in state cases. The defendant may be represented by private counsel or by a representative of the Public Defender's staff, who is a salaried defender used in all cases in which private counsel is not employed. Actually, because of the volume of work, his services are rather perfunctory. If the charges are proved, one of several dispositions is possible. (1) A serious felony charge, or a felony charge against a youth with a prior criminal record, may result in his being held for the grand jury and criminal court action. (2) In a felony case, the State's Attorney may, at his own discretion, change the charge to misdemeanor, over which the court has full jurisdiction. (3) If the defendant is found guilty in a case in which the court has jurisdiction, he may be (a) sentenced to the Cook County Jail or the Chicago House of Correction for a period not to exceed one year, or (b) placed on probation under supervision by the Adult Probation Department (Cook County and Chicago, serving all criminal courts), or (c) placed under the "supervision" of a private social agency, operated usually under sectarian auspices.

The jail and house of correction provide nothing but custody. Supervision, by far the most usual form of disposition, was used in nearly one-third of all cases in the latest year for which Boys' Court data were separately published. Significantly, the report comments: "From the reports of the agencies, the caseworkers have about 100 boys each under their supervision. It is impossible for any caseworker to

[10] See Burke, *Youth and Crime* (*Study of Chicago Boys' Court*); Worthington, *Men's Misdemeanants Division of the Municipal Court of Philadelphia*; Topping, *Women's Misdemeanants Division of the Municipal Court of Philadelphia*; Tappan, *Delinquent Girls in Court.*
[12] Braude, "Boys' Court."

work effectively with that large number of boys." [12] Not all agencies working with the Boys' Court currently have caseloads this high. Some of them are well staffed, but they do not "take" many cases. The Probation Department itself is utterly inadequate, politically dominated, and generally unreliable. Despite the rotation of judges in the court, two outstanding judges—Joseph J. Drucker and Jacob M. Braude—have served for long periods. But they have never been given decent resources. Without resources for diagnosis and treatment, the best judge is nearly helpless.

Until now the youth courts simply have not "caught on." Neither the examples of existing courts nor the Model Youth Court Act adopted by the American Law Institute have had much of an impact. Over forty years after the first youth court was created, only a scant half-dozen jurisdictions have tried to meet the challenge posed by youthful offenders in court.

Youth Courts in New York City

The youth courts of New York City deserve special attention, not because they provide an "answer" that may be applied elsewhere, but because they have received intensive scrutiny recently. Out of this may come a pattern that will be promising for use in other jurisdictions.[13]

The New York City courts dealing with youth present a strange, wonderful, and weird pattern that defies brief descriptive analysis. In part, the confusion, overlapping, and duplication found in the youth courts is due to the patchwork of total court organization itself. To a certain extent the problem stems from the fact that New York City embraces five counties, legally termed boroughs: Kings County (Brooklyn), the Bronx, Queens, Richmond, and New York County (Manhattan).

There are three distinct kinds of criminal courts in New York City. The Magistrates' Courts, which correspond to the police courts in most jurisdictions, are responsible for dealing with summary offenses. They have jurisdiction over initial or preliminary hearings which result either in disposition, if the offense falls within their purview, or holding the

---

[12] *Report on the Boys' Court,* p. 5.
[13] See *Justice for Youth;* and Gellhorn, *Children and Families in the Courts of New York City,* commonly called the Gellhorn study or Gellhorn report.

alleged offender for further proceedings in higher courts if there seems to be a *prima facie* case against him. The Court of Special Sessions, which is a city-wide court with limited criminal jurisdiction, is the trial court for most misdemeanors, and misdemeanors not within the jurisdiction of the Magistrates' Courts are transferred directly to Special Sessions. The County Court, which only in Manhattan has the special designation "Court of General Sessions," is the trial court for felonies. When the alleged felony offender is held after preliminary hearing in Magistrates' Court, the case must be sifted by the grand jury, which determines whether or not the evidence warrants further proceedings; if the decision is affirmative, a "true bill" is returned; if the evidence is insufficient, the case is dismissed when the grand jury returns "no bill." Both Magistrates' and Special Sessions Courts are New York City courts, but the County courts are state entities.

Following the customary pattern, the Magistrates' Courts—the poor people's courts—deal with the largest number of persons. The fifty-eight courts in the New York City Magistrates' Court system in 1953 handled 1,492,762 cases, of which 91.5 percent were summary offenses, 7.2 percent were misdemeanors, and 1.3 percent were felonies. From time to time, special Magistrates' Courts have been created to deal with special kinds of cases. Among these are the socialized courts—Adolescent Courts, Youth Terms, Girls' Term, and Narcotics Term; and the Home Term also has responsibility for certain types of youth cases.[14]

A startling picture of the dispersal of effort in the New York City situation is seen in this over-all summary of the youth courts:

> New York City has no less than eighteen courts and court divisions especially concerned with youth cases: a section devoted to Youthful Offender proceedings in each of the five County Courts, a court arrangement in each borough for Youthful Offender proceedings in the Court of Special Sessions, three Adolescent Courts, two Youth Terms, Girls' Term, Narcotics Term, and Home Term. Add to these courts the many other courts and court parts into which youths may be directed, and the number is considerably greater.[15]

This miscellany of courts and court proceedings may be described very cursorily as follows:

[14] *Justice for Youth*, pp. 6-7.
[15] *Justice for Youth*, pp. 42-43.

(1) The *Youthful Offender Law*, passed in 1943, permits the criminal courts (Court of Special Sessions and County Courts) to treat offenders between sixteen and nineteen as "youthful offenders," giving them a noncriminal status. Discretionary with the court and district attorney, determination rests upon probation investigation and sometimes clinical tests.

(2) The *Adolescent Courts*, in Brooklyn, Queens, and Richmond, after preliminary examination of an alleged offender between sixteen and eighteen years of age, with the consent of the assistant district attorney assigned to the court, may substitute a wayward minor complaint, under the Wayward Minor Act of 1923, for the criminal charge. The Wayward Minor Act itself applies to those between sixteen and twenty-one who are allegedly developing habits and associations that may lead to crime. The first Adolescent Court was established in Brooklyn in 1935; it was adopted in Richmond in 1953.

(3) *Youth Term* is a Magistrates' Court branch established in Manhattan and the Bronx for persons between sixteen and twenty and differs from the ordinary police court mainly in segregation of defendants from prisoners of other ages.

(4) *Girls' Term* is a city-wide Magistrates' Court branch with jurisdiction over girls from sixteen to twenty-one in the wayward minor category. Its procedures are similar to Children's Court, with informal hearings, probation investigations, and individualized planning.

(5) *Narcotics Term* is a Magistrates' Court branch established in 1952 to administer an Adolescent Drug Users Law. It may commit for treatment without a finding of criminality any person from sixteen to twenty-one years of age who is found to be a drug user.

(6) *Home Term* is a Manhattan court with jurisdiction over intrafamily controversies, which also deals with boys between sixteen and twenty-one under wayward minor proceedings.

All the courts described may use varied dispositions such as discharge, commitment, or probation.[16]

Within the Magistrates' Court system alone, there is uncertainty as to whether a person stops being young upon becoming nineteen (as in Adolescent Court) or twenty (as in Youth Term) or twenty-one (as in Girls' Term and Home Term). The overlap, confusion, and incon-

---

[16] This description was adapted and paraphrased from the chapter "Young People in Trouble," in the Gellhorn study.

sistency of approach is demonstrated by an example cited in the Gell-horn study. A girl under nineteen may be charged with being a shop-lifter and tried in Special Sessions as a criminal, or if the judge and assistant district attorney are impressed favorably, she may be dealt with as a youthful offender. But if she were over nineteen she would be tried as a criminal because the Youthful Offender law says she is no longer youthful after her nineteenth birthday. In that event, she might be tried in Girls' Term as a wayward minor rather than as a shoplifter.[17]

As a result of the dispersal previously described, the volume of youth cases is so low in each court that youth sessions are held only during parts of each week, sometimes only for an hour or two. Despite recent improvements, clinical services are hopelessly inadequate, and casework services through probation departments are not at all satisfactory. There are considerable disparities in the caliber of probation personnel, to a certain extent due to extreme salary differences from one court to another. The County Courts, being state courts, have a so-called mandatory budget. The budget of New York City must provide for them willy-nilly, but the other courts, being city courts, can be budgeted as the city fathers deem suitable—which usually means quite inade-quately.[18]

The Gellhorn study concluded that a new, integrated attack must be made on the problem of law administration as it affects young people. It was pointed out that youthful offenders, being neither juvenile nor adult, are uncertain, often unclear and confused about themselves, their obligations, and their status. And the report com-mented, "Certainly there is nothing in the present judicial or admin-istrative organization that is likely to diminish their confusion."[19]

The two studies relied upon here came to somewhat different con-clusions as to what should be done about the confused, crazy-quilt youth court pattern of New York City. In *Justice for Youth*, the Community Service Society makes specific reform proposals, rather too detailed for reproduction here, but essentially suggesting a city-wide Youth Court as a division of a new comprehensive Family Court. The Youth Court would be a single court for youths with both initial and final jurisdiction, and would feature extension of noncriminal adjudi-

---

[17] Gellhorn study, p. 153.
[18] *Justice for Youth*, p. 63.
[19] Gellhorn study, p. 157.

cations, elimination of the substitution aspects of present Youthful Offender and Wayward Minor procedures, mandatory investigations in all cases, and provision for flexibility in treatment. The Youth Court would have original and exclusive jurisdiction over neglect of minors sixteen to eighteen, waywardness of minors sixteen years and older, narcotics use or addiction in minors sixteen years and older, criminal offenses other than homicide by minors sixteen years and older, and those felony offenses committed by minors nineteen years and older specified by the legislature.[20] But the Gellhorn study, which had a much broader scope than youth courts, concluded that ". . . change either in law administration or in disposition and treatment of youths adjudged to be offenders, leads directly to reëxamination of the structure of criminal law enforcement in general." A separately focused study was considered advisable, but it was urged that this be done without delay because present methods were considered cumbersome, costly, and "insufficiently alive to the necessities of society and its young people." [21]

Regardless of what may prove to be the best solution for the problems described, one thing seems certain: the youth courts of New York City function as a model of what should not be done—not what ought to be done. Yet even the turbulent scene described has one bright feature: some attempt is made, however awkward it may be, to deal with youthful offenders in a specialized setting ostensibly devoted to their needs. That, at least, is a beginning. But the problem of providing adequate diagnostic and treatment resources will remain, even with "model" youth courts.

The Federal Juvenile Delinquency Act

Although it is customary to deal with federal jurisdiction over delinquents in conjunction with a discussion of juvenile courts, the Federal Juvenile Delinquency Act, which was signed by the President of the United States on June 16, 1938, is a modified criminal proceeding and is only roughly equivalent to juvenile court legislation in its basic concepts. Noncriminal procedures cannot be established for juveniles in the United States courts because the federal government does not stand in the relation of *parens patriae* to minors. Neither is it youth court

[20] *Justice for Youth*, pp. 124-126.
[21] Gellhorn study, p. 157.

legislation, properly speaking, because youth courts usually are envisaged as applying modified criminal court procedures to those beyond juvenile court jurisdiction but still under twenty-one. Nevertheless, as the New York City situation demonstrates, the upper age of youth court jurisdiction is sometimes eighteen, sometimes nineteen, and sometimes twenty, so it is not straining too far to discuss federal juvenile delinquency jurisdiction in a chapter devoted to the youthful offender, especially since over 70 percent of federal juvenile offenders are over sixteen. More extended attention is given to this problem here than is customary, for not only is this legislation important in dealing with youngsters who violate federal laws, but also some interesting intergovernmental relationships are involved; the youngster who violates a federal law has usually violated a state law at the same time, and there are issues as to who should take responsibility for applying corrective measures to him.

The Federal Juvenile Delinquency Act applies to all federal juvenile offenders under the age of eighteen, and it may be used in connection with all federal offenses not punishable by death or life imprisonment. A juvenile offender not turned over to the authorities of any state is "prosecuted" as a juvenile delinquent if "the accused" consents in writing. Prosecution is by information on the charge of juvenile delinquency, not by grand jury indictment; trial is without a jury; and the case may be heard in chambers. Under the Act, a juvenile so adjudicated has the status of a delinquent, not a criminal. He may be placed on probation or committed to the Attorney General, although the period of control must not exceed the delinquent's minority or the term for which he could have been sentenced if convicted under adult proceedings.

This description sounds pretty formidable. But, despite the quasi-criminal proceedings vis-à-vis the chancery proceedings in the traditional juvenile courts, the federal courts generally are extremely careful in juvenile delinquency proceedings to carry out the nonpunitive intent of the Act. In fact, the majority are far less formal than many juvenile courts.

The Attorney General may designate any public or private agency for the custody of the committed delinquent. The Act also contains provisions respecting detention of juveniles after arrest, requiring detention in a juvenile home or other suitable place of detention, but not permitting jail detention unless it is necessary to secure the custody of the juvenile or to insure his safety or that of others. There is provision for bail or release upon recognizance, or pending trial, the juvenile may be committed to the custody of the United States marshal, who is instructed to place him in a "suitable" detention facility, a jail being used as an alternative only when necessary. When in jail, the juvenile is to be kept in a room or other place apart from adults, if facilities for such segregation are available. A person committed under the Act may be released by the United States Board of Parole if there is "reasonable probability that . . . he will remain at liberty without violating the law." [22] Youngsters convicted under the Act and placed on probation are supervised by U.S. probation-parole officers appointed by the federal district courts. If committed to an institution designated by the Attorney General, the great majority of juvenile delinquents committed under the federal Act are housed in institutions operated by the U.S. Bureau of Prisons of the Department of Justice. During the year ended June 30, 1954, a total of 1,709 youngsters—1,622 boys and 87 girls—were dealt with by federal courts under juvenile delinquency procedure, while only 146—140 boys and 6 girls—were dealt with under regular criminal procedure. No court action was taken in 707 boys' and 66 girls' cases. The number reported diverted to state authorities during the year totaled 478 boys and 41 girls, *officially* diverted, that is; other diversions occur that are not reported upon. Altogether, 2,628 youngsters under eighteen, of whom 2,469 were boys and 159 were girls, were dealt with by federal courts during the year under scrutiny.[23] The chart reproduced on page 476 shows dispositions in cases of federal juvenile offenders over a twelve-year period. Several interesting trends are shown, particularly the 1954 rise in the number of commitments to custody (895), compared with the number placed on probation (855). This is quite different from the 1952 situation, when 728 were committed to custody and 891 placed on probation.

The whole question of federal treatment of juvenile offenders presents complications, not all of which can be considered here. Nevertheless, some issues stand out boldly and are sufficiently important to warrant some comment. Among the more perplexing questions are (1) the

---

[22] 18 *U.S. Code* 5031-5037, the Federal Juvenile Delinquency Act reproduced in Abbott, *The Child and the State*, II, pp. 435-437.

[23] *Federal Prisons: 1954*, table 26, p. 90.

CHART XIV

Disposition of Cases of Offenders Aged Under 18 Charged with Violation of Federal Laws, Fiscal Years Ended June 30, 1943 to 1954*

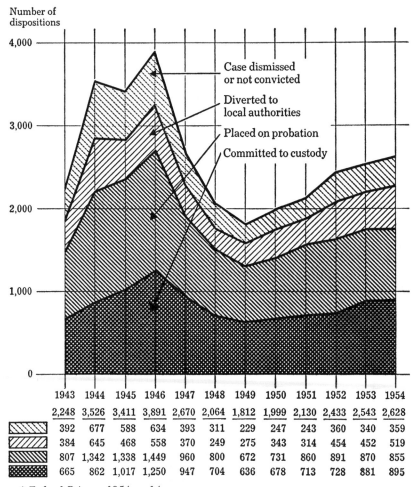

Number of dispositions

	1943	1944	1945	1946	1947	1948	1949	1950	1951	1952	1953	1954
	2,248	3,526	3,411	3,891	2,670	2,064	1,812	1,999	2,130	2,433	2,543	2,628
	392	677	588	634	393	311	229	247	243	360	340	359
	384	645	468	558	370	249	275	343	314	454	452	519
	807	1,342	1,338	1,449	960	800	672	731	860	891	870	855
	665	862	1,017	1,250	947	704	636	678	713	728	881	895

* *Federal Prisons: 1954*, p. 14.

detention problem, as it applies to youngsters who have violated federal laws; (2) the diversion of juveniles to state authorities; (3) the problems incident to probation; and (4) the vexing issue of institutional commitment to far-flung federal facilities for juveniles.

Detention Under the Federal Act

The detention of juvenile offenders against federal laws is complicated seriously by the high proportion of federal offenders apprehended some distance from their usual place of residence, a situation particularly evident in violations of the National Motor Vehicle Theft Act, the so-called Dyer Act. As the earlier discussion of detention problems indicated,[24] the youngster who is in flight is a logical candidate for detention, but it has also been shown that there are relatively few specialized detention facilities. Therefore, most youngsters violating federal laws who need to be detained must be detained in jail. Only about one-fourth of all jails in the nation are approved for federal prisoners, even on an emergency basis, and it is only realistic to assume that some of these "approved" jails are not suitable places for detention of youngsters under eighteen years of age. Many must be detained; in many cases they require detention for a relatively long period of time in order to ascertain from home communities, perhaps thousands of miles away, enough salient information to make it possible for the courts to make suitable dispositions. Very strenuous efforts are made to keep down the length of detention, and while it is still too long, in many cases it is less than detention in a child's own community is likely to be.

The latest available data indicate that for the year ended June 30, 1954, there were 1,781 juveniles under eighteen in "held-for-trial" detention status. The average length of stay in held-for-trial detention was over twenty days, and the median was over sixteen days. This does not mean that all these cases were ultimately tried in federal courts; some were diverted to local authorities.

The jail detention of juveniles charged with offenses against federal laws will remain an unsolved problem until local communities provide decent detention facilities. There is a fairly strong presumption that the average number of the youngsters in this category detained on any

[24] Compare Chap. 11, pp. 267 ff.

one day is less than one hundred, and it is quite out of the question for federal authorities to provide a national chain of detention facilities for a number such as this. Even an increase in the use of diversion to state and local authorities, discussed below, will not solve this problem entirely, because though virtually all offenses against federal laws are simultaneously offenses against state laws, many local communities are reluctant to take over responsibility for federal law violators who "belong elsewhere." If a seventeen-year-old steals a car in New York and is finally apprehended in the Middle West, it is clear that he has violated several laws—those affecting theft of an automobile where the car was taken, unlawful possession of an automobile where he is apprehended, and violation of the National Motor Vehicle Theft Act, which prohibits the interstate transportation of stolen automobiles.

But a small Midwestern community does not want a New York youngster "on its hands." It does not want to take responsibility for disposing of the case in the local courts, because almost inevitably any plan other than commitment that could be worked out would include his return to New York. But New York authorities might prove reluctant to "come and get him." Consequently, there is considerable pressure in these cases to have the federal district court take jurisdiction, and since there is clear violation of federal law, the federal court literally has no choice but to do so. Thus, the youngster becomes a "federal" detention problem. This takes the pressure off the local community; it avoids training school commitments to a state or local institution supported by the local taxpayers; and it also eliminates any question about who is responsible for transportation expenses to remove the youngster or return him to his home. This example shows how closely related detention and diversion are. The reasoning used here is common in many parts of the country, and it applies with equal force to both detention and diversion. In the case described, the youngster is above juvenile court age in New York.

It seems pretty clear that the federal courts will always have to deal with a certain number of juvenile offenders, and it seems equally clear that the problems associated with their detention pending disposition cannot be solved by the federal government but must be worked out by the provision of better detention facilities by state and local governments.

Diversion

The problem of diverting to the state and local authorities those who have violated federal laws is ostensibly a relatively simple one when the youngster has been apprehended in his own community or at least within his own state. Youngsters get involved in thefts from interstate commerce, whether from trucks or railroad cars, and they frequently violate the postal laws by theft from mailboxes. These cases do not seem to present the problems either of detention or of diversion that are characteristic of the youngster who may be hundreds or thousands of miles away from his home at the time of apprehension. But sometimes they do. Usually the need for detention itself is not particularly acute, and the violator of federal laws should be detained in accordance with the same principles that are applicable to the detention of other children. Long ago, the Wickersham Commission recognized the diversion problem, and in a report on the question of child offenders in the federal courts pointed out that during the six months ended December 31, 1930, there were 2,243 boys and girls of eighteen years and under held in jail for violations of the federal prohibition acts, immigration acts, the National Motor Vehicle Theft Act, the Anti-Narcotics Act, the Mann Act, and the postal laws. But, as the report pointed out:

> The great majority of juvenile offenders against the Federal laws are typical delinquency cases. It is only by accident that they have fallen within the Federal jurisdiction. Their offenses are such as call for the application of community guardianship. Any State would apply to them the usual technique of juvenile delinquency treatment.[25]

The Wickersham Commission strongly urged that the federal government be empowered to withdraw from the prosecution of juveniles and to leave treatment of their cases to the juvenile courts or other welfare agencies of their own states. The Congress speedily acted and in 1932 passed legislation enabling United States district attorneys to forego prosecution of any person under twenty-one years of age arrested and charged with the commission of any federal crime and to surrender

[25] Report on the Child Offender in the Federal System of Justice, pp. 2-3.

the offender to the state authorities under escort by a United States marshal, provided that the person signified his willingness to be returned, or the state in question completed appropriate extradition proceedings.[26] Although this was a clear mandate from Congress, and although later developments indicate that the Children's Bureau and the Department of Justice worked together on the theory that most of the cases involving children could be ultimately transferred to local juvenile courts, there were certain clear-cut barriers in the way. A high proportion of charges against juveniles in federal cases were filed in southern states, notably Alabama, Florida, Georgia, Louisiana, South Carolina, and Tennessee. By 1933, after only a year's experience, it was recognized that diversion would not be speedily realized. The crux of the problem was pointed out in the 1934 Annual Report of the Secretary of Labor, which stated:

> It is clear from the year's experience that the objectives will not be quickly realized. In the States selected for special work the State resources for care of juvenile delinquents are quite inadequate. Juvenile courts are often such in name only and lack provision for adequate probation service; there are sometimes no detention facilities for juveniles except the county jails, and some of the institutions are planned and operated in accordance with old theories of repression and punishment. . . . In such States the development of more adequate agencies must precede success in the program of transferring Federal delinquents to the care of home agencies.[27]

More recent information indicates that the states about which there was considerable concern are still unable to provide facilities, at least, federal courts rather than local courts and other facilities continue to be used. The latest available information shows that the federal district courts in the six states identified in 1933—Alabama, Florida, Georgia, Louisiana, South Carolina, and Tennessee—disposed of 515 juvenile cases; 186 offenders were committed to custody, and 115 were diverted to state authorities, a surprising increase from the 57 of the previous year. The other cases were either dismissed, or not convicted, or placed on probation. The 186 commitments to custody represented about 21

---

[26] 47 U. S. *Statutes at Large* 301 (approved June 11, 1932).

[27] *Twenty-First Annual Report of the Secretary of Labor for the Fiscal Year Ended June 30, 1933*, pp. 71-72; sections of which are in Abbott, *The Child and the State*, II, pp. 433-435.

percent of the juvenile commitments by all federal district courts.[28] During the same year, the federal district courts in the six New England states—Maine, Massachusetts, Vermont, New Hampshire, Rhode Island, and Connecticut—disposed of a total of five cases of federal juvenile offenders; of these, one was committed to custody, and one was diverted to state authorities.

This raises the interesting point that statistics of cases actually dealt with in federal courts do not give a true index of the extent that diversion is used. When the federal courts are being used for youthful offenders under the Federal Juvenile Delinquency Act in such large numbers in certain areas of the country and in such small numbers in other areas, it is quite evident that the key to the extent of diversion is the unofficial action that takes place when jurisdiction is assumed by local authorities with consent of the United States district attorney. Obviously, in the Southern states named a great many cases that might well have been dealt with under state laws are referred to the federal courts for disposition. This is interesting, because the states in question are strongly identified as "state's rights" states. In any case, these states, when a federal law is broken, seem to want a large number of juvenile cases dealt with by the federal courts rather than by the local community. This creates a serious dilemma, because the federal correctional facilities available when juveniles are committed to custody are hundreds and even thousands of miles away.[29]

It seems apparent that whenever possible these cases should be dealt with locally. When this does not happen, there ensues a senseless waste of the taxpayers' money, as well as thoroughly unsound planning for the youngsters in question. It should be made clear that the federal authorities are concerned about this problem and their official opinions have been expressed without equivocation. Nevertheless, the local authorities are not so clear, and in effect they "pass the buck" to the federal government. Presumably there will always be some cases in which diversion is not used because of a juvenile court upper age limit below that of the federal Act. Keeping federal control may avoid

[28] *Federal Prisons, 1954*, table 28, pp. 92-93.

[29] See *Interim Report*, Committee on the Judiciary, pp. 25-27, for a review by the Senate Subcommittee to Investigate Juvenile Delinquency of the diversion problem, and a strong criticism of the Department of Justice for failure to develop criteria for the United States attorneys. The Subcommittee acknowledged that a manual was in the course of preparation.

turning over a youngster for criminal court proceedings in the receiving community.

Probation of Federal Juvenile Offenders

Of 2,628 federal juvenile offenders whose cases were disposed of during the year ended June 30, 1954, 855 were placed on probation, compared with 895 committed to custody. In these probation cases, 170, or about one-fifth, were dealt with under the so-called "deferred prosecution" plan, or "Brooklyn plan," first used in the Eastern District of New York (Brooklyn) in 1938. This device, endorsed by Attorney General Tom C. Clark in 1946, involves the holding in abeyance by the United States district attorney of all legal processes during a period of unofficial supervision by a probation officer. Only "good risks" are chosen, based on a probation officer's study of all factors in the case. If the offender so treated makes a satisfactory adjustment, the case is closed without further action, and a court "record" is averted. If he gets into difficulty, the original complaint is prosecuted.[30] This method has interesting legal implications which cannot be discussed here, including the fact that its unwise use may deprive a person of his "day in court." Its use is increasing somewhat, from about one-tenth of all cases in 1947 to one-fifth in 1954.

This is not the place for an extended review of the work of the federal probation system, but the importance of this program is not measured simply by the number placed on probation, because in virtually all cases of federal juvenile offenders some service is provided, such as a presentence investigation by a federal probation officer. Therefore, taking this into account, the number affected by federal probation activities is around 2,500 annually at the present time.

Although there have been many improvements in recent years, the status of the federal probation program still leaves a great deal to be desired. Federal probation-parole officers are appointed by the federal district courts. Although the total service is under the general supervision of the Administrative Office of the United States Courts, which in turn reports directly to the Judicial Conference of the United States, the role played by the Division of Probation of the Administrative Office is mainly an advisory, consultative, and leadership one. This

---

[30] Printzlien, "Deferred Prosecution for Juvenile Offenders."

does not imply that the role described is unimportant. Actually, under the long-time direction of Richard A. Chappell, and more recently under the Chief of Probation, Louis J. Sharp, considerable strides have been made. The point is that this program, except for certain policy matters, is controlled by the federal district judges who appoint the probation staffs. There is no centralized control of the federal probation services.

The Administrative Office of the United States Courts, in coöperation with the Bureau of Prisons of the Department of Justice, publishes *Federal Probation*, considered by many as the outstanding journal devoted to correctional philosophy and practice.

In 1942, the Judicial Conference of the United States, comprising the senior judges of the various federal circuits and the Chief Justice of the United States, set up qualifications for the appointment of federal probation officers. In addition to certain character, health, and age traits, these specify the requirement of a liberal education at college level, and experience in personnel work for the welfare of others for not less than two years, or two years of specific training for welfare work in an appropriate school, college, or university. Certainly these standards are minimal; they are below the National Probation and Parole Association recommendations. But even the recommendations of the Judicial Conference may be ignored and are ignored by some members of the federal judiciary. As the Director of the Administrative Office of the United States Courts, Mr. Henry P. Chandler, pointed out in his 1954 Annual Report, sixteen new probation officers were appointed in 1954; fourteen met the educational requirements, but only eight met the qualifications of experience. A total of only eight officers —exactly half—met the standards of both education and experience. Two met neither requirement. As the Director tersely remarked, "This is a disappointing record." [31]

At the end of 1954, the number of authorized probation officer positions was 316, an increase of only four over the number at the end of 1953. Nevertheless, the average caseload for supervision of each probation officer increased during the year from ninety-two to ninety-four persons. When it is considered that the supervisory load probably should not exceed fifty, and that the officers in question averaged seven

[31] *Annual Report of the Director of the Administrative Office of the United States Courts: 1954*, p. 71.

and a half investigations per month, it is clear that the total load was exceedingly heavy. Using National Probation and Parole Association standards, which at present count each investigation as five points, and each case under supervision at a given time as one point, this works out to 133.5 units per worker, as against a recommended fifty units per worker under the Association's standards. It is unmistakably evident that moderate year-by-year increases in the number of federal probation personnel could not solve the total problem, nor could there be very much opportunity for careful, imaginative work with federal juvenile offenders without a service properly implemented by adequate numbers of qualified personnel. Although a substantial increase in diversion of juveniles to local authorities is highly desirable, it is certain that the utilization of appropriate local resources requires cultivation, which in turn demands that a considerable amount of time be devoted to each case.[32] In June, 1955, the Congress finally recognized the long-standing needs of the service, and the personnel authorized was increased by nearly one-fourth. This should produce real improvements in a relatively short time.

Despite the limitations suggested here, the federal probation service ranks very high with respect to the caliber of its personnel. Perhaps because appointments to the federal bench are lifetime appointments, the mine-run political upheavals characteristic of many state and local probation services have not jeopardized the federal system. Federal probation officers are not under civil service, although personnel practices and salary scales are in accordance with the various federal classification and salary acts. At the end of June, 1955, the annual entrance salary for federal probation officers was about $4,500. In relationship to other types of federal employment, the salary level is entirely too low, and this is bound to have effects upon recruitment and preparation for this important field.[33]

[32] One of the present writers (Flynn) has participated in federal probation officer three-day training programs conducted by the Administrative Office in various parts of the United States. Since January, 1950, a permanent training program for newly-appointed federal probation officers has been operated in Chicago under the direction of Ben S. Meeker, Chief Probation Officer for the Northern District of Illinois. By the end of 1954, sixty-one officers from forty-two courts had attended the two-weeks intensive program. For a description of this training program, see Meeker, "The Federal Probation Service Training Center."

[33] The qualifications of probation officers and their functions are discussed elsewhere in this book; see especially Chap. 14.

Commitment of Juveniles by the Federal Courts

Commitment procedures affecting federal juvenile offenders are susceptible to radical modification under the Federal Youth Corrections Act signed by the President on September 30, 1950. But certification that facilities and personnel were available to implement the Act did not come until January 15, 1954, and then only for the area east of the Mississippi River. The courts are not bound to use its provisions for the youthful offenders covered by the Act, namely those seventeen to twenty-one years inclusive. There is an overlap between the Federal Juvenile Delinquency Act and the Federal Youth Corrections Act affecting those who are seventeen but not yet eighteen. Use of either Act is within the discretion of the court, although the Youth Corrections Act is supposed to be used if a period of control longer than that available under the Juvenile Delinquency Act appears necessary, or if the current offense is serious and the offender has been previously committed to a penal or correctional institution.[34]

During the year ended June 30, 1953, 745 juveniles were sentenced under Federal Juvenile Delinquency Act procedures to "serve" more than one year. Of these, 45 percent had been committed previously to an institution of some kind, and 71 percent previously were committed to an institution as delinquents, or placed on probation, or both. As might be expected, interstate transportation of stolen automobiles was the most frequent offense in commitments—72 percent of all cases of juveniles committed to federal institutions. Other types of larceny, including postal thefts and thefts from interstate commerce, represented the second largest category.

Three institutional facilities are used for federal juvenile offenders: The National Training School for Boys at Washington, D.C., which provides care and treatment for both federal cases and District of Columbia cases; The Federal Correctional Institution at Englewood, Colorado; and Natural Bridge Camp, Greenlee, Virginia. During 1954 the National Training School for Boys had an average of 227 federal cases and 205 District cases; the Englewood institution had an average population of 387; and the Natural Bridge Camp had a population of 70.[35]

[34] Reed, "The Federal Youth Corrections Act in Operation."
[35] *Federal Prisons: 1954*, p. 11.

Like Alcatraz, the National Training School has been a thorny problem to the Federal Bureau of Prisons for many years. In its 1953 Annual Report, the Bureau commented as follows:

> Although a considerable amount of effort has been devoted to the development of a competent staff and the organization of a sound program at the National Training School during the fourteen years it has been under the jurisdiction of the Bureau, the institution still falls far short of providing the facilities necessary for effective care and treatment of juveniles. The earliest buildings were erected in 1872 and from that date forward units were added with little evidence either of long-range or short-range planning. The so-called cottages in which the boys live are without exception too large to lend themselves to constructive living. All of the buildings require a considerable expenditure for maintenance and repair, and few are suited to the purposes for which they are used. . . . we are badly handicapped by a makeshift, superannuated plant which is so located that a tremendous part of the staff's energies must be devoted to day-to-day problems of supervision of youngsters rather than to the creation of a more dynamic program.[36]

Although there is no question as to the wholehearted attempts that are being made by the United States Bureau of Prisons to cope successfully with the problem of committed federal juvenile offenders, the barriers to really adequate programs are extensive. Even though personnel quality is high—for example, the present superintendent of the National Training School is Dr. Louis Jacobs, a U. S. Public Health Service psychiatrist—and although personnel are recruited on a career basis and civil service operates in practically 100 percent of all positions, the acute problem of geographical distances related to the number of youngsters received from the courts makes it eminently clear that institutional treatment is primarily a responsibility that ought to be assumed by the states to whatever extent is feasible. Despite innuendos and even open declarations that the "federal government is trying to take over all problems" in various areas, the evidence in this field makes it very clear that the Federal Bureau of Prisons for a long time has been trying to get the states to take over their rightful responsibilities. Until this happens, the problem of dealing constructively with juveniles who violate federal laws will not be solved satisfactorily.

[36] *Federal Prisons: 1953*, pp. 17-18.

The Youth Authority Movement

One of the most controversial developments in recent years is the youth authority movement, which has been defined by one expert as "a *reorganizational movement,* concerned with renovation of a state's apparatus for dealing with juvenile delinquents or youthful criminal offenders." [37] This is a debatable definition, for many advocates of the youth authority plan would not agree with Mr. Rubin's tempered version of what the youth authorities actually are. Nevertheless, an analysis of the existing youth authority provisions in the states adopting such legislation seems to bear out in substance the Rubin statement. By the end of 1953, eight states and the federal government had enacted some form of youth authority legislation. But a close look at the laws passed by the legislatures of California (1941), Minnesota (1947), Wisconsin (1947), Massachusetts (1948), Texas (1949), Arizona (1951), Kentucky (1952), and Illinois (1953), and by the Congress of the United States in 1950, reveals their extreme dissimilarities one from the other. Rubin's definition seems to be virtually the only one that contains them all. Because of their striking differences rather than similarities, generalization about them is difficult, and a state-by-state review of the legislation enacted and implemented requires far more detailed analysis than would be justified here. Some picture of the diversity can be seen in Rubin's very useful chart of youth authority provisions in the first five states passing legislation, compared with the Model Act originally promulgated by the American Law Institute in 1940 but not followed completely in any state adopting this form of legislation. The differences between state laws and the Model Act are relatively enormous ones, and not matters of minutiae or minor modifications.[38]

In addition to the states actually passing youth authority legislation in one form or another, a number of other states which have considered youth authority legislation have adopted some kind of program dealing with the problems of youthful offenders, so the authority movement unquestionably has had an impact extending far beyond the states

[37] Rubin, "Changing Youth Correction Authority Concepts."
[38] See Table H, p. 488.

TABLE H: Youth Authority Provisions*

	MODEL ACT	CALIFORNIA	MINNESOTA	WISCONSIN	MASSACHUSETTS	TEXAS
NAME	Youth Correction Authority	Youth Authority	Youth Conservation Commission	Div. of Ch. Welf. and Youth Service in DPW	Youth Service Board	Youth Devel. Council
STAT. REF.	1940 Adopted American Law Institute	1941 ch. 937; Welf. & Insts. Code Div. 2.5, ch. 1	1947 ch. 595	1947 ch. 546, 560 (1949 ch. 376)	1948 ch. 310	1949 ch. 538
ADMIN. ORG.	3 man full time bd. apptd. by gov., 9 yr. staggered terms, bd. selects chmn.	3 man full time bd. apptd. by gov.; 2 from list of advisory panel (6 pres. of quasi-public prof. assns.) 4 yr. staggered terms, gov. selects chmn.	6 apptd. by gov. (3 pub. officials ex-off.; dir. of div. of insts., chmn. of parole bd., juv. ct. judge), staggered terms, gov. selects chmn.	Div. of DPW. Bd. may appt. citizen committee with gov.'s appvl. to advise on programs and problems, DPW dir. selects div. head	3 man full time bd., apptd. by gov. from list of adv. committee on children & youth (15 apptd. by gov.), 6 yr. staggered terms, gov. selects chmn.	6 apptd. by gov. and 8 state officers ex-off.; DPW dir. is chmn.
AGE JURIS.	16-21 from crim. or juv. ct.	Discretionary, 16-21 from crim. or juv. ct.	Minors convicted of crime, sentenced to less than life. Juv. ct. commitments to tr. schools	Minors sentenced to less than life, juvs. not released on probation	Juv. ct.; children convicted of crime after juv. ct. waiver (under 18)	Juv. ct.
TYPE COMMITMENT	Indeterminate	Indeterminate to 25, subject to max.	Indeterminate to max.	Definite (fixed by ct.), 1 yr. min.; or indeterminate to max.	Indeterminate to 21	Indeterminate to 21
PROB.	Granted by auth.	By ct.	By ct.	By ct.	By ct.	By ct.
ADMIN. OF FACILITIES	Auth. is mainly diagnostic; permitted to admin. facilities	Manages insts.	Manages state tr. schools	May be given management of treatment facilities	Manages insts.; may use other facilities	Manages insts.
DURATION OF CONTROL	To 25. Juv. ct. commitments to 21; if over 18, 3 yrs. Unlimited control on appvl. of ct. may continue where release is dangerous	To 25 for felons; 23 for misdems. Control may continue by ct. order but only to max. for offense. Juv. ct. commitments to 21	To 25, or max. for offense. To 21 for delinquents. Control may be trans. to another agency after 25 where release is dangerous	Unlimited, with appvl. of ct. Jury trial on dangerousness may be demanded. Juv. ct. commitments to 21	To 21; unlimited with appvl. of ct. Boy 14-18 convicted of crime may be committed to bd. to 23, or punished as adult	To 21
DISCH. PAROLE	At any time	At any time	At any time	2 yr. min. for felons, except with appvl. of ct.	At any time	At any time

* Rubin, "Changing Youth Authority Concepts."

immediately affected. New York, which has firmly resisted through the years efforts to enact youth authority legislation, in 1945 created a State Youth Commission, which has the fundamental purpose of stimulating local communities to act in connection with delinquency problems. Lowell J. Carr in 1950 called the New York program, which in its first five years had spent, or caused to be spent by the state-aid device, $7,000,000, and about $20,000,000 in nine years, "the most broadly conceived and the best financed delinquency control effort on a state-wide basis under way at mid-century." [39]

As a matter of fact, it is clear that the entire movement has arisen from the dissatisfaction with prevailing methods of dealing with youthful offenders. Enough has been said about the situation concerning youth and crime to demonstrate that public concern unquestionably has some justification in fact. Presumably this concern is directed not toward a particular age group but toward youth generally. When a community is alarmed about youthful offenders, it rarely thinks of the problem in terms of statutory age limits of juvenile court jurisdiction or the niceties of divisions of jurisdictional responsibility among state and local governments, but rather concentrates upon the undiluted fact that the community is faced with a difficult, even threatening situation for which some remedy ought to be found. Naturally, if this concern can be brought under control and diverted into constructive channels, this is all to the good. Despite certain misgivings about the youth authority movement that will be indicated, it would be less than fair to deny that it has transformed community alarm into specific action resulting in either nominal or extensive improvements in dealing with juvenile delinquents or youthful offenders. Whether these improvements would have taken place under some other set of circumstances and with a different kind of formula is impossible to know. In any case, with its various real hazards and potential harmful effects, the youth authority movement has been able to funnel anxiety and alarm into a device that has had some merit wherever it has been used.

Background of the Youth Authority Movement

Publication of *Youth in the Toils* (1938), based on a study conducted under the auspices of the Community Service Society of New York,

---

[39] Carr, *Delinquency Control*, p. 455; See also Capes, "New York State's Blueprint for Delinquency Prevention."

provoked considerable discussion and some consternation at the way youthful offenders above juvenile court age were treated in the New York City correctional "system." [40] Altogether, the book is a scathing denunciation of practices that prevailed at the time, and its exposure of conditions in the aptly named "Tombs," Manhattan's now abandoned detention facility for untried prisoners, produced sharp reaction. The authors recommended a Delinquent Minor Court for those aged sixteen to twenty-one, which would separate the judicial function from the disposition function. Thus, the question of guilt or innocence would be settled apart from determination of the form of treatment to be used for those found guilty, with treatment decisions being based on diagnostic examinations by experts in a dispositions board.

Obviously, this is a pretty radical proposal, cutting deeply into what has always been considered a judicial prerogative, and it has not been adopted anywhere in the way Harrison and Grant proposed. The idea of a dispositions tribunal or board itself is not a new one; Governor Alfred E. Smith of New York advocated such a board in 1929. The dispositions board approach seems to be a device for dealing with the sentencing dilemma faced by the courts.[41]

Subsequent to the Harrison and Grant study, the American Law Institute appointed a committee to consider the findings, and on the basis of the committee's recommendations the Institute established the Criminal-Justice Youth Committee, charged with responsibility for drafting a model statute, which after numerous revisions finally appeared as the Model Youth Correction Authority Act. (The same committee's Model Youth Court Act has not been put into effect anywhere.) The Model Correction Act, which removes from the courts even the power to place on probation, provides for the commitment of youthful offenders for disposition to a state panel known as the Authority, under a completely indeterminate sentence with neither minimum nor maximum. In effect, the dispositions function is transferred to a state agency, unlike the court panel suggested by Harrison and Grant. Some limitations were placed upon the Authority's action in holding an offender beyond a specified time, chiefly through judicial review. The Authority was authorized to use any facilities in the state as well

[40] Harrison and Grant, *Youth in the Toils.*
[41] See Chandler, "Latter-Day Procedures in the Sentencing and Treatment of Offenders in the Federal Courts"; and Campbell, "Developing Systematic Sentencing Procedures."

as to construct facilities as funds were appropriated. Particularly significant were the age limitations suggested—youths from sixteen to twenty-one committed by either the criminal or juvenile court. But in fact, in all the youth authority legislation adopted, with the single exception of the Federal Act, the great majority of cases coming under the jurisdiction of the authorities are those normally under juvenile court jurisdiction; and even the Federal Act overlaps with the Federal Juvenile Delinquency Act in the age bracket seventeen but not yet eighteen.

Professor John Barker Waite, a member of the committee responsible for the Act, has described it as follows:

> The proposed Correction Act, then, is not a radical offer of new and untried practices, supported only by theory. On the contrary *it does no more than gather together the practices actually in effect and accepted as wise* under the legislation of various states, and other practices—such as effective assistance in law-abiding conduct after release—which, though not yet in utilization under governmental authority, *have been followed by private agencies and are approved by all students of the problem.* Its essential value as a proposal for legislation is that it gathers together these desirable but scattered practices, not all of which are yet followed in any one state, and *integrates them into a coördinated procedure for diminishing that burden of repeated criminality from which the public now suffers.*[42]

Shortly after the adoption of the Model Act by the Institute, a special adviser, John R. Ellingston, was employed. For a decade, he was literally the "apostle" of the youth authority movement in this country. Mr. Ellingston's operations had an impact on a large number of states, far more than the number of states adopting the authority idea in one form or another would suggest. His missionary crusade was aided considerably by California's adoption of the Youth Authority plan in 1941, and it is interesting to observe that California's plan comes closer than any of the others to the Model Act. At least until the present time, California has been successful in implementing its youth authority plan, aided by the selection of top-flight persons for the Authority and its insistence upon the recruitment of adequate personnel. The result has been that California, generally speaking, provides a greater variety of treatment resources than other "authority" states, even though the

[42] Waite, "The Youth Correction Authority Act."

diagnostic phases of the program were not fully implemented until two new diagnostic and reception centers were completed in 1953.

While Mr. Ellingston's role presumably was that of consultant on the youth correction authority plan, he became in fact a consultant on juvenile delinquency. The American Law Institute always recognized that the plan would have to be adapted to the various states; but since it has taken on the general appearance of a program for juveniles as contrasted with older youthful offenders, it seems reasonable to question whether the deviations have not been so extreme as to vitiate the American Law Institute's plan. Instead of dealing with youthful offenders, the chief interest has been one of reorganizing services for juveniles. This is not said in condemnation of Mr. Ellingston's activities. As he himself explains it:

> It is to be noted that the decision to extend the Youth Authority plan to include all committed juveniles was not made by the American Law Institute. In fact, the decision was made not by individuals at all; it was made by the stubborn and irreducible fact of the failure of existing industrial schools to provide delinquent children effective individual treatment aimed at their rehabilitation. In the main, these schools for juveniles, like prisons for adults, provide custody and punishment to fit the crime. People who have discovered the chaotic and punitive nature of most correctional schools for delinquent children naturally feel that the place to begin applying the rational principle and procedures of the Youth Authority program is with these delinquent children.[43]

Although there are difficulties in generalizing about the youth authority movement, in most instances there is a pattern. Without interfering with the probation functions of the court, usually the juvenile court, a youngster is committed to a central state agency which presumably has facilities for reception, diagnosis, and classification as well as a variety of facilities available to which children may be appropriately sent for necessary treatment. This central state agency or "authority" has been given different names in the various states: California Youth Authority; Minnesota Youth Conservation Commission; Wisconsin Division for Children and Youth (prevention activities) and Division of Corrections (other "authority" functions), Department of Public Welfare; Massachusetts Youth Service Board; Texas Youth Development Council;

[43] Ellingston, "The Youth Authority Program."

Arizona Youth Authority; Kentucky Division of Youth Authority, State Department of Welfare; and Illinois State Youth Commission.

Usually the length of treatment is determined by the central agency, whose diagnostic and release functions are performed by a panel. Theoretically, treatment can be of any kind based upon the youngster's individual needs, and it can last for as long as the authority believes necessary. Usually the authority plan involves considerable attention to community services intended to prevent delinquency. In other words, it has important preventive as well as treatment goals.

Unfortunately, not all states, even those that have had experience with the use of the authority for five years or more, have fully implemented the basic notions involved. In some instances it is evident that not much more than a paper reorganization of state services has taken place. While this may be due to lack of leadership on the part of the authority itself, the most common cause is legislative penury. Reorganization itself, no matter how extensive it may be, cannot and does not provide the personnel and facilities needed to cope with the youthful offender problem.

While not all of the issues involved in the youth authority movement can be discussed here, certain problems deserve more extended consideration. In question form these are: (1) What has been done by the youth authority movement for youthful offenders in the sixteen-to-twenty-one age category? (2) What have been the effects of the movement on the treatment of juvenile delinquents, whether below sixteen years of age or overlapping with the sixteen-to-twenty-one age group? (3) What has been the impact of the youth authority movement on the organization of services for those affected by the various legislative enactments, whether juvenile delinquents or youthful offenders?

In considering these questions, it should be noted that there is available a substantial study of youth authority programs operating in five states—California, Massachusetts, Minnesota, Texas, and Wisconsin—conducted by Bertram M. Beck at the request of the American Law Institute, which wanted a ten-year evaluation of the Institute's work in this field. The Beck study is a candid, factual description of existing programs, particularly in terms of their relationship to the detailed provisions of the Model Act, and some of his findings are undoubtedly reflected in these comments, even when not specifically identified.[44]

[44] Beck, *Five States.*

The Youth Authority and Youthful Offenders

The impact of the youth authority movement on the group which originally aroused the interest and concern of the American Law Institute is relatively difficult to measure, simply because the youth authority states have applied the plan chiefly to juvenile delinquents. In two of the five youth authority states studied by Beck—Texas and Wisconsin—the authority deals only with juveniles; in Massachusetts, over 90 percent of the commitments were delinquents from juvenile courts; over a four-year period 80 percent of the admissions in California were juvenile delinquents committed by the juvenile court; and in Minnesota, which has a larger proportion of youthful offenders committed by the criminal court to the authority than any of the other states, 64 percent of all commitments in slightly more than two years were juvenile delinquents committed by juvenile courts.[45] Kentucky and Illinois, which have been added to the group of authority states since the Beck study, have jurisdiction over juvenile delinquents only.

Nevertheless, Beck concluded that in California and Minnesota, where the youth authority actually has dealt with youthful offenders, the results had been salutary. Because of the diversity of institutional facilities that had been developed, results were particularly notable in California; considerable progress also had been made in Minnesota, even though the institution to which youngsters in the youthful offender group were committed was not under the jurisdiction of the authority. About one-fourth of all those received and given diagnostic studies in Minnesota were released at the completion of the diagnostic period to return to the community under supervision. (The Minnesota Youth Conservation Commission reported in 1955 that in the six and one-half year period beginning March, 1948, it had effected savings of $726,225 by diagnostic studies that resulted in early return of youngsters to the community on probation. But such statements are to be taken with caution. The provision of state diagnostic facilities may result in more commitments by the courts because in "doubtful" cases the courts may resolve their doubts by commitments, knowing that the youth will be returned to the community if studies show this to be desirable. This is not a criticism of the over-all method, the Commis-

[45] Beck, *Five States*, pp. 55-56.

sion, or the courts—but rather a suggestion that the kind of savings actually made cannot, for the reason noted, be translated into dollar terms.) Inevitably, the conclusion must be that the youthful offender group has been benefited by the youth authority movement in the only places where the youthful offender group has received any significant amount of attention.

Whether this was because the states in question were ready for improvements for this group in any case or the improvements for the group are directly attributable to the youth authority plan simply cannot be answered one way or the other. The evidence available is quite inconclusive, particularly because California since the early 1940's has undergone a reformation in the whole corrections field that has brought it from one of the worst of the states to one of the best. The California situation is complicated further because the upper age of juvenile court jurisdiction is twenty-one, with the criminal courts having concurrent jurisdiction in certain kinds of cases from age eighteen to twenty-one. There were many interrelated factors: a serious crime problem; the careful selection of personnel appointed to the new program; the provision of real leadership by Governor Earl Warren and the Authority members; the impact upon the entire state correctional system of the development of an Adult Authority, which tries to do for adults what the Youth Authority does for youthful offenders—all these suggest that the apparent success of the youth authority plan could have resulted from other factors or that the improvements that have taken place might have occurred without the Authority plan.[46] All the evidence seems to indicate that the Minnesota situation has been improving, and Minnesota, unlike California, has not been the scene of spectacular upheaval in the corrections field.

On the basis of the very fragmentary indications available, and weighing rather heavily the entire logic of the youth authority plan itself, one is inclined to conclude that if given any kind of chance, this plan has real merit for dealing with those above juvenile court age limits. Certainly the plight of the youthful offender in this nation has not improved very much from the time that Harrison and Grant wrote their vivid report. While speculation as to what might have happened

[46] Ellingston, *Protecting Our Children from Criminal Careers*; see also the reports published from time to time by the California Youth Authority, Sacramento, and *California Youth Authority Quarterly*; also Freeman, "The California Youth Authority."

may seem idle, one cannot help but wonder whether setting the sights on the youthful offender group as a target and keeping them there might not have resulted in more constructive activity in a larger number of states.

Mr. Beck points out that from the time of the development of the Model Act, there was no continuing review of the work done by Mr. Ellingston, the Institute's special adviser. Because he was dealing with questions involving juvenile delinquents much of the time, and because it was necessary that he take a stand on some highly important and controversial issues, he represented the Institute in effect, even though the Institute itself was without a policy.[47]

The Youth Authority and Juvenile Delinquents

The Beck study concluded that the Youth Authority Movement bettered treatment facilities for thousands of juvenile delinquents committed to the care of the state.[48] But he also concluded that the youth authority plan was treading on dangerous ground. At first glance, it would seem that if the betterment of thousands of children had come about in the states with youth authority programs, the only thing necessary to do to better the conditions of other thousands of juvenile delinquents would be to extend the plan to other states. But there is no evidence to support the notion that improvements were made solely in youth authority states, or even that the youth authority states have advanced their programs for dealing with juvenile delinquents beyond those of comparable states. Certainly, there are no definitive studies that make valid comparisons possible. But it is important to keep in mind the fact that the youth authority movement is essentially a reorganization movement, and in some states this may mean little more than giving a newly created state agency powers that already have been vested in another state agency. As a matter of fact, the notion of a separate state plan for youthful offenders was predicated chiefly upon the need to provide integration of services for a group above juvenile court age, for whom services might be scattered among several state agencies. But this is not the case in a great many states with respect to state functions in treatment of juvenile delinquents.

[47] Beck, *Five States*, p. 138.
[48] Beck, *Five States*, p. 53.

An interesting example of this point is found in a report on youth authority legislation prepared by the Illinois Legislative Council in 1952:

> . . . in Illinois the welfare department has developed many of the component parts of a youth authority, and little would need to be added to make the practice in this state equal the best such program in any state. Major missing elements are commitments of youths to the department instead of to a specific institution, completion of a fully developed diagnostic center, and establishment of forestry and work camps. But for these lacks, Illinois has every service which is included in any state's youth authority program. . . .[49]

Of paramount importance is the point that may be made very emphatically: Commitment to a department instead of to a specific institution, the development of diagnostic centers, and the establishment of forestry and work camps do not require the creation of a new agency. Virginia has utilized commitment to a state department since 1922; diagnostic centers have been developed in New Jersey and New York; and forestry camps have been established in a number of states not having a youth authority.[50]

Therefore, it seems evident that the youth authority movement cannot be credited conclusively with improvements for services for juvenile delinquents that conceivably might have taken place without the movement. As far as juvenile delinquents are concerned, there is literally nothing new in the youth authority plan that makes a logical case for its application to this age group. Regardless of this, it should be admitted that because a new agency was created, because it was on the whole well publicized, and because it had certain ingredients that appealed to the public, some real improvements may have been brought about that otherwise might have been delayed indefinitely. Whether its virtues were exaggerated or not, there are some indications that the plan produced larger legislative appropriations for services for juvenile delinquents than otherwise would have been made available. However different from the

---

[49] "Youth Authority Legislation."

[50] In an unpublished report dated December 1, 1950, dealing with the Illinois training school population, Frank Flynn recommended a plan for commitment to the Department of Public Welfare, the development of a diagnostic center, and the establishment of forestry camps. For a strong statement making the case for centralized classification and allocation, see "Coordination of the Program of Institutional Care of Juvenile Delinquents in Pennsylvania."

original proposals it may have been in practice, the youth authority concept has a "new look," and this may have helped to improve services by providing better financing, although this is not proved completely. In a number of the "authority" states at least, state programs for dealing with juvenile delinquents were more or less in the doldrums, and in some of these states, child welfare services were badly neglected. In other words, the youth authority movement came into a vacuum of a sort and offered the state what seemed to be an opportunity to provide an integrated service for delinquents, but usually for delinquents only, not youthful offenders.

The Youth Authority Plan and Organization for Services

For the youthful offender group, as distinguished from the juvenile delinquents, the development of commitment to a central agency, the use of diagnostic services, and the creation of appropriate treatment programs and facilities aimed at rehabilitation rather than punishment would represent a considerable step forward in a substantial number of states—in fact, in nearly all of them. It is necessary to keep in mind that, generally speaking, this group is dealt with in precisely the same manner as adult criminals are, and while the use of commitment to a central agency, diagnosis, and specialized treatment facilities is not a new theoretical approach to the problem, extension in these directions would be desirable. In any event, no potential negative effects can be discerned.

New York State has been using a reception center for youthful offenders since November 1, 1945.[51] The problems of the Center are described by Beck.[52] The Center is regarded as "the cornerstone of the state treatment facilities for older adolescents." Currently the Center processes about 1,200 youths a year received from the courts for assignment to appropriate facilities.

With respect to juvenile delinquents, however, the general situation is altogether different. In the field of child welfare, the trend over many years has been in the direction of planning integrated services for children, whether they are delinquent, neglected, or dependent. This trend is notably true of state services. But what the youth authority movement

[51] Kendall, "The New York State Reception Center."
[52] Beck, *Youth Within Walls*, Chap. I.

does is to remove from the general child welfare field a special group of children labeled juvenile delinquents, and ostensibly create a new agency and set of services to deal with them. This is not true, however, in Wisconsin, where the functions of the youth authority, which is practically unrecognizable as a youth authority, actually are divided between the Division for Children and Youth and the Division of Corrections of the State Department of Public Welfare, or in Kentucky, where the Division of Youth Authority is in the State Department of Welfare.

When the Youth Authority is created as a separate state agency certain additional problems arise. The mere establishment of a new state agency does not automatically provide the personnel and facilities to implement it. As a matter of fact, by setting up duplicate services, it may have the opposite effect by thinning out existing personnel available in any state, because separate services for different types of children require separate staffs. Even if money is available, personnel may not be. Youth authorities the country over have been confronted by this dilemma.

Likewise, the proliferation of new agencies is generally frowned upon by public administration experts, and in state after state commissions looking into the organization of state government have recommended reductions in the number of agencies rather than the creation of new ones. In Massachusetts, for example, the state's "little Hoover Commission" criticized the authority program, stating:

> Instead of maintaining two agencies, one for the care of delinquent children, and the other for the care of dependent and neglected children, with top administrative officials directing both programs, a better and sounder program for the care of all children could be maintained under one agency with appropriate services such as institutional care, foster home services, community services, and services to the individual families.[53]

Too often, in states in which the various state child welfare functions are submerged within a large department of public welfare responsible for the mentally ill, for public assistance, and a host of other social welfare functions, the issue of a separate agency for delinquent children, as against unified services for all children who need them, is discussed in the light of existing programs. Actually, there is a growing belief that

[53] *Tentative Report on Study Unit No. 4*, p. 9, also cited by Beck, *Youth Within Walls*, p. 47.

in the larger states services for children might well be combined in a separate state agency. But, because of overlapping and duplication, it seems unnecessarily wasteful to carry this to the extreme of providing a separate state agency solely for delinquent children.

Any state considering the youth authority plan has an obligation to study existing services carefully in order to provide a rational basis for action. The Wisconsin plan, which provides integrated services for delinquents within the framework of an omnibus department of welfare, seems most suitable when the reorganization of state services for those of juvenile court age is required. But the state looking at the total question should be most concerned about its facilities for dealing with the youthful offender problem, which stands out as the major unsolved issue in nearly all the states. Because of the overwhelming importance of the youthful offender problem, it seems worthwhile to examine the pertinent federal legislation.

The Federal Youth Corrections Act

Although the Federal Youth Corrections Act was passed by the Congress in 1950 and signed by the President on September 30 of that year, implementation of the Act did not begin until January 19, 1954, when formal certification was forthcoming that facilities and personnel were available. As of July 1, 1955, about 425 persons had been committed as youthful offenders under the Youth Corrections Act, and about forty other youthful offenders had been referred to the Youth Correction Division for observation, study, and a report of findings to the court for its guidance in determining sentence.

The Federal Youth Corrections Act does not follow the recommendations of the American Law Institute's Model Act with respect to making mandatory the commitments to the Youth Correction Division, which corresponds to the Authority, or in removing from the courts the power to place convicted offenders on probation, or even in removing youthful offenders from the usual statutory penalties and placing them under completely indeterminate sentences. But it carries out in general the basic philosophy of the Model Act and, with respect to the ages covered, eliminates from consideration the greater proportion of those generally designated as juvenile delinquents, because the age range used is seventeen to twenty-one years inclusive, although there is no minimum statutory age limit. Judges may continue to place offenders on probation and may sentence them under the provisions of the usual federal criminal statutes applicable to adults, but the new Act has three important provisions:

(1) The court may commit to the Attorney General any young offender aged seventeen through twenty-one for an indefinite period up to six years. A person so sentenced may be released by the Youth Correction Division of the Board of Parole at any time; he must be released from custody under supervision at the end of four years.

(2) If the court believes that the youth requires treatment or supervision for a period of more than six years, it may commit him for an indefinite period not to exceed the statutory maximum penalty for the offense.

(3) The court is empowered, if uncertain as to how to proceed, to place the youth for sixty days in the custody of the Attorney General for study, diagnosis, and recommendation prior to the imposition of sentence.[54]

As procedure is presently envisaged, any youth sentenced under one of the new Act's provisions will be placed in a classification center for intensive study by specialists. Reports and recommendations will be forwarded to the Director of the Bureau of Prisons, who will recommend to the Youth Correction Division of the Board of Parole a program of treatment for the consideration of the Division. The Director determines the institutional program with the advice of the Board. The Bureau of Prisons submits periodic reports to the Youth Correction Division, and the Division, acting in its Parole Board capacity, determines when institutional treatment will be discontinued and decides upon conditions of release.[55] The "flow" chart on p. 502 gives a graphic description of operations under the Act.

There are numerous questions raised by the new federal program, such as the need for coöperation and integration of the work of the federal bureaus concerned, the great need for skilled personnel to implement the Act, and the requirement of varied treatment facilities if the purposes of the Act are to be fulfilled.

The Senate Subcommittee to Investigate Juvenile Delinquency em-

[54] 18 *U.S. Code* 5005-5025.
[55] See Bennett, "The Federal Youth Corrections Program"; also Reed, "The Federal Youth Corrections Act in Operation."

CHART XV *Flow Chart: Operations Under Federal Youth*

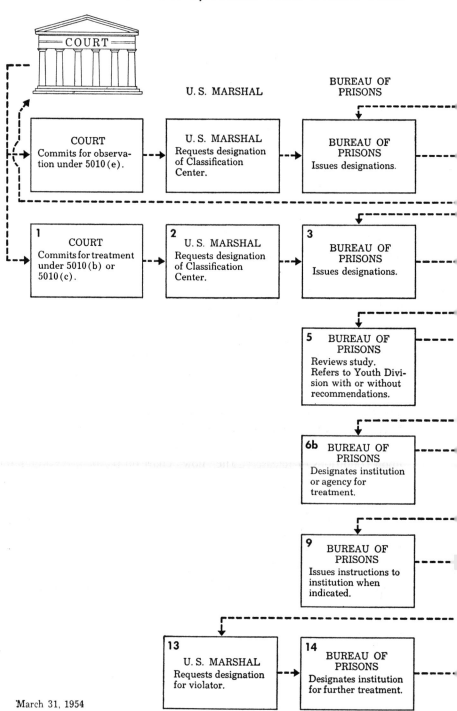

COURT

U. S. MARSHAL

BUREAU OF
PRISONS

COURT
Commits for observation under 5010(e).

U. S. MARSHAL
Requests designation of Classification Center.

BUREAU OF PRISONS
Issues designations.

1 COURT
Commits for treatment under 5010(b) or 5010(c).

2 U. S. MARSHAL
Requests designation of Classification Center.

3 BUREAU OF PRISONS
Issues designations.

5 BUREAU OF PRISONS
Reviews study. Refers to Youth Division with or without recommendations.

6b BUREAU OF PRISONS
Designates institution or agency for treatment.

9 BUREAU OF PRISONS
Issues instructions to institution when indicated.

13 U. S. MARSHAL
Requests designation for violator.

14 BUREAU OF PRISONS
Designates institution for further treatment.

March 31, 1954

Corrections Act

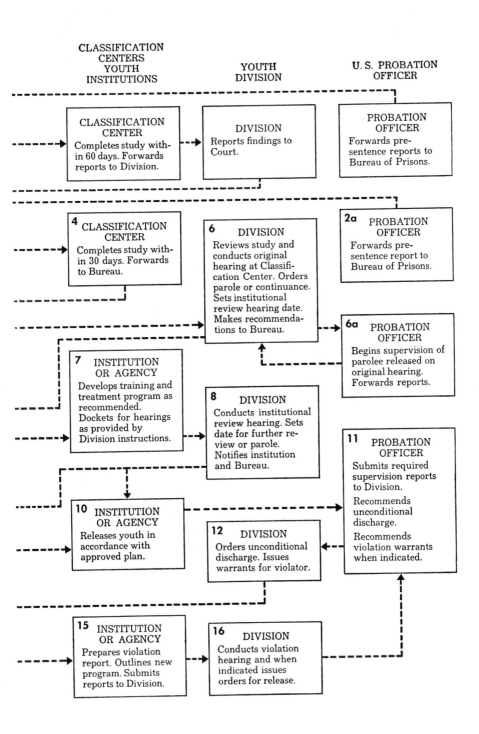

CLASSIFICATION
CENTERS
YOUTH
INSTITUTIONS

YOUTH
DIVISION

U. S. PROBATION
OFFICER

CLASSIFICATION
CENTER
Completes study within 60 days. Forwards reports to Division.

DIVISION
Reports findings to Court.

PROBATION
OFFICER
Forwards pre-sentence reports to Bureau of Prisons.

4 CLASSIFICATION
CENTER
Completes study within 30 days. Forwards to Bureau.

6 DIVISION
Reviews study and conducts original hearing at Classification Center. Orders parole or continuance. Sets institutional review hearing date. Makes recommendations to Bureau.

2a PROBATION
OFFICER
Forwards pre-sentence report to Bureau of Prisons.

6a PROBATION
OFFICER
Begins supervision of parolee released on original hearing. Forwards reports.

7 INSTITUTION
OR AGENCY
Develops training and treatment program as recommended. Dockets for hearings as provided by Division instructions.

8 DIVISION
Conducts institutional review hearing. Sets date for further review or parole. Notifies institution and Bureau.

11 PROBATION
OFFICER
Submits required supervision reports to Division.

Recommends unconditional discharge.

Recommends violation warrants when indicated.

10 INSTITUTION
OR AGENCY
Releases youth in accordance with approved plan.

12 DIVISION
Orders unconditional discharge. Issues warrants for violator.

15 INSTITUTION
OR AGENCY
Prepares violation report. Outlines new program. Submits reports to Division.

16 DIVISION
Conducts violation hearing and when indicated issues orders for release.

phasized the fact that the Youth Correction Division of the Board of Parole and the Bureau of Prisons, even though both are under the Attorney General, are two separate bureaus. The Subcommittee stated bluntly that the success of the entire operation will depend on how closely these two bureaus can coöperate. It pointed out that the question of proper implementation was a crucial issue, and cited testimony before the Subcommittee which indicated "that the facilities and personnel of the federal institutions which are to be utilized by the Youth Correction Division are inadequate, with inadequate salaries being paid for work which requires a high degree of skill. Lack of psychiatrists and inadequate parole staff are of particular concern." [56]

This also suggests the highly important question of the number and variety of facilities that will be created under this Act. There is no way of knowing in advance the extent to which the Act will be employed by the courts, since its use is entirely optional. But from the preceding comments by the Senate Subcommittee and a review of recent reports of the Federal Bureau of Prisons, it is evident that crucial personnel deficiencies may develop. At the same time, the diagnostic and classification functions inherent in this operation require an adequate number of highly specialized personnel strategically located. At the present time, the Correctional Institution at Ashland, Kentucky, is being used as a diagnostic and classification center. With only one institution available, and that east of the Mississippi, a special problem is created if a person committed for observation must be returned to the court for sentence. This might involve going from the Northern District of New York to Ashland, Kentucky; coming back to northern New York for sentence; and then winding up at Ashland, again, after commitment to custody.

One thing is perfectly obvious. With all the potential values of this Act for youthful offenders against federal laws, it will take all the skill and knowledge of the federal agencies concerned to make it operate effectively. There are real problems here, and the operations of the Act will be watched with interest. The delay of nearly four years in making a start, presumably affected by the change in administration in Washington, is cause for some concern, although with all the obstacles suggested, caution may have been highly desirable. In any event, unless Congress is willing to appropriate adequate funds for implementation of the excellent objectives of the Act, not very much will come of it. Federal

[56] *Interim Report*, p. 30.

activities on behalf of youthful offenders, and society as well, might be effective in breaking the stalemate that seems to block off really constructive action in this most important and most difficult segment of the crime problem.

Leonard V. Harrison ably summarizes this troublesome question in the Preface to the Community Service Society report, *Justice for Youth:*

> We are fully aware of the seriousness of youth crime. We could elaborate, fruitlessly we think, in speculation about causes. It is enough to say that youths are mature in physical strength, that they are often heedless, hostile and violent, and that they have brought large numbers of citizens within the shadow of great fear of their individual and group-mass attacks upon the public peace and public safety. . . . Unless an offending minor, branded and disabled for awhile by imprisonment, is to be discarded, so far as any hopeful expectations of him for the future are concerned, it becomes necessary to do our best in strengthening him to play the role of the useful citizen in the community. Life in confinement through formative years is a process of negative value, although it is the best that can be contrived in the case of some of the more difficult youths, under our present limited knowledge of how to straighten warped personalities.
>
> An erroneous belief, widely held by many adults who exercise the power to punish, is that a youth of abnormal behavior will react to punishment with normal, logical reasoning for his own benefit. . . . The central difficulty is that errant youth do *not* react in a normal pattern of thought and emotion as would the distinguished justice who recites his favorite lecture and pronounces sentence. The already bent twig does not sway in the same arc as does the straight one, not even in the same breeze.[57]

For Further Reading

OSWALD, RUSSELL G., "Correctional Treatment," in *Social Work Year Book. 1954* (New York, 1954), pp. 135-42.

> A brief but very knowledgeable article by one of the nation's foremost correctional agency administrators. It gives the reader considerable insight into problems of this field, and, although it deals chiefly with adult correctional programs, it must be remembered that the youthful offender normally is dealt with as an adult.

[57] *Justice for Youth,* pp. ii-iii.

Justice for Youth: The Courts for Wayward Youth in New York City,
Community Service Society of New York City, Bureau of Public Affairs
(New York, 1955).

> Prepared by Bernard C. Fisher under the general direction of Leonard
> V. Harrison, this survey is useful chiefly as a portrait of the confusion
> in the courts and the crazy-quilt pattern that has developed in a great
> metropolitan area.

GELLHORN, WALTER, *Children and Families in the Courts of New York
City,* The Association of the Bar of the City of New York (New York,
1954).

> This comprehensive review of the work of the courts contains an
> excellent chapter, "Young People in Trouble," which graphically de-
> picts the plight of youth before the courts in the nation's largest city.

PRINTZLIEN, CONRAD P., "Deferred Prosecution for Juvenile Offenders," in
Federal Probation, 12 (March, 1948), pp. 17-22.

> This is a detailed description of the so-called "Brooklyn plan" of hold-
> ing all legal processes in abeyance during a period of unofficial super-
> vision by a probation officer.

RUBIN, SOL, "Changing Youth Correction Authority Concepts," in *Focus,*
29 (May, 1950), pp. 77-82.

> This is a controversial but persuasive article which defines the youth
> authority movement as essentially a reorganizational movement.

CHANDLER, HENRY P., "Latter-Day Procedures in the Sentencing and Treatment of Offenders in the Federal Courts," in *Federal Probation,* 16 (March,
1952), pp. 3-12.

> This is an able review of the issues and problems in the area of sen-
> tencing by the director of the Administrative Office of the United
> States Courts.

BECK, BERTRAM M., *Five States: A Study of the Youth Authority Program
as Promulgated by the American Law Institute* (Philadelphia, 1951).

> A definitive and useful analysis of youth authority programs that pro-
> vides the only independent review of this development as it actually
> operates.

FREEMAN, DOROTHY, "The California Youth Authority," in *The Social
Service Review,* 22 (June, 1948), pp. 211-33.

> A careful review of the development of the first Youth Authority which
> sets forth both its interesting historical background and its earlier days
> of operation.

REED, GEORGE J., "The Federal Youth Corrections Act in Operation," in *Federal Probation*, 18 (September, 1954), pp. 10-15.

In this article, which is chiefly descriptive, the essential provisions of the Federal Youth Corrections Act are presented by the Director of the Youth Correction Division of the United States Board of Parole.

Part Four | PREVENTION

Chapter 17

THE RESPONSIBILITY
OF SOCIETY

In the introductory chapter to this review of treatment agencies, it was stated that the community's responsibility for a total program to deal with the delinquency problem included far more than specific services to children identified as delinquents. Consequently, it seems desirable to review some of the programs designed to deal with delinquency in its incipient or formative stage. Although comprehensive analysis is not feasible at this point, it is possible to identify and describe briefly the more significant preventive programs and to indicate some of the important problems of evaluation that emerge in the whole field of prevention.

What Is Prevention?

Any attempt to define preventive activities in the field of delinquency presents enormous hazards both because of differences in what various persons mean by prevention and because of the generally accepted fact that delinquency itself has multiple causes. The multiple causation theory itself poses certain complications, because most social scientists today agree that it must be applied to delinquency as a whole as well as to delinquent conduct in a particular child. Furthermore, a review of the pertinent literature suggests that those concerned with prevention define it in one of three ways: (1) the sum total of all activities that contribute to the adjustment of children and to healthy personalities in children; (2) attempts to deal with particular environmental conditions that are believed to contribute to delinquency; and (3) specific preventive services provided to individual children or groups of children.

These three ways of looking at prevention are definitely interrelated, and they are not mutually exclusive. Those who take the view that anything that contributes to healthy personalities in children prevents delinquency are concerned with the roles of the home, the church, and the school, and the general opportunities for children to make normal adjustments in the communities in which they live. Likewise, those concerned with a particular condition believed to contribute to delinquency are interested in a segment of the general activities that affect the over-all adjustment of children, such as bad housing, overcrowded schools, or conditions inimical to the welfare of minority groups. Similarly, those whose main preoccupation is with services to individual children or groups of children are interested in the impact of particular services upon the children served and therefore might well be concerned about the absence of a school social work program. Therefore, even though the emphases are different, the goal as well as the object of concern and action may join together at points.

As a matter of fact, the observable indications point definitely toward a trend in the direction of agreement upon the interrelatedness of various approaches and processes of prevention. It does not seem feasible at the present time to set up a simple dichotomy of prevention as between an environmental approach and an approach by services to individuals. Such segmentation seems logically unsound. The interrelatedness of various approaches to prevention is emphasized further by the fact that preventive services are sometimes included under treatment services designed to reduce the frequency or seriousness of delinquency in specific instances. Under such a view, for example, the services of probation officers and training school programs are identified as preventive services.

Bearing in mind the interrelatedness already described, it is feasible nevertheless to distinguish preventive programs on the basis of their primary emphasis. Thus, the primary emphasis of a mass recreational program is essentially environmental, and the primary emphasis of child guidance clinic services is essentially individual. Not all preventive programs present such clear-cut differences, and despite some lack of conceptual clarity it is possible to separate arbitrarily the various major preventive programs into those that are environmentally oriented, those that are geared to specific services to children or groups, and those that are primarily coördinating devices. Before discussing specific preventive programs, it seems desirable to suggest some of the problems and cautions that must be contended with in evaluating the effectiveness of preventive programs.

Evaluation of Preventive Programs

In the evaluation of preventive programs there are no simple proofs that may be utilized. In the public health field, for example, it is possible to show a relatively clear-cut relationship between mass x-ray programs and the early identification and treatment of tuberculosis. Unfortunately, the identification of delinquents from the mass of all children who are potentially delinquent is not susceptible to the same kind of diagnosis; that is, it is not possible to take a mobile x-ray unit into a high delinquency area and sort out the children who show indications of delinquency. Nor is it possible to use mass vaccinations that will protect or immunize children from delinquent conduct. Furthermore, regardless of the seductive quality of predictive and prognostic tests of one kind or another, there simply is no instrument, test, or series of tests that has been validated as a device for predicting which children out of a particular group will become delinquent. Therefore, this absence of knowledge creates the dilemma in which proponents of preventive programs do not really know what is being prevented. And it is this point, more than any other, that makes extremely hazardous any positive statements about preventive programs in terms of their actual value or success in preventing delinquency. Mention was made previously of a recreational program that seemed to be enormously successful in reducing delinquency in a particular area, but upon examination this was found to be due to the diversion of youngsters who got into the hands of the police to the recreational agency rather than to the juvenile court. This resulted in a reduction of delinquency as measured by juvenile court statistics, but it demonstrated nothing at all as far as delinquency itself was concerned.[1] This same dilemma holds true in the case of a child guidance clinic which may deal with an aggressive, acting-out youngster referred by a school. The child so treated may not become delinquent, but there is no proof available that he would have become delinquent if he did not receive treatment.

It seems clear that the role of any preventive agency is likely to be most difficult to assess. This is particularly true because delinquency results from a variety of causes and conditions, and it is unlikely that any given program can deal simultaneously with all of the potential factors that may lead to delinquency. Therefore, the focus of most programs tends to be upon only one or perhaps two elements of the total societal and individual configurations that may lead to delinquency. This also means that many programs that are aimed ostensibly at delinquency prevention are trying to use a one-shot panacea for delinquency. Yet many of the programs now in operation have never been evaluated, and some that have been evaluated have been reviewed by methods that are inadequate or even suspect. In a sense, this means that the public has been asked to support programs largely on faith and with little or no scientific evidence to demonstrate that the program in question actually has any effect upon delinquency one way or another. Inevitably, this means that the confusion is magnified to the extent that one group, for example, may be pressing for rigid enforcement of child labor laws as an answer to juvenile delinquency, while another group, equally well-intentioned, may be using delinquency as an argument for relaxing stringent child labor laws.

Although it is certainly true that a great deal of research is needed in connection with delinquency prevention programs, it is equally true that some of the problems presented may not be researchable by any known methods. If delinquency emerges from a welter of factors, and only one facet of the situation is being dealt with and evaluated, the uncontrolled and possibly uncontrollable other factors may be responsible for whatever takes place, whether it be an increase or a decrease in delinquency in the group under consideration. This is not meant to imply that efforts to test various types of preventive programs should be abandoned;

[1] See Chapter 8, pp. 203 ff. For a more critical example see Alinsky, "Heads I Win and Tails You Lose."

it is simply an attempt to emphasize some of the truly enormous difficulties that are involved in such testing.

In any event, this situation makes a relatively strong case for the development of prevention programs that are multiphasic in nature, that is, projects that employ a variety of techniques dealing with as many factors as possible. Of course, this does not lessen the difficulties of measurement; in fact, it tends to enhance them to a certain degree.

Three brief examples will serve to illustrate this problem of evaluation.

1. *A Boys' Club Referral.* Johnny and Tommy, both aged fifteen, are referred by the school counselor to a boys' club situated in a high delinquency area. Both youngsters are disciplinary problems in the school; they are doing failing work; and they are known to spend a great deal of time hanging around corners with generally disreputable youngsters of about their own age. In both instances the referrals are made after discussion with the boys and their parents and with club staff. Both boys plunge into club activities with great interest; their school behavior improves, and both begin to do passing work. All goes well for nearly a year, until Johnny is apprehended by the police after a wild chase while driving a stolen car which crashes and seriously injures two other boys. Johnny is sent to the state training school. Tommy, on the other hand, goes along quite uneventfully, leaves school when he is able to get his working certificate, and obtains a position as plasterer's apprentice. Several years later he is still doing well and ostensibly keeping out of trouble. Meanwhile, Johnny, released from the training school, is in the community only a few months when he is again apprehended in a stolen car and returned as a parole violator. When last heard from, he is serving a burglary sentence in the state reformatory.

The problem here is whether the club, situated in a high delinquency area, "failed" in the case of Johnny and "succeeded" in the case of Tommy. Actually, no one can give a definite answer to this question. There are too many possibilities to contend with, not the least of which is the one that Tommy—the nondelinquent—may have been involved in three or four stolen car escapades without having been caught. We know nothing of the strengths of their respective homes from the standpoint of emotional climate; we know nothing at all about the influences that played upon them outside of the club situation; we know nothing about their roles as leader or follower; and we have only a superficial knowledge of their personality characteristics as demonstrated by misbehavior at school and getting failing grades. Even if it is assumed that both made about the same adjustment in the club situation, and even if a great many other similarities are assumed, the presence of one significant difference between the two boys might be sufficient to account for the beginning of a criminal career by one and the formation of normal work habits on the part of the other.

2. *A Recreational Center and a Low Delinquency Rate.* A recreational center serves about one-half of the children aged ten to seventeen, corresponding to juvenile court age, in a community that year after year has a high delinquency rate. But the rate among youngsters being reached by the club is only one-fifth as high as that of the group not being reached by the club. Does this prove the efficacy of the club in question from the standpoint of its delinquency prevention role? Actually, the facts as given neither prove nor disprove the club's importance as a delinquency preventive. There is no way of knowing, for example, whether the youngsters who attend the club, by a process of natural selection or even by staff determination, are less prone to delinquency than those who do not attend the club. Even if the group attending the club were a good statistical cross section from the standpoint of racial and economic conditions or any other series of indices, salient information as to the extent of delinquency-proneness among the club and nonclub children would still be absent. Furthermore, if there were sound predictive or prognostic devices that indicated clearly that the two groups were evenly matched as to delinquency-proneness, the same general reasoning could be applied as in the cases of Tommy and Johnny. A great many other factors contributing to their total development certainly would not be controlled by the club situation *per se.*

3. *A "Big Sister" Volunteer Service.* Mary and Jane, both fifteen, are referred by a public assistance worker to a big-sister-type organization because they are known to have been staying out at night later than the approved standard in the community permits, and in general seem not to get along well at home. The volunteer "big sisters" assigned to the two girls apparently make excellent progress during the first six months. A good relationship is established, wholesome and worthwhile

activities are discussed and shared, and some amelioration in the home situations appears to occur. But after six months, Mary begins to back-slide; she stays away from home overnight on several occasions, she begins to run with a "wild gang" of boys; and finally she becomes pregnant and is committed by the juvenile court to the House of the Good Shepherd. Meanwhile, Jane continues her good adjustment, begins to develop an intense interest in her studies, and upon graduation from high school enters nurses' training and apparently is getting along very well.

Here are two distinctly dissimilar results, even though certain factors were relatively similar in each situation, and each included the development of a good relationship. Also, both of the "big sisters" were ostensibly equally skilled in getting along with teen-age girls. But Jane's desire for attention, especially attention from boys, may have been a strong motivation; it is even conceivable that her relationships with her family deteriorated because of the contrast between the well-groomed, poised "big sister" and her slovenly, unkempt mother. In fact, any number of potential differences could be explored here, but just as in the two examples given previously it is clear that the program in question cannot control all aspects of the lives of children.

These examples should make it clear that the evaluation of the results of any preventive program is likely to be highly speculative. This is meant neither to reflect upon the integrity of those involved in so-called preventive programs nor to question the worthwhileness of any of the programs themselves. But it does seem clear that any statistical demonstration of their usefulness is extremely difficult to measure. Probably the point needs to be made that it is not always necessary to wait for statistical proof that a program is effective before putting it into operation. As was mentioned earlier, the case for many of the programs commonly identified with delinquency prevention rests upon a somewhat different basis, namely, the need for children to have opportunities for normal growth and development.

In their excellent recent review of prevention programs, Witmer and Tufts give a very clear picture of the problems involved in evaluation. Although the report itself is concerned chiefly with a limited group of programs selected on the basis of evaluations that have been attempted, the authors have described in slogan form the programs dealt with as follows:

Give children a good place to play and good leadership in their recreational pursuits.

Increase neighborhood cohesiveness and sense of responsibility.

Identify potential delinquents and mobilize community resources in their behalf.

Give them psychiatric or social treatment.

Redirect the energy and interests of delinquent gangs.[2]

It seems clear that the value of the programs described in such general terms has a certain inherent logic. While this does not negate in any way the desirability of scientific measurement, it means that to some extent the development of such programs must be urged as desirable activities on behalf of children in this highly complex civilization, not as scientifically proved delinquency prevention devices. This is not begging the question, but it is separating the problem into two distinct parts: (1) the desirability of scientific measurement, and (2) the general consensus that these programs have a motivation and a rationale that on the whole seems to be sound. It seems better to recognize this separation, rather than to confuse the two.

Programs Designed to Deal Primarily with the Environment

Before discussing specific programs that may be grouped arbitrarily in various categories, some recognition should be given to the broad preventive aspects of sound family life, the significant possibilities inherent in religious programs, in properly conceived and adequately implemented school programs, and in wholesome community facilities of all kinds. Nevertheless, any extended analysis of the roles of these basic social institutions in their relationship to the problem under consideration is clearly beyond the scope of the present volume. At this point, it seems sufficient, therefore, to make clear the authors' convictions that anything that strengthens these institutions contributes to the wholesome and normal development of children; and conversely, anything that threatens or renders them impotent is likely to have deleterious effects upon children. Furthermore, it is difficult to see how substantial improvements in the present delinquency picture will be made unless there are large-scale improvements in basic social institutions as a whole, even in society

---

[2] Witmer and Tufts, *The Effectiveness of Delinquency Prevention Programs*, p. 7.

itself. Even so, the need for social reorganization of the very complex cultural structure, while probably desirable and even necessary, is a distracting will-o'-the-wisp to those who are concerned with the here-and-now.

Large-scale reform in our society, especially of the kind that would conceivably have a direct impact upon the behavior of children, seems simply not to be near at hand, and the immediate problems deserve consideration on the basis of what should be done at this time. It may well be argued that the programs actually discussed in this chapter represent trivia and minutiae and that the problem of prevention ought to be looked at mainly in terms of basic social institutions rather than in the segmented focus used here. Of course, this is a debatable issue, but the selection made is based upon the program having a major or primary emphasis upon delinquency prevention, and certainly it cannot be argued that the home, the church, the school, and the community exist primarily to prevent delinquency. This does not imply that the social institutions identified have no importance in a delinquency prevention program. As previously pointed out, their contributions are pervasive and their scope is too broad for inclusion here.

Recreation

Recreational programs of one kind or another have become involved in the delinquency prevention theme chiefly because it seemed at first glance that organized, supervised recreational facilities would perform a useful task in redirecting the energies of youth into acceptable channels. Back of this was the notion that either exuberant spirits or boredom and inactivity caused youngsters to get into trouble in a climate featured by a paucity of adequate leisure-time pursuits. Very simply stated, the argument went something like this: Our youngsters have no adequate opportunity for decent recreation; instead, they congregate in pool halls or loaf on street corners, and when this kind of activity or inactivity palls upon them they are likely to indulge first in mischievous pranks of one kind or another and then in more serious offenses. The solution, also simply stated, was simply to fill this vacuum with recreational programs that would both drain off energies and provide constructive opportunities for character development. This combination of the "surplus energy" and the "keep-them-off-the-street" theories became the standard argument for recreational programs as an antidote for delinquency. Logically, the general premises involved merit rather serious consideration, but it seems even more logical to consider suitable recreational facilities as a normal and desirable part of community living, rather than as a specific antidote to delinquency as such. The proponents of the recreational approach, nevertheless, tend to believe that, by simply increasing the available facilities and directing youngsters into suitable recreational outlets, the delinquency problem can be sharply curtailed if not eliminated entirely. How extensive the increase of facilities should be and how youngsters can be made to use them are two problems that have not been solved.

One of the real difficulties in discussing the role of recreational agencies in delinquency prevention is the lack of truly evaluative studies of the real impact of these programs upon children. This is not to minimize the difficulties in the design of evaluative studies in the face of the fact that delinquency-proneness itself is not measurable with existing tools and because recreational agencies do not reach all children. For various reasons, some children, both delinquent and nondelinquent, do not participate in supervised recreational facilities. This is true of the mass recreational programs such as public parks and playgrounds, and it is true of small club groups that have been developed on the theory that the natural "gang relationships" of youngsters should be used by directing activities into positive rather than into negative channels. The result, therefore, is that there is really no way of determining whether these programs actually are effective in reducing delinquency.

Actually very little has been done in an attempt to measure the influence of various kinds of recreational programs. In their recent definitive analysis of research in this field, Witmer and Tufts found only three not very recent studies that seemed pertinent: (1) a survey by Ethel Shanas and Catherine Dunning for the Chicago Recreation Commission in 1938-39; (2) a study by Frederic Thrasher undertaken at the suggestion of the Boys' Clubs of America during the period 1927-31; and (3) Ellery Reed's study of Cincinnati group work agency clientele in 1942.[3]

Even these three studies are relatively inconclusive. The Shanas-Dunning study showed that the total extent of participation in super-

[3] Witmer and Tufts, *The Effectiveness of Delinquency Prevention Programs*, pp. 19-24.

vised play by both delinquent and nondelinquent boys was dismayingly low. During any one season, between one-third and one-half of the participants spent less than ten hours in supervised activities, and on the average, delinquent and nondelinquent boys spent about twice as much time at the movies as in supervised recreation. Thrasher's study showed that even though the Boys' Club of New York University reached a larger proportion of delinquent and potentially delinquent youngsters than of the other kinds of children, which indicated that de-linquents take to supervised recreation, there was no indication that club membership reduced delinquency. As a matter of fact, the percent-age of members engaged in delinquency or truancy that brought them to the attention of the courts increased rather than declined as the boys continued membership in the club. Disturbing also was the fact that the duration of membership was relatively brief, with fully one-third of the boys who joined in any one year not enrolling in the next year. As Witmer and Tufts point out, while there have been no additional evaluative studies of boys' clubs, the national organization from time to time has gathered information which shows that in particular areas the number of recorded cases of delinquency declined after the establish-ment of a boys' club. Nevertheless, with all of the cautions that pre-viously have been suggested with respect to the use of recorded delin-quency statistics, it is clear that such general observations about reduc-tion of delinquency do not constitute the kind of studies on which any great reliance can be placed.

The Reed study of group-work agencies in Cincinnati suggested strongly something that has been reflected in the literature for a long time, namely, that the agencies studied were reaching a selected group of the population. In fact, Reed concluded a report of his study with this statement:

> The findings of this study, however, may suggest the question of whether some group-work agencies by the nature of their programs, atti-tudes, and methods do, in fact, screen out the boys and girls who are handicapped physically, mentally, economically, or racially; or who are emotionally maladjusted; or who have an unfortunate and unhappy family background. If this is true, are they failing to serve those who need their services most? Should they be giving more attention to the problem of serving more effectively the boys and girls who are most in danger of becoming delinquents and, ultimately, burdensome and dangerous mem-

bers of society? If group-work agencies could more effectively serve such, it would be of great value to society as well as to these unhappy children and their families.[4]

Bearing in mind that one of the chief difficulties is identifying those who are "in danger of becoming delinquents," it should be pointed out that there seems to be a distinct trend in two wholesome directions: (1) increasing awareness on the part of some of the so-called character building agencies, such as the Y.M.C.A. and Y.W.C.A. children's programs and the scouting program, in the direction of gearing programs to meet the needs of the less advantaged children of the community, both in program content and in leadership training which puts emphasis upon helping volunteer leaders deal with more difficult children; and (2) attempts to reach out to youngsters who have already formed natural groups or gangs and to work with these gangs as a unit. Both of these developments seem to be significant, but whether or not they will prove to be substantially effective remains to be seen.

The Area Project Approach

The area project approach, developed by Clifford R. Shaw and his associates, has been one of the most interesting developments of the past quarter-century. The projects, of which there are now ten in Chicago, attempt to develop a sense of neighborliness and mutual responsibility in specific slum communities. Certain premises underlie this method. In the first place, a central theme of the area project movement is that leadership must be developed within the community and not superimposed from without. Shaw has been extremely critical of the leadership techniques used by a great many traditional agencies, including settlement houses, boys' clubs, and the like, on the grounds that they involve the imposition of leadership and program ideologies from outside the community. In other words, Shaw's point is that somebody else decides what is good for the community, and that this must be replaced by the development of indigenous leadership.

A second concept is that the delinquency-breeding communities can help themselves by the development of an internal cohesiveness based upon activities rooted in concern about delinquency by natural community leaders. This means that through these natural leaders, who may

‹ Reed, "How Effective Are Group Work Agencies in Preventing Delinquency?"

be precinct captains, bartenders, truck-drivers, or local "self-made" businessmen, community deterioration can be halted by involving a substantial number of the people who live in slum areas in the kinds of activities that will improve community life and give children an opportunity to grow up in decent and wholesome surroundings.

In the Chicago area projects, the program, which is tailored to meet each community's needs, is centered in a recreational and educational facility. Paramount is the notion that the activities are not an end in themselves but a means of developing unity within the community itself. It is believed that the children drawn into various activities are susceptible to identification with the more conventional forms of American behavior, and that delinquency is largely social in nature, although not exclusively so. Delinquency is considered to be a reaction to a conflict of values in which children are exposed to widely diverse points of view, resulting in confusion and the failure to incorporate acceptable standards of any kind.

The area projects operate through various kinds of neighborhood and community committees which conduct a wide variety of activities, and in addition do some direct work with children of the counseling or person-to-person type. Again, the keynote is that only the person who has status in the community, even a former delinquent, is likely to have influence upon youngsters who live in such communities. Consequently, the use of outside leadership is minimal—chiefly to discover and develop local talent rather than to bring professional resources to bear upon the situation; although in certain instances, apparently relatively few in number, referral to psychiatric resources is made for the youngsters who seem to have deep underlying personality disturbances.

Naturally it is difficult to evaluate the area projects, and to measure what effect they have on the environment itself; even more difficult is the assessment of their specific contribution to community delinquency prevention. Shaw and those associated with him have been extremely careful not to make claims with respect to success of the projects. Nevertheless, a considerable amount of work has been done with individual youngsters, especially those released on parole from training schools, and some attempts are being made currently to determine the extent to which this type of work is successful. After reviewing the pertinent literature concerning the area projects, Witmer and Tufts make the following statements as to the facts at hand concerning the effectiveness of the projects in producing change in the neighborhoods themselves. According to their evaluation, there is evidence to indicate the following:

1. Residents of low income areas can and have organized themselves into effective working units for promoting and conducting welfare programs.

2. These community organizations have been stable and enduring. They raise funds, administer them well, and adapt the programs to local needs.

3. Local talent, otherwise untapped, has been discovered and utilized. Local leadership has been mobilized in the interest of children's welfare.[5]

The area projects obviously represent a reaction to conventional forms of community organization, especially in their emphasis upon local indigenous leadership. Another Chicago program, the Back-of-the-Yards Neighborhood Council, identified with Saul Alinsky, uses generally many of the bases of the area project approach but is oriented particularly in the direction of social action. Alinsky's ideological notion is that people must feel that they are creating and securing their own objectives and goals rather than being merely recipients of governmental benevolence of one kind or another. This approach recognizes that many of the problems which seem to be related to a local community actually arise out of forces far removed from the immediate community; thus, in addition to problems being related to one another, communities are related to one another; and a segmental approach in either direction will not be productive of good results.[6] Like Shaw, Alinsky places heavy reliance on the development of natural leadership in the community, but the Council is just as likely to organize a march on Springfield or a march on Washington as it is to talk to the local alderman about the need for improved play lots. Altogether, the break with the notion of "outside" leadership represents a refreshing and probably a highly desirable element in community organization. One can see certain limitations in this kind of development, because certainly some outside leadership is necessary. As Walter Reckless has pointed out, spontaneous generation of experimental action is simply not likely to take place. As he puts it, the ferment must be implanted by someone from without,

---

[5] Witmer and Tufts, *The Effectiveness of Delinquency Prevention Programs*, p. 15; see also Burgess, Lohman, and Shaw, "The Chicago Area Project."

[6] See Alinsky, *Reveille for Radicals*, for a statement of his rather pungent philosophy.

even though the local community "carries the ball" after action gets started.[7]

Community Organization and Coördination

The process of community organization for social welfare has been described as the joining together of people of communities either as individual citizens or representatives of groups to determine social welfare needs, to plan ways of meeting them, and to mobilize the necessary resources. The focus may be a functional field of social welfare, such as leisure time and recreation, or it may be a geographical area such as a neighborhood or city or county.[8] Obviously, in its simplest form this means that people recognize a need and band together to see that the need is met. The background for various kinds of community organization activities in this country is intimately related to the highly complex structure through which various services are performed in our society. As a matter of fact, the layman is appalled when confronted with the multiplicity and diversity of agencies of one description or another operating in various fields, whether under public or private sponsorship, and it is not at all difficult to make the case for some method of avoiding duplication and overlapping of services in the interests of efficiency and economy. But the agencies in question usually are autonomous, and there has crept into the picture the development of vested interests of one kind or another and even outright jealousies between and among agencies. This means that a great many of the things that need to be done simply do not get done because they are not properly planned for and because joint efforts are relatively infrequent.

In the delinquency field, one device that received considerable attention about twenty years ago and is still very much alive in certain areas on the West Coast is that of the coördinating council, which, as the name implies, tries to coördinate efforts in the direction of delinquency control through periodic meetings of the various agencies which have to do with delinquent children. Interestingly enough, the idea seems first to have been conceived by August Vollmer, Berkeley's famed chief of police, in 1919; it received further impetus from Kenyon J. Scudder

---

[7] Reckless, *The Crime Problem*, p. 524.

[8] See McNeil, "Community Organization for Social Welfare." The definitive work in this field is McMillen, *Community Organization for Social Welfare*.

when he was chief probation officer in the Los Angeles Probation Department; and in the 1930's the National Probation Association conducted a nationwide survey of coördinating councils under the direction of Kenneth S. Beam. At the time of the Beam survey, coördinating councils were found in operation in 163 cities and towns in twenty states.[9] A review of the pertinent literature indicates that the coördinating council seems to be most effective in small communities, although Los Angeles has had a number of useful, active councils for many years. The council is usually composed of many agencies that deal with delinquents or potential delinquents, including law enforcement bodies, representatives of the schools, family welfare and children's agencies, persons active in character-building organizations and civic groups, service clubs, and churches.

Emphasis is placed upon lay participation, although professional representation is included; and it is believed by many that professional leadership is a *sine qua non* of a successful coördinating council. As a matter of fact, the organization of various types of community groups interested in the prevention of delinquency under the auspices of the state youth authorities that have emerged in recent years, virtually all of which include some phase of delinquency prevention or control as a specific objective of their programs, features heavy reliance upon the use of professional personnel for development of leadership and planning. Both California and Wisconsin, classified as youth authority states, have put very strong emphasis upon the development of community councils of one kind or another, chiefly for the purpose of getting at the facts and bringing forth a plan of united action. In Wisconsin, this has been done chiefly through county surveys in which professional staff members of the Division of Children and Youth of the State Department of Public Welfare participate, but local citizen groups have been responsible for the general planning and carrying out of local surveys. It seems clear that this type of activity is highly desirable; unquestionably, sound community planning envisages the integration of the activities of a multiplicity of agencies so that their total strength can be brought to bear upon the delinquency problem. The absence of any reference to the coördinating, planning, and research activities of Councils of Social Agencies or Welfare Councils does not imply any failure to recognize their importance. Discussion of their

[9] Beam, "Community Coordination for Prevention of Delinquency."

role is omitted because their concern is not primarily with delinquency.

While emphasis in this discussion has been upon the coördination of agency activities primarily at the local level, it should not be assumed that the profusion and perhaps confusion suggested is found solely at the local level. In many state and national organizations, there is interest in delinquency expressed in one form or another, but on the whole they have borne little or no relationship to one another. The National Conference on the Prevention and Control of Delinquency, called by the Attorney General in November, 1946, helped to bring together some of the national organizations interested in the problem, and more recently the Special Juvenile Delinquency Project operated in conjunction with the United States Children's Bureau has devoted considerable attention to the problem of lay groups, especially national organizations. The Senate Subcommittee to Investigate Juvenile Delinquency in its *Interim Report*, dated March 14, 1955, urged strongly the need for coördination of the activities of national agencies of one kind or another and had actually taken steps in that direction as a result of its earlier hearings by bringing together about twenty organizations for a one-day meeting in Washington.[10]

Legal and Regulatory Efforts

It is probably trite to remark that if delinquency could have been legislated out of existence presumably it would have disappeared a long time ago. Nevertheless, one of the interesting characteristics of recent years has been the oft-repeated attempts to enact legislation of one kind or another or to devise regulations that would curtail the delinquency problem. In view of the fact that none of these seem to have had much effect in the intended direction, it seems fruitless to spend any considerable time at this point in analyzing the various kinds of efforts that have been made. Unfortunately, many of these devices come under the heading of panaceas, which as we have already seen are hopelessly inadequate to cope with so complex a problem. Nevertheless, some of the attempts to control problems that seem to be related to delinquency have a considerable degree of merit. Laws restricting the sale of liquor to juveniles or minors seem to have a valid purpose, and whenever properly enforced they have potentially useful effects. This is equally

[10] *Interim Report of the Committee on the Judiciary*, pp. 62-63.

true of restrictions on child labor, especially as child labor laws apply to street trades and other occupations which may bring children into contact with unwholesome and unsavory elements in the community. There is, nevertheless, some question as to the upper limits of child labor legislation; this is suggested in connection with the school-work plan mentioned later in this chapter.

But in recent years there have been a plethora of devices aimed at dealing with delinquency, ranging all the way from curfew laws which require children of stated ages to be off the streets at particular hours during the evening unless accompanied by an adult to the punishment of parents whose children are delinquent. In addition, there have been periodic attempts at censorship of the mass media of communication, although in more recent years this has taken the form of a concerted drive against the so-called comic books. While there seems to be no question about the desirability of using existing laws or even erasing the loopholes in existing laws with respect to pornographic literature, there is some indication that the emphasis of recent years on the comic book, television, radio, and movies really has no scientific foundation. The curfew laws, of course, have a certain seductive appeal, generally on the theory that offenses are committed late at night by youngsters who are roaming the streets without parental supervision of any kind. Nevertheless, it seems clear that the complete enforcement of curfew laws would require far more attention than police departments can give at the present time. Consequently, most of the existing laws are selectively enforced, and this may lead to a variety of abuses and difficulties.

Services to Individuals and Groups

Although the effectiveness of various programs designed to provide services to individuals and groups identified as incipient delinquents or even actual delinquents has not been completely tested by any means, it seems desirable at least to consider some of the ways in which communities have attempted thus to meet the problem of delinquency. These services are very numerous, and they only can be mentioned rather than described at this point. Among the major public agencies providing services, in addition to the previously discussed programs offered by the police, are those made available by the schools. The case for school activities in this direction seems to be strong, chiefly because virtually all of those labeled delinquent are in the age group served by the schools, and also because of the specific connection between truancy and delinquency. This latter connection seems to be fairly definite. A very high proportion of delinquents are truants, even though the converse is not necessarily true—that all truants are delinquents is apparently not the case. The school activities in this area range from the standard attendance officer or truant officer programs, many of which have been sadly deficient both in the quality and quantity of personnel provided, to the use of school social workers, a movement which has not gained as strong a foothold as its adherents had hoped after its early enthusiastic inception in 1906-07 in Boston, Hartford, and New York.

No exact statistics on the number of school social workers are available, but the membership of the American Association of School Social Workers, the professional organization in this field, is only about 650. School social workers attempt to help children whose problems in school stem from social and emotional causes in the child, his family, or his environment. They act as a kind of liaison between and among the school and home and the community. Some schools have developed rather extensive so-called pupil counseling and guidance services, most of which are oriented toward the better adjustment of children to the school situation, but this kind of program contributes to the prevention of the kind of maladjustments that result in delinquency.

In some communities, "big brother" and "big sister" organizations under one name or another have been organized, chiefly utilizing volunteers who develop personal relationships with youngsters likely to be from the groups of children in the community who get into trouble. These volunteers are assisted and trained to some extent in their work by professional staff members. Without trying to assess the effectiveness of these organizations at this point, it should be mentioned that one of the outstanding weaknesses has been the failure to utilize adequate numbers of professional persons to assist and guide the volunteers in their counseling efforts. Disturbed children can be seriously damaged by unskillful handling.

Child guidance clinics actually originated in connection with juvenile courts. The first clinic, known as the Juvenile Psychopathic Institute, was established in connection with the Cook County Juvenile Court in 1900; but in recent years the child guidance clinics have veered away from direct concern with delinquency, although it is reasonably safe to say that many of them deal with youngsters classifiable as potentially delinquent. Featuring the team organization of psychiatrist, clinical psychologist, and psychiatric social worker, the child guidance clinic accepts referrals from many sources, but in its modern version it is likely to draw the line between those children considered treatable, which very often requires the coöperation of parents, and those considered untreatable or at least not amenable to treatment. Unfortunately, a reality factor involved here, extending beyond the question of treatability and nontreatability, is that virtually all clinics today have far more applicants than they can conveniently serve. This inevitably results in the selection of patients on a basis that makes services available to those who can use them profitably.

The Gluecks' study in the 1930's of subsequent records of 1,000 boys who had been referred by the Boston Juvenile Court to the Judge Baker Foundation Clinic (now the Judge Baker Guidance Center) showed the dismaying result that 88 percent of the boys continued their misconduct. This challenge to the child guidance clinic approach had the effect of stimulating a shift from almost exclusively diagnostic services toward treatment services. But treatment services inevitably involve some selection of those to be treated, and it seems fairly conclusive on the basis of later studies by Healy and Bronner that youngsters with marked abnormal personalities do not respond particularly well to clinical services. Although the child guidance clinics have been severely criticized for "accepting only the good risks" and for "being too selective," the argument for selectivity seems to be a sound one.[11]

One of the most interesting experiments of recent years was the Cambridge-Somerville Youth Study under the aegis of Dr. Richard Cabot of Harvard University. This was an attempt to find out whether delinquent and potentially delinquent youngsters would develop into youths of good characters if provided with the friendship and counsel of deeply interested adults who could make available to them whatever community services they needed, whether in health, education, recreation, or welfare. Although a critique of the experiment cannot be attempted at this point, the final report on the project suggests that the technique of friendly counseling and the tapping of services by

[11] Glueck, *One Thousand Juvenile Delinquents*; Healy and Bronner, *New Light on Delinquency and Its Treatment*.

interested adults seems to have little if any effect upon delinquency as such. Witmer and Tufts summarize the situation as follows:

> In conclusion, then, this experiment seems to indicate that the provision of the kind of friendly guidance and other services . . . afforded will not reduce delinquent acts or keep chronic delinquency from developing. This is not to say such services are not useful to certain children, especially to nondelinquents. The services were especially ineffectual, however, with the kinds of boys who became chronic delinquents: slum boys with indifferent, neglectful parents; seriously neurotic boys, from various kinds of neighborhoods, who had even more emotionally unfavorable homes; and feebleminded or neurologically handicapped boys whose homes, too, were poor.[12]

Other recent attempts to deal with the delinquency problem have involved what might be termed "reaching the unreached," whether as individuals or as gangs. Based to some extent upon the work of Shaw and the earlier suggestions of Thrasher, the attempts to work with gangs have been interesting and possibly productive, but as yet there have been no conclusive evaluative studies of their effectiveness. The various projects that have been tried seem to take a relatively similar form. A group worker becomes acquainted with a gang in its natural habitat, whether the pool room or the street corner, gains the confidence of the leaders, and attempts ultimately and gradually to work the group around to sublimative, constructive activities rather than destructive acts.[13]

Similarly, in the casework field, the New York City Youth Board has been extremely active in what is known as "aggressive casework," which is to a certain extent a repudiation of the general stand taken by casework agencies that motivation and desire for help are extremely important if not the ultimate determining factors in casework treatment. Eleven areas in New York City with the highest rates of delinquency were selected for operations, and in each area a referral unit was set up in schools, usually operated by the Division of Child Welfare of the Board of Education. In order to provide adequate treatment services, the Youth Board contracted with some twenty voluntary agencies to provide services on a per capita payment basis to those

[12] Witmer and Tufts, *The Effectiveness of Delinquency Prevention Programs*, p. 30; for the complete report see Powers and Witmer, *An Experiment in the Prevention of Delinquency*.

[13] See Crawford, Dumpson, and Malamud, *Working with Teen-Age Gangs*.

referred. The chief characteristic of this operation is that when parents show resistance to referrals, the project workers persistently follow through. When families still refuse service of any kind, a special project, developed in conjunction with the City Department of Welfare, Bureau of Child Welfare, takes over and attempts literally to thrust services through the door. This is a complete reversal of standard social work practice, because the criteria used in the project for case acceptance are that the parents have no recognition of the problem or demonstrate no willingness to work with it. It is still too early to know what the results of this interesting effort will be.[14]

Where Do We Go from Here?

The foregoing brief review of some of the attempts that have been made to deal with the problem of delinquency prevention provides an admittedly diffused background for a summary statement on the problem of prevention attempting to indicate the general directions that the road to improvement must take. The earlier extended discussion of the etiology of delinquency and the review of the work of the official treatment agencies should have made it quite clear that the difficulties involved in the entire field of delinquency are vexatious, perplexing, and of great magnitude. Nevertheless, the problem is of sufficient importance to demand truly constructive efforts. In moving forward, the following considerations seem pertinent:

1) Each community represents a unique and different problem. This means that the approach must have many facets and a strategic focus upon the problems that are peculiar to or different in a particular community. Furthermore, the differences are not simply as between metropolitan centers and small towns. Each community represents a different situation, and one small community may differ from another even more than it differs from a much larger one.

2) Delinquency itself encompasses a wide variety of behavior patterns and deviations of behavior that are to a certain extent community-determined. Not only is the range of misbehavior a wide one, but to a large extent the youngsters involved have normal intelligence and their misconduct cannot be attributed to gross physical or hereditary defects.

3) It seems certain that a fairly substantial proportion of delinquency

[14] See Furman, ed., *Reaching the Unreached*.

reflects strains in the American social structure affecting different types of children and families in myriad ways. Despite its roots in individual differences, delinquency as a cultural phenomenon means that to a certain extent society is the patient. Unfortunately, the American social structure has a deceptive kind of rigidity and resistance to drastic change, so that anything that smacks of social planning is likely to be

CHART XVI

*The Cost of Preventive Programs**

SPENDING money or SAVING money?
. . . what $2,500 a year will pay for:

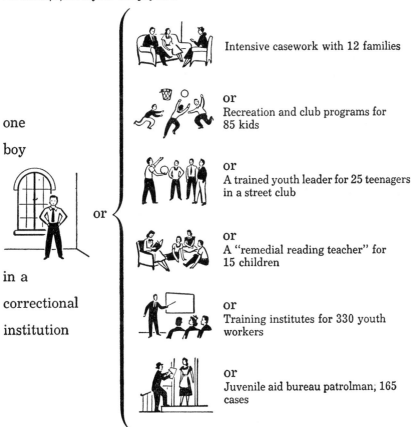

one

boy

or

in a

correctional

institution

Intensive casework with 12 families

or
Recreation and club programs for 85 kids

or
A trained youth leader for 25 teenagers in a street club

or
A "remedial reading teacher" for 15 children

or
Training institutes for 330 youth workers

or
Juvenile aid bureau patrolman; 165 cases

* *Exhibit* "B" (From Epstein, "Perspectives on Delinquency Prevention," p. 48).

regarded as radical socialism and social engineering may be considered a totalitarian device.

4) Despite this strong resistance to change, it is possible to alleviate focal points of tension which are generally productive of delinquency through more intelligent concerted action on community, state, and national levels.

5) There is a "hard core" of delinquency, which can become a major focus for attack. The studies of Bradley Buell and associates in St. Paul, Minnesota, and San Mateo County, California, demonstrate clearly that only a small proportion of the total number of families and children are involved in delinquent conduct.[15] In the San Mateo study, for example, only slightly more than 1,200 families, actually about 1.5 percent of the total number of families in the area, accounted for every detected and reported case of juvenile misbehavior as well as about half the petty crimes and misdemeanors in the entire county. This suggests the desirability of identification of the delinquent as early as possible and the use of a "saturation with services" technique. Essentially, the Buell findings document what has been known for a long time, but they may provide the kind of evidence that may result in action, which until now generally has not resulted from the observations of competent workers in the field.

6) The failure of the popular nostrums, which have become gestures to futility, should lead to a new frontal attack upon the delinquency problem. These futile efforts include the censorship of the mass media; the compulsory education of parents, as in San Francisco; the punishment of parents, as seen in numerous cities; the curfew laws; and the provision of more parks and playgrounds without any notion as to what the real need is.

7) A beginning must be made by knowing the pattern of causation. In this connection, sound research of an evaluative type, difficult though this is to work out in practice, must be expanded vastly.

8) There is need for concerted and coördinated community efforts to provide a network of preventive and treatment services available to the entire community. Coördination itself involves: (1) getting the facts; (2) promoting community understanding; (3) achieving balanced growth and maximum quality of service; (4) relating delinquency to other social problems; (5) using suitable mechanics of coördination,

---

[15] Buell and Associates, *Community Planning for Human Services.*

such as the Social Service Exchange, case conferences, and planning to avoid overlapping and duplication; and (6) movement toward a sustained, dynamic program for the over-all improvement of community conditions, especially those that seem to have some relationship to delinquency, even though our knowledge of the exact relationship is still uncertain.

9) In order to attain substantial improvements, there must be a strengthening of the agencies concerned with the total problem. An area of great promise would be to start with the so-called unofficial delinquents known to the schools and to the police. Both the schools and the police have a long way to go before it can be said that they provide really adequate services for difficult youngsters. In the case of the police, the "sidewalk dispositions" and repeated warnings unaccompanied by any other kind of service suggest that a great deal of improvement can be made. In the schools, there is a specific need for much more individualized work with youngsters who are having difficulties with reading, arithmetic, and the like, as well as the use of some scheme that will get the best teachers into the more difficult schools. In general, delinquents do not get along well in school.

10) There must be early identification of youngsters who are delinquency-prone and effective follow-through with appropriate treatment services. Although it is clear that we do not have prognostic tests that are accurate in determining which youngsters are likely to be delinquent, and this therefore tends to make the identification of the delinquency-prone quite difficult, there should be continued attempts to identify the youngsters as well as evaluative studies to determine what particular selection devices seem to have the greatest validity. This is a very hopeful area. The Gluecks' *Unraveling Juvenile Delinquency* showed that about one-half of the delinquents studied gave evidence of their delinquent traits before the age of eight and nearly 90 percent did so by the age of eleven.[16] While this does not mean that we can do an accurate prediction job at the present time, it suggests the need for further study along such lines.

11) Agencies national in scope concerned with this problem need far better support and implementation. The Child Welfare League of America, a privately sponsored standard-setting body, has made a substantial contribution to the improvement of children's services. The

[16] *Unraveling Juvenile Delinquency,* p. 257.

National Probation and Parole Association has performed a most useful task in providing consultation services to communities, especially in relationship to detention and to juvenile courts. Periodic conferences, such as the various White House Conferences that have been held since 1909, usually at intervals of a decade, and the National Conference on the Prevention and Control of Juvenile Delinquency held in 1946, have had an important impact upon the national scene. The Children's Bureau of the Department of Health, Education, and Welfare has received somewhat larger but still insufficient appropriations for work in the field of delinquency. The scope of the Bureau's services should be expanded greatly.

12) Citizen participation in this area deserves much greater consideration than has been given in the past. Too often the layman has been given a task for which he was ill equipped, such as counseling with delinquent or so-called predelinquent children. Actually the layman, through his individual efforts and through organizations of one kind or another, can make a far greater contribution than has been asked of him previously. As the layman becomes better informed about the problems of delinquency and more aware of the needs that exist as well as the deficiencies of present-day programs, he will be in a position to exert his influence in the direction of substantial improvement in existing agencies. The layman's potential has not been fully realized. While he cannot become a substitute for a probation officer, while his role as a counselor of delinquent youth is seriously open to question, and while he cannot be expected to take over responsibilities that do not become him, he can, through knowledge and awareness, be a vital force in the improvement of the important services that have been discussed.

It seems fitting to conclude this discussion with a presentation of ten priority programs proposed by Deputy Mayor Henry Epstein of New York City in his May 6, 1955, recommendations to Mayor Robert Wagner, called "Perspectives on Delinquency Prevention." This is an extraordinarily competent report which follows the general thesis of this chapter, namely, that knowledge must precede action. While the programs in question apply to New York City, they demonstrate the breadth of vision and the variety of perspectives required to deal with this whole question.

Ten Priority Programs

1. Provision of competent staff for recreational facilities already available in 27 public housing projects (for residents of projects and their neighbors); planning for staff in all the other projects not presently served.

2. Expansion of the remedial reading program in our schools to enable children to get 100 cent value on the education dollar.

3. Police services affecting juvenile delinquency.

4. Expansion of the Youth Board Street Club Project and its services to families and children.

5. Provision of programs under Youth Board contract to the three areas in Manhattan, Staten Island, and Queens where delinquency rates have increased alarmingly; contracts for casework, group work and recreation services from private as well as public agencies.

6. Reëxamination of teacher rotation policies, in an effort to assure placement of a larger proportion of our more highly experienced teachers in "difficult" schools.

7. Parent education programs centered around informal discussion groups.

8. Expansion of the "co-op" program which provides students an opportunity to complete their high school education while working half time in private industry at prevailing wages; more guidance services.

9. Inauguration of training services through the Youth Board to equip its own personnel to do an even more effective job, and to serve other departments which have approached the Youth Board for this kind of help; a fellowship study program for adding to the professional skills of workers on key projects in various city youth-serving agencies.

10. Provision for small, top-calibre units to do over-all planning and to be responsible for assessment.

For Further Reading

WITMER, HELEN L., AND EDITH TUFTS, *The Effectiveness of Delinquency Prevention Programs*, U.S. Department of Health, Education, and Welfare, Children's Bureau Pub. No. 350 (Washington, D.C., 1954).

Without question, this is the most discerning and penetrating statement of its kind. Essentially, the basic problems of evaluation are discussed, and a number of programs are described in some detail. The programs selected have been subjected to some attempts at evaluation, so in effect this is a report of where we now stand in delinquency prevention.

REED, ELLERY F., "How Effective Are Group Work Agencies in Preventing Delinquency?" in *The Social Service Review*, 22 (September, 1948), pp. 340-48.

This report of a study by an able researcher has the challenging implication that group work agencies reach a selected group of the child population and because of programs, attitudes, and methods tend to screen out the maladjusted and the handicapped.

BURGESS, ERNEST W., JOSEPH D. LOHMAN, AND CLIFFORD R. SHAW, "The Chicago Area Project," in *National Probation Association Yearbook, 1937*.

This is a good descriptive statement of the general objectives of the area projects. The area project approach, while not completely evaluated even now, may have important implications for delinquency prevention.

ALINSKY, SAUL D., *Reveille for Radicals* (Chicago, 1946).

Essentially, this is a statement of the pungent philosophy of a man with considerable experience in community organization who, like Shaw and his associates, relies heavily on the development of natural leadership in the community, breaking with the "outside leadership" tradition.

MCNEIL, C. F., "Community Organization for Social Welfare," in *Social Work Year Book, 1954* (New York, 1954), pp. 121-28.

A good summary of principles and practices in the field of community organization by a well-known social welfare specialist.

MCMILLEN, WAYNE, *Community Organization for Social Welfare* (Chicago, 1945).

This is the definitive work in this area by a distinguished scholar who has an excellent awareness of the human factors that are so significant in this field.

EPSTEIN, HENRY, *Perspectives on Delinquency Prevention* (New York, 1955).

This report, making recommendations to the mayor of New York, is a comprehensive, intelligent approach to a difficult and pervasive problem. Its implications are useful to many communities, and not only to metropolitan areas.

Appendixes

I. THE CASE OF GEORGE STONE

II. PAROLE SUPERVISION:
A CASE ANALYSIS

THE CASE OF GEORGE STONE

This is a New York case of sustained delinquency, lawbreaking, and maladjustment from which all identifying names and places have been deleted in order to protect the subject and innocent individuals associated with the case. The record incorporates contacts with and treatment procedures of private community agencies, a Children's Court, a state school for delinquent boys, an adult court, The Elmira Reception Center, Elmira Reformatory, and the State Division of Parole.

Face Sheet

NAME: STONE, George   COLOR: White   RELIGION: Protestant

DATE OF BIRTH: 10-22-29   BORN: Central City, New York

FATHER: Cyril Stone   ADDRESS: Whereabouts Unknown

STEPFATHER: Joseph Jansen   ADDRESS: 529 Sixth Avenue, Central City, N. Y.

MOTHER: Rose (Wheeler) Jansen   ADDRESS: same

SIBLINGS:

James Stone	Born 3-1-28	above
George Stone	Born 10-22-29	"
Robert Stone	Born 9-5-33	"

HALF SIBLINGS:

Joseph Jansen	Born 10-11-36	"
William Jansen	Born 4-14-38	"
John Jansen	Born 6-14-39	"
Brian Jansen	Born 10-24-40	"

Relatives

MATERNAL UNCLE	Michael Wheeler	Address: Springdale, N. Y.
MATERNAL GRANDMOTHER	Mrs. Mary Wheeler	Springdale, N. Y.
MATERNAL UNCLE	Vincent Wheeler	27 Third Street, Central City, N. Y.
MATERNAL UNCLE	Joseph Wheeler	Altman, N. Y.
MATERNAL AUNT	Mrs. Margaret Cannon	270 Peck St., Central City, N. Y.
MATERNAL AUNT	Mrs. Edward Smith	Solomon, N. Y.
MATERNAL COUSIN	Mrs. Raymond Rose	270 Peck St., Central City, N. Y.

CHILDREN'S COURT JUDGE: Hon. David Bellows   COURT: Central County

COUNTY COURT JUDGE: Hon. William Tower

COMMITTED TO INDUSTRY: 6-2-43   OFFENSE: Juvenile Delinquency (petit larceny)

PAROLED FROM INDUSTRY: 6-23-44 to mother

Committed to Elmira Reception Center	5-17-46 (Grand Larceny 2nd degree)
Received at Reception Center	5-28-46
Transferred to Elmira Reformatory	8-5-46
Paroled from Elmira	5-27-48
Discharged from parole	5-17-51 District X

GEORGE STONE (*Born 10-22-29*)
Chronology in relation to Police, Probation, Court, Detention and Private Agency Records: 1939 to 1943

DATE	POLICE	CHILDREN'S COURT—CENTRAL COUNTY			COMMUNITY AGENCIES
		PROBATION DEPT.	COURT ACTION	DETENTION DEPT.	
7-20-39	Boy warned & family advised re: Boy's entering B. Lumber Co. office				
7-22-39	Boy warned & family advised re: Boy's entering Beauty Parlor				
8-2-39	Boy arrested, breaking & entering X. Comp. Bldg. Returned home & delin. pet. filed (burglary)				
8-5-39		Prob. Invest. P.O. "A"			
8-22-39		Presented to Ch. Ct.	Mother & boy in court. No Adjud.-Disch. to Court Social Worker for foster home placement through Luth. Char. Detent. until home is found. Judge "…"	Placed in Sanford Foster Home by Worker "C" for detent. care 8-22-39 to 9-15-39	

Date				
8-28-39	Exam. at Guidance Center—Psychometric only—I.Q. 76			
8-30-39	Physical exam. Child. Hospit. Rec. Refraction & Dental care			
2-17-40				Boy taken into custody for begging; had been warned but persisted
2-19-40			George & mother in court; also Luth. Char. worker "C." Boy admitted offense. *Case held indefinitely.* Cont. in Luth. C. foster home	
2-21-40		Transfer to Schuster Foster Home by Worker "C" 2-21-40 to 2-23-40		
2-23-40	Placed by Luth. Char. in Lutz Fos. Home by Worker "D" 2-23-40—9-11-41			
7-11-41				Boy warned re panhandling

| | | CHILDREN'S COURT—CENTRAL COUNTY | | | |
DATE	POLICE	PROBATION DEPT.	COURT ACTION	DETENTION DEPT.	COMMUNITY AGENCIES
9-11-41				Referred by L. Char. Wkr. "E" for detention care—George had taken quantity of valuables from foster mother. Placed in Sanford home for care by Wkr. "C" 9-11-41	
9-12-41					Children's Hosp. physical recheck—Negative
9-15-41			George, mother & atty. in court. George admitted thefts of money & car tokens. Boy adjud. negl. Commit. to C. Boys' Farm & School —Judge "B"		Transferred by Worker "D" of Luth. C. to Boys' Farm & School 9-15-41 to 8-21-42
8-21-42				Transf. to Det. Dept. George, leader of boys steal. from cars, placed in Mercer foster home for deten. care by Wkr. "C" 8-21-42 to 9-15-42	

Date	Complaint	Court Action	Detention Care	Placement
9-9-42				
9-15-42		George & mother in court. Admitted taking money. Former order amended—commit. to L. C. for foster home placement		Placed in L. C. foster home by Wkr. "E" — Schlachter Home. 9-15-42 to 5-17-43. Ran away
5-24-43	Arrested for stealing chickens	George denies theft. Held to 6-2-43 for trial —Judge "B"	Placed in Mercer Foster Home for detention care 5-24-43 to 6-2-43	
6-2-43		George & mother in ct. George admits thefts. *Adjud. deling.* Commit. to N. Y. S. Agric. & Indus. School—Judge "B"	Placed in home of Mr. & Mrs. Gould for detention care. 6-2-43 to 6-7-43	
6-7-43			Transfer to Mercer foster home for detention care 6-7-43 to 6-12-43	
6-12-43				To Industry—N. Y. S. Agric. & Indus. School by Parole Officer "G" 6-12-43

GEORGE STONE

SUMMARY—Probation Investigation for Central County Children's Court (8-5-39).

Presented to Court 8-22-39.

OFFENSE   On 8-22-39 George Stone, aged nine years ten months, appeared in Central County Children's Court for the first time. Delinquency petition filed by Central City Police Department detective alleging that on 8-2-39 George broke into X Feed Company, 607 6th Avenue. Two other boys were with him.

PREVIOUS OFFENSES   On two previous occasions in July, 1939, George was warned by police and parents advised regarding his breaking and entering offices; also, stealing from cars. No known delinquencies prior to July.

DESCRIPTION OF CHILD   George is a nice-looking boy, light brown hair and eyes, dimple in chin, small for his age, clean cut, friendly, talkative, very active and full of life. Police describe him as a "bad kid, tough and impudent." Mother says George is becoming delinquent because she no longer has time nor strength to give him the loving attention that he used to get from her; stepfather does not like him and pushes him out to play; recently associating with other delinquent boys.

FATHER   George's father, Cyril Stone, born 10-19-03 in Central City of German parents, was reared by his parents until he was thirteen years of age when his mother died, and father, irresponsible and intemperate, deserted family. Subsequently lived with an aunt. At nine years of age he was a delinquent, later committed to industry and at age of 21 committed to Elmira Reformatory for theft of taxi. An unstable, irresponsible, chronic alcoholic, abusive to wife and children, he was arrested fifty-six times from 1912 to 1938. Married in 1928 at age of twenty-four. From 1930 to 1933 he was in City Court nine times for public intoxication, desertion, petit larceny, disorderly conduct and vagrancy. On probation and in penitentiary three times. Separated from family several times; permanent separation 1932. Since then lived in lodging and rooming houses. No contact with George for past six or seven years.

MOTHER   George's mother, Rose Wheeler Stone Jansen, was born in Central City on 2-9-11 of respectable German parents, completed eighth grade. Mother claims that she married Cyril Stone 3-22-27 at Immanuel Lutheran Church. Marriage date verified by Lutheran Charities as 3-22-28, three weeks after first child, James, born 3-1-28. She is a soft-spoken, fairly good-looking woman, interested in her children, has good understanding of their needs and of the unfairness of their situation. Tries to watch George but has not the physical strength to take proper care of the family. Wants to separate from Mr. Jansen, second husband, have him support his three children, and place three Stone children.

STEPFATHER   Joseph Jansen, born 4-8-05 in Central City, youngest in family, attended Vocational High School for two years, employed as truck driver for city for past eight years. Works nights. Described in Children's Aid Society record as good-looking with considerable charm. At age thirty-three married Mrs. Stone 3-29-38, two weeks before their second child was born. Resents supporting Stone children. Does not like George.

BROTHERS   Very good boys—no trouble, according to mother.

1929—BIRTH OF GEORGE   George was born on 10-22-29 in own home in Central City, the second of three male siblings born to Cyril and Rose Stone. Birth not recorded in Bureau of Vital Statistics—not verified other than by mother's statement. (On first court appearance mother claimed 1930 as year of his birth.)

He was a full term baby, normal delivery, bottle fed; dentition began at six months, walked and talked at thirteen months. Normal development, active, alert child. Had measles, mumps, chicken-pox, pneumonia and bronchitis during childhood.

1932—GEORGE THREE YEARS OF AGE   On 9-5-32 Robert, the third and last child of this marriage was born. (C. A. S. records gave 1933 as year of his birth.)

Father arrested three times this year. Parents permanently separated. Department of Social Welfare gave full and partial relief from 1930, when father first deserted family, to 1938 when mother married second time.

1934—GEORGE FIVE YEARS OF AGE   In 1934 mother was seriously injured in an automobile accident while driving in car with man, fracturing skull, nose and arm, and was in ill health for some time thereafter. (Record does not state who cared for children during this period.)

1936—GEORGE SIX YEARS, TEN MONTHS OF AGE   In September 1936 George started his schooling at Immanuel parochial school. One month later, on 10-11-36, mother gave birth to Joseph, born out of wedlock; father of child, Joseph Jansen. (Mother claims first marriage annulled and second marriage took place in April 1936.) No record of annulment in Central County Clerk's Office.

1938—APRIL, GEORGE EIGHT YEARS, SIX MONTHS OF AGE   Mother and J. Jansen married 3-29-38 by Justice of Peace (verified). Two weeks later William was born on 4-14-38. Department of Social Welfare closed case May, 1938.

1939—JUNE, GEORGE NINE YEARS, EIGHT MONTHS OF AGE.   On 6-14-39 mother gave birth to John, her sixth child, and the third by second husband. This month George completed the third grade at Immanuel School and was promoted. During school vacation he committed his first known delinquencies. In Children's Court in August, 1939.

HOME AND NEIGHBORHOOD   Upper flat in two-family dwelling, six rooms, $19.50 month rent; mother, stepfather, six children and mother's brother in home. Home clean and comfortable, but poorly furnished. Industrial and poor residential section, near railroad and viaduct. Boys' Club across the street.

ANALYSIS   George is product of unfavorable home environment from birth, due to father's alcoholism, instability and frequent desertions; later, due to mother's extra-marital relations culminating in apparent bigamous marriage; stepfather resents supporting Stone children and particularly George, whom he does not like; financial insecurity; socially impoverished neighborhood with high delinquency rate.

RECOMMENDATION   Foster home.

STONE, GEORGE

DATE OF BIRTH: 10-22-29
PLACE OF BIRTH: Central City, New York
RELIGION: Protestant   COLOR: White
COMMITTED: 6-2-43   ADMITTED: 6-12-43

George Stone was received at the State School on 6-12-43 from Central County Children's Court as a juvenile delinquent (petty stealing). He had been known to the police since 8-12-39 when he became involved in a burglary. He had several subsequent contacts with the Police Department but was warned and sent home. He was known as "Racket" and considered as a "tough kid" by the policemen in the precinct which was across the street from his home. He was placed in a succession of foster homes and later placed in a private home for boys but failed in each placement. In May of 1943, with other boys, stole a number of chickens. He was said to be known for his untruthfulness and general irresponsibility.

On admission George was placed in Oneida Reception Cottage where he remained until 7-7-43 when the Assignment Committee placed him in the open program, with assignment in Swenoga Cottage. He attempted to run away when he was placed in Swenoga. Since George appeared to be upset at this time he was placed the same day in Tayoga Cottage to permit closer supervision. On 7-21-43, he was again placed in Swenoga and again attempted to run away. He was replaced the same date in Tayoga Cottage where he remained until 8-18-43 when he was transferred to Ohadi Cottage and placed in a full-time academic program. He was placed in the 8th grade and reports showed considerable dissatisfaction. He was demoted to 7th grade where his attitude improved considerably.

In June 1943 on an Otis Intermediate test he received an I.Q. of 80. His total reading was 4.3 grade and total arithmetic 6.6 grade.

He was seen by the psychologist as a well-institutionalized boy full of platitudes and good intentions. On December 21, 1943, he received a home visit of one week over the Christmas holidays and he returned on time. On February 19, 1944, it was again necessary to place him in a closed program at Tayoga Cottage because George stole some keys and attempted to use them to enter cottage staff living quarters. George claimed he was trying to steal some cigarettes. He was returned to Ohadi Cottage and a full-time school program on 3-1-44 but shortly thereafter he became troublesome, irritable, touchy and quarrelsome. His day-by-day pattern of behavior, both in the cottage and in school, was unpredictable. In school, however, at times he was doing "A" work but would suddenly become "completely at odds with everything and everyone." He insisted on being with the oldest and most aggressive boys and met all efforts of friendliness with a disagreeable "smart-aleck" attitude. He sought to dominate the group and although things went along smoothly when under supervised recreation, if things did not go his way he would rebel. Frequently tried to stir up restlessness in the group. He was not seen by the psychiatrist but the clinic social worker described him as having some insight into his own situation and showing some feeling about the stepfather. In the clinic he revealed that he had been allowed to get away with too much in his own home and in the placement situations where he claims he deliberately stole whenever he was anxious to go home.

The medical history is normal—no defects or illnesses and rechecks showed normal gains.

A parole review was scheduled for February 1944, at which time the Committee noted that in some portions of his program, such as in school, definite gains had been made and that some of the staff had begun to see some changes in his attitude and behavior. It was felt that if continued improvement was sustained until the end of the academic year, he could be considered for a try-out in the community in June.

In June 1944 some improvements in the home situations were noted and because of George's continued improvement in the program, he was paroled to his own home June 23, 1944, to live with his mother and family. At that time the parents had reunited and were making some effort to create a home for their children. Although both parents were working, the mother planned to quit her job to devote all of her time to the home. It was felt that there were evidences of close family ties despite the irresponsibilities of the stepfather and the apparent weaknesses in the mother's makeup.

The summer following George's return home from industry was uneventful. In September 1944 George returned to P.S. 8 where he entered the 8th grade and graduated the following June. The school record reveals good scholarship and a Regents average of 85 and better for most subjects. Following graduation, George entered Vocational High School in September 1945, but quit a month later when he became 16 years of age. He joined a Boys' Club, became interested in basketball and baseball, and although he was above average in ability he was not a good sport. Although the family attended to their religious obligations only irregularly George managed to attend Sunday school every Sunday. While employed for a delivery concern George found access to stores and began stealing from counters, etc., which resulted in his dismissal from his job. There followed a year of no employment but with ample spending money provided by his mother. He found much time to spend at a local pool room, made new friends and severed his relationships with the normal recreational outlets. The associations George made subsequently led to more serious stealing habits and finally to his arrest for grand larceny in the second degree.

Unfortunately, George was without the continuous supervision of a parole agent throughout most of the after-care period. All supervision was done on an emergency basis by parole agents from other districts and, therefore, a continuing satisfactory relationship with an after-care agent was never developed.

Probation Summary

GEORGE STONE

George was sentenced to the Elmira Reception Center on May 24th, 1946, after having been found guilty in Central County Court, of the crime of grand larceny in the second degree.

George appeared in county court after having been arrested in company with Clarence R., also 16, and like George on parole from industry at the time of his arrest. (It is assumed the regular process of prosecution was followed in George's case. That is, upon arrest a defendant is arraigned before the City Court, a court of special sessions, for the purpose of holding a preliminary hearing to determine whether there was sufficient evidence to connect him with the crimes alleged by the police. The defendant can demand a hearing, or waive the hearing and have his case go to the Grand Jury. In the Grand Jury the evidence is presented by the police. In the interim the defendant can be admitted to jail. If he is unable to provide bail, he is held in the County Jail until the Grand Jury makes its report.)

George remained in jail for a period of ten days and then was released on bail until sentenced. (When the Grand Jury makes its report, it may render an indictment charging the defendant with the commission of one or more crimes, or it may return a "no bill." In George's case, two indictments were returned against him, charging him with the commission of six different crimes of burglary and larceny, in different degrees.

When the indictment is presented in County Court, there is an arraignment on the charges set forth in the indictment. The defendant is entitled to counsel, can demand a jury trial or plead guilty to the charges set forth in the indictment.)

George retained an attorney and pleaded guilty to count 4 of one indictment charging him with grand larceny in the second degree, in that he stole watches, jewelry, and sundry items valued at $244.50 in the home of Mrs. H.

The other three counts in this indictment alleged respectively, burglary, third degree; grand larceny, first degree; and burglary, third degree. The second indictment with its two counts of burglary, third degree, and grand larceny, first degree, remained pending against George as well as the three counts in the first indictment when he pleaded guilty to the above crime. In some of these crimes, in addition to Clarence H., his co-participants were Robert B. and John W.

Upon his plea of guilty, as in every case in Central County Court, the county judge ordered the Probation Department to make a complete investigation of George's criminal and social history. George was continued on bail pending the preparation of the probation report. A date was set for his sentence by the County Court. On that day, seven days after conviction, the court sentenced George to the Elmira Reception Center.

The probation report revealed substantially the same family social history reported by the probation department when George first appeared in Children's Court. The picture of family disintegration persisted. If anything, further deterioration had set in. George's mother and stepfather had separated. Prior to the separation Mrs. Jansen had Mr. Jansen in court for non-support on several occasions.

The probation report revealed a limited work record for George at odd jobs, such as snow shoveling and helper on a truck. His school history brought up to date showed that he had six weeks at a vocational high school. The other social history was generally a repetition of facts revealed in the earlier probation report.

The probation report devoted considerable space to the criminal activities of George since being released from industry. The offenses were highlighted and detailed at great length. In addition to the offense for which he was convicted, the report described in detail the offenses set forth in the other courts and indictments. Further criminal activities of George and his companions were described in a report of the other seven burglaries which he admitted to the police and for which he was not apparently indicted.

Outline of Correctional Experience of George Stone

RECEPTION CENTER (10 Weeks)

Date Received 5/28/46—Date Classified 7/27/46—Date transferred to Elmira Reformatory 8/5/46

I. *Reception, Orientation, Testing period (2 weeks)*

Transition from civilian to custodial life—

Orientation interviews—Receiving officer (cell assignment, physical check, shower, barber, clothing and supply issue, first letter, handbook), Chaplain, parole officer, identification officer.

Orientation talks—Director, Assistant Director, reception officer, company officer, parole officer.

Examinations—complete medical, psychometrics (group).

II. *Study and Observation (6 weeks)*

Group observation in General Education classes and exploratory Vocational shop—about 12 to 15 sessions of 2 hours each in the six week period. Psychiatric examination. Psychological interview.

Recreation period, Chaplain's interview and services, work details, etc. This period terminated with the *Classification* meeting.

III. *Transfer period (2 weeks)*

Awaiting approval of Center recommendations from Albany.

Work squads—supplementary interviews.

Arrangements for transfer—final details (clerical, administrative, etc.).

Classification—pooling of staff findings and recommendations.

STAFF SUMMARY Bad home situation—normal male physically, low average intelligence, 7th grade achievement, poor mechanical aptitude —normal (psychiatrist) with pronounced personality difficulties, egocentric and unstable—no strong academic interest, needs to learn to accept responsibility for his behavior, listens attentively to advice—slow thinking and acting in vocational area, interested in plumbing and farming—adjusted well in recreation area, played well in group and well-liked, ability as swimmer, good attitude—Chaplain found rare outside observance of religion, exposed to religious training in Lutheran school, attendance at Center satisfactory, real interest in religion lacking, no constructive plans for future—custodially works well under supervision and thorough when shown how, cell tidy, personal appearance neat, well-behaved, respects authority, mixes well with group, no disciplinary reports.

STAFF RECOMMENDATIONS Institution—Transfer to Elmira Reformatory Program—Social Education (a) to learn to be honest first with others, (b) to overcome unfortunate home environment. Vocational training conditional tryout in plumbing; otherwise, further consultation with guidance counsellor—possible maintenance.
Parole—According to progress in program.
Custodial—Caution—runaway from State School.

No special recommendations from physician, psychiatrist or psychologist. No unusual features.

ELMIRA REFORMATORY (21 months, 23 days)

Date Received from Reception Center 8/5/46
Date Paroled 5/28/48
(NB: Total time in Reception Center and Reformatory—exactly 2 yrs.)

I *Administrative Developments*

ASSIGNMENT BOARD 10/18/46
(11 weeks after Ref. reception—21 weeks after R.C. reception).
ACTION Dining room until 2/1/47. School all day until 4/1/47, then plumbing class. This follows Reception Center recommendation.

CLASSIFICATION BOARD 12/12/46
(18 weeks after Ref. reception—28 weeks after R.C. reception).
ACTION Given an "E" classification for his time. This set his minimum parole eligibility at 1/28/48 if approved by parole board. An "E" classification means 24 months (including 10 weeks at Reception Center) less 4 months off for good behavior if earned. Since George came to the Reception Center 5/28/46 his full minimum would have been 5/28/48. If all "good time" had been earned, his earliest possible parole date (if approved) would have been 4 months sooner or 1/28/48.

SCREENING BOARD (Initial Consideration)—10/9/47
(14 months after Reformatory reception).
ACTION Was held 2 months plus 48 days lost time. This means that he was not approved to see the December '47 Parole Board for release in January as originally planned. In effect this action did two things: (1) deferred his consideration for screening until Feb. '48 and (2) took two of his four months "good time" away from him as well as fining him 48 days "lost time."

SCREENING BOARD (Reconsideration)—2/6/48
(18 months after Reformatory reception).
ACTION Improvement in institutional record found. Certified or approved to meet April '48 Parole Board.

PAROLE BOARD APPEARANCE 4/5/48
(20 months after Reformatory reception).
ACTION Parole approved on or after 5/26/48—An "open date" case. This means that George can be released any time after 5/25/48 providing a satisfactory home and job are available.

II *Program*

(Received 8/5/46—Paroled 5/28/48—21½ months).

8/12/46—10/21/46 (10 weeks)—Physical training
10/21/46—2/3/47 (14 weeks)—Dining Room
2/3/47—4/1/47 (9 weeks)—School all day (Social Education)
4/1/47—4/30/47 (4 weeks)—Plumbing Class all day
4/31/47—5/28/48 (56 weeks)—School half day, Plumbing class half day

Parole Supervision—Summary

GEORGE STONE

Home Visits	—34
Collateral Visits	— 7
Office Reports	—82

This subject was released under parole supervision on May 28th, 1948. Since the residence with the mother had proven unsatisfactory during the course of an investigation and on the basis of previous history, he was not permitted to return to her home, but was released to the residence of an aunt who was considered a reputable person and one who would coöperate with the parole office.

On the basis of the parole officer's review of the parolee's previous history of recalcitrance and nonconformity in the community and in the institution, it was believed that there was a definite need for close and positive supervision in the home to supplement the parole officer's supervision.

During the parolee's residence with his aunt, his conduct was consistently satisfactory in the home and he got along well with the aunt and her husband. He paid his board regularly and accepted her supervision in the home.

On infrequent occasions, the parolee visited his mother and was visited by her. The situation relating to the mother had been frankly discussed with him and explained to the mother. She, at the time, was not on good terms with her husband, the parolee's stepfather, and had frequent altercations with him. She was attacked on several occasions by him and there were several City Court actions brought about by her against her husband. The parolee openly expressed hostility and resentment against the stepfather because of his treatment of the mother and trouble between the two could reasonably be expected if frequent visits were permitted. There was also the association with another man, presumably a paramour, and this added to a general unsatisfactory tone which made it advisable to keep the parolee away from the mother's residence.

Both the parolee and the mother accepted the restriction and in good grace after an explanation by the parole officer.

The parolee's employment record after a spotty and unsatisfactory beginning was generally satisfactory. He had a total of three different jobs within the first three months, working at the first one for two weeks, the second for one month and the third for about three weeks. Between each job the parolee was required to report daily to the parole office and to make continual efforts to secure employment himself.

During his incarceration in the institution, the parolee had been trained as a plumber. He had not been released to a plumbing job because a satisfactory one could not be located. After his release, however, he was given an opportunity to work at this trade, but was unable to do so.

In connection with his training as a plumber, the parolee made several efforts to obtain work in that capacity. It was not known until after he lost a position with the Alert Press Machine Service Company that he had been employed as a pipe fitter. Circumstances of his employment and discharge are as follows:

The parolee reported to the parole officer that he had obtained employment with the Alert Press Machine Service Company. After about three weeks' employment, he reported to the parole officer that he had been laid off. Explanation for the discharge was that he had rebelled against the constant abuse handed out by the employer and by his immediate supervisor. It was learned after investigation, however, that he had been employed upon the basis of his own claim that he was an experienced pipe fitter. When he could not do the work, he was discharged. The parolee admitted this falsification when he was faced with it.

About three months after his release, the parolee obtained steady employment at the Republic Steel Plant, Crestin, N. Y., through the efforts of the parole officer. This job was secured through the relationship previously established by the parole officer with the Personnel Department of the steel plant and the parolee's complete record was revealed to the employer and to the Chief of Police in the steel plant.

The parolee worked steadily at the Republic Steel Plant until his discharge from parole two years later with only intermittent periods of unemployment due to temporary shutdowns and strikes. In the latter part of his parole period, he obtained extra work cleaning a barber shop on Sundays. Employment at the Republic Steel Corporation was satisfactory and no adverse reports were entered against him by the employer. The parole officer checked with the police department of the plant and the Personnel Department on several occasions during the parolee's employment.

Consistently, during the parole period, earnings and employment attendance were verified by his weekly wage slips.

During the employment, the possibilities of advance were pointed out on frequent occasions by the parole officer. It was considered necessary to hold out this goal as a probable reward for services since parolee considered the job onerous and uninteresting in the beginning, and might have quit it without a specific objective.

Immediately after the parolee's release from the institution, he was encouraged to establish a savings account and did so. He deposited money regularly, but began to use it indiscriminately and carelessly. No bank control had been placed on the account in the beginning, but when the deposits became sporadic, a control was placed on the account. Deposits then became more regular while he was employed and, at the termination of his parole period, he had the total of approximately $750 in his savings account.

Although this account was under the control of the parole office from September, 1948, to the end of the parole period, the parolee was permitted to withdraw money when he presented a satisfactory reason for doing so. Some of the withdrawals were for recreational purposes and some for loans to his mother and for the purchase of clothing.

The development of habits of thrift was considered important in this case, since his early attitude toward savings and finances in general was thought to be a reflection of his earlier profligate ways. The matter of thrift and economy was the subject of frequent discussions with the parolee and part of the considered parole plan.

The parolee paid his board regularly while employed, and, during temporary layoffs, had enough money in the bank to pay his board.

During some of the periods of unemployment, the parolee showed definite resentment toward his aunt's insistence upon the payment of board. He described her attitude as unnecessarily mercenary and cold. Such feeling on the part of the parolee was considered by the parole officer to be a possible indication of the parolee's desire to be wanted and belong, in a secure family group.

During the early part of the parole period, the parolee frequently spoke of his former associates and of his old neighborhood. In view of the unsatisfactory nature of most of the associates, he was warned against them and directed to stay away from the scene of most of his former difficulties. It was necessary to reprimand him for a few incidents of corner lounging and for occasional returns to the neighborhood and association with individuals who were not considered suitable companions. He developed an early interest in a girl and, when he seemed on the point of becoming too involved, was cautioned by the parole officer because of his youth and lack of preparation for marriage.

Particular emphasis was placed by the parole officer on the dangers of sexual intimacies and he was warned about too frequent associations with this particular girl friend, who was investigated discreetly and was learned to have a good reputation and no record.

On one occasion, the parolee admitted sexual relations with a promiscuous girl in the area in which he lived.

After the association for about one year with the girl friend mentioned above, the parolee's interest waned and he became interested in several other girls in succession.

During the parole period, the only incidents of misconduct were the sexual relations reported above, the purchase of lottery tickets, the loss of $17 gambling, and an unauthorized visit to Canada.

Generally, the parolee showed a gradual satisfactory adjustment under parole supervision and his reporting status was changed after about six months from a weekly reporting basis to a bi-monthly reporting basis. Parolee never indicated any objection to his weekly reporting and, in fact, objected to a change, commenting that he might forget something if he did not report often enough.

Over the period of parole supervision, the parolee gradually developed a relationship with the parole officer where he could discuss his mother's problems, his own, and the problems of his relations with various girl friends without difficulty. He reported suspicious circumstances, such as questioning by detectives, charges of theft in the barber shop (later proven unfounded) without reservation. This might have been because of his belief that the parole officer would find them out anyway, but there is reason to believe that the relationship in general was a satisfactory one.

The parole officer's evaluation of this case is presented in the following final summary and closing summary:

FINAL SUMMARY

This final summary of the parolee's recent activities finds him still living in the home of his cousin, Mrs. Ross, and working for the Republic Steel Corporation, where his wages are fluctuating between $63 and $75 gross each week. He has continued his savings program without interruption and has on deposit at the time of his discharge $750. The writer has spent the last three interviews with this man in discussing the progress that he has made while under parole supervision and the vast change which seems to have occurred in him and particularly in his attitude in recent months. The parolee himself says that he does not seem nearly as tense as he used to and in his own words he states, "I feel more secure than I used to." He has no immediate plans except that he hopes for a deferment from Army service so that he can enjoy himself for a while as he has been under some form of restraint for so long a period that it will "feel good to do things the way I want to for a change." The parolee is still seeing his girl friend on an average of 2 or 3 nights a week, and mostly in the home of her sister on McCamley Street, although he occasionally visits her home on Ingham Avenue, Lackawanna, N. Y.

When this parolee was given his discharge papers on the evening of 5/21/51, he made the simple statement, "Thanks a lot for everything," and seemed to be genuinely appreciative of what had been done for him but at the same time most relieved that he would be under no further surveillance. In general appraisal of this man the writer would say that he is quite intellectually honest, very forthright in his manner, but a person who is inclined to live in the past too often.

CLOSING SUMMARY

George Stone was convicted of the crime of grand larceny, 2nd degree, on 5/24/46 in Central County Court at Central City, N. Y. He was sentenced to Elmira Reformatory with a 5-year maximum sentence because of his involvement in a series of burglaries which occurred in the general vicinity of the neighborhood where he lived. He was 16 years of age at the time that these depredations were committed and he had a lengthy history of juvenile delinquency preceding it.

Parolee comes from a background of deprivation and neglect with his father, a known alcoholic, having disappeared and the mother later remarrying an irresponsible stepfather who neglected the seven children of both marriages.

Considering the atrocious background of this case, the parolee was forbidden to return to his own family group at the time of his release, and from time of his arrival report on 5/28/48, he has made his home first with a maternal aunt and then with a maternal cousin.

A release program of employment failed in this case and the parolee was provided employment with the Republic Steel Corporation where he remained in steady employment until his discharge. He was regarded as an excellent employee and the writer has endeavored to convince this man of the prospect of advancement with this firm if he remains with them for an indefinite period.

The parolee's home situation was physically excellent at all times and yet the intensity of family feeling could not be found in either home in which he lived. There was undoubtedly an interest in the family and his affairs but little affection could be found in the relationship which existed between the parolee and the family group with whom he resided.

The writer feels that this parolee, through an effort on his own part and through thinking things through for himself, has formed certain concepts which were missing in his life before commitment. The writer has resorted to practically no threat in this case and in fact when the parolee was found in violation of his parole regulations in a rather serious manner on one occasion, the interpretation was one of pointing out to the parolee how he had failed in his promises and how, if he continued this pattern, his word would never be accepted. From that point on, the writer experienced no difficulty whatever with the parolee, although because of his unusual process of reasoning he continued to be a threat to himself up to the very day of his discharge. The writer feels that this parolee has not had the proper confidence in himself, and though he shows much more at the time of his discharge than he had when released, it is questionable if he could meet any serious situation without a great deal of counsel from some more mature individual.

The degree of success attained in this case is difficult to judge but the known factors of steady employment, of truthful recounting of his own experiences and the economic stability secured are indicative of a fair surface adjustment.

Appendix II

PAROLE SUPERVISION: A CASE ANALYSIS[1]

Carl Sullivan, age 18, when released on parole from the National Training School at Washington, D. C., was the sixth of seven children born to parents described as cultured, well-to-do, and socially prominent. The father, a successful banker, is distinguished in appearance, possesses many admirable traits, but is rigid, cold, domineering, and inflexible. The mother is a gracious person who is well-groomed, quiet-spoken, and self-contained. There are no indications of friction between the father and mother. The family are active members of the Catholic Church. Their home, located in one of the best residential sections of . . . , is large and beautifully furnished.

More youthful appearing than his years, Carl is a tall, thin boy with a ready smile and agreeable manners. His mouth is partly open much of the time, which tends to make him appear stupid. He has been marked as the "problem child" of the family for a long time. His early adjustment in parochial and public schools was poor. He was truant frequently, and he was given to lying and taking sums of money from the home. When he was 8 years old he was taken to a mental hygiene clinic by his parents for advice and guidance. After repeated failures in school adjustment, a progressive private day school was tried, but even the flexible curriculum and focus on individual interests failed to capture his sustained attention. A well-known psychiatric clinic examined Carl, and the parents were told that he had

[1] This case analysis (originally published in *Federal Probation,* June, 1951, pp. 36-42) is that of a parolee who was under the supervision of a federal probation officer. In the Federal Government the probation officer investigates and supervises both probationers and parolees. To protect the identity of the person studied, all names, dates, and other identifying data have been altered.

limited intelligence and probably would not achieve the college education and professional goals of the other children in the family.[2]

Carl had one interest—automobiles. He liked to drive them and to work on motors. At 15, he was arrested for operating an automobile without a driver's license, and at 16 persistent truancy and petty thefts brought him to the attention of the juvenile court, but no official record was made because the family arranged a plan for him. In March 1946 he was admitted to . . . , a well-known private training school, the father paying $1,400 a year tuition. Carl resented this action, and later contended that the only reason for it was that his father wanted to get rid of him.

His adjustment at the training school was fair for a time. He participated in the student government as a judge, and he did academic work at the eighth-grade level. Nevertheless, he ran away numerous times during the next 14 months. Early in May 1947, Carl and another boy made off with the car of the principal of the school. They were apprehended in Virginia, and returned. Both boys escaped from detention at the school a fortnight later, broke into the home of the principal, and departed in the same car, taking a watch, radio, cash, and clothing. They were apprehended in South Carolina. Neither the school authorities nor the father interceded this time and under the provisions of the Federal Juvenile Delinquency Act Carl was committed to the custody of the Attorney General for a period of 2½ years by the United States District Court for the Eastern District of South Carolina.

At the National Training School, tests revealed that Carl had high-average intelligence (I.Q. 112), high-average mechanical aptitude, and high-average manual dexterity. He was assigned to part-time school, in which his work was poor, and to part-time auto class, in which his progress was above average despite less effort than was regarded as desirable. In the National Training School evaluation this significant comment appears: "Much of this boy's future depends upon his family and their attitude toward him. So far, they have given him little affection and understanding. While he is a capable boy and has at least average abilities, he probably will never live up to the expectations of his parents."

Carl was received at the National Training School in late June 1947. In August, the admission summary was sent to the probation office, and in December the probation office was notified by telephone that Carl was granted parole effective at once and the school hoped he could be released before Christmas. There had been no parole planning. There had been some discussion of the possibility of working out a school program for him, and it was hoped something could be worked out with the parents.

The probation office summary of what happened is interesting and informative:

[2] Whether this is the parental version, or whether the statement is based on a clinic report is not clear. In either event, the parents are likely to be influenced negatively.

Upon initial contact, the father was obviously displeased that Carl had been granted parole. He felt the boy had been doing fairly well for the first time in his life and the same program should be continued for a longer period in order that settled work habits and attitudes might be firmly established. The boy had been at the National Training School only 6 months. It seemed very soon for him to come home. Furthermore, the parents had not been consulted. The father accepted the boy's return home as inevitable, but he was not prepared to offer any suggestions as to a parole plan. If we could make any arrangements about a school program, that would be satisfactory. We succeeded in having him participate to the extent of securing the services of a parish priest as the adviser. A tentative school plan was set up after conference with the director of vocational schools and a member of the guidance staff of the department of education. Carl was well known to these people because of their efforts to work out a plan for him a few years ago. If Carl could take an advanced course in automobile mechanics which would fit him for eventual work on a managerial level, he might gain status in the eyes of his family. In any event, Carl would have to participate in any plan decided upon, and he will be interviewed and tested after his return home.

Report of Supervision Progress[3]

Carl Sullivan was released on parole on December 21, 1947. On our first contact, he talked at length about the training school where he obviously felt "a sense of acceptance and belonging"; the school was a fine place and he was now a finished automobile mechanic. He was lukewarm about the possibilities of a school program now but agreed to withhold judgment until he had talked with Mr. Packard and Mrs. Greenbaum of the department of education, with whom he was already acquainted.

January 5, 1948.—The interviews at the department of education resulted in a decision by Carl to attend high school 4 nights a week to take algebra and mechanical drawing in order to have a better foundation in math before undertaking an advanced course in automobile mechanics. These classes would begin the first of February. In the meantime, Carl was to seek employment in a garage. Various possibilities were discussed with him.

There were a number of contacts during the first month. On January 19, Carl started work in a small garage near his home. His talk, however, centered on his experiences at the training school and tended to be boastful in tone about his achievements and the recognition he received. When he requested permission to visit the school one Saturday, it was given as

[3] Because of space limitations only those more pertinent chronological entries are included here. In some instances direct quotations are taken from the entries. Ellipses are used at those points where portions of the entries have been omitted. Statements not carried in quotes are summaries in the probation officer's own words of the highlights of each contact.

we felt that this might help him to orient himself. It was our impression that he felt happier at the school than he ever had at home. If he realized he was now only a visitor and no longer belonged there, some of the ties might be severed.

Carl quit his first job after a few weeks because, he said, the employer did not appreciate his abilities and did not pay high enough wages. He got another job in a service station but was dissatisfied because he felt he was fitted for more skilled work. He began school but complained almost at once that the algebra was too difficult.

February 20, 1948.—Mrs. Sullivan called. . . . She expresses concern about Carl. They are very doubtful that he is attending night school regularly. . . . She believes he is using the pretext of going to school in order to get out at night. . . . The job which the boy says he has at . . . does not seem to amount to much. . . .

We talked with Carl the same day. He thinks he may drop the algebra; he cannot see much use in it anyhow. Employment was also discussed. Carl's interest, however, centers on the unhappy home conditions. His father is constantly nagging; the family is always "riding" him. His father insists on his doing odd jobs that none of the others has to do because Carl should "earn his keep." It is difficult to find anything that Carl is really interested in. He sees a great deal of former friends and seems to have plenty of social life but this is aimless and disorganized.

March 12, 1948.—"Call from Carl's mother. The boy is still unemployed and seems to be making no effort to find work. He wants to go out at night all the time . . . there are many arguments about this because the father insists that Carl be in by 11:30 or 12:00. The boy often is out until 1:00 or 2:00 a.m. and even later and then wants to sleep until noon. He will not confide in either of his parents and will never satisfactorily answer their questions. Mrs. Sullivan feels that employment is the chief problem at this time."

Arrangements were immediately made for referral to the state employment service. An appointment was made and a letter of introduction given to Carl. We learned later that, although he went to the employment service, he did not persist in any follow-up because, he said, they could not do anything for him.

March 15, 1948.—Carl continues to talk primarily about the family and his father in particular. We have felt that it might help him to let him express his hostility freely and accept it. At the same time we have tried to interpret the father's attitudes. Carl wishes he could move into a room to himself and asks if this would be permitted. We told him that it might but that he would first have to secure a job and show that he could be self-supporting. While we do not feel that Carl is mature enough to live by himself, we did not want to discourage him, as a move may be the ultimate solution. A placement in some family would be a different matter but we know of no possibilities of such an arrangement.

April 1948.—The situation remained relatively quiet. Carl succeeded in getting a job as a bank runner and worked almost a full month. He was enthusiastic at first but this soon waned. He dropped algebra. He never seeks advice but acts on his decisions and tells us about them afterwards. We suggested that he have another talk with the guidance adviser at the department of education but he did not follow this up.

May 3, 1948.—"Mr. Sullivan called. He states that he is afraid Carl is 'back to his old tricks.' The other night his aunt's car was taken from her garage . . . and returned before morning. It was necessary to break into the garage to gain access to the car. Mr. Sullivan suspects Carl of participating in this affair because he knows about his aunt's car and she lives next door to a boy . . . with whom Carl constantly associates. . . . Carl is habitually untruthful, constantly telling fantastic tales . . . but they are so far-fetched that the brothers and sisters ridicule him about them."

We suggested to the father that Carl probably has to manufacture stories because he feels very insecure and a great deal of his trouble may come from his uncertain place in the household and in the family's affections. Although the father agrees with this readily, it has no effect because he feels that the attitudes toward Carl are only to be expected because of past experiences with him and you cannot expect all the members of a family to make themselves over for one.

Subsequently, Carl denied having anything to do with his aunt's car. He was not surprised we had learned of the incident but he assumed that the police had told us. Carl was never questioned by the police about it.

May to July 1948.—There were no specific complaints during this period although the situation remained much the same. Carl joined the National Guard, drilled weekly, and went away to camp for 2 weeks toward the end of July. This ended in a discharge from the National Guard because he had an accident with an Army vehicle and was antagonistic toward the officers.

Prior to leaving for camp, Carl obtained a job at the . . . aircraft plant, to begin work early in August. He started on August 16 as a turret lathe operator. There was some discussion about his obtaining a room near the plant or at the "Y."

September 9, 1948.—Mrs. Sullivan called. She is very disturbed about Carl. She has reason to doubt that he is still working at . . .'s and told us of the irregular hours he is keeping and his conflicting statements about his work. He has been riding around in a Model-A Ford which he claims is his, although his father forbade him to buy a car. A check with the commissioner of motor vehicles revealed that the Ford is still registered in the name of a boy with whom Carl is friendly.

The parents would like to see Carl get a room near the . . . plant but Mrs. Sullivan does not believe Carl has really tried.

There followed several contacts with Carl. He claimed positively to be working at . . . 's and said he had been transferred to the night shift. He does not like the work; it is not the kind he was promised at the plant. The hostility toward his father continues to occupy his whole attention and seems to prevent all other constructive activity. We tried to point out the advantages of working at a place like . . . 's; it is in keeping with his general interests, has prestige, and could lead to a good future.

September 16, 1948.—The mother called again. She is convinced Carl is not working. He has been remaining out all night and says he is on the night shift from 12:00 to 8:00 but was seen by the paper boy at 4:00 a.m. wandering the streets just last night.

We checked with the personnel office at the . . . plant. This was the fourth consecutive day that Carl has not reported for work. He had not been transferred to the night shift. If he would report back for work at once, he might be able to retain his job.

Visited the home. Mrs. Sullivan seems to wish to leave the full responsibility for Carl's troubles up to the probation officer. She has no suggestions.

We talked with Carl privately, telling him of our concern about him, particularly with reference to his staying out all night. He insisted that he has been on the night shift at . . .'s whether they have a record of it or not. Carl always has a ready explanation whenever questioned but his answers are either a flat denial or evasive. We told him that, regardless of what the situation at . . .'s might be, we would expect him to go back there and keep his job.

September 27.—Talked with Father Morris, the parole adviser. He is well acquainted with the family situation but seems inclined to feel that Carl has a tendency to make more of his father's attitude than is warranted. Carl's eldest brother has done everything he could to be helpful and has interceded on many occasions with the father. This brother has talked with Father Morris about it. Carl never attends Mass with any member of the family but always comes to a different service. He also attends a teen-age social held in the parish house every Sunday evening and Father Morris has noted that he seems to enjoy himself and gets along well with boys and girls.

Father Morris does not believe that Carl ever really wanted to move away from home. Whenever the possibility of doing so appeared to be close, Carl's enthusiasm waned. He may be gaining some satisfaction out of aggravating his father and the rest of the family.

September 30.—Carl quit his job at . . .'s on the 29th. He has decided to go to vocational school and take a part-time course in automobile mechanics.

October and November.—Very little employment and no apparent serious effort to locate work, but he states he is going to school 1 hour daily. In the latter part of November, Carl bought a 1933 Packard sedan for $18.00 and had an accident the first day. He claimed damages amounting to $160.00. He was found "not guilty" of reckless driving, but the operator of the other car was fined. Carl sold his car for $25.00 on the promise he would have the repairs made. He wanted to collect from the operator of the other car involved in the accident.

December 13.—"Mr. Sullivan called. Carl went out last Friday afternoon and did not return home until Saturday evening. Money has been disappearing from around the house constantly. Mr. Sullivan accuses Carl. The boy must get out and find a room. . . . Some time ago Carl got up one night at 1:30 a.m. Mr. Sullivan was aroused and saw some boys outside Carl's bedroom window. They had wakened him and wanted Carl to join them. One of Carl's brothers tried to persuade the boy not to go out but he did so and remained out the rest of the night."

Talked with Carl the same day. He said the boys had called for him because he had a temporary job delivering early morning papers and that was why he went out. He refused to offer his father this explanation.

Carl announced that he had located a room for $8.00 a week and he had already paid a week's rent. It is in a good neighborhood, directly across from the church where the parole adviser is located. Carl is convinced that once away from home, everything will be all right. He has no job but will find one. We told him to go to the employment office and report back to us.

We later talked to the father who is satisfied with Carl's move and offered to help financially at any time we feel there is a need but he hopes Carl may learn to be more responsible if he has to meet his own living expenses.

December 17.—Received a call from Mr. Sullivan to advise us that Carl had been arrested on a charge of breaking and entering and burglary. During the night of December 16 and 17 Carl had come to the home and taken the family car without the knowledge of anyone. He had picked up two friends and, toward morning, had broken into a restaurant at . . .

December 18.—Attended the magistrate's hearing. Carl pleaded guilty to the charge. One boy, age 15, was turned over to the juvenile court authorities. A third boy, age 18, claimed convincingly that he had tried to persuade Carl and the juvenile not to commit the offense and had not participated in it. Carl's testimony corroborated this boy's contentions and he was released. Cartons of cigarettes, cigars, a coin box, a slot machine, and money from the cash register were taken. All of these items were in the car when the boys were apprehended. Carl was held for the action of the grand jury and committed to jail.

When it was explained to Carl that this offense constituted a parole violation, he became very upset. He had thought that we would find some way to get him out of the trouble. He gave vent to his feelings about his father, saying he was to blame for everything, that he had never given him anything in his life and he intended to kill him the first chance he got.

A parole violator warrant was subsequently issued. We then discussed the case with the state's attorney who agreed to *nol. pros.* the new charge on condition that Carl be returned to a federal institution as a parole violator. Carl was returned to the National Training School on January 18, 1949.

In the meantime, we had visited Carl in the county jail. He seemed much less perturbed than at first. He brought out more hostile feelings about his father, going back into the more distant past than he ever had before. He said that his father had frequently taunted him by saying, "Why don't you get out; why don't you change your name and disappear?"

He had decided that when released this time, he is going to some entirely different part of the country. This is the only way he can get rid of all the unhappy associations he has surrounding the home. He hopes his parole adviser can help him in this plan.

General Comments by the Supervising Officer[4]

Problems and needs at time the parole warrant was issued.—At the time the parole warrant was issued, Carl had committed a new offense. His life had become completely disorganized, and we felt that this was directly attributable to a deep emotional conflict involving his relationship to his father and to his family in general. He was acting out his inner hostilities. There were feelings of rejection and "not belonging" which produced bitterness, resentment, and defiance of parental authority in an effort to retaliate. The family patterns of rejection and punishment for failure to conform were firmly fixed. The situation reached a point where Carl was incapable of making an adjustment in the community. He was in constant turmoil and the threat of overt antisocial behavior was ever present.

In our opinion, Carl was in need of intensive individual psychiatric counseling in an institutional environment in order to develop sufficient maturity to face his problems without the support and help of his family.

General factors contributing to failure to adjust. The family's rejection and Carl's reactions to it were the fundamental factors in the failure to adjust. The attitudes of the family should have been given greater consideration before the parole was granted. These attitudes dated back to the boy's early childhood and had become more firmly fixed through the years with Carl's continuing failure to adjust to any program attempted in his behalf. The family, and particularly the father, were not ready to have the boy at home again. The father felt that the boy was making progress for the first time in his life at the training school and he was convinced that this program should be continued for a longer time. The parole was forced on him and on the family with no participation on their part and without any request for their opinion about the boy. In effect, they were told that he was coming home and that they would have to accept him.

Contributing further to Carl's failure to adjust was his seeming lack of interest in any kind of program. He did not care either about work or school and made little real effort to occupy himself constructively. This increased the friction at home. He liked to drive cars, listen to the radio, and read comic books. He wanted to receive the care and affection of his family but was not able to give anything of himself to make this more possible.

---

[4] The three topics in this section of the case analysis are discussed by the probation officer who supervised Carl while on parole.

General principles which guided supervision.—Our endeavors throughout were directed toward establishing and maintaining a friendly, accepting, and nonpunitive relationship with the boy. We gave encouragement and praise in order to increase his self-esteem. We recognized with him the family problems and his difficult relationship with his father. We gave him opportunity to express his hostilities freely and endeavored, when possible, to interpret to him his emotions and the family attitudes. At the same time, we guarded against siding wholly with Carl against the family because we felt that he had to make an adjustment with the family before he could become independent of them. We followed the policy of being noncritical, nondemanding, and liberal in granting requests in order that Carl would not feel that we, like his family, rejected him. We counseled him regarding employment and school possibilities, at times taking the initiative in offering concrete and specific suggestions but generally leaving the action up to the boy. The general principles underlying supervision, therefore, were an accepting and nonpunitive relationship within which we attempted to give Carl an opportunity to work out and live through his many emotional conflicts and hostilities.

Analysis of Parole Supervision

Space limitations do not permit comment on all of the important aspects of this interesting case, and even thorough exploration of the areas chosen for discussion is out of the question. Nevertheless, an attempt is made to deal with some of the broader issues raised by this case material, especially those which have general relevance rather than those specific to the record itself. The writer had access to the probation officer's entire chronological record and also was informed of later developments in the case; he therefore has an advantage in commenting on it. Because of this, arrangements were made for a discussion of the case by a group of experienced workers who had access only to the information available when the "Report of Supervision Progress" ends. The areas selected for attention here are among those the group considered most important.[5]

The relationship of release planning to supervision.—This case demonstrated clearly and forcibly the importance of careful prerelease planning. Without attempting to assess the degree of responsibility of the parole

[5] With permission of the Administrative Office of the United States Courts, and with the coöperation of Mr. Russell G. Oswald, director of the Division of Corrections, Wisconsin Department of Public Welfare, the case was discussed by an in-service training group consisting of administrative assistants and case consultants of the Bureau of Probation and Parole, supplemented by one social service representative from each of five institutions. This group of 15 spent nearly 5 hours discussing various phases of the case. This suggests that it may be useful for other in-service training programs, and it also indicates the cursory nature of the treatment of it given here.

board, the institution, or the probation office, it is certain that some rather obvious danger signals were ignored. The training school staff recognized the important role of family attitudes in Carl's situation—much of his future depended on it. Yet release was planned without consulting the family. When the father was informed he was resistant and resentful. He reluctantly accepted the situation as inevitable, but he could not move into participation in planning for Carl, except that he obtained a priest as parole adviser. Older brothers and sisters may have been resources, but apparently they were not brought into the picture.

It is conceded that there are some dangers in delaying release after parole has been granted. Nevertheless, the importance of the family in relation to Carl's adjustment suggests that release should have been deferred for at least a month. Probably the proverbial warmth of the Christmas holidays was accorded too much weight. But Carl could have been somewhat of a problem during the holidays. The record indicates that he was a problem to the family for more than 10 years—probably much longer than that. Now he appears at Christmas—for his family it is party-time, and social-calling time. With his half-open mouth, he certainly is not an asset. In addition, school plans must be deferred until February, and a planless, aimless January does not offer much promise of getting him off to a good start.

The failure to enlist family coöperation before Carl's release unquestionably affected supervision here. As the record shows, the family failed to accept responsibility for him, and both the father and mother projected their own obligations on the supervisory officer. It may be argued that a plan for Carl away from the home was indicated because the pattern of parental rejection was both deep-seated and long-standing. The evidence is not very clear on this point; at any rate, alternatives were not explored. Inadequate planning made supervision very difficult.

The role played by the supervising officer.—At the outset it should be pointed out that a person reviewing the record is in a far different position from the one working with the case. Looking at another's work is done from a different perspective, and there are not the same emotional involvements which so frequently beset the person in day-by-day contact with the case. Consequently, it is easy to be critical and to sit in judgment when one is removed from the situation and when all the known facts are at hand. It should be added that the supervision of Carl is complicated by the fact that the causes of his difficulties are largely unknown. As a result, the tendency is to treat symptoms as they develop, and this is noted when the greatest activity, except for initial planning, seems to occur around crises, especially when the parents report that he is proving difficult. Finally it must be kept in mind that the supervision is being done by a worker with a heavy case load. This factor alone is a compelling one, when any evaluation of his efforts is attempted.

With all these factors under consideration, it must be admitted that the officer's work was of a high order. He operated at all times with a keen understanding of the dynamics of personality development. He attempted to interpret Carl's situation to the parents, and their reactions in turn were interpreted to him. He recognized the difficulties involved, but he was willing to carry on under what must have been discouraging conditions. Some readers of this record will be convinced that he lacked aggressiveness, and that the parents should have been confronted more consistently with their responsibility in the matter. We have a clear picture of the father— dominant, aggressive, positive, and righteous. The mother does not emerge so clearly. She complains of Carl's lack of progress; she seems to be the quiet, soft-spoken one; but one suspects that the mother's rejection of Carl is more profound, more complete than that of the father. She does not come into focus sufficiently for one to know precisely what part she is playing here. It would be helpful to know. The problem is that both parents are able to rationalize their conduct and project the blame on Carl or the officer. It is heavy going when one tries to interpret a Carl to parents who are self-satisfied and whose methods have been proved by rearing six children successfully—as measured by conformity at least.

The specific role of the supervising officer is described in his own words in the section "General principles which guided supervision." One sentence is especially important: "We followed the policy of being noncritical, nondemanding, and liberal in granting requests in order that Carl would not feel that we, like his family, rejected him." This, of course, is generally sound practice; in this situation it may have been carried too far. Carl is essentially an impulsive, hedonistic person who invariably fails to look before he leaps. He needs standards, and as long as he rejects those of his family —although he is ambivalent about it—he needs a relationship with a person who does represent standards. In other words, there are a good many reality factors here that need attention, and there is some danger in overpermissiveness in this and similar situations. This comment does not in any way recommend or condone punitive, aggressive treatment of Carl. As a matter of fact, such handling would cut off any chance for Carl to develop the kind of relationship he needs. But Carl is intelligent; he has learned to "use" people; there is a real possibility here that he can use the relationship with the supervisory officer in such a way as to evade responsibility. His "upset" reaction when confronted with the fact that breaking and entering and burglary constitutes a parole violation is very interesting. The "noncritical, nondemanding" approach may possibly have evoked this response.

One question that is bound to be raised here is whether the supervising officer might have used psychiatric services in dealing with Carl. While the family had prior contacts with clinics, which were not especially helpful, there is no evidence that psychiatric *treatment* as distinguished from psychiatric *diagnosis* was ever used in trying to deal with Carl's problems. Possibly, in view of the financial resources of the family and the urban setting, the attempt should have been made. Even at the diagnostic level, psychiatric services might have been used in order to provide consultation to the supervising officer. Probably the officer was conscious of the danger of "pushing" Carl, and giving the worker an opportunity to discuss his interviews with a psychiatrist might have given him more security and freedom in dealing with Carl, especially in setting limits that made more demands upon him.

This record displays critical thinking and the application of good case-work principles in what was at best a very difficult situation.

Later Career

The later career of Carl is not surprising. He remained at the National Training School for about a year after his return, made a fair adjustment, and was paroled with a plan which included employment in Washington, D. C., as a service station attendant. Although he received a great deal of attention from a prominent "big brother," the plan lasted only a few months. He wandered to California. With a companion he stole a car and returned East, committing numerous larcenies en route. They were finally apprehended after a series of thefts in Maryland, and although he admitted the charges, Carl asked that a brother, an attorney, be informed of his plight, because he thought there were some legal loopholes in the charges. The family did not wish to become involved, and in September 1950, a few days before his 21st birthday, Carl was sentenced to the state reformatory for a period not to exceed 4 years.

Bibliography

Abbott, Grace, *The Child and the State*, Vols. I and II (Chicago, 1938).

Ackerson, Luton, *Children's Behavior Problems: Relative Importance and Intercorrelations Among Traits*, Vol. II (Chicago, 1942).

Adler, Alfred, *The Case of Miss R.* (New York, 1930), Chap. 1.

———, *The Practise and Theory of Individual Psychology*, trans. by P. Radin (New York, 1925).

———, *Problems of Neurosis* (New York, 1930), Chaps. 2 and 3.

———, "A Study of Organ Inferiority and Its Physical Compensation," *Nervous and Mental Disease Monograph*, Series No. 24 (1917).

Adler, Herman M., and Myrtle R. Worthington, "The Scope of the Problem of Delinquency and Crime as Related to Mental Deficiency," in *Journal of Psycho-Asthenics*, 30 (1925), pp. 47-57.

Aichhorn, August, *Wayward Youth* (New York, 1935); original title, *Verwahrloste Jugend* (1925).

Alexander, Franz, and Hugo Staub, *The Criminal, the Judge and the Public* (New York, 1931).

Alexander, Paul W., "Of Juvenile Court Justice and Judges," in *Yearbook of the National Probation and Parole Association, 1947* (New York, 1948), pp. 187-205.

———, "What's This about Punishin Parents?" in *Federal Probation*, 1 (March, 1948), pp. 23-29.

Alinsky, Saul D., "Heads I Win and Tails You Lose," in *Yearbook of the National Probation and Parole Association, 1946* (New York, 1947), pp. 43-44.

———, *Reveille for Radicals* (Chicago, 1946).

Allaman, Richard, "Managing Misbehavior at the Detention Home," in *Federal Probation*, 17 (March, 1953), pp. 27-32.

Allport, F. H., "The J-Curve Hypothesis of Conforming Behavior," in *Journal of Social Psychology*, 5 (1934), pp. 141-83.

Allport, Gordon W., *Personality* (New York, 1937).

Alpert, Harry, *Émile Durkheim and His Sociology* (New York, 1939).

Alt, Herschel, "The Training School and Residential Treatment," in *Federal Probation*, 16 (March, 1952), pp. 32-35.

Annual Message of William N. Erickson, President, Board of Commissioners of Cook County, Illinois, for the Fiscal Year of Nineteen Hundred and Fifty-two (Chicago, 1953).

Annual Report, Hawthorne-Cedar Knolls School (Westchester County, New York, 1949).

Annual Report of the Director of the Administrative Office of the United States Courts: 1954 (Washington, D.C., 1955).

"Annual Report for the Fiscal Year 1 July, 1949, to 30 June, 1950, of the

Illinois State Training School for Boys" (unpublished), pp. 24-25.

Axelrad, Sidney, "Negro and White Institutionalized Delinquents," in *The American Journal of Sociology*, 57 (1952), pp. 569-74.

Bain, Read, "The Concept of Complexity in Sociology," in *Social Forces*, 8 (1929), pp. 222-31.

———, "Our Schizoid Culture," in *Sociology and Social Research*, 19 (1935), pp. 266-76.

Bakke, E. Wight, *The Unemployed Worker* (New Haven, 1940).

Banay, Ralph S., "Physical Disfigurement as a Factor in Delinquency and Crime," in *Federal Probation*, 17 (January-March, 1943), pp. 20-24.

Barnes, Harry E., and Negley K. Teeters, *New Horizons in Criminology* (2nd ed., New York, 1946).

Barron, Milton L., "Juvenile Delinquency and American Values," in *American Sociological Review*, 16 (April, 1951), pp. 208-14.

———, *The Juvenile in Delinquent Society* (New York, 1954).

Bartlett, Edward R., and Dale B. Harris. "Personality Factors in Delinquency," in *School and Society*, 43 (1936), pp. 653-56.

Bayley, N., and N. C. Jones, "Some Personality Characteristics of Boys with Retarded Skeletal Maturity," in *Psychological Bulletin*, 38 (1941), p. 603.

Beam, Kenneth S., "Community Coordination for Prevention of Delinquency," in *Yearbook of the National Probation Association, 1936*, pp. 89-115.

Beck, Bertram M., *Five States: A Study of the Youth Authority Program as Promulgated by the American Law Institute* (Philadelphia, 1951).

———, "Juvenile Delinquency," in *Social Work Year Book, 1954* (New York, 1955), pp. 301-302.

———, *Youth within Walls*, Community Service Society of New York (New York, 1950).

Beckham, Walter H., "Helpful Practices in Juvenile Court Hearings," in *Federal Probation*, 13 (June, 1949), pp. 10-14.

Belden, Evelina, *Courts in the United States Hearing Children's Cases*, U.S. Department of Labor, Children's Bureau Pub. No. 65 (Washington, D.C., 1920).

Bender, Dr. Lauretta, "Behavior Problems in the Children of Psychotic and Criminal Parents," *Genetic Psychology Monographs*, 19 (1937), pp. 229-338.

———, "Reactive Psychosis in Response to Mental Disease in the Family," in *Journal of Nervous and Mental Disease*, 83 (1936), pp. 143-289.

———, S. Kaiser, and P. Schilder, "Studies in Aggressiveness," *Genetic Psychology Monographs*, 18 (1936), pp. 357-564.

Benedict, Ruth, "Continuities and Discontinuities in Culture Conditioning," in *Psychiatry*, 1 (1938), pp. 161-67.

———, *Patterns of Culture* (New York, 1934).

Bennett, James V., "The Federal Youth Corrections Program," in *The Prison World*, 13 (January-February, 1951).

Berg, Charles, *The Case Book of a Medical Psychologist* (New York, 1948), "Anxiety—The Foundation of Nervous Illness."

Berman, Dr. Louis, Review of W. H. Sheldon *et al.*, "The Varieties of Human Physique" in *Saturday Review of Literature*, September 14, 1940, p. 17.

Black, Bertram J., and Selma J. Glick, *Recidivism at The Hawthorne-Cedar Knolls School*, Jewish Board of Guardians, Research Monograph No. 2 (New York, 1952).

Blake, Marilyn A., "Probation Is Not Casework," in *Federal Probation*, 12 (June 1948), pp. 54-57.

Blake, Robert Rogers, and G. V. Ramsey, eds., *Perception: An Approach to Personality* (New York, 1951), Chap. XII, "The Personal World through Perception."

Blatz, William E., *The Five Sisters* (New York, 1938).

Bloch, Donald A., "Some Concepts in the Treatment of Delinquency," in *Children*, 1 (March-April, 1954), pp. 49-55.

Bloch, Herbert A., *Disorganization: Personal and Social* (New York, 1952).

———, "Economic Depression as a Factor in Rural Crime," in *Journal of Criminal Law and Criminology*, 40 (Nov.-Dec., 1949), pp. 458-70.

———, "Social Change and the Delinquent Personality," in Marjorie Bell, ed., *Current Approaches to Delinquency, Yearbook of the National Probation and Parole Association, 1949* (New York, 1950).

———, "The Social Individual as a Primary Datum in Sociology," in *American Sociological Review*, 8 (October, 1943), pp. 499-512.

———, "Structured Roles and Anomie," in *Proceedings of the American Sociological Society* (Berkeley, Calif., 1953).

Blos, P., *The Adolescent Personality: A Study of Individual Behavior* (New York, 1941).

Blumer, Herbert, *Movies and Conduct* (New York, 1933).

———, and P. M. Hauser, *The Movies, Delinquency, and Crime* (New York, 1933).

———, ed., and others, "Symposium on Psychiatry and Sociology," in *American Journal of Sociology*, 42 (May, 1937), pp. 773-877.

Bonger, William A., *Criminality and Economic Conditions* (Boston, 1916).

Bossard, James H. S., *The Sociology of Child Development* (New York, 1948).

Bovet, Lucien, *Psychiatric Aspects of Juvenile Delinquency*, World Health Organization (Geneva, 1951).

Bowen, Mrs. Joseph T., "The Early Days of the Juvenile Court," in *The Child, The Clinic and The Court* (New York, 1925), p. 307.

Bowers, Father Swithun, "The Nature and Definition of Social Casework," in *Principles and Techniques in Social Casework* (New York, 1950), pp. 97-127.

Bowler, Alida C., and Ruth S. Bloodgood, *Institutional Treatment of Delinquent Boys, Part I*, U.S. Department of Labor, Children's Bureau Pub. No. 228 (Washington, D.C., 1935).

Braude, Jacob M., "Boys' Court: Individualized Justice for the Youthful Offender," in *Federal Probation*, 12 (June, 1948), pp. 9-14.

Breckinridge, S. P., "Legal Problems of the Juvenile Court," in *The Social Service Review*, 17 (March, 1943), pp. 12-14.

———, *Social Work and the Courts* (Chicago, 1934).

———, and Edith Abbott, *The Delinquent Child and the Home* (New York, 1912).

Brennan, James J., *The Prevention and Control of Juvenile Delinquency by Police Departments* (New York, 1952).

Bromberg, Walter, *Crime and the Mind* (Philadelphia, 1948).

Brown, J. F., *Psychology and the Social Order* (New York, 1936).

Buell, Bradley, and Associates, *Community Planning for Human Services* (New York, 1952).

Burgess, Ernest W., "The Individual Delinquent as a Person," in *American Journal of Sociology*, 28 (May, 1923), pp. 657-80.

———, Joseph D. Lohman, and Clifford R. Shaw, "The Chicago Area

Project," in *National Probation Association Yearbook, 1937.*

Burke, Dorothy Williams, *Youth and Crime,* U.S. Children's Bureau, Pub. No. 196 (Washington, D.C., 1930).

Burt, Cyril, *The Young Delinquent* (New York, 1925).

California Children in Detention and Shelter Care, California Committee on Temporary Child Care (Sacramento, Calif., 1954).

Campbell, Judge William J., "Developing Systematic Sentencing Procedures," in *Federal Probation,* 18 (September, 1954), pp. 3-9.

Cantor, Nathaniel, *Crime and Society* (New York, 1939).

Capes, Robert P., "New York State's Blueprint for Delinquency Prevention," in *Federal Probation,* 18 (June, 1954), pp. 45-50.

Care for Children in Trouble, Public Affairs Pamphlet No. 217 (New York, 1955).

Carr, Lowell J., *Delinquency Control* (New York, 1940); revised edition (New York, 1950).

Careers in Social Work, Council on Social Work Education (New York, n.d.).

Cavan, Ruth S., and Katherine H. Ranck, *The Family and the Depression* (Chicago, 1938).

Chandler, Henry P., "Latter-Day Procedures in the Sentencing and Treatment of Offenders in the Federal Courts," in *Federal Probation,* 16 (March, 1952), pp. 3-12.

Chapin, F. Stuart, *Experimental Designs in Sociological Research* (New York, 1948).

Chappell, Richard A., and Will C. Turnbladh, "Probation: Case Work and Current Status," in Paul W. Tappan, ed., *Contemporary Correction* (New York, 1952).

Charnyak, John, "Some Remarks on the Diagnosis of the Psychopathic Delinquent," in *The American Journal of Psychiatry,* 97 (May, 1941), pp. 1326-35.

Chase, Stuart, *The Proper Study of Mankind* (New York, 1948).

Chessman, Caryl, *Cell 2455 Death Row* (New York, 1954).

Chicago Recreation Survey, Vols. 1-5 (1937-40).

Children and Youth at the Midcentury: Fact Finding Report, a Digest, Midcentury White House Conference on Children and Youth (Washington, D.C., 1950).

Children and Youth in Illinois, Governor's Committee for Illinois on the Midcentury White House Conference (Springfield, Ill., 1951).

Children Served by Public Welfare Agencies and Institutions, 1945, Federal Security Agency, Children's Bureau Pub. No. 3 (Washington, D.C., 1947).

Children's Bureau, The: Yesterday, Today and Tomorrow, U.S. Department of Labor, Children's Bureau (Washington, D.C., 1937).

Clinard, Marshall, review of Glueck, *Delinquents in the Making,* in *Federal Probation,* 17 (March, 1953), pp. 50-51.

Cohen, Albert K., *Juvenile Delinquency and the Social Structure* (unpublished doctoral dissertation, Department of Social Relations, Harvard University, 1951).

———, *Delinquent Boys: The Culture of the Gang* (Glencoe, Illinois, 1955).

Cohen, Frank J., *Children in Trouble* (New York, 1952).

———, "Seventh Report of Executive Director to the Board of Directors, The Youth House, April 1, 1950 to March 31, 1952" (New York, 1952), p. 8.

Cole, Luella, *Psychology of Adolescence* (New York, 1948).

"Comic Books and Juvenile Delinquency," *Interim Report of the Subcommittee to Investigate Juvenile Delinquency,* Committee on the Judiciary, S.Res. 89 and S.Res. 190 (Washington, D.C., 1955).

Connecticut, State of, *Annual Report of the Juvenile Court, 1949* (Hartford, Conn., 1950).

Construction and Design of Correctional Institutions, The, U.S. Bureau of Prisons (Washington, D.C., 1949).

Controlling Juvenile Delinquency, U.S. Department of Labor, Children's Bureau Pub. No. 301 (Washington, D.C., 1943).

Coogan, Father John Edward, S.J., "The Myth Mind in an Engineer's World," in *Federal Probation,* 16:1 (March, 1952), pp. 26-30.

Cooley, E. J., *Probation and Delinquency* (New York, 1927).

"Coordination of the Program of Institutional Care of Juvenile Delinquents in Pennsylvania: A Report to the Department of Welfare, Commonwealth of Pennsylvania." Government Consulting Service, Institute of Local and State Government, University of Pennsylvania (Philadelphia, January, 1955; mimeographed).

Correction, New York State Department of Correction, 19 (Jan., 1954).

Costello, John B., "Institutions for Juvenile Delinquents," in *The Annals,* 261 (January, 1949), pp. 166-78; also in Tappan, ed., *Contemporary Correction.*

Cosulich, Gilbert, *Juvenile Court Laws of the United States,* 2d ed., National Probation Association (New York, 1939).

Coulter, Charles W., "Family Disorganization as a Causal Factor in Delinquency and Crime," in *Federal Probation,* 12 (Sept., 1948), pp. 13-17.

Crawford, Paul L., James R. Dumpson, and Daniel J. Malamud, *Working*

with *Teen-Age Gangs,* Welfare Council of New York City (New York, 1950).

Crime in California, 1953, State of California, Department of Justice, Bureau of Criminal Statistics (Sacramento, Calif., 1954).

Dai, Bingham, "Some Problems of Personality Development Among Negro Children," in C. Kluckhohn and H. A. Murray, eds., *Personality in Nature, Society, and Culture* (New York, 1948), pp. 437-58.

Davenport, Charles B., and Florence H. Danielson, *The Hill Folk* (Cold Spring Harbor, New York, 1912).

Davidoff, Eugene, and E. S. Noetzel, *The Child Guidance Approach to Juvenile Delinquency* (New York, 1951).

Davie, Maurice R., "The Pattern of Urban Growth," in G. P. Murdock, ed., *Studies in the Science of Society* (New Haven, 1937).

Davis, Allison, and John Dollard, *Children of Bondage,* American Council on Education (Washington, D.C., 1940).

———, and Robert Havighurst, *Father of the Man* (Boston, 1947).

——— ———, "Social Class and Color Differences in Child-Rearing," in *American Sociological Review,* 11 (Dec., 1946), pp. 698-710.

Davis, Kingsley, "Adolescence and the Social Structure," in *The Annals of the American Academy of Political and Social Science,* 236 (1944), pp. 9-16.

———, *Human Society* (New York, 1949).

———, "Mental Hygiene and the Class Structure," in *Psychiatry,* 1 (1938), pp. 55-65.

———, "The Sociology of Parent-Youth Conflict," in *American Sociological Review,* V (August, 1940), pp. 523-35.

Deardorff, Neva, "Central Registration of Delinquents," in *Probation*, 23 (June, 1945), pp. 141-48.

Delinquent Child, The, U.S. White House Conference on Child Health and Protection (New York, 1932).

Deutsch, Albert, *The Mentally Ill in America* (New York, 1949).

———, *The Trouble with Cops* (New York, 1954 and 1955).

———, *Our Rejected Children* (Boston, 1950).

Dobbs, Harrison Allen, "In Defense of Juvenile Courts," in *Federal Probation*, 13 (September, 1949), pp. 24-29.

DuBois, Cora, *The People of Alor* (Minneapolis, Minn., 1944).

Dugdale, Richard L., *The Jukes* (New York, 1877).

Dunn, C. V., "The Church and Crime in the United States," in *The Annals* (1926), pp. 246-47.

Durkheim, Émile, *The Rules of Sociological Method*, trans. by G. E. Simpson (Chicago, 1938).

———, *Le Suicide* (Paris, 1897).

Educational Leave in the Public Child Welfare Program, 1953, U.S. Children's Bureau, Statistical Series, No. 26. (Washington, D.C., 1955).

Eliasberg, W. G., "Psychopathy or Neurosis," in *Journal of Clinical Psychopathology*, 8 (Oct., 1946), pp. 274-75.

Ellingston, John R., *Protecting Our Children from Criminal Careers* (New York, 1948).

———, "The Youth Authority Program," in Paul W. Tappan, ed., *Contemporary Correction*, (New York, 1951), pp. 126-27.

Elliott, Mabel, *Correctional Education and the Delinquent Girl* (Harrisburg, Penn., 1929).

Estabrook, Arthur H., *The Jukes in 1915* (Washington, 1916).

———, and C. B. Davenport, *The Nam Family* (Cold Spring Harbor, New York, 1912).

Farnham, Marynia F., *The Adolescent* (New York, 1951).

Federal Prisons: 1950, 1952, 1953, and 1954, U.S. Department of Justice (Washington, D.C., 1951, 1953, 1954, and 1955, respectively).

Fenichel, Otto, *The Psychoanalytic Theory of Neurosis* (New York, 1945).

Fenton, Norman, *The Delinquent Boy and the Correctional School* (Claremont, California, 1935).

Final Report, United States White House Conference on Children in a Democracy (Washington, D.C., 1940).

Fink, Arthur E., *Causes of Crime* (Philadelphia, 1938).

Flesch, G., "Valor y limites del factor hereditario en la etiologia de la criminalidad" ("Value and Limits of the Hereditary Factor in the Etiology of Criminality"), *Revista Mexicana de Sociologia*, 1952, pp. 193-218.

Flynn, Frank T., "Courts and Social Work," in *Social Work Year Book, 1954* (New York, 1954), pp. 153-54.

———, "First Steps in Solving Training Needs of Court and Institutional Workers Who Treat Juvenile Delinquents," in *Training Personnel for Work with Juvenile Delinquents*, U.S. Department of Health, Education, and Welfare, Children's Bureau Pub. No. 348 (Washington, D.C., 1954), pp. 82-86.

———, "Judge Merritt W. Pinckney and the Early Days of the Juvenile Court in Chicago," in *The Social Service Review*, 28 (March, 1954), pp. 20-30.

———, "Parole Supervision: A Case Analysis," in *Federal Probation*, 15 (June, 1951), pp. 36-42.

Folsom, Joseph K., *The Family and Democratic Society* (New York, 1943).

For Every Child a Healthy Personality, U.S. Midcentury White House Conference on Children and Youth (Washington, D.C., 1950).

Forman, H. J., *Our Movie Made Children* (New York, 1933).

Frank, Lawrence K., *Society as the Patient* (New Brunswick, New Jersey, 1948).

——, "Structure and Growth," in *Philosophy of Science*, 2 (April, 1935), pp. 210-35.

Frazier, E. Franklin, *The Negro Family in Chicago* (Chicago, 1932).

——, *The Negro Family in the United States* (Chicago, 1939).

Freeman, Dorothy, "The California Youth Authority," in *The Social Service Review*, 22 (June, 1948), pp. 211-33.

Freud, Anna, and Dorothy Burlingham, *Infants without Families* (New York, 1944).

Fromm, Erich, "Individual and Social Origins of Neurosis," in *American Sociological Review*, 9 (1944), pp. 380-84.

Furman, Sylvan S., ed., *Reaching the Unreached*, New York City Youth Board (New York, 1952).

Gardner, George E., M.D., "American Child Guidance Clinics," in *The Annals*, 286 (March, 1953), pp. 126-35.

——, "The Institution as Therapist," in *The Child* (January, 1952), pp. 70-72.

——, "The Juvenile Court as a Child Care Institution," in *Federal Probation*, 16 (June, 1952), pp. 8-12.

Gellhorn, Walter, *Children and Families in the Courts of New York City: A Report by a Special Committee of the Association of the Bar of the City of New York and a Study by Walter Gellhorn, assisted by Jacob D. Hyman and Sidney H. Asch on*

The Administration of Laws Relating to the Family in the City of New York (New York, 1954).

Gesell, Arnold, and Frances L. Ilg, *The Child from Five to Ten* (New York, 1946).

——, *Infant and Child in the Culture of Today* (New York, 1942).

Gilpin, Ruth, "Foster Home Care for Delinquent Children," in *The Annals*, 261 (January, 1949), pp. 120-27.

Glueck, Sheldon, *Crime and Correction: Selected Papers* (Cambridge, Mass., 1952).

——, and Eleanor, *Juvenile Delinquents Grown Up* (New York, 1940).

—— ——, *One Thousand Juvenile Delinquents: Their Treatment by Court and Clinic* (Cambridge, Mass., 1934).

—— ——, *Unraveling Juvenile Delinquency* (New York, 1950).

Goddard, Henry H., *Juvenile Delinquency* (New York, 1921).

——, *The Kallikak Family* (New York, 1912).

Goldberg, Jacob A., and Rosamond W., *Girls in the City Streets* (New York, 1935).

Goldfarb, William, "Psychological Privation in Infancy and Subsequent Adjustment," in *American Journal of Orthopsychiatry*, 15 (April, 1945), pp. 254-55.

Goldman, Nathan, "The Differential Selection of Juvenile Offenders for Court Appearance" (unpublished Ph.D. thesis, The University of Chicago, 1950).

Goode, William J., and Paul K. Hatt, *Methods in Social Research* (New York, 1952).

Gorer, Geoffrey, *The American Character* (New York, 1947).

——, *The American People: A Study in National Character* (New York, 1948).

Goring, Charles, *The English Convict* (London, 1913).

Gough, Harrison G., "Sociological Theory of Psychopathy," in *American Journal of Sociology*, 53 (March, 1948), pp. 359-66.

Green, Arnold W., "The Middle Class Male Child and Neurosis," in *American Sociological Review*, II (Feb., 1946), pp. 31-41.

———, "Social Values and Psychotherapy," in *Journal of Personality*, 14 (1946), pp. 199-228.

Greenacre, Phyllis, "Conscience in the Psychopath," in *American Journal of Orthopsychiatry*, 15 (July, 1945), pp. 495-98.

Greenwood, Ernest, *Experimental Sociology* (New York, 1945).

Gross, Fred, *Detention and Prosecution of Children* (Chicago, 1946).

Guide to Planning for Training Schools for Delinquent Children, with Particular Reference to Clinical Facilities, A, American Psychiatric Association, Subcommittee on Standards for Training Schools (Washington, D.C., 1952).

Gula, Martin, "Study and Treatment Homes for Troubled Children," in *The Child*, 12 (November, 1947), pp. 66-70.

Hagan, Helen R., "Foster Care for Children," in *Social Work Year Book, 1954* (New York, 1954), pp. 225-32.

Hall, Robert J., "The Modern Approach to Mental Deficiency," in *Mental Hygiene News*, Department of Mental Hygiene, New York State, 19 (April, 1949), p. 5.

Halliday, James L., *Psychosocial Medicine* (New York, 1948).

Handbook of American Institutions for Delinquent Juveniles, The Osborne Association. Vol. I, 1938; Vol. II, 1940; Vol. III, 1940; Vol. IV, 1943.

Hanes, Ella Z., *Case Study of Three Delinquency Areas* (University of Michigan, Flint, Mich., 1937).

Hankins, F. H., "Organic Plasticity vs. Organic Responsiveness," in *Publications of the American Sociological Society*, 22 (1928), pp. 44-47, 49-50.

Harrison, Leonard V., and William Pryor Grant, *Youth in the Toils* (New York, 1938).

Hartshorne, Hugh, and Mark A. May, *Studies in the Nature of Character* (New York, 1928-30).

Hathaway, Starke R., and Elio D. Monachesi, eds., *Analyzing and Predicting Juvenile Delinquency with the MMPI*, especially Studies 1, 2, 5, and 6 (Minneapolis, 1953).

Havighurst, Robert J., and Hilda Taba, *Adolescent Character and Personality* (New York, 1949).

Healy, William, *The Individual Delinquent* (Boston, 1915).

———, and Augusta F. Bronner, *Delinquents and Criminals—Their Making and Unmaking* (New York, 1926).

——— ———, *New Light on Delinquency and Its Treatment* (New Haven, 1936).

——— ———, *Treatment and What Happened Afterward*, Judge Baker Guidance Center (Boston, 1939).

——— ———, Edith M. H. Baylor, and J. Prentice Murphy, *Reconstructing Behavior in Youth* (New York, 1929).

Hearings, Subcommittee to Investigate Juvenile Delinquency, Senate Judiciary Committee (S.Res. 89), June 5, Oct. 19 and 20, 1954 (Washington, D.C., 1955), p. 3.

Henderson, D. K., *Psychopathic States* (New York, 1939).

Hentig, Hans von, *Crime: Causes and Conditions* (New York, 1947).

———, *The Criminal and His Victim* (New Haven, Conn., 1948).

Hewitt, Lester E., and Richard L. Jenkins, *Fundamental Patterns of Maladjustment: The Dynamics of Their Origin* (Springfield, Ill., 1947).

Hirsch, Nathaniel, *Dynamic Causes of Juvenile Crime* (Cambridge, 1937).

Hollingshead, A. B., *Elmstown's Youth* (New York, 1949).

Hollis, Florence, "Social Casework," in *Social Work Year Book, 1954* (New York, 1954) pp. 474-80.

Hooton, E. A., *The American Criminal* (Cambridge, 1939).

——, *Crime and The Man* (Cambridge, 1939).

Horney, Karen, *Our Inner Conflicts* (New York, 1945).

Indiana, State of, *Report and Surveys of the State Penal and Correctional Survey Commission, 1948* (Indianapolis, 1949).

Interim Report of the Committee on the Judiciary, Subcommittee to Investigate Juvenile Delinquency, U.S. Senate, 83rd Congress, 1st Session, Report No. 1064 (Pursuant to S. Res. 89) (Washington, D.C., March 15, 1954).

Interim Report of the Committee on the Judiciary, Subcommittee to Investigate Juvenile Delinquency, U.S. Senate, 84th Congress, 1st Session, Report No. 61 (Pursuant to S. Res. 89 and S. Res. 190) (Washington, D.C., March 14, 1955).

Jersild, Arthur T., *Child Psychology* (New York, 1940).

Johnson, Adelaide M., "Sanctions for Superego Lacunae of Adolescents," in K. R. Eisler, ed., *Searchlights on Delinquency* (New York, 1949).

Justice and the Child in New Jersey, New Jersey Juvenile Crime Commission (Trenton, 1941).

Justice for Youth: The Courts for Wayward Youth in New York City, Community Service Society of New York, Bureau of Public Affairs, prepared by Bernard C. Fisher, under the general direction of Leonard V. Harrison (New York, 1955).

Juvenile Court Standards, U.S. Department of Labor, Children's Bureau Pub. No. 121 (Washington, D.C., 1923; reprinted, 1947).

Juvenile Court Statistics, 1946-1949, Federal Security Agency, Children's Bureau Statistical Series Pub. No. 8 (Washington, D.C., 1951).

Juvenile Court Statistics, 1950-1952, U.S. Department of Health, Education, and Welfare, Children's Bureau Statistical Series Pub. No. 18 (Washington, D.C., 1954).

Juvenile Court Statistics, 1953, U.S. Department of Health, Education, and Welfare, Children's Bureau Statistical Series Pub. No. 28 (Washington, D.C., 1955).

Juvenile Delinquency (Comic Books), U.S. Senate, Hearings before the Subcommittee to Investigate Juvenile Delinquency, Committee on the Judiciary, 83rd Congress, 2nd Session, S. Res. 190 (Washington, D.C., 1954).

Kahn, Alfred J., *A Court for Children: A Study of the New York City Children's Court* (New York, 1953).

——, *Police and Children: A Study of the Juvenile Aid Bureau of the New York City Police Department*, Citizens' Committee on Children of New York City (New York, 1951).

Kallmann, Franz J., *The Genetics of Schizophrenia* (New York, 1938).

Kardiner, Abram, et al., *The Psychological Frontiers of Society* (New York, 1945).

——, and Ralph Linton, *The Individual and His Society* (New York, 1939).

Karpman, Ben, "The Case of Walter Manson," in *Case Studies in the Psychopathology of Crime*, 2 (Baltimore, 1944), p. 35.

————, *Orthopsychiatry: Retrospect and Prospect, 1923-1948*, American Orthopsychiatry Association (New York, 1948).

————, "The Principles and Aims of Criminal Psychopathology," in *Journal of Criminal Psychopathology*, 3 (Jan., 1940), pp. 200-01.

Kendall, Glenn M., "The New York State Reception Center," in *Federal Probation*, 12 (Sept., 1948), pp. 42-47.

Kennedy, M., *Criminal Tribes of the Bombay Presidency* (Bombay, 1908).

Kennedy, R., "The Colonial Crisis and the Future," in Ralph Linton, ed., *The Science of Man in the World Crisis* (New York, 1945).

Kenney, John P., and Dan G. Pursuit, *Police Work with Juveniles* (Springfield, Illinois, 1954).

Kite, Elizabeth S., *The Pineys* (New York, 1913).

Klein, Alice C., *Civil Service in Public Welfare* (New York, 1940).

Klein, George S., "A Clinical Perspective for Personality Research," in *Journal of Abnormal Psychology*, 44 (1949), pp. 42-50.

————, "The Menninger Foundation Research on Perception and Personality, 1947-1952: A Review," in *Bulletin of the Menninger Clinic*, 17 (May, 1953), pp. 93-99.

————, and H. J. Schlesinger, "Perceptual Attitudes toward Instability," in *Journal of Personality*, 19 (1951), pp. 289-302.

———— ————, and David Meister, "The Effects of Personal Values on Perception," in *Psychological Review*, 58 (1951), pp. 96-112.

Kluckhohn, Clyde, and Henry A. Murray, *Personality in Nature, Society, and Culture* (New York, 1948).

————, Henry A. Murray, and David M. Schneider, *Personality in Nature, Society, and Culture* (2d ed., New York, 1953).

Knee, Ruth Irelan, "Psychiatric Social Work," in *Social Work Year Book, 1954* (New York, 1954), pp. 387-94.

Kobrin, Solomon, "The Conflict of Values in Delinquency Areas," in *American Sociological Review*, 16 (Oct., 1951), pp. 653-61.

Kolb, L., "Types and Characteristics of Drug Addicts" in *Mental Hygiene*, 9 (1935), p. 301.

Kostir, Mary S., *The Family of Sam Sixty* (New York, 1916).

Krech, David, "Notes towards a Psychological Theory of Personality," in *Journal of Personality*, 18 (Sept., 1949), p. 80.

Kretschmer, E., *Physique and Character*, trans. from *Körperbau und Charakter* by W. H. Sprott (New York, 1925).

Kvaraceus, William C., *Juvenile Delinquency and the School* (Yonkers-on-Hudson, New York, 1945).

LaBarre, Weston, "The Cultural Basis of Emotions and Gestures," in Douglas A. Haring, ed., *Personal Character and Cultural Milieu*, (Syracuse, 1948), pp. 487-506.

Lander, Bernard, *Towards an Understanding of Juvenile Delinquency* (New York, 1954).

Larkins, John R., "A Study of the Adjustment of Negro Boys Discharged from Morrison Training School," North Carolina State Board of Public Welfare, Information Bulletin No. 8 (Raleigh, N.C., 1947).

Lathrop, Julia C., "The Background of the Juvenile Court in Illinois," in *The Child, the Clinic and the Court* (New York, 1925).

Lecky, Prescott, *Self-Consistency: A Theory of Personality* (New York, 1945).

Lemkau, Paul, *Mental Hygiene and Public Health* (New York, 1949).

————, Christopher Tietze, and Morris Cooper, "Mental Hygiene Problems in an Urban District," in *Mental Hygiene*, 27 (April, 1943), pp. 28-29.

Lenroot, Katherine F., "The Juvenile Court Today," in *Federal Probation*, 13 (Sept., 1949), pp. 9-15.

Lenz, Marjorie W., "A Yardstick for Measuring Detention Homes," in *Federal Probation*, 6 (April-June, 1942), pp. 20-23.

Levy, David, "Maternal Overprotection," in Nolan D. C. Lewis and Bernard L. Pacella, eds., *Modern Trends in Child Psychiatry* (New York, 1945).

———, "Maternal Overprotection," in *Psychiatry*, 1 (1938), pp. 561 *et seq.*

———, "Maternal Overprotection and Rejection," in *Archives of Neurology and Psychiatry*, 24 (1931), pp. 886-88.

———, *Studies in Sibling Rivalry*, Research Monograph No. 2 (American Orthopsychiatric Association, 1937).

Levy, John, "A Quantitative Study of the Relationship between Basal Metabolic Rate and Children's Behavior Problems," in *American Journal of Orthopsychiatry*, 1 (1931), pp. 298-310.

Lewin, Kurt, *A Dynamic Theory of Personality* (New York, 1935).

Lindesmith, Alfred R., *Opiate Addiction* (Bloomington, Ind., 1947).

———, and Anselm L. Strauss, *Social Psychology* (New York, 1949).

Lindner, Robert M., *Rebel without a Cause* (New York, 1944).

Linton, Ralph, *The Cultural Background of Personality* (New York, 1945).

———, *The Study of Man* (New York, 1936).

Lippman, Hyman S., "The Role of the Probation Officer in the Treatment of Delinquency in Children," in *Federal Probation*, 12 (June, 1948), pp. 36-39.

Lombroso, Cesare, *Crime: Its Causes and Remedies* (New York, 1911), trans. by Henry P. Horton from *Uomo Delinquente* (Criminal Man), originally published in 1876.

Lott, George M., M.D., "The Juvenile Detention Home," in *Federal Probation*, 6 (Jan.-March, 1942), pp. 35-39.

Lou, Herbert H., *Juvenile Courts in the United States* (Chapel Hill, N.C., 1927).

Lundberg, George A., *Can Science Save Us?* (New York, 1947).

———, *Social Research* (New York, 1942).

MacGregor, Frances, "Some Psycho-Social Problems Associated with Facial Deformities," in *American Sociological Review*, 16 (Oct., 1951), pp. 629-38.

McKenzie, Roderick D., *The Metropolitan Community* (New York, 1933).

———, "The Rise of Metropolitan Communities," in *Recent Social Trends in the United States* (New York, 1933), Vol. I, pp. 443-96.

McMillen, Wayne, *Community Organization for Social Welfare* (Chicago, 1945).

McNeil, C. F., "Community Organization for Social Welfare," in *Social Work Year Book, 1954* (New York, 1954), pp. 121-28.

Mahler, Margaret S., "Ego Psychology Applied to Behavior Problems," in Nolan D. C. Lewis and Bernard L. Pacella, eds., *Modern Trends in Child Psychiatry* (New York, 1945), pp. 52-56.

Maisel, Albert Q., "America's Forgotten Children," in *Woman's Home Companion* (January, 1947).

Maller, J. B., "Juvenile Delinquency in New York City: A Summary of a Comprehensive Report," in *Journal of Psychology*, 3 (Jan., 1937), pp. 1-25.

May, Rollo, *The Meaning of Anxiety* (New York, 1950).

Mead, G. H., *Mind, Self and Society*, edited by Charles W. Morris (Chicago, 1934).

Mead, Margaret, *And Keep Your Powder Dry* (New York, 1942).

——, "Anthropological Data on the Problem of Instinct," in *Psychosomatic Medicine*, 4 (1942), pp. 396-97.

——, *Male and Female* (New York, 1949).

——, *Sex and Temperament in Three Primitive Societies* (New York, 1935).

Meeker, Ben S., "The Federal Probation Service Training Center," in *Federal Probation*, 15 (Dec., 1951), pp. 31-36.

——, "Probation is Casework," in *Federal Probation*, 12 (June, 1948), pp. 51-54.

——, "Training of Juvenile Court Probation Officers and Related Workers Who Cannot Attend Graduate School," in *Training Personnel for Work with Juvenile Delinquents*, U.S. Department of Health, Education, and Welfare, Children's Bureau Pub. No. 348 (Washington, D.C., 1954), pp. 23-43.

Merton, Robert K., "Social Structure and Anomie," in *Social Theory and Social Structure* (Glencoe, Ill., 1949), pp. 125-49.

——, *Social Theory and Social Structure* (Glencoe, Ill., 1949).

Metfessel, Milton, and Constant Lovell, "Recent Literature on Individual Correlates of Crime," in *Psychological Bulletin*, 39 (March, 1942), p. 148.

Meyer, Rev. James, O.F.M., ed., *Crime and Religion* (Chicago, 1936).

Michaels, Joseph J., "The Incidence of Enuresis and Age of Cessation in One Hundred Delinquents and One Hundred Sibling Controls," in *American Journal of Orthopsychiatry*, 8 (1938), pp. 460-65.

——, "Parallels between Persistent Enuresis and Delinquency in the Psychopathic Personality," in *American Journal of Orthopsychiatry*, 11 (1941), pp. 260-74.

——, "Psychobiologic Interpretations of Delinquency," in *The American Journal of Orthopsychiatry*, 10 (July, 1940), pp. 501-509.

——, and S. E. Goodman, "Incidence and Intercorrelations of Enuresis and Other Neuropathic Traits in So-Called Normal Children," in *American Journal of Orthopsychiatry*, 4 (1934), pp. 79-106.

——, and Arthur Steinberg, "Persistent Enuresis and Juvenile Delinquency," in *The British Journal of Delinquency*, 3 (Oct., 1952), pp. 1-10.

Mihanovich, Clement S., "Who Is the Juvenile Delinquent?" in *Social Science*, 22 (April, 1947), pp. 45-50.

Monachesi, Elio D., "Some Personality Characteristics of Delinquents and Non-Delinquents," in *The Journal of Criminal Law and Criminology*, 38 (Jan.-Feb., 1948), pp. 487-500.

Montagu, M. F. Ashley, "The Biologist Looks at Crime," in *The Annals*, 217 (1941), pp. 46-58.

Mowrer, Harriet J., *Personality Adjustment and Domestic Discord* (New York, 1935).

Murchison, Carl, *Criminal Intelligence* (Worcester, Mass., 1926).

Murphy, Gardner, *Personality: A Biosocial Approach to Origins and Structures* (New York, 1947).

——, "The Relationships of Culture and Personality," in S. Stansfeld Sargent and Marian W. Smith, eds., *Culture and Personality* (New York, 1949), pp. 13-30.

Murray, Raymond W., C.S.C., and Frank T. Flynn, *Social Problems* (New York, 1938).

Navin, R. B., W. B. Peattie, F. R. Stewart, *et al.*, *An Analysis of a*

Slum Area in Cleveland, Metropolitan Housing Authority (Cleveland, 1934).

Nelson, Edwin, *Prevailing Factors in Juvenile Delinquency in Brockton, Mass.* (unpublished master's thesis, Boston University, 1940).

Neumeyer, Martin H., *Juvenile Delinquency in Modern Society* (New York, 1949).

Newcomb, T. M., *Social Psychology* (New York, 1950).

Newell, H. A., "The Psychodynamics of Maternal Rejection," in *American Journal of Orthopsychiatry*, 4 (1934), pp. 387-401, and 6 (1936), pp. 357-401.

Nielsen, John M., and George N. Thompson, *The Engrammes of Psychiatry* (Springfield, Ill., 1948).

Norman, Sherwood, *The Design and Construction of Detention Homes for the Juvenile Court* (New York, 1947).

———, *The Detention of Children in Delaware* (Wilmington, Del., 1951).

———, *The Detention of Children in Michigan: A Study Requested by the Michigan Probate Judge's Association* (New York, 1952).

———, "New Goals for Juvenile Detention," in *California Youth Authority Quarterly* (Summer, 1951); substantially the same article, with the same title, appears in *Federal Probation*, 13 (December, 1949), pp. 29-33.

———, *Standards and Goals for the Detention and Shelter of Children, Part I: Detention* (New York, 1954).

———, and Helen Sherwood, "Detention for the Juvenile Court: A Discussion of Principles and Practices," (2d ed., New York, 1946; mimeographed).

Ormsbee, Mabel, *The Young Unemployed Girl* (New York, 1927).

Oswald, Russell G., "Correctional Treatment," in *Social Work Year Book, 1954* (New York, 1954), pp. 135-42.

Papanek, Ernst, "The Training School: Its Program and Leadership," in *Federal Probation*, 17 (June, 1953), pp. 16-22.

Parents and Delinquency, U.S. Department of Health, Education, and Welfare, Children's Bureau (Washington, D.C., 1954).

Park, Robert E., Ernest W. Burgess, and Roderick D. McKenzie, "The Ecological Approach to the Study of the Human Community," in *The City* (Chicago, 1925).

Parsons, Talcott, "Age and Sex in the Social Structure of the United States," in *American Sociological Review*, 7 (1942), pp. 604-16.

Pastore, Nicholas, "The Genetics of Schizophrenia," in *Psychological Bulletin*, 4 (July, 1949), pp. 285-302.

Patients in Mental Institutions, 1946, U.S. Dept. of Commerce, Bureau of the Census (Washington, D.C., 1949).

Pattern for Prevention, New York City Youth Board (Nov. 10, 1952).

Perlman, Richard I., "The Meaning of Juvenile Delinquency Statistics," in *Federal Probation*, 13 (Sept., 1949), pp. 63-67.

Phelps, H. A., "Cycle of Crime," in *Journal of Criminal Law and Criminology* (1929), pp. 107-21.

Police Services for Juveniles, U.S. Department of Health, Education, and Welfare, Children's Bureau Pub. No. 344 (Washington, D.C., 1954).

Polier, Justine Wise, *The Role of a Juvenile Court in 1948* (an address delivered at the Annual Meeting of the Illinois Children's Home and Aid Society, Chicago, Ill., January 30, 1948).

Pollack, Otto, and collaborators, *Social Science and Psychotherapy for Children*, Russell Sage Foundation (New York, 1952).

Porterfield, Austin L., *Youth in Trouble*, The Leo Potishman Foundation (Austin, Texas, 1946).

Pound, Roscoe, "The Juvenile Court and the Law," in *National Probation and Parole Association Yearbook, 1942* (New York, 1943).

———, "The Juvenile Court in the Service State," in *Yearbook of the National Probation and Parole Association, 1949* (New York, 1950).

Powdermaker, Hortense, "The Channelling of Negro Aggression by the Cultural Process," in C. Kluckhohn and H. A. Murray, eds., *Personality in Nature, Society, and Culture* (New York, 1948), pp. 473-84.

Powers, Edwin, and Helen Witmer, *An Experiment in the Prevention of Delinquency* (New York, 1951).

Pray, Kenneth L. M., "The Place of Social Case Work in the Treatment of Delinquency," in *Social Service Review*, 19 (June, 1945), pp. 235-44.

———, "The Principles of Social Case Work as Applied to Probation and Parole," in *Federal Probation*, 9 (April-June, 1945), pp. 14-18.

Printzlien, Conrad P., "Deferred Prosecution for Juvenile Offenders," in *Federal Probation*, 12 (March, 1948), pp. 17-22.

Probation and Parole Directory, National Probation and Parole Association (New York, 1952).

Progress Report of the Delinquency Control Institute, University of Southern California (Los Angeles, Calif., 1949).

Public Training Schools for Delinquent Children: Directory, May, 1955, U.S. Department of Health, Education, and Welfare, Children's Bureau (Washington, D.C., 1955).

Puttkammer, Ernst W., *Administration of Criminal Law* (Chicago, 1953).

Reckless, Walter C., *The Crime Problem* (New York, 1950).

———, "Training of the Correctional Worker," in Paul W. Tappan, ed., *Contemporary Correction* (New York, 1951), pp. 35-50.

———, "Training Probation and Parole Personnel," in *Focus* (March, 1948).

———, and Mapheus Smith, *Juvenile Delinquency* (New York, 1932).

Recommended Standards for Services for Delinquent Children, U.S. Department of Health, Education, and Welfare, Children's Bureau (Washington, D.C., 1953).

Redl, Fritz, "Group Emotion and Leadership," in *Psychiatry*, 5 (1942), pp. 573 ff.

———, "The Psychology of Gang Formation and the Treatment of Juvenile Delinquents," in *The Psychoanalytic Study of the Child* (New York, 1945).

———, and David Wineman, *Children Who Hate* (Glencoe, Ill., 1951).

——— ———, *Controls from within* (Glencoe, Ill., 1952).

Reed, Ellery F., "How Effective Are Group Work Agencies in Preventing Delinquency?" in *The Social Service Review*, 22 (Sept., 1948), pp. 340-48.

Reed, George J., "The Federal Youth Corrections Act in Operation," in *Federal Probation*, 18 (Sept., 1954), pp. 10-15.

Reed, Hugh P., *The Detention of Children in Illinois*, National Probation and Parole Association (New York, 1952).

———, *The Handling of the Neglected and Delinquent Child in Lincoln, Nebraska, 1955* (New York, 1955).

Reinemann, J. O., "The Truant before the Court," in *Federal Probation*, 12 (Sept., 1948), pp. 8-12.

Reiss, Albert J., "Social Correlates of Psychological Types of Delinquency," in *American Sociological Review*, 17 (Dec., 1952), pp. 710-18.

Report on the Boys' Court, The Municipal Court of Chicago (Chicago, 1948).

Report on the Child Offender in the Federal System of Justice, U.S. National Commission on Law Observance and Enforcement (Washington, D.C., 1931).

Report on Criminal Statistics, National Commission on Law Observance and Enforcement (Washington, D.C., 1931).

Report of the Division of Mental Deficiency, Commonwealth of Massachusetts (Boston, 1935), pp. 33-34.

Report on Institutional Treatment of Delinquent Juveniles, National Conference on Prevention and Control of Juvenile Delinquency (Washington, D.C., 1947).

Report on Juvenile Court Administration, National Conference on Prevention and Control of Juvenile Delinquency (Washington, D.C., 1947).

Report on Juvenile Detention, National Conference on Prevention and Control of Juvenile Delinquency (Washington, D.C., 1947).

Report on Role of Police, National Conference on Prevention and Control of Delinquency (Washington, D.C., 1947).

Ribble, Margaret A., "Anxiety in Infants," in Noland D. C. Lewis and Bernard L. Pacella, eds., *Modern Trends in Child Psychiatry* (New York, 1945), pp. 17-25.

Robinson, Louis N., *Jails: Care and Treatment of Misdemeanant Prisoners in the United States* (Philadelphia, 1944).

Robison, Sophia M., *Can Delinquency Be Measured?* (New York, 1936).

Rogers, Carl R., *The Clinical Treatment of the Problem Child* (Boston, 1939).

Rosanoff, A. J., *et al.*, "Criminality and Delinquency in Twins," in *Journal of Criminal Law and Criminology* (Jan.-Feb., 1934), pp. 923-24.

Rosenheim, F., "Character Structure of a Rejected Child," in *American Journal of Orthopsychiatry*, 12 (1942), pp. 486-94.

Rosenow, Kurt, "The Incidence of First Born among Problem Children," in *Journal of Genetic Psychology*, 37 (1930), pp. 145-51.

Rothschild, D., "Senile Pyschoses and Cerebral Arteriosclerosis," in *Mental Disorders in Later Life*, O. J. Kaplan, ed. (Stanford University, 1945).

Rotman, David B., "Alcoholism and Crime," in *Federal Probation*, 11 (Sept., 1947), pp. 31-33.

Rowe, A. W., "A Possible Endocrine Factor in the Behavior Problems of the Young," in *American Journal of Orthopsychiatry*, 1 (1931), pp. 451-75.

Rubin, Sol, "Changing Youth Correction Authority Concepts," in *Focus*, 29 (May, 1950), pp. 77-82.

———, "State Juvenile Court: A New Standard," in *Focus*, 30 (July, 1951), pp. 103-107.

——— "The Legal Character of Juvenile Delinquency," in *The Annals* (January, 1949).

"Salaries of Probation and Parole Officers in the United States, 1953-54," National Probation and Parole Association (New York, 1954, mimeographed).

Sauber, Mignon, *Personnel in Public Child Welfare Programs: 1953*, U.S. Department of Health, Education, and Welfare, Children's Bureau Statistical Series Pub. No. 20 (Washington, D.C., 1954).

Schachtel, Anna H., and Marjorie B. Levi, "Character Structure of Day Nursery Children as Seen through the Rorschach," in *American Journal of Orthopsychiatry*, 15 (April, 1945), pp. 213-22.

Schlapp, M. G., "Behavior and Gland Disease," in *Journal of Heredity*, 15 (1924), p. 11.

Schlapp, Max A., and Edward H. Smith, *The New Criminology* (New York, 1928).

Schramm, Gustav L., "Philosophy of the Juvenile Court," in *The Annals*, 261 (Jan., 1949), pp. 101-108.

Schreiber, Flora R., "Our Forgotten Children," in *Today's Woman* (Sept., 1953).

Schroeder, Paul L., "Behavior Difficulties in Children Associated with the Results of Birth Trauma," in *Journal of the American Medical Association*, 92 (1929), pp. 100-104.

Schulze, Susanne, ed., *Creative Living in a Children's Institution* (New York, 1951).

———, and Morris Fritz Mayer, "Training for Houseparents and Kindred Personnel in Institutions for Juvenile Delinquents," in *Training Personnel for Work with Juvenile Delinquents*, U.S. Department of Health, Education, and Welfare, Children's Bureau Pub. No. 348 (Washington, D.C., 1954).

Schwartz, Edward E., "A Community Experiment in the Measurement of Juvenile Delinquency," in *Yearbook of the National Probation Association, 1945* (New York, 1946), pp. 157-82.

———, "Statistics of Juvenile Delinquency in the United States," in *The Annals*, 261 (January, 1949), pp. 9-20.

Sellin, Thorsten, *Culture Conflicts and Crime* (New York, 1938).

———, ed., *Prisons in Transformation*, entire issue of *The Annals*, 293 (May, 1954).

———, "The Uniform Criminal Statistics Act," in *Journal of Criminal Law and Criminology*, 40 (March-April, 1950), pp. 679-700.

"Seventh Report of Executive Director to the Board of Directors, The Youth House," see Cohen, Frank J.

Shalloo, Jeremiah P., "Youth and Crime," in *The Annals*, 194 (1937), pp. 79-86.

Shanas, Ethel, *Recreation and Delinquency*, Chicago Recreation Commission (Chicago, 1942).

Shaw, Clifford, *Brothers in Crime* (Chicago, 1938).

———, *Delinquency Areas* (Chicago, 1929).

———, "Housing and Delinquency," in J. M. Gries and James Ford, eds., *Housing and the Community-Home Repair and Remodeling*, The President's Conference on Home Building and Home Ownership (Washington, D.C., 1932), pp. 15-16.

———, *The Jack-Roller* (Chicago, 1930).

———, *The Natural History of a Delinquent Career* (Chicago, 1931).

———, and Henry D. McKay, "Social Factors in Juvenile Delinquency," *Report on the Causes of Crime*, National Commission on Law Observance and Enforcement, II (1931), p. 266.

Sheldon, W. H., Emil M. Hartl, and Eugene McDermott, *Varieties of Delinquent Behavior* (New York, 1949).

———, S. S. Stevens, and W. B. Tucker, *The Varieties of Human Physique* (New York, 1940).

——— ——— ———, *The Varieties of Temperament* (New York, 1942).

Sherif, Muzafer, *Psychology of Social Norms* (New York, 1936).

Slawson, John B., *The Delinquent Boy* (Boston, 1926).

———, "The Use of the Authoritative Approach in Social Casework in the Field of Delinquency," in *American Journal of Orthopsychiatry* (October, 1938), pp. 673-78.

Smith, Sampson G., "The Schools and Delinquency," in *Yearbook of the National Probation and Parole Association, 1948* (New York, 1949).

Social Base Map, Local Neighborhood, New York City, 1931, prepared under the direction of Frederic M. Thrasher,

New York University (New York, 1931).

Social Statistics, U.S. Department of Labor, Children's Bureau (Washington, D.C., 1945).

Social Statistics, II, The Child, U.S. Department of Labor, Children's Bureau (Washington, D.C., 1946).

Social Work as a Profession, Council on Social Work Education (New York, n.d.).

Social Workers in 1950, U.S. Department of Labor, Bureau of Labor Statistics. Also published as a pamphlet by the American Association of Social Workers (New York, 1952).

Some Facts about Juvenile Delinquency, U.S. Department of Health, Education, and Welfare, Children's Bureau Pub. No. 340 (Washington, D.C., 1953).

Spitz, René A., "The Role of Ecological Factors in Emotional Development in Infancy," in *Child Development*, 20 (1949), pp. 145-56.

Standard Juvenile Court Act, A, National Probation and Parole Association (revised edition, New York, 1949).

"Standards for Selection of Probation and Parole Officers," National Probation and Parole Association (mimeographed, New York, 1952).

Standards for Specialized Courts Dealing with Children, U.S. Department of Health, Education, and Welfare, Children's Bureau Pub. No. 346 (Washington, D.C., 1954).

State and National Correctional Institutions, The American Prison Association (New York, 1954).

Steinberg, J., "Relation between Basal Metabolic Rate and Mental Speed," in *Archives of Psychology*, 39, No. 172 (1934).

Stone, C. P., and R. C. Barker, "The Attitudes and Interests of Pre-Menarcheal and Post-Menarcheal Girls," in

Journal of Genetic Psychology, 54 (1939), pp. 27-71.

Studt, Elliot, and Milton Chernin, "The Role of the School of Social Work in Educating and Training Personnel for Work with Juvenile Delinquents," in *Training Personnel for Work with Juvenile Delinquents*, U.S. Department of Health, Education, and Welfare, Children's Bureau Pub. No. 348 (Washington, D. C., 1954).

Studt, Ray, *Functions of Detention— Principles, Operation* (mimeographed, California, undated).

Suggested College Curricula as Preparation for Correctional Service, Committee on Personnel Standards and Training, American Prison Association (New York, 1954).

Sullenger, Thomas E., *Social Determinants of Juvenile Delinquency* (Columbia, Mo., 1929).

Sullivan, Harry Stack, *Modern Conceptions of Psychiatry*, The William Alanson White Psychiatric Foundation (Washington, D.C., 1945).

———, "Multidisciplined Coordination of Interpersonal Data," in S. Stansfeld Sargent and Marian W. Smith, eds., *Culture and Personality*, Viking Fund (New York, 1949), pp. 175-94.

———, "The Study of Psychiatry," in *Psychiatry*, 10 (1947), pp. 355-71.

Summary Report: Survey of Pennsylvania Training Schools for Juvenile Delinquents, Government Consulting Service, Institute of Local and State Government, University of Pennsylvania (mimeographed, Philadelphia, June, 1954).

Sussmann, Frederick B., *Law of Juvenile Delinquency: The Laws of the Forty-Eight States* (New York, 1950).

Sutherland, E. H., *Principles of Criminology* (Philadelphia, 1947, also 4th ed., New York, 1947).

Symonds, Percival M., *Adolescent Fantasy* (New York, 1949).

———, "A Study of Parental Acceptance and Rejection," in *American Journal of Orthopsychiatry*, 8 (1938), p. 686.

Szurek, S., "Genesis of Psychopathic Personality Trends," in *Psychiatry*, 5: 1 (February, 1942).

Taber, Robert C., "The Value of Casework to the Probationer," in *National Parole Association Yearbook, 1940* (New York, 1941), pp. 167-79.

Tappan, Paul W., *Comparative Survey on Juvenile Delinquency, Part I: North America*. United Nations Department of Social Affairs, Division of Social Welfare (New York, 1952), pp. 1-8.

———, ed., *Contemporary Correction* (New York, 1951).

———, *Delinquent Girls in Court* (New York, 1947).

———, *Juvenile Delinquency* (New York, 1949).

Teeters, Negley K., and John Otto Reinemann, *The Challenge of Delinquency* (New York, 1950).

Tentative Report on Study Unit No. 4 —Public Welfare, State of Massachusetts, Special Commission on the Structure of the State Government (Boston, 1951).

Tentative Standards for Training Schools, 1954, U.S. Department of Health, Education, and Welfare, Children's Bureau Pub. No. 351 (Washington, D.C., 1954).

Thomas, Dorothy Swain, *Social Aspects of the Business Cycle* (New York, 1925).

Thomas, W. I., *Primitive Behavior* (New York, 1937).

Thrasher, Frederic M., "The Boys' Club and Juvenile Delinquency," in *The American Journal of Sociology*, 42 (July, 1936), pp. 66-80.

———, "The Comics and Delinquency: Cause or Scapegoat," in *The Journal of Educational Sociology* (December, 1949), pp. 195-205.

———, *The Gang* (Chicago, 1927).

Thurston, Henry W., *Concerning Juvenile Delinquency* (New York, 1942).

———, *Delinquency and Spare Time, The Cleveland Recreational Survey* (Cleveland, 1918), pp. 105-18.

Topping, Ruth, "Case Studies of Aggressive Delinquents," in *American Journal of Orthopsychiatry*, 11 (1941), pp. 485-92.

———, *Women's Misdemeanants Division of the Municipal Court of Philadelphia* (Philadelphia, 1932).

Towle, Charlotte, "Social Casework," in *Social Work Year Book, 1947* (New York, 1947).

Training Personnel for Work with Juvenile Delinquents, U.S. Department of Health, Education, and Welfare, Children's Bureau Pub. No. 348 (Washington, D.C., 1954).

Tulchin, Simon H., *Intelligence and Crime* (Chicago, 1939).

Twenty-First Annual Report of the Secretary of Labor for the Fiscal Year Ended June 30, 1933, U.S. Department of Labor (Washington, D.C., 1934).

Uniform Crime Reports, XVI, U.S. Department of Justice, Federal Bureau of Investigation (Washington, D.C., 1946).

Uniform Crime Reports, XVIII, No. 2, U.S. Department of Justice, Federal Bureau of Investigation (Washington, D.C., 1948).

Uniform Crime Reports, XXIV, No. 2, U.S. Department of Justice, Federal Bureau of Investigation (Washington, D.C., 1954).

Uniform Crime Reports, XXV, No. 2, U.S. Department of Justice, Federal Bureau of Investigation (Washington, D.C., 1955).

Van Waters, Miriam, *Parents on Probation* (New York, 1931).

Virginia Welfare Bulletin 31, Virginia Department of Welfare and Institutions (October, 1953).

Vold, George B., "The Amount and Nature of Crime," in *American Journal of Sociology*, 40 (May, 1935), pp. 796-803.

Waite, John Barker, "The Youth Correction Authority Act," in *Law and Contemporary Problems*, IX, Duke University, (Autumn, 1942).

Wallace, E. W., "Physical Defects and Juvenile Delinquency," in *New York State Journal of Medicine*, 40 (1940), pp. 1586-90.

Warner, Florence M., *Juvenile Detention in the United States* (Chicago, 1933).

Warner, W. Lloyd, and Paul S. Lunt, *Democracy in Jonesville* (New York, 1949).

————— —————, *The Social Life of a Modern Community* (New Haven, Conn., 1941).

Wegrocki, Henry J., "A Critique of Cultural and Statistical Concepts of Abnormality," in *Journal of Abnormal and Social Psychology*, 34 (1939), pp. 166-78.

Weinberg, S. Kirson, *Society and Personality Disorders* (New York, 1952).

Weiss, H. R., and R. Sampliner, "A Study of Adolescent Felony Offenders," in *Journal of Criminal Law and Criminology* (March-April, 1944), pp. 377-91.

Weiss, Jerome S., "Criminals or Delinquents? Another Illinois Merry-Go-Round!" in *Chicago Bar Record* (January, 1953).

Wertham, Dr. Frederic, *Seduction of the Innocent* (New York, 1954).

Westlund, Norman, and Adelaide Z. Palumbo, "Parental Rejection of Crippled Children," in *American Journal of Orthopsychiatry*, 16 (1946), pp. 271-81.

Wetterdal, "Diagnosis for Children Delivered by Forceps: A Re-Investigation of 2,000 Children Delivered by Forceps and 2,000 Spontaneously Delivered," in *Child Development Abstract and Bibliography*, 3 (1929).

What's Happening to Delinquent Children in Your Town? U.S. Department of Health, Education, and Welfare, Children's Bureau Pub. No. 342 (Washington, D.C., 1953).

White, Leonard D., *Introduction to the Study of Public Administration* (3rd ed., New York, 1948).

White House Conference on Child Health and Protection: Report of Sub-Committee on Growth and Development (New York, 1932), pp. 220-25.

Wickman, E. K., *Children's Behavior and Teachers' Attitudes*, Commonwealth Fund (New York, 1928).

Wiese, Leopold von, and Howard Becker, *Systematic Sociology* (New York, 1932).

Wile, Ira S., and Rose Davis, "The Relation of Birth to Behavior," in *American Journal of Orthopsychiatry*, 11 (1941), pp. 320-34.

Williams, Frankwood, *Adolescence: Studies in Mental Hygiene* (New York, 1930).

Williams, Herbert D., "Foster Homes for Juvenile Delinquents," in *Federal Probation*, 13 (September, 1949), pp. 46-51.

Williams, Robin, *American Society* (New York, 1951).

Winslow, Emma A., "Relationships between Employment and Crime Fluctuations as Shown by Massachusetts Statistics," in *Report on Causes of Crime*, National Commission on Law Observance and Enforcement, (Washington, D.C., 1931), pp. 257-312.

Wirth, Louis, "Ideological Aspects of Social Disorganization," in *American Sociological Review*, 5 (August, 1940), pp. 472-82.

Witmer, Helen L., and Edith Tufts, *The Effectiveness of Delinquency Prevention Programs*, U.S. Department of Health, Education, and Welfare, Children's Bureau Pub. No. 350 (Washington, D.C., 1954).

Worthington, George E., *Men's Misdemeanants Division of the Municipal Court of Philadelphia* (Philadelphia, 1932).

Yardstick for Measuring Juvenile Courts, A, National Probation and Parole Association (New York, n.d.).

Yearbooks of the National Probation and Parole Association (New York)

Note: Yearbooks from 1936 to 1952 were edited by Marjorie Bell; since 1953 they have been edited by Matthew Matlin

Probation in the United States (1915; pub. 1915)

The Progress of Probation (1916; pub. 1916)

Social Problems of the Courts (1917; pub. 1918)

The Social Work of the Courts (1918; pub. 1919)

Social Courts and Probation (1919; pub. 1920)

Social Service in the Courts (1920; pub. 1920)

Social Treatment of the Delinquent (1921; pub. 1922)

The Social Service of the Courts (1922; pub. 1923)

Probation and the Prevention of Delinquency (1923; pub. 1924)

Community Treatment of Delinquency (1924; pub. 1924)

The Development of Juvenile Courts and Probation (1925; pub. 1925)

The Courts and the Prevention of Delinquency (1926; pub. 1926)

The Newer Justice and the Courts (1927; pub. 1927)

Proving Probation (1928; pub. 1928)

Probation, Juvenile Courts, Domestic Relations Courts, Crime Prevention (1929; pub. 1929)

Probation, Juvenile Courts, Domestic Relations Courts, Crime Prevention (1930; pub. 1930)

Probation, Juvenile Courts, Domestic Relations Courts, Crime Prevention (1931; pub. 1931)

The Yearbook of the National Probation Association (1932-33; pub. 1933)

The Yearbook of the National Probation Association (1934; pub. 1934)

The Yearbook of the National Probation Association (1935; pub. 1935)

The Yearbook of the National Probation Association (1936; pub. 1936)

Coping with Crime (1937; pub. 1937)

The Offender in the Community (1938; pub. 1938)

Trends in Crime Treatment (1939; pub. 1939)

Dealing with Delinquency (1940; pub. 1940)

Probation and Parole Progress (1941; pub. 1941)

Social Defenses against Crime (1942; pub. 1942)

Delinquency and the Community in Wartime (1943; pub. 1944)

Cooperation in Crime Control (1944; pub. 1945)

Social Correctives for Delinquency (1945; pub. 1946)

Society's Stake in the Offender (1946; pub. 1947)

Redirecting the Delinquent (1947; pub. 1948)

Bulwarks against Crime (1948; pub. 1949)

Current Approaches to Delinquency (1949; pub. 1950)

Advances in Understanding the Offender (1950; pub. 1951)

The Community and the Correctional Process (1951; pub. 1952)

Crime Prevention through Treatment (1952; pub. 1953)

Reappraising Crime Treatment (1953; pub. 1954)

Yepsen, Lloyd, "Where We Stand at Present in Care of Mentally Deficient," in *Welfare Reporter*, New Jersey Department of Institutions and Agencies (August, 1949).

Young, Pauline V., *Pilgrims of Russiantown* (Chicago, 1932).

——, *Scientific Social Surveys and Research* (2nd ed., New York, 1949).

——, *Social Treatment in Probation and Delinquency* (2nd ed., New York, 1952).

"Youth Authority Legislation," Illinois Legislative Council, Memorandum Report Pursuant to Proposal 366 (File No. 1-611, processed, Springfield, Ill., May, 1952).

Zimmerman, Carl C., *The Family of Tomorrow: The Cultural Crisis and The Way Out* (New York, 1949).

Znaniecki, Florian, *The Method of Sociology* (New York, 1934).

INDEX

NOTE: *q. = quoted*

H

I

V

W

U